# THE
# DEVELOPMENT
# OF LOGIC

# THE
# DEVELOPMENT
# OF LOGIC

BY

## WILLIAM KNEALE
F.B.A.,
WHITE'S PROFESSOR OF MORAL PHILOSOPHY
IN THE UNIVERSITY OF OXFORD

AND

## MARTHA KNEALE
FELLOW OF LADY MARGARET HALL
OXFORD

OXFORD
AT THE CLARENDON PRESS
1962

*Oxford University Press, Amen House, London E.C.4*

GLASGOW  NEW YORK  TORONTO  MELBOURNE  WELLINGTON
BOMBAY  CALCUTTA  MADRAS  KARACHI  LAHORE  DACCA
CAPE TOWN  SALISBURY  NAIROBI  IBADAN  ACCRA
KUALA LUMPUR  HONG KONG

PRINTED IN GREAT BRITAIN

# PREFACE

As its name indicates, this book is an account of the growth of logic, rather than an attempt to chronicle all that past scholars, good and bad, have said about the science. For the sake of continuity, and in order to give historical perspective to our story, my wife and I have included some references to work which does not deserve to be remembered for its own sake; and occasionally we have allowed ourselves to indulge an antiquarian curiosity, when we thought that the result might be of some interest to others. But our primary purpose has been to record the first appearances of those ideas which seem to us most important in the logic of our own day. Such a programme is based on judgements of value, and we realize that our selection of material and still more our comments, especially in the later chapters, may seem eccentric to some readers. In defence of our undertaking we can only say that we have followed the plan which our interests suggested, and that we could not have written in any other way.

The idea of attempting a history of logic on these lines occurred to me first in 1947 when I was asked to give a lecture in Cambridge on the centenary of Boole's *Mathematical Analysis of Logic*. Part of that lecture survives in Chapter VI of this book, where it is reprinted from *Mind*, lvii (1948), by permission of the editor. During the next ten years I gave to the project all the time I could spare from teaching and other more urgent work, and by 1957 I had a draft which covered most of the field but in a very uneven fashion. Some of the material now contained in Chapter IX, § 3, was published under the title 'The Province of Logic' in *Contemporary British Philosophy*, Third Series (George Allen & Unwin, 1956), from which it is reprinted here by permission of the publishers, but much of what I had written seemed to me unsatisfactory. As might be expected, the earlier chapters, which I had put together quickly in an impressionistic style, were those in need of most revision, and I soon came to the conclusion that they would have to be completely rewritten on a larger scale. At this stage the Leverhulme Trustees gave me a grant to make possible two terms' special leave from my tutorial duties in Exeter College. I am very grateful for their generous help, which enabled me to finish the chapters now numbered IV, V, and VI. But I am afraid that even so I might have lost heart, if my wife had not at the same time agreed to take charge of the Greek part and then devoted to it not only a term of sabbatical leave but also most of her leisure during the next two and a half years. Apart from the concluding section, on the Stoic System of Inference Schemata, the first three chapters, as they stand, are her work. In addition she has helped me with advice about the treatment of many subjects in the later chapters.

We have to thank Mr. John Lemmon, Mr. Brian McGuinness, Dr. Lorenzo Minio-Paluello, Dr. Richard Walzer, and Professor Hao Wang for reading parts of the work and suggesting corrections or improvements. Professor Arthur Prior, who read the whole in typescript, gave us a great many useful comments, and we are very grateful for the generosity with which he has allowed us to profit from his wide knowledge of the history of logic. Although we have gladly accepted most of the advice we have received, we have sometimes persisted in going our own way, and none of our friends are to be held responsible for faults that remain.

W. K.

*April 1960*

# CONTENTS

# I

## THE BEGINNINGS

### 1. *The Notion of Validity*

Logic is concerned with the principles of valid inference; and it is certain that men made inferences and criticized the inferences of others long before the time of Aristotle. This is not enough in itself to justify us in saying that there must have been a beginning of logic before the time of Aristotle; for men may perform various activities correctly (e.g. talk English) without formulating the rules for those activities explicitly. But it is clear from what we find in Plato and Aristotle and other sources that Greek philosophers had begun to discuss the principles of valid inference before Aristotle wrote those works which came to be known as the *Organon*. It is the purpose of this chapter to trace, as far as the evidence allows, the development of logical thought before Aristotle. This is not easy on the basis of the evidence alone, but it is possible to form reasonable conjectures about the origins of logical reflection and to show that these are supported to a certain extent by the evidence.

Since logic is not simply valid argument but the reflection upon principles of validity, it will arise naturally only when there is already a considerable body of inferential or argumentative material to hand. Not every type of discourse provokes logical inquiry. Pure story-telling or literary discourse, for example, does not provide a sufficient amount of argumentative material. It is those types of discourse or inquiry in which *proof* is sought or demanded that naturally give rise to logical investigation; for to prove a proposition is to infer it validly from true premisses. The conditions of proof are two: true premisses, or starting-points, and valid arguments. It is not easy to tell how soon it was realized that the two conditions are independent, but this was perfectly clear to Aristotle when he drew the distinction between apodeictic and dialectical reasoning in the *Topics*[1] and again in the *Prior Analytics*.[2] The latter passage is worth quoting in full because it throws light on the context in which the distinction was first drawn.

'The demonstrative premiss (ἀποδεικτικὴ πρότασις) differs from the dialectical, because the demonstrative is the assumption of one of

---

[1] *Topica*, i. 1 (100ᵃ25–30).    [2] *An. Pr.* i. 1 (24ᵃ22–24ᵇ12).

B

a pair of contradictory propositions (for the man who demonstrates assumes something and does not ask a question), but the dialectical premiss is a question as to which of two contradictories is true. But this makes no difference to the fact that there is a syllogism in each case. Both the man who demonstrates and the man who asks a question reason assuming that some predicate belongs or does not belong to something. So that a syllogistic premiss is simply the affirmation or denial of some predicate of some subject, as we have said, but it is demonstrative if it is true and accepted because deduced from basic assumptions, while a dialectical premiss is for the enquirer a question as to which of two contradictories is true and for the reasoner the assumption of some plausible or generally held proposition.'

The distinction between demonstrative and dialectical argument is introduced here by reference to the activities in which, according to Aristotle, the statement of the premisses properly plays its part. The demonstrative premiss is laid down by a teacher in the course of developing his subject. It is the premiss of what Aristotle calls in the *De Sophisticis Elenchis* a didactic argument.[1] The dialectical premiss, on the other hand, is one adopted in debate for the sake of argument. From the logical point of view, however, the important distinction is that the demonstrative premiss is true and necessary, while the dialectical premiss need not be so.[2] In demonstration we start from true premisses and arrive with necessity at a true conclusion: in other words, we have proof. In dialectical argument, on the other hand, the premisses are not known to be true, and there is no necessity that the conclusion be true. If there is an approach to truth through dialectic, it must be more indirect.

We may distinguish three types of discourse in which proof is sought and demanded. In pure mathematics we seek to prove abstract *a priori* truths, in metaphysics we seek to prove very general propositions about the structure of the world, and in everyday argument, especially political or forensic argument, we look for proofs of contingent propositions. Of these three only mathematics answers obviously to Aristotle's description of demonstrative argument, and mathematics provides the larger number of his illustrations of demonstration. Since it is likely that the first logical inquiries were stimulated by reflection on such reasoning, we shall consider this first.

## 2. *Geometrical Demonstration*

It seems probable that the notion of demonstration attracted attention first in connexion with geometry. It is well known that

[1] *De Soph. Elench.* 2 (165ᵇ1).　　[2] *An. Post.* i. 19 (81ᵇ18).

the Egyptians had discovered some truths of geometry empirically, e.g. a formula for calculating the volume of a pyramid, and the name 'geometry', which originally meant the same as 'land measurement', shows how the study was considered when it was introduced to Greece. The great achievement of the Greeks was to replace this empirical study by a demonstrative *a priori* science. Some stories give Thales (640–546 B.C.) the credit for *proving* the first theorem in geometry,[1] but the systematic study of the science seems to have begun in the Pythagorean school.

Pythagoras is said to have been born at Samos some time in the first half of the sixth century B.C. and to have emigrated to Croton, a Greek city in southern Italy, where he founded an ascetic order and taught the doctrine of metempsychosis. Here we have the origin of the notion of philosophy as a way of life. It is possible, indeed, that the word 'philosophy', meaning originally love of wisdom, was coined in the Pythagorean school to describe the way which the Master had shown when he called himself φιλόσοφος. Here also we have the beginning of intellectualism, the doctrine that the most important faculty of man is his intellect and that truths which can be learnt only by the use of the intellect are in some way more noble and fundamental than those learnt by observation. We may regret the evils of a *priori* metaphysics which were brought into the world by this doctrine, but it is only fair to say that it gained influence because the discovery of a *priori* knowledge naturally excites the admiration of intelligent men. For a while the order of Pythagoras was dominant in Croton, but there was presently a reaction, and Pythagoras went to live at Metapontum, where he died at the end of the sixth or the beginning of the fifth century. It has been conjectured that the final downfall of the order as a political force came about 450 B.C., and that it was this collapse which brought Pythagoreans to the mainland of Hellas. If we may take Plato's *Phaedo* as evidence, there were Pythagoreans living at Thebes when Socrates died in 399 B.C., but they were men who had dropped a good deal of the religious teaching of their founder, and in particular his theory of the transmigration of souls, in order to concentrate attention on the scientific side of the tradition.

Let us now consider what is involved in the customary presentation of elementary geometry as a deductive science. First of all, certain propositions of the science must be taken as true without demonstration; secondly, all the other propositions of the science must be derived from these; and, thirdly, the derivation

[1] Proclus, *In Primum Euclidis Elementorum Librum Commentarii*, ed. Friedlein, p. 65.

must be made without any reliance on geometrical assertions
other than those taken as primitive, i.e. it must be *formal* or independent of the special subject matter discussed in geometry.
From our point of view the third is the most important requirement: elaboration of a deductive system involves consideration
of the relation of logical consequence or entailment. Historically geometry was the first body of knowledge to be presented
in this way, and ever since Greek times it has been regarded as
the paradigm of deductive system-building. Hence, for example,
the title of Spinoza's work, *Ethica more geometrico demonstrata.*
It would be wrong, however, to suggest that all this was clear
to Pythagoras and his immediate followers. On the contrary, we
must suppose that for the first Greek geometers any procedure
was admissible which helped them to 'see' the truth of a theorem.
They probably used methods like those of some modern teachers
who find Euclid's work too academic; but they had the excuse
that they were still seeking the light, not sinning against it. This
point can be illustrated by consideration of the theorem about
the square on the hypotenuse of a right-angled triangle which is
always attributed to Pythagoras and was presumably discovered
in his school. The proof we find in Euclid is rather complicated,
in that it requires a number of lemmata, or preliminary theorems.
These other theorems may have been known to the early Pythagoreans, but it is hardly to be supposed that they discovered
things in the order in which they are presented by Euclid, and
it seems likely that the first 'demonstration' of Pythagoras'
theorem consisted in the construction of a figure from which the
theorem could be 'read off'. Modern editors of Euclid have suggested such a figure, or rather pair of figures:[1]

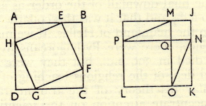

In the first of these, four equal right-angled triangles are arranged
in such a way that their hypotenuses enclose an area: in the
second, four triangles of the same dimensions are arranged to form
two rectangles with the sides OQ and PQ at right angles. It then
seems obvious that the area EFGH in the first figure is the square
on the hypotenuse and equal to the sum of the areas PQOL and

[1] T. L. Heath, *The Thirteen Books of Euclid's Elements*, i, p. 354.

MJNQ of the second figure, which are the squares on the other two sides of one of the right-angled triangles. But for a rigorous proof it would be necessary to show that the three areas just mentioned are indeed squares. By the beginning of the third century B.C. when Euclid wrote, the ideal of demonstration had become clear to geometers. No one can read Euclid's *Elements* without realizing that his aim was to put all his special geometrical assumptions at the beginning and to construct chains of demonstration in which the theorems followed from axioms by purely formal necessity. It is true that in the proof of the first proposition of his first book Euclid assumed that two equal circles each of which has its centre on the circumference of the other must intersect in two places, although he had laid down no explicit postulate from which this follows; but it seems clear that if anyone had brought this defect to his notice he would have tried to remove it by setting down a new postulate.

Unfortunately we have no complete work of geometry earlier than Euclid's *Elements*, and we cannot trace in detail the process by which the Greeks became aware of the requirements of demonstration; but we know that there were books of elements, i.e. deductive treatises, before Euclid's. Scraps of early proofs are preserved in the works of Plato and Aristotle,[1] and material from a history of geometry by Aristotle's pupil Eudemus is to be found in Proclus' commentary on Euclid. It is therefore safe to say that the ideal of a deductive system was known in the Pythagorean school and in the Platonic Academy, which continued some of its traditions. But there was probably a good deal of confusion in the minds of many who read the earliest books of elements. Aristotle tells us that some people said there could be no demonstration and others that demonstration could be circular.[2] In order to understand why queer views of this kind were current, we must realize that the earliest books of elements probably differed in their choice of axioms, since there may be many different ways of presenting geometrical propositions in a deductive system. If this was so, propositions which were derivative in one system would be primitive in another, and the project of demonstration might easily become suspect to the half-initiated.

Now if reflection of the kind we call logical began in this context, what parts of logic, as we know it, should we expect to find stressed in the earliest exposition? In the first place we should expect to find special attention paid to general propositions, that is to say, propositions about *kinds* of things. For in geometry we are not concerned with individuals. We may sometimes talk of

[1] T. L. Heath, *Mathematics in Aristotle*.     [2] *An. Post.* i. 3 (72$^b$5–18).

'the line AB' as though we were referring to a particular line, but it is always understood by geometers that this is just a way of speaking about all lines that satisfy a certain condition, e.g. that of being hypotenuse in a right-angled triangle. Secondly, among universal propositions (i.e. general propositions about *all* of a kind) we should expect to find special attention paid to those which are necessarily true. For when we do geometry in the Greek way, we must distinguish between universal propositions which must be true from the nature of the case and those which just happen to be true (e.g. that each book of the *Iliad* contains less than a thousand lines), and we suppose that the universal propositions of geometry are all of the first kind. It is not likely, of course, that the Greeks were able to formulate the distinction clearly as soon as they began to do geometry; as we shall see, it cost Aristotle some effort to reach this position. But a sure instinct guided them to pay special attention to those propositions which are in fact necessarily true. Thirdly, among universal propositions which are necessarily true we should expect definitions to receive special (but not exclusive) attention. A reader who is familiar with modern logic may perhaps deny that definitions are necessarily true propositions, and suggest that they are merely records of our determination to use certain abbreviations when we find it convenient to do so. To the Greeks, however, it did not seem that definitions were mere conventions. There is a great deal of muddle in the doctrine of real definition which started at this time, but it is easy to understand the Greek attitude if we remember that before the Greeks began to do demonstrative geometry words such as 'circle' had meaning only as standing for certain perceptual patterns. When a Greek said 'A circle is the locus of points equidistant from a given point', he was not introducing the word 'circle' for the first time, but rather giving it new connexions; and to himself he seemed to be expounding a truth of great importance about circles. Fourthly, we should expect to find great interest in the subsumption of specific varieties under general rules, since this seems to be the most common pattern of argument in geometry. Now all these features are to be found, as we shall see, in the logic of Aristotle, and some of them already in Plato's work or earlier. Aristotle tells us, for example, that Archytas, a Pythagorean mathematician who influenced Plato, had views about the proper form of definitions.[1] It is, therefore, reasonable to suppose that one trend in Greek logic was determined in large part by reflection on the problems of presenting geometry as a deductive system.

[1] *Metaphysica, H,* 2 (1043ª21).

## 3. *Dialectic and Metaphysical Argument*

The character of Greek logic cannot be explained wholly in terms of demonstration (ἀπόδειξις). As we have already seen, Aristotle in the first account of syllogistic considered that his study covered also dialectical arguments. The word 'dialectic' had a number of different shades of meaning even in the early stages of philosophy, and it is of particular interest to us as the first technical term to be used for the subject we now call logic. Aristotle's word 'analytics' refers to his treatises rather than to their subject-matter, and 'logic' itself does not appear with its modern sense until the commentaries of Alexander of Aphrodisias, who wrote in the third century A.D.

In its earliest sense the word 'dialectic' is the name for the method of argument which is characteristic of metaphysics. It is derived from the verb διαλέγεσθαι, which means 'discuss', and, as we have already seen, Aristotle thinks of a dialectical premiss as one chosen by a disputant in an argument.[1] Plato's dialogues give numerous illustrations of the method of argument intended. In the *Theaetetus*, for example, Theaetetus lays down the thesis that knowledge is perception, and from this premiss Socrates draws conclusions which eventually force Theaetetus to abandon it.[2] The same illustration serves also to bring out the more precise meaning which 'dialectic' has for Plato in the dialogues of his middle period. There it is the examination of propositions called 'hypotheses' by drawing consequences from them. If a consequence is unacceptable, the hypothesis from which it is derived must be rejected. It is clear that, in general, this procedure can lead only to negative results; for the argument will proceed in accordance with the logical schema, 'If P then Q; but not-Q; therefore not-P'. This is the standard argument-pattern of refutation (ἔλεγχος) and it was probably suggested to Plato not only by the practice of Socrates in refuting the uncritically held opinions of his contemporaries, but also by the use of the *reductio ad impossibile* argument in metaphysics by Zeno of Elea. In his *Parmenides* Plato makes Zeno claim to have written a book in which he defends the monism of Parmenides by drawing out the absurd consequences of the supposition that there is plurality.[3] It was perhaps to this remark that Aristotle referred when he said, as reported by both Diogenes Laertius[4] and Sextus Empiricus,[5] that Zeno was the inventor of dialectic.

---

[1] *An. Pr.* i. 1 (24ᵇ1).　　[2] *Theaetetus*, 151E ff.　　[3] *Parmenides*, 128D.
[4] *Vitae*, viii. 57 and ix. 25.
[5] *Adversus Mathematicos*, vii. 7.

In any case what Aristotle attributed to Zeno was presumably the discovery of the use of the *reductio ad impossibile* in metaphysics, and it is possible that this was suggested to Zeno himself by its use in Pythagorean mathematics. For the Pythagoreans are supposed to have discovered the incommensurability of the diagonal with the side of a square (in modern terminology, the irrationality of $\sqrt{2}$), and the proof of this proposition, preserved as an interpolation in our text of Euclid, has the form of a leading-away to the impossible (ἀπαγωγὴ εἰς τὸ ἀδύνατον).[1] When Aristotle has occasion to mention such reasoning, he cites this theorem as though it were the standard example.[2] In the proof it is first supposed for the sake of argument that $\sqrt{2}$ is rational, i.e. that there are two integers, say m and n, which are mutually prime and such that $m/n = \sqrt{2}$ or $m^2 = 2n^2$. From this it follows that $m^2$ must be even and with it m, since a square number cannot have any prime factor which is not also a factor of the number of which it is the square. But if m is even, n must be odd according to our initial supposition that they are mutually prime. Assuming that $m = 2k$, we can infer that $2n^2 = 4k^2$ or $n^2 = 2k^2$; and from this it can be shown by a repetition of the reasoning used above that n must be even. Our hypothesis, therefore, entails incompatible consequences, and so it must be false.

Once established by Zeno as a method of reasoning in philosophy, dialectic had a long history. Among the philosophers who are sometimes called Minor Socratics it was practised by Euclides of Megara. Evidently he stood close to Socrates, for Plato and some other Athenian friends went to stay with him in Megara immediately after the death of Socrates. But it is said that he was also a follower of Parmenides and Zeno. The members of his school were called dialecticians, and we read that Euclides himself 'attacked demonstrations not by the premisses but by the conclusion', which presumably means that he tried to refute his opponents by drawing absurd consequences from their conclusions. Apparently he found all this consistent with his admiration for Socrates; for he even tried to identify the Good of Socrates with the One of Parmenides.[3] But this is not surprising if Socrates himself had adopted the method of Zeno for his own purposes. It is difficult to reach any certainties about the teaching of the historical Socrates, but those passages of Plato's works which because of their dramatic quality seem most reliable as evidence in this connexion suggest that he was not merely a lover of philosophical conversation but one who practised a definite

---

[1] *Elements*, x. 117, relegated to an appendix in Heiberg's edition.
[2] *An. Pr.* i. 23 (41ᵃ26).   [3] Diogenes Laertius, ii. 106–7; Cicero, *Academica*, ii. 129.

technique of refuting hypotheses by showing them to entail incompatible or unwelcome consequences.

It seems, then, that the first precise meaning of the word 'dialectic' was *reductio ad impossibile* in metaphysics. It is to be noticed, however, that the Socratic elenchus differs from the Zenonian in that the consequences drawn from the hypothesis need not be self-contradictory but may on occasions be simply false. Thus in the *Meno* Socrates argues that if virtue were teachable good men would instruct their sons in it, but it is a well-known fact that Pericles, Themistocles, and Aristides did not succeed in making their sons virtuous.[1] Here the philosophical thesis 'Virtue is teachable' is refuted by the deduction from it of an empirical consequence which is known to be false. It is not clear whether Plato was aware of this distinction. In a passage of the *Phaedo* where he discusses the hypothetical method he seems to suggest that all refutation of hypotheses should proceed by deduction of self-contradictory consequences;[2] but not all the arguments in the dialogues fit this pattern exactly. Perhaps the name *reductio ad absurdum* may be allowed to cover those which are not strictly instances of *reductio ad impossibile*.

In the *Republic* Plato seems to have meant something more precise by 'dialectic', namely a method of argument involving refutation but leading eventually to positive results of high generality. This is difficult to understand, and the interpretation of the relevant passages is highly controversial.[3] Perhaps Plato himself was confused, so that no satisfactory account can ever be given of what he meant by 'dialectic' in the context. But in any case he drops the notion in his later works and transfers the name 'dialectic' to the method of division and collection (διαίρεσις καὶ συναγωγή) which is discussed in the *Phaedrus* and *Philebus* and illustrated in the *Sophist* and *Politicus*.[4] The process of collection is not clearly explained and remains obscure, but division is evidently the method of seeking definitions by dichotomy of notions beginning with the most general. In the *Sophist* Socrates illustrates it by producing a definition of an angler as a technician who practises an art of the acquisitive coercive sort through the hunting of living things that swim in the water by striking at them during the day with a hook. Here the string of determinants is obtained by selection of the first alternative at each stage in the following division:

[1] *Meno*, 93 ff.
[2] *Phaedo*, 101D: εἰ δέ τις αὐτῆς τῆς ὑποθέσεως ἔφοιτο ... οὐκ ἀποκρίναιο ἕως ἂν τὰ ἀπ' αὐτῆς ὁρμηθέντα σκέψαιο, εἴ σοι ἀλλήλοις συμφωνεῖ ἢ διαφωνεῖ.
[3] For a thorough discussion see R. Robinson, *Plato's Earlier Dialectic*, ch. x.
[4] *Phaedrus*, 266B; *Philebus*, 16C ff.; *Sophista*, 218E ff.; *Politicus*, 258E ff.

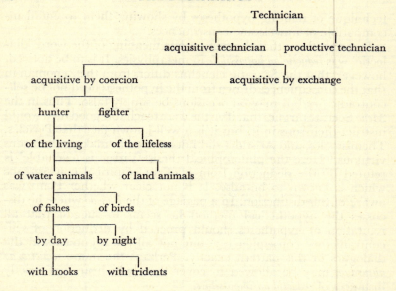

This method, which appears to us trivial and question-begging, is of some importance in the history of logic. The comic poet, Epicrates, gives us evidence that it was practised in the Academy as an exercise to the point of becoming a joke,[1] and the consideration of it undoubtedly influenced Aristotle in his invention of the syllogism.[2]

The only feature common to all Plato's uses of the term 'dialectic' seems to be that it signifies a co-operative method of philosophical investigation, involving a search for definitions, and approved by Plato at the time of writing.[3] In the middle period it is the hypothetical method of refutation together with some mysterious positive addition, while in the later period it is the method of division and collection.

It remained for Aristotle to generalize and weaken the sense of the word 'dialectic'. For him, as we have seen, it is a name for the science of argument from non-evident premisses. It is easy to see how its application could be still further widened to cover the study of valid argument in general.

Plato's contribution to formal logic is not confined to his attempt to work out a dialectical method. We find that from time to time he enunciates logical principles in the course of the dialogues. It is natural that he should do so, for they consist almost entirely of arguments on philosophical topics and it is

[1] Epicrates, fragment 11 in *Comicorum Atticorum Fragmenta*, ed. Kock ii, p. 287.
[2] See below, p. 67.          [3] R. Robinson, *Plato's Earlier Dialectic*, p. 70.

often convenient to strengthen an argument psychologically by adding an explicit statement of its principle. A person who is doubtful of the argument may nevertheless recognize its principle as sound and so be brought to admit the validity of the argument. If we continue in this way we shall in the end be led to enunciate a logical principle. Consider, for example, the following dialogue:

*A.* Plato was a philosopher, so he was vague.
*B.* I don't see.
*A.* All philosophers are vague.

In his second remark A has introduced the principle of his original argument. It is not, however, a principle of logic but an empirical statement. His argument now runs: 'All philosophers are vague, and Plato was a philosopher; therefore Plato was vague.' If B still refuses to admit the argument, which is unlikely in this case, A may further reinforce it by adducing the principle, 'If every M is L and S is an M, then S is L'; and this is a principle of logic, a formal principle whose truth does not depend on any special interpretation given to 'M', 'L', and 'S'.

In this way Plato enunciates a number of logical principles incidentally. One famous example is his formulation of the Law of Contradiction in the course of his argument in the *Republic* to prove that the soul has independent parts.[1] It is an interesting fact, however, that not all the general principles cited by Plato are sound. Thus in the first book of the *Republic* he adduces the principle that 'a man is of the nature of those whom he resembles',[2] and his use of the pronouncement shows that it is supposed to mean that, if a man resembles the members of some class in some respect, he must resemble them in all respects, which is plainly false. We cannot tell for certain whether Plato knew when he was adducing unsound principles. Since he uses the dialogue form, he is not committed to the statements made by any of his characters, and it may be that, whenever he makes one of them argue unsoundly, he is well aware of the fact. On the other hand, the explanation of his fallacious arguments may be simply that matters which are now perfectly plain were very difficult when they were first thought of. It appears, for example, that the ambiguity of the verb 'to be' gave serious trouble to Plato and his contemporaries,[3] although to us the puzzle it presented now seems childish. This is a matter which it is impossible to decide.[4]

Although it is clear that Plato discovered some valid principles of logic in the course of his argument, he is scarcely to be called

---

[1] *Resp.* 436B.    [2] *Resp.* 349D.    [3] *Resp.* 479B. *Sophista*, 243D, 249E ff.
[4] See R. Robinson, 'Plato's Consciousness of Fallacy', *Mind* li (1942), pp. 97–114.

a logician. For he enunciates his principles piecemeal as he needs them, and he makes no attempt to relate them one to another or to connect them in a system as Aristotle connected the various figures and moods of the syllogism. It is not unlikely that he would even have disapproved of logical investigations pursued for their own sake.

## 4. *Eristic and Sophistry*

The connexion of early logical thinking with the arguments of the law-courts and what Aristotle calls 'encounters' (ἐντεύξεις)[1] is not so easy to trace, and it is possible that our evidence is to some extent distorted. In what follows it is argued that some logical thinking had been done before Aristotle which had its source in the criticism of everyday factual argument, and that this helped to give rise to a tradition independent of Aristotle, that of the Megarians and the Stoics.

The first tentative steps towards logical thinking are taken when men try to generalize about valid arguments and to extract from some particular valid argument a form or principle which is common to a whole class of valid arguments. It is natural to think of this form as correctly expressed in a verbal pattern which can be detected in the argument. Aristotle, for example, collects a whole class of valid arguments under the principle 'If no B is $A$, then no $A$ is $B$'.[2] This highly natural way of thinking can, however, be misleading, for it is possible to find two arguments apparently of exactly similar verbal form, the one of which is valid, the other invalid. Consider, for example, the following arguments:

1. This is a pen; this is blue; therefore this is a blue pen.
2. That dog is a father; that dog is his; therefore that dog is his father.

The former appears to be perfectly valid, but the latter, which is adapted from Plato's *Euthydemus*, is a fallacy, since, if it is applied to some particular dog and some particular human being, the premisses may well be true, while the conclusion is obviously false.

Arguments which are like the second of the above in that they are fallacious and yet bear a misleading resemblance to valid arguments are called by Aristotle *sophisms*,[3] and he implies that there were men called Sophists who made their living by inventing such arguments and exhibiting them in public.[4] This seems

[1] *Topica*, i. 2 (101ª27).                       [2] *An. Pr.* i. 2 (25ª15).
[3] *Topica*, viii. 11 (162ª14).                   [4] *De Soph. Elench.* 1 (165ª19–37).

implausible, and yet it has the full support of Plato. For in his dialogue called *Euthydemus* he presents two sophists, Euthydemus and Dionysodorus, giving a sort of advertisement display in which they prove by means of sophisms such paradoxical propositions as that no one can tell a lie (284c), that Socrates knows everything (293c), and that the father of Ctesippus is a dog (298c).

Apart from the *Euthydemus* our best evidence concerning sophisms and their use is Aristotle's *De Sophisticis Elenchis*, an appendix to the *Topics*, which is generally regarded as one of the earliest of Aristotle's logical works. In the *Topics* he gives chiefly rules for conducting disputes by means of valid arguments, in the *De Sophisticis Elenchis* rules for the invention and detection of invalid arguments. The latter work resembles the *Euthydemus* (from which in fact about a tenth of its examples could have been drawn) in that most of the examples are not only fallacious but also trivial in subject-matter and unlikely to deceive an intelligent child for a moment. There are, however, a few serious examples drawn from mathematics and metaphysics.[1]

The *Euthydemus* and the *De Sophisticis Elenchis* present clear evidence that the practice of public dispute according to set rules was well established. In general only two persons take part in the dispute, one as questioner and the other as answerer. It is the part of the answerer to maintain a thesis, of the questioner to upset it by making the answerer admit that false or absurd consequences follow from it. Aristotle gives rules and hints for both questioner and answerer in the last book of his *Topics* and in his *De Sophisticis Elenchis*. What is not so clear is the purpose of these disputes, or why people should have been paid for instructing others in the art of disputation. We have evidence in Plato for the use of this method for two purposes, philosophical investigation and mere amusement. His own dialogues are themselves examples of the use of the method in philosophical investigation and it is interesting to observe that the conduct of the argument often follows the pattern suggested by Aristotle. In the *Republic*, however, Plato issues a warning against the use of the method of disputation, especially by the young, for mere amusement.[2] It appears from his description that the power of argument went easily to the heads of the Athenians.

Aristotle says in the *Topics* that what he teaches is useful for these two purposes (if we can identify his 'encounters' with Plato's 'amusement').[3] It is also possible, however, that those who taught the art of disputation had two other ends in view. In the

---

[1] e.g. squaring the circle in *De Soph. Elench.* 11 (171$^b$15) and the 'third man' ibid. 22 (178$^b$36).    [2] *Resp.* 498A and 539B.    [3] *Topica*, i. 2 (101$^a$27).

first place, they may have considered the use of argument for practical purposes. A little imagination will show that even the most preposterous examples of the *Euthydemus* or the *De Sophisticis Elenchis* could be used in a law court either to confute an opponent who produced a subtly fallacious argument or to confuse a jury faced with a sound one. The move would be 'You might as well say . . .'. Suppose a lawyer to argue, 'There is evidence to show that my client is a generous man. It is well known that he is the plaintiff's neighbour. Is it likely that a generous neighbour would do what my client is accused of doing?' The argument about the dog could be used to cast doubt on this. The traditional story of Protagoras and Euathlus[1] show that the notion of setting logical puzzles to juries did not seem absurd to the Greeks.

While it is quite likely that the earliest sophisms were invented in such practical contexts[2] and that it was the possibility of such practical application together with its amusement value which made the art of the sophists so popular, it is also possible (and this is of much greater interest for our purpose) that some of the teachers of the art were engaged in a serious attempt to discover principles of logic and to distinguish them from verbal formulae. One context in which ridiculous examples such as those of the *Euthydemus* abound is a logic course for beginners. It would be very easy to misinterpret a dispute undertaken for the sake of logical investigation as one undertaken for mere amusement, especially if attention were concentrated on the ridiculous examples. This is what Plato may have done when he wrote the *Euthydemus*, i.e. he may have misrepresented a logical investigation as a verbal exercise undertaken to amuse the spectators. It is not impossible even that such misrepresentation might be deliberate, for Plato would probably have been averse to logical investigation carried out for its own sake without the further aim of establishing moral or metaphysical truth.[3] He was certainly not opposed to all logical investigation as such, nor yet to the use of trivial examples, as we see from his account of the process of division in the *Sophist* and the *Politicus*; but while his dialogues contain much logical material, none of them is purely logical in content. It is significant that in the Peripatetic tradition, which throughout its history bears traces of its Platonic origin, logic never became a part of philosophy, a subject in its own right,

[1] Aulus Gellius, *Noctes Atticae*, v. 10.
[2] Cf. the stock charge against the sophists of 'making the worse appear the better reason'.
[3] Cf. his attitude to mathematics in the *Republic*, where this science is treated as essentially a propaedeutic to metaphysics. The same point is brought out very clearly in *Euthydemus* 290c.

but was treated as a capacity (δύναμις) which might be acquired or as an art (τεχνή) to be learnt.[1]

Against the suggestion that logical investigations of this nature were already being carried out in Plato's time or before, the evidence of Aristotle may be quoted. He claims at the end of the *De Sophisticis Elenchis* to be breaking entirely new ground. He says, contrasting his study with that of Rhetoric, 'Of this inquiry, on the other hand, it was not the case that part of the work had been thoroughly done before, while part had not. Nothing existed at all.'[2] Perhaps all he means is that there was no systematic treatise on the subject of argument; but if he means further that no one had tried to give principles as distinct from examples, he is refuted by his own words. For he says in the same work that there is no true distinction such as some people have made between arguments directed against expressions and arguments directed against thought,[3] and also that it is absurd to discuss refutation (ἔλεγχος) without discussing reasoning (συλλογισμός),[4] which implies that some people had done so.

It seems likely then that some logical discussion suggested by the puzzles arising in everyday discourse was already taking place before Aristotle wrote. It is natural to suppose that its centre was the Megarian school, of which the founder was Euclides, a disciple of Socrates and the elder contemporary of Plato. The Megarians were universally credited with skill at verbal controversy and according to Diogenes Laertius[5] were at one time called 'Eristics'. 'Eristic' is the invidious term applied by Plato and Aristotle to argument which they regard as frivolous. We know at least that the Megarians of the generations after Aristotle, Diodorus Cronus and Philo, showed a genuine understanding of logical problems, and it is difficult to see how they could have made the progress they did without previous preparation.

It is probable then that the early Megarians took part in, and were stimulated to logical discovery by, such disputes as we find satirized in Plato's *Euthydemus*. They must also have been influenced by reflection on metaphysical argument; for there is evidence of their connexion with the Eleatics. As we have already noticed, Euclides is said to have applied himself to the works of Parmenides[5] and to have criticized arguments by attacking their conclusions rather than their premisses,[6] which suggests that he

[1] Alexander, *In Aristotelis An. Pr. Lib. I Commentarium*, ed. Wallies, *Commentaria in Aristotelem Graeca*, ii (i), p. 1; Philoponus, *in Aristotelis An. Pr. Commentaria*, ed. Wallies, *C.I.A.G.* xiii (ii), p. 6. This series will be cited in future by the abbreviation '*C.I.A.G.*'          [2] *De Soph. Elench.* 34 (183ᵇ34–36).
[3] Ibid. 10 (170ᵇ12–14).          [4] Ibid. (171ᵃ1–2).
[5] *Vitae*, ii. 106.          [6] Ibid. 107.

was fond of the *reductio ad absurdum* method of Zeno. A combination of the two influences seems to have been at work on Eubulides, the successor of Euclides, when he invented the Liar and several other well-known sophisms which, as we shall see, are of considerable logical interest. The Liar is one of the many puzzles connected with the notions of truth and falsehood. These are of great importance to logic, because the fundamental notion of logic is validity and this is definable in terms of truth and falsehood.

Further evidence that pre-Aristotelian thinkers were seriously concerned with the notions of truth and falsehood is provided by the curious fragment called the *Dissoi Logoi*.[1] If genuine, this was written about the end of the fifth or the beginning of the fourth century B.C.; and it is in a Doric dialect, so that it may be of Megarian origin. It is obviously part of the protracted debate on the possibility of falsehood and contradiction. As the fragment is mutilated, it is impossible to be certain of its purpose, but the author seems to be arguing that it is possible not only to make contradictory statements (ἀντιλέγειν) but even to maintain in a variety of contexts two plausible theses which contradict each other. To this end he sets out a series of antinomies, each one with thesis and antithesis. Of special interest is the fourth antinomy in which the writer shows that it is possible to uphold either side of a contradiction about true and false discourse. In the thesis he tries to prove that true and false discourse are identical by quoting the example of a verbal form, e.g. 'I am an initiate', which is true when spoken by A but false when spoken by B. It is possible, however, to draw from this argument the conclusion that it is not the verbal expression (the sentence) which can properly be called true or false. These predicates must be applied to what is expressed by the sentence, i.e. the statement or proposition. We may have here the origin of the Stoic distinction between φωνή and λεκτόν.[2] This argument makes the same point about the notions of truth and falsity which the argument in the *Euthydemus* makes about validity, namely that they cannot be attached to verbal patterns as such.

We may conclude from this evidence, then, that there had been considerable reflection on topics of formal logic before Aristotle wrote the works now known as the *Organon*. This is not to belittle Aristotle's achievement; for the *Prior Analytics* is undoubtedly the first systematic treatise on formal logic.

---

[1] H. Diels, *Fragmente der Vorsokratiker* (7th ed.), vol. ii, pp. 405 ff. See also A. E. Taylor, *Varia Socratica*, 3.
[2] Sextus Empiricus, *Adversus Mathematicos*, viii. 11–12.

## 5. *Plato and the Philosophy of Logic*

Although, as we have seen, Plato was perhaps averse to the study of formal logic for its own sake, he is undoubtedly the first great thinker in the field of the philosophy of logic. He treats at some length three important questions which arise as soon as we begin to reflect on the nature of logic, namely:

(1) What is it that can properly be called true or false?
(2) What link is it that makes valid inference possible, or what is necessary connexion?
(3) What is the nature of definition and what is it that we define?

We shall discuss Plato's treatment of the questions in this order, trying to show how each arises and the nature of the relation between them. It must be understood, however, that Plato does not address himself directly to these questions, which seem central and important to us. They have emerged clearly only after centuries of reflection; and as we read Plato, it seems to us that they are still obscured for him by the metaphysical and epistemological questions with which they are inextricably interwoven. There are to be detected in his writings answers which anticipate later thinking, but when we extract them for separate discussion we may perhaps be presenting his thought in a guise which he would hardly recognize. For our purposes the most important texts are two dialogues of the later period, the *Theaetetus* and the *Sophist*, especially the *Sophist*.

The question 'What is it that can properly be called true or false?' arises in the *Theaetetus* in the attempt to define knowledge. Theaetetus' second attempt at definition identifies knowledge with true opinion (ἀληθὴς δόξα).[1] Opinion then is most naturally regarded by Plato as being true or false. But what is an opinion? Is it a psychological event peculiar to one person or something which may be shared by many? It appears that the same ambiguity infects the Greek as the English word. Later in the same dialogue Socrates gives an explanation of what it is to form an opinion. This he also treats, without appearing to notice the difference, as an explanation of what it is to think (διανοεῖσθαι):

'*Socrates.* Do you call thinking what I call thinking?
*Theaetetus.* What is that?
*Socrates.* The talk (λόγον) which the soul holds with herself on what she sees. It appears to me that, when she thinks, she is doing nothing else than conversing, asking questions and giving answers, affirming

[1] *Theaetetus*, 178B.

C

and denying. When she reaches a decision and is not in doubt, we call
that opinion. So what I call forming an opinion is talking (λέγειν)
and opinion is speech that is held not with someone else or aloud
(φωνῇ) but in silence with oneself.[1]

The identification of thought or opinion with talk or discourse
suggests the transference of the predicates, 'true' and 'false' to
talk or discourse. This thought is carried over into the *Sophist*
where Plato makes the same identification of thought with internal
speech. There the discussion as a whole is directed towards the
solution of the problem 'How can there be falsity?' and it
appears that Plato regards falsity as characterizing primarily
speech or sentence (λόγος)[2] and derivatively thought, opinion,
and fancy.[3] The same of course applies to truth. Can we conclude from this that Plato regards the form of words, the sentence,
as that which is true or false? In our consideration of the δισσοὶ
λόγοι we have already seen reason to doubt the complete satis-
factoriness of such a view. But Plato is by no means clearly committed to it. The Greek word λόγος is highly ambiguous. In the
present passage it seems sometimes to mean quite plainly 'sentence'; for Plato insists that a complete λόγος must be made up of
at least one noun and one verb,[4] and refers to the Greek equivalents of 'A man learns' and 'Theaetetus sits' as λόγοι.[5] On the
other hand, it comes most natural to him to think of that which
is true or false as arising *in the soul*,[6] and he could easily return to
the view that thought, opinion, and fancy are most properly
called true and false.

We can, then, detect at least two possible answers to our question in Plato. Sometimes it is suggested that the proper subject
of the predicates 'true' and 'false' is a sentence or verbal pattern.
And at other times it is suggested that the proper subject is a
psychological event which occurs when the verbal pattern is
formed or used by a person in overt or silent discourse. These
two answers recur constantly in the history of the philosophy of
logic. The former is in modern times associated with the word
'sentence', the latter with the word 'judgement'. For a formulation of a third possible answer, that associated with the word
'proposition', we must wait for the Stoics.

If we regard valid inference as the tracing of necessary connexions, it seems that the answer to our first question must carry
with it an answer to our second. That is to say, if it is sentences
that are true or false, then we trace necessary connexions between
sentences when we make valid inferences; if, however, it is

---

[1] *Theaetetus*, 189E–190A.    [2] *Sophista*, 263B.    [3] Ibid. 263D.
[4] Ibid. 262A.    [5] Ibid. 262C, 263A.    [6] Ibid. 263D.

thoughts, then in valid inference we find some sort of necessary connexion between thoughts. But the second view is obviously confused and inadequate. For 'necessary connexion between thoughts' suggests something that always holds when we think, and it is clear that we do not always infer validly. Historically recognition of this confusion and inadequacy has often led to rejection of the suggestion that it is judgements which may properly be called true or false. The first view is characteristic of conventionalists, i.e. of those philosophers who hold that necessary connexion, like the linguistic expressions between which it holds, is in some sense man-made and arbitrary. Plato, however, does not seem to accept either of the two doctrines. According to him necessary connexion holds between Forms ($\epsilon\tilde{\iota}\delta\eta$).

The Platonic doctrine of Forms has a whole literature devoted to it. However we interpret it, two negative points seem clear. Forms are neither things in the ordinary sense nor 'ideas' in the mind, but correspond in part at least to what later philosophers have called 'universals'. The theory is introduced in the following way in two passages of the *Republic*:

'The same holds of the just and the unjust, the good and the bad, and all the Forms. Each by itself is one, but as they appear everywhere through their communion with actions and bodies and with each other, each seems to be many.'[1]

'We have been accustomed to assume a single Form for each group of things to which we apply a common name.'[2]

These passages suggest that the Form is a character or set of characters common to a number of things, i.e. the feature in reality which corresponds to a general word. But Plato also uses language which suggests not only that the Forms exist separately ($\chi\omega\rho\iota\sigma\tau\acute{a}$) from all the particulars, but also that each Form is a peculiarly accurate or good particular of its own kind, i.e. the standard particular of the kind in question or the model ($\pi\alpha\rho\acute{a}\delta\epsilon\iota\gamma\mu\alpha$) to which other particulars approximate. Thus he frequently calls a Form 'the so-and-so itself', e.g. 'the man himself', 'the bed itself' ($\alpha\mathord{\mathaccent"712 \iota}\tau\grave{o}s$ $\acute{o}$ $\mathring{\alpha}\nu\theta\rho\omega\pi\sigma$, $\alpha\mathord{\mathaccent"712 \iota}\tau\grave{\eta}$ $\acute{\eta}$ $\kappa\lambda\acute{\iota}\nu\eta$). This is a mistake, if the Form is supposed to be also a general character. For general characters are not characterized by themselves: humanity is not human. The mistake is encouraged by the fact that in Greek the same phrase may signify both the concrete and the abstract, e.g. $\tau\grave{o}$ $\lambda\epsilon\upsilon\kappa\acute{o}\nu$ (literally 'the white') both 'the white thing' and 'whiteness', so that it is doubtful whether $\alpha\mathord{\mathaccent"712 \iota}\tau\grave{o}$ $\tau\grave{o}$ $\lambda\epsilon\upsilon\kappa\acute{o}\nu$ (literally 'the white itself') means 'the superlatively white

---

[1] *Resp.* 476A.       [2] Ibid. 596A.

thing' or 'whiteness in abstraction'. Some admirers have denied that Plato ever fell into the error of 'Platonism', but it is quite certain that Aristotle thought he did, and Aristotle's own thinking on the philosophy of logic was largely determined by his objections to Plato's Theory of Forms as he conceived it.

Both in the *Republic* and in the *Sophist* there is a strong suggestion that correct thinking is following out the connexions between Forms. The model is mathematical thinking, e.g. the proof given in the *Meno*[1] that the square on the diagonal is double the original square in area. For Plato necessary connexions hold between Forms, and inference is presumably valid when we follow in thought the connexions between Forms as they are. How is this view related to the theory which assigns truth and falsity to sentences made up of nouns and verbs? Plato seems to hold that a sentence is true if the arrangement of its parts reflects or corresponds to a connexion between Forms. Discourse is possible only on the supposition that there is connexion between Forms (συμπλοκὴ τῶν εἰδῶν),[2] and true discourse speaks of realities as they are (λέγει τὰ ὄντα ὡς ἔστι).[3] It is curious, however, that Plato gives a singular sentence, 'Theaetetus sits' as an illustration of true discourse, for this would certainly not in our way of thinking involve only Forms. But he never dealt clearly with the distinction between singular and general statements and we shall see later that even Aristotle did not pay sufficient attention to the difference.

Another part of the *Sophist* which was probably fruitful in logical theory is Plato's discussion of the role of the terms 'being', 'same', and 'other'.[4] He holds that the Forms signified by these words can 'communicate' with any other Forms, including contraries, such as motion and rest, and even their own contraries. Otherness, for example, is the same as itself, and sameness other than otherness. Thus we may justify the apparently contradictory sentences 'The same is other' and 'The other is the same'. These terms are in fact in a peculiar sense pervasive and do not serve, like ordinary common nouns or adjectives e.g. 'kangaroo' or 'red', to pick out classes of objects. There are no classes of existent objects, other objects, or same objects. Plato's discussion is rather confusing in that he refers to these three forms, together with motion and rest as 'five greatest kinds' (μέγιστα γένη). But he does not suggest that motion and rest have the same peculiar character as the other three. They are used rather as illustrations to exhibit the pervasiveness of the others. It would be wrong to

---

[1] *Meno*, 84D–85B.
[2] *Sophista*, 259E.
[3] Ibid. 263B.
[4] Ibid. 254B ff.

suggest that μέγιστον γένος means 'pervasive form' or that Plato
had a theory of pervasive forms, but this discussion directed
attention to them and may have suggested Aristotle's theory of
terms predicable in various categories.

Our third question concerns the nature of definitions. Many
of Plato's dialogues take the form of a search for definitions, and,
according to Aristotle, this interest in definitions is derived from
Socrates' attempt to define ethical terms.[1] But it is likely that
Plato was also impressed by the importance of definition in
mathematics. It is clear that he, like the earlier mathematicians,
regarded definition as both non-arbitrary and informative.
There is, he thinks, a right and a wrong answer to the question
'What is justice?' or 'What is colour?' and the rightness or wrong-
ness is not determined solely by the way the ordinary Greek used
the words δικαιοσύνη or χρῶμα. Plato knew, of course, that the
imposition of words was in a sense arbitrary or conventional, i.e.
that a different word could have been used in the very same way
in which the average Greek used the word χρῶμα; for the mere
existence of different languages shows this. But he held that definition is concerned with the thing to which the word refers rather
than with the word itself. What is defined is the Form or common
nature present in many particular things. This may be called
the 'realistic' theory of definition, and it is historically connected
with the phrase, 'real definition'. Aristotle was undoubtedly influenced by it in his account of definition and in his thinking on
logic in general, in spite of the fact that he rejected the Platonic
Theory of Forms. Because of his Platonic training he expected
to find as the ultimate object of intellect and the foundation of
valid inference a system or chain of Forms whose interrelation-
ships limit the possibilities of actual existence and determine the
correctness or incorrectness of scientific thought. Furthermore,
he tried always to obey the Platonic injunction to look to the
thing rather than to the word, and long after his time his followers,
the Peripatetics, used this misleading antithesis in their criticisms
of the Stoics, whom they despised as mere word-mongers.

Before leaving Plato we should mention his contribution to the
development of logic by the clearing up of two ancient puzzles.
From the time of Parmenides with his warning against entertaining the supposition that not-being is, the Greeks had found something mysterious in negation and consequently in falsehood. In the
*Theaetetus* and the *Sophist*[2] Plato examines these notions and solves
the puzzles concerning them by making it clear that discourse
(λόγος) is essentially that which can be true or false: that is to say,

[1] *Metaphysica*, A, 6 (987ᵇ1–4).     [2] *Theaetetus*, 187D ff.; *Sophista*, 237A ff.

no assertion is significant unless its denial is also significant. In the same passage he resolves the problem arising from the confusion between statements of identity and statements of predication.[1] This confusion had led some philosophers to deny the possibility of any predication other than identical predication. The views that non-identical predication and negation were nonsensical would have been serious stumbling-blocks to the development of logical theory. Plato's efforts enabled Aristotle to treat them as mere historical curiosities.[2] They certainly did not trouble him in his logical writings.

[1] On this passage see J. L. Ackrill, 'Plato and the Copula: *Sophist* 251–9', *Journal of Hellenic Studies*, lxxvii, part i (1957), pp. 1–6.    [2] *Physica*, i. 3 ($187^a3$ ff.).

## II

## ARISTOTLE'S *ORGANON*

### 1. *The Contents of the* Organon

WHEN Aristotle's writings were collected by his pupils after his death in 322 B.C., a number of his treatises on reasoning were grouped together, and the collection came in time to be called the *Organon*, or instrument of science. The word 'logic' did not acquire its modern sense until some 500 years later, when it was used by Alexander of Aphrodisias; but the scope of the study later called logic was determined by the contents of the *Organon*. Since, however, these writings do not form an ordered whole, having apparently been composed at different dates and without a single plan; it is necessary to say something about the various treatises.

It is in general very difficult to determine the dates, even the relative dates, of Aristotle's works. Many of them are in the form of lecture notes and Aristotle seems to have been in the habit of revising them constantly and inserting references to works written later. This applies to the works composing the *Organon*. It is generally agreed among scholars, however, that the treatise called the *Categories*, or at any rate its first draft, comprising chapters 1–8, is the earliest of these writings. Its doctrine, which is metaphysical rather than logical in a strict sense, appears as an integral part of the argument in all the other works. Although it has been extremely influential, it is very difficult to interpret with any confidence. On the face of it, it is a classification of types of predicate (κατηγορίαι). Aristotle gives a list of ten supreme predicates or types of predicate. These are substance (οὐσία), quantity (ποσόν), quality (ποιόν), relation (πρός τι), place (ποῦ), time (ποτέ), situation (κεῖσθαι), state (ἔχειν) action, (ποιεῖν), and passion (πάσχειν). The detailed interpretation of this work will be discussed later.

Next in order, or contemporary, is the work called the *Topics*, with its appendix the *De Sophisticis Elenchis*. This is of interest because it seems to spring directly from a consideration of the dialectical encounters we have already discussed. The subject-matter is stated to be 'dialectical reasoning', which is defined as 'reasoning which proceeds from opinions that are generally accepted' and opposed to demonstrative reasoning, i.e. reasoning from premisses which are true and primary.

Another early work is the *Peri Hermeneias*. The name means literally 'On Exposition', and since the Renaissance the book has been known by its Latin name, *De Interpretatione*. Aristotle's main purpose in this work is to determine what pairs of statements are opposed and in what ways. His interest in opposition is perhaps determined by the practical requirements of dialectical argument as described in the *Topics*. The development of the main theme is preceded by a discussion of the notion of statement, a brief contribution to the philosophy of logic, which occupies the first four chapters.

There remain two works, called the *Prior Analytics* and the *Posterior Analytics*, which contain Aristotle's most mature thought about logic. Of these the first is concerned with the analysis of arguments according to their forms, i.e. according to the various figures and moods of the syllogism, which is Aristotle's chief contribution to logic, and the second with the special requirements of demonstration. Aristotle opens the *Prior Analytics* with the statement that his subject in that treatise is demonstration, but he quickly corrects himself by saying that the contrast between demonstration and dialectic is irrelevant to the syllogism, since both the demonstrator and the dialectician argue syllogistically.[1] It is clear, then, that according to Aristotle's final view the formal theory of the syllogism is not especially connected with demonstration. But the close association of the *Prior Analytics* and the *Posterior Analytics* and the opening statement of the former suggest that he came to the doctrine of the syllogism by the investigation of reasoning which he called demonstrative (e.g. reasoning in mathematics), and that he valued this doctrine chiefly for the insight which he thought it gave into the structure of demonstration. It has even been conjectured that the *Posterior Analytics* was composed before the *Prior Analytics*.[2] This is obviously wrong if it is supposed to mean that the work was complete as we know it before any of the *Prior Analytics* was written; for it contains many references to the doctrine of the syllogism as something already expounded. But it seems not at all improbable that Aristotle began by trying to write a book or set of lectures which would do for demonstration what his *Topics* had already done for dialectic (as he understood it), and that the doctrine of the syllogism was elaborated in the course of this investigation. If he had finished the *Prior Analytics* at the time he started to work on the *Posterior*

*Analytics*, he would have ordered his material in a rather different way. But the point is of no great importance.

Aristotle's major discoveries, which constitute the 'Aristotelian system', are contained in the *De Interpretatione*, chapters 5 to 8 and 10, 11, and 14, and in *Prior Analytics*, i. 1–7. Before discussing these passages we shall give an outline of the earlier works of the *Organon* in their probable historical order.

## 2. *The Doctrine of the* Categories *and its Logical Consequences*

When the *Organon* was put together, the line between logical and non-logical studies was not, and could not be, precisely drawn. The compilers must have found something in common between all these works, but there is a considerable overlap between their content and the content of works not included in the *Organon*, e.g. between the *Topics* and the *Rhetoric* and between the *Categories* and the *Posterior Analytics* on the one hand and the *Metaphysics* on the other. Of all the decisions of the compilers, however, the decision to include the *Categories* in the *Organon* is the most diffi-cult to understand. All the other works are concerned directly or indirectly with the criticism of arguments at that level of generality indicated in the *Rhetoric* as characteristic of dialectic,[1] but much of the doctrine of the *Categories* must be regarded as metaphysical rather than logical. Its inclusion in the *Organon*, however, has ensured that it has been discussed in almost every textbook of logic until very recent times and this alone would make it necessary to consider the treatise here. Moreover, the theory itself, although not logical in a strict sense, has had con-siderable influence on logic, and that not entirely good.

The *Categories* is a work of exceptional ambiguity both in purpose and content. Two major ambiguities are especially note-worthy. In the first place it is unclear whether Aristotle is classify-ing symbols or what they symbolize, words or, in a very wide sense, things. This is a question which has exercised commen-tators since ancient times.[2] Secondly, it is not clear whether Aristotle is concerned with predicates only or with terms in general, including subjects. We shall give the main outlines of the work before attempting to resolve these ambiguities.

After drawing a distinction between homonyms, synonyms, and paronyms, Aristotle states that all expressions (λεγόμενα) are either simple or complex.[3] He further states that every simple expression

---

[1] *Rhetorica*, i. 2 (1358ᵃ10 ff.).
[2] e.g. Porphyry, *In Aristotelis Categorias Expositio per Interrogationem et Responsionem*, ed. Busse, *C.I.A.G.* iv(i), pp. 58–59.
[3] *Categoriae*, 2 (1ᵃ17).

signifies (σημαίνει) either substance or quality or one of the other categories.[1] Most of the rest of the work is devoted to the discussion of the individual categories, and among these substance, which is treated in chapter 5, and quality, which is treated in chapter 8, receive the fullest consideration. The last five chapters do not deal with the categories as such, but with a rather miscellaneous collection of very general terms (opposition, privation, priority, simultaneity, motion, and possession) and their ambiguities. These came to be known later as the *Post-Predicaments*.

In chapter 5 Aristotle draws an important distinction between primary substance (πρώτη οὐσία) and secondary substance (δεύτερα οὐσία):

'Substance in the most literal and primary and common sense of the term is that which is neither predicated of a subject nor exists in a subject, as for example, the individual man or horse. Those things are called secondary substances to which, as species, belong the things called substances in the primary sense and also the genera of these species. For example, the individual man belongs to the species man, and the genus of the species is animal. These, then, are called secondary substances, as for example both man and animal.'[2]

We may now attempt to resolve the ambiguities mentioned above. Is Aristotle here classifying linguistic expressions or what they symbolize? In favour of the first interpretation may be cited the use of the word κατηγορία, which sometimes occurs non-technically with the meaning of 'predicate'.[3] This, however, is far from decisive, since we cannot be sure that Aristotle meant by κατηγορία in the non-technical sense a linguistic expression rather than an attribute. Secondly, the way in which Aristotle introduces the doctrine, 'Expressions (λεγόμενα) which are in no way composite signify (σημαίνει) substance,' etc.[4] suggests that he is thinking primarily of symbols. On the other hand, immediately after introducing the distinction between simple and compound forms of speech he says, 'Of things themselves (τῶν ὄντων) some are predicable of a subject and are never present in a subject. Thus man is predicated of a subject, the individual man, but is present in no subject.'[5]

Aristotle was almost certainly unaware of the ambiguity that puzzles his commentators. He had almost certainly not asked himself the question. 'Does the sign ἄνθρωπος (in the original of the sentence quoted above) stand for the Greek word ἄνθρωπος or for some extra-linguistic entity?' He lacked two devices which

---

[1] *Categoriae*, 4 (1ᵇ25–2ᵃ4).                                    [2] Ibid. 5 (2ᵃ11–19).
[3] *Metaphysica*, Θ, 3 (1047ᵃ34).
[4] *Categoriae*, 4 (1ᵇ25 ff.).                                      [5] Ibid. 2 (1ᵃ20 ff.).

later logicians and philosophers have found indispensable in making their points clear, inverted commas and the free invention of abstract nouns. We can ask ourselves, 'Is Aristotle saying that "man" is predicated of the individual or that humanity is predicated of the individual?', but Aristotle had only one sign, namely, ἄνθρωπος to do duty for the three English signs, 'man', 'the word "man"', and 'humanity'. This deficiency of the Greek language had already been a source of trouble in Plato's philosophy, and the reproduction of it in Latin translations from Aristotle's works was later to be a difficulty for medieval philosophers when they discussed the theory of universals. It is true that Aristotle sometimes uses the neuter article τό followed by a word to stand for 'the word so and so';[1] but this is not his invariable practice, and so the absence of this device in the present passage is not decisive evidence that he is not thinking of words.

If, however, he had been able to ask the question, Aristotle would almost certainly have answered that he was dealing with things and not with words. The clearest proof of this is his coupling κατὰ τινὸς λέγεσθαι ('being predicated of something') and ἐν τινι εἶναι ('being in something') as he does in the characterization of substance quoted above. When he illustrates his notion of 'being in' by saying that a certain point of grammatical knowledge is in the mind,[2] he could scarcely conceive that he was talking of a linguistic expression. The true resolution of the ambiguity seems to be given by Porphyry when he says, 'For as things are, so are the expressions which primarily express them'.[3] Aristotle is classifying types of being (τὰ ὄντα), but he uses the differences between rules for different linguistic expressions as a clue to the differences between types of being.

The resolution of the second ambiguity follows from that of the first. If Aristotle is primarily concerned with types of being, it should be clear that he is not much concerned with the question whether the words which express them occur in the subject or in the predicate position in any given sentence. The belief that he is dealing primarily with predicates arises partly from his use of the word κατηγορία and partly from his emphasis on primary substance, which has suggested that the rest of the work must be concerned with the different kinds of things that can be said about a concrete individual. This view is supported also by some of his examples of the different categories.[4] For he seems to be concerned

---

[1] e.g. *De Int.* 1 (16ᵃ14), 12 (21ᵇ1–5), cf. 1 (16ᵃ16).    [2] *Categoriae*, 2 (1ᵃ25).
[3] ὡς γὰρ ἔχει τὰ πράγματα, οὕτως καὶ αἱ ταῦτα πρώτως δηλοῦσαι λέξεις. Op. cit. *C.I.A.G.* iv (i), p. 71.    [4] *Categoriae*, 4 (1ᵇ28 ff.).

with the differences between 'This is a man', 'This is white', 'This is shod', &c. On the other hand, this interpretation restricts the doctrine to a rather narrow application and excludes from consideration many propositions that interest Aristotle, e.g. 'White is a colour','Justice is a virtue', 'Virtue is a disposition',&c. Moreover, the restriction is not supported by all of his examples. For he cites yesterday and last year under the category of time, and these cannot be predicated of a concrete individual.

In any case the passage in the *Topics* in which he summarizes his doctrine of the categories shows that he had a wider theory in mind:

'It is clear, too, from a consideration of them that the man who signifies something's essence signifies sometimes a substance, sometimes a quality, sometimes one of the other categories. For when a man is set before him and he says that what is set before him is a man or an animal, he states its essence and signifies a substance; but when a white colour is set before him and he says that what is set there is white or is a colour, he states its essence and signifies a quality. Likewise also if a magnitude of a cubit is set before him and he says that what is set before him is a magnitude of a cubit, he states its essence and signifies a quantity. Likewise also in other cases. For each of these predicates if it is asserted of itself, or if its genus be asserted of it, signifies an essence; but if it is asserted of something else, it does not signify an essence but quantity or quality or one of the other categories.'[1]

Aristotle seems here to have two distinctions in mind, first that between giving the nature (οὐσία) of a primary substance and characterizing it in any other way, and second that between giving in whole or in part the essence or definition (τί ἐστι) of anything whatsoever and saying something of it which is not essential. He states as a general rule that when we predicate a term of itself or give its genus, we are giving its essence (τί ἐστι), though we may not be signifying substance (οὐσία) but one of the other categories. Thus not only 'This is a man' but also 'White is a colour' and 'A foot is a length' are statements of essence (τί ἐστι), though only the first expresses substance. When, however, we use a term in one category of a term in another, e.g. in saying 'The man is seated' or 'White is lighter than red', we do not give the essence of the subject.

Finally it may be remarked that to take the doctrine in its wider signification gives a better sense to those passages in Aristotle's other works in which he says that certain very general

---

[1] *Topica*, i. 9 (103<sup>b</sup>27–38).

terms are 'in' or 'applied in' all the categories. Thus in his
*Nicomachean Ethics* he says ' "Good" is used in as many different
contexts as "being" (τἀγαθὸν ἰσαχῶς λέγεται τῷ ὄντι). For it is
used in substance (ἐν τῷ τί), as for example of God and the intellect, and in quality of the virtues, and in quantity of the
moderate, etc.'[1] The wording of this passage is curious, but it may
be understood to mean that God, the intellect, the virtues, the
moderate, and Aristotle's other examples can all alike be called
good things, though they do not all belong to the same category.

We may take it, then, that the *Categories* is concerned with the
classification of things signified by terms, whether these terms
occupy subject or predicate positions in sentences. From this we
may go on to consider the nature of Aristotle's special interest in
the doctrine. Why did he take the trouble to state the theory of
the categories and what is its relation to his other doctrines,
especially to those of his logical works?

The most satisfactory answer to the first question is that the
theory is obviously true. An individual man differs from a time
(e.g. two o'clock today) or from a virtue in a way in which he
does not differ from another individual man or even from an
individual cat or dog. Inter-category distinctions are different
from intra-category distinctions, however difficult it may be to
formulate this fundamental difference precisely. This was a point
which presented itself to Aristotle's wide-ranging curiosity and
which he thought worth recording.

It may be acknowledged, however, that he had perhaps an
ulterior motive in formulating the doctrine. At least he often finds
it a very convenient stick with which to beat Platonism. His
objection to the Theory of Forms is twofold. In the first place, it
seems to him to be an over-simplified theory of meaning. Plato
is apparently committed to the thesis that every term has a single
signification, namely its appropriate Form, and Aristotle tries
to refute him, as in the passage we have quoted from the *Nicomachean Ethics* by adducing terms which may be applied in all the
categories and therefore cannot, according to him, have a single
meaning or definition. In the second place, Platonism seems to
him to involve a serious confusion between substance and the
other categories. It is his constant complaint that Plato treats the
Forms as substances, i.e. capable of independent existence, and
such, he thinks, they are plainly not.[2] For this reason it is of the
utmost importance to him to maintain that only primary substance is capable of independent existence and that the existence
of things falling under other categories is dependent. Thus he says:

[1] *Ethica Nicomachea*, i. 6 (1096ᵃ23 ff.).     [2] *Metaphysica, A*, 9 (991ᵇ1–4).

'Everything except primary substances is either predicable of
primary substances or present in them as subjects. This becomes
evident by reference to particular instances. Animal is predicated of
man, and therefore of the individual man; for if there were no individual man of whom it could be predicated, it could not be predicated of man at all. Again colour is present in body, therefore in some
individual body; for if it were not in some individual body, it could
not be present in body at all. Thus everything except primary substance is either predicated of primary substances or is present in them;
and if these last did not exist, it would be impossible for anything else
to exist.'[1]

If it is Aristotle's intention thus to oppose his doctrine of categories to Plato's theory of Forms, he does less than justice to the
later Plato; for his own theory of the predicates which are applicable in all the categories owes something to the Platonic doctrine
of the greatest kinds (μέγιστα γένη) in the *Sophist*.[2] Perhaps Aristotle has gone farther in distinguishing pervasive from non-
pervasive terms; for the predicates which he picks out as running
through all the categories,[3] 'one', 'being', 'same', 'other', 'opposite', seem (with the possible exception of 'opposite') to be rightly
regarded as pervasive in the sense discussed earlier.[4] His followers
in later times have sometimes wished to include 'good' among the
strictly pervasive (or transcendental) predicates; but in the passage
of the *Nicomachean Ethics* to which we have referred Aristotle says
only that it can be applied to things in all categories, not that it can
be applied to everything without exception, whether concrete or
abstract; and he did not in fact wish to hold that it was predicable
of everything. It is of course, obvious, but perhaps worth saying,
nevertheless, that the categories themselves are not pervasive terms.
They are supposed in general to be mutually exclusive, and are
therefore essentially classificatory.[5] But they differ from the simpler
kind of classificatory terms in that they do not serve to classify
primary substances. The connexion between categories and pervasive terms is that it is a necessary, though not a sufficient, condition of a term's being pervasive that it should be predicable of
objects falling under all the categories. It is therefore a mistake
to suggest, as some historians have done, that Plato's theory of
greatest kinds is an anticipation of the theory of the categories.
Rather it is an anticipation of the theory of pervasive terms which
is linked with the theory of categories in the way just explained.

[1] *Categoriae*, 5 (2ᵃ34 ff.).                    [2] See above, p. 20.
[3] *Metaphysica*, Δ, 10 (1018ᵃ35).                [4] See above, p. 20.
[5] In *Cat.* 8 (11ᵃ37) Aristotle allows that his categories of quality and relation may
not be mutually exclusive.

The consequences of the theory of categories for logic seem to be three.

First, Aristotle's emphasis on primary substance as the ultimate subject of predication led to an over-emphasis on the subject-predicate form of proposition which still restricted logical development at the time of Leibniz. If primary substance is the ultimate subject of predication, all basic truths are of the form 'This (primary substance) is (or is not) such and such', and other truths are derivative from or dependent on these. The most obviously dependent are those which apparently have the same form, i.e. the universal propositions of Aristotelian logic, and it is therefore not surprising that Aristotle regarded it as one of his first tasks in the *Prior Analytics* to explain the universal proposition in terms of the singular proposition: 'We say that one term is predicated of all of another whenever no instance of the latter can be found of which the former cannot be asserted.'[1]

It seemed then that the important differences between propositions were those marked by the occurrence or non-occurrence of the negative particle and by the quantifiers, 'all' and 'some'. In other words, concentration on the subject-predicate form led to the fourfold classification of the *De Interpretatione*. When once this is accepted, other differences between propositions, except on occasions those of modality, tend to be treated as differences between predicates and therefore insufficiently general to be germane to the general theory of argument. Furthermore, the tendency is encouraged by the interpretation of κατηγορία as 'predicate'. It seems likely that this over-simplified view of the nature of the basic proposition has been a hindrance to the development of the logic of relations and of multiply general propositions.

Secondly, Aristotle's use of the same term οὐσία to signify both primary and secondary substance blurs the all-important distinction between singular and general propositions. 'Socrates is a man' and 'Man is an animal' although for Aristotle admittedly different are in an important sense alike, because both subject terms fall under the category of substance. The admission of secondary substance as substance is, in fact, a survival in Aristotle of the Platonism from which he could never entirely free himself. Since a predication under secondary substance gives the essence of a primary substance in a way in which no other predication does, true propositions about connexions between secondary substances have the merit of being both basic and general. These are the materials of Aristotle's demonstrative syllogisms. Behind

[1] *An. Pr.* i. 1 (24$^{b}$28).

the theory lies the same fundamental doctrine of the chain of Forms which underlay Plato's theory of division.

Thirdly, the *Categories* seems to be the first attempt at what has recently been called a theory of type-distinctions, that is to say a theory in which entities are classified according to what can be said about them significantly. Plato had already remarked that to be capable of expressing a truth a linguistic formula must be complex, containing at least both noun and verb.[1] This is a necessary, but not a sufficient, condition of meaningfulness. Grammatically correct sentences may fail to have intelligible meaning, e.g. 'Socrates is the opposite of Thersites', 'Amoebae are opposite to men', 'They are both men but one is much more so'. These sentences may not strike the modern reader as entirely convincing examples of absurdity, but they are deliberately chosen as being excluded by rules which Aristotle lays down in his treatment of the individual categories. In each case he asks whether the terms which fall under the category in question admit of opposites or have degrees, and in the case of substance he denies both these possibilities. It cannot be said with certainty, however, that Aristotle is trying to make type-distinctions; for it is not clear from his language whether he holds that statements like those above are simply false or self-contradictory or nonsensical. Translated as literally as possible, what he says is as follows:

'It also belongs to substances that there is nothing opposite to them. For what should be opposite to primary substance, as for example the individual man or animal? Nothing is opposite. Nor is anything opposite to man or animal in general.'[2]

'Substance seems not to admit of more and less. I mean . . . that each substance is what it is and is not called more or less so. For example, if this substance is a man, it will not be more or less man either than itself at another time or than another similar substance.'[3]

These observations certainly imply that a sentence which appears to state that a given substance is the opposite of another substance or that it admits of more and less does not express a true proposition. But what further shall we say of such a sentence? Does it fail to express any proposition at all? Does it express an impossible proposition? Or does it express one that is merely false? This question touches on the foundation of logic; for it raises the problem of the correct formulation and the range of applicability of the law of excluded middle.

[1] Plato, *Sophista*, 262A; cf. *Categoriae*, 4 (2ᵃ5).
[2] Ibid., 5 (3ᵇ24).
[3] Ibid. (3ᵇ33).

## 3. *The* Topics

The *Topics*, as we have already said, is avowedly a handbook
for the guidance of those taking part in public debating contests.
The final book (viii) gives specific directions for both questioner
and answerer in such contests. The content, however, seems to be
largely determined by the exercises in classification and definition
performed in the Academy, and it is possible that the theory of
the Predicables which gives unity to the *Topics*, in so far as it has
unity, was already worked out in the Academy, for Aristotle introduces the key-terms (property, accident, genus, species, and
differentia) as already familiar. The *Topics* is the product of
reflection upon the dialectical method as applied to questions of
definition and classification. As it stands, it is a number of not
very well-ordered observations on matters logical, psychological,
and linguistic. It may be said, however, to hold a logical theory
in solution, the theory which appears crystallized in the *De Interpretatione* and the *Prior Analytics*.

It may be seen in general that the development is natural. In
the first place a *practical* interest in the winning of arguments leads
to a *theoretical* interest in valid inference; for among honest men
the surest way of winning argument is to present trains of valid
reasoning. It is true that Aristotle points out devices that may also
help in dishonest winning, e.g. the concealment of the direction
of the argument,[1] but this is part of the sediment which will drop
from the solution. Secondly, since the argument is to be carried
out in dialogue form with the speakers maintaining opposite
theses, there is great interest in the question. 'What statement
is the contradictory of a given statement?' For it is essential
to determine at what point one speaker has refuted his opponent. This leads to the doctrine of the square of opposition,
the main contribution of the *De Interpretatione* to logic. Thirdly,
since the speakers are trying to classify and define, the statements
considered are of the forms 'X is Y' and 'X is not Y'. More precise
versions of these and their contradictories are the materials of
Aristotle's syllogistic. After a brief outline of the contents of the
*Topics*, we shall consider in detail a few passages, of which some
are anticipations of syllogistic, while others put forward logical
theses outside the scope of that system. To continue our metaphor,
there is more in the solution of the *Topics* than Aristotle saw
crystallize out of it, not only the elaborate symmetrical flower of
syllogistic, but also the strong simple shapes of propositional logic
and the intricate patterns of the logic of relations.

---

[1] *Topica*, viii. 14 (163$^b$35).

D

The name *Topics* is derived from the Greek word which originally meant 'place' but later came to signify a 'commonplace', i.e. a recurrent theme or pattern in discourse. Aristotle explains his sense of the term in his *Rhetoric*:

'I mean that dialectical and rhetorical syllogisms are concerned with those things of which we speak of the *topoi*. These are common to questions concerning right conduct, to physical and political questions and to many others which differ in kind among themselves, as for instance the *topos* of more and less.'[1]

It appears from this that the *topos* is something which may occur in any argument, whatever its subject-matter. What Aristotle means by the word in the *Topics* can best be gathered from examples:

'One *topos* is to look and see if a man has described as an accident what belongs in another way.'[2]

'Another is to make definitions both of an accident and its subject, either of both separately or else of one of them, and then look and see if anything untrue has been assumed in the definitions.'[3]

It will be seen that the *topoi* are standard procedures or moves which can be made in argument on any subject. In fact what Aristotle does in the *Topics* is to give general tactical hints for the conduct of competitive argument.

At the beginning he draws a distinction between a *protasis* and a *problema*. These are both questions and the difference between them, says Aristotle, is merely one of form, i.e. the difference between 'Is animal the genus of man?' and 'Is animal the genus of man or not?'[4] This appears to be not very important, but the distinction is perhaps that between the thesis proposed for discussion, i.e. the starting-point of the argument, and a question put later in order to keep it going. We may suppose that the question for discussion is 'Is animal the genus of man?' This is the *protasis*, the starting-point. In the course of the argument, the questioner asks 'Is it or is it not a property of animals to be self-moving?' This would be a *problema*. In the *Prior Analytics*, on the other hand, the word *protasis* always means a statement, and in chapters 26 to 28 of the first book of that work, where Aristotle, returning partly to the manner of the *Topics*, gives practical suggestions for the conduct of arguments, *problema* also seems to mean a statement. His point of view has changed. He is concerned to find out how a given proposition can be proved rather than how a given question can be answered either in the affirmative

[1] *Rhetorica*, i. 2 (1358[a]10 ff.).    [2] *Topica*, ii. 2 (109[a]34).
[3] Ibid. ii. 2 (109[b]30).    [4] Ibid. i. 4 (101[b]28–33).

or the negative. In the *Topics* he has always the two disputants in mind. A consideration of etymology is perhaps helpful in following the changes of meaning undergone by these two words. *Protasis* is from προτείνω ('to hold forth or offer') and is therefore something offered for consideration at the beginning of the dispute, while *problema* from προβάλλω ('to throw forward or down') is rather something thrown down or out in the middle of the argument, i.e. a suggestion. What is proffered or thrown out may well take the form of either a question or a statement. The Latin *propositio* (from *propono*) has also the essential meaning common to both *protasis* and *problema*.

Every *protasis* or *problema* is said to indicate either the definition, a property, the genus, or an accident of the subject. The assumption is that the *protasis* or *problema* is concerned with a general statement, e.g. 'Man is a two-footed animal', 'Man is white'. The headings indicate the relation which the predicate may have to the subject in such propositions. In the first place it may be the *definition* (ὅρος) of the subject, i.e. the predicate phrase of our statement may give the essence of the subject, what it is to be a so-and-so. Secondly the predicate may be a *property* (ἴδιον) of the subject, i.e. something which is not the essence of the subject, yet belongs to that species alone and is predicated convertibly of it: 'Thus it is a property of man to be capable of learning grammar: for if he is a man, he is capable of learning grammar, and if he is capable of learning grammar, he is a man.'[1] Thirdly, the predicate may be the *genus* (γένος) of the subject, i.e. the larger kind to which the species in question belongs and within which it is distinguished by its specific difference (διαφορά). Fourthly, the predicate may be an *accident* (συμβεβηκός), i.e. a character which can belong to instances of the species, but need not so belong, e.g. whiteness in relation to men. Whereas the first two are convertible predicates (i.e. such that we can argue from 'X is Y' to 'Y is X'), the third and fourth are not. It will be seen that the theory of the predicables is based on two important distinctions, that between necessary and non-necessary, and that between convertible and non-convertible predication. These two distinctions play a considerable part in Aristotle's later thought.

After introducing the theory of the predicables, Aristotle proceeds to define more closely the nature of a dialectical question and to give general hints on the selection of propositions for discussion and on the examination of them. In the course of this discussion he recapitulates the theory of the categories[2] and draws some distinctions of considerable logical importance. For example

---

[1] Ibid. i. 5 (102ᵃ19–22).      [2] Ibid. i. 9.

he distinguishes three senses of identity (numerical, specific, and generic),[1] and gives here for the first time in extant literature the division of propositions into ethical, physical (i.e. concerned with physical science), and logical,[2] but the most interesting of his logical distinctions is that between induction (ἐπαγωγή) and reasoning (συλλογισμός), drawn in chapter 12. Of induction he says: 'Induction is the passage from particulars (τῶν καθ' ἕκαστα) to the universal. For example, if the skilled pilot is the best and also the charioteer, generally speaking the skilled is the best in each case.'[3] Although he uses the phrase καθ' ἕκαστα it is clear from his examples that he does not mean by induction the simple enumeration of actual individual cases but rather the bringing together and comparing of a number of specifically different cases.

Aristotle then proceeds to a consideration of questions involving accident. His discussion of this is concluded at the end of book iii. Book iv then deals with genus, book v with property, and book vi with definition. Book vii contains afterthoughts on definition which naturally lead to further remarks on identity, while book viii concludes with practical hints for questioners and answerers in dialectical debate.

There are many passages in the *Topics* which anticipate points in Aristotle's syllogistic. We shall discuss a few of these, pointing out the difference between the earlier and the later treatment of the same theme. In this connexion it will sometimes be convenient to anticipate our own exposition of syllogistic by mentioning technicalities which have not yet been explained.

When Aristotle says: 'When we have proved that an attribute belongs to all of a kind, we shall have proved that it belongs to some,'[4] he anticipates the theory of subalternation and makes a clear distinction between universal and particular statements. Both these points are characteristic of his later doctrine.

The following passage shows how near the *Topics* comes to stating syllogistic rules:

'In order to show that opposites belong to the same thing, we should consider the genus, e.g. if we wish to prove that correctness and error both arise in relation to perception, we say that, since perception is judgement and judgement may be either correct or incorrect, there will be correctness and incorrectness in the case of perception too. In this case the proof goes from genus to species; for judgement is the genus of perception, since the man who perceives judges in a way. Again we may proceed from species to genus; for what belongs to the

[1] *Topica*, i. 7 (103ᵃ6–14).
[3] Ibid. i. 12 (105ᵃ10–16).
[2] Ibid. i. 14 (105ᵇ20–25).
[4] Ibid. ii. 1 (109ᵃ3).

species belongs also to the genus. For example, if knowledge is good and bad, disposition is good and bad; for disposition is the genus of knowledge. The former *topos* is fallacious for establishing a proposition, the second is correct. For it is not necessary that what belongs to the genus should belong to the species; for animal is winged and four-footed but not man. But what belongs to the species must belong to the genus; for if man is good, then animal is good also. But with a view to refutation, the first is valid, the second invalid. For what does not belong to the genus does not belong to the species, but what does not belong to the species does not necessarily fail to belong to the genus.'[1]

The indefinite form of statement, e.g. 'Man is good', is charac-teristic of the *Topics*. The interpretation of it as existential, which is frequent with both editors and translators, is misleading to a modern reader, because it inevitably suggests an equivalence with the form 'Some man is good', an equivalence which Aristotle had not yet established. We may read into this passage the acceptance of two forms of syllogism and the rejection of two others. Those accepted are 'If some M is L and every M is S, then some S is L' (*Disamis* in the third figure) and 'If no M is L and every S is M, then no S is L' (*Celarent* in the first figure), those rejected are 'If some M is L and every S is M, then some S is L' (*IAI* in the first figure) and 'If no M is L and every M is S, then no S is L' (*EAE* in the third figure). But comparison with the relevant passages in the *Prior Analytics*[2] will show how far the *Topics* falls short of complete formalization of these principles. In comparison with the *Analytics*, the treatment here lacks both generality and pre-cision. No formal system lies behind it, there is no use of variables, and the vague use of the verbs εἶναι and ὑπάρχειν does not dis-tinguish between universal and particular statements, nor be-tween statements of fact and statements of possibility. For example, ζῷον μέν ἐστι πτηνόν (literally 'Animal is winged') might mean 'Every animal is winged', 'Some animal is winged', 'Every animal may be winged', or 'Some animal may be winged'.

On the other hand, the treatment of the *Topics* is in some ways more open than that of the *Analytics*. There is room for disjunctive predicates, such as 'correct or incorrect', which the later work excludes; and attention is given to many kinds of argument which cannot be reduced to syllogistic form. The arguments of the following passage, for example, could not be formalized as syllogisms:

---

[1] Ibid. ii. 4 (111ª14–32).
[2] *An. Pr.* i. 6 (28ᵇ7–11); i. 3 (25ᵇ40–26ª16); i. 4 (26ª30–34); i. 6 (29ª17).

'Since it is necessary that some one of the species should be predicated of everything of which the genus is predicated, and that things which possess the genus . . . must also possess some one of the species . . . (for instance if science is predicated of anything, then music or grammar or some other science must be predicated of it, and if anyone possesses science . . ., then he must possess music or grammar or one of the other sciences). . . .'[1]

The nearest we could get to a syllogistic analysis of these arguments would be 'If all science is either grammar or music or . . . and this is a science, then this is either grammar or music or . . . ' and 'If all science is either grammar or music or . . . and he has science then he has either grammar or music or . . . '. The first of these is only by courtesy a syllogism on account of the indefinite disjunctive major term. And the second is not a syllogism at all; for there is no middle term, the predicate in the minor premiss being 'having science' and not 'science'. The second is indeed similar to an argument mentioned by Aristotle in the *Prior Analytics*,[2] which he declares to be valid but not syllogistic.

Two passages of the *Topics* anticipate the doctrine of indirect reduction. The first runs: 'If the good is made the genus of pleasure, consider whether there is any pleasure which is not good; for if there is, it is clear that good is not the genus of pleasure; for the genus is predicated of everything that falls under a given species.'[3] Here an appeal is made in effect to a syllogism in *Barbara*, 'If every pleasure is good and X is a pleasure, then X is good' to validate reasoning in *Felapton*, 'If no X is good and every X is a pleasure, then some pleasure is not good'. There is a similar appeal in the following passage:

'Again consider whether the suggested species is true of something, but the genus not, as, for example, if the existent or the knowable is put forward as the genus of the opinable. For the opinable may be predicated of the non-existent (for many non-existent things are the objects of opinion), but it is clear that the existent or the knowable is not predicated of the non-existent. So that neither the existent or the knowable is the genus of the opinable.'[4]

Here the syllogism in *Ferison*, 'If no non-existent is existent and some non-existent is opinable, then some opinable is not existent,' is backed by appeal to a syllogism in *Darii*, 'If everything opinable is existent and some non-existent is opinable, then some non-existent is existent'. In both cases, as in the *Prior Analytics*, Aristotle refers to the first figure for support, but he

---

[1] *Topica*, ii. 4 (111ᵃ33–111ᵇ2.)    [2] *An. Pr.* i. 32 (47ᵃ–24 ff.).
[3] *Topica*, iv. 1 (120ᵇ17–20).    [4] Ibid. iv. 1 (121ᵃ20 ff.).

makes his points by examples and does not use variables. Overt generality is achieved by using the terminology of the predicables, as in the sentence 'The genus must be predicable of everything of which the species is predicable'. This does not, however, give complete *formal* generality, for a statement of the form 'Every X is Y' might be a statement of definition, genus, property, or accident. It may be that inferences in the *Topics* were not fully formalized because Aristotle was still unconsciously hesitating between two possible ways of classifying statements in which one general term is predicated of another. He inherited from Plato's method of division a way of expressing such statements without any signs of quantification ('some' or 'every'). Statements of this form which Aristotle calls 'indefinite' (ἀδιόριστοι λόγοι) appear to us highly ambiguous. They may be rendered precise in either of two ways, i.e. by adding one of the quantifiers 'every' and 'some' to the subject term or by making more explicit the relation expressed by 'is', i.e. by introducing different forms of copula. If we think of the general terms as names of classes we find that there are five possible relations between any two classes, X and Y: coincidence, inclusion of Y by X but not vice versa, inclusion of X by Y but not vice versa, overlap and total exclusion. The theory of the *Topics* to some extent foreshadows this classification. The inclusion of X in Y is expressed by saying that X is a species of Y, the reverse relation by saying that it is its genus, for Aristotle always insists that the genus must be wider than the species;[1] statements of definition and of property both express the relation of coincidence, while statements of accident correspond in a rather obvious way to overlap, in spite of the fact that Aristotle allows that an accident may be a relative or temporary property. In such a case the statement of accident would express the relation of coincidence.

Aristotle's fourfold scheme differs from the fivefold scheme of class-relationships partly because he is also concerned with the independent distinction between necessary and contingent and partly because, being concerned with affirmative statements, he does not explicitly recognize the relation of exclusion. His concern with necessity and contingency leads him to distinguish two different cases of coincidence (definition and property) and to define accident in terms of contingency.[2]

Although not fully conscious of the scheme, Aristotle does work out some of its characteristic laws, as for example, that if

---

[1] Ibid. iv. 1 (121ª13 f.); iv. 2 (122ᵇ35 f.).
[2] Ibid. i. 5 (102ᵇ20 ff.).

X includes and is included in Y, then not-X includes and is included in not-Y.[1]

That syllogistic rather than the logic of classes was developed at this stage is probably to be explained by the fact that Greek, like English, does not have a single expression for each of the class-relationships, so that the class-logic is difficult to develop without an artificial symbolism, a device which did not occur to logicians for many centuries. Already in the *Topics* we find Aristotle inclining towards the doctrine of the *De Interpretatione*. In the following passage, for example, he is conscious of the ambiguity of the indefinite statement and is showing the interest in contradiction which dominates the *De Interpretatione*:

'If the statement put forward is indefinite, it is possible to refute it in only one way, as for example, if he has said that pleasure is good or not good and not made the statement more precise in any way. For if he said that some pleasure is good, it would have to be shown universally that none is, if the suggestion were to be refuted. Likewise if he said that some pleasure was not good, it would have to be shown universally, that all is. It is not possible to refute the statement in any other way. For if we show that some pleasure is not good or good, the suggestion is not yet refuted. It is clear that it is possible to refute in one way only but to establish in two. For if we show universally that every pleasure is good, or if we show that some pleasure is good, the proposition put forward (i.e. that pleasure is good) will be demonstrated. Likewise if it were necessary to maintain in argument that some pleasure is not good, if we show that none is good or if we show that some is not good, we shall have established by argument in each case either by the particular or by the universal that some pleasure is not good. But if the thesis is definite, it is possible to refute in two ways, as for example if it were laid down that it belongs to some pleasure to be good but not to some other. For if it were shown that all pleasure is good or that none is, what is laid down would be refuted. But if he laid it down that only one pleasure is good, it is possible to refute the statement in three ways. For showing that all or that none or that more than one is good, we shall have refuted the proposition laid down. If the thesis is even more determinate, as for example that practical wisdom alone among the virtues is knowledge, it can be refuted in four ways. For if it were shown that all virtue is knowledge or that none is or that some other, e.g. justice, is or that practical wisdom itself is not knowledge, what is laid down would be refuted.'[2]

The end of this passage goes even farther than the *De Interpretatione* in recognizing differences of quantity and draws distinctions which play no part in the *Prior Analytics*.

While the theory of class-relationships is an alternative to the

---

[1] *Topica*, v. 6 ($135^b13$ ff.).    [2] Ibid. iii. 6 ($120^a6$–31).

theory of quantified propositions, the distinction between necessary and contingent, which plays an important part in the *Topics* is independent of both, a fact which Aristotle later realized when he tried to develop a theory of modal syllogisms as distinct from that of assertoric syllogisms.

In the following passage Aristotle anticipates the doctrine of the contraposition of the universal affirmative statements: 'In all cases a postulate of this sort should be made: e.g. "If the honorable is pleasant, what is not pleasant is not honorable, while if the latter is untrue so is the former"; likewise also "If what is not pleasant is not honorable, then what is honorable is pleasant".' Here, although he gives his rule only by means of an example, Aristotle makes it clear that he regards any statement of the form 'If anything is X it is Y' as equivalent to the corresponding statement of the form 'If anything is not Y it is not X'.

This thesis may be further generalized to yield the formula 'If the proposition that-P follows from the proposition that-Q, then the proposition that-not-Q follows from the proposition that-not-P'. Aristotle does not give precisely this formula, but he does give a still more general principle applicable to arguments with more than one premiss. It is characteristic of the *Topics* that such a principle should be found embodied in a hint for methods of practice:

'The best way to secure training and practice in such arguments is to get into the habit of transposing arguments. For in this way we shall be better able to deal with the matter in hand and shall thoroughly understand many arguments in the light of a few. Transposition is the refutation of one of the given propositions by considering the conclusion together with the other propositions in question; for if the conclusion is false, one of the premisses must be abandoned, if indeed it is the case that, if they are all true, then the conclusion must hold.'[2]

This says that if a number of propositions jointly entail a conclusion, then, if the conclusion is false, at least one of the premisses must be false. The thesis lies behind the theory of indirect reduction of syllogisms.

There are, however, some strictly logical passages in the *Topics* which Aristotle did not develop elsewhere. One of these is concerned with relations:

'The case of relative terms should be treated in like manner to that of a state and its privation; for the sequence of these as well is direct. Thus if three-times is a multiple, a third is a fraction; for

---

[1] Ibid. ii. 8 (113$^b$22).     [2] Ibid. viii. 14 (163$^a$29 ff.).

three-times is relative to a third, and so is a multiple to a fraction. Again, if knowledge be a conceiving, then also the object of knowledge is an object of conception; and if sight be a kind of perception, then the object of sight is an object of perception.'[1]

Aristotle is concerned here with two principles. In the first sentence quoted he considers the converses of relations and lays it down that if one relation entails another, as being-three-times entails being-a-multiple, the converse of the first must also entail the converse of the second. In the second sentence he goes on to maintain that, if one character entails another, then anything which has a certain relation to an instance of the first must also have that same relation to an instance of the second. Each of these theses is an interesting contribution to the theory of relations, but neither is presented in full abstraction, and after these promising beginnings Aristotle drops the subject.

Another subject to which Aristotle makes contributions incidentally in his *Topics* is the theory of identity. What he has to say on this is written in more abstract style:

'Again look and see if, supposing the one to be the same as something, the other also is the same as it; for if they be not the same as the same thing, clearly neither are they the same as one another. Moreover, examine them in the light of their accidents and of the things of which they are accidents; for any accident belonging to the one must belong also to the other, and if the one belong to anything as an accident, so must the other also. If in any of these respects there is a discrepancy, clearly they are not the same.'[2]

'Only to things that are indistinguishable and one in being is it generally agreed that all the same attributes belong.'[3]

Here we have first a version of the principle of the transitivity of identity, next a formulation of the principle of the indiscernibility of identicals, and finally a version of the principle of the identity of indiscernibles. Like the truths about relations noticed in the last paragraph, all these were destined to be reformulated much later by other philosophers without reference to Aristotle's work. In his text they occur without emphasis, and it is therefore not surprising that he does not generally get any credit for them.

The case is quite different with the theory of arguments *a fortiori*, or, as Aristotle says, 'from the more and the less'. This is a topic to which he refers many times and always in a way which suggests that he thinks of it as a well-recognized theme.[4]

---

[1] *Topica*, ii. 8 (114ª13).                                    [2] Ibid. vii. 1 (152ª30).
[3] *De Soph. Elench.* 24 (179ª37).
[4] *Topica*, ii. 10 (114ᵇ37); iii. 6 (119ᵇ17); iv. 5 (127ᵇ18); v. 8 (137ᵇ14); vi. 7 (145ᵇ34); vii. 1 (152ᵇ6); vii. 3 (154ª4).

It was natural, therefore, that he should wish to incorporate his views on the subject into his later work on logic, and it seems probable that this is what he had in mind when he spoke later of his intention to write on arguments 'according to quality' (κατὰ ποιότητα). We shall have occasion to refer to it again later in connexion with the theory of arguments 'from hypothesis' (ἐξ ὑποθέσεως) which was developed in Aristotle's school.

The reader of the *Topics* will find much beside formal logic, syllogistic or non-syllogistic. The distinction between formal and informal is not yet clearly drawn. Much of book iii, for example, is concerned with arguments about the preferable (τὸ αἱρετώτερον) and Aristotle lays down such theses as 'That which is more lasting and durable is preferable to that which is less so',[1] and 'That which is chosen for itself is preferable to that which is chosen for the sake of something else.'[2] Here we have a 'logic of ordinary language' rather than a formal logic, and the same is true of the following: '(although disposition is the genus of knowledge) knowledge is called knowledge of the object known, but the state or disposition is not said to be of the object known but of the soul'.[3]

Aristotle tries, however, to make his theses as general as possible, as when he generalizes for comparatives some of the rules he has worked out in relation to the preferable.[4]

In the last chapter of the *De Sophisticis Elenchis*, which is to be considered also as the conclusion of the *Topics*, Aristotle claims that in dialectic, as distinct from rhetoric, there was no systematic teaching before his time:

'On the subject of rhetoric there exists much that has been said long ago, whereas on the subject of reasoning (συλλογίζεσθαι) we had nothing of an earlier date to speak of at all, but were kept at work for a long time on experimental researches. If, then, it seems to you after inspection that from a start such as I have described the study has come to a satisfactory condition in comparison with the other enquiries which have been developed by tradition, it remains for you all, my students, to give me your pardon for the shortcomings of the enquiry and your warm thanks for the discoveries it contains.'[5]

Since we concede Aristotle's claim to be the first writer of a treatise on reasoning and wish also to count ourselves among his pupils, we must treat his work as he requests. But unlike the audience who heard the lectures, we have the opportunity of studying his later work, and we shall therefore spend no more

[1] Ibid. iii. 1 (116ª13).    [2] Ibid. iii. 1 (116ª29).    [3] Ibid. iv. 4 (124ᵇ33).
[4] Ibid. iii. 5.                                          [5] *De Soph. Elench.* 34 (184ª8).

time over his first attempt to bring order out of chaos. As part of the *Organon*, the *Topics* continued to influence students of philosophy until the seventeenth century, but we cannot in retrospect say that it has contributed much to the development of logic, except indirectly through the impulse it gave to the elaboration of the medieval theory of *consequentiae*.

Whereas in the *Topics* the word 'syllogism' was used in accordance with its etymology for any conclusive argument from more than one premiss, in the *Analytics* it is used in a narrower sense for a piece of reasoning that relates two general terms by means of a middle term; and in several passages of the *Prior Analytics* Aristotle claims that all proof, properly so called, involves such reasoning.[1] His elaboration of the rules of syllogistic is Aristotle's chief title to fame as a logician, but it must be recognized that the development to which we have just drawn attention represents a restriction of interest. Aristotle came to think that the study of syllogisms in his narrow sense was the central part of the study of reasoning, because he came to believe that in every statement worth serious consideration as a thesis of science one general term was asserted or denied of another, either universally or in part. Thus in the first of the passages mentioned above where he tries to explain the central importance of syllogistic he begins by saying: 'It is necessary that every demonstration and every syllogism should prove either that something belongs or that it does not, and this either universally or in part.'[2] If it is assumed also that statements admissible as premisses must be of the same general form, the rest follows, as we shall see when we examine his theory in detail. But it may be asked why in his later works he attached so much importance to general statements of the kind noticed here. Special attention to such statements is evident already in the doctrine of the predicables which Aristotle used throughout his *Topics*, and it is implicit in the Platonic doctrine of the interconnexions of forms, from which we must suppose that his inquiry began. When Aristotle asserted that nothing could count as proof unless it established a proposition of the kind noticed, he was merely stating dogmatically what he had generally assumed at an earlier date. But the hardening of the dogma seems to have occurred in connexion with the working out of the theory of science presented in the *Posterior Analytics*.

In what follows we shall be concerned chiefly with the doctrine of the *Prior Analytics*, though we shall have occasion to consider also what Aristotle says in his *De Interpretatione*.

---

[1] *An. Pr.* i. 23 (40ᵇ16); i. 29, 30 (45ᵃ23); ii. 23 (68ᵇ8).
[2] *An. Pr.* i. 23 (40ᵇ23).

## 4. *Aristotle's Theory of Meaning and Truth*

The introductory chapters of the *De Interpretatione* appear to be closely linked with Plato's discussion of truth and falsity in the *Sophist*; for Aristotle begins by saying that the terms 'noun' (ὄνομα), 'verb' (ῥῆμα), and 'proposition' or 'statement' (λόγος) must be defined. Like Plato he considers both the spoken words and the mental experiences (παθήματα) or thoughts (νοήματα) of which they are said to be the symbols. He implies that it is the thoughts to which the predicates 'true' and 'false' primarily belong, apparently on the ground that while the spoken words are different for different peoples, the thoughts and the things of which they are resemblances (ὁμοιώματα) are the same for all alike. The truth or falsity of the spoken word is derivative.[1]

Aristotle also follows Plato in two other contentions. First he says that every thought or part of discourse which is to be true or false must be composite. The noun or verb taken alone has significance (σημαίνει τι), but is not true or false.[2] Secondly, he recognizes that spoken words are significant by convention (κατὰ συνθήκην).[3] He distinguishes the noun from the verb by saying that the former is 'without time' (ἄνευ χρόνου)[4] while the latter 'signifies time in addition' (προσσημαίνει χρόνον).[5] It appears that he thinks of verbs as being always in some definite tense, past, present, or future, i.e. that he rejects the notion of timeless predication. This is not certain, however; for there is a distinction at the end of chapter 1 of the *De Interpretatione* between the use of the verb 'to be' 'simply' and 'according to time' (ἢ ἁπλῶς ἢ κατὰ χρόνον) which might be interpreted as a contrast between tensed and untensed assertion.[6] Possibly Aristotle wished to allow what has been called the omnitemporal use of the present tense (which covers the past and future as well as the present) but to deny any strictly timeless predication on the ground that this was bound up with the Platonic metaphysics of the realm of timeless Forms, which he had abandoned. If so, this step had serious consequences for his philosophy of logic, as we shall see later.

Aristotle distinguishes among sentences (λόγοι) a special class to which alone it belongs to be true or false. These are declarative sentences as distinct from prayers and other utterances which are not true or false, although they have complete meaning. Aristotle's technical name for the declarative sentence is ἀπόφανσις or λόγος

[1] *De Interpretatione*, 1 (16ᵃ9).
[2] Ibid. 1 (16ᵃ13).
[3] Ibid. 2 (16ᵃ19). Cf. Plato's *Cratylus*, 384D.
[4] *De Interpretatione* 2 (16ᵃ19).
[5] Ibid. 3 (16ᵇ6).
[6] Cf. also *An. Pr.* i. 15 (34ᵇ7).

ἀποφαντικός.[1] It has been usual among logicians to follow
Aristotle's lead here and to dismiss prayers, commands, &c., as
having only rhetorical interest. We shall see that there is some
confusion in this attempt to delimit the sphere of logic.

Although the notions of truth and falsity are essential to his
explanation of ἀποφαντικὸς λόγος, Aristotle does not commit himself to any definition of these in his logical writings. In the *Metaphysics*, however, we find the following: 'For it is false to say of
that which is that it is not or of that which is not that it is, and it is
true to say of that which is that it is or of that which is not that it
is not.'[2] Here again Aristotle follows the doctrine of Plato's
*Sophist*.

The first four chapters of the *De Interpretatione* are perfunctory.
Aristotle seems impatient to get on to his discussion of contradictory pairs and the formal classification to which it leads. Like
others who have made logical discoveries of the first importance,
he is somewhat impatient of the philosophy of logic; it is too
troublesome to be really clear about the preliminaries. Unfortunately the neglect of these can lead to some logical trouble. In
the case of Aristotle the result is the very odd and puzzling thesis
to which he commits himself in chapter 9 of the *De Interpretatione*.

Before giving an account of this, it is convenient to say here
that Aristotle accepts in general the principles which came to be
known later as the Law of Contradiction and the Law of Excluded
Middle. These are stated in the *Metaphysics* in the same passage as
the definitions of truth and falsity quoted above and run as
follows:

'The principles of demonstration . . . as for example that it is
necessary in every case either to affirm or to deny and that it is
impossible simultaneously to be and not to be.'[3]

'The firmest of all first principles is that it is impossible for the same
thing to belong and not to belong to the same thing at the same time
in the same respect.'[4]

'It is not possible that there should be anything between the two
parts of a contradiction, but it is necessary either to affirm or deny
one thing of any one thing.'[5]

The first and third of these passages offer alternative formulations
of the Law of Excluded Middle, while the first and second give
less and more elaborate forms of the Law of Contradiction.

In chapter 9 of the *De Interpretatione* Aristotle questions the

---

[1] *De Interpretatione*, 4 (17ᵃ2 ff.).          [2] *Metaphysica*, Γ, 7 (1011ᵇ26–27).
[3] *Metaphysica*, B, 2 (996ᵇ26–30).
[4] Ibid. Γ, 3 (1005ᵇ19–23).                     [5] Ibid. Γ, 7 (1011ᵇ23–24).

assumption that every declarative sentence is true or false. It might seem that he is clearly committed to this thesis already, but this is not so; for when he says that to be true or false belongs to declarative sentences alone, this may be taken to mean that only these are capable of being true or false not that they all necessarily are. The principle that every statement[1] is true or false is called the Principle of Bivalence and has been distinguished from the Law of Excluded Middle[2] which is generally formulated 'Either P or not-P', where 'P' marks a gap into which a declarative sentence may be inserted. Given the definitions of truth and falsity which we have quoted the principles are, however, obviously equivalent; for if 'It is true that P' is equivalent to 'P' and 'It is false that P' is equivalent to 'not-P', 'P or not-P' is plainly equivalent to 'It is true that P or it is false that P'. It is important to make the distinction here for what Aristotle appears to be doing in this chapter is to question the Principle of Bivalence while accepting the Law of Excluded Middle. It is not altogether surprising that he should do this for he approaches the main question of *De Interpretatione* by constructing the notion of a contradictory pair (ἀντίφασις). This is defined as a pair of statements in which the same thing is respectively asserted and denied of the same thing.[3] It is not obvious that in the case of every such pair, the one must be true and the other false. Aristotle finds one exception to this rule in the case of indefinite statements for, he says, 'Man is white' and 'Man is not white' are both true.[4] It is, therefore, quite conceivable to him that statements about the future should constitute another exception, although of a different kind.

He is puzzled by an argument which may be set out as follows. In accordance with the Law of Excluded Middle we can say today:

(1) Either there will be a naval battle tomorrow or there will not be a naval battle tomorrow.

And this seems to be equivalent to the assertion:

(2) Either the statement 'There will be a naval battle tomorrow' is true and its negation false or vice versa.

But it seems reasonable to say also:

(3) If it is true now that there will be a naval battle tomorrow, it is necessary in relation to this fact about the present that

---

[1] We use the word 'statement' here as conveniently ambiguous between the notion of a declarative sentence and another notion which will be explained below.

[2] By J. Łukasiewicz, appendix to 'Philosophische Bemerkungen zu mehrwertigen Systemen des Aussagekalküls', *Comptes rendus des séances de la Société des sciences et des lettres de Varsovie*, 1930, and *Aristotle's Syllogistic*, p. 82.

[3] *De Interpretatione*, 6 (17ᵃ34).          [4] Ibid. 7 (17ᵇ30).

there should be a naval battle tomorrow; and similarly if it is true now that there will not be a naval battle tomorrow, it is necessary in relation to this fact about the present that there should not be a naval battle tomorrow.

And from (2) and (3) taken together there follows the conclusion:

(4) What is to happen tomorrow is determined already in any case apart from anything we may do, and so all deliberation is useless.

There is clearly something wrong in this short proof of fatalism, and Aristotle does right to reject it; but his solution of the puzzle is not at all clear. He seems to admit (1) and (3) and the fact (4) follows from (2) and (3) taken together but to deny that (2) follows from (1). For while he asserts that 'everything must either be or not be, be about to be or not to be',[1] he also says: 'It is not necessary that of every affirmation and denial of opposed statements one should be true and the other false. For in the case of that which exists potentially but not actually the rule which applies to that which exists actually does not hold good.'[2] This appears to mean that the disjunction of a statement and its negation can be true without either the original statement or its negation being true. In other words Aristotle is trying to assert the Law of Excluded Middle while denying the Principle of Bivalence. We have already seen that this is a mistake, and it is especially surprising in a chapter where Aristotle has given explanations of truth and falsity that reveal the source of the error.[3] But it seems to have been widely held in antiquity that there is a connexion between the Principle of Bivalence and determinism. The Stoics, who were determinists, held strongly to the principle, whereas Epicurus thought he had to deny it in order to maintain the doctrine of free-will.[4] Though Aristotle does not say so, it may be that when he wrote there was already current a sophistic objection to deliberation such as these later philosophers discussed under the name of 'the lazy argument' (ὁ ἀργὸς λόγος).[5]

What is wrong with the argument for fatalism set out above is not (2) but (3) and the transition from (3) to (4). The mistake here arises from confusion concerning the nature of truth and

---

[1] *De Interpretatione*, 9 (19ᵃ27–30).
[2] Ibid., 9 (19ᵃ39–19ᵇ4).
[3] Ibid., 9 (18ᵃ39–18ᵇ2).
[4] Cicero, *De Fato*, 21 and 37.
[5] We here follow the customary interpretation of this chapter as given, for example, by Boethius (*Commentarii in Librum Aristotelis Περὶ Ἑρμηνείας, Secunda Editio*, ed. Meiser, pp. 248–9). It was rejected by Abelard (*Dialectica*, p. 22), and has recently been attacked by Miss G. E. M. Anscombe in *Mind*, lxv (1956), pp. 1–15.

falsity. We have already seen in discussing Plato's views that there is a natural tendency to suppose that the predicates 'true' and 'false' can properly be applied to sentences or forms of words, i.e. to λόγοι in Plato's terminology, which is followed by Aristotle. This springs naturally from language; for we say that what people say is true or false, and what they say (in one sense of 'say') is obviously a sentence. This way of thinking and speaking leads us to talk of something 'becoming true', 'remaining true for some time', or 'being true at one time but not at another'. For if we consider such a sentence as 'I am sitting by a stove', it is tempting to say at a given time that it is true at that time, but was not true earlier and will not be true later. Aristotle himself notices and explicitly adopts the usage in another place.[1]

A little reflection shows that this account of the proper subject for the predicates 'true' and 'false' is unsatisfactory. Two persons may utter the above sentence simultaneously, one speaking truly and the other falsely. This fact had already puzzled the author of the δίσσοι λόγοι. It is not the sentence or form of words which is true or false, but what is expressed by it. The word 'proposition' has often been used in modern times to convey this notion and it is, on the whole, the most convenient for the purpose. In order to avoid all confusion it is necessary, however, to distinguish here a number of interrelated notions.

(1) A *token-sentence* is a sentence in that sense in which we may say 'He hesitated in the middle of his first sentence' or 'The sentence on the blackboard is badly written'.[2] A sentence in this sense is a particular set of sounds or marks occurring at a definite time or existing for a definite period.

(2) A *type-sentence* is a sentence in that sense in which the same sentence may be said to occur many times. When grammarians talk of sentences, they commonly refer to type-sentences. A sentence in this sense is a complete pattern of sounds or marks having meaning. It is not the sounds or marks in abstraction from the fact that they have meaning; for we should not call a set of sounds or marks a sentence unless we at least believed that it had meaning. Nor, on the other hand, is it a meaning or content considered in abstraction from all determinate marks; for we cannot speak properly of the same sentence in different languages, but only of corresponding sentences.

(3) A *statement in the grammarian's sense* is an indicative or declarative sentence, where 'sentence' means 'type-sentence'. In

---

[1] *Cat.* 5 (4ª23).
[2] Cf. C. S. Peirce's distinction between token-word and type-word in *Collected Papers*, iv. § 537.

this sense statements are distinguished from prayers, commands, &c., just as Aristotle distinguished ἀποφαντικοὶ λόγοι from all other λόγοι.

(4) To *make a statement* is to utter an indicative sentence for the purpose of asserting something and the meaning of 'statement' in this context is not the same as the grammarian's sense noticed above. For, as we have seen, persons who utter the same indicative sentence do not necessarily make the same statement, and one person may make different statements by uttering the same indicative sentence on different occasions, e.g. by saying on different days 'Today I am sitting in front of a stove'. On the other hand, a man may utter two different indicative sentences at different times and thereby make the same statement twice, e.g. by saying on successive days 'I am sitting by a stove today' and 'I was sitting by a stove yesterday'. Moreover, it is not the case that the speaking or writing of an indicative sentence is always the making of a statement. Acting, fiction-writing, and reporting other people's statements are obviously exceptions. It should further be noticed that when we make a complex (e.g. conditional) statement, we do not thereby make all the statements which we should make by using the subordinate clauses alone as complete sentences. Thus someone who says 'If Charles entered for the race, James didn't come in last' does not state that Charles entered or deny that James came in last, although there is certainly something expressed by each of the subordinate clauses.

(5) A *proposition* or *propositional content* is that which is asserted in the making of a statement or expressed without assertion in the production of a subordinate clause such as those we have just considered. Clearly it is to propositions that the predicated 'true' and 'false' apply fundamentally. For in order that these words should have application it is not necessary that any particular sentence should have been spoken or written nor yet that any statement should have been made previously. What is expressed by the protasis or apodosis of a conditional statement may rightly be characterized as true or false. The notion of a proposition has given rise to some philosophical difficulties which will be noticed later, but there can be no serious doubt of the facts of usage reported here. Sentences and clauses which express propositions may both alike be described as propositional signs. In medieval Latin *propositio* was used in the sense of 'propositional sign' and 'proposition' sometimes has this meaning in older English, but in modern usage it is equivalent to 'propositional content.'

(6) A *designation of a proposition* is a 'that' clause or some linguistic equivalent. Such linguistic devices must be allowed to the

logician if he is to discuss propositions, which he plainly must in order to elucidate the notion of validity. In modern European languages the device of inverted commas is sometimes used as a means of designating the proposition which could be expressed by the use of the indicative sentence inside the inverted commas, e.g. 'He said, "I didn't hear you", which was true enough'. This use of inverted commas is to be distinguished from their use to form the designation of a type-sentence, e.g. 'He said, "Ah've not 'eerd thi", which she didn't understand'. The distinction is made clear by the consideration that in translating the first sentence, we can translate the part inside inverted commas without altering the sense, or affecting the point, of the whole, whereas we cannot do this with the quotation in the second sentence.

Having made these distinctions, it is possible to show clearly where Aristotle made his mistakes in the *De Interpretatione*. The argument in chapter 9 is faulty because he thinks of the predicates 'true' and 'false' as applicable to something (probably a sentence) at a certain time. What puzzles him is the fact that we can say, 'It is *now* true that there will be a naval battle tomorrow'. But the 'now' is superfluous. It may seem at first sight peculiarly uninformative to say, as Aristotle himself does in his *Metaphysics*, 'He speaks truly who says of what is that it is and of what is not that it is not'. But it is just this feature that has commended Aristotle's definition to later logicians who are anxious to avoid unnecessary metaphysical puzzles concerning the nature of truth. And their approval is justified; for Aristotle's definition gives the most important fact about the predicate 'true', namely that, if 'P' is any propositional sign, the proposition that-P and the proposition that it is true that-P mutually entail each other. This holds also when the propositional sign is a sentence in the future tense. For it is true that there will be a naval battle tomorrow if, and only if, there will be a naval battle tomorrow. By introducing the phrase 'it is true that' we make no assumption about determinism which is not made by use of the simple sentence in the future tense. We mislead ourselves, however, when we speak, as Aristotle does, of its being true *now* that there will be a naval battle tomorrow, for we thereby induce ourselves to suppose that *this* will not be true tomorrow evening, when the battle is over, but something else will, i.e. 'There has been a naval battle today'. Two different *sentences* are plainly involved here, but they both express the same proposition in the sense that to convict any person who uttered either of error would also be to convict of error any person who uttered the other at the appropriate time.

The system of tenses in a language is a device whereby we

indicate the temporal relation of our spoken or written sentence (i.e. token-sentence) to the events of which we speak or write. A verb with a tense is, therefore, like the demonstratives, a 'token-reflexive' word, i.e. on each occasion of use it indicates the object of discourse by relating it to the token of itself which is then uttered or written.[1] To say 'He walked' is to indicate that the walking occurred before the utterance of the sentence, while 'He walks' indicates that it is contemporaneous, and so on. Tenses or some similar device are therefore indispensable for the complete expression of singular propositions, i.e. those about unique events; for any system of dating which may be offered as an alternative must be explained by reference to the time of the utterance through which it is introduced.

The phrase 'to be true' is used in all tenses and there are somewhat complicated rules which govern its combination with the tenses of the subordinate clause. Thus we have, for example, 'It was true that there would be a naval battle', 'It is true that there has been a naval battle', and 'It is true that there will be a naval battle'. The important thing to note is that in all cases the verb 'to be' with 'true' can be eliminated in such a way as to leave a sentence expressing a proposition which entails and is entailed by the proposition expressed by the original sentence. Thus the first of the sentences above can be replaced either by 'There is a naval battle' or by 'There was a naval battle', according to circumstances, the second by 'There has been a naval battle', and the third by 'There will be a naval battle'. The use of 'is true' or 'was true' is determined by conditions of appropriateness other than the truth of the proposition designated by the 'that' clause. It adds no further information. Consequently, 'It is true that there will be a naval battle' does not refer to the time of utterance in any way in which 'There will be a naval battle' does not. In short, no argument for determinism can be drawn from this form of expression, and Aristotle is not obliged to find here any exception to the Principle of Bivalence.

Having made a distinction between sentences and propositions, we can also see why it was unnecessary for Aristotle to exclude prayers, commands, &c., from logical consideration. The linguistic expressions for these are not statements in our first sense of the word, nor do we in uttering them make statements in the second sense of the word. But we cannot formulate a prayer, command, &c., without expressing a proposition, and that proposition must be true or false. Thus in the command 'Shut the door' there is expressed the proposition that the door will be shut, and that is

[1] See H. Reichenbach, *Elements of Symbolic Logic*, p. 284.

in fact true or false. This consideration explains the fact, which is obvious on reflection, that commands or prayers may stand in logical relations to each other and be of various logical forms. If one person says 'Shut the door' and another says 'Don't shut the door', both speaking to the same hearer and in quick succession, they contradict each other. Similarly, there may be conditional requests, e.g. 'Please come, if it is fine', existential questions, e.g. 'Are there people on Mars?', &c.

Statements, commands, requests, &c., are to be distinguished by their different functions in social life. The function of statements is mainly, although not solely, to convey information, that of commands and requests to induce people to do things, and so on. Connected with the fact that a given type of utterance has a certain function is the fact that an utterance not only expresses a proposition but also manifests or evinces an attitude towards the proposition expressed. When we make statements we manifest belief in the propositions expressed; when we give orders we manifest a wish that the propositions expressed should be true. We may be insincere in manifesting any of these attitudes. If we evince belief insincerely we are said to lie, but the notion of lying is not extended to other forms of utterance, except doubtfully to promises. It is because the function of statements is mainly to convey information, i.e. to induce others to accept certain propositions as true, that they are evaluated mainly as true or false, whereas commands are evaluated as wise or unwise, and not solely by consideration of whether or not they are fulfilled. For this reason it is usual to characterize statements in both senses as true or false.

It will be convenient here to enumerate various different uses of 'true' and 'false' and to explain how they are related:

(1) Propositions are true or false in the basic sense.

(2) Token sentences are true when they express true propositions.

(3) Type-sentences of the statement variety are true when they express true propositions. It is the fact that a given type-sentence containing a token-reflexive may express at one time and in one context a true, and at another time or in another context, a false proposition, which led to the puzzle of the δισσοὶ λόγοι and also to that of chapter 9 of the *De Interpretatione*. It should be noticed that a sentence containing a token-reflexive taken out of context expresses no proposition at all and should not be called true or false, e.g. the sentence 'There will be a naval battle tomorrow' as used in this chapter, being purely illustrative, does not express

any proposition. Such sentences are puzzling because we can say of them that they 'become true', 'remain true for some time', and 'cease to be true', e.g. 'The reigning British monarch is a Queen' has been true at various times in history, is now true and will again cease to be true. This means that at certain times the situation is such that the sentence then expresses a true proposition.

(4) A person makes a true statement when he utters a declarative sentence which expresses a true proposition. He need not be sincere: for it is possible to make a true statement by mistake, believing oneself to be lying.

(5) Beliefs, thoughts, or opinions are true when their expressions would be the expressions of true propositions.

From this account it will be seen that Aristotle made two mistakes in the *De Interpretatione*. In the first place, he was misled by the confusion of sentence and statement on the one hand with proposition on the other into a faulty argument about determinism and so to an unnecessary limitation of the Principle of Bivalence. Secondly, by confining his attention to declarative sentences, he suggested falsely that there cannot be logical relations between utterances of other types. These mistakes are of considerable philosophical interest, but fortunately not of great logical importance. The first is of no importance to Aristotle, because, as we have noticed in our consideration of the *Topics*, he tends to confine his attention to general sentences. The puzzles concerning tenses and token-reflexives do not arise in connexion with general sentences of science, which, if they ever express true propositions, always express true propositions, provided only that the meanings of their constituent symbols remain unaltered. Consequently Aristotle's mistake in chapter 9 of the *De Interpretatione* has no serious consequences for his logic as developed in other parts of the *De Interpretatione* and in the *Prior Analytics*. The second mistake has also no serious consequences, since logic is concerned with the relations between propositions, and once these are worked out, the results can be applied to sentences other than statements.

## 5. *The Four Forms of General Statement*

Aristotle is concerned in the *De Interpretatione* to group statements in pairs such that the second is the denial of the first. Generally, but as we have seen not always, the one will also be the contradictory of the other in the sense that one must be true and the other false. Apart from the dubious case of statements about the future, the obvious exception to this rule is the in-definite statement, e.g. 'Man is white'. The only way to deny this is to say 'Man is not white', but as Aristotle points out these two statements may be true together.[1] The indefinite statement now drops out of logical consideration. Aristotle says in the *Prior Analytics* that for purposes of syllogistic it is equivalent to the particular statement,[2] i.e. he treats it, according to the doctrine foreshadowed in the *Topics*,[3] as a disjunction of the universal and particular and so equivalent in inferential force to the latter. This provides some justification for treating it as existential.

Putting aside the indefinite statement, Aristotle recognizes three forms of statement which affirm a predicate of a subject, the singular, the universal, and the particular. In a singular statement the subject term is the name of an individual that cannot itself be predicated of anything else, e.g. 'Callias'. In a general statement, on the other hand, the subject term is said to be a symbol for a kind, e.g. 'man' and such that it may be predicated of many individuals. Further, statements which concern kinds may be distinguished according as they are or are not universal in scope. Thus 'Every man is white' is universal because it is about all instances of humanity, and it must be distinguished from the particular statement 'Some man is white'. The most important and influential part of his theory is concerned with the opposition of universal and particular statements.

Combination of the distinction between universal and particular with the distinction between affirmative and negative yields a fourfold classification of general statements according to the following scheme, in which each type is illustrated by Aristotle's own example:

*Universal Affirmative (A)*  
Every man is white

*Universal Negative (E)*  
No man is white

contrary

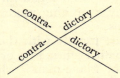

*Particular Affirmative (I)*  
Some man is white

*Particular Negative (O)*  
Some man is not white

[1] *De Interpretatione*, 7 (17ᵇ30).    [2] *An. Pr.* i. 7 (29ᵃ27).  
[3] *Topica*, iii. 6 (120ᵃ15–17).

For ease of reference we have added the vowels by which the four types have been distinguished since the Middle Ages, but these are, of course, no part of Aristotle's work. The figure, which is commonly called the square of opposition, is also not to be found in Aristotle's text, but it provides a useful summary of his doctrine. According to his explanations, statements are opposed as *contradictories* (ἀντιφατικῶς) when they cannot both be true and cannot both be false, but as *contraries* only (ἐναντίως)[1] when they cannot both be true but may both be false. Sometimes for the particular negative he uses the form 'Not every man is white',[2] which makes it quite clear that this is to be regarded as the simple negation of the universal affirmative. The two particular statements have been said by later logicians to be *subaltern* to the universal statements under which they occur in the figure and *sub-contrary* to each other. Although he does not use these expressions, Aristotle is interested in the relations so described, and assumes that subcontraries cannot both be false though they may both be true. This is shown, by his description of them as contradictories of contraries. He also assumes that each universal statement entails its subaltern. Let us consider what is involved in his theory of opposition.

The need for distinguishing between the contraries and the contradictories of general statements shows that these have a logical complexity not to be found in singular statements. Although 'Every man is white' and 'Some man is white' are grammatically similar in certain respects to 'Socrates is white' and 'Plato is white', 'every man' and 'some man' are not symbols of the same kind as 'Socrates' and 'Plato'. That is to say, if one of these phrases is substituted for 'Socrates' in the sentence 'Socrates is white', the result differs from the original in a way in which 'Plato is white' does not. This difference is ignored when it is said without further qualification that general statements have the same subject-predicate form as singular statements. Attempts have therefore been made in recent times to reform Aristotle's doctrine by exhibiting more clearly the complexity of general propositions.

These attempts start usually with the observation that particular statements, whether affirmative or negative, are assertions of existence. Instead of 'Some man is white' let us write 'There exists something which is both a man and white', or for short '!(M&W)', and instead of 'Some man is not white' the corresponding formula '!(M&$\overline{\text{W}}$)' in which the horizontal stroke is used to make the negation of the expression over which it occurs.

---

[1] *De. Int.* 7 (17$^b$16–25).          [2] Ibid. 8 (18$^a$5).

Then, assuming that the universal affirmative is to be taken as the contradictory of the particular negative and the universal negative as the contradictory of the particular affirmative, we obtain the following scheme of opposition:

| *Universal Affirmative* | *Universal Negative* |
|:---:|:---:|
| $!(\overline{M\&\overline{W}})$ | $!(\overline{M\&W})$ |
| *Particular Affirmative* | *Particular Negative* |
| $!(M\&W)$ | $!(M\&\overline{W})$ |

This method of symbolization has the merit of bringing out two points of considerable interest.

In the first place universal negative and particular negative statements are grouped together as negative only because each contains a negative particle of some sort, and it is wrong to treat them both as negative in the same sense as 'Socrates is not white'. In a sentence such as 'Some man is not white' the word 'not' must be taken together with the word 'white'. By the device which is called *obversion* we can, if we like, write the sentence in the form 'Some man is not-white' to bring out the fact that as a whole it is no less affirmative than 'Some man is white'. Similarly 'No man is white' can be replaced without alteration of sense by 'Every man is not-white', which has the same status as 'Every man is white'. Aristotle considered the use of privative terms and allowed that 'Every man is not-white' could be said to entail 'No man is white',[1] but rejected the converse entailment, which is required for obversion, on the ground that 'is not-white' might be taken in a narrower sense than 'is not white'.[2] It is true that privative terms such as 'unjust' tend to acquire a positive sense of their own which makes them contrary, rather than contradictory, to the positive terms from which they are constructed; but we need not be worried by this in the present context, since the purpose of our hyphen is merely to show logical relevance and not to create new expressions for ordinary use.

Secondly, particular affirmative and universal negative statements are *convertible* without alteration of sense. That is to say, 'Some man is white' is strictly equivalent to 'Some white thing is a man' and 'No man is white' to 'No white thing is a man'. In our symbolization of the two forms of statement this is shown by the fact that 'M' and 'W' play precisely similar roles, except that one appears before and the other after the sign of conjunction. Universal affirmatives and particular negatives, on the other

---

[1] Ibid. 10 (20ᵃ20).                    [2] *An. Pr.* i. 46 (51ᵇ8).

hand, cannot be converted, because their terms play different roles, as may be seen from the distribution of negation signs in our symbolism. In the passage where he discusses conversion[1] Aristotle notices that there is a difference, but maintains that the universal affirmative is partially convertible, i.e. that we can argue from 'Every pleasure is good' to 'Some good thing is a pleasure'. This doctrine is obviously connected with his assumption that universal statements entail their subalterns. For if we can pass from 'Every pleasure is good' to 'Some pleasure is good', we can certainly go on to say 'Some good thing is a pleasure'. But it still remains to be considered whether inference to subalterns is valid within the scheme now under consideration.

Here we come to a difficulty. If general statements conveyed no more than we have allowed for in our new rendering, it would undoubtedly be incorrect to argue from a universal statement to the corresponding particular statement; for the existence of a thing of a certain kind does not follow from the non-existence of things of another kind. Nor is this the only way in which our new scheme differs from that of Aristotle. So far as logic is concerned, it is quite possible that '$!\overline{(M\&\overline{W})}$' and '$!\overline{(M\&W)}$' should both express true propositions and similarly that '$!(M\&W)$' and '$!(M\&\overline{W})$' should both express false propositions. If we assume that the statements in the first row of our table have the relation of Aristotle's contraries and the statements in the second row the relation of his sub-contraries, that is only because we assume that there are men, which is a contingent fact. It has therefore been suggested that for Aristotle, and perhaps also for the ordinary user of a natural language, universal statements always have *existential import* which can be expressed in our new symbolism by writing '$!\overline{(M\&\overline{W})}$ & $!M$' for the affirmative and '$!\overline{(M\&W)}$ & $!M$' for the negative. It would, of course, be pointless to add '$!M$' to the expression of a particular statement, since an assertion of the existence of a man who is white, or not-white, as the case may be, already involves an assertion of the existence of a man. This suggestion has the merit of providing a justification for what Aristotle says about subalternation and contrariety, but it does not agree with his account of contradictory opposition. For the strict negation of '$!\overline{(M\&\overline{W})}$&$!M$' is not '$!(M\&\overline{W})$' but rather the disjunction of this and '$!\overline{M}$'. And conversely, from the falsity of the proposition expressed by $!(M\&\overline{W})$' we cannot infer the truth of the proposition expressed by '$!\overline{(M\&\overline{W})}$&$!M$'. Are we

---

[1] *An. Pr.* i. 2 (25ᵃ5).

then to say that Aristotle's teaching is inconsistent and to reject that part which seems to require an assumption of existential import for universal statements?

For many centuries all the relations asserted by Aristotle were accepted without much questioning by the thousands who studied his work. It is therefore very likely that his work is a faithful reflection of the normal usage for sentences constructed with words like 'every' and 'some'. And even according to the analysis of general statements in terms of existence and non-existence his doctrine can easily be justified as a whole, if we suppose that he was dealing only with terms that have application. When we confine attention to what is explicit in our symbolism, we cannot maintain that the proposition expressed by '$!(M\&\overline{W})$' entails that expressed by '$!(M\&W)$' and excludes that expressed by '$\overline{!(M\&W)}$'; but it is quite proper to assert these relations *under the tacitly assumed condition that there is at least one man*. If after hearing the conversation of Mrs. Gamp someone said that Mrs. Harris was wise and another said that she was not, a third who also believed in the existence of a person called Mrs. Harris might properly say that the two remarks were in contradiction. When it had been established that there was no Mrs. Harris, there would no longer be any point in talking about the relation of the two remarks, since both were based on the assumption of her existence and ceased to serve any useful purpose as soon as that assumption was abandoned. But this is not to say on the one hand that the remarks were consistent, nor yet to say on the other hand that they included as part of their meaning an assertion of the existence of Mrs. Harris. So, too, a certain use of a general term may be based on the assumption that there is something answering to the term, though no assertion of existence is made by the use of the term. The cases are not exactly parallel, because the assumption of application for a general term cannot properly be identified with an intention to refer to an individual or individuals, but the analogy is close enough to be helpful in an explanation of the square of opposition.

When the difficulties of Aristotle's theory of opposition were first realized, attention was concentrated chiefly on the question whether universal statements could properly be said to entail their subalterns, and the notion of existential import was introduced as something required especially for the understanding of universal statements within the Aristotelian scheme. But it is a mistake to suppose that all can be set right by consideration of the way in which Aristotle used statements of this form. Unless we tacitly assume that there is at least one man, we are not entitled to assert with Aristotle that of the particular statements 'Some man is white' and 'Some man is not white' one or other must be true. Nor is it enough to say that for Aristotle's purposes the general terms must be assumed to have application when they appear as the subjects of statements. For it is part of Aristotle's doctrine that particular affirmative and universal negative statements can both be converted simply, which implies that in these cases the predicate terms must be assumed to have application as well as the subject terms. In particular affirmative statements the fulfilment of the requirement is automatic: if any-one asserts that some man is white, he commits himself thereby to the assertion that there is at least one white thing. But when Aristotle claims the right to pass from 'No man is white' to 'No white thing is a man' and from this in turn to 'Some white thing is not a man', he reveals that he assumes not only the existence of at least one man but also the existence of at least one white thing, where the second assumption is independent of the first.

In order to justify Aristotle's doctrine as a whole it is necessary, then, to suppose that he assumed application for *all* the general terms with which he dealt. To a modern logician this seems a rather curious restriction of the scope of logic. For it is not at all difficult to construct a general statement in which at least one of the terms lacks application, e.g. 'No mathematician has squared the circle'; and once this has been realized, it becomes clear that there are advantages in a system where postulates of existence occur only explicitly. How was it that Aristotle failed to notice this? The explanation may be that he was interested already in the project of a syllogistic system where every term is capable of occupying either the subject or the predicate position in a state-ment. General terms which occur in the subject position must be nouns or noun phrases, and existential import (in the sense of a suggestion or implication, as distinct from an explicit assertion) attaches naturally to these. If we try to convert 'No mathematician has squared the circle', we must begin by rewriting it in the form 'No mathematician is a person who has squared the circle' and then go from this to 'No person who has squared the circle is a mathematician'. But the second form of words suggests already, as the first did not, that someone has squared the circle. So strong is the suggestion of application or reference conveyed by the use of nouns that when we want to use a noun without existential import we must provide specially for the cancelling of the suggestion. We may, for example, employ the conditional form of the verb, as in the sentence 'A dragon would be a dan-gerous pet', or we may employ a prefix which combines the notion of conditionality with that of universality, as in the sentence 'Any person who thinks he can swim the Atlantic is a fool'.

It is perhaps worth noticing that in some modern versions of Aristotle's doctrine the difficulties of his account of opposition are unnecessarily aggravated by use of examples and formulae in the plural. For the sentences 'All men are white' and 'Some men are white' suggest not only that the word 'man' has application but that there are in fact several men. Such examples are not normal in Aristotle's own work.

The method of exposition in the *Prior Analytics* differs in two notable respects from that in the *De Interpretatione*. In the first place, Aristotle uses letters as term-variables, that is as signs to mark gaps which may be filled by any general terms we choose, provided gaps marked by the same letter are filled by the same term in any one statement. This is a new and epoch-making device in logical technique. It is used for the first time without explanation in the second chapter of the *Prior Analytics*,[1] which deals with conversion, and it seems to be Aristotle's invention. In earlier works generality is indicated by a rather clumsy use of pronouns or by examples in which it is left to the reader to see the irrelevance of the special material. Both methods are used by both Plato and Aristotle. An example of the former from the *Republic* is: 'When things are of such a nature as to be relative to something, then those that are of a certain sort are relative to something of a certain sort.'[2] The latter is used by Aristotle in the *De Interpretatione*: 'The denial proper to the affirmation, "Every man is white" is "Not every man is white", that proper to the affirmation "Some man is white" is "No man is white".'[3] Plato's statement would be almost unintelligible without the illustrations which he adds, and Aristotle requires the reader to understand that the particular terms, 'man' and 'white' are irrelevant to the point he is making. In both cases the use of variables would have given greater clarity and conciseness. For the statement of more complicated logical rules, such as those of the syllogism, their use is almost indispensable.

It is natural to ask whether Aristotle's great innovation was suggested by any earlier practice. A device which may have suggested it is the use of two letters to name a line in geometry. This occurs in Aristotle's own work,[4] and it may have been derived from Eudoxus; for it is to be found in Euclid's *Elements*, book v, which is said to be his work. It was difficult for the

---

[1] *An. Pr.* i. 2 (25$^a$14.)    [2] *Respublica*, 438$_B$.    [3] *De. Int.* 7 (18$^a$4).
[4] *Ethica Nicomachea*, v. 4 (1132$^b$6).

Greeks to use letters as numerical variables, since they used these already as numerals. Diophantus, who was probably active in the second century A.D., introduced a special sign for the unknown in algebra, and this seems to be the first appearance of anything like a numerical variable in mathematics.

Instead of a simple variable, e.g. '*A*', Aristotle sometimes writes the phrase 'that to which *A*' (ἐφ' ᾧ *A*) or 'that of which *A*' (ἐφ' οὗ *A*). To us this appears to be a different convention in which the symbol '*A*' is *mentioned* instead of being *used* as a substitute for an ordinary noun or adjective. But Aristotle seems not to be aware of any difference, since he passes straight from one to the other.[1]

The second innovation in the *Prior Analytics* is the almost total supersession of the simple form of expression '*B* is *A*' by the more complicated forms '*A* belongs (ὑπάρχει) to *B*' and '*A* is predicated (κατηγορεῖται) of *B*'. In the *De Interpretatione* Aristotle uses the simple Greek predicative form with or without the copula ἐστι, and this he also uses at times in the *Prior Analytics*, but the other forms are much more common. It seems clear that the following four forms are regarded as equivalent:

(1)  *A* is predicated of *B*.
(2)  *A* belongs to *B*.
(3)  *B* is *A*.
(4)  *B* is in *A* as in a whole.

All these expressions are used interchangeably in the *Prior Analytics*, but (1) predominates. This fact is probably connected with the introduction of variables; for their use with the ordinary predicative form leads to awkwardness and even ambiguity in Greek, where the word-order is not fixed. For instance, Aristotle uses as an illustration of the simple conversion of a universal negative proposition, εἰ μηδεμία ἡδονὴ ἀγαθόν, οὐδ' ἀγαθὸν οὐδὲν ἔσται ἡδονή, ('If no pleasure is a good, neither will any good thing be a pleasure').[2] Here ambiguity is prevented by difference of gender; but all variables are treated as neuter, and had he attempted to state this rule by means of variables, he would have had, εἰ μηδὲν *A* *B*, οὐδὲ *B* οὐδὲν ἔσται *A*, which is ambiguous. When he uses ὑπάρχειν or κατηγορεῖσθαι, however, subject and predicate are in different cases, so that ambiguity is avoided. The rule will run, εἰ μηδενὶ τῷ *B* τὸ *A* ὑπάρχει, οὐδὲ τῷ *A* οὐδενὶ ὑπάρξει τὸ *B*. This form of expression is used in the proof of the rule.[3]

It seems likely that the use of ὑπάρχειν with a noun or neuter

---

[1] e.g. *An. Pr.* i. 31 (46ᵇ12–14) 35 (48ᵃ34 ff.).    [2] Ibid. i. 2 (25ᵃ6).
[3] Ibid. i. 2 (25ᵃ14 ff.). Aristotle does sometimes write τὸ *A B* or ἡ *A B* to indicate the premiss in which *A* is the predicate and *B* the subject, cf. *An. Pr.* i. 9 (30ᵃ33).

adjective as subject is an unconscious invention of Aristotle's, made in order to facilitate the use of variables. For it is difficult to believe that ἄνθρωπος οὐ παντὶ ζῴῳ ὑπάρχει[1] ('Man does not belong to every animal') was natural Greek for 'Some animal is not a man', and it is noticeable that when Aristotle gives concrete examples he tends to slip back to the ordinary predicative form of expression.[2] There is a natural use of ὑπάρχειν with an abstract, sometimes an infinitive, as subject. This occurs, for example, in a passage of the *Topics* where it is said that to sleep belongs to man and also to other things,[3] and it is possible that when Aristotle uses 'man', 'animal', &c., as subjects to the verb ὑπάρχειν he means us to understand 'being a man', 'being an animal', &c.[4] But, although this makes the use of ὑπάρχειν fairly easy and natural, it is not an interpretation which can be thought through consistently. For, as we have seen, it is essential to Aristotle's system, that the interchange of terms in any general statement should yield another general statement, and this is not so if one term is read as 'being $A$' and the other simply as '$B$'. Thus the principle of simple conversion for particular affirmative propositions is expressed in the form, 'If $A$ belongs to some $B$, then $B$ belongs to some $A$'.[5] But the simple operation of interchanging nominative and dative cannot be performed if we understand the first clause as an abbreviation for 'If being $A$ belongs to some $B$'. In fact it may be said that, on account of the peculiarities of the Greek language, the price paid for the technical advance brought by the use of variables was a philosophical obscurity which affected logic for many centuries.

For his purposes Aristotle needs a theory of statements and a manner of expressing them which fulfil the following conditions: (i) It must be natural within this theory to regard singular and general statements as co-ordinate species of a genus. The copula and the predicate should have the same function in both cases and the kinds differ only in the nature of the subject-term. This seems to be the initial line of thought in the *De Interpretatione*.[6] (ii) Every general term must be capable of occurring either as subject or as predicate without change of meaning. (iii) The copula should retain the same meaning in all four forms of general statement. (iv) The use of variables must not lead to ambiguity or awkwardness in Greek. (v) All the inferences of the Aristotelian system must hold good. It is impossible, however, that all these conditions should be fulfilled together as may be seen from

---

[1] Ibid. i. 2 (25ᵃ25).    [2] Ibid. i. 10 (31ᵇ9).    [3] *Top.* i. 5 (102ᵃ23).
[4] Compare the form τινὶ . . . ὑπάρχειν ἡδονῇ ἀγαθῷ εἶναι (*Top.* iii. 6 (120ᵃ22)).
[5] *An. Pr.* i. 2 (25ᵃ21).    [6] *De Int.* 7 (17ᵃ38 ff.).

consideration of the various possible interpretations of Aristotle's four forms. Most of the interpretations which follow are suggested by his terminology or incidental remarks.

(1) The subject-term may be taken to indicate or refer to a number of individuals distributively by expressing a property or group of properties which these individuals have in common. The copula then expresses the not further analysable notion of predication and the predicate simply expresses the property which it is the function of the whole sentence to ascribe to the individuals indicated by the subject-term. This may be called the predicative interpretation and is probably the most obvious reading both of the English sentence 'Some (every) man is white' and of the corresponding Greek ἄνθρωπός τίς (πᾶς) ἐστι λευκός. It is natural on this interpretation to quantify the subject, i.e. to add 'every' or 'some' in order to make clear whether the statement made holds good of all or only of some of the individuals indicated by the subject-term. On the other hand, the quantification of the predicate yields a meaningless sentence. This is possibly what Aristotle means when he says that statements with universally quantified predicates are never true,[1] but he may have another interpretation in mind. On the predicative interpretation subject and predicate cannot be interchanged without change of their meanings.

(2) The copula may be taken to express identity while both subject and predicate terms are supposed to refer to individuals by expressing properties. In this case the predicate term of an affirmative statement must be assumed to be implicitly preceded by 'some', not used, however, as a quantifier but rather as expressing the same notion as 'a certain', 'some or other'. This interpretation is very natural in the case of an English sentence which has as a predicate a noun with the indefinite article. For example, 'Every man is an animal' can easily be read as 'Every man is identical with some animal'. It seems likely that the interpretation was equally natural in the case of a Greek sentence with a noun-predicate. It is possible that Aristotle has this interpretation in mind in the passage mentioned above. 'Every man is identical with every animal' may seem false rather than meaningless, since it would have been true had there been only one man and one animal.

(3) The subject term may be interpreted as above but the predicate may be regarded as naming rather than expressing a property, that is it may be supposed to be an abstract term. This interpretation is almost inevitable if we translate Aristotle's

---

[1] *De. Int.* 7 (17ᵇ12). In *An. Pr.* i. 27 (43ᵇ20) he seems to say that they are absurd (ἄχρηστον καὶ ἀδύνατον).

formulation with ὑπάρχειν at all literally, and it seems likely that the Greek form also suggests it, but since Greek is frequently ambiguous as between abstract and concrete,[1] it was probably not clear to Aristotle that his new formulation involved the use of a new type of term. This interpretation does not allow for the free interchangeability of subject and predicate terms.

(4) Both subject and predicate may be taken as names of classes and the copula to mean 'is included in' in the universal affirmative statement. This interpretation is naturally suggested by Aristotle's formulation with ἐν ὅλῳ εἶναι. It has the advantage of allowing full interchangeability of terms, but the disadvantage that the copula must have different meanings in statements of different forms. 'All men are animals' is taken to mean 'The class of men is included in the class of animals' but 'Some men are white' to mean 'The class of men overlaps with the class of white things.' Moreover, sentences understood in this way cannot have singular terms as subjects. It was the development of this interpretation of Aristotelian formulae which eventually led to the recognition of the five possible relations between classes already mentioned in connexion with the *Topics*.

(5) The subject term may be understood as in (1) to (3) above while the predicate term is regarded as the name of a word which is properly applied to or predicated of the individuals referred to by the subject term. This interpretation is suggested by Aristotle's formulation τὸ Α κατηγορεῖται τοῦ Β and its English translation 'A is predicated of B', although perhaps less strongly in Greek than in English, because of a common failure to distinguish between the use and mention of a word. On this interpretation the terms are obviously not freely interchangeable.

(6) Both subject and predicate may be interpreted as abstract terms. In this case they are freely interchangeable, but the copula must mean 'entails' in the universal and 'is compatible with' in the particular. This interpretation is natural for the universal, but artificial for the particular statement. A concrete singular term cannot be the subject of a statement of this sort.

(7) The statements may be interpreted as positively and negatively existential. This interpretation gives free interchangeability of terms, and keeps a constant meaning for the copula, but distinguishes sharply between general and singular propositions. The latter indeed are not expressible in the symbolism appropriate to this interpretation. Further, it does not allow those Aristotelian inferences which depend on giving existential import to universal statements. This interpretation is suggested

---

[1] See above, p. 19.

by one formulation of the particular affirmative ἔστι τις ἄνθρωπος λευκός,[1] which is naturally read existentially.

None of these interpretations fulfils all the conditions listed above. Those which are most naturally expressed by the use of the verb εἶναι ('to be') are incompatible with the fourth condition, for it is this formulation which gives rise to awkwardness and ambiguity in Greek. It should be noted that there are no similar difficulties arising from the use of 'to be' in English with a fixed word-order. Interpretations suggested by formulations devised to meet these difficulties do not fulfil the condition of free interchangeability of terms, except in the case of the class interpretation, which does not fulfil the first and third conditions, i.e. this interpretation cannot be applied to singular sentences and it does not allow the copula to retain the same meaning in statements of all four forms.

Aristotle, of course, was not aware of these complications. He chose the formulations which allowed him to complete his technical task and left the philosophical interpretation obscure. But he was not entirely blind to the difficulties in his use of the verb ὑπάρχειν, as is shown by a discussion in *Prior Analytics*, i. 36, where he points out that on many occasions we cannot regard its subject as equivalent to an ordinary predicate, since we may say that one science belongs to opposites (that the science of opposites is one), without meaning that opposites are one science.

Fortunately philosophical obscurity is not an insuperable bar to logical progress. On all possible interpretations we find that all the Aristotelian inferences are valid, except those which rest on the existential import of universal propositions. Their correct formulation, however, would be more complicated than Aristotle allows. For example, the rule allowing the simple conversion of universal negative statements would be formulated as follows under the different interpretations:

(1) If none of the X things is Y, then none of the Y things is X.

(2) If no X thing is identical with any Y thing, then no Y thing is identical with any X thing.

(3) If none of the X things has the property Y then none of the Y things has the property X.

(4) If the class of X things is totally excluded from the class of Y things, then the class of Y things is totally excluded from the class of X things.

(5) If none of the X things is describable by the word 'Y', then none of the Y things is describable by the word 'X'.

---

[1] *De. Int.* 7 (17ᵇ19).

(6) If the property X is incompatible with the property Y then the property Y is incompatible with the property X.

(7) If nothing is both X and Y, then nothing is both Y and X.

## 6. *The Doctrine of the Syllogism*

Aristotle's account of general propositions prepares the way for his doctrine of the syllogism. At the beginning of the *Prior Analytics* he defines a syllogism as a discourse in which from certain propositions that are laid down something other than what is stated follows of necessity.[1] This formula is wide enough to cover almost any argument in which a conclusion is inferred from two or more premisses; and it had already been used with that inclusive sense in the *Topics*.[2] But when he discusses syllogisms in detail, Aristotle considers almost exclusively arguments in which both premisses (now called προτάσεις) and conclusion (συμπέρασμα) are simple in his sense and general; and when he is speaking more precisely, he says that every syllogistic conclusion follows from two premisses which relate the terms (ὅροι i.e. literally 'limits'), of the conclusion to a third term, called the middle.[3] According to his narrower usage we may not apply the name 'syllogism' to such an argument as 'If it rains the ground will be wet; but it will rain; therefore the ground will be wet', nor to any other argument with a compound statement as a premiss. It has also been said that he does not allow that a syllogism may have a singular statement as premiss, but he does in fact in a later passage give an example of a syllogism with such a premiss.[4] This is in accordance with his official view that singular statements are co-ordinate with universal and particular statements. Singular terms, however, have the peculiarity that they can occur only as subjects, so that Aristotle is led not only by a sound logical instinct, but also by the desire to have all his terms interchangeable to concentrate his attention on arguments consisting entirely of general statements.

His interest in working out the forms of argument that depend on the relations between general terms is due, no doubt, to his interest in demonstrative science. But it seems very probable that the way in which he presented his theory was determined by reflection on Plato's method of division.[5] This is mentioned by him in both the *Prior*[6] and the *Posterior Analytics*,[7] and he points out correctly in the former passage that it is not a method of proof. For,

---

[1] *An. Pr.* i. 1 (24ᵇ18).  [2] *Top.* i. 1 (100ᵃ25).  [3] *An. Pr.* i. 25 (41ᵇ36).
[4] Ibid. ii. 27 (70ᵃ27).  [5] See above, p. 44.
[6] *An. Pr.* i. 31 (46ᵃ31).  [7] *An. Post.* ii. 13 (96ᵇ25).

to use his own example, if we start with the genus animal, assume every animal to be mortal or immortal, and then put man in the division of the mortal, we take for granted that part of the final definition which states man to be a mortal animal, i.e. we beg the question. Plato's method, therefore, is simply one of exposition or clarification by which we may articulate our thought. But it seems to have suggested to Aristotle the general outline of syllogistic reasoning. In the passage to which we have just referred he remarks that division is so to speak a weak syllogism which begs what it ought to prove, and he suggests that in demonstration the major, or most general, term is shown to be predicable of the middle, which is itself predicable of the minor. Obviously he has in mind a chain of forms, say X-ness, Y-ness, and Z-ness so arranged that we can say 'Because X-ness belongs to every Y and Y-ness belongs to every Z, X-ness must belong to every Z.' This pattern is in fact peculiar to one of the syllogistic forms he recognizes, but it supplies the terminology for the whole system.

Before developing the theory of syllogism in detail, he explains how statements ($\pi\rho o\tau\acute{a}\sigma\epsilon\iota\varsigma$) of the $A$, $E$, and $I$ forms may be converted and why statements of the $O$ form cannot be.[1] This is an essential preliminary to the doctrine of reduction. It is in this passage that he first uses term-variables.

According to Aristotle there are three figures ($\sigma\chi\acute{\eta}\mu\alpha\tau\alpha$) of syllogism distinguished by the different relations in which the middle term stands to the extremes. In the first figure the middle term is subject to one and predicate to the other; in the second figure it is predicate in both; and in the third figure it is subject to both. The figures may be represented by the following patterns:

| (1) | (2) | (3) |
|-----|-----|-----|
| $A$–$B$ | $M$–$N$ | $\Pi$–$\Sigma$ |
| $B$–$\Gamma$ | $M$–$\Xi$ | $P$–$\Sigma$ |
| $A$–$\Gamma$ | $N$–$\Xi$ | $\Pi$–$P$ |

Here each pair of Greek capitals is supposed to exhibit the skeleton of a general statement (whether affirmative or negative, universal or particular) with the first letter in each case marking the place for the predicate in Aristotle's usual formulation. In each case the predicate of the conclusion is called by Aristotle the major term ($\tau\grave{o}$ $\mu\epsilon\hat{\imath}\zeta o\nu$), and the subject the minor ($\tau\grave{o}$ $\check{\epsilon}\lambda\alpha\tau\tau o\nu$), while the middle term is taken to be the one common to both premisses. The terminology seems to have been originally suggested by the fact that in a syllogism in the first mood of the first figure, the

---

[1] *An. Pr.* i. 2. (25$^a$1)

predicate of the conclusion generally has the widest extension, but the artificiality of the terminology as applied to the second and third figures is easy to show. Let us consider, for example, the following syllogism in the second figure: 'No newt is a mammal; but some organism is a mammal; therefore some organism is not a newt.' According to Aristotle's explanations 'organism' is the minor term and 'newt' the major term, and 'mammal', which is the middle term, comes before either of them in order of generality; but in fact 'organism' is obviously more general than the others, and there is no basis for a comparison between 'mammal' and 'newt', since the characters they connote do not belong to one chain of forms. But the difficulties of his terminology are not confined to his account of the second and third figures; they appear also in connexion with three of the four kinds of syllogisms he distinguishes in the first figure. Let us suppose, for example, we have to analyse the following argument: 'No bees are ants; but some gregarious creatures are bees; therefore some gregarious creatures are not ants.' It belongs to the first figure, and so according to Aristotle the terms 'ant', 'bee', and 'gregarious creature' should be in descending order of generality; but again the facts do not fit his description.

The source of the trouble seems to be that he tries to talk of the terms of all general statements in a way which is appropriate only to the terms of universal affirmative statements. Already in antiquity commentators were puzzled by the difficulty of finding any definitions of 'major' and 'minor' which would be suitable for all contexts. But in fact Aristotle defines 'major' and 'minor' separately for each figure according to the positions the term occupies in a standard formulation or description of syllogisms in that figure. Only in his definitions for the first figure is there any reference to the comparative extension of the application of the terms. He says there: 'I call the major term that in which the middle is contained, the minor that which falls under the middle':[1] But in his account of the middle term in this figure he introduces another notion: 'The middle is that which is included in another and itself includes another, which in position ($\theta\acute{\epsilon}\sigma\epsilon\iota$) is also middle'.[2] Here the last clause refers apparently to position in either formulation of the general pattern of first figure syllogisms. In both cases, given the correct arrangement of premisses, the middle term is mentioned after the major and before the minor.[3]

Aristotle uses this notion of position again to distinguish the major and minor terms in the second and third figures, realizing

[1] Ibid. i. 4 (26$^a$21).                     [2] Ibid. (25$^b$35–36).
[3] Ibid. (25$^b$32–35 and 37–39).

presumably that the notion of comparative extension is inapplicable. He says of the second figure : 'The major is that which lies next to the middle, the minor that which is further from the middle'.[1] This remark refers to the general method of formulating a syllogism in the second figure, e.g. 'Let $M$ be predicated of none of $N$ but of all of $\Xi$',[2] or again 'If $M$ belongs to all $N$ but to no $\Xi$'.[3] In each case the major term, $N$, is mentioned after the middle in the exposition. In describing the third figure Aristotle says; 'The major term is that which is farther from the middle, the minor that which is nearer'[4] and this again refers to such a formulation as 'When $\Pi$ and $P$ alike belong to all $\Sigma$'.[5] Here $\Pi$ in virtue of its position, which is farther from the middle term, is said to be the major. Aristotle always follows this order in giving shorthand directions for constructing pairs of premisses for the different figures. For example, 'Terms: animal, substance, raven',[6] occurring in the discussion of the second figure, means that we are to construct a pair of premisses appropriate to that figure with 'animal' as the middle, 'substance' as the major, and 'raven' as the minor term. The order given for the first figure is major–middle–minor,[7] and for the third major–minor–middle.[8] But although he uses his notion of position in formulation as an explanatory device, always putting the major term before the minor, this can scarcely be all that he had in mind; for it would give a quite artificial importance to the order of the premisses, and Aristotle rightly saw nothing sacrosanct in their order. Alexander of Aphrodisias suggest that the major term is, in fact, predicate of the 'problem' whose provability is to be investigated by the construction of the syllogism.[9] This suggestion has a good deal in its favour; for Aristotle shows in the later chapters of the *Prior Analytics*[10] that he sometimes thinks of syllogistic as a way of solving problems of this sort. It may in fact be the case that Aristotle always had in mind the predicate of the conclusion when he spoke of the major term; but it would not occur to him to use this as a definition, because his way of approaching the question of the validity of a given form is not to construct a complete syllogism, but rather to offer a pair of premisses and ask what conclusion, if any, can be derived from them. He must therefore have some way of at least apparently determining the major term without reference to the conclusion. On the other

---

[1] *An. Pr.* i. 5 (26ᵇ37–38).          [2] Ibid. (27ᵃ5).
[3] Ibid. (27ᵃ9).          [4] Ibid. i. 6 (28ᵃ14).
[5] Ibid. (28ᵃ18).          [6] Ibid. i. 5 (27ᵇ5).
[7] Ibid. i. 4 (26ᵃ8).          [8] Ibid. i. 6 (28ᵃ32).
[9] *In Aristotelis An. Pr. Lib. I Commentarium*, ed. Wallies, *C.I.A.G.* ii (i), p. 75.
[10] e.g. i. 28 (44ᵃ36).

hand, it is not impossible for him to speak of a syllogism in which the minor is predicated of the major term.[1]

It appears, then, that the meaning of the terms 'major' and 'minor' changes as Aristotle's thought develops. The *words* express the relation which he believed to hold between the extensions of terms in the first figure; and since in a syllogism in *Barbara* with true premisses, which is his model, the term with greatest extension is in fact the predicate of the conclusion, this is the notion which Aristotle uses in adapting his terminology to the second and third figures. He defines 'major term', however, by reference to the position of the term in a standard formulation of premisses, according to which it is always mentioned before the minor. By the time he came to write the summary in chapter 7 of the *Prior Analytics*, this is the *meaning* of 'major term', so that when he asks himself if premisses of the form 'Some $N$ is $M$', 'No $\mathcal{Z}$ is $M$' yield a conclusion, he says that we cannot conclude 'Some $\mathcal{Z}$ is not $N$' but can conclude 'Some $N$ is not $\mathcal{Z}$', i.e. predicate the minor of the major. The major here is simply the term mentioned first.

The whole question, however, is of merely antiquarian interest, since all medieval and later writers adapted the expedient put forward by John Philoponus, that the major term be *defined* as the predicate of the conclusion. Philoponus clearly recognizes that this is an arbitrary decision; he says:

'It is possible to define this [the major term] both in a way common to all the figures and in a way peculiar to the first figure. By the definition which is peculiar to the first figure, the major term is that which is predicated of the middle, and the minor that which is subject to the middle. But since in neither of the other two figures have the extremes a different position in relation to the middle, it is clear that this definition will not apply to them. We must therefore apply to the figures the common rule that the major term is the predicate of the conclusion.'[2]

Aristotle's insistence on the arrangement of the three terms of a syllogism in a linear order suggests that instead of the patterns of letters and lines given above he may perhaps have used for his three figures diagrams of the following kinds (see p. 72), which are in fact like some to be found in manuscripts of ancient commentaries.[3] Here each upper link between letters is to be taken as representing a relation of terms expressed in a premiss, and each lower

---

[1] *An. Pr.* i. 7 (29ᵃ23).
[2] Philoponus, *In Aristotelis An. Pr. Commentaria*, ed. Wallies, *C.I.A.G.* xiii (ii), p. 67.
[3] e.g. Ammonius, *In Aristotelis An. Pr. Lib. I Commentarium*, ed. Wallies, *C.I.A.G.* iv (vi), p. x.

link as representing a relation expressed in a conclusion. If his thought was guided by such diagrams, it is easy to see why he assumed that there could be only three syllogistic figures. For obviously there are only three ways in which the middle term can be ordered with respect to the two extremes, given that the major must always precede the minor.

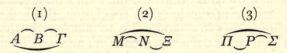

$$(1) \qquad (2) \qquad (3)$$

$$A \; B \; \Gamma \qquad M \; N \; \Xi \qquad \Pi \; P \; \Sigma$$

In later times the various ways in which syllogisms may be constructed within the figures came to be called moods. Using this terminology for convenience, we may say that Aristotle distinguishes fourteen valid moods, apart from derivative patterns to be noticed presently. For each he formulates a principle in the form of a conditional statement, using the letters mentioned above as variables. In the table which follows we have abandoned Aristotle's own letters in favour of a uniform scheme in which 'M' always marks the place of the middle term, 'S' the place of the minor (i.e. smaller) term, and 'L' the place of the major (i.e. larger) term. On the other hand, we have put before the principles of each figure a note of the order in which the terms are supposed by Aristotle to occur in that figure: this is a substitute for his device of using consecutive letters. The numbers and the medieval mood names which have been added for ease of reference are, of course, no part of Aristotle's work. The order, however, is his, and it is to be understood that each of the following formulae were conceived by him as a pattern for statements of necessary connexion.

First Figure: *L, M, S.*

    1.1. *If every M is L and every S is M, then every S is L* (Barbara).
    1.2. *If no M is L and every S is M, then no S is L* (Celarent).
    1.3. *If every M is L and some S is M, then some S is L* (Darii).
    1.4. *If no M is L and some S is M, then some S is not L* (Ferio).

Second Figure: *M, L, S.*

    2.1. *If no L is M and every S is M, then no S is L* (Cesare).
    2.2. *If every L is M and no S is M, then no S is L* (Camestres).
    2.3. *If no L is M and some S is M, then some S is not L* (Festino).
    2.4. *If every L is M and some S is not M, then some S is not L* (Baroco).

Third Figure: *L, S, M.*

3. 1. *If every M is L and every M is S, then some S is L* (Darapti).
3. 2. *If no M is L and every M is S, then some S is not L* (Felapton).
3. 3. *If some M is L and every M is S, then some S is L* (Disamis).
3. 4. *If every M is L and some M is S, then some S is L* (Datisi).
3. 5. *If some M is not L and every M is S, then some S is not L* (Bocardo).
3. 6. *If no M is L and some M is S, then some S is not L* (Ferison).

For interest, we give two examples of Aristotle's formulation of these principles in Greek. It will be noticed that in neither case does he use the simple predicative form of expression which we have used in English. Corresponding to 1. 1 (*Barbara*) he has εἰ γὰρ τὸ Α κατὰ παντὸς τοῦ Β καὶ τὸ Β κατὰ παντὸς τοῦ Γ, ἀνάγκη τὸ Α κατὰ παντὸς τοῦ Γ κατηγορεῖσθαι, i.e. literally 'If *A* is predicated of all *B* and *B* is predicated of all *Γ*, then it is necessary that *A* should be predicated of all *Γ*'.[1] And corresponding to 2. 3 (*Festino*) he has εἰ γὰρ τὸ Μ τῷ μὲν Ν μηδενί, τῷ δὲ Ξ τινί, ὑπάρχει, ἀνάγκη τὸ Ν τινὶ τῷ Ξ μὴ ὑπάρχειν, i.e. literally 'If *M* belongs to no *N* but to some *Ξ*, then it is necessary that *N* should not belong to some *Ξ*'.[2]

Anyone who argues in the first figure proves his conclusion by showing that a sufficient condition is fulfilled. This is the only figure in which general statements of all four kinds can be proved. Its special rules are (i) that the major premiss (i.e. the premiss containing the major term) must be universal, and (ii) that the minor premiss must be affirmative. Aristotle thinks that only syllogisms of the first figure are perfect or complete (τέλειος). His reason is presumably that only in the first figure, when the terms are arranged in his usual order, is the transitivity of the connexion between the terms obvious at a glance.[3] This peculiar character of the first figure is hidden when the verb 'to be' is used in premisses and conclusion, as in textbooks written in Latin and in many of the European languages, a fact which has led to much futile speculation as to the meaning of τέλειος in Aristotle. When stating the rule for the first figure in terms of the phrase ἐν ὅλῳ εἶναι Aristotle reverses the usual order of premisses in order to make this relation clear. It is instructive to compare two formulations of the principle of Barbara:

'When the terms are so related to each other that the last is in the middle as in a whole and the middle is in the first as in a whole, there will necessarily be a perfect syllogism connecting the extremes.'[4]

[1] *An. Pr.* i. 4 (25$^b$37).   [2] Ibid. i. 5 (27$^a$32).
[3] G. Patzig, *Die Aristotelische Syllogistik*, chapter 3.
[4] *An. Pr.* i. 4 (25$^b$32–35).

'If *A* is predicated of all *B* and *B* is predicated of all *Γ*, it is necessary that *A* should be predicated of all *Γ*.'[1]

Anyone who argues in the second figure proves his conclusion, which must be negative, by showing that a necessary condition for the application of the predicate to the subject is not fulfilled. The special rules for this figure are (i) that the major premiss must be universal, and (ii) that one premiss must be negative.

Anyone who argues in the third figure proves his conclusion, which must be particular, by showing that instances can be adduced. This is essential because a particular statement is an assertion of existence, as we have seen, and existence cannot be established without reference to instances. Apart from the requirement that the conclusion shall be particular the only special rule of this figure is that the minor premiss must be affirmative. But it should be noticed that the first two moods according to Aristotle's order (*Darapti* and *Felapton*) are valid only on the assumption of existential import for the universal statements used as premisses. If in a syllogism of either of these moods one of the universal premisses entails the particular statement said to be its subaltern, we can obviously construct a syllogism with the same terms and the same conclusion in one of the other four moods of the figure, i.e. the syllogism with two universal premisses is unnecessarily strong for the task it has to perform. On the other hand, if neither of the universal premisses entails its subaltern, the conclusion does not follow from the premisses. In a theory of syllogism which did not involve the assumption of existential import these two moods could be excluded by a further special rule requiring that one premiss in this figure should be particular.

Although the two first moods of the third figure are the only syllogistic patterns in Aristotle's list which depend on the assumption of existential import, it is clear that with that assumption particular conclusions can be derived from any premisses that warrant universal conclusions, that is to say, we may add the following principles:

1. 11. *If every M is L and every S is M, then some S is L* (Barbari).
1. 21. *If no M is L and every S is M, then some S is not L* (Celaront).
2. 11. *If no L is M and every S is M, then some S is not L* (Cesaro).
2. 21. *If every L is M and no S is M, then some S is not L* (Camestros).

These subaltern moods (as they were called in the Middle Ages) were not recognized by Aristotle. Their chief interest is that they level up the number of moods in the three figures recognized by

[1] *An. Pr.* i. 4 (25ᵇ37–39).

him. Apart from existential import there are four and only four valid moods in each figure; but if existential import is assumed, there are six valid moods in each figure.

In the course of his exposition Aristotle enunciates some general rules for all syllogisms, e.g. that at least one premiss must be universal and at least one premiss affirmative.[1] But he does not attempt to derive the whole theory from a set of general rules as some of his successors have done. His procedure is to consider what pairs of premisses yield valid syllogisms, i.e. entail conclusions in the figure under examination, and then to exclude non-probative pairs of premisses. In this connexion he frequently supplies material to show that the pair of premisses in question does not yield a conclusion. His method has been called proof by contrasted instances.[2] It would perhaps be better called rejection by contrasted instances.[3] For it consists in the production of two triads of terms such that in each the relations of the extremes to the middle are of the kinds under investigation, though in one the major belongs to all of the minor and in the other to none of the minor. Obviously the first triad is a counter-example to show that the specified relations do not allow for inference to a negative conclusion, whether universal or particular, while the second triad is a counter-example to show that the relations do not allow for inference to an affirmative conclusion, whether universal or particular. Together they suffice to show that the specified relations allow no conclusion at all. Aristotle's own first example will make this clear.

'If the first follows all the middle, but the middle belongs to none of the last, there will be no syllogism of the extremes. For things being thus, nothing necessarily follows. For the first may belong either to all or to none of the last, so that neither the particular nor the universal is necessary. And nothing being necessary as a consequence of these statements, there will be no syllogism. Terms for belonging to all: animal, man, horse; for belonging to none: animal, man, stone.'[4]

Aristotle here invites us to consider the two pairs of true statements, 'Every man is an animal' and 'No horse is a man' and 'Every man is an animal' and 'No stone is a man', and further to consider that every horse is an animal and that no stone is an animal. From these relations it follows that a pair of statements of the forms 'Every M is L' and 'No S is M' is consistent with statements of all four forms, 'Every S is L', 'No S is L', 'Some S is L' and 'Some S is not L'. This method may appear at first sight

---

[1] Ibid. i. 24 (41$^b$6 ff.).
[2] W. D. Ross, *Aristotle's Prior and Posterior Analytics*, p. 30.
[3] J. Łukasiewicz, *Aristotle's Syllogistic*, pp. 67 ff.          [4] *An. Pr.* i. 4 (26$^a$2–9).

over-ingenious, but it is comparatively economical, since it rejects four invalid forms of reasoning together.

The purpose of the special rules that Aristotle states in his discussion of the various figures is to summarize his results and dispose of the invalid moods in groups. It would be a mistake, however, to suggest that his exposition is unsystematic; for his doctrine of reduction from one figure to another, to which he recurs continually, provides a unifying plan in what would otherwise be a mere catalogue of separate principles. After the statement of each principle for a valid mood in the second or the third figure he shows how it can be validated directly or indirectly through a syllogism in the first figure.

In origin the doctrine of reduction is connected with the view that only syllogisms of the first figure are perfect in themselves, that is to say, evidently conclusive without supplementary argument.[1] For most of the moods in the imperfect figures such supplementary argument takes the form of conversion. Thus, for example, 2. 2 (*Camestres*) can be validated as follows through 1. 2 (*Celarent*) and two conversions of universal negative statements:

$$\frac{\text{Every L is M} \quad \dfrac{\text{No S is M}}{\text{No M is S}}}{\dfrac{\text{No L is S}}{\text{No S is L}}}$$

There are, however, two moods, namely 2. 4 (*Baroco*) and 3. 5 (*Bocardo*) which cannot be validated in this way, and for them Aristotle uses the procedure which was later called reduction *per impossibile* or indirect reduction. Let us take for an example 2. 4 (*Baroco*) of which the principle is:

*If every L is M and some S is not M, then some S is not L.*

In order to validate this Aristotle takes the contradictory of the conclusion (i.e. 'Every S is L') together with the first of the premisses and argues in accordance with 1. 1. (*Barbara*) that this combination entails the contradictory of the other premiss, i.e.

*If every L is M and every S is L, then every S is M.*

This is as much as to say that any one who accepted the two premisses of the original syllogism but denied the conclusion would be involved in self-contradiction. Aristotle suggests in one

[1] *An. Pr.* i. 1(24$^b$22); i. 4 (26$^b$28); i. 5 (28$^a$4); i. 6 (29$^a$14).

place that his argument is like the famous proof of the incommensurability of the diagonal and the side of a square.[1]

In order to avoid confusion we use the English word 'reduction' for Aristotle's ἀναγωγή, which is validation of a syllogism in one figure by construction of a syllogism in another figure, and the Latin *reductio* for his ἀπαγωγή, which is argument in the style of Zeno. Thus reduction *per impossibile* is a case of reduction in which the new syllogism amounts to a *reductio ad impossibile* of the denial of the conclusion of the old syllogism. It is possible, however, to regard reduction *per impossibile* as a particular application of the logical rule that, if two propositions entail a third, the falsity of the third together with the truth of the first (or the second) entails the falsity of the second (or the first). Aristotle comes very near to stating this principle in application to the syllogism when he says: 'It is clear then that if the conclusion is false it is necessary that either all or some of the premisses should be false.[2] But his purpose here is different.

Apart from conversion and reduction *per impossibile*, Aristotle uses a process called *ecthesis* (ἔκθεσις), or exposition, to establish some of his formulae. The notion first occurs, although the name is not used, in connexion with simple conversion: 'If A belongs to no B, neither will B belong to any A; for if it did belong to any A, say Γ, it would not be true that A belonged to no B; for Γ is one of B's.'[3] *Ecthesis* is the name for the production of the extra term, Γ. Aristotle uses the word itself in connexion with the third-figure mood *Darapti*: 'It is possible to prove this *per impossibile* and by *ecthesis* (τῷ ἐκθέσθαι). For if both Π and P belong to Σ, if one of the Σ's is taken, e.g. N, both Π and P will belong to this, so that Π will belong to some P.'[4] He states also that *ecthesis* can be used for the proof of *Disamis* and *Datisi*[5] and gives direction for its use in the proof of *Bocardo*: 'It can be proved without *reductio* if one of the Σ's is taken to which Π does not belong.'[6] The meaning of these passages has been much disputed from ancient times. The point at issue is whether the new term introduced (e.g. Γ in the first passage) is to be thought of as naming an individual or a sub-class under B. The point seems impossible to settle. It is almost certain that in the proof of *Darapti* Aristotle had an individual in mind; for as Alexander remarks, the argument would otherwise be circular.[7] But in the other cases, a sub-class would fit the argument better. Fortunately the matter is of little

[1] Ibid. i. 23 (41ᵃ26).  [2] Ibid. ii. 4 (57ᵃ36).
[3] Ibid. i. 2 (25ᵃ15–17).  [4] Ibid. i. 6 (28ᵃ22–24).
[5] Ibid. (28ᵇ14).
[6] Ibid. (28ᵇ20–21).
[7] *In Aristotelis An. Pr. Lib. I Commentarium*, ed. Wallies, *C.I.A.G.* ii (i), p. 99.

importance. Aristotle himself omits any reference to *ecthesis* in his summary of syllogistic, and the only place in which it is essential to his argument is in the proof of two modal syllogisms.[1] But here, too, a better theory of modality would enable him to dispense with it.

Many critics have objected that reduction of any kind is unnecessary since syllogisms in the second and third figures are quite satisfactory as they stand. This is fair comment on the suggestion that no one can see the force of these arguments without going through the procedure of reduction. But it is difficult to believe that Aristotle was slower than his critics to see implications, and in any case if reduction were supposed to be merely a procedure for helping men to intellectual insight, the question whether it is necessary would belong to psychology, not to logic, as Aristotle seems to hold. It seems therefore that he must have supposed the first figure to be the most fundamental in some objective sense. As we have already seen he was probably influenced by the consideration that it is the only figure in which the middle term can appear as intermediate in a chain of predicates such as Plato had considered. But however that may be, he certainly developed the doctrine of reduction in a way which would have been quite pointless if he merely wished to convince himself and his readers of the validity of syllogisms in the second and third figures. He showed, for example, that reduction *per impossibile* could be applied universally (i.e. not only to the cases which eluded direct reduction), and he even discussed the reduction of syllogisms in the first figure to syllogisms in the second or third. In this connexion his most interesting result is a proof that all syllogisms can be reduced to the syllogisms of the first figure with universal conclusions.[2] The essential point of the proof is that syllogisms of the first figure with particular conclusions can be reduced *per impossibile* to syllogisms of the second figure, which are reducible in turn, but by conversion, to syllogisms of the first figure with universal conclusions. As he himself remarks, the complete reduction of a syllogism in the third figure with a particular premiss involves three stages: (i) reduction to a syllogism of the first figure with a particular conclusion, (ii) reduction from this to the second figure *per impossibile*, (iii) reduction from the second figure to a syllogism in the first figure with a universal conclusion.[3] The man who wrote this was obviously not worrying about the

---

[1] For *ecthesis* see further Alexander, *op. cit.*, pp. 32–33, 99–100, 104; Sir David Ross, *Aristotle's Prior and Posterior Analytics*, p. 32; J. Łukasiewicz, *Aristotle's Syllogistic*, pp. 59–67; G. Patzig, *Die Aristotelische Syllogistik*, pp. 166–80.

[2] *An. Pr.* i. 7 (29$^b$1) and i. 23 (40$^b$17).

[3] Ibid. i. 7 (29$^b$6).

cogency of syllogisms in the second or the third figure. His interest was the same as that of a geometer who tries to construct a deductive system with a small number of axioms and those the most 'natural'.

Reduction *per impossibile* is especially interesting because it links the moods in groups of three, one from each figure. Thus each of the following moods can be reduced to either of the others mentioned in the same triad:[1]

| | |
|---|---|
| 1. 1, 2. 4, and 3. 5 | (*Barbara, Baroco,* and *Bocardo*) |
| 1. 2, 2. 3, and 3. 3 | (*Celarent, Festino,* and *Disamis*) |
| 1. 3, 2. 2, and 3. 6 | (*Darii, Camestres,* and *Ferison*) |
| 1. 4, 2. 1, and 3. 4 | (*Ferio, Cesare,* and *Datisi*) |

And similar triads can be constructed for the moods which involve existential import. By making use of this procedure, together with conversion and obversion (which was not admitted by Aristotle), we can reduce any one of the eighteen valid moods in Aristotle's three figures to any other and therefore to 1. 1 (*Barbara*). Granted obversion, the truth that all valid moods can be reduced to 1. 1 follows from the result of Aristotle noticed in the last paragraph. For the principle of 1. 2 (*Celarent*) can be rewritten in the form:

*If every M is not-L and every S is M, then every S is not-L*

which is obviously a special case of 1. 1. But for the reduction of moods which involve existential import it is necessary, of course, to allow the inference from universal statements to their subalterns. In short, the principles of the various moods need not be regarded as independent by any one who accepts the various logical principles used in reduction.

In recent centuries there have been many discussions about the essence of syllogistic reasoning, and odd passages of Aristotle that have nothing to do with his doctrine of syllogism have been cited in support of this or that generalization. The most widely accepted formula is the *dictum de omni et nullo*; 'What is predicated of any whole is predicated of any part of that whole.'[2] But there has been argument in favour of the tag *Nota notae est nota rei ipsius*, or 'What qualifies an attribute qualifies a thing possessing it'.[3] Neither of these dicta is satisfactory even for the first mood of the first figure; but it is useless to discuss them in detail, since the whole debate arises from a misunderstanding. Aristotle formulated a separate principle for each of his fourteen moods, and then

---

[1] This result is worked out by Aristotle in *An. Pr.* ii. 8–10.
[2] Supposed to be derived from ibid. i. 1 (24$^b$26).
[3] This has been said to come from *Categories*, 3 (1$^b$10).

showed in his doctrine of reduction from one figure to another how the last twelve moods could be derived from the first two. Those who ignore his doctrine of reduction but insist on asking for a single principle of syllogistic reasoning seem to have no clear idea of what they want.

Throughout his logical writings Aristotle followed the practice of expressing the principle of each syllogistic mood in a conditional statement such as 'If every M is L and every S is M, then every S is L'. In later antiquity admirers like Galen and Boethius presented his work as a theory of inference schemata, i.e. as a theory in which rules of inference are taught by means of skeleton arguments such as 'Every M is L, and every S is M; therefore every S is L', and this custom has been followed by most modern expositors. There is therefore some interest in returning, as we have done, to Aristotle's own practice. But it would probably be a mistake to lay much emphasis on the distinction. For in the detailed application of his theory Aristotle reasons as though his conditional statements were in effect rules of inference rather than theses. Thus when he explains his method of reduction *per impossibile*, he does *not* try to show that one of his conditional statements follows from another in accordance with the general principle

*If (if P and Q then R) then (if P and not-R then not-Q).*

Rather he tries to show that if anyone rejects a certain pattern of inference while accepting a certain other pattern he can be led into self-contradiction. That is the point of his comparison between this method of reduction and the argument which establishes the incommensurability of the diagonal with the side of a square. There are indeed very few remarks *about* the conditional form of statement to be found in Aristotle's work, though there is very frequent *use* of that form to express entailment.

In recent times Łukasiewicz has tried to present Aristotle's syllogistic as a deductive system (that is to say, in the manner of Euclid's *Elements*) with four special axioms, namely two syllogistic principles, 1. 1 (*Barbara*) and 3. 4 (*Datisi*), and two laws of identity, 'Every X is X' and 'Some X is X'.[1] The result is something of great interest, but very different from Aristotle's own conception of his work; and for an understanding of the history of logic it is important to record the differences.

In the first place, although Aristotle propounded his syllogistic principles in statements of the conditional form, it seems certain that he regarded use of this form as no more than one device

---

[1] J. Łukasiewicz, *Aristotle's Syllogistic* (1st ed. 1951).

among others for saying that certain premisses allow inference to certain conclusions. Unlike Łukasiewicz, he did not think of his syllogistic theory as presupposing a more fundamental part of logic which deals with the notions of conditionality and negation. And when he talked of the reduction of all syllogisms to 1. 1 (*Barbara*) and 1. 2 (*Celarent*), what he had in mind was a procedure like that we have illustrated above by a complex derivation in tree form, rather than the deduction of one conditional thesis from another.

Secondly, Aristotle did not, like Łukasiewicz, think of his task as that of formulating axioms to delimit the sense of relational signs such as the medieval *A* and *I*. For him the universal affirmative and the particular affirmative had no special priority among his four forms; and although he undoubtedly assumed application for all his general terms, he would probably have been surprised and puzzled if told that his theory presupposed Łukasiewicz's second law of identity.

Thirdly, it is evident from the way in which Aristotle introduces conversion that he regarded it as a form of argument independent of syllogism. Whereas Łukasiewicz derives the principles of conversion from axioms which appear at first sight to have nothing to do with conversion, Aristotle presents these principles in the second chapter of his *Prior Analytics* as evident to anyone familiar with the procedure of *ecthesis* and the notion *reductio ad impossibile*. It is true that the order of his argument in this chapter is not very clear, and that the commentator Alexander of Aphrodisias thought he might have intended use of a third-figure syllogism rather than simple *ecthesis*. But the kind of proof which Łukasiewicz gives for principles of conversion seems to have been conceived first in the Middle Ages (perhaps by the English logician Kilwardby), and its adoption is inconsistent with Aristotle's programme of taking 1. 1 (*Barbara*) and 1. 2 (*Celarent*) as the basic principles of syllogistic. For such proof involves use of a second- or third-figure syllogism which cannot itself be reduced to one of Aristotle's two primary syllogistic patterns except by use of conversion.

## 7. *Aristotle's Modal logic*

Together with the theory of pure (or assertoric) general statements and syllogisms constructed from them, Aristotle elaborated a theory of modal statements and modal syllogisms. A modal statement is one containing the word 'necessary' or the word 'possible' or some equivalent of one of these, and a modal syllogism is one in which at least one of the premisses is a modal statement. Statements of the form 'It is necessary that-P' were later called apodeictic, statements of the form 'It is possible that-P' problematic, and statements lacking either qualification assertoric. We shall use this terminology for convenience.

The theory of modal statements is developed in *De Interpretatione*, chapters 12 and 13, and in *Prior Analytics*, i. 3 and 13; that of modal syllogisms in *Prior Analytics*, i. 8–22. In the earlier passage Aristotle does not explain why he treats of modality, or how it is germane to the general theme of his work; but at the beginning of his discussion of modal syllogisms he says:

'Since there is a difference between belonging, necessarily belonging, and being able to belong (for many things belong but not necessarily, others neither necessarily nor at all, but are able to belong), it is clear that there will be syllogisms in each of these cases, and that terms will not be related in the same way, but in the one case the premisses will assert necessity, in the second actuality, and in the third possibility.'[1]

We can see from this why Aristotle thinks that the theory of modality belongs to the formal theory of argument. The notions of possibility and necessity have that complete generality which is stated in the *Rhetoric* to be characteristic of rhetorical and dialectical *topoi*.[2] Any statement on any theme may be qualified by 'possibly' or 'necessarily'. Furthermore, the distinction between necessary and non-necessary predication is basic in the theory of the predicables, where an accident (συμβεβηκός) is defined as a character that may (ἐνδέχεται) or may not belong to some given thing, e.g. as being seated may or may not belong to a man.[3]

Before discussing whether Aristotle was right in thinking that the theory of modality should be included in the theory of argument, we must ask what he meant by necessity and possibility; and before attempting to answer this question, we must give in outline the contents of the relevant sections.

In chapter 12 of the *De Interpretatione* Aristotle considers two questions, 'What is the proper contradictory of a modal statement?' and 'Does the modal word modify the predicate of a sentence or the whole sentence?' The second question is not clearly stated, but an answer to it emerges incidentally in the course of the discussion of the first.

Aristotle's answer to the first question is that the contradictory of 'It is possible that-P' is 'It is not possible that-P' and not 'It is

---

[1] *An. Pr.* i. 8 (29ᵇ29–35).
[2] See quotation above, p. 34.    [3] *Topica*, i. 5 (102ᵇ6).

possible that-not-P'. A similar statement holds of 'It is necessary that-P' and other modal assertions.[1] This is obviously correct.

He includes 'True: not-true' in his list of contradictory pairs. This is probably the first instance of the treatment of truth as a quasi-modal notion.

His answer to the second question is that the modal words must be taken as modifying the whole sentence in which they occur and not any single word or phrase in it. The statement of this is not very clear, but Aristotle's thought seems to be that we should regard the subordinate clause as the subject of the modal sentence, which as a whole is used to affirm or deny possibility or one of the other modal notions of what is expressed by the subordinate clause. A modal expression such as 'is possible' is to be regarded as analogous to the verb 'to be' used existentially. It is used to make an assertion about what is expressed by the subordinate clause, and in order to deny this assertion, we must attach the negative particle to the modal expression and not to the clause, just as the denial of 'There is a man' is 'There is not a man' and not 'There is a not-man'.[2] So far the analogy with existential statements is helpful to Aristotle's argument, but consideration of assertoric sentences containing the verb 'to be' tempts him to make the generalization that contradictories are always formed by attaching 'not' to that verb when it occurs. Modal phrases and statements form an exception to this rule. For the contradictory of 'the possibility that X should be' is 'the impossibility that X should be' and not 'the possibility that X should not be'. Aristotle is therefore led to realize that in a modal statement the modal expression forms the main predicate of the sentence and is, as it were, external rather than internal to the rest. He makes this same point about 'It is contingent' in the *Prior Analytics*,[3] so that it appears to be his considered opinion, although, as we shall see, he sometimes deviates from it.

In this point, too, he seems to be clearly right and for this reason we shall throughout the discussion of modality use the rather artificial forms 'It is possible that-P', &c., where 'P' marks a gap suitable for a propositional sign. In Greek and English alike there are many alternative idiomatic ways of expressing modal statements; e.g. alternative expressions to 'It is necessary that X is Y' are 'X must be Y' and 'X is necessarily Y'. These forms may be misleading, especially the latter, which suggests that the modal term modifies the predicate. For a person using Greek this false suggestion is particularly liable to arise in connexion

---

[1] *De. Int.* 12 (22ᵃ12).                   [2] Ibid. (21ᵇ26–32 and 22ᵃ8–11).
[3] *An. Pr.* i. 3 (25ᵇ19–25).

with apodeictic statements, because these are often expressed by the use of the adverbial phrase ἐξ ἀνάγκης ('of necessity'). Problematic propositions are not so easy to read in this way, as there is no adverb corresponding to the English 'possibly', and, in Aristotle at least, the most common way of expressing a problematic statement is by the use of the verb ἐνδέχεσθαι ('to admit', 'to be possible').

In chapter 13 of the *De Interpretatione* Aristotle is concerned to make clear the logical relations between 'It is possible (δυνατόν) that-P', 'It is contingent (ἐνδεχόμενον) that-P', 'It is necessary (ἀναγκαῖον) that-P', their several contradictories, and the corresponding expressions with negative subordinate clauses, e.g. 'It is possible that-not-P', &c. The discussion is very difficult to follow, and the main source of the difficulty seems to be that Aristotle is at first trying to combine two contradictory theses, namely (i) that 'It is possible that-P' and 'It is contingent that-P' mutually entail each other[1] and (ii) that 'It is possible that-P' is equivalent to 'It is not necessary that-not-P'.[2] The contradiction arises in the following way. 'It is contingent that-P' entails 'It is contingent that-not-P', so that if we identify possibility with contingency, 'It is possible that-P' entails 'It is possible that-not-P'. Now 'It is necessary that-P' obviously entails 'It is not necessary that-not-P', i.e. according to the second thesis 'It is possible that-P'. This according to the first thesis entails 'It is possible that-not-P'. We therefore have the contradictory conclusion that 'It is necessary that-P' entails 'It is possible that-not-P'. As a solution to this difficulty Aristotle finally lays down the rule that 'possible' (δυνατόν) is to be regarded as compatible with 'necessary'. Indeed, 'it is possible' follows from 'it is necessary', although of course not everything that is possible is also necessary.[3]

It would have been convenient if Aristotle had used different words to express the two notions of that which is not impossible and that which is neither impossible nor necessary. He does not, however, take this course, but in the *Prior Analytics* uses predominantly ἐνδεχόμενον and its related verbal forms, treating it as synonymous with δυνατόν, and allowing it to have two senses, a stricter in which it means 'neither impossible nor necessary' and a looser in which it means simply 'not impossible'. The following passages are clear on this point: 'I call to be possible (ἐνδέχεσθαι) and the possible (τὸ ἐνδεχόμενον) that which is not necessary, but from which, if we suppose it to exist, nothing impossible follows. The necessary is said to be possible homony-

---

[1] *De. Int.* 13 (22ᵃ15).
[2] Ibid. (22ᵇ20).                                    [3] Ibid. (23ᵃ17).

mously.'[1] Here τὸ ἐνδεχόμενον is defined, in effect, as that which
is neither necessary not impossible; for the impossible follows
only from the impossible. But in the last clause Aristotle allows
an extended sense in which the necessary may also be said to be
possible. The second passage runs as follows: 'So that A possibly
belongs to no B. This syllogism does not conclude to the possible
in our defined sense, but in the sense that it does not necessarily
belong to any B (τοῦ μηδενὶ ἐξ ἀνάγκης).'[2] Here Aristotle points
out that the conclusion of the syllogism in question, 'It is possible
that no B is A', means simply 'It is not necessary that any B is A',
i.e. 'It is not impossible that no B should be A', and not 'It is
neither necessary nor impossible that no B should be A'. He keeps
his two notions distinct, although he uses the same word. We
shall in general follow Sir David Ross and express Aristotle's
stricter notion by 'it is contingent that', while reserving 'it is
possible that' for 'it is not impossible that'.

In the *Prior Analytics* ἐνδεχόμενον when occurring in a premiss
always means 'it is contingent that', but when occurring in a
conclusion, as we have just seen, it sometimes means 'it is possible that', but when this is so Aristotle always states the fact.
Sometimes also when used with οὐδενί it means 'is possible',
e.g. ἄνθρωπον οὐδενὶ ἵππῳ ἐνδέχεται[3] ('It is not possible for any
horse to be a man'). These cases are generally clear from the
context.

Aristotle was probably determined by metaphysical considerations to make contingency, rather than possibility, the leading
notion in his theory of problematic syllogisms; for in his metaphysics the distinction between the necessary and the impossible
on the one hand and the merely factual on the other is of fundamental importance. But his choice, though understandable, is
unfortunate from a logical point of view, since a statement of
contingency is, as we have seen, a disguised conjunctive statement and all statements occurring in syllogisms should be simple
in Aristotle's sense.

No analysis of either necessity or possibility is attempted in
either the *Prior Analytics* or the *De Interpretatione*, but it is shown that
either term may be defined in terms of the other with the help of
negation. We have already seen that the possible may be defined
as the 'not-necessarily-not'. Alternatively the necessary may be
defined as the 'not-possibly-not'. The contingent may then be
defined as what is possible and not necessary. Thus all the
modal notions may be defined beginning with either necessity or

---

[1] *An. Pr.* i. 13 (32ᵃ18–21).                [2] Ibid. i. 15 (34ᵇ25).
[3] Ibid. (34ᵇ13).

possibility and negation. The relations between them may be set out simply in a square of opposition as follows:

It is necessary that-P        It is impossible that-P

It is possible that-P        It is not necessary that-P

It is contingent that-P

Within the square the relations of contradiction, contrariety and subalternation are maintained as in the assertoric square of opposition, and 'It is contingent that-P' is defined as the conjunction of the two subcontraries.

The Aristotelian theory of modal syllogisms is generally recognized to be confused and unsatisfactory, and it has been conjectured that it is a late and unfinished work, inserted into the *Prior Analytics* long after the completion of the rest of the book. But it is not necessary to suppose this in order to account for its unsatisfactoriness. Aristotle was hampered not only by his choice of an unnecessarily difficult definition of possibility, but also by the absence of a logic of propositions, such as the Stoics developed in the next century, and by the lack of any perspicuous symbolism. His method of work is to go through the valid assertoric moods, testing the new syllogisms which result when one at least or may be both of the assertoric premisses are replaced by modal propositions. The number of possible combinations is large $(8 \times 14 = 112)$, and though many can be taken together (as when Aristotle accepts on the basis of a single argument modal syllogisms with two apodeictic premisses corresponding to all assertoric moods except *Baroco* and *Bocardo*[1]), the amount of argumentation involved is still considerable, so that the reader of these chapters inevitably has the feeling that there are too many trees for the wood to be plainly seen. Furthermore, it has been recognized since the time of his immediate successors, Eudemus and Theophrastus, that some of the arguments are doubtful.

Before considering his treatment of modal syllogisms we shall consider Aristotle's theory of the conversion of modal statements. Here he is guided almost entirely by the insight of the *De Interpretatione* that the modal word qualifies a whole proposition. It seems obvious from this that, if one proposition entails another, the necessity, or possibility, of the first extends also to the second. Aristotle adheres to this rule in his theory of the conversion of

[1] *An. Pr.* i. 8 (29$^b$35 ff.).

apodeictic statements, saying that they convert in precisely the same way as the corresponding assertoric statements.[1]

His theory of the conversion of problematic statements has two peculiarities. In the first place, he allows a new kind of conversion, called by Sir David Ross complementary conversion.[2] This is the inference from 'It is contingent that-P' to 'It is contingent that-not-P'.[3] We may also infer that, given that a proposition is contingent, its contrary is contingent. In the light of the definition of contingency, this is sound.

But Aristotle also maintains that the problematic universal negative does not convert simply, if it is taken as a statement of contingency, arguing as follows:[4] 'It is contingent that every S is L' entails by the rule of complementary conversion 'It is contingent that no S is L'. If this is taken to entail 'It is contingent that no L is S' which in turn entails by complementary conversion 'It is contingent that every L is S', then 'It is contingent that every S is L' would entail 'It is contingent that every L is S'. This Aristotle thinks is obviously not the case, presumably because 'Every S is L' does not entail 'Every L is S'. This is a weak argument; for from the fact that 'It is contingent that-P' entails 'It is contingent that-Q' it certainly does not follow that 'P' entails 'Q'. For, as we have seen, 'It is contingent that-P' entails 'It is contingent that not-P'. Aristotle, however, reinforces his argument by an example. He says that it is contingent that no man should be white, but not contingent that no white thing should be a man, because many white things are necessarily not men. By 'many white things' Alexander says he means for example snow and swans.[5] If Alexander is right, Aristotle's position is very strange; for if the converted proposition is false because snow and swans exist, the original proposition should be equally false because negroes exist. Both propositions in fact appear to be true; for it is equally contingent that no swans should exist and that no negroes should exist.

It would be ungracious, tedious, and unprofitable to subject the whole of Aristotle's doctrine of modal syllogisms to detailed criticism. We shall deal with two points only at some length, because they are the origins of further logical development.

Aristotle seems to have been almost wholly mistaken in his theory of syllogisms with problematic premisses. He says, for example, that first-figure syllogisms corresponding to *Barbara* are valid and yield a problematic conclusion when both premisses

[1] Ibid. i. 3 (25ª27–35).     [2] *Aristotle's Prior and Posterior Analytics*, p. 298.
[3] *An. Pr.* i. 13 (32ª35 ff.).                    [4] Ibid. i. 17 (36ᵇ35.).
[5] *In An. Pr. Lib. I Commentarium*, ed. Wallies, *C.I.A.G.* ii(i), p. 220.

are problematic or when the major is problematic and the minor assertoric. That this is not so may be shown by the following pairs of premisses:

(1) It is contingent that every triangle should be blue.
    It is contingent that every red thing should be a triangle.
(2) It is contingent that every animal should be a biped.
    Every man is an animal.

In each case the conclusion we should draw by the Aristotelian rules is plainly false, though the premisses are true.

Aristotle gives very few examples in these sections, so that it is difficult to trace the source of his mistake. It may be that in spite of his official view, he thinks of contingency as internal to the proposition and is misled by the consideration of an argument such as the following:

For every mammal it is contingent that it should have reddish hair.
Every man is a mammal.
Therefore for every man it is contingent that he should have reddish hair.

This argument is valid and in English can be understood more easily in the form:

Every mammal either may or may not have reddish hair.
Every man is a mammal.
Therefore every man either may or may not have reddish hair.

It should be noted, however, that the major premiss is not equivalent to the proposition 'It is contingent that every mammal should have reddish hair', which may still be true even though some mammals, e.g. foxes, necessarily have reddish hair. Moreover, even with this analysis of the problematic proposition, the syllogism with two problematic premisses is invalid, as may be seen by considering the following pair of premisses:

Every triangle may or may not be blue.
Every red thing either may or may not be a triangle.

This formulation shows clearly the two fallacies involved in drawing a universal affirmative problematic conclusion from a pair of premisses of this form. The first is the fallacy of four terms; for 'being capable of being a triangle' is a different term from 'being a triangle'. The second is the assumption that, if premisses are severally possible, they must be jointly possible. Aristotle rightly observes that what is entailed by the possible must itself be possible,[1] but it does not follow from this that what is entailed by the conjunction of a number of severally possible premisses must itself be possible.

It appears that Aristotle was aware that the fallacy of four terms might arise; for he seems to be trying to avoid it by suggesting that sometimes, but not always, 'Every $B$ is possibly $A$' should be understood to mean 'Everything which is contingently $B$ is contingently $A$',[2] and he perhaps intends the premisses of syllogisms with two problematic premisses to be understood in this way. According to this direction our first syllogism would be expanded as follows:

Everything which may or may not be a triangle may or may not be blue.
Everything which may or may not be red may or may not be a triangle.
Therefore everything which may or may not be red may or may not be blue.

It might be argued that the conclusion is here true and the syllogism valid, but this move will not overcome all Aristotle's difficulties; for the syllogism with an assertoric minor premiss remains invalid even if the major premiss is interpreted in this way.

The second point we shall discuss is Aristotle's treatment of syllogisms with one apodeictic and one assertoric premiss. This has puzzled logicians since the time of Eudemus. For convenience of reference let us write $A^n$ for an apodeictic universal affirmative proposition and $E^n$ for an apodeictic universal negative proposition.[3] Then what Aristotle asserts in his *Prior Analytics*, i. 9, is in effect that a syllogism of the form $A^nAA^n$ in the first figure is valid, though one of the form $AA^nA^n$ is invalid, and similarly that a syllogism of the form $E^nAE^n$ is valid, though one of the form $EA^nE^n$ is invalid. This is surprising. Consider the examples:

(1) It is necessary that no male cat should be female.
Every ginger cat is a male cat.
Therefore it is necessary that no ginger cat should be female.

(2) No female cat is ginger.
It is necessary that every mother cat should be a female cat.
Therefore it is necessary that no mother cat should be ginger.

An. Pr. i. 15 (34ᵃ25–33).　　　　　　　　　　² Ibid. i. 13 (32ᵇ25 ff.).
³ We are here following the notation of Sir David Ross in his edition of *Aristotle's Prior and Posterior Analytics*. See especially the table opposite p. 286.

It seems that (2) is as valid as (1) or (1) as invalid as (2). In fact
Aristotle should have rejected both; but he rejects (2) only, on
the ground that by combining the conclusion with the minor
premiss in a modal syllogism of the third figure corresponding to
*Felapton* it is possible to infer 'It is necessary that some female cat
should not be ginger', which is objectionable because it takes us
beyond the merely factual connexion of characteristics stated in
the major premiss. This move is not possible in the case of (1)
because the combination of the major premiss and the conclusion,
which are both negative, gives no inference. It is possible, however, to construct a plausible, although not entirely syllogistic,
argument to show that if we accept the conclusion of (1) we must
go beyond its minor premiss in the same way in which Aristotle
found it objectionable to go beyond the major premiss in (2).
We begin with the plausible proposition 'It is necessary that every
cat should be either male or female' and from this derive 'It is
necessary that every non-female cat should be male'. This together with the obverted form of the conclusion of (1), 'It is
necessary that every ginger cat should be non-female', yields in
accordance with the wholly apodeictic syllogism corresponding
to *Barbara* 'It is necessary that every ginger cat should be male'. If
then we should reject (2) on the grounds that to accept its conclusion would be to accept an apodeictic statement not entailed
by its major premiss, we should also reject (1) because, if we accept
its conclusion, we must accept an even stronger apodeictic statement not entailed by its minor premiss. Aristotle should, therefore,
have rejected both syllogisms alike, a course which is certainly
favoured by intuition. What mistaken reasoning, then, led him
to accept syllogism (1)? He says:

'If *A* is taken as necessarily (ἐξ ἀνάγκης) belonging or not belonging
to *B* and *B* as merely belonging to *Γ*; if the premisses are taken in this
way, *A* will necessarily belong or not belong to *Γ*. For since *A* belongs
to all *B* of necessity and *Γ* is among the *B*'s, it is clear that one or other
of the relations will necessarily hold of *Γ*.'[1]

It seems that here, as in the case of syllogisms with problematic
premisses, Aristotle has been misled by his adverbial formulation
to think of the modal qualification as internal to the proposition,
i.e. that he has in mind a syllogism of the following form:

Every *B* is necessarily-*A*.
Every *Γ* is *B*.
Therefore every *Γ* is necessarily-*A*.

[1] *An. Pr.* i. 9 (30ª18 ff.).

This line of thought is not, however, carried through consistently; for it leads to the conclusion that premisses of the form 'Every *B* is *A*' and 'Every *Γ* is necessarily-*B* should give no conclusion (and not, as Aristotle says, an assertoric one), since they contain four terms.

It appears that in general in his theory of the conversion of modal statements, Aristotle takes what may be called the external view of modality, while in treating of modal syllogisms he is inclined to the internal interpretation. There is therefore a certain incoherence between the two parts of his theory,[1] and the latter part is clearly wrong. If modal words modify predicates, there is no need for a special theory of *modal* syllogisms. For these are only ordinary assertoric syllogisms of which the premisses have peculiar predicates. On the other hand, if modal words modify the whole statements to which they are attached, there is no need for a special modal *syllogistic*, since the rules determining the logical relations between modal statements are independent of the character of the propositions governed by the modal words. To put this in another way, all modal statements may be regarded not only, as Aristotle saw, as affirmative, but also as singular; or more strictly, distinctions of quantity do not apply to them. For this reason Aristotle was mistaken when, elated by the discovery of the syllogism, he tried to use it as a guide in his investigation of modal logic.

The necessary basis for a modal logic is a logic of unanalysed propositions such as was developed by the Stoics.[2] Lacking this, Aristotle had no clear thread to guide him, but it is interesting to see that it is in connexion with modal logic that he first uses propositional variables, i.e. letters which may be replaced by propositional signs and not by terms, almost as if the exigencies of the subject-matter were driving him to adopt the necessary symbolism. The passage runs:

'We must first say that if when *A* is, it is necessary that *B* should be, then if *A* is possible, it is also necessary that *B* should be possible. For let us suppose that what we call *A* (τὸ ἐφ'ᾧ *A*) is possible, what we call *B* impossible. If then the possible, since it is possible, should come to be and the impossible, being impossible, should not come to be, then it would be possible for *A* to come to be without *B*, and if to come to be then to be. . . .

Moreover when we say that, if *A* is, *B* must be, we must not take it

---

[1] A. Becker, *Die Aristotelische Theorie der Möglichkeitschlusse*. For further discussion of Aristotle's modal syllogistic see also I. M. Bochenski, *La Logique de Théophraste*, pp. 67 ff.; J. Łukasiewicz, *Aristotle's Syllogistic*, pp. 133 ff.; and J. Hintikka, 'Necessity, Universality, and Time in Aristotle', *Ajatus*, xx (1957), pp. 65–90; and 'An Aristotelian Dilemma, ibid. xxii (1959), pp. 87–92.

[2] J. Łukasiewicz, *Aristotle's Syllogistic*, p. 133.

that *A* is a single thing, for nothing follows of necessity from a single thing, but from two at least, as for example when the premisses are as we have stated according to the syllogism. For if *Γ* holds of *Δ* and *Δ* of *Z* then *Γ* will necessarily hold of *Z*. And if both are possible the conclusion will be possible. So that if one calls the premisses *A* and the conclusion *B*, it will result not only that *B* will be necessary if *A* is necessary, but also that it will be possible if *A* is possible.'[1]

Aristotle here states two important modal theses, i.e. that what follows from the necessary is necessary and that what follows from the possible is possible. It is in reliance on the first of these theses that he develops his theory of syllogisms with two apodeictic premisses, the only undoubtedly correct part of his modal syllogistic. The second thesis is not similarly helpful in developing the theory of syllogisms with problematic premisses; for while the conjunction of two necessary propositions is itself necessary, the conjunction of two possible propositions is not always possible.

The passage just quoted is noteworthy not only for the use of propositional variables, but also for the fact that Aristotle acknowledges explicitly that two premisses can be considered as forming a single statement. At the same time it shows his weaknesses. His preoccupation with syllogism leads him to say that nothing can follow from a single premiss and he assumes that the conjunction of two possible propositions is always possible. But such a passage is a promising beginning for modal logic and similar modal theses are to be found in Aristotle's works outside the *Organon*. He says, for example, in the *De Caelo*:

'It is not the same thing to make a false and to make an impossible hypothesis. The impossible follows from the impossible. A man has at the same time the power to sit and the power to stand, because when he has the one he also has the other, but not in such a way that he can both sit and stand at the same time.'[2]

Here we have a modal thesis formally derivable from the second thesis in the last quoted passage. It can be more accurately stated as 'If "P" entails "Q" and it is impossible that-Q, then it is impossible that-P'. Aristotle also clearly recognizes in this passage that two propositions which are severally possible need not be jointly possible and that consequently a distinction may be drawn between absolute and relative possibility parallel to the distinction between absolute and relative necessity which he draws in the following passages:[3]

'It is not the same that everything should be of necessity when it is and that it should be simply of necessity.'[3]

---

[1] *An. Pr.* i. 15 (34ᵃ5–24).                    [2] *De Caelo*, i. 12 (281ᵇ14–18).
[3] *De Interpretatione*, 9 (19ᵃ25–27).

'One might show by an exposition of the terms that the conclusion is not necessary simply (ἁπλῶς), although it is necessary in relation to the premises (τούτων ὄντων).'[1]

The recognition of the distinction between absolute and relative possibility is implicit in an historically influential passage of the *De Sophisticis Elenchis* which explains the fallacy of composition:

'The fallacy of composition arises in connection with such statements as "The man who is sitting can walk" and "The man who is not writing can write". For it doesn't mean the same to say that it is possible for a sitting man to walk if one takes the phrase in division (διελών) and in composition (συνθείς). Similarly if one takes in composition "The man who is not writing can write"; for it means that he has the capacity to write while not writing; but if it is not taken in composition, it means that when he is not writing he has the power of writing.'[2]

It is clear that a distinction between the absolute and relative uses of the modal terms should be drawn, because what is necessary in relation to something else need not be necessary in itself, and what is possible in itself need not be so in relation to all other statements. In both Greek and English the same words are used to express both absolute and relative necessity and possibility, and this is natural; for every case of relative necessity or possibility can be expressed as a case of absolute necessity or possibility. In syllogistic, for example, if a conclusion is necessary in relation to certain premises, it is absolutely necessary that if the premises are true, the conclusion should be true also. Similarly, if the truth of 'P' is possible in relation to 'Q', it is absolutely possible that 'P and Q' should be true. But this use, though natural, may give rise to confusion, because statements of relative necessity or possibility are often made elliptically and may for this reason be misunderstood as statements of absolute necessity or possibility. Aristotle is partially aware of these facts. He explicitly draws the distinction between absolute and relative necessity, and there is no evidence that he confuses these in practice. The passage of the *De Interpretatione*, 'If it is true to say that it is white or not white then it is necessary that it should be white or not white',[3] which has sometimes been cited as an instance of such confusion,[4] is ambiguous, and the ambiguity is resolved in the passage already quoted. On the other hand, the distinction between absolute and relative possibility, although at times clearly recognized, does, as we have seen, cause Aristotle difficulty in practice. And he

---

[1] *An. Pr.* i. 10 (30ᵇ32–33).    [2] *De Sophisticis Elenchis*, 4 (166ᵃ22–30).
[3] *De Interpretatione*, 9 (18ᵃ39–18ᵇ1).
[4] e.g. by J. Łukasiewicz, *Aristotle's Syllogistic*, p. 152.

never says explicitly that relative necessity and possibility involve absolute necessity and possibility.

The enterprise of constructing a theory of syllogisms with apodeictic premisses is otiose if a necessary proposition cannot be distinguished from one which is universally true. We therefore expect Aristotle to explain the distinction between necessity and universal truth. This is done in the *Posterior Analytics* where necessary predication is characterized as not only universal (κατὰ παντός) but also essential (καθ' αὐτό).[1] Predication κατὰ παντός is defined here as predication that holds in every instance, which agrees with the definition of the same term in the *Prior Analytics*.[2] But it must be admitted that the instances he gives of predication κατὰ παντός, namely 'Every man is an animal' and 'Every line contains a point', are necessary propositions. Predication καθ' αὐτό is defined as that which states an essential connexion,[3] and Aristotle's examples show that he has in mind statements which are either definitions or based on definitions; for 'point' is essentially connected with 'line', and 'odd' and 'even' similarly with 'number'. He still holds to the distinction put forward in the *Topics* between definition and property, essential and non-essential connexion.

On consideration of these facts a reader who is familiar with later philosophy may be tempted to conclude that Aristotle meant by 'necessary' what some modern logicians have meant by 'analytic'. Such a suggestion would be misleading because the word 'analytic' has acquired in recent times an association with linguistic convention that is quite foreign to Aristotle's notion of necessity. His theory of definition is not entirely clear, but it is certain that, like Plato, he assumes definition to be of something objective, and that for him any proposed definition is either correct or incorrect. A correct definition is a true proposition and can be used as a premiss in demonstration. Demonstration, he says, does not imply Platonic Forms, but it does imply a universal, a common nature:

'So demonstration does not necessarily imply the being of Forms nor a One beside the Many, but it does necessarily imply the possibility of truly predicating one of many; since without this we cannot save the universal (τὸ καθόλου), and if the universal goes, the middle term goes with it, and so demonstration becomes impossible. We conclude then that there must be a single identical term unequivocally predicable of a number of individuals.'[4]

---

[1] *An. Post.* i. 4 (73^b25–28).    [2] *An. Pr.* i. 1 (24^b28).
[3] *An. Post.* i. 4 (73^a34 ff.).
[4] Ibid. i. 11 (77^a5 ff.).

It is this universal or common nature which is, for Aristotle, the object of definition. Here, as in Plato's work, we have the picture of a chain of universals connected by definitions, and their necessary connexions are supposed to make possible the demonstrative, syllogistic reasoning of science.

We have seen that Aristotle distinguishes between a universal premiss which is simply true and one which is necessary. Similarly, when he uses the word ἀνάγκη to mark the connexion between premisses and conclusion, he does not mean simply that, in all cases where premisses of the kinds indicated are true, a conclusion of the kind indicated is likewise true. There is no evidence that he held such a view. He probably correctly took the word ἀνάγκη to have the same meaning whether it occurs in a premiss or marks the connexion between premiss and conclusion. But although this is correct, there is an important difference between the two uses which Aristotle does not make explicit.

Consider the syllogism:

Every animal is necessarily mortal;
Every man is necessarily an animal;
Therefore necessarily every man is necessarily mortal.

On the Aristotelian theory the adverb 'necessarily' within the premisses marks the essential connexions between animality, mortality, and manhood, and it is easy to think the 'necessarily' which introduces the conclusion is simply another mark of this. If, however, we replace the terms by variables, as Aristotle himself does, we see that this cannot be the case:

Every M is necessarily L.
Every S is necessarily M.
Therefore necessarily every S is necessarily L.

For the 'necessarily' which now introduces a schematic conclusion cannot be the expression of any connexion between the terms of the special example with what we stated. It would be appropriate if any other terms were introduced to replace the variables; and if the modal premisses were replaced by merely assertoric premisses, it would still be appropriate. It is justified, then, not by any definitional connexion between the terms, but by the nature of the logical connexion signified by 'every . . . is' and in the case of the modal syllogism by the subordinate occurrences of 'necessarily'. In other words we are here dealing with a formal rather than a material necessity. Although Aristotle *uses* this distinction (it is involved in his use of variables), he seems not to have reached the point of formulating it.

It seems clear from this account that Aristotle is right in includ-ing the study of modality in his logical inquiries for two reasons. In the first place, since we can draw a distinction between the merely *de facto* and the necessarily true and between the merely false and the impossible and these distinctions, like that between the true and the false, apply to all propositions alike, whatever their subject matter, the theory of inferences which depend on the modal characters of propositions is part of the general theory of valid inference, that is, of logic. Secondly, we cannot consider logic itself without using modal terms. For the formal connexions which we consider in logic are naturally described as *necessary*; and when we try to explain what is meant by the validity of a syllogism, we commonly say that it is *impossible* for the premisses to be true while the conclusion is false. Even if the study of these notions as *used* in logic were assigned to a different science, called, for instance, meta-logic, this would still be a natural extension of logic. Aristotle has the credit of initiating such study, and the faulty detail of his theory is not surprising in a work which breaks completely fresh ground.

## 8. *Non-syllogistic Logic in the* Analytics

We have seen that Aristotle does not provide any theory of conditional statements as a sub-structure for his syllogistic, but there are in his *Prior Analytics* two pronouncements which have sometimes been cited as theses about the conditional form. They can better be treated as logical truths about entailment or relative necessity, however this may be expressed. In modern terminology we may say that they are principles of contraposition and tran-sitivity. The first is introduced in the course of a discussion of the dictum that true premisses cannot entail a false conclusion though false premisses may entail a true conclusion. It is one of the few passages in Aristotle's work involving the use of propositional variables, and it can be rendered as follows:

> *If given that-P it is necessary that-Q, then given that-not-Q it is necessary that-not-P.*[1]

The second is presented by means of an example, but it too can be formulated with propositional variables as follows:

> *If given that-P it is necessary that-Q and given that-Q it is necessary that-R, then given that-P it is necessary that-R.*[2]

With the help of these two principles, considered as rules of inference, Aristotle tries to show that a proposition and its

[1] *An. Pr.* ii. 2 (53^b12).      [2] Ibid. ii. 4 (57^b6).

contradictory cannot both entail the same conclusion.[1] His argument seems out of place in the passage where it occurs. It is also
somewhat obscure, because it is stated by means of an example;
but it can be formalized as follows. Let us suppose

(1) Given that-P, it is necessary that-Q

and

(2) Given that-not-P, it is necessary that-Q.

Then from (1) we can obtain by the principle of contraposition
the consequence

(3) Given that-not-Q, it is necessary that-not-P.

And from this together with (2) we can obtain by the principle of
transitivity the further consequence

(4) Given that-not-Q, it is necessary that-Q.

But this, Aristotle thinks, is absurd, and so he says that (1) and
(2) cannot both be true. The derivation of (4) from (1) and (2)
is, of course, perfectly valid, but Aristotle is mistaken in thinking
that (4) is absurd. On the contrary, the establishment of (4)
would be a very interesting achievement, because it would
amount to a demonstration of the absolute necessity that-Q. Such
demonstration has played an important part not only in philosophy but also in mathematics, and we shall see in the next
chapter that it was studied with great care by the logicians of the
Stoic school. There is nothing in the passage of Aristotle we have
just considered to show that it had been discussed by anyone
before him, but it is tempting to suppose that his irrelevant ex-
cursus is directed against a doctrine of the Megarians. For what
he attacks is in effect the positive counterpart of Zeno's *reductio
ad impossibile*, and the tradition of Zeno's dialectic was preserved
in his day by this group of his philosophical opponents. On the
other hand, the best-known example of such reasoning before the
date of the *Prior Analytics* comes not from a Megarian source but
from Aristotle's own early work called the *Protrepticus*. Wishing
to show that we cannot escape from the need to study philosophy,
he writes there: 'Either we ought to philosophize or we ought
not. If we ought, then we ought. If we ought not, then also we
ought [i.e. in order to justify this view]. Hence in any case we
ought to philosophize.'[2]

---

[1] Ibid. (57ᵃ36–57ᵇ17).
[2] *Aristotelis Fragmenta*, ed. V. Rose, frag. 51; W. D. Ross, *Select Fragments of
Aristotle*, p. 27. This fragment and the passage of *An. Pr.* ii. 4. mentioned in the last
note are discussed by W. Kneale in 'Aristotle and the *Consequentia Mirabilis*', *Journal
of Hellenic Studies*, lxxvii, part i (1957), pp. 62–66.

That Aristotle did not recognize the conditional form of statement and argument based on it as an object of logical inquiry comparable to the syllogism may be inferred safely from his discussion of certain arguments said to be 'from hypothesis'. (ἐξ ὑποθέσεως). Here the subject-matter seems to demand an explicit discussion of the varieties of argument with one conditional premiss, but Aristotle draws distinctions on other grounds. The basic forms of argument involving one conditional premiss are those which were later called the *modus ponendo ponens* and the *modus tollendo tollens*, i.e. arguments of the forms. 'If P then Q; but P; therefore Q' and 'If P then Q; but not-Q; therefore not-P'. The second is obviously exemplified by a *reductio ad impossibile* such as the proof that the diagonal of a square is incommensurable with the side. In three places Aristotle says that such *reductio* is a kind of reasoning from hypothesis,[1] and in the first and the third of these places he explains the difference between *reductio* and other reasoning from hypothesis. If it is not *reductio*, reasoning from hypothesis, he says, begins with an agreement that if a certain proposition is true the desired conclusion follows. The proposition thus introduced as a substitute (μεταλαμβανόμενον) for the conclusion is then proved syllogistically and the conclusion thereby established ἐξ ὑποθέσεως. It is agreed, for example, that if there is not always one potentiality of opposites there is not always one science of opposites, and then it is proved syllogistically that there is not always one potentiality of opposites.[2] Apparently the hypothesis is the conditional statement agreed at the beginning. With this he contrasts *reductio ad impossibile*,[3] saying that in the latter case no prior agreement is necessary, but assent is secured 'because the falsity is obvious' (διὰ τὸ φανερὸν εἶναι τὸ ψεῦδος). Again he has in mind the argument to the incommensurability of the diagonal with the side of a square.

This is strange and confused. Arguments with a conditional statement as premiss may no doubt be distinguished in more ways than one. The important logical distinction is between that form in which the second premiss is the affirmation of the antecedent of the conditional premiss and that form in which it is the denial of the consequent (*ponendo ponens* and *tollendo tollens*). But other distinctions, which are epistemological rather than logical may be drawn with respect to the reasons for accepting the premisses. Aristotle seems to be ignoring the purely logical distinction and contrasting a case in which the conditional premiss must be conceded in advance with a case in which the second

---

[1] *An. Pr.* i. 23 (40ᵇ25), i. 29 (45ᵇ15), and i. 44 (50ᵃ32).
[2] Ibid. i. 44 (50ᵃ29).                                      [3] Ibid. (50ᵃ31 ff.).

premiss (i.e. that an odd is not equal to an even number) is an obvious truth.

The source of the confusion is that he is concerned throughout to establish how many stages of a given argument can be reduced to syllogistic form. In an earlier passage he has argued that all valid arguments involve syllogistic reasoning, even if they are not entirely reducible to it,[1] and 'hypothesis' seems here to be his general name for a statement which plays an essential role in an argument but not as any part of a syllogism nor yet as the conditional formulation of a syllogism. Thus we have for example:

(1)  If there is not always one potentiality of opposites, there is not always one science of opposites. (*Hypothesis supposed to be conceded in advance.*)

There is not always one potentiality of opposites. (*Provable syllogistically.*)

Therefore there is not always one science of opposites. (*Conclusion drawn non-syllogistically.*)

(2)  If the diagonal is commensurate with the side, an odd will be equal to an even number. (*Abbreviated summary of a syllogism in conditional form.*)

It is not the case that an odd is equal to an even number. (*Denial of obviously false hypothesis.*)

Therefore the diagonal is not commensurate with the side. (*Conclusion drawn non-syllogistically.*)[2]

Although Aristotle was aware that there are several kinds of valid argument which cannot be reduced to syllogistic form, he did not, so far as we know, succeed in giving a formal analysis of any of them. He promises a fuller account of the varieties of argument from hypothesis (in the wide sense of 'hypothesis' which we have just explained),[3] and in one place he distinguishes two forms, arguments κατὰ μετάληψιν and arguments κατὰ ποιότητα;[4] but he does not discuss them further in his surviving works, and we cannot be sure that these phrases have for him the same meaning as they have for his pupil, Theophrastus. Aristotle has no word for a conditional statement. He does not use the word ὑποθετικός or make a contrast between hypothetical and categorical statements or syllogisms. The theory of those arguments whose validity depends on the meaning of conditional or other complex sentences was in antiquity the work of the Stoics.

---

[1]  Ibid. i. 23 (40ᵇ23).
[2]  Ibid. (41ᵃ28).
[3]  Ibid. i. 44 (50ᵃ39).
[4]  Ibid. i. 29 (45ᵇ17).

Aristotle and his school, fascinated by the achievement of the syllogism, made little progress in that direction, though, as we shall see in the last section of this chapter, they did something to redeem Aristotle's promise.

## 9. *Aristotle's School: Theophrastus*

After his death Aristotle's works were collected and edited by his pupils. The chief editor was presumably Theophrastus, who succeeded him as head of the Lyceum. This philosopher also wrote works of his own on logic. None of them has survived, but from references in later commentators it seems clear that they were concerned chiefly with the development of Aristotle's doctrine and its presentation in improved form. Some of his contributions have been incorporated into the tradition which derives from Aristotle, and they deserve to be noticed here.

In the first place, Theophrastus is said to have added five indirect moods to the first figure of syllogism.[1] These are moods in which the middle term is subject of one premiss and predicate of the other, but the major term appears as subject and the minor term as predicate in the conclusion. Their principles are:

1.5. *If every M is L and every S is M, then some L is S* (Baralipton).
1.6. *If no M is L and every S is M, then no L is S* (Celantes).
1.7. *If every M is L and some S is M, then some L is S* (Dabitis).
1.8. *If every M is L and no S is M, then some L is not S* (Fapesmo).
1.9. *If some M is L and no S is M, then some L is not S* (Frisesomorum).

As the commentator Alexander of Aphrodisias said, these are only elaborations of some incidental remarks made by Aristotle in his *Prior Analytics*,[2] and it is not to be supposed that Theophrastus thought he was doing more than systematizing the teaching of his master. In later times his five moods were assigned to a fourth figure in which the middle term is the predicate of the premiss containing the predicate of the conclusion and the subject of the other premiss. In order to present his principles in the form required by this innovation we need only transpose the premisses and change the variables 'L' and 'S' consistently:

4.1. *If every L is M and every M is S, then some S is L* (Bramantip).
4.2. *If every L is M and no M is S, then no S is L* (Camenes).
4.3. *If some L is M and every M is S, then some S is L* (Dimaris).
4.4. *If no L is M and every M is S, then some S is not L* (Fesapo).
4.5. *If no L is M and some M is S, then some S is not L* (Fresison).

[1] *In Aristotelis An. Pr. Lib. I Commentarium*, ed. Wallies, *C.I.A.G.* ii (i), pp. 69 f.
[2] *An. Pr.* i. 7 (29$^a$19) and ii. 1 (53$^a$8).

If we add the subaltern mood with the principle:

4. 21.  *If every L is M and no M is S, then some S is not L* (Camenos).

we get six valid moods in this figure, as in each of those recognized by Aristotle, but the number of moods which require the assumption of existential import (4. 1, 4. 21, and 4. 4) is here three, instead of two.

Much energy has been spent in disputes about the existence of a separate fourth figure, but it is not at all clear what the disputants wish to prove or disprove. Sometimes they talk as though the question at issue were about the way men naturally argue. If this is the problem, the proper way to solve it is to hold a large-scale empirical inquiry, but we must then contemplate the possibility that the fourth figure exists for some people and not for others! That the arguments which some logicians assign to a fourth figure are valid was expressly stated by Aristotle himself, and the answer to the question whether they belong to a separate figure must surely depend on our definition of a figure. If figures are to be distinguished by the roles which the subject and the predicate of the conclusion have in the premisses, there are undoubtedly four figures. But this was not Aristotle's conception of the distinction. According to his view the subject of the conclusion was minor and the predicate of the conclusion major in order of generality. We have seen that his way of describing matters is unsatisfactory in any case for all syllogisms except those in the first mood of the first figure; but it is quite obviously incompatible with recognition of a fourth figure where the predicate of the conclusion appears as subject in its premiss and the subject of the conclusion as predicate in the other premiss. It is this feature which accounts for the 'unnaturalness' of the figure; for we do not commonly present our premisses in such a way that *both* terms of the conclusion appear there with reversed roles. If we nevertheless accept the figure as a distinguishable form of argument, we find that for the same reason it is somewhat apart from the others, in that the reduction of its moods *per impossibile* does not lead outside the figure.

Secondly, Theophrastus is remembered for an interesting attempt to simplify the theory of modality. From several passages in Alexander's commentary on the *Prior Analytics* it appears that Theophrastus saw the difficulties in Aristotle's treatment of the subject and offered a definition according to which 'It is possible that-P' would not entail 'It is not necessary that-P'. He therefore rejected complementary conversion as invalid.[1] This was plainly

[1]  *In Aristotelis An. Pr. Lib. I Commentarium*, ed. Wallies, *C.I.A.G.* ii (i), p. 159.

necessary since he was dealing with statements of possibility and not of contingency. He also maintained against Aristotle that the universal negative problematic proposition is simply convertible. In this too he is right, and his argument as reported by Alexander is interesting:

'If it is possible for $A$ to belong to no $B$, then it is possible for $B$ to belong to no $A$. For since it is possible for $A$ to belong to no $B$, then, when it does not belong to any, it is possible for $A$ to be separated (ἀπεζεῦχθαι) from all of the $B$'s (τῶν τοῦ $B$). In this case $B$ will be separated from $A$.'[1]

This argument seems to be suggested by some sort of spatial diagram, and it may perhaps reflect the first use of such diagrams as an aid to logical reflection.

Tradition also attributes to Theophrastus a simplification of the doctrine of modal syllogisms. According to Alexander he maintained that in any modal syllogism the conclusion has the same character as the weaker of the two premisses.[2] Here it must be understood that a statement of actuality is supposed to be weaker than a statement of necessity and a statement of possibility weaker than a statement of actuality. Alexander notes for purposes of comparison that a syllogism with a particular premiss must have a particular conclusion and a syllogism with a negative premiss a negative conclusion. This is the first appearance of the rule *Sectetur partem conclusio deteriorem*. Theophrastus's reform eliminates those theses of Aristotle's modal logic which seem unsatisfactory and produces a notable simplification of the whole.

Unfortunately the modifications which he introduced render his own system incoherent;[3] for it is impossible to maintain that the rule *Sectetur partem conclusio deteriorem* always holds, that the Aristotelian principle of indirect reduction is universally applicable, and that certain moods recognized by Theophrastus are valid. According to Alexander, Theophrastus applied indirect reduction to some modal syllogisms at least,[4] and it would have been strange indeed if he had not recognized the general applicability of the principle. But he also recognized the validity of certain moods with one assertoric and one problematic premiss, of which the conclusion should be, according to the *deteriorem* rule, problematic.

We use the same symbolism as before to represent the two first-figure forms specifically mentioned by Alexander.[5] 'Sa$^n$L'

[1] *In Aristotelis An. Pr. Lib. I Commentarium*, ed. Wallies, *C.I.A.G.* ii (i), p. 220.
[2] Ibid., p. 124.
[3] I. M. Bochenski, *La Logique de Théophraste*, p. 101.
[4] *In Aristotelis An. Pr. Lib. I Commentarium*, ed. Wallies, *C.I.A.G.* ii (i), p. 123.
[5] Ibid., p. 173.

stands for a universal affirmative apodeictic proposition, '$So^pL$' for a particular negative problematic proposition, and so on. We then have the following forms of syllogism:

|  |  |  |  |
|---|---|---|---|
| (1a) | $Ma^pL$ | (2a) | $MaL$ |
|  | $SaM$ |  | $Sa^pM$ |
|  | $Sa^pL$ |  | $Sa^pL$ |

The inconsistency arises as follows. Since the contradictory of a proposition of the form '$Sa^pL$' is of the form '$So^nL$', by the rule of indirect reduction the syllogisms set out above should yield the following:

|  |  |  |  |
|---|---|---|---|
| (1b) | $So^nL$ | (2b) | $MaL$ |
|  | $SaM$ |  | $So^nL$ |
|  | $Mo^nL$ |  | $So^nM$ |

Each of these, however, breaks the rule that the conclusion follows the weaker premiss. It is clear therefore that we cannot retain together this rule, the principle of indirect reduction, and the validity of the original syllogisms. Obviously the way out of the difficulty is to reject the original syllogisms, and it is easy to construct counter-examples to show that they are not, in fact, valid forms. Thus we have:

(1a) All ponies may be black.
All Palominos are ponies.
Therefore all Palominos may be black.

(2a) All members of the Cabinet are over forty.
All members of Parliament under forty may be members of the Cabinet.
Therefore all members of Parliament under forty may be over forty.

This solution raises the question of the interpretation of the *deteriorem* rule. It may be taken in a strong sense as giving a reliable means of deriving modal from purely assertoric syllogisms, i.e. as meaning 'Given any valid assertoric syllogism, a corresponding syllogism with any modal qualification of premisses is valid, provided that the conclusion agrees in modality with the weaker premiss'. Understood in this sense, the rule provides an immense simplification of the theory of modal syllogisms, but leads, as we have seen, to inconsistancy. On the other hand, it may be taken, like the corresponding *deteriorem* rule for the assertoric syllogism, as a necessary, but by no means sufficient, condition for the validity of modal syllogisms. Possibly Theophrastus thought of it in this way and devised it in the course of his rejection of the Aristotelian form $A^nAA^n$ discussed above. Taken in this sense, it simplifies the theory only to the extent of providing another limitation on possible valid forms and gives no clear rule for finding them. A much more precise understanding of the modal notions was required before the problem of finding such a rule could be solved.

It remains to ask why Theophrastus should have accepted the doubtful syllogisms set out above, if he did not take the *deteriorem* rule in the strong sense. A possible answer is that he was deceived by plausible examples and by the confusion between absolute and relative possibility. To show how both these factors may be misleading, let us consider the following syllogism, which is of the same form as the invalid example (1*a*) above:

All micro-organisms are possibly harmful to human beings.
All moulds are micro-organisms.
Therefore all moulds are possibly harmful to human beings.

Without regard to the complications of modality regarded as an internal qualification, 'possible' may be taken here in two senses. In the first place it may be taken to qualify the conclusion as it stands alone, e.g. it may mean 'self-consistent'. In this sense the conclusion is true, but it is not formally derivable from the premisses, as we showed by the counter-example, in which from two premisses, each of which is self-consistent, we derived, by the same rule, an inconsistent conclusion. Yet it is only this sense of 'possible' which is relevant to the theory of modal syllogism, as the conclusion of a syllogism is *proved* only if it can be stated in detachment from the premisses. If, however, we think of 'possible' in the second sense as meaning 'possible in relation to the premisses', i.e. consistent with them, then the conclusion is certainly that, but so is any other proposition which is not inconsistent with the premisses, and we could as well conclude our syllogism:

Therefore all cheese is possibly edible.

We have already noted a parallel distinction between absolute and relative necessity. The parallelism is brought out if we consider a syllogism which is equivalent by the rule of indirect reduction to our invalid syllogism (2*a*):

All members of the cabinet are over forty.
Necessarily some members of parliament under forty years of age are not over forty years of age.
Therefore necessarily some members of parliament under forty years of age are not members of the cabinet.

This again is plausible, but it owes its plausibility to the ambiguity of 'necessarily' in the conclusion. The conclusion without the 'necessarily' is necessary in relation to the premises, but so is the conclusion of any valid syllogism. It is not necessary in itself nor has it been proved to be so. Aristotle, as we have noticed above, made the same point in relation to the second figure form $EA^nE$. We are unconsciously influenced by the fact that the statement is relatively necessary to accept it as absolutely necessary.

Theophrastus may have made a third noteworthy contribution to logic by developing the doctrine of hypothetical syllogism from the hints dropped by Aristotle in his discussion of arguments from hypothesis. We cannot assess his contribution with certainty, for the evidence is scanty and confused. Some of the discoveries mentioned under this head may have been made by Aristotle himself, but not published, while others may be due to Eudemus or others of the Aristotelian school. In commenting on Aristotle's discussion of arguments from hypothesis, Alexander says that Theophrastus mentioned the varieties of hypothetical argument in his *Analytics*, and that other pupils of Aristotle, including Eudemus, wrote about them.[1] Alexander uses the word ὑποθετικός both of premises[2] and of arguments,[3] and contrasts it with κατηγορικός. It does not, however, mean for him what 'hypothetical' means for us (i.e. 'conditional'), but as applied to premises 'complex' and as applied to arguments 'having at least one complex premiss'. Hypothetical arguments in his sense of the phrase are stated to be of the following kinds:

(1) from a conditional premiss (διὰ συνεχοῦς, ὃ καὶ συνημμένον λέγεται);
(2) by subsumption of a third term (τῆς προσλήψεως ὑποθετικούς);
(3) from a disjunctive premiss (διὰ τοῦ διαιρετικοῦ τε καὶ διεζευγμένου);
(4) from a denial of a conjunction (διὰ ἀποφατικῆς συμπλοκῆς);
(5) by analogy or similarity of relations (ἐξ ἀναλογίας);
(6) by degrees of a quality (κατὰ ποιότητα or ἀπὸ τοῦ μᾶλλον καὶ ἧττον καὶ ὁμοίως).

What exactly Aristotle and his pupils worked out under (1), (3), and (4) we cannot say. But they cannot have gone far, since the study of these parts of logic was regarded in later antiquity as a Stoic innovation and Boethius says expressly that they did not produce much in this field.[4] That they did something, however, is confirmed by the existence of a separate non-Stoic terminology

---

[1] *In Aristotelis An. Pr. Lib. I Commentarium*, ed. Wallies, *C.I.A.G.* ii (i), pp. 389 ff.
[2] Ibid., p. 324.  [3] Ibid., p. 390.
[4] *De Syllogismo Hypothetico*, i. ed. Migne, col. 831C.

for the discussion of conditional and disjunctive statements. In the list quoted in the last paragraph Alexander gives both technical terms together, putting the Stoic second as though it were better known. And Galen tells us that the non-Stoic terms were current among the older logicians, i.e. those before the Stoics.[1] This must mean that they were introduced by Aristotle or his pupils.

Alexander gives an account of arguments κατὰ ποιότητα.[2] They are *a fortiori* arguments with a general conditional premiss. Alexander's example is:

> If that which appears to be more sufficient for happiness is not in fact sufficient, neither is that which appears to be less sufficient.
> Health appears to be more sufficient for happiness than wealth and yet it is not sufficient.
> Therefore wealth is not sufficient for happiness.

The theory of arguments κατὰ ποιότητα was probably an attempt to systematize what Aristotle says of *a fortiori* arguments in various passages of his *Topics*.

The subject of arguments κατὰ πρόσληψιν is very confused. In commenting on the passage in which Aristotle casually mentions arguments κατὰ μετάληψιν as a variety of arguments from hypothesis, Alexander identifies πρόσληψις with μετάληψις, saying that the Aristotelians called μετάληψις what the moderns (i.e. the Stoics) called πρόσληψις.[3] But in another place he says that the Aristotelians thought of μετάληψις as implying less novelty than πρόσληψις.[4] Both words can have the meaning 'something taken in addition', and for the Stoics the πρόσληψις was the additional premiss in an argument with a complex leading premiss, e.g. in an argument of the form 'If the first, then the second; but the first; therefore the second' the statement indicated by the 'the first' would be the πρόσληψις. In the passage where he identifies the meanings of the two words Alexander has an argument of this form in mind, as is shown by his example:

> If the soul always moves, the soul is immortal.
> The soul always moves.
> Therefore the soul is immortal.

In accordance, however, with the practice of the Aristotelians of stressing the importance of syllogism, he points out that the

---

[1] *Institutio Logica*, ed. Kalbfleisch, pp. 8 and 32.
[2] *In Aristotelis An. Pr. Lib. I, Commentarium*, ed Wallies, *C.I.A.G.* ii (i), p. 265.
[3] Ibid., p. 324.                                        [4] Ibid., p. 263.

πρόσληψις is proved syllogistically by introducing the middle term 'self-moving'. If this were all that is meant by arguments κατὰ πρόσληψιν, they would be identical with arguments of type (1) and there would be no point in the separate heading. In this passage, however, Alexander does not mention Theophrastus, and in the passage in which he specifically mentions him in connexion with premisses and arguments κατὰ πρόσληψιν, the argument intended seems to be of a different sort; for he says that the premiss which Theophrastus called κατὰ πρόσληψιν is of the form 'A is predicated of everything of which B is predicated universally'.[1] He explains that such premisses contain a third term potentially, though this is not made definite and clear. They are presumably called κατὰ πρόσληψιν because the third term is added in the other premiss. He also says that, according to Theophrastus, premisses κατὰ πρόσληψιν differed only in expression (τῇ λέξει μόνον) from ordinary categorical premisses. This statement is also made by an anonymous scholiast who reports that Theophrastus maintained that such premisses are potentially equivalent to categorical premisses.[2] This scholiast also tells us that Theophrastus constructed syllogisms in three figures from such premisses, but he gives only the form of the leading premiss in each case. Only in one place have we a complete syllogism of this kind. This occurs in a scholium on Aristotle attributed to the school of Ammonius, an Alexandrian commentator of the sixth century A.D., which bears the interesting title 'On all Forms of Syllogism'.[3] The syllogism κατὰ πρόσληψιν in the first figure is:

> Substance is predicable universally of whatever is predicable of man.
> But animal is predicable universally of man.
> Therefore substance is predicable universally of animal.

This is an argument of the form which later logicians have called argument by substitution and detachment. It cannot be reduced to syllogistic form, although it has some connexion with the syllogism:

> Every animal is a substance.
> Every man is an animal.
> Therefore every man is a substance.

It can be derived from the syllogism by first making the middle term indeterminate and combining the two premisses into one

[1] Ibid., p. 378.  [2] *Scholia in Aristotelem*, ed. Brandis, 189<sup>b</sup>43.
[3] Ammonius, *In Aristotelis An. Pr. Lib. I. Commentarium*, ed. Wallies, *C.I.A.G.* iv (vi), Praefatio, p. xii.

new leading premiss. The new second premiss then reintroduces the middle term by substituting it for the indeterminate 'whatever' of the new leading premiss, and the conclusion is equivalent to the major premiss of the original syllogism. The scholiasts seem to have thought that Theophrastus derived the other two figures by performing similar operations on second- and third-figure categorical syllogisms; for it is said that in each case it is the middle term which is indeterminate and the forms given for the new leading premisses are:

*Fig.* 2. That which is predicated of *A* is predicated also of *B*.
*Fig.* 3. Of that of which *A* is predicated *B* is also predicated.[1]

These forms suggest a superficial resemblance to second- and third-figure syllogisms, but they could also have been derived from a first-figure syllogism by making indeterminate respectively the major and the minor terms. Thus corresponding to the example given by the Ammonian writer we should have:

*Fig.* 2. That which is predicated of animal is predicated of man.
Substance is predicated of animal.
Therefore substance is predicated of man.

*Fig.* 3. Of that of which animal is predicated substance is also predicated.
Animal is predicated of man.
Therefore substance is predicated of man.

We cannot in any case be certain of the details of Theophrastus' work; for he may have been misunderstood by the commentators. But it is clear that these three arguments are valid, and that the first at least is not reducible to ordinary syllogistic form. Moreover, they open a new field for logical investigation in that they involve explicit general statements about properties or classes rather than about individuals. This becomes clear if we contrast the arguments with another argument by substitution and detachment, which both Aristotle and Theophrastus would probably regard as an ordinary categorical syllogism:

Whatever is a man is mortal.
Socrates is a man.
Therefore Socrates is mortal.

The gap indicated by 'Whatever' must here be filled by the name of an individual, and when it is so filled we have an argument by substitution and detachment of the same general form as the

[1] *Scholia in Aristotelem*, loc. cit.

syllogism κατὰ πρόσληψιν, but with different content. In modern practice it is usual to indicate the gap in which substitution can be made by the use a letter or other symbol called a 'free variable'. It is interesting that neither Aristotle nor Theophrastus uses this device. Letters are used by them simply as abbreviated illustrations, and for the free variable they still use the demonstrative and relative pronouns. There is still an incomplete grasp of the potentialities of the use of variables. The first premiss of Theophrastus' syllogism κατὰ πρόσληψιν could have been expressed much more clearly in the form 'Substance is predicable of $A$, if $A$ is predicable of man'.

When it is realized that generalizations can be made about properties and classes as well as about individuals, it will be seen that statements of many interesting new forms can be constructed. For instance, we can speak of all the classes all of whose members have a certain property and of all the classes some of whose members have a certain property. Aristotle saw this distinction in that chapter of his *Prior Analytics* on which the Theophrastean discussion is based. He wrestles here with the ambiguities of '$A$ belongs to all $B$'. It may mean, he says, either '$A$ belongs to all of that to which $B$ belongs' or '$A$ belongs to all of that to which $B$ belongs universally', and he finally explains that it is to be taken to mean '$A$ is predicated of all those things of which $B$ is predicated' (καθ᾽ ὅσων τὸ $B$ λέγεται, κατὰ πάντων λέγεσθαι καὶ τὸ $A$).[1] But he goes on to say that of these things $B$ may or may not be predicated universally. The things in question, therefore, are not individuals but rather the classes all or some of whose members have the property $B$. We may have arguments then involving either of the two premisses:

(1) $A$ is predicated of all of which $B$ is predicated universally.
(2) $A$ is predicated of all of which $B$ is predicated but not universally.

An example of an argument with a premiss of type (2) is:

All animals some of which are tame are mammals.
Some cats are tame.
Therefore cats are mammals.

However we interpret this argument, it is clear that it cannot be regarded as equivalent to an ordinary categorical syllogism, since the first premiss is not equivalent either to 'All tame animals are mammals' or to 'Some tame animals are mammals'.

Aristotle seems to have been more aware of these interesting

[1] *An. Pr.* i. 41 (49$^b$27).

possibilities than Theophrastus, who, if we are to believe our authorities, maintained that premisses κατὰ πρόσληψιν were equivalent to ordinary categorical premisses[1] and that 'A is predicated of all B' must mean always and only 'A is predicated of all of that of which B is predicated universally',[2] which is to obliterate the distinction made by Aristotle. It seems clear in any case that the complexities of the syllogism κατὰ πρόσληψιν were not further developed in antiquity and we may conjecture that failure to develop them was partly due to failure to develop an adequate symbolism.

Another interesting entry in Alexander's list of hypothetical syllogisms is (5) and about this he gives us more information in another place.[3] Sometimes the arguments under this heading were called totally hypothetical syllogisms (δι᾽ ὅλων ὑποθετικοί), or syllogisms with three hypothetical propositions (διὰ τριῶν). Theophrastus is said to have arranged them in three figures and to have given the following five examples of arguments belonging to his figures:

1.1. *If A then B; if B then Γ; therefore if A then Γ.*
1.2. *If A then B; if B then Γ; therefore if not Γ then not A.*
2.1. *If A then B; if not A then Γ; therefore if not B then Γ.*
2.2. *If A then B; if not A then Γ; therefore if not Γ then B.*
3.1. *If A then Γ; if B then not Γ; therefore if A then not B.*

Alexander cites as an illustration of 1.1 the argument 'If a man exists an animal exists; if an animal exists a substance exists; therefore if a man exists a substance exists'. The same argument had been given by Aristotle himself as a specimen of reasoning not in ordinary syllogistic form.[4] And so it seems reasonable to say that here, too, Theophrastus was only elaborating the work of his master, perhaps even that he was reducing to order the unwritten teaching of Aristotle's last years. This impression is confirmed by a more detailed consideration of the formulae. For it seems clear that they have been inspired by reflection on the figures of the categorical syllogism set out by Aristotle. The first formula corresponds in an obvious way to a syllogism in the first mood of the first figure, and the formula assigned by Theophrastus to his third figure corresponds in a no less obvious way to a categorical syllogism in the first mood of the second figure. It is indeed rather surprising that Theophrastus did not try to emphasize this latter correspondence by numbering his figures

---

[1] Alexander, *In Aristotelis An. Pr. Lib. I Commentarium*, ed. Wallies, *C.I.A.G.* ii (i), p. 378.                        [2] *Scholia in Aristotelem*, ed. Brandis, 189ᵇ43.
[3] Op. cit., *C.I.A.G.* ii (i), p. 326.                        [4] *An. Pr.* i. 32 (47ᵃ28).

like the figures of categorical syllogisms. It is interesting to notice that the variables in Theophrastus' formulae are apparently intended to mark places which can be filled by general terms, with some such word as 'exists' understood, if not expressed. Alexander tells us that Theophrastus called all such arguments 'syllogisms by analogy' either because of the similarity in form between the three propositions involved in each of them or because they yielded only conditional conclusions and were therefore not syllogisms in that sense in which, according to Aristotle, a syllogism must prove that something is the case or that something is not the case.[1] Neither reason is very good; but if Theophrastus thought of the first, he must have recognized what modern logicians call the transitivity of implication. In any case it is clear he was not referring to arguments by analogy in the modern sense of that expression.

According to Alexander's account Theophrastus used inference schemata in his doctrine of totally hypothetical syllogisms. When talking of categorical syllogisms, Aristotle had formulated a principle for each mood in a conditional statement. Many modern expositors write 'Every M is L; and every S is M; therefore every S is L'. But this is not Aristotle's idiom: it seems to have been introduced by Theophrastus, for Aristotle kept to his own method even here, if we may judge from the single example mentioned above. The two methods are, of course, equivalent in effect, since Aristotle's conditional statements are to be understood as principles necessarily true on logical grounds, while Theophrastus' inference schemata are to be understood as though they were preceded by the preamble 'Any argument of one of the following forms is valid'. Whichever we use, we make a second-order statement, i.e. a statement about other statements. But the difference is important for certain later developments of logic.

All the contributions of Theophrastus mentioned so far appear to be elaborations of the teaching of Aristotle, but a scholiast says that he disagreed with his master on one small point of some interest.[2] Aristotle had maintained that a word such as 'every' cannot properly be attached to the predicate of a proposition.[3] In commenting on this the scholiast says that Theophrastus argued that if no additional distinction ($\pi\rho\sigma\sigma\delta\iota\sigma\rho\iota\sigma\mu\delta\varsigma$) such as we now call a quantifier were ever allowed in the predicate we should sometimes be unable to make our meaning clear, e.g. if we had to say 'Phaenias does not possess knowledge' instead of

---

[1] Cf. ibid. 23 (40ᵇ23).
[2] *Aristotelis Organon Graece*, ed. Waitz, i, p. 40.  [3] *De Interp.* 7 (17ᵇ16).

'Phaenias does not possess *all* knowledge'. It is clear that he was not advocating quantification of the predicate as preached by Sir William Hamilton in the middle of the nineteenth century, but the much more interesting thesis that a quantifier may be attached to a general word or phrase which is neither subject nor predicate in the statement in which it occurs. Aristotle might have replied that the proposition of Theophrastus could be expressed by the statement 'Some knowledge is not possessed by Phaenias', where the quantifier is attached to the subject; but this device cannot be applied where two distinct quantifiers are required, as in the statement '*Some* man does not possess *all* knowledge', and multiply general statements are quite common in science and philosophy, e.g. '*Every* event has *a* cause'. In short, Aristotle's theory of general statements is concerned only with those which have a superficial resemblance to the subject-predicate pattern of singular statements such as 'Socrates is white', although there may be many different forms. But this moral was not drawn until many centuries later.

# III

# THE MEGARIANS AND THE STOICS

## 1. *The Megarian Philosophy and the Origins of Stoic Logic*

THROUGHOUT later antiquity two great schools of logic were distinguished, the Peripatetic which was derived from Aristotle, and the Stoic which was developed by Chrysippus from the teaching of the Megarians. It is tantalizing that tradition has preserved so little of the work of these latter philosophers; for what remains suggests that they were highly intelligent and deserving of better treatment than they have received from historians.

Whereas Aristotle's logical theorizing appears to have been prompted mainly by thought about demonstration as it occurs, for example, in geometry, the Megarians seem to have concentrated their attention on Zenonian dialectic and on the everyday argumentative encounters which gave rise to what Plato and Aristotle call eristic. It is, at least, easy to see how the characteristic features of their argument could have arisen from such concentration, and we have evidence of an inheritance from the Eleatic school. Euclides, the founder of the Megarian school, is said to have applied himself to the works of Parmenides,[1] and Diodorus Cronus, one of its prominent members, to have constructed arguments against the possibility of motion.[2] It is also significant that the Stoic logic was known as dialectic.[3]

Euclides was a slightly older contemporary of Plato. Among his pupils were Eubulides, the inventor of many paradoxes,[4] and Stilpo or Stilpo's teacher.[5] Stilpo was the master of Zeno, the founder of the Stoic school.[6] One of the pupils of Eubulides was Apollonius Cronus,[7] the master of Diodorus Cronus, who was active as a teacher at the end of the fourth century B.C. According to a foolish tradition preserved by Diogenes Laertius, Diodorus committed suicide because he was not able immediately to solve a logical puzzle propounded to him by Stilpo in the presence of Ptolemy Soter.[8] This is obviously a common-room story from

[1] Diogenes Laertius, ii. 106.
[2] Sextus Empiricus, *Adversus Mathematicos*, x. 85.
[3] Diogenes Laertius, vii. 43.      [4] Ibid. ii. 108.
[5] Ibid. ii. 113.      [6] Ibid. ii. 114.
[7] Ibid. ii. 111.      [8] Ibid. ii. 111–12.

one of the Athenian colleges, but it is good enough to date the activities of Diodorus; for Ptolemy conquered Megara in 307 B.C.

The Megarians made three important contributions to the development of logic, the invention of a number of interesting paradoxes, the re-examination of the modal notions, and the initiation of an important debate on the nature of conditional statements. We shall have occasion to consider the second and third of these in detail later, but we may conveniently say something here about the first.

From the explanations given by various writers of later antiquity it appears that some of the seven paradoxes specifically attributed to Eubulides[1] were merely variants of others and that the list can probably be reduced to the four following items:

(1) *The Liar.* 'A man says that he is lying. Is what he says true or false?'[2]

(2) *The Hooded Man, the Unnoticed Man, or the Electra.* 'You say you know your brother. But that man who came in just now with his head covered is your brother, and you did not know him.'[3]

(3) *The Bald Man, or the Heap.* 'Would you say that a man was bald if he had only one hair? Yes. Would you say that a man was bald if he had only two hairs? Yes. Would you . . . , etc. Then where do you draw the line?'[4]

(4) *The Horned Man.* 'What you have not lost you still have. But you have not lost horns. So you still have horns.'[5]

Paradoxes of the first type show the oddity of trying to make a statement say something about its own truth or falsity. Those of the second type raise questions about different uses of the word 'know' and about the propriety of assuming that, if X is identical with Y, whatever can be said truly of X can also be said truly of Y. Those of the third type reveal the essential vagueness of some of our common expressions. And these of the fourth type show that if a statement (e.g. 'You have lost horns') involves a presupposition (e.g. that you once had horns) it may be negated either in a restricted way with acceptance of the same supposition or in an unrestricted way without acceptance of that presupposition. All are interesting, and it is incredible that Eubulides produced them in an entirely pointless way, as the tradition suggests. He must surely have been trying to illustrate some theses of Megarian

[1] Diogenes Laertius, ii. 108.
[2] Cicero, *De Divinatione*, ii. 11, *Academica*, ii. 96.
[3] Lucian, *Vitarum Auctio*, 22.
[4] Diogenes Laertius, vii. 82; Cicero, *Academica*, ii. 49; Horace, *Epistulae*, ii. 1 (45).
[5] Diogenes Laertius, vii. 187.

philosophy, though it may be impossible for us to reconstruct the debates in which he introduced them. We shall find that even in the mangled form in which it was transmitted this part of Megarian teaching has been of some importance in the later history of logic.

It seems probable, however, that Eubulides' work had another and more unfortunate effect on the history of logic. Diogenes Laertius says that he was strongly opposed to Aristotle and attacked him at length.[1] We do not know whether this was the beginning of the hostility between the Peripatetics and the Megarians; but it is certain that, inherited by the Stoics from the Megarians, the quarrel continued for many centuries and had a bad effect on the development of logic. For, although Aristotelian and Stoic theories are in fact complementary, they were treated as alternatives. By the time it became clear that they should be amalgamated, the intellectual impetus of the ancient world was spent, and there was no one of the requisite stature for the task.

The Stoics were the first to work out in detail a theory of arguments involving the conditional and other forms of complex propositions. For reasons we shall notice presently an interest in conditional statements was natural among philosophers who practised dialectic in the tradition of Zeno the Eleatic, and the Stoics acquired this interest through their connexion with the Megarians.

Zeno of Citium, the founder of Stoicism, who died in 264 B.C., studied under Stilpo[2] and possibly also under Diodorus,[3] and it is not fanciful to see traces of Eleatic monism in the pantheist, but nevertheless materialist, metaphysics of the Stoic school. Diogenes Laertius tells us that Zeno had Philo for a fellow-pupil, that he used to dispute carefully with him, and that he respected him as much as he did Diodorus.[4] It is true that this Zeno was not as much interested in dialectic as his namesake had been, but he is reported to have said that it was important in education because it enabled students to solve the paradoxes.[5] This seems to confirm the view that the Megarian study of paradoxes was a serious affair and not mere perversity. The influence of Megarian logic was very strong with Chrysippus (280–207) who succeeded Cleanthes, himself the successor of Zeno, as head of the Stoic school. His voluminous writings fixed the doctrines of the school, and it was even said, 'If there had been no Chrysippus, there would have been no Stoa'.[6] His work in dialectic was greatly admired by later Stoics and much discussed by other writers of

[1] Ibid. ii. 109.   [2] Ibid. vii. 2.   [3] Ibid. vii. 16.   [4] Loc. cit.
[5] Plutarch, De Stoic. Repugn. 8 (1034 E).   [6] Diogenes Laertius, vii. 183.

late antiquity. Diogenes Laertius records a saying, 'If there were dialectic among the gods, it would be none other than that of Chrysippus',[1] a saying which proves incidentally that his system was regarded as one distinct from that of Aristotle. When Clement of Alexandria wishes to mention one who is master among logicians, as Homer is master among poets, it is Chrysippus, not Aristotle, whom he names. He regards Aristotle as the master of scientists and Plato as the master of philosophers.[2] Cicero connects Chrysippus with Philo and Diodorus in a reference to the debate on conditionals:

'What a great dispute there is about that elementary point of logical doctrine, how we should judge of the truth or falsity of a complex statement such as "If it is day, it is light"? Diodorus has one view, Philo another, and Chrysippus yet a third.'[3]

We do not know for certain what view Chrysippus defended in the controversy, but it is clear that the theory of conditional propositions was central in his logic, and also that this system was derived from the dialectic of Zeno the Eleatic by a line of inheritance quite independent of Aristotle. This independence is shown in the use of separate terminology even for concepts with which Aristotle had dealt.

Unfortunately, all we know about Stoic logic is to be found in fragments preserved by writers of other schools, some of them hostile; but on many points these fragments confirm each other, and we can reconstruct the main features, though there must be some conjecture about the connexions and relations of the items. In what follows we shall often speak of the Stoics rather than of Chrysippus, because it is not easy to distinguish for certain between his views and those of his successors. Although it is clear that he laid down the general lines which they all followed, there is evidence for some diversity of opinion among his successors on details. This is very natural, since the Stoic school was still vigorous in the time of Marcus Aurelius (d. A.D. 180) and it is unlikely that a single wholly consistent body of doctrine was maintained throughout its history.

The chief sources for Stoic logic are late. In the second century A.D. Apuleius and Galen incorporated some Stoic material into their manuals of logic, and in the next century Sextus Empiricus and Diogenes Laertius preserved some interesting parts of the tradition. Sextus, who was a sceptic, gave an account of the doctrine only to refute it, but he nevertheless reported it intelli-

---

[1] Diogenes Laertius, vii. 180.     [2] *Stromateis*, vii. 16 (323).
[3] *Academica Priora*, ii. 143.

gently, although perhaps not always with complete honesty. Diogenes, who wrote a series of gossipy lives of the eminent philosophers, gave a conspectus of Stoic philosophy, including logic, in the course of his life of Zeno. Since he is generally not very reliable as an expositor, it is fortunate that in this section he drew largely on a handbook of Stoic doctrine prepared by Diocles of Magnesia, a scholar of the first century B.C. Sextus and Diogenes often confirm each other. For other knowledge of Stoic logic we must draw on scattered sources of late antiquity.

## 2. *Megarian and Stoic Theories of Modality*

Aristotle tells us that the Megarians of his day maintained there was no distinction to be drawn between potentiality and actuality.[1] In spite of its strangeness, this thesis is natural enough among Eleatics, since, as Aristotle goes on to say, it is equivalent in effect to a denial of motion or change of any kind. But if it were correct, the modal words 'possible' and 'necessary' would both alike be superfluous. It is therefore rather surprising to find that Megarians of the generation after Aristotle discussed questions of modal logic very seriously. It is possible that what they were trying to do was to find a place for the modal notions while denying the Aristotelian theory of real potentiality. This at least seems to have been the aim of Diodorus Cronus in a later generation. To Aristotle it would appear to be a denial of the distinction between the possible and the actual. In this section we shall consider together the definitions of the modal notions which were put forward by Diodorus and Philo and the variants of these which are attributed to the Stoics. For it is certain that the Stoic discussion continued that of the Megarians, and our ancient authorities often mention them together.

The most original theory is that of Diodorus Cronus. The only authority who gives us a complete account of it is Boethius, but what he says agrees with earlier incomplete accounts, in particular that of Cicero, and we may regard him as trustworthy. He tells us:

'Diodorus defines the possible as that which either is or will be (*quod aut est aut erit*), the impossible as that which, being false, will not be true (*quod cum falsum sit, non erit verum*), the necessary as that which, being true, will not be false (*quod cum verum sit, non erit falsum*), and the non-necessary as that which either is already or will be false (*aut jam est aut erit falsum*).'[2]

[1] *Metaphysica*, Θ. 3 (1046ᵇ29).
[2] *Commentarii in Librum Aristotelis Περὶ Ἑρμηνείας, Secunda Editio*, ed. Meiser, p. 234.

Since the last three definitions all contain references to truth and falsehood, it seems likely that truth was mentioned also in the original text of the first, and Cicero does in fact say: 'Placet igitur Diodoro id solum fieri posse quod aut verum sit aut verum futurum sit.'[1] The form of these definitions makes it clear that Diodorus does not think of *events* as possible, impossible, necessary or non-necessary, for he assumes that the modal adjectives apply to the same subjects as the predicates, 'true' and 'false'. It is difficult, nevertheless, to characterize these subjects exactly. We cannot say with certainty whether in his view that which is called true or false, necessary or impossible is an indicative sentence, a proposition in the modern sense, or some third thing distinct from either of these. The Greek and Latin languages, with their free use of neuter adjectives as nouns, lend themselves peculiarly well to the maintenance of such ambiguity. In our exposition of Diodorus' theory we shall use the non-committal word 'statement' in order to leave the issue open.

It also follows from the form of the definitions that Diodorus is not defining necessity *simpliciter* but rather necessity-at-a-time, and similarly with the other terms. If statements change their truth-values, then according to Diodorus' definitions, they must also change their modalities. For consider such a statement as 'There was a French revolution'. This is now necessary according to Diodorus' definition, but was not so before 1789.

Not all changes of modality, however, are permissible in Diodorus' system. A statement can be at one time possible and at a later time necessary, as we have just shown; or it can be at one time possible and at a later time impossible, e.g. 'The solar system will disintegrate'. Again, it may be at one time non-necessary and at a later time necessary, e.g. 'There will be no more men'; or it may be at one time non-necessary and at another time impossible, e.g. 'There have been exactly 1,000,000,000 men up till now'. But once a statement is necessary or impossible, it cannot again change either its truth-value or its modality; for since the necessary at a given time is defined as what will at all subsequent times be true, it follows that it will at all subsequent times be necessary. Similarly with the impossible.

Two further points about the views of Diodorus may be stated with certainty. First, that they are connected with the famous 'Master Argument' (κυριεύων λόγος), and, secondly, that they were regarded in antiquity as involving determinism or fatalism.[2]

According to Alexander, Diodorus constructed the Master

---

[1] *De Fato*, 17. Cf. Benson Mates, *Stoic Logic*, p. 37.
[2] e.g. Cicero, *De Fato*, 17; Boethius, op. cit., p. 235.

Argument in order to establish his own definition of possibility,[1] but a modern scholar has suggested that the title refers to the overmastering power of fate.[2] Epictetus gives us our only complete account of it:

'The Master Argument seems to have been formulated with some such starting points as these. There is an incompatibility between the three following propositions, "Everything that is past and true is necessary", "The impossible does not follow from the possible", and "What neither is nor will be is possible". Seeing this incompatibility, Diodorus used the convincingness of the first two propositions to establish the thesis that nothing is possible which neither is nor will be true.'[3]

To the modern reader only one statement in this argument is unexceptionable. This is the second proposition, a recognized thesis of modal logic, which, as we have seen, was already known to Aristotle. It is difficult to understand either why the first statement should have been found generally acceptable or why the first two should have been held to entail the denial of the third.

To establish the first point Diodorus probably appealed to the platitude that the past is unalterable. This is expressed as follows by Aristotle in the *Nicomachean Ethics*:[4] 'No-one deliberates about the past, but about what is to come and is possible, whereas the past cannot not have come about; so that Agathon is right when he says: "Of this power alone even God is deprived, the power of making what has been done not to have happened."'
It seems plausible to say 'What has come to be is necessarily as it is, because it cannot now be otherwise'. As Aristotle saw in the *De Interpretatione*, this is a relative necessity, but it seems plausible to attribute some sort of absolute necessity to the past when the notion of necessity is not carefully examined. It is important, however, to notice that, as put forward in the Master Argument, the thesis has an ambiguity, which we have tried to preserve by an awkward translation. It may mean either 'Every true statement about the past is necessary' or 'Every true statement in the past tense is necessary'. If we take the assertion in the second sense, it is not true according to the interpretation of 'necessary'

---

[1] *In Aristotelis An. Pr. Lib. I Commentarium*, *C.I.A.G.* ii (1), p. 184.
[2] P. M. Schuhl, *Le Dominateur et les possibles*.
[3] *Dissertationes*, ed. Schenkl. ii. 19. 1. The original is as follows: Ὁ κυριεύων λόγος ἀπὸ τοιούτων τινῶν ἀφορμῶν ἠρωτῆσθαι φαίνεται· κοινῆς γὰρ οὔσης μάχης τοῖς τρισὶ τούτοις πρὸς ἄλληλα, τῷ πᾶν παρεληλυθὸς ἀληθὲς ἀναγκαῖον εἶναι καὶ τῷ δυνατῷ ἀδύνατον μὴ ἀκολουθεῖν καὶ τῷ δυνατὸν εἶναι ὃ οὔτ᾽ ἔστιν ἀληθὲς οὔτ᾽ ἔσται, συνιδὼν τὴν μάχην ταύτην ὁ Διόδωρος τῇ τῶν πρώτων δυεῖν πιθανότητι συνεχρήσατο πρὸς παράστασιν τοῦ μηδὲν εἶναι δυνατὸν ὃ οὔτ᾽ ἔστιν ἀληθὲς οὔτ᾽ ἔσται.
[4] *Eth. Nic.* vi. 2 (1139b7–11).

given by Diodorus; for there are many statements in the past tense which are at one time true and at a later time false, e.g. 'It was fine yesterday' and in general all those in which the identification of the subject or subjects is achieved by explicit or implicit reference to the time of utterance.

On the other hand, we can produce a convincing argument for the second point about entailment only if we interpret πᾶν παρεληλυθὸς ἀληθές as 'every true statement in the past tense'. It is true we can begin without distinguishing senses. For it follows from the first proposition that every false proposition in the past tense (or, with the alternative interpretation, every false statement about the past) is impossible, because the contradictory of a necessary statement is impossible. If we can show, therefore, that every false statement in the present or future tense (or about the present or future) entails some false statement in the past tense (or about the past), we shall have shown according to the second proposition of the Master Argument that all such statements are also impossible. Here, however, the ambiguity becomes very important. First consider the statement 'I have a scar on my left hand' uttered by a speaker who has not and never will have a scar on his left hand. The statement 'I had a wound on my left hand' made by this same speaker may be said to be impossible according to one interpretation of the first proposition of the Master Argument, since it is a false statement about the past; and it may reasonably be said to follow from the statement 'I have a scar on my left hand', which is therefore also impossible.[1] In this particular case the argument is plausible, but it can be made perfectly general only by begging the question at issue. For consider a false statement about the future which applies to a case where Aristotle would have found real potentiality, e.g. a false prediction of some human voluntary action as 'He will resist the temptation'. There is no reason other than a dogmatic determinism to suppose that such a statement entails a false statement about the past; for we are not in fact in a position to fill in the gap in the sentence 'If he is to resist the temptation, then it must have been the case that . . . '. But we can construct a perfectly general argument to show that any false statement in the present or future tense entails a false statement in the past tense. For example, from the statement that a given shell now on the ocean bed is being or will be seen it would generally be taken to follow that a corresponding statement in the future tense, i.e. 'The shell will be seen' was true in the past. If the statement 'The shell will be

---

[1] For the illustration see Sextus Empiricus, *Adv. Math.* viii. 254, where it is used in a discussion of the Stoic σημεῖον, a topic closely related to that of 'following'.

seen' is in fact false, the past-tense statement which follows from
it, namely 'It was true that the shell would be seen', is also false,
and so according to the first proposition of the Master Argument
impossible.[1]

If he used this second argument, Diodorus seems to have over-
reached himself; for being perfectly general, it shows that every
false statement in the present or future tense is impossible, and
every true statement necessary. It follows from this that the
possible, the true, and the necessary coincide as do the non-
necessary, the false, and the impossible. There can therefore be
no change of truth-values. But Diodorus' definitions of the
modal notions are based on the assumption that truth-values
change. The ambiguity which gives rise to this confusion has
already been pointed out. Only if we take πᾶν παρεληλυθὸς
ἀληθές to mean 'every true statement (i.e. proposition) about the
past' is the first proposition of the Master Argument plausible.
What is true about the past remains so and cannot be altered.
But a statement which is about the past in this sense need not be
expressed in an indicative sentence in the past tense. It may be
expressed in a sentence whose main verb is in the future tense,
e.g. 'It will always be true that Queen Anne is dead'. Similarly,
a statement in the past tense may be about the future, e.g. 'It has
always been true that I shall be in Oxford tomorrow, i.e. on
18 April 1960'. Diodorus claims that statements of this sort
are necessary because he wants to be able to say that they trans-
mit their necessity to the propositions expressed by their subordinate clauses in the future tense. The Master Argument thus
depends on an ambiguity. What is said to be necessary in the
first proposition is not the same sort of thing that is said to be
impossible in the second. Every true statement about the past is
necessary in relation to the fact that what it states to have happened
has in fact happened. But it is not a statement about the past in
this sense that follows from a false statement about the future,
but simply a statement in the past tense. There is no more reason
for attributing impossibility to such a statement than there is for
attributing impossibility to the future-tense statement from which
it was derived. As an argument for determinism, then, the Master
Argument fails. It also fails in the purpose for which Alexander
says it was designed; for far from making it plausible to define
the possible as 'What is or will be true', it demolishes the alternatives that give point to this definition.

[1] Cf. A. N. Prior, 'Diodoran Modalities' in *The Philosophical Quarterly*, v (1955),
pp. 205–13. The illustration is from Philoponus, *In Aristotelis An. Pr. Commentaria*, ed.
Wallies, *C.I.A.G.* xiii (ii), p. 169.

The confusions of the Master Argument arise from a failure which we have already noticed in Aristotle to distinguish between an indicative sentence and the proposition it expresses. Diodorus probably began by noticing the difference between such sentences as 'It is day' (a common Megarian example), which are said loosely to be sometimes true and sometimes false, and sentences in the past tense, e.g. 'Plato founded the Academy', which do not change their truth-value. He then wrongly assumed that the platitude about the unalterability of the past was equivalent to the false statement that true past-tense sentences do not change their truth value. He thought he had thus found a way to refute the Aristotelian theory of potentiality on the grounds of a thesis recognized by Aristotle himself. For it is likely that the Master Argument is directed against chapter 9 of the *De Interpretatione*. However that chapter is interpreted, Diodorus contradicts it, but he shares with Aristotle the mistake of assuming that it is sensible to talk about truth-at-a-time. It is likely that this dispute stimulated the Stoics to distinguish between sentences and what they express and to consider seriously the problem of changes in truth-value.

In opposition to Diodorus' doctrine Philo is said to have defended the view that a state of affairs may be called possible in 'virtue of the bare suitability of the subject' (κατὰ ψιλὴν τὴν ἐπιτηδειότητα τοῦ ὑποκειμένου) even though its realization is prevented by external constraint, as for example the burning of a piece of wood is prevented by circumstances when it is at the bottom of the ocean.[1] Boethius expounds his four definitions of modal terms as follows:

'Philo says that the possible is that which by the intrinsic nature of the assertion admits of truth (*quod natura propria enuntiationis suscipiat veritatem*), as when for example I say that I shall read the *Bucolics* of Theocritus again to-day. If no external circumstance prevents this, then, considered in itself (*quantum in se est*), the thing can be affirmed truly. In the same way this same Philo defines the necessary as that which, being true, can never, considered in itself, admit of falsity. The non-necessary he explains as that which, considered in itself, can admit of falsity, and the impossible as that which by its intrinsic nature (*secundum propriam naturam*) can never admit of truth.'[2]

Unfortunately we have no more detailed information about his views, but it seems clear that he took possibility as the basic modal notion and identified it with self-consistency.

[1] Alexander, loc. cit. Cf. also Philoponus, loc. cit., and Simplicius, *In Aristotelis Categorias Commentarium*, ed. Kalbfleisch, *C.I.A.G.* viii, pp. 195–6.
[2] Boethius, op. cit., p. 234.

The view attributed to the Stoics is rather more complicated and it is possible that it has been imperfectly reported. It is expressly distinguished from that of Philo by Boethius,[1] although it obviously has something in common with the earlier doctrine. We have essentially the same account in two widely separated sources. Diogenes Laertius gives the Stoic definitions as follows:

'The possible is that which admits of being true (τὸ ἐπιδεικτικὸν τοῦ ἀληθὲς εἶναι), provided that external circumstances do not prevent it from being true (τῶν ἐκτὸς μὴ ἐναντιουμένων πρὸς τὸ ἀληθὲς εἶναι), as for example "Diocles is alive". The impossible is that which does not admit of being true, as for example "The earth is flying". The necessary is that which is true and does not admit of being false, or, admitting of being false, is prevented from being false by external circumstances, as for example "Virtue is beneficial". The non-necessary is that which is true and may be false if external circumstances do not prevent, as for example "Dion is walking".'[2]

And Boethius reports of the first three items:

'The Stoics have declared that to be possible which is susceptible of true affirmation (*quod susceptibile esset verae praedicationis*) when things which, although they are external, happen together with it do not in any way prevent it (*nihil his prohibentibus quae, cum extra sint, cum ipso tamen fieri contingunt*). The impossible is that which never admits of any truth, since other things, apart from its own outcome, prevent it (*aliis extra eventum ipsius prohibentibus*). The necessary is that which when it is true does not in any way admit of false affirmation (*quod cum verum sit falsam praedicationem nulla ratione suscipiat*).'[3]

The discussion by Boethius is similar to an argument in Cicero's *De Fato* in which the views of Chrysippus are contrasted with those of Diodorus.[4] Perhaps Boethius drew on Cicero, but it is also possible that they had a common source in some Stoic handbook; for Cicero writes as if he had such a handbook before him. In any case the view called 'Stoic' by Boethius can safely be attributed to Chrysippus, although he was probably not the only one to hold it.

It will be noticed that the definition of 'necessary' as given by Diogenes covers two alternatives. The necessary is either that which does not admit of falsehood *simpliciter* or that which is true but nevertheless might have been false if external circumstances had not prevented it from being so. The first alternative is the only one illustrated; for a Stoic could scarcely have conceived that in certain circumstances 'Virtue is beneficial' might be false.

---

[1] Boethius, op. cit., p. 234.
[3] Boethius, op. cit., pp. 234-5.

[2] Diogenes Laertius, vii. 75.
[4] *De Fato*, 12-20.

But it seems clear that there is an intention to distinguish between absolute and relative necessity in the way suggested above.[1] And we have some other evidence to show that Chrysippus made this distinction. Cicero ascribes to him a contrast between simple and complex facts (*simplicia* and *copulata*).[2] Chrysippus, it seems, argued that certain simple facts (e.g. that Socrates would die on a given day) were predetermined independently of other facts, whereas other facts (e.g. that Oedipus would be born to Laius) were predetermined only in conjunction with associate facts (e.g. that Laius would have intercourse with his wife). Connected events, says Cicero, were called by Chrysippus 'condestinate' (*confatalia*). Clearly a proposition about the happening of one of them would be necessary in relation to a proposition about the happening of the other in the second sense of 'necessary' given in the Stoic definition. Thus it is true that Oedipus was born, but it would have been false had not external circumstances, i.e. the intercourse between Laius and Jocasta, prevented it from being so.

If the definition of necessary is complex in this way, the definition of the other modal notions should have a corresponding complexity. This may have dropped out in the account given by Diogenes, which is extremely compressed, or it may even be that some seemingly repetitious phrases have been dropped by copyists. If all the definitions had this internal complexity, they would run as follows:

> The possible is that which admits of truth or that which, while admitting of truth, is not prevented from being true by external circumstances.

> The impossible is that which does not admit of truth or that which, while admitting of truth, is prevented from being true by external circumstances.

> The necessary is that which is true and does not admit of falsehood or that which, while admitting of falsehood, is prevented by external circumstances from being false.

> The non-necessary is that which admits of falsehood or that which, while admitting of falsehood, is not prevented from being false by external circumstances.

It will be noticed in Diogenes' version the definition of the non-necessary requires that it be true. If this was part of the Stoic definition, it was a mistake. What is essential to a non-necessary proposition is that it *can* be false. This condition is satisfied if the proposition is in fact false, but proof of its non-necessity is then less interesting.

[1] See pp. 92–93.                            [2] *De Fato*, 30.

If regarded as *explanations* of the modal notions, the definitions given by Philo and the Stoics are circular, for the key words 'admitting of' (ἐπιδεκτικός) and 'prevent' (ἐναντιοῦσθαι) both involve modal notions, i.e. the notion of being *able* to receive and the notion of being rendered *unable*. This circularity is obvious in Boethius' formulation of Philo's definition: 'Impossibile vero, quod secundum propriam naturam nunquam possit suscipere veritatem.'[1] Such circularity is not necessarily a fault. If the modal notions are in some sense fundamental, it may well be that we cannot explain them without using them covertly. Of the three sets of definitions mentioned by Boethius only that of Diodorus is non-circular, and we have seen that it has its own difficulties.

All three sets of definitions conform to the logical requirements for the relationship of the modal notions, i.e. they make it possible to form a square of opposition. In the case of Diodorus, the square is:

|  |  |
|---|---|
| It is true and will not<br>be false that-P | It is false and will not<br>be true that-P |
| It is true or will be<br>true that-P | It is false or will be<br>false that-P |

Since the assertions of possibility and non-necessity are contradictory to the assertions of impossibility and necessity respectively, and these latter are both conjunctive propositions, the former are disjunctive propositions. Again, the contradictory of an impossible proposition is a necessary proposition and vice versa. For if it is false and will not be true that-P, it is true and will not be false that not-P, which makes it necessary by definition that-not-P. For Philo's definitions the square is as follows:

|  |  |
|---|---|
| The statement that-P does not<br>admit of falsehood | The statement that-P does not<br>admit of truth |
| The statement that-P admits<br>of truth | The statement that-P admits<br>of falsehood |

In the case of the Stoic definitions, if we have interpreted them correctly, the matter is more complicated. Since each of the terms is defined by means of a disjunction, no two of the defining

---

[1] Boethius, op. cit., p. 234.

terms can stand in the relation of contradiction to each other. But the definitions give rise to two separate squares of opposition, one for the modal terms understood absolutely, which is identical with the Philonian square, the other for the terms understood as relative, which is as follows:

| | |
|---|---|
| The statement that-P is prevented by external circumstances from being false | The statement that-P is prevented by external circumstances from being true |
| The statement that-P is not prevented by external circumstances from being true | The statement that-P is not prevented by external circumstances from being false |

According to either of the Stoic squares the contradictory of a necessary proposition is an impossible proposition in the relevant sense. This makes all the more surprising the one additional piece of information we have about the views of Chrysippus on possibility, namely that he denied the second premiss of the Master Argument and said the impossible could follow from the possible.[1] This is apparently inconsistent with the definitions, according to which, as we have seen, the contradictory of an impossible proposition must be necessary. For if the proposition that-P, which is impossible, follows from the proposition that-Q, which is possible, then by the law of contraposition, which was well known to the Stoics, the proposition that-not-Q follows from the proposition that-not-P. But the proposition that-not-P is necessary, and so by a generally agreed principle the proposition that-not-Q should be necessary too, which is plainly inconsistent with the initial assumption of possibility for the proposition that-Q.

Chrysippus defends his curious view by the use of the example 'If Dion is dead, this man is dead'. He holds that this sentence spoken in the presence of Dion expresses a sound conditional (ὑγιὲς συνημμένον)[2] in which the consequent follows from the antecedent, but that the antecedent is possible, since Dion is mortal, while the consequent is impossible, since when Dion is dead there is no longer anything to which the demonstrative applies and the proposition (ἀξίωμα) is accordingly destroyed.[3]

[1] Alexander, *In Aristotelis An. Pr. Lib. I Commentarium*, ed. Wallies, *C.I.A.G.* ii (i), p. 177; Epictetus, *Diss.* ii. 19. 1.
[2] For this phrase, see the discussion in the next section.
[3] Alexander, loc. cit.

The argument is as strange as the view it is supposed to support, but there are two possible explanations which make it seem less surprising.

In the first place it may have been simply an *argumentum ad hominem* against Diodorus. Chrysippus himself almost certainly held, as we shall see, that the words 'true', 'false', 'necessary', &c., applied to propositions (λεκτά) and not to sentences. But he may have tried to refute Diodorus by pointing out that if the latter talks of sentences, as he seems to do in the first premiss of his Master Argument, his second premiss does not hold, since a *sentence* that can plausibly be called impossible may plausibly be said to follow from one which is properly called possible. The technique of refutation by drawing unpalatable consequences was part of the Stoic inheritance from the Megarians, and it could easily give rise to misunderstanding. For the conclusion of an *argumentum ad hominem* is sometimes mistakenly regarded as the view of the inventor of the argument.

A second and more interesting hypothesis is that Chrysippus made a distinction between kinds of necessity or impossibility apart from that between relative and absolute suggested above. According to Cicero he denied the universal validity of the rule that what follows from the necessary is itself necessary: *Chrysippo non videtur valere in omnibus*.[1] This denial agrees, as we have seen, with the contention that the impossible may follow from the possible, and its phrasing suggests that Chrysippus thought he had found some special cases of necessity and impossibility which required to be excepted from the ordinary rules. Now the Stoics reserved the special name 'definite' (κατηγορευτικά) for assertions with demonstratives as subjects,[2] and these assertions may, it seems, be necessary and impossible in a rather peculiar way. To consider a famous example; 'I exist' has been said to be necessary and 'I do not exist' to be impossible in this way. From 'I exist' spoken by Descartes it follows that Descartes exists, but 'Descartes exists' is not necessary. Similarly, from 'Descartes does not exist' spoken by Descartes there follows 'I do not exist', which is accounted impossible in this peculiar sense, though 'Descartes does not exist' is not impossible in any sense at all. Perhaps it was this distinction Chrysippus had in mind when he said that the impossible might follow from the possible. If so, he would have modified Aristotle's rules to read:

An impossible cannot follow from a possible proposition, unless the consequent is a definite proposition impossible in the sense peculiar to definite propositions.

[1] Cicero, *De Fato*, 14.                    [2] Diogenes Laertius, vii. 70.

What follows from a necessary proposition is itself necessary, unless the antecedent is a definite proposition necessary in the way peculiar to definite propositions.

It may be objected to this that 'having a demonstrative as subject' is a characteristic of sentences and not of propositions. This is an important point which will be discussed later, but the Stoics apparently thought that definiteness in the sense explained above was a characteristic of propositions as well as of sentences.[1]

### 3. *The Debate on the Nature of Conditionals*

According to our evidence the first logicians to debate the nature of conditional statements were Diodorus Cronus and his pupil Philo. This development may be due to the Megarian connexion with Zeno the Eleatic. If, as we have suggested, Aristotle was interested primarily in reasoning such as we find in geometry, it would be natural for him to concentrate his attention on general propositions and definitions. Nothing in his favourite examples of demonstration would force him to consider the meaning of 'if . . . then . . .'. And we have seen that in fact he ignored the conditional form of statement in his classification of propositions, although he used it in his *Prior Analytics* for the presentation of the principles of the various syllogistic moods. But the dialectical arguments which Zeno used were of the form 'If P then Q, and if P then not-Q; therefore it is impossible that-P', and a logician who started from consideration of such arguments might be expected to pay special attention to conditional statements. Sextus Empiricus refers three times to a debate on this topic between Diodorus and his pupil Philo. Other logicians added their suggestions and the dispute became so well known in antiquity that Callimachus wrote an epigram saying 'Even the crows on the roofs caw about the nature of conditionals'.[2]

In the first place where he mentions the dispute Sextus lists four views which had been held about the nature of conditionals. In the translation which follows they are distinguished by numbers.

'[1] Philo says that a sound conditional (ὑγιὲς συνημμένον) is one that does not begin with a truth and end with a falsehood, e.g. when it is day and I am conversing, the statement "If it is day, I am conversing". [2] But Diodorus says it is one that neither could nor can begin with a truth and end with a falsehood. According to him the conditional statement just quoted seems to be false, since when it is day and I have become silent it will begin with a truth and end with

---

[1] Diogenes Laertius, vii. 69.          [2] Sextus Empiricus, *Adv. Math.* i. 309.

a falsehood. But the following statement seems to be true: "If atomic elements of things do not exist, then atomic elements of things do exist." For he maintains it will always begin with the false antecedent (ἡγούμενον) "Atomic elements of things do not exist" and end with the true consequent (λῆγον) "Atomic elements of things do exist". [3] And those who introduce the notion of connexion (συνάρτησις) say that a conditional is sound when the contradictory of its consequent is incompatible with its antecedent. According to them the conditionals mentioned above are unsound, but the following is true: "If it is day, it is day." [4] And those who judge by implication (ἔμφασις) say that a true conditional is one whose consequent is contained potentially in its antecedent. According to them the statement "If it is day, it is day" and similarly every conditional which is repetitive (διφορούμενον) will apparently be false; for it is impossible for a thing to be contained in itself."[1]

Unfortunately we know nothing more about the arguments that were used in this debate. And although we can take it that the objections mentioned by Sextus were in fact put forward at some time, we cannot safely assume that the order of appearance of the four views was precisely that of his list. For he may well have arranged them according to the strictness of their requirements, in the hope of making the relations between them more easily intelligible. Even the names of the authors of the third and fourth views have been lost, though their identities may perhaps be guessed. A passage in Cicero suggests that the third view may be that of Chrysippus.[2] For it is argued that, if Chrysippus allows the truth of the conditional statement 'If Fabius was born at the rising of the dog-star, then Fabius will not die at sea', he must also allow that 'Fabius was born at the rising of the dog-star' and 'Fabius will die at sea' are incompatible (*pugnant*). This view is also attributed to the Stoics by Diogenes Laertius.[3] The fourth view, on the other hand, is probably Peripatetic. This is suggested both by the use of the word 'potentially' (δυνάμει) and by the rejection of the form 'If P then P', which the Peripatetics regarded as a piece of useless Stoic verbalism.[4]

Whoever their authors may have been, it is interesting to examine the views as they have been reported and to conjecture the motives of the principal characters.

When Philo said that a conditional statement was sound if, and only if, it did not begin with a truth and end with a falsehood, he was offering what would now be called a truth-functional

---

[1] Sextus, *Pyrrhoneiae Hypotyposes*, ii. 110–12.
[2] *De Fato*, 12.    [3] *Vitae*, vii. 73.
[4] Alexander, *In Aristotelis An. Pr. Lib. I Commentarium*, ed. Wallies, *C.I.A.G.* ii (i), p. 20.

definition of 'if . . . then . . .', that is to say, a definition according to which the truth or falsity of a conditional statement is determined by the truth or falsity of its antecedent and its consequent. In a second reference to his views Sextus says:

'So according to him there are three ways in which a conditional may be true, and one in which it may be false. For a conditional is true when it begins with a truth and ends with a truth, like "If it is day, it is light"; and true also when it begins with a falsehood and ends with a falsehood, like "If the earth flies, the earth has wings"; and similarly a conditional which begins with a falsehood and ends with a truth is itself true, like "If the earth flies, the earth exists". A conditional is false only when it begins with a truth and ends with a falsehood, like "If it is day, it is night".'[1]

Writing 'P' to mark the place of the antecedent and 'Q' to mark that of the consequent, we may present this explanation in a truth-table as given here. The device of tabulation was not introduced until recently, but the idea of truth-functional dependence was obviously quite clear to Philo. Why did he think 'if . . . then' could be defined in this way? On the face of it, his account of the meaning of the phrase is

| P | Q | If P then Q |
|---|---|---|
| t | t | t |
| t | f | f |
| f | t | t |
| f | f | t |

not very plausible; for we do not ordinarily make a conditional statement which we can defend only by saying that it satisfies his requirement of having either a false antecedent or a true consequent. The example attributed to him by Sextus shows the strangeness of his view; for no one would naturally say 'If it is day, I am conversing' merely because it was day and he was conversing. It seems almost as though Philo had deliberately chosen to insist on the correctness of this queer statement because he was committed to an extension of ordinary usage. But what was his motive?

If, as we suppose, Philo began by considering the use of 'if . . . then . . .' in arguments, he may have wished to draw attention to the fact that the conjunction of a conditional statement with its antecedent is always held to entail the consequent. This is indeed essential to the meaning of the phrase. Whatever else we may say about it in various contexts, we must allow the validity of the inference schema 'If P then Q; but P; therefore Q'. Now Philo's interpretation is the weakest which satisfies this requirement. That is to say, any other interpretation which was plausible could differ from his only by imposing some additional requirement or by not allowing the truth of a conditional in some case

[1] *Adv. Math.* viii. 113.

or cases in which he allows it. If we define a conditional as any complex statement containing two propositional signs and such that its conjunction with the first entails the second, we commit ourselves to Philo's view. And he apparently wished to insist on this definition even when it led him to claim truth for some rather strange-looking statements.

To the philosophers of the Megarian school Philo's definition may have seemed even more curious than it does to most modern readers. For they were accustomed to the use of conditional statements in the formulation of arguments *ad absurdum*. When a follower of Zeno wishes to refute some common assumption that-P, he produces an argument of the form 'If P then Q; and if P then not-Q; therefore it is impossible that-P'. In this context he cannot assert his conditionals on the sole ground that they satisfy Philo's requirement. Admittedly he believes that their common antecedent is false, which is enough to guarantee the truth of both according to Philo's criterion; but he puts them forward as premisses in an argument to *prove* the falsity of the antecedent, and he must therefore expect his opponent to concede them for some reason which is independent of the truth or falsity of the antecedent or the consequents. It seems that when he says 'If P then Q' he means not merely 'It is not the case that-P-and-not-Q' but rather 'It is impossible that-P-and-not-Q'. Perhaps Diodorus was trying to allow for this when he put forward his account of the meaning of 'if . . . then . . .'. But we have seen that he had curious views about modality, and we must consider how these affected his theory of conditional statements.

The objection which he urged against Philo's example and the phrase 'neither could nor can begin with a truth and end with a falsehood' which he used in stating his own view show that here, as in the Master Argument, Diodorus was working with a notion of statements, or forms of words, which may be true at one time but not at another. When he said that a sound conditional neither could nor can begin with a truth and end with a falsehood, he evidently meant to imply that a conditional form of words such as 'If it is day, I am conversing' might conceivably satisfy Philo's requirement at one time but not at another, and to say that it would not be sound according to his own theory if it failed to satisfy Philo's requirement at any time, past, present, or future. In short, he was not defining 'If . . . then . . .' by reference to necessity as we ordinarily understand it, but rather declaring that he would not recognize a conditional statement as sound unless not only it but all the other statements made by utterance of the same form of words at different times were sound in the sense of Philo's definition. For a form of words whose reference did not depend in any way on the occasion of utterance his criterion would coincide with Philo's, because utterances of the words at different times would not constitute different statements. But it is not to be supposed that he realized this. On the contrary, his construction of the Master Argument suggests that he did not fully appreciate what he was about when he spoke of a form of words as true at one time and false at another.

One of the curiosities of Diodorus' statement (if it is his statement) of his view is the introduction of the phrase 'is not possible' in addition to ' was not possible'. This is redundant, for, according to his definition of possibility, if it was not possible for the antecedent to be true and the conclusion false, then it *is* not possible. If it was ever the case that 'P and not-Q' would not in the future be true, then it is now the case that it will not in the future be true. It would be more intelligible if the order of the verbs in the statement had been reversed and Diodorus had said 'is not and was not possible', for the second clause would then tighten the condition imposed by the first. If he had simply said 'It is not possible for the antecedent to be true and the conclusion false', then according to his view of possibility, any pair of true statements in the past tense would have formed a sound conditional in either order; for it is not now and never will be true that the one is true and the other false. This paradox is avoided by the addition of 'was not possible', because for most pairs of true statements in the past tense there was some time when one was true and the other false.

Diodorus' view, however, still involves the following paradoxes:

(*a*) Any pair of true statements in the past tense which became true simultaneously form a sound conditional in either order.

(*b*) From any pair of true statements in the past tense which did not become true simultaneously we can construct a sound conditional by taking the one which became true later as antecedent and the one which became true earlier as consequent, since it can never have been true that the first would be true and the latter false.

(*c*) Any pair of true statements in the future tense which will become false simultaneously form a sound conditional in either order.

(*d*) From any pair of true statements in the future tense which do not become false simultaneously we can construct a sound conditional by taking the one which becomes false first as antecedent and the other as consequent.

(*e*) Any conditional with a true general statement as consequent or a false general statement as antecedent is sound.

Diodorus could have avoided two of these paradoxes, namely (*b*) and (*d*), by adding the phrase 'was true' to his queer definitions of the modal notions, i.e. by defining the necessary as what is true and *was true* and will not be false and the possible as what *was*, is, or will be true. This change, however, would not remove the other paradoxes, for no redefinition of the modal notions along these lines will remove the paradoxes (*a*) and (*c*). If Caesar said *Et tu, Brute* at the moment when Brutus stabbed him, there was not and never will be any time at which it is true that Caesar said *Et tu, Brute* but false that Brutus stabbed him, or vice versa.

The final paradox of Diodorus' position is less disturbing, but only because it is likely that any certainly true general proposition will be necessary in a stronger sense than he allows and that any certainly false general proposition will be impossible in a stronger sense than he allows. For when we think of necessity and impossibility in this stronger sense, it seems not absurd to say that, if any proposition whatsoever is true, then a necessary proposition is true and, conversely, that if an impossible proposition were true, then any proposition whatsoever would be true.

It is a further consequence of Diodorus' view that sound conditionals cannot, like simple statements, change their modality. According to the definition of necessity, they will not only always be necessary, they must always *have been* necessary. If there was no time at which it was true to say that 'P and not-Q' would be true, then at all times it was true to say that 'Either P and Q, or not-P and Q, or not-P and not-Q' would always be true, i.e. what is stated in a sound conditional is necessary at all times.

The logical views of Diodorus, both on modality and on conditionals, probably had some connexion in his mind with a metaphysical thesis akin to Eleaticism, i.e. with the denial of real contingency. This seems to have been the point of the Master Argument, and it is possible that his work is directed especially against Aristotle's thesis in chapter 9 of the *De Interpretatione*. However that thesis may be interpreted, Diodorus contradicts it. For he maintains that all true statements about the future are necessary, and he tries to make this a consequence of what is admitted by Aristotle, namely the necessity of the past. The aim of his programme is probably to prove that all true statements without exception are necessary, but he is defeated by his passionate determination to take tenses seriously and by his unclarity about the nature of the subjects to which he applies the predicates 'true' and 'necessary'.

It is much more difficult to detect any connexion between Philo's views on modality and his account of the sound conditional or between either of these and any metaphysical position. It may be that his definition of the sound conditional was a *reductio ad absurdum* of Diodorus' views, i.e. that he said in effect 'With your view of necessity, there is no distinction between necessity and truth, between impossibility and falsehood, so that, instead of saying that a conditional is sound if it cannot begin with a truth and end with a falsehood, you might as well say that it is sound if it does not begin with a truth and end with a falsehood. In order to make the difference between a sound and an unsound conditional, you need a real notion of necessity, which I will now expound.' This, however, is pure conjecture. For all we know, Philo may have developed his various views independently.

The third and fourth of the views listed by Sextus are obviously attempts to present conditionals as statements of necessary connexion, and it seems likely that they were formulated by philosophers who had in mind the use of conditionals in place of entailment statements. When Zeno or one of his followers produced a statement beginning 'If there is motion . . .', he thought of the consequent as something that followed logically from the antecedent. This is a fairly common use of the conditional form. We have seen it already in Aristotle's formulation of the principles of syllogistic reasoning, and we shall meet it again. But it is a mistake to suppose that 'if . . . then . . .' is always used in this way, and much confusion has been produced in logic by the attempt to identify conditional statements with expressions of entailment. If one statement entails another we can always make a true conditional with the first as antecedent and the second as consequent, but we cannot properly assume that the antecedent of every true conditional entails its consequent. The philosophers who talked of implication (ἔμφασις) seem to have been more deeply committed to this erroneous view than those who talked of connexion (συνάρτησις); but the difference between them was small. The objection which the partisans of implication brought against the theory of connexion is not of a fundamental kind. If we are content to admit repetitive conditionals as limiting cases of necessary connexion, we can equally well allow ourselves to speak of a statement as contained potentially in itself. Such extensions of usage for the purpose of simplicity are not uncommon in mathematics.

Assuming that the rival views were as we have represented them, what are we to say on the question at issue, that is, on the meaning of 'if . . . then . . .'? In recent times, as in antiquity, it has often been suggested that we must choose between Philo's theory and a theory of necessary connexion. But neither is satisfactory as a general account of all conditional statements; for there are several distinguishable uses of this form of speech.

Let us begin by considering the occurrence of 'if' in sentences other than statements. When a man promises to do something if a certain condition is fulfilled, it is clear that he does not institute a necessary connexion by his act, and it is equally clear that his utterance cannot be explained by any adaptation of Philo's theory. We say that he keeps his promise if the condition is fulfilled and he does what he said he would do in that contingency. But we do not say that he keeps his promise if the condition is not fulfilled. Similarly, we do not say that a soldier obeys a conditional order from his superior officer when the condition contained in the order is not fulfilled. In all such cases we say rather that the conditional utterance has no application. Since these are obviously primitive uses of the conditional form of speech, it seems safe to say that the primary purpose of an 'if' clause is to select for attention a possibility about whose fulfilment the speaker is uncertain, and that what is said in the other clause is said with regard to the selected possibility alone.

This interpretation can be applied also to some statements in the conditional form. Suppose, for example, that the rowing correspondent of a newspaper predicts that Oxford will win the boat race if the water is calm, but there is in fact a considerable wind on the appointed day: no one says that the prediction is verified simply because its condition is not fulfilled. On the other hand, if we learn that the water was calm and Oxford won the race, we think it quite natural to say that the correspondent was right. Admittedly we cannot now use the conditional sentence 'Oxford won if the water was calm', because that would imply uncertainty on our part about the weather, but we can properly say that the correspondent's prediction has been proved true. In short, Philo was right in maintaining that the truth of such a conditional statement may be established by the discovery that its antecedent and its consequent are both true, but he was wrong in trying to provide as he did for the truth of conditional statements whose antecedents are false. We may perhaps describe the situation by saying that a conditional statement of the primitive kind appears to be a defective truth-function of its

antecedent and its consequent. The suggestion can be understood most easily from consideration of a truth-table in which no

| P | Q | If P then Q |
|---|---|-------------|
| t | t | t |
| t | f | f |
| f | t | .. |
| f | f | .. |

truth value is assigned to the conditional
for those two contingencies which involve
the falsity of its antecedent.

It must be admitted, however, that this
interpretation involves two consequences
which are at variance with the common
assumptions of logicians. In the first place,
conditional statements, so interpreted, are not subject to the principle of bivalence, which was strongly defended by the Stoics.
This does not mean that they may have some mysterious third
value between truth and falsity, but simply that we may sometimes
have to say they are neither true nor false because they have no
application. We can put the same point in another way by saying
that according to this view a conditional has no proper negative.
'If P then not-Q' is true when 'If P then Q' is false, and false
when 'If P then Q' is true, but it is not the contradictory of the
other, because it may turn out that neither is true and neither
false. And if we try to identify the negative of 'If P then Q' with
the propositional sign which is false when 'If P then Q' is true
but otherwise true, we allow no difference between 'If P then Q'
and the conjunction 'P and Q'. Secondly, according to the interpretation given above, conditionals are not subject to the principle
of contraposition, i.e. 'If P then Q' is not equivalent to 'If not-Q
then not-P'. For these two agree only in being false in the same
contingency: when either is true the other has no application.
Thus in the example considered earlier we can scarcely say that
the prediction of the newspaper correspondent is verifiable by
the failure of Oxford on a windy day, although that would be
enough to verify a prediction of the form 'If Oxford does not win,
it will be on a day when the water is not calm'.

If there are indeed conditional statements which satisfy neither
the principle of bivalence nor the principle of contraposition,
why has this curious fact been overlooked by logicians? The
answer seems to be that even conditional statements of the
primitive kind we have just considered suggest something more
than we have allowed so far in our analysis. Although a statement
of this kind is said to be verified when its antecedent and its consequent are both found to be true, the speaker is always assumed
to have some reason for saying what he does other than knowledge
of the facts which suffice to verify it. For when the antecedent and
the consequent are both known to be true, the conditional form
no longer seems appropriate. If the speaker is pressed to give his

reason, he may say that it is impossible for the antecedent to be true while the consequent is false. Here the word 'impossible' need not be taken to mean the same as 'absolutely impossible'; for the original assertion is justified if it can be shown that the conjunction of the antecedent with the negation of the consequent is impossible in relation to some fact which can be known before the truth-values of the antecedent and the consequent are discovered. But the connexion which is expressed in this way may also be expressed by the conditional form itself with the addition of some modal word to the consequent. Thus if the newspaper correspondent of our example were asked why he had written what he had, he might reply in irritation 'Oxford cannot fail to win if the water is calm'. He would be more informative if he spoke about the evidence for this statement, but the new statement as it stands is not a mere repetition of his original assertion. For in making it the correspondent commits himself to something more than a defective truth-function of the old antecedent and the old consequent. What he says entails his former remark, but it cannot itself be verified by Oxford's victory in calm water, and it is not thought to lack all application if the day of the race turns out to be windy. For in these latter circumstances it commits the correspondent to the assertion that Oxford would have won if the water had been calm. Such a subjunctive conditional is indeed equivalent to a repetition of the modal conditional with an admission that its antecedent is false.

Sometimes necessary connexion is expressed by the conditional form without the addition of any modal words. This is especially common in statements of a scientific kind, e.g. 'If you take vitamin C in large quantities at the beginning of an influenza attack, you will escape the exhaustion which often follows that illness'. Here the clauses which would be described by a grammarian as protasis and apodosis are not complete propositional signs: for the word 'you' is obviously intended to function in this context as a variable, and the whole might be paraphrased by the statement 'Anyone who takes vitamin C in large quantities at the beginning of an influenza attack will escape the exhaustion which often follows that illness'. It should also be noticed that in this example the necessitation asserted by the speaker is not of the formal kind studied in logic. But we can use the conditional form to assert logical necessity, and it is perhaps not surprising that logicians, with their special interest, have sometimes written as though this were the sole function of such statements.

When we use 'if . . . then . . .' in a modal sense, our conditional statements are subject to the principle of bivalence and the principle of contraposition, and so create no scandal for the tidy minds of logicians. On the other hand, since they are not truth-functions of their antecedents and consequents, they cannot be verified from knowledge of the truth-values of those propositional signs, even in the case in which both are true. But the possibility of such verification is essential to conditional statements of the most primitive kind. It is impossible, therefore, to bring all the usages of 'If . . . then . . .' under one simple rule. This is not to say, however, that the expression is ambiguous; for the context usually shows whether a conditional statement is to be taken as a defective truth-function or as an assertion of necessary connexion. And the fact that anyone who utters a statement of the first kind is always assumed to believe a proposition of the second kind makes it easy for us to understand a transition from one usage to the other. If the water is not calm on the day of the boat race, it is thought quite natural for the newspaper correspondent of our example to say 'Well, Oxford would have won if the water had been calm'.

If anyone is worried by the need to admit conditional statements which are not subject to the principle of bivalence and the principle of contraposition, his distress may perhaps be relieved by the reflection that these utterances differ in another important way from ordinary statements. When we allow that a remark in the conditional form can be verified by the discovery that its antecedent and its consequent are both true, we think of it as giving advice rather than information; i.e. advice on what to expect in certain circumstances. And we understand by 'verification' in this context only the justification of the speaker's advice by circumstances, i.e. without regard to the ground, if any, which he had for offering it. Some modern logicians have maintained that all conditional statements give advice rather than information; but in saying this they overlook the distinction to which we have tried to draw attention. A conditional statement which purports to express a necessary connexion cannot be verified in the special sense we have just explained, because it is not even a defective truth-function. And if it is introduced in a context where advice would be appropriate, it is regarded as an attempt to formulate the ground for giving such advice rather than the advice itself.

## 4. *The Stoic Theory of Meaning and Truth*

In their study of logic the Stoics were more self-conscious than any of their predecessors. For they assigned a definite place to the

science in their scheme of human knowledge and held a definite
theory about the nature of its subject-matter. According to
Diogenes, Zeno, their founder, was the first to divide philosophical
doctrine into three parts—physics, ethics, and logic.[1] This division
corresponds verbally with a classification of propositions and
problems made by Aristotle in his *Topics*,[2] but explicit recognition
and use of it in teaching seems to be a novelty of the Stoics. In
later antiquity it was a commonplace that they treated logic as
a *part* of philosophy, whereas the Peripatetics regarded it rather
as a *tool* (ὄργανον).[3]

The Stoics elaborated their division of philosophy by the use
of picturesque metaphors:

'They liken philosophy to an animal, comparing logic to the bones
and sinews, ethics to the flesh, and physics to the soul. Or again to an
egg: logic is the outermost part, further in is ethics, and the inmost
part is physics.'[4]

There was disagreement among them about the sub-divisions of
logic:

'Some say that the logical part of the system is divided into two
sciences, rhetoric and dialectic, while others would add a part
dealing with definitions and one dealing with canons and criteria;
others again omit the part concerning definitions.'[5]

'Dialectic' is the Stoic term most closely corresponding to our
'logic', although they included under it a good deal which we
should refer to epistemology on the one hand or to grammar and
linguistics on the other.

According to Diogenes, the Stoics further divided dialectic into
a part which is concerned with things signified (τὰ σημαινόμενα)
and a part which is concerned with things signifying (τὰ σημαί-
νοντα), or elements of speech.[6]

Apparently they gave considerable thought to the latter. They
distinguished, for example, between voice (φωνή), which may
be mere noise, speech (λέξις), which is necessarily articulate but
may be meaningless, and discourse (λόγος), which is meaningful
utterance.[7] Again, they distinguished three applications of the
word 'letter', namely to a sound, to its written symbol, and to its
name, e.g. 'alpha'.[8] The most original part of their theory,

---

[1] Diogenes Laertius, vii. 39.                    [2] *Topics*, i. 14 (105$^b$19).
[3] Alexander, *In Aristotelis An. Pr. Lib. I Commentarium*, ed. Wallies, *C.I.A.G.* ii (i),
p. 1; Philoponus, *In Aristotelis An. Pr. Commentaria*, ed. Wallies, *C.I.A.G.* xiii (ii), p. 6.
[4] Diogenes Laertius, vii. 40.                    [5] Ibid. 41.
[6] Ibid. 43, 62.
[7] The first distinction had been noticed already by Aristotle in his *Historia Ani-
malium*, iv. 9 (536$^b$19), and the second by Plato in his *Theaetetus*, 163B.
[8] Diogenes Laertius, vii. 56–57.

however, concerns things signified or expressed, which they commonly called *lekta* (λεκτά). The doctrine of these is an important novelty in the philosophy of logic and deserves careful attention. Unfortunately, the evidence is insufficient for us to determine exactly how the Stoics arrived at their views or how they would have answered certain important questions concerning the nature of *lekta*.

First we shall give the most important passages in which *lekta* are discussed. In these the word will be transliterated, rather than translated, in order to avoid prejudging issues; but it may be helpful to remember that the Greek verb λέγειν, from which λεκτόν is derived, means 'to mean' as well as 'to say', and that 'what is meant' is probably the most literal translation of *lekton*. Then we shall give an account of the Stoics' classification of *lekta* and compare it with their classification of parts of speech. Next it will be necessary to consider the Stoic account of truth and falsehood. And after this we shall be in a position to give a tentative interpretation and evaluation of the theory.

Sextus gives the most complete account:

'The Stoics say that three things are linked together, that which is signified, that which signifies, and the object; of these that which signifies is speech, as for example, "Dion", that which is signified is the thing itself which is revealed by it and which we apprehend as subsisting with our thought but the barbarians do not understand, although they hear the spoken word, while the object is that which exists outside, as for example, Dion himself. Of these two are corporeal, that is, speech and the object, while one is incorporeal, that is the thing which is signified, i.e. the *lekton*, which is true or false.'[1]

The end of this passage is misleading in that not all *lekta* are true or false. For example, whatever is meant by the word 'Dion' is not true or false, as Sextus himself immediately goes on to point out. Later he tells us:

'They say that the *lekton* is that which subsists according to a rational presentation, and a rational presentation is one in which what is presented can be conveyed in speech.'[2]

And this definition is confirmed by Diogenes:

'Of presentations some are rational, others irrational. The rational are those of rational animals. . . . They say that the *lekton* is that which subsists according to a rational presentation.'[3]

[1] Sextus, *Adv. Math.* viii. 11, 12.
[2] Ibid. 70.
[3] Diogenes Laertius, vii. 51 and 63.

Finally, Seneca gives an account of matter in Latin:

'Video Catonem ambulantem. Hoc sensus ostendit, animus credidit. Corpus est quod video, cui et oculos intendi et animum. Dico deinde: "Cato ambulat." "Non corpus", inquit, "est quod nunc loquor sed enuntiativum quiddam de corpore, quod alii effatum vocant, alii enuntiatum, alii dictum." '[1]

Here *effatum, enuntiatum, dictum* are various attempts to render λεκτόν in Latin.

Three important points emerge from these passages; that *lekta* are signified in meaningful discourse, that they are incorporeal, and that an important class of *lekta* are called true or false. In being incorporeal, *lekta* are exceptional in Stoic metaphysics; for in general the Stoics were materialists who believed that even the soul was corporeal.[2]

After explaining the Stoic use of the word *lekton* Sextus tries to show that their theory involves two serious contradictions, and the passage in which he does so is worth considering in some detail not only for the additional information which it yields, but also because it gives a fair example of Sextus' methods in dealing with his opponents.[3] He begins with an account of natural signs (σημεῖα) which appears to be part of Stoic epistemology. The Stoics say that a sign of this kind is a proposition (ἀξίωμα, a kind of *lekton*) and therefore intelligible rather than sensible: according to their definition it is the true antecedent in a sound conditional serving to reveal the consequent.[4] He next proceeds to discuss the nature of a sound conditional and attributes to the Stoics the view we associate with Philo. He points out, however, that only in the case where the antecedent is true, could it possibly be regarded as a sign, and that even there a further condition must be fulfilled, namely that it serves to reveal the consequent. Thus in the conditional 'If it is day, it is light', the antecedent is not a sign, since 'It is light' is clear of itself. A proper example of the antecedent as sign is 'If she has milk in her breasts, she has conceived'. The Stoics say, moreover, that both sign and signified must be 'present'. It might seem otherwise; for when we consider 'If he has a scar, he has had a wound' and 'If he has a wound in his heart he will die', we are inclined to say that the things signified, namely the wound and the death, are respectively past and to come. But, say the Stoics, although the wound is past and done with, his having had the wound (τὸ δὲ ἕλκος ἐσχηκέναι τοῦτον),

[1] *Epistulae*, 117. 13.  [2] Diogenes Laertius, vii. 56–57.
[3] *Adv. Math.* viii. 243–65.
[4] ἀξίωμα ἐν ὑγιεῖ συνημμένῳ καθηγούμενον, ἐκκαλυπτικὸν τοῦ λήγοντος, *Adv. Math.* viii. 245.

which is a proposition, is present (ἀξίωμα καθεστηκός, ἐνέστηκεν), although it is pronounced about something past. Similarly, the death is in the future, but the proposition that he will die is present (τὸ δὲ ἀποθανεῖσθαι τοῦτον ἀξίωμα ἐνέστηκεν), although it is pronounced about what is to be, and is now true (νῦν ἐστιν ἀληθές).[1]

Up to this point Sextus is probably reporting fairly. No doubt he is correct also when he points out that not everyone agrees with the Stoics in asserting the existence of such things as *lekta* and that even some Stoics, such as Basilides have denied their existence. But he then goes on to produce a typical sceptical argument to show that the existence of *lekta* cannot be proved without begging the question. Proofs, he says, consist of propositions, which are *lekta*, and it is just the existence of these which is in question. Further, he argues, *lekta* are supposed to be incorporeal, and therefore according to the Stoics they cannot do or suffer anything. But to reveal or make clear, which is the function of a sign, is to do something. This is the first contradiction. The second follows immediately after. Things signifying are supposed to be sounds and things signified *lekta*, which includes propositions. But if this is so, says Sextus, since all propositions are things signified as distinct from things signifying, it is impossible that a natural sign (σημεῖον) should be a proposition.[2]

The last two points show Sextus' complete lack of intellectual conscience in the formulation of criticisms. In the first place, although the Stoics seem to have allowed that everything active is a body,[3] they could very easily answer his first argument by saying that revealing is not acting in the appropriate sense. Secondly, when he tries to produce a contradiction between Stoic epistemology and semantic theory, he blandly ignores the fact that different, though similar, terminologies are used in these two theories. The relation between σημαῖνον and σημαινόμενον is that between language and what it expresses, while the relation between σημεῖον and σημειωτόν is that between what is known first and what is known through it.[4] There is no contradiction at all in the assumption that a proposition may be signified by an indicative sentence and yet also act as a sign in serving to reveal a further proposition to one who knows it. Now Sextus is our best single authority for Stoic logic. It is therefore not surprising that it has often been misunderstood and is still unclear. The theory of *lekta*, especially, seems soon to have caused considerable confusion. For instance, of the late Aristotelian

[1] *Adv. Math.* viii. 255–6.          [2] Ibid. 262–4.
[3] Diogenes Laertius, vii. 56.
[4] For the theory of signs see Sextus, *Adv. Math.* viii. 143.

commentators, Simplicius says that *lekta* are thoughts,[1] while Philoponus says they are sounds.[2]

Although *lekta* are to be distinguished from any spoken sounds, words, or sentences, it is clear that a *lekton* can be identified only by use of a word or sentence which expresses it, and it is not surprising that the divisions of *lekta* should correspond fairly closely with the divisions of speech. Diogenes gives the following account of the division of λόγος, i.e. articulate, intelligible utterance. He states that a certain Diogenes of Babylonia and Chrysippus distinguish five parts of speech, name (ὄνομα), common noun or appellation (προσηγορία), verb (ῥῆμα), connective or conjunction (σύνδεσμος), and article (ἄρθρον). To these Antipater added a sixth called the mean (μεσότης).[3] The common noun (προσηγορία) is defined as a part of speech which signifies a common quality, e.g. 'man', 'horse'. A name is a part of speech signifying an individual quality (ἰδία ποιότης), e.g. 'Diogenes', 'Socrates'. A verb is a part of speech signifying an uncompounded predicate (ἀσύνθετον κατηγόρημα) or, according to others, an undeclined element of speech signifying something that can be attached (συντακτόν) to one or more things, e.g. 'I write', 'I speak'. A conjunction is an undeclined part of speech joining together the parts of discourse. The ἄρθρον is simply the article. Diogenes gives us no more light on the μεσότης, but it is probably what Dionysius Thrax (*c.* 100 B.C.) in his book on grammar calls the μετοχή, i.e. the participle, so called because it partakes (μετέχει) of the nature of both noun and verb.[4]

It is interesting to notice that the Stoics seem to have been the first to make a systematic study of what we now call grammar. The terminology of Dionysius Thrax is obviously derived from Stoic sources. He defines λόγος as 'a combination of speech in prose or verse revealing a complete thought' and distinguishes eight parts of λόγος, noun, verb, participle, article, pronoun (ἀντωνυμία), preposition (πρόθεσις), adverb (ἐπίρρημα), and conjunction. That he is here modifying a Stoic source is shown by the fact that he apologizes for not including the προσηγορία, saying that it is a species of ὄνομα. The word 'complete' (αὐτοτελής) used in the definition is also a typical piece of Stoic terminology.

The list of parts of speech given by Diogenes Laertius surprises us by its obvious omissions. There seems to be no place for the preposition, pronoun, or adverb. That the Stoics had not overlooked

---

[1] Simplicius, *In Aristotelis Categorias Commentarium*, ed. Kalbfleisch, *C.I.A.G.* viii. p. 10.

[2] Philoponus, *In Aristotelis An. Pr. Commentaria*, ed. Wallies, *C.I.A.G.* xiii (ii), p. 243.                                    [3] Diogenes Laertius, vii. 57–58.

[4] *Anecdota Graeca*, ed. Bekker, ii, p. 634.

these, however, is shown by a passage of Priscian, the Latin grammarian, who wrote in Constantinople in the sixth century A.D.

'Secundum Stoicos vero quinque sunt eius partes: nomen, appellatio, verbum, pronomen sive articulus, coniunctio. Nam participium connumerantes verbis participiale verbum vocabant vel casuale; nec non etiam adverbia nominibus vel verbis connumerabant et quasi adiectiva verborum ea nominabant; articulis autem pronomina connumerantes finitos ea articulos appellabant; ipsos autem articulos, quibus nos caremus, infinitos articulos dicebant vel, ut alii dicunt, articulos connumerabant pronominibus et articularia eos pronomina vocabant;... praepositionem quoque Stoici coniunctioni copulantes praepositivam conjunctionem vocabant.'[1]

Priscian was extremely influential in the Middle Ages, and the word *appellatio*, his translation of προσηγορία, reappears in medieval logical terminology.

We now turn to Diogenes' classification of *lekta*. This is more or less systematically developed in a long passage[2] and repeated almost identically by Sextus.[3] The main division of *lekta* is into complete (αὐτοτελῆ) and defective (ἐλλιπῆ): 'Those are defective of which the expression is unfinished (τὰ ἀναπάρτιστον ἔχοντα τὴν ἐκφοράν), for example "writes"; for we ask "Who?"'. The complete are those of which the expression is finished, for example "Socrates writes".'[4] Deficient *lekta* seem to have been divided into predicates (κατηγορήματα) and subjects (πτώσεις, 'cases'). Diogenes gives two definitions of κατηγόρημα. According to the first the predicate is something said of something, or a thing combinable with some thing or things (πρᾶγμα συντακτὸν περί τινος ἢ τινῶν); according to the second it is a defective *lekton* combinable with a nominative case to produce a proposition.[5] The subdivisions of κατηγορήματα are a little obscure. Diogenes' distinctions seem to correspond to those between transitive verbs, passive verbs, intransitive verbs, and reflexive verbs and are expressed entirely in grammatical terms. Thus a direct predicate is said to be one which combined with an oblique case makes a complete predicate, e.g. 'fears', 'sees', 'converses'. And Diogenes later says that the oblique cases are the genitive dative, and accusative.[6]

Complete *lekta* are divided according to Diogenes into *axiomata* (ἀξιώματα), questions (ἐρωτήματα), inquiries (πύσματα), commands (προστακτικά), oaths (ὁρκικά), prayers (ἀρατικά),

[1] *Grammatici Latini*, ed. Keil, ii, p. 54.    [2] Diogenes Laertius, vii. 63–83.
[3] *Adv. Math.* viii. 70 ff. and 93 ff.    [4] Diogenes Laertius, vii. 63.
[5] Ibid. 64.    [6] Ibid. 65.

suppositions (ὑποθετικά), addresses (προσαγορευτικά), and things similar to *axiomata* (πράγματα ὅμοια τοῖς ἀξιώμασιν).[1] Sextus gives a similar list except that he uses the expression εὐκτικά instead of ἀρατικά and calls the things similar to *axiomata* 'more than *axiomata*'.[2] These last are of special interest. Sextus gives the better explanation of them. He says that they are more than *axiomata* and not *axiomata*. For instance, if we say 'The cowherd is like Priam's sons', the *lekton* is an *axioma* and true or false; but the addition of a single word in the sentence 'How like Priam's sons the cowherd is!' causes it to express something which is not an *axioma* and not true or false, since these properties are said to belong to *axiomata* alone.

*Axiomata* are obviously of the greatest logical importance. The word ἀξίωμα is connected with the verb ἀξιοῦν, which means to put forward a claim and 'assertion' would perhaps be the most literal translation. It has been rendered by 'judgement' and by 'proposition'. For the present we shall simply transliterate in order to avoid misleading associations. Diogenes gives the following definition:

'An *axioma* is that which is true or false, or a complete thing declaratory in itself (πρᾶγμα αὐτοτελὲς ἀποφαντὸν ὅσον ἐφ' ἑαυτῷ).'[3]

This is repeated almost identically by Sextus[4] and by Aulus Gellius, quoting a Stoic handbook.[5] It is clear that the Stoics regarded every *axioma* as either true or false, and Cicero says that Chrysippus laid great stress on this point.[6]

*Axiomata* are classified as simple and non-simple. The simple consist of one *axioma* alone, the non-simple of several *axiomata* or of one *axioma* duplicated. An example of the first kind is 'If it is day, it is light', and of the second 'If it is day, it is day'.[7] The duplicated *axioma* is technically called a διφορούμενον.[8] The fact that complex *axiomata* are said to consist of simple *axiomata* suggests that the Stoics did not distinguish between an assertion or statement and the proposition or propositional content expressed when we make an assertion. Both the name and the definition of the *axioma* suggest that it is an assertion, but it is not true that more than one assertion is made when we use a conditional sentence. We do not assert either what is expressed by the protasis or what is expressed by the apodosis.

---

[1] Ibid. 66.  [2] *Adv. Math.* viii. 73.  [3] Diogenes Laertius, vii. 65.
[4] *Pyrrh. Hyp.* ii. 104.  [5] *Noctes Atticae*, xvi. 8.
[6] *De Fato*, 38.  [7] Diogenes Laertius, vii. 68–69.
[8] This is a rare word in other contexts and is naturally corrupted by the copyists to διαφορούμενον, which has led to great confusion in texts and translation. On the textual point see Prantl, *Geschichte der Logik*, i, p. 445, n. 122.

Diogenes' division of simple *axiomata* proceeds on two different principles, although he does not expressly recognize this. The one yields the threefold classification, categorical (κατηγορικόν), definite (καταγορευτικόν), and indefinite (ἀόριστον), while the other gives the distinction between the affirmative and various kinds of negative.[1] Using the first principle, Sextus also gives a threefold classification, but he uses the terminology 'definite', 'indefinite', and 'intermediate' (ὡρισμένα, ἀόριστα, μέσα).[2] The definite *axioma* here seems to correspond to Diogenes' καταγορευτικόν: Sextus' examples are 'This man is walking' and 'This man is sitting'. Similarly the indefinite *axiomata* are the same for both authors. Sextus' examples of the intermediate are 'Man is sitting' or 'A man is sitting' and 'Socrates is walking'. He explains that the indefinite is said to be true when the definite is found to be true and argues that unless the definite is true no proposition can be true,[3] which suggests that the Stoics regarded the definite *axioma* as basic.

Two peculiarities of this classification may be noted. First no distinction is made between *axiomata* expressed by sentences having proper names and those expressed by sentences having common nouns as subjects. This is in accordance with the Stoic view that words of these types both signify qualities, and therefore differ only inessentially. Secondly, there is no place here among simple *lekta* for the Aristotelian universal proposition. No example is given with the word πᾶς or πάντες. In one passage, however, Sextus attributes to the Stoics the view that a definition differs only in expression from a universal *axioma* (καθολικόν), and explains this by saying they thought that 'Man is a rational mortal animal' equivalent to 'If anything is a man, it is a rational mortal animal' (εἴ τί ἐστιν ἄνθρωπος ἐκεῖνο ζῷόν ἐστι λογικὸν θνητόν).[4] Chrysippus is mentioned as offering a similar analysis of 'Things are either good, bad, or indifferent'; and so we may assume that we have here his analysis of the universal proposition. This passage also throws some light on a curiosity of Diogenes' exposition, namely that he gives 'He is in motion' (ἐκεῖνος κινεῖται) as an example of an indefinite and not, as we should expect, of a definite *axioma*. If the Stoics were in the habit of using ἐκεῖνος in such sentences as 'If anyone is a man, then *he* is mortal', they might think of it first in this rather than in its demonstrative use.

According to the second principle of classification, Diogenes distinguishes three kinds of *axiomata* apart from the affirmative, namely the negative, the denial, and the privative.

---

[1] Diogenes Laertius, vii. 69.　　[2] *Adv. Math.* viii. 96.
[3] Ibid. 98.　　[4] Ibid. xi. 8.

Of the negative (ἀποφατικόν), he gives the example 'It is not day (οὐχὶ ἡμέρα ἔστιν), and he writes as if all negatives were simple *axiomata*; but Sextus' discussion of contradictories (ἀντικείμενα) makes it clear that the Stoics knew that any *axioma*, however complex, could be negated. They insisted that the contradictory of an *axioma* is formed by prefixing the negative particle, οὐχί, to the whole:

'They say that contradictories are such that the one exceeds the other by the negation (ἀποφάσει), as for example "It is day" "It is not day" (οὐχ ἡμέρα ἔστιν). For the *axioma* "It is not day" exceeds the *axioma* "It is day" by the negation, i.e. by the particle "not" (οὐχί), and for this reason it is its contradictory. But if this is what a contradictory is, such as these will also be contradictory: "It is day and it is light" and "It is day and it is not light". But according to them these are not contradictories. Therefore the fact that the one exceeds the other by negation, does not make them contradictories. Yes, they say, but they are contradictories on this condition, that the negation is placed before the whole of the one. For then it governs (κυριεύει) the whole *axioma*, but in "It is day and it is not light", being a part of the whole, it does not govern it so as to make the whole negative. It was necessary, then, we shall say, to add to the notion of contradictories that they are contradictories not simply when the one exceeds the other by negation, but when the negation is placed before the whole *axioma*.'[1]

This passage is noteworthy for the idea of a particle governing the whole or a part only of a proposition. We have here the first appearance of the notion of the scope of an operator. The Stoics also recognized the double negative (ὑπεραποφατικόν) and said that it was equivalent to the original affirmative.[2]

The denial (ἀρνητικόν) differs from the negative in not containing a negated affirmative. It consists of a denying particle and a predicate, e.g. 'No one is walking'.[3] It seems from the definition that denials must have 'no one' or 'nothing' as subject. We do not know how the Stoics would have classified propositions expressed by sentences containing the words, 'never' or 'nowhere'. The privative (στερητικόν) has what might be called a privative predicate, e.g. 'He is unkind'.[3]

Of non-simple *axiomata* Diogenes distinguishes the following kinds:

(1) The conditional (συνημμένον) formed by means of the connective 'if' (εἰ);
(2) the inferential or modified-conditional (παρασυνημμένον) formed by means of the connective 'since' (ἐπεί);

[1] Sextus, *Adv. Math.* viii. 89–90.　　[2] Diogenes Laertius, vii. 69.
[3] Ibid. 70.

(3) the conjunctive (συμπεπλεγμένον) formed by means of the connective 'and' (καί);

(4) the disjunctive (διεζευγμένον) formed by means of the connective 'or' (ἤ, ἤτοι);

(5) the causal (αἰτιῶδες) formed by means of the connective 'because' (διότι);

(6) the *axioma* formed by means of the connective 'rather than' (μᾶλλον . . . ἤ);

(7) the *axioma* formed by means of the connective 'less than' (ἧττον . . . ἤ).[1]

The exact meaning of some of these compound forms will be discussed later. The following points may be made here.

If we may judge from this list, the Stoics do not seem to have been aware of a sharp and important distinction between compound statements which are truth-functional and those which are not truth-functional. A truth-functional compound statement, as we have seen, is one of which the truth or falsity is determined solely by the truth or falsity of its constituent propositions; in Philo's view the conditional is such a compound statement. Diogenes seems to give a truth-functional definition of one of the forms in his list, the disjunctive, when he says:

'This connective ['either'] shows that one of the *axiomata* is false.'[2]

But his remark can scarcely be taken as a definition, since the more important function of the connective he mentions is to indicate that one of the disjoined propositions is true. The remark is probably intended only to make clear that strong or exclusive disjunction is intended. He gives a partly truth-functional account of the inferential form, when he says:

'This connective ['since'] say that the second member follows from the first and that the first is true.'[3]

Sextus, on the other hand, gives a truth-functional definition of conjunction,[4] which is further elaborated by Aulus Gellius, quoting a Stoic handbook:

'In omni autem coniunctione si unum est mendacium, etiamsi cetera vera sunt, totum esse mendacium dicitur.'[5]

This view was apparently in need of defence; for opponents who failed to understand that a conjunctive statement should be treated as *one* said that it would be naturally described as 'no more true than false' if some of its constituents were true and

[1] Diogenes Laertius, vii. 71–74.                    [2] Ibid. 72.
[3] Ibid. 71.          [4] *Adv. Math.* viii. 125–7.          [5] *Noctes Atticae*, xvi. 8.

others false, though they allowed that it might perhaps be called true 'if most of its components were true'.[1] For the conditional Diogenes gives a definition which is in accordance with the third view listed by Sextus in his account of the controversy over conditional propositions:

'A conditional is true in which the contradictory of the consequent is incompatible with the antecedent.'[2]

According to the general theory of the relation between language and *lekta* we should expect the divisions of speech and of *lekta* to correspond more closely than they do. A verb is said to signify a predicate (κατηγόρημα) which is a *lekton*; but both common and proper names are said to signify properties (ποιότητες), which do not occur anywhere in the list of *lekta*. Their place is taken by 'cases', if by anything. The conjunction or connective (σύνδεσμος) is mentioned both as a part of speech and as an essential part of the compound *lekton*. Without further evidence it would be idle to conjecture how the Stoics would have dealt with these discrepancies. A possible explanation is that in their theory of *lekta*, they were mainly interested in the complete *lekta*, *axiomata*, questions, &c., while in grammatical theory they thought of the minimal units of meaning, i.e. words. When they considered words in connexion with the theory of *lekta*, they thought of their functions in sentences and described them as signifying subjects, predicates, and the like. In grammatical theory, on the other hand, they tended to think of the signification of a word as something out of relation to the significations of other words. The common noun, for example, could be grammatically either subject or predicate, and in either case it might be held to signify a quality; but the incomplete *lekton* which it signified would not be the same in each case, since it would play a different part in a complete *lekton*.

We now turn to the Stoic theory of truth. They distinguished the truth (ἡ ἀλήθεια) from the true or what is true. This is explained by Sextus in two passages, of which the shorter runs as follows:

'The true is said to differ from the truth in three ways, in essence (οὐσίᾳ), in constitution (συστάσει), and in meaning (δυνάμει): in essence, since the true is incorporeal (for it is an *axioma* and a *lekton*) whereas truth is a body (for it is knowledge declarative of all true *axiomata*, and knowledge is the leading part in a certain state, just as the fist is the hand in a certain state, and the leading part is a body, for, according to them, it is breath); in constitution, since the true is

---

[1] Sextus, loc. cit.     [2] Diogenes Laertius, vii. 73.

something simple, e.g. "I converse", but truth consists of many true cognitions (γνώσεων); in meaning, since truth is connected with knowledge, but the true not invariably so, for which reason they say that truth is only in a good man, but the true may be in a bad man, as the bad man can say something true.'[1]

By the 'leading part' Sextus here means the intellect, which is part of the soul and therefore, for the Stoics, material. They held, then, that 'truth' refers to a complete body of knowledge as it may be possessed by a person or persons, while 'true' is an adjective applied to an *axioma*. This linguistic distinction appears to be a little eccentric, but is perfectly intelligible. We shall not be further concerned with the truth in the Stoic sense.

They applied the predicates 'true' and 'false' to subjects of three different kinds, *axiomata* (ἀξιώματα), presentations (φαντασίαι), and arguments (λόγοι). But the use of 'true' and 'false' in reference to *axiomata* was probably regarded as basic. There are two reasons for thinking this. The first is that Sextus gives it as the characteristic doctrine of the Stoics that truth and falsity are about the signified ((περὶ) τῷ σημαινομένῳ): 'There was another difference of opinion in that some supposed that truth and falsehood were about the signified, others about speech, and yet others about the movement of thought. The Stoics defended the first view.'[2] Secondly, the truth of arguments was defined in terms of the truth of propositions, and it is very likely that this was done also for the truth of presentations. A true argument is said to be one which is valid and has true premisses.[3] The case of true presentations is not quite so clear. Sextus says: 'True presentations are those of which it is possible to make a true predication (κατηγορία), as, for example, "It is day" or "It is light" at the present moment.'[4] If we take κατηγορία here as equivalent to ἀξίωμα then Sextus is defining the truth of presentations in terms of the truth of *axiomata*. This identification is plausible, but there seems to be only one other occurrence of the term κατηγορία in Sextus' writings and he nowhere discusses its meaning.

The theory of presentations belongs to the epistemology rather than to the logic of the Stoics. Roughly speaking, they seem to have meant by a presentation a sense-impression or a mental image. But they were much exercised about the criterion of truth in presentations, and this fact makes it doubtful whether they were absolutely clear that the basic use of the word 'true' is its application to *axiomata*. They might consistently have held that

[1] *Pyrrh. Hyp.* ii. 81 ff. Cf. *Adv. Math.* vii. 38 ff.
[2] Ibid. viii. 11.
[3] Sextus, *Pyrrh. Hyp.* ii. 138; Diogenes Laertius, vii. 79.
[4] *Adv. Math.* vii. 244.

for purposes of definition the true proposition is basic, but epistemologically the true presentation. That is to say, they might have held that we can explain what is meant by 'true' only by explaining the truth of *axiomata*, but that we can recognize that a particular *axioma* is true only in virtue of having a true presentation. There is no decisive evidence, however, that they held such a view. There is another interesting passage in Sextus which may reflect a Stoic argument to the effect that presentations are not true in the basic sense. It immediately precedes the passage in which he distinguishes the three views about what is to be called 'true' and 'false', and it runs as follows:

'The Stoics say that some sensibles and some intelligibles are true, but the sensibles not directly (ἐξ εὐθείας) but by reference to their corresponding intelligibles (κατ' ἀναφορὰν τὴν ὡς ἐπὶ τὰ παρακείμενα τούτοις νοητά). For according to them the true is what is real (τὸ ὑπάρχον) and is the contradictory of something, while the false is what is not real and is the contradictory of something. And this is an incorporeal *axioma* and is intelligible.'[1]

The verb ὑπάρχειν, here translated by 'be real', is an extremely difficult one to render, because it is ambiguous between 'exist' of objects and 'be true' of propositions. It must not be thought, however, that the Stoic argument represented in this passage is an attempt to define the truth of *axiomata* by means of this notion. It is here used simply as a means of indicating in a convenient way the difference between truth and falsehood. The point of the passage seems to be that anything which can be called true or false must have a contradictory. For everything said to be true it is possible to indicate something which is false. This is the function of the particle 'not' in language. But sensibles as such have no contradictories, and sensibles include, of course, presentations and also the things described by Sextus in his discussion of the three views as 'movements of thought'; for according to the Stoics thinking is a physical activity and so perceptible.

We have a reason, then, both for the Stoic view that the truth of presentations is a derivative type of truth and also for their rejection of the third view mentioned by Sextus as to the proper subject for the predicates 'true' and 'false'. But we must now ask ourselves why they rejected the second view. Why are truth and falsehood not to be found in language? Sextus discusses this question and produces two arguments probably drawn from Stoic sources. Their origin is indicated by the examples used, especially the form βλίτυρι as an instance of an articulate but

---

[1] Ibid. viii. 10.

unintelligible sound; for this same example occurs in Diogenes' résumé of Stoic logic.[1] Sextus argues first that, if truth is in speech (φωνή), it is either in significant or non-significant speech. The second is obviously impossible, but so is the first; for no speech as such is significant (οὐδεμία γὰρ φωνὴ ὡς φωνὴ σημαντική ἐστιν). If it were, everyone who apprehended the speech, both Greeks and barbarians, would apprehend what was signified by it. This brief argument goes to the heart of the matter, but it is followed by another which seems much less satisfactory. Of sections of speech (τῶν φωνῶν) some are simple and some complex, e.g. 'Dion' and 'Dion walks'. Truth cannot lie in the simple, since only *axiomata* are true and they are complex. But it cannot lie in the complex, since complex speech (λέξις) as such, e.g. 'Dion walks', cannot exist; for when we say 'Dion' we do not say 'walks', and so on.[2] The argument which forms the second horn of this dilemma appears futile and trivial to us; and it is so, in so far as it implies the impossibility of making any predication of a thing which can exist only over a period of time. The same argument would make it impossible for us to say anything of Dion himself; for he certainly cannot exist in an indivisible moment. It may, however, have a serious point here. As a previously quoted passage has shown, the Stoics wished to insist that an *axioma* which is to be described as true or false must somehow be present when it is so described.[3] And common usage gives some support to this suggestion. Sometimes at least we wish to say 'What he said *is* true', and this is a queer idiom if we are talking about the utterance which took place at a definite time. If in such contexts we referred solely to utterances or token-sentences, we should always say 'What he said was true', just as we always say 'The war of 1914–18 *was* a great disaster', not '*is* a great disaster'.

The first argument in any case must be taken seriously; and this applies against the view that speech can be true or false in its own right; whether we think of speech as consisting of token-sentences or of type-sentences. If the barbarians cannot understand the Greek token-sentence, neither can they be said to understand the Greek type-sentence; for tokens are significant only as instances of types used in certain circumstances.

For the Stoics, then, the *axioma* is true or false in the basic sense, and a simple definite *axioma* is said to be true 'when the predicate belongs to the thing which falls under the demonstrative' (ὅταν τῷ ὑπὸ τὴν δεῖξιν πίπτοντι συμβεβήκῃ τὸ κατηγόρημα).[4] Diogenes gives a simpler explanation by means of an example.

[1] Diogenes Laertius vii. 59.          [2] *Adv. Math.* viii. 133 ff.
[3] Ibid. 254–6.          [4] Ibid. 100.

The *axioma* signified by 'It is day' is true if it is day; if it is not day, it is false.[1] This account is very close to the Aristotelian,[2] except that it proceeds by example. But the definition given by Sextus is more complicated and suggests that the true *axioma* has a structure corresponding to a similar structure in the object described. And unlike the Aristotelian definition, it applies directly only to simple *axiomata*. The truth of other *axiomata* would have to be defined in terms of the truth of these.

We are now in a position to attempt to interpret the Stoic theory of *lekta* and more particularly of *axiomata*. We have argued earlier[3] that it is necessary to distinguish the proposition, which is true or false in the primary sense, from the sentence in which it is expressed. It seems likely that the Stoics were convinced in a similar way that *lekta* must be distinguished from the sentences which express them. It is not the case, however, that any type of *lekton* can be identified simply with the proposition. It is the *axioma* which, for the Stoics, is primarily true or false, but the *axioma*, as we have seen, is the proposition as asserted rather than the proposition in itself. This is further made clear by the way in which Sextus discusses the 'thing-more-than-an-*axioma*'. He does not seem to detect any element which is common to this and to the *axioma* and which is true or false. Again questions, commands, &c., are for the Stoics species of *lekta* co-ordinate with *axiomata*. They did not in fact abstract from the attitude of speaker or writer in forming the concept of the *lekton*, but merely from the linguistic expression. For this reason *lekta* have moods.

*Axiomata* differ, moreover, from propositions in having tenses. It is unfortunate that no work of the Stoics dealing with tenses survives. They were interested in the subject; for Chrysippus, according to Diogenes, wrote a work 'On Temporal Expressions' and another 'On *Axiomata* in the Perfect Tense',[4] and Priscian gives the Stoics credit for distinguishing a use of the present tense in which it expresses what is expressed in English by the continuous present.[5] The passage of Sextus in which he says that the Stoics regarded *axiomata* about the past and future as themselves present clearly implies that *axiomata* have tenses. 'He has been wounded' and 'He will die' are regarded as expressing different *axiomata* from those expressed at any time by 'He is being wounded' and 'He is dying'.[6] Since *axiomata* have tenses, we should expect that their truth-value may change, and it seems that the Stoics allowed for this in the case of certain *axiomata*

---

[1] Diogenes Laertius, vii. 65.  [2] *Metaphysica*, Γ, 7 (1011ᵇ26–27).
[3] See pp. 49 ff.  [4] vii. 190.
[5] *Grammatici Latini*, ed. Keil, ii, p. 415.  [6] *Adv. Math.* viii. 255.

which they called μεταπίπτοντα (changing). These are mentioned
by Sextus, who shows how the Stoics used them to solve an
apparent paradox,[1] and Dionysius of Halicarnassus states that
Chrysippus wrote about them in a work 'On the Combination
of the Parts of Arguments' (περὶ τῆς συντάξεως τῶν τοῦ λόγου
μερῶν), which was 'about the combination of *axiomata*, true and
false, possible and impossible, contingent and changing'.[2] It
appears from this that the capacity for change was thought of as
a property of *axiomata*, like truth, falsity, possibility, and impossibility. Alexander gives as an example of a changing *axioma*
the conditional 'If Dion is alive, Dion will be alive'.[3] The Stoics,
he says, mention that there will be a time when this conditional
will be false, because the antecedent will be true when the consequent is false.

The last and perhaps most surprising way in which Stoic
*axiomata* differ from propositions is that they may cease to exist
and presumably also (though this is not stated) begin to exist
at definite times. Chrysippus as reported by Alexander allows that
*axiomata* may be destroyed (φθείρεσθαι). This emerges in his argument against Diodorus to show that the impossible can follow
from the possible.[4] He maintained that 'This man is dead' is
impossible', while 'Dion is dead' is possible, although in the case
where 'this' refers to Dion, the first follows from the second. The
argument is complicated and difficult to follow, but Alexander
several times uses the notion that the *axioma* 'This man is dead',
is destroyed (φθείρεται) after Dion's death,[5] and this seems to be
different from its being false or impossible. Chrysippus apparently
argued that, while Dion is alive, the *axioma* 'This man is dead' is
impossible, because self-contradictory, and that after his death
it does not exist, so that the question of its truth or falsity does not
arise. From this it would follow that 'Dion is dead' could never
be true while 'This man is dead' was false, so that the conditional
having the former as antecedent and the latter as consequent
would be sound according to the definition of Diodorus and also
according to that of Chrysippus himself. It will be noticed that
the *axioma* 'Dion is dead' is apparently not destructible. The word
'Dion' signifies an individual quality, which is always expressible,
while what is expressed by the word 'this' on some particular
occasion cannot be expressed under altered circumstances. The
destruction of an *axioma* is its ceasing to be expressible. Detached

---

[1] *Pyrrh. Hyp.* ii. 234.          [2] *De Compositione Verborum*, ed. Reiske, 31–32.
[3] Apud Simplicium, *In Aristotelis Physic. Libros Quattuor Post. Commentarium*, ed.
Diels, *C.I.A.G.*, x, p. 1299.
[4] Alexander, *In Aristotelis An. Pr. Lib. I Commentarium*, ed. Wallies, *C.I.A.G.* ii (i),
pp. 177 ff.          [5] Ibid., pp. 178, 179, 181.

from the picturesque way in which it is expressed, the view of Chrysippus is not startling; for we are familiar with the notion that a form of words which can be used to express a proposition on one occasion cannot be so used on another occasion. For example, the words, 'My left eye-tooth is aching', spoken by a given person at one time will express a proposition true or false, but at a later time, if uttered by the same person, may not express any proposition. On the Stoic view, according to which the means of referring to the subject are included in the *lekton*, this means that the *axioma* formerly expressed by the words is no longer expressible, i.e. is destroyed, whereas later philosophers have for the most part maintained that a proposition is always expressible in some way, although at certain times it may not be expressible in certain ways, e.g. by means of a demonstrative.

In all these ways, then, the complete *lekta* of the Stoics differ from propositions as we conceive them. The last two features in which they differ, the change in truth-value and what may be called the 'mortality' of *lekta*, arise from the fact that token-reflexives are assigned to the *lekta* themselves as well as to the means of expression. In general, it may be said that when sentences are distinguished from what they express, two extreme positions may be adopted. We may say that sentences express the same proposition when they are verified or falsified by the same situation or state of affairs. This is admittedly somewhat obscure, since the notion of the same situation or state of affairs needs to be clarified; but it is evident that on this view we could, for example, allow differently tensed sentences to express the same proposition. It is characteristic of this point of view to assign token-reflexives to the means of expression, while excluding them from the proposition expressed, and this involves an element of paradox; for it seems very strange to allow that 'There will be a naval battle' and 'There was a naval battle' ever *mean* the same. We are inclined to think that the temporal relation of the battle to the utterance is part of what is meant or expressed and not merely something involved in the means of expression. In reaction to this paradox we may adopt the other extreme position and allow sentence-meanings, which we call propositions for convenience, to proliferate, until we finally reach the position that the same singular proposition can never be expressed twice. Every serious use of tenses involves at least a tacit 'now' and so 'My left eye-tooth is aching now' will not express the same proposition twice. Thus singular propositions become as fugitive as token-sentences. They do not change their truth-value but they are extremely short-lived. The Stoics seem to have taken a middle course between these two extreme positions. On the one hand, they brought token-reflexives into *lekta*; but on the other they allowed that repetitions of a given form of words would for a certain time at least express the same *lekton*, for the *axioma* expressed by 'If it is day, it is day' is said to consist not of two *axiomata*, but of the same *axioma* repeated.[1]

Athough for the reasons we have seen, *axiomata* cannot be simply identified with propositions, they resemble the latter in several important respects. They are expressed by complete indicative sentences; they are true or false in the basic sense; they are abstract or, as the Stoics perhaps rather unhappily put it, incorporeal; and they exist in some sense whether we think of them or not. The last point needs to be argued. The definition of a *lekton* as 'that which exists according to a rational presentation' suggests that there is no *lekton* if there is no corresponding presentation, i.e. that all *lekta* must be objects of thought, and in one place Sextus clearly assumes that *lekta* exist only when they are expressed or meant.[2] This may, however, be a mere *argumentum ad homines*. For there is one central Stoic doctrine which certainly implies that *lekta* exist even when we do not think of them. According to the theory of natural signs considered above,[3] an *axioma* which is a sign reveals another *axioma* which is its significate. The latter must therefore exist in order to be revealed. Again Sextus' remark that, while truth is necessarily connected with knowledge, the true is not[4] implies that true *axiomata* may exist although they are not known. It seems, therefore, to be consistent with the greater part of Stoic theory to maintain that *lekta* may exist which are neither expressed nor thought.

There is much in common, then, between what the Stoics expressed by the word ἀξίωμα and what we express by the word 'proposition', and when we consider general sentences the notions coincide. By a 'general' sentence we mean here a sentence expressing unrestricted universality or an existential sentence with its verb in the present tense understood timelessly. As long as the meaning of their constituent words remains the same, such sentences cannot change their truth-value or cease to have one, nor does their meaning or truth-value change with the person uttering them or the circumstances of utterance.

In the case of sentences containing token-reflexives, however, the Stoic *axioma* differs from the proposition. The reason for this difference appears to be that the Stoics came to their theory by examining the notion of meaning, whereas we approached the

---

[1] Diogenes Laertius, vii. 68.    [2] *Pyrrh. Hyp.* ii. 109.
[3] p. 141.    [4] *Pyrrh. Hyp.* ii. 82.

notion of the proposition by asking what it is that can be called true or false. Now the word 'mean' in English has two uses which it is important to distinguish in this connexion. We can ask what a person means and we can ask what a sentence means. The Stoics, on the other hand, had two different words where we have only one; for Greek uses λέγειν of persons, σημαίνειν of sentences. But they deliberately identified *semainomena* with *lekta*. Sextus says in the passage in which he discusses *lekta* most fully: 'But one is incorporeal, that is the thing signified (τὸ σημαινόμενον) and meant (λεκτόν), which is true or false'.[1] What a sentence means, then, in their view is what a person means when he utters it. And what a person means when he utters a sentence includes what he expresses by mood and tense. He would not be said to mean the same in making a statement and in uttering the corresponding command, e.g. in saying 'The door is shut' and 'Shut the door'. Nor again would he be said to mean the same when uttering with the appropriate interval between his times of utterance 'I shall be in London tomorrow' and 'I was in London yesterday'.

In keeping close to the common-sense notion of what a person means, the Stoics were forced, therefore, to allow that *lekta* have mood and tense. On the other hand, they cut across ordinary usage in not allowing that a person could mean the same by saying 'Dion is dead' and 'He is dead', when 'He' refers to Dion. In making a distinction of *lekta* here, the Stoics were presumably influenced by the fact that no one would say that the two sentences, taken out of context, had the same meaning. 'Meaning the same' has a different use as applied to persons and applied to sentences. One or more persons may use different sentences to mean the same thing, or the same sentence to mean different things; but a given sentence has always the same meaning, and, when two sentences are said to mean the same, this does not entail that two different persons could use them to mean the same. For example, the sentences 'I am cold' and *J'ai froid* mean the same, but they could not be used by two persons to mean the same. The sentences 'I am cold' and 'You are cold' can be so used, but they would never be said to have the same meaning. The Stoics seem to have allowed both notions of meaning to act as principles of differentiation among *lekta*. That is to say, they held that, whenever a person or persons could be said to mean different things, then at least two *lekta* were involved, and also that, whenever two sentences could be said to mean different things, then at least two *lekta* are involved. They thus achieved in their theory almost the

---

[1] *Adv. Math.* viii. 12.

maximum multiplicity. For them difference of verbal form in the
same language was almost always an indication of difference of
meaning; and it was probably this fact that led the Peripatetics
to say that they paid too much attention to verbal form and
therefore gave different names to arguments which were identical
from the Peripatetic point of view. The complaint is made in two
passages of Alexander. In the first he says that the Stoics,
although allowing that the two forms, 'Some S is not L' and 'Not
every S is L' were equivalent (ἰσοδυναμοῦντα), yet distinguished
between the two arguments:

(1)  Every L is M                    (2)  Every L is M
     Some S is not M                      Not every S is M
     Therefore some S is not L            Therefore not every S is L.

calling the first a syllogism and the second a hyposyllogism.[1]
Later he says:

'The moderns who follow expressions (ταῖς λέξεσιν) and not what
they mean (τοῖς σημαινομένοις) say that the same result does not arise
in the substitution for terms of their equivalent expressions (τὰς
ἰσοδυναμούσας λέξεις). For while "If A then B" means the same as "B
follows from A", they say that there is a syllogistic argument if we
take the expression "If A then B; but A; therefore B", but that "B
follows from A; but A; therefore B" is not syllogistic but concluding
(περαντικόν).'[2]

We may infer from these passages that the Stoics made a distinction between identity of meaning and equivalence which seemed
unimportant to the Peripatetics. Unfortunately we do not know
what criterion of equivalence the Stoics recognized.

Whenever the Stoics would say that two token-sentences or
type-sentences express the same complete *lekton*, we should say
that they express the same proposition, but the converse does not
hold. A *lekton* is the result of abstraction from particular forms of
linguistic expression. It is what remains constant in translation
from one language to another. But a proposition is the result of
a further abstraction from the time and circumstances of utterance.
It is what remains constant through transformation of means of
expression, i.e. token-reflexives, in the same language.

## 5. *The Stoic System of Inference Schemata*

In their account of reasoning Chrysippus and the Stoics
generally concentrated attention on valid inference schemata
(συνακτικὰ σχήματα). Whereas Aristotle had used the conditional

form of statement in presenting the principles of the various moods of categorical syllogism, the Stoics set out skeleton arguments such as 'If the first, then the second; but the first; therefore the second'. This method had been used already by Theophrastus in his account of totally hypothetical syllogisms, and it may be assumed that the Stoics adopted it as a general method from the desire to avoid the complicated sentences which result when we try to formulate conditional propositions about the relation of conditional propositions. They were well aware of the truth that the principle of a valid inference schema can be presented in a conditional statement, such as 'If if-the-first-then-the-second and the first, then the second'. Indeed they sometimes said that the validity of an inference schema depended on the truth of the corresponding conditional. There are a number of passages in which Sextus Empiricus refers to this, although, as might be expected, some which involve one condition within another have been corrupted by copyists.[1] The fact that the Stoics did not bother to speak of the *logical necessity* of a conditional proposition corresponding to a valid inference pattern suggests strongly that they thought of all conditional statements as assertions of necessary connexion. Anyone who had adopted the Philonian definition of 'if . . . then' could scarcely fail to remark that a formula like that quoted above was a very special case among conditionals.

It is an interesting point that the Stoics did not follow Aristotle in using letters as variables when they were talking of the forms of propositions, but introduced ordinal numbers instead. We have given an example of this usage in the previous paragraph. It is to be found in all the Stoic fragments where it is appropriate, and where it occurs without reference to author or school it may be taken conversely as a sign of Stoic origin. For in antiquity it was already regarded as a Stoic peculiarity. Apuleius says: *Stoici porro pro literis numeros usurpant.*[2] But it is important to realize that a numeral occurring in a Stoic text as a variable marks a gap to be filled by a *propositional* sign, not by a term. Failure to understand this difference between the Stoic and Aristotelian systems was responsible until recently for a great deal of confusion in the history of logic.

Before treating valid inference schemata in detail, we shall consider again the various kinds of complex propositions which are essentially involved in them.

---

[1] *Pyrrh. Hyp.* ii. 113, 137, 139; *Adv. Math.* viii. 416, 421. Benson Mates has emended the text in an article on 'Stoic Logic and the Text of Sextus Empiricus', *American Journal of Philology*, lxx (1949), pp. 290–8.
[2] *De Philosophia Rationali*, 279.

The Stoics phrased their definition of complex propositions in such a way that it did not cover negative propositions, but they seem to have realized that a negative proposition could not properly be treated as co-ordinate with the proposition of which it was the negative. According to Apuleius, *solum abdicativum vocant cui negativa particula praeponitur*.[1] That is to say, they held that in order to obtain the negative of any given statement we should place a negative particle in front to operate upon the whole. And Apuleius goes on to say they argued that *Voluptas non est bonum* was affirmative because it was equivalent to *Evenit cuidam voluptati bonum non esse*. This is not easy to understand, but the point may be that 'Some pleasure is not good' should not be treated as a negative statement. If this is the right interpretation, they seem to have been protesting against the Aristotelian classification of general propositions, and for reasons which were explained in the last chapter. The interpretation is supported by a passage of Boethius where he says that the Stoics wanted to put negation signs on some names.[2] For this might well be a way of describing the analysis which resolves 'Some man is not white' into 'Some man is not-white'.

Of conjunction the Stoics had not much to say. They defined a conjunctive proposition (συμπεπλεγμένον) as one which was true if both the conjoined propositions were true and otherwise false. And they recognized that the conjoined propositions might themselves be complex.[3]

A disjunctive proposition (διεζευγμένον), i.e. a proposition such as we express by the use of 'or', was said to involve a complete opposition (τέλεια μάχη) of its disjuncts.[4] But later Stoics recognized also the possibility of a 'quasi-disjunction' (παραδιεζευγμένον) which was true if either of its disjuncts was true and false only if they were both false.[5] It is interesting to notice here the beginning of a fruitless dispute which has engaged the attention of many later logicians. In ordinary speech we sometimes use 'or' and similar words in a non-adversative sense, as when, for example, we say that hail or heavy rain has beaten down the crops, not wishing to exclude the possibility that both have fallen and done damage. But at other times we intend to convey that one and only one of the alternatives is true, as when we say (with a stress on the word 'either') that an earthwork was built either by the ancient Britons or by the Romans. And there are many

---

[1] *De Philosophia Rationali*, 266.
[2] *Commentarii in Lib. Arist. Περὶ Ἑρμηνείας, Sec. Ed.*, ed. Meiser, pp. 261-2.
[3] Sextus Empiricus, *Adv. Math.* viii. 124.
[4] Ibid. 162.
[5] Galen, *Institutio Logica*, ed. Kalbfleisch, p. 12.

occasions when we wish it to be clearly understood that two alternatives *could not* be true together, as when we say that a medicine will either kill or cure. Once these different usages have been recognized, it is clear that we cannot speak of a single meaning for the word 'or', although for certain purposes we may find it convenient to concentrate attention on the first, as being the simplest and presupposed by the other two. But Chrysippus and his followers seem to have assumed that the third and strongest sense was the only proper one. The expression which we have translated by 'complete opposition' must surely be understood to mean incompatibility, i.e. more than mere *de facto* separation. In view of this and their metaphysical interest in determinism, it is not surprising to find that the Stoics were eager to defend the principle of excluded middle and also the principle of bivalence. According to Boethius they criticized Aristotle for denying the latter.[1]

It is rather surprising, however, that Chrysippus recognized 'not both . . . and . . .' as a distinct form for complex propositions. Greek, like English, contains no single particle for the notion of separation, and it is to be assumed therefore that he admitted this form because he thought that it was needed in reasoning. We shall notice later a consideration which may have led him to this conclusion. Apparently he thought of the form as expressing *de facto* separation rather than incompatibility, and he may perhaps have used it to supply in a round-about way the lack of a weak or non-adversative 'or' in his system. For 'The crops have been beaten down by hail or heavy rain' is equivalent to 'It is not the case both that the crops have not been beaten down by hail and that the crops have not been beaten down by heavy rain'. It is possible also that he used the form for defining Philonian conditionals.[2]

In a passage of Cicero quoted above Chrysippus is mentioned with Diodorus and Philo as a disputant in the famous controversy about conditionals, and the phraseology implies that he had a view of his own, different from either of the Megarian views. We know also from Diogenes Laertius that he wrote against Philo on meanings and on moods of argument.[3] It is tempting therefore to suppose that he was the author of the third doctrine mentioned by Sextus, namely, the doctrine that the negation of the consequent is incompatible with the antecedent in any sound conditional. He can scarcely have held the fourth view, at least with the corollary given by Sextus, since he is supposed to have used

[1] *Commentarii in Lib. Arist. Περὶ Ἑρμηνείας, Sec. Ed.*, ed. Meiser, p. 208.
[2] Cicero, *De Fato*, 15.  [3] *Vitae*, vii. 191, 194.

repetitive conditionals in some of his arguments. In support of this conjecture we may cite passages of Sextus[1] and Diogenes[2] which seem to imply that the Stoics required incompatibility between the antecedent and the negation of the consequent in a conditional. On the other hand there is a statement by Sextus that they adopted Philo's definition.[3] Perhaps we should draw the conclusion that at some times the Stoics favoured Philo's definition and at other times the stricter definition by reference to incompatibility.

In a review of the varieties of propositions Galen says that the disjunctive statement 'Either it is day or it is night' is equivalent to 'If it is not day it is night'.[4] The example and the context suggest that he is drawing on Stoic sources, but, as it stands, his assertion does not allow for complete opposition of disjuncts which we know the Stoics usually maintained. Possibly his expression is loose and he means to say that the disjunctive statement is equivalent to the bi-conditional 'It is not day if, and only if, it is night'. For the assertion of such an equivalence would indeed be in keeping with the Stoic doctrine of disjunction, provided always that the conditional is understood to convey necessary connexion. We shall see reason to believe, however, that the Stoics were not much interested in a reduction of the number of logical constants.

On the other hand, we have evidence to show that Chrysippus and his followers were interested in calculating the number of distinct complex propositions that could be constructed from a given number of simple propositions. According to a statement of Plutarch, Chrysippus said that more than a million conjunctions (συμπλοκαί) could be made from ten simple propositions, but all the mathematicians were against him, and one of them, Hipparchus, maintained that, whereas affirmation gave 103,049 conjunctive propositions (συμπεπλεγμένα), negation gave 310,952.[5] It is difficult to make any satisfactory sense of the passage, but it shows at least that there was some interest in the *ars combinatoria* at this time.

Among valid inference schemata Chrysippus recognized five as basic. These are listed by a number of ancient authorities[6] as the indemonstrable moods (ἀναπόδεικτοι τρόποι) and they are as follows:

[1] *Pyrrh. Hyp.* ii. 190.    [2] *Vitae*, vii. 73.
[3] *Pyrrh. Hyp.* ii. 104. It has been said that Cicero attributes the definition to Chrysippus himself, but the passage in question, *De Fato*, 15, seems to suggest the opposite view.    [4] *Institutio Logica*, ed. Kalbfleisch, p. 9.
[5] Plutarch, *De Stoic. Repugn.* 1047C.
[6] e.g. Sextus, *Pyrrh. Hyp.* ii. 157f. and *Adv. Math.* viii. 224 f.

1. *If the first, then the second; but the first; therefore the second.*
2. *If the first, then the second; but not the second; therefore not the first.*
3. *Not both the first and the second; but the first; therefore not the second.*
4. *Either the first or the second; but the first; therefore not the second.*
5. *Either the first or the second; but not the second; therefore the first.*

It will be noticed that an argument in any of these moods must have two premisses. According to Chrysippus and his immediate followers this was essential for the simplest sort of reasoning. When Antipater, who was head of the school about 159–130 B.C., recognized inference from one premiss ($\mu o \nu o \lambda \acute{\eta} \mu \mu a \tau o s$ $\dot{\epsilon} \pi \iota \phi o \rho \acute{a}$), his usage was regarded as an innovation.[1] Furthermore, of the two premisses required for an argument in one of Chrysippus' indemonstrable moods one must be complex. This was usually set out first in a formal exposition, and was called the leading premiss ($\dot{\eta} \gamma \epsilon \mu o \nu \iota \kappa \grave{o} \nu$ $\lambda \hat{\eta} \mu \mu a$). Presumably it had the place of honour because it determined the distinctive character of the whole argument. By way of contrast the second premiss was called the additional assumption ($\pi \rho \acute{o} \sigma \lambda \eta \psi \iota s$).[2] In a particular application of an indemonstrable mood the second premiss might no doubt have some internal complexity; but if so, any complexity it had (other than the possession of a negation sign) was irrelevant to the nature of the argument.

Since they distinguished arguments by the forms of their leading premisses, it was natural that the Stoics should try to provide for arguments involving all the different kinds of complex propositions they had recognized. But it is not easy to understand why they supposed their list of five indemonstrable moods to be at once exhaustive and irreducible. In the first place the list contains no mood for an argument with a conjunctive leading premiss. Probably the reason for this omission was that such a mood, if it existed, would require no second premiss. In Stoic terminology it would have the form 'Both the first and the second; therefore the first', and Chrysippus, as we have seen, did not think that such a pattern of speech could properly be said to express inference. On the other hand, he did recognize a special mood for arguments with leading premisses of the form 'Not both the first and the second', although there seems at first sight to be only a verbal distinction between this and the disjunctive mood which follows it in his list. As we have suggested in an earlier paragraph, his reason for regarding 'Not both the first and the second' as a special form of a complex premiss may have been that he did not

---

[1] Sextus, *Adv. Math.* viii. 443.    [2] Diogenes Laertius, vii. 76.

admit a truth-functional interpretation for 'Either the first or the second'. If this was so, he certainly had need of a special mood for arguments in which the evidence did not satisfy the requirements of disjunction, as he understood that form. But the need is not so obvious that it has been recognized by all logicians who reject the truth-functional interpretation of disjunction, and we may properly ask what brought it to his attention. The answer can be found, if at all, only by consideration of the purpose Chrysippus had in mind when he made his list. Again, it is curious that he thought it necessary to provide separately for conditional and disjunctive arguments. For he could scarcely have failed to see that 'or' might be defined in terms of 'if' and 'not' or 'if' in terms of 'or' and 'not'—unless indeed he held that one of these connectives was to be understood in the truth-functional fashion but the other not, and that is very unlikely. Here too it seems that for further explanation of the list of indemonstrable moods we must consider the uses for which Chrysippus compiled it.

No doubt he intended in the first place to provide a list of moods which are required for ordinary reasoning in history and science, that is to say, reasoning from first-order premisses which are not themselves in any sense truths of logic. But when he called his five moods indemonstrable, he seems to have had in mind another project, namely, that of constructing a deductive system within which a great many demonstrable moods can be derived from a few primitive patterns. If we may judge from the remarks of ancient authorities such as Cicero[1] and from the titles of the works attributed to him by Diogenes Laertius,[2] he did in fact elaborate a host of theorems or derivative moods, from his five indemonstrables. Sometimes in late antiquity these derivative moods were called in a rather confusing way non-simple indemonstrables, but Sextus Empiricus implies that in Chrysippus' own work ἀναπόδεικτος had the meaning of 'self-evident'.[3] Apparently Chrysippus carried through his programme in rigorously formal style, proving even theorems which everyone else was ready to take for granted. When Prantl, the nineteenth-century historian of logic, spoke of the *blödsinniger Formalismus* of the Stoics, he was only echoing ancient criticisms by the followers of Aristotle. Alexander, for example, says in several places that the Stoics were too fussy about form and carried rigour in the analysis of arguments beyond what was useful for

[1] *Topica*, 57.
[2] *Vitae*, vii. 194–6.
[3] *Adv. Math.* viii. 223, 228–9. It is rendered by *indemonstrabilis* in the Latin of Apuleius, *De Philosophia Rationali*, 277.

the ordinary concerns of life.[1] And Galen complains that they attended to expression (λέξις) more than to things.[2] To modern logicians who have learnt from mathematics the importance of form and rigour these criticisms may appear as recommendations; but they were unfortunately so damaging in late antiquity, when theology and rhetoric were more highly esteemed than mathematics, that the works of Chrysippus have all disappeared. From the host of theorems which he proved only six have been discovered so far in the works of other ancient authors, four in the writings of Sextus Empiricus, one in Alexander's *Commentary on the Prior Analytics*, and one in Origen's tract *Against Celsus*. Of these six, two (both of them in the writings of Sextus) are accompanied by detailed proofs, and two others are so simple that it is easy to construct proofs for them in analogous fashion, but the remaining two, which are by far the most interesting, cannot be proved by the procedures of which we have examples, and it is a fascinating problem to discover what more we must assume in the method of demonstration introduced by Chrysippus.

Apart from the facts already mentioned in this chapter the only relevant evidence is to be found in some ancient references to *themata* (θέματα) which were used by the Stoics in the analysis of complicated arguments. If the reconstruction which we have to suggest is satisfactory, it should not merely furnish proofs of the interesting theorems mentioned above but also enable us to fit our fragmentary account of the *themata* into a coherent scheme, together with our other scraps of information, so that details which would otherwise seem arbitrary become intelligible. For convenience of reference all theorems will be expressed in the standard Stoic phraseology and numbered consecutively after the indemonstrables to indicate that they are of the same general character, but those for which there is no ancient authority will be distinguished by asterisks.

It is natural to begin by considering the theorems which have been preserved by Sextus Empiricus with their proofs.

6. *If the first, then if the first then the second; but the first; therefore the second.*[3]

Here the two premisses yield 'If the first, then the second' in accordance with indemonstrable 1. And this together with the second premiss yields 'The second' in accordance with indemonstrable 1 again.

---

[1] *Alexander, In Aristotelis An. Pr. Lib. I. Commentarium*, ed. Wallies, *C.I.A.G.* ii (i), p. 284.
[2] *Institutio Logica*, ed. Kalbfleisch, p. 11.
[3] *Adv. Math.* viii. 230–3.

7. *If the first and the second, then the third; but not the third; on the other hand the first; therefore not the second.*[1]

Here the first two premisses yield 'Not both the first and the second' in accordance with indemonstrable 2. And this together with the third premiss yields 'Not the second' in accordance with indemonstrable 3.

It will be seen that each of these theorems is proved in two steps. In the first case the two steps are of the same kind, in the second of different kinds. But as Sextus remarks, both proofs illustrate a traditional principle for the analysis of arguments, namely:

> *When we have premisses which entail a certain conclusion, we also have potentially the conclusion involved in them, though it may not be explicitly stated.*

In other words, what is entailed by the premisses of an argument, or by any selection of them, may itself be used as a premiss for further reasoning. So far all is clear. But there is something rather curious in the procedure of these proofs which seems to have escaped the notice of the historians of logic, ancient and modern.

When we undertake to derive a mood of argument from others, we propose in effect to show that certain general statements of the second order about entailment follow from simpler statements of the same order. For to say that a mood is valid is the same as to say that any set of propositions which exhibit certain specified forms entail a proposition which exhibits a certain other form related to the first in specified fashion. Now we can, if we choose, derive entailment statements from other entailment statements in a straightforward fashion, relying on such principles as the transitivity of entailment. Chrysippus, however, works in a different way. He tries to derive complicated moods from simple moods by arguments within those simple moods, and for this purpose he treats expressions such as 'If the first and the second, then the third' as though they were premisses, although in strict parlance they are not statements at all but only patterns for statements. When he says 'If the first and the second, then the third; but not the third; therefore not both the first and the second', he is really engaged in a kind of make-believe deduction with dummy premisses. We do not mean by this that his method is invalid; on the contrary, it is a sound method which has been used at some time or other by every teacher of logic. But it works only because it leads us to a position in which we are able to say that any genuine set of premisses of certain forms *would* entail a conclusion of a certain other form. Like the use of examples in

[1] *Adv. Math.* viii. 234–6.

logic, it is a technique for helping men to make intuitive inductions about entailment. Probably Chrysippus adopted it as his
official method because he was interested in the practical applic-
tion of logic and thought that the derivation of a complicated
mood was essentially the same task as that of persuading a doubter
to accept a conclusion established in that mood by true premisses.

It is now easy to find proofs for two other theorems attributed
to Chrysippus.

8. *If the first, then the first; but the first; therefore the first.*[1]

Here the conclusion follows directly from the premisses in accordance with indemonstrable 1. As Alexander said, the theorem is
a mere triviality, but we shall see later that Chrysippus may have
had a good reason for including it in his voluminous works.

9. *Either the first or the second or the third; but not the first; and not
the second; therefore the third.*[2]

Here, it seems, we must think of the words 'the second or the
third' as bracketed together in the disjunctive premiss; for the
conclusion can then be obtained by two applications of indemonstrable 5. If this procedure is correct, the disjunction may indeed
be made as long as we please, since the conclusion can always be
proved by a number of applications of the same indemonstrable.
Chrysippus himself is reported to have said that his argument
from a disjunction with three members was used by a dog when
it came to a cross-roads and after sniffing at the entries to two of
the new ways went down the third way without sniffing because
it knew that its quarry must be there.

By application of the procedures we have noticed so far it is
possible to prove a great many more theorems, including some
of considerable complexity, but not those which are most interesting among the small number preserved from the work of
Chrysippus, namely, 'If the first, then the second; and if the first,
then not the second; therefore not the first' and 'If the first, then the
first; if not the first, then the first; but either the first or not the
first; therefore the first'. For as they stand, neither of these contains the material required for any application of an indemonstrable. If, then, we wish to repeat the enterprise of Chrysippus,
we must cast about and try to supplement our very meagre stock
in trade from sources which are known to have been open to him.
And since there is no evidence at all to suggest that the early
Stoics introduced any basic patterns of inference other than the
five indemonstrables, it is natural to consider whether there are

---

[1] Alexander, *In Aristotelis An. Pr. Lib. I Commentarium*, ed. Wallies, *C.I.A.G.*
ii(i), p. 20.                              [2] Sextus, *Pyrrh. Hyp.* i. 69.

any logically necessary truths which Chryippus might have used as supplementary premisses. For truisms of this sort can be invoked to make good a shortage of inference patterns; and if Chrysippus used them so, he would have been justified in not mentioning them explicitly among the premisses of any derivative mood which he proved by their means, since what is true on logical grounds should not be treated as though it were a special assumption which might conceivably be false.

In this connexion it is interesting to notice that the Stoics are reported to have said that introduction of superfluous material among the premisses of an argument was a defect in reasoning. But apparently they had in mind only saying 'It is day and Dion is walking' when it would be enough to say 'It is day'.[1] And in later times they themselves were accused of introducing unnecessary complications, because they gave as a premiss the conditional statement 'If it is day, it is light' instead of arguing direct from the antecedent to the consequent, i.e. by the argument 'It is day; therefore it is light'.[2] We must admit therefore that we have no clear evidence of Stoic views about the use of logical truisms as premisses, but we know that they attached great importance to the principle of excluded middle in the form 'Either the first or not the first' and it is easy to see how they could have used it to prove two important theorems.

*10. *Either the first or not the first; but the first; therefore not not the first.*

Here the conclusion follows directly from the premisses by indemonstrable 4.

*11. *Either the first or not the first; but not not the first; therefore the first.*

Here the conclusion follows directly from the premisses by indemonstrable 5.

Together these two theorems allow us to assert the equivalence of any proposition to the negation of its negation, provided only we accept the truism 'Either the first or not the first'. But it should be noticed that theorem 10 depends on the use of 'or' in an exclusive sense. Just because the earlier Stoics insisted on this interpretation, the principle 'Either the first or not the first' could play for them the role which logicians commonly assign to the principle of non-contradiction. Furthermore, we can find here a reason why Chrysippus should wish to have indemonstrables 4 and 5 in his list as well as 1 and 2. If he had omitted

[1] Sextus, *Pyrrh. Hyp.* ii. 147; *Adv. Math.* viii. 431, 439.
[2] Sextus, *Pyrrh. Hyp.* ii. 159 ff.; *Adv. Math.* viii. 440 ff.

them, he would have been unable to obtain the two rules of double negation by any methods which he recognized. He might, of course, have added these rules as independent inference patterns; but to do so would have been contrary to his doctrine that every simple inference pattern must involve two premisses. However that may be, there is a passage of Diogenes Laertius which leaves no doubt that the Stoics discussed the double negative, or super-negative (ὑπεραποφατικόν), as they called it, and formulated the appropriate rules.[1]

Are there any other logically necessary truths which Chrysippus might have used as supplementary premisses? Galen[2] and Alexander[3] tell us that the Stoics had four *themata* (θέματα) for use in the analysis of complex arguments. Of these only the first and the third have been preserved, but it is possible from consideration of them to guess the nature of the theory to which they belonged. The first is the principle assumed by Aristotle in this indirect reduction of syllogisms:

> *If two propositions entail a third, then either of these two together with the negation of the third entails the negation of the remaining one.*[4]

And the third is the principle:

> *When two propositions entail a third and one of those two is itself established by further premisses, then the other proposition and the further premisses together entail the original conclusion.*[5]

Apparently the second and the fourth were something like the third, for Alexander says that the Stoics, with a passion for useless detail, elaborated these three out of a single principle of composition which had been handed down in the Peripatetic school. Possibly the principle mentioned by Sextus Empiricus in his account of theorem 6 is the second *thema*. At any rate it seems clear that the *themata*, unlike the principle of excluded middle, were not conceived as supplementary premisses to be worked into arguments in any of the indemonstrable moods but rather as second-order rules governing the procedures followed by Chrysippus in his derivation of complicated moods. In the Latin of Apuleius θέμα is translated by *constitutio vel expositum*, which sounds like a phrase of the Roman imperial administration; perhaps 'guiding principle' or 'directive' is the nearest English equivalent. But how could the first *thema* be said to express a guiding prin-

---

[1] Diogenes Laertius, vii. 69.    [2] *De Hipp. et Plat. Plac.* ii. 3 (92).
[3] *In Aristotelis An. Pr. Lib. I Commentarium*, ed. Wallies, *C.I.A.G.* ii(i), p. 284.
[4] Apuleius, *De Philosophia Rationali*, 278.
[5] Alexander, op. cit., p. 278. Cf. Simplicius, *In Arist. de Caelo Commentaria*, ed. Heiberg, *C.I.A.G.* vii, p. 236.

ciple of the method followed by Chrysippus? It seems that he must have had a procedure which allowed him to pass from a mood with the general plan 'The first; and the second; therefore the third' to a mood with the general plan 'The first; but not the third therefore not the second'. And most fortunately theorem 7, which has been preserved with its proof by Sextus Empiricus, shows how this might be done. According to that theorem we can always argue in the pattern 'If the first and the second, then the third; but not the third; on the other hand the first; therefore not the second'. Suppose now that in some application of this mood the conditional premiss has been obtained by the device of expressing the principle of a valid mood in a conditional statement: obviously it can be omitted without effect on the validity of the new argument. For it is a logically necessary truth, and not an assumption which might conceivably have been false. But this simplification leaves us with a mood which is related to the source of the conditional premiss in the way described by the first *thema*. It seems very probable, therefore, that in such contexts Chrysippus allowed himself the use of supplementary premisses which had been derived from already accepted moods by the principle of conditionalization.[1]

If in fact he argued so when constructing proofs in accordance with the first *thema*, there is no reason why he should not have followed the same procedure whenever it was convenient to do so for his purpose of demonstrating complicated moods by arguments framed within the indemonstrable moods, and it may that this was the gist of the fourth *thema*. There can be no doubt that the principle of conditionalization was familiar to the Stoics, and its use in the way we have described would explain their special interest in complex propositions of the form 'Not both the first and the second'. For the conditional statement corresponding to a mood with two premisses has a conjunction in its antecedent, and when it is introduced to serve as leading premiss in an argument according to indemonstrable 2 the conclusion of the step is inevitably the negation of a conjunction. If that is to be used as leading premiss for another argument, it is essential that a mood like 3 should be included among the indemonstrables.

Let us now consider some theorems which show at least what Chrysippus could have achieved by this method. Since the proofs

---

[1] This most important step in the reconstruction was suggested by Benson Mates in a doctoral dissertation of 1948 on *The Logic of the Old Stoa* and elaborated in his *Stoic Logic* (*University of California Publications in Philosophy*, vol. 26). The suggestion that the principle of conditionalization might be the fourth *thema* was considered by O. Becker in *Zwei Untersuchungen zur antiken Logik* (*Klassisch-Philologische Studien*, Heft. 17), p. 43, but not adopted by him.

are more complicated than any we have considered so far, it will
be convenient to set them out in tabular style with some abbreviations. In what follows the Greek letters α and β are used, as
Chrysippus himself might have used them, in place of 'the first'
and 'the second' respectively, and the notes at the ends of lines
indicate the articulation of the argument. Thus '(a) (b), 1' means
that what precedes is obtainable from (a) and (b) by means of
mood 1, and '1, cond.' means that what precedes is a conditionalization of mood 1. For the sake of simplicity it is assumed
that references to theorems 10 and 11 are sufficient to justify the
introduction and elimination of double negatives without more
ado, but if it is thought that Chrysippus would have disapproved
of this manœuvre, on the ground that it looks like inference
from one premiss, the proofs of 'theorems 14 and 15 below can
be amplified by citations of the principle of excluded middle in
appropriate form.

*12. *If the first then not the second; but the first; therefore not if the
first then the second.*

| | | |
|---|---|---|
| (a) | If α then not β. | Hyp. |
| (b) | α. | Hyp. |
| (c) | Not β. | (a) (b), 1 |
| (d) | If (if α then β) and α, then β. | 1, cond. |
| (e) | Not [(if α then β) and α]. | (d) (c), 2 |
| (f) | Not (if α then β). | (e) (b), 3 |

*13. *If not the first then the second; but not the second; therefore not if
the first then the second.*

| | | |
|---|---|---|
| (a) | If not α then β. | Hyp. |
| (b) | Not β. | Hyp. |
| (c) | Not not α. | (a) (b), 2 |
| (d) | If (if α then β) and not β, then not α. | 2, cond. |
| (e) | Not [(if α then β) and not β]. | (d) (c), 2 |
| (f) | Not (if α then β). | (e) (b), 3 |

14. *If the first then the second; if the first then not the second; therefore
not the first.*

| | | |
|---|---|---|
| (a) | If α then β. | Hyp. |
| (b) | If α then not β. | Hyp. |
| (c) | If (if α then not β) and α, then not (if α then β). | 12, cond. |
| (d) | Not not (if α then β). | (a), 10 |
| (e) | Not [(if α then not β) and α]. | (c) (d), 2 |
| (f) | Not α | (e) (b), 3 |

*15. *If the first then the second; if not the first, then the second; therefore the second.*

| | | |
|---|---|---|
| (a) | If $\alpha$ then $\beta$. | Hyp. |
| (b) | If not $\alpha$ then $\beta$. | Hyp. |
| (c) | If (if not $\alpha$ then $\beta$) and not $\beta$, then not (if $\alpha$ then $\beta$). | 13, cond. |
| (d) | Not not (if $\alpha$ then $\beta$). | (a), 10 |
| (e) | Not [(if not $\alpha$ then $\beta$) and not $\beta$]. | (c) (d), 2 |
| (f) | Not not $\beta$. | (e) (b), 3 |
| (g) | $\beta$. | (f), 11 |

There is no known mention of theorems 12 and 13 in any ancient authority, but theorem 14, which we have now proved by means of a conditionalization of theorem 12, is one of the two Stoic theorems for which we were formerly unable to find a proof. Its survival has a special interest for us because it is the pattern of the *reductio ad absurdum* used by the Eleatics and their Megarian successors. Apparently the Stoics held it in high esteem, for it is mentioned several times by ancient authorities under the special name of 'the theorem with two complex premisses' (τὸ διὰ δύο τροπικῶν θεώρημα).[1] We may reasonably suppose that the Stoics possessed also theorem 15, since this can be proved by similar steps; but it has not so far been found as a derivative rule in any of our sources for Stoic logic, and it can scarcely have been famous, since, if it had been, the special name, 'theorem with two complex premisses' would not have been appropriate for theorem 14.[2]

By substitution of 'the first' for 'the second' in theorems 14 and 15 it is possible to obtain the two theorems:

*16. *If the first then the first; if the first then not the first; therefore not the first.*

17. *If the first then the first; if not the first then the first; therefore the first.*

But there is some evidence to suggest that Chrysippus obtained these by the long way, that is to say, without use of any lemmata which involve 'the second'. For if he adopted that course in his proof of theorem 16, he would have to prove a preliminary mood like theorem 12, i.e. 'If the first then not the first; but the first;

[1] e.g. Origen, *Contra Celsum*, vii. 15, and Sextus Empiricus, *Pyrrh. Hyp.* ii. 3.
[2] The rule which we have called theorem 15 appears in the scholium 'On All Forms of Syllogism' printed in *Commentaria in Aristotelem Graeca*, iv (vi), p. xi, ll. 13–26 but it is treated there as a basic rule of inference and is not explicitly attributed to the Stoics, though it is given in company with the five indemonstrables of Chrysippus.

therefore not if the first then the first', and for that he would need a conditionalization of theorem 8, which the Peripatetics ridiculed as a foolish triviality.

It may perhaps be thought curious that theorem 17 has been preserved by Sextus in a version which includes the principle 'Either the first or not the first'.[1] For if our reconstruction of Stoic logic is correct, that principle is never more than a supplementary premiss which can be omitted without loss of rigour. It appears, however, from what Sextus says in his first mention of the theorem that some unspecified Stoics justified it by an argument which amounts in effect to assumption of our theorem 15, and it is easy to see that anyone who wishes to reason in this way without going back to the five indemonstrables of Chrysippus may find it natural to introduce the disjunctive premiss. Thus when Aristotle in his *Protrepticus* used the pattern of theorem 17, he said explicitly 'Either we should philosophize or we should not philosophize'. Nevertheless, in his second mention of the theorem Sextus indicates that some Stoics were in fact worried by an appearance of redundancy in their formulation. And well they might be; for when we examine this remarkable theorem carefully, we find that *it requires no ordinary premisses*. If we omit 'Either the first or not the first', we may just as well omit 'If the first then the first', and we are then left with 'If not the first then the first' as our sole premiss. Certainly this is not a truism, as it stands, and for that reason it is essential to the argument in a way in which the other two premisses are not. But in reality it is a pattern for propositions, not a proposition in its own right; and it is easy to see that we can never be entitled to assert a genuine proposition of this form except as the conditionalization of some entailment. The theorem therefore amounts to this: any proposition which is entailed by its own negation is true. Considered as a mood of reasoning, it is a device for establishing necessarily true propositions, that is to say, propositions which follow from any assumptions whatever.

To the Stoics, however, theorem 17 seems to have been interesting chiefly for its use in confuting sceptics. Several generations earlier Plato had used a version of theorem 16 for the refutation of relativism, when he made Socrates say that the theory of truth put forward by Protagoras must be false because it entailed its own contradictory.[2] In a somewhat similar fashion the Stoics argued against the scepticism of their day that there must be proof because the attempt to prove that there was no proof

---

[1] *Adv. Math.* viii. 281–4 and 292–6.
[2] *Theaetetus*, 171A.

showed that there was.[1] Close parallels to their reasoning can be found in various works of St. Augustine,[2] and although we have no conclusive evidence on the point, it seems quite likely that their discovery of theorem 17 had some influence on Augustine and through him on Descartes. But it is interesting to notice that all these opponents of scepticism overstate their case by claiming that the proposition in which they are interested follows from its own contradictory; in fact the proposition is verified only by *the occurrence of an attempt to establish its contradictory*. Examples of argument which fit the Stoic scheme exactly can nevertheless be found. In antiquity this pattern of reasoning was used by the mathematicians Euclid[3] and Theodosius,[4] and at the Renaissance it had a new lease of life as the *consequentia mirabilis*. We shall see in a later chapter that it gave the inspiration for a remarkable development of mathematics.

There are several passages of ancient authors which imply that the Stoics believed their list of five indemonstrables to be complete in the sense of containing all that is required for reasoning. It is said, for example, in one place that according to Chrysippus every argument is constructed out of them,[5] and in another place that all other arguments are thought to be validated by reference to them.[6] Obviously a claim of completeness was made by the Stoic school, but it seems very unlikely that any member of the school ever gave a precise definition of completeness or considered how the property could be proved to belong to a system of rules for deduction such as theirs. It can be shown that the Stoic system as we have presented it (i.e. with the principle of analysis mentioned by Sextus as second *thema* and the principle of conditionalization as fourth) is complete in a strict modern sense with respect to conjunction and negation.[7] But in order to achieve this result it is necessary to admit by the back door arguments from one premiss, which, as we have seen, were explicitly excluded by Chrysippus; and in any case the result is not very important if, as we have argued, the early Stoics did not think of conditional and disjunctive statements as definable by reference to conjunctions and negations.

Whether or not our reconstruction is correct in detail, it is clear that the Stoics had a well-elaborated body of logical doc-

---

[1] Sextus, *Pyrrh. Hyp*, ii. 186, and *Adv. Math.* viii. 281, 466.
[2] e.g. *De Civitate Dei*, xi. 26.
[3] *Elementa*, ix. 12.
[4] *Spherica*, i. 12.
[5] Diogenes Laertius, vii, 79.
[6] Sextus, *Pyrrh. Hyp.* ii. 156-7, 166-7, 194.
[7] O. Becker, op. cit., p. 46.

trine. And it is clear also that some Aristotelians such as Alexander regarded Stoic teaching on logic as hostile to that of their master. But this can scarcely have been because the Stoics denied the validity of Aristotle's syllogistic. For there is nothing in the positive doctrine of the Stoics which could have led them to reject Aristotle's moods, and we have no evidence to suggest that they did so. The testimony of Galen[1] and Alexander[2] suggests rather that the Stoics annoyed the Peripatetics by claiming priority for their own dialectic and pointing to Aristotle's unacknowledged use of its principles in such parts of his syllogistic as the theory of reduction. What in fact is the relation between the two systems?

In an earlier paragraph we drew attention to the fact that the variables in Stoic logic mark gaps to be filled by propositional signs. This is the key to the understanding of their work. Whereas Aristotle had concentrated attention on inferences which involve relations between general terms, the Stoics tried to deal with inferences which depend only on the notions expressed by the connectives in complex statements. As Łukasiewicz first remarked,[3] we have here the beginning of what is now called the calculus of propositions, that is to say the most fundamental part of logic without which the calculus of propositional functions or general terms cannot be elaborated systematically. Unfortunately the recognition of this fact has led recently to several attempts to express Stoic theorems in modern symbolism. Such attempts are misleading, first because they suggest improperly that the Stoics accepted a truth-functional interpretation of all the propositional connectives, and secondly because they obscure the peculiar character of the reasoning by which Chrysippus derived complex moods of argument from his indemonstrables. But the intention is good, and it is just to give honour to the Stoics for an important discovery about the structure of logic.

The logic of propositions, which they studied, is more fundamental than the logic of general terms, which Aristotle studied, not in the sense that it includes the second, but rather in the sense that it is presupposed by the second. Sometimes its special importance has been emphasized by the title 'theory of deduction'.[4] But it is more satisfactory to describe it as primary logic, because it must come at the beginning in any systematic development. If we adopt this practice, we may then reserve the title

[1] *Institutio Logica*, ed. Kalbfleisch, p. 17.
[2] Alexander, *In Aristotelis Topicorum Libros Octo Commentaria*, ed. Wallies, *C.I.A.G*, ii(ii), p. 218.
[3] 'Zur Geschichte der Aussagenlogik' in *Erkenntnis*, v (1935), pp. 111–31.
[4] A. N. Whitehead and B. Russell, *Principia Mathematica*, i, p. 90.

'general logic' for that study in which we are concerned not only with the notions of negation, conjunction, disjunction, &c., but also with the notions of generality expressed by 'every' and 'some'. General logic, so defined, includes primary, or non-general, logic, and cannot be developed without it, whereas primary logic can be presented as an independent theory. Within this scheme Aristotle's syllogistic takes its place as a fragment of general logic in which theorems of primary logic are assumed without explicit formulation, while the dialectic of Chrysippus appears as the first version of primary logic.

# IV

## ROMAN AND MEDIEVAL LOGIC

### 1. *From Cicero to Boethius*

FOR some centuries after Stoic logic had been formulated by
Chrysippus we find discussion of the merits of his system and
that of Aristotle, then a gradual fusion, or perhaps we should
say confusion, which was completed at the end of classical
antiquity in the work of Boethius. When the study of logic was
resumed after the Dark Ages, the writings of Boethius were better
known than those of Aristotle and his reputation as high. Some
part of the Stoic contribution remained, therefore, in what we
now call traditional logic, though weakened later by a revival
of interest in Aristotle, which led sometimes to a kind of Aristotelian purism. In this section we shall try to trace the transmission from Greek antiquity to the Middle Ages giving names
and dates where these are likely to be useful. But we shall not
attempt to treat even the famous philosophers of this long period
in detail, since our purpose is only to give perspective to our view
of antiquity and the Middle Ages.

During the last two centuries B.C. and the first century A.D. the
philosophical schools in Athens existed side by side, competing
for pupils with doctrines which followed more or less closely those
of their founders; but the Stoics and the Epicureans were the
most influential. Plato's Academy became presently a home of
scepticism with Carneades as its most famous member, and Aristotle's influence was not very strong. If we may judge from the
writings of Cicero, the Stoic school was the dominant one in his
day. No doubt there were developments in that school after
the time of Chrysippus, but we cannot now separate them from
his work, because the ancient tradition is not full enough. Later
writers such as Galen, Alexander, and Boethius speak constantly
of the Stoics or 'the moderns' (οἱ νεώτεροι) without troubling to
distinguish individuals.

Cicero made no original contribution to the development of
logic, but his writings preserve some scraps of information about
the teaching of the Stoics, and in this, as in other fields of philosophy, he did a useful service by inventing Latin equivalents for
Greek technical terms. *Propositio*, for example, was introduced

by him, but not with exactly the same sense as that it commonly
has in later Latin. In his terminology it means the leading premiss
of an argument ($\tau\grave{o}$ $\dot{\eta}\gamma\epsilon\mu o\nu\iota\kappa\grave{o}\nu$ $\lambda\hat{\eta}\mu\mu\alpha$), and is used to make a contrast with *assumptio*, which means the additional premiss ($\dot{\eta}$ $\pi\rho\acute{o}\sigma$-
$\lambda\eta\psi\iota s$).[1] This special sense is to be found later in the logical
writings attributed to Apuleius and Martianus Capella, but
already before the end of the first century A.D. the word was
used by Quintilian, the rhetorician, in the more general sense of
'statement' or 'indicative sentence' which it retained throughout
the Middle Ages.

Cicero's word for a conclusion in the passage we have just
noticed is *complexio*, which means literally 'a knitting together',
but it is interesting to notice that the same word occurs elsewhere
in the book with the sense of 'dilemma': 'Complexio est in qua,
utrum concesseris, reprehenditur ad hunc modum: *Si improbus
est, cur uteris? Si probus, cur accusas?*'[2] No doubt such reasoning was
popular with the Hellenistic rhetoricians from whom Cicero took
his material, and it may have been cultivated by them rather
than by the Stoic logicians, who first studied conditional and disjunctive arguments. The 'theorem with two complex premisses'
which we noticed in our section on the system of Chrysippus is,
of course, a special case of the kind of argument called by later
logicians a simple constructive dilemma (i.e. in Stoic terminology
'If the first, then the third; if the second, then the third; but
either the first or the second; therefore in any case the third'),
and the paradox of the crocodile and the baby, which Lucian
attributes to Chrysippus,[3] involves an argument of similar pattern.
So there can be no doubt that the Stoics were familiar with this
development of their logic. On the other hand, according to
Chrysippus all good arguments are $\delta\iota\lambda\acute{\eta}\mu\mu\alpha\tau\alpha$ in the original sense
of 'arguments with two premisses'; and there is no evidence of
the use of the word $\delta\iota\lambda\acute{\eta}\mu\mu\alpha\tau o\nu$ in the modern sense of 'dilemma'
before the second century A.D., when it occurs in the work of the
rhetorician Hermogenes with an explanation like that given by
Cicero for *complexio*, namely by reference to two questions, both
equally awkward to answer.[4]

Among Cicero's philosophical works there is a small treatise
called *Topica* which has had considerable influence on the teaching of logic because it was highly regarded in late antiquity, when
logic was associated with rhetoric in the way he thought proper.
This book professes to be an adaptation of Aristotle's *Topics* for
the use of a friend called Trebatius, but it shows little trace of

[1] *De Inventione*, i. 57 ff.                                    [2] Ibid. 45.
[3] *Vitarum Auctio*, 22.                      [4] Hermogenes, *De Inventione*, iv. 6.

direct borrowing from Aristotle's work. It is conceived as a
manual for the training of Roman orator and is therefore furnished
with illustrations from Roman jurisprudence. Probably the plan,
such as it is, was derived from some Hellenistic manual; for the
topics discussed here are mentioned in the same order in the *De
Oratore*,[1] as though they were in fact commonplaces of that age.
Some topics, it is said, are connected intrinsically with the
subject to be discussed (*in eo ipso de quo agitur haerent*), e.g. those
concerned with definition, genus, species (or in Cicero's terminology *forma generis*), while others are brought in from without
(*assumuntur extrinsecus*), e.g. that which involves appeal to authority.
With some elaborations this simple classification was retained as
long as men thought there was anything to be learnt from the
study of topics.

Near the beginning of his *Topica* Cicero remarks that Stoic
treatises on dialectic concentrated attention on questions about
the validity of reasoning and neglected the problem of finding
arguments, which is commonly treated under the heading 'topics'.
And later he says that the rules of inference given by the dialecticians are not necessary for the kind of instruction that interest
him. But he does, nevertheless, list here some such rules, which he
says are sufficient for the derivation of innumerable others, and
this passage is the most interesting part of the book.[2]

After explaining the five indemonstrables in the usual order,
but without mention of Chrysippus, Cicero goes on 'Deinde
addunt coniunctionum negantiam sic: *Non et hoc et illud; hoc
autem; non igitur illud.* Hic modus est sextus. Septimus autem:
*Non et hoc et illud; non autem hoc; illud igitur.*' Here the sixth is no
more than a reformulation of the third, while the seventh is
plainly invalid as it stands. We may perhaps suppose that Cicero
was muddled, since the subject is not one on which he could be
expected to shine and his examples of the use of the third indemonstrable suggest in fact that he did not understand it very
well, but the phraseology of the passage shows clearly that he was
following some manual in which dialectic was said to have seven
basic rules of inference, and we have independent evidence to
show that such a doctrine was current in later antiquity. For
Martianus Capella,[3] who wrote at the beginning of the fifth
century A.D. and used the Stoic terminology of *primum* and *secundum* (not found at this point in Cicero's text) and the author of the
scholium 'On All Forms of Syllogism',[4] who probably wrote in

---

[1] *De Oratore*, ii. 162–73.                              [2] *Topica*, 54–57.
[3] *De Nuptiis Philologiae et Mercurii*, iv. 414–21.
[4] Ammonius, *In Aristotelis An. Pr. Lib. I Commentarium*, ed. Wallies, *C.I.A.G.*
iv(vi), Praefatio, p. xi.

the sixth century A.D., both report seven kinds of hypothetical syllogisms. Furthermore, each of these authors gives a list agreeing with that of Cicero as to the first, second, fourth, fifth, and sixth entries, and each describes the seventh rule in a way which is clearly defective. Martianus Capella's formula for this last commits the same fallacy as that of Cicero, while the scholiast's account breaks off without the presentation of a complete inference schema, but both say enough by way of comment to indicate that the seventh rule was something like the fifth. In the text of the scholium it is called the παραδιεζευγμένος, or quasi-disjunctive. On the other hand, Martianus Capella and the scholiast both give for a third rule something different from their own sixth and therefore different also from Cicero's third. In Martianus Capella's Latin the third rule has the form: 'Non et primum et non secundum; primum autem; igitur et secundum.' But in the scholiast's Greek the rule with this number is called the παρασυνημμένος, or quasi-conditional, and it turns out to be the simple constructive dilemma which we have proved as a theorem in our attempt to reconstruct a portion of the system of Chrysippus.

These facts suggest that already before the time of Cicero some philosopher, probably a member of the Stoic school, had offered a set of seven basic rules for hypothetical syllogisms (other than those of the totally hypothetical kind cultivated by Theophrastus) and that his list contained the five indemonstrables of Chrysippus as its first, second, fourth, fifth, and sixth items but had in the third and the seventh places two new rules which were sufficiently like the third rule of Chrysippus, now renumbered as sixth, to be capable of being confused with it and yet sufficiently unlike to be thought worthy of separate mention. Furthermore, we may suppose that the first three rules were all in a large sense rules of conditional inference and the last four all in a large sense rules of disjunctive inference. For all three of our authorities say something which implies a division of this kind. Perhaps the original scheme of seven rules had the following form:

(1) *If the first then the second; but the first; therefore the second.*

(2) *If the first then the second; but not the second; therefore not the first.*

(3) *Not both the first and not the second; but the first; therefore the second.*

(4) *Either the first or the second; but the first; therefore not the second.*

(5) *Either the first or the second; but not the first; therefore the second.*

(6) *Not both the first and the second; but the first; therefore not the second.*

(7) *Not both not the first and not the second; but not the first; therefore the second.*

Here (3) is taken directly from Martianus Capella, while (7) differs in effect from his text (and so from that of Cicero) only by the insertion of two negatives which could easily have been omitted by a copyist. It is clear indeed from the manuscripts that some copyist had difficulty already with the placing of the negatives in rule (2), though in that case the preceding explanation by Martianus Capella is clear enough to leave no doubt of the correct reading.

If our conjecture is right, the logician who worked out the original scheme of seven rules probably had in mind the plan of showing completely by rules (3), (6), and (7) what could be done with the two notions of conjunction and negation. We have seen reason to believe that Chrysippus understood the Greek words for 'if' and 'or' in a strong sense which cannot be analysed except by use of modal words such as 'necessary' or 'impossible' and that this may have been one of the reasons why he thought it proper to consider also premisses of the form 'Not both the first and the second'. Once the distinction between strong (or modal) and weak (or non-modal) connectives was appreciated, it was natural to consider what more, if anything, could be achieved by means of the weak connectives alone, and this seems to be the idea behind the scheme given above. For the leading premiss of rule (3) is in effect a weak conditional such as Philo the Megarian had discussed, while the leading premiss of (7) is the corresponding weak disjunction, i.e. the disjunction which holds merely because one or other of the disjuncts is true. In his account of the seven rules Cicero seems to have been misled by a recollection of the system of Chrysippus, but the deviation which the scholiast makes in this place from the relatively simple system reported by Martianus Capella cannot be explained as an oversight. We must therefore suppose that at some date the rule given by the scholiast under the name παρασυνημμένος was seriously considered as a basic rule in place of the third suggested above, although the name seems more appropriate to the latter. If Chrysippus provided for the development of his system in the way we suggested in our last chapter, no such supplementary rules were needed, since they could all be derived from his indemonstrables. But it seems clear that we must in any case suppose some attempt to improve upon his work.

From the second century A.D. we have a little manual which treats in Latin of Aristotelian and Stoic logic together and notices the peculiarities of each. This is the *De Philosophia Rationali sive Peri Hermeneias* attributed to Apuleius, who flourished in the time of the Antonines, about A.D. 140. The real origin of the work is

unknown; for it can scarcely belong to the work *De Dogmate Platonis*
of which it forms the third part in our manuscripts of Apuleius.
There is no reason, however, to doubt that it comes from the
second century A.D., and it is a valuable source of information
about Stoic logic.

A much better-known writer on logic from the second century
is the physician Galen, who lived from about 129 to 199. According to his own catalogue of his works he wrote a great deal about
logic from the point of view of an Aristotelian. But apart from a
little tract on fallacies, the only logical work which has survived
is an *Introduction to Dialectic* (Εἰσαγωγὴ διαλεκτική) *not* mentioned in
his catalogue. It was first published in 1844, a few years after it had
been discovered in a monastery on Mount Athos, and Prantl who
wrote on the history of logic in the second half of the nineteenth
century, thought that it was not by Galen, but his view is no longer
accepted. In any case the work is of great interest for the history
of logic because it shows the mingling of the two streams.

Galen uses the technical terms of both schools, sometimes with
an explanation, sometimes without. Thus he talks of the moods
of Aristotle's first figure as indemonstrables.[1] And when he comments on the two sets of technical terms, he implies that it does
not matter which we use. On the question whether the categorical
or the hypothetical syllogism is prior in the order of nature, he
notes that Boethus, the eleventh head of the Peripatetic school
after Aristotle had allowed the priority of the hypothetical syllogism, but says he does not think the dispute important, because
we must in any case learn both. His own view seems to be that
each logic has its own field of application. Categorical syllogisms,
mostly from the first figure, are required for checking the reasoning of the geometers, e.g. the calculations of Eratosthenes about
the size of the earth,[2] while hypothetical syllogisms are needed
for the investigation of such questions as 'Is there Fate?' 'Are
there Gods?' 'Is there Providence?'[3] This distinction is interesting
because it suggests that Aristotelian logic was still associated at
this time with geometrical demonstration and Stoic logic with
use of dialectic for settling metaphysical questions.

The following are some other points of interest in this little
manual.

First, we find the word 'hypothetical' firmly established here
as a generic name for complex statements, whether conditional,
disjunctive, or conjunctive. Galen assumes that disjunctive statements should, properly speaking, involve complete opposition of

---

[1] *Institutio Logica* ed. Kalbfleisch, p. 19.
[2] Ibid., p. 26.                                                    [3] Ibid., p. 32.

the disjuncts, but says we sometimes find statements of disjunctive form in which there is no such opposition and tells us that these are called quasi-disjunctives ($\pi\alpha\rho\alpha\delta\iota\epsilon\zeta\epsilon\upsilon\gamma\mu\acute{\epsilon}\nu\alpha$).[1] He suggests also that a disjunctive statement is equivalent to a conditional with a negative antecedent (i.e. that 'P or Q' is equivalent to 'If not-P, then Q').[2] In fact this equivalence holds only if the disjunction is taken in a non-separative sense. Taken in a separative sense it would be equivalent to the conjunction of two conditionals (i.e. of 'If not-P, then Q' and 'If P, then not-Q').

Secondly, after expounding the Aristotelian figures of syllogism and showing how arguments in the second and the third can be reduced to the first, Galen goes on to say that there are no other figures and cannot be, as he had shown in his *Notes about Demonstration* (now lost).[3] This is interesting because it shows that the tradition which ascribes the doctrine of a fourth figure to Galen must be false. But it is puzzling to know when the doctrine was first introduced and by whom. The Renaissance scholar Zabarella in the opening of his work *De Quarta Syllogismorum Figura* noticed that it was ascribed to Galen by the Arabian philosopher Averroës in his comment on Aristotle's *Prior Analytics*, i. 8, and he assumed that Averroës found it in some work of Galen which had been lost in the intervening centuries.[4] We know now that Zabarella's assumption was mistaken; and from the manner in which Galen claims to have proved that there cannot be more than three figures we may perhaps conclude that someone had at least raised the question before his time. But it is curious that we have no trace of anyone who defended the doctrine of four figures before the end of the Middle Ages.

On the other hand, we have some external evidence about Galen's logical work which explains how he may have come to be credited (or debited) with the introduction of a fourth figure. In the scholium 'On All Forms of Syllogism' to which we have already referred the opening sentences read as follows:

'There are three kinds of syllogism: the categorical, the hypothetical, and that which involves an additional assumption ($\kappa\alpha\tau\grave{\alpha}\ \pi\rho\acute{o}\sigma\lambda\eta\psi\iota\nu$). Of the categorical there are two kinds: the simple and the compound. Of the simple syllogism there are three kinds: the first, the second, and the third figures. Of the compound syllogism there are four kinds: the first, the second, the third, and the fourth figures. Aristotle says there are three figures because he considers simple syllogisms constructed with three terms. Galen, however, in his own *Apodeictic* says

[1] Ibid., p. 12.   [2] Ibid., p. 9.
[3] Ibid., p. 26.
[4] Averroës returns to the subject in his comment on *An. Pr.* i. 23, and mentions Galen again, but with no more detail.

there are four figures because he considers compound syllogisms constructed with four terms, having found many such in Plato's dialogues.'[1]

From the explanation which follows it appears that Galen numbered his figures according to the following plan:

| Galen's figures of Compound Syllogism | | Aristotle's figures of Simple Syllogism |
|---|---|---|
| I | combining | I and I |
| II | ,, | I and II, or II and I |
| III | ,, | I and III, or III and I |
| IV | ,, | II and III, or III and II |

It might naturally be thought that each compound syllogism was considered as a type of argument in which the conclusion of a simple Aristotelian syllogism (containing two of the three premisses of the compound syllogism) served as a premiss for a second simple Aristotelian syllogism (containing the third premiss of the compound syllogism). But this hypothesis does not accord with the scholiast's statement that Galen's scheme did not allow for the combination of II with II or III with III. As reason for the exclusion of such combinations the scholiast cites the general rules of syllogistic that no conclusion follows from two negative or two particular premisses. This explanation is almost certainly mistaken, since it implies that the simple Aristotelian syllogisms in each pair mentioned above are to be considered as pro-syllogisms to a third and final Aristotelian syllogism, whereas a set of four terms is manifestly not large enough for such a structure. But we must assume that Galen's scheme did in fact recognize only the combinations mentioned in the table above, and the only way left in which to make sense of the scholiast's account is to suppose that Galen thought of each compound syllogism as a combination of the two simple syllogism which might be made by taking the middle premiss (i.e. the premiss which contains neither the subject nor the predicate of the conclusion) first with the minor premiss and then with the major premiss of the whole argument, or vice versa first with the major premiss and then with the minor premiss. This is a curious way of analysing a complex train of reasoning, and not to be commended for imitation; but it is easy to see how misunderstanding of it by some Arabian philosopher who had access to Galen's *Apodeictic* could have given rise to the tradition that Galen added a fourth figure to Aristotle's syllogistic theory.

[1] Ammonius, *In Aristotelis An. Pr. Lib. I Commentarium*, ed. Wallies, *C.I.A.G*, iv (vi), Praefatio, p. ix. This passage is discussed by J. Łukasiewicz in *Aristotle's Syllogistic*, § 14.

Thirdly, Galen says at the end of his *Introduction to Dialectic* that there are arguments which fit neither the Aristotelian nor the Stoic scheme, e.g. 'Theon has twice as much as Dio, and Philo twice as much as Theon; therefore Philo has four times as much as Dio' or 'Sophroniscus is father to Socrates; therefore Socrates is son to Sophroniscus'.[1] He calls these relational syllogisms (κατὰ τὸ πρός τι) and suggests that it is possible to give general principles by which their validity can be checked, but he does not attempt to carry out this programme. Clearly he had some ideas, found perhaps in Theophrastus or Eudemus, from which a general theory of relations might have been developed.

Among writers of the beginning of the third century Sextus Empiricus and Alexander of Aphrodisias deserve special mention as two of our most reliable sources of information about Greek logic. Being himself a Sceptic, Sextus was impartial in his dislike for Peripatetics and Stoics, but sufficiently conscientious to reproduce some arguments from each school in detail when he tried to show the futility of all system-making. Alexander was a partisan of Aristotle and the best of all ancient commentators on his works, but also an acute and honest critic of Stoic doctrines who thought it necessary to discuss some of the enemy's pronouncements in detail. The importance of the evidence about antiquity which these authors have preserved is shown by the references in the last chapter. It is possible, but not certain, that Sextus also had a direct influence on the development of medieval logic, since his short work on the *Outlines of Pyrrhonism*, which contains some information about Megarian and Stoic logic, was translated into Latin during a formative period and may have been read by some of the leaders of thought, even though it was never widely circulated. The influence of Alexander, on the other hand, is certain but indirect. His commentaries were used as a mine by later scholars, and some of his learning reached the Latin west through Boethius or other intermediaries. A curious, though not very important, example is his comment on Aristotle's *Prior Analytics*, i. 28.

In the chapter under consideration Aristotle suggests a technique for finding syllogisms to prove conclusions of the four different kinds. When we want to prove a universal affirmative conclusion with two given terms, we should consider characters which entail the predicate of the proposed conclusion and characters which are entailed by the subject of the proposed conclusion. When we want to prove a particular affirmative we should consider characters which entail the predicate and characters which

[1] *Institutio Logica*, ed. Kalbfleisch, p. 38.

entail the subject. When we want to prove a universal negative we should consider characters which are incompatible with the predicate and characters which are entailed by the subject or conversely characters which are entailed by the predicate and characters which are incompatible with the subject. And finally, when we want to prove a particular negative we should consider characters which are incompatible with the predicate and characters which entail the subject. If in the two groups of characters that we are directed to consider for any of these cases we find a common member, we can then construct a syllogism in one or other of the three figures. For some reason which is not clear Aristotle assigned a distinctive letter to each of the six groups of characters mentioned above, and this suggested to Alexander (or possibly to some earlier scholar) the

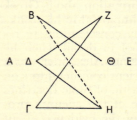

making of a diagram (διάγραμμα) in which the desired link between two groups of characters can be indicated by a line joining two points marked with Aristotle's letters.[1] The diagram which Alexander describes is not preserved in our text of his work, but it can easily be reconstructed as shown. According to Aristotle's lettering, *A* is the predicate of the conclusion, *B* the group of characters entailed by *A*, *Γ* the group of characters that entail *A*, *Δ* the group of characters incompatible with *A*, *E* the subject of the conclusion, and *Z*, *H*, *Θ* the groups of characters related to it in the same way as the groups opposite are related to *A*. We have inserted five continuous lines to represent the five cases noticed above (two for the proof of universal negative conclusions) and a dotted line to represent the case (*Baralipton*) in which we can prove a particular affirmative conclusion from premisses that would suffice to prove the universal affirmative with transposed terms. The diagram recurs, complete with Alexander's examples, in the commentary of the sixth-century Christian scholar John Philoponus,[2] and is to be found not only in our oldest Greek manuscript of the *Prior Analytics* but also in a scholium to an early Latin translation of that work. The Latin manuscript which contains the scholium dates from the second half of the twelfth century, but the translation and the scholium itself may well be the work of Boethius who lived in the sixth century.[3] In the later Middle Ages this diagram (with

[1] Alexander, *In Aristotelis An. Pr. Lib. I Commentarium*, ed. Wallies, *C.I.A.G.* ii (i), p. 301.
[2] Philoponus, *In Aristotelis An. Pr. Commentaria*, ed. Wallies, *C.I.A.G.* xiii (ii), p. 274.
[3] L. Minio-Paluello, 'A Latin Commentary (? Translated by Boethius) on the

accompanying mnemonic verses to distinguish good connexions from bad) was used extensively for the teaching of syllogistic and came to be known as the *pons asinorum*. Possibly the triangular figures which are used in medieval manuscripts and early printed books to explain syllogisms and their reduction *per impossibile* are also of ancient origin. For they are to be found already in the twelfth-century manuscript mentioned above and in manuscripts of the commentary of John Philoponus.[1]

From the end of the third century we must notice Porphyry, not only for his share in the transmission of ancient learning, of which we shall have occasion to say more later when we consider the work of Boethius, but also because he is the source of a misinterpretation of Aristotle's doctrine of the predicables which produced some confusion in later times. Apart from certain passages of the *Categories* and *De Interpretatione*, Aristotle's logic was concerned with general propositions. When he formulated the doctrine of the predicables, he was trying to set out the different relations in which a predicate might stand to a subject in a general statement, i.e. a statement about a kind or species. The predicate, he said, might be the definition of the subject or a part of this, the genus, or it might be a property or an accident. We may think these distinctions less valuable than Aristotle held them to be, but we can at least make sense of them when we remember that Aristotle was talking of the relation of a predicate to another general term. In his work called the *Eisagoge* (or *Introduction*, i.e. to the *Categories* and logic in general) Porphyry added *species* as one of the heads of classification requiring explanation. If this innovation is taken to imply that the distinction of predicables can be used in connexion with an individual subject, it is unfortunate, since nothing is essential or accidental to an individual as such. Here, however, we have the origin of the medieval doctrine of the *quinque voces* (species, genus, differentia, property, and accident).

In the fourth century Aristotle's *Categories* and *De Interpretatione* and Porphyry's *Eisagoge* were translated into Latin by Marius Victorinus. This rhetorician also composed commentaries on Cicero's *De Inventione* and *Topica*, and wrote works of his own called *De Definitionibus* and *De Syllogismis Hypotheticis*. Of these only the treatise *De Definitionibus* and the commentary on Cicero's *De Inventione* survive. Marius Victorinus was not only a teacher of

*Prior Analytics*, and its Greek Sources', *The Journal of Hellenic Studies*, lxxvii, part i (1957), pp. 93–102.

[1] See the article of Minio-Paluello mentioned in the preceding note and the edition of Philoponus mentioned in the note before that, pp. vii and xxxvii.

St. Jerome and a writer who influenced St. Augustine, but also himself a convert to Christianity and the author of some theological treatises. These facts made him acceptable in later times as an authority on the learning of the ancient world, and it is to them rather than to any novelty of doctrine that he owes his place in the history of logic.

Among the works which have been attributed to St. Augustine there is an essay called *Principia Dialecticae* and a little treatise called *Categoriae Decem ex Aristotele Decerptae*. The latter is an exposition of Aristotle's doctrine by some Latin writer who followed the commentator Themistius, and it deserves notice here only because its insertion among the works of the saint helped to secure great influence for this part of Aristotle's philosophy in early medieval times, when works of pagan learning were still very scarce. The former, on the other hand, seems to be a genuine work of Augustine, since it contains a passage in which the author uses his own name for purposes of illustration, but it is very slight, no more in fact than an introduction to the *scientia bene disputandi* by means of a few reflections on words, thoughts, and things and the need for avoiding equivocation. Its most interesting feature seems to be its use of the word *dicibile*. This is explained by the remark: 'Quod dixi, *dicibile*, verbum est, nec tamen verbum sed quod in verbo intelligitur et in animo continetur significat.'[1] And it is contrasted with *dictio* in a way which suggests that the author was trying to render the Greek terms λεκτόν and λέξις. In any case this is a passage which may have stimulated medieval logicians to work out again for themselves the Stoic theory of propositional contents.

During the fourth century ancient civilization was already in decline, and at the beginning of the fifth century, when St. Augustine was active, large parts of the Roman empire in the West were overrun by barbarians. In the same period Martianus Capella wrote his work *De Nuptiis Philologiae et Mercurii*, of which the fourth book is called *De Arte Dialectica*. It is a dull manual and written in a high-flown style, but it is interesting for our purposes because it shows clearly that something of the Stoic tradition was still alive at this date. In the verses with which the fourth book opens Aristotle and Chrysippus are mentioned together as the chief authorities on logic, and in the body of the work there is an account of hypothetical syllogisms which has obviously been derived, directly or indirectly, from Stoic sources, since it uses the words *primum* and *secundum* as propositional variables. We have seen already that it throws light on a puzzling passage in Cicero's *Topica*.

---

[1] *Principia Dialecticae*, 5.

Boethius is the last philosopher of Latin antiquity to be mentioned here, but the most important for his influence on the Middle Ages. He was a Christian who lived from 470 to 524 and wrote extensively not only on logic but also on arithmetic, music, and theology. For the most part he was content to compile material from Greek handbooks and commentaries, but he was at least a patient scholar, and his works therefore became a valuable storehouse of learning to the men who tried to rebuild civilization in the West after the Dark Ages. His Latin versions of the *Categories* and the *De Interpretatione* were indeed the only texts of Aristotle generally available to philosophers of the early medieval period. Recent research suggests that the translations of the *Prior Analytics*, the *Topics*, and the *De Sophisticis Elenchis* which were attributed to him in the first printed edition of his works are also authentic, but it appears that these were not widely circulated until a later date.[1] Apart from translations, his extant works on logic consist of two commentaries on Porphyry's *Eisagoge* (one based on the translation of Marius Victorinus, the other on his own), a commentary on Aristotle's *Categories*, two editions of a commentary on Aristotle's *De Interpretatione*, a treatise *De Syllogismo Categorico*, with an *Introductio ad Syllogismos Categoricos*, a treatise *De Syllogismo Hypothetico*, a treatise *De Divisione*, a commentary on Cicero's *Topica*, and a treatise *De Differentiis Topicis*.

The little work *Introductio ad Syllogismos Categoricos* is interesting because it contains what appears to be the first record of that distinction between five possible relations of general terms which we noticed in our discussion of Aristotle's *Topics*. As its name implies, this tract of Boethius deals with the preliminaries to syllogistic, and the material of which it is composed seems to be derived chiefly from Aristotle's own writings, though some may perhaps have been taken from another compilation. Near the beginning, when explaining the distinction between predication which is convertible (*reciproca*) and that which is not, Boethius says that it is impossible for the subject-term of any proposition to have a wider application than the predicate: 'Ut vero id quod subiectum est maius possit esse praedicato nulla prorsus enuntiatione contingit: ipsa enim natura praedicata minora esse non patitur.'[2] This is the assumption which led Aristotle to talk of major and minor terms as he did in his *Prior Analytics*. But later, when discussing the results of inserting negative signs before the

---

[1] Minio Paluello, 'Note sull' Aristotele latino medievale', vi, *Rivista di filosofia neo-scolastica*, xliv (1952), pp. 398–401, and 'Les traductions et les commentaires aristotéliciens de Boèce', *Studia Patristica*, ii (1957), pp. 358–65.

[2] *Introd. ad Syll. Cat.*, 768D. All detailed references are to the columns of Migne's *Patrologia Latina*, vol. lxiv.

terms of propositions, Boethius silently abandons the confusing old dogma and operates with the following classification of predicates:

1. *quod de subiecto nequeat segregari, ut ab homine rationabilitas;*
2. *quod a subiecto quidem recedere queat sed subiecti naturam non possit aequare, ut homini grammaticus;*
3. *quod numquam subiecto valeat convenire, ut lapis homini;*
4. *quod conveniens a [subiecto] possit abscedere cum sit maius et universalius subiecto, ut iustitia homini;*
5. *quod et semper [subiecto] copuletur neque tamen subiectum possit excedere, ut risibile homini.*[1]

The examples are all Aristotelian, and it is evident that the classification was inspired by thought about Aristotle's doctrine of the predicables; but Boethius does not discuss its origin, and there is nothing in his text to indicate who was the first to formulate it. All we can say is that Boethius' explanations and his repeated use of the same five examples show clearly enough his own recognition of the principle involved. With regard to the fourth case, for instance, he says 'Item propositio *Omnis homo iustus est* falsa est, cuius sequitur falsitatem *Omnis non homo non iustus est.* Nam divinis substantiis adest semper iustitia, cum non sit humanitas.'[2]

When he takes notice of controversies between the Aristotelians and the Stoics, Boethius favours the Aristotelians. Thus in his commentary on the *De Interpretatione* he says that the Stoics were mistaken in their attacks on Aristotle's remarks about future contingents, and maintains that of a proposition about the future and its contradictory neither need be true definitely (*definite*) though the disjunction of them is true.[3] And in a later passage of the same work he shows himself impatient when defending Aristotle's identification of possibility and contingency against the Stoic view that the necessary may be accounted possible.[4] In his theory of modality he professes to follow Theophrastus for whom he has great admiration,[5] but he does not attempt to introduce any account of modal syllogisms, either Aristotelian or Theophrastean, into his work *De Syllogismo Categorico.*

The main ideas of the *De Syllogismo Hypothetico* are also derived from Theophrastus, who is mentioned at the beginning together with Eudemus, and even the tedious elaboration, which seems at first sight to be Boethius' own work, may be derived from

[1] *Introd. ad Syll. Cat.,* 779C–781A.       [2] Ibid.
[3] *In Lib. de Int. Ed. Sec.* iii. 498B.
[4] Ibid. v. 587B.                          [5] Ibid. 585C.

Porphyry.[1] This treatise is concerned chiefly with complex hypo-thetical syllogisms of such forms as:

*Si est A, est B; si est B, est C; ergo si est A, est C.*

And it recognizes three figures like those attributed to Theo-phrastus by Alexander of Aphrodisias. The distinction and enumeration of moods on which Boethius prides himself is made by ringing the changes on affirmative and negative in the various clauses of the various premisses. But all this is done without con-sideration of examples, and it is not clear how Boethius intends the reader to understand a schema such as *Si est A est B*. If the theory is supposed to apply to conditional propositions of all kinds, the letters must be assumed to represent propositional signs and the word *est* must be taken to mean 'it is the case that'. But since the theory is derived from a Peripatetic source, it seems more likely that the letters are to be taken as representatives of common nouns, such as *homo* and *animal*, and that *est* means either 'it is' or 'there is'.

There are some clear traces of Stoic influence at the beginning of the *De Syllogismo Hypothetico* in the discussion of arguments which are not totally hypothetical (like that cited above). And we find there an example which is almost certainly as old as the Megarians:

*Si dies est, lucet; atqui dies est; lucet igitur.*[2]

But Boethius can scarcely have been following a Stoic original when he said that the negative of *Si est A, est B* was *Si est A, non est B*,[3] nor yet when he offered as a pattern of valid reasoning the scheme: *Si est A, cum sit B est C; atqui cum sit B non est C; non est igitur A*.[4] If, as seems likely, the word *cum* is intended to be no more than a stylistic variant for *si*, we have in the second passage a mistake which follows naturally from the mistake in the first passage. But it is at least possible that the argument of the second passage may have seemed acceptable because the clause *cum sit B* was not completely equated with *si est B*. For if this clause is taken in its more normal sense as meaning 'since there is a B thing', the argument is indeed valid, though rather unnatural.

The Stoic indemonstrables are preserved by Boethius in his commentary on Cicero's *Topica*, as in the original, but his remarks on the third and the seventh of the patterns of argument listed by Cicero are not very helpful.[5] His text of the third contains between the two premisses a phrase (*et his alia negatio rursus*

---

[1] *De Syll. Hyp.* i. 831D. J. Bidez, 'Boèce et Porphyre', *Revue belge de philologie et d'histoire*, ii (1923), pp. 189 ff.    [2] *De Syll. Hyp.* i. 833C.
[3] Ibid. 843D.    [4] Ibid. 851C.    [5] *In Top. Cic. Comm.* v. 1142C and 1144D.

*adiungitur*) which is unintelligible in the context but may conceivably be derived from a gloss that reported an original rule rather like that in the text of Martianus Capella. In part of his commentary Boethius does in fact try to extract from Cicero's words a rule like that of Martianus Capella, although he has difficulty in making it square with Cicero's own examples. His version of the seventh of Cicero's rules and the comment which he adds show that in his time the text was already defective in the same way as the text of the seventh rule in our manuscripts of Martianus Capella.

Although Boethius is important chiefly as an agent in the transmission of classical culture to the Middle Ages, there is one point in his treatise on hypothetical syllogisms which may be new and is certainly deserving of attention because it is a possible source for one of the most interesting developments of medieval logic. This is a distinction among conditional statements according to the kind of *consequentia* involved.[1] Boethius' word *consequentia* is presumably a translation for ἀκολούθησις and ἀκολουθία, which were used by Aristotle and the Stoics respectively in the sense of 'following from'.[2] According to him the truth of a conditional statement may involve no necessary connexion but be only *secundum accidens*. This can be noticed especially in conditional statements constructed with *cum* instead of *si*, for example in the statement 'Cum ignis calidus sit, coelum rotundum est'.

On the other hand, there are conditional statements which involve a *consequentia naturae*, and these are subdivided again by Boethius in the following passage:

'Harum quoque duplex modus est, unus cum necesse est consequi ea tamen ipsa consequentia non per terminorum positionem fit, alius vero cum fit consequentia per terminorum positionem. Ac prioris quidem modi exemplum est, ut ita dicamus: *Cum homo sit, animal est.* Haec enim consequentia inconcussa veritate est subnixa, sed non idcirco animal est quia homo est. Non enim idcirco genus est quia species est, sed fortasse a genere principium ducitur, magisque essentiae causa ex universalibus trahi potest, ut idcirco sit homo quia animal est; causa enim speciei genus est. At qui dicit *Cum homo sit, animal est,* rectam et necessariam consequentiam facit; per terminorum vero positionem talis consequentia non procedit. Sunt autem aliae hypotheticae propositiones in quibus et consequentia necessaria reperietur et ipsius consequentiae causam terminorum positio facit hoc modo: *Si terrae fuerit obiectus, defectio lunae consequitur.* Haec enim consequentia rata est, et idcirco defectio lunae consequitur quia terrae intervenit obiectus. Istae igitur sunt propositiones certae atque utiles ad demonstrationem.'

[1] *De Syll. Hyp.* i. 835B.          [2] e.g. *Analytica Priora*, i. 46 (52$^b$29).

In his translation of Aristotle's *Prior Analytics* Boethius uses the phrase *positio terminorum* to mean what we should mean in English by 'position of the terms', i.e. the order in which they occur in the premisses of a syllogism,[1] and it looks as though he may conceivably have understood the phrase in much the same way here, thinking that a *consequentia naturae* is established *per terminorum positionem* if and only if the antecedent gives the *causa*, or ground of being, for that which is expressed by the consequent. The example which he uses to illustrate this is Aristotelian,[2] and it is probable that he is only using the language of *consequentia* here to summarize the old Aristotelian doctrine that true science is knowledge of things through causes. But it must be confessed that the phrase *consequentia per terminorum positionem* is rather curious. Perhaps Boethius has in mind the syllogistic apparatus of the *Posterior Analytics*, though this is not strictly relevant to the example as he expresses it here.

Conditional statements which assert necessary connexions, though not always *per terminorum positionem*, can be obtained in Boethius' view from the *loci* discussed by Aristotle and Cicero. A *locus* according to Cicero is a *sedes argumenti*. When we formulate the principle in general terms, the result is a *maxima propositio*:

'Ideo et universales et maximae propositiones loci sunt dictae, quoniam ipsae sunt quae continent ceteras propositiones et per eas fit consequens et rata conclusio. Ac sicut locus in se corporis continet quantitatem, ita hae propositiones quae sunt maximae inter se omnem vim posteriorum atque ipsius conclusionis consequentiam tenent, et uno quidem modo locus, id est sedes argumenti, dicitur maxima principalisque propositio fidem ceteris subministrans.'[3]

The interest which Boethius shows in *loci* and even the content of his doctrine come to him from the Aristotelian tradition and the teaching of the schools of rhetoric, rather than from any Stoic legacy. But we may perhaps trace a Stoic influence in his use of the word *consequentia* to cover both the relation of a conclusion to its premisses and the relation of the consequent to the antecedent in a conditional statement. It is true that Aristotle had used the conditional form of sentence to express his principles of syllogistic reasoning, but he seems to have done so without reflection on the nature of conditional statements. The Stoics, on the other hand, explicitly equated the notion of entailment with that of the correctness of a conditional statement, and their assumption seems to underly the way in which Boethius talks of *consequentia*. It is

---

[1] *Prior. An. Arist. Interp.* i. 35, 676D.
[2] *Analytica Posteriora*, ii. 2 (89ᵇ36–90ᵃ34).
[3] *De Diff. Top.* ii. 1185D.

possible even that what he says of *consequentia secundum accidens* derives from some Stoic memory of the debate between the Megarians Philo and Diodorus, though the phrase *secundum accidens* has an Aristotelian ring.

As we have seen, the Stoics, unlike the Peripatetics, listed dialectic as one of the main branches of philosophy, but they treated it in close connexion with their theory of language, and in later antiquity the study was commonly associated with rhetoric. It is therefore not surprising that Boethius talks of logic as though it were generally admitted to be concerned with language. But for an understanding of the theories to which his work gave rise in later centuries it is important to notice what he says when explaining this view.

In his commentary on Aristotle's *Categories* he writes *Omnis ars logica de oratione est* in order to make clear why that work is properly taken as the starting-point for the study of logic and so for all philosophy.[1] Logic is concerned with syllogisms; but syllogisms are composed of propositions, and propositions of simple signs. The *Categories* being a classification of the things which can be signified by simple signs, is entitled for this reason to first place in logic, and because it is orderly in its consideration of kinds of things, it is also of great value to those who will proceed later to Aristotle's natural philosophy or to moral philosophy. For in treating of signs we inevitably treat also in a certain way of things signified, but it is proper to begin with the signs: 'Res enim et rerum significatio iuncta est, sed principalior erit illa disputatio quae de sermonibus est, secundo vero loco illa quae de rerum ratione formatur.' When, however, he says that logic is concerned with speech (*oratio*), Boethius does not mean that logic is part of grammar or what we should now call philology. For it appears in his second commentary on Aristotle's *De Interpretatione* that he uses the word *oratio* as a rendering for the Greek λόγος and includes under it not only the speaking or writing of words but also that discourse which is composed of thoughts (*intellectus*).[2]

At the beginning of his *De Interpretatione* Aristotle had said that written words were signs of spoken words and these in turn signs of mental modifications (παθήματα τῆς ψυχῆς) which were common to all men because they were resemblances of things. According to Boethius this pronouncement had been developed by the Peripatetics into a theory of three kinds of discourse, written, spoken, and mental. He mentions Porphyry in particular as an authority for this doctrine, and Porphyry's commentary on the

[1] *In Cat. Arist.* i. 161c.      [2] *In Lib. de Int. Ed. Sec.* i. 407B.

*Categories* (which survives in a single Greek manuscript) does in fact contain a reference to that discourse in the understanding (ὁ ἐν τῇ διανοίᾳ λόγος) which takes place even when we are silent.[1] Considered by itself, Porphyry's phrase might be understood to mean only image-speech (i.e. what is sometimes called thinking-in-Greek or thinking-in-English, as the case may be), but it is clear from what Boethius says that mental discourse was supposed to be the same for men of different nations because it consisted of mental modifications which were in some way copies of non-mental things and therefore natural signs for these latter. That there are such signs is a theory which can be derived very easily from what Aristotle says in his *De Anima* about the ability of an intellectual soul to receive forms into itself. But it has also a natural plausibility, and it has been retained in recent centuries by many who ridicule Aristotle's psychology.

Since he writes in Latin, Boethius usually takes written Latin words as his examples of signs, but he follows Aristotle in asserting that such signs are significant only because they are conventionally connected with conceptions which are themselves natural signs:

'Sicut nummus quoque non solum aes impressum quadam figura est ut nummus vocetur sed etiam ut alterius rei sit pretium, eodem quoque modo verba et nomina non solum voces sunt sed positae ad quandam intellectuum significationem. Vox enim quae nihil designat, ut est gargulus, licet eam grammatici figuram vocis intuentes nomen esse contendant, tamen eam nomen philosophia non putarit nisi sit posita ut designaret aliquam animi conceptionem, eoque modo significare aliquid rerum possit.'[2]

When discussing in detail the notion of linguistic convention, he takes over from Porphyry[3] (who himself probably got it from some predecessor) a distinction between names of first and second imposition (θέσις), that is to say, between names which designate extra-linguistic entities and names which designate other names: 'Est prima positio ut nomina rebus imponerentur, secunda vero ut aliis nominibus ipsa nomina designarentur.'[4] But apparently he thinks that second imposition is something characteristic of the writings of grammarians; for he says that use of names of second imposition is especially connected with discussion of the shapes of names of first imposition, and he goes on to maintain (here again following Porphyry) that the purpose of the *Categories* (on which he is commenting at the time) is to treat of names of

[1] Porphyry, *In Aristotelis Categorias Expositio*, ed. Busse, *C.I.A.G.* iv (i), p. 101.
[2] *In Lib. de Int. Ed. Sec.* i. 408c.
[3] Porphyry, *In Aristotelis Categorias Expositio*, ed. Busse, *C.I.A.G.* iv (i), p. 57.
[4] *In Cat. Arist.* i. 159c.

first imposition with respect to their role as signs ('de vocibus res significantibus in eo quod significantes sunt pertractare'). Obviously the point of this remark is to make a distinction between logic as he understands it and grammar.

Aristotle's philosophy of logic would have been clearer than it is if he had forced himself to consider more carefully what he wanted to say about words and what he wanted to say about things. When, for example, he says 'The individual man exists in the species man, and the genus of the species is animal (ὁ τὶς ἄνθρωπος ἐν εἴδει μὲν ὑπάρχει τῷ ἀνθρώπῳ, γένος δὲ τοῦ εἴδους ἐστὶ τὸ ζῷον)', he seems to mean that individual men exemplify the species mankind, membership of which is indicated by application of the word 'man', and likewise the genus animal-kind, membership of which is indicated by application of the word 'animal'. But his language suggests that he thinks there is a species named 'man' and a genus named 'animal', and he does in fact go on to say that man and animal are called secondary substances (δεύτεραι οὖν αὗται λέγονται οὐσίαι, οἷον ὁ ἄνθρωπος καὶ τὸ ζῷον). This queer way of talking was current throughout later antiquity, and through the writings of Boethius it produced the puzzle about universals which exercised the minds of medieval philosophers.

The passage of Boethius that was most influential in this connexion occurs at the beginning of his commentary on his own translation of Porphyry's *Eisagoge*. Porphyry had written at the opening of his own work:

'As for genus and species, I beg to be excused from discussing at present the question whether they exist in reality or have their place simply and solely in thoughts, and if they exist, whether they are corporeal or incorporeal, and whether they are separable or exist only in sensible things and dependent upon them. For such a study is very deep and requires another and larger inquiry.'[2]

But Boethius felt called upon to deal with these problems in a way which would, he thought, set his reader's mind at rest without introducing too long a digression.[3] According to his doctrine universals subsist in sensible corporeal things, but are themselves incorporeal and separable in thought from corporeal things; for a *species* or a *genus* is just a similarity which may be collected by the mind from various individuals, e.g. the *similitudo humanitatis* which may be collected *ex singulis hominibus*. This, he tells us, is the view of Aristotle, which we may accept for the purposes of the main inquiry, without presuming to decide definitely against

---

[1] *Categoriae*, 5 (2ᵃ16–18).
[2] Porphyry, *Isagoge*, ed. Busse, *C.I.A.G.* iv (i), p. 1.
[3] *In Porph. Comm.* i. 83A.

Plato's view that universals are not only thinkable apart from bodies but capable also of existing in separation.

It is worth noticing that in this account of universals Boethius rightly gives *humanitas* rather than *homo* as the name of a species. But the influence of the other usage, which Boethius followed in many places, was so great that *Homo est species* continued to be used as a tag so long as men discussed philosophy in Latin. It is therefore not surprising that some modern philosophers who are impatient of all talk about universals have tried to dismiss the whole doctrine as an illusion created by the assumption that general terms are significant in the same way as proper names. Even when he tries seriously to explain the difference, Aristotle, as we have seen, sometimes uses language which fosters such misunderstanding. In his *De Interpretatione*, for example, he writes: 'Some things are universal, others individual. I call that universal which is naturally fitted to be predicated of many things, and that individual which is not. Thus man is a universal (ἄνθρωπος μὲν τῶν καθόλου), Callias an individual.'[1] If it began with a reference to words instead of things, this passage could be accepted as a useful and satisfactory explanation of the difference between the words ἄνθρωπος and Καλλίας, but it is presented as an account of two kinds of things (πράγματα), and as such it lends itself to misunderstanding. In his comment Boethius tries to make sense by supposing that just as the word *homo* in his Latin translation may be supposed to do duty here in a philosophical idiom for the word *humanitas*, so the word *Plato* (which he substitutes for the less familiar *Callias*) may be supposed to do duty for the word *Platonitas*, i.e. for the name of a quality predicable correctly of Plato but of nothing else.[2] It is unlikely that Aristotle had any such notion in mind, but it is easy to see how his words could suggest such an interpretation. In any case we have here the beginning of another confusion which has bedevilled the theory of individuals and universals. Instead of falling into the absurdity of treating the word *homo* as though it differed from a proper name only by standing for something general, Boethius has adopted the equally curious course of treating the word *Plato* as though it differed from a common noun only by being limited in its application, and in this he is followed by some later philosophers.

In the history of western culture Boethius' works are important because he wrote at the end of classical antiquity before polite

---

[1] *De Interpretatione*, 7 (17ᵃ38ff.).
[2] *In Lib. de Int. Ed. Sec.* ii. 463A. This seems to be a reminiscence of the Stoic ἰδία ποιότης.

learning was overwhelmed by barbaric vigour. If we are disposed to be gloomy, we may reflect that the time which separates us from him is about the same as that which separated him from the Trojan war and the destruction of Minoan civilization. In the history of Greek and Levantine thought the writings of his contemporaries such as Ammonius and the author of the scholium 'On All Forms of Syllogism' have no comparable importance. For the reworking of old themes, to which they all alike devoted themselves, was continued in the East for many more centuries by an uninterrupted succession of scholars. Even within the part of the Byzantine empire which the Arabs conquered the work did not stop for long. Soon Arabian scholars became students of classical philosophy, and through them the West later recovered part of what it had lost. After the Greek commentaries on Aristotle their works are the most promising mine for further discoveries about the logical tradition of later classical antiquity.

## 2. *From Alcuin to Abelard*

When learning began to revive at the end of the eighth century, the texts used in the study of logic were the more easily available writings of the Latin authors mentioned in the last section. Alcuin, who taught at York about 778, records that in his time the library there contained Aristotle, Victorinus, and Boethius,[1] but we do not know for certain how much was included in this Latin version of Aristotle. Until the twelfth century the only works of Aristotle generally available in the West were the *Categories* and the *De Interpretatione*. These with Porphyry's *Eisagoge* and the treatises of Boethius were the best texts for study, but they had to be eked out with material from other sources, and even Martianus Capella did some service at this time. For the Irish monks who were then leaders of learning had copies of his work and brought it back into the schools.

The first medieval treatise on logic was Alcuin's own *Dialectica*. This was presumably composed for use in the *trivium* (grammar, dialectic, and rhetoric), which he re-established as the basis of education when he became master of the palace school of Charlemagne, and it has the curious form of a dialogue between himself and the emperor in which Charlemagne is made to ask questions like a good child in *The Swiss Family Robinson*. Aristotle's categories (as expounded in the Pseudo-Augustinian *Categoriae Decem*) receive a disproportionately large amount of attention,

---

[1] *Poema de Pontificibus et Sanctis Ecclesiae Eboracensis*, vv. 1547–9. (ed. Migne, ii. 843c).

and the space given to consideration of arguments is very small indeed. There is no detail about syllogisms. For a time this work was widely used in teaching, but it fell into oblivion when knowledge grew.

Johannes Scotus Erigena, who lived from about 810 to 877, is said to have been the first medieval writer to use syllogistic trains of reasoning, but it was long before the fashion became general. For most scholars logic was no more than a curiosity to be found in the literary remains of Christian Rome. In the tenth century, however, Boethius' translations of Aristotle's *Categories* and *De Interpretatione* and Porphyry's *Eisagoge* began to circulate more widely, and Gerbert, who taught from 972 onwards at Rheims and died in 1003 as Pope Sylvester II, is said to have worked also on Cicero's *Topica* and the writings of Victorinus and Boethius. Abbo of Fleury and Notker Labeo of St. Gall were other influential teachers of the period.

The new interest in logic went together with a lively interest in grammar, and sometimes the result of this association was unfortunate. In the *Dialectica* of Garland the Computist (i.e. author of a *computus*, or treatise on the calculation of almanacs), which may have been composed in Liège a little before 1040, the predicables are discussed under the heading *De Vocibus Incomplexis* and said to be themselves *voces* because they can be predicated in propositions.[1] The reader may at first think that Garland is talking of the words *genus*, *species*, *differentia*, *proprium*, and *accidens*, which are often called the *quinque voces*, but the confusion goes much deeper. In the sections on accidents, for example, it is said: 'Accidens est quod adest et abest praeter subiecti corruptionem. . . . Quod totum est dicere: illa vox appellatur accidens quae consignificat adventicio modo substantivae voci.'[2] Possibly one source of the muddle is Aristotle's talk of man as a species and animal as a genus. For Garland says in one place: 'Ista *Animal est genus* de hac sola voce quae est *animal* agit.'[3] And later he produces the remarkable assertion:

'Videndum est itaque quod in omni propositione categorica vera affirmativa aut praedicatus et subiectus consignificant (ut hic, *Omnis homo est animal*) aut significatum subiecti consignificat significato praedicati (ut hic, *Species est genus*, id est *Homo est animal*) aut significatum subiecti consignificat praedicato (ut *Species est animal*, id est *Homo est animal*) aut significatum praedicati consignificat subiecto (ut *Homo est genus*, id est *animal*) aut alterum significat alterum, id est praedicatus subiectum (ut hic, *Animal est genus*) vel subiectus praedicatum (ut in ista *Genus est animal*).'[4]

---

[1] *Dialectica*, ed. L. M. de Rijk (Assen 1959), p. 3.      [2] Ibid., pp. 10–11.
[3] Ibid., p. 44.                                              [4] Ibid., p. 115.

Here *consignificat* means 'signify the same', and *species* is apparently taken to be a name for the word *homo*, while *genus* is taken to be a name for the word *animal*.

The bland way in which Garland expounds his doctrine and his omission of any special reference to the opening of Boethius' commentary on Porphyry's *Eisagoge* suggest that at the time he wrote philosophers had not yet begun the great debate about universals which was to divide the schools for four centuries. But we may safely assume that the *moderni* who rejected Aristotle's doctrine of universals developed their theses in linguistic discussions such as we find in Garland's work. Since they insisted repeatedly that a *homo* could be nothing but a *res discreta* or individual, it seems that they were properly suspicious of the statement *Homo est species* and wished in the first place to get rid of the misleading suggestion of Platonism conveyed by the language of the *antiqui*. Peter Abelard (1079–1142) put the point very clearly when he wrote: 'Singuli homines discreti ab invicem . . . in eo . . . conveniunt quod homines sunt; non dico *in homine*, cum res nulla sit homo nisi discreta, sed *in esse hominem*. Esse autem hominem non est homo nec res aliqua.'[1] But this justifiable irritation with an unfortunate idiom of ancient philosophy sometimes led them on to maintain the absurd thesis of nominalism, namely that *species* and *genera* and with them all *universalia* are nothing but words, or *flatus vocis* as Roscellin is reported to have said. Since some dogmas of the Church, in particular the doctrine of the Trinity, had been expounded in the language of philosophical realism, this positive theory was thought to be theologically dangerous, and in 1092 Roscellin was condemned at the instance of Anselm on a charge of tritheism. In 1121 and again in 1140 Abelard also was censured for his theological views, though his modernism was more subtle than that of Roscellin. Writing about these matters in 1159, John of Salisbury noted that the trouble all began with the debate on the opening of Porphyry's *Eisagoge*:

'Naturam tamen universalium hic omnes expediunt, et altissimum negotium et maioris inquisitionis contra mentem auctoris explicare nituntur. Alius ergo consistit in vocibus, licet haec opinio cum Rocelino suo fere iam evanuerit. Alius sermones intuetur et ad illos detorquet quicquid alicubi de universalibus meminit scriptum. In hac autem opinione deprehensus est Peripateticus Palatinus Abaelardus noster, qui multos reliquit et adhuc quidem aliquos habet professionis

---

[1] *Logica Ingredientibus*, p. 19 in *Peter Abaelards Philosophische Schriften*, ed. B. Geyer, *Beiträge zur Geschichte der Philosophie und Theologie des Mittelalters*, xxi (1919–33). Cf. also the pronouncements of the *moderni* as reported by Anselm in *De Fide Trinitatis*, chap. ii (ed. Migne, 265A).

huius sectatores . . . Rem de re praedicari monstrum ducunt, licet Aristoteles monstruositatis huius auctor sit.'[1]

So far from dying out, as John of Salisbury seems to have expected, the party of the *moderni* grew to great strength in the centuries after Abelard, and we shall have occasion to notice their doings later. But for the moment what concerns us is the new spirit of self-confidence which inspired philosophers. John of Salisbury tells us, for example, that a certain William of Soissons to whom he taught the elements of logic 'later produced an engine for capturing, as his friends say, the citadel of the old logic, building up unexpected links of argument, and demolishing the opinions of the ancients' ('ad expugnandam, ut aiunt sui, logicae vetustatem et consequentias inopinabiles construendas et antiquorum sententias diruendas machinam postmodum fecit').[2] It has been thought recently that this William anticipated Jevons's invention of a logical machine, but almost certainly his invention was some novel pattern of argument which his friends likened to a siege engine, much as a general method of intellectual attack might be called in our time a bulldozer. How exactly he set to work we do not know; but apparently he proved (though not to the satisfaction of John of Salisbury) that from one impossible all impossibles follow, and it looks as though he also argued against Aristotle that the same consequence might follow from contradictory hypotheses ('idem esse ex contradictione, cum Aristoteles obloquatur'). The first thesis, as we shall see, was maintained by his older contemporary Abelard, and the second came to be generally accepted in later times.

So great, indeed, was the spirit of intellectual adventure at the end of the eleventh and the beginning of the twelfth century that even Anselm, who described the *moderni* as heretics of dialectic and said that they were to be hissed away (*exsufflandi*) from discussion of spiritual questions,[3] introduced in his own theology one of the most notable of all dialectical heresies. For in his *Proslogion* he tried to prove the existence of God by an argument (later called the ontological) in which existence is assumed to be an attribute adding to the perfection of the things that have it. God, he tells us, may be defined as that than which nothing greater can be conceived, and according to this definition God exists so truly that he cannot even be thought not to exist:

'Nam potest cogitari esse aliquid quod non possit cogitari non esse, quod maius est quam quod non esse cogitari potest. Quare si id quo

---

[1] *Metalogicon*, ii. 17 (ed. Migne, 874B).      [2] *Metalogicon*, ii. 10 (ed. Migne, 868c).
[3] *De Fide Trinitatis Contra Blasphemias Ruzelini sive Roscelini*, 2 (ed. Migne, 265A).

maius nequit cogitari potest cogitari non esse, id ipsum quo maius cogitari nequit non est id quo maius cogitari nequit; quod convenire non potest. Sic ergo vere est aliquid quo maius cogitari non potest ut nec cogitari possit non esse.'[1]

So far as we know, this attempt to prove God's existence by discovery of a contradiction in the supposition that he does not exist was Anselm's own invention. But another argument, which is given by Anselm in his *Monologion*, suggests strongly the influence of Stoic logic, exercised perhaps through St. Augustine:

'Denique si veritas habuit principium vel habebit finem, antequam ipsa inciperet verum erat tunc quia non erat veritas, et postquam finita erit verum erit tunc quia non erit veritas. Atqui verum non potest esse sine veritate. Erat igitur veritas antequam esset veritas, et erit veritas postquam finita erit veritas, quod inconvenientissimum est. Sive igitur dicatur veritas habere sive intelligatur non habere principium vel finem, nullo claudi potest veritas principio vel fine. Quare idem sequitur de summa natura, quia ipsa summa veritas est.'[2]

It was probably this argument (of the pattern later called the *consequentia mirabilis*) which St. Thomas had in mind when, writing his *De Veritate*, he supposed that an opponent might say:

'Omne illud cuius esse sequitur ad destructionem sui esse est aeternum, quia sive ponatur esse sive ponatur non esse sequitur quod erit, et oportet secundum unumquodque tempus ponere de unoquoque quod sit vel quod non sit. Sed ad destructionem veritatis sequitur veritatem esse, quia, si veritas non est, veritatem non esse est verum, et nihil potest verum nisi veritate. Ergo veritas est aeterna.'[3]

The first half of the twelfth century was the time when medieval philosophy took the shape it was to retain until the Renaissance, and one of the most powerful influences in the formation of the tradition was Abelard's work *Sic et Non*. In this he set out the conflicts of authorities on questions of theology, not, as some rationalist of our day might think, in order to discredit the study, but rather because he gloried in finding subjects of high importance for the exercise of human reason. In the works of later writers who are accounted most orthodox, e.g. St. Thomas Aquinas, this method persists. All philosophy and theology and even jurisprudence is studied by consideration of *quaestiones*. At the beginning of each *quaestio* authorities who oppose, or seem to oppose, each other are set in array, and then the teacher shows his mastery by producing distinctions of meaning that suffice to solve the problem and dispose of all the difficulties. In the universities, which were first

---

[1] *Proslogion*, 3.
[2] *Monologion*, 18. Cf. *De Veritate* 1.          [3] *De Veritate*, qu. 1, art. 5 (2).

organized during the twelfth century, even the students were
expected to acquire debating skill; for the examinations were disputations in which the candidates showed their ability to continue the work of their masters. Since the medieval schoolmen
had to reach conclusions consistent with revelation, their activity
was not dialectic as the Greeks knew it. But they were justified
in using that word, because they were trying to discover the truth
by discussion which would reveal the unacceptable consequences
of various suggestions. And there can be no doubt of their enthusiasm for this method. Abelard spoke of dialectic as *dux
universae doctrinae*,[1] and it was his confidence in reason, rather than
any particular heresy, that he communicated to the hundreds
who crowded to hear him. There were some critics who said that
Christians should have nothing to do with secular learning, and
some who attacked logic in particular, but this illiberal view did
not prevail. On the contrary, it became an assumption of the
organization of universities that, as Abelard had said, *veritas
veritati non est adversa*.[2]

Abelard composed four works on logic: (1) *Introductiones Parvulorum*,[3] which consists of short glosses on Porphyry's *Eisagoge*
and Aristotle's *Categories* and *De Interpretatione*; (2) *Logica Ingredientibus*[4] (so called because *ingredientibus* is the first word of its
text), which consists of longer glosses on the texts covered by the
previous work together with Boethius' *De Differentiis Topicis* and
was probably written while Abelard was teaching in Paris before
1120; (3) *Logica Nostrorum Petitioni* (so called because *nostrorum
petitioni* are the first words of its text), which consists of longer
glosses on the *Eisagoge* and may date from the time of his teaching
at the hermitage of the Paraclete; (4) *Dialectica*,[5] which has the
form of an independent work about the subjects covered by
Boethius' logical writings and Victorinus' treatise *De Definitionibus* and seems to contain materials from different periods of
Abelard's life but probably did not reach its final form until a
late date, perhaps the time of his stay at Cluny shortly before his
death. Of these the second and the fourth are the most valuable.

[1] *Dialectica*, ed. L. M. de Rijk, p. 470.                    [2] Ibid., p. 469.
[3] Edited by M. Dal Pra under the title *Pietro Abelardo, Scritti Filosofici, Editio
super Porphyrium*, &c. (Milan, 1954). The name given above is that by which
Abelard himself refers to the work in his *Dialectica*, p. 329.
[4] Edited, together with the next work, in our list, by B. Geyer in *Peter Abaelard's
Philosophische Schriften, Beiträge zur Geschichte der Philosophie und Theologie des Mittelalters*, xxi (1919–33). The end of the commentary on the *De Interpretatione* in
Geyer's edition appears to be not by Abelard, but Abelard's own text has been
restored from another manuscript by L. Minio-Paluello in *Abaelardiana Inedita,
Twelfth Century Logic, Texts and Studies*, ii (Roma, 1958).
[5] Edited by L. M. De Rijk (Assen, 1956).

The *Dialectica* indeed, though based, like that of Garland, chiefly on the works of Boethius and written with the prolixity which was all too common among medieval authors, is an original composition of great importance for the development of logic. Abelard's mind was the keenest (though not in all respects the most admirable) that had been devoted to the subject for more than a thousand years, and he approached his task with the belief that it was still possible to make discoveries: 'Non enim tanta fuit antiquorum scriptorum perfectio ut non et nostro doctrina indigeat studio, nec tantum in nobis mortalibus scientia potest crescere ut non ultra possit augmentum recipere.'[1] The *Dialectica* survives in a single manuscript which lacks the opening sections. Excerpts from it were published by Victor Cousin in 1836 in his *Ouvrages inédits d'Abélard*. But unfortunately the text was not printed in full until 1956, and before that date it was therefore not possible to appreciate the magnitude of Abelard's contribution to the doctrines we regard as characteristically medieval. In what follows we shall survey the contents of this work, mentioning not only the principal novelties but also some of the doctrines of Boethius to which he gave new life.

The text is divided into five *tractatus* which correspond to groups of Boethius' writings and are called respectively: I *Liber Partium*, II *De Categoricis*, III *Topica*, IV *De Hypotheticis*, and V *De Divisionibus et Definitionibus*. Of these the first is subdivided into three *volumina* dealing with the *antepraedicamenta* (or *quinque voces* of Porphyry), the *praedicamenta* (or categories of Aristotle), and the *postpraedicamenta* (or questions about meaning raised in the *De Interpretatione*).[2] But our sole surviving manuscript lacks the whole of the first *volumen* and the opening of the second. This is unfortunate, since the missing part probably contained Abelard's last thoughts about universals. We can be reasonably sure also that it contained an account of the distinction between words of first and words of second imposition, since this was mentioned by Boethius in his commentary on the *Categories* and is taken for granted later by Abelard.[3]

In that part of his treatment of the *Categories* which survives quantity receives a fuller discussion than any of the other headings; and this discussion includes a section on *oratio*, or speech, which Aristotle had mentioned as a process taking time. Abelard's

---

[1] *Dialectica*, p. 535.
[2] In later times the name *antepraedicamenta* was used (more naturally) for the subjects treated by Aristotle in his *Categories*, 1–3 (i.e. equivocal and univocal naming, simple and complex expressions, &c.), and the name *postpraedicamenta* for the subjects treated by Aristotle in his *Categories*, 10–15 i.e. kinds of opposites, kinds of priority, &c.).                      [3] *Dialectica*, p. 122.

interest in this was due, of course, to his belief that logic had to do with *oratio* as the vehicle of reasoning. The section leads up to the conclusion that, since a spoken utterance is finished and no longer existent by the time its whole meaning has been conveyed, its being significant cannot be a property or form belonging to it in its own right, but must consist simply in its generating a thought. In this connexion Abelard notices, however, that the word *oratio* may be used to cover more than spoken utterances, and mentions the old doctrine of the three kinds of discourse, written, spoken, and mental.

The third part of the first *tractatus* and the first two books of the second (*De Partibus Categoricarum* and *De Specierum Differentiis Categoricarum*) may conveniently be taken together, since they deal with the contents of the *De Interpretatione* and the theory of propositions presupposed in the doctrine of the categorical syllogism. Abelard defines a *propositio* (i.e. a propositional sign) as an *oratio verum falsumve significans*.[1] This formula is obviously derived from a definition of *enuntiatio* given by Boethius in various passages of his works with slight changes of wording,[2] but Abelard, unlike Boethius, is well aware of an interesting implication of the definition, namely that truth and falsity belong primarily to the contents signified by propositional signs. He is quite prepared to speak of propositions themselves (i.e. propositional signs) as true or false, and even to say that they may change from truth to falsity, or vice versa, according to change of circumstances.[3] But he holds that when we speak of a proposition as true we must mean either that it generates a true thought or that it propounds what is in fact the case (*proponit id quod in re est*), and he argues that of these two notions the second is the more fundamental. For although signs may be said to signify in two different senses, one concerned with thoughts and the other with things, what interests us in propositions when we do logic is their signification of states of affairs. When, for example, we say that one proposition entails another, we do not mean that the thought conveyed by the first is impossible without the thought conveyed by the second, since the one may very well occur without the other: 'Cum enim dicimus *Si est homo est animal*, si ad intellectus propositionum consecutionem referamus, ut videlicet de ipsis intellectibus agamus, nulla est consequentiae veritas, cum scilicet alter intellectuum sine altero omnino subsistat.'[4] It is clear therefore that in the definition of a proposition '*verum* et *falsum* nomina sunt earum existentiarum rerum quas

---

[1] Ibid., p. 153.  [2] *In Lib. de Int. Ed. Sec.* ii. 451D; *De Diff. Top.* i. 1174B.
[3] *Dialectica*, p. 53.  [4] Ibid., p. 154.

ipsae propositiones loquuntur'.[1] And it is this usage which we have in mind when we construct such sentences as *Socratem currere verum est*. For the accusative and infinitive of such a remark make up something like a name of what would be expressed by the corresponding nominative and indicative (*quasi nomen illius quod propositione exprimitur*).[2] In the language of the *Logica Ingredientibus* they stand for the *dictum* of the corresponding proposition.[3]

These reflections lead Abelard to the question 'utrum illae existentiae rerum quas propositiones loquuntur sint aliquae de rebus existentibus', and he concludes that what a proposition expresses cannot be an existing thing precisely because it is the existence of a thing or at any rate a way in which things may be related to each other:

'Esse autem rem aliquam vel non esse nulla est omnino rerum essentia. Non itaque propositiones res aliquas designant simpliciter quemadmodum nomina, immo qualiter sese ad vicem habent, utrum scilicet sibi conveniant annon, proponunt; ac tunc quidem verae sunt cum ita in re est sicut enuntiant, tunc autem falsae cum non est in re ita. Et est profecto ita in re sicut dicit vera propositio, sed non est res aliqua quod dicit. Unde quasi quidam rerum modus habendi se per propositiones exprimitur, non res aliquae designantur.'[4]

As might be expected there is a close resemblance between this account of propositional contents and the pronouncement of Abelard on universals which was quoted above. That which all men have in common is being-a-man, and this is not a thing such as we indicate by words like *Socrates* and *homo*. Similarly that which is signified by *Socrates est homo* is Socrates'-being-a-man, and this again is not a thing (*res*) in Abelard's view, though it is presumably something (*aliquid*) in that sense in which according to him the word may be applied even to a non-existent object of thought.[5] In each case the abstract entity under consideration is brought to attention by use of the verb 'to be', and so this *verbum substantivum*, as the Latin grammarians called it (translating from their Greek predecessors), deserves special attention.

In his *De Interpretatione*[6] Aristotle says that a statement is composed of a noun and a verb, but he also remarks incidentally that a verb such as 'walks' may be replaced by a phrase such as 'is walking', and it is clear that for his theory of syllogism he assumes in every general proposition two terms of the same kind, that is to say, each capable of being a subject and each capable of being a predicate. Pursuing these suggestions, Abelard treats the verb

[1] *Dialectica*, p. 156.                    [2] Ibid., p. 150.
[3] *Logica Ingredientibus* (ed. Geyer), p. 275.     [4] *Dialectica*, p. 160.
[5] Ibid., p. 137.                           [6] *De Interpretatione*, 12 (21ᵇ9–10).

'to be' as the *copula*, or link, which joins the subject and the predicate of a categorical proposition.[1] He recognizes, of course, that
statements can be made without the use of that verb, but he says
that other verbs can be expanded in the way indicated by Aristotle,
and argues that what distinguishes verbs in general from nouns
is not, as Aristotle said, that they contain an indication of time,
but rather that they can effect the joining (*copulatio*) required for
the constitution of a proposition.[2] When the verb *est* occurs *tertium adiacens*, as in the proposition *Socrates est homo*, it is merely a
link between two explicitly formulated terms. But it can also occur
*appositum subiecto* and without any explicit predicate, as in
*Socrates est*, and then it is to be understood as an abbreviation for
the phrase *est ens*.[3]

This account of the two uses of the verb *est* implies, of course,
that when the verb occurs as a mere *copula* it does not involve a
predication of existence. For as Abelard saw, if it did, *Socrates est
ens* could be expanded again to *Socrates est ens ens* and so on *ad
infinitum*, and *Chimaera est opinabilis* (where *opinabilis* means
'imaginary') would be plainly false.[4] But in its original use the
verb was applied only to existing things,[5] and so there was no
difficulty. When it occurs in a proposition such as *Chimaera est
opinabilis*, we have a *locutio* which is *impropria* in the same sort of
way as a phrase containing *oppositio in adiecto*. For just as use of the
phrase 'dead man' may suggest incorrectly that we are talking
about a man of a certain kind, so use of the proposition *Chimaera
est opinabilis* may suggest incorrectly that we are committed to the
truth of the proposition *Chimaera est*. In either case the trouble
arises from trying to take separately words which are not intended to be taken so.[6] According to Abelard it was the view of
one of his masters (possibly William of Champeaux) that
*Chimaera est opinabilis* was a *figurativa atque impropria locutio* because
its construction suggested the attribution of a property to a non-
existent chimaera when the real sense to be conveyed was that
given by the more complex proposition *Anima alicuius opinionem
habet de chimaera*.[7] Abelard does not entirely reject this account of
the matter, but he says that we can solve the problem more simply
by making clear that the copula is never to be understood as a
sign of existence: 'Nec quidem, quantum ad eius interpreta-
tionem pertinet, ex eo quod dicitur *Petrus est homo* inferri potest
*Petrus est*, sed fortasse quantum ad praedicationem *hominis*, quod
existentis rei tantum nomen est.'[8]

[1] *Dialectica*, p. 161.          [2] Ibid., p. 123.          [3] Ibid., pp. 161–2.
[4] Ibid., pp. 137, 162.         [5] Ibid., p. 137.          [6] Ibid., p. 138.
[7] Ibid., p. 136.                                            [8] Ibid., p. 137.

Abelard is usually credited with introduction of the word *copula* as a technical expression of logic, but it is clear from what he says that before his time there had been discussion about the role of the verb 'to be' in categorical propositions, and that some philosophers had said it signified a relation of inherence between the predicate and the subject. Obviously this view went together with a doctrine of universals which Abelard disliked, and it was often expressed by a barbarous use of general terms as though they were proper names of universals. For those who were prepared to say *Homo est species* were also prepared to say *Homo inhaeret Socrati* instead of *Humanitas inhaeret* (or *inest*) *Socrati*. Abelard did not altogether reject talk of inherence; but he insisted that it was useless as an explanation of the meaning of the verb 'to be', and he argued that, if it were taken seriously, it would lead to absurdity, in particular to the absurdity of an infinite regress:

'Si per *esse* inhaerentiam necesse sit attribui, et cum dicitur *Inhaerentia est inhaerentia* inhaerentiam quoque in inhaerentia per verbum copulamus, in adiacentia scilicet sicut in aliis propositionibus. Si enim in essentia attribueretur per verbum inhaerentia inhaerentiae, superflue subderetur post verbum nomen *inhaerentiae*. Quodsi per *est* verbum inhaerentia secundum adiacentiam attribuatur inhaerentiae, et rursus cum de illa quae attribuitur vere dicitur quia est inhaerentia, in ipsa quoque rursus inhaerentiam oportet esse, ita ut ini nfinitum ratio procedat.'[1]

In opposition to all this Abelard insists that *est* is an intransitive link, that is to say, a link by which something is related only to itself: 'Oportet autem praedicatum subiecto intransitive copulari, ut videlicet in eadem re ipsius impositio in subiecto inveniatur; veluti cum dicitur *Homo est animal* . . . et *homo* et *animal* . . . eiusdem nomina esse oportet.'[2] In short, he takes the *copula* as a sign of identity.

This analysis of the uses of the verb 'to be' does not, as we had hoped, do much to clarify Abelard's doctrines of universals and propositional contents, and it is not easy to reconcile with what he says later about the existential import of categorical propositions. For all his subtlety and shrewdness Abelard seems to have failed to appreciate the great importance of the difference between referring to an individual by means of a proper name or demonstrative sign and characterizing it by means of a general term or descriptive phrase, though he was of course quite well able to use the distinction in ordinary discourse and even to talk

---

[1] *Dialectica*, pp. 158–9.        [2] Ibid., p. 166.

about it intelligently when he was not dealing with those controversial problems for the solution of which it is essential. His
teaching was nevertheless very influential, and many of his successors who did not agree with his account of universals accepted
his view that an affirmative categorical proposition was true if
and only if the subject term and the predicate term both stood
for the same thing or things. Out of this doctrine there grew in
the next hundred years the theory of *suppositio terminorum*, that is
to say the theory of the different ways in which the terms of propositions may stand for things.

Since we shall have to consider later the tracts *De Proprietatibus
Terminorum* in which the theory of *suppositio* is presented, a detailed discussion would be out of place here, but it may be useful
to notice some theses of Abelard which reappear in the fully developed doctrine. In the first place there is his remark that verbs,
unlike nouns, can link themselves directly to subjects. In later
times the *copulatio* which he mentions in this connexion was
reckoned as one of the *proprietates terminorum*, together with *significatio*, *suppositio*, and *appellatio*. Admittedly neither the word *suppositio* nor the word *appellatio* occurs in his *Dialectica* with the
technical sense which it acquired later, but the phrase *proprietates terminorum* has a close resemblance to the phrase *proprietates
nominum iuxta significationem* which he uses in a discussion of the
grammatical peculiarities of nouns.[1] Secondly, Abelard notices
that subject-terms stand primarily for things existing at the time
of speech, and argues that for this reason propositions in a past or
a future tense cannot be converted as simply as those in the
present tense. When Socrates is old, it may be said truthfully
'Socrates was a boy', but not 'A boy was Socrates'. If we wish to
provide a converse for the former proposition, we must put the
mark of past time into the predicate before reversing the order
of the terms, so that we get 'Something which was a boy is
Socrates'.[2] Problems of this kind became prominent later in the
discussions of *suppositio*. Thirdly, when explaining his notion of
the *copula* as an intransitive link, Abelard objects to the remarks
of some grammarians that a proposition like *Homo est nomen* involves a transitive construction (*transitivam grammaticam*) because
it deals at once with a sign and what it signifies. The subject word
*homo*, he agrees, is a name for itself, but in his view this admission
requires no departure from his account of the function of the
*copula*. For it is still true to say that the subject and the predicate
stand for the same thing, namely for the subject word: 'Quodsi vox
subiecta se ipsam nominat ac rursus praedicata ipsa nominatur,

---

[1] Ibid., p. 124.                     [2] Ibid., p. 139.

profecto praedicata vox et subiecta in eadem re conveniunt atque hoc modo consignificant.'[1] This seems to be the origin of the doctrine of *suppositio materialis*.

After treating of terms and the *copula* Abelard excuses himself from writing about the square of opposition and the rules of conversion on the ground that he has dealt with these carefully in his *Introductiones Parvulorum*, but says that he wishes to consider some deeper questions about negation. The point which interests him especially is the difference of sense which may result from a change in the position of the negation sign, e.g. the difference between *Non quidam homo est iustus* and *Quidam homo non est iustus*. And the thesis which he wishes especially to defend is that the proper negation of any proposition, whether categorical or hypothetical, results from the placing of the negation sign in front of the whole: 'Manifestum est autem ex suprapositis omni affirmationi eam in contradictionem recte opponi negationem tamquam propriam dividentem quae negatione praeposita totam eius sententiam perimit.'[2]

This is good Stoic doctrine, but Abelard seems to have thought it out for himself, and he derives from it a rather surprising conclusion that is at variance with the ordinary account of the square of opposition, which he himself had apparently accepted in the earlier work mentioned above. While he admits that *Nullus homo est albus* can be regarded as the contradictory of *Quidam homo est albus* because *nullus* is merely an abbreviation of *non ullus*,[3] he now refuses to allow that *Quidam homo non est albus* is the contradictory of *Omnis homo est albus*, as Boethius had maintained, and says that Aristotle dealt with the question more subtly when he offered *Non omnis homo est albus* as the contradictory. It is true, of course, that Aristotle wrote Greek words corresponding to *Non omnis homo est albus*,[4] but it seems clear that he did not intend to convey by these words anything different from the doctrine later attributed to him by Boethius. Abelard, on the other hand, thinks that *Non omnis homo est albus* is something distinct in meaning from the particular negative proposition *Quidam homo non est albus*, and therefore outside the usual scheme of four categorical forms.[5] His reason for introducing this complication is that he assumes existential import for *Omnis homo est albus*, though apparently not for *Nullus homo est albus*. The assumption seems curious after his explicit statement that the word *est* occurring as pure *copula* involves no assertion of existence; but there can be no doubt of his

---

[1] *Dialectica*, p. 166.                                              [2] Ibid., p. 178.
[3] Ibid., p. 177.                              [4] *De Interpretation*, 7 (17$^b$16–19).
[5] *Dialectica*, p. 184.

doctrine on this point, since he insists that even the seeming tautology *Omnis homo est homo* would be false if there were no men:
'Cum autem *Quidam homo non est homo* semper falsa sit atque *Omnis
homo est homo* homine non existente, patet simul easdem falsas esse:
unde nec recte dividentes dici poterunt.'[1] We must therefore
suppose that in his view it is the word *omnis* which introduces
existential import.

Later medieval logicians did not follow Abelard in trying to
distinguish between *non omnis* and *quidam non*; but a recent writer
on Medieval logic has said that they assumed existential import
for affirmative propositions only and then preserved the customary
square of opposition by giving to *quidam non* the sense which
Abelard reserved for *non omnis*.[2] No decisive evidence has been
cited in support of this statement and it is difficult to believe
that anyone could suppose *Quidam homo non est albus* to mean
'Either there are no men or there is a man who is not white'.
But if it were true, it would be additional confirmation of the
importance of Abelard's influence in the formation of medieval
logic. In any case he should have the credit of being the first
to worry about the traditional square of opposition, though
he did not work out all the consequences of the change he
advocated.

From negation Abelard goes on to consider the *signa quantitatis*,
*omnis*, *quidam*, and *nullus*. The last, as we have seen, he takes to be
an equivalent for *non quidam*, and so the problem for him is what to
say of the other two. It is clear that *omnis* is not what Priscian the
grammarian calls a *nomen appellativum*; that is to say, when we
have to do with a phrase such as *omnis homo* we cannot treat
*omnis* as applicable to each of the men covered by *homo*. On the
contrary its function is to collect the various individuals for attention in somewhat the same way as they might be collected by their
various proper names, while conveying that none is excluded:
'... in *omnis* non solum singula colliguntur, verum etiam innuitur
quod nullum excipiatur.'[3] We may perhaps say therefore that
the phrase *omnis homo* is a composite name standing for each individual man without exception, whereas the phrase *quidam homo*
is a composite name standing indeterminately for some man or
other.[4] And since such a phrase can occur in the predicate place
of a proposition just as well as in the subject place, we should
allow for two kinds of universality and two kinds of particularity
in propositions, with corresponding relations of opposition:

[1] Ibid., p. 176.
[2] E. A. Moody, *Truth and Consequence in Medieval Logic*, pp. 52–53.
[3] *Dialectica*, p. 187.                              [4] Ibid., p. 188.

'Potest quoque in propositionibus duplex universalitas aut particularitas accipi signis quantitatis tam subiecto quam praedicato appositis.'[1] It will be seen that in all this Abelard thinks of terms as names of things, i.e. that he takes what came to be called later an extensional view of categorical propositions.

In many places Abelard's manner of argument shows that he is attacking the views of predecessors or contemporaries, and sometimes he says explicitly that a thesis which he criticizes has been put forward by another logician. This happens in his discussion of modality. For he tells us that one of his masters (perhaps William of Champeaux) maintained that every modal proposition was about the sense of another proposition, so that to say *Possibile est Socratem currere* was to predicate possibility of the *sensus* of the proposition *Socrates currit*.[2] Abelard does not deny that expressions containing *possibile* and similar words may be interpretable in this way. On the contrary, he points out that this interpretation agrees well with what he has said earlier about truth as a property of propositional contents.[3] And he seems to have this interpretation in mind when he says: ' . . . *verum* . . . antecedit quidem ad *possibile*, sequitur vero ad *necessarium*; *falsum* autem ad *impossibile* tantum sequitur.'[4] But he holds that a proposition which bears this interpretation is not strictly speaking modal, since it involves no modification of the propositional link between things, but is merely the simple application of a special kind of adjective to a simple propositional content. A genuinely modal proposition, he thinks, is one which involves modality *secundum expositionem de rebus*.[5] This may be constructed by means of an adverb such as *possibiliter*, but it may on the other hand be constructed by means of a modal adjective with an accusative and an infinitive. For although *Nullum hominem possibile est esse album* may be taken to be a true singular affirmative proposition with the meaning 'It is possible that no man should be white', it may also be taken to be a false universal negative proposition with the meaning 'No man can be white' or 'It is impossible that any man should be white', and according to Abelard it is not really a modal proposition unless taken in the second sense, when the modal word qualifies the link and may therefore be said to express a mode or manner of union.

In this contrast between *expositio de sensu* and *expositio de rebus* (which appears also in Abelard's commentary on the *De Interpretatione* as a distinction between *expositio per compositionem* and *expositio per divisionem*, with a reference to the *De Sophisticis*

---

[1] *Dialectica*, p. 190.    [2] Ibid., p. 195.    [3] Ibid., p. 205.
[4] Ibid., p. 204.                              [5] Ibid., p. 206.

*Elenchis*[1]) we have an attempt to draw that distinction between external and internal qualification which we considered in an earlier chapter as a possible justification for some strange features in Aristotle's theory of modal syllogisms. Some later medieval logicians talked of a distinction between modality *de dicto* and modality *de re*, assuming thereby that propositions *de dicto* could properly be accounted modal. But some at least followed Abelard in saying that genuinely modal propositions never involved application of modal adjectives to propositional contents. This particular feature of Abelard's doctrine is unfortunate. For it now seems obvious that the use of modal words *de dicto* is fundamental, and that, if modal words are sometimes used in such a way as to convey a qualification which is inextricably internal, this should not be taken as a simple and basic usage, but rather as evidence of the complexity of the discourse in which it occurs. In some respects modal words are like negative particles. As Abelard rightly says, to obtain the negative of a given proposition we must introduce a negative particle in such a position that it can operate upon the whole of the original. But a negative particle may nevertheless occur within a complicated proposition at some position in which it does not operate upon all the rest and from which it cannot be extracted by any ingenuity of paraphrase. It would obviously be foolish in this case to say that only complicated propositions of the second kind are truly negative. On the contrary, it is more reasonable to say, as Abelard does in effect, that a proposition of the second kind need not be negative as a whole. So too a proposition which involves modality *de re* need not be modal as a whole; and denial of the name to propositions of the form 'It is possible that no man should be white' seems to be no more than pedantic adherence to the misleading suggestions of the word *modus*. Some of the later Schoolmen came near to realizing the point, but in general the influence of tradition was too strong for them.

Near the beginning of his treatment of modality Abelard says that *possibile* and *contingens* are equivalent.[2] This remark is derived, of course, from Aristotle, but it seems clear that Abelard uses it as a new definition of *contingens* rather than for the restriction of *possibile* to what is not necessary. For although he regards *necessarium*, *possibile*, and *impossibile* as the three basic modal words whose relations he should discuss, he says that *Necesse est Socratem esse album* entails *Possibile est Socratem esse album*, which would not be true if *possibile* were taken to mean what *contingens* usually means.[3]

[1] L. Minio-Paluello, *Abaelardiana Inedita, Twelfth Century Logic, Texts and Studies*, ii, pp. 13 ff.        [2] *Dialectica*, p. 193.        [3] Ibid., pp. 198–9.

From modality Abelard goes on to the problem of future contingents. And here, as might be expected, he uses the word *contingentia* in something like its ordinary sense. For he says that the contingent is what may or may not happen and contrasts it with the *necessarium* and the *naturale*, giving as an example of the latter the proposition that a man will die.[1] The past and the present, he tells us, are determinate; for although we do not know whether the number of the stars is odd or even, it is certainly one or the other.[2] And true propositions about the past or the present are determinately true because their truth can in principle at least be ascertained from knowledge of the facts which they state. No proposition *de contingenti futuro* can be either determinately true or determinately false in the same sense, but this is not to say that no such proposition can be true or false. On the contrary, any such proposition is true if the outcome is to be as it states, even though this is unknown to us ('si futurum sit ut propositio dicit, etsi ignoratum nobis sit').[3] What Aristotle wished to maintain in his *De Interpretatione* was that, while a true proposition is necessarily true when it is true, it is not therefore necessarily true simply and always.[4] On the question of free will an opponent might perhaps still argue, like the Stoics, that human judgements and actions are themselves necessary events and therefore not excluded by the doctrine of universal necessity, but possibly this issue was not one which Aristotle wished to discuss.[5]

This passage is apparently an attempt to defend Aristotle against the charge of having denied the universal validity of the principle of bivalence, and up to a point it is a plausible explanation of a very obscure text. But it involves an attempt to take seriously the notion that a proposition can be true at one time but not at another. Abelard does not expressly define a necessary proposition as one which is true at all times and a contingent proposition as one which is true only at some time, but he seems here to identify absolute necessity with truth at all times and in several other places he mentions it as a special mark of necessary truths, and in particular of *consequentiae* such as *Si est homo, est animal*, that they are *verae ab aeterno*. The suggestion that contingent truths may be true at one time but not at another does not accord well with the doctrine that truth belongs primarily to propositional contents rather than to the propositional signs which express them. But Abelard failed to notice the difficulty, and his practice of talking about truth-at-a-time was followed by many of his successors.

[1] *Dialectica*, p. 211.        [2] Ibid., p. 212.        [3] Ibid., p. 213.
[4] Ibid., p. 221.                           [5] Ibid., pp. 216 and 222.

After these elaborate preliminaries, which occupy 180 pages
of our printed text, it is rather surprising that the whole theory of
syllogistic is presented in 18 pages. The account of the figures and
the moods and of the reduction of moods of the second and the
third figures to the first is satisfactory, so far as it goes, but rather
thin. There is very little, for example, about modal syllogisms,
and nothing at all about the philosophy of deductive reasoning.
This may be due in part to the direction of Abelard's interests:
he was probably more interested in metaphysics than in the
theory of deductive systems. But it seems likely that his allocation
of space was determined primarily by the character of the logical
texts in general use at his time. In the whole of the *Dialectica* there
are only three references to Aristotle's *Prior Analytics*, as compared
with more than 250 to the *Categories* and the *De Interpretatione*,
which were widely circulated and well known. We must not conclude, however, that Abelard himself had never seen any Latin
version of the *Prior Analytics*. For it so happens that two at least of
Abelard's quotations from this work cannot be derived from any
known secondary source such as Boethius' work *De Syllogismo
Categorico*.[1] Possibly he had seen a copy of Boethius' translation
in some library, but had not studied it closely and could not
assume that it was available to his hearers or readers.

As in Boethius' writings, so here the study of *loci*, or topics,
receives a great deal of space. In fact Abelard gives to it more
pages than he has given to all the surviving parts of the first two
tracts, and it must be admitted that a good deal of what he has to
say seems tedious to the modern reader who is looking for evidence
of the development of formal logic. But this part of the work contains his account of *consequentiae*, from which there grew one of
the most interesting novelties of medieval logic.

In Abelard's usage the word *consequentia* does not mean, as it
did for Boethius, the way in which one proposition follows from
another. When he wishes to talk of that relation, he uses instead
the word *consecutio*,[2] because he regards *consequentia* as reserved
for the sense of 'conditional proposition'. From the way in which
he explains this usage we may safely conclude that it has been
adopted by others before him.[3] As he says, it seems to be based on
the use of the word *consequens* to signify the second part of a conditional proposition. But there can be no doubt that for him the
word still suggests following in that sense in which the conclusion
of a valid argument is said to follow from the premisses. He tells

---

[1] B. Geyer, 'Die ältesten lateinischen Übersetzungen der Analytik, Topik, und
Elenchik', *Philosophisches Jahrbuch der Görresgesellschaft*, xxx (1917), pp. 25–43.
[2] *Dialectica*, pp. 163 and 472.                        [3] Ibid., p. 165.

us that some people, including one of his own masters (perhaps William of Champeaux), thought mere probability good enough to secure the truth of a conditional proposition, but that in his view nothing less than *necessitas consecutionis* is implied by use of this form.[1] In short, he assumes that conditional statements, or at any rate those which he calls *consequentiae*, are statements of necessary connexion such as we sometimes offer in justification of inferences, and that is why he finds it desirable to consider them in detail when investigating the theory of topics. Furthermore, since they profess to be statements of necessity, he thinks that they must, if true at all, be true *ab aeterno*.[2]

Some arguments, he says, are perfect in the sense that their premisses suffice by themselves for the establishment of their conclusions. If we construct a conditional statement which has for its antecedent the conjunction of the premisses of such an argument and for its consequent the conclusion, the result is a *consequentia* true *secundum complexionem*, that is to say, in virtue of its formal structure. For an example we may take : 'Si omnis homo est animal et omne animal est animatum, omnis homo est animatus.' We may replace the terms as we please by others, but what we get will always be a true *consequentia*, provided only that the pattern of the whole is preserved. There are, however, other arguments which we must call imperfect because they do not satisfy this condition but require for their justification some supplement *ex rerum natura*. The truth of the *consequentia* corresponding to such an argument depends upon the nature of the things named by the terms in a way in which the truth of a *consequentia* corresponding to a perfect argument does not. For if we replaced the terms by others, the result might perhaps be a false proposition :

'Istae ergo consequentiae recte ex natura rerum verae dicuntur quarum veritas una cum rerum natura variatur; illae vero veritatem ex complexione, non ex rerum natura, tenent quarum complexio necessitatem in quibuslibet rebus, cuiuscumque sint habitudinis, aeque custodit, sicut in syllogismis vel in consequentiis quae formas eorum tenent ostenditur.'[3]

Now a *locus* has been defined by Cicero as a *sedes argumenti*, and in view of the distinction we have just drawn we may say also that it is the *vis inferentiae* of an imperfect argument.[4] Thus when we proceed from the premiss *Socrates est homo* to the conclusion *Socrates est animal*, we use the *locus a specie* whose *maxima propositio* is *De quocumque praedicatur species, et genus*. If, however, we try to

[1] *Dialectica*, pp. 253 and 271–4.        [2] Ibid., pp. 160 and 279.
[3] Ibid., p. 256.        [4] Ibid., p. 253.

set out in detail what the *locus* contributes in this particular case, we get a *consequentia* which is true *ex rerum natura*, namely, *Si Socrates est homo est animal*. And so the *maxima propositio* of the *locus* may be described as the principle which contains in itself the sense of all such *consequentiae*.[1] It was suggested by Boethius that there are *maximae propositiones* also for syllogisms,[2] and it is true that we can bring each syllogism under some general rule such as: 'Si aliquid praedicatur de alio universaliter et aliud prae-dicetur de praedicato universaliter, illud idem praedicatur et de subiecto universaliter.'[3] But rules of this kind should not be con-fused with maxims. For syllogisms are already perfect by reason of their structure (*complexio*) and require no justification from without.[4] Admittedly syllogisms of the second and third figures have been said to be imperfect, but in Abelard's view this remark refers to their clarity (*evidentia*), not to their conclusiveness (*in-ferentia*), which is perfect, though we cannot detect it as quickly as we should if the terms were in the right order.

Not content with insisting that the conditional form must be taken to express necessary connexion, Abelard goes on to say that even the phrase *consecutionis necessitas* is insufficient as a formulation of his requirement, because it can be understood in a loose sense which involves awkward consequences (*inconvenientia*). Some people say that a *consequentia* is necessarily true if it is im-possible that the antecedent should be true without the con-sequent. At first sight such an interpretation seems reasonable, but it commits us to accepting as a true *consequentia* the para-doxical assertion: *Si Socrates est lapis, est asinus*. For it is impossible that Socrates should be a stone, and so impossible that he should be a stone without being an ass. We must therefore under-stand *consecutionis necessitas* in a stricter sense according to which the antecedent of a true conditional statement requires the con-sequent intrinsically (*ex se ipso exigit*).[5] This very interesting con-tention of Abelard seems to be the beginning of a long medieval debate about paradoxes of implication. For it can scarcely be an accident that later logicians who take part in the debate commonly mention as an example of the impossible a man's being an ass and sometimes also, like Abelard, use *Brunellus* as a name of an ass.[6] But the way in which Abelard applies his strict definition of necessary connexion seems unfortunate. He tells us that the *consequentia* which he cites so often as an example, *Si est homo est animal*, is satisfactory because it is a case of proceeding

---

[1] Ibid., p. 263.  [2] *De Differentiis Topicis*, i. 1173ᴮ.
[3] *Dialectica*, p. 261. The subjunctive is in the printed text.
[4] Ibid., p. 261.  [5] Ibid., pp. 283–5.  [6] Ibid., p. 293.

from the less general (*inferius*) to the more general (*superius*), which, as Priscian said, is understood in the former. On the other hand, he thinks that we have departed from the highest standard of rigour as soon as we put forward a *consequentia* which involves the assumption of two distinct substances, for example, *Si homo est, lapis non est* or *Si paternitas est, filiatio est*. For he says that in such a case the sense of the consequent is not contained in the sense of the antecedent, and that the truth of the whole can be established only by special knowledge of nature ('posterius ex naturae discretione et proprietatis naturae cognitione').[1]

It is difficult to find any satisfactory interpretation for this passage. On first inspection a modern reader may be inclined to think that it is an attempt to make a distinction between *a priori* truths, certifiable by consideration of the meanings of the words in which they are expressed, and *a posteriori* or empirical truths which can be discovered only by attention to experience. But this suggestion is almost certainly an anachronism. For there is nothing to show that Abelard had any conception of what we now call inductive method; and apart from that, the examples cited above are quite unsuitable for such a theory. The point seems to be rather that when we have to talk about relations of any kind (including that of incompatibility between characters perceived in different things), we cannot rely solely on familiarity with definitions *per genus et differentiam*, since these are plainly inadequate to settle the questions which may be raised. We may know, for example, that a man is by definition a rational animal and similarly that a stone is by definition a solid mineral, but these items of information will not by themselves enable us to say that if anything is a man it is not a stone. And again, since it is impossible to introduce the notion of fatherhood by any definition in non-relational terms, it is obvious that no such definition can be cited in proof of Abelard's second example. It seems as though for a moment he recognizes here a severe limitation of the Aristotelian conception of science which he has inherited from Boethius, but does not understand properly how to overcome it. Instead of trying (*a*) to find a place in formal logic for the theory of relations and (*b*) to draw a line of demarcation between *a priori* and empirical studies, he retains the Aristotelian scheme while suggesting that there should be developed in addition a new non-formal logic which will deal with all consequentiae true *gratia terminorum*, that is to say, in virtue of their terms as distinct from their structure.

[1] *Dialectica*, p. 284.

He explains this enlarged view of logic in the following passage:

'Hoc autem logicae disciplinae proprium relinquitur, ut scilicet vocum impositiones pensando quantum unaquaque proponatur oratione sive dictione discutiat. Physicae vero proprium est inquirere utrum rei natura consentiat enuntiationi, utrum ita sese, ut dicitur, rerum proprietas habeat vel non. Est autem alterius consideratio alteri necessaria. Ut enim logicae discipulis appareat quid in singulis intelligendum sit vocabulis, prius rerum proprietas est investiganda. Sed cum ab his rerum natura non pro se sed pro vocum impositione requiritur, tota eorum intentio referenda est ad logicam. Cum autem rerum natura percontata fuerit, vocum significatio secundum rerum proprietates distinguenda est, primo quidem in singulis dictionibus, deinde in orationibus quae ex dictionibus iunguntur et ex ipsis suos sensus sortiuntur.'[1]

Taken by themselves, the first two sentences might be thought to imply a modern-sounding distinction between logic as the study of meanings and physics as the study of facts. For Abelard says that it is the business of the science of logic to reflect on the conventions which give words their meanings and so to consider how much is propounded by various expressions, while it is the business of physics to inquire whether things have the characters ascribed to them in various propositions. But he goes on immediately to add that the student of logic must investigate the nature of things to find out what should be understood by the various words, and he maintains that all this activity is for the making of conventions about the use of words (*pro vocum impositione*). The suggestion seems to be now that language might be so improved and regularized that the learning of it would give a mastery of all science. If Abelard did indeed hold such a view, he was the first of a distinguished but rather wild company. Unfortunately the passage is too short to make his opinions clear.

Most of the maxims which Abelard enunciates for his various topics may be omitted here, but in his discussion of *consequentiae* he naturally has occasion to use various rules of formal logic, and it will be interesting to set out some of these. Occasionally they too are called maxims.

First there is the rule for what came to be called later the *modus ponendo ponens*:

(1) *Posito antecedente ponitur consequens,*

and secondly the rule for the *modus tollendo tollens*:

(2) *Perempto consequente perimitur antecedens.*

Each is cited from time to time in other words, but the versions given above are the shortest.[2] When presenting them, Abelard

[1] Ibid., pp. 286-7.   [2] Ibid., p. 288.

says that either can be derived from the other, because it is possible
to argue from *Si est homo est animal* to *Si non est animal non est homo*
and conversely. His proof of equivalence is by *reductio ad impossibile*. For if anyone admits the first of the *consequentiae* noticed
above while doubting the second, he says in effect that there
might be no animal although there was a man. But by the first
*consequentia*, which he admits, there must be an animal if there is
a man. And so the objector is convicted of saying that there might
be no animal although there was an animal. A similar contradiction results if the objector accepts the second *consequentia* while
rejecting the first.

Immediately after the foregoing Abelard offers a number of
negative rules, namely that there can be no formally valid argument (*a*) from the affirmation of the antecedent to the denial of
the consequent, or (*b*) from the denial of the antecedent to the
denial of the consequent, or (*c*) from the denial of the antecedent
to the affirmation of the consequent, or (*d*) from the denial of
the consequent to the affirmation of the antecedent, or (*e*) from
the affirmation of the consequent to the affirmation of the antecedent, or (*f*) from the affirmation of the consequent to the denial
of the antecedent. And he mistakenly tries to derive the first of
these from (2) above by use of the Aristotelian argument which
purports to show that a proposition and its negation cannot both
entail the same conclusion.

Next we have what is called in modern times the principle of
transitivity for entailment. This also is presented from time to
time in various forms, but the simplest is:

(3) *Si aliquid infert aliud quod inferat aliud, primum inferens infert
ultimum.*[1]

Then for the relations of truth and falsity with affirmation and
negation there are the two maxims:

(4) *Si vera est affirmatio, falsa est negatio,*
(5) *Si vera est negatio, falsa est affirmatio.*[2]

And for the relation of the various modalities (including truth
and falsity) with the notion of entailment there are the rules:

(6) *Si antecedens possibile est esse, et consequens,*
(7) *Si antecedens verum est esse, et consequens,*
(8) *Si antecedens necessarium est esse, et consequens,*
(9) *Si consequens esse impossibile est, et antecedens,*
(10) *Si consequens esse falsum est, et antecedens.*[3]

[1] *Dialectica*, p. 297.      [2] Ibid., p. 395.      [3] Ibid., pp. 361–2.

Again there are some variants. We have, for example, *Nullum verum infert falsum* cited in one place as a principle.[1]

After the tract on topics comes that on hypotheticals. At this time the word 'hypothetical' was still used to cover both conditional and disjunctive propositions, and for purposes of contrast under the general heading the former were sometimes called conjunctive. Since he offers his tract as a reworking of the contents of Boethius's *De Syllogismo Hypothetico*, Abelard retains the old terminology, but he has a tendency to equate 'hypothetical' in meaning with 'conditional',[2] and he justifies its application to disjunctive propositions by showing that the latter can be reduced to conditionals.[3] Natural and proper hypotheticals (*naturales et rectae hypotheticae*) are the *consequentiae* with which he has dealt at length in his previous tract, and he does not find it necessary to discuss their truth conditions again. But he notices here, rather perfunctorily, the distinction which Boethius had drawn between conditionals true *per positionem terminorum* and the rest.[4] In his opening remarks the most interesting novelty is his treatment of temporal propositions constructed by use of *cum*. Boethius had regarded these as conditionals which did not involve the notion of necessity and might therefore be said to be accidentally true. Abelard, on the other hand, refuses to allow that they can properly be called hypothetical or conditional, since they involve only *comitatio*, as distinct from *necessitas consecutionis*, but he gives three rules by which they may be related to *naturales consequentiae*:

(i) *Quorumcumque antecedentia sese comitantur, et consequentia,*
(ii) *Existente antecedente existunt simul quaelibet eius consequentia,*
(iii) *Existente antecedente cum quolibet, existit quodlibet eius consequens,*

Examples of the application of these rules are said to be:

(i) *Si cum est homo est medicus, cum est animal est artifex,*
(ii) *Si est homo, cum est animatum est animal,*
(iii) *Si cum est animatum est homo, est animal.*[5]

It is noticeable, however, that even here, where he tries to improve upon the work of Boethius, Abelard still thinks it proper to give examples composed of clauses like *si est homo*, i.e. clauses such as Theophrastus had used centuries before in his doctrine of totally hypothetical syllogisms.

The same conservatism runs through Abelard's account of hypothetical arguments. For although he makes a change of order

[1] Ibid., p. 287.                                     [2] Ibid., pp. 287 and 484–5.
[3] Ibid., p. 488.          [4] Ibid., pp. 472–3.          [5] Ibid., pp. 482–4.

in his exposition[1] and corrects the questionable argument of
Boethius which we noticed in the last section,[2] he follows his
authority closely through the various complex moods. And here,
where Boethius had used letters as variables, he too allows himself
that device, but always still in schemata such as *Si est A est B*,
where they mark places to be filled by general terms. Two
hundred years later Walter Burleigh still thought it proper to
follow this usage in his account of the Boethian system, though
he did not employ variables at all elsewhere. On the other hand,
Abelard gives no special attention to the scrap of Stoic logic preserved by Boethius in his commentary on Cicero's *Topica*. Perhaps
Cicero's account of the matter was too obscure to be of any help to
medieval logicians even when they were most dependent on the
Boethian corpus.

As we noticed earlier, Abelard holds that the proper negation
of any proposition is made by the placing of a negation sign in
front of the whole. In conscious opposition to Boethius he declares
that if a negation sign is inserted into either of the clauses of a
conditional proposition, the result is not the negation of the
original but a new proposition.[3] Thus *Si non est A est B* means the
same as *Aut est A aut est B*. And similarly *Aut non est A aut est B* means
the same as *Si est A est B*. In Abelard's view it is a mistake to say,
as some had done, that for the truth of a disjunction it is sufficient
that one of the disjuncts should be true, and a mistake also to say,
as others had done, that it is sufficient that one but only one of
the disjuncts should be true. For the real sense of a disjunction we
must always go, as Boethius did, to the associated conditional
which involves the notion of necessity. But according to Boethius
the two members of a disjunction are necessarily incompatible,
which is as much as say that *Aut est A aut est B* is not equivalent to
*Si non est A est B* but rather to the conjunction of that proposition
with *Si est A non est B*. Abelard rejects this stricter requirement for
the truth of a disjunctive proposition and with it the argument
from affirmation of one member of a disjunction to denial of
the other, i.e. what was later called the *modus ponendo tollens*.[4] Since
he regards a disjunction as equivalent to a conditional with a
negative antecedent, the *modus tollendo ponens* of disjunctive reasoning is for him naturally a special case of the *modus ponendo ponens*
of conditional reasoning.

When he abandons the requirement that the members of a
disjunction should be incompatible, Abelard begins a retreat from
the very strong interpretation of the disjunctive particle which

---

[1] *Dialectica*, p. 515.        [2] Ibid., p. 507.        [3] Ibid., pp. 485 ff.
[4] Ibid., pp. 489, 491, 499, 531. Cf. Boethius *De Syll. Hyp.* ii. 876c.

was introduced, as we believe, by Chrysippus. And this is not
the only step he takes towards a simplification of propositional
logic. Although he insists that a disjunction of two members should
be understood as equivalent to a statement that the negation of
either entails the other, he recognizes that this interpretation
cannot be extended to disjunctions of more than two members.
As he puts it, the true proposition *Aut est calidum aut frigidum aut
tepidum* cannot properly be supposed equivalent to the proposition
*Aut est vera haec disiuncta 'Est calidum aut frigidum' aut est tepidum,*
nor yet to the proposition *Aut est calidum aut vera est illa disiuncta
'Est frigidum aut tepidum'*, since these latter are obviously both false,
if we interpret *aut* both inside and outside the quotation by
reference to necessary connexion. The only escape from the difficulty is to allow a weaker sense of disjunction, and this Abelard
does, saying that it is to be found already in the use of *aut* or *vel*
to make complex predicates for categorical propositions. According to his new interpretation the original disjunction of three
members is equivalent to the proposition *Si non est calidum est
frigidum vel tepidum* (where *vel* has this weak sense) and, of course,
to the other two propositions which may be made in the same
pattern by permutation of the three terms.[1] It is a mark of
Abelard's acuteness that he noticed this difficulty and tried to
resolve it in a promising fashion. For a full solution of the puzzle
it is sufficient to add the remark that the weak sense of disjunction
which Abelard finds only in certain complex predicates may be
taken as fundamental, since the strong modal sense can always
be conveyed by the prefixing of the phrase 'it is necessary that'
to operate *de sensu* of the whole weak disjunction.

According to Abelard, temporal and disjunctive proposition
can be converted by simple rearrangement of their clauses, but
conditional propositions only by contraposition in accordance
with the rule: 'Si aliquid antecedit ut aliud consequatur, si id
quod consequitur non fuerit, nec illud quidem quod antecedit
erit.' Apparently some logicians objected to use of the word
'conversion' in this connexion, and Abelard therefore thinks it
necessary to collect such scraps of authority as he can find for his
extended usage.[2] The point is interesting only because it shows
once more that there had been detailed debates in the logic
schools before Abelard's time.

The last tract, *De Divisionibus et Definitionibus*, contains little of
importance for the development of logic though much that is interesting for the general history of philosophy. Roscellin is said
here to have maintained the *insana sententia* that nothing can

---

[1] *Dialectica,* pp. 492–3.          [2] Ibid., p. 496.

consist of parts since every part is naturally prior to its whole and a whole which just was its parts would therefore have to be prior to itself. Apparently this paradoxical contention may have had something to do with the controversy about universals; For Abelard says of Roscellin in this connexion: 'Sicut solis vocibus species, ita et partes adscribebat.'[1] Immediately after this passage comes a notice of the doctrine of the *anima mundi* and a statement of the reasons for which Abelard at the time of writing thought it inconsistent with the Catholic faith.

### 3. *The Logic of the Universities*

It is conceivable that in some medieval manuscript there may still survive a work of William of Champeaux or some other predecessor of Abelard, but it seems unlikely that anything we can hope to discover will alter very much the general outline of our picture of the development of logic before Abelard or lead us to revise our estimate of his importance. When we turn to consider the later history of medieval logic, we find a very different situation. After centuries of neglect or contempt (e.g. by Prantl in the third and fourth volumes of his *Geschichte der Logik*) those achievements of medieval logicians which are accessible in printed books from the end of the fifteenth or the beginning of the sixteenth century have been reconsidered in the light of discoveries by modern logicians, and works which were once condemned as tedious and trifling are now praised as brilliant anticipations of recent innovations. Such sudden revaluation leads almost inevitably to exaggeration and loss of perspective. Thus authors of the fourteenth century have received credit for observations which were made first by Abelard 200 years before, and phrases which come from Boethius or from some Arabic commentator on Aristotle have sometimes been quoted as though they were gems of medieval Christian wisdom. But in literary history, as contrasted with archaeology, the forays of enthusiasts do not destroy the evidence. On the contrary, they may provide the stimulus to research by which their own errors can be corrected. And so it has proved in this case. For it is now established that apart from the printed texts there exist scores of manuscript treatises on logic from the twelfth and later centuries. Until these have all been edited, or at least analysed and described, by experts in medieval studies, there can be no hope of determining correctly the various strata of the great deposit.[2] In this section, therefore,

---

[1] *Dialectica*, p. 555.
[2] M. Grabmann gave some information about eleven early treatises in his article 'Bearbeitungen und Auslegungen der Aristotelischen Logik aus der Zeit von

we shall not try to give more than a rough sketch of the history of logic in the high Middle Ages with references to some of the more famous persons who wrote about it then. But in order to give some indication of the great wealth of material which needs to be sifted we shall try to collect in the following sections information about two of the more interesting novelties which appeared in the exposition of logic during the period of about 250 years from the death of Abelard.

Soon after the middle of the twelfth century the whole of the *Organon* was in circulation, either in the old version of Boethius or in newly made translations, and within the next half century most of the rest of Aristotle's writings became available in Latin. Some translations were made at this time in Spain from Arabic versions and some in Italy by scholars who were in touch with Byzantine learning. That translations were made at this time in either way is to be explained by the intellectual awakening of the western world, rather than by any historical accident; for men who had heard of the learning of the Arabs made long journeys to find what they wanted. In 1126, for example, Adelard of Bath brought to the West the trigonometrical tables of al-Khowara-zmi, whose name, in the form 'algorism', was later used to mean 'reckoning' much as 'Euclid' was used to mean 'geometry'. Those parts of Aristotle's *Organon* which now came into the schools for the first time, either in new translations or in the versions of Boethius, namely all except the *Categories* and the *Peri Hermeneias*, were known for long after as the *ars nova*. Henceforward the standard logical works for study at Paris, Oxford, and the other universities were the *Organon*, Porphyry's *Eisagoge*, Boethius' *De Divisionibus* and *De Differentiis Topicis*, and the *Liber de Sex Principiis* of Gilbert de la Porrée. The last named was a treatise, composed about the middle of the twelfth century, which supplemented Aristotle's *Categories* by dealing with those heads that Aristotle had not discussed in detail.

The first medieval work which takes account of the whole *Organon* is the *Metalogicon* of John of Salisbury, written in 1159. This professes to be a defence of logic (conceived as *loquendi vel disserendi ratio*) against the attacks of an ignorant critic, but its chief value is in the information it gives us about the state of learning in the twelfth century. In 1136, when he was still a boy, John studied logic at Paris, and was much impressed by the

Peter Abaelardb is Petrus Hispanus', *Abhandlungen der Preußischen Akademie der Wissenschaften*, 1937, Nr. 5. But L. Minio-Paluello has collected photographic copies of many more works of this period, and has begun the publication of a series of texts and studies under the general title *Twelfth Century Logic* (Rome, 1956–).

brilliance of the masters whose lectures he attended. Abelard had then returned for a time to teaching, but there were others too who delighted in dialectic. When he went back twelve years later, John found many of them still debating the same questions as though they had learned nothing but had unlearned moderation. 'And thus', he wrote, 'experience taught me a manifest conclusion, that, whereas dialectic furthers other studies, so, if it remains by itself, it remains bloodless and barren, nor does it quicken the soul to yield fruit of philosophy, except the same conceive elsewhere.'[1]

When this was written, Aristotle's *Physics* and *Metaphysics* had not yet been incorporated into the university curriculum, as they were half a century later, and the philosophical instruction may well have seemed thin. But during the next 200 years the enthusiasm of the dialecticians led to a remarkable development of philosophy. We shall not try to decide here whether the result justified the great intellectual effort that produced it. Perhaps the systems of St. Thomas Aquinas and John Duns the Scot deserve only the reluctant admiration we give to the pyramids of Egypt and the palace of Versailles. And it may be that the thousands of young men who wrestled with subtle abstractions at the medieval universities would have been better employed in the literary studies which were then thought fit only for grammar schools. On the other hand, it is arguable that the exercises of the medieval universities prepared the way for modern science by sharpening men's wits and leading them to think about the methods of acquiring knowledge. For it is certainly a mistake to suppose that all the philosophers of the Middle Ages believed in systems of deductive metaphysics, and that experimental science began quite suddenly when Galileo or some other Renaissance worthy made an observation for the purpose of refuting a generalization of Aristotle or Galen, just as it is wrong to suppose that Luther was the first to suggest reform of the Church.

When the works of Aristotle and his Arabian commentators had been translated into Latin, the philosophers of the West set themselves to digest and assimilate the new material, producing for the purpose not only commentaries but *tractatus* on special subjects and *summulae*, or systematic compendia, of their own. In formal logic the work of Aristotle which made the biggest impression on logicians of the twelfth century was not, as we might perhaps expect, the *Prior Analytics*, but the *De Sophisticis Elenchis*. The reason was that this latter work filled a gap in their collection of texts. They already knew about topics and syllogisms from what

---

[1] *Metalogicon*, ii. 10 (ed. Migne 869B).

they read in Boethius' own writings, but they had not hitherto been able to read a text on sophisms and what they found here was much to their taste. In syllogistic theory they had to struggle with the doctrine of modal syllogisms, which was new and difficult, but it seemed at first that there was little, if anything, they could add here to what Aristotle had said. On the other hand, just as in Abelard's time the theory of topics, being less perfect than that of syllogisms, gave scope for innovations, so now sophistic, or the study of sophisms, incited philosophers to exercise their ingenuity in making and solving new puzzles. Even before the spread of the *ars nova* this interest appears in the *Ars Disserendi* which was written in 1132 by the Englishman Adam of Balsham (also called Parvipontanus because he lectured at the Petit Pont in Paris). According to this author, who deliberately avoided traditional terminology and prided himself on his originality, one of our main aims in studying logic is to gain a mastery of language so that we cannot be deceived by sophisms.[1] Such an enterprise naturally involves examination of the various ways in which sophisms may arise, and so leads men to spend much time and effort in elucidating the subtleties of ordinary usage. One very interesting paradox which Adam of Balsham notices incidentally is that of the possibility of a set of things having a proper sub-set equal in size to itself.[2] In later times, when the appetite had been stimulated by reading of Aristotle's *De Sophisticis Elenchis*, the liking for sophisms became so great that they were introduced in all sorts of contexts. Walter Burleigh, for example, who wrote his *De Puritate Artis Logicae Tractatus Longior* in the fourteenth century, peppers them so freely over the latter part of his work that in some sections they occupy more than half the space. There were even collections of *aurea sophismata* for teaching purposes. But piquant flavours are apt to pall, and in the end what had seemed fascinating came to seem stupid and tedious. To men of the Renaissance sophistical logic-chopping was perhaps the most contemptible part of medieval education.

Among *sophismata* a group which attracted special attention were variants of the Liar paradox, then called *insolubilia*. Adam of Balsham mentions as something well known the puzzle of the man *qui se mentiri dicit*,[3] and later many treatises were written

---

[1] See L. Minio Paluello, 'The *Ars Disserendi* of Adam of Balsham, Parvipontanus', *Mediaeval and Renaissance Studies*, iii (1954), pp. 116–69, and also his *Twelfth Century Logic*, i (1956), where the text is printed in full for the first time. Adam is mentioned by John of Salisbury in his *Metalogicon*, ii. 10.

[2] *Ars Disserendi*, ed. L. Minio Paluello, p. 92. See I. Thomas, 'A Twelfth Century Paradox of the Infinite', *Journal of Symbolic Logic*, xxiii (1958), pp. 133–4.

[3] *Ars Disserendi*, ed. L. Minio Paluello, p. 107.

about this, but so far little work has been done on the surviving
texts, and we cannot even say yet when or how the study of *insolubilia* began. The Liar paradox is not formulated in the works
of Aristotle; and although a passage in his *De Sophisticis Elenchis*,
where he speaks of 'the story about the same man's lying and
telling the truth at one and the same time', may perhaps refer to
this puzzle, it is not enough to enable anyone to reconstruct the
puzzle without a good deal of fresh ingenuity.[1] St. Paul does indeed
refer to the Epimenides version, but apparently without realizing
that it is a paradox; for he writes 'One of themselves . . . said
"The Cretans are always liars . . ." This witness is true'.[2] It may
be, therefore, that the paradox was discovered afresh in the twelfth
century. In any case medieval logicians were not satisfied with
simple versions such as *Ego dico falsum*, but invented complicated
variants like 'Socrates says "What Plato says is false", and Plato
says "What Socrates says is true", and neither says anything else.
Is what Socrates says true or false?' It was realized that the trouble
arose from the attempt to produce a certain sort of self-reference,
and an *insolubile* was defined as a 'propositio habens super se
reflexionem suae falsitatis aut se non esse veram totaliter vel
partialiter illativa.'[3] But there was no single agreed doctrine
about the bearing of such paradoxes on the theory of meaning
and truth. On the contrary, various medieval logicians suggested
various ways of dealing with the trouble. In an anonymous
manuscript from the beginning of the fourteenth century it is
said:

'Est autem triplex oppositio circa insolubilia, scilicet: cassatio, restrictio, solutio secundum quid et simpliciter. . . . Cassantes autem
dicunt quod dicens se dicere falsum nihil dicit. . . . Restringentes dicunt
quod littera *falsum* non potest supponere pro hac oratione cuius est
pars, nec similiter pars pro toto.'[4]

*Cassatio*, or the doctrine of nullity, seems to be the correct view,
though given here (i.e. in the printed excerpt) without reasons.
*Restrictio*, which is phrased in the language of the theory of *suppositio terminorum*, seems on the other hand to be too restrictive,
since it wrongly excludes harmless self-reference such as that of
the sentence 'What I am now saying is a sentence of English'.

---

[1] *De Sophisticis Elenchis*, 25 (180ᵇ2–7).      [2] *Epistle to Titus*, i. 12–13.
[3] Paul of Venice, *Logica Magna*, p. 194v.ʙ; quoted in part by Prantl, *Geschichte
der Logik*, iv, p. 139.
[4] *Bibliothèque Nationale, Cod. Lat.* 16617, formerly *Codex Sorbonnensis* 1797; quoted
in Prantl's *Geschichte der Logik*, iv, p. 41. M. Grabmann thinks this treatise may be
by William of Shyreswood, in which case it was probably composed before the
middle of the thirteenth century. The word *littera* in Prantl's excerpt is presumably
a quotation mark like the common medieval *li* or *ly*.

The third view is an unsatisfactory suggestion extracted from the passage of Aristotle mentioned above. At the beginning of the fifteenth century the voluminous writer Paul of Venice listed fifteen different attempts which had been made to solve the puzzle, some of them not impressive and others mere variants of well-known suggestions such as that of Aristotle. Of the fifteen, ten could not be traced by Prantl to their authors; and of these ten, one (fifth in Paul's list) seems to be the theory of cassation mentioned above, while another (eighth in Paul's list) is the similar suggestion 'that no *insolubile* is true or false, because nothing of this kind is a proposition'.[1] Since Prantl was at least a very industrious compiler of references, it may be that what he could not find will never be found. On the other hand, there may be a detailed discussion of cassation still waiting to be edited. In the present state of medieval studies it is impossible to say for certain what remains of medieval logic and what has been lost.

When Aristotle's non-logical works were translated, they were at first suspect because they came into circulation with the pantheistic interpretation of the Arabic philosopher Averroës (Ibn Roshd, 1126-98), who lived and worked in Spain. But in the course of the thirteenth century they were freed from suspicion and reconciled with Christianity by Albert the Great (1193-1280) and St. Thomas Aquinas (1225-74). In the controversies of this period the doctrine of Aristotle's *De Anima* about the intellectual soul was of central importance, and attention was therefore directed to Aristotle's assertion that the soul becomes aware of things by receiving their forms (*species*) into itself. This account of mental life was very naturally taken to be an elaboration of the familiar teaching of the first chapter of the *De Interpretatione*, where it is said that the soul has states or modifications which are in some sense copies of external things; and so the old theory of three kinds of discourse, written, spoken, and mental, received new life. Thought, it was generally held, proceeds by means of *propositiones mentales* formed from natural signs in the soul, and here again Arabic influence was important in the detailed elaboration of the theory. In the Arabic of Avicenna (Ibn Sina, 979-1037) a form in the soul was identified with a *ma'na*, i.e. a meaning or notion, and when Avicenna's works were translated into Latin, *ma'na* was rendered in all contexts by *intentio*, which thus came to have in medieval epistemology the technical sense of 'natural sign in the soul'. Furthermore, as Porphyry had distinguished between words of first and second imposition, so Avicenna

---

[1] *Logica Magna*, p. 192r.B,e.s; quoted in Prantl's *Geschichte der Logik*, iv, pp. 138-9.

distinguished between natural signs of first and second understanding, saying that the latter were abstract notions, such as those
of *genus* and *species*, which men applied to the former. Logic, he
held, was concerned only with *ma'ani* of second understanding,
as these were used in reasoning from the known to the unknown:

'Subiectum vero logicae, sicut scisti, sunt intentiones intellectae
secundo, quae apponuntur intentionibus primo intellectis, secundum
quod per eas pervenitur de cognito ad incognitum, non in quantum
ipsae sunt intellectae et habent esse intelligibile, quod esse nullo modo
pendet ex materia, vel pendet ex materia sed non corporea.'[1]

This is the origin of that discussion of first and second intentions
which continued until the end of medieval logic. The distinction
is essentially a development of the old theory of three kinds of
discourse, which was never far from the thoughts of medieval
logicians and should always be remembered as an assumption
underlying their description of logic as a *scientia sermocinalis*.
Avicenna himself spoke of forms-in-thought as having logical
features which they could not possess as forms-by-themselves nor
yet as forms-in-individuals:

'In eis autem quae sunt extra non est essentialitas nec accidentalitas
omnino, nec est aliquod complexum nec incomplexum nec propositio
nec argumentatio nec cetera huiusmodi. Cum autem volumus con-
siderare ad hoc ut sciamus eas, necesse est eas colligere in intellectu,
et tunc necessario accident illis dispositiones quae sunt propriae tantum
intellectui.'[2]

In later times the analogy between thought and language was
sometimes taken so seriously that mental propositions were
thought to have a grammar like that of spoken or written propositions. Pierre d'Ailly (1350–1425), for example, says that mental
terms in the proper sense of that phrase can be distinguished as
nouns and verbs, and that the nouns among them have cases:

'Terminorum mentalium proprie dictorum aliqui naturaliter
significant nominaliter et tales naturaliter sunt nomina, aliqui naturaliter significant verbaliter et tales sunt naturaliter verba, et sic de aliis
partibus orationis. . . . Item aliquis naturaliter est nominativi casus,
alter genitivi, et sic de aliis.'[3]

Each of the mental terms of which he speaks here is supposed to
be a *conceptus naturaliter significans aliquid vel aliqua*, and it is called a

---

[1] *Avicennae Opera*, ed. Venice, 1508, *Philosophia Prima*, i. 2, p. 70*v*.A; quoted by
Prantl, *Geschichte der Logik*, ii, p. 328, but with omission of *non* before *in quantum*.
[2] *Avicennae Opera*, ed. Venice, 1508, *Logica*, p. 2r.B; quoted by Prantl, *Geschichte
der Logik*, ii, p. 328.
[3] *Conceptus*, quoted by Prantl, *Geschichte der Logik*, iv, p. 109. This is *not* the same
as the Stoic assignment of cases to parts of λεκτά.

mental term *proprie dictus* in order to distinguish it from the image
of a spoken or written word. Such an image may be described as
a natural sign of the word of which it is an image, but just because
it is a copy of the word it can also be described as a conventional
sign of that which is conventionally signified by the word:

'Terminus mentalis improprie dictus est conceptus vocis vel scriptu-
rae . . . et, licet significet naturaliter proprie vocem vel scripturam,
cuius est naturalis similitudo, potest tamen cum hoc significare ad
placitum et subordinari alteri conceptui . . . v. gr. conceptus huius
vocis *homo* naturaliter proprie significat illam vocem *homo*, sed, ad
placitum significat omnes homines et sic subordinatur in significatione
illi conceptui qui naturaliter est repraesentativus omnium hominum.'[1]

Pierre d'Ailly declares further that the adjectives 'true' and 'false'
are applicable in their basic sense to mental propositions properly so called; but this was not universally accepted. For some
of his contemporaries followed Gregory of Rimini (died 1358)
in holding that truth and falsity belonged properly to propositional
contents, which they called *complexe significabilia*.[2] Thus questions
raised by Abelard were still under discussion 300 years later.
If John of Salisbury had lived through ten generations instead
of two, he would have found that the subjects of debate among
logicians were still recognizably the same as they had been in
his youth.

Among manuals of logic written after the spread of the *ars nova*
the oldest which has been printed so far is the *Introductiones in
Logicam* or *Summulae* of William of Shyreswood.[3] This little work,
which comprises only seventy-five pages in the modern printed
text, was composed by an Englishman in the first half of the
thirteenth century and probably at Paris. It is divided into six
parts which deal respectively with propositions, predicables, syllogisms, dialectical topics, *proprietates terminorum*, and fallacies.

In the part on propositions it is said that for the truth of a conjunctive proposition (*copulativa*) it is necessary that both of its
parts should be true, while for the truth of a disjunctive proposition it is enough that one of its parts should be true and for the
truth of a conditional proposition *quod cum sit antecedens sit consequens*. The relations of the quantifiers, *omnis*, *quidam*, and *nullus*,
and the ways in which they can be combined with *non* are also

---

[1] Ibid.
[2] For details see Paul of Venice, *Logica Magna*, i. 10 (*De Significato Propositionis*),
pp. 162r.A–167v.B.
[3] Edited by M. Grabmann in *Sitzungsberichte der Bayerischen Akademie, Phil.-Hist.
Abteilung*, 1937, Heft 10. His introduction contains information about the author
and the manuscript (*Bibliothèque Nationale, Cod. Lat.* 16617, formerly *Codex Sorbonnensis* 1797).

discussed here, and the results of the discussion are summarized in the mnemonic verses:

> Aequivalent *omnis, nullus-non, non-aliquis-non.*
> *Nullus, non-aliquis, omnis-non* aequiparantur.
> *Quidam, non-nullus, non-omnis-non* sociantur.
> *Quidam-non, non-nullus-non, non-omnis* adhaerent.[1]

When he comes to write of modality the author follows Abelard in distinguishing between propositions which ascribe *modi* (necessity, possibility, or impossibility) to *dicta* and propositions which ascribe characters modally (i.e. in a qualified way) to subjects other than *dicta*. But he goes on to say that a proposition which is of the first kind *secundum constructionem* (and so not modal in the strict sense, but rather *de modo*) may be regarded nevertheless in certain contexts as modal *secundum rem*, e.g. in the context of syllogistic reasoning when it is accounted universal or particular in respect of a subject other than a *dictum*.

In the part on the doctrine of the predicables there appears the scheme of division commonly called Porphyry's tree, that is to say, a table in which we can descend by dichotomous division at each stage from *substantia* through *corpus, corpus animatum, animal, animal rationale* to *animal rationale mortale*, or *homo*, which represents the *species infima* containing Socrates, Plato, and other individual men. This was suggested by a passage of Porphyry's *Eisagoge*,[2] and it was presumably used in exposition of Boethius's commentary. In the edition of Boethius's works which was printed at Basle in 1570 there is a tree which has at the bottom not only *Plato* as the name of an individual man but also, rather inappropriately, *Brunellus* as the name of an individual ass.

In the part on syllogisms the famous mnemonic verses *Barbara celarent* make their first appearance, and in the form:

> Barbara celarent darii ferio baralipton
> Celantes dabitis fapesmo frisesomorum;
> Cesare campestres festino baroco; darapti
> Felapton disamis datisi bocardo ferison.

Here each word is to be taken as the formula of a valid mood and interpreted according to the following rules: the first three vowels indicate the quantity and quality of the three propositions which go to make a syllogism, *a* standing for the universal affirmative, *e* for the universal negative, *i* for the particular affirmative, and *o* for the particular negative; the initial consonant of each formula

---

[1] In the third and fourth lines of Grabmann's printed text, p. 39, *ullus* appears instead of *nullus*.

[2] *Commentaria in Aristotelem Graeca*, iv(i), ed. A. Busse, p. 4, ll. 21–25.

after the first four indicates that the mood is to be reduced to that mood among the first four which has the same initial; *s* appearing immediately after a vowel indicates that the corresponding proposition is to be converted simply during reduction, while *p* in the same position indicates that the proposition is to be converted partially or *per accidens*, and *m* between the first two vowels of a formula indicates that the premisses are to be transposed; *c* appearing after one of the first two vowels indicates that the corresponding premiss is to be replaced by the negative of the conclusion for the purpose of a reduction *per impossibile*. The verses, as given here, have the defect that the division of lines does not correspond exactly to the division of figures, and many later authors have exercised their ingenuity in suggesting improvements. In spite of his interest in modality and his acquaintance with the *Prior Analytics* William makes no attempt to deal with modal syllogisms.

Topics are discussed according to the customary divisions and maxims are stated in the usual style, but there is no mention of *consequentiae* as in Abelard's work. Application of a maxim to a case is always supposed to produce an argument of some such form as: 'Socrates est homo, ergo Socrates est animal.' And when the argument is thought to require a supplementary premiss, this is supplied in such a form as to make possible a categorical syllogism.

In the part *De Proprietatibus Terminorum* we have a medieval novelty which must be reserved for separate consideration, and in the part *De Fallaciis* we have the Aristotelian account of sophisms presented with new examples which show the lively interest excited by this subject. For an illustration of equivocation we have the entertaining syllogism: 'Quicumque sunt episcopi sunt sacerdotes; isti asini sunt episcopi; ergo isti asini sunt sacerdotes.' Asses, and Brunellus in particular, were always a favourite subject with medieval logicians.

In the manuscript which contains the only known medieval text of the *Introductiones* there are also some other logical works which have been thought to be by William of Shyreswood, namely tracts on *syncategoremata*, *insolubilia*, and *obligationes*, all subjects on which there exist numerous separate writings by medieval authors. *Syncategoremata* are words such as 'and', 'or', 'not', 'if', 'every', 'some', 'only', and 'except' which cannot function as terms but are of special importance in logic because they show the forms of statements. We have already noticed a passage in the *Introductiones* where William of Shyreswood considers the results of combining quantifiers with the sign of negation. The fact that medieval logicians found it worth while to write separate treatises about such words shows that they appreciated their importance for formal logic. But it is probably a mistake to suppose that these signs were universally recognized as formal in a very strict sense. For the words *incipit* and *desinit* (meaning 'begins' and 'stops') were sometimes included among *dictiones syncategorematicae*, although they are concerned with temporal distinctions.[1] *Insolubilia* have been noticed already. The treatise thought to be by William is that which contains an account of the three views, *cassatio*, *restrictio*, and *solutio secundum quid et simpliciter*. *Obligationes* are obligations assumed by a party to a disputation, or conditions within which such a discussion must be conducted. The logicians of the period considered in detail what was involved in making this or that concession for the purposes of argument, e.g. that a certain proposition was doubtful, and insisted on maintaining consistency between the principles assumed during any discussion. Little, if any, modern work has been devoted so far to the investigation of this part of medieval logic, but it may perhaps be compared with Aristotle's treatment of debate in his *Topics* and *De Sophisticis Elenchis*.

William of Shyreswood seems to have had a fair measure of success in his own time, and in 1267 Roger Bacon, writing of him as though he were still alive, said that he was a better philosopher than Albert the Great. Although this judgement may perhaps be inspired by prejudice, since Roger was a Franciscan and Albert a Dominican, we must agree that William was a good logician. But a few years later Peter of Spain, who became Pope John XXI and died in 1277, wrote a manual called *Summulae Logicales* which had much more influence on later thought. This work came to be accepted as the standard textbook of logic through all the later Middle Ages and was still in use as late as the beginning of the seventeenth century, by which time there had been no less than 166 printed editions.[2] Its greater success may be due to the fact that it contains more and better mnemonic verses than William of Shyreswood's work. In the fifteenth century it was even translated into Greek, verses and all, with the curious result that Prantl writing 400 years later supposed the translation to be a Byzantine original and elaborated a wholly gratuitous theory about the influence of the East on the West in the thirteenth century.[3] The *Summulae* consists of twelve tracts, six about Aristotle's themes

[1] Walter Burleigh, *De Puritate Artis Logicae Tractatus Longior*, ed. Ph. Boehner, *Franciscan Institute Publications*, No. 9 (1955), p. 191.
[2] J. P. Mullaly, *The Summulae Logicales of Peter of Spain*, Publications in Mediaeval *Studies*, viii (1945), pp. 133–58.
[3] *Geschichte de Logik*, iii, p. 33.

(propositions, predicables, categories, syllogisms, topics, and fallacies) and six about specifically medieval themes (supposition, relatives, ampliation, appellation, restriction, and distribution). In some editions the latter are grouped together under the title *De Terminorum Proprietatibus* or *Parva Logicalia*. In general the treatment is very similar to that of William of Shyreswood, from which it may have been derived. Aristotle's *Posterior Analytics* are ignored, and the system is purely formal in the sense that it contains no epistemological considerations about demonstration as Aristotle understood it. But there are some interesting differences between the two manuals. Peter, like Abelard, understands conditional statements as assertions of necessary connexion : for the truth of a conditional, he says, it is required *quod antecedens non possit esse verum sine consequente*, and so *omnis conditionalis vera est necessaria*.[1] On the other hand, he does not, like William, follow Abelard in the theory of modal propositions.

Another interesting logician of the same generation was Robert Kilwardby, a Dominican who became Archbishop of Canterbury. He did not produce an influential manual, but what has so far been published of his commentary on the *Prior Analytics* shows that he was an acute thinker. In particular he gives the first known proof of a principle of conversion by means of a syllogism with two terms. In order to defend Aristotle's treatment of conversion against a charge of circularity, which had been brought against it already in antiquity, he first explains Aristotle's use of ecthesis and then goes on:

'Alio modo potest idem declarari per syllogismum in quarto primae et per hoc primum principium *Non de eodem simul vera est affirmatio et negatio* sic. Si nullum B est A et aliquid A est B ex hypothesi, ergo aliquid A non est A, quod est contra primum principium. Hypothesis ergo non potest stare cum prima, quia ex positione eius sequitur maximum inconveniens, ut negatio eiusdem a se.'[2]

Possibly this way of reasoning was suggested by the juxtaposition in Aristotle's own argument of the two propositions which here serve as premisses for a syllogistic *reductio ad impossibile*. But once the possibility of such reasoning had been recognized, it was not difficult to see that a principle of conversion could be proved directly in a syllogism which had for one of its premisses the familiar principle of identity. Writing later in the same century, Albert the Great tells us that some logicians of his time tried to justify

---

[1] *Summulae Logicales*, ed. I. M. Bochenski, §1. 23.
[2] I. Thomas, 'Kilwardby on Conversion', *Dominican Studies*, vi (1953), pp. 56–76.

conversion as an enthymeme, or abbreviated syllogism, and says of the first case discussed by Aristotle:

'Efficitur syllogismus per additionem minoris propositionis sic: *Nullum B A; omne A A; ergo nullum A B* . . . . et est iste syllogismus primus secundae figurae . . . . Similiter est de enthymemate quod est conversio universalis affirmativae, . . . et fit syllogismus primus tertiae figurae per additionem maioris sic; *Omne B A; omne B B; ergo aliquid A B.*'[1]

Albert himself did not approve of this procedure, because he thought it circular. Conversion, he said, was supposed to be perfected by syllogisms in the second and third figures, and yet these syllogisms had to be perfected by reduction to the first figure through the device of conversion. As we have seen, conversion is not in fact necessary for reduction of second- or third-figure syllogisms to the first figure, since Aristotle himself showed that such reduction could always be achieved by the indirect method. But it is necessary for the execution of Aristotle's full programme of reducing every syllogism to *Barbara* or *Celarent*.

Views about modality like those of Abelard and William of Shyreswood can be found again in Albert the Great's commentary on the *Prior Analytics* and in the works of St. Thomas Aquinas. Since the latter has come to be regarded by many as the chief Christian philosopher, whose works are second in importance only to the Bible, it is interesting to notice his treatment of this question of formal logic and the use which he later made of his results in theology. In his little tract *De Modalibus*[2] St. Thomas says that modal propositions may be either *de dicto* or *de re*. By a modal proposition *de dicto* he means, of course, a second-order statement such as we may express in the form 'It is possible that Socrates is running', and it seems likely that he got the terminology from William of Shyreswood or Peter of Spain. Unfortunately medieval philosophers rarely acknowledge borrowings from men of their own age, though they gladly cite Aristotle and the fathers of the church in support of their opinions. By a modal proposition *de re*, on the other hand, St. Thomas understands one in which the modal sign is essentially internal. This sign may be an adverb, as in 'Socrates is possibly running', but in Latin at least it may also be a predicative phrase displaced towards the middle, as in *Socratem possibile est currere*. Unlike

---

[1] Albertus Magnus, *Liber I Priorum Analyticorum, Tractatus I*, cap. viii (*Opera*, ed. Borgnet, i, p. 470).

[2] Edited by I. M. Bochenski in 'Sancti Thomae Aquinatis de Modalibus Opusculum et Doctrina', *Angelicum*, xvii (1940), pp. 180–218. The tract is not universally admitted to be a work of St. Thomas.

Abelard and William of Shyreswood, St. Thomas does not suggest that either of the forms he distinguishes is more properly modal than the other, but he follows William in pointing out that a modal proposition *de dicto* is always singular, since it has a *dictum* for its subject, whereas a modal proposition *de re* may be universal or particular according to the sign of quantity.

The examples by which St. Thomas illustrates his distinction in the tract *De Modalibus* are not very illuminating, but there is more to be learnt about it from a passage of his *Summa Contra Gentiles* where he uses it to dispose of an objection against God's knowledge of future contingents:

'Si unumquodque a Deo cognoscitur sicut praesentialiter visum, sic necessarium erit esse quod Deus cognoscit, sicut necessarium est Socratem sedere ex hoc quod sedere videtur. Hoc autem non necessarium est absolute, vel, ut a quibusdam dicitur, necessitate consequentis, sed sub conditione, vel necessitate consequentiae. Haec enim conditionalis est necessaria: *Si videtur sedere, sedet.* Unde et, si conditionalis in categoricam transferatur ut dicatur *Quod videtur sedere necesse est sedere*, patet eam de dicto intellectam et compositam esse veram, de re vero et divisam esse falsam. Et sic in his et in omnibus similibus quae Dei scientiam circa contingentia oppugnantes argumentantur secundum compositionem et divisionem falluntur.'[1]

The general sense of this passage is clear. If God has foreknowledge of a proposition about the future, that proposition is necessary in relation to the fact of its being foreknown, but not therefore absolutely or unconditionally necessary. For when a predicate belongs to a subject with unconditional necessity, the fact that it can be said to belong to the subject necessarily does not depend on the way in which the subject is described, e.g. as a person of whom God foreknew that he would be seated at a certain time. And only then can the modal statement be said to be *de re*. Any statement of necessity which is true when understood *de re* will also, it seems, be true when understood *de dicto*, but the converse does not hold. The point St. Thomas makes here is a good reply to the objection he has proposed for consideration, but we may well doubt whether any character (other than a triviality such as being-square-or-not-square) could ever belong to anything with a necessity which was altogether unconditional, if this last phrase is supposed to mean 'independent of every other character or set of characters by which the thing in question might be identified'. We shall have occasion to return to this question in a later chapter when we discuss the development of modal

---

[1] *Summa Contra Gentiles*, i. 67. Cf. also his *De Veritate*, qu. 2, art. 12, ad 4.

logic during the twentieth century. It is interesting, however, to notice that while explaining his distinction St. Thomas uses the word *consequentia* in the same way as Abelard.

The problem of future contingents and divine foreknowledge which St. Thomas discussed in the passage we have quoted from his *Summa Contra Gentiles*, involves not only the theory of modality but also those questions about truth and the principle of excluded middle which exercised Aristotle when he wrote the famous chapter in his *De Interpretatione* about the naval battle. It is therefore not surprising that this problem was the subject of a great deal of discussion among medieval logicians. During the period of intense philosophical activity which lasted for about a century after the death of St. Thomas all the great schoolmen contributed opinions on the question at issue. But it can scarcely be said that the debate produced any new light on the puzzles that worried Aristotle, since it proceeded in accordance with his assumption that we can talk sensibly about a proposition as true at a certain time. And it is a mistake to say, as one historian has done, that the idea of a three-valued logic was introduced by Ockham at this time. There were indeed some philosophers who accepted Aristotle's view according to which a proposition about the future is neither determinately true nor determinately false though the disjunction of the proposition and its negation is true. But Ockham was not one of the number; and the most he can be said to have contributed to the development of a three-valued logic is the working out of what Aristotle could say about the conditional propositions 'If God knows that A will happen, then A will happen' and 'If A will happen, then God knows that A will happen' on various suppositions about the truth, falsity, or indeterminateness of the antecedent and the consequent.[1]

In the same period discussions of divine omniscience led to differences of opinion on the question whether that which was once true must be true for all time. Writing just before the middle of the twelfth century, Peter Lombard asks in his *Sentences* (which became the chief theological textbook of the Middle Ages), 'An ea quae semel scit Deus vel praescit semper sciat et praesciat et semper scierit et praescierit', and he answers that what God

[1] The statement that Ockham had a three-valued logic was made by Michalski in 'Le problème de la volonté à Oxford et à Paris au XIVᵉ siècle', *Studia Philosophica*, ii (1937), p. 299. It has been examined carefully by Philotheus Boehner in *The Tractatus de Praedestinatione et de Praescientia Dei et de Futuris Contingentibus of William Ockham, Franciscan Institute Publications*, No. 2 (1945), pp. 58 ff. His discussion contains a useful summary of the views of the most distinguished medieval logicians on the problem raised by Aristotle in his *De Interpretatione*. See also L. Baudry, *La Querelle des futurs contingents (Louvain 1465–1475), Textes inédits* (Paris, 1950).

knows is true timelessly though in talking of it we have to use different tenses according to our different positions in time. The prophets foretold the birth of Christ, and that same truth which they announced in the future tense is now declared by Christians in the past tense:

'Nam quod futurum tunc erat nunc praeteritum est, ideoque verba commutanda sunt ad ipsum designandum, sicut diversis temporibus loquentes eandem diem modo per hoc adverbium *cras*, dum adhuc futura est, designamus, modo per *hodie*, dum praesens est, modo per *heri*, dum praeterita est.... Tempora enim, ut ait Augustinus, variata sunt et ideo verba mutata sunt, non fides.'[1]

This thesis was probably suggested by the doctrine of Augustine and Boethius that God, being not in time, knows all historical facts with equal immediacy, much as a human being may see things spread out before at one time in space,[2] but it seems to have been supported by grammatical considerations. According to John of Salisbury it was a received doctrine in the school of Bernard of Chartres, a contemporary of Abelard, that words such as *albus*, *album*, *albedo*, and *albet*, which differ only in grammatical terminations, all signify the same form,[3] and apparently it was concluded from this that the time said to be *consignificatum* by a verb was no part of that which was stated by a sentence and capable of truth or falsity. Later philosophers tell us in their commentaries on the *Sentences* that the upholders of this view were called *nominales*. Since Bernard of Chartres was a Platonist, it must not be supposed that this description applied to his followers had anything to do with nominalism, and in fact St. Bonaventura tells us: 'Dicti sunt nominales quia fundabant positionem suam super nominis unitatem.'[4]

Those who rejected the view of Peter Lombard did not, of course, wish to dispute the traditional doctrine of God's immutable omniscience, but rather to separate it from the thesis 'Quod semel est verum semper est verum'. St. Thomas, for example, writes:

'Antiqui nominales dixerunt idem esse enuntiabile Christum nasci et esse nasciturum et esse natum, quia eadem res significatur per haec tria, scilicet nativitas Christi, et secundum hoc sequitur quod Deus quidquid scivit sciat, quia modo scit Christum natum quod significat idem ei quod est Christum esse nasciturum. Sed haec opinio falsa est,

---

[1] *Sententiarum Lib. I*, dist. 41, cap. 3. The reference is to St. Augustine, *In Ioannis Evangelium*, xlv. 9.    [2] Cf. Boethius, *De Consolatione Philosophiae*, v. 6.
[3] *Metalogicon*, iii. 2.
[4] *In I Sent.*, dist. 41, a.2, q.2. The story has been reconstructed by M. D. Chenu in his article 'Grammaire et théologie aux XIIᵉ et XIIIᵉ siècles', *Archives d'histoire doctrinale et littéraire du moyen âge*, 1936, pp. 5–28, from which we have derived most of our references.

tum quia diversitas partium orationis diversitatem enuntiabilium causat, tum etiam quia sequeretur quod propositio quae semel est vera esset semper vera, quod est contra Philosophum, qui dicit quod haec oratio *Socrates sedet* vera est eo sedente et eadem falsa est eo surgente. Et ideo concedendum est quod haec non est vera, *Quidquid Deus scivit scit*, si ad enuntiabilia referatur. Sed ex hoc non sequitur quod scientia Dei sit variabilis. Sicut enim absque variatione divinae scientiae est quod sciat unam et eandem rem quandoque esse et quandoque non esse, ita absque variatione divinae scientiae est quod scit aliquod enuntiabile quandoque esse verum et quandoque esse falsum. Esset autem ex hoc scientia Dei variabilis, si enuntiabilia cognosceret per modum enuntiabilium, componendo et dividendo, sicut accidit in intellectu nostro.'[1]

As often happens in philosophy, the parties in this debate were at cross-purposes. For a settlement of their dispute it is necessary to keep in mind a distinction to which we drew attention in our account of Stoic logic, namely that between what men assert and what forms of words signify. What the *nominales* call true in the basic sense is what a speaker asserts or might assert by uttering a token indicative sentence, and they rightly observe that there is a usage according to which men may be said to assert one and the same thing at different times by uttering at those different times indicative sentences with different tenses. Thus after the birth of Christ a Christian may defend the truth of old prophecies by saying 'Christ has been born, as the prophets foretold'. It is somewhat strange, however, to say, as the *nominales* appear to do, that *Christus nasciturus est* and *Christus natus est* mean the same. For while tokens of the two type sentences may refer to the same event, it is clear that they do so in different ways and there is a well-established usage according to which speakers of the tokens can properly be said to make different assertions. When reporting what the prophets asserted we must still use a phrase such as 'that Christ would be born', rather than 'that Christ has been born'. On the other hand, St. Thomas and those who agree with him appear to hold that truth belongs in the basic sense to a type-sentence, or to something in an intellect which can be signified by such a sentence, and so they are naturally led on to say with Aristotle that what is true at one time may be false at another. St. Thomas's use of the word *enuntiabile* is obscure and uncertain, but it seems clear that he sometimes understands by it a form of words or other signs, since he speaks of *enuntiabilia in voce* or *in intellectu*,[2] and it is noteworthy that in the passage we have quoted he slips from talking of the truth of an *enuntiabile* to talking of the

[1] *Summa Theologica*, I. xiv. 15. Cf. also his *Quodlibetalia*, 4 (17).
[2] See especially *Summa Theologica*, I. xvi. 7.

truth of a *propositio* or *oratio*. Since, however, what God knows of history cannot be a form of words or even what is signified by such, St. Thomas finds himself compelled to say that what God knows is that certain *enuntiabilia* are true at certain times and false at others. In the context this obviously implies that the possession of truth by an *enuntiabile* at a time is itself an unchanging fact, and so we are led back to a position like that we outlined above in our criticism of the *nominales*. For to say that the phrase 'Christ will be born' was true in the time of the prophets is only to say in a roundabout way, by reference to a form of words, what the prophets themselves asserted directly, namely that Christ would be born after their time, and this is timelessly true, though we in talking of it as we have done must now use the construction 'would be born'.

Roger Bacon (1214–92) and Raymond Lull (1235–1315) stand apart from the general line of development, but they cannot be overlooked in any account of the logic of the period.

Roger Bacon is remembered chiefly as the forerunner of Francis Bacon in the advocacy of empirical method, and for this reason he has often been mentioned with honour in order that his contemporaries may be damned. It is true that his writings on the magnet and the rainbow made no great stir, and that he achieved nothing with the great work by which he hoped to interest the Pope in a plan for experimental research; but his interest in nature was not unique. The study of the *quadrivium* (arithmetic, geometry, astronomy, and music) and of Aristotle's *Physics*, however elementary and repetitive it may have been, kept alive the notion of science discovered by the Greeks, and there were some philosophers, especially among the English Franciscans, who tried to improve on what they inherited. Even before Bacon there was Robert Grosseteste, lecturer of the Franciscan school in Oxford about 1224 and later Bishop of Lincoln. The chief obstacle to steady scientific progress was not the influence of Aristotelian logic or anything else derived from Greece, but a lack of sustained curiosity about things which were not mentioned by ancient authors and did not appear to contribute in any way to salvation. It was easier to get the support of Pope and Emperor for an *inquisitio haereticae pravitatis* than for an *inquisitio naturae*.

Raymond Lull was a Catalan who turned from soldiering to religion and died while trying to convert the Moors in Africa. But his fame rests chiefly on his invention of a system for combining concepts in a mechanical fashion so as to exhaust all alternatives. He seems to have had the curious idea that this would help to confute the Mohammedans and spread the truth of the

Christian religion. Signs for the most important concepts in certain groups were to be set out round circles like the points of the compass, and various combinations were to be produced by the rotation of the circles about a common centre. His selection of fundamental concepts did not show great philosophical ability; and his method of combining them has not produced any results, either in the conversion of the Moors or in the advancement of science. But his system, which his followers called the *Ars Magna*, has nevertheless had some influence on the development of logic. It was never entirely forgotten during the Middle Ages, and in the seventeenth century it inspired various attempts to work out a philosophical language in which all complex ideas could be expressed by the combination of certain fundamental signs. In particular, it probably suggested to Leibniz, either directly or indirectly, his plan for a *characteristica universalis* based on the principles of an *ars combinatoria*.[1]

Among commentaries on the classical texts there is one of special interest called *In Universam Logicam Quaestiones*. It was formerly attributed to John Duns the Scot (1266–1308), and may be found in the first volume of the edition of his works published by Luke Wadding in 1639, together with another interesting treatise called *De Modis Significandi sive Grammatica Speculativa*. But the latter is now supposed to be by Thomas of Erfurt, who flourished in the first half of the fourteenth century, and the *Quaestiones* have been ascribed, rather quaintly, to a Pseudo-Scot. Even though he may not have been the *doctor subtilis* himself, this author was a very able logician, and his work is not a mere paraphrase of the ancient texts, but a series of discussions on questions suggested by Porphyry's *Eisagoge* and Aristotle's *Organon* (apart from the *Topics*). Some of the problems are remote from anything considered by ancient authors. Thus *quaestio* 4 on the first book of the *Prior Analytics* is whether every proposition is universal, particular, indefinite, or singular in quantity. The author points out correctly that the distinction cannot be applied to all hypothetical (i.e. complex) propositions, though the parts of these may be said to have quantity according to the ordinary scheme. This remark contrasts favourably with the muddled classification of judgements according to quality, quantity, relation, and modality which Kant took for granted in his *Critique of Pure Reason*.

In his *quaestiones* 25–33 and 36 on the first book of the *Prior Analytics* the Pseudo-Scot gives the most ingenious discussion of

---

[1] Some details of the *Ars Magna* may be found in Martin Gardner's *Logic Machines and Diagrams* together with further information about Lull's life.

modal logic so far discovered in a medieval text. He does not talk of modal propositions *de dicto* and *de re*, but like St. Thomas and Abelard before him he distinguishes a *sensus compositus* and a *sensus divisus*, and he uses this distinction for the elaboration of a new theory of conversion and syllogistic reasoning with modal propositions. In particular he tries to justify the disputed part of Aristotle's theory by maintaining in *quaestio* 28 that 'ex maiore de necessario in sensu diviso et minore de inesse valent modi primae figurae directe concludentes'. Furthermore, apart from the strictly logical modalities of necessity, possibility, contingency, and impossibility he considers others expressed by words such as *dubium*, *scitum*, *opinatum*, *apparens*, *volitum*, and *dilectum*; and he finds that some, but not all, of these are subject to rules like those holding for logical modalities.[1] Thus a proposition with the modal word *scitum* may be converted like one with *necessarium* and may be used in the same way as a premiss for syllogistic reasoning. Perhaps these were the complications which led medieval students of logic to say: *De modalibus non gustabit asinus*.

Some of the most striking passages of the work occur in *quaestio* 10 on the first book of the *Prior Analytics* and *quaestio* 3 on the second book. These deal with *consequentiae*, which were also the subject of many separate tracts by medieval logicians, and we shall reserve them for detailed consideration in a later section.

William Ockham (*c.* 1295–1349) has been mentioned already in connexion with the debate about future contingents. In our time his political writings against the claims of the papacy have been republished, and he is remembered as an influential nominalist, but his popular fame as a great logician rests chiefly on the maxim known as Ockham's razor: *Entia non sunt multiplicanda praeter necessitatem*. No doubt this represents correctly the general tendency of his philosophy, but it has not so far been found in any of his writings. His nearest pronouncement seems to be *Numquam ponenda est pluralitas sine necessitate*, which occurs in his theological work on the *Sentences* of Peter Lombard.[2] His most important contributions to logic were his *Expositio Aurea super Artem Veterem* and his *Summa Totius Logicae*. The latter was reprinted in Oxford as late as 1675 for use as a textbook, and it is noteworthy as being apparently the first attempt to present the whole of logic,

---

[1] Modalities in an extended sense were considered already by St. Anselm. See F. S. Schmidt, *Ein neues unvollendetes Werk des heiligen Anselms von Canterbury, Beiträge zur Geschichte der Philosophie des Mittelalters*, xxxiii. 3 (1936), and D. P. Henry, 'St. Anselm on the Varieties of "Doing"', *Theoria*, xix (1953), pp. 178–83.

[2] *Super Quattuor Libros Sententiarum* (ed. Lugd., 1495), i, dist. 27, qu. 2, K. In his *Summa Totius Logicae*, i. 12, Ockham cites the principle of economy, *Frustra fit per plura quod potest fieri per pauciora*.

including medieval novelties, in one systematic exposition. The work is divided into three books which deal respectively with terms, propositions, and arguments; and the third book is subdivided into four parts which deal with syllogism, demonstration, *consequentiae*, &c., and fallacies. There are things of interest to be found throughout the work, e.g. in the theory of modal syllogisms, which is more complicated even than that of the Pseudo-Scot, since it provides for arguments in which one premiss is taken *in sensu composito* and the other *in sensu diviso*. But the chapters on universals and on *suppositio* in the first book and the whole of the third part of the third book are especially valuable to a reader who wishes to learn about what was peculiar to medieval logic. In addition to a detailed discussion of *consequentiae* the third part of the third book contains seven chapters on *obligationes* and one on *insolubilia*. Ockham's views on the *suppositio terminorum*, and therefore on universals, will be noticed in the next section, and his contributions to the theory of *consequentiae* will be examined in the last section of this chapter.

After Ockham there were a number of logicians who attained European reputation in the fourteenth century: Walter Burleigh, who wrote also an adaptation of the work of Diogenes Laertius on the lives of the ancient philosophers; Jean Buridan, Rector of the University of Paris in 1328 and 1340 and author of a theory of physical impulse; Richard Swineshead (in Latin Suisseth), a Fellow of Merton College, Oxford, in 1348, who was often called the Calculator because of his interest in mathematics; Albert of Saxony, Rector of the University of Paris in 1353; Marsilius of Inghen, first Rector of the University of Heidelberg; William Heytesbury (in Latin Hentisberus or Tisberus), a Fellow of Merton College in 1370; Ralph Strode, another Mertonian; Richard Ferrybridge (in Latin Ferabrich or Ferebrich or Feri-Brigus). These were not all followers of Ockham. Burleigh, for example, was a defender of old views about universals. But Ockham's influence was dominant among them, and this period in which logic was studied most intensely was also the period in which scholastic metaphysics began to decline because Ockham had convinced many philosophers of the impossibility of getting rational proof or even support for theological doctrines. But it was Ockham's theory of knowledge which led men to scepticism about metaphysics on the one hand and to an interest in formal necessity on the other. Unfortunately the constructive influence seems to have been short-lived. After about 1380 there is little of interest to report about medieval logic. Philosophers continued to write about *insolubilia*, *consequentiae*, and the rest, but without producing anything radically new, though logic was studied at this time by more first-class intellects and more intensively than ever before or after. Perhaps this failure to advance is not surprising. The step required next was a big one, and even after Leibniz had announced his projects in the seventeenth century there was to be an interval of two centuries before the achievements of Frege.

Throughout the period after Abelard in which the universities flourished and multiplied there was debate about universals. In the twelfth and thirteenth centuries this did not much affect the teaching of formal logic, but we shall see in the next section that the division between *antiqui* and *moderni* showed itself in the working out of the doctrine of *proprietates terminorum*. In the fourteenth and fifteenth centuries the *moderni* (or *nominales terministae*, as they were sometimes called) were the more active in elaboration of logical subtleties, and in reaction the *antiqui* (or *reales in metaphysica*) became a party who wished to base education on the *ars vetus* (in particular the *Categories*) and *philosophia realis* (i.e. physics and metaphysics, either Thomist or Scotist) rather than on the newer developments of logic, which they thought tedious and profitless. In theology the *moderni* of this period prided themselves on their orthodoxy, and it is interesting to notice that some of the more famous precursors of the reformation, in particular Wycliffe and Savonarola, were *antiqui*. There were in effect two educational programmes for the first degree, a *via antiqua* and a *via moderna*, and at the end of the fifteenth century some of the newly founded German universities tried to get the best of both worlds by maintaining two rival faculties of arts, each with its own dean and its own teachers.[1]

A hundred years after their triumphs in Oxford the Merton logicians were still being studied in Italy. In 1486 the statutes of the University of Padua provided for lectures on the work of Strode and Heytesbury and on the writings of the Italian teachers Paul of Venice and Paul of Pergolae who had commented on them earlier in the fifteenth century.[2] A generation later the demand for information about this sort of logic was enough to justify the publication at Venice in 1517 of an omnibus volume called *Consequentiae Strodi cum commento Alexandri Sermonetæ, Declarationes Gaetani in easdem consequentias, Dubia magistri Pauli Pergolensis, Obligationes eiusdem Strodi, Consequentiae Ricardi de Ferabrich, Expositio Gaetani super easdem, Consequentiae subtiles Hentisberi,*

---

[1] C. Prantl, *Geschichte der Logik*, iv, pp. 38, 148, 187–91, 230.
[2] H. Rashdall, *The Universities of Europe in the Middle Ages*, ed. Powicke and Emden, i, p. 247.

*Quaestiones in consequentias Strodi perutiles eximii artis doctoris domini Antonii Frachantiani Vicentini.* But the rise of humanism and of new philosophical interests connected with natural science led gradually to the neglect of formal logic, and we hear little of *consequentiae* from the famous philosophers of the seventeenth century, although, as we shall see presently, they had not been entirely forgotten when Leibniz began the next great advance.

## 4. *Proprietates Terminorum*

The theory of the *proprietates terminorum*, which is very prominent in later medieval logic, took shape in the second half of the twelfth century, and it seems to have grown out of the discussions of Abelard and his contemporaries about the structure of categorical propositions. Since, however, it is not yet possible to trace the details of this development, we shall begin our consideration with the earliest printed version of the theory, namely that of William of Shyreswood in his *Introductiones in Logicam*.[1] From the manner in which this is presented and from its occasional references to other views we may safely conclude that the general doctrine was already well known when the author wrote.

The fifth part of the *Introductiones* opens as follows:

'Quattuor sunt proprietates terminorum quas ad praesens intendimus diversificare. Harum enim cognitio valebit ad cognitionem termini et sic ad cognitionem enuntiationis et propositionis. Et sunt hae proprietates significatio, suppositio, copulatio, et appellatio. Est igitur significatio praesentatio alicuius formae ad intellectum. Suppositio autem est ordinatio alicuius intellectus sub alio. Et est copulatio ordinatio alicuius intellectus supra alium. Et notandum quod suppositio et copulatio dicuntur dupliciter, sicut multa huiusmodi nomina, aut secundum actum aut secundum habitum. Et sunt istae definitiones earum secundum quod sunt in actu. Secundum autem quod sunt in habitu, dicitur suppositio significatio alicuius ut subsistentis (quod enim tale est natum est ordinari sub alio) et dicitur copulatio significatio alicuius ut adiacentis (et quod tale est natum est ordinari supra aliud). Appellatio autem est praesens convenientia termini, i.e. proprietas secundum quam significatum termini potest dici de aliquo mediante hoc verbo *est.* Ex his patet quod significatio [non] est in omni parte seu dictione orationis. Suppositio autem in nomine substantivo tantum vel pronomine vel dictione substantiva; haec enim significant rem ut subsistentem et ordinabilem sub alio. Copulatio autem in omnibus adiectivis et participiis et verbis. Appellatio autem in omnibus substantivis et adiectivis et participiis, et non in pronominibus, quia non significant formam aliquam sed solam substantiam, nec in verbis, quia

---

[1] Ed. M. Grabmann in *Sitzungsberichte der Bayerischen Akademie der Wissenschaften, Phil.-Hist. Abteilung,* 1937, Heft 10.

verbum non significat aliquod quod apponitur per verbum substantivum, quia sic esset extra ipsum. Nulla autem istarum trium, scilicet
suppositio, copulatio, appellatio, est in partibus indeclinabilibus, quia
nulla pars indeclinabilis significat substantiam aut aliquid in substantia.'[1]

As its name implies, the theory of the *proprietates terminorum* is
intended to provide an account of the different roles that words
or phrases can have when they appear as terms in propositions.
But it is assumed in this theory that a word or phrase which is
capable of serving as a term must first have *significatio* in the sense
of conveying or presenting, as William says, a form. There is, of
course, a non-technical usage in which words such as *et* and *cum*
may be said to have *significatio*; but these words cannot serve
as terms, and so their *significatio* is not relevant here. It is a little
surprising, however, that all terms should be assumed to signify
forms, and we may perhaps take this assumption as an indication
that the theory was first conceived as a doctrine about general
terms such as *homo* and only later extended to singular terms such
as *Socrates* and *ille*. There is in fact no place in the theory for
these latter except in connexion with one of the subdivisions of
*suppositio* which we shall notice presently. For William tells us
that *copulatio* is peculiar to adjectives, participles, and verbs,
which are all general, and that *appellatio* cannot be ascribed to
pronouns because they do not signify forms but only substances.
It is true that his definition of *appellatio* as the present applicability
(*praesens convenientia*) of a term to something might be held to
justify us in saying that the proper name *Socrates* had *appellatio*
in 400 B.C.; but if the pronoun *ille* is disqualified from having
*appellatio* because it never signifies a form, there seems to be no
good reason why the proper name *Socrates* should not be disqualified also on the same ground.

The notion of *appellatio* seems to be derived from Priscian's use
of the phrase *nomen appellativum* for a term which applies to all
the several things it covers, and it is not surprising to learn
from William of Shyreswood that some logicians thought *appellatio*
peculiar to terms in the predicative position. For it may be said
that a common noun, adjective, or participle occurring in this
position is in fact applied by the copula *est*, whereas a general
term occurring in the subject position is at best only applicable.
But it seems rather curious that no term is said to have *appellatio*
unless it is applicable to something existing at the time of

---

[1] Ibid., pp 74–75. The *non* which we have printed in square brackets destroys
the sense. In the next to the last sentence Grabmann has *in omnibus substantiis*,
and at the end he has *substantiam et aliquid in substantia*.

speaking; for while it may be important to distinguish in logic between terms which have application to something, past, present, or future, and those which have no application at all, it is not so obviously important to draw a line where William of Shyreswood and other medieval logicians draw their line between terms which have *appellatio* and those which do not. For understanding of this feature of the theory we must consider the rest in more detail, but we may suppose that medieval logicians thought of *appellatio* as involved primarily in such statements as 'This is a man', when we *call* a present individual by a general term.

The word *copulatio* comes from Abelard's discussions of terms; and since William of Shyreswood says that the property which it indicates can belong only to adjectives, participles, and verbs, it seems clear that the word still suggests to him, as it did to Abelard, the notion of grammatical dependence. But in the definition which we have quoted from the beginning of William's discussion there is a different metaphor; for *suppositio* and *copulatio* are here said to be respectively the subordination and the superordination of one thought (*intellectus*) to another. William does not say explicitly that the technical usage of *suppositio* was derived from this metaphor, but he seems to assume that it was introduced with the sense of 'placing under'. In any case it seems that nouns and in general all *dictiones substantivae* are said to have *suppositio* because they are thought to stand for the substances which support the accidents expressed by adjectives, participles, and verbs.[1] But the philosophical distinction of substance and accident is historically derivative from that of subject and predicate, and so the notion of *suppositio* is especially associated with the appearance of substantives as subjects in propositions. When a substantive appears in the predicate role, as for example in the proposition *Omnis homo est animal*, there is said to be a harmless and insignificant reduplication of the reference to a substance or substances which is made by the subject:

'Omne enim nomen significat solam formam, et non absolute sed inquantum informat substantiam deferentem ipsam, et sic aliquo modo dat intelligere substantiam. Nomen ergo in praedicato dat intelligere formam, dico, ut est forma substantiae subiecti. Et ideo cum illa substantia intelligatur in subiecto, non intelligetur iterum in praedicato. Unde praedicatum solam formam dicit.'[2]

Since, however, logicians sometimes wish to convert categorical propositions, they find it interesting to consider just what commitment is involved in the use of a substantive as predicate, and

---

[1] *Introductiones*, p. 82.                              [2] Ibid., p. 78.

so there is discussion of the *suppositio* of predicate terms in various kinds of propositions. This is probably what William of Shyreswood has in mind when he talks of habitual (i.e. dispositional) as opposed to actual *suppositio*. For he says later in a discussion of *appellatio*:

'Dicunt igitur quidam quod terminus ex parte subiecti supponit et ex parte praedicati appellat. Et sciendum quod ex parte subiecti supponit secundum utramque definitionem suppositionis, ex parte autem praedicati supponit secundum habitualem suam definitionem.'[1]

So much is fairly clear, but it is not so easy to determine the precise force of the verb *supponere* in passages like that just quoted. Sometimes the past participle *suppositum* is used of an individual which has the form signified by a term, as when William writes a few lines later *Suppositum et appellatum sunt quandoque idem*; and in one place the present passive *supponitur* is used of a *res deferens formam significatam per nomen*.[2] But this is not the only use, nor even that which appears to be basic. William often says that a term *supponit pro* such an individual, and when he is writing most carefully he puts in as object to the verb *formam* or *significatum*. Probably the key to the whole of his terminology is to be found in the passge where he defines the most common kind of *suppositio*, namely that called *personalis*: 'Personalis autem [est suppositio] quando [dictio] supponit significatum sed pro re quae subest, ut *Homo currit*. Cursus enim inest homini gratia alicuius singularis.'[3] In this context it seems clear that William ascribes *suppositio* to a common noun or similar substantive occurring as subject in a proposition because he thinks that it subordinates its meaning (i.e. the form it signifies) to that of the predicate. No doubt this account of predication is unsatisfactory for any but universal affirmative propositions such as *Omnis homo est animal*. But it should not surprise us that a logician of the early Middle Ages sometimes spoke as though it were universally valid; for we have found that an assumption of the same kind underlies Aristotle's talk of major and minor terms in syllogistic theory. And in the passage just quoted we find that William goes some way to meet objections by saying that the form which a subject-term expresses may be subordinated only for, or in respect of (*pro*), some individual or individuals which have it. Furthermore, from such a usage there is an easy transition to talking of the individuals which have the form as *supposita*, since each can be said to be metaphorically under its form. Thus we have the two usages, *Iste terminus communis 'homo' supponit humanitatem pro Socrate* (or more shortly *supponit pro Socrate*) and *Socrates supponitur per istum terminum*.

[1] Ibid., p. 82.   [2] Ibid., p. 76.   [3] Ibid., p. 75.

Against all this we must set the fact that the successors of William of Shyreswood define *suppositio* quite simply as the *acceptio termini substantivi pro aliquo* and constantly use the phrase *supponere pro* without any accusative, as though *supponere* were in their view an intransitive verb like *stare* in the equivalent phrase *stare pro*.[1] Conceivably their usage could have grown out of that we find in the work of William of Shyreswood; but if so, William's use of phrases such as *supponit significatum pro re quae subest* must have been old fashioned even when he wrote. For he himself often omits the accusative *significatum* after *supponere*, and there seems to be little, if any, trace of it after his time, although some references to *suppositio* by other writers (e.g. by Peter of Spain) cannot be more than a few years later than his own. On the other hand, the absolute use of *supponere pro* might perhaps have started as a vulgarism like the use of 'substitute for' in English where it would be more correct to write 'serve in place of'. In classical Latin the phrase *supponere aliquid pro aliquo* had the sense of 'substitute something for something', and a transition from this to the technical usage noticed above would be no more surprising than many developments that have undoubtedly occurred in the history of the language. If, however, this was what happened, the explanations of William of Shyreswood could be no more than private fancies suggested by false etymologies. It is perhaps a point in favour of this hypothesis that William finds difficulty in applying his account to any varieties of *suppositio* other than the *suppositio personalis* of general terms. But it may be replied that such difficulty would be natural if the technical terminology had been elaborated first with the sense which William gives to it in this case and then extended inappropriately to other cases. Moreover, William writes as though the *dubitationes* which he tries to solve had been raised by other people, not by himself; and it is at least conceivable that they might have been the occasion for the adoption of the simplified usage whereby *supponere* is treated as an intransitive verb. In defence of William's authority as an historical witness we may say that he does not show elsewhere any disposition to fanciful theorizing.

The truth of the matter seems to be even more complicated than either of the hypotheses we have considered. The word *suppositum* occurs already in Priscian's work in a passage where it seems to mean the same as 'individual',[2] and throughout medieval philosophy it often recurs with this sense. It was probably introduced first as a translation for the Greek ὑποκείμενον, i.e. to signify

---

[1] Peter of Spain, *Summulae Logicales* (ed. Bochenski), § 6.03. Cf. Ockham, *Summa Totius Logicae*, i. 63.          [2] *Institutiones Grammaticae*, xvii. 23.

an entity of the kind that underly all other entities and are, as we might say in modern English, presupposed by talk of qualities, positions, relations, and the rest. As late as 1710 the French derivative *suppôt* was used by Leibniz with this sense when he was trying to explain how body and mind had been said to constitute one person.[1] But in the passage of Priscian to which we have referred *suppositum* might also be translated by 'subject', and there can be no doubt that the word came to have this sense in medieval writings on grammar, where it is commonly contrasted with *appositum*, or predicate. In this context a *suppositum* is defined as *id de quo fit sermo* and an *appositum* as *illud quod dicitur de supposito*; and although grammarians sometimes say that a noun in the nominative case *supponitur verbo*, they tend in general to use the active verb *supponere* in the sense of 'act as grammatical subject'.[2] Originally the verb may have been used in the active voice with an accusative understood, i.e. as though it meant 'posit something or other', but in time it came to be regarded as intransitive. When therefore logicians say that a term *supponit pro* something which is under discussion, they are probably adapting this usage to their own purposes. But it seems clear that for William of Shyreswood the word *suppositio* has not yet lost its metaphorical force, and that his various usages reveal different notions which the word could suggest to a man of his time.

At the opening of one of the sections of his *Summulae Dialectices* William's younger contemporary and admirer Roger Bacon distinguishes four meanings of *suppositio* which we may perhaps call the epistemological, the onomastical, the metaphysical, and the grammatical:

'Sumitur autem supposito multipliciter. Dicitur in uno modo petitio alicuius vel acceptio sine probatione cum indigeat probari vel possit. Alio modo dicitur suppositio substantiva rei designatio, sicut dicimus quod substantiva nomina supponunt rem suam, id est, substantive designant. Tertio modo dicitur proprietas termini communis per comparationem ad individua quae sunt eius supposita, secundum quod dicimus quod nomen commune, ut *homo*, significat qualitatem cum substantia, sive humanitatem, et supponit individua, scilicet Socratem et Platonem et alia. Quarto modo dicitur suppositio proprietas termini subjecti, sive termini in quantum alii supponit et subicitur in oratione.'[3]

None of these meanings corresponds exactly to the definition given by William in the long passage quoted above, but we have

[1] *Theodicée*, § 59.
[2] The evidence is collected by Ch. Thurot in *Notices et extraits de divers manuscrits latins pour servir à l'histoire des doctrines grammaticales au moyen âge, Notices et extraits des manuscrits*, xxii. 2 (1868), pp. 217–18.
[3] *Opera Hactenus Inedita Rogeri Baconi*, Fasc. xv, ed. R. Steele, 1940, p. 268.

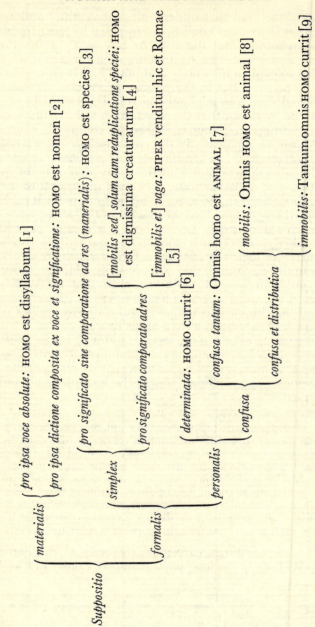

*Suppositio*

*materialis*
- *pro ipsa voce absolute:* HOMO est disyllabum [1]
- *pro ipsa dictione composita ex voce et significatione:* HOMO est nomen [2]

*formalis*
- *simplex*
  - *pro significato sine comparatione ad res (materialis):* HOMO est species [3]
  - *pro significato comparato ad res*
    - [*mobilis sed*] *solum cum reduplicatione speciei:* HOMO est dignissima creaturarum [4]
    - [*immobilis et*] *vaga:* PIPER venditur hic et Romae [5]
- *personalis*
  - *determinata:* HOMO currit [6]
  - *confusa*
    - *confusa tantum:* Omnis homo est ANIMAL [7]
    - *confusa et distributiva*
      - *mobilis:* Omnis HOMO est animal [8]
      - *immobilis:* Tantum omnis HOMO currit [9]

seen that the second, third, and fourth are all to be found in his work, and we shall notice presently a passage in which William writes of existential import as though he thought that the *suppositio personalis* of general terms necessarily involved a presupposition or assumption of the existence of examples of a form. It seems impossible to find any English translation for *supponere* which will convey all these suggestions at once, but that is no reason for doubting that they could all be conveyed by the Latin word at the beginning of the thirteenth century, and William's work is especially interesting because it contains evidence of them all.

Apart from one pair to be noticed later, all the varieties of *suppositio* distinguished by William of Shyreswood are shown in the accompanying table together with the examples by which he illustrates them. In each example we have used small capitals to distinguish the substantive which has the kind of *suppositio* under consideration, but it is to be understood that the word has that kind of *suppositio* only in the context of a proposition like the example. The descriptions of the different varieties are all taken from William's text, but the words *mobilis* and *immobilis* occur first in his account of [8] and [9]. We have introduced them in the descriptions of [4] and [5] for purposes of brevity.

If we take *supponere pro* to mean 'stand for', it is easy to make some sense of the various distinctions with the help of William's examples, but as soon as we begin to ask more searching questions about the relationship he intends to indicate by the word *suppositio* and the propriety of his classifications we encounter difficulties. Thus it is clear that in [1] and [2] we have to do with the occurrence of a word either as a sign for itself or for its sound, i.e. with that sort of occurrence which in modern writing and printing is commonly indicated by inverted commas. William explains its difference from all the other varieties of *suppositio* by saying:

'Est igitur suppositio quaedam materialis, quaedam formalis. Et dicitur materialis quando ipsa dictio supponit vel pro ipsa voce absolute vel pro ipsa dictione composita ex voce et significatione, ut si dicamus, *Homo est disyllabum, Homo est nomen.* Formalis est quando dictio supponit suum significatum.'[1]

Presumably the name *materialis* is intended to indicate that this kind of *suppositio* is concerned with the matter of a word (i.e. its sound) and not with the subordination of one form to another, but in that case it cannot differ from *suppositio formalis* in anything like the way in which two varieties of the latter are said to differ from each other. In the passage just quoted William

seems to admit as much by using the verb *supponere* first intran-
sitively and then transitively. Later he says explicitly that doubts
have been raised on this score:

'Dubitatur de prima divisione suppositionis. Videtur enim quod non
sit diversus modus supponendi sed potius significandi, quia significatio
est praesentatio alicuius formae ad intellectum. Ergo diversa praesentatio diversa significatio. Sed cum dictio supponit materialiter,
praesentat aut se aut suam vocem; cum autem formaliter, praesentat
suum significatum. . . . Hoc tamen non verum est, quia dictiones
semper suum significatum praesentant quantum de se est, et si praesentant suam vocem, hoc non est secundum se sed ex adiunctione cum
praedicato.'[1]

The criticism is well-conceived and William's reply is unsatisfactory. For when in speech or writing we say that *homo* is a noun,
we are not using the word *homo* in the ordinary way at all, but
mentioning it and talking about it by a linguistic device which
involves production of its sound or shape. Instead of writing, for
example, as we could, 'the word which is spelt with an *h* and an *o*
and an *m* and an *o*' we put these letters down in the proper order
and then (as William of Shyreswood rightly remarks) trust to the
rest of the sentence to show that we intend to refer to the word
which could have been indicated by the long description given
above. Similarly when we talk orally about the word, we produce
the sounds which constitute the word and leave it to be understood from the context that we do so for the purpose of referring
to the word they constitute. In each case we produce a specimen
of a pattern to which convention has assigned a meaning in certain contexts, but in this context our specimen does not convey
that meaning any more than the drill sergeant expresses respect
to the recruit when he shows him how to salute.

There are similar difficulties also about [3], i.e. about *suppositio
simplex pro significato sine comparatione ad res*, or *suppositio simplex
absoluta*, as it was called by some later logicians. The example
makes clear that this is the much-disputed philosophical usage
whereby a general term such as 'man' is treated as a name for a
species; and the discussion which follows later shows that even
among logicians who were prepared to tolerate this way of talking
there were some who thought it could not properly be said to
differ from other usages of the word by a special kind of *suppositio*.
For William writes:

'Similiter dubitatur de hac divisione: *Alia simplex, alia personalis.*
Videtur enim quod haec diversitas facit equivocationem, quia cum

_____
[1] *Introductiones*, p. 76. In the fourth sentence Grabmann has *autem se aut suam
vocem.*

supponit simpliciter praesentat ad intellectum formam significatam per nomen, cum autem personaliter praesentat rem deferentem formam. Ad hoc potest responderi sicut ad primum, vel potest dici quod semper idem supponit, scilicet significatum suum, sed hoc dupliciter, aut pro significato, et tunc simpliciter, aut pro re significata, et tunc personaliter.'[1]

Again the criticism is sound and William's reply inadequate. For if we use the word *homo* as a substitute for the word *humanitas*, we give it a new sense. But William refuses to admit this, and produces instead an incoherent account of two kinds of *suppositio*. It is presumably no more than an unfortunate slip when he says that *suppositio personalis* is *pro re significata* (using *re significata* here to mean something quite different from *significato*); but even if we substitute what his argument seems to require, namely the phrase *pro re deferente formam significatam per nomen*, the result is a muddle. For the sense in which the notion of humanity may perhaps be said to be subordinated in its own right to the notion of a species by the remark *Homo est species* seems to be quite different from that in which the notion of humanity may be said to be subordinated in respect of an individual man to the notion of running by the remark *Homo currit*. So far from explaining anything, the use of the one word *suppositio* for the two relations is a source of unnecessary perplexities. If the phrase *supponere pro* is used only to mean the same as 'stand for', we may perhaps say that the subject-term *supponit pro forma* in the sentence *Homo est species*, whereas the subject term *supponit pro re deferente formam* in the sentence *Homo currit*, but William confuses this by trying to provide an accusative for *supponere* in each case, and so reaches the curious result we have just noticed.

In a later note William remarks that the term *homo* of the example *Homo est species* is sometimes said to have *suppositio manerialis, quia supponit pro ipsa manerie speciei*.[2] The word *maneries* (or rather *maneria*) appears in Abelard's work with the sense of 'variety' or 'sort',[3] and the phrase *ipsa maneries speciei* must be supposed to mean here 'the specific character in itself'. The two kinds of *suppositio simplex pro significato comparato ad res*, which are numbered [4] and [5] in our table, are apparently betwixt-and-between cases. When we say *Homo est dignissima creaturarum*, we are, it seems, talking primarily of the species, but not of the species in abstraction from all individuals, and the *suppositio* of the word *homo* is *mobilis*, because what we say can

[1] Ibid., p. 77.
[2] Ibid. Grabmann has *materialis*. We owe the correction to L. Minio-Paluello.
[3] *Dialectica*, pp. 93 and 95.

be repeated of the individuals of the species, provided always that it is applied to them solely in virtue of their specific nature. Thus we can say of an individual man, *Iste homo, inquantum homo, est dignissima creaturarum*. On the other hand, when we say *Piper venditur hic et Romae*, the *suppositio* of the word *piper* is *immobilis*, because our statement does not imply that each individual particle of pepper is sold both here and at Rome, and the *suppositio* is called *vaga*, because we are concerned only with the species in respect of its relation to some-individual-or-other. Since there can be no doubt that we do in fact use words as they occur in these two examples, it is interesting to have the usages noticed and docketed, though we may doubt whether either can properly be said to involve *suppositio pro significato*.

The use of the word *personalis* as a title for all the remaining varieties of *suppositio* is curious, since they are not all concerned with persons, and the most plausible explanation is that this fashion started in a theological context such as consideration of Boethius' work *De Persona et Duabus Naturis Contra Eutychen et Nestorium*. When a Christian says *Deus factus est homo*, he does not mean by this that the form of deity has been identified with the form of humanity, but that a person who already had the first came at a certain time to have also the second; and this distinction is so important in Christian thought that it may well have provided the name for the second big division of *suppositio formalis*, and we may reasonably suppose that the contrast of *suppositio simplex* and *suppositio personalis* was one of the first to be drawn by medieval logicians.[1]

When he introduces this contrast William remarks that it is also possible to divide the whole field of *suppositio formalis* between *suppositio communis* and *suppositio discreta*[2], but he does not explain in detail how the one distinction is related to the other. If, as he says, *suppositio communis* is made by a general term and *suppositio discreta* by a singular, it should be possible to find instances of the latter which are also instances of *suppositio materialis* according to his criteria, e.g. that of *Socrates* in *Socrates est nomen proprium*. He does not discuss this point, but he explicitly rejects the argument that *Homo est species* may be described as a singular proposition because its subject is to be taken as the proper name of a species,[3] and he writes in one place as though he thought that a singular term, no less than a general, might be used either with *suppositio personalis* or with *suppositio simplex*:

---

[1] In his *Formale Logik*, § 27.20 I. M. Bochenski draws attention to the use of the distinction by St. Thomas in his *Summa Theologica*, III. xvi. 7.
[2] *Introductiones*, p. 75.  [3] Ibid., p. 78.

'Volunt enim quidam quod haec divisio *Alia simplex alia personalis* sit divisio communis suppositionis, quia non cadit haec diversitas in discreta suppositione. Non enim est ibi nisi personalis. Semper enim supponitur individuum in tali, scilicet in discreta, suppositione. Dicendum quod hoc non facit personalem suppositionem, scilicet quod supponitur individuum, sed quod supponitur res deferens formam significatam per nomen, et hoc potest accidere in nomine proprio cum significat substantiam cum qualitate, ut, cum dico *Socrates currit*, respicitur pro sua re, cum dico *Socrates est praedicabile de uno solo*, respicitur pro forma significata per nomen.'[1]

Here again we find our author trying to extend the application of notions which seem appropriate only in connexion with the *suppositio personalis* of general terms. It is true that he does not here use the phrase *supponit formam*, but he insists very strangely that a proper name can be said to signify a form and that this is essential to its having *suppositio*. As Aristotle rightly remarked in his doctrine of primary substance, Socrates is not predicable of anything. If William's last example means anything at all, it must mean either that being-called-Socrates is predicable of only one thing or that being-identical-with-Socrates is predicable of only one thing, and in neither case is a form of Socraticity involved. On the other hand, those against whom he argues apparently equate *suppositio* with 'standing for' and suggest for this reason that *suppositio discreta* should not be regarded as a subdivision of *suppositio personalis* but taken earlier on its own.

If the account of *suppositio* which William tries to apply to all the varieties in his list is not his own innovation but the original sense of the terminology, the doctrine of *suppositio* must have started with the cases [6] to [9] which we have still to consider. For it does not properly fit any of the earlier cases [1] to [5], and it is scarcely credible that it could have been elaborated by anyone who had them in mind from the beginning. On the other hand, it is easy to see how they could be included when the notion of subordinating one form to another was not stressed and the phrase *supponere pro* was taken to mean only the same as 'stand for'. In any case the doctrine of *suppositio personalis*, to which we must now turn, is the best developed part of the whole theory, as that is preserved in the surviving documents.

In *Homo currit* (which is to be understood here in the sense of the English sentence 'A man is running') the word *homo* is said to have *suppositio determinata* because it could be explained by reference to one individual (*potest locutio exponi per aliquod unum*).[2]

---

[1] Ibid., p. 76. In the third sentence Grabmann has *Semper enim supponit*.
[2] Ibid., p. 75.

But as William remarks, from another point of view we might call this *suppositio indeterminata*, because the proposition does not indicate definitely which man is running. By contrast *suppositio confusa* is so called because it involves either many individuals or one individual taken many times in a context where there might be many different individuals under consideration. The second part of this explanation is inserted to allow the word *hominem* to have *suppositio confusa* in the proposition *Omnis homo videt hominem* even though there be only one man, say Socrates, whom everybody sees.[1] If, furthermore, a substantive stands for everything which has the form it signifies, its *suppositio* is not only *confusa* but also *distributiva*. This is the case for the subject of a universal affirmative proposition, but not for the predicate. Finally, if the proposition containing a term with *suppositio confusa et distributiva* allows for inference to propositions concerning all the several individuals covered by the term, the *suppositio* of the term is said to be also *mobilis*. It may perhaps be thought that the condition must always be fulfilled, but this is not so. For although we may argue correctly from *Omnis homo currit* to *Socrates currit*, we cannot from *Tantum omnis homo currit* (i.e. 'Every man is running, but nothing else is') derive *Tantum Socrates currit* (i.e. 'Socrates is running, but nothing else is').

*Suppositio confusa* is said to be due always to a preceding distribution, that is to say, to the occurrence of a sign of universality or something with the same force. But *suppositio confusa tantum* differs from *suppositio confusa et distributiva* in a very important way, and in order to make this clear William lays down the following five rules about their relations to each other and to *suppositio determinata*. Some of his examples are designed to show the significance of word-order in Latin sentences, and for this reason are difficult to translate, but it is possible to reproduce the sense in English by using the passive voice in some places where he uses the active.[2]

(i) Every distributive sign (i.e. sign with the sense of 'all' or 'none') gives *suppositio confusa et distributiva* to the term to which is directly adjoined, and a negative sign does the same also for the remote term, but an affirmative sign gives *suppositio confusa tantum* to the remote term. This is why we can argue correctly 'No man is an ass; therefore no man is this ass', but not 'Every man is an animal; therefore every man is this animal'.

(ii) There is no valid inference from *suppositio confusa tantum* to

---

[1] *Introductiones*, p. 80.
[2] Ibid., pp. 80–81. The punctuation of the examples in Grabmann's text is so erratic as to destroy the sense.

*suppositio confusa et distributiva*. For when each man sees himself alone, it is not correct to argue 'For every man a man is not seen; therefore every man sees not a man' (*Omnis homo hominem non videt; ergo omnis homo non videt hominem*).

(iii) There is no valid inference from many cases of *suppositio determinata* to one of *suppositio determinata*, but only to one of *suppositio confusa*. For when each man sees himself alone, it is not correct to argue 'A man is seen by Socrates, and a man is seen by Plato, and so on; therefore a man is seen by every man', though we may conclude 'Therefore every man sees a man'.

(iv) There is no valid inference from *suppositio determinata* to *suppositio confusa et distributiva*, but only to *suppositio confusa tantum*. For it is not correct to argue 'A man is not seen by Socrates; therefore Socrates does not see a man', though it is correct to argue 'A man is seen by every man; therefore every man sees a man'.

(v) There is a valid inference from *suppositio confusa et distributiva* to *suppositio determinata*, but not from *suppositio confusa tantum*. For it is correct to argue 'Socrates does not see a man; therefore a man is not seen by Socrates',[1] but not to argue 'Every man sees a man; therefore a man is seen by every man'.

There are two puzzling features in this doctrine. In the first place, apart from *suppositio confusa et distributiva sed immobilis*, which may perhaps be neglected in this connexion, the scheme of classification involves three possible kinds of *suppositio communis*, although there are only two kinds of quantification for general terms in traditional logic, namely universal and particular (or existential). Secondly, the kinds of *suppositio* which William calls *determinata* and *confusa tantum* seem to be both associated with existential quantification, but the second is here labelled *confusa* like the third, although this latter is associated with universal quantification. The explanation of these two oddities is in part highly creditable to the logicians who devised the scheme. They had realized already the need for a theory of multiple quantification and had begun to work out some of the details, not only for the comparatively dull case which was later to be called quantification of the predicate, but also for the much more interesting theory of relations. In effect the fourth of the rules reproduced above provides that a doubly general proposition with an existential quantifier in front of a universal quantifier implies the corresponding doubly general proposition with quantifiers transposed, while the fifth rightly rejects the converse implication. On the other hand, the logicians who drew up the classification of

[1] The negation is omitted from the conclusion in Grabmann's text.

kinds of *suppositio* were unduly impressed by considerations about the number of individuals for which a term might be said to stand; for this reason they assigned *suppositio confusa* not only to every term with universal quantification but also to every term which occurred with existential quantification after the universal quantification of another term. By contrast a term which occurred with existential quantification and not preceded by any term with universal quantification was said to have *suppositio determinata* because it could be described as standing for a single individual.

This way of looking at things is bound up with the fundamental assumption that a general term, like a proper name or a unique description, must stand for an individual or individuals. At the end of his section on the *proprietates terminorum* William tells us that, when it occurs without special qualification, each general term stands for its *appellata*, that is to say, for the individuals which are present examples of the form it signifies; and he justifies this assumption as follows: 'Et dico quod ille terminus *homo* supponit pro praesentibus de se, quia significat formam in comparatione ad suas res. Haec autem comparatio tantum salvatur in existentibus. Solum enim est suum significatum forma existentium et proprie pro his supponit de se.'[1] In other words, *suppositio* depends first on *significatio*, and that which the general term *homo* signifies is a form to be realized in existing things; so unless special provision has been made to the contrary, it is to be assumed that *homo* stands for men existing at the time of speech. But special provision can be made to the contrary, as William recognizes in more explicit fashion when he writes: 'Terminus communis non restrictus habens sufficientiam appellatorum et supponens verbo de praesenti non habenti vim ampliandi supponit tantum pro his quae sunt.'[2] It is interesting to consider in turn, as he does, the various qualifications noticed here.

In the first place, a general term such as *homo* may be restricted by some qualifying phrase such as *qui fuit* and so be made to stand for the non-existent. This is a simple case which seems to require no further comment.

Secondly, it may happen that a general term has not enough *appellata* to satisfy the requirements of the sentence in which it occurs, and in this case again it will stand for the non-existent, as William tries to show by the following very curious argument:

'Hoc membrum *habens sufficientiam appellatorum* apponitur quia, si non habet, potest supponere pro non-enti. Et intellige quod sufficientia

---

[1] *Introductiones*, p. 85.
[2] Ibid., p. 82. Grabmann has *suppositiones* in place of *supponens*, which we have restored from William's self-quotation on p. 84.

appellatorum in tribus consistit ad minus. Unde, si non sint tot appellata, potest terminus supponere pro non-enti, ut, si sint tantum duo homines, haec est falsa, *Omnis homo est*. Probatio: Hoc signum *omnis* imponitur ad distribuendum pro summa multitudine, et hoc signum *uterque* pro minima. Cum ergo minima multitudo sit in binario, hoc signum *uterque* distribuit pro duobus tantum. Maior autem multitudo est in ternario et superioribus numeris. Unde hoc signum *omne* distribuit pro tribus ad minus. Cum igitur in hoc casu sint duo supposita existentia et vult iste sermo quod praedicatum insit tertio, vult quod insit non-existenti, et sic haec falsa est, *Omnis homo est*, et sua contradictoria vera, *Aliquis homo non est*. Ergo homo non est. Sed non esse non dicitur de existenti. Ergo ly *homo* supponit pro non-existenti.'[1]

The example is unfortunate because *Omnis homo est* and *Aliquis homo non est* are both alike senseless. And apart from that it is very fanciful to suggest that anyone who utters a universal proposition constructed with *omnis* commits himself to belief in the existence of three examples of the form signified by his subject term. But there can at least be no doubt that William holds to the doctrine of existential import for universal propositions and that he is prepared to describe a universal proposition as false if its subject term applies to nothing at all.

Thirdly, a term which occurs together with a verb in the past or the future tense may have *suppositio* for something not existing at the time of speech. As William puts it:

'Hoc membrum *supponens verbo de praesenti* apponitur quia, si terminus communis verbo de praeterito et futuro supponeret, posset supponere pro non-enti, ut hoc *Homo cucurrit* verum est pro Caesare. Et solet assignari talis regula: Terminus communis supponens verbo de praeterito supponit tam pro praesentibus quam pro praeteritis, et similiter supponens verbo de futuro supponit tam pro praesentibus quam pro futuris.'[2]

Fourthly, there are some verbs which can be used correctly even in the present tense of things which do not exist at the time of speaking, and these according to William exercise a power of *ampliatio* upon their subjects: 'Hoc autem membrum *non habenti vim ampliandi* apponitur quia, si sit verbum amplians, potest subiectum supponere pro non-enti, ut *Homo laudatur* haec est vera pro Caesare. Et est verbum amplians cuius res potest inesse non-enti.'[3] Other passive verbs with the power of *ampliatio* are 'mentioned', 'considered', 'feared', 'desired'. What all of this

---

[1] Ibid., p. 83. The suggestion that 'all' presupposes at least three probably comes from Aristotle's *De Caelo*, i. 1 (268ª16).
[2] *Introductiones*, p. 84. Grabmann has *Homo currit*, but the sense requires a past tense.   [3] Ibid., p. 84.

group have in common as an element of their meaning is the notion of being thought about. Clearly it is not necessary that anything of which we think should exist when we think of it or indeed at any other time. Another group of verbs to which William ascribes the power of *ampliatio* is that which consists of *potest* and similar signs of possibility. When we say 'Some day a man may land on the moon', we do not necessarily intend to refer to one of the men now living.

When William of Shyreswood says *Potest subiectum supponere pro non-enti*, his examples show that at the moment he has in mind only the possibility of a term's standing for something which does not exist at the time of speaking. But his theory seems to commit him also to the assertion that terms may stand for things which do not exist, have not existed, and will not exist. For he assumes that the subject of a categorical proposition always has *suppositio* for something, and so he must say that the word 'chimaera' *supponit pro non-enti* when it occurs in the proposition 'A chimaera is mentioned by Homer'. Is this defensible? If we define the phrase 'stand for' in such a way that anything a term stands for must exist at some time, it is obviously absurd to assert later that some terms stand for things which do not exist at any time. No doubt we can avoid this absurdity by explaining that we do not use 'stand for' with any implication that the things for which terms are said to stand must exist at some time. In ordinary English conversation a man who says that the word 'chimaera' stands for a monster which is part lion, part goat, and part serpent is not thought to have committed himself to belief in the existence of such a monster at any time. But if we announce that we intend to use the phrase 'stand for' in this way, we can no longer use it to make a contrast with 'mean'. For to say that the word 'chimaera' stands for a monster of the sort just described is to say in effect that the word means the same as our longer description. William of Shyreswood, however, insists very strongly that *suppositio* is not reducible to *significatio*, and so he cannot avail himself of this line of defence. Some philosophers of a later date, in particular Alexius Meinong and Bertrand Russell at one period of his life,[1] have said that terms like 'chimaera' and 'golden mountain' stand for objects which possess being of a kind, though not existence. There is no such suggestion in William's *Introductiones*; but if he tried to apply his theory of *suppositio* to cases of the kind we have just considered, he might find himself committed to some such extravagance.

In later accounts of the *proprietates terminorum* we find little new

[1] *Principles of Mathematics*, p. 449.

about *significatio, copulatio,* and *appellatio,* but there is a good deal of variety in the detail of what is said about *suppositio.* Thus Peter of Spain presents the following scheme.[1]

$$
Suppositio
\begin{cases}
discreta \\
communis
\begin{cases}
naturalis \\
accidentalis
\begin{cases}
simplex \\
personalis
\begin{cases}
determinata \\
confusa
\begin{cases}
necessitate\ signi \\
necessitate\ rei
\end{cases}
\end{cases}
\end{cases}
\end{cases}
\end{cases}
$$

Here the distinction between *suppositio materialis* and *suppositio formalis* is completely omitted, while the distinction between *suppositio discreta* and *suppositio communis* is introduced in a way which William of Shyreswood had considered only to reject. On the other hand, the distinction between *suppositio naturalis* and *suppositio accidentalis* is new. The first of the pair is said to be that *suppositio* which a term has when it is used to stand for all the things of which it is predicable, e.g. the *suppositio* of the word 'man' when it is used to stand for all men past, present, and future. Peter does not give an example, but perhaps he has in mind the use of the word *homo* in the formulation of a scientific law such as *Omnis homo est mortalis,* where the word *est* is not taken to involve any restriction to the time of speaking. Because Peter, unlike William of Shyreswood, starts with the assumption that if the context allows a general term will stand for past and future instances of the form it signifies as well as for those existing at the time of speech, he is led to think of the tenses of verbs as restricting rather than amplifying the *suppositiones* of their subjects. This is perhaps an improvement on William's doctrine, but it is curious that *suppositio simplex* should be included with these cases under the heading of *suppositio accidentalis.* The reason is apparently that a word acquires *suppositio simplex* from its context. In this place, however, Peter seems uncertain about the scope of *suppositio simplex.* For he says that the term *animal* has this kind of *suppositio* in the proposition *Omnis homo est animal,* although later on he cites the same example to illustrate *suppositio confusa necessitate rei.* In defence of his thesis that the predicate has *suppositio simplex* he says that it stands only for the nature of the genus (*solummodo supponit pro natura generis*), and it may be that he has in mind the barbarous old paraphrase *Animal inest omni homini* on which we have remarked in an earlier section. But it is clear that in the example

[1] *Summulae Logicales* (ed. Bochenski), § 6.04 ff.

which he cites the word *animal* is not a substitute for *animalitas*, although the sentence as a whole is equivalent to *Animalitas inest omni homini*.

In a later section, where he is discussing *appellatio*, Peter produces the interesting remark that for singular terms such as *Petrus* and for general terms such as *homo* when they occur with *suppositio simplex* there are no separate objects of *significatio*, *suppositio*, and *appellatio*.[1] When he wrote this he realized that a general term occurring with *suppositio simplex* is used as though it were the proper name of a kind; and by pointing out that the distinctions of the doctrine of the *proprietates terminorum* could not be applied usefully in the cases just mentioned he showed that, however the doctrine may have originated, it had become primarily a theory of the uses of general terms with *suppositio personalis pro suis inferioribus*.

In the part of his *Summulae* called *De Distributionibus* Peter argues against the thesis of William of Shyreswood that the word *omnis* requires the existence of at least three instances for the term to which it is attached, and he concludes sensibly that if the universal sign is put in front of the word *phoenix*, which is supposed to apply to one and only one thing at a time, it distributes the term solely with respect to that individual ('non distribuit ipsum nisi pro unico supposito').[2] What happens in the case where the subject-term applies to nothing at all, he does not say. But we may safely assume that he, like Abelard before him, would regard *Omnis chimaera est chimaera* as false because there are no chimaeras. For this is the common medieval doctrine.

At a later date attempts were sometimes made to elaborate the doctrine by use of the distinction between *suppositio naturalis* and *suppositio personalis*. In his work of 1372 called *De Suppositionibus Dialecticis* the Spanish Dominican friar St. Vincent Ferrer (1350–1419) maintains that a universal proposition whose subject has *suppositio naturalis* may be true even though there are no existent things to which the subject term applies.[3] His examples are *Rosa est odorifera* and *Pluvia est aqua guttatim cadens*. Since, however, the first of these is a scientific generalization based on observation of roses in the past, he may intend only to make clear that use of the present tense with a subject having *suppositio naturalis* does not commit the speaker to assertion of the present existence of things to which the subject term applies. In medieval Latin the

---

[1] *Summulae Logicales*, §§ 10.02 and 10.03.
[2] Ibid., §§ 12.17–12.19.
[3] *De Suppositionibus Dialecticis*, ch. 3, in *Œuvres de Saint Vincent Ferrier* (ed. Fages, 1909), i. The relevant passages are quoted and discussed by I. Thomas in 'St. Vincent Ferrer's De Suppositionibus', *Dominican Studies*, v (1952), pp. 88–102.

verb *existere* is not commonly used in the timeless (or omnitem-poral) way now customary among logicians, and we cannot safely conclude that because St. Vincent Ferrer would be prepared to count *Rosa est odorifera* as true even if there were no roses, he would also be prepared to count it as true if there never had been and never would be any roses. Unfortunately the second of his examples does not help to resolve any doubts there may be about his inten-tions, since it appears to be a definition. Perhaps if pressed he would be prepared to say that it would have been true even if there never had been and never were to be any rain. But in order to estimate the importance of such a concession it would then be necessary to discover what he thought was asserted in the formulation of a definition. In any case neither he nor any other medieval logician known to us goes so far as to suggest that 'Every A thing is B' means simply 'There are no A things which are not B' and must for that reason be true if there are no A things at all.

In spite of their differences William of Shyreswood and Peter of Spain are both realists in that they believe general terms to signify universals, or characters which things may have in com-mon. This is obvious enough in the explanations of William which we have quoted, and there are passages of the *Summulae Logicales* in which Peter talks similar language, e.g. his definition of *sup-positio simplex* as *acceptio termini communis pro re universali figurata per ipsum.*[1] When we turn to the account of terms in Ockham's *Summa Totius Logicae* we find a very different theory. In his view all signs, whether natural or conventional, represent individual things, because there is nothing else in the world of which they could be signs. It is absurd, he holds, to say that a universal is something existing in many individuals to which we apply a common name:

'Item, si illa opinio esset vera, nullum individuum posset creari, sed aliquid individui praeexisteret, quia non totum caperet esse de nihilo si universale quod est in eo prius fuit in alio. Propter idem etiam sequitur quod Deus non posset unum individuum substantiae an-nihilare nisi cetera individua destrueret, quia si annihilaret aliquod individuum, destrueret totum quod est de essentia individui, et per consequens destrueret illud universale quod est in eo et in aliis et per consequens alia non manerent, cum non possint manere sine parte sua, quale ponitur illud universale. . . . Item, sequitur quod aliquid de essentia Christi esset miserum et damnatum; quia illa natura communis existens realiter in Christo realiter existit in Iuda et est damnata; igitur in Christo et in damnato, quia in Iuda. Hoc autem absurdum est.'[2]

---

[1] *Summulae Logicales*, § 6.05.    [2] *Summa Totius Logicae*, i. 15.

This modernism is more far-reaching and much less plausible than that of Abelard.

According to Ockham, if we talk at all about universals, we must identify them with those signs which represent many things. This, he says, is the teaching of Avicenna:

'Dicendum est igitur quod quodlibet universale est una res singularis et ideo non est universale nisi per significationem, quia est signum plurium. Et hoc est quod dicit Avicenna quinto *Metaphysicae*: *Una forma apud intellectum est relata ad multitudinem, et secundum hunc respectum est universale quoniam ipsum est intentio in intellectu cuius comparatio non variatur ad quodcumque acceperis.* Et sequitur: *Haec forma quamvis in comparatione individuorum sit universalis, tamen in comparatione animae singularis in qua imprimitur est individua; ipsa enim est una ex formis quae sunt in intellectu.* . . . Verumtamen sciendum quod universale duplex est. Quoddam est universale naturaliter, quod scilicet naturaliter est signum praedicabile de pluribus . . .; et tale universale non est nisi intentio animae. . . . Et de tali universali loquar in sequentibus capitulis. Aliud est universale per voluntariam institutionem . . . quia scilicet est signum voluntarie institutum ad significandum plura. Unde sicut vox dicitur communis, ita potest dici universalis.'[1]

This is Ockham's nominalism, or perhaps we should say rather his conceptualism; for he holds that natural signs are primary and always prefers to talk about them rather than about words in this connexion.

In an earlier chapter of the *Summa Totius Logicae* these natural signs in the soul are identified with the mental modifications of which Aristotle spoke at the beginning of the *De Interpretatione*:

'Illud autem existens in anima quod est signum rei, ex quo propositio mentalis componitur ad modum quo propositio vocalis componitur ex vocibus, aliquando vocatur intentio animae, aliquando conceptus animae, aliquando passio animae, aliquando similitudo rei. Et Boethius in commento super libros *Perihermenias* vocat intellectum.'[2]

It is to be assumed, therefore, that when an *intentio* signifies many things it resembles them all in a certain way in which they also resemble each other, and Ockham in fact frequently makes this assumption. But to talk of the possibility of things resembling each other in a certain way is to allow all that any realist can wish, unless he has fallen into the errors of Plato. For to say that several things have a common character is not, as Ockham suggests in the

---

[1] *Summa Totius Logicae* i. 14. The passage of Avicenna to which Ockham refers can be found in *Avicennae Opera* (Venice, 1508), fol. 87r.B.
[3] *Summa Totius Logicae*, i. 12.

criticisms we have quoted, the same as to say that they have a common part about which we can make remarks of the sort we make about the individuals themselves. Rather it is to say that they resemble each other in some respect. And so the assertion that there are universals independent of human minds is no more than a declaration in the language of metaphysics to the effect that there are ways in which things can be like each other and that there would be such ways even if no one knew anything about them. The technical terminology is useful precisely because it enables us to direct attention to the obvious which would otherwise be taken for granted without remark. But it is sometimes mistaken for a revival of Platonism and therefore opposed with a fervour which is wholly inappropriate. When this happens, the critics are liable to commit the absurdity of denying what they assume (and must assume) in all their own thinking.

In Ockham's logic and theory of knowledge the immediate effect of his modernism was an impoverishment of the doctrine of the *proprietates terminorum*. William of Shyreswood and Peter of Spain, assuming that a general term always signified a form, had said that such a term could *supponere pro suo significato* only in the peculiar case of *suppositio simplex*. But Ockham rejected all this and made *suppositio* the basic notion in his theory of terms. For first of all he says that, in the sense in which he uses the word, *suppositio* includes *appellatio* as a variety;[1] and then he goes on to declare that in *suppositio personalis*, which he takes to be the normal case, a term stands for the things it signifies: 'Exemplum . . . sic dicendo *Omnis homo est animal*, li *homo* supponit pro suis significatis, quia *homo* non imponitur ad significandum nisi istos homines. Non enim significat aliquod commune eis, sed ipsosmet homines, secundum Damascenum.'[2] He does right, of course, to reject the view of Peter of Spain that a concrete term such as *albus* occurring as the predicate of a proposition *supponit pro forma* and also in giving as his reason that it is wrong to say *Albedo est alba*.[3] But by denying that a general term signifies anything which may be common to various individuals he commits himself to the mistaken

[1] Ibid. 62.
[2] Ibid. 63. The reference is apparently to chapter 5 of the *Dialectica* of St. John of Damascus (ed. Migne, 542 B), where the substantive 'man' is said to signify all particular men. But immediately afterwards it is said that men are all called men because they do not differ in species or nature. St. John, who was famous as an opponent of the iconoclasts, died about 752, and his *Exposition of the Orthodox Faith* was translated into Latin in the twelfth century by Burgundio of Pisa. His *Dialectica* (or *Philosophical Chapters*) was available to Ockham in a translation by Robert Grosseteste. Like some other early works called *Dialectica* (e.g. St. Augustine's and Alcuin's) it is chiefly about the predicables and the categories.
[3] *Summa Totius Logicae*, i. 62.

view that a general term is merely a substitute for a list of proper names. This commitment becomes evident in his later development of the theory. For he adopts the various subdivisions of *suppositio communis* mentioned by William of Shyreswood, and then tries to explain them by an enlargement of the notion of logical descent to individuals. In the work of William of Shyreswood the phrase *descendere ad supposita* is used to describe an argument such as 'Every man is running; so Socrates is running', where it is to be assumed, of course, that Socrates is a man.[1] But Ockham says that from *suppositio personalis determinata* we can make a logical descent to individuals by means of a disjunctive proposition: 'Est igitur regula certa quod, quando sub termino communi contingit descendere ad singularia per propositionem disiunctivam et ex qualibet singulari infertur talis propositio, tunc ille terminus habet suppositionem personalem determinatam.' And he distinguishes *suppositio confusa tantum* by saying that in this case we can make a logical descent to particulars only by means of a disjunctive predicate (e.g. by passing from *Omnis homo est animal* to *Omnis homo est hoc animal vel illud vel illud et sic de singulis*), whereas from *suppositio confusa et distributiva* it is possible *aliquo modo descendere copulative*.[2] Clearly what he means by descent in each of these cases is a transition to an equivalent statement which does not contain the original general term but contains instead singular terms linked either conjunctively or disjunctively. It is impossible, however, even in principle to make such a descent. For if every general term were merely an abbreviation for a list of proper names linked by 'and' or by 'or', every statement would be necessarily true or necessarily false, which is absurd. When we say 'Socrates is a man' we do not mean that 'Socrates is either Socrates or Plato or Aristotle or . . . '. On the contrary we mean that he has a certain character, and our use of the word 'man' to signify or express that character is logically prior to our use of the word to stand for any individual man. Although it is worth notice that Ockham here treats universal propositions as indefinitely large conjunctions, and existential propositions as indefinitely large disjunctions, we should not let this interesting novelty blind us to the fact that his real concern is not to explain quantifiers, but rather to show how general terms may be said to stand for individuals.

Ockham assumes, as we have seen, that *suppositio personalis* is the normal case, and he even goes so far as to say that, whatever the proposition may be in which it occurs, a term can always have *suppositio personalis* if it is not confined to some other kind of

---

[1] *Introductiones*, p. 81.          [2] *Summa Totius Logicae*, i. 68.

*suppositio* by the will of those who use it ('nisi ex voluntate utentium arctetur ad aliam').[1] Thus we can, if we like, understand *homo* to have *suppositio personalis* in each of the propositions, *Homo est nomen* and *Homo est species*; but if we do so, we must say that these propositions are both false. What is peculiar about these two propositions is that they have predicates which enable us to interpret them differently when we wish to do so. In order to obtain the other interpretations we must take the word *homo* without regard to its signification (*non significative*) and let it stand in the first case for the spoken or the written word and in the second case for the corresponding *intentio animae*. Thus we get *suppositio materialis* and *suppositio simplex* respectively.[2] Unlike the *moderni* of 200 years earlier, Ockham does not protest against the use of the word *homo* in *Homo est species*, but he rejects the explanation given by William of Shyreswood and treats *suppositio simplex* as a special usage which is similar to *suppositio materialis* in being concerned with a sign instead of with things signified. When we write *Homo est vox disyllaba*, we make the written sign *homo* stand for the corresponding sign of speech, but there is no special name by which to distinguish this kind of *suppositio materialis* from the usage in which we write *Homo est dictio scripta* and so make the written sign stand strictly for itself. Similarly, when we write *Homo est species*, we make the written sign *homo* stand for the corresponding mental sign, but this time we have a special name, *suppositio simplex*, by which to distinguish our usage.

When presenting his account of the proposition *Homo est species* Ockham might have derived some advantage from the fact that medieval philosophers used the word *species* quite freely as a synonym for *intentio*, but he does not choose to dwell on the Aristotelian theory of the reception of forms into the soul. On the contrary, he prefers to think of *intentiones* by analogy with spoken and written terms, and he even says that they admit all the distinctions of the theory of *suppositio*: 'Sicut autem talis diversitas suppositionis potest competere termino vocali et scripto, ita etiam potest competere termino mentali, quia intentio potest supponere pro illo quod significat et pro seipsa et pro voce et pro voce et scripto.'[3] If, as many of his remarks seem to imply, the *intentio animae* corresponding to the word *homo* is an image of a man, it is difficult to see how this could stand for the written word *homo* in a mental proposition to the effect that this written word has four letters. Unfortunately Ockham gives no further explanation of his curious statement.

When he first introduces the notion of *suppositio*, Ockham says

[1] Ibid. 64.    [2] Ibid. 63.    [3] Ibid.

that, unlike *significatio*, which he has already discussed, it belongs to terms only in the context of propositions.[1] But we have seen that in the normal cases he distinguishes *suppositio* from *significatio* only by its conjunctive or disjunctive character, and that in the abnormal cases he allows *suppositio* to words which occur *non significative*. It seems, therefore, that *suppositio* is the basic notion for him, and that *significatio* as he understands it could be defined by reference to the normal or primary *suppositio* of a term. Furthermore, in his account of truth he leaves no doubt that he takes the notion of *suppositio* as basic. For he says that a singular affirmative categorical proposition is true if, and only if, the subject term and the predicate term stand for the same thing:

'Ad veritatem istius *Iste est angelus* . . . sufficit et requiritur quod subjectum et praedicatum supponant pro eodem. . . . Et ideo non denotatur quod hic habet angelitatem vel quod in isto sit angelitas vel aliquid huiusmodi, sed denotatur quod hic sit vere angelus, non quidem quod sit illud praedicatum, sed quod sit illud pro quo supponit praedicatum.'[2]

No doubt he had some justification for his contempt of talk about *angelitas* and similar forms, but in his anxiety to be tough-minded he brought himself to the absurd position of saying that all history (and perhaps also all science) is nothing but the linking of signs with identical reference.

In the period after Ockham much attention was given to the formulation of rules of *distributio*, &c., like those we have noticed in the work of William of Shyreswood. A good example of this interest can be found in the *Perutilis Logica* of Albert of Saxony. But there was also debate about the philosophical questions raised by Ockham. The *Summa Totius Logicae* was probably finished in 1325, and in 1328 or thereabouts Walter Burleigh wrote his *De Puritate Artis Logicae Tractatus Longior*, which contains a defence of the old view of *significatio* and *suppositio simplex* against Ockham's attacks:

'Aliqui tamen reprehendunt illud dictum, scilicet quod suppositio simplex est quando terminus supponit pro suo significato; dicunt enim reprehendendo antiquiores quod illud est falsum et impossibile. Immo dicunt quod suppositio personalis est quando terminus supponit pro suo significato vel suis significatis et suppositio simplex est quando supponit pro intentione vel intentionibus animae. . . . Sed sine dubio illud est valde irrationabiliter dictum. . . . Nam certum est, quod secundum Philosophum in *Praedicamentis*, quod *homo* est nomen secundae substantiae; ergo iste terminus *homo* significat secundam substantiam et . . . speciem; ergo accipiendo *hominem* pro eo quod significat

---

[1] *Summa Totius Logicae*, i. 62.                    [2] Ibid. ii. 2.

haec erit vera *Homo est species*. . . . Item hoc nomen *homo* significat aliquid primo, et non significat primo Socratem nec Platonem, quia sic audiens hanc vocem et sciens quid per hanc vocem significaretur determinate et distincte intelligeret Socratem, quod est falsum. Ergo hoc nomen *homo* non significat primo aliquid singulare. Ergo significat primo commune, et illud commune est species. Sed sive illud commune sit res extra animam sive sit conceptus in anima, non curo quantum ad praesens.'[1]

By his reference to the *Categories* Burleigh proves no more than the historical respectability of his own view, but in the argument which begins with *Item* he gives a conclusive refutation of Ockham's account of *significatio*. If *homo* signified, that is to say, meant, Socrates and other individual men, no one could learn the meaning of the Latin word without learning that it applied to Socrates, which is plainly false.

Burleigh does not follow William of Shyreswood in supplying *formam* or *significatum* as an accusative to the verb *supponere*, but his account of the divisions of *suppositio* is nearer to William's than to either of the others we have noticed. It differs indeed only by containing more items. One of these is a division at the very beginning between *suppositio propria*, in which a term stands for something by the virtue of the expression (*de virtute sermonis*) and *suppositio impropria*, in which a term stands for something by metaphor or by special custom (*ex transsumptione vel ex usu loquendi*).[2] It is difficult to see how this distinction could be applied with any precision, but there is even less to be said in favour of Burleigh's attempt to distinguish varieties of *suppositio materialis*. For he says that we have this sort of *suppositio* when a term stands either for itself or for another expression not inferior to it (*pro alia voce quae non est inferior ad illam*) and gives as an example of the second *Hominem esse animal est propositio vera*.[3] The example is interesting because it suggests that Burleigh, who was very well read in his subject, either did not know or did not understand Abelard's account of the phrase *hominem esse animal* as a quasi-name for what is expressed by the proposition *Homo est animal*. Apparently the device of accusative and infinitive was sometimes used at the time where direct quotation would have been more appropriate.

On the other hand, Burleigh makes a good point when he distinguishes a special *suppositio personalis confusa et distributiva singulata* for the word *se* as it occurs in *Omnis homo videt se*.[4] As he says, the important thing about this case is that from *Omnis homo videt se* we can infer *Socrates videt Socratem*. Similarly he starts

---

[1] *De Puritate Artis Logicae Tractatus Longior* (ed. Ph. Boehner in *Franciscan Institute Publications*, 1955), pp. 7–8. The historical information given above is taken from Boehner's preface.    [2] Ibid., p. 2.    [3] Ibid.    [4] Ibid., p. 31.

something interesting when he remarks that *Equus tibi promittitur* may mean either 'Someone says with regard to some determinate horse that he will give it to you' or 'Someone says that he will give you some horse or other'.[1] For in the second case, where the promise itself is supposed to involve the notion expressed in English by 'some', the word *equus* must apparently stand for all horses though indeterminately and disjunctively. Here we have two further examples of the way in which medieval logicians developed their doctrine of *suppositio personalis* as a substitute for what modern logicians call quantification theory. Both involve relational notions, and the second involves also what is now called an intensional context. Although medieval logicians never doubted the primary importance of the subject-predicate pattern which they found in Aristotelian logic, they tried at times to cope with logical problems not considered by any ancient authors, and their work is interesting at least because it shows the difficulty of making progress in these new fields without specially designed symbolism.

Complicated as Burleigh's classification may seem, the distinctions which he offers are only a selection from those which he might have given. For he tells us at the beginning of his treatise: 'Plurimas divisiones suppositionis in iuventute mea memini me scripsisse, sed in praesenti opusculo nolo tot membra ponere, quia ad praesens propositum sufficiunt pauciora.'[2]

Of all this elaborate edifice erected by mediaeval logicians nothing has survived into modern times except the doctrine of *distributio terminorum*, which has been found useful for the presentation of rules of syllogistic. In its earliest usage by logicians the word *distributio* seems to have meant the prefixing of a universal quantifier. Thus Peter of Spain says 'Distributio est multiplicatio termini communis per signum universale facta, ut, cum dicitur *Omnis homo currit*, iste terminus *homo* distribuitur seu confunditur pro quolibet suo inferiori per hoc signum *omnis* et sic est ibi multiplicatio.'[3] But it came later to indicate the property which a general term is supposed to have when it is used to stand for all the individuals to which it is applicable. Thus the Pseudo-Scot says 'Distributio est acceptio alicuius communis pro quolibet eius supposito quorum quodlibet est ipsum.'[4] Using the word in this sense he finds it convenient to explain the *dici de omni* and the *dici de nullo* (which were commonly supposed to be the basic principles of all syllogistic reasoning) by saying that the essential

[1] *De Puritate Artis Logicae Tractatus Longior*, p. 15.          [2] Ibid., p. 2.
[3] *Summulae Logicales*, ed. Bochenski, §12.01.
[4] *Super Libros Elenchorum, quaestio* xiv (3).

feature of a syllogism is *sumptio sub termino distributo*, i.e. the sub-ordination of the subject-term of the conclusion to a middle term which is distributed in at least one of the premisses.[1] And with the same usage he remarks in another place, 'Ex non distributo num-quam sequitur distributum gratia formae.'[2] From these begin-nings there were then developed two rules of syllogistic which logicians came to regard as fundamental. At the end of the *Modernorum Summulae Logicales*, compiled by the regent masters of the University of Mainz from late medieval authors and printed in 1489, there occurs a list of miscellaneous rules *ad discernendos syllogismos a fallaciarum paralogismis*, which includes the following:

'Prima: In quolibet syllogismo non expositorio oportet medium complete distribui in praemissis, aut in ambabus teneri collective. Et si sint partes aeque principales, sic oportet medium complete distribui in altera praemissarum. . . . Octava: In nullo syllogismo debet argui a non distributo ad distributum. . . . Nona: In nullo syllogismo debet committi peccatum . . . contra aliquam regulam logicam.'

An expository syllogism is one in which the middle term cannot be distributed because it is singular (e.g. 'Socrates died of drinking hemlock; Socrates was a philosopher; so a philosopher died of drinking hemlock'), but for simplicity in the formulation of rules medieval logicians sometimes tried to get rid of this exception by writing *omne quod est* in front of the singular term.[3] Furthermore, a syllogism in which the middle term is taken collectively is also in effect a syllogism with a singular middle term. The second sentence of the first rule is obscure, but it seems to refer to the second figure, where the middle term is predicate in both premisses and so cannot be distributed more than once. A hundred years later the Jesuits of Coimbra give the rules in final form:

'Ad haec [i.e. the older rules of syllogistic] duo quaedam documenta adiungunt recentiores. Alterum est medium terminum in altera saltem praemissarum complete distribuendum esse, hoc est accipiendum pro omni re pro qua accipi potest. . . . Alterum documentum est nullum terminum qui non fuerit distributus in antecedente distribuendum esse in consequente.'[4]

How can we explain the almost complete disappearance of a study which once seemed important to a number of serious and highly intelligent men? Three different interests were served by this part of medieval logic. The first was an interest in the making of a general theory of language and the elucidation of such notions as meaning, application, and reference. The second was an

---

[1] *Super Librum I Analyticorum Priorum, quaestio* vii (5).
[2] Ibid., *quaestio* xi (9).                                                   [3] Ibid. (5).
[4] *Commentarii Collegii Conimbricensis e Societate Jesu in Universam Dialecticam Aristotelis* (Cologne, 1607), *In Lib. de Priori Resolutione*, i. 7 (p. 355).

interest in the precise description of various idioms of the natural language used for philosophizing. And the third was an interest in the elaboration of rules for valid inference in general logic, or quantification theory, as it is sometimes called. All are respectable, and each has its devotees in our time, but we no longer think it profitable to cultivate them all together in one theory, because we are no longer under the influence of certain prepossessions which influenced medieval logicians.

The distinction between *significatio* and *suppositio*, which may perhaps have been suggested by some of Abelard's reflections about the use of general terms, was a good beginning. But the notion of *suppositio* was never sufficiently clarified. For the word was used to mean both the designation of an individual by a proper name or definite description and also the use of a general term in such a way as to cover certain individuals. The same ambiguity belongs in English to the phrase 'stand for'. Thus we may say that 'the philosopher who drank the hemlock' stands for Socrates and also perhaps that 'man' in 'Every man is mortal' stands for Socrates among others. The unclarity might have been harmless if no great emphasis had been laid on the word, but it became a serious matter when the old notion of *significatio* was rejected by Ockham. For now the whole theory of language was made to rest on an imperfectly conceived metaphor. And the trouble was worse because the doctrine of *suppositio* had been extended to cover on the one hand oddities like *Homo est nomen* and *Homo est species* and on the other hand the distinctions of universal and existential quantification. In each case the extension was suggested by peculiarities of the Latin in which philosophers conducted their thinking. If Aristotle had not started a queer fashion in the use of general terms, there would have been no problem of *suppositio simplex*. And similarly if Latin had possessed an indefinite article there might have been no theory of *suppositio determinata*. For when *Homo currit* must be understood in an existential sense, it is not surprising that the whole mystery of existential assertion should be assumed to be contained somehow in a special use of the word *homo*, nor yet that within the theory of *suppositio* this term should be said to stand disjunctively for all men. But to those who are not obsessed by the notion of *suppositio* and the peculiarities of the Latin language the explanation is no explanation at all.

## 5. *Consequentiae*

The basic doctrine of the numerous fourteenth-century treatises on *consequentiae* is obviously derivative from that of Abelard in his

*Dialectica*, but how Abelard's influence was transmitted, whether directly or through an intermediary, we do not know, nor yet who it was that introduced the innovations characteristic of the later treatises. It is a natural conjecture that some one logician of considerable ability was responsible for the reformulation; for the principal novelties of doctrine and terminology all appear together in those surviving treatises which seem to be earliest, and are explained with the help of certain fanciful examples whose recurrence suggests strongly the influence of a single mind. But unlike Abelard's *Dialectica* and John of Salisbury's *Metalogicon*, these treatises, which technically are among the most interesting achievements of medieval logic, are written in the impersonal and unhistorical manner of a school textbook of mathematics. Presumably some at least of the authors whose works have reached us knew the outline of the development of logic between Abelard's time and their own, but none of them has thought it worth recounting.

We have seen that the word *consequentia* is used by St. Thomas Aquinas in his *Summa Contra Gentiles* in a passage where it seems to have the sense of 'conditional proposition', as in Abelard's work. The same usage is to be found also in the work of his contemporary and fellow Dominican, Robert Kilwardby, who became Archbishop of Canterbury in 1272 and died in 1277. Commenting on the passage of the *Prior Analytics*, ii. 4, where Aristotle says that the same conclusion cannot follow both from a proposition and from its negative Kilwardby writes:

'Dubitatur de maiore propositione suae rationis. Videtur enim ad idem esse et non esse sequi idem, quia si tu sedes deus est et si tu non sedes deus est, quia necessarium sequitur ad quodlibet. Adhuc si tu sedes, alterum istorum est verum, te sedere, te non sedere; et si tu non sedes, alterum eorum est verum. Adhuc disiunctiva sequitur ad utramque suae partem, et hoc naturali consequentia, quia sequitur *Si tu sedes tu sedes vel tu non sedes* et *Si tu non sedes tu sedes vel tu non sedes*, et ita naturali consequentia sequitur idem ad idem esse et non esse, et ita ex necessitate. Ad primum dicendum quod duplex est consequentia, scilicet essentialis vel naturalis, sicut quando consequens naturaliter intelligitur in suo antecedente, et consequentia accidentalis. Talis autem est consequentia secundum quam dicimus necessarium sequi ad quodlibet et de tali non intelligendum est sermo Aristotelis. Ad secundum dicendum quod idem potest sequi ad idem dupliciter: scilicet aut gratia eiusdem in ipso, et sic non sequitur idem ad idem affirmatum et negatum, et hoc intendit Aristoteles; aut gratia diversorum in ipso, et sic potest sequi idem ad idem affirmatum et negatum, et sic non intendit Aristoteles. Sic autem procedit oppositio. Per hoc etiam solvitur tertium, quia disiunctiva sequitur ad utramque suae partem non gratia eiusdem in ea sed gratia diversorum. Intendit Aristoteles quod ad idem esse et non esse non sequitur aliquid ex necessitate naturali consequentia et gratia eiusdem.'[1]

Here Kilwardby suggests that *Si tu sedes deus est* and *Si tu non sedes deus est* are both true because the necessary follows from anything. This paradoxical thesis, which he produces as though it were well known, is a counterpart to Abelard's thesis (to be noticed by Kilwardby a few sentences later but without mention of Abelard) that anything follows from the impossible, and it can be proved in a similar fashion. If, for example, it is necessary that God exists, then it is not possible that God should not exist, and so not possible either that you should be seated and God not exist or that you should not be seated and God not exist. Furthermore, just as Abelard said that his paradox showed the need for distinguishing between a stricter and a looser sense of *necessitas consecutionis*, so Kilwardby tries to answer the objection to Aristotle's assertion by saying that the necessary does not follow from everything in a *consequentia essentialis vel naturalis* but only in a *consequentia accidentalis*; and his requirement for a *consequentia naturalis* (namely that the consequent be understood in its antecedent) is the same as Abelard's stricter requirement for necessary connexion. Next Kilwardby presents in two slightly different ways the objection that even by the standards of a *consequentia naturalis* a proposition and its negation can entail the same proposition, since they certainly both entail in this way the proposition which is the disjunction of them both. And in reply to this he maintains that Aristotle was not thinking of such cases, since he meant only to deny that the same conclusion could follow in virtue of the same part of itself both from a given proposition and from the negation of that proposition. The passage as a whole shows a continuing interest in analysis of the notion of entailment, and the third objection (beginning with *Adhuc disiunctiva sequitur*) shows that at least one new rule or scheme of formally valid *consequentiae* had been formulated since Abelard's time. For the principle that a disjunctive proposition follows from either of its parts is not to be found in the works of Abelard, and anyone who accepts it must not only, like Abelard, abandon the view that the truth of a disjunction requires the falsity of one of its disjuncts, but also, unlike Abelard, reject the old assumption that disjunction is a modal notion to be explained by reference to the necessary connexion expressible in conditional statements.

[1] Ivo Thomas, 'Maxims in Kilwardby', *Dominican Studies*, vii (1954), pp. 129–46. The passage quoted consists of his extracts (28)–(33) from a manuscript in Merton College, but the italics are not in his printed text.

Although Kilwardby uses the word *consequentia*, as Abelard had done, for 'conditional statement', it clearly suggests to him the validity of an argument. That is why in his formulation of the third objection he falls into the queer construction of applying the verb *sequitur* to a *consequentia*: at the back of his mind there is a memory of that usage in which men say *Sequitur* to show approval of argument and *Non sequitur* to show disapproval. In later times the word *consequentia* is commonly applied to a piece of reasoning of some such form as 'Tu sedes, ergo tu sedes vel tu non sedes'. But the influence of tradition is still so strong that an argument of this kind is still often described as a hypothetical (i.e. complex) proposition and treated as though it differed from a conditional statement only in its use of a new connective. Thus the Pseudo-Scot writes in *quaestio* x on the first book of the *Prior Analytics*: 'Consequentia est propositio hypothetica composita ex antecedente et consequente mediante coniunctione conditionali vel rationali quae denotat quod impossibile est ipsis, scilicet antecedente et consequente, simul formatis quod antecedens sit verum et consequens falsum.' And from what follows it is clear that he means by a *coniunctio rationalis* an inferential particle such as *ergo* or *igitur*. This is a muddled way of speaking and not properly defensible, though it can be understood and perhaps even excused as a concession to tradition.

Although the Pseudo-Scot speaks of a *consequentia* as a proposition and talks sometimes of its truth, as Abelard would have done, he more often treats a *consequentia* as a piece of reasoning to which he may give approval (when approval is deserved) by saying that it is *bona* (i.e. sound). Later writers sometimes express the same thought by saying instead *Valet consequentia* (i.e. 'The argument is valid'). The change of fashion is something like that from Aristotle's presentation of syllogistic theory by means of conditional statements to Boethius' presentation by means of inference schemata; but it is made without a clear change of technical terminology and therefore leads to some confusion. Even when logicians cease to think of *consequentiae* as hypothetical propositions, they still continue to talk in general of their antecedents and their consequents, rather than of their premisses and their conclusions. This is a small point, but one of some importance. We shall see presently that the Pseudo-Scot and later writers are willing to apply the word *consequentia* to a piece of reasoning with more than one premiss; but because they still talk of *consequentiae* in the language appropriate to conditional statements, they sometimes formulate general rules about transitivity and the possibility of contraposition in such a way that these apply only to *consequentiae* with single premisses. Walter Burleigh notices this fault of his predecessors when he writes:

'Et dixi quod haec regula, videlicet ex opposito consequentis debet inferri oppositum antecedentis, est intelligenda in consequentia enthymematica et universaliter in consequentia non-syllogistica, quia in consequentia syllogistica, videlicet in syllogismo, antecedens non habet oppositum, quia antecedens syllogisticum est propositiones plures inconiunctae et tale antecedens non habet oppositum, cum nec sit propositio simpliciter nec propositio coniunctione una. Sed in consequentia syllogistica ex opposito conclusionis, scilicet ex contradictorio conclusionis, cum utraque praemissarum sequitur oppositum alterius praemissae. Et . . . isto modo probat Aristoteles suos syllogismos.'[1]

But even while he is explaining the need to restrict the rule of contraposition given by his predecessors, Burleigh himself uses the terminology which led them into error. Hence the oddity of his remark *Antecedens syllogisticum est propositiones plures inconiunctae*. Later, when he goes on to remark that Aristotle's procedure of indirect reduction depends on the principle that the premisses and the negation of the conclusion of any valid syllogism form together an inconsistent triad (or antilogism as it has sometimes been called), he rightly abandons talk of antecedent and consequent.

After giving the definition of a *consequentia* quoted above the Pseudo-Scot goes on to distinguish various kinds of *consequentiae*, and the passage deserves to be quoted in full as being the clearest account of the matter available in any medieval author:

'Consequentia sic dividitur: quaedam est materialis, quaedam formalis. Consequentia formalis est illa quae tenet in omnibus terminis stante consimili dispositione et forma terminorum. Et vocantur termini in proposito subiecta et praedicata propositionum, vel partes subiecti et praedicati. Sed ad formam consequentiae pertinent omnia syncategoremata posita in consequentia, ut coniunctiones, signa universalia, particularia, et huiusmodi. Secundo ad formam consequentiae pertinet copula propositionis, et ideo non est eadem forma consequentiae ex propositionibus quarum copula est de inesse et quarum est de modo. Tertio ad formam pertinet multitudo praemissarum, affirmatio et negatio propositionum, et huiusmodi, et ideo non est eadem forma arguendi ex affirmativis et negativis, et ita de aliis. Consequentia formalis subdividitur, quia quaedam est cuius antecedens est una propositio categorica, ut conversio, aequipollentia, et huiusmodi, alia est cuius antecedens est propositio hypothetica; et quilibet istorum modorum potest subdividi in plures alios modos. Consequentia materialis est illa quae non tenet in omnibus terminis retenta consimili dispositione et forma ita quod non fiat variatio nisi terminorum. Et talis est duplex, quia quaedam est vera simpliciter et alia est vera ut nunc. Consequentia vera simpliciter est illa quae potest reduci ad formalem per assumptionem unius propositionis necessariae. Et sic est ista consequentia materialis bona simpliciter, *Homo currit, igitur animal currit*; et reducitur ad formalem per istam necessariam, *Omnis homo est animal*. Et ista subdivitur in multa membra secundum diversitatem locorum dialecticorum. Consequentia materialis bona ut nunc est illa quae potest reduci ad formalem per assumptionem alicuius propositionis contingentis verae. Et sic, posito quod Socrates est albus, illa consequentia est bona ut nunc, *Socrates currit, igitur album currit*, quia reducitur ad formalem per istam contingentem *Socrates est albus*.'

This classification can be presented in tabular form as follows:

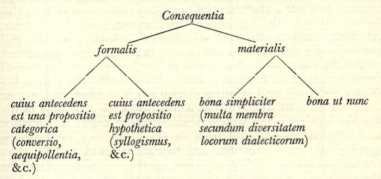

If for the moment we leave out of account *consequentiae materiales bonae ut nunc*, the division is like one made by Abelard. For a formal *consequentia* is either what he calls a perfect argument or the corresponding conditional proposition which is true *secundum complexionem* (i.e. in virtue of its structure as determined by the syncategorematic signs it contains and the number and ordering of its other elements), while a *consequentia materialis bona simpliciter* is either what he calls an imperfect argument or the corresponding conditional proposition which is true *gratia terminorum* (i.e. in virtue of the special meanings of its terms). Admittedly the Pseudo-Scot does not talk of perfect and imperfect arguments, but it is clear that he has such a distinction in mind, since he defines a *consequentia materialis* as one which can be reduced to formal validity by assumption of an additional premiss. Furthermore he says that *consequentiae materiales bonae simpliciter* are to be subdivided according to the diversity of dialectical commonplaces, as though he wished to connect this part of his doctrine explicitly with what Abelard had written about *consequentiae* in his discussion of topics.

By contrast with the other items in the classification the notion of a *consequentia materialis bona ut nunc* is new, but here again we can find a link with Abelard's work and even perhaps with that of Boethius. Once it is admitted that an argument can be enthymematic, or imperfect in the sense of requiring for its validity some unexpressed premiss, there is no good reason to deny that an argument may be imperfect for lack of a contingent premiss. When everyone knows that Socrates is white, it is natural to say with the Pseudo-Scot 'Socrates is running, therefore a white thing is running'. According to his own principles Abelard would have to refuse to admit the truth of the corresponding conditional proposition 'If Socrates is running, a white thing is running', because it is not a statement of necessary connexion; but in this he would be plainly at variance with common-sense. If, however, Abelard could be brought to agree that such a conditional proposition was a genuine *consequentia* in his sense, he would undoubtedly wish to say that it was at best *vera ut nunc*, i.e. true at present or true as things are. For in his view the distinction between necessary and contingent truth is a distinction between truth for all time and truth at a time. So even that part of the Pseudo-Scot's scheme which Abelard would reject is described in a terminology he could approve. If on the other hand we disapprove of that terminology and hesitate to speak in English of truth-at-a-time or validity-at-a-time, we shall not misrepresent the Pseudo-Scot's thought by writing 'contingently valid' for his *bona ut nunc*. Although he uses a phrase which suggests Abelard's theory, he explains it in a way which contains no reference to time, and he contrasts it with *bona simpliciter*, for which we may write 'absolutely valid'. Perhaps he (or the logician who first suggested the notion, if that was not the Pseudo-Scot himself) took courage to make the innovation from consideration of what Boethius had written about conditional propositions which are true only *secundum accidens*.

We shall see presently that according to the Pseudo-Scot's definition a propositional *consequentia materialis vera ut nunc* must be a Philonian conditional. On encountering this notion once more in the context of a debate about the requirements for validity of inference it is natural to ask whether medieval writers about *consequentiae* learnt anything from their Megarian and Stoic predecessors; but it is not at present possible to give a definite answer. There were fragments of Megarian and Stoic logic available to them in the works of Cicero and Boethius, but much more important as a possible source of information about the non-Aristotelian logic of antiquity was a Latin translation of the *Outlines of Pyrrhonism* by Sextus Empiricus. This was certainly in existence in the thirteenth century, since one of the two manuscripts in which it survives is a miscellaneous collection of philosophical treatises copied about 1300; and it may be quite early, since the other writings of the collection are twelfth-century works.[1] On the other hand, the manner in which the Pseudo-Scot introduces his account of *consequentiae materiales verae ut nunc* is entirely free from all parade of ancient learning. He defines them in a fashion which seems quite natural after his account of *consequentiae materiales verae simpliciter*. When he goes on to notice their paradoxical properties, he makes these appear as the inevitable consequences of his original definition, so that he (or the originator of the doctrine, if that was a different person) may be said to reveal for the first time how Philonian junction is related to entailment and why it deserves the attention of logicians. If it is proper for historians of philosophy to search for evidence of the influence of Sextus Empiricus in the Middle Ages, the reason is not that the doctrines which might be derived from reading of his work are extraordinary or such as medieval philosophers could not have evolved for themselves, but simply that it would be interesting to know what really happened.

Immediately after the classification of *consequentiae* quoted above the Pseudo-Scot goes on to state and prove the following five theses:

1 (*a*)  *Ad quamlibet propositionem implicantem contradictionem de forma sequitur quaelibet alia propositio in consequentia formali.*

2 (*a*)  *Ad quamlibet propositionem impossibilem sequitur quaelibet alia propositio non consequentia formali sed consequentia materiali bona simpliciter.*

2 (*b*)  *Ad quamlibet propositionem sequitur propositio necessaria bona consequentia simplici.*

3 (*a*)  *Ad quamlibet propositionem falsam sequitur quaelibet alia propositio in bona consequentia materiali ut nunc.*

3 (*b*)  *Omnis propositio vera sequitur ad quamcumque aliam propositionem in bona consequentia materiali ut nunc.*

The proof of 1 (*a*) runs as follows:

'Ad istam *Socrates est et Socrates non est*, quae implicat contradictionem de forma, sequitur *Homo est asinus* vel *Baculus stat in angulo* et sic de

---

[1] The manuscript is *Cod. Paris. Bibl. Nat. Lat.* 14700. See H. Mutschmann, *Sexti Empirici Opera*, vol i, p. x, and L. Minio Paluello, *Adam Balsamiensis Parvipontani Ars Disserendi* (*Twelfth Century Logic: Texts and Studies*, i), p. xv.

quocumque. Probatur, quia sequitur *Socrates est et Socrates non est, igitur Socrates non est*, quia a copulativa ad alteram eius partem est consequentia formalis. Tunc reservetur illud consequens. Postea sequitur *Socrates est et Socrates non est, igitur Socrates est* per eamdem regulam. Et ad istam *Socrates est* sequitur *Igitur Socrates est vel homo est asinus*, quia quaelibet propositio infert se ipsam formaliter cum quacumque alia in una disiunctiva. Tunc arguitur ex consequente: *Socrates est vel homo est asinus, sed Socrates non est* (ut reservatum fuit prius), *igitur homo est asinus*. Et sicut arguitur de ista, ita potest argui de quocumque alia; omnes enim consequentiae sunt formales.'

Using a horizontal line to indicate the transition represented in Latin by *igitur*, we may reproduce the whole proof in the following tree of derivation:

| Socrates exists and Socrates does not exist | Socrates exists and Socrates does not exist |
|---|---|
| | Socrates exists |
| Socrates does not exist | Socrates exists or a man is an ass |

A man is an ass

As the Pseudo-Scot says, each of the *consequentiae* used in the derivation is formally valid; and so, paradoxical as it may seem, no one can reject it without rejecting something essential to primary logic.

For a first proof of 2(*a*) the Pseudo-Scot uses this result. That is to say, he assumes that the *consequentia* 'A man is an ass and a man is not an ass, therefore you are at Rome' is formally valid. Then, since it is impossible that a man should be an ass, he remarks that it is necessary that a man should not be an ass, and concludes that the *consequentia materialis* 'A man is an ass, therefore you are at Rome' is *bona simpliciter*, being reducible to a formally valid *consequentia* by addition of a necessarily true premiss. But he notices also that his thesis can be proved without the use of 1(*a*) by a derivation of the following pattern, in which 'A man is not an ass' is supposed to be a necessarily true proposition:

| A man is an ass | |
|---|---|
| A man is an ass or you are at Rome | A man is not an ass |

You are at Rome

For 3(*a*) the Pseudo-Scot gives a proof dependent upon 1(*a*) in the same way as the first proof of (2*a*), but it is obvious that we can also construct a proof like the second for 2(*a*) by putting a contingently false proposition in place of 'A man is an ass' and its contradictory in place of 'A man is not an ass'.

For the proof of 2(*b*) the Pseudo-Scot applies the principle of contraposition, 'In omni bona consequentia oppositum consequentis infert oppositum antecedentis'. If from an impossible proposition there follows in a *consequentia simplex* any proposition we may choose, then from the negation of any proposition we may choose, and so in effect from any proposition we may choose, there follows in the same way a necessary proposition which is the negation of the impossible proposition. *Mutatis mutandis* 3(*b*) is derived in the same way from 3(*a*). For a proof of the principle of contraposition itself, which is the nominal subject of the whole *quaestio*, the Pseudo-Scot relies on his definitions of the various kinds of *consequentiae*.

It is curious that the author of these proofs, who was obviously a logician of great ability, made no attempt in this *quaestio* to prove or even to state the thesis which would be 1(*b*) in our numbering, namely 'Any proposition which is itself formally necessary as being the disjunction of two contradictories follows formally from any proposition whatever'. Although he numbers his five theses consecutively in the order in which they have been given above, he can scarcely have failed to notice that there might be a thesis related to his first as his third is to his second and his fifth to his fourth. We must therefore suppose that he thought our 1(*b*) in some way less clear and satisfactory than the others. But he came nearer to a formulation of it in *quaestio* iii on the second book of the *Prior Analytics*.

The subject of this later *quaestio* is 'Utrum ad utrumque contradictoriorum possit sequi idem', and it opens with an argument like that of Kilwardby to show that Aristotle's denial was too sweeping because there is at least one proposition which follows from a proposition and from its contradictory, namely the disjunction of them both. But this is not all. By reference to his five paradoxical theses about *consequentiae* (which he restates and reproves here without any important change) the Pseudo-Scot goes on to show in more detail what is wrong with Aristotle's denial. Clearly any proposition follows from itself in a valid *consequentia* of each of the three kinds which have been distinguished. But if a proposition is true, it follows *ut nunc* from its own negation, since by 3(*b*) it follows *ut nunc* from anything; therefore a true proposition can follow *ut nunc* from each of two contradictories. Similarly if a proposition is necessary, it follows *simpliciter* also from its own negation, since by 2(*b*) it follows *simpliciter* from anything; therefore a necessary proposition can follow *simpliciter* from each of two contradictories. Finally, if a proposition is one whose negation is self-contradictory, it follows by 1(*a*) *formaliter* from that negation; therefore a proposition whose negation is self-contradictory can follow *formaliter* from each of two contradictories. The most, then, that can be said in favour of Aristotle's doctrine is that a simple categorical proposition cannot follow *formaliter* both from a proposition and from the negation of that proposition. So far there is no addition to the set of five paradoxical theses, but in dealing with the last of the three cases which he distinguishes the Pseudo-Scot seems to recognize the possibility of extending his own doctrine. For he asserts here not only the objection to Aristotle which we have just noticed but also the rather wider principle: 'Ad utrumque contradictoriorum sequitur idem formaliter ubi consequens est disiunctiva facta ex duobus contradictoriis ut ista *Socrates currit vel Socrates non currit*.' This he proves by the consideration that the contradictory of such a disjunction, being self-contradictory, would entail everything *gratia formae*, and therefore would entail incidentally any pair of contradictories, which according to the principle of contraposition for *consequentiae* is as much as to say that the disjunction follows *formaliter* from each of a pair of contradictories. He could, indeed, assert quite simply that a disjunction of contradictories follows *formaliter* from anything we may choose, since its negation formally entails the negation of anything we may choose. But he does not take this step.

For the argument which we have just stated it is essential that the negation of a disjunction of contradictories is itself a conjunction of contradictories, and it is possible that the Pseudo-Scot was held up for a while by failure to recognize this. But whatever the reason for his delay, it is interesting to notice that the procedure which he follows in his final argument, like that used earlier in his proofs of 2(*b*) and 3(*b*), involves the second-order principle of contraposition for all *consequentiae*, which he restates here in the form: 'Quando ad antecedens sequitur consequens, ad oppositum consequentis sequitur oppositum antecedentis'. For it is no mere accident that he did what he did in this fashion, as anyone may confirm who tries to prove 1(*b*) by first-order *consequentiae* alone, i.e. in some such way as the Pseudo-Scot proved 1(*a*). The fact that 1(*a*) can be proved directly by simple first-order *consequentiae*, but not 1(*b*), is connected with the fact that any argument may have several premisses but only one conclusion.

In earlier discussions of *consequentiae* the theses 2(*a*) and 2(*b*) were derived from the suggestion that a conditional statement was true if and only if it was impossible that its antecedent should be true and its consequent false; and it was argued that their paradoxical nature showed the need for a stricter definition of conditional dependence. The Pseudo-Scot, on the other hand, offers all five of his paradoxical theses as true statements which seem curious only because they have to do with unfamiliar applications of the notion of following. So far as 1 (*a*) is concerned, this line is clearly justified. For the first paradox is proved solely by reliance on three rules of formal entailment which no one can plausibly call in question, namely (i) the rule that a conjunctive proposition entails each of its parts, (ii) the rule that a disjunctive proposition is entailed by each of its parts, and (iii) the rule that a disjunctive proposition and the negation of one of its parts together entail the other part. It is true, of course, that there can be no inference from a self-contradictory proposition if by 'inference' we mean a transition from the known to the previously unknown; and for this reason the word *igitur* is rather absurd in the formula: 'Socrates est et Socrates non est, igitur baculus stat in angulo.' But if the theory of *consequentiae* is taken to be an account of the derivability of propositions from other propositions, there is nothing absurd in 1 (*a*). On the contrary it is quite good sense to say that anyone who commits himself to formal self-contradiction can no longer reject anything. Furthermore, 1 (*b*), which the Pseudo-Scot did not formulate, is also beyond criticism, since it can be derived from 1 (*a*) by the unexceptionable principle of contraposition. But what of the other four paradoxical theses? For proof of them the Pseudo-Scot relies on his definitions of the two kinds of *consequentiae materiales*, and it may perhaps be suggested that his definitions are discredited by the results he derives from them.

It is rather unfortunate that in the Pseudo-Scot's system material *consequentiae* are all treated as imperfect arguments. For in the ordinary sense of the word 'perfect' a *consequentia materialis bona simpliciter* is perfectly valid as it stands; and even from a psychological point of view there is nothing to be gained by reduction of it to a *consequentia formalis*, since anyone who doubts its validity will doubt also the truth of the supplementary premiss required for converting it into a *consequentia formalis*. But a *consequentia materialis bona ut nunc* is really an imperfect argument in the ordinary sense of the phrase, because the conclusion does not follow from the expressed premiss or premisses alone. It is, so to say, a *consequentia* by courtesy, as being the offspring of that genuine *consequentia* which results from addition of a suppressed premiss. Now in the first case the definition given by the Pseudo-Scot, although misleading for the reason just noticed, does not vitiate his proofs of the paradoxical theses 2(*a*) and 2(*b*). For it is certainly the case that a *consequentia materialis* is *bona simpliciter* if and only if it can be reduced to a *consequentia formalis* in the way he indicates. But the definition of a *consequentia materialis bona ut nunc* which the Pseudo-Scot uses in his proofs of the paradoxical theses 3(*a*) and 3(*b*) involves a stretch of the meaning of the word *consequentia*, and this makes 3(*a*) and 3(*b*) not merely surprising (which is what we commonly mean by 'paradoxical') but also unacceptable to those who wish to retain ordinary usage. For when we agree that 'Socrates is running, so a white thing is running' would be a satisfactory argument in certain circumstances, we do not thereby commit ourselves to the assertion that any argument may be called contingently valid if it can be reduced to formal validity by addition of some contingently true premiss, even though that be the contradictory of the original premiss. And to suppose that we do intend this is to misunderstand the way in which our ordinary usage is related to its context. Similarly when we say that the form of words 'If Socrates is running, a white thing is running' could be used in certain circumstances to make a true statement, we do not wish to include among the circumstances in question that of Socrates' not running or that of there being a white thing other than Socrates running. This indeed is what distinguishes the ordinary conditional from the Philonian.

Although the Pseudo-Scot does not use his paradoxes to discredit any account of the nature of *consequentiae* (even when he might legitimately do so), he discusses various alternatives before offering the general definition quoted above. It is not clear whether what he says in this connexion is a report of a debate among his predecessors or merely a piece of dialectic invented by him for purposes of exposition, but he declares that there are three possible accounts (*triplex est modus dicendi*) and that against each there is an argument (*arguitur*) from a counter-example.

According to the first account it is necessary and sufficient for the validity of a *consequentia* that it should be impossible for the antecedent to be true and the consequent false. But against this we have the counter-example 'Every proposition (i.e. propositional sign or indicative sentence) is affirmative, so no proposition is negative'. Here the *consequentia* as a whole is obviously valid, and yet the antecedent might conceivably be true though the consequent must be false because it is refuted by the mere existence of itself.

According to the second account the necessary and sufficient condition for validity of a *consequentia* is that it should be impossible for things to be as signified by the antecedent without also being as signified by the consequent. Presumably this formula was designed to avoid the difficulty about self-refuting sentences which we have just noticed. But against it we have the counter-example 'No chimaera is a goat-deer, so a man is an ass'. Here the *consequentia* as a whole is said to be invalid because the antecedent is true (by the principle that the truth of a negative proposition requires only the non-realization of the state of affairs signified by the contradictory affirmative) and the consequent is false. Yet, contrary to the suggestion under consideration, it is said to be impossible for things to be as signified by the antecedent without being also as signified by the consequent, which is as much as to say that things cannot in any circumstances be as signified by the antecedent. This is very strange indeed. Perhaps the point is that the state of affairs signified by the antecedent would involve the existence of a chimaera. But if so, it seems that the existence of a chimaera would be required also for the truth of the antecedent, since according to ordinary usage its truth is the same as the realization of the state of affairs which it signifies and we cannot reasonably deny existential import in the one context while accepting it in the other. The Pseudo-Scot makes no comment on the argument, and his silence presumably means that the argument is his own or at least one he approves.

According to the third account a *consequentia* is valid if and only if it is impossible that the antecedent should be true and the consequent false when they are both formulated together (*antecedente et consequente simul formatis*). Here the addition of the qualifying clause seems to be another attempt to escape from the objection brought against the first account. If 'Every proposition is affirmative' is formulated at the same time as 'No proposition is negative', they are both contingently false, and they are therefore able to appear as antecedent and consequent respectively in a valid *consequentia*. But against the new suggestion we have the counter-example 'God exists, so this *consequentia* is invalid'. If the antecedent is assumed to be necessarily true, it can be concluded that the *consequentia* as a whole must be invalid, since the hypothesis that it is valid leads to a self-contradiction. But this is as much as to say that the consequent is necessarily true, and so we have an invalid *consequentia* satisfying the suggested condition of validity. Again the Pseudo-Scot offers no detailed comment, but contents himself with adding to the third account a new clause 'except for the single case in which the sense of the consequent is inconsistent with the sense of the inferential particle (*igitur*) which marks the existence of a *consequentia*'. And even so he makes little use of the qualification later. For he omits it when giving a definition of a *consequentia* in his next paragraph (i.e. the definition we have quoted above), and he mentions it only once again, namely in his first version of the paradoxical thesis 2(*b*), where he seems to think it specially relevant.

Since the notion of entailment is at least as simple and clear as that of impossibility, there is nothing much to be gained from talking of the validity of arguments in any of the ways contemplated by the Pseudo-Scot. But of all the suggestions he considers, including that which he finally adopts, the second seems to be the most satisfactory, because it makes the validity of an argument consist in a connexion between certain propositional contents rather than in any relations between truth-values of propositional signs (or forms of words). And it is therefore not surprising to find that the criticism brought against this suggestion turns out to be very flimsy. But it is interesting to notice that logicians who favoured this view found it necessary to meet an objection something like that brought against the first suggestion in the Pseudo-Scot's list. As Buridan pointed out, it is a mistake to suppose that a *consequentia* must be valid if it is impossible that when the *consequentia* is formulated the state of affairs signified by the antecedent should be realized without the state of affairs signified by the consequent.[1] For the *consequentia* 'No proposition is negative, so some proposition is negative' is obviously invalid, and yet it is certainly impossible that when this *consequentia* is formulated the state of affairs signified by the antecedent should be realized at all. Rather we should say that a *consequentia* is valid if, for the state of affairs signified by the antecedent and the state of affairs signified by the consequent, it is impossible that the first should be realized without the second. This condition differs from that we have rejected in being a formula of impossibility *in sensu diviso*. That is to say, the impossibility which it requires is not merely impossibility in relation to the contingent fact that the two states of affairs which it mentions have been signified in the *consequentia*.

When we turn to Ockham's treatment of *consequentiae* in his *Summa Totius Logicae*, we find the same terminology but with different explanations. In several respects his version of the theory seems less satisfactory that of the Pseudo-Scot, and it may conceivably be earlier; for it is not easy to discover from internal

---

[1] *Sophismata*, ch. 8, soph. 2; cited by I. M. Bochenski in *Formale Logik*, § 30.18 after E. Moody.

evidence how they are related. Ockham begins by saying that *consequentiae* differ from syllogisms in being enthymemes (i.e. elliptic arguments), and then sets out a number of distinctions that may be made among them.[1] His manner of listing the distinctions suggests that he thinks they are for the most part independent, but we shall see that this cannot in fact be the case.

First he distinguishes between *consequentiae simplices* and *consequentiae ut nunc* strictly by reference to the time for which they are valid. If the antecedent cannot at any time be true without the consequent, the *consequentia* is *simplex*; but if at some time, though not at the time of speaking, the antecedent can be true without the consequent, the *consequentia* is only *ut nunc*. This emphasis on truth-at-times is unfortunate for reasons we have noticed in our discussion of Aristotle's argument about the naval battle. On the other hand, it is a good feature of Ockham's treatment that he puts the distinction of absolute and contingent validity first. For, however we may define *consequentiae ut nunc*, it is clear that they are only *consequentiae* by courtesy and therefore to be separated at the beginning from absolute *consequentiae*.

Next Ockham goes on to distinguish between *consequentiae* which hold *per media intrinseca* and others which hold *per media extrinseca*. The noun *medium* seems to be new in this connexion, but the adjectives 'intrinsic' and 'extrinsic' come from the theory of topics. Ockham explains that he means by a *medium intrinsecum* a proposition formed from terms contained in the *consequentia* and by a *medium extrinsecum* a general rule which is no more concerned with the terms of the *consequentia* than with any others. For an example of the first kind of *consequentiae* he gives the argument 'Socrates is not running, so a man is not running', which holds by the *medium* 'Socrates is a man', and for an example of the second kind the argument 'Only a man is an ass, so every ass is a man', which holds by the general rule 'An exclusive affirmative proposition is equivalent to a universal affirmative proposition with terms transposed' and needs no support from any proposition including the terms 'man' and 'ass'. Syllogisms, he tells us, hold *per media extrinseca*, and any *consequentia* which holds *per medium intrinsecum* may be said to hold also *per medium extrinsecum* but less directly. From this it appears that the distinction is that between arguments which Abelard called imperfect and those he called perfect. The latter are valid by virtue of their structure and therefore fall under general rules of the kind Ockham describes, but the former need supplementary premisses to bring them into perfect form. In admitting perfect arguments as *consequentiae*

---

[1] *Summa Totius Logicae,* iii (iii). 1.

Ockham departs from his original description of *consequentiae* as enthymemes, but instead of recognizing this he misleadingly groups general rules together with supplementary premisses as *media* through which *consequentiae* hold.

Thirdly, Ockham distinguishes between *consequentiae formales* and *consequentiae materiales*, but with new senses for the two phrases. Instead of saying (as the Pseudo-Scot would have done if he had talked of *media*) that only those *consequentiae* are formal which hold in virtue of *media extrinseca* concerning the forms of their propositions, he includes among formal *consequentiae* also those which hold directly *per medium intrinsecum* and indirectly *per medium extrinsecum* ⟨*non*⟩ *respiciens conditiones generales propositionum, scilicet veritatem, falsitatem, necessitatem, impossibilitatem*; and he cites as examples of the two kinds of *consequentiae* which he recognizes the same two arguments that he used to illustrate the distinction of the previous paragraph. A *consequentia materialis*, he then says, is one that holds *praecise ratione terminorum et non ratione alicuius medii extrinseci* ⟨*non*⟩ *respicientis praecise generales conditiones propositionum*; and the only specimens he gives under this head are the two obviously paradoxical arguments, 'A man is running, so God exists' (where the consequent is supposed to be necessary) and 'A man is an ass, so God does not exist' (where the antecedent is supposed to be impossible). From the examples by which he illustrates his distinction it is clear that Ockham wishes to call a *consequentia* formal if, and only if, it involves a necessary connexion in the stricter sense of which Abelard spoke, and that a material *consequentia* is for him always a paradoxical argument. But if, like Ockham, we ignore 1(*a*) and 1(*b*) in the scheme of paradoxical theses given above, we can say that paradoxical *consequentiae* differ from humdrum arguments in involving no *media extrinseca* except such as have to do with the general status of their propositions, e.g. the rule that an impossible proposition entails everything. And this, it seems, is what Ockham intends to convey by his phrase about the *conditiones generales propositionum* in the two definitions quoted above.[1]

---

[1] The text of this passage as printed in the early editions, without *non* before *respiciens* and *respicientis*, is unintelligible. In an article first published in *Przeglad Filozoficzny*, xxxviii (1935), but translated after his death as 'Die Aussagenlogik bei Wilhelm Ockham', *Franziskanische Studien*, xxxii (1950), pp. 97–134, J. Salamucha has suggested that after *conditiones generales propositionum* we should read *non veritatem vel falsitatem, necessitatem vel impossibilitatem*. This has some manuscript support but is still unsatisfactory; for it seems clear that the *conditiones generales propositionum* of which Ockham speaks are to be contrasted with the internal forms of propositions and that they must be truth, falsity, necessity, and impossibility, as the commonly received text implies. Insertion of *non* before *respiciens* and *respicientis* restores the required sense, gives point to the second occurrence of *praecise* (which Salamucha omits), and produces a text that is just sufficiently complicated to have been corrupted easily.

After these general distinctions Ockham goes on to consider *consequentiae* according to the logical characters of their consequents (e.g. according to the universality or particularity of those propositions) and formulates various special rules. But in his concluding chapter on the subject he reverts to first principles and gives eleven general rules[1] which recur with variations and additions in many later works:

(1) *The false never follows from the true.*
(2) *The true may follow from the false.*
(3) *If a consequentia is valid, the negative of its antecedent follows from the negative of its consequent.*
(4) *Whatever follows from the consequent follows from the antecedent.*
(5) *If the antecedent follows from any proposition, the consequent follows from the same.*
(6) *Whatever is consistent with the antecedent is consistent with the consequent.*
(7) *Whatever is inconsistent with the consequent is inconsistent with the antecedent.*
(8) *The contingent does not follow from the necessary.*
(9) *The impossible does not follow from the possible.*
(10) *Anything whatsoever follows from the impossible.*
(11) *The necessary follows from anything whatsoever.*

Of these (7), (8), and (9) are rightly said to hold only for absolute *consequentiae*. But the same restriction applies also to (6). And it is worth noticing that (3), (4), and (5) hold for contingently valid *consequentiae* only if the second occurrence of the word 'follow' is taken to indicate the sort of following appropriate to such *consequentiae*. For a proposition which follows absolutely from the consequent of a contingently valid *consequentia* need only follow contingently from the antecedent. The first five and the ninth can all be extracted from Aristotle's works, while the sixth, seventh, and eighth are at least of a kind that he would have accepted. But the last two belong to a different tradition. Of them Ockham says rather strangely 'But such *consequentiae* are not formal, and so these rules are not in common use'. It is true, of course, that they are not formal in his special sense of that word, but we have seen that the Pseudo-Scot succeeded in proving by unexceptionable first-order rules that according to a more natural sense of the word 'formal' anything whatsoever follows formally from the formally impossible. And if (10) and (11) look surprising, the reason is merely that they serve no useful purpose in

[1] *Summa Totius Logicae*, iii (iii). 37.

ordinary straightforward inference, however interesting they may be for the general theory of entailment.

Unlike Ockham, Ralph Strode and Richard Ferrybridge are content with one main distinction among *consequentiae*, that between the formal and the material. But Strode at least interprets this in much the same way as Ockham. According to him every valid material *consequentia* allows for inference (*illatio*) from the antecedent to the consequent, but a formal *consequentia* involves in addition a connexion of meaning or understanding (*intellectio*) between the antecedent and the consequent. Thus 'if anyone understands that you are a man, he understands that you are an animal', because the second follows from the formal understanding (*de formali intellectu*) of the first. From these definitions he draws the interesting conclusion that every formal *consequentia* is material but not vice versa. As an example of a *consequentia* which is merely material (*materialis tantum*) he cites 'A man is an ass, so a stick is standing in the corner', and for general rules of material *consequentiae* he gives only (10) and (11) of Ockham's list.[1] The chief novelty in this account of the distinction is that Strode entirely ignores the notion of form in the purely logical sense and introduces instead the notion of understanding. But the latter was already implicit in Abelard's talk of strict connexion. Ferrybridge's treatment of the subject is similar in some respects, but he seems to wish to combine Ockham's view of formality with a view like that of the Pseudo-Scot. For near the beginning of his little treatise he says that non-formal *consequentiae* are either (1) arguments from the impossible to something not specially relevant, or (2) arguments to the necessary from something not specially relevant, or (3) arguments which do not hold if the terms are changed. And after (2) in this list he adds the note 'But I do not consider that kind of argument valid'.[2]

The occasion for all these curious deviations from the comparatively simple doctrine of the Pseudo-Scot was probably a debate about the paradoxes. Perhaps Ockham and Strode were trying to find a sense of 'formal' which would be in one way stricter and in another way more inclusive than that of the Pseudo-Scot. It is curious that they wanted to use the same word for their new purpose; but in medieval Latin *formalis* seems to have some of the associations which 'proper' has in modern English. However that may be, the result of their innovations was confusion in the terminology for talking about *consequentiae*. In the early years of the fifteenth century Paul of Pergolae, trying

---

[1] *Consequentiae Strodi cum Commento Alexandri Sermonete*, &c. (Venice, 1517), pp. 1r. and v., 4v.          [2] Ibid., p. 93v.

to work all the various distinctions into one scheme, produced the following table:[1]

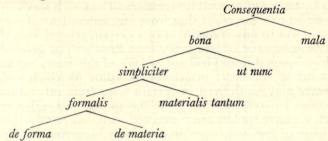

Here *formalis* is to be taken in the sense of Strode, on whose work Paul of Pergolae was commenting, and the *tantum* after *materialis* is to be understood as a limitation required by Strode's doctrine that formal *consequentiae* are also material. Given this interpretation for the fourth line of the table, the entry below, which would otherwise be very puzzling, becomes intelligible. It is in effect the Pseudo-Scot's distinction of formal and material, but expressed in a new terminology because his adjectives have been used for another purpose.

Although the word *consequentia* was commonly reserved by later writers for arguments expressed with *igitur* or *ergo*, there was always supposed to be a close connexion between the validity of a *consequentia* and the truth of a conditional statement. It is therefore not surprising that some of the formulae which were evolved as stipulations for the validity of *consequentiae* reappear in the work of Paul of Venice as stipulations for the truth of conditional statements.[2] In a list of ten suggestions which he notices without naming the authors the first is the first of the views considered by the Pseudo-Scot and the eighth the view of Strode, while the second appears to be conceived as a direct denial of the view of Buridan noticed above. It is not possible as yet to say who first thought of the other suggestions or even to understand clearly what they all mean; but it is reasonable to assume that most of them were put forward in the course of a debate about the validity of *consequentiae*.

As it started with consideration of topics, so the theory of *consequentiae* continued to be associated with this branch of the older logic. But most logicians who wrote on *consequentiae*, including Ockham, gave a good deal of attention to *consequentiae* of the kind called formal by the Pseudo-Scot. Unlike Aristotle and the Stoics,

[1] Ibid., p. 48*v*.                    [2] *Logica Magna*, ii. 9; 134r.A–135r.A.

they did not commonly use variables for the purpose of exhibiting the logical forms which interested them, but formulated their rules by means of general descriptions. Thus each special rule is a statement to the effect that from any antecedent of a certain logical form to any consequent of a certain related logical form *valet consequentia* or *est bona consequentia formalis*. The general rules we have quoted from Ockham are not of this kind, but some of them are second-order principles according to which valid *consequentiae* may be derived in certain ways from other valid *consequentiae*. In contrast with these the special first-order rules of which we have spoken are concerned with *consequentiae* that hold in virtue of the syncategorematic words occurring in the antecedent or the consequent or both.

In theory the study of *consequentiae* was sometimes taken to cover the whole of deductive logic, including the doctrine of the conversion of categorical propositions and the doctrine of the syllogism. Such a comprehensive view may be found, for example, in the accounts of *consequentiae* given by the Pseudo-Scot and Walter Burleigh and also in the *Perutilis Logica* of Albert of Saxony. But in practice tracts on *consequentiae* are usually regarded as supplements to the Aristotelian tradition. After dealing with topical arguments such as those *a superiori distributo ad inferius distributum* (e.g. from 'All animals are mortal' to 'All men are mortal')[1] and rules of conversion they give rules allowing *consequentiae* of such kinds as the following:

(1) *From a conjunctive proposition to either of its parts.*

(2) *From either part of a disjunctive proposition to the whole of which it is a part.*

(3) *From the negation of a conjunctive proposition to the disjunction of the negations of its parts, and conversely.*

(4) *From the negation of a disjunctive proposition to the conjunction of the negations of its parts, and conversely.*

(5) *From a disjunctive proposition and the negation of one of its parts to the other part.*

(6) *From a conditional proposition and its antecedent to its consequent.*

(7) *From a conditional proposition and the negation of its consequent to the negation of its antecedent.*

(8) *From a conditional proposition to the conditional proposition which has for antecedent the negation of the original consequent and for consequent the negation of the original antecedent.*

[1] Ockham, *Summa Totius Logicae*, iii (iii). 2.

(9) *From a singular proposition to the corresponding indefinite proposition.*

(10) *From any proposition with an added determinant to the same without the added determinant.*

(11) *From necessity to actuality.*

(12) *From actuality to possibility.*

(13) *From the negation of necessity to the possibility of negation, and conversely.*

(14) *From the negation of possibility to the necessity of negation, and conversely.*

Of the rules in this list, which are no more than a selection from the available material, (1) to (8) belong to what we have called primary logic. Most of this first group have been noticed already, but (3) and (4), which are commonly known today as De Morgan's rules after the logician who rediscovered them in the nineteenth century, are new and interesting. They are presupposed by the Pseudo-Scot and they occur explicitly in Ockham's work, though not in his treatment of *consequentiae*.[1] For a systematic treatment of general logic (9) is of great importance, but such an enlargement of general logic beyond the bounds of syllogistic is not to be found in the medieval treatises so far printed. This rule is mentioned casually by Ockham in his first chapter on *consequentiae* as the rule by which we construct such arguments as 'Socrates is running, so something is running'.[2] In general logic again (10) is an analogue to (1). But, as most medieval logicians knew, Ockham's version, which we quote, is defective if it is supposed to apply to propositions in ordinary language;[3] for while it is correct to say 'A white man is running, therefore a man is running', it is certainly not correct to say 'I have an imitation pearl, therefore I have a pearl'. In modal logic (11) and (12) are basic principles formulated already by Abelard, but (13) and (14) are more complicated rules given by Peter of Spain and paraphrased here from Ockham's *Summa*.[4] They correspond in an interesting way to (3) and (4) above and also to the rules of William of Shyreswood whereby *non omnis* is equivalent to *quidam non* and *non aliquis* to *omnis non*.

As in the doctrine of *suppositio terminorum*, so here some of the more subtle theses asserted by medieval logicians belong to what modern logicians call quantification theory. Thus from the principle 'Quod sequitur ad consequens sequitur ad antecedens' Burleigh derives the theorem:

---

[1] Ibid. ii. 32.       [2] Ibid. iii (iii). 1.

[3] Ibid. 6.       [4] Ibid. 13.

'In conditionali cuius antecedens est propositio particularis vel indefinita subiectum antecedentis supponit confuse et distributive respectu consequentis, ita quod ad talem conditionalem cuius antecedens est propositio particularis vel indefinita sequitur conditionalis in cuius antecedente subicitur aliquod inferius ad subiectum primae conditionalis. Verbi gratia sequitur enim: *Si animal currit, substantia currit; ergo si homo currit, substantia currit.*'[1]

In another place the same author sets out the thesis 'Quando aliqua consequentia est bona terminis acceptis sine distributione, e converso est bona terminis acceptis cum distributione'.[2] As it stands this is not altogether clear, but from his explanations it appears that what he has in mind is the rather complicated principle of argument κατὰ πρόσληψιν which might be expressed in the form 'If whatever is predicable of some A is predicable of some B, then whatever is predicable of every B is predicable of every A'. And in a third place he remarks correctly that from the fact that anything with every quality of a certain range (*qualelibet*) has a given character we cannot properly conclude that any thing with some quality of that range (*aliquale*) has the same character, since *qualelibet* is *inferius* in relation to *aliquale*.[3] Here the point is that the word *qualelibet*, although a sign of universality, restricts the class of things under discussion, because its distributive force does not apply to the things themselves but rather to the qualities by which they are selected for attention. These passages are impressive and of considerable historical interest because they show clearly the difficulties of expression with which logicians had to contend before the invention of a simple but adequate notation for quantification theory.

In his proof of the paradoxical thesis 1(*a*) the Pseudo-Scot had shown that he knew how to validate a *consequentia* by reference to others in the way that Chrysippus had followed when deriving theorems from his indemonstrables. And in his proofs of the paradoxical theses 2(*b*) and 3(*b*) he had shown that he knew how to derive one *consequentia* from another by application of a second-order rule such as the principle of contraposition for *consequentiae*. Both methods of proof are to be found in the works of later writers on *consequentiae*, in particular those of Walter Burleigh and John Buridan. There seems, however, to have been no elaborate system of derivative rules such as Chrysippus is said to have produced and therefore no very long train of reasoning in this sort of work. What these authors tried to do at their most

---

[1] *De Puritate Artis Logicae Tractatus Longior* (ed. Boehner), p. 68.
[2] Ibid., p. 211. This passage comes from the *Tractatus Brevior*, printed by Boehner as an appendix.
[3] Ibid., p. 258. This is also from the *Tractatus Brevior*.

systematic was to set out the principles of primary, or propositional, logic presupposed by syllogistic theory, and in this they
very largely succeeded. But there is no single work of medieval
logic which has established itself as a classic, and it is significant
that modern writers who try to present the medieval contribution
in comprehensive and orderly fashion find it necessary to collect
pieces from various sources.[1]

[1] E. Moody has made an interesting attempt of this kind in his *Truth and Consequence in Mediaeval Logic*, §15.

# V

# LOGIC AFTER THE RENAISSANCE

## 1. *Humanism and the Rise of Natural Science*

WHEN we turn to consider what men made of traditional logic at the Renaissance and after, we find so much complexity in the history of ideas that it no longer seems profitable to maintain strictly chronological order in the mention of the various items that have to be noticed.

In the first place it is important to realize that there was no sharp break between the Middle Ages and the later period. Peter of Spain's textbook, the *Summulae Logicales,* was still studied in the seventeenth century. It was included, for example, in an anthology of philosophy for the use of students which was printed at Paris in 1605 under the title *Gymnasium Speculantium.* And in 1618 Robert Sanderson of Oxford devoted a chapter of his *Logicae Artis Compendium* to explaining *suppositio terminorum.* His account is brief and not well articulated, but it mentions all the main distinctions, and it has some importance because the *Compendium* continued to be used in English universities until the nineteenth century and was reprinted as late as 1841. Except for talk about the distribution of terms, the doctrine of *suppositio* disappeared from newly composed textbooks before the end of the seventeenth century, but in H. Aldrich's *Artis Logicae Compendium* of 1691 there still survive a distinction between *consequentiae formales* and *consequentiae materiales* and a short account of *sophismata* and *insolubilia.* Furthermore, this book remained in use until the second half of the nineteenth century and was reprinted with Mansel's notes in 1862. But long before Sanderson wrote attacks had been made on the medieval tradition and even on logic itself. Although the subject survived in the elementary instruction of universities, it no longer attracted the attention of many of the best minds. From the 400 years between the middle of the fifteenth and the middle of the nineteenth century we have in consequence scores of textbooks but very few works that contain anything at once new and good.

Among the manuals of the sixteenth century *The Rule of Reason* by Thomas Wilson (1551), *The Arte of Reason, rightly termed Witcraft* by Raphe Lever (1573), and *The Arte of Logicke* by Thomas

Blundeville (1599) are interesting as being the first attempts to present the subject in English. Wilson dedicated his work to Edward VI, and we may suppose that he wrote in English because he thought it important that secular learning, no less than theological, should be available to his countrymen in their own language; but he was content to use Anglicized versions of the Latin technical terms, e.g. 'proposition'. Lever on the other hand was determined to be as Anglo-Saxon as he could, and produced such novelties as the pronouncement 'Gaynsaying shewsayes are two shewsayes, the one a yeasaye and the other a naysaye, changing neither foreset, backset nor verbe'. Three hundred years later the Dorsetshire dialect poet William Barnes made a similar effort in *An Outline of Redecraft* (1880), but with no more effect on the practice of English-speaking logicians. Neither Wilson nor Lever professes to be very profound, and Blundeville's book is confessedly a work of popularization, published for the benefit of ministers of religion who have not been brought up in any university. But the standard of scholarship is no better in the Latin *Dialectica* of John Seton (1545) or in the manual which John Argall published in 1605 under the title *Ad Artem Dialecticam Introductio brevis et perspicua, salibus et facetiis undique aspersa, pro tyronibus et novitiis elaborata*. Seton sided with Rome in the ecclesiastical troubles of age, but his work continued in use at the English universities and went through many editions. Argall, on the other hand, was a Protestant who liked nothing better than a quip against Romanists, and he prides himself on having freed logic from the useless medieval subtleties of Hispanus, Scotus, &c., while rendering it into more elegant Latin. It has been suggested that the use of 'argal' intead of 'ergo' (then pronounced like 'argo') by the first clown in *Hamlet*, Act V, scene i, is a joke on his name.[1] Since the play was printed in 1604 with the reading 'or all', which is obviously a corruption of 'argal', it cannot owe anything to Argall's book, but the joke may nevertheless be a pun. In the preface to his book Argall says that he lectured on logic at Christ Church many years before, and it seems clear that his text is based on the script of his old lectures, since it contains jokes directly addressed to Oxford undergraduates, in particular an elaborate passage about the prison of Bocardo *apud nos Oxonienses*.[2] It would not be at all surprising if he had gained a reputation as a university wit and 'argal', as used by Shakespeare's

---

[1] The suggestion was made by Mr. A. F. E. Shields, a pupil of Prof. G. Ryle, to whom we owe the information.
[2] P. 148. The Bodleian copy contains a written dedication to Sir Thomas Bodley in which Argall describes himself as *plus quam sexagenarius*.

clown, had become a catchword among smart young men some years before the composition of *Hamlet*.

In form at least the curriculum of studies in most universities was the same at the end of the seventeenth century as it had been two or even three hundred years before; and, as in the Middle Ages, so then, disputations were required before graduation. For many students of logic these were, no doubt, the chief occasions on which they could exhibit their skill. It is, therefore, not surprising that some of the jargon of disputations became current in ordinary academic Latin. One of the most interesting examples of this is the use of the word *implicat* as an abbreviation for *implicat contradictionem*. In philosophical debate it was the ambition of each participant to show that his adversary's thesis could be reduced to absurdity, and the procedure was so well known that at the end, where we should say in English 'which is absurd', it was enough for general understanding to say *quod implicat*. Even Spinoza, who, being a Jew, did not receive the ordinary education of a university, was familiar with the practice and used *implicat* as short for *implicat contradictionem* in his *De Intellectus Emendatione*[1] of 1662 and his *Cogitata Metaphysica*[2] of 1663. There are also some passages from this period in which he uses *implicantia* in the sense of 'contradiction' or 'impossibility'.[3]

The first blow to the prestige of logic came from the humanists, or classical scholars, of the Renaissance, i.e. in the fifteenth century. Their objection to scholasticism, and to medieval logic in particular, was not that it was false in any details, but rather that it was barbarous in style and unattractive in content by contrast with the rediscovered literature of antiquity. Who but a dullard would devote his life to the *proprietates terminorum* when he might read the newly found poem of Lucretius *De Rerum Natura* or learn Greek and study Plato? To some scholars such as Rabelais the pretensions of the philosophers were plainly ridiculous, and it is clear enough from the learned works of the time that logic in particular no longer attracted the best minds. In general education the writing of elegant Latin was now the chief accomplishment to be learnt, and for this Cicero and Quintilian were the authorities. From them the men of the Renaissance acquired the Roman attitude to scholarship, with the result that genuine logic was neglected for rhetoric and books which purported to be on logic quoted Cicero as often as Aristotle. Laurentius Valla, who exposed the forged donation of Constantine, and Rudolphus Agrippa were two writers who started the corruption. But the most

---

[1] *Opera*, ed. van Vloten and Land, i, p. 16.
[2] Ibid. iv, p. 205.                    [3] Ibid. iii, p. 39, and iv, p. 196.

famous logician of this tendency was Petrus Ramus, or Pierre de la Ramée (1515–72).

It is said that when Ramus took his master's degree in 1536 the thesis he chose to defend was that everything Aristotle had taught was false. This is probably a misrepresentation; but in his *Aristotelicae Animadversiones* of 1543 he charges Aristotle with confusion and obscurity, and there can be no doubt that he made many enemies by the vigour of this attack on Aristotelianism and also by the cocksureness with which he put forward his own views in his *Dialecticae Partitiones* of the same year (later called *Institutiones Dialecticae*). So bitter indeed was the opposition that in 1544 his enemies obtained from Francis I a royal decree in which he was described as 'rash, arrogant, and impudent' and forbidden to teach philosophy. In the next year, however, he received an invitation to the Collège de Presle in the University of Paris, and in 1547 Henri II cancelled the decree of condemnation at the instance of the Cardinal of Lorraine, then a patron of Ramus. During these years Ramus worked so effectively that his reputation as a polymath was established, and in 1551 he was appointed to a professorship of eloquence and philosophy at the Collège Royal. There he was very active in making plans for the improvement of teaching in the liberal arts and produced works in all parts of this big field, including Greek grammar, rhetoric, and mathematics. The scope of his learning can be seen most easily in the collection of his *Scholae in Liberales Artes* which was published in 1569. This includes twenty books of *Animadversiones Aristotelicae* which had been published already in 1556 but are not to be confused with the short book of 1543. He became best known, however, through his *Dialectique* of 1555, the first work on logic in the French language, and his Latin *Dialectica* of 1556. His popularity is obvious from the number of editions through which his books passed in his lifetime, and his success as a public figure is shown by his appointment in 1559 to a commission for the reform of the University of Paris. This project was dropped, however, on the death of Henri II, and Ramus's future became uncertain when he turned Protestant in 1561. During the latter part of his life he had to spend about half of his time away from Paris because of the wars of religion, and in the end he was killed in the massacre of St. Bartholomew's Day 1572. It is said that his murderers were incited by a professional rival called Charpentier, and that after they had stabbed him they threw his body from the window of his study on the fifth floor of the Collège de Presle.

In the long run France and the Roman Catholic Church were the chief sufferers from the terrible deeds of St. Bartholomew's

Day, but one minor consequence unfortunate for Britain and the other northern countries was that Ramus won the glory of a Protestant martyr and so came to enjoy in those countries a greater influence than he deserved. As early as 1574 Robert MacIlmaine of the University of St. Andrews produced an English translation of the *Dialectica* under the title *The Logike of the moste Excellent Philosopher P. Ramus Martyr*. And in 1592 Christopher Marlowe included the death of Ramus (together with some speeches about the peculiarities of Ramist logic) in his chronicle play *The Massacre at Paris*. Since we can find little of value either in Ramus's criticisms of Aristotle or in his original work, it is difficult for us to understand what made his admirers enthusiastic; but if we may judge from the references of Marlowe and other writers of the time, what attracted most attention was his passion for simplicity and order.

In his reform of the liberal arts Ramus took as his guide three principles which he found in Aristotle's *Posterior Analytics*, i. 4, namely (1) that a scientific statement should be true in all instances, (2) that it should be true essentially, i.e. by a necessary connexion of the predicate with the subject, and (3) that it should be reciprocal, i.e. have a predicate commensurate with its subject. From these propositions (which his followers called fancifully the laws of truth, justice, and wisdom) Ramus concluded in a way which is not very clear that everything merely probable must be banished from science, that every science must have a precisely delimited field, and that the method of exposition should always be a descent from the more general to the less general. There was nothing very new in these assertions, nor yet in the use of epitomes and the practice of dichotomous division for which he was evidently famous at the time Marlowe wrote his play; but the scheme was presented with a vigour that made converts, and it may have prepared men's minds for the more revolutionary changes of thought that were to come. In logic, however, it involved a specious rearrangement of the old material, which was no gain.

According to Ramus, logic is the *ars bene disserendi* and should include all that concerns the invention and disposition of arguments, while rhetoric (contrary to the views of Cicero) is to be confined to discussion of style and delivery. The distinction between invention and disposition is assumed in Aristotle's *Topics*, where the first seven books deal with the first and the eighth with the second subject, and it is stated explicitly in Cicero's *Topics* and Boethius' *De Differentiis Topicis*, where *dispositio* is identified with *iudicium*, but Ramus seems to have derived it more immediately from Rudolphus Agrippa. In his *Dialectica* he gives one book to each subject. Passing over Aristotle's categories, predicables, and topics as useless or confused, he offers first nine *loci*, or places in which arguments may be found artificially (i.e. by rules of technique). These are cause, effect, subject, adjunct, opposite, comparative, name, division, and definition, and the discussion of them with their subdivisions (e.g. efficient, material, formal, and final causes) make up nearly half of his logic. It will be seen that many items in the list are taken from Aristotle, and that the result is no more systematic than the parts of Aristotle's logic that it is supposed to replace. After these, at the end of the first book, comes a short consideration of inartificial argument, of which a prime example is the direct testimony given by a witness in a court of law. Evidently this distinction caught the attention of readers, since the remark *Argumentum testimonii est inartificiale* appears in Marlowe's play.

In the second book of his *Dialectica* Ramus crowds all that he has to say about the rest of logic. In his preliminary account of kinds of statement he introduces *axioma* as a technical term instead of *propositio*, presumably because he wishes to use *propositio* later in its Ciceronian sense of 'major premiss'. For the minor premiss he uses the word *assumptio* and for the conclusion *quaestio*. This terminology shows the nature of his reading, and from what he says in his bigger works, e.g. in the first book of his large *Animadversiones Aristotelicae*, it is clear that he knew a good deal about the history of logic. He was familiar, for example, with what had been said in antiquity about the question whether conditional and disjunctive statements involve the notion of necessity, and he argues for the view that they do, with references to Diodorus and Chrysippus. But in his account of categorical statements, which he calls *axiomata simplicia*, he departs from tradition by introducing the division:

$$\text{Axioma simplex} \begin{cases} \textit{generale} \\ \textit{speciale} \begin{cases} \textit{particulare} \\ \textit{proprium} \end{cases} \end{cases}$$

Here an *axioma generale* is what we ordinarily call a universal statement and an *axioma particulare* one in which the predicate is not ascribed to the whole subject or, as he puts it with a curious adaptation of terminology from another part of logic, *consequens non omni antecedenti attribuitur*, while an *axioma proprium* is one which has for *antecedens*, or subject, a proper name or other singular term. It is indeed one of Ramus's chief claims to novelty in logic that he makes explicit provision throughout for statements of the last kind which were almost ignored by Aristotle in his *Analytics*, but it will be noticed that by an unintelligent application of his principle of dichotomy he has put particular and singular propositions together under the uninformative heading 'special' instead of adopting the more reasonable scheme:

$$\text{Categorical statement} \begin{cases} \textit{singular} \\ \textit{general} \begin{cases} \textit{universal} \\ \textit{particular} \end{cases} \end{cases}$$

which could be derived from Aristotle's *De Interpretatione*.

In his earlier accounts of syllogistic Ramus is content to include moods with singular terms in each of the Aristotelian figures, but in the edition of the *Dialectica* which was published in the year of his death he made a more radical break with tradition and offered the following dichotomous division of categorical syllogisms, or *syllogismi simplices* as he called them in distinction from conditional and disjunctive arguments:

$$\text{Syllogismus simplex} \begin{cases} \textit{contractus} \\ \textit{explicatus} \begin{cases} \textit{speciei primae} \\ \textit{speciei secundae} \end{cases} \end{cases}$$

Here *syllogismi contracti* are arguments from examples which Aristotle would have presented in his third figure. According to Ramus even Aristotle acknowledged in his practice that they are better set out in the simple fashion of *Quaedam confidentia est virtus, ut constantia* or *Quaedam confidentia non est virtus, ut audacia*. His *syllogismi explicati*, on the other hand, are fully articulated arguments such as Aristotle would include in his first and second figures, but subdivided in a new way. At the outset Ramus, for no obvious reason, makes Aristotle's second figure his first and Aristotle's first his second. Possibly his use of the words *antecedens* and *consequens* in the senses explained above and his separation of the first two figures of syllogism from the third were intended to suggest a correspondence between certain categorical syllogisms and certain conditional arguments. If so, he had an interesting point to make, but he does nothing to explain it here. On the contrary, his alteration of the order of the first two figures tends rather to obscure it. Next he assumes that all the statements involved in syllogisms of these two figures must be universal or singular and thus omits all syllogisms with particular premisses or particular conclusions. Then, ringing the changes on the per-missible combinations of premisses, he constructs in his first figure three variants of each of the two moods *Cesare* and *Camestres* and in his second three variants of each of the moods *Barbara* and *Celarent*. When both premisses are universal, the syllogism as a whole is called *generalis*; and when both premisses are singular, the syllogism as a whole is called *proprius*; but when one premiss is universal and the other singular, the syllogism as a whole is called, in a rather misleading way, *specialis*. Thus there are six varieties of syllogism in each figure, but not the six moods which can be obtained by adding subaltern moods to those of Aristotle. For a specimen of a *syllogismus specialis* in his first figure which according to the old classification would be a version of *Camestres* Ramus gives 'Saltator est luxuriosus; Muraena non est luxuriosus; Muraena igitur non est saltator'. And for a specimen of a *syllo-gismus proprius affirmativus* in his second figure he has 'Octavius est haeres Caesaris; ego sum Octavius; sum igitur haeres Caesaris'. Here and throughout examples are taken from ancient authors, in particular Terence, Cicero, Horace, and Ovid.

In his account of *syllogismi compositi* Ramus follows tradition more closely, but confines his attention to the four moods of Chrysippus which had become commonplaces and takes no account of the great development of primary logic in the Middle Ages. Finally, Ramus asserts that the method of exposition should normally be from the more general to the less general, and claims the support of Aristotle for this principle, but adds that in certain contexts it may be expedient to adopt a *methodus prudentiae* which allows for digressions acceptable to the audience.

Discussion of the merits of Ramus's reforms continued for a long time. In his *Institutiones Logicae* of 1626 Franco Burgersdyck divided logicians into Aristotelians, Ramists, and Semi-Ramists (sometimes called Philippo-Ramists because they tried to make a compromise between Ramist teachings and those of Philip Melanchthon, the humanist friend of Luther, who had written a manual based on Aristotle's works). The debate was still going on in England at the end of the century.[1] In 1672 John Milton, the poet, published a small volume which he had composed forty years earlier under the title *Artis Logicae Plenior Institutio ad Petri Rami methodum concinnata*, and in 1687 John Wallis, the mathe-matician, published a textbook called *Institutio Logicae* with an appendix, dating from 1631, in which he tried to show that Aristotle's authority justifies us in treating singular terms as though they were general terms considered with respect to the

---

[1] See W. S. Howell, *Logic and Rhetoric in England, 1500–1700*.

whole of their possible application. This explanation was widely accepted, and it appears in many later works (e.g. Euler's *Lettres à une Princesse d'Allemagne* of 1761) as something well established. It is to be found even in some elementary textbooks of the twentieth century. The work of Wallis which has just been mentioned is interesting also because it contains an attempt to bring conditional statements within the Aristotelian scheme by treating them as universal. According to Wallis, '*Si* universaliter sumendum est, quasi tantumdem valens atque *omni casu quo*'.[1]

Even Wales was affected by the teaching of Ramus the Martyr. For as early as 1595 his principles were expounded by Henry Perry in *Egluryn Phraethineb* (i.e. *An Elucidation of Wit*) and it seems that Welsh puritan divines continued to apply them in sermonmaking until the Methodist revival of the eighteenth century brought new ideas of pulpit eloquence.[2]

Not all the humanists of the Renaissance despised Aristotle. Some such as Pomponazzi thought he had been in part misrepresented by the scholastics, and these tried to apply to his work the methods of what we now call historical scholarship. In logic the most famous writer who adopted this point of view was Zabarella (1538–89), a professor of the University of Padua. In his commentary on the *Posterior Analytics* and in his other logical works such as his treatises *De Quarta Syllogismorum Figura* and *De Methodis* he shows knowledge of medieval authors (in particular Averroës, for whom he has great respect), but he does not discuss in detail those parts of medieval logic which now seem to us most interesting. His work is that of a classical scholar who does not expect to find much of value after the classical period, and his subjects are almost all such as might be suggested by close reading of Aristotle. Unlike Ramus, he may still be studied with some profit, but his writings do not give the impression that the teaching of formal logic was very lively in his time.

Perhaps the most important service of Zabarella was his discussion of the distinction between the compositive (or synthetic) and the resolutive (or analytic) method. In his usage a method is a way of acquiring knowledge, and is not to be confused with an order of exposition. We can, indeed, speak of compositive and resolutive orders. As Aristotle and other distinguished authors, such as Galen, Avicenna, and Averroës, have shown, exposition of a theoretical science must proceed compositively from first principles, which are relatively simple and most easily knowable,

---

[1] *Institutio Logicae*, ii. 10.
[2] R. Tudor Jones 'Rhesymeg y Piwritaniaid', *Efrydiau Athronyddol*, 1950, pp. 19–37. We are indebted to Prof. R. I. Aaron for information about this article.

to their consequences, which are more complicated and less easy to grasp, but an art or practical discipline must start from consideration of an end and then work back to the means by which the end may be achieved. Thus Aristotle says in his *Metaphysics* that the activity of a builder must be preceded by a regressive study in which the acts to be done are shown to be relevant to the production of the building desired.[1] But the distinction of compositive and resolutive method is something different.[2] The compositive method is the method of demonstration properly so called, and it is expounded by Aristotle in his *Posterior Analytics* according to the resolutive order, as indeed it must be, since the making of a demonstration is a practical activity guided by the conception of an end to be achieved.[3] The resolutive method, on the other hand, is that kind of reasoning in which we argue *a posterioribus ad priora*, that is to say from what is later or derivative in the order of nature to what is earlier or more original, and it has two forms: (*a*) reasoning from effects or signs to causes, and (*b*) induction or reasoning from singulars to universals.[4] Both are recognized by Aristotle in various places and shown to be capable of being presented in syllogistic form. Of the two the first is the more powerful, since it can lead to knowledge of something radically new, whereas the second gives only confirmation of what is implicit in our knowledge of individual cases. Zabarella does not profess to add anything here to Aristotle's doctrine, and he does not consider how we may acquire the major premiss for an argument from effect to cause. So it can hardly be said that he has indicated a new programme for scientific advance. But his terminology seems to have inspired Galileo's procedure in the analysis of mechanical problems, and for this reason it deserves to be remembered.[5]

Although the teaching of logic became impoverished at this time by neglect of some medieval subtleties, there was no widespread movement of Aristotelian purism. And the excessive attention of educators to Cicero and Ovid was not enough by itself to produce the marked decline of interest in formal logic which occurred during the seventeenth and eighteenth centuries. Another cause is to be found in the rise of modern physics (i.e. the physics of Galileo) and the recognition that logic was not an instrument of discovery, as had sometimes been supposed. For the rise of physics three things were necessary: first a development

---

[1] *Metaphysica*, Z, 7 (1032ᵃ32–1032ᵇ31).  [2] *De Methodis*, iii. 1.
[3] Ibid. iv. 19.  [4] Ibid. iii. 4 and 19.
[5] J. H. Randall, 'The Development of Scientific Method in the School of Padua', *The Journal of the History of Ideas*, i (1940), pp. 177–206.

of mathematics, secondly a theory of perception which would delimit a profitable field of study for the physicist, and thirdly a willingness to learn from experience. Of these the first two were supplied indirectly by the humanist renaissance. Already in the fifteenth century the study of Plato had become fashionable among the learned of Italy. Academies were founded in imitation of Plato's society, and there was even at one time a wild suggestion by Gemistus Pletho for the establishment of a new religion with elements drawn from Platonism. This enthusiasm was due no doubt to the charm of Plato's style and the poetic qualities of his work. But Plato had said that the study of mathematics was a necessary preparation for illumination, and so some members of the academies set themselves to learn geometry. Another ancient system of philosophy which interested the scholars of the renaissance was Epicureanism. Here again the first reason for study was probably aesthetic rather than scientific; for the poem of Lucretius *De Rerum Natura* was rediscovered in 1417 and published in 1473. But the system of Epicurus rests on the atomism of Democritus, and that in turn involves the distinction of primary and secondary qualities which is now fundamental in our scientific view of the world. The third requisite for the development of physics, namely an empirical approach to nature, had been recommended already by many philosophers of antiquity and the Middle Ages: it was necessary only that their precepts should be taken seriously.

It may, nevertheless, be thought surprising that logic was divorced at this time from mathematics with which it had been associated in its origin. The explanation is to be found in the fact that mathematical development now took a new line. The mathematical legacy of Greece was chiefly geometrical; for even questions about primes, such as we now assign to the theory of numbers, had been treated in Euclid's *Elements* among problems of geometry. But the discoveries of the mathematicians of the seventeenth century were not merely corollaries to Greek theorems. It is true that they used the word 'geometer' much as we use the word 'mathematician', but the novelties which occupied their attention belonged to the parts of mathematics now called algebra and analysis. The fundamental notion in their thinking was that of functional dependence, although they could not at first express it with abstract generality, and they were inspired throughout by the desire to solve problems in mechanics, as is shown by the terminology of 'variables' which they have bequeathed to us.

Now there was a very important difference between geometry and these new branches of mathematics in the manner of their development. Geometry was conceived from the beginning as a science in which theorems were derived from axioms according to principles of logical entailment. It was supposed that the axioms were truths known by extra-logical intuition, but that, when once the axioms had been accepted, there need be no use of intuition other than that required for seeing a logical entailment. Algebra and analysis, on the other hand, were not elaborated in axiomatic fashion, and are not so presented even now in elementary teaching. These studies grew out of arithmetic, and were conceived originally as techniques for the manipulation of symbols according to special rules, e.g. the rules for brackets, signs, and indexes. It is possible, of course, to recast an algebraic argument in such a way that all the special principles of algebra appear as premisses or definitions; but this was not the way in which the mathematicians of this time conceived their work. They thought of their novelties as new procedures for reckoning, and the language of modern mathematicians still retains from this time a number of words like 'operation' and 'calculus' (Latin for 'stone' or 'piece') which suggest an analogy with the use of the abacus. No doubt the mathematicians of the sixteenth and seventeenth centuries would have maintained that their procedures were based on an intuitive understanding of the notions with which they dealt; but in fact they often allowed themselves to extend the application of these notions without realizing exactly what they were doing (e.g. when they talked of the sum of an infinite series), and it may be that they could not have made their advances in any other way. But the result was that they came to think of their new methods as independent of traditional logic. The old geometrical style of presentation, or the synthetic method, as it was sometimes called, was still considered to be the ideal in exposition, but the new branches of mathematics were supposed to contain a technique of discovery. Descartes wrote about a mysterious method of analysis which had been known to Pappus and Diophantus but not properly formulated until his own time.[1] And Newton seems to have looked upon his infinitesimal calculus as a dodge, rather than as an addition to mathematics in the old sense. For when he wrote his *Principia Mathematica Philosophiae Naturalis*, he took great trouble to present his results in the geometrical style without reference to the methods by which he had reached them.

The first modern attempt to formulate a doctrine of scientific method was Bacon's *Novum Organum* of 1620. As its title implies, this work was written in opposition to Aristotle. Bacon realized that the traditional logic was not an instrument of scientific

[1] *Regulae ad Directionem Ingenii*, 4.

discovery, as some had supposed, and he tried to lay down new rules by which the making of discoveries could be reduced to a simple task. But he did not suggest any development of logic in that sense of the word which interests us, and we need not consider his theory of induction, or indeed any put forward by his successors. In his *Discourse of Method* (1637) and his unfinished *Regulae ad Directionem Ingenii* Descartes also tried to lay down rules for discovery, though of a very different kind. He was so much impressed by the development of mathematics that he thought of all science as a kind of mathematics and tried to generalize the notion of analytic method to which we have referred above. Again we need not consider the merits of his doctrine. For our purpose it is sufficient to notice that his influence, like that of Bacon, tended to make philosophers neglect formal logic in favour of the new study of heuristic methodology.

Descartes's talk of ideas is commonly accounted one of the more important novelties in seventeenth-century philosophy, and so indeed it is. But it should be remarked here that the novelty was one of terminology rather than of substance. In the Middle Ages the word *idea* was still reserved for a form as that was understood in the Christian Platonism of St. Augustine, i.e. for an archetypal concept in the mind of God. Thus St. Thomas asks in his *Summa Theologica*, i. xv. 1, *Utrum ideae sint* and replies *Necesse est ponere in mente divina ideas*. At that time the forms which were supposed to exist in human minds were described as *species* or *intentiones*, and there were debates between philosophers who followed Aristotle in thinking that *species intelligibiles* were all derived by abstraction from *species sensibiles* and others who followed St. Augustine in thinking that *species intelligibiles* could be acquired only by divine illumination. During the humanist renaissance the word *idea* became fashionable because of its Greek origin and was sometimes used in a loose way as an equivalent for *imago*.[1] When Descartes and Locke used it as a substitute for the medieval *species* and *intentio*, their chief purpose was no doubt to free themselves from medieval entanglements, but Descartes had in mind also the Augustinian precedent. For in reply to a criticism of Hobbes he declares: 'I employed this term because it was the term commonly used by philosophers for the forms of perception of the Divine mind.'[2] That is to say, by his doctrine of innate ideas he deliberately assimilated the human mind to the divine mind as that was described by theologians in the Augustinian tradition.

---

[1] C. C. J. Webb, 'Idea' in *Hasting's Dictionary of Religion and Ethics*.
[2] *Replies to Objections*, iii. 5.

Thomas Hobbes is remembered chiefly for his political philosophy, but of the famous philosophers of the age, apart from
Leibniz, he had most of interest to say about logic. In his youth
he acted as amanuensis to Bacon, but he did not discover his
vocation to philosophy, and to logic in particular, until at the age
of forty he accepted an invitation to travel on the continent as
tutor to a nobleman's son. And then the first stimulus came
from geometry. According to his friend John Aubrey, he chanced
one day to find a copy of Euclid lying open in a gentleman's
library at the page containing Pythagoras' theorem:

'He read the proposition. "By God," sayd he, "this is impossible."
So he reads the demonstration of it, which referred him back to such
a proposition; which proposition he read. That referred him back to
another, which he also read. *Et sic deinceps* that at last he was de-
monstratively convinced of that trueth. This made him in love with
geometry.'[1]

Hobbes came indeed to think of himself as an authority on the
subject, and rashly maintained against Wallis that he had found
a way of 'squaring the circle'. It might be thought that one who
had so lively an appreciation of mathematical discovery would
be tempted to talk of it as entry into a Platonic heaven; but when
once he had mastered, as he thought, the science of geometry,
Hobbes put forward a very different theory of demonstration.
Already in the *Objections* printed in 1641 with the first edition of
Descartes's *Meditations* he wrote:

'But what shall we say now, if reasoning chance to be nothing
more than the uniting and stringing together of names or designations
by the word 'is'? It will be a consequence of this that reason gives us
no conclusion about the nature of things, but only about the terms
that designate them, namely, whether or not there is a convention
(arbitarily made about their meanings) according to which we join
these names together.'[2]

In the first part of his *De Corpore* of 1655, which has the separate
title *Computatio sive Logica* and is intended as an introduction to
his whole system, he is more explicit. He writes there:

'The first truths were arbitrarily made by those that first of all
imposed Names upon Things, or received them from the imposition
of others. For it is true (for example) that *Man is a Living Creature*; but
it is for this reason, that it pleased men to impose both those names on
the same thing. . . . Now *Primary Propositions* are nothing but Definitions, or parts of *Definitions*, and these onely are principles of

<hr>

[1] *Brief Lives*, ed. Clark, vol. i, pp. 332 and 396.     [2] *Objections*, iii. 4.

Demonstration, being Truths constituted arbitrarily by the Inventors of Speech, and therefore not to be demonstrated.'[1]

Euclid's axioms, e.g. 'The Whole is greater than the Part thereof', are not principles of demonstration, he tells us, i.e. not truths to be accepted without proof, but propositions which are themselves demonstrable from definitions.[2] They must therefore be distinguished from the laws of physics, which are not made by arbitrary definitions.[3]

This is the beginning of the conventionalist theory of necessary truth. In the development of Hobbes's philosophy it is connected with the doctrine that our thinking is only the manipulation of signs, and the title *Computatio sive Logica* suggests that he thought reasoning might be reduced to a species of calculation. His writings contain in fact no attempt to work out such a project; but the suggestion was taken up by Leibniz together with the theory that demonstration proceeds from definitions. Being himself a mathematician who had made great discoveries, Leibniz could not accept the conventionalist theory of necessity, but his younger contemporary Berkeley thought that it was a natural consequence of his own empiricist philosophy and wrote in his notebook:

'The reason why we can demonstrate so well about signs is that they are perfectly arbitrary and in our power—made at pleasure. The obscure ambiguous term *relation*, which is said to be the largest field of knowledge, confounds us, deceives us. Let any man show me a demonstration, not verbal, that does not depend either on some false principle or at best on some principle of nature which is the effect of God's will and we know not how soon it may be changed. *Qu*: What becomes of the *aeternae veritates*? *Ans*: They vanish.'[4]

And a little later he added:

'Take away the signs from Arithmetic and Algebra, and pray what remains? These are sciences purely verbal, and entirely useless but for Practice in societies of men. No speculative knowledge, no comparing of ideas in them.'[5]

But these suggestions were not published until the end of the nineteenth century, and the close alliance of conventionalism and empiricism was not established until our own time.

Locke had little or no interest in formal logic, and so long as his influence was dominant few philosophers thought the subject worthy of serious study. He was prepared, indeed, to admit that

---

[1] *Elements of Philosophy Concerning Body* (English translation, published 1656), ch. iii, §§ 8 and 9.     [2] Ibid., ch. vii, § 25.     [3] Ibid., ch. xxvi, § 1.
[4] *Philosophical Commentaries* (in *Works*, ed. Luce and Jessop, vol. i), 732–5. 'Relation' is Locke's word.     [5] Ibid., 767–8.

all deductive reasoning could be reduced to Aristotle's rules, but he thought that what was important in the rules would in any case be obvious to a normal healthy mind. For 'God has not been so sparing to men to make them barely two-legged creatures, and left it to Aristotle to make them rational'.[1] A country gentle-woman that has never heard of Aristotle can reason well enough about her own affairs. Syllogisms are useless for discovery, and serve only for verbal fencing. As for identical statements of the form 'A is A' and statements in which part of any complex idea is predicated of the whole, they are but trifling.[2] Real instructive knowledge, such as we have in mathematics, cannot be gained by mere explication of definitions, but must be derived from intuition of relations between ideas.

When he had occasion to mention scholastic philosophy, Locke wrote with contempt. But what he has to say about the generality of ideas, and indeed the whole of his doctrine of ideas as signs, is very similar to Ockham's account of *intentiones* which was noticed in the last chapter. Since Ockham's *Summa Totius Logicae* was reprinted at Oxford in 1675 while Locke was forming the opinions he later expressed in his *Essay*, it is difficult to believe that the similarity can be mere coincidence. But detailed examination of Locke's numerous notes and drafts may perhaps make it possible to settle the question beyond all doubt.

Although the well-known philosophers of the seventeenth century gave no detailed expositions of formal logic and sometimes decried the study, there were plenty of textbooks available to their readers, and it may be useful to conclude this section with an account of some of the best of these. For an understanding of the intellectual life of an age it is necessary to know not only the authors who have been remembered as innovators, but also those who were influential in their time, either as representatives of tradition or as popularizers of new ideas.

In this connexion we may notice first the *Logica Hamburgensis* published by Joachim Junge in 1638. The book went through several editions, and its author was highly praised by Leibniz on many occasions. Apart from the customary subjects, it contains some novelties which look like anticipations of later developments, in particular a discussion of some properties of relations. Further-more, under the heading of *consequentiae* there is mention of argu-ment by inversion of a relation and argument *a recto ad obliquum* (e.g. 'A circle is a figure; therefore anyone who draws a circle draws a figure'). In a passage on *entia per aggregationem* Junge distinguishes an *ens aggregativum per ordinem* from an *ens mere aggregativum*. On

[1] *Essay Concerning Human Understanding*, IV. xvii. 4.　　　[2] Ibid. viii.

the other hand, there is little in the book that can be supposed to have inspired the work for which Leibniz is famous.

Next there is *Logica Fundamentis Suis a quibus hactenus collapsa fuerat Restituta*, which was published by Arnold Geulincx in 1662. As its title suggests, this book is an attempt to restore logic from the state of decay into which it seemed to have fallen, and it contains competent summaries of some medieval doctrines which were disappearing from the knowledge of contemporary philosophers. Thus at the beginning there is a distinction between varieties of *suppositio* or *acceptio terminorum* according to the following scheme:[1]

$$
Suppositio
\begin{cases}
ordinaria
\begin{cases}
singularis: \text{PETRUS est doctus.} \\
communis: \text{MUS rodit caseum.}
\end{cases} \\
extraordinaria
\begin{cases}
logica: \text{MUS subalternatur animali.} \\
grammatica: \text{MUS est syllaba.}
\end{cases}
\end{cases}
$$

The divisions are, of course, medieval, but the names by which they are introduced appear to be new. Geulincx then goes on to distinguish varieties of *suppositio ordinaria communis* in the usual way, and explains *distributio* as *acceptio copulativa cum enumeratione laxa subiectorum* (i.e. the old *suppositio confusa et distributiva*)[2] with a view to using it later in his account of syllogistic for the formulation of rules.[3] In this connexion there appears the new notion of an antisyllogism with the example: 'Petrus non est animal, ergo non et Petrus est homo et omnis homo est animal.[4] In his theory of *consequentiae* Geulincx preserves the common distinctions and enumerates some of the well-known principles, including the paradoxical rules that the impossible entails everything and the necessary follows from everything.[5] In his distinction of formal and material arguments he says that the latter, which he calls also *argumenta physica* and *argumenta topica*, do not depend on the *affectiones logicae*.[6] It is especially interesting that he makes a clear distinction between *argumenta in enuntiationibus* and *argumenta in terminis* and that in his account of *argumenta formalia in enuntiationibus* (i.e. propositional logic) he holds it to be sufficient and necessary for the truth of a disjunctive proposition that one of its parts should be true. From this latter thesis he derives quite correctly the two principles which are now commonly called De Morgan's rules and the need for rejecting the argument *ponendo tollens*, which

---

[1] *Logica*, &c. (in *Opera Philosophica*, ed. J. P. N. Land, 1891), i. ii. 4.
[2] Ibid. 6.          [3] Ibid. III. ii. 5.          [4] Ibid. 6.
[5] Ibid. II. ii. 6 and 7.                    [6] Ibid. i. 9 and 11.

depends on taking disjunction in the exclusive sense.[1] Finally in a chapter called 'De ratione a priori et a posteriori' he discusses the two phrases of the title in a way which shows that they were still used in his time in the old sense we have noticed in our account of Zabarella's essay *De Methodis*.[2]

In the same year as the *Logica* of Geulincx there appeared a much more famous work *La Logique ou l'Art de penser*. This is often called the *Port Royal Logic* because it was composed by Antoine Arnauld and Pierre Nicole, two leaders of the Port Royal movement, and manifests the distinctive tone of earnest piety for which the movement became famous. As might be expected, the authors have little patience with medieval subtleties. In their view talk of second intentions is useless trifling and scholastic authorities can be safely neglected. On the other hand, they have no respect for Ramus. For they not only ridicule his attempts to draw exact boundaries between the sciences and his passion for dichotomies, but reject his conception of logic as the *ars bene disserendi*. According to their definition at the beginning of the book, logic is the art of managing one's reason aright in the knowledge of things, both for the instruction of oneself and for the instruction of others. They are certainly interested in clear exposition, but not in forensic skill or academic prestige. Augustine and Pascal are their models of style, and Montaigne, with his egoism and his affectation of scepticism, is their chief abomination.[3] Nor are they Aristotelian purists, though they think that the *Prior Analytics* is the chief source of formal logic. They mention Aristotle's list of categories and his classification of topics, but only to dismiss them both as unprofitable. In the clash between Aristotelianism and the new science their sympathies are all for the modern, and they explain in the first of their preliminary discourses that they have deliberately chosen some of their examples with a view to introducing the reader to the correct philosophy of nature and of mind, just as they have chosen others to spread correct views on moral and religious questions. On the other hand, they show no understanding of the role of experiment in the growth of natural science, and they mention induction only to say that it is unreliable.[4] Their notions of method seem to be derived entirely from consideration of geometry, and they are so far from a truly scientific attitude in any field that they think of all scientific study as pointless unless it helps to perfect the reason. Good sense and sound judgement ('le bon sens et la justesse de l'esprit dans le discernement du vrai et du faux') are, they declare, infinitely more

---

[1] Ibid. ii. 1; iii. iii. 1, 2, and 4.
[2] Ibid. iv. ii. 7.
[3] *Logique*, iii. 19.
[4] Ibid. 18, iv. 6.

estimable and more important than any theoretical knowledge that may be gained by devotion to the most genuine and solid of sciences.[1] In short, they are followers of Descartes, but followers who are interested in his philosophy chiefly because they see it as a revival of Augustinian thought and therefore an ally of their own kind of theology. Having said this, we must add that their book nevertheless deserves its high reputation. It is written with a fresh vigour that distinguishes it from the common run of text-books, and although it is the source of a bad fashion of confusing logic with epistemology, it contains some novelties that are worth study.

The epistemological interest of the authors is shown by their division of the work into four parts which are said to treat respectively of conception, judgement, reasoning, and method. In their discussion of conception they follow closely what Descartes says of ideas (e.g. his account of innate ideas), but they try to include also some of the themes commonly discussed under the heading of terms. In so doing they are naturally led to talk of ideas as signs and to treat them as what medieval logicians called *termini mentales*. Thus they say that there are singular ideas, each of which represents an individual, and common or general ideas which represent many things, and after connecting these two sorts with proper and common nouns they declare that the phrase 'general term' may be used equally for universal ideas and for common nouns.[2] But they add that one of the most frequent sources of confusion in thinking is uncertainty in the connexions between words and ideas. For this the proper remedy in their view is the fixing of the connexions by our own act. Such fixing is nominal definition (*definitio nominis*), and it must be distinguished from real definition (*definitio rei*), which is by no means arbitrary but explicates the idea already attached to a word, i.e. reveals what other ideas are contained in it.[3] The reader may perhaps be inclined to think that by 'real definition' the authors mean only the explanation of the meaning assigned to a word in ordinary usage, but apparently that is not so. For they go on to talk separately of this third sense of definition and introduce here some interesting remarks about the difference between the principal and the accessory ideas attached to words. By accessory ideas they mean the suggestions that give words their emotional flavours and make them polite or offensive, reverent or obscene. In their second and third parts, on the other hand, the authors do not raise many psychological questions about judgement and reasoning but content themselves for the most part with dis-

[1] *Logique*, Premier Discours.    [2] Ibid. i. 6.    [3] Ibid. 12–13.

cussing propositions and arguments as pieces of spoken or written discourse. The word *iudicium* was not commonly used in the Middle Ages for the mental counterpart of assertion, but the phrase *actus iudicativus* had been used by Ockham in this sense,[1] and the word *jugement* may perhaps have seemed less strange in a seventeenth-century book of logic than *idée*. In their account of complex propositions the authors make the interesting remark that phrases such as 'I hold that' and 'it is true that' should not always be taken as signs of separate assertions.[2]

In spite of their titles the first three parts of the *Port Royal Logic* correspond to customary divisions of treatises on logic, but the fourth part of the work is an innovation, and here the authors give all their attention to the questions about clear thinking which are their main interest. They begin, it is true, with some mention of the old distinction between reasoning *a priori* and reasoning *a posteriori*, but they remark that it is necessary to extend the application of these phrases a little (i.e. beyond their usual senses of 'reasoning from causes' and 'reasoning from effects') if it is to be supposed that between them they cover all kinds of demonstration,[3] and then they go on to discuss at length the advice given by Descartes in his *Discours de la méthode* and by Pascal in his *Esprit géométrique*. What they mean by 'method' can be understood best from the eight rules in which they summarize their results:

'1. To leave no term at all obscure or equivocal for lack of a definition.

2. To employ in definitions only terms which are known perfectly or already explained.

3. To require as axioms only things which are perfectly evident.

4. To receive for evident that which needs only a little attention to be recognized as true.

5. To prove all propositions which are at all obscure, using in the proof of them only preceding definitions, agreed axioms, and propositions already demonstrated.

6. Never to be misled by equivocation of terms through failing to make mental substitution of the definitions which restrict and explain them.

7. To treat things, so far as possible, in their natural order, starting with the most general and the most simple and explaining what belongs to the nature of the genus before passing to the various species.

8. To divide, so far as possible, each genus into all its species, each whole into all its parts, and each difficulty into all its cases.'[4]

---

[1] *Super Quattuor Libros Sententiarum, Prolog., quaestio* i, O. See Prantl, *Geschichte der Logik*, iii, p. 333.  [2] *Logique*, ii. 8.
[3] Ibid., iv. 1.  [4] Ibid. 11.

These maxims seem to be drawn up with special reference to mathematics, but the authors make it clear in their opening remarks that one of the chief lessons to be learnt from mathematics is humility in dealing with the infinite, and so they find all this indirectly relevant to the treatment of religious faith with which they close the work.

The best remembered contribution of the *Port Royal Logic* is its distinction between the comprehension and the extension of a general term. At their first introduction of these technical words the authors speak of the comprehension and the extension of a general idea,[1] but in some other places they assign both to terms, and we cannot do wrong in following this practice, since ideas are terms according to their usage. The comprehension of a general term, then, is the set of attributes which it implies, or, as the authors say, the set of attributes which could not be removed without destruction of the idea. Thus the comprehension of the idea of triangle includes extendedness, shape, having three sides, having three angles, and having its interior angles equal to two right angles. The extension of a term, on the other hand, is the set of things to which it is applicable, or what the older logicians called its inferiors. This distinction may perhaps be intended to replace the medieval distinction of *significatio* and *suppositio*; but it does not exactly correspond, since the comprehension and the extension of a term are not properties of it, but rather sets of entities to which it is related in certain ways. Furthermore, the new technical words have given rise to new puzzles. Since *compréhension* means in ordinary French the same as 'understanding' does in 'English', it is natural to assume that Arnauld and Nicole intend to refer here to what we understand by a term, i.e. its *significatum* or meaning. But their definition and their example do not support this view. For having interior angles equal to two right angles is said by them to be included in the comprehension of the idea of a triangle, and this character is indeed something which the character implies in a large sense (*enferme en soi*); but it is certainly not part of the meaning of the word 'triangle'. Since the middle of the nineteenth century English writers have commonly followed Sir William Hamilton in replacing 'comprehension' by 'intension', which has no use in ordinary language, but it is not always clear that they have made up their minds how much this should be taken to include. Again, according to Arnauld and Nicole, the extension of a general term is the set of its inferiors, but it is not clear whether the inferiors of which they speak are supposed to be species or individuals. When working out their example, they

[1] *Logique*, i. 6.

say that the idea of a triangle in general extends (*s'étend*) to all the various species of triangles, but in the next paragraph they make the point that the extension of a term, unlike its comprehension, might be cut down without destruction of the idea ('on peut la reserrer quant à son étendue . . . sans que pour cela on la détruise), and this is not true of the set of species falling under a genus. We cannot continue to talk sensibly of triangles while denying that triangularity covers the possibility of equiangular triangularity, though we may without any difficulty say while pointing to an individual triangle 'Let us suppose that there were no triangle here'. Almost certainly the authors, if pressed on this point, would have said that they meant by 'extension' the set of individuals to which a general term applies. The confusion of their exposition seems to be due to their use of the word 'inferiors', which is itself metaphorical and unclear. It will be remembered that in medieval representations of Porphyry's tree individuals such as Socrates, Plato, and Brunellus were often mentioned at the bottom of a table in which all the other entries were general terms.

Having introduced their distinction, Arnauld and Nicole say that in certain contexts a term may not be considered according to its whole extension (*selon toute son étendue*) either because it is qualified by an indefinite restriction such as 'some' or because it occurs as predicate in an affirmative proposition and so is restricted to the scope of the subject to which it is attached.[1] Obviously they are here translating into their own terminology what medieval logicians said of *termini non complete distributi*. But they abstain from all use of the word 'distribution', presumably because they think it belongs to a mystifying jargon, and they allow themselves to treat singular propositions as similar to universal propositions on the ground that the subject of a singular proposition is necessarily taken in its whole extension.[2] This is an unhappy dodge which muddles the account of extension still further by blurring the distinction between singular and general terms, but it is no worse than the medieval assumption that both sorts of terms have *suppositio*. On the basis of their own doctrine, and the medieval rules of distribution which it has been made to include, they then proceed to work out rules of conversion[3] and rules of syllogistic[4] with a degree of rigour which is creditable but somewhat surprising. Their quasi-mathematical treatment of these subjects may indeed be the first of its kind, as it is certainly the source from which most later writers of logic manuals derive

[1] Ibid. ii. 3 and 17.   [2] Ibid. 3.
[3] Ibid. 18–20.   [4] Ibid. iii. 3–11.

the details of their formal theory, e.g. their determination of the valid moods of syllogism and their proofs of the special rules of the various figures. It is characteristic, however, of Arnauld and Nicole that before each of their passages dealing with details of formal logic they tell the reader that he may omit what follows since it is necessary only for pure theory.

A small point of some interest in their treatment of reasoning is a remark that, when only one premiss of a valid syllogism is known to be true, the other premiss may be introduced as a condition to the conclusion. Given, for example, that no matter thinks, we may go on to infer that, if everything which feels pain thinks, no matter feels pain. And when neither premiss is known to be true, we may even present them both as conditions in hypothetical statement.[1] Here we have in effect a version of the principle of conditionalization (or 'deduction theorem') which was taken for granted by Aristotle and explicitly used by the Stoics.

Some features of the *Port Royal Logic* reflect special interests of Arnauld and Nicole which could not be expected to spread far beyond their own circle; but the general conception of logic which they expounded in this book was widely accepted and continued to dominate the treatment of logic by most philosophers for the next 200 years. To follow in detail the transmission of their influence would be tedious and not very profitable. In the rest of this chapter we shall therefore consider instead another line of thought which has in the end proved much more fruitful, though for a long time it produced little effect in the academic teaching of logic. This is the line which Leibniz started as a boy, a few years before the writing of the *Port Royal Logic*.

## 2. *The Interests of Leibniz*

Although, as we have seen, few famous thinkers of the seventeenth and eighteenth centuries gave much attention to formal logic, Gottfried Wilhelm Leibniz, who was born in 1646 and died in 1716, deserves to be ranked among the greatest of all logicians. That his work on logic had little influence for nearly 200 years after he wrote was due in part to the dominance of other interests, connected with the rise of natural science, but also in part to the defects of his own character. He was a universal genius who conceived many projects and made many beginnings but brought little to fruition. When he died, his fame rested on his discovery of the infinitesimal calculus and his defence of the metaphysical doctrine that this is the best of all possible worlds. But the admirers

---

[1] *Logique*, iii. 13.

of Newton said that he had stolen the idea of the calculus from their master, and the unmetaphysical minds of the eighteenth century found his *Théodicée* and his *Monadologie* (published after his death) fantastic: he was the butt of Voltaire's wit in *Candide*. From short pieces published in journals, letters written to some of his many correspondents, and references scattered through his *Nouveaux Essais sur l'entendement humain* (a detailed criticism of Locke, first published in 1765) it became known that he claimed to have made great discoveries in logic, but there was little available to substantiate this claim. For years Leibniz had written copiously on his many projects, but in the form of notes or memoranda, and most of what he had written remained unpublished in the library at Hanover, where he had served the Elector as historian, scientific adviser, and expert on international law. During the nineteenth century various selections from his papers were published, but there was no complete (or nearly complete) catalogue until 1895,[1] and even now there is no complete text; for the definitive edition in forty volumes projected by the Berlin Academy (of which he was the first president) has been delayed by anti-semitism and war.

There are many different facets to Leibniz's thought about logic. He was a man who took great delight in intellectual synthesis; and just as he praised his metaphysical theory of monads for connecting many things which would otherwise be disconnected (e.g. teleology and mechanism, substance and energy, mind and matter, the infinitesimal calculus and microbiology), so too he valued his logic because it seemed to him like a jewel that can throw light in many different directions. For an explanation of his thought it will therefore be necessary to consider a number of his interests in turn, and we propose to treat briefly of the following: (1) his respect for traditional logic, (2) his notion of an *ars combinatoria*, or general theory of arrangements, (3) his plans for an ideal language, (4) his scheme for the coordination of knowledge in an encyclopaedia, and (5) his hope for a general science of method. Each of these interests he shared with some of his contemporaries, but the remarkable feature of his thought is the way in which he tried to relate them together. The order in which we shall deal with them is that which helps most to an understanding of their connexions in Leibniz's mind. It corresponds in part to the order of development of his thought, for (1) and (2) came very early and (5) later; but we do not attach much importance to this, since it is not yet possible to trace

---

[1] E. Bodemann, *Die Leibniz-Handschriften der Königlichen Öffentlichen Bibliothek zu Hannover.*

the history of his thought in detail, and it is clear in any case that he retained all these interests to the last.[1]

(1) According to his own statement Leibniz read Zabarella with pleasure at the age of twelve and at the age of fourteen had the idea that all propositions might be arranged according to the order in which they gave matter for syllogisms, i.e. in a deductive system like that which Euclid elaborated for geometry.[2] This enthusiasm for Aristotle's theory of the syllogism remained with him still when he wrote the *Nouveaux Essais*. For he there describes Aristotle's doctrine as 'one of the most beautiful discoveries of the human spirit', and says it is an 'art of infallibility' which can be developed into 'a sort of universal mathematics'.[3] These remarks are directed, of course, against Locke's depreciation of formal logic. In a note of 1715, not intended for publication, he was more outspoken: *Lockius aliique qui spernunt non intelligunt*.[4] But it is interesting to consider Leibniz's views on a number of points of syllogistic theory; for he was by no means an Aristotelian purist.

In the first place, he did not believe that all arguments could be brought into syllogistic form. The examples of non-syllogistic reasoning which he liked to cite were the arguments by inversion of relations and the arguments *a recto ad obliquum* discussed by Junge in the *Logica Hamburgensis*. But he can scarcely have intended to suggest that these were the only forms not covered by Aristotle's doctrine; for he sometimes insisted that an enlarged theory of deduction would allow for many different calculi, and apart from that he was well aware of the impossibility of reducing conditional and disjunctive arguments to syllogistic form. He held, nevertheless, that there is a common principle of all deduction, namely, substitution of equivalents.[5]

Secondly, he maintained the existence of four figures of syllogism, each with six moods. This view appears already in his *De Arte Combinatoria*, written in 1666, when he was only nineteen years of age, and it obviously attracted Leibniz because of its tidy symmetry. He saw that the ordinary Aristotelian doctrine of fourteen moods, distributed between three figures, was due to an arbitrary notion of what was natural in reasoning, rather than to any consistent theory of syllogistic form. In accepting the doc-

---

[1] In giving references to works which have not been published separately we use 'P' for *Die philosophischen Schriften von G. W. Leibniz* and 'M' for *Leibnizens mathematische Schriften*, both edited by Gerhardt, and 'O' for *Opuscules et fragments inédits de Leibniz*, edited by L. Couturat. The plan and much of the material of this section came from Couturat's *Logique de Leibniz* (1901).        [2] *P*, vii, p. 126.
[3] *Nouveaux Essais*, iv. xvii. 4. We shall use '*N.E.*' for the title of this work.
[4] *P*, vii, p. 481.        [5] *Leibnitii Opera* (ed. Dutens 1768), vi (i), p. 32.

trine of twenty-four moods he committed himself quite explicitly to the assumption of existential import for all universal state- ments. We shall see that in spite of misgivings he never succeeded in freeing himself from this entanglement and that it was probably one of the factors which prevented him from producing a really satisfactory calculus of logic.

Thirdly, he preferred to reduce syllogisms to the first figure *per impossibile* rather than by conversion, because he held that the method usually called indirect was really simpler. But he saw that syllogisms in the fourth figure could not be reduced at all without principles of conversion (or at any rate without the prin- ciple of identity which he used for proofs of the principles of conversion in the second or third figures), and that in this respect at least the tidiness of his scheme was compromised.[1] The remarks which he makes in this connexion show how carefully he had studied the history of logic, and it is therefore rather strange that he tries to justify indirect reduction by the principle of non- contradiction alone, i.e. without the principle of primary logic which the Stoics called the first thema.

Fourthly, he defended the view (which we have noticed already in Wallis's work) that singular statements may be classed as universal for the purposes of syllogistic theory.[2] If this were only a dodge for allowing us to treat arguments with singular premisses as though they were syllogisms, it would be harmless enough. For although these arguments are different in character from Aristotelian syllogisms, their rules have a similarity to those for syllogistic reasoning which can be brought out by the device just mentioned. We think it is clear, however, that Leibniz went farther than this and accepted the assimilation of singular to universal statements because it seemed to him there was no fundamental difference between the two sorts. Such a conclusion is implied by his often repeated assertion that in every true affir- mative proposition, whether universal or singular, necessary or contingent, *praedicatum inest subiecto*,[3] and it is so important in his thought that it requires special notice.

Lord Russell argued in his book on *The Philosophy of Leibniz* that this principle was the chief source of the curious metaphysical doctrines to which Leibniz found himself committed. We can now see that it was equally fateful in the development of Leibniz's logic. It may perhaps be paraphrased in English by the remark 'Every true affirmative statement ascribes to the thing denoted by its subject term an attribute which really inheres in that thing'.

---

[1] *N.E.* iv. ii. 1.  [2] *N.E.* iv. xvii. 8.
[3] *O*, p. 16; *O*, p. 51; *O*, pp. 518–19; *Discours de métaphysique*, §8; *P*, ii, p. 46.

Taken in this way, it would probably have been accepted by Aristotle; for his account of general statements is based on a notion of predication derived from consideration of singular statements. But the application of the subject-predicate way of talking has usually tended to make philosophers think of general propositions in a way appropriate only to singular propositions. In particular they have assumed that the subject-term of a universal statement must refer to something, and so have accepted without question the doctrine of existential import. Leibniz sometimes followed this line of thought, as we have noticed; but the peculiarity of his philosophy is due in large part to the fact that he also fell into the opposite mistake of trying to treat propositions about individuals as though they were like the laws we express by universal statements. When he used the phrase *Praedicatum inest subjecto*, he thought not only of the sense in which wisdom may be said to inhere in Socrates, but also of the sense in which animality may be said to be contained in humanity; and the second predominated so far that he often talked as though there were a concept or essence of each individual which necessarily involved all the attributes predicable of that individual. This is the origin of his principle of the identity of indiscernibles. Just as St. Thomas Aquinas held that every angel was of a distinct species, because they all lacked matter, by which ordinary things are individuated, so Leibniz maintained that every individual differed from every other in some attribute.[1] For him the distinction between history and science disappeared, and the assimilation of singular to universal statements was no longer merely a dodge for economy of rules in the criticism of arguments, but the expression of a profound truth.

His respect for the Aristotelian logic of subject and predicate had another unfortunate effect on Leibniz's thought, namely, that of making him try to explain away propositions of a relational form. His mention of Junge's argument by inversion of relations (e.g. from 'Titus is bigger than Caius' to 'Caius is smaller than Titus') shows that he was aware of the need for an enlargement of logic by a theory of relations; but he was never able to admit that the addition would be more than a gloss on the theory of attributes. According to him, 'Titus is bigger than Caius' means the same as 'Titus is big in as much as Caius is small', i.e. relational facts can be resolved into conjunctions of attributive facts.[2] This doctrine is certainly untrue, and we shall see that it hampered Leibniz seriously in the development of his own ideas;

[1] *Discours de métaphysique*, § 9.
[2] *O*, p. 280. Cf. *Fifth Letter to Clarke*, § 47 (*P*, vii, p. 401).

but he did a service to philosophy by trying to state it in un-
compromising form. The strenuousness of his efforts to preserve
the old theory that every statement ascribes an attribute to a
subject shows his own uneasiness, and has stimulated later
logicians to shake themselves free from this part of the tradition.

The most fruitful idea that Leibniz derived from his study of
Aristotelian logic was the notion of formal proof. This is emphasized in the criticism of Locke noticed above, and it recurs
again and again in his writings. He says, for example, that Descartes's rules of method are psychological advice of no great
value,[1] and that Descartes's weakness as a writer on method was
his failure to understand the importance of logical form.[2] He
recognized, of course, that the use of syllogisms in scholastic disputations could degenerate into stupid pedantry; but he saw
also that there could be no rigour without formality, and he
insisted rightly on the importance of presenting new developments of mathematics in such a way that their necessity could
be seen to depend on their form. This interest of his was un-
fashionable when he wrote, and remained so for a long time
afterwards, but it has been amply justified in the past century.

(2) The theory of permutations and combinations was developed first in the seventeenth century, primarily for its use in
connexion with the calculus of probabilities, and it attracted
Leibniz's attention while he was still in his teens. Indeed his
first considerable work was the *De Arte Combinatoria*[3] mentioned
in an earlier paragraph. In later life he was annoyed by the
republication of this tract without his permission; the ground for
his objection, however, was not that he had abandoned its theses,
but rather that he did not wish to have his immature work printed
as though it were a recent composition.[4] To the end of his life
he thought of the theory of combinations as something more
fundamental than ordinary logic; but he meant by the phrase
*ars combinatoria* more than the rules for calculating the number of
sub-sets of a certain constitution which may be formed from the
members of a given set. In his teens he had conceived already
the idea of an alphabet of human thought with which all possible
thinkables might be constructed by suitable combinations and
by which reasoning might be reduced to the quasi-mechanical
operation of going through a list.[5] His inspiration came from the
*Ars Magna* of Raymond Lull and the *Computatio sive Logica* of
Hobbes (i.e. the first part of *De Corpore*).[6] But he realized that in

---

[1] E. Bodemann, *Die Leibniz-Handschriften*, p. 82.    [2] *P*, iv, p. 276.
[3] *P*, iv, p. 27.    [4] *N.E.* iv. iii. 18.
[5] *P*, vii, p. 185.    [6] *P*, iv, p. 64.

order to make the method useful two things were needed which neither Lull nor Hobbes had provided: (*a*) an assurance that the 'alphabet' was really ultimate and complete, and (*b*) a procedure for making sure that *all possible* combinations were considered. In his early work so much space was given to the calculation of the numbers of combinations permissible in certain circumstances that these points were obscured; but even there he made it clear that he was trying to work out a logic of discovery (*logica inventiva*), and he achieved at least one interesting result by showing that there could be just twenty-four valid forms of syllogism.

In the tract *De Arte Combinatoria* Leibniz tries to show how the composition of complex geometrical notions could be exhibited concisely by a code in which integral numerals were made to stand for *termini primi* (e.g. '1' for *punctum* and '2' for *spatium*) and fractional numerals for other terms which have been introduced by definition and arranged in various classes (e.g. '$\frac{1}{2}$' for the first term of the second class, which happens to be *quantitas*). With this apparatus he produced such definitions as *Circulus est* $\frac{1}{12}$.8 *ab* 18.21 *habens* τὴν 16.$\frac{2}{3}$ τοῦ 19 *alicuius* 1 *ab* 18.6. But he did not try to show how such a code might help in the enterprise with which he was mainly concerned, and the fact that he never made any use of it in later works suggests that he soon realized its inadequacy as an instrument of logical analysis. It is in fact no more philosophical than a telegraph code, and it is interesting chiefly because it shows in a clear light the difficulties of the project Leibniz had in mind.

In the first place, Leibniz's list of twenty-seven *termini primi* for geometry is not compiled on any intelligible principle. Some of the items, such as *punctum* and *dimensio*, seem to be peculiar to geometry, while others, such as *unum*, *possibile*, and *omne*, have application outside that study; and of the geometrical terms it is by no means clear that all are indispensable. Secondly, the need for auxiliary expressions such as *ab*, *habens*, *alicuius*, and the inflected Greek articles in the formulation of definitions is a sign of the insufficiency of Leibniz's analysis. In order to carry out his programme satisfactorily it would be necessary (*a*) to distinguish sharply between the common signs of logical syntax and the peculiar signs of geometry and (*b*) to consider carefully what sorts of complexity can occur in definitions, or, in other words, what is to be understood by the 'combination' of simple geometrical notions. Leibniz's failure to produce a convincing example of his method was due mainly to his obsession with the idea that all complexity must arise from the conjunction of attributes. When he talked of combination he thought of such complexes as we express by putting together adjectives or common nouns, e.g. in the definition 'A triangle is a three-sided rectilinear figure', and he failed to understand that the complexity of the world cannot be explained in this way alone. We shall have occasion to consider this point again, and we mention it here only because it is interesting to notice that one of Leibniz's chief difficulties was implicit in his early treatment of the *ars combinatoria*.

(3) Many writers of the seventeenth century put forward suggestions for the construction of an artificial language; in Leibniz's day such ideas flourished especially in England, where Wilkins and Dalgarno each advocated a system of his own. The chief arguments of the inventors were like those advanced in recent times for Esperanto, namely, that communication would be much easier and the spread of ideas more rapid if all men, or at least all learned men, had at their disposal a language constructed on simple principles and strictly regular in its grammar. Leibniz was not indifferent to such considerations. For he believed firmly in the importance of establishing peace and order throughout the world, and he held that the advancement of science depended on intellectual co-operation between men of different nations. He therefore advocated at one time the use of a basic regular Latin (presumably something like the *Latino sine flexione* used by Peano at the beginning of this century in his *Formulario Mathematico*).[1] But his interest in the construction of an ideal language went much farther than this. He wanted a scientific language which would help not merely in the communication of thoughts but also in thinking itself, and this he called a *lingua philosophica* or *characteristica universalis*.[2]

The fundamental principle in Leibniz's theory of symbolism is that our expressions should mirror the structure of the world. Although the basic signs which stand for simple elements may be chosen arbitrarily, there must be an analogy, in the strict sense of that word, between their relations and the relations of the elements they signifiy,[3] so that the name of each complex thing is its definition and the key to all its properties.[4] We cannot escape from the use of signs in thinking, but our ordinary systems fall short of the ideal, and this is the chief source of the difficulty of intellectual work: 'In signis spectanda est commoditas ad inveniendum, quae maxima est quoties rei naturam internam paucis exprimunt et velut pingunt; ita enim mirifice imminuitur cogitandi labor.[5] In mathematics the importance of good symbolism is already established by the discoveries which it has made possible

---

[1] *P*, vii, p. 28.  [2] *P*, vii, p. 184.  [3] *P*, vii, p. 192.
[4] *O*, p. 152.  [5] *M*, iv, p. 455.

(e.g. Leibniz's own discovery of the infinitesimal calculus), but we need a thread of Ariadne to guide us through the labyrinth of other studies,[1] and this we can get only from the *characteristica universalis*. With such a help to thought we shall be free from the snares of the evil genius imagined by Descartes, because all will be clear and there will be no danger of false memory.

In order to carry out Leibniz's programme, or any part of it, we should have to provide (*a*) symbols for all the notions to be taken as ultimate or unanalysable, and (*b*) suitable devices for expressing such formal notions as predication, conjunction, disjunction, negation, conditional connexion, universality, and existence. In most ordinary languages there are special symbols (called syncategorematic) to signify some of the formal notions, but it is not essential that these should always be expressed by separate words. In ancient Greek, for example, the notion of predication could be expressed by the placing of an adjective before a noun with the definite article, as in μέγας ὁ ἀνήρ, and in English we can express conjunction by the simple juxtaposition of words, as in the phrase 'a round red apple'. Furthermore, even non-formal notions may sometimes be expressed by the arrangement of other symbols. This is most obvious in the making of maps, when the relative positions of the various natural features are shown by the relative positions of marks associated with the names of those features. But it can occur also in oral language, as when Julius Caesar said *Veni, vidi, vici*, meaning that his arrival, his inspection, and his conquest happened in the order of the verbs he used to announce them. How exactly Leibniz wished to construct his *characteristica universalis* is not clear; for he never produced a detailed scheme or even discussed the alternatives noticed above. But he probably thought of it most often as a script in which the non-formal notions would be represented by signs other than words. Sometimes he says that it would be like algebra, and sometimes that it would be an improved version of the Chinese ideographic system.[2] And he certainly intended it to exhibit the logical form of propositions in a simple and more regular way than any natural language. For he often asserts that a philosophically constructed grammar will make formal reasoning easy by providing the framework for a *calculus ratiocinator* (i.e. a quasi-mechanical method of drawing conclusions) in which even the non-syllogistic arguments of Junge may be brought under a few simple rules of procedure. And he prophesies that, when the new language is perfected, men of good will desiring to settle a controversy on any subject whatsoever will take their pens in their hands and say *Calculemus*.[3]

There were two reasons why Leibniz never succeeded in producing a definite system. The first was the impossibility of drawing up a dictionary for the new language until the work of scientific research had been brought to completion, or at least nearer to completion than it was in Leibniz's own day. We cannot provide an explanatory symbolism for chemistry until chemistry already exists as a science. Descartes had made this point earlier in the century against a proposal of Mersenne,[1] and it did not escape the attention of Leibniz. His enthusiasm for the project of an encyclopaedia was due in part to his hope that it would help to make possible the production of a *characteristica universalis*. But there was a second reason, unknown to Leibniz, why he could make little progress in the construction of an ideal language, and that was his failure to shake himself free from the subject-predicate dogma of traditional logic.

We have seen already how Leibniz failed in his early attempt to apply the *ars combinatoria* to geometrical notions. The limitation of his thought which made failure inevitable on that occasion was certain also to prevent him from working out a system of symbolism in which the name of each thing would be its definition and the key to all its properties. For the notion of complexity with which he worked was always that of the conjunction of attributes, and this is not sufficient to account for the diversity of thinkables. A typical suggestion to which he recurred on several occasions was that simple ideas might be expressed by different prime numbers and complex ideas by products of primes.[2] Since there is only one way in which any given natural number can be decomposed into primes, this plan would enable a person who had mastered the system to read off, or at least to work out in unambiguous fashion, the definition of each derivative term; Leibniz was dissatisfied with it only because he hoped for some system in which even the primitive terms would be intelligible without a dictionary, i.e. a kind of picture writing which would be not only independent of the spoken language (as Chinese characters are) but also very easy to learn.[3] But such a system would not allow for the expression of complexities outside a very restricted range. Let us consider for an example the meaning of the common term 'grandparent'. This is obviously complex, and Leibniz could scarcely wish to express it in his numerical system by a prime number; but it is not the notion of a thing with two or more attributes conjoined. When we say that X is a grandparent, we mean that there are two persons Y and Z such that X is a parent

[1] Descartes, *Œuvres* (ed. Adam et Tannery), i, p. 76.
[2] *P*, vii, p. 292.                    [3] *N.E.* iii. i. 1 and iv. vi. 2.

of Y and Y a parent of Z. We have here what might be called a second power of an asymmetrical, intransitive, two-termed relation. Leibniz could not fit it into his scheme, because he never took relations seriously.

(4) We have seen that Leibniz was interested in the making of an encyclopaedia because he hoped that a systematic collection of knowledge would make it possible to construct a *characteristica universalis*. But he had other reasons of a more obvious kind for his interest. In the first place he was himself a polymath with a strong desire to extend his learning yet farther and bring it all into a single system. His works and his correspondence show the enormous range of his curiosity. Logic, mathematics, physics, engineering, biology, philology, history, politics, jurisprudence, metaphysics, and theology were all for him congenial studies; and in nearly all of them his knowledge was at least equal to that of the most learned of the age. Since he died there has been no man for whom the same distinction could be claimed; and his writings show that his interest in the making of an encyclopaedia was due in large part to his realization of a growing tendency to the fragmentation of knowledge.[1] Secondly, he believed that the safety of all society depended on the maintenance of good order in the intellectual realm, and he sometimes thought of an encyclopaedia as an instrument for uniting scholars of all groups. He was especially interested in the reconciliation of the churches, and himself devoted much care to the exposition of the doctrines which had to be brought into harmony.

Like his other leading ideas, the project of an encyclopaedia remained with Leibniz from his youth until his death, but it took somewhat different forms at different dates. When he was about twenty, he thought of it only as an *opus Photianum*, or series of extracts from the best writers on all the various subjects. Thus the logic would be taken mainly from Junge and the physics mainly from Hobbes.[2] At this date mathematics had no more than a minor place in his scheme, because he himself had not yet made much progress in that science. But he insisted already that the material should be presented in a logical order of development. At a later date the mathematical ideal became dominant in his thought, and he not only gave a bigger place to mathematics in his scheme but wished to have the whole prepared in the demonstrative form of Euclid's *Elements*. When his plans were most ambitious, he proposed to include the knowledge of nature which had been accumulated by craftsmen but not hitherto written down for students to read. This idea may have been suggested to

---

[1] *P*, vii, p. 160.    [2] Couturat, *La Logique de Leibniz*, pp. 570–1.

him by some of the work which he did for his employer, the Elector of Hanover. But at a still later date he abandoned such schemes in favour of a proposal that the encyclopaedia should include only the first principles of the various sciences, and towards the end of his life seems to have limited his project to the presentation of a unified world-view, at once scientific and religious. His tract called *Principes de la nature et de la grâce* and his *Monadologie* were written for this purpose.

The planning of the encyclopaedia was usually linked in Leibniz's thought with schemes for co-operative research in learned academies. At various times he sent proposals to the Royal Society of London, Louis XIV of France, Frederick I of Prussia, and Peter the Great of Russia. With the King of Prussia he had some success; for his initiative led to the founding of the Prussian Academy with himself as president for life. But in general the response to his proposals was not encouraging, and the last years of his life must have been a time of disappointment. He had hoped to accompany George I to England, but he was ordered to stay in Hanover, perhaps because of the dispute about the discovery of the differential calculus. When he died, there was little prospect that science would be perfected and civilization made secure by a college of *illuminati*.

(5) Projects for an encyclopaedia contributed to the formation of Leibniz's logical theory only in so far as they led him to think about the possibility of organizing knowledge in a deductive system. But his reflections on scientific method were of the greatest importance for his logic. Like Bacon and Descartes before him, he thought it was possible to describe a procedure for the rapid enlargement of knowledge, and he sometimes wrote as though the work of research might be completed in his lifetime and made available to all men by an order of missionaries (*Ordo Pacidianorum* or *Societas Theophilorum*) devoted to that purpose.[1] For there was in his thinking an element of that mysticism which makes men look for the consummation of history in a millenium. When he wrote his *De Arte Combinatoria*, he had already the idea of a logic of discovery, and in his later work this becomes the dominant theme under which his other interests can all be organized. We can see this most clearly from a number of fragments about a work on General Science, i.e. the science of method, which he planned to produce under the pseudonym 'Guilielmus Pacidius'.[2] One of these fragments, from which we reproduce selections below, is especially interesting because it mentions all the various interests of Leibniz and shows by its style what sort of man he was.

[1] *O*, pp. 3–8.  [2] From *Pax Dei*: *O*, p. 4.

'Guilielmi Pacidii

## PLUS ULTRA,

sive initia et specimina Scientiae Generalis de instauratione
et augmentis scientiarum ac de perficienda mente rerumque
inventione ad publicam felicitatem.

1. Rationes quae autorem ad scribendum impulerunt, ubi et cur
nomen dissimulavit. Magnorum principum familiaritas et cogita-
tiones concordes....

7. De scientiarum instauratione, ubi de Systematibus et Repertoriis
et de Encyclopaedia demonstrativa condenda. De linguis et Grammatica rationali.

8. Elementa veritatis aeternae et de arte demonstrandi in omnibus
disciplinis ut in Mathesi.

9. De novo quodam Calculo generali cujus ope tollantur omnes
disputationes inter eos qui in ipsum consenserint et Cabbala sapientium.

10. De Arte Inveniendi.

11. De Synthesi seu Arte combinatoria.

12. De Analysi.

13. De Combinatoria speciali seu scientia formarum sive qualitatum
in genere sive de simili et dissimili.

14. De Analysi speciali seu scientia quantitatum in genere seu de
magno et parvo.

15. De Mathesi generali ex duabus praecedentibus composita....

21. Dynamica seu de Motuum Causa seu de Causa et Effectu ac
potentia et actu....

32. De Medicina. Medicina provisionalis....

De Jurisprudentia, ubi de Jure Naturae ac Gentium, itemque legibus
positivis variis, imprimis de jure Romano et de jure Ecclesiastico. De
jure publico ac re faeciali. De optima republica....

De concordia Christianorum et conversione Gentilium,

De societate Theophilorum.'[1]

At the beginning of his discussions Leibniz assumes a distinction between the method of exposition, which is synthetic, and
the method of discovery, which is analytic;[2] but this disappears
in time from his writings, and it is interesting to see why.

For Leibniz, as for Hobbes, all necessary truths are guaranteed
by the definitions of their terms, and there are no absolutely
indemonstrable axioms except the principle of identity.[3] To prove
a proposition is to show that its predicate concept is contained in
its subject concept, and for this purpose we must analyse the two
concepts far enough to make their relations clear. That is to say,
the essential procedure in the construction of a proof is the setting
forth of a chain of definitions by reference to which we can see

---

[1] P, vii, p. 49.   [2] O, p. 572.   [3] O, p. 518; P, i, p. 188.

that the proposition to be proved is a virtual identity. Thus, given the definitions:

$$\text{(i)} \quad 2 = 1+1$$
$$\text{(ii)} \quad 3 = 2+1$$
$$\text{(iii)} \quad 4 = 3+1,$$

we can assert:

| | |
|---|---|
| $2+2 = 2+2$ | by the principle of identity |
| $= 2+(1+1)$ | by definition (i) |
| $= (2+1)+1$ | |
| $= 3+1$ | by definition (ii) |
| $= 4$ | by definition (iii).[1] |

But if all reasoning, syllogistic and non-syllogistic, is just the replacement of expressions by other expressions which are equivalent according to definition, it does not matter whether we start with an identity and proceed synthetically from that by successive steps to the demonstrandum, as in the example given above, or start with the demonstrandum and reduce analytically it by successive steps to an identity. The difference of order does not amount to a difference of method; for in either case we must use a chain of definitions, and discovery consists in the marshalling of these, or, at a more fundamental level, in the survey of possible combinations of predicates.

This account of demonstration is unsatisfactory because it is based on the assumption that in every affirmative truth *praedicatum inest subiecto*. As always, Leibniz is thinking of complexity as arising solely from the conjunction of attributes. The definition of a term is supposed to be something like the factorization of a number, and the existence of a necessary connexion something like the divisibility of one number, corresponding to the subject, by another number, corresponding to the predicate.[2] Every term has just one adequate definition which is the factorization of it into prime notions; but for purposes of demonstration it is not always necessary to proceed so far, and if we stop short of this, there may be several equivalent definitions of a term, one appropriate in one context and another in another according to the property of the definiendum which it is desired to demonstrate. We have seen already that complexity may arise in other ways, and it follows from this that demonstration need not always be the straightforward procedure it seemed to Leibniz. Since Fermat died in 1665 no mathematician has been able to prove his

---

[1] *N.E.* IV. vii. 10. Leibniz does not notice, however, that the transition from the second to the third line depends on the associative law for addition, i.e. the law that $x+(y+z) = (x+y)+z$, which itself requires proof.          [2] *P*, vii, p. 292.

famous 'last theorem', i.e. the proposition that there are no four natural numbers, x, y, z, and n, all greater than o and such that $x^{n+2} + y^{n+2} = z^{n+2}$. And it seems mere foolishness to say that we can get a decision by expanding the expression in accordance with definitions. For, although the signs of addition and exponentiation can be defined by reference to more fundamental notions, the definitions are such that we cannot always eliminate the signs from a formula which contains variables. But this objection is derived from considerations that did not occur to Leibniz. For the understanding of his thought it is more interesting to consider how he tried to deal with two difficulties of a more obvious kind.

In the first place, it seems paradoxical to say that all necessary truths depend on definitions which we ourselves have made. Leibniz admits this, but says the argument has no force against his own theory, because he, unlike Hobbes, does not regard definitions as wholly arbitrary. A real, as distinct from a nominal, definition contains, he thinks, an implicit assertion of the possibility of that which is defined. This possibility is not established by our conventions for the use of words, and without it there can be no demonstration.[1] It is correct, then, to say with the scholastic philosophers that an axiom is evident to one who understands its terms; but the understanding of a term, or the having of a real idea, involves the recognition of the possibility of that which is signified.[2]

Leibniz is right in his protest against the conventionalism of Hobbes, but his account of real definition is confused. For it is surely untrue that a phrase cannot occur in a genuine demonstration unless it signifies something possible. In order to prove that there are infinitely many prime numbers we may properly begin by saying 'Suppose there were a largest prime number', and then go on to show that this supposition involves an absurdity though it sounds reasonable at first hearing. Furthermore, it is not clear what the word 'possible' means in this context. Since for Leibniz a necessary truth is apparently one whose negation would be formally self-contradictory,[3] it is natural to assume that for him 'possible' means the same as 'free from formal self-contradiction'. And he tells us in fact that all purely positive terms are compossible.[4] But if nothing is impossible except what is excluded by the principle of non-contradiction, how are we to explain any ordinary true remark of the kind 'A is not B'? It is not sufficient to say in Leibnizian phraseology that the nature of A includes not-B-ness. For a negative character is not simple, and

---

[1] *P*, vii, pp. 191–2; *M*, iv, p. 462.       [2] *P*, iii, p. 443; *N.E.* ii. xxxii.
[3] *P*, iii, p. 400.                           [4] *P*, vii, p. 195. Cf. *M*, iii, p. 574.

Leibniz did not wish to say that it was. On the other hand, we are not allowed to say that the nature of A includes some character C-ness which is incompatible with B-ness though neither is the negation of the other or the conjunction of that negation with one or more simple characters. For this would be tantamount to an admission that purely positive terms may be incompossible.

The second difficulty concerns empirical science. Leibniz professes to give a general theory of method, but how can what he says about demonstration have any application in physics? He boldly maintains that all true propositions, including even singulars, are virtual identities, though God alone can know them all *a priori*. There is indeed a distinction between truths of reason, which hold for all possible worlds, and truths of fact, which are in a sense contingent because they depend on the will of God and hold only for the actual world. But the principle of sufficient reason assures us that even truths of fact are necessary inasmuch as nothing happens without a ground.[1] In *every* true proposition the subject concept contains the predicate concept, and the difference between truths of reason and truths of fact is simply that the latter cannot be demonstrated without reference to that superiority of the actual which determined God to choose it from among all possible worlds. Sometimes Leibniz goes so far as to suggest that study of the *ars combinatoria* would enable us to work out *a priori* which combinations must be realized, because the largest system of compossibles is that which contains most perfection.[2] But he never tried to deduce anything in this way except theses of metaphysics which cannot be tested empirically. More often he was prepared to regard the discovery of order in nature as like the solution of a cryptogram.[3] Mere empirical generalization is not enough for science, and since we cannot in this context argue to first principles by the regressive method of Pappus (i.e. cannot say that there is only one system of possibilities consistent with the facts of experience), we must use hypotheses. These are probable according as (i) they are simple and explain a great number of phenomena by a small number of postulates, and (ii) they allow us to predict new phenomena or explain new observations.[4]

What Leibniz says of hypotheses is interesting, but his general account of natural science is unsatisfactory because it leaves no place for the knowledge on which this must be based, i.e. the knowledge we get by observation. Like Spinoza, he maintains the unintelligible doctrine that experience is confused thinking,

---

[1] *P*, vii, p. 309.  [2] *Discours de métaphysique*, §6; *N.E.* iv. ii. 7.
[3] *N.E.* iv. xii. 13.  [4] *P*, i, pp. 195–6.

and talks of nature as though it were a piece of pure mathematics which we must try to reconstruct from fragments. In one place he even says 'My metaphysics is so to say all mathematics, or could become so'.[1] But we need not consider the difficulties of these views any further. For our purpose his notion of fundamental mathematics is more important than his superstructure.

### 3. *Leibniz's* Calculus de Continentibus et Contentis

While explaining the interests which directed Leibniz's thought, we have commented freely on the defects or absurdities of some theses which he took for granted, and the reader may perhaps wonder why we have described him as one of the greatest of all logicians. We must therefore try now to present as well as we can the new view of logic which he derived from all these considerations. He never succeeded in expressing it to his own satisfaction, and the account we give must therefore be a conflation of fragments.

Although he used different terminology on different occasions, it seems clear that Leibniz had conceived the possibility of elaborating a basic science which would be like mathematics in some respects but would include also traditional logic and some studies as yet undeveloped. Having noticed that logic, with its terms, propositions, and syllogisms, bore a certain formal resemblance to algebra, with its letters, equations, and transformations,[2] he tried to present logic as a calculus, and he sometimes called his new science universal mathematics. But he did not wish to suggest that logic should be absorbed into mathematics as that was commonly understood. For the accepted mathematics dealt only with relations of quantity, and although Descartes had developed the algebra of Vieta in such a way that it could deal with notions derived from geometry, his study was not, as the Cartesians supposed, the most fundamental kind of mathematics that could be conceived. There might be calculi concerned with abstract or formal relations of a non-quantitative kind, e.g. similarity and dissimilarity, congruence, inclusion : 'Non omnes formulae significant quantitatem, et infiniti modi calculandi excogitari possunt.'[3] What he had in mind was a general theory of structures that could provide the syntax for his *characteristica universalis*. Of this theory he wrote *Doctrina Formarum continet Logicam et Combinatoriam.*[4] It would cover the theory of series and tables and all forms of order, and be the foundation of other branches of mathematics such as geometry, algebra, and the

---

[1] *M*, ii, p. 258.    [2] *M*. vii, p. 54.    [3] *O*, p. 556.    [4] *O*, p. 525.

calculus of chances.[1] But most important of all it would be an instrument of discovery. For according to his own statement it was the *ars combinatoria* which made possible his own achievements in mathematics (e.g. the infinitesimal calculus and the series for $\pi/4$) and in engineering (e.g. the calculating machine which he exhibited to the Royal Society in 1673).[2] In retrospect we can see that Leibniz was striving for the sort of generality which is to be found in Galois's theory of groups and in modern abstract algebra. We may even find hints of these developments in his work. But of the *infiniti modi calculandi* of which he wrote he developed only two in any detail, one a calculus of identity and inclusion, and the other a geometrical calculus of similarity and congruence. The second was an attempt to treat of geometrical structure without the use of co-ordinates, and it anticipated Grassmann's *Ausdehnungslehre* of 1844, much as the first anticipated Boole's *Mathematical Analysis of Logic* of 1847. In what follows we shall consider only Leibniz's attempts to work out a calculus of identity and inclusion. This applies to part of the field of traditional logic and illustrates in a relatively simple fashion what Leibniz had in mind when he spoke of a general theory of forms.

Among Leibniz's papers there are many different projects for a calculus of inclusion. When he began, he intended, no doubt, to produce something wider than traditional logic. For he says in one place that the theory of inclusion had been studied in part by Aristotle in his *Prior Analytics*.[3] But although he worked on the subject in 1679, in 1689, and in 1690, he never succeeded in producing a calculus which covered even the whole theory of the syllogism. On the other hand, he did succeed in presenting some fragments in an abstract fashion, i.e. in such a way that they would admit various interpretations. For he realized quite early that there was an isomorphism, or identity of form, between some assertions which are made in logic and some assertions which may be made in geometry about the relations of lines, areas, or volumes, and he frequently used geometrical illustrations of the kind usually associated with the name of his successor Euler. He also realized that the calculus he wished to elaborate was distinguished by two special principles which may be expressed in the formulae $ab = ba$ and $aa = a$. This is the point of his remark, 'Calculus de continentibus et contentis est species quaedam calculi de combinationibus, quando scilicet nec ordinis rerum nec repetitionis ratio habetur.'[4]

The first attempt was based on the analogy between composite concepts and composite numbers to which we have already drawn

[1] *M*, iv, p. 460; *P*, vii, p. 298.    [2] *M*, v, p. 89; *P*, i, p. 58.
[3] *M*, vii, p. 261.    [4] *O*, p. 256.

attention.[1] Each simple term was to be represented by a prime number, and each composite term by a product of prime numbers. A universal affirmative proposition would then be true if the subject number was divisible by the predicate number, i.e. if $S = yP$ or $S/P = y$, with y an integer, and a particular affirmative proposition would be true if $xS = yP$ or $S/P = y/x$, with x and y integers but $y/x$ not necessarily an integer. This scheme, however, did not provide for negative propositions. It was therefore necessary to represent each term by two numbers, one positive and one negative.[2] If the positive number of any term had a common factor with the negative number of any other term, those two terms would be mutually exclusive, i.e. a universal negative proposition would be true. Leibniz became dissatisfied with this complicated system, but he never abandoned his theory that the predicate concept must be contained in the subject concept in any true proposition. As we shall see, he developed a calculus which can be interpreted in extension, that is as a series of statements about the relations of classes, but he always thought first of the intensional interpretation according to which the meaning of the predicate term is contained in the meaning of the subject-term, e.g. animality in humanity. And he retained throughout the principle that if A contains B then $A = yB$.

In a later attempt, preserved in his *Specimen Calculi Universalis* and its *Addenda*, he lays down the following:

'Propositions true of themselves: (1) *A is A*; (2) *AB is A*; (3) *A is not not-A*; (4) *Not-A is not A*; (5) *Whatever is not A is not-A*; (6) *Whatever is not not-A is A*.

*Consequentia* true of itself: *A is B and B is C, therefore A is C*.

Principles of the calculus: (1) Anything included in certain undetermined letters (*in literis quibusdam indefinitis*) is to be understood as concluded (*conclusum*) in any others whatsoever which are subject to the same conditions, e.g. since *AB is A* is true, *BC is B* will also be true. (2) Transposition of letters in the same term makes no difference, i.e. *AB* is equivalent to *BA*. (3) Repetition of the same letter in the same term is useless, e.g. in *B is AA*. (4) One proposition can be made from any number of propositions by combining all the subjects into one subject and all the predicates into one predicate, i.e. from *A is B* and *C is D* and *E is F* we can get *ACE is BDF*. (5) From any proposition whose predicate is composed from several terms it is possible to make several propositions each of which has the same subject as the original but a predicate which is part of the predicate of the original, i.e. given *A is BCD*, we have *A is B* and *A is C* and *A is D*.'[3]

For the further development of his calculus Leibniz tried to

---

[1] *O*, p. 54.                                           [2] *O*, p. 70.
[3] *P*, vii, p. 224. We have abbreviated Leibniz's exposition and substituted capitals for small letters.

express Aristotle's four types of general propositions by reference to the combination of attributes and considered the following schemes:

| Type | First Scheme | Second Scheme |
|------|------|------|
| Every A is B | A non-B est non-ens | AB = A |
| Some A is not B | A non-B est ens | AB ≠ A |
| No A is B | AB est non-ens | AB ≠ AB ens |
| Some A is B | AB est ens | AB = AB ens. |

Here *ens* and *non-ens* may perhaps be rendered by 'something' and 'nothing', but it is clear that Leibniz wishes to allow an interpretation whereby *ens* means something *in regione idearum*, i.e. a possibility. In his *Difficultates Quaedam Logicae*[1] where the two schemes occur he recognizes that we cannot argue correctly from 'Everything that laughs is human' to 'Something human is laughing', if the premiss is supposed to state a relation of concepts and the conclusion a contingent matter of fact, but he maintains that the conversion of a universal affirmative statement *per accidens* is valid for a conceptual interpretation as well as for one in terms of actual individuals, provided (*a*) the simple terms involved in the universal statement represent possibilities (just as for the interpretation *secundum individua* they must have application to something actual), and (*b*) the particular statement which results from conversion is understood to be concerned with the possibility of a certain combination of characters rather than with the existence of an actual instance. Since he holds in general that the predicate of an affirmative proposition is contained in the subject, he naturally inclines to the intensional interpretation, and he claims that it has good authority: 'Aristotle himself seems to have followed the way of ideas (*viam idealem*); for he says that animal is in man, i.e. notion in notion, though elsewhere it is more usual to say that men are in [i.e. among] animals.'

Leibniz is right in thinking that it is possible to construct a symbolism which can be interpreted either intensionally or extensionally, but he is wrong in holding that, as ordinarily used, a phrase of the form 'Some A is B' can properly be taken as an assertion of the compatibility of two characters, and he is mistaken when he says that *ens* is to be treated as a term involved in all others (*in omnibus tacite assumitur terminum ingredientem esse ens*). A character's having application is a second-order character, and so too is a character's being such as might have application; but in neither case can the second-order character be properly conceived as conjoined with the first-order character. This in effect is what Leibniz assumes in the paper under consideration. His mistake is

[1] *P*, vii, p. 211.

naturally more obvious in the second of the two schemes set out above, where he tries to present statements of all the four traditional patterns as equalities or inequalities, but it is implicit also in the first.

When he returned to the attack some years later, Leibniz made more progress in the elaboration of a calculus, but only by abandoning all reference to existential propositions. At the same time he made a small change of notation. Instead of the juxtaposition of letters, which in algebra signifies multiplication, he now used the sign of addition to express the combination of concepts, although from time to time he lapsed into his older usage in the middle of a paper. This innovation does not imply any radical change of outlook, but it suggests the possibility of introducing the inverse operation of subtraction. In his *Non Inelegans Specimen Demonstrandi in Abstractis*[1] Leibniz says that $A-B = C$ if, and only if, $A = B+C$ and B and C have nothing in common. The second part of the condition is essential, because if B and C were allowed to have anything in common the operation of subtraction would not give a unique result. We might, for example, have not only $A-(L+M) = N$ but also $A-(L+M) = M+N$, since $L+M+N = L+M+M+N$ according to the principle that repetition of a letter in a complex term makes no difference. Leibniz tells us that in application to concepts subtraction is not the same as negation. For Man not Rational=Impossible, but Man—Rational =Brute.[2] It seems, therefore, that when he asserts $A-A = $ nil, he means by 'nil' the absence of all determination, i.e. what he would have expressed by the numeral 1 when he tried to represent the combination of concepts by the multiplication of numbers.

The attempt to use the sign — together with the sign + in a calculus where $A + A = A$ proved unfruitful, and Leibniz abandoned it in his last scheme. Here he continues to use the sign of addition for the combination of concepts, but as though to mark the fact that it is not to be taken in its ordinary numerical sense he puts it inside a circle. The resulting calculus is the most highly developed of the many suggestions which he put forward, and we shall therefore reproduce it in some detail.

'DEF. 1. Terms are the same or coincident which can be substituted one for another wherever we please without altering the truth of any statement. $A = B$ signifies that A and B are the same.

DEF. 2. Terms which are not the same, i.e. terms which cannot always be substituted one for another, are different. $A \neq B$ signifies that A and B are different.

PROP. 1. *If* $A = B$, *then also* $B = A$. For since $A = B$ (by hyp.), it follows (by def. 1) that in the statement A = B (true by hyp.) B can be substituted for A and A for B; hence we have B = A.

PROP. 2. *If* A $\neq$ B, *then also* B $\neq$ A. Otherwise we should have B = A, and in consequence (by the preceding prop.) A = B, which is contrary to hypothesis.

PROP. 3. *If* A = B *and* B = C, *then* A = C. For if in the statement A = B (true by hyp.) C be substituted for B (by def. 1, since B = C), the resulting statement will be true.

PROP. 4. *If* A = B *and* B $\neq$ C, *then* A $\neq$ C. For if in the proposition B $\neq$ C (true by hyp.) A be substituted for B, we have (by def. 1, since A = B) the true proposition A $\neq$ C.

DEF. 3. A is in L, or L contains A, is the same as to say that L can be made to coincide with a plurality of terms taken together of which A is one. B$\oplus$N = L signifies that B is in L and that B and N together compose or constitute L. The same thing holds for a larger number of terms.

AXIOM 1. B$\oplus$N = N$\oplus$B.

POSTULATE. Any plurality of terms, as A and B, can be added to compose a single term A$\oplus$B.

AXIOM 2. A$\oplus$A = A.

PROP. 5. *If* A *is in* B *and* A = C, *then* C *is in* B. For in the proposition A is in B (true by hyp.) the substitution of C for A (by def. 1, since by hyp. A = C) gives C is in B.

PROP. 6. *If* C *is in* B *and* A = B *then* C *is in* A. For in the proposition C is in B the substitution of A for B (since A = B) gives C is in A.

PROP. 7. A *is in* A. For A is in A$\oplus$A (by def. 3). Therefore (by prop. 6) A is in A.

PROP. 8. *If* A = B, *then* A *is in* B. For (by the preceding) A is in A, that is (by hyp.) A is in B.

PROP. 9. *If* A = B, *then* A$\oplus$C = B$\oplus$C. For if in A$\oplus$C = A$\oplus$C (true of itself) B be substituted for A in one place, we have A$\oplus$C = B$\oplus$C.

SCHOLIUM. This proposition cannot be converted—much less the two which follow.

PROP. 10. *If* A = L *and* B = M, *then* A$\oplus$B = L$\oplus$M. For since B = M, A$\oplus$B = A$\oplus$M (by the preceding), and putting L for the second A (since by hyp. A = L), we have A$\oplus$B = L$\oplus$M.

PROP. 11. *If* A = L *and* B = M *and* C =N, *then* A$\oplus$B$\oplus$C = L$\oplus$M$\oplus$N. And so on.

PROP. 12. *If* B *is in* L, *then* A$\oplus$B *is in* A$\oplus$L. For L = B$\oplus$N (by def. 3) and A$\oplus$B is in B$\oplus$N$\oplus$A (by the same), that is, A$\oplus$B is in L$\oplus$A.

SCHOLIUM. This proposition cannot be converted.

PROP. 13. *If* L$\oplus$B = L, *then* B *is in* L. For B is in L$\oplus$B (by def. 3) and L$\oplus$B = L (by hyp.); hence (by prop. 6) B is in L.

PROP. 14. *If* B *is in* L, *then* L$\oplus$B = L. For if B is in L, then (by def. 3) L = B$\oplus$P. Hence (by prop. 9) L$\oplus$B = B$\oplus$P$\oplus$B, which (by ax. 2) = B$\oplus$P, which (by hyp.) = L.

PROP. 15. *If A is in B and B is in C, then A is in C.* For A is in B (by hyp.), hence $A \oplus L = B$ (by def. 3). Similarly, since B is in C, $B \oplus M = C$, and putting $A \oplus L$ for B in this statement (since we have shown that they are coincident), we have $A \oplus L \oplus M = C$. Therefore (by def. 3) A is in C.

COROLLARY. *If $A \oplus N$ is in B, then N is in B.* For N is in $A \oplus N$ (by def. 3).

SCHOLIUM. This proposition cannot be converted, and much less can the following.

PROP. 16. *If A is in B and B is in C and C is in D, then A is in D.* And so on.

PROP. 17. *If A is in B and B is in A, then A = B.* For if A is in B, then $A \oplus N = B$ (by def. 3). But B is in A (by hyp.); hence $A \oplus N$ is in A (by prop. 5). Hence (by coroll. to prop. 15) N is in A. Hence (by prop. 14) $A = A \oplus N$, that is A = B.

PROP. 18. *If A is in L and B is in L, then $A \oplus B$ is in L.* For since A is in L (by hyp.), $A \oplus M = L$ (by def. 3). Similarly, since B is in L, $B \oplus N = L$. Putting these together, we have (by prop. 10) $A \oplus M \oplus B \oplus N = L \oplus L$. Hence (by ax. 2) $A \oplus M \oplus B \oplus N = L$. Hence (by def. 3) $A \oplus B$ is in L.

PROP. 19. *If A is in L and B is in L and C is in L, then $A \oplus B \oplus C$ is in L.* And so on.

SCHOLIUM. It is obvious that these two propositions and others of the same kind can be converted.

PROP. 20. *If A is in M and B is in N, then $A \oplus B$ is in $M \oplus N$.* For A is in M (by hyp.) and M is in $M \oplus N$ (by def. 3). Hence (by prop. 15) A is in $M \oplus N$. Similarly, since B is in N and N is in $M \oplus N$, then also (by prop. 15) $A \oplus B$ is in $M \oplus N$.

SCHOLIUM. This proposition cannot be converted—much less can the following.

PROP. 21. *If A is in M and B is in N and C is in P, then $A \oplus B \oplus C$ is in $M \oplus N \oplus P$.* And so on.

SCHOLIUM TO DEF. 3. We say that the concept of the genus is in the concept of the species, the individuals of the species in [i.e. among] the individuals of the genus, a part in the whole, and indeed the ultimate and individual in the continuous, as a point in a line, although a point is not part of a line. Likewise the concept of the attribute or predicate is in the concept of the subject. And in general this concept is of the widest application. . . . We are not here concerned with the [special] manner in which those things that are contained are related to each other and to that which contains them. Thus our demonstrations cover also those things which compose something in the distributive sense, as all the species together compose the genus. . . . The same thing can be composed in many different ways if the things of which it is composed are themselves composite. Indeed if resolution could be carried to infinity, the variations of composition would be infinite. Thus all synthesis and analysis depends upon the principles here laid down.

SCHOLIUM TO AXIOMS 1 AND 2. Since the general theory of forms (*speciosa generalis*) is nothing but the representation of combinations by means of symbols, and their manipulation, and the discoverable laws of combination are various, it results that various modes of computation arise. In this place, however, we have nothing to do with the theory of the variations which consist simply in change of order, and $A \oplus B$ is for us the same as $B \oplus A$. And also we have taken no account of repetition, that is, $A \oplus A$ is for us the same as A. Thus wherever these laws just mentioned can be used, the present calculus can be applied. It is obvious that it can be used in the composition of absolute concepts, where neither laws of order nor laws of repetition obtain; thus to say, "warm and light" is to say the same as "light and warm", and to say "warm fire" or "white milk", after the fashion of the poets, is pleonasm. . . . The same thing is true when certain given things are said to be contained in certain things. For the real addition of the same is a useless addition. . . . Accordingly I here denote this real addition by $\oplus$, as the addition of magnitudes is denoted by $+$."[1]

The two notes at the end of this quotation show clearly Leibniz's interest in the abstractness of his calculus, that is to say, in the possibility of interpreting it in various ways. He thought primarily of the combination of attributes, but he illustrated many of his theorems by drawings of lines contained in other lines, and he recognized explicitly that they could all be applied to the constitution of classes. It is important, however, to notice that the sense of the symbol $\oplus$ alters according to the kind of interpretation given to the letters A, B, &c. Thus when Leibniz is thinking of attributes, he understands $\oplus$ as a symbol of conjunction, but when he is thinking of classes, he understands it as a symbol of disjunction. For if we say that the class of men is contained in the class of animals, we mean that anything which is an animal is *either* a man *or* a horse *or* a dog and so on. And the sense of 'is in' alters in a similar fashion. To say that an attribute is contained in another is to say that the first is entailed by the second, whereas to say that one class is contained in another is to say that the first is a sub-class of the second.

If throughout Leibniz's calculus we replace the phrase 'is in' by some artificial symbol, say $\dashv$, we get an even more general calculus which admits two additional interpretations, one in-

---

[1] This piece, published by Gerhardt in *P*, vii, p. 236, has no name. The version given above is abbreviated with some slight changes from the translation of C. I. Lewis in his *Survey of Symbolic Logic*, p. 379. We have substituted the modern sign of equality for Leibniz's $\infty$ and inserted $\oplus$ where it had been omitted in the final scholium. Otherwise the symbolism is unaltered. The passages we have omitted contain three problems, and a number of definitions, comments, and examples which are not required for the formal development of the theorems we have reproduced.

tensional (in terms of attributes), the other extensional (in terms of classes). We can set out the four interpretations for attributes and classes as follows:

| $A, B$, &c. | $\oplus$ | $\dashv$ |
|---|---|---|
| attributes | conjunction | is entailed by |
| attributes | disjunction | entails |
| classes | conjunction | is a super-class of |
| classes | disjunction | is a sub-class of |

The first and the fourth interpretation, in which the symbol $\dashv$ can be rendered by 'is in', are those noticed by Leibniz. In an earlier fragment on his project for a calculus of inclusion he suggested that the consequent of a conditional proposition might be said to be contained in the antecedent.[1] He does not refer to this in his exposition of the calculus we are now considering, but it is clear that we can interpret his formulae as assertions about the relations of propositions. In order to obtain the required senses for the special symbols we need only put 'propositions' instead of 'attributes' in the first two lines of the table given above. And there is nothing far-fetched in this interpretation. For when we say that one proposition *implies* another, we use a metaphor which depends on recognition of formal similarity between this logical relation and the relation of spatial inclusion.

Leibniz's geometrical illustrations in which lines are said to be contained in other lines is a special case of the fourth interpretation listed above; for a line may be considered as a class of points. If, however, the end of the first sentence of the scholium to definition 3 is intended to suggest that the calculus might be applied to the inclusion of points in lines, this is a mistake. For the sense in which an individual is contained in a class as a member is quite different from the sense in which one class is contained in another as a sub-class, and the first relation has not the same logical properties as the second. Thus from the fact that A is a member of B and B is a member of C it does not follow that A is a member of C. We can say that Lord Tomnoddy is a member of the peerage and that the peerage is one of the estates of the realm, but we cannot say that Lord Tomnoddy is one of the estates of the realm. That Leibniz did not see this was due to his excessive respect for the Aristotelian doctrine according to which singular and general statements share the same categorical form.

We have discussed the possibility of different interpretations because the most interesting feature of Leibniz's calculus is its

[1] *O*, p. 377.

abstract formality. What he produced was certainly much less than he hoped to produce. For the last scheme, lacking as it does any provision for negation or for the consideration of conjunction and disjunction together, is still a fragment. So far from including all Aristotle's syllogistic theory as a part, it contains no principle of syllogism except the first (which appears as proposition 15). The meagreness of the result was due, as we have seen, to Leibniz's preoccupation with the conjunction of attributes and his inability to provide a satisfactory account of existential statements. But it is important to stress in conclusion the novelty of what he produced. Here for the first time there was an attempt to work out a piece of abstract mathematics, i.e. mathematics that is not specially concerned with space or numbers. The calculus covers in fact part of the field of logic, but it can be manipulated without regard to any interpretation.

## 4. *From Saccheri to Hamilton*

Leibniz is by far the most important of the mathematicians who interested themselves in logic during its decline as a branch of philosophy, but there are others who deserve mention, and one of the most interesting of these is Gerolamo Saccheri, an Italian Jesuit who in 1697 published a little book called *Logica Demonstrativa* and later produced the first theorems in non-Euclidean geometry. The book must have had some success when it first appeared; for there was a second edition in 1701 and a third in 1735, two years after the author's death. But it was forgotten during the eighteenth and nineteenth centuries, and when Vailati drew attention to it at the beginning of this century there were few remaining copies.[1]

The book is divided according to the Aristotelian scheme into four parts which deal respectively with *Analytica Priora*, *Analytica Posteriora*, *Topica seu Dialectica*, and *Sophismata*; but its most interesting novelties are derived from reflection on the requirements of geometrical proof. In the preface Saccheri says that he intends to proceed 'severa illa methodo quae primis principiis vix parcit nihilve non clarum, non evidens, non indubitatum admittit'. This means that he wishes to apply the strict standards of geometry to logic itself and so reduce to a minimum the number of first principles. In chapter 4, however, he remarks that

---

[1] G. Vailati 'Di un' opera dimenticata del P. Gerolamo Saccheri' and 'A proposito d'un passo del Teeteto e di una dimostrazione di Euclide' in his collected *Scritti*. For what follows we have used the copy of the *Logica Demonstrativa* preserved in the Stadtsbibliothek of Cologne. This is said to be the only surviving specimen of the third edition; but there is now a microfilm of it in the Bodleian Library, Oxford.

for certain purposes it seems necessary to assume a principle not explicitly stated by previous logicians, namely that terms do not all stand in relations of mutual implication or incompatibility but are some of them subordinate to others and some of them independent of others. This assumption is clearly true for the world we know; but since it cannot be proved by logic alone, it must be treated in logic as a mere assumption, if we are to proceed with the rigour proper to demonstrative science (*ut scientifice procedamus*). In chapter 9, which deals with *consequentiae leges*, he uses the assumption in order to show by means of counter-examples that certain combinations of premisses are not permissible in certain figures of syllogism, but he thinks that the demonstration of such negative rules is unsatisfactory so long as it rests on an extralogical assumption, and in chapter 11 he undertakes to confirm his results by a nobler procedure:

'It is now my intention to follow another and, as I think, a very beautiful way of proving these same truths without the help of any assumption. I shall proceed as follows: I shall take the contradictory of the proposition to be proved and elicit the required result from this by straight-forward demonstration (*ostensive ac directe*). This method of proof has been applied by Euclid (ix, 12), by Theodosius (*Spherica* i, 12), and by Cardan (*De Proportionibus* v, 201), whom Clavius reproves (in his scholium to Euclid ix, 12) for boasting that he was the first to discover this kind of proof.'

An example will make the method clear. In order to prove that there cannot be a valid syllogism in the first figure with a universal affirmative major premiss, a universal negative minor premiss, and a universal negative conclusion (i.e. of the pattern traditionally called *AEE*) Saccheri constructs the following argument:

Every syllogism with a universal major and an affirmative minor premiss yields a conclusion in the first figure.
But no syllogism of the pattern *AEE* has a universal major and an affirmative minor premiss.
Therefore no syllogism of the pattern *AEE* yields a conclusion in the first figure.

This argument is itself a syllogism of the kind under consideration, and the two premisses are obviously true. If the pattern *AEE* is valid in the first figure, the conclusion must therefore be true. But the conclusion is a statement that the pattern *AEE* is invalid in the first figure. And so the desired result is seen to follow even from its own negation, which is as much as to say that it must be true. Saccheri gives half a dozen examples of this kind, and remarks at the end of the chapter that the method can be applied more widely. Thirty-six years later in his *Euclides ab Omni Naevo Vindicatus*, which we shall have occasion to notice in the next chapter, he refers back to the *Logica Demonstrativa* and says that his researches confirm the view that every prime verity can be deduced from its own contradictory.

Clearly the method which Saccheri uses is the same as that devised by the Stoics for the confutation of sceptics. But we have found no evidence to suggest that he got the idea from reading about Stoic logic. Nor does he connect it with medieval discussions of *consequentiae*, although he uses the word *consequentia* and reproduces a few medieval results in his book (e.g. the principle that the contradictory of a conjunction of propositions is the disjunction of the contradictories of the same propositions). Almost certainly the source of his inspiration was the widely read edition of Euclid published in 1574 by Clavius, a mathematician who worked out later the calculations required for the Gregorian calendar. And his attention may have been directed to the relevant scholium by his Jesuit teachers. For Clavius himself had belonged to the Society of Jesus, and it seems that the argument on which he wrote his comment had a vogue among the members in the seventeenth century as the *consequentia mirabilis*.[1]

It is interesting, however, to notice that Cardan (1501–76), who was the first to use this kind of argument in modern times and even claimed to have invented it, was well aware of its connexion with Stoic discoveries. In the passage of his *De Proportionibus* (1570) mentioned by Saccheri he praises it by saying:

'And this has never been done by anyone; nay, it seems clearly impossible, and is the most wonderful thing that has been discovered since the beginning of the world, namely to prove something from its opposite, in a demonstration which does not lead to an impossibility, and in such a way that it could not be demonstrated by that demonstration except through the supposition of the contrary of the conclusion, just as if one demonstrated that Socrates is white because he is black and could not demonstrate it otherwise; and for that reason it is far greater than the Chrysippaean syllogism (*et ideo est longe majus Chrysippaeo Syllogismo*).'

There is nothing else in the passage to indicate what argument of Chrysippus he had in mind, and we have not been able to discover in logic texts of the period any use of the phrase 'Chrysippaean syllogism' for a special kind of argument; but it seems probable that he meant some form of reasoning with which his

[1] Professor J. Łukasiewicz gives references to two Polish Jesuits of the time in a note to his 'Philosophische Bemerkungen zu mehrwehrtigen Systemen des Aussagenkalküls', *Comptes rendus des séances de la Société des sciences et des lettres de Varsovie, Classe III*, xxiii (1930), p. 67.

own might be compared, and the most likely is the Stoic retort to intellectual scepticism.[1] For the point on which he lays stress in the preceding explanation is that his conclusion follows directly from its opposite and could not be obtained in any other way. Unlike the refutation of scepticism, his argument is indeed a genuine example of the pattern 'If the first, then the first; if not the first, then the first; but either the first or not the first; therefore the first'. But he had been anticipated in the construction of such an argument by Euclid and Theodosius, as Clavius remarked.

Apart from its use of the *consequentia mirabilis*, Saccheri's *Logica Demonstrativa* is noteworthy as being perhaps the first book to deal with the fallacy of complex definition. In the last chapter of the work Saccheri distinguishes between nominal and real definition, or *definitio quid nominis* and *definitio quid rei*. A purely nominal definition is just a licence to abbreviate and raises no special problem; but a real definition postulates the existence or at least the possibility of that which is defined and so requires justification. Now trouble occurs when a definition which has been introduced without any existence theorem is used in such a way as to convey an assumption of existence. Some geometers, for example, have tried to simplify Euclid's exposition by defining parallels as straight lines equidistant at all points, but they have omitted to notice that their convention for the use of the word 'parallel' does not by itself entitle them to assume that, given a straight line and a point not in the line, it must be possible to draw one line through the point which is at once straight and equidistant at all points from the given line. This example is given by Saccheri himself in his *Euclides ab Omni Naevo Vindicatus* (p. 100) with a reference back to his *Logica*. The point is obviously of great importance for the philosophy of mathematics and it is interesting to notice that Saccheri and Leibniz thought of it independently about the same time.

So far as we know, Saccheri owed nothing to Leibniz, but there can be little doubt of Leibniz's influence on Johann Heinrich Lambert and Gottfried Ploucquet, who helped to keep mathematical logic alive in the eighteenth century. Lambert, who died in 1777, was a distinguished mathematician and his *Sechs Versuche einer Zeichenkunst in der Vernunftlehre* (in his *Logische und philosophische Abhandlungen*, edited by Johann Bernoulli in 1782) contain some ingenious analogies between logic and ordinary algebra, but none that provides the basis for a satisfactory calculus. His most interesting novelties were a suggestion for the systematic

---

[1] Unless possibly he meant the paradox of the crocodile and the baby, attributed to Chrysippus by Lucian in *Vitarum Auctio*, 22.

quantification of the predicate and a beginning of the theory of relations. In connexion with the first he used expressions such as $mA = nB$, where the small letters were supposed to stand for indeterminate characters conjoined with the determinate characters represented by large letters. That is to say he still thought of all propositions in intension and tried to regard 'some A' in 'some A is some B' as though it were the sign of a subspecies of A-ness. In connexion with the second he introduced the notion of a power of a relation, i.e. he suggested that if x was R to y and y was R to z, x might be said to be $R^2$ to z. This was to prove important later, but at the time it led to no important development. Ploucquet's work (which was published in several editions under different names and appeared for the last time in 1782 as *Expositiones Philosophiae Theoreticae*) has less originality. It is indeed little more than a code for the abbreviation of syllogisms. But it is interesting to notice that he too advocates quantification of the predicate: 'Secundum sensum logicum cum omni termino iungendum est signum quantitatis.' In his symbolism distributed terms are represented by large letters and undistributed terms by small letters.

Leonhard Euler's *Lettres à une Princesse d'Allemagne* (which were written in 1761 and published at St. Petersburg in 1768) must also be mentioned among works of the eighteenth century that contributed something to mathematical logic. Those letters which deal with logic contain no attempt to work out a calculus, though Euler was a great mathematician; but they popularized Leibniz's device of illustrating logical relations by geometrical analogies, and this had some influence on thinkers in the next century. In particular it directed attention to the extensional or class interpretation of general statements; for Euler represented (or rather illustrated) the four Aristotelian forms of statement by three relations of closed figures according to the following scheme,[1]

Every a is b   (a) b

No a is b   (a)   (b)

Some a is b   (a)b)

Some a is not b   (a( )b)

in which 'some' has the sense of 'some but only some'.[1] If for the truth of any universal affirmative statement it is necessary that

[1] *Lettres à une Princesse d'Allemagne*, lettre ciii (p. 101).

something connected with the subject-term should be a part of something connected with the predicate-term, obviously this something must be the extension.

In Euler's version of logic the chief role of spatial figures is to make the principles of syllogistic seem intuitively evident, and there is no attempt to survey all possible relations of extensions; but fifty years later the French mathematician J. D. Gergonne developed from Euler's work a new theory which may be described as a substructure for syllogistic.[1] At the opening of his article Gergonne remarks that Aristotelian logic had fallen into general discredit during the eighteenth century, 'though still taught in some Gothic academies', and that it had been revived in his own time only because the conservatism of the age demanded a 'return to the old studies'. But he notes with approval a suggestion of Condorcet that Aristotle's idea of reducing arguments to rules might be regarded as a first step towards the still unachieved perfection of the art of reasoning,[2] and he says later that in his view the ultimate perfection of the art would be a method by which we could get our results in purely mechanical fashion. What he offers, however, is not a machine but a theory within which the principles of syllogistic can be proved rigorously.

If, in the fashion of Euler, we represent the extensions of two ideas by closed figures such as circles, we can easily establish that there are five and only five ways in which they may be related. For each of these relations (which were known already to Boethius) Gergonne introduces a letter in accordance with the adjoining scheme. Here H is to suggest *est hors de*, X *s'entre-croise avec*, I *est identique à*, C *est contenu dans*, and Ↄ *contiens*. And as the first three letters are symmetrical, so are the relations they represent. In terms of these the four Aristotelian forms can be defined as follows:

aHb
aXb
aIb
aCb
aↃb

Every a is b      . . . aIb or aCb.
No a is b          . . . aHb.
Some a is b      . . . aXb or aIb or aCb or aↃb.
Some a is not b . . . aHb or aXb.

Conversely we may, if we wish, define the new relations by use of the Aristotelian forms as follows:

---

[1] 'Essai de dialectique rationelle', *Annales de Mathématiques*, vii (1816–17), pp. 189–228.

[2] *Esquisse d'un tableau historique des progrès de l'esprit humain*, v. This optimistic work was written in 1793, while Condorcet was in hiding from the Terror.

aHb . . . No a is b.
aXb . . . Some a is b and some a is not b and some b is not a.
aIb . . . Every a is b and every b is a.
aCb . . . Every a is b and some b is not a.
a⊃b . . . Every b is a and some a is not b.

But it is then obvious that Gergonne's relations are more narrowly defined than those of Aristotle. Furthermore, they are at once exhaustive and exclusive. That is to say, between any two extensions, provided only that neither is null, one and only one of Gergonne's relations holds. And for the purposes of reasoning these have also the advantage of enabling us to dispense with the complications of the Aristotelian figures. Since the first three are all symmetrical and the fourth is the converse of the fifth, it is sufficient to choose some standard arrangement of terms, say that of Aristotle's first figure

$$
\begin{array}{l}
m \;.\;.\;.\; b \\
a \;.\;.\;.\; m \\
\hline
a \;.\;.\;.\; b
\end{array}
$$

and then to consider the results of inserting Gergonne signs in the gaps. Gergonne himself does just this and discovers that of the $5 \times 5 \times 5$ conceivable distributions of his signs in the figure given above only 54 represent possible states of affairs. Since he is interested chiefly in providing a substructure for Aristotelian syllogistic, he then goes on to derive the customary rules from his table. But by setting out the results in another way it is possible to work out a new theory of Gergonne syllogisms.[1] In the following table

m.....b

|   | H | X | I | C | ⊃ |
|---|---|---|---|---|---|
| **H** |  | T ⊐ | H / T ⊐ | T ⊐ | H |
| **X** | T ⊐ | X | H̄ / T ⊐ | T ⊐ | T ⊐ |
| **I** | H | X | I | C | ⊃ |
| **C** | H | T ⊐ | C | C |  |
| **⊃** | T C̄ | T C̄ | H̄ / ⊃ | H̄ | ⊃ |

(a.....b, read down the left-hand column)

the presence of a letter in a compartment indicates that a conclusion of the kind signified by the letter can be derived from premises

[1] J. A. Faris, 'The Gergonne Relations', *The Journal of Symbolic Logic*, xx (1955), pp. 207-31.

corresponding to the letters at the sides, while the presence of a letter with a stroke over it indicates that we can infer the negation of the relation which would be signified by the letter alone. There are thus 13 Gergonne syllogisms with positive conclusions and 19 with negative conclusions. But each positive conclusion is equivalent to the conjunction of 4 negative conclusions (because the 5 Gergonne relations are exhaustive and exclusive), and so our table accounts for all the 71 cases excluded by Gergonne's table of compatibility.

Since the Gergonne relations are in a certain sense simpler than those expressed by the several Aristotelian forms of statement, it is natural to ask why they cannot be expressed in ordinary language without a good deal of complication. The reason cannot be anything to do with the assumption that all general terms have application (i.e. with the exclusion of null classes); for that, as we have seen, was made by Aristotle himself in the elaboration of his syllogistic. But it is connected with the fact that Gergonne relations are relations of extensions. In natural language words such as 'every' and 'some' may be used in many contexts other than those of the four Aristotelian forms of statement. We can say, for example, 'Every man is a son of some woman', which cannot be classified in the Aristotelian scheme with respect to both its quantifiers at once. If, however, we wish to concentrate attention on what is relevant to the rules of Aristotle's syllogistic, we can for convenience combine expression of universality or particularity with expression of predication or negation of predication. This is done in the scholastic notation of $A$, $E$, $I$, and $O$, but in such a way that we can return to ordinary language in one move, whenever we choose to do so. With the introduction of Gergonne's notation of H, X, I, C, and ⊃ we take another step away from ordinary language, and there are undoubtedly advantages to be gained from employment of this symbolism when we want to talk about relations of extensions. But they are to be had only by loss of direct connexion with that notation of quantifiers which we can use for dealing with many other situations. Ordinary language may seem cumbrous in contrast with a symbolism specially designed for talking about relations of extensions and nothing else, but it has the very great merit of being useful in indefinitely many different contexts.

Failure to appreciate this point was the source of the troubles into which Sir William Hamilton (of Edinburgh) fell when he tried to improve on Aristotle's system by including provision for quantification of all predicates.[1] According to his 'New Analytic

[1] *Lectures on Logic*, ii, appendix v, especially p. 277.

of Logical Forms', first announced in 1846, we should distinguish
for purposes of syllogistic, and presumably for all science, eight
different forms of statement, namely:

    (1) All a is all b.
    (2) All a is some b.
    (3) Some a is all b.
    (4) Some a is some b.
    (5) Any a is not any b.
    (6) Any a is not some b.
    (7) Some a is not any b.
    (8) Some a is not some b.

Obviously the word 'some' is to be understood here in the sense
of 'some but only some', since it is contrasted with 'all' and 'any'.
If, further, we suppose that 'all' is to be understood in a collective
sense (so that 'all a' is an ungrammatical abbreviation for 'the
whole class of a things'), (1)–(4) in this list may be identified with
Gergonne's 'aIb', 'aCb', 'aⅅb', and 'aXb' respectively; and this, no
doubt, is the interpretation that Hamilton intended. For although
he seems to have known nothing of Gergonne's work, he too was
trying to talk precisely about relations of extensions. But what are
we to say of the rest of the items in his list? Perhaps we may
understand (5) as equivalent for Gergonne's 'aHb', but in that
case the remaining three items cannot represent independent
possibilities, since Gergonne's set of five relations is known to be
exhaustive.[1] And apart from this difficulty, there is something
radically wrong in a scheme which involves a switch from the
collective 'all' to the distributive 'any'. Hamilton thinks, no doubt,
that his change from one word to the other is merely a trick of
English style which has no logical significance. In fact the transition from collective to distributive is indispensable for his attempt
to work out the second half of the table, since if 'All a is not all b'
meant anything at all it would presumably mean the same as
'the whole class of a things is not the whole class of b things' and
that, being the contradictory of (1), would be equivalent to the
disjunction of the other four items in Gergonne's scheme, provided
always that null classes are excluded from consideration.

But the truth is that Hamilton never thought out completely
what he was trying to do and never succeeded in making clear
what should be understood by the negation of any of the items in
his list. It is not surprising, therefore, that his ill-considered claims
led to a controversy in which he was thoroughly trounced by

[1] W. Bednarowski, 'Hamilton's Quantification of the Predicate', *Proceedings of the Aristotelian Society*, lvi (1956), pp. 217–40.

Augustus De Morgan.[1] His failure to work out a satisfactory scheme for systematic quantification of predicates is interesting, nevertheless, because it shows that the quantifiers of ordinary speech are not, as he apparently thought, merely incidental features of a symbolism for talking about relations of classes, but signs which have a life outside that context. It is by no means an accident that his suggestion breaks down at the point where he tries to combine his universal quantifier with a negative sign and is therefore unable to take it collectively without abandoning the pretence that he is developing Aristotle's classification of propositions, or, in his own words, placing 'the keystone in the Aristotelic arch'. In this connexion it is worth remarking that according to his own meticulous account of the history of his innovation he began by considering his first four items in 1833 and only proceeded some seven years later to the quantification of the predicate in negative propositions.[2]

While following the line of development from Leibniz we have passed over the work of Kant, and for completeness we must now turn back to consider his relation to the development of logic. If we compare his writings with those of other philosophers of the eighteenth century, we find an appearance of greater interest in formal logic. In an essay of 1762, *Von der falschen Spitzfindigkeit der vier syllogistischen Figuren*, he tried to defend the view that all syllogistic reasoning depends on the single principle *Nota notae est nota rei ipsius*. We have seen that there is a mistake in trying to find one formula for syllogistic reasoning without taking account of the procedure of reduction elaborated by Aristotle; but Kant's discussion of the question suggests at least that he had more interest in traditional teaching than some of his recent predecessors such as Hume. This impression is confirmed by the use he makes of formal logic in his *Critique of Pure Reason*, in particular by his attempt to derive a table of categories from the classification of forms of judgement. But when we look closer, we find that Kant's interest is superficial. In the book *Logik*, which was compiled from his lecture notes in 1800 by B. G. Jäsche, he says little of value about syllogistic and shows no sympathy with efforts to improve upon the legacy of Aristotle. Of Lambert's work in particular he says that it contains nothing but useless subtleties. And in the *Critique of Pure Reason* he discusses formal logic only in order to distinguish it from transcendental logic, which is supposed to be concerned with the possibility and validity of knowledge.

[1] 'Logic' in *The English Cyclopaedia* (*Arts and Science Division*), v (1860), pp. 340–54.
[2] *Lectures on Logic*, ii, p. 249.

In the Preface to the second edition of the *Critique of Pure Reason* Kant writes:

'That logic from the earliest times has followed this sure path [i.e. of a science] may be seen from the fact that since Aristotle it has not had to retrace a single step, unless we choose to consider as improvements the removal of some unnecessary subtleties or the clearer exposition of its doctrine, both of which refer to the elegance rather than to the solidity of the science. It is remarkable also, that to the present day it has not been able to advance a step and is thus to all appearance complete and perfect. If some modern philosophers have thought to enlarge, by introducing *psychological* chapters on the different faculties of knowledge . . . , *metaphysical* chapters on the origin of knowledge or the different kinds of certainty according to the differences in the objects. . . , or *anthropological* chapters on prejudices, their causes and remedies, this could only arise from their ignorance of the peculiar nature of logical science. . . . The limits of logic are quite precisely determined: it is a science concerned solely with the exhaustive exposition and strict proof of the formal rules of all thought.'[1]

The concern which Kant shows here for the purity of logic is difficult to reconcile with his own practice in the body of the work. For it was he with his transcendentalism who began the production of the curious mixture of metaphysics and epistemology which was presented as logic by Hegel and the other Idealists of the nineteenth century. But it is more interesting to notice that he was apparently unaware of the value of any contributions made to logic after the time of Aristotle, and that the doctrine which he regarded as the complete and perfect discovery of Aristotle was in fact a peculiarly confused version of the traditional mixture of Aristotelian and Stoic elements. The second point is worth explaining at some length, because Kant's authority has led many philosophers to think of his scheme as classical.

In a section of his *Critique of Pure Reason* with the title 'Of the Logical Function of the Understanding in Judgements' Kant gives the following table for the classification of judgements:[2]

| I | II | III | IV |
|---|---|---|---|
| *Quantity* | *Quality* | *Relation* | *Modality* |
| Universal | Affirmative | Categorical | Problematic |
| Particular | Negative | Hypothetical | Assertoric |
| Singular | Infinite | Disjunctive | Apodeictic |

The fact that he is able to provide three species under each heading is obviously a matter of accident. For the species in any one set are not really co-ordinate, and there is no common principle

---

[1] *Critique of Pure Reason*, B. viii.      [2] Ibid., B. 95.

requiring trichotomy. But Kant seems to attach some importance to the symmetry of his scheme, and he apparently holds (*a*) that every judgement can be placed in one of the three divisions under each heading, and (*b*) that each division under one heading can be combined with each division under each of the others. These assumptions are mistaken. We cannot, for example, have a negative hypothetical judgement. For the presence of negation in either the antecedent or the consequent of a hypothetical judgement does not make the whole negative, and the negation of the whole is not itself hypothetical. Nor again is it sensible to talk of a particular disjunctive judgement. For while each or any of a number of disjuncts may be particular according to Aristotle's classification, the whole has no subject in Aristotle's sense, and so cannot be brought in any way under the heading of quantity. These confusions result from a failure to think out the relations between the Aristotelian and the Stoic contributions to logic—a failure not surprising in one who assumed that all the valuable part of traditional logic had come from Aristotle. But there is a muddle also in Kant's account of modality, where his basic ideas are derived from Aristotle alone. He tells us that modality 'contributes nothing to the content of a judgement (for besides quantity, quality and relation there is nothing that constitutes the content of a judgement), but concerns only the value of the copula in relation to thought in general'. And he seems to mean by this cryptic remark that a modal adverb such as 'possibly' represents only a way of thinking the thought enunciated by the rest of the sentence in which it occurs. For he says that the three 'functions of modality' which he distinguishes represent three 'moments of thought' which form a series. If this is indeed his doctrine, it is a bad instance of the corruption of logic by psychology and epistemology. When a man says 'Possibly the train will be late', he does not commit himself to an assertion that the train of which he speaks will be late. What he asserts is the second-order proposition that it is possible (in relation to what he knows) that the train will be late. It would be absurd, of course, to say that the word 'possibly' helped to express a thought content in the same way as an ordinary adverb like 'quickly'. But no one who had a proper understanding of the complexities that may be found in a proposition would suppose that any such absurdity was involved in an objectivist theory of modal distinctions.

Similar defects are to be found in Kant's distinction between analytic and synthetic judgements. According to his definition a judgement of the subject-predicate form is analytic if there is nothing contained in the predicate which was not already thought in the concept of the subject; otherwise it is synthetic.[1] The idea of the distinction seems to be derived from Locke's discussion of trifling and instructive propositions, but in Kant's system the distinction is of fundamental importance and must therefore be examined with special care. As it stands, Kant's explanation refers only to judgements of the subject-predicate form; but he can scarcely have intended his distinction to be limited to them in its application, for he goes on to talk as though he were dealing with the whole field of possible knowledge. Perhaps he fell into the mistake of assuming that all judgements are of the subject-predicate form, e.g. when he wrote of the judgement that $7+5 = 12$ as though it were synthetic. But he has nowhere discussed the application of his distinction to hypothetical or disjunctive judgements, e.g. to that expressed by 'Queen Anne is dead or Queen Anne is not dead'. If he had been questioned about this example he might have said that it was analytic, but in order to justify that answer he would have had to fall back on another way of defining the key-word 'analytic'.

In one place he says that the fundamental and sufficient principle of all analytic judgements is the Law of Contradiction.[2] This seems to mean that a judgement is analytic if, and only if, its negation is a conjunction of contradictories. Such a characterization of analytic judgements is undoubtedly more suitable for Kant's purposes than that with which he began, since it is possible with this definition to divide all true judgements between the headings 'analytic' and 'synthetic'. But it is a mistake to suppose, as many philosophers have done, that the class of analytic judgements so defined includes all judgements that are true on logical grounds alone. The principle of a syllogism of the first mood of the first figure is assuredly true on logical grounds, if any statement is, and yet it cannot be derived from the principle of non-contradiction alone. Admittedly consequences which are mutually incompatible can be obtained from the negation of a statement of the form 'If every M is L and every S is M, then every S is L'. But in order to obtain them we must first assume the principle of the syllogism. And this is as much as to say that the principle of non-contradiction is not a sufficient foundation for all logic.[3] Kant, indeed, did not say explicitly that it was; but if it has to be allowed that, according to his best definition of the terms 'analytic' and 'synthetic', the principle of a syllogism in *Barbara* is a synthetic truth, it is difficult to find any clear sense

---

[1] *Critique of Pure Reason*, B. 10; *Prolegomena to any Future Metaphysic*, § 2.
[2] *Critique of Pure Reason*, B. 190. 'Law of non-contradiction' would be a better name.   [3] This point was made by J. S. Mill in his *System of Logic*, II. vi. 5.

for his famous question 'How are synthetic *a priori* judgements possible?' For there is nothing especially surprising in the suggestion that the principle of a syllogism is *a priori* in the Kantian sense of the phrase, i.e. non-empirical.[1]

Already in 1844 the mathematician Gauss, writing to a friend about the absurdity of the pronouncements on mathematics by Schelling, Hegel, and a number of other philosophers, said : 'But even with Kant it is not much better; in my opinion his distinction between analytic and synthetic propositions is one of those things that either run out in a triviality or are false.'[2] The word 'analytic' has nevertheless some associations which make philosophers loth to abandon it, and we find it in many modern works with an explanation which makes it a synonym for 'true on logical grounds alone'. This usage can be defended by the argument that it maintains contact with tradition and renders Kant's intention better than he ever succeeded in doing for himself. But the associations of the word may easily mislead us when we discuss the foundations of logic itself, and it is in fact not difficult to find passages in recent literature where philosophers have sought to explain the nature of logical truth by use of the word 'analytic', although the only precise modern definition of the word refers back to logic.

After these strictures on Kant's logic it is important to give him credit for one great achievement, the exposure of the ontological argument for the existence of God. This argument was put forward first by St. Anselm in the eleventh century and revived by Descartes in the seventeenth. In its simplest form it is just the assertion that God must exist because existence is involved by definition in the essence of divinity. To this Kant replied that existence is not an attribute or determination of anything and so cannot be involved in the essence of anything.[3] The point had been made already by Gassendi in his objections to Descartes's *Meditations*, but it had been overlooked or forgotten, and Kant has the credit of making the criticism generally understood. Unfortunately he did not give any satisfactory account of existential propositions. If he had gone on to investigate this matter further, he could not have remained content with the poor version of traditional logic which he used.

## 5. *Bolzano and Mill*

Kant's purpose in the writing of his *Critique of Pure Reason* was to make an end of metaphysical philosophy as it had been before

---

[1] This new sense was popularized by Kant, but it is to be found already in Leibniz's fifth contribution to the *Leibniz–Clarke Correspondence* (1716), § 129.
[2] Letter of 1 November 1844 to Schumacher, *Werke*, xii, p. 62.
[3] *Critique of Pure Reason* B. 625.

his time, but he did not succeed. Among those who rejected his work and continued to philosophize in what Kantians called a pre-critical fashion one of the most interesting, though not very influential, was Bernard Bolzano (1781–1848).[1] Because he was a Roman Catholic priest and professor of the philosophy of religion in the University of Prague (until deposed in 1819 for expressing liberal opinions on questions of politics), it has sometimes been supposed that his reaction against Kant in his *Wissenschaftslehre* of 1837 and his *Paradoxien der Unendlichkeit* (which was not published until after his death) must have been inspired by reading of medieval authors. On one occasion he does in fact quote a not very helpful passage from a work *De Demonstratione* formerly attributed to St. Thomas Aquinas,[2] on another he mentions the treatment of *insolubilia* in Savonarola's *Compendium Logicae*,[3] and on a third he uses the German word *Consequenz* in what appears to be the same sense as the medieval *consequentia*.[4] But he seems to have known little of the achievements of medieval logicians, and the references in his *Wissenschaftslehre* suggest that he spent much more time in reading the ancients (e.g. Sextus Empiricus) and the moderns from Descartes onwards. If there is any one predecessor whose work he may be said to follow with admiration, that is 'the great Leibniz'.[5] But it may be that when he called his chief work *Wissenschaftslehre* he had in mind both the medieval account of logic as *ars artium* and also Leibniz's talk of a *scientia generalis* that would deal with the organization of the sciences. For the title means 'theory of science' rather than 'theory of knowledge' (*Erkenntnislehre*), and the sub-title of the original edition explains that the work is 'an attempt at a detailed and in large part new presentation of Logic with constant reference to those who have worked on it hitherto'. But the work is not concerned solely with formal logic. On the contrary it professes to deal with 'all the rules to be observed in the division of the whole realm of truth into separate sciences and in the presentation of these same sciences in special treatises'.[6] Towards the end of the fourth volume there is even a section on the composition of title-pages[7] and after that another in which the author of more than 2,300 pages mentions prolixity as a common failing of the writers of textbooks.[8] It is rather curious perhaps that an admirer of Leibniz should have called all this logic, but the explanation

---

[1] Some detailed information about his life and writings can be found in the historical introduction to his *Paradoxes of the Infinite*, translated and edited by D. A. Steele, 1950.                                    [2] *Wissenschaftslehre*, § 27.
[3] Ibid., § 19.                                                    [4] Ibid., § 254.
[5] Ibid., § 104, Anm. 3.        [6] Ibid., § 1.        [7] Ibid., § 696.
[8] Ibid., § 697.

seems to be that discontent with Kant's talk of a distinction between form and matter had made Bolzano doubtful of the
possibility of drawing any clear line between the two.[1] He wished
to separate logic from psychology and rhetoric and to insist that
possibility is not to be confused with conceivability,[2] but he
thought that logic must take account of the different ways in
which we come to knowledge and that it could not consist solely
of analytic truths, as those were conceived by Kant, since such
truths would not be important enough to make a science.[3] There
is, he holds, a sense in which logic may be described as formal
because it deals with forms or patterns of inferences,[4] but this
does not justify us in excluding from the scope of logic such distinctions as that between judgements *a priori* and judgements
*a posteriori* (in the sense which Kant gave to those phrases).[5]

According to Bolzano a science in the objective sense of that
word is a sum of objective truths. If it is set forth in a treatise,
the truths of which it consists must, of course, be known to
some man, but truths are not in general to be identified with
truths known to men. On the contrary it is reasonable to suppose
that the great majority of them are known only to God. For an
objective truth is a true proposition-in-itself (*Satz-an-sich*), that
is to say, a true propositional content, something thinkable or
expressible but not necessarily thought or expressed.[6] Often the
word 'judgement' is used in this sense, but it is not suitable as a
technical term because it is sometimes used also for the act as
opposed to the content of judging; and apart from that it would
be misleading if applied to a content which was not believed but
merely considered as an hypothesis. 'Judgement' is in fact just
one of many words that we can use to refer to propositional contents in special contexts. Others are 'premiss' and 'conclusion',
which logicians introduced as descriptions for sentences occurring
in certain positions in arguments but used later as though they
were designations for propositional contents.

The passages from earlier writers which Bolzano cites in support
of his account of *Sätze-an-sich* (and *Wahrheiten-an-sich* in particular)
are not very good for his purpose. He does not notice the Stoic
doctrine of λεκτά and the medieval doctrine of *dicta propositionum*
or *complexe significabilia*, but mentions instead ancient and modern
assertions that being and truth may be identified.[7] And the writings of Leibniz which he cites, namely the *Dialogus de Connexione
inter Res et Verba et Veritatis Realitate* and the *Nouveaux Essais*, IV. v,

---

[1] *Wissenschaftslehre*, § 186.   [2] Ibid., § 7.   [3] Ibid., §§ 12–13.
[4] Ibid., § 254.   [5] Ibid., § 12.   [6] Ibid., § 19.
[7] Ibid., § 27. In § 23 he quotes from Sextus Empiricus, *Adv. Math.* viii. 12,
where the word λεκτόν occurs, but does not comment on it.

are not exactly what he needs.[1] For while Leibniz insists in these places that there can be truths which no one knows and goes on to make fun of the suggestion that truths are sets of signs which may be classified according to the ink in which they are printed, he seems to hold that the property of being true belongs to possible thoughts or signs. In the dialogue mentioned above he makes one of the speakers say 'Vides ergo veritatem esse propositionum seu cogitationum, sed possibilium', and what he adds later about the relations of signs to things does not imply belief in *Sätze-an-sich*.[2] But Bolzano is fully entitled to say that his doctrine is implicit in many remarks made by philosophers and plain men alike. Apart from 'premiss' and 'conclusion' which he mentions, we have the words 'question', 'theorem', 'suggestion', 'theory', 'tenet', 'dogma', which are all used as descriptions for *Sätze-an-sich* in special contexts.

In German the word *Satz* from which Bolzano makes his technical term can be used either as a grammatical term covering the ranges of both the English words 'sentence' and 'clause' or as a word like 'premiss' and the rest but without a link to any special context of thought except that of exposition. Thus theorems in a book of mathematics may be called *Sätze*, and it is even possible to use the phrase *der zweite Satz der Wärmelehre* where we in English should say 'the second law of thermodynamics'. In this respect its history is very like that of the Latin *propositio*. For although medieval logicians always defined *propositiones* as complex signs of a certain sort, they commonly applied to them adjectives such as *necessaria* and *impossibilis* which are appropriate only to propositional contents. And in ordinary Latin it became customary also to use the word in talking of theses in mathematics, law, or theology without regard to the particular words used by the persons who put them forward. In English we have the special words 'sentence' and 'clause' for purely grammatical purposes, and it is therefore not surprising that for us 'proposition' has come to mean exactly what Bolzano meant by *Satz-an-sich*. Until recently writers of textbooks on logic preserved the tradition of defining a proposition as the verbal expression of a judgement; but what they said did not correspond to common usage and the old definition has now been abandoned by most logicians. Since this differentiation in modern English between 'sentence', 'clause', and 'proposition' is obviously advantageous, we shall always use 'proposition' in what follows as an equivalent for Bolzano's

[1] *Wissenschaftslehre*, §§ 21 and 27.
[2] *Philosophische Schriften*, ed. Gerhardt, vii, p. 190. Couturat has published since in *Opuscules et fragments inédits de Leibniz*, p. 512, a note in which Leibniz ascribes truth to a *cogitabile complexum*.

*Satz-an-sich*, unless historical considerations require a temporary and easily recognized return to the older usage. Unfortunately the differentiation has sometimes been ignored in translations from German, where *Satz* has to do duty for all three notions. Thus the English phrase 'propositional calculus', which signifies properly the part of logic in which the variables mark gaps for signs (i.e. expressions) of propositions, has been rendered into German by *Satzkalkül* and this in turn has been incorrectly rendered back by 'sentential calculus', although it should be clear to any one familiar with English that the letters $P$ and $Q$ in a formula such as *If P then Q* do not mark gaps for signs of sentences nor yet for sentences themselves in the proper sense of that word.

Having explained how he uses the phrase *Wahrheiten-an-sich*, Bolzano undertakes to show that there are infinitely many of them and even that we know infinitely many. His arguments here are of the same sort as those used by the Stoics against the Sceptics. Thus he begins by showing that it is self-refuting to say 'No proposition is true' and then argues that it is impossible to stop at this or any other point in a sequence of such propositions. Furthermore, he knows the history of the kind of reasoning he uses, and he gives references in this connexion to Sextus Empiricus, St. Augustine, and Descartes.[1] The reader who is not already convinced by earlier considerations will probably think this passage sophistical; but we need examine it no further, since we accept the main thesis.

It is one thing, however, to recognize with Bolzano that there are propositions expressed by the signs of many different languages or perhaps not expressed at all, and another thing to agree with all that he proceeds to say about them. For some of his pronouncements on this subject are very curious indeed. He asserts, for example, that, although there are such things, they do not have real existence (*wirkliches Dasein*).[2] When he says this, he realizes that statements of the form 'An X exists' are often made as substitutes for statements of the form 'There is an X'; but he thinks that this usage is metaphorical and that, contrary to what Kant said, existence is properly to be described as an attribute.[3] Since, however, he maintains also that this attribute is simple and undefinable, it is difficult to understand what he means by his denial that propositions can have it. Apparently the remark is intended to disarm opposition by letting it be known that propositions are not in space and time. For he writes in explanation: 'They have no real existence, i.e. they are not of such a sort as to

---

[1] *Wissenschaftslehre*, §§ 31, 33, and 44.
[2] Ibid., §§ 19, 25, and 30.                    [3] Ibid., § 142, Anm. 2.

be in any place or at any time or in any other manner as anything real (*d. h. sie sind nicht solches, das in irgend einem Orte, oder zu
irgend einer Zeit, oder auf sonst einer Art als etwas Wirkliches bestände*).'[1]
And elsewhere he declares that all created substances, including
spirits, are in space and time.[2] But the language he uses suggests
that he does not want to *identify* existence with being in space
and time; and so, while we may agree that propositions have
neither places nor dates, we cannot understand his doctrine as a
whole.

Another curiosity of Bolzano's theory is that he thinks *Sätze-
an-sich* must be composed of *Vorstellungen-an-sich* much as sentences are composed of words.[3] The phrase *Vorstellung-an-sich*
means literally 'idea in itself', but the reader must not suppose
that Bolzano is thinking of a *Satz-an-sich* as a *propositio mentalis*
composed of *termini mentales*. On the contary, a *Vorstellung-an-sich*
is said to be in no way mental; for like a *Satz-an-sich* it is not even
a real existent.[4] Perhaps the best way of describing it is to say
that it is an ideal content or an idea in that sense in which many
people may be said to have the same idea. As Leibniz remarked
in his *Nouveaux Essais*, II. i. 1, ideas in this sense do not come to
be or cease to exist with the changes in our mental life. Furthermore, according to Bolzano, if they are purely conceptual, i.e.
free from any sensory elements, those objective ideas are the
universals about which philosophers quarrelled in the Middle
Ages. The nominalists were right in saying that they are nothing
existent, but the realists were right in saying that they are not
mere names.[5] Part of this is good sense, but part is very queer.
We may agree with Bolzano that propositions involve universals
(or objective concepts) and that the status of the latter is similar
to that of the former. But we must insist also that propositions
can be about individuals in space and time, and that there is
something wrong with any theory which denies this. It is difficult
to understand exactly what Bolzano wishes to say about the
subject of the historical proposition that Socrates died from
drinking hemlock, but it seems sometimes as though he were
committed to the doctrine that the subject is a timeless entity
distinct from the real Socrates. This is surely a mistake. Propositions may reasonably be described both as timeless and as
composite, but this should not be taken to mean that they are
composed of timeless constituents just as steel ships are composed
of steel plates.

While considering *Vorstellungen-an-sich* in the second main

---

[1] Ibid., § 25.                       [2] *Paradoxien der Unendlichkeit*, § 55.
[3] *Wissenschaftslehre*, § 48.        [4] Ibid.                  [5] Ibid., § 51.

division of his work Bolzano makes some interesting remarks about properties and relations. A relation, he says, is a character (*Beschaffenheit*) of a whole whose parts do not themselves have that character, though either, of course, may be said to have the extrinsic character of being related by the relation in question to the other part.[1] In contrast a property, or intrinsic character, is a character which does not in any way involve a relation. Here and in other places Bolzano seems to be in danger of confusing a whole of parts with a set of members,[2] but what he says is nevertheless a good start for a theory of relations. In the same section he goes on to notice also the distinction between symmetrical and asymmetrical relations and to consider the possibility of relations which have more than two terms or less than two terms.

Later in this part there is a discussion of relations between general ideas in respect of extension, and a number of theorems are set out with illustrative diagrams and proofs.[3] Most of them are taken, as Bolzano says, from J. G. E. Maass's *Grundriß der Logik* of 1793. As an example we give the last (23). When A and B are a pair of concatenated (*verkettete*) ideas (i.e. have extensions related in the way Gergonne indicated by the sign X), not-A and not-B are also concatenated if, and only if, the extensions of A and B do not together exhaust the domain of the widest possible idea, that of Something. For in order that not-A and not-B should be concatenated it is necessary and sufficient that there should be (i) something which falls under both, (ii) something which falls under not-A without falling under not-B, and (iii) something which falls under not-B without falling under not-A. But the first condition is satisfied if the extensions of A and B do not together exhaust the universe, and otherwise not. And the second and third conditions are satisfied in any case, because it follows from the concatenation of A and B that there is something falling under A which does not fall under B but does fall under not-B, and similarly that there is something falling under B which does not fall under A but does fall under not-A.

In contexts like this Bolzano makes free use of the notion of extension, which he renders by *Umfang*, and he remarks that since the publication of the *Port Royal Logic* it has been mistakenly asserted in nearly all books of logic that comprehension and extension vary inversely.[4] Obviously this doctrine is wrong if it is supposed to mean that there could not be more men (than there have been, are, and will be) without a reduction of the set of attributes which belong necessarily to all men. But Bolzano bases

---

[1] *Wissenschaftslehre*, § 80.                    [2] Ibid., § 66.
[3] Ibid., § 105.                                  [4] Ibid., § 120.

his objection on different considerations. According to him the comprehension (*Inhalt*) of an idea is not, as Arnauld and Nicole said, the set of attributes belonging necessarily to anything falling under the idea, but rather the set of concepts involved in its specification.[1] Thus he maintains that the idea of a man-who-knows-all-living-European-languages has a greater comprehension than the idea of a man-who-knows-all-European-languages and at the same time also a greater extension. In defence of his new definition of comprehension he says that it is required for Kant's distinction of analytic and synthetic judgements. But this seems to be a poor argument, since he himself offers another account of the distinction between analytic and synthetic.

In order to understand Bolzano's new definition of analytic propositions it is necessary to begin by considering his notion of a class of propositions each of which may be obtained from some given proposition by substitution for one or more constituents of that proposition.[2] According to his own example, when we start with the proposition expressed by 'The man Caius is mortal' and consider as replaceable only its constituent Caius, we determine a class whose other members are propositions like those expressed by 'The man Sempronius is mortal' and 'The man Titus is mortal'. If, furthermore, as in this example, all the members of the class are true, or at any rate all those which may be called *gegenständlich* because they deal with real objects, Bolzano says that the original proposition is universally valid with respect to that constituent or those constituents for which substitution has been considered. If, on the other hand, all the members of the class are false, he says that the original proposition is universally invalid. And if some of the class are true while others are false, he says that the proposition has an intermediate degree of validity equal to the proportion of true propositions in the class : this notion of degree of validity proves important later in his theory of probability. Finally, if a proposition is either universally valid or universally invalid, he says that it is analytic with respect to the constituents for which substitution is considered, but otherwise synthetic. Thus the proposition expressed by 'A morally bad man deserves no honour' is analytic with respect to the constituent signified by 'man', because substitution for that constituent yields only true propositions, but the proposition expressed by 'A triangle contains two right angles' is synthetic, because it has no constituent for which substitution yields only true propositions or only false propositions. Bolzano admits that the notion of an analytic proposition which he has defined is much wider than

[1] Ibid., § 56.　　　　　　　　　　　　　[2] Ibid., § 147.

that of Kant, and he says that if the part of an analytic proposition which is considered invariant (i.e. not open to substitution) contains only logical notions, it may perhaps be useful to describe the whole proposition as logically analytic, or analytic in the stricter sense. Apparently he thinks that this is something like the sense intended by Kant; but he does not attach much importance to it, because he does not think it possible to draw a clear line between logical and non-logical notions.[1]

There are a number of curious features in this passage of Bolzano's work. The first is a purely verbal point. Bolzano has so defined the word 'analytic' that it can be applied to false propositions. This is contrary to Kant's usage, but it is easy to see why Bolzano thought it reasonable. He wanted to use the two words 'analytic' and 'synthetic' as exhaustive of the realm of propositions, and he noticed that according to the Kantian usage self-contradictory propositions would be neither analytic nor synthetic. The practice of later philosophers has followed Kant's lead rather than Bolzano's and it seems that we must either reconcile ourselves to saying that 'analytic' and 'synthetic' are not contradictory opposites or try to secure the exhaustiveness of the division by applying it only to truths. Secondly, Bolzano's account of analytic propositions seems to be based on the very naïve assumption that a proposition must contain distinguishable constituents corresponding to all the distinguishable constituents of a sentence that expresses it, and vice versa. It is true that he sometimes cautions us against classifying propositions by their linguistic expressions and points out in one place that sentences like 'War is war' may be used to express synthetic propositions.[2] But in practice he often slips into naming sentences when according to his general theory he should be talking about propositions, and in one place he says that the proposition 'The sum of all the angles of a regular quadrilateral amounts to four right angles' is analytic with respect to the concept *regular* though it would not be recognized as such by a person ignorant of geometry.[3] Apart from its curious expression, this example is very puzzling. For Bolzano seems to hold that if the word 'regular' were omitted the sentence which he gives would express a synthetic proposition, but that with this superfluous word it expresses an analytic proposition. Thirdly, Bolzano has given a definition of 'analytic' such that a proposition can be analytic by virtue of natural laws or even by virtue of mere accidents. Consider, for example, the sentence 'Kant was not an eighteenth-century philosopher who died on the anniversary of his birth'. If it so happens that no

---

[1] *Wissenschaftslehre*, § 148.     [2] Ibid., Anm. 1.     [3] Ibid., § 367.

eighteenth-century philosopher died on the anniversary of his birth, all the sentences that can be made from this by substitution of other names for 'Kant' express true propositions, and so the proposition expressed by the original sentence is analytic according to Bolzano's definition.

The most interesting and valuable element in Bolzano's discussion of the distinction between analytic and synthetic propositions is his recognition of the fact that there are certain characters which belong to propositions in virtue of their structure. According to his way of talking a proposition may be universally valid with respect to substitution for certain constituents but not with respect to substitution for others. This is intelligible but rather confusing, and it seems preferable to say that universal validity (or validity, as it is sometimes called for short by later logicians) belongs primarily to certain propositional patterns and only secondarily to the propositions which exemplify them. Similar paraphrases can be supplied also for what he goes on to say about compatibility and derivability.

If among the constituents of the various propositions of a group there are some for which substitution can be made throughout the group in such a way as to leave only true propositions, Bolzano says that the original propositions of the group are compatible with respect to the constituents for which substitution has been considered, but otherwise incompatible.[1] In the language which we have suggested this means that a group of propositional patterns are compatible, or, as modern logicians sometimes say, simultaneously satisfiable, if they are in fact exemplified together by a group of true propositions, and that, when this is the case, *any* group of propositions which exemplifies the group of patterns may be described as compatible in a secondary sense. The notion of compatibility is, of course, closely connected with the notion of possibility applicable to single propositions, and it is therefore not surprising to find that Bolzano later defines a possible proposition as one compatible with all purely general truths (*Begriffswahrheiten*).[2] Since at the same time he defines a necessary truth as one whose negation is incompatible with purely general truths, he is apparently committed to saying that the proposition expressed by 'Kant was not an eighteenth-century philosopher who died on the anniversary of his birth' is not necessary, though it may be analytic with respect to the constituent Kant.

The notion of a proposition's following from one or more other propositions is discussed by Bolzano immediately after his account of compatibility and in a similar fashion. According to his own

[1] Ibid., § 154.  [2] Ibid., §§ 119 and 182.

way of describing the matter, the propositions M, N, O, . . .
follow, or are derivable (*ableitbar*), from the propositions A, B,
C, D, . . . with respect to the constituents i, j, . . . if any set of ideas
which yield a set of true propositions when substituted for i, j, . . .
in A, B, C, D, . . . do the same also when substituted for i, j . . .
in M, N, O . . . .[1] In other language this means that a proposition
called a conclusion is entailed by a set of propositions called premisses if the argument constituted by the association of the premises
and the conclusion exemplifies a pattern of argument for which
all exemplifications with true premises also have true conclusions.
In recent times a similar thought has been expressed by the
stipulation that a formula may be described as a consequence of
other formulae if, and only if, every interpretation which verifies
them (i.e. turns them into true statements) also verifies it. But the
notion of consequence defined in this way is not now identified
with that of derivability. The reason why it has recently been
found necessary to make a distinction cannot be explained fully
until later, but it is possible already to see that there is something
wrong in the use of the word 'derivability' for the relation defined
by Bolzano. For a proposition cannot properly be said to be
derivable from a set of premises unless it is possible to establish
that if the premises are true the proposition is also true without
first establishing whether or not the premises and the proposition
are true. But the relation defined by Bolzano might hold when
this condition was not fulfilled. Just as according to his definitions
a proposition can be analytic by accident, so too one proposition
may follow from another by accident, that is to say in such a way
that the truth of the universal proposition about the results of
substitution can be known only by examination of all the individual results. This can be seen most easily from consideration
of the limiting case where the proposition called a consequence
has no constituents in common with any of the premises. For
then, according to Bolzano's definition, its being a consequence
of the premises depends solely on its being true. He does not
make this point explicitly in his section on derivability, but in the
previous section on compatibility he says that a false proposition
which contains none of the constituents for which substitution
may be made in a certain set of propositions is incompatible with
those propositions,[2] and according to his own account of the connexion between the two sections this is just another way of saying
what we have said above. Perhaps Bolzano overlooks it because
he wants to think of the relation of consequence as holding always
in virtue of a general rule. For he says in a note at the end of this

---

[1] *Wissenschaftslehre*, § 154.     [2] Ibid., § 154 (20).

section that when Aristotle uses the phrase συμβαίνει ἐξ ἀνάγκης ('it follows of necessity') to describe the relation of the conclusion to the premisses in a valid syllogism,[1] even though premisses and conclusion may be all alike false, he must surely mean that *every* argument of the form exemplified leads to a true conclusion if only the premisses are true.[2]

The fact that the relation which he calls *Ableitbarkeit* (and we shall call that of being a consequence) may hold between false propositions distinguishes it, according to Bolzano, from the relation of having something as ground, since the latter can hold only between truths.[3] But that is not the only difference between them; for the second, unlike the first, is asymmetrical[4] and intransitive.[5] That is to say, if A is the ground of B, it cannot be the case that B is also the ground of A, nor yet that, if B is the ground of C, A is also the ground of C. The ground of a truth is what Aristotle called its διότι and what some scholastic philosophers called its *principium essendi*, as distinct from the various *principia cognoscendi* by which we may come to know it.[6] The notion which Bolzano discusses here is of great interest in metaphysics and in the philosophy of natural science, but it need detain us no longer, since it can scarcely be said to belong to logic.

After defining the relation which we call that of being a consequence Bolzano proceeds in the same section to formulate a number of general principles concerning it and to prove them from his definitions. He makes a slip when he says that no proposition can have its own negation as a consequence because no substitution or set of substitutions which made the first true could make the second true also. For in the special case where the proposition under consideration has the form of a self-contradiction no substitutions whatsoever can turn it into a truth, and so it is established in a trivial way that no substitutions can turn it into a truth without turning every other proposition into a truth. On the other hand, he makes the proper correction of Aristotle when he says that no proposition *other than one which is universally valid* can be a consequence both of a proposition and of the negation of that proposition. And he enunciates the more general thesis that if a proposition is a consequence both of the premisses A, B, C, D, ..., X and also of the premisses A, B, C, D, ..., not-X, it is a consequence of the premisses A, B, C, D, ..., alone. Other interesting theorems proved in this section are the principle of the transitivity of the relation of being a consequence and a

---

[1] *An. Priora*, i. 1 (24ᵇ19), but see *An. Pr.* ii. 4 (57ᵃ36–40) against this.
[2] *Wissenschaftslehre*, § 154, Anm. 1.
[3] Ibid., and § 198.
[4] Ibid., § 162.          [5] Ibid., § 203.          [6] Ibid., § 198, Anm.

generalization of the principle for the indirect reduction of syllogisms, namely the theorem that if M is a consequence of
A, B, C, D, . . ., then not-A is a consequence of B, C, D, . . .,
not-M. If a proposition is a consequence of a set of propositions
but not of any selection from among them, Bolzano calls the
relationship of consequence exact or adequate, and he proves
that in this case neither the consequence nor any of the premises
can be universally valid. This consideration, like some of the foregoing, suggests very strongly that a universally valid proposition
may be described in the inexact sense as a consequence of any
set of premisses; but Bolzano does not make this point.

In a later section Bolzano introduces the convention that the
figure

$$\frac{A, B, C, D, \ldots}{M}$$

may be used to represent the fact that the proposition M is a consequence of the propositions A, B, C, D, . . . .[1] Then, using this
notation, he enunciates the theorem that from

$$\frac{A, B, C, D, E, F, G, \ldots}{M}$$

we may conclude

$$\frac{A, B, C, D, \ldots}{\text{If E, F, G, } \ldots \text{ then M}}.$$

This is a generalization of the principle of conditionalization
which was first formulated by the Stoics but assumed already by
Aristotle. Another of Bolzano's theorems can be expressed in the
same notation by the statement that from

$$\frac{A, B, C, D, \ldots}{M} \quad \text{and} \quad \frac{H, J, K, \ldots}{\text{Not-M}}$$

we may conclude

$$\frac{A, B, C, D, \ldots}{\text{Not both H and J and K and } \ldots}.$$

Since his definition of the relation of consequence (which he
identifies with derivability) allows for patterns of inference corresponding to all the various laws of nature that may ever be
discovered, Bolzano disclaims any intention to enumerate all
types of valid argument. But he recognizes that in a work described
as a treatise on logic he must give some account of types commonly

---

[1] *Wissenschaftslehre*, § 223.

said to belong to formal logic, and this he does under thirteen heads.[1] The result is not easy to follow, and can scarcely be said to have contributed to the advancement of the science. Since, as we have already noticed, Bolzano did not think it possible to draw a clear line between the formal and the material, it is not surprising that what he puts down here is not organized according to any clear principle. But it is interesting to ask why a philosopher who was so obviously gifted for logical studies should have failed to make progress in this part of his work.

The explanation seems to be that Bolzano, like Leibniz, was obsessed by a certain pattern into which he tried to force all propositions. Every proposition, he says, must have a subject, a predicate, and copula (*Unterlage*, *Aussageteil*, *Bindeglied*), but he thinks of the predicate as a character (*Beschaffenheit*) which is to be represented in language by an abstract noun, and he therefore talks of *having* as the copula which may be found in all propositions without exception.[2] According to his analyses 'God exists' signifies that God has existence, 'Socrates was wise' that Socrates-in-past-time has wisdom, 'Alcibiades was not wise' that Alcibiades-in-past-time has lack-of-wisdom, 'Some man is wise' that the idea of a man who has wisdom has realization (*Gegenständlichkeit*), 'Goldbach's conjecture is probably true' that the proposition that Goldbach's conjecture has truth has probability, and so on.[3] In the working out of his reductions Bolzano shows great ingenuity, and some of his incidental remarks (e.g. about perceptual and conceptual propositions) may be valuable in epistemology, but it is obvious that his programme must lead to a blurring of the distinction between matter and form made by previous philosophers. For by insisting that all propositions shall be considered as examples of a single pattern Bolzano has produced two curious results. In the first place he has made that pattern useless for the classification of propositions. And secondly he has made it necessary to express notions which are usually regarded as formal (e.g. those of negation and particularity) by signs which enter his reductive formulae in the same way as signs which would ordinarily be said to express material notions (e.g. that of wisdom). It is understandable therefore that he cannot find any clear principle by which to determine what is formal and what is material.

As Bolzano may be said to continue some of the interests of Leibniz, so John Stuart Mill (1806–73) may be said to represent another pre-Kantian tendency. His *System of Logic*, which is described in the sub-title as 'a connected view of the principles of

---

[1] Ibid., §§ 225–53.                                    [2] Ibid., § 127.
[3] Ibid., §§ 132–44. The examples given here are not all from Bolzano's text.

evidence and the methods of scientific investigation', had great
influence from the date of its first publication in 1843, because it
was a serious attempt to expound logic in a way consistent with
the empiricist tradition of British philosophy. As might be expected, the greater part of the work is devoted to an account of
induction and the methodology of the natural and the social
sciences. But in the first two books, where he deals with names,
propositions, and reasoning, Mill gives a systematic account of
formal logic instead of dismissing it with contempt as most of his
empiricist predecessors had done. And just as in his later work
*Utilitarianism* he found it necessary to modify the ethical hedonism
which he had inherited from Bentham and his father, so here he
tried to improve empiricism (or experientalism, as he preferred to
call it) by freeing it from the nominalism with which it had been
entangled since the time of Locke and by working out a theory of
syllogistic which would leave it a respectable though subordinate
part of logic. He was certainly not inclined to abandon any of
the essentials of the empiricist philosophy, and in some respects,
as we shall see, he was more radical that any other philosopher
of his school; but he was in all things a liberal who wanted to do
justice to the opinions of philosophers outside his own tradition.
As mottoes for his first book he quotes passages in which Condorcet and Hamilton write of the debt which the modern world
owes to scholasticism for its standards of precision and subtlety,
and in his text he says that the schoolmen, 'notwithstanding the
imperfections of their philosophy, were unrivalled in the construction of technical language' and that their 'definitions, in
logic at least, though they never went more than a little way
into the subject, have seldom . . . been altered but to be
spoilt'.[1]

When he speaks of nominalism, Mill thinks particularly of the
*Computatio sive Logica* of Hobbes, whom he describes as 'one of the
clearest and most consecutive thinkers whom this country or the
world has produced'; and the feature of that work which he finds
especially unsatisfactory is the doctrine 'that in every proposition
what is signified is the belief of the speaker that the predicate is
the name of the same thing of which the subject is a name' (that
is to say, the doctrine of Ockham and perhaps also of Abelard).
He is prepared, indeed, to admit that what Hobbes says is 'the only
analysis that is rigorously true of all propositions without exception', but he goes on to say:

'The only propositions of which Hobbes' principle is a sufficient
account are that limited and unimportant class in which both the

[1] *System of Logic*, 1. ii. 4.

predicate and the subject are proper names. . . . But it is a sadly inadequate theory of any others. That it should ever have been thought of as such, can be accounted for only by the fact that Hobbes, in common with the other Nominalists, bestowed little or no attention upon the *connotation* of words and sought for their meaning exclusively in what they *denote*; as if all names had been (what none but proper names really are) marks put upon individuals; and as if there were no difference between a proper and a general name, except that the first denotes only one individual and the last a greater number.'[1]

In Mill's usage terms are all alike called names and said to denote the things of which they are the names (i.e. to which they refer, if they are singular terms, or to which they apply, if they are general terms). But general terms like 'man' and 'wise', as distinct from proper names like 'Socrates' and singular abstract names like 'wisdom', not only denote things but connote, or imply, attributes of those things.[2] Mill remarks in a footnote that the Latin *connotare* meant in medieval logic 'to mark in addition', and he may perhaps intend his new technical word to suggest that the implication of attributes by general names is something additional to the work of denotation which all names perform. But he makes it clear that his connotation is what we ordinarily call meaning, and that in the general terms to which it belongs it is logically prior to denotation: 'when mankind fixed the meaning of the word wise, they were not thinking of Socrates'.[3] In short, 'denotation', as he uses the word, covers what medieval logicians called *suppositio personalis*, while 'connotation' corresponds to their word *significatio* as used in connexion with *termini communes*.

According to Mill definitions proper are always nominal definitions, i.e. declarations of the meanings of general names in cases where such meanings admit of analysis, and what some philosophers have called real definitions, or definitions of things, are only nominal definitions accompanied by assumptions of matters of fact:

'The definition is a mere identical proposition, which gives information only about the use of language, and from which no conclusions affecting matters of fact can possibly be drawn. The accompanying postulate, on the other hand, affirms a fact which may lead to consequences of every degree of importance. It affirms the actual or possible existence of things possessing the combination of attributes set forth in the definition, and this, if true, may be foundation sufficient on which to build a whole fabric of scientific truth.'[4]

[1] Ibid. v. 2.  [2] Ibid. ii. 5.
[3] Ibid. v. 2.  [4] Ibid. viii. 5.

Here the point which Mill makes is similar to points of Leibniz and Saccheri which we have already noticed, but it is expressed in more downright fashion and its influence has been much greater. After Mill's book little was heard of the doctrine of real definition.

Mill defines a proposition as a portion of discourse in which a predicate is affirmed or denied of a subject,[1] and tries to justify the apparent narrowness of his definition by saying that the disjunctive pattern can be reduced to the conditional and this in turn to the subject-predicate pattern, since a sentence of the form 'If A is B, C is D' can be understood as an abbreviation for an assertion of the form 'The proposition C is D is a legitimate inference from the proposition A is B' and so assimilated in logical character to various other assertions in which propositions appear as subjects.[2] Here and elsewhere much of what he says about propositions is applicable only to propositional contents.

Among propositions there are some which Mill calls merely verbal. By this title he does not mean to convey that they are expressed in words as opposed to other signs, nor yet that they are about words in the same way as the assertions of philologists, but rather that 'they can be evolved from the meaning of the terms used', i.e. that they can be asserted safely without investigation of non-linguistic facts. They are what older philosophers called essential propositions, i.e. assertions such as 'Man is rational' where the predicate is the definition or part of the definition of the subject. But Mill tells us that, so far from being of supreme importance, as the older philosophers appear to have thought, these propositions either give no information or give it respecting names not things.[3]

Obviously verbal propositions are supposed to be those which Locke called trifling and Kant analytic, but the name 'verbal' and the suggestion that they may give information about names introduces an unfortunate confusion. If the form of words 'Man is rational' is ever in fact used to give information about the meaning of either of the words 'man' and 'rational', the proposition which it then expresses is not analytic and trifling, but synthetic and instructive, or, in Mill's phraseology, real. For the words 'man' and 'rational' are in a certain sense things, and the fact that we use them as we do is contingent. Nor is this the only respect in which Mill departs from the position of the two predecessors whom he professes to follow in his account of verbal propositions. Whereas they both think that some instructive propositions can be known intuitively, he holds that all such propositions are learnt by induction. Even the principle of non-contradiction, he tells us, is not, as Sir William Hamilton and the Germans consider, an *a priori* law of thought, nor yet, as the Nominalists declare, a merely verbal proposition, but 'like other axioms, one of our first and most familiar generalizations from experience'.[1] But if this is empirical, there cannot, it seems, be any non-empirical truths.

When he turns to consider ratiocination, Mill is content to identify it with syllogism,[2] just as he was content to assume that all propositions are of the subject-predicate pattern. But he rejects the whole of the traditional philosophy of formal logic. First he says:

'Those who considered the *dictum de omni* as the foundation of the syllogism, looked upon arguments in a manner corresponding to the erroneous view which Hobbes took of propositions.'[3]

And later he adds:

'It must be granted that in every syllogism, considered as an argument to prove the conclusion, there is a *petitio principii*. When we say,

All men are mortal,
Socrates is a man,
therefore
Socrates is mortal;

it is unanswerably urged by the adversaries of the syllogistic theory, that the proposition, Socrates is mortal, is presupposed in the more general assumption, All men are mortal.'[4]

From the second assertion it follows that syllogistic reasoning cannot be inference, properly so called, and Mill does not hesitate to draw this conclusion:

'All inference is from particulars to particulars. General propositions are merely registers of such inferences already made, and short formulae for making more. The major premise of a syllogism, consequently, is a formula of this description; and the conclusion is not an inference drawn *from* the formula, but an inference drawn *according* to the formula; the real logical antecedent or premise being the particular facts from which the general proposition was collected by induction. Those facts, and the individual instances which supplied them, may have been forgotten; but a record remains, not indeed descriptive of the facts themselves, but showing how these cases may be distinguished, respecting which, the facts, when known, were considered to warrant a given inference. According to the indications of this record we draw

[1] Ibid. ii. vii. 5.                    [2] Ibid. ii. 1.
[3] Ibid. 3.                             [4] Ibid. iii. 2.

our conclusion; which is, to all intents and purposes, a conclusion from the forgotten facts. For this it is essential that we should read the record correctly; and the rules of the syllogism are a set of precautions to ensure our doing so.'[1]

These passages about syllogistic have often been attacked by critics of Mill, and it must be admitted that they are full of confusions. First Mill seems to say that the theory of syllogism expressed in the *dictum de omni et nullo* is mistaken because it pays attention only to the denotation of terms and represents inference as asserting about individual members of a class what one already knows to hold true for all members. From this beginning we might expect him to go on to say that a universal statement is useful as a premiss for inference only if it conveys information about a necessary connexion between the attributes connoted by its terms, and in some places he does in fact come near to saying this.[2] But in the second of the passages we have quoted, instead of taking this line, he reverts to the mistaken view that a universal statement is never more than a summary of the cases which it covers. And then in the third passage he seems to try to combine both views by saying that universal statements are at once compendious records of past observations and laws or principles in accordance with which we may reason from particulars to particulars. In some way the rules of syllogism are supposed to regulate our use of universal statements in such inference; but it is not at all clear what benefits they are supposed to confer, and we may suspect that at this point Mill became confused about the interpretation of his own phrase 'inference from particulars to particulars'. For while the opening of the third passage suggests that he means argument such as we may express by saying 'Socrates is a man; therefore Socrates is mortal', the continuation suggests that he has in mind rather argument such as we may express by saying 'All other recorded men, including, for example, Thales, Solon, and Pythagoras, have been found to be mortal; therefore Socrates, who is a man, is mortal'. In an argument of the first kind a singular conclusion is drawn from a singular premiss in accordance with an assumed law, or non-formal principle, but any one who chooses to add the law as a major premiss can convert the argument into a piece of formally valid reasoning of the sort Mill calls a syllogism. In an argument of the second kind a record of observations is cited as evidence for a singular conclusion, but the conclusion does not follow, either formally or non-formally, from that record, unless it can be shown that the record justifies

---

[1] *System of Logic*, II. iii. 4.  [2] Ibid. I. v. 2 and III. v. 6.

assumption of a law which will serve as principle for an argument of the first kind.

The unclarity of Mill's theorizing cannot be denied, but here as in many other places the trouble arises from his failure to realize the incompatibility of a good new insight with a bad old tradition in which he had been educated. Like a convert from paganism to Christianity who cannot bring himself to believe that his ancestors are all damned, he mixes old and new in bizarre confusion. Thus he rightly rejects both the conventionalist account of logic which he read in Hobbes and the psychologistic talk about laws of thought which he heard from German Idealists and their English followers, but he then finds himself unable to account for the objectivity of the principles of logic without suggesting that they are empirical generalizations. In the empiricist tradition it has often been assumed that no non-empirical statement can give information of any sort about the world, and we shall see later that some modern philosophers who reject conventionalism and psychologism follow Mill in trying to treat logic as an empirical science. On the other hand, when he comes to treat of ratiocination, Mill realizes that he has to give some account of syllogistic which will distinguish it from induction, and he suggests that rules of formal logic should be regarded as principles about the use of those non-formal principles of inference which we accept on inductive grounds. This is inconsistent with the suggestion that principles of formal logic are themselves first-order generalizations from experience, but it makes good sense if the distinction between first-order and second-order principles is carried through carefully. For then it appears that our knowledge of the principles of formal logic, though not empirical in the ordinary sense, can properly be said to be based on experience, since we have learnt them by finding them implicit in rules of language which we have unconsciously adopted during the course of our experience and without which we could not practise induction deliberately as a scientific policy. We should claim too much if we said that Mill ever explicitly described formal logic as a science whose propositions are themselves second-order principles about principles of inference; but such a view is at least suggested by some of his remarks, and we believe that it is correct.

In this section and the one before it we have been able to report some interesting discoveries made in the century and a half after the time when Leibniz worked intensively on his project of a logical calculus. But it must be admitted that there was no steady progress during the period, and it has sometimes been suggested that this was due to the dominance of Hume, Kant, and Hegel. We hold no brief for any of these philosophers, but we think the charge against them is unfair. No doubt their influence was hostile to mathematical logic, but other conditions also were unfavourable. Although Leibniz had put forward a number of brilliant suggestions, it was not possible to make sure progress until mathematics had developed so far that the sort of abstraction he desired seemed natural and easy. When logic was revived in the middle of the nineteenth century, the new vigour came from mathematicians who were familiar with the progress of their own speciality, rather than from philosophers who were occupied with the controversies of idealism and empiricism. In our next chapter we propose therefore to consider the development of mathematical abstraction, in so far as this is relevant to our main theme, and for this purpose we shall have to range rapidly from Greek to modern times.

# VI

## MATHEMATICAL ABSTRACTION

### 1. *Geometry and Axiomatics*

FOR the Greeks the most important part of mathematics was geometry, and in Euclid's *Elements* vii–x we find even theorems of pure arithmetic, e.g. about prime numbers, presented as propositions about the commensurability or incommensurability of lines. It has been suggested that the comparative neglect of other branches of mathematics by the Greeks was due to the deficiency of their system of numeration; but it seems more likely that geometry was developed first because the effort of abstraction which it requires is not so great as that needed for algebra and analysis. We shall see presently that even mathematicians of a much later age have had difficulty in freeing themselves from excessive reliance on spatial intuition. However that may be, for many centuries Euclid's *Elements* set the standard of rigour in all demonstration, and we must begin by considering the pattern of his work, although our main concern in this chapter will be with later developments.

Obviously Euclid did not discover all the theorems which he presents in the *Elements*. There were treatises on geometry before the beginning of the third century B.C. when he worked, and we know, for example, that the beautiful theory of proportion which he uses in book v comes from Eudoxus, a younger contemporary of Plato. But he achieved fame by his masterly attempt to derive all previous discoveries from a relatively small number of common notions (κοιναὶ ἔννοιαι) and postulates (αἰτήματα). The common notions are propositions said to be fundamental in all sciences, e.g. that the whole is greater than the part; and the postulates are five propositions, peculiar to geometry, which we are asked to concede at the beginning. In later times the two sets of primitive propositions were sometimes put together under the name of axioms. It must be admitted that in various places Euclid assumes geometrical propositions which are neither included among his axioms nor proved to follow from these, as when, for example, he takes it for granted in the proof of the first proposition of book i that circles drawn about the two ends of a straight line with radii equal in length to that line must intersect in two points. But there

can scarcely be any doubt that he intended to put all his extra-
logical assumptions at the beginning and then to derive the
theorems from them by logic alone. For anything else would be
a compromise inconsistent with that desire for rigour which is
obvious throughout his work. The use of a figure may help us to
concentrate our attention when we are following a proof, and for
psychological reasons it may even be necessary in the process of
discovery; but if we accept propositions merely because they
seem evident to us when we consider a figure, we are in effect
adding to our axioms without due notice, and this is contrary
to the whole spirit of Greek geometry.

Euclid and all his successors until last century assumed that
his postulates were universal and necessary truths about physical
space. But there is one among them which has always seemed
more complicated than the rest. This is the famous parallels
postulate: 'If a straight line falling on two straight lines makes
the interior angles on the same side less than two right angles,
the two straight lines, when produced indefinitely, meet on that
side on which are the angles less than two right angles.' In
antiquity Ptolemy and Proclus both tried to show that this proposition should not appear as a postulate because it could be
demonstrated as a theorem, and many similar attempts to improve on Euclid's work were made by later geometers.[1] One of
the most interesting was that of Saccheri in his book of 1733 called
*Euclides ab Omni Naevo Vindicatus*. This is based, as he himself
says,[2] on the principle of the *consequentia mirabilis* which he used
in his *Logica Demonstrativa*; and although it does not succeed, as
he thought, in establishing the necessary truth of the parallels
postulate, it deserves fame as the first work containing theorems
of non-Euclidean geometry.

Most of the earlier geometers who claimed that they had proved
the parallels postulate assumed as an explicit or implicit premiss
some other proposition with the same deductive force as that they
were trying to prove. John Wallis, for example, assumed that for
any given figure it is possible that there should exist a similar
figure of any size whatsoever. Saccheri's enterprise was much
bolder: he wished to show that the parallels postulate was a
necessary truth because it followed even from its own negation.
In order to get this negation into a convenient form he considered not Euclid's statement of the postulate but an equivalent
suggested by a figure in Clavius's edition of Euclid. From the
ends of a straight line AB two perpendiculars of equal length, AC

---

[1] T. L. Heath, *The Thirteen Books of Euclid's Elements*, i, pp. 202 f., gives an
account of noteworthy attempts.    [2] P. 99.

and BD, are erected on the same side, and the points C and D are then connected by a straight line. In the resulting quadrilateral the angles at C and D must be equal, and it can be shown that Euclid's parallels postulate is equivalent to the assumption that they are both right angles. Saccheri therefore examines the two other conceivable hypotheses, namely, (i) that the angles are obtuse and (ii) that they are acute. These correspond respectively to the two forms of non-Euclidean geometry later distinguished as elliptic and hyperbolic; and in the course of his investigation he proves some characteristic theorems of those geometries. He shows, for example, in proposition ix that on the hypothesis of the obtuse angle the internal angles of a triangle are always together greater than two right angles, and that on the hypothesis of the acute angle they are always less. But his attempt to prove the parallels postulate from consideration of the two distinguishable alternatives covered by its negation is not so happy. For the first case he seems to achieve the desired result easily by showing in proposition xii that the hypothesis of the obtuse angle entails the parallels postulate (and is therefore self-contradictory, since the parallels postulate itself entails the hypothesis of the right angle). But he does so only by assuming tacitly that a straight line can be produced to any desired length. This assumption is in fact inconsistent with the hypothesis he is considering, since in elliptic geometry there must be a maximum length for a straight line. The other hypothesis gives him much more trouble, and although he speaks later as though he had relied throughout on the *consequentia mirabilis*, he does not even try to show that this alternative entails the parallels postulate. But he claims to prove in proposition xxiii that it involves a self-contradictory consequence. If his proof were satisfactory, it would, of course, suffice with proposition xii to establish the truth of the parallels postulate; but there is a flaw in his reasoning.

It is not known for certain whether Saccheri's work had any influence on the mathematicians who developed non-Euclidean geometry in the nineteenth century, but the book found its way into a number of libraries and was noticed in some works of reference such as Montucla's *Histoire des mathématiques* of 1758 and Klügel's *Conatuum Praecipuorum Theoriam Parallelarum Demonstrandi Recensio* of 1763.[1] In this way it may have come to the attention of Gauss (1777–1855), who was the first to recognize the possibility of developing non-Euclidean geometry in a

---

[1] Corrado Segre, 'Conjetture intorno all'influenza di Girolamo Saccheri sulla formazione della geometria non-euclidea', *Atti della R.A. delle Scienze di Torino*, xxxviii (1903).

consistent fashion and regarded it as a question to be settled by observation whether the interior angles of a triangle in physical space are or are not equal to two right angles. But in this field of mathematical research, as in many others in which he made brilliant discoveries, Gauss published nothing. The first printed work to develop a form of non-Euclidean geometry for its own sake was a paper of Lobachevsky published in 1826. This dealt with the hypothesis of the acute angle (that is to say, with hyperbolic geometry in which there are two lines through a given point parallel to a given straight line). The development of the hypothesis of the obtuse angle (that is to say, of elliptic geometry in which there are no lines through a given point parallel to a given straight line and every straight line returns on itself when produced) had to wait for Riemann. Indeed it was not until the posthumous publication in 1867 of Riemann's inaugural lecture of 1854 *Über die Hypothesen welche der Geometrie zu Grunde liegen* that non-Euclidean geometry was taken seriously by pure mathematicians; and even after that the speculations of Riemann and his disciple Clifford about the possibility of using non-Euclidean geometry in physics went unregarded for more than a generation.

These advances in geometry are important to the logician chiefly because of the attention which they drew to axiomatics, or the theory of postulate sets. If it had been shown that a contradiction was introduced by the negating of Euclid's parallels postulate in a system which retained all his other axioms, it would have been proved by *reductio ad absurdum* that the parallels postulate followed from those other axioms. On the other hand, mere failure to discover a contradiction does not suffice by itself to prove the consistency of a non-Euclidean geometry. For that it would be necessary to establish that no contradiction could ever be derived. This is a very large requirement, and, as we shall see later, by no means easy to satisfy. But without going so far, we may do something to establish the respectability of a non-Euclidean geometry by showing that it cannot be inconsistent unless Euclidean geometry is also inconsistent; and this result was in fact achieved in the last century by the discovery of ways of representing non-Euclidean geometry within Euclid's system. In the best known of these we suppose that when a phrase from the left in the following list occurs in elliptic geometry it is to have the same sense as the corresponding phrase on the right has in Euclidean geometry:

| | |
|---|---|
| plane | surface of a sphere |
| straight line | arc of a great circle |
| angle between two straight lines | angle between the planes of two great circles. |

If the other phrases used in elliptic geometry of two dimensions are allowed to retain the meanings customary for such phrases in Euclidean geometry, the system as a whole is then transformed into the geometry of the surface of a Euclidean sphere, a study familiar to navigators, and all the peculiar propositions of elliptic geometry of two dimensions are found to hold true in the new interpretation. Through a given point no line can be drawn parallel to a given straight line; there is a maximum length for a straight line; and the interior angles of any triangle are together greater than two right angles. From this it follows that if Euclid's geometry is consistent so too is elliptic geometry of two dimensions.[1] By suitable interpretations of a rather more complicated kind Felix Klein and others have shown that both elliptic and hyperbolic geometry of three dimensions can be represented within Euclidean geometry. This does not mean that non-Euclidean geometries are identical with parts of Euclidean geometry, but only that they can be *mapped* within Euclidean geometry in a sense somewhat like that in which the surface of France may be mapped on part of the surface of England.

What are we to say then of the status of Euclid's parallels postulate? If Euclid's geometry is consistent, there is clearly no *logical* contradiction involved in the denial of this postulate nor yet in the conjunction of its negation with the other axioms of Euclid, which is as much as to say that it is logically independent of those other axioms. If anyone wishes to insist that the postulate is true of straight lines in physical space, he may perhaps do so; but the pure mathematician need not concern himself with this question. For the development of non-Euclidean geometries has inevitably produced a change of attitude among mathematicians towards all geometry, including that of Euclid. Since there are alternatives, all worthy of study, it cannot be the business of the mathematician to assert the axioms which make any one of the alternatives what it is. His task is to say what follows *logically* from a given set of axioms. Consideration of traditional geometry in this fashion has naturally led to the demand for an explicit formulation of all its presuppositions, that is, for the rigorous carrying out of the programme we have attributed to Euclid; and the results can be seen in modern presentations of Euclid's geometry, e.g. in Hilbert's *Grundlagen der Geometrie* of 1899. But this way of looking at geometry has also led to a kind of abstraction which is far removed from the interests of Euclid.

---

[1] Sometimes the title 'elliptic' is reserved for a geometry in which antipodal points are identified. The system considered above is then called spherical geometry.

When one proposition follows logically from another, it should be possible to formulate the two propositions in such a way that their relation can be seen to depend on their form alone, that is to say, on their logical structure as opposed to their special subject-matter. Now this can be done for the propositions of geometry. In the customary presentations of Euclidean geometry the form of the axioms is not easy to grasp because we use a number of special signs such as 'point', 'line', 'plane', 'lies on', 'between', 'parallel', and 'congruent', but we can write all the axioms we need for ordinary Euclidean geometry without using any special signs except the word 'point' and the phrase 'A is at the same distance from B as C is from D', which expresses congruence as a four-termed relation between points. Thus instead of 'C is collinear (lies on the same straight line) with A and B' we may say 'If P and Q are any two points such that A is at the same distance from P as A is from Q and B is at the same distance from P as B is from Q, then C also is at the same distance from P as C is from Q'. And instead of 'C is between A and B' we may say 'C is collinear with A and B and there are three points P, Q, and R such that (i) P is collinear with A and B, (ii) P is at the same distance from A as P is from B, (iii) Q is at the same distance from P as P is from A, (iv) R is at the same distance from P as P is from A, (v) C is collinear with Q and R, and (vi) C is at the same distance from Q as C is from R'. And instead of 'The line AB is parallel with the line CD' we may say 'The class of points collinear with A and B and the class of points collinear with C and D have no member in common'. Even the word 'point' need not be used; for we may safely leave it to be understood that the things or elements to which we refer by single letters are those things, whatever they may be, which are suitable in nature to be terms of the four-termed relation mentioned in the axioms. It is obviously tedious to write in this style a set of axiom formulae sufficient for ordinary Euclidean geometry, but when the task has been done, it is clear that apart from the expression 'A is at the same distance from B as C is from D' the only words used are those we reserve for expressing form, e.g. 'and', 'or', 'not', 'if', 'any', 'there is', and letters serving as variables. And since the theorems can also be expressed in this notation, it is possible to establish beyond doubt that the entailment of the theorems by the axioms does not depend on the meaning which the phrase 'A is at the same distance from B as C is from D' has in application to the things we perceive.

Having come so far, we may go a step farther and say that for pure geometry the ordinary meaning of the phrase is quite irrelevant. If there were any other phrase with four gaps which could be substituted for it consistently in all the axiom formulae, then the same phrase could be substituted for it also in the theorem formulae without change in the relations of the latter to the former. What the geometer asserts is the highly abstract proposition that any four-termed relation which satisfies all the logical conditions prescribed in the axiom formulae must also satisfy each of the logical conditions formulated in the several theorem formulae; and he may if he likes make this clear by using a letter in place of the phrase given above, much as Aristotle used letters in formulating his principles of syllogistic. The conditions expressed in the various formulae of geometry by the other signs are of a complexity not considered by Aristotle, but for all that they are purely logical.

Sometimes it is said that the axiom formulae of a system of geometry together amount to an *implicit definition* of the special geometrical signs which they contain. This way of speaking, which was introduced by J. D. Gergonne as early as 1818,[1] is useful, but it can lead to misunderstandings. The axiom formulae of a geometrical system define an extra-logical expression which they contain only in the sense of delimiting the logical range within which the meaning of that expression must lie. For they impose only formal conditions; and although a geometer using the phrase 'A is at the same distance from B as C is from D' in his professional work need not concern himself with anything but the formal conditions satisfied by this relation of congruence, in ordinary usage the phrase has a meaning which is not exhausted by those conditions. If this were not so, there would be no sense in speaking of the application of geometry to the world we perceive. For such application depends on the finding of a perceptible relation which satisfies a set of formal conditions without being exhausted by them. In short, a pure intelligence with no perception of things in physical space might conceivably study geometry in abstract fashion, but its knowledge of geometry would not be a substitute for the perception which it lacked. When this point has been made clear, it can be seen that the development of non-Euclidean geometry does not, as some philosophers have supposed, disprove the old view of Euclid and Kant according to which the parallels postulate is a necessary truth about perceptual space. For it is at least arguable that the logical conditions prescribed by the axioms of Euclidean geometry hold necessarily of the perceptible relation of congruence. If, however, they do so

---

[1] 'Essai sur la théorie des définitions', *Annales de mathématiques*, ix (1818), pp. 1–35, especially p. 23.

hold, the statement that they hold is not a truth of formal logic, and so not a truth of geometry in the sense in which the word 'geometry' is now used by pure mathematicians. For the purposes of mathematics it is sufficient that the conditions prescribed by the axioms of a non-Euclidean geometry are consistent, i.e. do not lead to a self-contradiction, and the procedure of representation or mapping has shown that there cannot be an inconsistency in the axioms of either elliptic or hyperbolic geometry unless there is also an inconsistency in the axioms of Euclidean geometry.

When 'space' and words of similar origin occur in pure mathematics, they refer to abstract patterns of ordering which may conceivably be exemplified by widely differing systems of objects. Geometrical studies began, of course, with thought about relations in physical space, but they have progressed to the consideration of patterns which cannot be visualized. This tendency to abstraction can be detected already in the non-Euclidean geometries which have been mentioned, but it is even more obvious in geometries of many dimensions. Such geometries can be constructed in the 'synthetic' fashion of Euclid, but the easiest approach is by extension of the notions involved in Descartes's 'analytic' geometry. When we draw graphs, we think of each point on our squared paper as determined by two numbers, one a value for the variable $x$ and the other a value for the variable $y$, and we say that a line on the paper corresponds to a certain functional relationship between these variables. Thus a straight line is the graph of some equation of the form $y = ax+b$, because each point on that line is associated by the frame of reference with a couple of numbers which satisfy such an equation. Here we have an interpretation for Euclidean geometry of two dimensions according to which points are number couples and relations between points are relations of the kind studied in algebra. Such an interpretation can easily be applied also to Euclidean geometry of three dimensions. And we need not stop there. Applying the analogy in the opposite direction, we may, if we wish, use the language of geometry to describe a system in which the related entities are sets of values for four or more variables. Thus if $(x_1, y_1, z_1, w_1)$ and $(x_2, y_2, z_2, w_2)$ represent two sets of values for the four variables $x$, $y$, $z$, and $w$, we may perhaps find it convenient to use the word 'distance' for the quantity represented by

$$\sqrt{[(x_1-x_2)^2+(y_1-y_2)^2+(z_1-z_2)^2+(w_1-w_2)^2]}.$$

Whether or not they approach multi-dimensional geometry by the route which Descartes opened, mathematicians rely on a numerical interpretation of axiom formulae for the proof of the consistency of any geometry they construct in axiomatic fashion. Admittedly elliptic and hyperbolic geometry of three dimensions can be shown to be consistent on the assumption that Euclidean geometry of three dimensions is consistent, and it may be thought an excess of caution to ask for a proof of the consistency of this latter. But it is by no means obvious that physical space is Euclidean in the sense of satisfying all Euclid's axioms. We can scarcely maintain, for example, that we perceive either an outward infinity of points beyond points for ever or an inward infinity of points between points for ever; and if we say that physical space is nevertheless Euclidean in the fullest sense, we must claim to know this as a necessary truth revealed in spatial intuition. During the nineteenth century such claims became suspect, and attempts were therefore made to free geometry from the last traces of dependence on sense experience. For the mathematician proofs of the consistency of axiom sets by means of numerical interpretations have the great merit of remaining entirely within the mathematical domain.

Consistency is the prime requisite of any axiom set. For a conjunction of inconsistent propositions entails any proposition whatsoever, as the writers on *consequentiae* remarked in the Middle Ages, and there is nothing to be learnt from study of a system in which the negation of every theorem is also a theorem. Mutual independence of axioms is not essential in the same way. That is to say, a deductive system is not shown to be worthless when it is discovered that one axiom can be derived from the others. But it is obviously inelegant to introduce as an axiom something which can be proved as a theorem; and apart from that, proofs of independence are required for a proper understanding of the structure of any system under investigation. Both points are illustrated clearly by the history of the parallels postulate. Now to prove that an axiom is independent of the other axioms of a set it is sufficient to show that its negation is consistent with those other axioms, and for this purpose the geometer relies once more on the method of numerical interpretation.

If two different interpretations of any kind for the extra-logical signs in a set of axiom formulae both yield truths and the systems of things described by the formulae in these interpretations are so related that for every item in the one there is a single corresponding item in the other, the two interpretations are said to be isomorphic. If, further, *all* the results of possible interpretations (or models, as they are sometimes called) for a certain set of axiom formulae are isomorphic one to another, the set of axioms is said to be categorical or monomorphic. This notion was familiar to Dedekind in 1887,[1] but the name 'categorical' was introduced by Veblen in 1904 on the suggestion of the logician Dewey.[2] Probably Veblen and Dewey had in mind a contrast between categorical and disjunctive propositions; but in origin 'categorical' means 'predicative', rather than 'non-disjunctive', and apart from that the word has the disadvantage of being much over-worked in other contexts. It therefore seems better to follow Carnap in talking instead about a contrast between monomorphic and polymorphic sets of axioms.[3]

A monomorphic set of axioms can be said to carry out completely the programme of implicit definition. For although the formulae in which it is presented may admit many different interpretations, these latter must all have the same logical structure and so be indistinguishable by purely formal criteria. If a set of axioms is monomorphic, it is useless to attempt further specification of the meanings of the extra-logical signs in its formulae by addition of any more axiom formulae in the same symbolism. For whatever formula we choose, either it or its negation is already a consequence of the axiom formulae in the sense of being true for every interpretation they admit. This is not to say, however, that a monomorphic set of axioms can never be usefully enlarged in any way. Monomorphism is always relative to a certain apparatus of primitive concepts, as may be seen most clearly in consideration of another geometrical example.

During the nineteenth century geometry developed not only by consideration of alternatives to Euclid's parallels postulate and by removal of his restriction to three dimensions, but also by distinction of different levels of geometrical properties. It had been known for a long time that there were some properties of figures which survived even when the figures were subjected to transformations of certain kinds. Thus Pascal (using methods suggested by Desargues, in particular the assumption of points at infinity) prove in the seventeenth century that if a hexagon is inscribed in a conic section the three points in which its opposite sides intersect must lie in a straight line. Since the theorem holds not only of a hexagon inscribed in a circle but also of any hexagon obtained by projection of that figure on a plane from a point, it is clear that we have to do here with a projective as opposed to a metrical property; that is to say, the theorem belongs to a level of geometry in which we consider relative positions without regard

---

[1] *Was sind und was sollen die Zahlen?*, § 134.
[2] 'A System of Axioms for Geometry', *Transactions of the American Mathematical Society*, v (1904), pp. 343–81.
[3] *Einführung in die symbolische Logik*, § 42 C.

to measurements. There are other properties of figures which survive transformations even more drastic than projection. If, for example, we draw a square within a circle on a sheet of rubber and then stretch the rubber in any way we please, the figure which was originally inside remains inside, although it may cease to be square or even to be rectilinear. Here we have to do with a property belonging to the yet deeper level of topology, where not only distance but even the difference between a straight line and a curve may be ignored. In the definition of a geometry of given level it is convenient to use the language of Klein and say that the geometry studies all properties which are invariant under the operations of a certain group. By 'operations' we mean here transformations such as displacements and rotations in space, projections, whether parallel or central, and the distortions described above; and by 'group' we mean a set of operations such that (*a*) the result of the successive applications of any two operations of the set is itself an operation of the set and (*b*) the inverse of any operation of the set is also an operation of the set. Incidentally, this notion of a group, first conceived by Galois (1811–32), is one of those high abstractions which now find application in many different fields of mathematics.[1]

For our present purpose the important point is that the axiom set of a geometry of lower level may be monomorphic although it certainly does not entail all the theorems belonging to geometries of higher level. We have seen that the propositions of ordinary Euclidean metrical geometry can all be formulated by use of a single special sign for the four-termed relation of congruence. In the paper in which he introduced the word 'categorical' to describe certain axiom sets, Veblen showed that all the propositions of a deeper system called descriptive geometry could be formulated by use of a single special sign for the three-termed relation of betweenness or serial order. Since betweenness can be defined in terms of congruence and metrical geometry contains theorems which do not occur in descriptive geometry, it may be thought that a set of axioms for the latter must inevitably be polymorphic. But this is not so. Veblen's set of axioms for descriptive geometry is monomorphic *with respect to betweenness*. If his axioms were all rephrased by use of the definition for betweenness mentioned above, the resulting set would indeed be polymorphic but *with respect to congruence*.

Since for the purpose of specification a monomorphic set of

---

[1] In the abstract theory of groups, where elements are not assumed to be always operations, it is necessary to specify separately that combination is associative and that there exists an identity element.

axioms cannot be usefully enlarged by means of new axioms expressed in the same symbolism, it is in a sense complete. But there is a stronger sense of the word 'complete' in which a deductive system with a monomorphic set of axioms may still be incomplete. In order to understand this we must think of completeness as defined by reference to proof and related to the principle of excluded middle in much the same way as consistency is related to the principle of non-contradiction. Let us choose any proposition which requires for its expression no primitive extra-logical signs but those of a given axiom set. Then if the axiom set is to be consistent, it must not allow both the proof of that proposition and also for the proof of its negation. And if it is to be complete in the strong sense we are now considering, it must provide either for the proof of the proposition or for the proof of its negation. At first sight this requirement for completeness looks like a requirement for monomorphism which we mentioned above, namely that the axioms should have either the proposition or its negation as a consequence, but it is really more stringent. For there may perhaps be a proposition expressible in the symbolism of a monomorphic axiom set which is a consequence of the axioms and yet not provable by deduction from them because the derivation would have to be infinitely long and therefore not a proof. We shall see later that this is in fact the situation in some very important parts of mathematics.

## 2. *Numbers and Functions*

We have seen that for proofs of consistency geometers commonly use numerical interpretations of their axiom sets. In doing so they hope to free their science from all extra-mathematical assumptions. But what is the basis of the part of mathematics that deals with number? In order to give a satisfactory numerical interpretation of any system of geometry which involves the notion of continuity we must make use of numbers such as $\sqrt{2}$ and $\pi$, and these gave rise to perplexity already in antiquity.

By some argument which is not now clear to us the Pythagoreans convinced themselves that they had found the key to the understanding of the universe in the notion of ratio, i.e. in the concept of a relation between two natural numbers. No doubt they were impressed by the importance of ratio in music, and they may perhaps have been influenced by the fact that λόγος, the Greek word for a ratio, is also the common word for reason or explanation. Alternatively they may have been the first to use λόγος in a mathematical sense. But whatever the ground of their metaphysical claims may have been, they were greatly disturbed by the discovery of the incommensurability of the diagonal with the side of a square. For here in a very simple case it was shown that talk of the ratio between the lengths of two lines led to contradiction, although common sense seemed to support philosophy in insisting that there must be some determinate relation : obviously the diagonal was more than a third bigger than the side, but not so much as a half bigger. Eudoxus saved the situation by providing a general account of proportion which was sufficient for geometry, and his theory (preserved in book v of Euclid's *Elements*) is a remarkable piece of work on the philosophy of mathematics. The essence of it is a new definition of the equality of ratios between magnitudes :

'The first of four magnitudes is said to have the same ratio to the second that the third has to the fourth, when any equimultiples whatever of the first and the third being taken, and any equimultiples whatever of the second and the fourth, if the multiple of the first be less than that of the second, the multiple of the third is also less than that of the fourth, and if the multiple of the first be equal to that of the second, the multiple of the third is also equal to that of the fourth, and if the multiple of the first be greater than that of the second, the multiple of the third is also greater than that of the fourth.'

This means in effect that where we cannot speak of a ratio in the strict Pythagorean sense (i.e. of a certain relation between natural numbers) we may nevertheless speak of a ratio in an extended sense, if it can be shown that every ratio in the strict Pythagorean sense is either too small or too large. In other words, the existence of a ratio in the extended sense is identified with the possibility of distributing all Pythagorean ratios between the mutually exclusive classes of the too small and the too large. We shall see presently that this suggestion is still used in mathematical analysis, i.e. the branch of mathematics which deals with continuously varying magnitudes ; but in order to get the subject into proper perspective we must first consider the development of the number concept since Greek times.

The earliest numerals were probably adjectives like 'one', 'two', 'three'. In Greek and many other languages such words, or at any rate some of them, are declined like ordinary adjectives, but it is obvious that they cannot qualify nouns in the same way as other adjectives do. For although a man who says that he has two large dogs intends to convey that each of the dogs is large, he certainly does not mean that each of them is two. This is slightly puzzling, but it is even more curious that in some languages, including English, the same sounds or marks are often used as proper names. We say, for example, 'Two is the smallest prime'. This usage belongs to talk of numbers as objects distinct both from the sets of things we count and also from the numerals we use in counting them; for what is true of the number two cannot even be denied sensibly of a pair of dogs or of a word. And there can scarcely have been any such talk before the development of arithmetic as a calculus. We have, indeed, some evidence to show that it did not come easily to Greeks of Plato's time. In the *Theologumena Arithmeticae*, formerly attributed to Iamblichus, there is a quotation from Plato's pupil Speusippus which shows a remarkable uncertainty of language.[1] The passage is about the Pythagorean doctrine of the perfection of the number ten, and within a few paragraphs it contains no less than four different designations for the number ten, namely, $\tau\grave{\alpha}$ $\delta\acute{\epsilon}\kappa\alpha$, $\acute{o}$ $\tau\hat{\omega}\nu$ $\delta\acute{\epsilon}\kappa\alpha$ $\mathring{\alpha}\rho\iota\theta\mu\acute{o}s$, $\acute{o}$ $\delta\acute{\epsilon}\kappa\alpha$, and $\delta\acute{\epsilon}\kappa\alpha$. The first means literally 'the ten [things]', the second 'the number of the ten [things]', the third 'the [number] ten', and the fourth just 'ten'. Furthermore, when Speusippus wishes to say that four is a multiple of two, he produces a strange sentence in which the symbol for four is treated as neuter plural and the symbol for two as masculine singular.

Apart from adjectives like 'one', 'two', 'three', even the most primitive languages have numerical terms such as 'a half', 'a third', 'a quarter'; but the usage whereby signs (such as $-1$, $\frac{3}{2}$, $\sqrt{2}$, and $\sqrt{-1}$ are said to stand for numbers is a product of the last few centuries. Like the use of numerals as proper names, this development is connected with the elaboration of mathematical calculi. It has been inspired in particular by Descartes's application of algebraic symbolism to geometry.

Let us suppose first that consideration of some problem has led us to formulate the equation $x+3 = 2$. It may be, for example, that we want to know how much money a man had in the bank before he brought his balance to £2 by paying in £3. Clearly the equation cannot be solved at all in terms of natural numbers, but if we allow ourselves to talk of negative numbers, we may write $x = -1$. And we can represent such numbers conveniently by placing marks on a line at equal intervals to the left of a point labelled o:

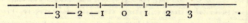

Secondly, numbers such as $\frac{3}{2}$ must be recognized if we are to talk of solving equations like $2x-3 = 0$. With these we have an

[1] Ed. de Falco, 82. 10 ff., reprinted in *Greek Mathematical Works*, ed. Ivor Thomas, i, pp. 75 ff.

enormous addition to the numbers which can be represented by points on a line. For between any two fractions it is always possible to find another; and this is as much as to say that there is an infinity of fractions in any finite interval such as that between the numbers 0 and 1. We must not assume, however, that with this enlargement we have recognized numbers corresponding to all the points on a line: if we construct a square whose side is one unit in length and then lay off its diagonal along the line from the origin, the end point is not one among those to which we have so far assigned numbers. But this gap and infinitely many others are closed by a third enlargement of the number concept to cover algebraic irrationals such as $\sqrt{2}$ and transcendental (or non-algebraic) irrationals such as $\pi$. With the former we are entitled to talk of solving algebraic equations like $x^2-2 = 0$, and with the latter we can complete the linear continuum. Finally a fourth enlargement commits us to recognizing the 'imaginary' number $\sqrt{-1}$ as a proper root of the equation $x^2+1 = 0$. Here the impulse to enlargement seems to have come entirely from formal algebra. There is no point on the straight line corresponding to $\sqrt{-1}$, and the mathematicians of the eighteenth century who used imaginaries did so only in order to make their calculations simpler and more general. But so long as imaginaries were admitted for this reason alone, their status was thought to be very mysterious. If a pupil asked for a justification of their use, there was little his teacher could say except that faith comes with works. This appearance of mystery was dissipated when Wessel in 1797 and Argand in 1806 showed a way of connecting imaginaries with motion in a plane. In Descartes's analytical geometry numbers are correlated with points according to the *distance* of these latter from certain co-ordinates; but it is possible also to think of a number as a vector or measure of the *displacement* through which a particle must go to reach a point, and within this scheme multiplication of a vector by $-1$ obviously represents reversal of the direction of motion. What could be more natural and satisfactory than to say that multiplication of a vector by $\sqrt{-1}$ represents rotation through a right angle, i.e. an operation whose repetition produces complete reversal? So at least most students of mathematics have thought from that day to this, and the fact that we can still derive pleasure from this interpretation gives some indication of the discomfort mathematicians must have felt when there was yet no known way of connecting the symbol with spatial intuition.

When we speak of successive enlargements of the number concept, we are inclined to think that the history can be summarized in a scheme of the following kind, where the names printed in italics stand for new kinds of numbers added to our original store:

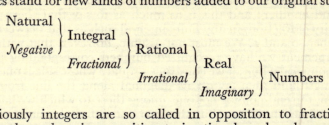

Obviously integers are so called in opposition to fractions, rational numbers in opposition to irrational, and real numbers in opposition to imaginary; and the system of naming naturally suggests a classification of species within a genus. But this way of describing the development is mistaken. We should speak rather of an hierarchy of five different types of numbers in which each higher type contains a sub-set corresponding to each lower type. In the following scheme each type is represented by a horizontal line, and correspondences are indicated by dotted vertical lines:

Complex numbers
Real numbers
Rational numbers
Signed integers
Natural numbers

The positive integer $+2$ is not the same as the natural number 2, and our custom of writing the symbol 2 instead of the symbol $+2$ is justified only by the fact that our rules for calculating with positive integers correspond exactly to our rules for calculating with natural numbers. Similarly the rational number $+2/+1$ must be distinguished in strict theory from the positive integer $+2$ and from the natural number 2, although we shall not fall into mistakes if we ignore the difference when we calculate. In the equation:

$$1 + \tfrac{1}{2} + \tfrac{1}{4} + \tfrac{1}{8} + \ldots = 2$$

we use the same sign 2 in yet another way, namely for a real number. And in certain contexts we may also make it serve as an abbreviation for the longer sign $2 + 0\sqrt{-1}$, that is for the symbol of a complex number in which the imaginary part is nil.

At each higher level in our diagram the whole of the type represented by a horizontal line is radically new, though mathematicians, failing to recognize this, have sometimes devised a new name only for that part of the type which is represented by the projecting portion of the line. And, except in one respect, the order of the development is fixed, that is to say, we could not have a calculus of complex numbers before we had a calculus of real numbers or a calculus of real numbers before we had a calculus of rational numbers. The exception concerns signed numbers: we could, if we wished, delay the distinction of positive and negative numbers until after the introduction of rational numbers or even until after the introduction of real numbers. And it seems that men had in fact a special notation for fractions before they spoke of negative numbers. But the scheme suggested above is the simplest because it makes the order of the appearance of negative, fractional, and irrational numbers correspond to the customary order of the inverse operations with which they are historically connected, i.e. subtraction, division, and extraction of roots.

The field of natural numbers is closed under the operations of addition, multiplication, and exponentiation, that is to say, except for certain special cases involving o, we always get a natural number as result if we add one natural number to another, or multiply one by another or raise one to the power of another. But this field is not closed under the operation of subtraction. The field of signed integers, on the other hand, is closed under all four of the operations mentioned so far, but not under the operation of division. For a field in which it is always possible to carry out that operation we must go on to consider rational numbers. But in this field we cannot always carry out the operation of extracting a root. And so we are led on to consider the field of real numbers, in which all positive numbers have roots of all desired degrees, and finally that of complex numbers, in which all the operations we have mentioned can be carried on without restriction. Apart from these there are other operations (such as that of taking the limit of a convergent infinite sequence) which may be applied already in the field of real numbers, but the field of complex numbers is especially interesting because here the notion of a *function* has its widest application.

In mathematical language the word 'function' is used to indicate an operation which when applied to some number called its argument (or to an ordered set of numbers, if it is a function of more than one argument) yields some number described (rather curiously) as the value of the function for that argument. Or if the word 'operation' suggests too strongly the intervention of men, we may say that mathematical talk of a function is equivalent to talk of a relationship in which a number (normally unique) called a value of the function may stand to a number called an argument of the function. Very often the relationship is expressed by a functional equation of the form $y = f(x)$ in which the letter $x$ is the independent variable, taking as its values the arguments of the function, and the letter $y$ the dependent variable, taking as its values the values of the function for the various possible arguments. Sometimes also a function is said to be *from* a certain class which is the range of possible arguments of the function *to* a certain class which is the range of possible values of the function.

This modern definition[1] is so drawn that it can be applied already within the field of natural numbers. We may say, for example, that the function expressed by $n^2$ takes the value 4 for the argument 2. But the terminology is derived from mechanics and associated historically with thought of continuous variation. Originally the word 'variable', now used to refer to letters occurring in certain ways in mathematical texts, was applied to physical magnitudes which varied with time, e.g. the distance of one particle from another or the pressure of a gas, and in formulae of the kind $y = f(x)$ the letters $x$ and $y$ were regarded as abbreviations for phrases such as 'the time elapsed' and 'the distance traversed'. When pure mathematicians began to talk of variables and functions, they did so because they were interested in the mathematical patterns exhibited by some physical laws; but they could no longer say that the letters they used were abbreviations for phrases like those just mentioned, and the usages which they then adopted, in particular the custom of calling the letters themselves variables, have given rise to a great deal of confusion and perplexity.

Sometimes it has been said that the letters called variables denote variable numbers, and at other times it has been said that they denote variably and ambiguously all the numbers which are their values. Neither explanation makes good sense. For numbers do not vary, and such variations as there may be in the denotation of signs are of no interest to mathematicians. Again it has been said: 'One variable $y$ is a function of another variable $x$ if for every determinate value of $x$, or at least for every determinate value within some range, there is at least one value of $y$ correlated with it according to a rule.' This explanation might have been satisfactory when the word 'variable' was used to refer to a physical magnitude; but it is very unsatisfactory when the word is used to refer to a letter, since it suggests that a function is a letter, or at any rate a symbol of some sort, although it is quite clear that the mathematicians who write about the theory of functions are not engaged in a branch of philology.

---

[1] The essentials are taken from A. Church's *Introduction to Mathematical Logic*, § 03.

Probably no mathematician engaged in his ordinary concerns has ever been seriously misled by remarks such as these, and in any case it is too late to think of abandoning the old terminology which gives rise to the trouble. But the point seems worth noticing, because the use of the word 'function' has been extended still farther in modern logic and has undoubtedly led to some serious misunderstandings there.

For the same reason it is worth remarking that there are at least two different ways in which a functional expression may occur with a variable in a mathematical text. When a mathematician writes

$$\tan x = \frac{\sin x}{\cos x},$$

the letter $x$ is part of a symbolism of universality by means of which he makes a statement about all numbers. The symbolism is extremely useful for its purpose, because it *suggests* what is in fact the case, namely, that replacement of the letter $x$ throughout the equation by any numeral will yield another true statement. Moreover, we can safely reason with the equation in most contexts *as though* $x$ were itself a numeral. When, however, a mathematician says in his letter-press 'We shall now discuss the function $\tan x$', the letter $x$ does not express universality, and it is not clear what grammatical role we should assign to the whole complex symbol $\tan x$. If, as is sometimes said, the letter $x$ serves here merely to mark a gap, the expression $\tan x$ can scarcely be the name of a function, any more than 'father of —' is the name of a relationship in ordinary English. But we can speak sensibly of the function *expressed by* the complex symbol $\tan x$ just as we can speak of the relationship expressed by 'father of —', and the common mathematical phrase quoted above may perhaps be regarded as an abbreviation for this way of talking. We shall see later that failure to appreciate this point has sometimes caused bewilderment among logicians who have adopted the language of functions for their own purposes.

Obviously we cannot use number expressions of higher types in the same way as we use ordinary numerals: it makes no sense to say there $5+3 \sqrt{-1}$ men in the room. Why then do we continue to talk of *numbers* throughout this development? It seems that our enlargement of the number concept is really an extension of the usage of the word 'number' to cover entities of various types, and that this is justified only by the possibility of calculating with symbols for these various entities according to the same basic rules of algebra, i.e. the commutative rules:

$$x+y = y+x \quad \text{and} \quad xy = yx,$$

the associative rules:

$$(x+y)+z = x+(y+z) \quad \text{and} \quad (xy)z = x(yz),$$

and the distributive rule:

$$x(y+z)=xy+xz.$$

A system of numbers in the extended sense is indeed just a set of entities for which all these laws hold *with suitable definitions of addition and multiplication*. The last point is important, since the notions of addition and multiplication appropriate in the calculus of natural numbers cannot be applied in a calculus of numbers of another type. If, for example, we wish to speak of multiplication of signed integers, we must first explain how we use the word 'multiplication' in this context, i.e. according to the rules:

$$(+a)(+b) = +ab, \quad (+a)(-b) = -ab, \quad (-a)(-b) = +ab.$$

This is as much as to say that the basic rules of algebra are systematically ambiguous, or better, that they give in abstract fashion certain logical conditions to be satisfied by the operations of any calculus which we call a calculus with numbers.

Up to and including the introduction of complex numbers the development was unconscious in the sense that mathematicians extended their use of the word 'number' without realizing exactly what they were doing. They were guided, no doubt by respect for what G. Peacock in 1833 called 'the principle of the permanence of equivalent forms',[1] that is to say by a desire to retain the general rules of algebra stated above; but they thought of each successive novelty as something they were forced to adopt in order to solve problems posed at the previous stage, and they did not consider algebra in abstraction from its exemplifications or try to invent new calculi for the sake of carrying development as far as it could go. In the nineteenth century the situation changed. In the first place, a number of distinguished mathematicians began to think of algebra in an abstract fashion. Peacock has been mentioned already, but there were others. D. F. Gregory, for example, wrote a paper 'On the Real Nature of Symbolical Algebra' in 1838,[2] and De Morgan published a series of four papers about 'The Foundations of Algebra' between 1839 and

---

[1] 'Report on the Recent Progress and Present State of Certain Branches of Analysis', *Report of the Third Meeting of the British Association for the Advancement of Science, held in 1833*, pp. 185–352, especially pp. 198–207.
[2] *Transactions of the Royal Society of Edinburgh*, xiv (1840), pp. 208–16.

1844.[1] Secondly, there were attempts to invent new calculi. H. Grassmann, for example, produced in 1844 a book on *Ausdehnungs-lehre* which carries out Leibniz's project of a geometrical calculus. And from 1844, when he published his first paper on quaternions, Sir William Rowan Hamilton of Dublin devoted a great deal of energy to perfecting a new algebra of hyper-complex numbers. It is interesting, however, to notice that Hamilton did not work entirely in the void. His efforts were all inspired by a desire to elaborate a calculus which would do for motion in three-dimensional space what the theory of complex numbers seemed to do very satisfactorily for motion in a plane. As complex numbers are expressible in the form $x+yi$ where the letter $i$ is an abbreviation for $\sqrt{-1}$, so his quaternions are expressible in the form $x+yi+zj+wk$ where the letters $i, j$, and $k$ represent rotations in three mutually perpendicular planes. But, unlike the theory of complex numbers, his system does not satisfy all the basic rules of algebra. In order to retain the other rules he had to abandon the commutative law for multiplication and declare $ij = -ji$. For this reason quaternions are not universally recognized as numbers. And the same can be said of other suggestions, e.g. matrices, which may perhaps be thought to provide an extension of the number concept beyond the domain of complex numbers. For it is now known that there can be no such extension without sacrifice of some one of the rules which determine the meaning of the word 'number' as that has been used hitherto in mathematics. This is not to say that it is foolish to talk of hyper-complex numbers, but that if we do so our usage is justified only by a partial analogy.

What did the mathematicians think of this progress from natural to complex numbers while it was taking place? At first each step produced a feeling of uneasiness, and then after a while each seemed inevitable. So far at least as real numbers, the progress was guided by spatial considerations; and even imaginary numbers, which had been introduced originally to preserve the generality of certain patterns of calculation, were accepted as fully respectable subjects of mathematical discourse only after they had been incorporated into a theory of complex numbers with a spatial interpretation. But very soon after the main development had been completed doubts began to arise about the reliability of spatial intuition as a basis for assertions about the continuum of real numbers. These doubts were not due to any difficulties in the application of mathematics, nor yet to the

---

[1] *Transactions of the Cambridge Philosophical Society*, viii, pp. 173–87, 287–300; viii, pp. 139–42, 241–54.

influence of non-Euclidean geometry, but arose rather from discoveries within mathematical analysis itself. It was shown, for example, by Bolzano in 1830, and later also by Weierstrass, that some continuous functions are not differentiable.[1] In geometrical language this seems to mean that there may be continuous curves without tangents. And paradoxes even more surprising were to follow. One of the most striking is concerned with the density of the rational points in a line. Let us suppose that the numbers 0 and 1 have been assigned to two points on a line, and that we decide to place a little canopy over each of the intervening points which have thus been made to correspond to rational numbers:

Since there are infinitely many fractions between any two fractions we may select, it seems natural to assume that every canopy will overlap with others and that the sum of their lengths will inevitably exceed one unit, however small the individual canopies may be. But this is not so. For if we consider the fractions between 0 and 1 in the order

$$\frac{1}{2}, \frac{1}{3}, \frac{2}{3}, \frac{1}{4}, \frac{3}{4}, \frac{1}{5}, \frac{2}{5}, \frac{3}{5}, \ldots$$

and then assign to the first a canopy of length equal to $\frac{1}{10}$ of a unit, to the second a canopy of length equal to $\frac{1}{10^2}$ of a unit, to the third a canopy of length equal to $\frac{1}{10^3}$ of a unit, and so on, the sum of the lengths of all the canopies will be only

$$\frac{1}{10} + \frac{1}{10^2} + \frac{1}{10^3} + \ldots = \frac{1}{9}.$$

Admittedly we cannot draw all the canopies with a pencil, but it is evident that our rule of procedure assigns a determinate length of canopy to each distinguishable fraction, since each such fraction has a place in our order.

When once doubt had been thrown on the reliability of spatial intuition as a source of mathematical knowledge, it became necessary to re-examine all the currently accepted proofs, and the result was a radical reconstruction of mathematics by such men as Cauchy (1789–1857) and Weierstrass (1815–97). It has been said, indeed, that nothing was satisfactorily proved in analysis before the nineteenth century. Now in analysis, just as in geometry, rigour requires the explicit formulation of everything essential to a demonstration; and so we find attention directed in the nineteenth century to the formulae which provide implicit definitions of the various types of numerical expressions. Whether these formulae are regarded as special rules of calcula-

---

[1] Bolzano's proof in his essay *Funktionenlehre* was not published until 1930.

tion or as axioms from which theorems are to be derived in accordance with the general laws of logic is of no great importance, provided they are set out fully and recognized to be fundamental. But it is natural to ask why we should have just these formulae. Is there some inherent necessity in the course of development which has led us to adopt them? Or are they conventions of our own making, suggested indeed by an interest in the description of nature or by a desire for abstract generality in mathematics itself, but incapable of proof precisely because they are just conventions? These questions were raised in the nineteenth century and are still debated in our own day. Perhaps the proper way of dealing with the problem is to show that the antithesis of discovery and invention has been wrongly conceived. For it is certain that mathematicians may construct calculi to serve their special interests, and it is equally certain that they are not entirely free in their choice of conventions. We can say, if we like, that Hamilton invented quaternions, but we must allow that neither he nor anyone else could make a system of hypercomplex numbers which satisfies all the laws of algebra valid for complex numbers. However that may be, the first step towards the clarification of the issue was the exact formulation of the rules of the various calculi which had already won recognition, and this was taken in the nineteenth century.

At each stage in the enlargement of the number concept we have to do with entities of a new type defined implicitly by the rules of operation of a new calculus. But in some contexts where we commonly speak of signed integers or of rational numbers it is possible to say all we want to say without talk about numbers of a new type. Thus instead of the equation $3-5 = -2$ we can write $3+2 = 5$, and instead of $\frac{5}{3} = \frac{10}{6}$ we can write $5 \times 6 = 10 \times 3$. And even when we find it convenient to reckon with signed integers or rational numbers we may regard these as ordered pairs of numbers selected from the next lower type and subjected to special rules of operation. The calculus of signed integers, for example, can be developed from rules such as:

$$(a, b) = (c, d) \text{ if and only if } a+d = b+c,$$
$$(a, b)+(c, d) = (a+c, b+d),$$
and
$$(a, b)(c, d) = (ac+bd, ad+bc).$$

At first sight this seems unfamiliar, but in order to obtain the usual method of representation we need only write $+a$ and $-a$ as abbreviations for the two standard forms $(a, 0)$ and $(0, a)$ to which our new numerical expressions are reducible in accordance with our special rules of equality. The special rules of the calculus of rational numbers are different, of course, but no more complicated. Nor is this the end of the possibilities of explanation by means of ordered pairs; for in 1835 Hamilton showed that the calculus of complex numbers could be presented as a calculus of ordered pairs of real numbers with suitably devised rules of equality, addition, multiplication, &c. If it could be shown that talk about real numbers was related in somewhat similar fashion to talk about rational numbers, the chain would be complete and we should be able to say in the terminology of Lord Russell that all numbers of higher types were logical constructions from natural numbers. That is to say, it would no longer be necessary to introduce numbers of higher types as new entities discovered by intuition of spatial or temporal continuity, since talk about them would be equivalent in principle to rather complicated talk about natural numbers and their properties. This programme, which has provided the inspiration for much later philosophy, is called the arithmetization of analysis.

Unfortunately real numbers have proved as troublesome to modern mathematicians as they were to the school of Pythagoras. The reason is that the calculus of real numbers cannot be presented as a calculus with any *finite* sets of rational numbers. As soon as we begin to reckon with real numbers, we commit ourselves to talk about infinity with all the difficulties that entails. This may be seen clearly from consideration of two theories of real numbers which were formulated last century.

The first was suggested by Weierstrass and developed by Cantor. In effect it amounts to identifying a real number with an infinite sequence of rational numbers which are commonly said to be successive approximations to it. In elementary arithmetic we have, for example, a procedure for extracting square roots, and by continued application of this we can work out the value of $\sqrt{2}$ to as many places of decimals as we desire. Since $\sqrt{2}$ is irrational, the procedure never leads to a conclusion, that is to a decimal expression which is completed by noughts or by a recurring period of digits, though our use of the phrase 'working out the value of $\sqrt{2}$' may tempt us to think that there is some complete decimal expression, i.e. that $\sqrt{2}$ is of the same nature as the numbers we call our approximations. According to Cantor the real number $\sqrt{2}$ may be identified with the sequence 1·4, 1·41, 1·414, 1·4142, &c., through which we proceed when we work first to one place of decimals, then to two, then to three, then to four, and so on. The sequence is potentially infinite, but we are able to lay down rules for reckoning with it as a number because the succession of its terms is fixed by a law.

The second theory of real numbers, which was put forward by Dedekind in his *Stetigkeit und irrationale Zahlen* of 1872, is a modern version of Eudoxus's theory of proportions. Although we cannot find any rational number whose square is equal to 2, we can divide the rational numbers exhaustively into those whose squares are less than 2 and those whose squares are greater than 2. According to Dedekind $\sqrt{2}$ is just the cut by which the rational numbers are divided in this way. If this sounds too paradoxical, we may say that $\sqrt{2}$ is the infinite set of rational numbers whose squares are not greater than 2; for the place of the cut is uniquely determined by the constitution of the lower set, and this formulation has the advantage of making it easier to compare the definition with other definitions of numbers of higher types. For as signed integers, rational numbers, and complex numbers are all defined as sets of numbers of the next lower type, so too are real numbers in this theory; but here, as in the scheme of Cantor, the set used for definition of a real number must be infinite. The two theories of real numbers are equivalent in the sense that a calculus of infinite sequences constructed to the prescription of Cantor has the same structure as a calculus of cuts constructed to the prescription of Dedekind. And this is not surprising, for a convergent infinite sequence is the appropriate instrument for locating a Dedekindian cut.

The definition of real numbers by means of infinite sets of rational numbers seems satisfactory in the sense that it gives us what we expect in the calculus of real numbers and relates this to the calculus of rational numbers which precedes. But it does not allow for the arithmetization of analysis, if we mean by that phrase, as apparently Kronecker did, the reduction of all mathematical statements to statements about natural numbers. For a statement which refers to an *infinite* set of rational numbers cannot be reduced in the strict sense, as a statement which refers only to a finite set of particular rational numbers may be. And if we give up the programme of complete reduction, we have still to face the difficulty of proving the consistency of the special rules we adopt for our calculus of real numbers. How is this to be done without begging the question at issue, namely the existence of the numbers which the rules are supposed to define? Although these criticisms were not worked out in detail during the nineteenth century, they were sufficiently well understood to produce misgivings in the minds of some mathematicians. Frege, for example, like Kronecker, was never completely satisfied by the theories of real numbers current in his time. In later chapters we shall have occasion to consider some of the difficulties in more detail.

### 3. *Boole and the Algebra of Logic*

Geometry and algebra have contributed in different ways to the development of mathematical logic. Geometry, as we saw in the first section of this chapter, has provided a field for the working out of the notions of axiomatics, while algebra has furnished a model for imitation in the making of a logical calculus. Leibniz realized already in the seventeenth century that there is some resemblance between disjunction and conjunction of concepts on the one hand and addition and multiplication of numbers on the other, but he did not find it easy to formulate the resemblance precisely and then to use it as the basic of calculus of logic. It was this that George Boole (1815–64) achieved in his *Mathematical Analysis of Logic*.[1] The idea that algebraic formulae might be used to express logical relations occurred to him first when he was still in his teens, working as an usher in a private school at Lincoln and educating himself by extensive reading. But the renewed interest in logic which led him to write this little book in 1847 was due to the appearance in periodicals of letters on the once famous controversy in which Sir William Hamilton of Edinburgh claimed priority in adoption of the doctrine of the quantification of predicates, charged Augustus De Morgan with plagiarism, and made foolish remarks against mathematics as an element in education. Before publishing his work Boole wrote to De Morgan, whose interests he shared, but the latter was finishing his *Formal Logic* at the time and suggested that they should both publish before consulting on their results. The two books appeared at about the same time; according to one story they reached the shops on the same day.

Although Boole's interest in mathematical logic was stimulated by an ephemeral dispute, it was surely no accident that there had been considerable discussion of the nature of algebra shortly before he wrote. We can safely assume that he had read some of the papers of Peacock, Gregory, De Morgan, and Sir William Rowan Hamilton which were mentioned in the last section. Gregory, the editor of the *Cambridge Mathematical Journal*, was a personal friend who had given him confidence in his powers as a mathematician. And apart from that Boole's aesthetic interest in mathematics led him to value very highly all attempts to achieve abstract generality. His reputation had been established by an essay of 1844 on *A General Method in Analysis*, in which he contributed to the generalization of algebraic reasoning by making free use of

[1] W. Kneale has given an account of Boole's life in 'Boole and the Revival of Logic', *Mind*, lvii (1948), pp. 149–75.

the calculus of operators, or separation of symbols, as it was then called.

From works which had already been published it was possible for Boole to collect two important discoveries: (i) that there could be an algebra of entities which were not numbers in any ordinary sense, and (ii) that the laws which hold for types of numbers up to and including complex numbers need not all be retained together in an algebraic system not applicable to such numbers. With his genius for generalization he saw that an algebra could be developed as an abstract calculus capable of various interpretations. The view of logic which he derived from this insight is clearly stated in the opening section of his *Mathematical Analysis of Logic*:

'They who are acquainted with the present state of the theory of Symbolical Algebra, are aware that the validity of the processes of analysis does not depend upon the interpretation of the symbols which are employed, but solely upon the laws of their combination. Every system of interpretation which does not affect the truth of the relations supposed, is equally admissible, and it is thus that the same processes may, under one scheme of interpretation, represent the solution of a question on the properties of numbers, under another, that of a geometrical problem, and under a third, that of a problem of dynamics or optics. . . . We might justly assign it as the definitive character of a true Calculus, that it is a method resting upon the employment of Symbols, whose laws of combination are known and general, and whose results admit of a consistent interpretation. That to the existing forms of Analysis a quantitative interpretation is assigned, is the result of circumstances by which those forms were determined, and is not to be construed into a universal condition of Analysis. It is upon the foundation of this general principle, that I purpose to establish the Calculus of Logic, and that I claim for it a place among the acknowledged forms of Mathematical Analysis, regardless that in its objects and in its instruments it must at present stand alone.'

Specimens of the first edition of Boole's pamphlet are now scarce, and it cannot be supposed that many were sold. In the following year, however, he published a short account of his Calculus of Logic in the *Cambridge and Dublin Mathematical Journal*, and this may have been more widely read among mathematicians. It adds nothing to the theory of the pamphlet, but it is somewhat easier to follow, and it ends with a paragraph which summarizes Boole's position very clearly:

'The view which these enquiries present of the nature of language is a very interesting one. They exhibit it not as a mere collection of signs, but as a system of expressions, the elements of which are subject to the laws of the thought which they represent. That these laws are as rigorously mathematical as the laws which govern the purely quantitative conceptions of space and time, of number and magnitude, is a conclusion which I do not hesitate to submit to the exactest scrutiny.'

In 1849 Boole was appointed to the chair of mathematics in Queen's College, Cork, then newly founded, and immediately began the preparation of a larger book about his logical theory. Of this period of his life he said that mental science was his study and mathematics his recreation. This does not mean that he was unproductive in mathematics (he composed notes on quaternions at this time), but that he spent a great deal of energy in familiarizing himself with what had been written by philosophers about the foundations of logic. The result of his labour was *An Investigation of the Laws of Thought on which are founded The Mathematical Theories of Logic and Probabilities*. This work, which was published in 1854 at the expense of Boole and a friend, did not sell very well, but it was read by many who had not seen the *Mathematical Analysis of Logic*, and it is often regarded as Boole's masterpiece. The chief novelty of the book is its application of his ideas to the calculus of probabilities. This is well done; but for the rest, the book is not very original. There is no important change on the formal side, and it cannot be said that the main ideas are presented more lucidly than in the earlier work. There are, however, some elaborate examples and some metaphysical passages which are interesting, if only for the light they throw on Boole's reading.

Towards the end of his life Boole said that he was dissatisfied with the exposition and arrangement of his *Laws of Thought* and wished he had spent twice as long in working out the ideas first presented in his *Mathematical Analysis of Logic*. In the year before his death he told Jevons in a letter that he was kept busy by the preparations for a new edition of his book on differential equations, but hoped to write again on logic as soon as he was free and therefore proposed to defer reading Jevons's work in order that there might be no possibility of misunderstanding about the origin of any views he later expressed. It is interesting to speculate on the changes he might have made in a revision of the *Laws of Thought*, but the selections which have been published from his drafts of the last few years suggest that what he had in mind was a development of his epistemological views rather than any alteration of the formal side of his work. In these papers he mentions in particular a distinction between the Logic of Class (i.e. his calculus of logic) and a higher, more comprehensive, logic that cannot be reduced to a calculus but may be said to be 'the Philosophy of *all* thought which is expressible in signs, whatever the object of that thought'.[1] It seems unlikely therefore that he would have produced a better book by working longer. For he was on a wrong track when he began to look for the basis of logic in the constitution of the human intellect. It is indeed one of his chief titles to fame that he freed logic from the dominion of epistemology and so brought about its revival as an independent science. The first break with the confused tradition of the seventeenth and eighteenth centuries had been made by Bolzano, himself a philosopher-mathematician, but it was Boole's work which showed clearly by example that logic could be studied profitably without any reference to the processes of our minds. He believed no doubt that he was dealing with laws of thought in some psychological sense of that ambiguous expression, but he was in fact dealing with some of the most general laws of thinkables.

In the exposition of Boole's system it will be convenient to begin with that interpretation from which, in all probability, he obtained his conception of a calculus of logic. Let us suppose that letters such as $x$ and $y$ stand for classes and that the use of the symbol $=$ between two class symbols indicates that the classes concerned have the same members. Then the intersection or overlap of two classes, that is to say, the class consisting of all the things which belong to both these classes, may be represented by a complex symbol such as $xy$. This convention is suggested by the way in which we string adjectives together when we are trying to specify some narrowly defined class. We may speak, for example, of the class of large, red, square things. Boole, indeed, does not distinguish very sharply between adjectives and class symbols; sometimes he calls the letters $x, y, z$, &c., *elective* symbols, thinking of them as symbols which elect (i.e. select) certain things for attention.

Among all distinguishable classes there are, however, two limiting cases for which it is convenient to have special symbols. These are the *universe* class, or the class of which everything is a member, and the *null* class, or the class of which nothing is a member. In Boole's symbolism they are represented respectively by the symbols 1 and 0. This usage may have been suggested to him by the conventions for the measure of probabilities, but it

[1] *Studies in Logic and Probability*, by George Boole (ed. by R. Rhees), 1952, p. 14. Apart from short works published in his lifetime, e.g. the *Mathematical Analysis of Logic*, this collection contains extracts from the papers in the possession of the Royal Society and in particular a draft 'On the Mathematical Theory of Logic and on the Philosophical Interpretation of its Methods and Processes'. Apparently Boole was not sufficiently satisfied with any of these papers to send it to a periodical, and De Morgan, who saw them after Boole's death, decided against publication. We are grateful to Dr. W. Mays for copies of correspondence between Boole and Jevons in 1863 and 1864.

had the great merit of according well with his desire to retain as much as possible of the normal algebraic formalism in his new calculus of logic. For the two equations $1x = x$ and $0x = 0$ are as valid in the class interpretation which has just been explained as they are in the ordinary numerical interpretation. But the appropriateness of this notation should not blind us to the fact that the introduction of the notions of the universe class and the null class involves an interesting novelty. Aristotle, as we have seen, confined his attention to general terms which were neither universal in the sense of applying to everything nor yet null in the sense of applying to nothing. When Boole wrote of the universe class and the null class, he made an important extension of the ordinary use of the word 'class'. If he had developed his new usage consistently, he would have been led farther away from the Aristotelian scheme than he ever wished to go. And since his time it has been discovered that the unrestricted use of the notion of the universe class can lead to serious paradoxes. In practice Boole takes his sign 1 to signify what De Morgan called the *universe of discourse*, that is to say, not the totality of all conceivable objects of any kind whatsoever, but rather the whole of some definite category of things which are under discussion. Thus in a context where the terms 'Briton' and 'alien' are supposed to determine complementary classes, the universe of discourse is mankind.[1]

Since there are obvious resemblances between Boole's symbolism for the intersection of classes and the long-established symbolism for the multiplication of numbers, it has become customary to describe the intersection of two classes as their logical product. There is a very important peculiarity, however, in the rules of the symbolism for intersection, which is not to be found in the rules for numerical multiplication. If $x$ denotes a class, the intersection of that class with itself is the same class, i.e. we have $xx = x$ as a basic equation. In his *Mathematical Analysis of Logic* Boole often expresses this truth by the formula $x^n = x$, saying that it is the distinguishing feature of his calculus. We shall meet it again presently in another shape.

Division appears in numerical algebra as the inverse of multiplication, but Boole does not in general allow an operation analogous to division when he is talking of classes. He points out that if the letters $x, y$, and $z$ denote classes we cannot argue from the equation $xz = yz$ to the equation $x = y$. The class of bachelor archdeacons may perhaps be coextensive with the class of red-haired archdeacons, but it does not follow from this that all

[1] A. De Morgan, *Formal Logic*, p. 55.

bachelors are red-haired. It should be remembered, however, that even in numerical algebra there are limits to the proper use of the operation of division. We cannot argue from the equation $2 \times 0 = 3 \times 0$ to the equation $2 = 3$. So far, then, it may be possible after all to find some analogue of division in the theory of classes, and Boole himself has suggested that the analogue may be abstraction (which Leibniz at one time represented by subtraction). Let us suppose that $x$, $y$, and $z$ denote classes related in the way indicated by the equation $x = yz$. The suggestion is that we should write $x/y = z$ as an expression for the fact that $z$ denotes a class we reach by abstracting from the membership of the class called $x$ the restriction of being included in the class called $y$. Thus we might perhaps say that, as the class of men is the logical product of the class of rational beings and the class of animals, so in this new notation

$$\frac{\text{the class of men}}{\text{the class of rational beings}} = \text{the class of animals.}$$

But it is important to notice two limits to this convention. First the expression $x/y$ can have no meaning at all in the calculus of classes if the class denoted by $x$ is not in fact a part of the class denoted by $y$. This is like the observation that the expression $x/y$ can have no meaning in the algebra of integers if the number denoted by $x$ is not a multiple of the number denoted by $y$. Secondly, the expression $x/y$ is generally indeterminate in the calculus of classes; for there may be many different classes whose intersections with the class denoted by $y$ are all coextensive with the class denoted by $x$. Instead of the example given above we might just as well write:

$$\frac{\text{the class of men}}{\text{the class of rational beings}} = \text{the class of primates,}$$

although the class of primates is certainly not identical with the class of animals. This is a much more serious limitation of the use of the suggested notation, and it probably accounts for Boole's statement that the expression $x/y$ cannot be interpreted in logic.

In the algebra of classes the complex sign $x + y$ may be used to signify the class of things which belong either to the class denoted by $x$ or to the class denoted by $y$. But the word 'or' has two distinguishable meanings in ordinary English; it is used sometimes in an inclusive and sometimes in an exclusive sense. Most of Boole's successors in mathematical logic have taken $x + y$ as a sign for the union, or logical sum in an inclusive sense, of the

classes called $x$ and $y$, i.e. so that the class called $x+y$ contains
the class called $xy$. This convention has considerable advantages
from the formal point of view, since it allows us to assert the
equation $x+x = x$ and so to work out the whole calculus in
accordance with a principle of duality for union and intersection.
In particular we can adopt De Morgan's two rules

$$\overline{xy} = \overline{x}+\overline{y}$$
$$\overline{x+y} = \overline{x}\,\overline{y}$$

in which the sign $\overline{x}$ stands for the complement of the class called
$x$, i.e. for the class of all things which do not belong to the class
called $x$. But Boole assumes always that if the letters $x$ and $y$ stand
for classes we are not to write $x+y$ unless the classes are mutually
exclusive, and in order to make clear that the condition is satisfied
he sometimes expresses a logical sum in the form $x+\overline{x}y$, where $\overline{x}$
has the sense explained above.[1] The effect of this restriction is to
bar from his system the equation $x+x = x$ and with it the two
general rules noticed above. It is not correct, however, to say
that he adopts an exclusive sense for the sign $+$, if by this assertion
it is meant that he introduces $x+y$ as a sign for the class of all
things which belong to the class called $x$ or to the class called $y$
but not to the class called $xy$. Rather he assumes that, if it is
correct to write $x+y$, the equation $xy = 0$ must be true.

Boole's reason for adopting the restriction we have just noticed
in his use of the symbol $+$ was probably a wish to be able to use
the symbol $-$ as its inverse. We have here a situation something
like that explained above in connexion with division. When $x$, $y$,
and $z$ denote classes it is tempting to suppose that from the
equation $x = y+z$ we can derive another equation $x-y = z$.
But there are two limitations to this usage in the algebra of classes.
In the first place we can attach no meaning to the expression
$x-y$ if the class denoted by $y$ is not part of the class denoted by $x$.
This is like the observation that the expression $x-y$ is meaningless
in the calculus of natural numbers if the number denoted by $y$ is
greater than the number denoted by $x$. Secondly, the expression
$x-y$ will be indeterminate if the symbol $+$ is taken in an inclusive
sense without the special assumption that the signs between which
it occurs stand for non-overlapping classes. For the equation
$x = y+z$ may then be quite compatible with the equation
$x = y+w$ although the letters $z$ and $w$ do not stand for coextensive classes. Whatever his motive, Boole adopts the convention
that the symbol $+$ may occur only between signs for mutually

[1] *Mathematical Analysis of Logic*, p. 52; *Laws of Thought*, pp. 33, 48, 55–56, 119.

exclusive classes and makes free use of the symbol—as its inverse. In particular he writes $1-x$ for the complement of the class denoted by $x$, and introduces the sign $\bar{x}$ merely as an abbreviation. This usage enables him to express the special principle of his system in the formula $x(1-x) = 0$. Sometimes he derives this from the equation $x = x^2$, which is a special case under his index law; but sometimes he prefers to regard it as basic, remarking that it is a formulation of the principle of non-contradiction, which Aristotle and Leibniz both described as the most fundamental of all principles.

This system of notation is sufficient, as it stands, for expression of the $A$, $E$, $I$, and $O$ propositions of traditional logic, provided that $A$ and $E$ propositions are taken without existential import.[1] Supposing the letter $x$ to stand for the class of X things and the letter $y$ for the class of Y things, we have the following scheme:

| | |
|---|---|
| Every X is Y . . . | $x(1-y) = 0$ |
| No X is Y . . . | $xy = 0$ |
| Some X is Y . . . | $xy \neq 0$ |
| Some X is not Y . . | $x(1-y) \neq 0$ |

Each of the four propositions can be represented in various other ways which are algebraically equivalent to these but not so simple. It will be noticed, however, that in this scheme particular propositions are expressed by inequalities, whereas universal propositions are expressed by equations. Boole prefers to express all the traditional types of categorical propositions by equations, and therefore writes instead of the last two lines of the scheme printed above:

| | |
|---|---|
| Some X is Y . . . | $xy = v$ |
| Some X is not Y . . | $x(1-y) = v$ |

The letter $v$, which he introduced here for the special purpose of expressing particular propositions, seems to correspond to the English word 'some'; but it is said to stand for a class 'indefinite in all respects but one', namely that it contains a member or members (i.e. is not coextensive with the null class). This explanation is not very satisfactory. If some X thing is Y, the class denoted by $xy$ does indeed contain at least one member. But we cannot assert this by equating the class called $xy$ with a class whose sole defining characteristic is that of containing a member or members; for there is no such class.

[1] Such an account of universal propositions was given by Franz Brentano in his *Psychologie vom empirischen Standpunkt* (1874), ii, ch. 7, and the consequences were developed in detail by his pupil F. Hillebrand in *Die neuen Theorien der kategorischen Schlüsse* of 1891.

Within Boole's system the letter $v$ can be manipulated in some respects as though it were a class symbol. But this is a defect rather than a merit of the notation, because it suggests mistaken inferences. We may be tempted, for example, to suppose that the equations $ab = v$ and $cd = v$ together entail the conclusion $ab = cd$. Boole himself does not fall into such fallacies, but that is because he observes restrictions on the use of the letter $v$ which are inconsistent with his own description of it as a class symbol. He says, for example, that we may pass from the equation $x(1-y) = 0$, which means 'Every X is Y', to the equation $vx(1-y) = 0$, and that the second may then be interpreted as meaning 'Some X is Y', but only on the assumption that the equations $v(1-x) = 0$ and $v(1-y) = 0$ are true, i.e. that the class denoted by $v$ is contained as a sub-class in each of the two classes denoted by $x$ and $y$. Since $v$ is supposed to denote a class which has at least one member, his condition of interpretation amounts in effect to an assumption that the classes denoted by $x$ and $y$ are not null. Obviously his purpose in all this is to provide for those Aristotelian inferences which depend on existential import, but he has chosen an unfortunate device. If the letter $v$ stood for a class, even in the enlarged sense in which the symbols 0 and 1 may be said to stand for classes, there would be no need to lay down special rules for its interpretation in the various contexts where it is used. It is interesting, however, to notice that at one time Leibniz had a similar idea.[1]

For the interpretation of the system in terms of classes and operations on classes it is clear that the following formulae, which are explicitly or implicitly assumed by Boole as premisses, all express true propositions:

(1) $xy = yx$         (5) If $x = y$, then $xz = yz$
(2) $x+y = y+x$     (6) If $x = y$, then $x+z = y+z$
(3) $x(y+z) = xy+xz$     (7) If $x = y$, then $x-z = y-z$
(4) $x(y-z) = xy-xz$     (8) $x(1-x) = 0$

Of these the first seven are similar in form to rules of ordinary numerical algebra. What distinguishes the system is the eighth formula. But Boole has pointed out that even this can be interpreted numerically with a suitable restriction of the values for the variable $x$. He states his discovery in the following words:

'Let us conceive, then, of an Algebra in which the symbols $x, y, z$ etc. admit indifferently of the values 0 and 1, and of these values alone. The laws, the axioms, and the processes, of such an Algebra will be identical in their whole extent with the laws, the axioms, and the processes of an Algebra of Logic. Differences of interpretation will alone divide them. Upon this principle the method of the following work is established.'[1]

This passage, and others like it, have led some commentators to describe Boole's system as a two-valued algebra. That description is a mistake; for when we treat the system as a calculus of classes, we do not assume that every class is coextensive either with the universe class or with the null class. It is possible, indeed, to turn Boole's system into a two-valued algebra by adding a new principle:

$$(9) \quad \textit{Either } x = 1 \textit{ or } x = 0.$$

The resulting calculus can still be interpreted numerically (i.e. by taking the symbols 1 and 0 in their ordinary numerical senses); but it no longer admits an interpretation in terms of classes. Boole does not distinguish sharply between his original system and the narrower system which involves (9). This may be seen from the fact that he gives two other logical interpretations of his formulae without remarking that one satisfies (9) while the other does not. These other interpretations have great interest for their own sake, and deserve to be mentioned here.

In the *Mathematical Analysis of Logic* and again in the *Laws of Thought* Boole suggests a convention whereby the equation $x = 1$ may be taken to mean that the proposition X is true and the equation $x = 0$ to mean that X is false. In accordance with this usage the truth-values of more complicated propositions can be represented by combinations of small letters, e.g. the truth-value of the conjunction of the propositions X and Y by the combination $xy$ and the truth-value of the exclusive disjunction of X and Y by the combination $x + y$. It will be seen that we have here all that is needed for an interpretation of Boole's system in terms of the truth-values of propositions with the symbols 1 and 0 standing respectively for truth and falsity. And this interpretation, like the numerical one, satisfies principle (9).

The interpretation by reference to propositions is worked out by Boole in the way just noticed, though without use of the phrase 'truth-value', which was invented later by Frege. But it is introduced on each occasion by remarks which might lead us to expect something different and perhaps more interesting. In his *Mathematical Analysis of Logic* Boole writes:

'To the symbols X, Y, Z, representative of Propositions, we may appropriate the elective symbols $x, y, z$, in the following sense. The hypothetical Universe, 1, shall comprehend all conceivable cases and conjunctures of circumstances. The elective symbol $x$ attached to any subject expressive of such cases shall select those cases in which the Proposition X is true, and similarly for Y and Z. If we confine ourselves to the contemplation of a given Proposition X, and hold in abeyance any other consideration, then two cases only are conceivable, viz. first that the given Proposition is true, and secondly that it is false. As these two cases together make up the Universe of the Proposition, and as the former is determined by the elective symbol $x$, the latter is determined by the elective symbol $1-x$. But if other considerations are admitted, each of these cases will be resoluble into others, individually less extensive, the number of which will depend on the number of foreign considerations admitted. Thus if we associate the Propositions X and Y, the total number of conceivable cases will be found as exhibited in the following scheme.

|  | Cases | Elective expressions |
|---|---|---|
| 1st | X true, Y true . . . . | $xy$ |
| 2nd | X true, Y false . . . . | $x(1-y)$ |
| 3rd | X false, Y true . . . . | $(1-x)y$ |
| 4th | X false, Y false . . . . | $(1-x)(1-y)$ |

. . . And it is to be noted that however few or many those circumstances may be, the sum of the elective expressions representing every conceivable case will be unity.'[1]

In the *Laws of Thought* Boole abandons this very promising suggestion and proposes instead that the letter $x$ should be taken to stand for the *time* during which the proposition X is true. This is a return to an unsatisfactory account of truth put forward by some ancient and medieval logicians, and it may have been suggested to him by what he read in metaphysical and theological books about eternal verities. But in both works he seems to be preparing the way for a scheme in which the symbols 1 and 0 would not stand merely for truth and falsity but represent rather necessary truth and impossibility. Like the class interpretation, this model would not satisfy principle (9), since it does not require that every elective expression be equated either to 1 or to 0.

At the end of the *Mathematical Analysis of Logic* Boole says rather obscurely that the theory of hypothetical propositions could be treated as part of the theory of probabilities, and in the *Laws of Thought* several chapters are devoted to the application of the new algebra to probabilities. This amounts in effect to yet another interpretation of the calculus according to which the letter stands for the probability of the proposition X in relation to all the available information, say K. Adapting and simplifying Boole's symbolism we have

[1] *Mathematical Analysis of Logic*, pp. 49–50.

$$\text{Prob}_{\kappa}(X \text{ and } Y) = xy$$

if X and Y are independent, given K, and

$$\text{Prob}_{\kappa}(X \text{ or } Y) = x+y$$

if X and Y are mutually exclusive. Clearly this scheme does not satisfy principle (9); for we cannot allow that every probability is equal to 1 or 0.

In a passage of the *Laws of Thought* which was quoted above Boole states that his method is founded on the identity of the calculus of logic with a numerical algebra of 0 and 1. Later in the same book he says emphatically:

'We may in fact lay aside the logical interpretation of the symbols in the given equation; convert them into quantitative symbols, susceptible only of the values 0 and 1; perform upon them as such all the requisite processes of solution; and finally restore to them their logical interpretation.'[1]

We have seen that the numerical algebra of 0 and 1 is a narrower system than the algebra of classes, since it involves principle (9), which does not hold for classes. But for anything which can be proved in the algebra of 0 and 1 without the use of principle (9) as a premiss there will, of course, be an analogue in the algebra of classes; and Boole does not in fact use principle (9), or anything which implies it, when he manipulates the symbols of his calculus. If he sometimes allows himself to think of his symbols as numerical, that is merely a concession to custom, something which makes him feel at home with them. The essence of his method is really the derivation of consequences in abstract fashion, i.e. without regard to interpretation. He made this clear in the opening section of his *Mathematical Analysis of Logic*, though he sometimes wrote later as though he had forgotten it.

The fundamental process in the formal elaboration of Boole's system is one which he calls *development*. Let us suppose that the expression $f(x)$ is an abbreviation for an expression involving the letter $x$ and possibly other elective symbols but apart from them only the usual algebraic signs we have already discussed. Then for suitable coefficients $a$ and $b$ we have $f(x) = ax+b(1-x)$. And in order to determine the values of $a$ and $b$ we need only suppose $x$ to take the values 1 and 0. For then we obtain by substitution the equations $f(1) = a$ and $f(0) = b$ from which we can infer

$$f(x) = f(1)x+f(0)(1-x).$$

This formula is said to give the development of the expression

---

[1] *Laws of Thought*, p. 70. The whole sentence is italicized in the original.

$f(x)$ with respect to $x$. In the *Mathematical Analysis of Logic* Boole treats it as a degenerate case under Maclaurin's theorem about the expansion of functions in ascending powers, but he relegates this rather fanciful notion to a footnote in the *Laws of Thought*.[1]

Let us now suppose that the expression $\phi(x, y)$ is an abbreviation for an expression which apart from the elective symbols $x$ and $y$ involves only the usual algebraic signs. Regarding this first as a functional sign with $x$ in the argument place, we can say

$$\phi(x, y) = \phi(1, y)x + \phi(0, y)(1-x).$$

Considering the result as a functional sign with $y$ in the argument place we can then go on to write

$$\phi(x, y) = \phi(1, 1)xy + \phi(1, 0)x(1-y) + \\ + \phi(0, 1)(1, x)y + \phi(0, 0)(1-x)(1-y),$$

which is the complete development of the expression $\phi(x, y)$. It is easy to see how functional expressions with a larger number of elective symbols may be developed in a similar fashion. If, for example, we have to do with an elective function of three arguments, the development will contain $2^3 = 8$ terms, each consisting of a coefficient equal to 0 or 1 and a product expression from the list: $xyz$, $xy(1-z)$, $x(1-y)z$, $x(1-y)(1-z)$, $(1-x)yz$, $(1-x)y(1-z)$, $(1-x)(1-y)z$, $(1-x)(1-y)(1-z)$. Those terms whose coefficients are equal to 0 can naturally be omitted without alteration to the sense of the whole expression.

Since any elective equation can be brought into the form $\phi(x, y, \ldots) = 0$, it is clear that it can also be expressed by the equation of a sum of terms to 0. From such an equation it can then be inferred that each of the terms included in the sum is separately equal to 0, since terms with negative values are not admissible in this calculus. On the other hand, if we have two elective equations $\phi(x, y, \ldots) = 0$ and $\psi(x, y, \ldots) = 0$, their full force can always be rendered in one equation $\chi(x, y, \ldots) = 0$ which includes among the terms of its developed form every term included in the developed form of either of the other two. It is then said that the two given equations have been *reduced* to one.

On this basis it is possible also to define another operation of importance, namely *solution*. Let us suppose that the given information is all contained in one equation $f(x) = 0$, where the expression $f(x)$ is an abbreviation for an expression involving elective symbols other than $x$, and that it is desired to find an equation of the form $x = \phi(y, z, \ldots)$, where $y, z$, &c., are the

[1] *Mathematical Analysis of Logic*, p. 60; *Laws of Thought*, p. 72.

other elective symbols. Developing our original equation with respect to $x$, we have

$$f(1)x + f(0)(1-x) = 0.$$

This can be rewritten in the form

$$[f(1) - f(0)]x + f(0) = 0,$$

and it is then easy to infer

$$x = \frac{f(0)}{f(0) - f(1)}.$$

It will be noticed that Boole introduces here the operation of division to which he has so far assigned no fixed interpretation in his calculus of logic. In order to make general provision for the solution of elective equations he therefore lays down some rules of decoding based on the assumption that here at least the symbolism of division may be taken to signify abstraction. The task is not so difficult as it might appear at first sight. When an expression of the form $\dfrac{f(0)}{f(0) - f(1)}$ is developed with respect to the elective symbols it involves, the result is a sum of products, and the sign of division appears only in the various coefficients, each of which must have one of the four forms: $\dfrac{1}{1}, \dfrac{0}{0}, \dfrac{0}{1}, \dfrac{1}{0}$. The first and the third of these are fairly easy to understand, because they can be reduced to 1 and 0 respectively, not only in ordinary numerical algebra, but also in a system where the sign of division indicates abstraction. Similarly the fourth is not very troublesome, since it can be shown not to occur except as coefficient to a product which is separately equal to 0. But the second is curious. Boole says that it is a perfectly indeterminate symbol of quantity, corresponding to 'all, some, or none'. Sometimes he equates it with the symbol $v$ which he uses in the expression of particular propositions, but this is unsatisfactory, since the letter $v$ is supposed to stand for a class which is not null. We may perhaps use the letter $w$ instead as an abbreviation. Thus if the application of the rules of solution has produced a result of the form

$$x = \frac{1}{1}p + \frac{0}{0}q + \frac{0}{1}r + \frac{1}{0}s,$$

where $p$, $q$, $r$, and $s$ are the various product expressions to be considered for inclusion in the final expression, we can write

$$x = p + wq.$$

E e

According to the class interpretation this means that the class denoted by $x$ consists of the class denoted by $p$ together with an indeterminate part (all, some, or none) of the class denoted by $q$. In one of the late drafts which he did not publish Boole said that the four possible coefficients noticed above should be taken to represent respectively the four categories of universality, in-definiteness, non-existence, and impossibility, which might, he thought, be adopted with advantage in place of the Kantian list.[1]

Finally, Boole lays down rules for *elimination*. Let us suppose that our information is represented in abbreviated form by the equation $f(x) = 0$ and that it is desired to find what relations, if any, hold independently of the class denoted by $x$ between the other classes symbolized in the full version of $f(x)$. By the process of solution we get

$$x = \frac{f(0)}{f(0)-f(1)}$$

and from this we can obtain also

$$1-x = -\frac{f(1)}{f(0)-f(1)}.$$

But by one of the basic rules of the calculus we have

$$x(1-x) = 0,$$

and from this, taken together with our two results of solution, we can infer according to Boole

$$-\frac{f(0)f(1)}{[f(0)-f(1)]^2} = 0,$$

i.e.
$$f(0)f(1) = 0.$$

If the working out of the left side of this equation yields only $0 = 0$, the original equation covers no relations independent of the class denoted by $x$. If, however, it yields something of the form $\phi(y, z, \ldots) = 0$, we have established that the full version of the equation $f(x) = 0$ covers some relation or relations in-dependent of the class denoted by $x$.

This argument, given by Boole in the chapter on elimination in the *Laws of Thought*, is bewildering because it involves use of expressions for which there is no logical interpretation. But the same result can be proved by an argument which is intuitively more satisfactory. Since development of the functional expression $f(x)$ with respect to $x$ gives $f(1)x+f(0)(1-x)$, where $f(1)x$ is short for the sum of those terms in the complete expansion which have

$x$ as a factor and $f(0)(1-x)$ short for the sum of those terms which have $(1-x)$ as a factor, $f(1)$ and $f(0)$ must each represent a sum of terms which are expressible without the symbol $x$, and $f(1)f(0)$ must be an abbreviation for their common part, i.e. for the sum of those terms which appear in both totals. If in fact the full versions of $f(1)$ and $f(0)$ have no common part, it is obvious that the equation $f(x) = 0$ covers no relation independent of the class denoted by $x$. If, however, the full versions of $f(1)$ and $f(0)$ have a common part, the equation of this to 0 must indicate a relation independent of the class denoted by $x$.

By various combinations of these processes of calculation Boole could give algebraic representations of all the kinds of reasoning recognized in traditional logic. Syllogistic reasoning, in particular, might be presented as the reduction of two class equations to one, followed by elimination of the middle term and solution for the subject-term of the conclusion. Thus, to take a simple example, if $h$ stands for the class of human beings, $a$ for the class of animals, and $m$ for the class of mortals, the premisses 'Every human being is an animal' and 'Every animal is mortal' can be replaced by the equations

$$h(1-a) = 0$$
$$a(1-m) = 0.$$

Reducing these to one we get

$$h-ha+a-am = 0$$

and from this in turn by development with respect to $a$ we get

$$(h-h1+1-1m)a+(h-h0+0-0m)(1-a) = 0$$

or

$$(1-m)a+h(1-a) = 0.$$

Then by eliminating $a$ in accordance with the rules we can conclude

$$(1-m)h = 0.$$

This equation is already in such a form that it can be interpreted to mean 'Every human being is mortal', but for an exercise in Boole's methods we may continue according to his rules for solution:

$$h = \frac{(1-m)0}{(1-m)0-(1-m)1}$$

$$= \frac{(1-1)0}{(1-1)0-(1-1)1}m + \frac{(1-0)0}{(1-0)0-(1-0)1}(1-m)$$

$$= \frac{0}{0}m + 0\,(1-m) = wm + 0(1-m).$$

In words our result means that the class of human beings consists of an indeterminate selection (which may perhaps be null) from the class of mortals together with a null selection from the class of immortals; in order to exclude the possibility of a null selection from the class of mortals it would be necessary to include among our premisses explicit provision for the existential import of the term 'man'. Obviously the nut from which this kernel has been obtained could have been cracked with a lighter hammer, but it is interesting to see that the methods Boole introduced can be applied in a mechanical fashion. In effect he has given what is now called a decision procedure.

## 4. *Later Developments of Boolean Algebra*

The chief novelty in Boole's system is his theory of elective functions and their development, or, as we should now say, his theory of truth-functions and their expression in disjunctive normal form. Philo of Megara discussed particular elective functions and explained how they could be developed, but Boole should have the credit of being the first to treat these two topics in general fashion. We have quoted a passage of the *Mathematical Analysis of Logic* from which it was a short step to Frege's use of truth-tables (i.e. tabulations of alternative truth-possibilities) in his *Begriffsschrift* of 1879 for the clear exhibition of Boolean developments.[1] In a paper of 1885 the American logician C. S. Peirce added the remark that a necessarily true formula was one which remained true under all assignments of truth-values to its constituents: 'To find whether a formula is necessarily true substitute **f** and **v** for the letters and see whether it can be supposed false by any such assignment of values.'[2] And with these two notions we have all the essentials for the tabular method in primary logic which was popularized by Post and Wittgenstein in 1920.

In his *Symbolic Logic* of 1881 J. Venn, another admirer of Boole, used diagrams of overlapping regions (i.e. topological models) to illustrate relations between classes or the truth-conditions of propositions. His diagrams differ from those of Euler in that he first represents all possible combinations by distinct areas and then indicates by marks within the various areas which combinations must be null and which not null for the holding of a given

---

[1] In his *Elementary Lessons in Logic* of 1870 and later works, W. S. Jevons produced tabulations of permissible combinations of general terms and showed how these could be used for logical calculations.

[2] *Collected Papers*, iii, § 387. In what follows this series of volumes will be cited as *C.P.*

proposition. Like Jevons, he thought that what he was trying to elucidate was one of the principal discoveries of Boole, and his diagrams may in fact be regarded as illustrations of the theory of development by which Boole justified his various processes of calculation. Thus the example considered at the end of the last section can be presented without Boole's fearsome apparatus of numerical coefficients by means of the figure to the right in which the square represents the universe of discourse and the areas of the three circles represent the three classes of human beings, animals, and mortals. Shading of an area indicates emptiness of the corresponding class as stipulated in a premiss, e.g. the class of human beings who are not animals, and the placing of an asterisk in an area indicates that the corresponding class is not empty. In his *Symbolic Logic* of 1896 Lewis Carroll used a somewhat similar scheme in a procedure which he introduced for determining the validity of syllogisms.

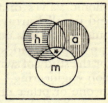

Because Boole's methods can be reduced to rules of thumb, they lend themselves to mechanization. Jevons was the first to realize this, and in 1869 he succeeded in constructing a logical machine which he exhibited next year to the Royal Society.[1] In one description he said that its appearance was like that of a very small upright piano, but to modern eyes it looks more like a cash register, since signs indicative of various possible combinations of elements (either classes or propositions) are made to appear and disappear by the pressing of keys. In 1885 Allan Marquand suggested an electrical analogue of Jevons's machine, and in 1947 an electrical computer of different design was constructed at Harvard by T. A. Kalin and W. Burkhart specially for the solution of Boolean problems involving up to twelve logical variables (i.e. proposition or class letters).[2]

Any modern electronic computer designed for general purposes must be capable of dealing with Boolean algebra. For if it is to follow the logical articulation of ordinary mathematical calcula-

[1] *The Substitution of Similars*, 1869; 'On the Mechanical Performance of Logical Inference', *Philosophical Transactions of the Royal Society*, clx (1870), pp. 497–518. There is an account of the machine, together with a picture, in *The Principles of Science* which Jevons published in 1874. The machine itself is preserved in the Museum of the History of Science at Oxford. W. Mays and D. P. Henry have given a summary of Jevons's work in 'Jevons and Logic', *Mind*, lxii (1953), pp. 484–505.
[2] B. V. Bowden, *Faster Than Thought*, pp. 333 f. This work on electronic computers contains particulars of other logical machines, but the fullest account of the subject is given by Martin Gardner in his entertaining book *Logic Machines and Diagrams*, which begins with Raymond Lull.

tion, it must be able to take account of conjunction, disjunction, negation, and conditional dependence. Its instructions may be, for example, that, if conditions A and B are both fulfilled in the carrying out of a certain process, it is to do C, and that then, if the result of C is either D or E, it is to go on to do F, but otherwise to do G, and so forth. All this is achieved by the use of thermionic valves or transistors, in various combinations of serial and parallel arrays, as switches for the routing of electrical impulses; and it is not very surprising that the appropriate circuits can be produced, since Boolean algebra was used as early as 1936 for the study of switch and relay circuits in electrical communication engineering.[1] If the putting-on of a switch, which must be in one or other of two states, is likened to the affirmation of a proposition, its putting-off may be likened to the denial of the same proposition, and the arrangement of two switches in series may be likened to the conjunction of two propositions, while the arrangement of switches in parallel may be likened to the connexion of two propositions by 'or'. When a complex circuit of switches and relays has been described in accordance with these analogies by the appropriate Boolean expression, it is possible to determine algebraically whether certain paths will be open in certain conditions, and through algebraic transformations of the expression it may even be possible to find a circuit that will produce the same results with less apparatus.

Although Boole's system lends itself in some ways to easy manipulation, we must admit that it contains not only a defect of elegance in the restriction whereby we may not write $x+y$ unless we know the truth of the equation $xy=0$, but also some defects of rigour such as the use of the letter $v$ for the expression of existential propositions, the admission of numerical coefficients other than 1 and 0, and the use of the operation of division to which no constant meaning has been assigned in logic. In the course of the half century after the publication of his *Laws of Thought* these shortcomings were all removed by his followers. Jevons began the reform in 1864 with his *Pure Logic, or the Logic of Quality apart from Quantity*, in which he suggested the use of the symbol + in the sense of the inclusive 'or' without any restriction on the signs between which it may occur. This made possible a great simplification, and was therefore welcomed by all later writers on the algebra of logic except Venn. As C. S. Peirce pointed out in a paper of 1867, it produces an exact parallelism between theorems including logical addition and

---

[1] C. E. Shannon, 'A Symbolic Analysis of Relay and Switching Circuits', *Transactions of the American Institute of Electrical Engineers*, lvii (1938), pp. 713-23.

theorems involving logical multiplication.[1] This advantage was most fully exploited by E. Schröder when he set out such theorems in parallel columns of his *Vorlesungen über die Algebra der Logik* (1890–5). In a paper of about 1880 Peirce went even farther in the direction of simplification and showed how all the elective functions of Boole could be expressed by use of a single primitive sign with the meaning of 'neither . . . nor . . .'.[2] But like many other discoveries of Peirce, this passed unnoticed at the time: no use was made of the possibility of such reduction until it had been rediscovered by H. M. Sheffer in 1913.[3] Peirce should also have credit for the reintroduction of a sign with the sense of Leibniz's *inest*; his idea, though not his sign, was adopted by Schröder.

The most important development, however, is the presentation of the calculus in a strictly axiomatized form. Whereas Boole had been content to characterize his system by the single principle in which it seemed to differ from ordinary numerical algebra, his successors tried to make all their assumptions explicit. The results of this endeavour can be studied best in two papers of E. V. Huntington on 'Sets of Independent Postulates for the Algebra of Logic'.[4] Although Huntington speaks of the algebra of logic, he presents his postulates in abstract fashion, i.e. without reference to any special interpretation, and it is interesting to notice that this reformed version of Boolean algebra has in fact a considerable interest for modern mathematicians apart from its use in logic. For convenience of comparison the first, second, and fourth of Huntington's sets are given below in the symbolism of Boole, so far as that is appropriate. It should be remembered, of course, that the various signs, including 1 and 0, have only the sense assigned to them by the postulates.

Huntington's first set is adapted from one given by A. N. Whitehead in his *Universal Algebra* of 1898, and is the nearest to Boole's system in that it takes the two operations of addition and multiplication as primitive. These are supposed to be applicable to any pair from a class of things which may be called for short the elements of the algebra. When we wish to give a logical interpretation to the postulates we take these elements to be either classes or propositions.

Ia.    *If $a$ and $b$ are elements, so too is $a+b$.*
Ib.    *If $a$ and $b$ are elements, so too is $a \times b$.*
IIa.   *There is an element $0$ such that $a+0 = a$ for every element $a$.*

[1] *C.P.* iii, §§ 1–19.          [2] *C.P.* iv, §§ 12–20.
[3] *Trans. Amer. Math. Soc.* xiv (1913), pp. 481–8.
[4] Ibid. v (1904), pp. 288–309, and xxxv (1933), pp. 274–304, 557–8, 971.

IIb.    *There is an element* 1 *such that* $a \times 1 = a$ *for every element a.*

IIIa.   $a+b = b+a$ *for all elements a and b whose combinations here mentioned are also elements.*

IIIb.   $a \times b = b \times a$ *for all elements a and b whose combinations here mentioned are also elements.*

IVa.    $a+(b \times c) = (a+b) \times (a+c)$ *for all elements a, b, and c whose combinations here mentioned are also elements.*

IVb.    $a \times (b+c) = (a \times b)+(a \times c)$ *for all elements a, b, and c whose combinations here mentioned are also elements.*

V.      *If the elements* 0 *and* 1 *exist and are unique, there is an element $\bar{a}$ such that* (i) $a+\bar{a} = 1$ *and* (ii) $a \times \bar{a} = 0$.

VI.     *There are at least two elements x and y such that* $x \neq y$.

It will be noticed that these postulates are framed in such a way as to bring out the correspondence between addition and multiplication in the system. The independence of each postulate from the rest can be proved by the construction of a model which satisfies all the others without satisfying the postulate under consideration. Some conditions which seem at first sight to be redundant are included for the special purpose of preserving independence. Thus IIa or IIb can be false when V is satisfied merely by the non-fulfilment of its condition.

Huntington's second set is similar to suggestions of Leibniz, Peirce, and Schröder in that it deals with a relation of inclusion between elements, as distinct from any operation on elements. The sign we shall use for this relation is employed in numerical mathematics with the sense of 'is less than', but it is to be understood here in such a sense that the formula $a < b$ does not exclude the formula $a = b$. If, as is usual, the elements of the algebra are supposed to be classes, the sign may be taken to mean inclusion in that sense in which a sub-class is included in a super-class, but *not* membership.

1.  $a < a$ *for every element a.*
2.  *If* $a < b$ *and* $b < a$, *then* $a = b$.
3.  *If* $a < b$ *and* $b < c$, *then* $a < c$.
4.  *There is an element* 0 *such that* $0 < a$ *for every element a,* $\neq 0$.
5.  *There is an element* 1 *such that* $a < 1$ *for every element a,* $\neq 1$.
6.  *If* $a \neq b$ *and neither* $a < b$ *nor* $b < a$, *there is an element s such that* (i) $a < s$, (ii) $b < s$, *and* (iii) *if y,* $\neq s$, *is such that* $a < y$ *and* $b < y$, *then* $s < y$.
7.  *If* $a \neq b$ *and neither* $a < b$ *nor* $b < a$, *there is an element p such that* (i) $p < a$, (ii) $p < b$ *and* (iii) *if x,* $\neq p$, *is such that* $x < a$ *and* $x < b$, *then* $x < p$.
8.  *If the elements* 0 *and* 1 *exist and are unique, then for every*

*element a there is an element $\bar{a}$ such that* (i) *if $x < a$ and $x < \bar{a}$, then $x = $ o, and* (ii) *if $a < y$ and $\bar{a} < y$, then $y = $ 1.*

9.  *If postulates* (1), (4), (5), *and* (8) *hold and it is not the case that $a < \bar{b}$, then there is an element $x$, $\neq$o, such that $x < a$ and $x < b$.*

10.  *There are at least two elements, $x$ and $y$, such that $x \neq y$.*

In this set postulates (1) to (7) are independent among themselves, and (8) and (9) are independent of the first seven, but either (6) or (7) can be deduced from the rest. Both are retained here for the sake of symmetry. The letters $s$ and $p$ used in the statement of them are intended, of course, to suggest 'sum' and 'product' respectively.

Postulates (4) and (8) for inclusion bring out explicitly a principle of the theory of classes which has often caused bewilderment, namely, that the null class is a sub-class of all classes. At first hearing there is something curious in any talk of a class with no members, but when once this technical extension of the use of the word 'class' has been accepted, the principle just mentioned is natural and easily intelligible. For it is a truism that the intersection of any two classes is a sub-class of each of them, and from this it follows directly that the class designated by $a \times \bar{a}$, i.e. the null class, must be a sub-class of the class designated by $a$, whatever that may be.

Huntington's fourth set is constructed to show how the whole system can be formulated with the operations of addition and taking the complement as the sole undefined notions. Other notions such as the operation of multiplication and the relation of inclusion can be introduced by definition, if required.

(i)   *If a and b are elements, so too is $a+b$.*
(ii)  *If a is an element, so too is $\bar{a}$.*
(iii) *$a+b = b+a$ for all elements a and b whose combinations here mentioned are also elements.*
(iv)  *$(a+b)+c = a+(b+c)$ for all elements a, b, and c whose combinations here mentioned are also elements.*
(v)   *$\overline{\bar{a}+\bar{b}}+\overline{\bar{a}+b} = a$ for all elements a and b whose combinations here mentioned are also elements.*

This and the corresponding set for the operations of multiplication and taking the complement are perhaps the simplest of the kind that can be constructed.

By the device of Peirce and Sheffer mentioned above it is possible, however, to produce a set of postulates which is simpler in that it involves only one primitive operation.

1. *There are at least two distinct elements.*
2. $a|b$ *is an element for all elements* $a$ *and* $b$.
3. $(a|a)|(a|a) = a$ *for every element* $a$ *whose combinations here mentioned are also elements.*
4. $a|\{b|(b|b)\} = a|a$ *for all elements* $a$ *and* $b$ *whose combinations here mentioned are also elements.*
5. $\{a|(b|c)\}|\{a|(b|c)\} = \{(b|b)|a\}|\{(c|c)|a\}$ *for all elements* $a$, $b$, *and* $c$ *whose combinations here mentioned are also elements.*

This set is to be found in the paper of Sheffer noticed above, and the expression $a|b$ is often called Sheffer's stroke function. Admittedly the last three postulates seem rather complicated when written, as here, in full, but they come to seem more natural when the expression $a|b$ is taken to mean either $\bar{a}\times\bar{b}$ or $\bar{a}+\bar{b}$ and the sign $\bar{a}$ is introduced as an abbreviation for $a|a$. The fact that the stroke can be interpreted equally well in two different ways is an interesting consequence of the principle of duality.

More recently A. Tarski has given several equivalent sets of postulates for an extended system of Boolean algebra in which there are two operations of a non-finitary character, namely that of taking the logical sum or union of all the elements of some specified set of elements and that of taking the logical product or intersection of all the elements of some specified set of elements.[1] This extended system is closely related to a theory of the part-whole relationship developed by S. Leśniewski under the name of 'mereology'.[2] In fact the difference is simply that Leśniewski's system excludes the possibility of a null element included in every other element.

It is a common feature of all these sets of axioms that they involve use of ordinary English words such as 'if' and therefore presuppose a system of logic containing rules for inference from one proposition or set of propositions to another. This fact is not sufficient reason for denying that Boole's algebra may itself be interpreted as a system of logic, but it suggests that it cannot be the simplest or most fundamental part of logic. If the elements of the algebra are supposed to be classes, there must clearly be a more basic theory about the derivation of propositions from other propositions. But that more basic theory cannot be Boolean algebra interpreted in the other way with propositions for elements, because the other version of the algebra involves precisely the same assumptions as the algebra of classes. Frege's

---

[1] 'Zur Grundlegung der Booleschen Algebra', *Fundamenta Mathematicae*, xxiv (1935), pp. 177–98. There is an English translation in the collection of his papers called *Logic, Semantics, Metamathematics*, pp. 320–41.
[2] 'O podstawach matematyki', *Przegląd Filozoficzny*, xxxiii (1930), pp. 77–105.

*Begriffsschrift* of 1879 was the first treatise of logic in which the science was developed in a thoroughly comprehensive fashion with a calculus of propositions, something like that of Chrysippus, at the beginning and then in due order a calculus of classes. But already in 1877 H. McColl had put forward suggestions for a calculus of propositions in which the asserted principles would be implications rather than equations, and he should therefore have credit for priority in this regard, though the system which he produced was not complete like Frege's calculus of propositions.[1]

## 5. *The Theory of Relations: De Morgan and Peirce*

Boole's success in constructing an algebra which included all the theorems of traditional logic led some logicians to assume that all logic must be capable of presentation in algebraic form, and attempts were made in the next generation to work out a logic of relations in the same fashion as the logic of classes. The most detailed development of this line of thought is to be found in Schröder's *Vorlesungen über die Algebra der Logik* (vol. iii, 1895), but the original idea and most of the interesting propositions were first suggested by Peirce in a series of papers written between 1870 and 1903 which are now available in the third volume of his *Collected Papers*. Unfortunately Peirce was like Leibniz, not only in his originality as a logician, but also in his constitutional inability to finish the many projects he conceived.

In earlier chapters we have noticed a number of sporadic attempts to deal with arguments which depend on the properties of relations, but sustained interest in this subject dates from a paper written by Augustus De Morgan in 1859.[2] In this he says that the doctrine of the syllogism, which he had discussed in his *Formal Logic* of 1847 and in earlier papers, is only a special case in the theory of the composition of relations, and that he wishes to go on to a more general treatment of the subject. The canons of syllogistic reasoning are in effect a statement of the convertible and transitive character of the relation of identity. A relation is convertible when it is the same as its own converse (e.g. the relation of resemblance); and it is transitive when a relative of a relative in respect of this relation is a relative of the same kind (e.g. the relation of being an ancestor). Here the word 'convertible' expresses what is meant by 'symmetrical' in the writings of later logicians. The distinction was not new; for, as

---

[1] 'The Calculus of Equivalent Statements', *Proceedings of the London Mathematical Society*, ix (1878), pp. 9–10, 177–86; x (1879), pp. 16–28; xi (1880), pp. 113–21.
[2] 'On the Syllogism IV and on the Logic of Relations', *Cambridge Philosophical Transactions*, x (1864), pp. 331–58.

Peirce pointed out, Ockham had written of such relations as equiparant in opposition to disquiparant relations like that of being father.[1] By the word 'relative' which he uses in his definition of transitive relations De Morgan means what some logicians have called a relative term, i.e. a term which applies to something only in respect of its being related to something else. He and Peirce and Schröder always think of relationships as expressed in some such form as '— is an ancestor of ...' and conceive their task to be that of showing how relative terms may be combined with each other and with non-relative terms.

In the body of his paper De Morgan suggests symbols for the converse and the contradictory (he says 'contrary') of a relative and for three different ways in which a pair of relatives may be combined. Having shown that the converse of the contradictory and the contradictory of the converse are identical, he then goes on to set out in a table the converse, the contradictory, and the converse of the contradictory of each of the three combinations. His notation is not very satisfactory and need not be reproduced here. The three modes of combination which he discusses are those which could be expressed by phrases of such patterns as (i) *x is an l of an m of y* (e.g. 'John is a lover of a master of Peter'), (ii) *x is an l of every m of y*, (iii) *x is an l of none but an m of y*. And he shows that the converse or the contradictory or the converse of the contradictory of each such combination is itself a combination of one of the kinds discussed, but a combination in which a simple relative may be the converse or the contradictory or the converse of the contradictory of a simple relative in the original combination. Thus the converse of the contradictory of the combination 'lover of a master of' is 'non-servant of every beloved of' or 'servant of none but a non-beloved of'.

In his first paper on the logic of relatives, published in 1870, Peirce says of De Morgan's work:

'This system still leaves something to be desired. Moreover Boole's logical algebra has such singular beauty, so far as it goes, that it is interesting to inquire whether it cannot be extended over the whole realm of formal logic, instead of being restricted to that simplest and least useful part of the subject, the logic of absolute terms, which, when he wrote, was the only formal logic known. . . . In extending the use of old symbols to new subjects, we must of course be guided by certain principles of analogy, which, when formulated, become new and wider definitions of these symbols.'[2]

---

[1] *Summa Totius Logicae*, i, ch. 52, quoted by Peirce in *C.P.* iii, § 136. The term *aequiparantia* occurs already in the *Summulae Logicales* of Peter of Spain (ed. Bochenski, § 3. 19).

[2] *C.P.* iii, §§ 45-46.

Possibly the idea of an algebra of relatives was suggested by De Morgan's convention of writing *lm* as an abbreviation for *l of an m of*; for Peirce continued to use juxtaposition of relative signs in this way and spoke of it as expressing a relative product. In what follows we shall use the symbol $l \times_R m$ instead of *lm* in order to make clear the novelty of the conception and the danger of supposing that relative multiplication is commutative, i.e. that from *x is a lover of a master of y* we may infer *x is a master of a lover of y*. Pursuing the same analogy, Peirce later introduced the notion of a relative sum. Since his special sign is difficult to reproduce, we shall express this by the symbol $l +_R m$. There was nothing in ordinary usage or the conventions of previous logicians to suggest an interpretation for such a sign, and Peirce's choice seems to have been guided by the desire to preserve the pattern of De Morgan's rules for logical sums and products of the non-relative kind. For he said that the relative sum of 'lover' and 'master' was to be 'lover of every non-master of'. This is a combination which would scarcely occur to anyone as a suitable candidate for the title of sum, but it has the merit of allowing us to assert the two equations

$$\overline{l +_R m} = \overline{l} \times_R \overline{m}$$

and

$$\overline{l \times_R m} = \overline{l} +_R \overline{m}.$$

The relative products and relative sums which Peirce defines in this way must, of course, be distinguished carefully from ordinary logical products and sums of relatives. The sign $l \times m$ may be taken to mean 'lover and master', where both the relations under consideration have the same terms; but the sign $l \times_R m$ means 'lover of a master of', where the relations are combined only in the sense that an after-term of the first is a fore-term of the second. This distinction inevitably leads to complications in the new calculus. We have, for example, not only

$$a \times_R (b \times_R c) = (a \times_R b) \times_R c,$$

but also

$$a \times_R (b \times c) < (a \times_R b) \times (a \times_R c)$$

where $<$ has the sense of 'is included in' and the terms between which it occurs are supposed to stand for classes.

Is the result a natural extension of Boolean algebra? Besides the three operations of addition, multiplication, and negation (or taking the complement) which occur in ordinary Boolean algebra, this new system contains the operations of relative addition, relative multiplication, and conversion; and although there are some analogies between the three new and the three old operations, anyone who studies the details in the work of Schröder may well doubt whether this attempt to present the theory of relations as an algebra is worth the trouble it involves. It is true, as Schröder said, that the notion of relative product is important for the study of series, e.g. in Dedekind's *Was sind und was sollen die Zahlen?* (1888). For in a series each earlier object is related to each later by a transitive relation, that is to say, by a relation whose powers are all equivalent to itself because it satisfies the condition $t \times_R t = t$. But the part of the theory of relations which can be presented in this way is only a small fragment of the whole, and even for that fragment the style of presentation seems inappropriate. When his earlier suggestions had been worked out in detail by Schröder, Peirce himself came to appreciate this point.

In a paper of 1883, printed as an appendix to *Johns Hopkins Studies in Logic*, he began to use subscript indices with his relational signs to show what terms were supposed to be related by each relation and in what order.[1] Thus the compound sign $l_{ij}$ was to mean that the person called $i$ was a lover of the person called $j$. This notation has very great advantages. If, for example, we want to talk about a man's loving himself, we can do very simply by writing $l_{ii}$, where the occurrence of the same letter in the two index places shows that we have to do with the reflexive, or, as Peirce called it, the self-relative, use of the relational sign. And if we wish to speak, as Peirce sometimes did, of relations with more than two terms, we may construct expressions such as $a_{ijk}$ and $b_{ijkl}$. But the most important use of these indices is that in which they are combined with the $\Sigma$ and $\Pi$ which Peirce introduces in the same article. These quantifiers, as he calls them, are operators with the meanings of 'some' and 'every', and they are intended, of course, to suggest logical addition and logical multiplication over all the objects of a certain range, although, as he explained later, they cannot stand for addition and multiplication in a strict sense if the individuals of the universe are innumerable.[2] With these devices it is possible to give very clear and simple definitions for the notions of relative product and relative sum, namely,

$$(l \times_R m)_{ij} = \Sigma_x (l_{ix} \times m_{xj})$$
and
$$(l +_R m)_{ij} = \Pi_x (l_{ix} + m_{xj}).$$

For the moment this was perhaps the chief service Peirce expected from his new notation, but he wrote of it at greater length

[1] *C.P.* iii, §§ 328–58.  [2] Ibid., § 393.

two years later,[1] and in the course of time he came to see that it could be employed to deal with all sorts of problems which could not be expressed in the language of relative multiplication and relative addition. In 1897 we find him writing of his own algebra of dyadic relatives:

'Professor Schröder attaches, as it seems to me, too high a value to this algebra. That which is in his eyes the greatest recommendation of it is to me scarcely a merit, namely that it enables us to express in the outward guise of an equation propositions whose real meaning is much simpler than that of an equation. Besides the algebra just described, I have invented another which seems to me much more valuable. . . . In this algebra every proposition consists of two parts, its quantifiers and its Boolian. Its Boolian consists of a number of relatives united by non-relative multiplication and aggregation. No relative operators are required (though they can be introduced if desired). Each elementary relative is represented by a letter on the line of writing with subjacent indices to denote the hecceities [i.e. individuals] which fill its blanks. An obelus is drawn over such a relative to deny it. To the left of the Boolian are written the quantifiers. Each of these is a $\Pi$ or a $\Sigma$ with one of the indices written subjacent to it to signify that in the Boolian every object in the universe is to be imagined substituted successively for that index and the non-relative product (if the quantifier is $\Pi$) or the aggregate (if the quantifier is $\Sigma$) of the results taken. Thus

$$\Pi_i \Sigma_j \, l_{ij} = (l_{11} + l_{12} + l_{13} + \text{etc.}) \cdot (l_{21} + l_{22} + l_{23} + \text{etc}) \cdot \text{etc.},$$

will mean everything loves something. But

$$\Sigma_j \Pi_i \, l_{ij} = l_{11} \cdot l_{21} \cdot l_{31} \cdot \text{etc.} + l_{12} \cdot l_{22} \cdot l_{32} \cdot \text{etc.} + \text{etc.}$$

will mean something is loved by all things.'[2]

In his paper of 1883 and his more detailed study of 1885 Peirce gives the credit for these new devices to O. H. Mitchell. This pupil of his had indeed used relational signs with indices and the operators $\Pi$ and $\Sigma$ in his contribution to *Johns Hopkins Studies in Logic*, but not in conjunction or with the senses which Peirce gave to them. What Peirce created was a symbolism adequate for the whole of logic and identical in syntax with the systems now in use. He himself called his invention the General Algebra of Logic;[3] but it is not an algebra in the same sense as Boole's, and recent custom has reserved the title 'algebra of logic' for that part of logical theory which can be presented without the use of quantifiers. This includes all primary logic and a fragment of non-primary logic which is isomorphic with primary logic, namely, the theory of attributes or of classes. When we have to deal with

---

[1] Ibid., §§ 359–403.   [2] Ibid., §§ 498–502.   [3] Ibid., § 499.

propositions which would be expressed in Peirce's final symbolism
by formulae such as $\Pi_i(a_i < b_i)$, we can drop the indices and
quantifiers without ambiguity; but some such devices are essential
for the general theory of relations, and it is a mark of Peirce's
greatness as a logician that he realized this. It is noteworthy
also that he formulated some very important principles for the
use of quantifiers in deduction. He saw, for example, that every
proposition could be expressed in a way which brought all the
quantifiers to the beginning; and he advised that existential
quantifiers should, so far as possible, be brought to the left of
universal quantifiers, thus anticipating in a remarkable way the
advantages of what is now called a Skolem prenex normal form.[1]
We cannot, it is true, give Peirce the credit of being the first to
conceive a comprehensive theory of general logic; for that honour
must go to Frege, who published his *Begriffsschrift* in 1879. But so
far as is known, Peirce had never heard of Frege when he published his paper on *The Logic of Relations* in 1883, and his achievement therefore deserves commemoration.

Because he had been led to his more comprehensive view of
logic by his study of the theory of relations, Peirce attached
special importance to the notion of a relation in his later logical
writings and sometimes tried to enlarge the terminology of his
theory in a slightly paradoxical way. Not content with talking
of *polyadic* relatives, i.e. relative expressions which in his notation
require more than two subscripts, he went on to say that an
attributive expression such as '... is wise' might be called a
*monadic* relative and a complete propositional expression without
blanks a *medadic* relative.[2] For certain purposes this way of talking
may offer the advantage of theoretical simplification, and it has
in fact been adopted for that reason by some later logicians, but
it can scarcely be said to give philosophical illumination. On the
other hand, there is some increase of understanding to be gained
from Peirce's remarks about two different ways in which his
notation of relatives may be connected with older talk of subjects
and predicates:

'In the statement of a relationship, the designations of the correlates
ought to be considered as so many *logical subjects* and the relative itself
as the *predicate*. The entire set of logical subjects may also be considered
as a *collective subject*, of which the statement of relationship is *predicate*.'[3]

Another interesting development of Peirce's theory of relations
was what he called second-intentional logic, i.e. the theory of
notions such as identity and inherence. He introduces it as follows:

    [1] *C.P.* iii, § 505.          [2] Ibid., § 465.          [3] Ibid., § 467.

'Let us now consider the logic of terms taken in collective senses. Our notation, so far as we have developed it, does not show us even how to express that two indices, $i$ and $j$, denote one and the same thing. We may adopt a special token of second intention, say $1$, to express identity, and may write $1_{ij}$. But this relation of identity has peculiar properties. The first is that if $i$ and $j$ are identical, whatever is true of $i$ is true of $j$. This may be written

$$\Pi_i \, \Pi_j \, \{\overline{1}_{ij} + \overline{x}_i + x_j\}.$$

The use of the general index of a token, $x$, here, shows that the formula is iconical. The other property is that if everything which is true of $i$ is true of $j$, then $i$ and $j$ are identical. This is most naturally written as follows: Let the token, $q$, signify the relation of a quality, character, fact, or predicate to its subject. Then the property we desire to express is

$$\Pi_i \, \Pi_j \, \Sigma_k \, (1_{ij} + \overline{q}_{ki} \, q_{kj}).$$

And identity is defined thus

$$1_{ij} = \Pi_k(q_{ki} \, q_{kj} + \overline{q}_{ki} \, \overline{q}_{kj}).$$

That is, to say that things are identical is to say that every predicate is true of both or false of both. It may seem circuitous to introduce the idea of a quality to express identity; but that impression will be modified by reflecting that $q_{ki}q_{kj}$ merely means that $i$ and $j$ are both within the class or collection $k$. If we please, we can dispense with the token $q$, by using the index of a token and by referring to this in the Quantifier just as subjacent indices are referred to. That is to say, we may write

$$1_{ij} = \Pi_x(x_i \, x_j + \overline{x}_i \, \overline{x}_j).\text{'[1]}$$

In this passage the word 'token' does not have the special sense of 'particular utterance' which he gave to it later but means any general symbol of the sort he often calls a relative, while 'index' means any sign whose sole task is to direct our attention to something and 'icon' any sign which represents by picturing.[2] Thus when he says that a certain formula is iconical because it contains the general index of a token, he intends to convey that it gives the pattern of many possible formulae and is therefore, as we should now say, schematic. The letter $q$ which he uses here to signify the relation of a character to a subject or that of a class to a member is obviously a constant sign of great importance. He introduces it in order to allow himself to generalize over the whole range of possible predicates of $i$ and $j$ without departing from the conventions that quantifiers refer only to subjacent indices; but he then goes on to say that we may, if we wish, abandon this convention and allow a quantifier to refer to an index of a token, which is as much as to say in modern terminology

---

[1] C.P. iii, § 398. Cf. C.P. iv, §§ 80–84.    [2] C.P. iii, §§ 361 ff.

that we may employ quantifiers to bind predicate variables. In later chapters we shall have occasion to examine more carefully the implications of Peirce's two ways of generalizing over qualities or classes. For the moment we need only remark that Peirce showed remarkable penetration when he distinguished his new study from the rest of logic by calling it second-intentional. It is a beginning of what we now call the theory of sets.

# VII

## NUMBERS, SETS, AND SERIES

### 1. *Frege and his Contemporaries*

AFTER the work of Boole the next great advance in logic was made by Gottlob Frege (1848–1925). But whereas Boole wished to exhibit logic as part of mathematics, Frege wished to show that arithmetic is identical with logic. On first consideration the two programmes seem to be opposed, and philosophers who are unsympathetic to both have sometimes pointed derisively to the apparent clash. But there is no real inconsistency. When Boole wrote of the mathematical analysis of logic, he meant only the presentation of logic as a calculus similar in certain respects to numerical algebra. Like Leibniz, he thought that the distinctive feature of mathematical science was the construction of calculi and that there might be interesting calculi which could be interpreted without reference to number or quantity. Frege did not wish to deny this. On the contrary, he went much farther than any of his predecessors in his demand for formal rigour within the study of logic, and the deductive system or calculus which he elaborated is the greatest single achievement in the history of the subject. But he tried also to show that numbers can be defined without reference to any notions other than those involved in the interpretation of his calculus as a system of logic. If he was right in this, logic includes arithmetic and with it all those branches of mathematics which can be reduced to arithmetic in the sense that they can be shown to involve only notions already available in arithmetic or logic.

The suggestion that arithmetic is an elaboration of logic had been made by other writers before Frege, as he well knew.[1] But no one had ever shown in detail how logic could be developed into a system which might also be called arithmetic, and Frege realized quite early that the thesis could not be satisfactorily established until two improvements had been made in the presentation of logic. First, the traditional material and the newer contributions of Leibniz and Boole must be organized in such a way as to make clear the structure of the science and the

---

[1] *Die Grundlagen der Arithmetik*, §§ 15–17. This work, which will be cited as *Gl.*, has been translated by J. L. Austin under the title *The Foundations of Arithmetic*.

great variety of the propositional forms to be considered in general logic. Secondly, everything which is required for the proof of the theorems must be set out explicitly at the beginning and the procedure of deduction must be reduced to a small number of standard moves so that there may be no danger of our unconsciously smuggling in what we ought to prove.[1] It was in order to meet these two requirements of system and rigour that Frege in 1879 produced his *Begriffsschrift, eine der arithmetischen nachgebildete Formelsprache des reinen Denkens*. As its name implies, this pamphlet is a manual of ideography or concept-script. In his preface Frege says that the relation of the script to ordinary speech is like that of the microscope to the eye, and claims for it the merits which had been predicted by Leibniz and others in the seventeenth century for a *calculus philosophicus et ratiocinator*. It is one of the tasks of philosophy, he tells us, to break the dominion of the word over the human mind, and his invention has already done something towards this by freeing logic from too close attachment to the grammar of ordinary language. In particular it is to be expected that the ambiguous and confusing terminology of 'subject' and 'predicate' will now give place in logic to a more satisfactory distinction of propositional forms according to the doctrine of functions. By addition of a few extra signs for intuitable relations the new script might be extended to make a geometrical calculus of the kind mathematicians desiderate when they speak of *analysis situs*; but it is his intention to show presently that it is adequate as it stands for the presentation of arithmetic, and the third part of the little book is to be taken as a preliminary communication on this programme.

Unfortunately Frege's epoch-making little book was neglected by mathematicians and philosophers alike. As he remarked later, there was no hope of understanding from the many mathematicians who, whenever they came across logical expressions like 'concept', 'relation', 'judgement', said *Metaphysica sunt, non leguntur*, nor yet from the many philosophers who on seeing a formula said *Mathematica sunt, non leguntur*.[2] In 1884 he therefore produced a book called *Die Grundlagen der Arithmetik* which gave an informal exposition of his views together with criticisms of current ideas about the nature of arithmetic. He did not claim here to have done more than render his thesis probable,[3] and though he was much discouraged by the neglect of his earlier work, he still hoped to produce a rigorous demonstration of the

---

[1] *Gl.*, §§ 90–91.
[2] *Grundgesetze der Arithmetik*, i, p. xii. This work, which has not been translated in full, will be cited as *Gg*.      [3] *Gl.*, § 87.

identity of arithmetic and logic. Somewhere about the end of the decade he returned to this task, and in 1893 there appeared the first volume of his masterpiece, *Die Grundgesetze der Arithmetik*. While working on this he modified his earlier notions of the philosophy of logic in certain respects, and some of his results were published in three important articles, 'Über Funktion und Begriff' (1891),[1] 'Über Begriff und Gegenstand' (1892),[2] 'Über Sinn und Bedeutung' (1892).[3] So far as they are relevant, these novelties are incorporated in his large work, but for a full understanding of his thought it is still necessary to refer back to the original publications. Again the reception of Frege's work was discouraging, and he did not produce the second volume of his *Grundgesetze* until 1903. This is concerned especially with the theory of real numbers, but a good deal of the space is taken up by criticism of current views, and at the end Frege allows that there is more to be done before real numbers can be properly defined. In a *Nachwort*, or appendix, written after most of the work had been printed, he sadly admits the ruin of his work by Bertrand Russell's discovery of a contradiction implicit in his premisses; but he still maintains that his general conception of the relation between arithmetic and logic is correct, and considers methods by which the damage might be repaired.

In the last twenty-two years of his life Frege continued to work at the philosophy of logic and mathematics, but published little, presumably because he could find no satisfactory solution to his problems. Some articles on the foundations of geometry which he published in 1906 show a lack of sympathy, and perhaps even a lack of understanding, for the development of axiomatic method by Hilbert.[4] On the other hand, some comments which he made on Russell's work in 1910,[5] and some papers which he published in later years on epistemological questions, show that his intellect remained vigorous and critical. It is unfortunate, therefore, that his literary executors have not yet given an account of the unpublished material in their keeping.

We shall consider in the next chapter those logical discoveries

[1] *Berichte der Jenaischen Gesellschaft für Medizinische und Naturwissenschaftliche Forschung*, 1891.
[2] *Vierteljahrschrift für wissenschaftliche Philosophie*, xvi (1892), pp. 192–205.
[3] *Zeitschrift für Philosophie und philosophische Kritik*, c (1892), pp. 25–50. These articles have been translated into English by P. Geach and M. Black in *Translations from the Philosophical Writings of Gottlob Frege*. These translations contain the original page numbers, which will be used in later references.
[4] 'Über die Grundlagen der Geometrie', *Jahresbericht des Deutschen Mathematiker Vereins*, xv (1906), pp. 293–309, 377–403, 423–30.
[5] P. E. B. Jourdain, 'The Development of the Theories of Mathematical Logic and the Principles of Mathematics', *The Quarterly Journal of Pure and Applied Mathematics*, xliii (1912), pp. 237–69.

of Frege which are respected even by his philosophical or mathematical opponents. But before entering into details it will be useful to notice here the general outlines of his programme, as he himself expounded it in his most popular work, *Die Grundlagen der Arithmetik*, and to compare it with the views of his distinguished contemporaries, J. W. R. Dedekind (1831–1916), G. Cantor (1845–1918), and G. Peano (1858–1943). Dedekind, who was the oldest and the first to attain fame, published his *Stetigkeit und irrationale Zahlen* as early as 1872, but Cantor was the only one of the group who put forward a 'logical' theory of arithmetic before Frege, and we must therefore start with him.

## 2. *Cantor's Theory of Sets*

The introduction of the theory of real numbers is a momentous step, not only because it involves talk about infinite sets of rational numbers, as we noticed in an earlier chapter, but also because it seems to require recognition of a new kind of infinity. Whereas the rational numbers can be put in one-to-one correspondence with the natural numbers and are therefore said to form a denumerably infinite set, even the sub-set of real numbers contained within an interval such as that from 0 to 1 apparently exemplifies a higher order of infinity. This was first shown by Cantor with his famous diagonal procedure. For simplicity let us think of the real numbers between 0 and 1 as infinite decimals, taking $\frac{1}{4}$ to be $0 \cdot 24\dot{9}$, $\frac{1}{2}$ to be $0 \cdot 4\dot{9}$, &c.; and let us suppose that there is some prescription for arranging them all in an infinite table of the form

$$0 \cdot a_1\, a_2\, a_3\, \ldots$$
$$0 \cdot b_1\, b_2\, b_3\, \ldots$$
$$0 \cdot c_1\, c_2\, c_3\, \ldots$$
$$\cdot \quad \cdot \quad \cdot \quad \cdot \quad \cdot$$

so that it is proper to speak of the first, the second, the third, and so on. Then it is possible to indicate a real number within the interval from 0 to 1 by putting in the first decimal place any digit we like except $a_1$, 0, or 9, in the second place any digit we like except $b_2$, 0, or 9, in the third place any digit we like except $c_3$, 0, or 9, and so on. But this real number cannot be identical with any one of those in the table, because it differs from each of them in at least one of its decimal places. And this is as much as to say that the table does not contain all the real numbers in the interval, or in other words that the totality of real numbers in the interval is not denumerable.

In order to deal with this situation Cantor elaborated between the years 1874 and 1897 a new mathematical discipline called the theory of sets. His work has won passionate admiration from many mathematicians, and equally passionate condemnation from others. Since, as we shall see later, debates about the development of the theory are very closely connected with some important questions about logic, it is necessary to consider here some of the principal ideas which he put into circulation.

According to Cantor's own definition a set (*Menge*) is 'a collection into one whole of definite, distinct objects of our perception or our thought, which are called the elements of the set'.[1] In his earlier papers he sometimes used instead the term 'manifold' (*Mannigfaltigkeit*) and his successors have used the words *Ensemble*, 'totality', 'aggregate', and 'class'. A set is said to contain its elements (or members), and they in turn are said to belong to it. A sub-set of a given set S is one whose elements are all elements of S; and this, in distinction from the elements, may be said to be a part of S. A set may be indicated either by the listing of its elements, e.g. the set {Peter, Paul}, or by the giving of some general description appropriate to all its elements and to nothing else; but in either case sets which have the same elements are to be accounted identical, since according to the definition a set is just a collection of elements. So far Cantor's theory of sets is like Boole's theory of classes, but there are further complications to come.

Two sets S and T are said to be equivalent if there exists a one-to-one correspondence between them, i.e. if there is some relation such that each element of S is correlated by the relation with one and only one element of T and each element of T has one and only one element of S correlated with it by the relation. Thus the set of husbands is equivalent in this technical sense to the set of wives in a monogamous society.

The power (*Mächtigkeit*), or cardinal number, of a set can then be introduced as that which it has in common with all equivalent sets but with no others. According to Cantor it is 'the general concept which with the aid of our active intelligence results from a set when we abstract from the nature of its various elements and from the order of their being given', and it can be represented by the sign '$\overline{\overline{S}}$', in which the two horizontal strokes indicate the double abstraction. If S is finite, $\overline{\overline{S}}$ is some natural number; but the theory is intended to cover also infinite sets, whose powers are certainly not natural numbers, and this extension can be

---

[1] 'Beiträge zur Begründung der transfiniten Mengenlehre', i, *Mathematische Annalen*, xlvi (1895), pp. 481–512, reprinted in *Gesammelte Abhandlungen*, ed. Zermelo, p. 282.

achieved most easily by a new definition of infinity. A set is infinite, we now say, if and only if it can be put in one-to-one correspondence with a proper sub-set (i.e. with a sub-set that is not identical with the set itself). Thus the set of the positive integers, 1, 2, 3, &c., can be put in one-to-one correspondence with the set of the squares of the positive integers, 1, 4, 9, &c., although the square numbers are only some among the positive integers. This definition was first formulated explicitly by Cantor's friend Dedekind in 1888,[1] but in 1885 C. S. Peirce had defined a finite set as one which could not be put in one-to-one correspondence with a proper sub-set,[2] and there are interesting anticipations of the idea to be found in Plutarch,[3] Proclus,[4] Adam of Balsham (who has been mentioned earlier), Galileo,[5] and Bernard Bolzano.[6]

As finite sets may be compared in respect of their cardinal numbers, so too may infinite sets. For any set S has a smaller cardinal number than a set T if S is equivalent to some sub-set of T but not to T itself. Thus N, the set of natural numbers, has a smaller transfinite cardinal number than C, the set of real numbers (sometimes called the continuum), i.e. $\bar{\bar{N}} < \bar{\bar{C}}$, because N is equivalent to a sub-set of C but not to the whole.

Next we define a number of operations by which sets may be constructed out of sets. In each case the sets to which the operation is applied may be either finite or infinite. (1) $S+T$, which is called the logical sum (or union or join) of S and T, contains those things which are elements either of S or of T and nothing else. (2) $ST$, which is called the inner product (or intersection or meet) of S and T, contains those things which are elements both of S and of T and nothing else. These are both Boolean notions, but what follows is new. (3) $S \times T$, which is called the outer (or Cartesian or cross) product of S and T, is that set whose elements are all the possible pairs containing one element from S and one element from T. (4) $S^T$, sometimes called the insertion set of S into T, is the set of all possible arrangements (or single-valued functions) by which elements of S may be assigned to all the various elements of T, when (a) T is not null, (b) it is allowed that one element of S may be assigned to more than one element

---

[1] *Was sind und was sollen die Zahlen*, § 5, 64.
[2] *Collected Papers*, iii, § 402.
[3] *De Communibus Notitiis*, § 38 (= *Moralia* 1079A).
[4] *In Primum Euclidis Elementorum Librum Commentarii*, Def. xvii.
[5] *Discorsi e dimostrazioni matematiche intorno a due nuove scienze*, i (*Opera*, ed. nazionale, vol. viii, p. 78).
[6] *Paradoxien der Unendlichkeit*, § 20. The historical introduction to the English translation of this work by D. A. Steele contains some interesting material, including the references to Plutarch and Proclus given above.

of T, and (c) two arrangements are counted as different if there is at least one element of T to which they assign different elements of S. Thus if T is a set of test-tubes and S a set of chemical substances, $S^T$ is the set of possible ways of inserting the substances into the tubes so that no tube contains more than one substance.

Among sets constituted by insertion into S there is one of special importance called the power set (*Potenzmenge*) of S. This is the set of all sub-sets of S (where among sub-sets of S we include both S itself and the null set), and it is often represented by '$\mathscr{U}$S', in which the letter '$\mathscr{U}$' is taken from the German *Untermenge*. In order to see that $\mathscr{U}$S is in fact a set constituted by insertion into S, we need only reflect that a sub-set of S is determined as soon as it has been decided for each of the elements of S whether or not it should be included in the sub-set under consideration. In short, $\mathscr{U}$S = {in, out}$^S$, where {in, out} is the set of possibilities open for each element of S during the selection of a sub-set.

Now Cantor declares that $\mathscr{U}$S has a higher cardinal number than S, whatever S may be; and this proposition is so important in his theory that it has been distinguished by the name 'Cantor's Theorem'. Obviously S is equivalent to a part of $\mathscr{U}$S, namely to the set of all unit sets whose elements are drawn from S, and it is therefore sufficient for Cantor's purpose to prove that S is not equivalent to the whole of $\mathscr{U}$S. Let us suppose for the sake of argument that S and $\mathscr{U}$S are equivalent. This is as much as to say that there is some scheme of correlation in which the elements of S are correlated one-to-one with the elements of $\mathscr{U}$S. Now the elements of $\mathscr{U}$S are all sub-sets of S, and so we may reasonably ask of any element of S whether or not it is an element of its correlate in this scheme. Let us then consider the set that contains all those and only those elements of S which are not elements of their correlates. This must itself be an element of $\mathscr{U}$S, say u*, and so according to the hypothesis we are investigating it must have correlated with it some element of S, say s*. Is s* an element of u*? If we say 'Yes', we fall into self-contradiction; for according to our definition u* contains only those members of S which are not elements of their correlates. But if we say 'No', we fall likewise into self-contradiction; for according to our definition any element of S not contained in u* must be an element of its correlate. But this is absurd, and so we must reject the supposition that S is equivalent to $\mathscr{U}$S. In short, $\overline{\overline{\mathscr{U}S}} > \overline{\overline{S}}$. The proof is similar in general conception to the proof that real numbers are not denumerable, since it shows the impossibility of a certain proposed correlation of elements by showing that this would permit the definition of an element it could not cover. For that reason the argument is sometimes said to exhibit Cantor's diagonal procedure, though the extra case which it introduces to refute the hypothesis of equivalence is not literally a diagonal sequence.

As their symbols suggest, the operations by which sets may be constituted out of sets are introduced in order to prepare the way for a general arithmetic of cardinal numbers. Thus if S and T are mutually exclusive (or disjoint), $\overline{\overline{S+T}} = \overline{\overline{S}} + \overline{\overline{T}}$ where the second use of '$+$' signifies addition of cardinal numbers. Similarly $\overline{\overline{S \times T}} = \overline{\overline{S}} \times \overline{\overline{T}}$ and $\overline{\overline{S^T}} = \overline{\overline{S}}^{\overline{\overline{T}}}$. So long as we confine our attention to finite sets, the results are in no way surprising. But when we take into account infinite sets, the arithmetic to which the definitions lead is inevitably different in many respects from the arithmetic of natural numbers. We have, for example,

$$\aleph_0 = \aleph_0 + n = n\aleph_0 = \aleph_0{}^n,$$

where $\aleph_0$ is the cardinal number of the set of natural numbers and n is any natural number greater than o. On the other hand $2^{\aleph_0} > \aleph_0$, just as $2^n > n$ for any natural number n; and in general $2^c > c$ for any cardinal c, whether finite or transfinite. This is an immediate corollary of Cantor's Theorem. For $\overline{\overline{\mathcal{U}S}} > \overline{\overline{S}}$ and $\overline{\overline{\mathcal{U}S}} = 2^{\overline{\overline{S}}}$, so that $2^{\overline{\overline{S}}} > \overline{\overline{S}}$, whatever S may be. We have therefore an unending succession of ever greater transfinite cardinals (or alephs), $\aleph_0$, $2^{\aleph_0}$, $2^{2^{\aleph_0}}$, &c. The first of these is by definition the cardinal number of N, the set of all natural numbers, and the second can be shown to be the cardinal number of C, the set (or continuum) of all real numbers, which we considered at the beginning of this section. But it is not known whether $2^{\aleph_0}$ is $\aleph_1$, i.e. the *next* transfinite number after $\aleph_0$. Cantor conjectured that it was, and Gödel has shown that the generalized continuum hypotheses, i.e. the proposition that $2^{\aleph_n} = \aleph_{n+1}$ for any ordinal number n, is at least consistent with some widely accepted axioms of set theory;[1] yet so far no one has proved the impossibility of a set which is equivalent neither to N nor to C but has a sub-set equivalent to N and is itself equivalent to a sub-set of C.

Like all great mathematicians, Cantor thought of his work as the discovery of laws not made by man. He was, he said, only a faithful scribe with no claim to merit except for his style and the economy of his exposition.[2] But his admirers have sometimes talked of his theory of sets as though it were a dream creation like Coleridge's *Kubla Khan*, and his enemies have treated it as a nightmare. That which above all else fascinates or repels is his

---

[1] *The Consistency of the Axiom of Choice of the Generalized Continuum-hypothesis with the Axioms of Set Theory* (*Annals of Mathematics Studies*, no. 3).
[2] *Gesammelte Abhandlungen*, pp. 282, 477, 480.

doctrine of the unending succession of transfinite cardinals; and this, as we have seen, depends on his theorem about power sets. The proof of that theorem is an argument *ad absurdum* constructed by means of Cantor's characteristic diagonal procedure, and it is therefore not surprising that suspicion of the general theory has led some mathematicians to cast doubt on the unrestricted use of arguments *ad absurdum* to prove existence.

### 3. *Frege on his Predecessors*

Frege was one of the few who admired Cantor's work when it first appeared. In his *Grundlagen* he writes:

'It is only recently that infinite Numbers have been introduced in a remarkable work by G. Cantor (*Grundlagen einer allgemeinen Mannichfaltigkeitslehre*, 1883). I heartily share his contempt for the view that in principle only finite Numbers ought to be admitted as actual. Perceptible by the senses these are not, nor are they spatial—any more than fractions are, or negative numbers, or irrational or complex numbers; and if we restrict the actual to what acts on our senses or at least produces effects which may cause sense-perceptions as near or remote consequences, then naturally no number of any of these kinds is actual. But it is also true that we have no need at all to appeal to any such sense-perceptions in proving our theorems. . . . While in this I agree, as I believe, with Cantor, my terminology differs to some extent from his. My Number he calls a "power", while his concept of Number has reference to arrangement in an order. . . . For us, because our concept of Number has from the outset covered infinite numbers as well, no extension of its meaning has been necessary at all.'[1]

And then, after some comments on Cantor's ideas of ordinal numbers, which were not mentioned in the last section, he goes on:

'Nothing in what I have said is intended to question in any way their legitimacy or their fertility. On the contrary, I find special reason to welcome in Cantor's investigations an extension of the frontiers of science, because they have led to the construction of a purely arithmetical route to higher transfinite Numbers (powers).'[2]

These remarks are especially noteworthy because they occur towards the end of a book which contains much hostile criticism of other writers. The objections which Frege has to bring against previous accounts of arithmetic are in fact so many that it would be impossible to summarize them all here. But in order to make clear the direction of his thought and to show why he sided with Cantor we must consider what he has to say against three rival

---

[1] *Gl.*, § 85.   [2] *Gl.*, § 86.

philosophies of arithmetic, namely that of J. S. Mill, that of Kant, and that of the formalists.

Since Greek times it has been accepted almost universally that mathematics is an *a priori* science, that is to say, a science in which all the propositions can be established without appeal to experience for information about particular objects. It was, indeed, reflection on the nature of this study which first led philosophers to conceive the possibility of learning without experience. But in the nineteenth century J. S. Mill went even beyond the empiricism of Hume and tried to maintain that arithmetic rests on inductions from facts about particular groups of things. He allowed that for proof of the equation '$5+2 = 7$' we may rely on the axiom that 'whatever is made up of parts is made up of the parts of those parts' and on the definitions '$7 = 6+1$' and '$6 = 5+1$'; but he said that the axiom, being 'obvious to the senses in all cases which can be fairly referred to their decision and so general as to be coextensive with nature itself', was to be considered 'an inductive truth or law of nature of the highest order'; and he argued that even the definitions involved assertion of physical facts about the existence of collections decomposable in certain ways.[1] Frege therefore thought it necessary to begin his *Grundlagen* by maintaining the *a priori* character of arithmetic.

Against Mill's account of definition Frege points out that, if knowledge of some special physical fact were required for correct use of the definition of each small number, such knowledge would be necessary also for the correct use of the definition of each large number. We could not, for example, put

$$1,000,000 = 999,999+1$$

unless we had observed a collection of a million things split up in precisely that way; and a man who calculated properly with nine-figure numbers would deserve the highest honour for his knowledge of nature.[2] Against the suggestion that general laws of arithmetic are inductive truths he makes the objection that induction itself seems to require some general propositions of arithmetic, since, in that usage in which it is supposed to be a method of science and not a mere process of habituation, it depends on the theory of probability.[3] But his most telling criticism of the whole empiricist theory is that it involves the confusion of supposing the plus sign to refer to physical addition.[4] When we say that $5+2 = 7$, we do not mean that if we pour 2 unit volumes of liquid onto 5 unit volumes of liquid we shall have 7 unit

---

[1] *A System of Logic*, III, xxiv, § 5.       [2] *Gl.*, § 7.
[3] *Gl.*, § 10.       [4] *Gl.*, § 9.

volumes of liquid. For the latter statement is at best an application of the mathematical proposition and holds good only under the proviso that no alteration of volume occurs as a result, say, of some chemical reaction. Other applications of the formula may be to numbers of events, or virtues, or roots of equations, where there can be no question of physical aggregation.

Having disposed of the empiricist theory, Frege goes on to consider whether the laws of arithmetic are synthetic or analytic. The question was raised first by Kant, and Frege regards Kant as the chief exponent of the view that mathematical propositions are synthetic, but he does not accept Kant's account of the distinction between the two kinds of judgement. According to his own account, a truth is analytic if for the proof of it we need refer back only to general logical laws and to definitions, but synthetic if for the proof of it we must use premisses which are not of a general logical nature.[1] Kant came near to suggesting this when he tried to connect the truth of analytic judgements with the principle of non-contradiction,[2] but he unfortunately worked with a conception of logic that was too narrow. When he asked whether the predicate concept was or was not contained in the subject concept of a judgement, he used a criterion that is applicable only to universal affirmative judgements of the Aristotelian scheme. For in singular and in existential judgements there is no subject concept. And he seems to have thought of the definition of a complex concept as a mere list of characters, whereas the really important definitions of mathematics, e.g. that of the continuity of a function, are not of this kind.[3] Here Frege lays his finger on a defect of the traditional logic which had not been noticed even by those among his predecessors whose interests were nearest to his own. Leibniz, for example, had thought of concepts and propositions in the way presupposed by Kant's account of analytic truths; that, as we have seen, was the main reason why he never succeeded in producing a convincing specimen of the great development that he proclaimed in his writings on logic. Boole too had been content to investigate those relatively simple patterns of structure that can be represented by Euler's circles. Frege could more plausibly make large claims for logic precisely because he allowed for much greater complexity of logical form than any of his predecessors had been able to conceive. In his work 'analytic' is to be understood by reference to his own logic, and it is by no means a synonym for Locke's 'trifling'.

[1] Gl., § 3.　　[2] The Critique of Pure Reason, B. 191.
[3] Gl., § 88.

Although Frege criticizes Kant's way of distinguishing between analytic and synthetic truths and rejects his account of arithmetic, he writes towards the end of the *Grundlagen*:

'I have no wish to incur the reproach of picking petty quarrels with a genius to whom we must all look up with grateful awe; I feel bound, therefore, to call attention also to the extent of my agreement with him, which far exceeds any disagreement. To touch only upon what is immediately relevant, I consider Kant did great service in drawing the distinction between synthetic and analytic judgements. In calling the truths of geometry synthetic and *a priori*, he revealed their true nature. And this is still worth repeating, since even to-day it is often not recognized. If Kant was wrong about arithmetic, that does not seriously detract, in my opinion, from the value of his work. His point was that there are such things as synthetic judgements *a priori*; whether they are to be found in geometry only, or in arithmetic as well, is of less importance.'[1]

In an earlier passage he tells us that geometry is indeed founded on intuition, as Kant said, and that its axioms govern everything which is spatially intuitable, including even the wildest visions of delirium and the boldest inventions of poetry:

'Conceptual thought alone can after a fashion shake off their yoke, when it supposes, say, a space of four dimensions or positive curvature. To study such conceptions is not useless by any means; but it is to leave the ground of intuition entirely behind. . . . For purposes of conceptual thought we can always suppose the contrary of some one or other of the geometrical axioms, without involving ourselves in any self-contradictions when we proceed to our deductions, despite the conflict between our suppositions and our intuition. The fact that this is possible shows that the axioms of geometry are independent of one another and of the primitive laws of logic and consequently are synthetic.'[2]

From these explanations it appears that Frege did not wish to deny the possibility of non-Euclidean geometries (in a large sense of the word 'geometry'); and if pressed, he would presumably have said that the assertions made by mathematicians who study such systems are analytic truths, since according to his account of the matter they can be no more than conditional statements guaranteed by their logical form. From this he might have been led on to admit that even Euclidean geometry, considered as a branch of pure mathematics, is analytic. For the truth, if it is a truth, that Euclid's axioms apply necessarily to relations in intuited space is irrelevant to the study of the system of order which they determine. But he followed the old fashion of using

[1] *Gl.*, § 89.      [2] *Gl.*, § 14.

the phrase 'truths of geometry' to cover axioms and theorems as well as statements of their connexion, and this accounts for the distinction of status which he drew between geometry and arithmetic. If anyone claims to know that Euclid's geometrical axioms are necessarily true in the sense in which Euclid intended them to be taken, i.e. as general statements about relations in ordinary space, he commits himself to a doctrine of intuition such as Frege took over from Kant. Conversely, anyone who rejects all talk about intuition as a source of *a priori* knowledge should realize that he is not entitled to retain the old view of *any* of Euclid's axioms. In short, the thesis which interested Frege is not refuted by an alteration of the usage of the word 'geometry'.

It must be admitted, nevertheless, as Frege himself says, that 'we are all too ready to invoke inner intuition when we cannot produce any other ground of knowledge'.[1] And it is difficult to attach any clear sense to what Kant says about intuition in his account of arithmetic. In one of his most explicit pronouncements he asserts that in order to add together the numbers 7 and 5 we must go beyond their concepts 'by calling to our aid the intuition corresponding to one of them, say our five fingers' and concludes, 'Arithmetical judgements are therefore always synthetic, and the more plainly according as we take larger numbers'.[2] But it is surely absurd to maintain that we can establish the truth of the equation

$$135,664 + 37,863 = 173,527$$

by calling to our aid an intuition of 173,527 fingers. Are we then to say that Kant's doctrine applies only to small numbers, in spite of his own explicit statement? But there is no fundamental distinction between small and large numbers. If formulae involving numbers from, say, 10 onwards are provable without intuition, why not those which involve smaller numbers?[3] And again what is this supposed intuition corresponding to a number? Arithmetic is not about fingers as geometry may be said to be about points, lines, and planes; and there is no intuition that can guarantee the applicability of arithmetical truths to everything numerable. Furthermore, if any truths of arithmetic were derivable only from intuition, they would presumably be independent of one another and of laws of logic, just as the axioms of Euclid have been found to be. But if we try denying any of the fundamental propositions of the science of number, the result is not an alternative system of arithmetic but complete confusion.[4]

---

[1] *Gl.*, § 12.  [2] *Prolegomena to any Future Metaphysic*, § 2.
[3] *Gl.*, § 5.  [4] *Gl.*, § 14.

From these considerations Frege draws the conclusion that the basis of arithmetic must lie deeper than that of any of the empirical sciences and deeper even than that of geometry as he conceives it. The domain of the numerable is the widest domain of all; for it is not confined to the intuitable, nor even to the existent, but includes everything thinkable. Is it not reasonable then to suppose that the laws of number may be connected very intimately with the laws of thought? When Frege asks this question, he certainly does not wish to suggest that arithmetic is a branch of psychology. For again and again he insists that logic, and with it arithmetic, which he wishes to exhibit as a development of logic, is completely independent of psychology. In the Preface to his *Grundlagen,* for example, he lays it down as the first guiding principle of his work that the logical should always be kept separate from the psychological. And in the Preface to his *Grundgesetze* he attacks explicitly all attempts to present the laws of thought as psychological generalizations, saying that he hopes his work will help to free logic from the infection which seems to have contaminated all the recent books on the subject. What he suggests by the question quoted above he expresses also in another place by saying that the laws of arithmetic are not laws of nature, but laws of the laws of nature, i.e. fundamental principles about the thinkable.[1]

Frege's thesis, then, is that truths of arithmetic are analytic because we require for their proof only laws of logic and definitions. But there were many mathematicians in his day who might have accepted this dictum and yet defended a theory of arithmetic which Frege rejected. The point at issue between them concerned the nature of definition in mathematics, and Frege evidently regarded it as of the utmost importance; for the space that he devotes to it in his *Grundlagen* and his *Grundgesetze* is more than he gives to the criticism of all other theories of mathematics.

When mathematicians of the nineteenth century surveyed the progress of their science since the Renaissance, they sometimes had the impression that the novelties were products of human construction rather than discoveries. As their name implies, imaginary numbers were conceived in this way from an early date; but presently it occurred to some mathematicians that all higher types of numbers, and even the natural numbers themselves, might be regarded in the same fashion. This view appealed to the positivist, or anti-metaphysical, temper of the age. In his *Theorie der complexen Zahlensysteme* of 1867 Hankel wrote:

[1] *Gl.,* § 87.

'Number to-day is no longer a thing, a substance, existing in its own right apart from the thinking subject and the objects which give rise to it, a self-subsistent element in the sort of way it was for the Pythagoreans. The question whether some number exists can therefore only be understood as referring to the thinking subject or to the objects thought about, relations between which the numbers represent. As impossible in the strict sense the mathematician counts only what is logically impossible, that is, self-contradictory. That numbers which are impossible in this sense cannot be admitted, needs no proof. But if the numbers concerned are logically possible, if their concept is clearly and fully defined and therefore free from contradiction, then the question whether they exist can amount only to this : Does there exist in reality or in the actual world given to us in intuition a sub-stratum for these numbers, do there exist objects in which they— that is, intelligible relations of the type defined—can become phenomenal?'[1]

The expression of this passage is not very clear, but the sense seems to be that in pure as opposed to applied mathematics questions about existence are out of place because the whole subject is a free construction of the human mind, subject only to the restrictions of logic.

Against such teaching Frege maintains that it is absurd to talk of creative definition :

'We might just as well say this : among numbers hitherto known there is none which satisfies the simultaneous equations

$$x + 1 = 2$$
$$x + 2 = 1,$$

but there is nothing to prevent us from introducing a symbol which solves the problem. Ah, but there is, it will be replied : to satisfy both the equations simultaneously involves a contradiction. Certainly, if we are requiring a real number or an ordinary complex number to satisfy them; but then all we have to do is to widen our number system, to create numbers which do meet these new requirements. Then we can wait and see whether anyone succeeds in producing a contradiction in them. Who can tell what may not be possible with our new numbers? . . . And why not create still further numbers which permit the summation of diverging series? But that will do,—even the mathematician cannot create things at will, any more than the geographer can; he too can only discover what is there and give it a name.'[2]

The source of the illusion is to be found in the history of mathematics. When they were already familiar with the operation of subtracting 2 from 3, mathematicians began to talk of the

---

[1] Pp. 6–7, quoted by Frege in *Gl.*, § 92.  [2] *Gl.*, § 96.

operation of subtracting 3 from 2, and introduced the symbol '−1' for the result of this operation. And again later, when they were already familar with the notion of the square root of a positive real number, they began to talk of the square root of a negative number, and introduced the symbol 'i' as an abbreviation for '√−1'. In each case it seemed that the scope of mathematics had been widened by the postulation of something not given before, and there was a temptation to say that new numbers had been created by the rearrangement of old signs. But this way of talking involves a serious mistake about definitions. Anyone who thinks he has fully explained his use of the symbol 'i' by writing 'i = √−1' must assume a meaning for the sign '√', and yet there was nothing in the original explanation of the use of this sign to justify its use in the new context. If, however, we say that the creative definition of imaginary numbers involves also enlargement of the definition of '√', we reduce everything to uncertainty. For this doctrine of the piecemeal definition of the mathematical signs implies that the square-root sign was not fully defined in its earlier uses. And 'so long as it is not completely defined, or known in some other way, what a word stands for, the word may not be used in an exact science—least of all with a view to further development of its own definition'.[1]

It is easy to understand why mathematicians have retained such symbols as '+' and '−' throughout the development of mathematics, while giving them different senses at the successive stages. For each lower calculus is in a sense reproduced in each higher calculus. But the practice has led to some confusion, and in his *Grundgesetze* Frege argues that we should do well to avoid it, at least for philosophical purposes.

'Instead of first defining a symbol for a limited domain and then using it for the purpose of defining itself in regard to a wider domain, we need only choose different signs, confining the reference of the first, once for all, to the narrower domain; in this way the first definition is now complete and draws sharp boundary lines. This in no way prejudges the relation between the reference of one sign and that of another; we can investigate this, without its being possible that the result of the investigation should make it questionable whether the definitions were justified. It really is worth the trouble to invent a new symbol if we can thus remove not a few logical difficulties and ensure the rigour of the proofs. But many mathematicians seem to have so little feeling for logical purity and accuracy that they will use a word to stand for three or four different things, sooner than make the frightful decision to invent a new word.'[2]

---

[1] *Gg.* ii, § 57.  [2] *Gg.* ii, § 60.

Again those who talk of creative definition reveal the confusion of their thought when they say that we must be careful to avoid self-contradiction while introducing novelties. They are obviously on the side of the angels in their desire to avoid inconsistency, but how do they propose to prove the consistency of their constructions? 'Strictly, of course, we can only establish that a concept is free from contradiction by first producing something that falls under it. The converse inference is a fallacy.'[1] And if we are in a position to indicate something that falls under a concept, it is obviously absurd to talk as though our definition of the concept were a creation. In practice, however, the mathematicians who use such language merely assume consistency because they have not hitherto found any inconsistency, and then go on to assume also the existence of examples. Sometimes indeed they try to justify the fallacy by saying that in mathematics 'existence' just means the same as 'consistency'; but if Frege is right, this defence is an aggravation of their fault, because it implies that consistency can never be proved at all.

According to his view each numerical calculus deals with a certain set of objects, not of course physical objects such as stones, nor yet psychical objects such as feelings, but nevertheless objects independent of all language. And when he speaks of the definition of a concept in mathematics, he means nothing like the constructive activity assumed by his opponents, but simply the delimitation of the field of application of a general term by means of an equivalence. Thus complex numbers may be defined as ordered pairs of real numbers, and operations on complex numbers may be defined by reference to operations on the real numbers in such pairs. That we use certain sounds or shapes as defined terms is obviously arbitrary, but there is nothing arbitrary about the truths which we enunciate by means of them after we have defined them. For it is possible in principle to eliminate all terms which have been defined explicitly. In the practice of mathematical thinking we need them only because we should find it difficult to focus our attention properly without them. They are, so to say, instruments of selection. In the philosophy of mathematics, on the other hand, we are especially interested in definitions precisely because the setting forth of a satisfactory chain of definitions shows the possibility of eliminating all the defined terms. That which is valuable from one point of view as a licence to abbreviate is valuable also from another point of view as an elucidation. Furthermore, it is Frege's view that when a satisfactory chain of definitions has been set forth

[1] *Gl.*, § 95.

it will be clear that the only undefined notions required for the presentation of arithmetic are notions of formal logic. In particular he wishes to show that talk about natural numbers can be reduced to talk about sets, classes, or manifolds, which in the terminology of logicians are the extensions of concepts, and he says explicitly that the objects of arithmetic are logical objects.[1]

If it is allowed that mathematical symbols have meanings and that mathematical formulae are used to make statements, Frege's attack on the theory of creative definition cannot be resisted, though his attempt to reduce mathematics to logic may still be questioned. But the suggestion that mathematical novelties are creations rather than discoveries has often been coupled with a rejection of the view that mathematicians as such make statements about any objects whatsoever, and Frege therefore devotes much space to proving that mathematics cannot properly be considered as a game with meaningless marks. Naturally no one ever denied that the application of arithmetic involved assignment of meanings to the arithmetical symbols, but mathematicians who call themselves formalists have tried to maintain that in pure mathematics there is no need to go beyond the symbols and their rules of combination, that is to say, beyond material over which we ourselves have complete control. At the beginning of his *Elementare Theorie der analytischen Functionen eines complexen Veränderlichen*, published in 1898, J. Thomae expressed the view as follows:

'The formal conception of arithmetic accepts more modest limitations than does the logical conception. It does not ask what numbers are and what they do, but rather what is demanded of them in arithmetic. For the formalist, arithmetic is a game with signs, which are called empty. That means they have no other content (in the calculating game) than they are assigned by their behaviour with respect to certain rules of combination (rules of the game). The chess player makes similar use of his pieces; he assigns them certain properties determining their behaviour in the game, and the pieces are only the external signs of this behaviour. To be sure, there is an important difference between arithmetic and chess. The rules of chess are arbitrary, the system of rules for arithmetic is such that by means of simple axioms the numbers can be referred to perceptual manifolds and can thus make important contribution to our knowledge of nature. . . . The formal standpoint rids us of all metaphysical difficulties; this is the advantage it affords us.'[2]

In the second volume of his *Grundgesetze*, published in 1903, Frege argues against this new enemy in detail, maintaining that it is impossible to present the arithmetic we know without assuming references for its signs.[3]

[1] *Gg*. ii, § 147.          [2] *Gg*. ii, §§ 88–89.          [3] *Gg*. ii, §§ 86–137.

In the first place, he points out that formulae which are merely combinations of meaningless marks cannot properly be said to have any applications. There would be no sense in talking of the application of chess unless we had *already* assigned a representative function to the pieces and their moves, e.g. by deciding that the movement of a pawn in a game was to represent the advance of a scouting patrol in a battle between armies. Now if, as the formalists seem to admit, it is the possibility of application which distinguishes mathematical thinking from the playing of games and entitles us to call it pursuit of knowledge, when does the assignment of meanings occur? It is presupposed in applied mathematics, and yet apparently it has no place in pure mathematics. Frege does not deny that it might be possible to carry out all the moves required for the derivation of a formula in his own deductive system without thinking of the meanings of the signs; but he says that, so far from producing a great simplification, such refusal to interpret the signs would make the problem harder. Since the interest of mathematical formulae lies in the possibility of applying them, let us be frank with ourselves and admit that our rules of calculation are not chosen arbitrarily but depend on the meanings we have assigned to our symbols. If a game were devised for playing on paper with meaningless marks according to arbitrary rules, it would certainly not be called a branch of mathematics.

Secondly, Frege draws attention to the fact that at certain critical points formalists unconsciously smuggle in meanings for marks that were supposed to be meaningless. The most interesting example of such self-deception in Thomae's work is a passage where he says that the rules for his calculating game are contained in a set of seven formulae such as 'a+b = b+a' and 'a+(b+c) = (a+b)+c'. From what he does later, however, it appears that these formulae are also to be taken as initial dispositions in the calculating game, i.e. something like the arrangement of the pieces on the board at the beginning of a game of chess. But how can a rule be given by an arrangement of meaningless marks? It would be thought very odd if anyone pointed to an arrangement of pieces on a chess-board and said that it was one of the rules of the game of chess. Obviously Thomae intends us to understand that any combination of marks which appears on one side of an identity sign in one of his formulae may be substituted for the combination of signs which appears on the other side of the same identity sign, or rather something more complicated, namely, that every combination of marks which occurs on one side of an identity sign in a formula that is structurally, though not perhaps alphabetically, similar to any of his seven may be substituted for the combination which appears on the other side of the same identity sign. In short, the identity sign, as he uses it here, expresses the equivalence of certain things for the purposes of his game, and the letters are variables which express generality. For a proper understanding of the situation we must distinguish between the game and the theory of the game. Whereas the former may be only a manipulation of meaningless marks, the latter, which deals with the rules and their consequences, cannot be formulated without meaningful signs. Indeed it involves arithmetic of the ordinary kind, and Thomae himself seems to admit as much in a curious passage where he says that his numerals sometimes 'have more than a mere formal reference even within pure arithmetic, e.g. in the sentence "this equation is of degree three" '. Now all Thomae's *theorems* and their proofs must belong to the theory of his calculating game, not to the game itself. Why then does he think that he has escaped from the restrictions of ordinary meaningful arithmetic?

Thirdly, Frege shows with many examples that the formalists persistently confuse numbers with numerals. Some of them explicitly identify numbers with sensible signs, and others give the same impression without committing themselves to a clear declaration. In mathematical texts we often find the authors writing as though there were no difference between 's is the smallest root of the equation' and 's designates the smallest root of the equation'. Such failure to distinguish between the *use* and the *mention* of a symbol may be harmless enough in many contexts, but in a discussion of the foundations of mathematics, and particularly in an exposition of formalist doctrine, it is extremely dangerous. For it encourages formalists to think that they can say about numerals what is significant only in reference to numbers. Thus Thomae writes about numbers at one moment as though they were marks on paper and at another moment as though they formed an infinite sequence in order of magnitude. Numbers do indeed form an infinite sequence, and this is essential for the development of arithmetic, e.g. for the theory of irrationals. But the set of particular numerals written or printed on paper is, and always will be, finite. It may be added that, if a formalist tried to answer Frege by saying that he was not thinking of what Peirce would call token numerals, but rather of what Peirce would call type numerals (e.g. of '2' in the sense in which '2' can be written or printed many times),[1] he would not improve his case. For while we may say that there are infinitely many numerals in this

---

[1] C. S. Peirce, *Collected Papers*, iv, § 537.

sense, our warrant for the assertion is our understanding of the infinity of the sequence of natural *numbers*. Given any type numeral we can conceive a successor constructed by means of the suffix '+1', but only because there is no limit to the theoretically possible number of such suffixes.

Fourthly, Frege shows that the rules given by Thomae are quite inadequate for his purpose of reproducing arithmetic without reference to the meanings of its signs. The seven formulae mentioned above are supposed to cover all numerals alike, and suitably interpreted they are unobjectionable as general rules, but they provide no clue to the distinctive features of the several numerals. It is as though a writer on chess gave some rules applicable to all pieces alike but omitted mention of the existence of pawns, bishops, and the rest. True, Thomae remarks on some peculiarities of the number 0, but what he has to say is very curious reading in an exposition of formalism. According to him, we must exclude combinations of marks such as '2/0', because division by zero cannot be 'performed uniquely (i.e. consistently)' and 'a quotient whose denominator is 0 has no meaning'. If manipulations of marks in which '0' is allowed to appear on the right of a division sign lead to results such as '1 = 2', why should this worry a formalist? And what special objection can there be to the combination '2/0' in a system where all the combinations of marks are meaningless? For Thomae the only proper course is to introduce a new rule which expressly forbids the placing of the mark '0' after (or under) a line. But even this is not enough. If he wishes to make his system resemble ordinary meaningful arithmetic in its external features, he must exclude also such combinations as '2/(3−3)' and '2/(2+1−3)', in short every combination in which there appears after a solidus a set of marks that can be replaced by the single mark '0'. Clearly he cannot exclude them all separately, and yet he has given no criterion for recognizing what sets of marks can be replaced by '0' in his system.

The criticisms are fatal to Thomae's philosophy of arithmetic, but we shall see later that a stronger case than his can be made for some kind of formalism. In accordance with our plan we must now go on to consider Frege's own doctrine.

## 4. *Frege's Definitions of the Natural Numbers*

Frege accepts the view of Leibniz, Mill, and others that all the natural numbers greater than 1 are to be defined by reference to their predecessors, i.e. by equations such as '2 = 1 + 1', '3 = 2+1', &c. But he remarks that these definitions remain

incomplete so long as the number 1 and the notion of increase by
1 are themselves undefined, and he draws attention also to the
fact that general propositions are needed for the full development
of arithmetic.[1] In order to gain a deeper understanding of the
subject he therefore decides to investigate the general concept of a
natural number. It would take too long to notice all the confusions
about this which he finds in the works of predecessors, including
even those of great mathematicians from Euclid to Cantor, but he
himself has summarized the results of his historical review in the
following passage:

'Number is not abstracted from things in the way that colour,
weight, and hardness are, nor is it a property of things in the sense that
they are. But when we make a statement of number, what is that of
which we assert something? This question remained unanswered. . . .
Number is not anything physical, but nor is it anything subjective (an
idea). Number does not result from the annexing of thing to thing. . . .
The word "one", as the proper name of an object of mathematical
study, does not admit of a plural. Consequently, it is nonsense to make
numbers result from the putting together of ones. The plus symbol in
$1 + 1 = 2$ cannot mean such a putting together.'[2]

The answer to the outstanding question is revealed in the next
section, where Frege says that numbers are properly assigned to
concepts, not to objects:

'This is perhaps clearest with the number 0. If I say "Venus has
0 moons", there simply does not exist any moon or agglomeration
of moons for anything to be asserted of; but what happens is that a
property is assigned to the *concept* "moon of Venus", namely that of
including nothing under it. If I say "the King's carriage is drawn by
four horses", then I assign the number four to the concept "horse that
draws the King's carriage".'[3]

For an understanding of this it must be remembered that in
Frege's terminology a concept is something signified by a general
word or phrase such as we might use in the predicate position of
a statement, whereas an object is something that can be named
by a proper name and said to fall under a concept or to have a
concept as a property. The opposition is not that between mental
and material, nor yet that between ideal and real, but more like
that between universal and individual; and yet it does not correspond exactly to the last of these traditional antitheses, because

---

[1] *Gl.*, § 18.                                                    [2] *Gl.*, § 45.
[3] *Gl.*, § 46. When Frege wrote 'the concept "moon of Venus" ', he meant presumably to refer to the concept expressed by the words 'moon of Venus'; for he
certainly did not think that the concept was a set of words.

the phrase 'moon of Venus' could scarcely be said to signify a universal.

There is an appearance of circularity in a definition according to which the number o belongs to a concept if no objects fall under the concept. For the word 'no' seems to be only a variant of the numeral 'o'. But we can avoid this objection by saying 'The number o belongs to the concept F if, for every x, x does not fall under F'. In similar style we can say also that the number $n+1$ belongs to the concept F if there is an object x falling under F and such that the number n belongs to the concept 'falling under F but not identical with x'. With this apparatus it is obviously possible to explain in the way suggested by Leibniz what it means to say that 1, 2, 3, or any other definite number belongs to a concept. But Frege is still not satisfied. It is an illusion, he tells us, to suppose that we have defined the numbers in this way. In reality we have only fixed the sense of such expressions as 'the number o belongs to ...' and 'the number 1 belongs to ...'. As yet we have no authority 'to pick out o and 1 as self-subsistent objects that can be recognized again'. But to do so, he thinks, is essential for arithmetic, since the numerals are used there as nouns. Admittedly the numerals occur in ordinary speech as adjectives. But 'Jupiter has four moons' can be replaced by 'the number of Jupiter's moons is four', where 'four' is a noun and 'is' has the sense of an identity sign; and the second expression is better articulated than the first. For although the adjective 'four' is said by the grammarians to agree with the plural noun 'moons', the moons are not severally four. There is indeed no property signified by the word 'four' which anything, whether an individual or a collection, may be said to possess. A number is not a concept but an object.

Frege is undoubtedly in the right when he maintains that we can think of objects which are neither sensible nor imaginable. But is he right when he says that numbers are objects in his special sense, i.e. not concepts? We must allow that numerical adjectives do not behave like ordinary attributive phrases: although it is correct to say that Jupiter has four moons, it is absurd to say that each of these moons is four, and also strange at the very least to say that the set of them is four. Furthermore, when the word 'four' is used as a noun, e.g. in the statement 'four is an even number', it seems to behave, as Frege says, like a proper name. It would be silly to say that the roots of two equations were both fours, though we can speak of fours in the plural when the context shows that we are talking of numerals as distinct from numbers. On the other hand, there are some definite nouns of multitude, such as 'pair' and 'dozen', which must be classed among common nouns, since they can be used in the plural; and these may appear as predicates for sets. It is quite sensible to say that the group of Jesus's disciples was a dozen. Whether we express numerical propositions by this device or in one of the other ways mentioned above seems to be a matter of linguistic accident. In Latin *mille* is an adjective but *milia* is a noun, and in English 'hundred' is still a noun though 'a hundred and one' is a complex adjective. Why then should we not identify numbers with pairhood, dozenhood, &c., or, to use Frege's terminology, with the concepts 'pair', 'dozen', &c.? This suggestion seems to be what Cantor had in mind when he talked of *Mächtigkeiten*, and it has the great merit of simplicity. Everyone must admit that there are sets of various sizes, and according to the proposed definition a number would be just the common character of all sets of the same size. Or, if it is thought better to say, as Frege does, that numbers belong to concepts, why should we not identify numbers with second-level concepts such as that of having a pair of instances?

Frege's reason for rejecting such a view is inadequate. He writes:

'In the proposition "the number o belongs to the concept F", o is only an element in the predicate (taking the concept F to be the real subject). For this reason I have avoided calling a number such as o or 1 or 2 a *property* of a concept. Precisely because it forms only an element in what is asserted, the individual number shows itself for what it is, a self-subsistent object. I have already drawn attention to the fact that we speak of 'the number 1', where the definite article serves to class it as an object. In arithmetic this self-subsistence comes out at every turn, as for example in the identity $1 + 1 = 2$.'[1]

When he says that o is only an element of the predicate, he seems to imply that if o were a property of the concept F it would be possible to say 'the concept F is o'. But this is a mistake. If o is indeed a concept, then to say 'o belongs to the concept F' is a perfectly proper way of saying that o is a property of the concept F. For according to this view 'o' is just an abbreviation for 'the concept of having no instances', and in certain contexts Frege allows himself to talk as though he recognized such a concept. He says, for example:

'By properties which are asserted of a concept I naturally do not mean the characteristics which make up the concept. These latter are properties of the things which fall under the concept, not of the concept.

[1] *Gl.*, § 57.

Thus "rectangular" is not a property of the concept "rectangular triangle"; but the proposition that there exists no rectangular equilateral rectilinear triangle does express a property of the concept "rectangular equilateral rectilinear triangle"; it assigns to it the number nought. In this respect existence is analogous to number. Affirmation of existence is in fact nothing but denial of the number nought. Because existence is a property of concepts the ontological argument for the existence of God breaks down.'[1]

Since the existence of which he speaks here is not, strictly speaking, the existence of concepts, but the existence of objects falling under them, the property of concepts with which he identifies it must be that of having an instance or instances. It is probable, therefore, that when Frege refused to regard numbers as second-level concepts he was moved chiefly by the thought that numbers have a self-subsistence which is impossible for concepts. If so, he was misled by one of his own doctrines about concepts which we shall have to examine later. But we must in any case go on to consider the nature of the objects with which he tries to identify the natural numbers.

In the introduction to his *Grundlagen* Frege had laid it down as the second of his three guiding principles that the meaning of a word was never to be sought in isolation but only in the context of a significant utterance. Following this principle, he now undertakes to obtain a definition of natural numbers in general by first fixing the sense of a numerical identity. If numbers are self-subsistent objects, but not perceptible, it is obviously of the greatest importance to make clear how we can recognize them, which is as much as to say, how we can establish numerical identities. The procedure suggested is rather like that of defining the direction of a line by first defining identity of direction, or parallelism, and then abstracting the notion of direction. Frege's main task, it seems, is to explain the sense of 'The number which belongs to the concept F is the same as the number which belongs to the concept G' without making use of such expressions as 'the number which belongs to the concept F'; and this he proposes to do by means of the notion of one-to-one correlation. The suggestion that identity of numbers could be defined in this way was at least as old as Hume,[2] but when Frege wrote it had recently become fashionable among mathematicians, as he himself remarked.[3] Cantor in particular had used it in his *Grundlagen einer allgemeinen Mannichfaltigkeitslehre* of 1883, and Frege, as we have seen, admired Cantor's work, though he sometimes found occasion to charge him, with other mathematicians, of talking loosely about 'ideal constructions'.

Now the objects falling under two concepts F and G may be said to be correlated with each other by the relation $\phi$ if (i) every object falling under the concept F stands in the relation $\phi$ to an object falling under the concept G, and (ii) for every object falling under the concept G there is an object falling under the concept F which stands to it in the relation $\phi$. And it may be understood that these conditions are satisfied vacuously when no objects fall under either of the concepts. In order to make such correlation one-to-one (*beiderseits eindeutig*) we must add two further conditions: (iii) that for all x, y, and z, if x stands in the relation $\phi$ to y and also to z, then y and z are the same; and (iv) that, for any x, y, and z, if x and y both stand in the relation $\phi$ to z, then x and y are the same. It will be noted that all four conditions are expressed in the terminology of formal logic (if that is allowed to include 'same'), and that one-to-one correlation can be explained in this fashion without use of the word 'one'.

On this basis Frege builds a structure of three definitions:

(1) 'The concept F is like-numbered (*gleichzahlig*) with the concept G' is to mean the same as 'there exists a relation $\phi$ which correlates the objects falling under the concept F one-to-one with the objects falling under the concept G'.

(2) The number which belongs to the concept F is the extension of the concept 'like-numbered with the concept F'.

(3) 'n is a number' is to mean the same as 'there exists a concept such that n is the number which belongs to it'.[1]

In (1) the artificial word 'like-numbered' is intended, of course, to suggest identity of the numbers belonging to the concepts to which it is applied, but the meaning of the phrase 'number belonging to the concept' is not fixed until we come to (2), and so for the purposes of strict theory 'like-numbered' is to be taken as a unitary expression with just the sense given to it by (1), i.e. concepts are to be called like-numbered if their extensions are equivalent according to the technical phraseology of the theory of sets. In (2) likewise the phrase 'the number which belongs to the concept F' is intended to suggest the ordinary use of the word 'number', but there is no circularity involved in the use of the phrase before the word 'number' is defined in (3). For in the strict theory (2) is merely an explanation of the usage of the whole phrase 'the number which belongs to the concept F', and it is not until we reach (3) that we have a rule for talking about a

[1] *Gl.*, § 72.

number without mention of this or that concept to which it
belongs.

This system of definitions is a very remarkable achievement of
philosophical ingenuity, and it is easy to see why Frege thought
he had at least made it probable that arithmetic could be reduced
to logic. But we must ask whether the definitions provide a satisfactory account of the natural numbers, and for this purpose
we must consider each in turn.

If at the first step Frege were merely stipulating that the expression 'like-numbered' might be used as a substitute for a longer
expression about one-to-one correspondence, there could, of
course, be no objection. But it is clear from his preliminary
explanation that he thinks his definition gives a correct analysis
of the sense which anyone would attach to the compound adjective if he met it without a special stipulation. That is the point of
Frege's statement that he intends to obtain the concept of number
by first finding the sense of a numerical identity. Now when it is
considered as an elucidation of ordinary usage, definition (1) involves a difficulty. For while it is obvious that any two concepts
whose instances are correlated in the way described must be like-
numbered in the sense that each has just as many instances as
the other, it is not so obvious that there must be such a correlation
between the instances of concepts which are like-numbered in
that sense.

Let us consider an example supplied by Frege. He says correctly:

'If a waiter wishes to be certain of laying exactly as many knives
on a table as plates, he has no need to count either of them; all he has
to do is to lay immediately to the right of every plate a knife, taking
care that every knife on the table lies immediately to the right of a
plate.'[1]

But his argument proves only that one-to-one correlation is a
sufficient condition of numerical identity, not that it is also a
necessary condition. Perhaps we may go farther than Frege does
in expounding his example, and say that two concepts cannot
be *proved* to be like-numbered unless there is a one-to-one correlation between their instances. For when we count the objects
falling under each concept, we establish such a correlation by
our assignments of ordinal numbers; and when in some special
case we are able to recognize a numerical identity without
counting, because the members of one set of things are arranged

---

[1] *Gl.*, § 70.

in the same pattern as the members of another, like the signs on playing cards of equal value, the important consideration is that each member of one set is related to one and only one member of the other set by the relation of similarity of position within the pattern. But even so there is no patent absurdity in the suggestion that the number of knives on a table might be the same as the number of plates though the knives were not correlated one-to-one with the plates in the waiter's way or by any other method such as the drawing of lines. According to Frege's doctrine the fact, if it is a fact, that the number of knives is the same as the number of plates requires the existence of *some* relation by which the knives are correlated one-to-one with the plates; and yet it seems that correlation of any special kind we choose to mention could be lacking without any alteration of the numbers.

If the number of knives is the same as the number of plates, it is certainly *possible* that the knives should be correlated one-to-one with the plates, whereas there can be no such correlation between the objects falling under concepts which are not like-numbered. And there, no doubt, is a reason why the difficulty of Frege's definition has been overlooked by many mathematicians. For the notion of one-to-one correlation first gained serious attention in connexion with Cantor's theory of transfinite numbers, and the only sets which can be cited as plausible illustrations of that theory are from within mathematics itself, that is to say, from a realm where we do not commonly distinguish between possibility and fact. Thus, for example, it is of no importance whether we say that the rational numbers *can be* correlated one-to-one with natural numbers or that they *are* so correlated by a functional relation. Outside pure mathematics the situation is very different; and yet, if Frege is right, from the mere fact that the number of knives on a table is the same as the number of plates it follows that there is some relation by which the knives *are* correlated one-to-one with the plates and will always be so correlated, whatever may happen, provided only that their number is not changed. How can this be explained?

If indiscernibles are identical, as Leibniz asserted, the various objects falling under a concept must have distinguishing attributes. Let us suppose that the objects falling under the concept F are distinguishable by the attributes $F_1$, $F_2$, and $F_3$, each of which entails F, and that the objects falling under G are likewise distinguishable by the attributes $G_1$, $G_2$, and $G_3$, each of which entails G. Further, let us agree to say that x has the relation R to y if, and only if, x and y satisfy the condition expressed by the complex formula:

(x has $F_1$ and y has $G_1$) or (x has $F_2$ and y has $G_2$)
$$\text{or (x has } F_3 \text{ and y has } G_3).$$

Then the objects falling under F are correlated by this relation one-to-one with the objects falling under G. That is to say, according to the explanation given above, every object falling under F has R to one and only one object falling under G, while for every object falling under G there is one and only one object falling under F which has R to it. For simplicity we have used the same numerical subscripts to indicate the distinguishing attributes under the two concepts and have then paired attributes with the same subscript when composing the long expression by which we define R, but there is nothing essential in this use of numerals. The distinguishing attributes under each concept may be indicated in any convenient way and paired as we please with attributes under the other concept, provided each distinguishing attribute appears in one and only one of the conjunctions we take for our alternatives. It is essential to the argument, however, that the only extra-logical signs contained in the definition are expressions for the distinguishing attributes of the objects which fall under the two concepts F and G. If anyone objects that what we have defined is not what men ordinarily call a relation, we may agree, but we must insist that this is the only kind of relation which suffices in all circumstances for one-to-one correlation between the objects falling under like-numbered concepts.

It may perhaps be thought that a suitable co-ordinating relation can always be defined more simply and without assumption of Leibniz's principle of the identity of indiscernibles by some such formula as:

(x = A and y = K) or (x = B and y = L)
$$\text{or (x = C and y = M),}$$

where 'A', 'B', and 'C' are supposed to be proper names of the objects falling under F and 'K', 'L', and 'M' proper names of the objects falling under G. But there are two mistakes in this objection. In the first place, our aim is not just to define relations for the co-ordination of classes whose members happen to have been named. We wish rather to indicate kinds of relations which suffice for the co-ordination of classes even though their members have not been named and perhaps never will be. Without Leibniz's principle there can be no assurance of the existence of such relations. Secondly, even when the objects falling under a concept all have proper names, it is clear that they must be distinguishable in some way without names, since otherwise they could not have been named. And so even for this special case our assumption of Leibniz's principle is not superfluous.

At stage (2) in his systematic construction Frege undertakes to define the number which belongs to the concept F, and he says that it is the extension of the concept 'like-numbered with the concept F'. Since the expression 'like-numbered with the concept F' can be applied with truth only to concepts, the extension of the concept which it expresses must be a set of concepts. And so Frege, after objecting to the suggestion that a number is a concept, seems to have committed himself to the view that a number is a set of concepts. But this is not the only curious consequence of his definition. For he wants to say that the concept F has a number belonging to it, and according to the definition which we have quoted this is as much as to say that the concept F has a set of concepts belonging to it, namely, the set of concepts whose instances are correlated one-to-one with its own instances. It is difficult to find any usage of the word 'belong' (*zukommen*) which makes this claim seem natural. We may perhaps say that the concept F belongs as a member to the set of concepts like-numbered with itself, or that the concept 'like-numbered with the concept F' belongs as a property to the concept F, but not that the set of concepts like-numbered with the concept F belongs to the concept F in either of these senses. Perhaps Frege realized that his phraseology was curious; for he says in a footnote that he believes the phrase 'extension of the concept' could be replaced in definition (2) by the single word 'concept'.[1] It is obvious, however, that in making this concession he did not intend to retract his earlier statement that individual numbers are objects, as distinct from concepts; for he says that he is convinced he could explain away the apparent contradiction, though to do so would take him too far afield. We do not know how he would have proceeded in the alternative development of his theory, but another remark in the footnote shows what was at the back of his mind when he chose the formulation given in his text.

Apart from an apparent contradiction with his earlier statements, there is according to Frege another difficulty to be met by the alternative development, namely, 'that concepts can have identical extensions without themselves coinciding'. In order to appreciate the point of this remark we must consider what is involved in the situation where the number belonging to the concept F is the same as the number belonging to the concept G. Clearly the two concepts are like-numbered, and so whatever is like-numbered with the one is like-numbered with the other, i.e.

[1] *Gl.*, § 68.

the extension of the concept 'like-numbered with the concept F' is identical with the extension of the concept 'like-numbered with the concept G'. But this does not mean that the concept 'like-numbered with the concept F' is identical with the concept 'like-numbered with the concept G'. On the contrary, it is obvious that they are distinct. And if we define the number belonging to the concept F as the concept 'like-numbered with the concept F' and similarly the number belonging to the concept G as the concept 'like-numbered with the concept G', we are committed to the paradoxical position that one and the same number is two distinct concepts. Obviously for one who wishes to maintain a theory like Frege's the easiest way out of the trouble is to define the number belonging to the concept F as the *extension* of the concept 'like-numbered with the concept F'. Frege admits that the definition seems strange at first, but he defends it by arguing that the extension to which he refers has the properties and relations expected of the number belonging to a concept.

At stage (3) in his construction Frege tries to explain how we can talk about numbers in general without referring to any particular concepts to which they belong, and for this purpose he lays it down that 'n is a number' is to mean the same as 'there exists a concept such that n is the number which belongs to it'. If we can accept what precedes, we need not cavil at this definition. For it is obvious that in order to practise arithmetic we must be able to talk about numbers without reference to particular concepts, and Frege's account of the matter shows how we can do so while retaining a connexion with the usage according to which numbers are said to belong to concepts. But the definition just quoted is not by itself enough for the foundation of arithmetic, since it provides only an explanation of the expression 'n is a number'. We still need definitions of the individual numbers, or rather a general scheme which provides for the definition of infinitely many numbers and so allows us to prove all the commonly accepted theorems of arithmetic.

Now within Frege's theory the only way of indicating an individual number is to speak of it as the number belonging to a certain concept. But it is his intention to exhibit arithmetic as a development of logic, and so he cannot introduce the individual numbers by reference to empirical concepts, e.g. by saying that 5 is the number belonging to the concept 'continent' and 12 the number belonging to the concept 'apostle'. Furthermore, reference to empirical concepts would not guarantee the existence of an infinite sequence of numbers such as we require for the higher development of arithmetic. It is essential, therefore, that

Frege should provide for definitions of the individual numbers by reference to standard concepts from within logic itself. Taking o as the start of the series, he offers the following scheme:

o is the number belonging to the concept 'not identical with itself'
1  „    „    „    „    „    'identical with o'
2  „    „    „    „    „    'identical with o or with 1'
3  „    „    „    „    „    'identical with o or with 1 or with 2'

. . . . . . . . . . . .

Here the concept 'not identical with itself' is supposed to come from pure logic; and obviously there can be no object falling under it. So the first definition apparently satisfies all the appropriate requirements. But if the first definition is free from extralogical concepts, so too are all the others; and the plan according to which they are constructed allows for continuation *ad libitum*. It seems, therefore, that Frege has succeeded in his enterprise and shown how arithmetic can be reduced to logic.

In the first volume of his *Grundgesetze* Frege goes through the same argument giving references back to the appropriate passages of his *Grundlagen*. But in accordance with the general policy of his later work he formulates his definitions wherever possible by means of class signs instead of functional expressions; and although he still says in his German text that numbers belong to concepts, in his symbolism the sign which has the sense of 'the number of' always appears in front of a class sign.[1] If we allow ourselves to talk of classes, we may accept this version of the theory as a reasonable simplification. For concepts which determine the same class must obviously be like-numbered according to Frege's way of speaking, and the number which he says they have in common may more naturally be said to belong to the class they determine. This way of speaking has in addition the merit of connecting Frege's definition of number with Cantor's theory of sets or classes. For the one-to-one correlation of which Frege speaks is the relation between sets which Cantor calls equivalence, and in Cantor's language the novelties of Frege's work can be summarized very simply by the two following statements:

(i)  The cardinal number of a set is the set of all sets equivalent to it.

(ii) For the natural numbers, o, 1, 2, 3, &c., considered as sets of equivalent sets, we may take as exemplars, or standard members, certain sets defined in purely logical fashion,

[1] See, for example, the definition of o in *Gg.* i, § 41.

namely, for 0 the set of things not identical with themselves, for 1 the set whose sole member is the number 0, for 2 the set whose members are the numbers 0 and 1, for 3 the set whose members are the numbers 0, 1, and 2, and so forth.

It is a curious fact, however, that neither Frege nor Cantor ever committed himself explicitly to this account of numbers. In his *Grundlagen* Frege said that the *Anzahl* which he defined was the same as the *Mächtigkeit* of sets in Cantor's theory,[1] but in a review of that work for the *Deutsche Literaturzeitung* Cantor denied this and found fault with Frege's definition.[2] While professing to agree with the programme of basing arithmetic on logic alone, he objected to some of Frege's subtleties and in particular to his talk of a number as the extension of a concept because, as he said, this latter might be 'quantitatively indeterminate'. It looks as though the difference was due merely to misunderstandings about technical usages. Such at least was the view of Whitehead and Russell, who accepted the definition of number given above, although for reasons which will become clear in a later chapter they could not accept Frege's way of guaranteeing the infinity of the series of natural numbers.

## 5. *The Number Series: Dedekind and Peano*

In order to carry out his programme of exhibiting arithmetic as identical with logic Frege must first define all the notions of arithmetic in an acceptable fashion without using any extra-logical terminology and then show that with these definitions all arithmetical reasoning can be reduced to logically valid patterns. In particular, he must show that nothing more than logic is required for the validity of mathematical (or recursive) induction, that is to say, the argument in which we conclude that, because a property belongs to the number 0 and also to the successor of any number which has it, it must therefore belong to all natural numbers. For those who wish to maintain that arithmetic is not identical with logic commonly point to this as a peculiarity of arithmetical reasoning, and say that it presupposes some in-tuition of extra-logical necessity. In his *Grundlagen* Frege did not attempt to deal with the second part of his programme in a detailed fashion, perhaps because he thought that the task was too difficult for a work of popular character. What he says about it seems, therefore, rather obscure and perfunctory. But he shows clearly enough that he is aware of the need for an analysis of

---

[1] *Gl.*, § 85.    [2] *Gesammelte Abhandlungen*, ed. Zermelo, p. 440.

mathematical induction, when, after quoting from the account of serial order which he gave at the end of his *Begriffsschrift*, he writes: 'Only by means of this definition of following in a series is it possible to reduce the argument from n to $(n+1)$, which on the face of it is peculiar to mathematics, to the general laws of logic.'[1] And he has in fact provided all that is needed for the purpose, although he has not indicated the connexions between his points in such a way as to make the reader's task easy.

First of all Frege says that 'n follows in the series of natural numbers directly after m' is to mean the same as 'There exists a concept F and an object x falling under it, such that the Number which belongs to the concept F is n and the Number which belongs to the concept "falling under F but not identical with x" is m'. This definition is easily intelligible from consideration of the definitions of particular numbers given near the end of the last section. As Frege says, it is also not difficult for the reader to see that the relation so defined is a one-to-one relation and that every number except o is related by this relation to some other number.[2] Then Frege goes on to sketch a proof of a proposition which he considers not so obvious, namely, that for every number in the series of natural numbers there is a number which follows directly after it; and it is while engaged on this enterprise that he mentions incidentally the possibility of reducing mathematical induction to the general laws of logic.

In the passage of his *Begriffsschrift*, to which he refers here, Frege had explained how, given a relation $\Phi$, we could define another relation expressible in the formula 'y follows in the $\Phi$-series after x', e.g. how, given the relation expressed by 'y is a child of x', we could define the relation expressed by 'y is a descendant of x'. In ordinary life we should probably explain the meaning of the word 'descendant' by saying 'A man's descendants are his children and the children of his children and the children of the children of his children and so on'. But Frege was not content with this, because he thought that for his purpose of reducing arithmetic to logic it was necessary to find a way of eliminating the phrase 'and so on'. He therefore suggested in effect that 'y is a descendant of x' might be taken to mean the same as 'y has all the attributes which belong to x and are invariably transmitted to his children by a parent who has them'. At first hearing this proposal may be received with some doubt. For we are inclined to say that, while a descendant of x must undoubtedly have all the attributes which are hereditary in the family started by x, it is not obvious that anyone who has all

[1] *Gl.*, § 81.  [2] *Gl.*, §§ 76–78.

those attributes must be a member of the family. But it can be answered that one of the attributes hereditary in the family is precisely membership of the family, so that anyone who possesses *all* the hereditary attributes must have this.

Applying Frege's technique to the number series, we may say that 'y follows in the series of natural numbers after x' is to mean the same as 'y has all those attributes which (i) belong to x and (ii) are such that if they belong to any particular number they belong also to the number which follows in the series of natural numbers directly after it'. In effect this is what Frege does for his special purpose in the *Grundlagen*. But in order to exhibit the argument by mathematical induction as a piece of logical reasoning we must go a step farther and say that 'n is a natural number' is to mean the same as 'n is identical with o or n has all the attributes which (i) belong to o and (ii) are such that if they belong to any object m they belong also to whatever follows-in-the-series-of-natural-numbers-directly-after m'. For the propriety of this definition it is essential, of course, that the words which we have hyphenated together should be understandable as one sign according to the explanation quoted above from Frege. But once this is granted, the rest is simple. For the ordinary formulation of the principle of mathematical induction can now be regarded as an abbreviation for the logical truism 'If P is an attribute which (i) belongs to o and (ii) is such that if it belongs to any object m it belongs also to whatever follows-in-the-series-of-natural-numbers-directly-after m, then P belongs to everything which is either identical with o or endowed with all the attributes which (i) belong to o and (ii) are such that if they belong to any object m they belong also to whatever follows-in-the-series-of-natural-numbers-directly-after m'. In other words, the validity of the principle of mathematical induction is made to depend on the fact that the series of natural numbers can be defined as the proper field for mathematical induction. It should be noticed, however, that this supposed reduction of arithmetical reasoning to logic involves talk of all the attributes or properties of numbers. In what follows we shall have occasion to return to this point.

In his little book *Was sind und was sollen die Zahlen?* first published in 1888, Dedekind reached somewhat similar conclusions, working independently from a different starting-point and using different terminology. According to his way of speaking a system (or set) of things S may be said to have another system S′ as its map or image (*Bild*) if there is a projection or rule of mapping (*Abbildung*) φ which assigns to every element of S something or other as its image and S′ is the totality of these images of elements of S. If the projection always assigns different images to different elements of S, it is said to be similar (*ähnlich*). Obviously this is what other mathematicians have called a one-to-one correlation. Next a system K is said to be a chain (*Kette*) with respect to a certain projection if it contains as a part (i.e. as a sub-system) K′ which is a map of itself according to that projection, i.e. if K′cK where 'c' signifies inclusion-in.[1] Probably Dedekind's reason for introducing this rather curious terminology was a wish to draw attention to the fact that the map contained in such a system must in turn contain a map of itself according to the same projection. For his first theorem about chains is that the map of a chain is itself a chain. Another of his theorems which can be proved very easily is that any chain which contains a system A as a part must also contain A′. Further, if A is a part of a chain S, the intersection or greatest common part (*Gemeinheit*) of all those chains, including S itself, which have A for a part is called the chain of A, or for short $A_0$. Again it can be shown easily that any chain which contains A as a part must also contain $A_0$. When A has only one element 1, Dedekind allows himself to call its chain $1_0$, though if he followed his own definition strictly he ought to write $\{1\}_0$. But whatever A may be, it should be remembered that A′ and $A_0$ are both determined by some particular projection $\phi$. With this apparatus of technical terms we can now say that a system N is *simply infinite* if there exists for it a projection $\phi$ and a basic element 1 satisfying the four conditions:

$\alpha$. N′cN.

$\beta$. N = $1_0$.

$\gamma$. 1 is not an element of N′.

$\delta$. The projection $\phi$ is similar.

And finally, if we concentrate attention upon the structure of the system N, disregarding the special nature of the elements in so far as that is not determined by the conditions listed above, we may say that N is the system of ordinal numbers.[2]

According to Dedekind arithmetic is just the science of the relations or laws which can be derived from the conditions mentioned above, and one of the most important of such laws is the principle of mathematical induction, for which we may write 'If 1 is an element of P and (NP)′cP, then NcP', though Dedekind himself does not use the Boolean notation of juxtaposed letters for an intersection. To prove this theorem we argue as follows.[3] Since 1 is an element of N and by hypothesis also of

[1] Dedekind himself uses a variant of the sign ' < ' which looks something like the numeral '3'.     [2] *Was sind und was sollen die Zahlen?*, § 6, 71–73.
[3] Ibid., § 4, 59–60, and § 6, 80.

P, it may be assumed that the system NP is not empty. Now evidently

$$NP \subset N$$

from which it follows in accordance with the definition of mapping that

$$(NP)' \subset N'.$$

But we know that

$$N' \subset N$$

from condition $\alpha$, and so we have

$$(NP)' \subset N.$$

By the second part of the hypothesis, however, we have also

$$(NP)' \subset P,$$

and from these two relations taken together it follows that

$$(NP)' \subset NP,$$

i.e. that NP is a chain. Then since 1 is an element of this chain and $1_0$ is the greatest common part of all chains of which 1 is an element, we can assert

$$1_0 \subset NP.$$

But by condition $\beta$

$$N = 1_0,$$

and so we may conclude

$$N \subset NP,$$

which is equivalent to

$$N \subset P.$$

The basis of this proof is the fact that N, the set of numbers over which we want to generalize, has been declared to be a chain and in particular that chain which is the greatest common part of all chains having 1 as an element. As in Frege's argument, so here the validity of the principle of mathematical induction is secured by a definition of number which has reference to all properties hereditary in a series. For to say that N is the greatest common part of all chains having 1 as an element is to say in effect that N is contained as a part in every chain P which satisfies the hypotheses of the principle of mathematical induction, and this is another version of Frege's account of the matter. Dedekind himself noticed the correspondence when he first read Frege's *Grundlagen*, about a year after the publication of his own book, and he drew attention to it in the preface to his second edition (1893). In the preface to his third edition (1911) he said that, although he still held to his original view, according to which arithmetic, algebra, and analysis are all parts of logic, he had to allow some force to objections which had been raised between 1893 and 1903. This means presumably that he made common cause with Cantor and Frege, whose work had been subjected to criticism at the time mentioned.

The chief difference between Frege's work and that of Dedekind is that the former, unlike the latter, connects numbers with the extensions of concepts. Although Dedekind started with general considerations about systems or sets, he ended with a purely ordinal theory of numbers. Frege was equally interested in the ordering of the items of the number series, but thought that it could be explained by the definition which he gave for 'n follows in the series of natural numbers directly after m'. It is not clear whether Dedekind wished to reject that part of Frege's theory which went beyond his own, but there are passages which suggest that he did not think it proper to make the theory of ordinal numbers rest on a theory of cardinal numbers. When he first announces that the elements of his system may be called numbers, he writes:

'If in the consideration of a simply infinite system N which is ordered by a projection $\phi$ we disregard entirely the special nature of the elements, retain merely their distinguishability, and conceive only the relations in which they are set one to another through the ordering projection $\phi$, then these elements are called *natural numbers* or *ordinal numbers* or simply *numbers*, and the basic element 1 is called the *basic number* of the *number series*. Having regard to this abstraction, or freeing of the elements from every other content, we may rightly describe the numbers as a free creation of the human mind. The relations or laws which are derived solely from the conditions $\alpha$, $\beta$, $\gamma$, $\delta$ in 71, and are therefore always the same in all ordered simply infinite systems (cf. 134), constitute the immediate object of the *science of number* or *arithmetic*.'[1]

In the later passage mentioned here he proves that all simply infinite systems can be mapped upon each other by similar projections, and then, with a reference back to the passage quoted above, goes on to say:

'It is clear at the same time . . . that every statement about the numbers, i.e. about the elements n of the simply infinite system N which is ordered by the projection $\phi$, every statement, that is, in which the special nature of the elements is disregarded and mention made only of those concepts which have their origin in the ordering $\phi$, possesses completely general validity for any other simply infinite

[1] *Was sind und was sollen die Zahlen?*, § 6, 73.

system $\Omega$ ordered by a projection $\theta$ and for its elements $\nu$, and that the transition from N to $\Omega$ (which is also the translation of an arithmetical statement from one language to another) takes place through the projection $\psi$ ... which transforms every element n of N into an element $\nu$ of $\Omega$ which is $\psi(n)$. This element $\nu$ can be called the nth element of $\Omega$, and by the same token the number n is itself the nth element of the number series N.'[1]

These pronouncements suggest that Dedekind thinks of arithmetic as a science whose subject is implicitly defined by the four conditions $\alpha$, $\beta$, $\gamma$, $\delta$, taken as axioms or postulates, and that he is not worried by the possibility of various interpretations for his basic signs, because he believes this has no importance for mathematics. It is true that he does not use the language of axiomatics, but he seems to say in effect that it is foolish to ask for more than a monomorphic axiom set.

In 1889, the year after Dedekind's work appeared, Peano published his *Arithmetices Principia Nova Methodo Exposita*, in which arithmetic is based explicitly on a set of nine axioms expressed in the new logical notation. Four of these are truths about equality, but the other five are the following special postulates:

(1) 1 is a number.
(2) The successor of any number is a number.
(3) No two numbers have the same successor.
(4) 1 is not the successor of any number.
(5) Any property which belongs to 1 and also to the successor of any number which has it belongs to all numbers.

In later versions of this attempt to characterize the number series Peano starts, like Frege, with the number 0; but his general conception of number is always ordinal, like Dedekind's, and there is a close similarity between his axioms and the conditions stated by Dedekind. Thus (2) corresponds to $\alpha$, (3) to $\delta$, and (4) to $\gamma$, while (1) and (5) together do the work of $\beta$. The axioms are independent one of another, as may be seen from consideration of models which satisfy four but not five of them,[2] and it can be shown by an adaptation of Dedekind's argument that they form a monomorphic set.

Peano was interested primarily in the clear presentation of mathematical results, and it was for this purpose, rather than for philosophical analysis, that he composed his *Notations de logique mathématique* of 1894. In the years 1895–1908 he produced five successive versions of a *Formulaire de mathématiques*, using his five axioms each time (but with 0 in place of 1) as a foundation for

---

[1] Ibid., § 10, 134.      [2] G. Peano, *Formulaire de mathématiques*, iii, p. 44.

arithmetic, and in the last version, where the non-symbolic part
was written in a new international language of his own invention
called *Latino sine flexione*, he introduced them with the remark:

'Quaestio si nos pote defini $N_o$ significa si nos pote scribe aequalitate
de forma

$N_o$ = expressione composito per signos noto, ∪, ∩, —, . . . , ᾿,

quod non es facile. Ergo nos sume tres idea $N_o$, o, + ut idea primitivo
per que nos defini omni symbolo de Arithmetica. Nos determina valore
de symbolo non definito per systema de propositio primitivo sequente.'[1]

The first group of signs to which he refers in this passage are of
course the purely logical signs of his *Arithmetices Principia* and later
works, while the other three mean respectively 'number', 'nought',
and 'successor'. It is clear, therefore, that at this date Peano still
had an open mind about the project of Frege, but thought it
possible to proceed without waiting for a settlement of the question about ultimate foundations.

Although their diction was sometimes loose and extravagant,
the formalists of the nineteenth century made an interesting suggestion when they said that arithmetic should be presented as an
axiomatized system in which the characteristically arithmetical
notions receive implicit definitions from the formal conditions
to which they are made subject. Admittedly Thomae's pronouncements were unsatisfactory in detail for the reasons given
by Frege, but we may well feel that in this contest Frege triumphed
too easily; for at the time he wrote Peano had already carried
out Thomae's programme in a much more impressive fashion.
On the one hand, Peano's set of axioms is not open, like Thomae's,
to the charge that it fails to provide for the several natural numbers, since we can introduce 1 as the successor of o, 2 as the
successor of 1, and so on. On the other hand, Peano's axioms,
taken together with suitable definitions of the operations of
addition and multiplication, are sufficient for the proof of all the
general laws of number set out by Thomae. Thus, for example,
we may define addition recursively by the two stipulations:

(i) $a + o = a$,
(ii) $a + n' = (a + n)'$,

where 'n'' is an abbreviation for 'the successor of n', and then
prove the associative law for addition as follows. First we show
that

$$a + (b + o) = (a + b) + o.$$

[1] *Formulario Mathematico*, p. 27.

This is done by successive applications of (i) above; for

$$a+(b+o) = a+(b+o)$$
$$= a+b$$
$$= (a+b)+o.$$

Next we show that if

$$a+(b+n) = (a+b)+n$$

it must also be the case that

$$a+(b+n') = (a+b)+n'.$$

This is done by successive applications of (ii) and by use of the hypothesis; for

$$a+(b+n') = a+(b+n')$$
$$= a+(b+n)'$$
$$= [a+(b+n)]'$$
$$= [(a+b)+n]'$$
$$= (a+b)+n'.$$

And finally from these two results taken together with Peano's fifth axiom we get the conclusion that

$$a+(b+c) = (a+b)+c.$$

Why then should we not be content with Peano's formulation of arithmetic and say that his primitive notions are sufficiently defined by the axioms in which they are mentioned?

If the suggestion is sound, the mathematician need worry himself no more about the metaphysical question 'What is a number?' When teased by a philosophical colleague or by his own conscience, he can reply that he regards mathematical axioms as implicit definitions and that all his professional demands are included in Peano's set. The proposal is, nevertheless, unsatisfactory, because it does not provide for that connexion with the ordinary use of numerals which is essential to any formal system worthy of the name of arithmetic. If the signs for 'number', 'nought', and 'successor' have only the sense required by Peano's axioms they are in effect variables for which we may substitute any expressions that turn all the axioms into true statements. Now the axioms are all verified when the signs 'o' and 'number' are taken in their usual senses and 'successor' is understood to mean the same as Frege's 'following in the series of natural numbers directly after'; but, as Peano himself remarked, they can all be verified by many other interpretations.[1] Thus the formal conditions are satisfied

---

[1] *Formulaire de mathématiques*, iii, p. 44.

when we put the numeral '1' for '0', 'member of the sequence $1, \frac{1}{2}, \frac{1}{4}, \frac{1}{8}, \ldots$' for 'number', and 'half' for 'successor'. In short, Peano's set of axioms, considered as an implicit definition, gives only the common logical characteristics of all progressions. In spite of all that Dedekind and Peano say in defence of their approach, we cannot be wholly satisfied with a basis for arithmetic which does not distinguish the sequence of natural numbers from any other progression. Even within pure mathematics we have occasion to use the numerals in their normal sense, as for example when we say 'There are *four* prime numbers less than 10'.

Nor is this the only reason for saying that Peano's axioms are inadequate by themselves as a foundation for arithmetic. The system which they form is monomorphic, as we have seen, but for this merit it seems to be essential that the fifth axiom contains a generalization over all properties. Such a generalization amounts in effect to assumption of the wide notion of a property or set used by Cantor in his theory of sets, and it must therefore be regarded with suspicion by those who are sceptical about Cantor's theory. Furthermore, it is apparently the breadth of this talk about all properties which allows for interpretation of the axioms by reference to progressions other than the natural number series. If we wish to avoid the dangers of over-wide generalization and to direct attention to the number series as distinct from other progressions, it seems, therefore, that we must try to replace Peano's single axiom of mathematical induction by a sequence of inductive axioms each dealing with some specified property of numbers. But the Norwegian mathematician Thoralf Skolem has shown that even with a denumerably infinite sequence of such axioms our new system must remain as a whole polymorphic (i.e. non-categorical). In his own words:

'The number series is completely characterized . . . by Peano's axioms, if we regard the concept "set" or "propositional function" as something given in advance with an absolute meaning independent of all principles of generation or axioms. But if one wishes to carry the axiomatic treatment through consistently, so that reasoning with sets or propositional functions is also axiomatized, then the unique or complete characterization of the number series is impossible.'[1]

This discovery is closely akin to Gödel's theorem on the incompletability of formal arithmetic, which we shall have occasion to notice later, and it was, of course, unknown to Frege. But

[1] Über die Nicht-charakterisierbarkeit der Zahlenreihe mittels endlich oder abzählbar unendlich vieler Aussagen mit ausschließlich Zahlvariablen', *Fundamenta Mathematicae*, xxiii (1934), pp. 150–61.

Frege had no sympathy for the postulational approach, because he was convinced that rules for the use of numerical expressions should be derived from definitions of the numbers and not vice versa. It was this conviction which inspired his efforts to present arithmetic as an extension of logic.

# VIII

## FREGE'S GENERAL LOGIC

### 1. *The Begriffsschrift*

WE must now consider the development of logic by which Frege hoped to carry out his programme with full rigour, and it will be natural to review his works in the order of their composition, reserving all major comments until we have the whole story before us.

In his first work, the *Begriffsschrift*, Frege's chief concern is the construction of a formalized language of pure thought, that is to say, a system of symbolism more regular than ordinary language and better adapted for ensuring accuracy in deduction because it allows only for what is essential, namely conceptual content as opposed to rhetorical emphasis. In his sub-title he says that this new script is to be modelled on the language of arithmetic, but it soon appears that the chief resemblance is in the use of letters to express generality. Frege was not, of course, the first logician to think of this device; for Aristotle had used it long before the invention of algebra. But Frege was the first to show its full possibilities, and we shall see presently that he distinguished clearly between several different notions that had been confused together in older talk about variables. Other signs of arithmetic such as '$+$' were not used by Frege with any special logical sense, because he wished to retain them for use in their normal mathematical sense together with his new logical signs. When Schröder objected to his departure from Boole's notation, Frege replied that he wanted to produce a script for the analysis of mathematical reasoning and therefore deliberately avoided Boole's adaptation of algebraical symbolism, convenient as that might be for certain limited purposes.[1]

The first of the special signs which he introduces is intended to express judgement or assertion. It has the form '$\vdash$' and is written to the left of the sign or complex of signs in which the content of the judgement is given. If the little vertical stroke at the beginning is omitted, the horizontal stroke which remains is called the content-stroke, and it serves to show that the content

---

[1] 'Über den Zweck der Begriffsschrift', *Sitzungsberichte der Jenaischen Gesellschaft für Medicin und Naturwissenschaft*, 1882, pp. 1–10.

expressed by the following sign or signs is under consideration without affirmation or denial by the author. Thus if ' $\vdash \varGamma$' is an abbreviation for the statement 'Unlike magnetic poles attract each other', ' $— \varGamma$' is to convey only the thought of mutual attraction between unlike magnetic poles, without any judgement of the correctness of that thought. Frege tells us that we may, if we like, read the horizontal stroke as though it meant 'the proposition that', and he emphasizes that the content of what follows the stroke must always be a permissible content of judgement, not a mere idea such as that of a house. In the example given above the Greek capital '$\varGamma$' is an abbreviation for the expression of such a content, and we have here an example of one way in which Frege uses letters for logical purposes. Greek capitals are always to be understood as abbreviations, but sometimes they may be introduced without any special explanation, and then the reader is to assign any sense he chooses, provided that he retains the same sense throughout the context in which the letter occurs. For the sake of clarity we shall use only Greek capitals which are unlike Latin letters, though Frege himself does not always follow this practice in his first work.

According to most earlier logicians there could be no adequate representation of a judgement without a distinction between subject and predicate, but Frege rejects this dogma. There may indeed be a rhetorical difference between 'The Greeks defeated the Persians' and 'The Persians were defeated by the Greeks'; but the *conceptual content* of the two statements is the same, because either can be substituted for the other as a premiss without effect on the validity of our reasoning, and this is all we need consider when we try to make a language for the purpose he has in mind. Let us imagine a variant of ordinary language in which an assertion that Archimedes perished at the capture of Syracuse would be expressed by the sentence 'The violent death of Archimedes at the capture of Syracuse is a fact', that is to say, a language in which the whole content of a judgement is expressed by a subject phrase. There will then be one and the same predicate phrase for all statements, namely 'is a fact'; but it will not be like ordinary predicate phrases, since its work will be simply to present the subject content in the form of a judgement. Frege tells us that his symbolic language is of this kind, and says that if we insist on looking for predicates we are to take the symbol '$\vdash$' as the common predicate sign of all judgements. This way of speaking commits him, of course, to the view that the distinction between universal and particular and the notion of negation both apply to possible contents of judgements, rather than to judgements as such, since they are connected with the relations of entailment, inconsistency, &c., which can hold between contents that are not asserted. On the other hand, he says that the distinction which logicians commonly draw between categorical, hypothetical, and disjunctive judgements is merely grammatical, as will appear from the later development of his system; and he argues that the distinction in respect of modality may be ignored because it refers to grounds rather than to contents of judgements. When we say that something must be the case, we indicate that we know some general truth from which it may be inferred; and when we say that something may be the case, we indicate that we are not acquainted with any laws from which the negation of the proposition would follow (unless, indeed, we use the language of possibility to express what is ordinarily called a particular affirmative judgement, as when we say 'A chill may result in death', meaning that some chills are fatal).

Having disposed in this way of the traditional analysis of judgements, Frege now introduces a complex expression '$\vdash\!\!\begin{array}{l}\rule{1em}{0.5pt}\Gamma\\[-2pt]\rule[0.5em]{0.5pt}{0.5em}\!\!\rule{1em}{0.5pt}\Delta\end{array}$' for the judgement that $\Gamma$ is not to be denied while $\Delta$ is affirmed. Clearly the content $\begin{array}{l}\rule{1em}{0.5pt}\Gamma\\[-2pt]\rule[0.5em]{0.5pt}{0.5em}\!\!\rule{1em}{0.5pt}\Delta\end{array}$ is what we have learnt to call a Philonian conditional with $\Delta$ as antecedent and $\Gamma$ as consequent. Frege says nothing about the history of the notion, and he may have had no knowledge of its use by earlier logicians, but he explains it in exactly the same way as Philo, i.e. by distinguishing the four different possibilities:

(i) $\Gamma$ affirmed, $\Delta$ affirmed,
(ii) $\Gamma$ affirmed, $\Delta$ denied,
(iii) $\Gamma$ denied, $\Delta$ affirmed,
(iv) $\Gamma$ denied, $\Delta$ denied,

and saying that his new complex sign stands for the judgement that the third possibility is not realized but one of the other three is. On the other hand, he recognizes, as Philo did not, that such a sign does not express the full force of the word 'if'. For while he uses the name 'condition stroke' for a vertical line linking horizontals he says that such a line cannot properly be rendered by 'if' unless $\Gamma$ is connected with $\Delta$ according to some law so that we can make the judgement $\vdash\!\!\begin{array}{l}\rule{1em}{0.5pt}\Gamma\\[-2pt]\rule[0.5em]{0.5pt}{0.5em}\!\!\rule{1em}{0.5pt}\Delta\end{array}$ without knowing whether $\Gamma$ and $\Delta$ are to be affirmed or denied separately. He goes too far in suggesting that the connexion must be causal; for we can certainly say 'If this field is a right-angled triangle, the square on its longest side is equal to the sum of the squares on its other two sides'. But he is right in maintaining that ' $\vdash\!\!\!\begin{array}{c}\Gamma\\\Delta\end{array}$ ' is not equivalent to 'If $\Delta$ then $\Gamma$' when it is asserted merely because $\Gamma$ is known to be true or $\Delta$ known to be false.

Frege's interest in Philonian junction is connected with his interest in deductive rigour. He remarks that the two judgements $\vdash\!\!\!\begin{array}{c}\Gamma\\\Delta\end{array}$ and $\vdash\Delta$ together entail the judgement $\vdash\Gamma$, because $\vdash\!\!\!\begin{array}{c}\Gamma\\\Delta\end{array}$ excludes the third of the four possibilities listed above while $\vdash\Delta$ excludes the second and the fourth; and he proposes to reduce all inference to this one simple pattern, the *modus ponens* of traditional logic, or detachment, as it is called by some modern logicians. If n is the number of a judgement $\vdash\!\!\!\begin{array}{c}\Gamma\\\Delta\end{array}$ in his deductive system, he expresses the inference shortly by writing

$$\text{'(n)}:\frac{\vdash\Delta}{\vdash\Gamma}\text{'}.$$

Most earlier logicians had exhibited a series of inference patterns, and Frege does not deny that in ordinary practice men use many distinct patterns; but he says that if we allow more than one there is no reason for stopping at any particular number. Now an increase in the number of rules increases the danger of mistakes in application, whereas a decrease makes for greater perspicuity and so for greater security. It is therefore desirable to get along with a single form of inference, if that is possible; and it can be done, provided we have at our disposal a sufficient number of logical formulae for use as premisses. We shall presently have occasion to notice the formulae chosen by Frege for this purpose, and it will then be easier to understand what is involved in his claim to reduce all inferences to one pattern; but we may remark here that he uses in fact a procedure of substitution as well as that of detachment. He himself admits as much; for after his claim to use only one kind of inference he adds the qualification '—at any rate in all cases where a new judgement is derived from more than one judgement'.

Negation is to be expressed by a small vertical stroke attached to the lower side of content stroke, as in the complex sign ' $\vdash\!\!\!\top\!\!\!-\Gamma$ ' which means 'It is not the case that $\Gamma$'. But in order to allow for the role of the content stroke as explained earlier ' $-\!\!\top\!\!\!-$ ' may be understood as a conflation of the signs '———', '$|$', and '———'. By combining the content, condition, and negation strokes in various ways we can now express various other notions of logic. Thus '⊢──┬──$\Gamma$' means 'The case in which the negation of $\Gamma$ is to be └──$\varDelta$ denied and $\varDelta$ affirmed does not occur' or 'It is not the case that both $\Gamma$ and $\varDelta$'. And the negation of the whole content of this judgement gives '⊢──┬──$\Gamma$' which means '$\Gamma$ and $\varDelta$'. When we say └──$\varDelta$ '$\Gamma$ but $\varDelta$', we add to mere conjunction the suggestion that $\varDelta$ is unexpected, but this is something for which Frege does not profess to have made provision in his symbolism. For '$\Gamma$ or $\varDelta$', where 'or' has the inclusive sense favoured by Frege, we have '⊢──┬──$\Gamma$ └─┬─$\varDelta$ which means literally 'The case in which $\Gamma$ is to be denied and the negation of $\varDelta$ affirmed does not occur'. And the negation of the whole content of this judgement gives in turn '⊢──┬──$\Gamma$ └─┬─$\varDelta$ which means 'Neither $\Gamma$ nor $\varDelta$'. For '$\Gamma$ or $\varDelta$' in the exclusive sense (sometimes rendered by 'either $\Gamma$ or $\varDelta$') we must conjoin the contents of the first and the third of these new compounds, and the result is the expression:

'⊢──┬──┬────$\Gamma$
        │  └──┬─$\varDelta$
        └───┬─$\Gamma$
            └────$\varDelta$'

As Frege points out, each of the judgements expressed in his stroke symbolism selects one or more of the four possibilities represented in the table given above and rejects the rest. The last, for example, leaves open the two possibilities

(ii) $\Gamma$ affirmed, $\varDelta$ denied,
(iii) $\Gamma$ denied, $\varDelta$ affirmed.

And if we wish to get to what is essential to the content of any such judgement, it is this selection from among possibilities we should consider, rather than any special form of expression. Thus if we had started with a basic sign for conjunction (i.e. for the selection of the first of the possibilities represented in our table and the rejection of all the rest), we could have defined the Philonian junction of $\varDelta$ and $\Gamma$ as the negation of the conjunction of $\varDelta$ with the negation of $\Gamma$. In some ways this would have been more natural, since our ordinary use of 'and' corresponds more closely to the notion of conjunction than our use of 'if' does to the notion of Philonian junction. But Frege explains that he has chosen to begin with his condition stroke because it simplifies the formulation of inferences. In other words, he thinks that there is a gain of elegance and clarity when the notion involved in his single rule of inference is represented by a single sign and in such a way that the consequent can be distinguished immediately from the antecedent. In his own scheme inference is indicated simply by the dropping of the lower clause in a conditional complex, i.e. by the passage from $\vdash\!\!\!\begin{array}{c}\rule{0pt}{0pt}\Gamma\\ \Delta\end{array}$ to $\vdash \Gamma$.

Frege now introduces a symbol for identity of content. Taking the letters '$\Gamma$' and '$\Delta$' as names of any kind, i.e. not necessarily propositional signs, he lays it down that '$\vdash(\Gamma \equiv \Delta)$' is to mean 'The name $\Gamma$ and the name $\Delta$ have the same conceptual content, so that $\Gamma$ can always be replaced by $\Delta$ and conversely'. It will be noticed that according to this explanation the judgement $\vdash(\Gamma \equiv \Delta)$ is about names. Frege himself puts the point in a curious way by saying that names joined by his new symbol are not mere proxies for their contents but appear *in propria persona*. And he goes on to argue that a symbol for identity of content is required because the same content may be given or determined in different ways. When this happens, the existence of different names for the same content is no triviality of usage but an essential feature of our language without which we should be unable to make some important judgements of the kind Kant called synthetic. We can perhaps illustrate his argument by an example which he himself used in later discussion. According to his way of talking at this date, 'the morning star' and 'the evening star' are both names for the same content; but when we say 'The morning star $\equiv$ the evening star' we are giving important information, since the two names correspond to different ways of determining the content. Another reason for introducing the symbol is that we require it for the formulation of definitions.

The next notion of the *Begriffsschrift* is that to which Frege attaches most importance in his preface, and he explains it as follows:

'Suppose that a simple or complex symbol occurs in one or more places in an expression (whose content need not be a possible content of judgement). If we imagine the symbol as replaceable by another (the same one each time) at one or more of its occurrences, then the part of the expression that shows itself invariant under such replacement is called the function; and the replaceable part, the argument of the function.'[1]

[1] *Bs.*, § 9.

Thus if our language contains the expression 'the circumstance of carbon dioxide's being heavier than hydrogen' and we think of this in such a way that the word 'hydrogen' might be replaced by the word 'oxygen' to make an expression of the same general kind as the first, we then treat 'hydrogen' as an argument of the function 'the circumstance of carbon dioxide's being heavier than . . . '. This way of talking commits us, of course, to saying that 'oxygen' is another argument of the same function. But we may equally well think of 'carbon dioxide' as the replaceable part in our original expression, and we shall then be led to talk of the function 'the circumstance of ——'s being heavier than hydrogen'. Or we may regard both 'carbon dioxide' and 'hydrogen' as replaceable and speak of 'the circumstance of ——'s being heavier than . . .' as a function of two arguments. Nor is this the end, since a continuation of the same line of thought leads us to recognize the possibility of functions with more than two arguments.

In a natural language a word or phrase which occupies the subject place in a sentence is usually intended to be taken as the argument, or at any rate as the principal argument, but we must guard against the assumption that every subject phrase can be treated as an argument. In the statement 'Every positive integer can be represented as the sum of four squares' we are indeed concerned, as we shall see later, with the function '—— can be represented as the sum of four squares', i.e. with a function of which 'the number 20' can be said to be an argument in 'The number 20 can be represented as the sum of four squares'. But according to Frege the phrase 'every positive integer', unlike 'the number 20' is not a possible argument of this or any other function, because it gets a sense only from its context in the sentences where it occurs, and by itself conveys no complete idea.

Frege's terminology of function and argument is derived, of course, from mathematics, and so too is the functional notation which he introduces. Thus he says that the complex sign '$\Phi(\Gamma)$' is to express an indeterminate function of the argument '$\Gamma$', and '$\Psi(\Gamma, \Delta)$' a function (not further determined) of the two arguments '$\Gamma$' and '$\Delta$' taken in that order. If the functions are supposed to be of the sort which when completed by arguments express possible contents of judgement, we may read '$\vdash\Phi(\Gamma)$' as '$\Gamma$ has the property $\Phi$' and '$\vdash\Psi(\Gamma, \Delta)$' as '$\Gamma$ stands in the relation $\Psi$ to $\Delta$'. For Frege the chief merit of such symbolism is that it allows for the expression of generality in a way more satisfactory than any supplied by ordinary languages. But it does so only when used together with a new device which later logicians have called the notation of bound variables; and in order to distinguish the role which his letters have when they are used as part of this notation Frege now introduces gothic type.

In the expression of a judgement by means of his script a complex symbol to the right of the assertion sign may always be regarded as a function of one of the symbols that occur in it. Let us replace this symbol by a gothic letter and insert the same gothic letter over a concavity in the content stroke so that we have for example '⊢—𝖆—$\Phi(\mathfrak{a})$'. Then according to Frege 'this signifies that the function is a fact whatever we take its argument to be'.[1] There must be a mistake in his phraseology here, for according to the explanation which he gave earlier a function is a part of an *expression*, i.e. something which cannot possibly be a fact. Nor is this the only passage of the *Begriffsschrift* where Frege seems to confuse symbols with what they symbolize. Other examples may be found among our quotations. But we need not dwell on that for the moment. He makes his meaning clear when he goes on to say that from such a judgement as that mentioned above we can always derive any number of judgements with less general contents by omitting the concavity with its gothic letter and substituting various definite symbols for the gothic letter inside the brackets. In short, the expression given above is equivalent to 'Everything is $\Phi$', but it is so constructed that we are in no danger of confusing its form with that of the expressions which arise from it by substitution.

It should be noticed, however, that in this context the word 'everything' is subject to no qualification except the implicit condition that any admissible substitution in the function must yield an expression for some possible content of judgement. If we wish to use our new script for the expression of a judgement to the effect that everything of certain kind is so-and-so, we must put the restriction into the symbolism which follows the concavity. Thus for 'Every living thing perishes' we must write

'⊢—𝖆—$\begin{matrix}\Pi(\mathfrak{a})\\\Lambda(\mathfrak{a})\end{matrix}$' treating '$\begin{matrix}\Pi(\ )\\\Lambda(\ )\end{matrix}$' as one complex functional sign.

This rendering means literally 'Everything does not live without perishing', and it makes clear the fact that the concavity with its gothic letter governs the whole following expression; but it does not allow for the existential import which attaches to statements of ordinary language such as that we are trying to translate. No doubt Frege was aware of the latter point, but he does not mention it explicitly.

[1] *Bs.*, § 11.

So far we have considered only cases where the concavity with its gothic letter comes immediately after the judgement stroke. But the universal quantifier, as it has been called by Peirce and later logicians, can occur in other positions in the expression of a judgement, as for example when we write

'⊢——𝔞—Φ(𝔞)'  or  '⊢———————Γ
                      └—𝔞——Φ(𝔞)  '

or

'⊢—𝔞———————Φ(𝔞)
        └—𝔢—Ψ(𝔞, 𝔢)  '

And this is of great importance because it allows for the making of a great many interesting kinds of statement in the new script. Thus when the universal quantifier is preceded by the negation stroke, as in our first example, we have an expression for the existence of something not satisfying the functional expression which follows, and in order to assert the existence of something satisfying a functional expression we need only insert another negation stroke between the universal quantifier and the functional expression as when we write '⊢—𝔞——Φ(𝔞)' for 'There is at least one philosopher'. As William of Shyreswood said, '*Quidam, non-nullus, non-omnis-non* sociantur'. If the scope of the universal quantifier is confined to the condition of the whole judgement, as in our second example, we have a way of rendering such statements as 'If everything is wet, we cannot light a fire', which is quite different, of course, from 'Mention what you like: if that thing is wet, we cannot light a fire'. And when one universal quantifier is included in the scope of another, as in our third example, we have a kind of complexity that was never considered in detail by earlier logicians, though it is to be found in ordinary speech and is essential for scientific discourse. To take examples which are slightly more complicated than that cited by Frege,

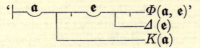

would serve for a rendering of 'Every cat fears some dog' and

'⊢—𝔢————𝔞———Φ(𝔞, 𝔢)'
              └K(𝔞)
        └————————Δ(𝔢)

for a rendering of 'There is some dog that every cat fears'. Obviously the two assertions are different, and both defy classification in the Aristotelian scheme. There is indeed no limit to the possible complexity of the assertions that may be expressed in Frege's script. For although he has only three basic signs which are of importance in this connexion, namely the condition stroke, the negation stroke, and the universal quantifier, these can be combined in infinitely many different ways. Whereas earlier logicians had talked as though it were possible to give a complete list of absolutely specific forms for propositions, he offers a scheme which is at once simpler than any previous suggestion and yet in a certain sense inexhaustible.

But the possibility of including one quantifier within the scope of another makes it necessary to use caution in the choice of gothic letters. Whereas in general it is legitimate to replace one gothic letter by another throughout the whole expression in which it occurs, it is important that *differences* of lettering should be preserved when one quantifier is included within the scope of another. Thus if '𝖊' were replaced by '𝖆' or '𝖆' by '𝖊' at any place in either of our last examples, the result would be either nonsense or something quite different from what we intended. The reason for this restriction on our liberty of choice is easy to understand. If a functional sign has several argument places which are to be filled in the same way, it is important to indicate this fact somehow, and the obvious method, now universally adopted, is to mark such places, but no others, by the same letter. For with this convention it is clear that the two argument places in a sign such as '𝖆 fears 𝖆' must be filled by the same argument if they are filled at all, though the two places in '𝖆 fears 𝖊' need not necessarily be filled by different arguments. And so when one quantifier occurs within the scope of another and there is a possibility of confusion we are committed to the distinction of lettering mentioned above.

Although the richness of Frege's system is due largely to the fact that his universal quantifier need not always occur immediately after his judgement stroke, those cases in which it does so occur are especially important, because they alone admit substitution. To take a parallel from ordinary language which we have already considered, a man who says 'If everything is wet, we cannot light a fire' does not thereby commit himself to all such assertions as 'If the grass is wet, we cannot light a fire'. For any of these latter may be false though what he said was true. In order to mark those cases which admit substitution and at the same time to simplify his notation Frege introduces a second way of expressing universality, namely, by means of an italic letter without a preceding quantifier. Thus instead of ' ⊢—𝖆—𝛷(𝖆)' we may write ' ⊢𝛷(a)', whenever it is convenient to do so; and from the latter we may, if we wish, pass back to the former, but when we replace an italic letter by a gothic letter we must make sure that the gothic letter we choose does not already occur in any part of our statement. This caution is necessary because our new quantifier will be so placed that it includes in its scope any other quantifiers there may be in the expression. The essential point is that when universality is expressed in a script like Frege's by letters without quantifiers (i.e. by free variables, as they are called in the terminology of modern logicians) each letter has for its scope the whole of the expression in which it occurs. The notation is at least as old as Aristotle, but Frege was the first to analyse it carefully and to realize that some other device is required for the expression of universality within a limited scope, as for example after a negation sign.

Having explained his symbolism, Frege goes on to set out some logical theses. There are, he says, some principles which cannot be expressed in his script because they are presupposed by it. These are rules for the use of the signs and rules of inference. But there are principles of pure thought which can be expressed in the script, and he proposes to give some examples and trace their connexions. In other words, he wishes to show in outline how logic can be presented as a deductive system, and for this purpose he tries to find some logical principles which together possess the force of all the others. As might be expected by anyone who knows something of the history of axiomatization in geometry, he discovers that various arrangements are possible; but he decides in favour of a scheme which contains nine axioms, all fairly simple and obvious. The first three are concerned solely with the notion expressed by the condition stroke, and the next three introduce the notion of negation. Two are concerned with identity of content, and one with universality as expressed by a gothic letter in a concavity. Set out in his script and with the numbers which they have in his system, they are as follows:

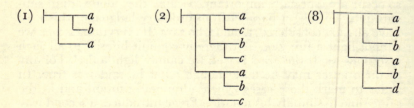

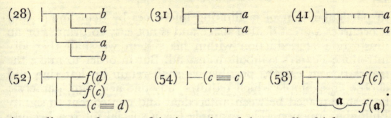

According to the use of 'primary' and 'general' which was explained and adopted in earlier sections, the first six of these belong to primary logic, and the ninth is an addition required for general logic, but the seventh and eighth belong to the still wider theory of identity.

It will be seen that all the axioms are formulated by use of italic letters (i.e. free variables). According to Frege's explanations this device is merely an abbreviation for expression by means of gothic letters and universal quantifiers, and we must suppose that he thought it appropriate here merely because it would facilitate substitution. But this can scarcely be a sufficient account of the matter. For if gothic letters were used throughout, we should lose the interesting and important difference between the first six axioms, which in their present form do not involve universal quantification, and the ninth, which does. That is to say, primary logic would no longer appear as an independent proper part of general logic, and the ninth axiom would cease to have the peculiar status which it now possesses. We shall return to this point later. For the present it is enough to notice the fact that in demonstration of theorems from his axioms Frege needs a principle of substitution in addition to the principle of detachment which he likes to regard as his sole rule of inference. Nor are these two the only rules which he employs. For his statement that we can if we wish return from an italic letter to a gothic letter with a quantifier amounts in effect to a third rule of inference. And during his explanation of the use of italic letters he introduces also a fourth rule, that from $\vdash\!\!\!\begin{array}{l}\!\!\!-\!\!-\Phi(a)\\ \!\!\!-\Gamma\end{array}$ we may deduce

$\vdash\!\!\!\begin{array}{l}\!\!\!-\mathfrak{a}\!\!-\Phi(\mathfrak{a})\\ \!\!\!-\Gamma\end{array}$ if '$\Gamma$' is an abbreviation for an expression in which '$a$' does not occur and '$a$' occupies only argument positions in the full version of '$\Phi(a)$'.[1] Taken with these four rules his axioms are indeed a complete set in the technical sense of that phrase, though their sufficiency could not be demonstrated in Frege's day.

Frege's script has the advantages which he claims for it, and

[1] *Bs.*, § 11.

in particular that of facilitating inferences by detachment, but it occupies a great deal of space and is not easy to print. For an illustration of deduction within his system we shall therefore introduce Peano's symbolism instead. But in order to make the translation as easy as possible we shall retain his lettering and choose an example which requires only one new sign, namely a horseshoe placed between antecedent and consequent to signify Philonian junction. The example has a special interest because it shows in a striking way the complexity which can result from simple beginnings. Starting with Frege's first two axioms as premisses, we shall deduce his third, and so prove incidentally that his system can be simplified still further. In what follows all the propositions from [3] to [8] inclusive were established by Frege himself, but the rest of the proof is due to Łukasiewicz,[1] and the numbering is our own. Various devices have been introduced by Frege and his successors for the abbreviation of such proofs, but for the convenience of the reader we shall set out each step in full with its justification. Thus the reference after [3] indicates that it is derived from [1] by substitution of the expression in front of a solidus for the letter standing after that solidus, and the reference after [4] indicates that it is derived from [3] and [2] by detachment, or the *modus ponens*.

[1]  $a \supset (b \supset a)$                                        Axiom.

[2]  $[c \supset (b \supset a)] \supset [(c \supset b) \supset (c \supset a)]$                          Axiom.

[3]  $\{[c \supset (b \supset a)] \supset [(c \supset b) \supset (c \supset a)]\} \supset ((b \supset a) \supset \{[c \supset (b \supset a)] \supset [(c \supset b) \supset (c \supset a)]\})$
        From [1]: $[c \supset (b \supset a)] \supset [(c \supset b) \supset (c \supset a)]/a; \, b \supset a/b.$

[4]  $(b \supset a) \supset \{[c \supset (b \supset a)] \supset [(c \supset b) \supset (c \supset a)]\}$
                                From [3] and [2].

[5]  $((b \supset a) \supset \{[c \supset (b \supset a)] \supset [(c \supset b) \supset (c \supset a)]\}) \supset (\{(b \supset a) \supset [c \supset (b \supset a)]\} \supset \{(b \supset a) \supset [(c \supset b) \supset (c \supset a)]\})$
        From [2]: $b \supset a/c; \, c \supset (b \supset a)/b; \, (c \supset b) \supset (c \supset a)/a.$

[6]  $\{(b \supset a) \supset [c \supset (b \supset a)]\} \supset \{(b \supset a) \supset [(c \supset b) \supset (c \supset a)]\}$
                                From [5] and [4].

[7]  $(b \supset a) \supset [c \supset (b \supset a)]$              From [1]: $b \supset a/a; \, c/b.$

[8]  $(b \supset a) \supset [(c \supset b) \supset (c \supset a)]$            From [6] and [7].

[9]  $\{(b \supset a) \supset [(c \supset b) \supset (c \supset a)]\} \supset \{[(b \supset a) \supset (c \supset b)] \supset [(b \supset a) \supset (c \supset a)]\}$            From [2]: $b \supset a/c; \, c \supset b/b; \, c \supset a/a.$

[10]  $[(b \supset a) \supset (c \supset b)] \supset [(b \supset a) \supset (c \supset a)]$            From [9] and [8].

---

[1] 'Zur Geschichte der Aussagenlogik', *Erkenntnis*, v (1936), pp. 111–31, especially p. 127.

[11] $\{[(c \supset b) \supset a] \supset [b \supset (c \supset b)]\} \supset \{[(c \supset b) \supset a] \supset (b \supset a)\}$

From [10]: $c \supset b/b$; $b/c$.

[12] $[a \supset (b \supset a)] \supset \{c \supset [a \supset (b \supset a)]\}$ From [1]: $a \supset (b \supset a)/a$; $c/b$.

[13] $c \supset [a \supset (b \supset a)]$  From [12] and [1].

[14] $[(c \supset b) \supset a] \supset [b \supset (c \supset b)]$

From [13]: $(c \supset b) \supset a/c$; $b/a$; $c/b$.

[15] $[(c \supset b) \supset a] \supset (b \supset a)$  From [11] and [14].

[16] $\{[(c \supset b) \supset a] \supset (b \supset a)\} \supset (\{d \supset [(c \supset b) \supset a]\} \supset [d \supset (b \supset a)])$

From [8]: $(c \supset b) \supset a/b$; $b \supset a/a$; $d/c$.

[17] $\{d \supset [(c \supset b) \supset a]\} \supset [d \supset (b \supset a)]$  From [16] and [15].

[18] $\{[c \supset (b \supset a)] \supset [(c \supset b) \supset (c \supset a)]\} \supset \{[c \supset (b \supset a)] \supset [b \supset (c \supset a)]\}$

From [17]: $c \supset (b \supset a)/d$; $c \supset a/a$.

[19] $[c \supset (b \supset a)] \supset [b \supset (c \supset a)]$  From [18] and [2].

[20] $[d \supset (b \supset a)] \supset [b \supset (d \supset a)]$  From [19]: $d/c$.

The last step is, of course, a trivial change which serves only to restore the lettering Frege happened to use in the formulation of his third axiom. But the discovery of the substitutions which make possible the other steps is by no means a trivial achievement. Using horizontal lines to indicate derivations, whether from one or from two premisses, we may represent Frege's part of the proof by the first of the following figures and the continuation by the second:

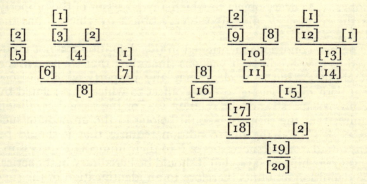

So far Frege has succeeded in developing his system without the use of any definitions for purposes of abbreviation, except that by which italic letters are introduced. But in the third part of his little book he recognizes the practical necessity of using some definitions and says that they are to be given in the form

'$\Vdash \Gamma \equiv \Delta$' with the new expression in each case following the identity sign. The purpose of the two vertical strokes at the beginning is to make clear that definitions are not judgements but conventions about symbolism. For our present purpose, however, it is not necessary to consider the third part of the *Begriffsschrift* in detail. Frege's intention there is to show in a preliminary way how his script can be used for the exact formulation of notions required by mathematics, and he chooses for his example the general theory of series. The example is interesting because, as we saw in the last chapter, mathematical induction depends on the serial ordering of the natural numbers and that ordering cannot be explained without the theory of relations which Frege first incorporated satisfactorily into logic.

For any relation $\Phi$ we may define another relation $\Phi'$ such that $\Gamma$ has $\Phi'$ to $\Delta$ if, and only if, $\Gamma$ has $\Phi$ to $\Delta$, or else to something which has $\Phi$ to $\Delta$, or else to something which has $\Phi$ to something which has $\Phi$ to $\Delta$, or else ... &c. In the language of later logicians $\Phi'$ is said to be the *proper ancestral* of $\Phi$, since if $\Phi$ is the relation of parent to child $\Phi'$ is the relation of ancestor to descendant. Frege himself does not use this terminology but expresses the derivative relation by saying '$\Delta$ follows $\Gamma$ in the $\Phi$-series', and the problem to which he addresses himself is that of defining the derivative relation by a finite expression, i.e. without using the 'etcetera' idiom, which itself presupposes an understanding of serial order. He achieves the desired result by saying that '$\Delta$ follows $\Gamma$ in the $\Phi$-series' means the same as '$\Delta$ possesses every property which belongs (i) to every object to which any possessor of the property has the relation $\Phi$ and (ii) to every object to which $\Gamma$ has the relation $\Phi$'.

The two conditions mentioned in this definition are not numbered as they are in later versions (including that we used in the last chapter), but it is clear that any property which satisfies them both must belong to every object to which $\Gamma$ is related by the proper ancestral of the relation $\Phi$. For the second condition requires that the property should belong to the immediate successors of $\Gamma$, and the first condition requires that it should be transmitted from all successors of $\Gamma$ to their immediate successors, or, as Frege himself says, that it should be hereditary in the series. The definition amounts therefore to an identification of the successors of $\Gamma$ in the $\Phi$-series by their possession of *all* properties which are hereditary in the series from $\Gamma$. There may no doubt be some properties which are hereditary in a series and yet belong also to some objects not in the series, just as a long nose may be hereditary in a family and yet belong also to persons not in the family. But we have seen that this cannot be true of *all* hereditary properties, since there is at least one such property, namely that of being a successor in the series, which belongs only to members of the series. It should be noticed, however, that Frege's definition covers only the successors of $\Gamma$ in the $\Phi$-series. If we wish to use the phrase '$\Phi$-series' in such a way as to include $\Gamma$ itself, we must define a member as an object which is either identical with $\Gamma$ or a successor of $\Gamma$ in the $\Phi$-series. Sometimes the word 'ancestral' is used for the relation which $\Gamma$ has to all members including itself, and that is the reason for speaking of the *proper* ancestral in connexion with Frege's theory.

When expressed in full by means of Frege's script, i.e. without use of the abbreviations which he introduces in propositions (69) and (76), a statement to the effect that $\Delta$ follows $\Gamma$ in the $\Phi$-series takes the form:

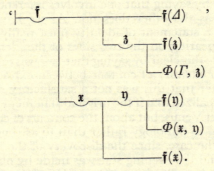

This is a good example of the use of quantifiers of different scope, and it shows also how in certain contexts a function may itself be treated as an argument to a function of higher order. For the gothic letter '𝔣' corresponds to the phrase 'every property' in the English paraphrase. When introducing his notation for quantification in the first part of the *Begriffsschrift*, Frege notices this possibility, and remarks that if an italic letter occurs as a functional symbol we must take due account of the fact in making substitutions. But he does not think it necessary to make any special provision for such cases when formulating the axioms of logic in his second part.

## 2. *Sense and Reference: Objects and Functions*

In his *Grundgesetze* Frege retained all the symbols of his *Begriffsschrift* except '≡', which he now replaced by the ordinary mathematical sign of equality. In itself the alteration of notation is trifling, but it marks a change in Frege's views about meaning, and explanation of this will serve conveniently as an introduction to his later doctrines. He himself started here when he wrote his paper called *Über Sinn und Bedeutung*.

Near the beginning of his *Begriffsschrift* Frege made a distinction between a judgement or assertion and something else which he called a content. He did not specify exactly how this last word was to be understood, but he obviously thought that a content was to be contrasted not only with a judgement but also with the signs by which it was expressed, and he used the second contrast in his explanation of such statements as 'The morning star is identical with the evening star'. Obviously this remark is quite different in force from 'The morning star is identical with the morning star'; and yet if the morning star is in fact identical with the evening star, we cannot explain the difference between the two statements by saying that one involves reference to the evening star whereas the other does not. As we have seen, Frege suggested that a statement of identity must really be about the expressions appearing on the two sides of the identity sign, and he tried to make this clear by saying that '$\equiv$' was to be understood as a symbol for identity of content between expressions. But he came to see later that this was not a satisfactory solution of the puzzle. For he realized that if the original statement was not really about the planet Venus, but about the contents of certain phrases, it would belong to philology rather than to astronomy, which is obviously not the case, since the discovery of the identity of the morning star and the evening star was made by observation and calculation, not by reflection on the use of words. We might add that even in philology the difficulty would break out again as soon as we tried to apply the proposed solution. For if we say that the phrase 'the morning star' has the same content as the phrase 'the evening star', is not this equivalent to an assertion that the content of the phrase 'the morning star' is identical with the content of the phrase 'the evening star'? And if it is, must we not go on to say that our original statement is not about the phrases 'the morning star' and 'the evening star' but about the phrases 'the content of the phrase "the morning star" ' and 'the content of the phrase "the evening star" '? But even that is not enough; for the proposed solution involves an infinite regress.

In his later work Frege tries to escape from the difficulty by abandoning his talk of content and making a new distinction between sense (*Sinn*) and reference (*Bedeutung*). When we say that the morning star is identical with the evening star, our descriptions refer to the same thing, but they do so in different ways, because they have not the same sense. In making the statement we use the two descriptions in exactly the same way as we should in any other astronomical statement, and there is no need to devise a new sign of identity which will suggest by its novelty that we are really talking about words instead of things. For the sign of identity that is used in mathematics has precisely the meaning we require. When it is said that $2 + 2 = 4$, '$2 + 2$' and '$4$' are both used to refer to a number. They are indeed proper names of a number, but names with different senses, and the only important difference between this statement and our astronomical example is that here the truth of what is asserted can be established *a priori*.

In ordinary German the words which we have translated by 'sense' and 'reference' are not used to make a contrast such as Frege intends. *Sinn* has the same wide range of usages as the English 'sense', and *Bedeutung* corresponds almost exactly to 'meaning'. In many contexts there could be none but stylistic reasons for preferring one to the other. But the simple verb *deuten*, from which *bedeuten* and *Bedeutung* are derived, can be used for 'point', at least in the metaphorical sense of that English word, and Frege seems to have seized on this peculiarity as a justification for his technical usage of *bedeuten*. He does not explain his reasons, since he never admits that his usage is a departure from ordinary German; but he reveals the movement of his thought when he says in one place that, though a gothic or italic letter *bedeutet* nothing, it nevertheless *andeutet* the argument of a function.[1] For *andeuten*, which means 'hint at', is another derivative of *deuten*, and Frege apparently thought that some importance could be attached to this fact. But whatever his motives may have been for using the word *Bedeutung* as he did, there can be no doubt that he gave it a special significance which it does not possess in ordinary German, and this naturally makes it difficult for us to find a suitable translation. We cannot use the word 'meaning', because it is not good English to say that the phrase 'the morning star' has for its meaning one of the heavenly bodies, though we can say that a person who uses the phrase means (i.e. intends) to refer to one of the heavenly bodies. 'Nominatum'[2] and 'denotation'[3] have been suggested, and there is something to be said in favour of each. For whenever Frege talks of the *Bedeutung* of a symbol, he seems prepared to maintain that the symbol under consideration is a name, or at any rate a quasi-name; and we

---

[1] *Gg.*, i, § 17.  [2] R. Carnap, *Meaning and Necessity.*
[3] Alonzo Church, 'The Need for Abstract Entities in Semantic Analysis', *Proceedings of the American Academy of Arts and Sciences*, lxxx (1951), pp. 100–12.

can certainly say that the phrase 'the morning star' denotes a heavenly body. But neither seems quite satisfactory. 'Nominatum' is too obviously artificial, and 'denotation' may be misleading because it has been used as a technical term by John Stuart Mill to make a contrast with connotation which is not exactly the same as that of Frege between *Bedeutung* and *Sinn*. 'Reference' is also not wholly satisfactory, since it is slightly queer to talk of a thing as the reference of a sign, but this translation is not likely to give rise to any misunderstanding. And we can vary our way of speaking from time to time. Frege himself explains his distinction in one place by saying that a proper name (which may be a single word or sign or a combination of such) *expresses* its sense, but *stands for* or *designates* its reference.

In the ordinary use of language for making statements, asking questions, giving orders, &c., it is to be assumed that every distinguishable complete sign has both sense and reference. The reference is an object of some kind, but not necessarily a perceptible object; for Frege is always anxious to controvert the view that nothing exists except what can be perceived, and he expressly includes among his objects such things as numbers, places, instants, and periods of time. The sense, on the other hand, is something by which the object may be singled out for attention. It is not an idea, if by that we mean an image or something private to an individual thinker. For all communication depends on the expression of sense by one man to another, and in special circumstances signs may have a public sense even though they lack all reference. This happens, for example, when words are used in fiction. A novelist may assure us in the preface of his book that the work contains no reference to a real person, but we are able, nevertheless, to understand what he has written. And there is something similar when a man reports the statements of another without himself ascribing any references to the words used by that other. Thus a classical scholar may use the words 'Zeus' and 'Athena' quite intelligibly in an account of Greek mythology though neither he nor his readers believe that there ever were persons such as he describes under those names. But these are special cases. In speech of the ordinary kind all names are supposed to have references, and in a logically perfect language designed for the purposes of science every expression constructed to work like a proper name would indeed have reference. For fallacies arise when phrases which presuppose the truth of existential statements are used without proof of those statements. Thus the phrase 'the least rapidly convergent series' has a sense, but it refers to nothing, and a sentence containing it fails for that reason to serve any useful purpose. We cannot even maintain that anyone who utters it makes a false statement, since presupposing is not the same as asserting.

So far there is nothing very controversial in Frege's theory. Some readers may perhaps be surprised by his use of the phrase 'proper name' to cover such expressions as '2+2', but anyone who objects on this score may substitute 'designation' for 'proper name' without altering anything essential to the doctrine. The case is different when Frege goes on to argue that sentences have both sense and reference. For this involves treating sentences as though they were names or designations, which is undoubtedly strange. He himself recognizes that it is curious to talk of the reference of a sentence, but he argues that we must do so for the following reason. An intelligible sentence undoubtedly has a sense, and this is the thought it expresses, not of course the subjective performance of thinking in the speaker or the hearer, but its objective content which can be thought by many thinkers. But among intelligible sentences there are some that contain designations with no reference, or at any rate designations for which we cannot guarantee a reference. Let us consider, for example, the sentence 'Odysseus was set ashore at Ithaca while sound asleep'. So long as we are content to treat this as part of a work of art, it is no matter of concern to us whether the name 'Odysseus' has a reference, but if we think of it as a serious statement we must assume that the name 'Odysseus' designates something of which the predicate can be affirmed or denied. Now the thought remains the same whether 'Odysseus' has reference or not, and so the demand which we make in the second case for reference as well as sense must be connected in some way with our search for truth. According to Frege it indicates that we expect a reference for the sentence as a whole, namely its truth-value, or the circumstance that it is true or false. In short 'every declarative sentence concerned with the reference of its words is . . . to be regarded as a proper name, and its reference, if it has one, is either the True or the False'.[1]

In his *Begriffsschrift* Frege had suggested that his judgement stroke might be taken as equivalent to the common predicate of all judgements, namely, ' . . . is a fact'. But he now rejects this view.

'One can indeed say "The thought that 5 is a prime number is true". But close examination shows that nothing more has been said than in the simple sentence "5 is a prime number". The truth claim arises in each case from the form of the declarative sentence, and when

---

[1] *Über Sinn und Bedeutung*, p. 34.

K k

the latter lacks its usual force, e.g. in the mouth of an actor upon the stage, even "The thought that 5 is a prime number is true" contains only a thought, and indeed the same thought as the simple "5 is a prime number". It follows that the relation of the thought to the True may not be compared with that of subject to predicate. . . . A truth-value cannot be part of a thought, any more than, say, the sun can, for it is not a sense but an object.'[1]

But a truth-value, he argues, can be the reference of a sentence. For it evidently depends on the references of the parts of the sentence, and it remains unaltered when any of these components is replaced by another expression with the same reference. As Leibniz said, 'eadem sunt quae sibi mutuo substitui possunt salva veritate'. Indeed, 'what else but the truth-value could be found that belongs quite generally to every sentence if the reference of its components is relevant and remains unchanged by substitutions of the kind in question?'[2]

All this, however, applies only to complete sentences used in the ordinary fashion. When a form of words which might be used to make a statement appears as a subordinate clause after 'say' or 'believe' or any similar verb, the situation is changed. For it now refers to what would be its sense in the context of direct speech. Let us consider, for example, the complex sentence 'Copernicus believed that the planetary orbits are circles'. Obviously the truth of the whole is not altered if we substitute after 'that' some other expression of the same thought. But the truth-value of the whole would not necessarily remain unaltered if we substituted after 'that' a form of words which expressed a different thought but happened to have the same truth-value as the 'the planetary orbits are circles'. For the truth or falsity of the statement about Copernicus does not depend on the truth or falsity of what he is said to have believed, but solely on his having believed or not having believed what is designated by the subordinate clause, and according to Frege that is a thought.

It must be admitted, however, that in certain circumstances a phrase may refer to a truth-value as well as to a thought. This occurs if some one says 'Copernicus believed rightly that the planetary orbits are circular'; for then the words after 'that' are used in effect twice, once as a subordinate clause, and once as an independent sentence. Nor is this the only complication of the doctrine. For if, as Frege holds, no name can have reference

---

[1] *Über Sinn und Bedeutung*, p. 34.
[2] Ibid. p. 35. Frege seems to be quoting from memory the opening of the *Non Inelegans Specimen Demonstrandi in Abstractis*, where Leibniz wrote 'Eadem sunt quorum unum potest substitui alteri salva veritate', *Philosophische Schriften* (ed. Gerhardt), vii, p. 228.

without having sense, even a subordinate clause which works solely as such should express something distinguishable from the thought it designates; and yet there is nothing in his theory to indicate what this can be. Perhaps he ignored the difficulty because subordinate clauses of the kind we have been considering, i.e. noun clauses, do not appear in the logical formulae of the *Grundgesetze*; but in any case we need not discuss it further at present.

Although Frege extended the usage of the phrase 'proper name' in a rather surprising way, he did not wish to maintain that all signs were of the same kind. On the contrary, he insisted strongly on a distinction between proper names and names or signs of functions, and at this stage he meant by a sign of a function what he had formerly called a function, i.e. an 'incomplete' or 'unsaturated' expression which can be completed by one or more proper names to make a new proper name. Thus '$(\ )^2$' and 'the father of . . .' are functional signs in which the gaps are indicated by empty brackets and dots. But for convenience of exposition Frege introduces a new convention that gaps are to be indicated by small Greek letters. Unlike the other letters of his script, these are not to be understood as abbreviations or as parts of a notation for universality, but simply as marks by which we keep places open for genuine argument signs. Thus we must write 'tan $\xi$ is a trigonometrical function' when we are talking about the function as distinct from its values, though we may write 'tan $x = \dfrac{\sin x}{\cos x}$,' when we wish to say that for any argument the value of tan $\xi$ is identical with the ratio between the value of sin $\xi$ for the same argument and the value of cos $\xi$ for the same argument. The reason for insisting on this way of writing is to make clear that the function itself is something incomplete or unsaturated. Mathematicians sometimes use the word 'function' when it would be more proper to speak either of a functional sign or of a value of a function; but things symbolized should never be confused with symbols, and among things symbolized functions should never be confused with objects. For according to Frege's usage objects include all things that are not functions, i.e. not only sticks and stones and men, but also numbers and truth-values. If we ask what a function is, he tells us that its essence is to be found in a certain connexion or co-ordination between the objects which are its arguments and those which are its corresponding values. But for functions whose values according to his theory are truth-values he has a special terminology. Thus the function represented by the sign '$\xi$ is a man' is often described as the concept 'man' or the concept *Man* and the function with two argument places represented by the sign '$\xi$ is father of $\zeta$' is said to be a relation.

When Frege speaks of a function in writings later than the *Begriffsschrift*, he always means something independent of thought and language. For he does not use the word 'concept' as a psychological term; and although he introduces the general notion of a function by talking first of functional signs, he regards this procedure as merely a device of exposition. But he admits, nevertheless, on several occasions that he finds a serious difficulty in making his meaning clear. He says for example:

'In logical discussions one quite often needs to assert something about a concept and to express this in the form usual for such assertions, viz. to make what is asserted of the concept into the content of the grammatical predicate. Consequently one would expect that the reference of the grammatical subject would be the concept; but the concept as such cannot play this part in view of its predicative nature; it must first be converted into an object, or speaking more precisely, represented by an object.'[1]

And again:

'By a kind of necessity of language, my expressions, taken literally, sometimes miss my thought; I mention an object when what I intend is a concept. . . . Someone may think that this is an artificially created difficulty . . . that one might . . . regard an object's falling under a concept as a relation in which the same thing could occur now as object, now as concept. The words "object" and "concept" would then serve only to indicate the different positions in the relation. This may be done. But anyone who thinks the difficulty is avoided in this way is much mistaken; it is only shifted. For not all parts of thought can be complete; at least one must be unsaturated or predicative; otherwise they would not hold together. . . . We now get the same difficulty for the relation that we were trying to avoid for the concept.'[2]

Some of these remarks may perhaps suggest that the difficulty is peculiar to talk about functions of the sort called concepts and relations, but Frege goes on to say that the same trouble occurs in any attempt to explain clearly the notion of function which is used in mathematical analysis. When we have to discuss that which is essentially incomplete or unsaturated,[3] we cannot avoid a certain inappropriateness of linguistic expression.

A philosopher is in a very awkward position when he finds himself driven to say that his thought cannot be expressed

---

[1] *Über Begriff und Gegenstand*, p. 197.  [2] Ibid., pp. 204–5.
[3] Cf. the Stoic notion of a predicate as an incomplete *lekton*.

adequately, and we shall argue presently that Frege's worry is due to a serious defect in his theory of language. But it is interesting to see how he tries to avoid some of the difficulties of talking about a function $\Phi(\xi)$ by talking instead about its range or course of values (*Wertverlauf*) $\dot{a}\Phi(a)$. In this new notation the small Greek vowel within the bracket marks an argument place as usual, but the corresponding vowel which appears in front with a smooth breathing is supposed to operate in such a way as to make the whole a name for an *object*. Unfortunately it is not easy to understand exactly what this object is. When he first introduces the notion, Frege considers a simple mathematical function $\xi^2-4\xi$ and remarks that the way in which various possible values of this function are associated with different possible arguments can be represented by a curve on graph paper.[1] Since the function $\xi(\xi-4)$ always has the same value as $\xi^2-4\xi$ for the same argument, it obviously determines the same curve, and Frege announces that he will express this state of affairs by saying the two functions have the same range of values. In general, whatever $\Phi(\xi)$ and $\Psi(\xi)$ may be, the statement that $\dot{a}\Phi(a) = \acute{\epsilon}\Psi(\epsilon)$ is to be understood to have the same reference as the statement that $\underset{\frown}{\quad a\quad}\Phi(\mathfrak{a}) = \Psi(\mathfrak{a})$, though the first is a singular statement of identity between two objects whereas the second is a universal statement to the effect that for every argument the value of one function is identical with that of another. From this explanation it seems natural to conclude that a range or course of values is, so to say, the extension of a function. For if we conceive a function as something which correlates objects, namely, those which are its arguments and those which are its values, we may perhaps think of the completed correlation as itself a new object, namely, a set of ordered pairs. Now Frege does indeed use the word 'extension' (*Umfang*) in this connexion, but not exactly as we have suggested. He tells us that for a concept (i.e. a function of one argument whose values are all truth-values) the range is the extension in the ordinary sense of the logicians, i.e. the set of all objects that fall under it. And for other functions he undertakes to indicate the appropriate ranges when they are introduced, giving as his reason for this piecemeal procedure the fact that the basic condition for recognizing the identity of two ranges is not enough by itself to determine what a range is. We must therefore beware of reading too much into Frege's terminology. When he speaks of fixing the range or course of values, what interests him especially is the discovery of an *object* which for certain purposes can represent all functions that have the same values for the same

[1] *Über Funktion und Begriff*, p. 9.

arguments, and within the limits imposed by this condition he thinks the choice of an object is a matter of convenience.

Whatever it may be, the object Frege calls a range of values is certainly not to be confused with the set of values which the function can take for various arguments. This is clear from the fact that a concept can take for value only one or other of the truth-values, whereas its range according to Frege is the set of objects falling under it. Nor should the range of a function as he understands it, be confused with the set of all possible arguments which can be mentioned in the argument place of the functional sign. For in Frege's view *every* object must be considered as a possible argument to the function represented by the sign. Thus the sentence '2 is a man' has a sense, and the worst that can be said of it is that it designates the false. He even maintains that a mathematical function such as $\xi+1$ should be defined in such a way as to allow for arguments other than numbers. He admits, of course, that he finds no use for such a phrase as 'the sun$+1$', but he insists that in a logically perfect language we must provide some reference for it, because otherwise concepts such as $\xi+1 = 10$ will not be sharply defined and logical laws such as the principle of excluded middle will not apply to them with full rigour. What rule we lay down for the wild cases is a matter of comparative indifference, but we must place them in some limbo in order to make sure that our concepts are well defined and every proper name has a reference. An interesting application of this principle may be found in Frege's treatment of the sign which he introduces as substitute for the definite article of ordinary speech.

One important use of the definite article is for the construction of descriptions like 'the man who discovered the elliptical orbits of the planets', and it is this which interests Frege. In his theory of sense and reference he recognizes that the utterance of such a phrase presupposes the existence of one and only one thing falling under a certain concept, but he refuses to say that a speaker of the phrase asserts the presupposition. Now for his purpose it is not sufficient that a phrase which works like a proper name should have reference only when there is a single thing falling under a certain concept, and he therefore introduces a function $\backslash\xi$ defined by the following stipulations: (i) for any argument identical with a range $\acute\epsilon(\epsilon = \varDelta)$, where $\varDelta$ is some object, the value of the function is $\varDelta$; (ii) for any argument not satisfying this condition the value of the function is just the argument. Of these two cases it is the first which corresponds to the ordinary usage of the definite article. For suppose $\varPhi(\xi)$ is a concept under which there falls one and only one object $\varDelta$. Then obviously the value of $\varPhi(\xi)$ for any argument is the same as the value of the function $\xi = \varDelta$ for the same argument. But this justifies us in saying that $\grave{a}\varPhi(a) = \grave{\epsilon}(\epsilon = \varDelta)$, and so we have the desired result

$$\backslash\grave{a}\varPhi(a) = \backslash\grave{\epsilon}(\epsilon = \varDelta) = \varDelta,$$

i.e. $\backslash\grave{a}\varPhi(a)$ is the sole member of $\grave{a}\phi(a)$ if this latter is what later logicians have called a unit-class. In order to preserve the principle of excluded middle it is necessary, however, to provide some reference for '$\backslash\grave{a}\varPhi(a)$' in the case where $\varPhi(\xi)$ is not a function under which there falls one and only one object, and this is achieved by the second stipulation. For since *ex hypothesi* there is no $\varDelta$ such that $\grave{a}\varPhi(a) = \grave{\epsilon}(\epsilon = \varDelta)$, we have $\backslash\grave{a}\varPhi(a) = \grave{a}\varPhi(a)$. Thus if English were reformed in accordance with Frege's legislation for his own script, anyone who said 'The king of France is bald' could be charged with making a false statement. For although he could *not* be said to assert by implication that there is one and only one king of France, he could be said to make a remark which in present political circumstances is equivalent to 'The class of kings of France is bald'; and this last (which must be distinguished, of course, from 'Kings of France are bald') is certainly untrue according to Frege's way of thinking, whether or not there are any kings of France.

## 3. *The Logic of the Grundgesetze*

Having expounded his notion of function with full generality, Frege makes it basic in his account of logic, and the new programme involves some reinterpretation of the signs which he introduced in his *Begriffsschrift*. Admittedly the judgement stroke is not a functional sign according to his new view, since it can no longer be interpreted as an abbreviation for the predicate 'is a fact'; but there is also a sense in which it may be said to stand outside logic. For its purpose is simply to show what the author asserts; and logic is not concerned with asserting, but with that which may be asserted. The grammar of the system requires, however, that the judgement stroke should be succeeded by a horizontal of the kind formerly called a content stroke, and this is certainly a functional sign. For when its argument is the True, ——$\xi$ has the True for its value, and in all other cases the False. Thus '——$2+2 = 4$' is not properly speaking a statement, but rather a name for the True, and '——$2+ 2 = 5$' and '——$2$' are both names for the False. The last example may seem somewhat surprising, but we have here another application of Frege's principle that any object must be considered as a possible argument of any function if it is grammatically possible to put its name in the argument place of the functional sign. Frege himself does not speak of grammatical possibility in this connexion, but the need for such a notion can be seen from consideration of the two functional signs which appear next in the construction of his system, namely, the negation stroke and the condition stroke. These both have the peculiarity that they cannot occur except in connexion with horizontals, and so the functions they represent can take only truth-values for their arguments. Since these functions have truth-values also for their own values, they are, so to say, functions from truth-values to truth-values, just as $\xi^2$ is a function from numbers to numbers; and for this reason they have sometimes been called truth-functions by later logicians. On the other hand, $\xi = \zeta$ is a function which can take objects of any kinds as arguments.

So far we have mentioned only functions which take one or more objects as arguments, but Frege recognizes that there may be functions of the second level, or functions of functions, and cites as examples $-^{\mathfrak{a}}\!\!-\phi(\mathfrak{a})$ and $\dot{\epsilon}\phi(\epsilon)$. It will be noticed that in naming these he indicates the argument place by means of a small Greek letter from the part of the alphabet usually reserved for abbreviations of functional signs. Another example of a second-level function is $-_{\mathfrak{a}}\!\!-\phi(\mathfrak{a})$, which is sometimes called existence but should more properly be called possession of an instance or having the True as value for some argument. Already in his *Grundlagen* Frege had remarked that the ontological argument for the existence of God was fallacious because it confused a second-level concept with a first-level concept which another first-level concept might involve as one of its marks or features.[1] In order to appreciate the justice of this criticism we need only reflect that Descartes tried to prove his point by saying that divinity entails existence just as triangularity entails the having internal angles equal to two right angles.

But it was not until he wrote the *Grundgesetze* that Frege devised a notation for talking in general about functions of the second level. And then he wrote:

$$`\!\!\!\begin{array}{l} \rule{1cm}{0.4pt}M_\beta(f(\beta))\,' \\ \rule{0.5cm}{0.4pt}\mathfrak{f}\rule{0.2cm}{0.4pt}M_\beta(\mathfrak{f}(\beta)) \end{array}$$

for 'Every function of the second level which holds of all functions of the first level with one argument holds of any function of the first level with one argument.' This corresponds, of course, to the axiom

which he had stated in the *Begriffsschrift* for functions of the first level, but it is more complicated in expression because it has to provide not only for a distinction of functions according to level but also for a distinction of functions according to the number of their arguments. The small Greek letter within the innermost pair of brackets serves as usual to mark an argument place and its occurrence here is important because it shows that the functions of first level which we now consider as arguments are such as themselves have only one argument. The large italic '*M*' is a free variable which indicates that we are talking about functions of the second level, and its small Greek subscript serves to show that the functions in question are such as can hold of functions of the first level with one argument. If we wished to generalize about second-level properties (such as transitivity) which can belong only to two-termed relations (i.e. functions with two arguments whose values are always truth-values), we should have to write two small Greek letters within the innermost brackets and two subscripts to the italic capital. Nor is this the end of the complexities which suggest themselves when we begin to discuss

functions of functions. For we may regard $-\overset{\mathfrak{f}}{\smile}-\mu_\beta(\mathfrak{f}(\beta))$ and $-\overset{\mathfrak{f}}{\smile}-\mu_{\beta,\gamma}(\mathfrak{f}(\beta,\gamma))$ as functions of the third level and then try to elaborate a notation for talking about all such functions. Or again, we may consider functions of uneven level such as that of falling under a concept. Frege notes these possibilities but does not discuss them in detail. It is clear, indeed, that he dislikes even the complication involved in his symbolism for universal statements about second-level functions of first-level functions with one argument. For he makes only one use of the special axiom stated above and congratulates himself that he has been able to avoid further complication by talking of ranges instead of the functions which determine them.[1]

For Frege his introduction of the notation for ranges was the most important of all the innovations he made in his *Grundgesetze* because it freed him from the embarrassments of talking about functions of various levels and allowed him to say what he wanted to say by reference to objects.[2] Admittedly most of

[1] *Gg.*, i, § 25.        [2] *Gg.*, i, §§ 9 and 25.

the objects to which he refers are not perceptible, but, unlike functions, they are all *complete* entities, and in his view it is just a weakness of the flesh to assume that there can be no objects except those we see or touch.

In order to get the full benefit of his notation for ranges he finds it necessary, however, to introduce another function with the following definition:

$$\text{'}\Vdash\backslash \grave{a}\left(\begin{array}{c} \underline{\phantom{xx}\mathfrak{g}\phantom{xx}}\quad \mathfrak{g}(a) = a \\ \underline{\phantom{xxxx}}\, u = \grave{\epsilon}\mathfrak{g}(\epsilon) \end{array}\right) = a \cap u.\text{'}$$

As always in Frege's definitions, the *definiendum* appears here on the right, and since it is a functional sign with two argument places it is written with two italic letters which occur also on the left. In words, the effect is to provide (i) that for any object $\varDelta$ and any function $\varPhi(\xi)$ the expression '$\varDelta \cap \grave{\epsilon}\varPhi(\epsilon)$' shall have the same reference as '$\varPhi(\varDelta)$', and (ii) that for any object $\varDelta$ and any object $\varGamma$ which is not a range the expression $\varDelta \cap \varGamma$ shall be a name for the null class. Thus if we disregard the second stipulation, which is merely a provision for waste cases, the expression '$\xi \cap \zeta$' corresponds fairly closely to '$\xi$ is a member of $\zeta$'. But we must be careful not to identify them, since in Frege's scheme the function $\varPhi(\xi)$ need not be a concept. It may, for example, be the numerical function $\xi^2$, in which case $3 \cap \grave{\epsilon}(\epsilon^2) = 3^2$. Or again it may be the function $\grave{\epsilon}(\xi > \epsilon)$ whose values are themselves ranges, in which case one of the arguments of the new function will be a *double* range of values, say $\grave{a}\grave{\epsilon}(a > \epsilon)$. The second of these examples is especially important because Frege uses his new notation as a way of expressing relations. For

$$3 \cap \grave{a}\grave{\epsilon}(a > \epsilon) = \grave{\epsilon}(3 > \epsilon)$$

and so
$$2 \cap (3 \cap \grave{a}\grave{\epsilon}(a > \epsilon)) = 2 \cap \grave{\epsilon}(3 > \epsilon)$$
$$= 3 > 2.$$

Obviously there is nothing to be gained from this way of writing in a case as simple as that we have chosen for illustration, but it seems to offer the great advantage of simplicity in cases where the alternative way of writing would involve application of quantifiers to relational functions of higher level, and for this reason Frege uses it extensively in the later development of his system.

For our present purpose it is not necessary to consider the details of the structure that Frege erects on the foundation we have described, but the axioms and rules in which he formulates the logic of the *Grundgesetze* deserve special notice.

For axioms or basic laws Frege sets out the following seven assertions:[1]

I. $\vdash$ ⌐⌐ $a$
      $b$
      $a$
    IIa. $\vdash$ ────── $f(a)$
               $\mathfrak{a}$ $f(\mathfrak{a})$
    IIb. $\vdash$ ────── $M_\beta(f(\beta))$
               $\mathfrak{f}$ $M_\beta(\mathfrak{f}(\beta))$

III. $\vdash$ $g\left(\begin{array}{l}\mathfrak{f}\\ \mathfrak{f}(a)\\ \mathfrak{f}(b)\end{array}\right)$
       $g(a = b)$
    IV. $\vdash$ $(\text{─── } a) = (\text{─── } b)$
             $(\text{─── } a) = (\text{─┬─ } b)$

V. $\vdash (\acute{\epsilon}f(\epsilon) = \acute{a}g(a)) = (\text{─}\mathfrak{a}\text{─}f(\mathfrak{a}) = g(\mathfrak{a}))$

VI. $\vdash a = \backslash\acute{\epsilon}(a = \epsilon)$

It will be noticed that, apart from the horizontal stroke, which is required for the expression of any assertion in the script, each basic sign has a single axiom assigned for the determination of its use, and that the order of introduction is apparently one of increasing complexity. Thus IV occurs where it does because Frege now thinks it proper to fix the meaning of his negation stroke by the help of the sign of identity introduced in III. But he lays no stress on this arrangement, and the only axiom on which he makes any lengthy comment is V. Of this he remarks that it must be accepted as a distinct law of logic because it is essential for the development of his system and cannot be derived from any other basic laws. Whenever logicians talk of the extensions of concepts they assume it, though usually without realizing what they are doing. It is fundamental in any attempt to construct a calculus of logic after the manner of Leibniz or Boole, and it is equally important for an account of the foundations of arithmetic, because numbers of all types, including even natural numbers, are to be defined as the extensions of concepts.[2]

Apart from its provision for functions not mentioned in the *Begriffsschrift*, this set of axioms for logic differs from Frege's earlier set in that it is not designed to be used with the *modus ponens* and the principle of substitution as the only rules of inference. For practical convenience and brevity in the making of deductions Frege now replaces some of his old axioms and even some of his theorems by new rules of inference. But he presents these latter as items in a general collection of rules for the use of his script, and in order to show the exactitude of his thought we shall summarize all these, except the last six, which are merely conventions about the use of brackets.[3] In what follows the word 'statement' should be understood as referring always to a statement of the system (i.e. an axiom or a theorem derived from the axioms), the phrases 'lower clause' and 'upper clause' as referring respectively to a condition and that of which it is a condition, and the phrase 'italic schema' as referring to an expression which contains one or more italic letters and could be converted into a name (either for an object or for a function, as the case may be) by suitable substitutions for these.

1. *Amalgamation of horizontals.* The horizontals which go with the negation stroke, the condition stroke, and the universal quantifier may be amalgamated with each other or with a simple horizontal in the same line.

2. *Rearrangement of conditions.* The order of the lower clauses of a statement may be changed at will.

3. *Contraposition.* A lower clause and an upper clause may always be interchanged if the truth-values of both are altered at the same time (i.e. by negation).

4. *Amalgamation of similar conditions.* A lower clause which appears several times in the same statement need not be written more than once.

5. *Change from an italic to a gothic letter.* An italic letter may be replaced throughout a statement in which it occurs by one and the same gothic letter, that is an object letter by an object letter and a function letter by a function letter, provided that the gothic letter is introduced at the same time in a concavity before an upper clause outside of which the italic letter did not occur. If, however, this upper clause contains the whole scope of a gothic letter and the italic letter occurred within that scope, the new gothic letter must be chosen to be different from the old.

6. *Inference (a).* If a statement has a lower clause which differs from another statement only in the absence of the judgement stroke, we may assert as a conclusion the statement which results from the first by suppression of the lower clause.

7. *Inference (b).* If the same collocation of signs (proper name or italic object schema) occurs in one statement as upper clause and in another as a lower clause, we may assert as a conclusion a statement which has for upper clause the upper clause of the second and for lower clauses all the lower clauses of both except that already mentioned. In the transition lower clauses which are similar may be amalgamated according to rule (4).

8. *Inference (c).* If two statements have the same upper clause and a lower clause of one differs from a lower clause of the other only by the prefixing of a negation stroke, we may assert as a conclusion a statement which has for upper clause the upper clause of both and for lower clauses all the lower clauses of both except the two mentioned above.

9. *Citation of statements with substitution for italic letters.* When we cite a statement we may at the same time make a simple inference either

by substituting the same proper name or italic object schema through-out for any italic object letter or by substituting the same name of a function or italic function schema for any italic function letter, pro-vided that in the latter case we preserve the level and the number of arguments of the function at which the original italic function letter hinted.

10. *Citation of statements with replacement of gothic letters.* When we cite a statement, we may replace a gothic letter in a concavity and in all argument places of the connected function by another gothic letter of the same kind (i.e. an object letter or a function letter, as the case may be), provided that we do not thereby destroy any difference of lettering in the original where the scope of one letter contained the scope of another and the first letter itself occurred within the scope of the second.

11. *Citation of statements with replacement of Greek vowels.* When we cite a statement, we may replace a Greek vowel under a smooth breath-ing and in all argument places of the connected function by another Greek vowel, subject to the same provision as in the preceding rule.

12. *Citation of definitions.* When we cite a definition, we may replace the definition stroke by the judgement stroke and carry through the alterations permissible in the citation of statements according to the last three rules.

According to Frege all the truths of arithmetic can be derived from his axioms by the application of his rules. But it is obvious that arithmetic deals with notions, in particular with that of number, for which there are no simple expressions among his basic signs. It is therefore essential for the success of his enterprise that he should show how these notions can be defined by com-plexes of his basic signs, and for clarity of exposition it may be necessary that he should construct a sequence of definitions in which each later item presupposes the earlier. But it is well known that fallacies may be committed in the making of definitions, as in the making of inferences, and with his usual care for rigour Frege tries to guard against this danger by laying down seven principles to be observed whenever new expressions are introduced into his system by definition.[1] Three of them are quite general and the other four are concerned with various special cases which occur in his system. Again we summarize:

1. Every name correctly constructed out of the defined names must have a reference, since otherwise questions about the applicability of signs would be left indeterminate.

2. The same sign must not be defined in two different ways, since it may then be doubtful whether the two definitions are in agreement.

3. A defined name must be simple, i.e. not composed of other names,

---

[1] *Gg.*, i, § 33.

since otherwise it might be doubtful whether the explanations of these names were in agreement.

4. A proper name introduced by definition must be replaceable at all its occurrences by the definiens, and it must never be used as a name of a function, since from such use there could be no return to the basic names.

5. A name which is introduced for a function of the first level with one argument must contain only one argument place, since if there were several argument places they might be filled differently with the result that the name came to stand for a function of several arguments. In the definition all the argument places of the definiens must be filled with one and the same italic letter, which is to be used also to indicate the argument place of the definiendum.

6. Similarly a name which is introduced for a function of the first level with two arguments must contain two and only two argument places. In the definition all the connected argument places of the definiendum must be filled by one and the same italic letter, which is to be used also to indicate one of the two argument places of the definiendum; and argument places which are not connected must be filled with different letters.

7. It follows that a definition must never contain on either side an italic letter which does not appear also on the other. If the substitution of proper names for italic letters in the definiens turns the latter into a properly constructed proper name, then according to the conventions of the system the function name which appears as definiendum always has a reference.

## 4. Frege's Achievement

Frege's *Begriffsschrift* is the first really comprehensive system of formal logic. Aristotle was interested chiefly in certain common varieties of general propositions. He did indeed formulate the principles of non-contradiction and excluded middle, which belong to a part of logic more fundamental than his theory of the syllogism; but he failed to recognize the need for a systematic account of primary logic. Such an account was supplied, at least in part, by Chrysippus; but neither he nor the medieval logicians who wrote about *consequentiae* succeeded in showing clearly the relation between primary and general logic. Leibniz and Boole, recognizing a parallelism between primary logic and certain propositions of general logic about attributes or classes, worked out in abstract fashion a calculus that seemed to cover both; but neither of these enlarged the traditional conception of logic to include the theory of relations. Working on some suggestions of De Morgan, Peirce explored this new field, and shortly after the publication of the *Begriffsschrift* he even produced independently a doctrine of functions with a notation adequate for expressing all the principles formulated by Frege; but he never reduced his thoughts to a system or set out a number of basic principles like those given in the last section. Frege's work, on the other hand, contains all the essentials of modern logic, and it is not unfair either to his predecessors or to his successors to say that 1879 is the most important date in the history of the subject.

Of all the novelties which Frege introduced his use of quantifiers was the most important. In our account of Peirce's contribution to logic we have already drawn attention to the significance of this step, but it is proper at this point to emphasize once more that use of quantifiers to bind variables is the main distinguishing feature of modern logical symbolism and the device which gives it superiority not only over ordinary language but also over symbolism of the algebraic type used by Boole. With this we are at last able to understand and to present clearly in one simple rational scheme a host of complications which puzzled logicians of earlier ages and were solved if at all only by *ad hoc* theories such as that of arguments κατὰ πρόσληψιν, that of modalities *de re* and *de dicto*, that of *suppositio personalis confusa et distributiva singulata* and many other varieties of *suppositio*, that of Boole's *v* symbol, and that of the algebra of relatives. Furthermore, even the supposedly simple theory of the four kinds of categorical statement becomes more easily intelligible when it is realized that, whatever else it may convey, 'Every man is mortal' entails the universal closure of the functional expression 'if x is a man x is mortal'. And when this has been clarified, the relation of Aristotle's logic to that of the Stoics becomes clear for the first time. In short, it is no exaggeration to say that use of quantifiers to bind variables was one of the greatest intellectual inventions of the nineteenth century.

With the possible exception of his *Grundlagen*, Frege's works have never been widely read. No doubt some who have opened his books have been deterred by his symbolism. Lord Russell, for example, confesses that on first acquaintance with volume I of the *Grundgesetze* he failed for this reason to grasp its importance or even to understand its contents.[1] But the forbidding appearance of his script can scarcely be the sole or even the chief cause of the delay of logicians in recognizing Frege's great merits. The truth seems to be rather that he presented too many difficult novelties at once, and with too few concessions to human weakness. Most of the German text of his logical writings is clear, but his exposition of his own views, in contrast with his criticism of the views of others, is very condensed, and an unsympathetic reader may

[1] *Principles of Mathematics*, p. vi.

easily get the impression that he was very critical of the use of language by others but curiously blind to the puzzling nature of many of his own statements on such subjects as truth-values, functions, and ranges. Like other innovators in logic he has often been regarded as a purveyor of unprofitable subtleties. But this is not to say that his work has been without influence. On the contrary, his writings are a mine from which at various periods his successors have drawn new material.

When he was finishing his own *Principles of Mathematics* (of which the first and only volume was published in 1903), Lord Russell made a more careful study of Frege's logic and wrote an appendix which is perhaps the first sympathetic large-scale review of his work from the *Begriffsschrift* to the first volume of the *Grundgesetze*. In volume I of *Principia Mathematica*, published by A. N. Whitehead and B. Russell in 1910, the influence of Frege is obvious, and even those doctrines of Russell in which he disagreed with Frege (e.g. his theory of descriptions and his theory of types) were at least suggested by difficulties in Frege's work. A little later Ludwig Wittgenstein became an admirer, with results which may be seen at various places in his *Tractatus Logico-Philosophicus* (first published in 1921 as an article in Ostwald's *Annalen der Naturphilosophie*). And quite recently Frege's doctrine of sense and reference, which was for many years considered the most unprofitable part of his work, has been reconsidered sympathetically by Rudolf Carnap[1] and Alonzo Church[2].

It seems that logicians have recognized the merits of Frege's ideas only when they themselves became ready to discuss the questions he raised. This is not to say that the history of logic in the twentieth century is merely a record of the gradual assimilation of his work into the body of accepted doctrine; for there have been some very important innovations of which he never dreamt. But his achievement was so great that a large part of what comes after can be reviewed most conveniently in relation to his work.

In the next chapter we shall consider formal developments in logic after Frege's time, opening each topic with a brief reminder of his position. Then we shall go on to discuss some problems in the philosophy of logic which have been raised by his work; in particular questions about sense and reference. And in the third chapter after this we shall take up again the history of the philosophy of mathematics, starting from the publication of the second volume of the *Grundgesetze* with its *Nachwort* on Russell's discovery of a contradiction in Frege's system.

---

[1] *Meaning and Necessity*, especially § 8 and §§ 28–30.
[2] *Introduction to Mathematical Logic*, vol. i, §§ 01–04.

# IX

## FORMAL DEVELOPMENTS AFTER FREGE

### 1. *Varieties of Symbolism*

THE details of the apparatus which Frege invented for the presentation of logic are extremely ingenious. His script is admittedly cumbersome, but his use of type from different founts enables him to distinguish the different roles of letters which are often confused together under the technical name 'variable', and his insistence on the distinction between the use and the mention of symbols is admirable. In this section we shall consider changes which have been made since his day for purposes of simplicity and clarity, and it will be convenient to begin with the conventions of quotation.

Although Frege's purpose in elaborating his script is to provide a *substitute* for ordinary language in the presentation of mathematics, he has to introduce it by means of ordinary language, and at this stage he does not hesitate to treat it as a *supplement* to ordinary language. That is to say, just as chemists mingle their special signs with the words of their mother-tongue, so Frege often writes sentences in which he *uses* his special signs together with German words. In this context, naturally, the signs appear without quotation marks. When, on the other hand, Frege wishes to *mention* his special signs in the course of a German sentence, he encloses them within quotation marks, just as he would enclose German words when he had to talk about them. In order to give a correct impression of his work we have followed this practice throughout our exposition of his logic in the last chapter. It is a mistake, however, to suppose that introduction of quotation marks is the only way, or even the best way, of avoiding confusion between use and mention of special symbols. A simpler method is to renounce at the beginning all use of the special symbolism as a supplement to ordinary language and so to make it clear that whenever the special symbols occur they must be taken as quoted. Classical scholars commonly adopt this practice when discussing the words of a classical text (though sometimes they also allow themselves to *use* Greek or Latin words, as we have done in our earlier chapters where there was no real possibility of confusion), and an example of its application to logic (which is very near to Boole's own practice) can be found in our section on the Algebra of Logic. In all such cases it is a help if the signs under discussion are distinguished typographically from those of ordinary language, e.g. if the letters of the special symbolism are all printed in italic. But the simplicity of this device has to be paid for by circumlocution in certain cases, where Frege's technique would seem more natural. Thus instead of saying '$a+b$ is the class which has for members all things that are members either of the class $a$ or of the class $b$' we must say '$a+b$ designates the class which has for members all things that are members either of the class designated by $a$ or of the class designated by $b$'. The choice between the two methods is a matter of taste. In the remainder of this book we shall follow the practice of our section on the Algebra of Logic, rather than that of Frege, since the former seems more economical for what we have to do. But in an attempt to get the best of both worlds we shall occasionally allow ourselves to combine English words with special signs of logic; and when we do so, we shall print the English words in italic type to show that they are temporarily seconded to the special script under discussion.

Frege's use of letters in special type for the exposition of the basic rules of his system is a very convenient device which may be adopted with advantage by all logicians, whatever their views about quotation. He tells us, for example:

'From the two statements "$\vdash \overset{\Gamma}{\underset{\Delta}{\rule{0pt}{1em}}}$" and "$\vdash \Delta$" we may derive the statement "$\vdash \Gamma$".'[1]

Here the letters are obviously free variables which have for their scope the whole statement in which Frege formulates his *modus ponens*. But, as he says, they do not belong properly to his concept script. Their work is not to express universality in statements of that script, but rather to express universality in statements about statements of that script. And for that reason they must have the peculiar property of over-riding the quotation marks within which they are enclosed. This has shocked some critics who think that quotation marks can be used only for the purpose of making a name of what occurs within them. But to object is to take too narrow a view of the possibilities of language. If we make clear in advance, as Frege does, that Greek capitals have this relation to the quotation marks with which they occur in our text, there is nothing at all improper in his device. Quotation marks were made for man, not man for quotation marks.

---

[1] *Grundgesetze der Arithmetik*, i, § 14.

In practice we shall dispense with quotation marks for the reason given above and use italic capitals in place of Frege's Greek capitals. The italic style is to suggest kinship with the special script we use for logic (i.e. a kinship that might have been indicated in another convention by inclusion within the same quotation marks), but the employment of capitals is to suggest the over-riding power we have just noticed. Since their chief use is in the presentation of rules by means of schemata such as

$$\frac{P \quad \textit{If P then Q}}{Q},$$

it seems most illuminating to follow W. V. Quine in describing them as schematic letters.[1] In any such case as that mentioned the form under consideration might be indicated by reference to the common features of a number of genuine examples set out in detail, but the use of schematic letters makes for perspicuity while leaving it open to the reader, as Frege says, to supply a genuine example by interpretation of the letters whenever he finds it convenient to do so. Perhaps these capital letters may be said to *represent* signs of the script, not in the sense of being designations of such signs (for they are certainly not that), but rather in the sense in which dummy guns are said to represent real guns during a tactical exercise.

In *Grundzüge der theoretischen Logik* by Hilbert and Ackermann and also in *Grundlagen der Mathematik* by Hilbert and Bernays gothic letters are used for the same purpose, but with an additional refinement whereby large letters represent *expressions* of propositions and propositional functions and small letters represent *designations* of all kinds. Since, as we shall see in the next chapter, confusion has arisen from failure to recognize the distinction between expressions (in a strict sense) and designations, it is an improvement of Frege's technique to introduce some convention for distinguishing the letters by which they are represented, but this end can be achieved more economically by reserving letters from certain parts of the alphabet for certain purposes. In what follows we shall use the letters $P$, $Q$, $R$, $S$, and $T$ as representatives for propositional expressions, the letters $F$, $G$, $H$, $J$, and $K$ as representatives for expressions of propositional functions, and the letters $X$, $Y$, $Z$, $V$, and $W$ as representatives for designations. If we wish to consider a common pattern shared by formulae of a script which differ only in respect of the variables of the script

---

[1] *Methods of Logic*, pp. 22, 91 f. Quine does not adopt the convention of Frege whereby schematic letters are always capitals and therefore typographically distinct from variables of the special script.

which they contain (e.g. in Frege's script the common pattern of —$\overset{\mathfrak{x}}{\smile}$—$\mathfrak{x}+1 = 1+\mathfrak{x}$ and —$\overset{\mathfrak{y}}{\smile}$—$\mathfrak{y}+1 = 1+\mathfrak{y}$), we may represent these also by special letters of the same status as our schematic letters, provided we make clear in some way that the signs represented are variables of the script. If, however, we are content to treat variables of the script as part of its formal apparatus and significant only of linkages between gaps, we may confine ourselves to the varieties of schematic letters just noticed, since these will suffice for the pronouncements we have to make as logicians.

For a proper understanding of the use of schematic letters it is essential to recognize that they are neither variables of the special script under investigation nor yet symbols of the sort which many modern logicians introduce under the name of syntactical or metalinguistic variables (i.e. symbols which mark gaps appropriate for designations of signs of the basic script).[1] Schematic letters are to be considered rather in the way Frege suggested, as abbreviations for any signs or sign-complexes of suitable type which the reader may select from the basic script. They are indeed variables, but of a peculiar kind. Although they occur within quotation marks (or at any rate in passages where these might have been used), they are never themselves quoted (i.e. mentioned), even when alone, unless, as in the last paragraph, they are expressly called letters. For the gaps they mark are to be treated as though made within the quoted material *after it has been quoted*. From this it follows that they are a device of second-order discourse and that the universality they can express belongs to such discourse rather than to that quoted. This usage involves a special convention about quotation, but one which is simple and natural. It is in fact the convention followed by the Stoics in their presentation of primary logic with the help of phrases such as 'the first' and 'the second' and again by the successors of Aristotle when they explain the theory of syllogistic by means of skeleton arguments.

Within Frege's script the basic device is the use of a Gothic letter to mark a gap in an expression. As he expounds it, this device is inseparable from the use of a gothic letter in a concavity of a horizontal stroke as a universal prefix or quantifier. But we can easily conceive a modification of his script in which there would be not only universal quantifiers but also prefixes of other kinds. Thus Frege might have written —$\overset{\frown}{\mathfrak{a}}$—$\Phi(\mathfrak{a})$ for the existential closure of a propositional function, i.e. as an equivalent

[1] R. Carnap, *The Logical Syntax of Language*, § 4; W. V. Quine, *Mathematical Logic*, §§ 4–6.

for —————$\mathfrak{a}$—————$\varPhi(\mathfrak{a})$. And again he might have used gothic letters instead of small Greek vowels in his notation for ranges. He might, for example, have put $\hat{\mathfrak{a}}\varPhi(\mathfrak{a})$ instead of $\dot{a}\varPhi(a)$ as a sign for the class to which a thing belongs if and only if it has the character expressed by $\varPhi$. Such modifications are in fact to be found in the script used by Whitehead and Russell for *Principia Mathematica*. According to the convention followed by them and most of their successors gap signs are small italic letters ($p$, $q$, $r$, $s$, and $t$ in gaps to be filled by propositional expressions, $f$, $g$, $h$, $j$, and $k$ in gaps to be filled by functional expressions, and $x$, $y$, $z$, $v$, and $w$ in gaps to be filled by designations) and there are various prefixes by which these letters may be bound with the results shown in the following table:

| | |
|---|---|
| $(x)F(x)$ . . . . . | *Whatever you please, F(it).* |
| $(\exists x)F(x)$ . . . . . | *There is something F(which).* |
| $\hat{x}F(x)$ . . . . . | *The class of all things F(which).* |
| $(\imath x)F(x)$ . . . . . | *The single thing F(which).* |

In each of the first two examples the complex sign made by addition of the prefix is an expression, but in the third and in the fourth it is a designation. Clearly the use of one style of type for the marking of gaps in all these cases brings with it no disadvantage, but on the contrary a gain in clarity.

By the queer-sounding translations in the table above we have tried to bring out the point that italic letters serve here not only to mark gaps but also to link them with prefixes. As W. V. Quine has said, their work in symbolic logic is rather like that of pronouns in ordinary language.[1] Sometimes logicians try to make this clear by reading $(x)F(x)$ as though it were an abbreviation of *For any x, F(x)* and offering similar expansions for the other composite signs listed above. As a technical device such phraseology may be harmless and convenient, but it is unsatisfactory as an explanation because it involves an unfortunate mixture of technical symbolism with natural language. When we read in ordinary English 'for any . . . ' we think of the gap as one to be filled by a general term such as 'man', but that is not at all what is wanted in any place marked by $x$. On the other hand, if we allow ourselves to think of $F$ as a general term, e.g. an adjective, we can get versions which sound natural, namely, *Everything is F, Something is F, The class of all F things*, and *The single F thing*. But even these renderings are not quite sound, since a functional expression is not a general term like 'square', but rather something like ' . . . is square'.

---

[1] *Mathematical Logic*, § 12.

When he wishes to talk about a function (i.e. to make it the subject of his discourse), Frege uses a composite sign of the form $\Phi(\xi)$, in which the small Greek letter is again a gap sign intended to show the unsaturated nature of the function and at the same time to indicate the way in which the function enters into the discourse. He fails, however, to notice that the whole sign $\Phi(\xi)$ must be a *designation* of a function and therefore not itself incomplete in the manner of a functional *expression*. In similar contexts Whitehead and Russell use the composite sign $F(\hat{x})$. This has the merit of retaining the ordinary style of gap sign but with a modification to show the special service which the whole sign now has to perform. The situation would be even clearer if the functional expression were allowed to appear in its ordinary guise but with a prefix introduced explicitly for the purpose of building up designations. Corresponding to the class abstractor noticed above we might have a function abstractor $\check{x}$. Thus $\check{x}\,F(x)$ would be short for *the function satisfied by anything $F(which)$*, and no one who used it would be in any danger of supposing, as Frege does, that talk of functions must inevitably involve bad grammar. In what follows we shall nevertheless follow the practice of Whitehead and Russell for the sake of uniformity.[1]

In all the contexts we have considered so far gap signs occur within functional expressions which themselves occur as parts of still larger complex signs; here each variable, as they are commonly called, has a prefix or other sign to bind it. But in the context for which he reserved italic type Frege used gap signs to express universality without prefixes. According to his explanation an expression containing italic letters is to be regarded as an abbreviation for an expression which is similar except for containing gothic letters in place of italic and having universal quantifiers at the beginning to govern the whole. The same account of real variables (i.e. free variables used to express universality) is to be found in Russell's introduction to the second edition of *Principia Mathematica*. It follows that an expression containing real variables can never occur as a mere part of a larger propositional expression (unless distinguished by quotation marks or some similar device), or to put the matter in another way, the scope of the universalization expressed by the use of a free variable must be the whole of the expression in which it occurs. Since this is so, it is not strictly necessary to use a special style of printing for gap signs which express universality without the help of prefixes. The fact that they have the additional role is shown already by the fact that expressions in which they occur appear

---

[1] A. Church uses the notation $\lambda x F x$ in the desired sense.

as complete sentences. Thus whenever it is clear from the context that an expression $F(x)$ is to be taken as a sentence, we are to understand it as an abbreviation for $(x)F(x)$. If, however, $F(x)$ were often cited in quotation marks or as it is here, we might find it tedious to indicate on each occasion what exactly was cited, and in such circumstances it would be useful to adopt a convention that $x$ remained a mere gap sign unless modified in some way (e.g. by printing in bold face) to indicate that it had the additional role of expressing universality. But even this is unnecessary in Frege's works and in *Principia Mathematica*, where Whitehead and Russell follow Frege's practice of putting an assertion sign before all their symbolic statements. For the presence of this sign is sufficient to show that any free variables contained in the following expression must be understood as though they were bound by universal quantifiers placed at the beginning of the whole expression. It has been suggested, indeed, that this is the only useful role of the assertion sign, and that it might be taken as an abbreviation for 'The expression which results from the following when universal quantifiers are prefixed to bind all the free variables is a theorem'.[1]

Although the use of letters to express universality without the help of quantifiers appears in Frege's account of his script as a device of abbreviation, it is historically the earliest use of variables in logic and mathematics, and that is why letters which appear in this role have been called real variables, whereas those bound by prefixes have been called apparent variables. The great merit of this notation is that it allows for the construction of universal statements which can safely be manipulated in many respects as though they were singular statements. And this is probably one of the reasons why it has sometimes been said that a real variable denotes ambiguously any and all of its values, i.e. any and all of the things denoted unambiguously by the signs appropriate for filling the gap it marks. The phrase is unfortunate, but it is true that a real variable can be treated for many purposes as a representative of signs appropriate to its place. We have already taken advantage of this fact in our use of italic capitals. Indeed the only difference between capitals and small letters used as real variables is that the former are reserved for use in second-order statements; but this carries with it the consequence that they have supreme scope and may even over-ride quotation marks, when that is necessary for the sense of the whole, considered as a universal statement.

If we tried to formulate a rule such as that of the *modus ponens*

<hr>

[1] W. V. Quine, *Mathematical Logic*, § 16.

by means of small letters, we should fall into serious confusion. It would be absurd, for example, to offer the pattern

$$\frac{p \quad \textit{If p then q}}{q}$$

since, according to the conventions which govern the use of small letters, $p$ occurring by itself in a place appropriate to a sentence must be taken as a universal statement equivalent to $(p)\ p$, i.e. to the assertion of all propositions whatsoever. Obviously the variables we need for the formulation of the rule must have as their scope the whole of the sentence in which the rule is presented, and this is the distinguishing feature of our capital letters. In certain contexts, however, the distinction between small letters and capitals may be ignored with impunity. Thus in mathematics the equation

$$1+2+3+\dots+n = \frac{n(n+1)}{2}$$

may be taken as a universal statement about numbers, but it may equally well be taken as a validating schema, that is to say, the enunciation of it may be regarded as a licence to replace any sign of the form $1+2+3+\dots+\mathcal{N}$ by a sign of the form $\dfrac{\mathcal{N}(\mathcal{N}+1)}{2}$. If we set down the formula as a conclusion or as a premiss for further reasoning in the theory of numbers, we understand it in the first way. If, on the other hand, we refer to it as something which sanctions a transition from a statement containing $1+2+3+\dots+100$ to a statement containing $\dfrac{100\ (100+1)}{2}$

in place of the sum, we understand it in the second way. There is no danger in using the one formula for the two purposes, because the context shows clearly enough which interpretation we need.

Frege's symbolism is cumbrous not only because of the variety of types which it requires, but also because it involves the disposition of formulae in two dimensions, and it has now been superseded by scripts which require no more than the linear arrangement of a comparatively small number of signs. The system most widely accepted is that introduced by Peano in his *Notation de logique mathématique* of 1894, used by him in the successive editions of his *Formulaire de mathématiques*, and then developed by Whitehead and Russell in their *Principia Mathematica* of 1910. But there are other systems in use, and for convenience we shall therefore present the principal signs of the best-known systems in one table, using capital letters for gap signs except in the last column where it is necessary to preserve Łukasiewicz's use of small letters in order to avoid confusion with the letters which he uses as operators.

| | Peano-Russell | Hilbert | Variants | Łukasiewicz |
|---|---|---|---|---|
| Negation | $\sim P$ | $\bar{P}$ | $- P, \urcorner\, P$ | $Np$ |
| Conjunction | $P.Q$ | $P \,\&\, Q$ | $PQ, P \wedge Q$ | $Kpq$ |
| Disjunction | $P \vee Q$ | $P \vee Q$ | $PQ$ | $Apq$ |
| Conditional | $P \supset Q$ | $P \rightarrow Q$ | | $Cpq$ |
| Bi-conditional | $P \equiv Q$ | $P \sim Q$ | $P \leftrightarrow Q$ | $Epq$ |
| Universal Quantification | $(x)F(x)$ | $(x)F(x)$ | $\forall x F(x), \wedge x\, F(x)$ | $\Pi x \Phi x$ |
| Existential Quantification | $(\exists x)F(x)$ | $(Ex)F(x)$ | $\exists x\, F(x), \vee x F(x)$ | $\Sigma x \Phi x$ |

The truth function listed here as the conditional is of course the Philonian conditional.

In order to reduce the need for brackets (or equivalent punctuation by dots) to a minimum it is agreed by users of the notations which appear in the first three columns that the negation sign (when printed before other signs) shall be understood to operate only on the immediately succeeding expression unless the contrary is shown by means of brackets, and that conjunction, disjunction, conditional, and bi-conditional signs shall be understood to bind in that order of strength, so that we may, if we wish, write

$$\sim P.Q \vee R \supset S \equiv T$$

instead of

$$\{[(\sim P.Q) \vee R] \supset S\} \equiv T.$$

Use of Hilbert's sign for negation makes possible the omission of other brackets, since the length of the super-imposed stroke shows clearly enough the extent of the expression to be negated; and small further economies may be made by writing $(x)Fx$ or $\forall x\, Fx$ instead of $(x)[F(x)]$, where the quantifier has for its scope only the immediately succeeding functional sign. But even so the piling up of necessary brackets may become troublesome, and there is therefore a strong motive for trying to devise a notation which requires no brackets at all. This has been done by

Łukasiewicz. Each of the capital letters which he uses as a connective or operator precedes the symbols to which it applies, and provided the number of these is clear from the definition of the operator, there can be no ambiguity about the interpretation of a well-formed formula. Thus $CKCpqpq$ can be read only as an equivalent for $[(p \supset q).p] \supset q$ because the second $C$ requires for its application two complete symbols which must be the adjoining $p$ and $q$ and $K$ similarly requires for its application two complete symbols which must be the adjoining $Cpq$ and $p$. But this advantage is gained at the expense of a radical departure from the style of construction used in natural languages, and must therefore be paid for by difficulty in reading. No doubt the difficulty can be overcome by practice, but most logicians have been content to go on using notations which require brackets, and in what follows we shall employ only the best known, that of Peano, Whitehead, and Russell, but with the rules about variables set out in this section.

A much more far-reaching change of logical symbolism was suggested in 1924 by M. Schönfinkel.[1] This has given rise to a quite new way of considering logic, and might therefore have been reserved for a separate section; but we shall notice it here, because we cannot hope to do more than indicate the most interesting features of the new symbolism.

Schönfinkel begins by remarking that Sheffer's attempt to reduce the number of logical constants can be carried a step farther if $Fx \mid^x Gx$ is introduced with the sense of $(x) \sim (Fx. Gx)$. For obviously the sign $\mid^x$ must mean the same as the simple stroke when it is written between expressions neither of which contains $x$ free; and when it is allowed to occur between expressions which contain $x$ free, it can be used to build up equivalents for all the quantified expressions of general logic. He goes on, however, to claim that he has discovered a way of simplifying the symbolism of logic even more drastically by getting rid of all variables, whether propositional, functional, or individual. The variables which are commonly used in the writing of logical formulae are no more than auxiliary signs for making cross references, and if we can find some other way of doing what is required, we may abandon them all. No doubt the use of variables will continue in practice, but it is theoretically interesting to see how they can be eliminated.

According to Schönfinkel we must first extend our notion of a

---

[1] 'Über die Bausteine der mathematischen Logik', *Mathematische Annalen*, xcii (1924), pp. 305–316. For later developments see H. Curry and R. Feys, *Combinatory Logic* (vol i, 1958).

function in such a way as to allow that the values of variables and the values of functions may themselves be functions. Thus for $F(x, y)$ we may write $(Fx)y$, or more shortly $Fxy$, thinking of the $Fx$ in this complex as a sign for an operation which is itself the result of applying an operation signified by $F$ to an argument signified by $x$. Unless the contrary is indicated by use of brackets, it is to be assumed that the operation indicated by the first sign is to be applied to the object indicated by the second sign and the result then applied to the object indicated by the third and so on. Next we introduce a number of special functions or operations defined by the equations:

$$(1) \quad \mathsf{I}x = x$$
$$(2) \quad \mathsf{C}xy = x$$
$$(3) \quad \mathsf{T}fxy = fyx$$
$$(4) \quad \mathsf{Z}fgx = f(gx)$$
$$(5) \quad \mathsf{S}fgx = fx(gx).$$

Here $\mathsf{I}$ signifies the identity operation which leaves its argument unchanged, $\mathsf{C}$ the function of two arguments whose value is always equal to its first argument, $\mathsf{T}$ the operation of transposing the arguments of a function (i.e. what in the theory of relations is commonly called conversion), $\mathsf{Z}$ that operation of compounding functions by which, for example, the notion of an uncle is compounded from the notion of a brother and the notion of a parent, and $\mathsf{S}$ that function of three arguments whose value is calculated by letting the first and the second arguments operate separately in turn upon the third and then letting the result of the first operation operate upon the result of the second. Of these five the second and the fifth are the least familiar concepts, but they are especially interesting because the other three functions can be defined in terms of them by the equations:

$$\mathsf{I} = \mathsf{SCC}$$
$$\mathsf{Z} = \mathsf{S(CS)C}$$
$$\mathsf{T} = \mathsf{S(ZZS)(CC)}.$$

We have, for example:

$$\begin{aligned}
\mathsf{Z}fgx &= \mathsf{S(CS)C}fgx \\
&= \mathsf{C}Sf(\mathsf{C}f)gx \\
&= \mathsf{S(C}f)gx \\
&= \mathsf{C}fx(gx) \\
&= f(gx).
\end{aligned}$$

If we now write $\mathsf{U}fg$ as an abbreviation for $fx|^xgx$, we can express any logical truism in terms of $\mathsf{C}$, $\mathsf{S}$, and $\mathsf{U}$, with each variable occurring once only and at the end of its formula, where it may be dropped as no longer essential to the fixing of the sense of the whole. Even U itself may be omitted, since it too can be reduced to one occurrence at the end, where its only remaining role is to show that we are writing logic. What is distinctive in each truism can then be expressed by an arrangement of the two signs C and S. We have for example:

$$
\begin{aligned}
p\,|^x(p\,|^x p) &= \mathsf{U}p(\mathsf{U}pp) \\
&= \mathsf{U}p(\mathsf{U}p(\mathsf{C}p(\mathsf{C}p))) \\
&= \mathsf{U}p(\mathsf{U}p(\mathsf{SCC}p)) \\
&= \mathsf{U}p(\mathsf{SU}(\mathsf{SCC})p) \\
&= \mathsf{SU}(\mathsf{SU}(\mathsf{SCC}))p \\
&= \mathsf{SU}(\mathsf{SU}(\mathsf{C}(\mathsf{SCC})\mathsf{U}))p \\
&= \mathsf{SU}(\mathsf{SS}(\mathsf{C}(\mathsf{SCC}))\mathsf{U})p \\
&= \mathsf{SS}(\mathsf{SS}(\mathsf{C}(\mathsf{SCC})))\mathsf{U}p.
\end{aligned}
$$

By introducing a new special function D which is defined directly by the equation

$$\mathsf{D}fx = fxx$$

or indirectly (i.e. in terms of C and S) by the equation

$$
\begin{aligned}
\mathsf{D} &= \mathsf{SS}(\mathsf{C}\mathsf{I}) \\
&= \mathsf{SS}(\mathsf{C}(\mathsf{SCC}))
\end{aligned}
$$

we can reduce the whole to SSD. But it has never been claimed that combinatory logic, as this study is now called, provides formulae of great intuitive clarity. So far Schönfinkel's technique is important chiefly for the light it throws on the role of variables and the notion of substitution in the symbolism of mathematical logic. Conceivably it may prove useful also in the exact analysis of patterns in natural languages, but at present that is mere conjecture.

## 2. *Methods of Presentation: Axioms and Rules*

In modern symbolism Frege's first set of axioms for general logic (without the theory of identity) can be written as follows:

(1) $p \supset (q \supset p)$
(2) $[p \supset (q \supset r)] \supset [(p \supset q) \supset (p \supset r)]$
(3) $[p \supset (q \supset r)] \supset [q \supset (p \supset r)]$
(4) $(p \supset q) \supset (\sim q \supset \sim p)$
(5) $\sim \sim p \supset p$
(6) $p \supset \sim \sim p$
(7) $(x)f(x) \supset f(y)$.

He says in his *Begriffsschrift* that he uses only one principle of inference in the derivation of theorems from these axioms, but we have seen that in fact he uses four. Of these (i) is a principle of substitution for real variables like that given in rule (9) of his *Grundgesetze* and the other three correspond to the following schemata:

(ii) $$\frac{P \quad P \supset Q}{Q}$$

(iii) $$\frac{F(x)}{(x)F(x)}$$

(iv) $$\frac{P \supset F(x)}{P \supset (x)F(x)},$$ provided that $x$ does not occur free in $P$.

Most later logicians have included in their systems axioms or rules which correspond closely to (7), (iii), and (iv), though (iii), as we shall see later, is redundant. But primary logic, which is determined by (1)–(6), (i), and (ii), has been presented in a number of different ways under such titles as 'the theory of deduction', 'the calculus of propositions', 'the theory of elementary propositions', 'the theory of truth functions', and 'the theory of statement composition'. These variations in style of presentation deserve attention, because some at least are of importance for the philosophy of logic.

We have seen already that the third of Frege's axioms is redundant, since it can be derived from the first two. In the presence of these two it is also possible to replace the last three by a single new axiom for negation, namely

$$(\sim p \supset \sim q) \supset (q \supset p).$$

Even more interesting is the possibility of replacing all Frege's axioms for primary logic by the following complete set of three axioms:

(1) $(p \supset q) \supset [(q \supset r) \supset (p \supset r)]$
(2) $(\sim p \supset p) \supset p$
(3) $p \supset (\sim p \supset q).$

For the first of the new set is the principle of the transitivity of the Philonian conditional connexion, the second is a version of the *consequentia mirabilis*, first formulated by the Stoics, and the third a reformulation of one of the paradoxical theses, formerly attributed to John Duns the Scot, namely that according to which any proposition may be derived from a self-contradictory conjunction. These discoveries and a number of other very interesting results (such as an axiom which is sufficient by itself, though not very perspicuous) are all due to Łukasiewicz and his pupils, who since the twenties of this century have investigated primary logic very carefully with special reference to systems based on Frege's two primitive notions, negation and the Philonian conditional.[1] But the system which has attracted most attention in this century is not Frege's but that of *Principia Mathematica*.

Whitehead and Russell worked like Frege with two principles of inference for primary logic, namely the principle of substitution and the principle of detachment (i.e. the *modus ponens* for the Philonian conditional), but they took the notions of negation and disjunction as their primitives and produced the following set of axioms:

(1) $(p \lor p) \supset p$
(2) $q \supset (p \supset q)$
(3) $(p \lor q) \supset (q \lor p)$
(4) $[p \lor (q \lor r)] \supset [(p \lor q) \lor r]$
(5) $(q \supset r) \supset [(p \lor q) \supset (p \lor r)]$.

In 1926 Bernays proved that (4) could be derived from the others and was therefore superfluous.[2] Apart from that, however, there is a certain inelegance in this well-known system. If the logical signs of negation and disjunction are to be taken as primitive, they should surely be used in the formulation of the axioms and rules of inference to the exclusion of all other signs. In this system it is permissible, of course, to replace $P \supset Q$ wherever it occurs by $\sim P \lor Q$, but when that is done in the axioms and rules the result is something more complicated than the systems of Frege and Łukasiewicz.

As we saw in our chapter on the algebra of logic, Peirce and Sheffer recognized the possibility of defining negation and all the connectives of primary logic by reference to one primitive notion. Taking $P|Q$ (in the sense of *Not both P and Q*) as undefined, Nicod showed in 1917 that the whole calculus could be based on the single axiom

$$[p|(q|r)]|([t|(t|t)]|\{(s|q)|[(p|s)|(p|s)]\})$$

with
$$\frac{P \quad P|(Q|R)}{R}$$

[1] J. Łukasiewicz and A. Tarski, 'Untersuchungen über den Aussagenkalkül', *Comptes rendus des séances de la Société des sciences et des lettres de Varsovie, Classe III*, vol. xxiii (1930), pp. 30–50. The work of this school is reported fully in A. N. Prior's *Formal Logic*.
[2] 'Axiomatische Untersuchungen des Aussagenkalküls der *Principia Mathematica*', *Mathematische Zeitschrift*, xxv (1926), pp. 305–20.

as a rule of inference in place of the traditional *modus ponens*.[1] In his introduction to the second edition of *Principia Mathematica*, published in 1925, Russell suggested that this formulation should be substituted for the system of the first edition noticed above, but it can scarcely be said that the reduction achieved by Nicod is a simplification which makes the theory easier to grasp.

If what is wanted is perspicuity and naturalness in the presentation of arguments, the best set of axioms for use with the principles of substitution and detachment is that given by Hilbert and Bernays in 1934.[2]

$$\text{I.} \quad (1) \ p \supset (q \supset p)$$
$$(2) \ [p \supset (p \supset q)] \supset (p \supset q)$$
$$(3) \ (p \supset q) \supset [(q \supset r) \supset (p \supset r)]$$
$$\text{II.} \quad (1) \ p.q \supset p$$
$$(2) \ p.q \supset q$$
$$(3) \ (p \supset q) \supset [(p \supset r) \supset (p \supset q.r)]$$
$$\text{III.} \quad (1) \ p \supset p \vee q$$
$$(2) \ q \supset p \vee q$$
$$(3) \ (p \supset r) \supset [(q \supset r) \supset (p \vee q \supset r)]$$
$$\text{IV.} \quad (1) \ (p \equiv q) \supset (p \supset q)$$
$$(2) \ (p \equiv q) \supset (q \supset p)$$
$$(3) \ (p \supset q) \supset [(q \supset p) \supset (p \equiv q)]$$
$$\text{V.} \quad (1) \ (p \supset q) \supset (\sim q \supset \sim p)$$
$$(2) \ p \supset \sim\sim p$$
$$(3) \ \sim\sim p \supset p$$

Here axioms are grouped together according to the signs they involve. First come those which involve only the Philonian conditional sign, next those which involve the conjunction sign as well as the conditional sign, and so forth. The privileged position of the conditional sign, which occurs as sole sign in the first group and as one of the two signs in each of the other groups, is due, of course, to the fact that it occurs also in the rule of detachment. In the presence of that rule each axiom takes the place of an additional rule of inference. The first, for example, is equivalent in power to the rule whose schema is

$$\frac{P}{Q \supset P}.$$

Admittedly the number of axioms in this system is large; but that is no disadvantage, since each distinguishable sign is introduced

[1] 'A Reduction in the Number of the Primitive Propositions of Logic', *Proceedings of the Cambridge Philosophical Society*, xix (1917), pp. 32–41.
[2] *Grundlagen der Mathematik*, i, p. 66.

in an easily intelligible fashion, e.g. that for disjunction by a group of three axioms dual to the three axioms for conjunction. We can reduce the number of axioms, if we like, by defining some of the signs in terms of others; but there is no real gain in perspicuity from this procedure, since a definition is in effect only a pair of rules of inference connecting a defined with an undefined sign. As they stand, these axioms are all independent, and it is interesting to notice that I (1), V (1), V(2), and V (3) come from Frege's system, I (3) from Łukasiewicz's, and III (2) from *Principia Mathematica*.

In all these systems a principle of substitution is required for the derivation of theorems from axioms. That such a principle can be formulated rigorously is undeniable, but there seems nevertheless to be an impropriety in putting forward anything of this kind as a rule of primary logic comparable with the rule of detachment. When we derive one statement from another by a process of substitution, the validity of our inference depends on the universality of the premiss, but in primary logic the subject of study is reasoning which does not involve the notion of generality, and it is therefore inappropriate that the axioms for such a theory should be universal propositions. This is not to say that in primary logic the logician should abstain from all generalization and confine himself to the giving of examples. He may as a logician produce universal statements, but in this part of his work they should be only statements of the second order such as that any argument of the pattern

$$\frac{P \quad P \supset Q}{Q}$$

is valid. In particular, if he talks of axioms for primary logic, he should not, like Frege, assume that these must be universal in character and finite in number, but rather be prepared to admit as axioms any propositions which exhibit certain validating forms, as for example the form $P \supset (Q \supset P)$, which corresponds to Frege's first axiom $p \supset (q \supset p)$. This device of giving axiom schemata rather than axioms is due to J. von Neumann,[1] but it may be said to carry out Frege's original intention of presenting logic, or at any rate primary logic, with only one rule of inference. Unfortunately the simplification offers no *practical* advantage to the user of logic, since the task of determining whether a statement can be admitted as an axiom under the new dispensation involves

[1] 'Zur Hilbertschen Beweistheorie', *Mathematische Zeitschrift*, xxvi (1927), pp. 1–46.

exactly the same difficulties as that of determining whether a statement can be derived from an axiom under the old dispensation. But the reform has the great philosophical merit of distinguishing clearly between first-order and second-order statements.

Probably Frege and those who followed him in using a principle of substitution were influenced by the analogy of algebra in which, as we have seen, one and the same formula may be used sometimes as a universal statement about numbers and at other times as a licence to make certain transformations. But they sometimes declare that the expression of universality by means of free variables is only an abbreviation for the expression of universality by means of bound variables, and if this way of describing the notation is taken seriously, the theory of logic becomes a great deal more complicated than they have admitted in their original accounts. For if the axiom formula $p \supset (q \supset p)$ is to be understood as an abbreviation for $(p)(q)[p \supset (q \supset p)]$, the simplest case of derivation from it must be in effect an application of a rule of general logic corresponding to the schema $\dfrac{(p)F(p)}{F(Q)}$.

But the only conclusions we can reach by this method are such statements as *The earth is flat* $\supset$ (*the moon is made of green cheese* $\supset$ *the earth is flat*), i.e. exemplifications of our logical principle in non-logical material, and logicians who rely on a principle of substitution are not commonly interested in results of that kind. Most often the theorems they profess to establish by substitution for variables are new universal statements such as $r.s \supset (\sim t \supset r.s)$, which cannot be derived by application of the simple rule mentioned above but require much more complicated reasoning in general logic. No doubt the necessary procedure can be strictly formalized,[1] but it is more illuminating to adopt von Neumann's device of axiom schemata and argue as follows;

Every statement of the form $P \supset (Q \supset P)$ is necessarily true.
But every statement of the form $R.S \supset (\sim T \supset R.S)$ is of the form $P \supset (Q \supset P)$.
Therefore every statement of the form $R.S \supset (\sim T \supset R.S)$ is necessarily true.

Admittedly this reasoning depends on a principle of general logic (the principle of a syllogism in *Barbara*), but it is unobjectionable in its context, because there can be no doubt that

---

[1] The problem was first taken seriously by S. Leśniewski. The most easily accessible account of his logic is to be found in his 'Grundzüge eines neuen Systems der Grundlagen der Mathematik', *Fundamenta Mathematica*, xiv (1929), pp. 1–81.

it belongs to argument about primary logic rather than to primary logic itself.

Similar considerations may be urged against Frege's account of the use of functional variables in the formulation of axioms for general logic. If the formula $(x)f(x) \supset f(y)$ is to be understood as an abbreviation for $(f)[(x)f(x) \supset f(y)]$, it is impossible to present the theory of first-level functions without trespassing on the theory of second-level functions. In short, the only way of making clear the articulation of logical theory is to use special variables like our capitals for the purpose of expressing generality in the logician's own discourse as distinct from that he analyses.

It must be confessed, however, that there is something strange in talk about axioms of logic, whether these are supposed to be few, as in Frege's system, or infinitely many, as in von Neumann's. Before Frege's day logicians thought it their business to consider how theorems followed from axioms in studies such as geometry, but they did not commonly try to present logic itself as a deductive system with axioms and theorems. Frege was not, of course, the first to maintain that some logical principles could be derived from others. For Aristotle reduced all valid syllogisms to *Barbara* or *Celarent*, and Chrysippus deduced complex moods from his indemonstrables. But Frege, following some suggestions of Leibniz and Boole, offered a system in which the axioms and theorems are not truths about what follows from what but logical truisms of the same status as the law of non-contradiction and the law of excluded middle. If we wish to use his logic in the construction of a deductive system of the ordinary kind, that is to say, one in which the axioms are not logical truisms, we must first add his axioms to our stock as supplementary premisses and then make all our inferences in accordance with the principle of substitution, the principle of detachment, or one of his two rules for reasoning with quantifiers. It is true that when he came to write his *Grundgesetze* he decided for reasons of practical convenience to adopt additional patterns of inference which would allow him to dispense with all his axioms for primary logic except the first, but he never explained clearly why logic should have any axioms at all. Perhaps he, and Whitehead and Russell after him, thought it natural to have some axioms because otherwise there would seem to be no sense in talking of arithmetic as a development of logic. But however that may be, after a short period in which the programme of presenting all logic as a deductive system was accepted without question, logicians recognized that truisms of primary logic could be certified for such without derivation from axioms.

The basis of the new method is the systematic enumeration of truth possibilities for a number of simple propositions, i.e. enumeration of the possible combinations of truth-values for these propositions. Thus for one proposition we have two possibilities, for two propositions four, and in general for n propositions $2^n$ possibilities. With a table showing the two possibilities for a single proposition we can define negation simply by putting 'f' under $\sim P$ opposite the 't' under $P$ and 't' under $\sim P$ opposite the 'f' under $P$. In antiquity Philo of Megara applied the same method in his account of conditional statements. For he said that any such statement was true if either its antecedent and its consequent were both true or its antecedent was false and its consequent true or its antecedent and its consequent were both false, but false if its antecedent was true and its consequent false. This amounts to a definition of the connective 'if' like that given for the horseshoe sign in the following series of tabular definitions:

| $P$ | $\sim P$ |
|---|---|
| t | f |
| f | t |

| $P$ | $Q$ | $P.Q$ | $P \lor Q$ | $P \supset Q$ | $P \equiv Q$ |
|---|---|---|---|---|---|
| t | t | t | t | t | t |
| t | f | f | t | f | f |
| f | t | f | t | t | f |
| f | f | f | f | t | t |

But so far as we know, lists of possibilities were not constructed in tabular form until the last century, when Boole used them to explain the process of development by which any expression of his system could be transformed into a sum of products (i.e. a disjunction of conjunctions) and Frege used them explicitly for definition of the various truth-functions. If there are two and only two propositions to be considered (as in the definitions which have been given above), the possibilities can be represented by the various places in a square matrix like that shown here and a definition constructed by filling these places in appropriate fashion, but tabulation in lines has the advantage that it can be applied to any number of propositions and then used for the purposes of calculation in a way to be explained presently.

|  | | $Q$ | |
|---|---|---|---|
| $\supset$ | | t | f |
| $P$ | t | t | f |
| | f | t | t |

Beginning with the simplest table of possibilities, which is sufficient for the definition of negation, since that is a truth-function involving only one argument, we can construct each more complicated table by writing down the immediately preceding table twice first with a 't' in front of each line and then with an 'f' in that place. Other arrangements are possible and have been used, but it is essential to follow some regular plan by which we can make sure of allowing for each possible combination of truth values once and once only. It will be noticed that in our examples we have used capitals as argument letters. This is to suggest that the construction of a tabular definition of a truth function is in effect the simultaneous formulation of a number of rules of inference. Thus the construction of the tabular definition given above for conjunction is equivalent to formulation of the rules expressed by the following three inference schemata :

| P | Q | R |
|---|---|---|
| t | t | t |
| t | t | f |
| t | f | t |
| t | f | f |
| f | t | t |
| f | t | f |
| f | f | t |
| f | f | f |

$$\frac{P \quad Q}{P.Q} \qquad \frac{P.Q}{P} \qquad \frac{P.Q}{Q}.$$

For in order to obtain any of these three from the tabular definition we have only to look for the lines in which the premiss or both the premisses, as the case may be, have 't' and verify that in all those lines the conclusion has 't'.

It is not difficult to find in Boole's work the notion that a necessarily true proposition should reveal itself as such in the process of development, and about the year 1920 it occurred to several logicians independently that when truth-functions had been defined by means of truth tables a rule-of-thumb calculation would suffice to determine whether a complex proposition expressed by the use of truth-functional signs was necessarily true, necessarily false, or contingent. The best known account of such a *decision procedure* for primary logic is perhaps that given by L. Wittgenstein in his *Tractatus Logico-Philosophicus*, first published in 1921, but there is a more straightforward discussion of the technique in an article published by E. L. Post in the same year.[1] For an example let us consider the proof of Frege's first axiom, or rather of the corresponding axiom schema.

|   |   |   | (1) | (3) | (1) | (2) | (1) |
|---|---|---|---|---|---|---|---|
| P | Q | P | ⊃ | (Q | ⊃ | P) |
| t | t | t | t | t | t | t |
| t | f | t | t | f | t | t |
| f | t | f | t | t | f | f |
| f | f | f | t | f | t | f |

[1] 'Introduction to a General Theory of Elementary Proportions', *The American Journal of Mathematics*, xliii (1921), pp. 163–85. The method was known also to Łukasiewicz at this date.

There are here just four possible cases to be distinguished, since only two argument letters are involved. In order to assign a truth value to the consequent of the schema in each of the four cases we need only consult the tabular definition of the Philonian conditional, which is of course a specification of conditions for truth and for falsity, and when this operation, indicated by (2), has been performed, another application of the definition, indicated by (3), is sufficient to show that the schema as a whole yields truth in all possible circumstances, or, as Wittgenstein says, that it is tautological.

Obviously the method can be applied mechanically (i.e. literally by a machine) to any formula constructed by means of the truth-functional signs of primary logic, and when it gives a proof, the validity of the result does not depend on the correctness of any special formulae previously selected to serve as axioms. But it is a mistake to suppose that the method requires only arbitrary definitions of the truth-functional signs. For the discovery that application of the definitions yields 't' under the main connective of a formula in all the lines of our table amounts to a proof of the necessary truth of the formula only when it is already established that the lines of the table exhaust all the possibilities with respect to the truth or falsity of the propositions which are arguments of the truth-function expressed by the formula. That a table constructed in the way explained above does indeed exhaust the possibilities is obvious, but only to one who understands the principle of construction and realizes that every proposition must be true or false.

The truth-table method of certifying truisms may perhaps be regarded as a refinement of von Neumann's technique, though it appeared earlier in time. For instead of specifying a number of axiom schemata we can use the word 'tautology' as a general, but nevertheless effective, description of all propositions that are to be admitted as axioms in primary logic. This is the procedure followed by W. V. Quine in his *Mathematical Logic*.[1] If, however, anyone objects that it is not properly the task of a logician to certify truisms as such, whether by Frege's method or by any modern alternative procedure, but rather to formulate those principles of inference which are valid for all possible studies, we can adapt our presentation of truth tables to meet his demand. For to say that one proposition entails another is to say that any possible state of affairs which would count as a verification for the first would count as a verification for the second, and this is something that may be read off from truth tables, if the entailment belongs to primary logic. We can see, for example, that in

[1] § 16, *100.

any row in which there is a 't' under the heading $P.Q$ in our table of definitions there is also a 't' under the heading $P \vee Q$. We may indeed take entailment, or relative necessity, as the basic notion to be expounded by means of truth tables, and say that truisms, or absolutely necessary propositions, are just propositions entailed by any propositions whatsoever. We have seen already that the tabular definitions of the truth-functions can be understood as compendious formulations of rules, and there is much to be said in favour of this way of regarding them, first because it accords well with the traditional conception of logic, and secondly because the notion of implicit definition by means of rules of inference is applicable also in that part of general logic which cannot be presented by means of truth-tables. A universal proposition is in some respects like a conjunction and an existential proposition is in some respects like a disjunction, but the range of possibilities from among which we select when we formulate a general proposition of either kind may be infinite, and when that is so the technique of tabulation is useless.

In his *Logische Syntax der Sprache*[1] (first published in 1934) R. Carnap made the illuminating comment that there is no difference of principle between logicians who offer both rules and axioms for logic and those who offer only rules of inference. As he remarked, any formula which is to be taken as axiomatic must be presented with an explanation of its role, and this explanation will amount in effect to a rule whereby the proposition which the formula expresses may be inferred from any proposition whatsoever, or, in his technical terminology, from the null class of premisses, which is the common part of all classes of premisses. In short, logic is essentially a science consisting of second-order principles.

Combining this suggestion with von Neumann's device of axiom schemata, we may take the following set of six rules as a simple alternative to the version of logic given by Frege in his *Begriffsschrift*:

1. $$\dfrac{P \supset Q \quad P}{Q}$$
2. $$\dfrac{*}{P \supset (Q \supset P)}$$

3. $$\dfrac{*}{[P \supset (Q \supset R)] \supset [(P \supset Q) \supset (P \supset R)]}$$
4. $$\dfrac{*}{(\sim P \supset \sim Q) \supset (Q \supset P)}$$

5. $$\dfrac{*}{(x)Fx \supset FY}$$
6. $$\dfrac{P \supset Fx}{P \supset (x)Fx}$$
   provided that $x$ does not occur free in $P$.

[1] §§ 31 and 47.

In this system the asterisk printed above the line in certain inference schemata marks a place where we may put any premiss we choose, and its introduction is therefore equivalent to an announcement that propositions of the patterns indicated below the line in those inference schemata may be asserted without more ado. If anyone dislikes this way of talking, he may follow von Neumann in describing such propositions as axioms; but, apart from other considerations, the name seems rather unfortunate here, because it is commonly thought that axioms should be independent of each other, whereas these propositions cannot all be independent of each other in the presence of the *modus ponens*. If, for example, $R$ and $S$ are any propositional signs, rule (2) above allows us to make the following three assertions among many others:

$$R \supset (S \supset R)$$
$$(S \supset R) \supset [R \supset (S \supset R)]$$
$$[R \supset (S \supset R)] \supset \{(S \supset R) \supset [R \supset (S \supset R)]\}.$$

And the second of these can be inferred from the first and the third by rule (1). It is better therefore to content ourselves with calling all such assertions *truisms* of logic.

In an application of logic to extra-logical subject-matter the capital letters of our inference schemata would be replaced by genuine expressions for propositions about that subject-matter, and the inferences licensed by the rules would be drawn. But when we are concerned with the elaboration of logic itself, our aim is not to derive consequences from premisses belonging to other sciences, but rather to derive new and perhaps more complicated rules of inference from those with which we start. Since the rules are themselves second-order pronouncements which can be cast in the form of principles about the relations of propositions, derivation of rules from rules must involve principles of the third order, but it can nevertheless be presented in a simple fashion by the device of schematic deduction which Chrysippus used in his elaboration of elementary logic. Here, for example, is a proof of the simple rule $\dfrac{Fx}{(x)Fx}$ which we have adapted to this procedure from the original demonstration of Bernays:[1]

$$\cfrac{\cfrac{Fx \qquad \cfrac{\overset{*}{\overline{Fx \supset \{[R \supset (S \supset R)] \supset Fx\}}}}{}(2)}{\cfrac{[R \supset (S \supset R)] \supset Fx}{[R \supset (S \supset R)] \supset (x)\,Fx}(6)}(1) \qquad \cfrac{\overset{*}{\overline{R \supset (S \supset R)}}}{}(2)}{(x)Fx}(1)$$

---

[1] Hilbert und Ackermann, *Grundzüge der theoretischen Logik*, ch. iii, § 6, rule γ′.

The numerals at the ends of horizontal lines show what basic schemata are used in the various transitions, and it is therefore clear that in order to prepare the way for the use of rule (6) in the middle of the proof we must suppose at the beginning that the letters $R$ and $S$ are not abbreviations for expressions which contain $x$ free. But there is no other restriction on the interpretation of the schematic letters (except, of course, the general restrictions required for preserving sense), and so the whole skeleton argument amounts to a justification of the rule $\dfrac{Fx}{(x)Fx}$.

For use of this rule must be correct, if it is correct, as it obviously is, to use rules (1), (2), and (6) in the manner indicated above.

Apart from the method of its proof, our example is interesting because it is concerned with passage from free to bound variables in the expression of universality. Since the universality in question belongs properly to the propositions of the argument under consideration, there is no departure here from the programme of using schematic letters wherever possible, but the reader may reasonably ask how we are supposed to get formulae with free variables from which we can argue in accordance with the rule noticed above. The answer is that for the purposes of general logic formulae in which free variables have been substituted consistently for designations may be treated as examples of the same patterns as their originals. When first considered, this rule for interpreting the phrase 'of the same pattern' is rather surprising, since a formula which expresses universality by means of a free variable is obviously very different in logical character from any of the singular formulae it entails. But we are justified in relying here on the fact that they are grammatically alike in all respects other than the use of free variables, as may be shown by more detailed examination of the example given above. According to rule (2) we can assert any proposition expressible in the form $P \supset (Q \supset P)$ and so, of course, any expressible in the form $P \supset \{[R \supset (S \supset R)] \supset P\}$. But all propositions whose expressions differ from each other only as $FX \supset \{[R \supset (S \supset R)] \supset FX\}$ and $FY \supset \{[R \supset (S \supset R)] \supset FY\}$, where $X$ and $Y$ designate different things, are also of that form, and it is therefore permissible to use the expression $Fx \supset \{[R \supset (S \supset R)] \supset Fx\}$ for the purpose of asserting them conjointly. Just because each of them may be asserted by virtue of rule (2), so also may the universal proposition expressed by introduction of a free variable in place of a designation. It is probably the occurrence of such reasoning in mathematics that has led mathematicians to speak sometimes of a variable as denoting ambiguously all its different values. We can explain the merits of the notation more correctly by saying that it is a very appropriate expression for the results of intuitive induction. For precisely that feature of the singular propositions which justifies our generalization is represented by the pattern we preserve in our expression of the generalization.

In order to take advantage of the device in other contexts we may properly assume that rule (5) allows us to assert all propositions expressible in the form $(x)Fx \supset Fy$. That is to say, whenever it seems convenient, we may write a free variable instead of a genuine designation in the place indicated by the schematic letter $Y$ of this rule. If, *mutatis mutandis*, we allowed ourselves a similar liberty in relation to *all* our schematic letters, we should in effect re-establish a calculus of the kind offered by Frege, Whitehead and Russell. For we might then write:

$$p \supset (q \supset p)$$
$$[p \supset (q \supset r)] \supset [(p \supset q) \supset (p \supset r)]$$
$$(\sim p \supset \sim q) \supset (q \supset p)$$
$$(x)fx \supset fy$$

as expressions for propositions obtained by use of rules (2), (3), (4), and (5), and go on to derive all other assertible formulae from these taken as premisses. In this context the customary rules of substitution would, of course, be available as derivative rules, since every formula which results from substitution for a free variable must be an instance of any schema of which that given formula is an instance and must therefore be itself certifiable as a truism if the given formula is certifiable as such in virtue of its pattern. It may perhaps be objected that this way of obtaining a calculus of logic with free variables involves the questionable device of allowing two kinds of instances for our basic schemata, namely formulae without free variables and formulae with free variables. But it is important to realize that some such device is required in any case by Frege's method of presenting logic. For, as we have seen, in his system and those of his successors substitution for formulae which contain free variables may lead either to formulae without free variables or to other formulae which contain free variables. When logic is considered as an abstract theory without regard to application, only substitution of the second kind is considered; but whenever the calculus is to be applied in the proof of extra-logical assertions, substitution of the first kind is essential. If we object to such duplicity, our proper course is to abandon the programme of presenting primary logic as a theory involving universal propositions of the first order and content ourselves with universal *rules* such as those formulated above. For free variables will then appear in our logic only as they occur in rule (6) and the specimen derivation set out above, i.e. for the purpose of marking that use of intuitive induction which is necessary for quantification theory, or general logic, but not required in primary logic. But we may still ask ourselves what system of rules is most obvious and natural.

### 3. *Natural Deduction and Development*

In 1934 a system of rules for natural deduction was produced by G. Gentzen.[1] In a later part of the same paper Gentzen showed that any proof in a certain related system of logic can be brought into a normal form which lacks an operation called 'cut' and is in a certain sense the most direct possible. This theorem, which he calls his main thesis (*Hauptsatz*), is important in connexion with his later proof of the consistency of number theory, and its interest led perhaps at one time to neglect of the first system. In the symbolism which we have adopted the rules of this first system are as follows:

$$(1)\ \frac{P \quad Q}{P.Q} \qquad\qquad (2a)\ \frac{P.Q}{P} \quad (2b)\ \frac{P.Q}{Q}$$

$$(3a)\ \frac{P}{P \vee Q} \quad (3b)\ \frac{Q}{P \vee Q} \qquad (4)\ \frac{P \vee Q \quad P/R \quad Q/R}{R}$$

$$(5)\ \frac{P/\dagger}{\sim P} \qquad\qquad (6a)\ \frac{P \quad \sim P}{\dagger} \quad (6b)\ \frac{\sim \sim P}{P}$$

$$(7)\ \frac{P/Q}{P \supset Q} \qquad\qquad (8)\ \frac{P \quad P \supset Q}{Q}$$

$$(9)\ \frac{Fx}{(x)Fx} \qquad\qquad (10)\ \frac{(x)Fx}{FY}$$

$$(11)\ \frac{FY}{(\exists x)Fx} \qquad\qquad (12)\ \frac{(\exists x)Fx \quad Fx/P}{P}$$

Here each rule is presented by means of a schema and those on the left are rules for the introduction of formal signs, while those on the right are rules for elimination. For the most part the rules are easy to understand, but there are some points that require comment.

The obelus in rules (5) and (6a) stands for 'the false' (or, perhaps it is better to say, for 'the absurd'), and it has a single additional schema $\frac{\dagger}{P}$ which according to Gentzen's explanation

[1] Untersuchungen über das logische Schliessen', *Mathematische Zeitschrift*, xxxix (1934), pp. 176–210, 405–31.

means 'If the false holds, then so does any proposition whatso-ever'. The $Y$ in rules (10) and (11) is a schematic letter like the other capitals, but the $x$ above the line in rule (9) and similarly the $x$ in $Fx/P$ of rule (12) are free variables whose scope does not extend across the horizontal line. The solidus which we have used in the formulation of rules (4), (5), (7), and (12) may be taken as an abbreviation for 'entails'. It is intended, of course, to suggest the horizontal line of an inference schema; but since it has the grammatical role of a verb, the signs to the left and to the right of it must be understood as nouns, i.e. as designations for propositions. A full rendering of an entailment statement would therefore have the form $\S P/\S Q$; where the sign $\S$ is an abbreviation for 'that' or 'the proposition that'; but it is convenient to adopt the conven-tion that $\S$ may be absorbed by the solidus much as 'that' is absorbed by 'says' in the English sentence 'He says it is hot'. In either case we get simplification without ambiguity. Gentzen, who uses the notation $\dfrac{[P]}{Q}$ instead of $P/Q$, speaks of the letter in square brackets as standing for a supposition from which a consequence is derived.[1] But the sense is the same; for what we sometimes call the derivation of a consequence from a supposition is really the process of convincing ourselves that the supposition entails the consequence.

It seems clear that Gentzen has in fact presented logic in a fashion more natural than that of Frege, Whitehead, and Russell. Admittedly the number of his rules is greater than the number of rules and axioms in *Principia Mathematica*, but here each sign is introduced separately and it is possible to prove the equivalences which are used in *Principia Mathematica* as definitions for the signs not taken as primitive. Furthermore, by a simple procedure like that which Chrysippus followed in the elaboration of his system of elementary logic the basic inference schemata can be made to yield others. Thus we can prove that $P.Q/P \vee Q$ by setting out the skeleton argument

$$\dfrac{\dfrac{P.Q}{P}\,(2a)}{P \vee Q}\,(3a)$$

[1] In the same year S. Jaśkowski produced independently a paper 'On the Rules of Supposition in Formal Logic', *Studia Logica*, no. I (Warsaw, 1934), which is an elaboration of results obtained as early as 1926 in the seminar of J. Łukasiewicz. Later accounts of natural deduction follow Jaśkowski's method of exposition rather than that of Gentzen, but Gentzen's procedure suggests the theory of development explained below.

where the numerals at the ends of horizontal lines show which basic schemata have been used in the transitions. And when we wish, we can derive a truistic statement pattern from an inference schema, whether basic or derived, by application of rule (7), which is the principle of conditionalization, also used by Chrysippus.

Against all this, however, it must be admitted that there is something awkward in the system. Rules (4), (5), (7), and (12) all depend in a certain way on other rules. For what follows from a supposition must follow in accordance with some rule, and obviously this cannot be the rule formulated by means of the supposition. Why then did Gentzen find it necessary to introduce such a complication in just these places? The answer can be found from a comparison between the rules for conjunction and those for disjunction. It is well known that in the algebra of logic the conjunction and disjunction signs are dual to each other, and yet rule (4), which provides for elimination of the disjunction sign, does not correspond to rule (1), which provides for introduction of the conjunction sign, in the same way as (3a) and (3b), the rules for introducing the disjunction sign, correspond to (2a) and (2b), the rules for eliminating the conjunction sign. If we tried to write something which would correspond in the required way, we should get

$$\frac{P \vee Q}{P \quad Q},$$

i.e. an arrangement of signs which cannot be interpreted as an inference schema since it has two propositional expressions below the line. There might, of course, be a convention whereby an arrangement of signs like that printed above could be taken as a conflation of two inference schemata, i.e. as a way of saying that each of the propositional expressions below the line could be inferred from that above. But this is not at all what we want, since it confuses $P \vee Q$ with $P.Q$. In short, the curious features of Gentzen's system seem to be forced on him by the obvious fact that an inference cannot have more than one conclusion though it may have two or more premisses. Probably it was this that prevented the Pseudo-Scot from completing his account of paradoxical *consequentiae* with a simple proof that a formally necessary proposition can be derived formally from any proposition.[1]

If we wish to improve on Gentzen's result, we must follow up an idea suggested by the second part of his paper and treat derivation or deductive inference as a special case of something

[1] See above, pp. 283–4.

we shall call development. Unfortunately there is no recognized terminology for talking about this, but it may be described meta-phorically as setting out the field within which the truth must lie if certain premises are to be accepted. When a man after consideration of certain premises, expressed perhaps by $P$ and $Q$, remarks that certain other propositions, expressed perhaps by $R$ and $S$, cannot all be false if his premises are all true, he may be said to be engaged in the development of those premises. Neither of the propositions expressed by $R$ and $S$ is a conclusion of inference, but they may perhaps be called the limits of develop-ment up to date. Though for convenience we may suppose that they are expressed by sentences in the indicative mood, it must be understood that neither is asserted in the context of develop-ment. In order to make this clear we may, if we choose, write question marks after their expressions, but this will not be necessary in what follows, because the formulae of unasserted limits will always be recognizable as such by their position in the tables of development which we construct.

A very simple development may have the form

$$\frac{P \quad Q}{R \quad S},$$

but between the initial formulae which express the premises and the end formulae which express the limits there may be many intermediate expressions, i.e. expressions that occur both above and below lines. If a development has only one end formula, though this may be repeated many times at the bottom of different descending branches, it is a derivation of the proposition ex-pressed by that end formula. Obviously a development that is not a derivation can always be continued in such a fashion that it becomes a derivation, namely, by the addition to each descending branch of a formula which is the disjunction of all the existing end formulae. If a derivation has no premises, or, to speak more strictly, no premises that cannot equally well be replaced by others, it is a demonstration. These relations will become clear when a few examples have been worked.

Just as a derivation is said to be valid if the premises entail the conclusion, so a development may be said to be valid if the premises *involve* the limits to which the development leads. Here we follow Carnap, who in his *Formalization of Logic* introduced the name 'logical involution' for the relation that holds between two sets of propositions when it is impossible that all of the first should be true and all of the second false. Entailment is then to be regarded as involution of a set containing only one member;

and just as an assertion of entailment takes some such form as $P, Q/R$, so an assertion of involution other than entailment takes some such form as $P, Q/R, S$, where the commas before and after the solidus serve to separate expressions of propositions of the relevant sets. In what follows we shall make free use of the convention that a solidus can absorb prefixes of the form § which would otherwise be attached to all the expressions of propositions written before or after it, but it is important to realize that when we write the solidus between expressions without prefixes we do not thereby transform it into a grammatical particle or connective as distinct from a verb. In short a formula of the pattern $P, Q/R, S$ is merely an abbreviation for a formula of the pattern $\{§P, §Q\}/\{§R, §S\}$ and so for an English sentence like *The set consisting of the proposition that-P and the proposition that-Q involves the set consisting of the proposition that-R and the proposition that-S*. Since, however, it is possible to omit both braces and prefixes without ambiguity, we shall always do so and even allow ourselves the liberty of reserving braces for a special use to be noticed presently.

The basic development schemata required for general logic are as follows:

$$(1)\ \frac{P \quad Q}{P.Q} \qquad\qquad (2a)\ \frac{P.Q}{P} \quad (2b)\ \frac{P.Q}{Q}$$

$$(3a)\ \frac{P}{P \vee Q} \quad (3b)\ \frac{Q}{P \vee Q} \qquad (4)\ \frac{P \vee Q}{P \quad Q}$$

$$(5)\ \frac{*}{P \quad \sim P} \qquad\qquad (6)\ \frac{P \quad \sim P}{*}$$

$$(7a)\ \frac{*}{P \quad P \supset Q} \quad (7b)\ \frac{Q}{P \supset Q} \qquad (8)\ \frac{P \quad P \supset Q}{Q}$$

$$(9)\ \frac{\{Fx\}}{(x)Fx} \qquad\qquad (10)\ \frac{(x)Fx}{FY}$$

$$(11)\ \frac{FY}{(\exists x)Fx} \qquad\qquad (12)\ \frac{(\exists x)Fx}{\{Fx\}}$$

The asterisk used in the formulation of rules (5), (6), and (7a) is something like the joker in card games. For it may be taken as a substitute for any propositional expression. It would have been possible to use a capital letter, say $R$, instead, but the asterisk serves the additional purpose of drawing attention to these rules, which are of special importance in demonstration. Apart from this usage, the only novelties here are the occurrence of two expressions below the line in rules (4), (5), and (7a) (i.e. in three of the places where Gentzen found it necessary to introduce suppositions), and the use of the sign $\{Fx\}$ in rules (9) and (12) to represent the set of all possible values of the function called $F\hat{x}$. But these changes are enough to secure symmetry and allow for the introduction and elimination of each formal sign by the rules which seem most natural. Thus rules (5) and (6) are versions of the principles of excluded middle and non-contradiction, and with one exception the others are all obvious.

Rule (7a), which looks a little curious at first sight, is equivalent in effect to the principle that a Philonian conditional is entailed by the negation of its antecedent. If we wish, we can easily get the latter as a derivative role.

(13)  $\sim P/P \supset Q$.
*Proof.*

$$\frac{\sim P \quad \overline{P}\,(6) \quad \overset{*}{\phantom{P}} }{\underset{*}{P \supset Q}}(7\text{a}).$$

But (7a) is preferable as a basic rule, because elegance requires that each formal sign should be introduced alone, i.e. that no basic rule should be concerned with more than one sign.

In general, a new development schema can always be derived from one already given by transferring a propositional expression to the other side of the horizontal line and adding or taking away a negation sign at the same time. Here, for example, is a new principle of development derivative from rule (4).

(14)  $\sim Q/P, \sim(P \vee Q)$.
*Proof.*

$$\frac{\overline{P \vee Q} \qquad\qquad \overset{*}{\phantom{x}} }{P \quad \underset{*}{\underset{}{Q}}(4) \quad \sim Q}(6).$$

$$\sim(P \vee Q)\,(5)$$

The comma which we have inserted between the two expressions after the solidus is intended, of course, to show that they are taken from the ends of separate descending branches. Similarly a comma placed between two expressions before a solidus shows that they are to be considered as taken from the tops of separate ascending branches.

In the working out of developments it is essential that token formulae which are already connected, either directly by one single horizontal line or indirectly through several horizontal lines, should not be connected again in any way. For otherwise we may obtain such absurd patterns as

$$\frac{P \vee Q}{\dfrac{P \qquad Q}{P.Q}}.$$

Similarly, if $Fx$ is introduced below $(\exists x)Fx$, it must not itself be followed by $(x)Fx$. For the absurd pattern

$$\frac{(\exists x)Fx}{\dfrac{Fx}{(x)Fx}}$$

involves the same mistake of linking items below which are already linked above, namely those formulae which express values of the function called $F\hat{x}$. Development is a generalization of the technique which mathematicians call proof by cases, and cases which have once been distinguished as alternatives must never be considered in conjunction.

The principle of conditionalization, which occurs as a basic rule in Gentzen's system, can be proved very simply within this new system. For it requires only that the proposition expressed by $P \supset Q$ shall be demonstrable if the proposition expressed by $P$ entails the proposition expressed by $Q$, and this is shown as follows:

(15) *If $P/Q$ then $*/P \supset Q$.*

*Proof.*

$$\frac{\dfrac{\overset{*}{\overline{\quad}}}{\dfrac{P}{Q}\text{(Hyp)} \qquad P \supset Q}{(7a)}}{P \supset Q}(7b).$$

For an extended illustration of the method of development it will be convenient to prove the rules and axioms of a well-known version of general logic. First we show the equivalence of $P \supset Q$ and $\sim P \vee Q$, i.e. the equivalence which is used in *Principia Mathematica* for the definition of the Philonian conditional. This can be done by two derivations.

(16) $P \supset Q/\sim P \vee Q$.

*Proof.*

$$\frac{\dfrac{P \supset Q \quad P}{Q}(8)}{\sim P \vee Q}(3b) \qquad \frac{\dfrac{\overset{*}{\overline{P}}}{\sim P}(5)}{\sim P \vee Q}(3a)$$

(17) $\sim P \vee Q / P \supset Q$.

*Proof.*

$$\dfrac{\dfrac{\sim P \vee Q}{\sim P}}{P \supset Q}(13) \qquad \dfrac{\dfrac{}{Q}(4)}{P \supset Q}(7\mathrm{b}).$$

Next we check that we have the *modus ponendo ponens*, or rule of detachment, for the Philonian conditional as one of our basic rules, namely (8). Thirdly, we construct demonstrations of the four independent axioms chosen by Whitehead and Russell for elementary logic, or rather we show the validity of the corresponding axiom schemata.

(18) $*/(P \vee P) \supset P$.

*Proof.*

$$\dfrac{\dfrac{P \vee P}{\dfrac{P}{(P \vee P) \supset P}(7\mathrm{b})}}{\phantom{x}} \qquad \dfrac{\dfrac{}{\dfrac{*}{(P \vee P) \supset P}}(7\mathrm{a})}{\dfrac{P}{(P \vee P) \supset P}(4)}(7\mathrm{b}).$$

(19) $*/P \supset (P \vee Q)$.

*Proof.*

$$\dfrac{\dfrac{P}{\dfrac{P \vee Q}{P \supset (P \vee Q)}(3\mathrm{a})}}{\dfrac{\dfrac{*}{P \supset (P \vee Q)}(7\mathrm{a})}{\phantom{x}}}(7\mathrm{b}).$$

(20) $*/(P \vee Q) \supset (Q \vee P)$.

*Proof.*

$$\dfrac{\dfrac{P}{\dfrac{Q \vee P}{(P \vee Q) \supset (Q \vee P)}(3\mathrm{b})}}{\phantom{x}}(7\mathrm{b}) \qquad \dfrac{\dfrac{P \vee Q \quad \dfrac{*}{(P \vee Q) \supset (Q \vee P)}(7\mathrm{a})}{\dfrac{Q}{Q \vee P}(4)}(3\mathrm{a})}{(P \vee Q) \supset (Q \vee P)}(7\mathrm{b}).$$

(21) $*/(Q \supset R) \supset [(P \vee Q) \supset (P \vee R)]$.

*Proof.*

$$\dfrac{\dfrac{\dfrac{Q \supset R}{\sim Q \vee R}(16) \quad \dfrac{*}{(Q \supset R) \supset [(P \vee Q) \supset (P \vee R)]}(7\mathrm{a})}{\sim Q \quad \dfrac{R}{\dfrac{P \vee R}{(P \vee Q) \supset (P \vee R)}(3\mathrm{b})}(4)}(7\mathrm{b})}{(Q \supset R) \supset [(P \vee Q) \supset (P \vee R)]}(7\mathrm{b})$$

N n

$$\frac{\dfrac{\dfrac{\sim Q}{\dfrac{P}{P \vee R}\,(3\text{a})}}{(P \vee Q) \supset (P \vee R)}\,(7\text{b})}{(Q \supset R) \supset [(P \vee Q) \supset (P \vee R)]}\,(7\text{b}). \qquad \frac{\dfrac{\dfrac{\sim(P \vee Q)}{(P \vee Q) \supset (P \vee R)}\,(13)}{(Q \supset R) \supset [(P \vee Q) \supset (P \vee R)]}}{}\,($$

And finally we construct proofs for the two additional axiom schemata and the two additional rules of inference required for a version of general logic like that of Hilbert and Ackermann but with axiom schemata in place of axioms.

(22)  $*/(x)Fx \supset FY$.

*Proof.*

$$\frac{\dfrac{(x)Fx}{FY}\,(10) \qquad (x)Fx \supset FY\,(7\text{a})}{(x)Fx \supset FY}\,(7\text{b}).$$

(23)  $*/FY \supset (\exists x)Fx$.

*Proof.*

$$\frac{\dfrac{FY}{(\exists x)Fx}\,(11) \qquad FY \supset (\exists x)Fx\,(7\text{a})}{FY \supset (\exists x)Fx}\,(7b).$$

(24)  If $P$ does not contain $x$ free, then $P \supset Fx/P \supset (x)Fx$.

*Proof.*

$$\frac{\dfrac{\dfrac{P \supset Fx \quad P}{Fx}\,(8)}{(x)Fx}\,(9) \qquad P \supset (x)Fx\,7(\text{a})}{P \supset (x)Fx}\,(7\text{b}).$$

(25)  If $P$ does not contain $x$ free, then $Fx \supset P/(\exists x)Fx \supset P$.

*Proof.*

$$\frac{\dfrac{Fx \supset P \quad \dfrac{(\exists x)Fx}{Fx}\,(12)}{P}\,(8) \qquad (\exists x)Fx \supset P\,(7\text{a})}{(\exists x)Fx \supset P}\,(7\text{b}).$$

All the derivations are straightforward, except those for (24) and (25), which require some explanation. When we enunciate rule (9) in the form $\dfrac{\{Fx\}}{(x)Fx}$ and rule (12) in the form $\dfrac{(\exists x)Fx}{\{Fx\}}$,

we use the braces to make clear that we are dealing with the class of all propositions that are values of the function expressed by $Fx$, i.e. what we write are abbreviations for

$$\frac{Fx_1 \quad Fx_2 \quad Fx_3 \quad \&c.}{(x)Fx}$$

and

$$\frac{(\exists x)Fx}{Fx_1 \quad Fx_2 \quad Fx_3 \quad \&c.}$$

where $Fx_1, Fx_2, Fx_3$, &c., are supposed to represent various values of the function. But it is obviously impossible to construct tables of development with more than a finite number of branches. How then can we ever make use of our non-finitary rules? Clearly the only possibility is to prove something with complete generality of all the values of the function expressed by $Fx$, using the sign $Fx$ for this purpose *as though it were the expression of such a value* rather than the expression of the function. This is the method of reasoning with free variables to which we drew attention in the last section. If we can show in this way that the proposition expressed by $P$ entails every value of the function expressed by $Fx$ we can prove that $P/(x)Fx$ by the development

$$\frac{\dfrac{P}{Fx_1} \quad \dfrac{P}{Fx_2} \quad \dfrac{P}{Fx_3} \quad \&c.}{(x)Fx}.$$

Similarly, if we can show in this way that every value of the function expressed by $Fx$ entails the proposition expressed by $P$, we can prove that $(\exists x)Fx/P$ by the development

$$\frac{(\exists x)Fx}{\dfrac{Fx_1}{P} \quad \dfrac{Fx_2}{P} \quad \dfrac{Fx_3}{P} \quad \&c.}.$$

In either case it is, of course, essential that the letter $P$ should be really the expression of a proposition and not an abbreviation for another expression containing $x$ free, i.e. as it occurs in $Fx$. All this is allowed for in the formulation of (24) and (25) above, with the result that these principles look a good deal more complicated than rules (9) and (12).

In his *Methods of Logic*, which is a recent attempt to improve the techniques of logical investigation, Quine uses a variant of the truth-table method for propositional logic but provides for the additional requirements of general logic by four rules like those given above. In particular he gives a Rule of Universal Generalization and a Rule of Existential Instantiation which resemble respectively our rules (9) and (12) (except that they do not contain braces to indicate reference to all the values of a function) and prescribes a drill to prevent illicit transitions such as that in the schema:

$$\frac{(\exists x)Fx}{\overline{\phantom{xx}Fx\phantom{xx}}}$$
$$\overline{(x)Fx}.$$

When used together with the device of suppositions introduced by Gentzen and Jaśkowski, these rules undoubtedly simplify the construction of proofs. But Quine himself talks of his procedure as the entry to a looking-glass world;[1] and so it must seem, unless it is explained as a way of getting the advantages which are to be had at the earlier stage of logic from the construction of developments with many branches.

## 4. *Modal Logic*

In his *Begriffsschrift* Frege dismissed modal distinctions as irrelevant to his purpose. According to his explanation anyone who says that something must be so uses the word 'must' to hint that he possesses knowledge of a universal truth from which the proposition in question can be deduced, and similarly anyone who says that something may be so concedes that he knows nothing from which the negation of the proposition follows. If Frege is right, words like 'must' and 'may', 'necessary' and 'possible', involve a covert reference to human knowledge for which there is no place in pure logic, and it is a mistake to suppose with Aristotle and his followers that it is any part of the logician's task to set forth rules of inference applicable only to modal propositions. Many of Frege's successors in logic have agreed with this view, but others have argued that Frege's work should be supplemented by a theory of modality because the notions of necessity and impossibility do not belong, as he thought, to epistemology, or indeed to any special science except logic itself. In this section we shall consider whether there is need for such a supplement.

Modern interest in modal logic begins with the work of C. I. Lewis, first published in book form in his *Survey of Symbolic Logic*

[1] *Methods of Logic*, (first edition) p. 161.

of 1918. This theory is commonly called the logic of strict implication, because it was originally put forward in opposition to an account of implication which Lewis thought mistaken. In their informal comments on their own system of logic Whitehead and Russell used the phrase *P materially implies Q* as a rendering for $P \supset Q$ and tried to justify this way of speaking by pointing out that

$$\frac{P \quad P \supset Q}{Q}$$

was undoubtedly a valid inference schema. The phrase is misleading, because it suggests wrongly that the horseshoe sign expresses a connexion of meaning between the propositional signs which are its antecedent and consequent. Those who use it commit themselves to the paradoxes that a false proposition, merely because it is false, implies every proposition and a true proposition, merely because it is true, is implied by every proposition. Lewis, on the other hand, said that one proposition implied another in the strict sense of the word if, and only if, it was *impossible* that the first should be true and the second false, and he wrote $P \rightarrow Q$ to express this relation between the propositions expressed by $P$ and $Q$. In his definition of implication he followed H. McColl, who had included some suggestions for modal logic in *Symbolic Logic and its Applications*, published in 1906; and, like McColl, he admitted that according to this definition an impossible proposition must imply every proposition and a necessary proposition be implied by every proposition. But he maintained that these two consequences were not really paradoxical and did nothing to discredit his view that the relation he called strict implication was the relation which justified inference from a premiss to a conclusion in deductive argument. Some critics said that his strict implication was not the same as entailment (i.e. the converse of following-from) because it could hold between propositions in a purely external way revealed by the paradoxes. But none of them ever succeeded in excluding these so-called paradoxes without also excluding at the same time arguments which everyone regards as valid, e.g. those by which the Pseudo-Scot proved the paradoxes in the Middle Ages. And apparently none of those who took part in the debate were aware of the close resemblance of their doctrines to contentions which had been put forward in antiquity and again in the Middle Ages.

Lewis's latest account of modal logic is to be found in the book called *Symbolic Logic* which he published with C. H. Langford in 1932. Here $\Diamond$ is taken as an undefined symbol and $P \rightarrow Q$

introduced as an abbreviation for $\sim\!\Diamond(P.\sim\!Q)$. The other undefined symbols are those for negation and conjunction, and the axiom formulae which he uses in his deductions are as follows:

B1. $p.q \prec q.p$

B2. $p.q \prec p$

B3. $p \prec p.p$.

B4. $(p.q).r \prec p.(q.r)$

B5. $p \prec \sim\!\sim\!p$.

B6. $[(p \prec q).(q \prec r)] \prec (p \prec r)$

B7. $[p.(p \prec q)] \prec q$

B8. $\Diamond(p.q) \prec \Diamond p$

B9. $(\exists p,q)[\sim\!(p \prec q).\sim\!(p \prec \sim\!q)]$

The letter B in the title of each postulate shows that it belongs to Lewis's second set as distinct from his *Survey* system. Apart from substitution for variables and interchange of strictly equivalent expressions there are two permitted methods of derivation, one in accordance with the schema

$$\frac{P \quad P \prec Q}{Q},$$

and the other in accordance with the schema

$$\frac{P \quad Q}{P.Q}.$$

The first of these is, of course, the pattern of detachment or *modus ponens* with $P \prec Q$ in place of $P \supset Q$, and the second, which Lewis calls adjunction, is required in the system because of the change in the first. In *Principia Mathematica*, which allows inference from $P$ and $P \supset Q$ to $Q$, it is possible to dispense with Lewis's rule of adjunction because $p \supset [q \supset (p.q)]$ is a theorem. But Lewis, while admitting this theorem in his own system, cannot use it as a premiss for the derivation of $P.Q$ from $P$ and $Q$, because the holding of a so-called material implication is not enough, in his view, to justify deduction and $p \prec [q \prec (p.q)]$ is not a theorem of his system. In the presence of the rule of detachment noticed above each of his axioms takes the place of a rule of inference from one premiss. Thus B2 when taken with Lewis's version of the *modus ponens* corresponds to rule 2(a) of the systems presented in the last section.

The first seven of the propositions listed above may be called the basic axioms of Lewis's modal logic, because they constitute the system S1, which he considers his strictest, and appear also as axioms or theorems in all the variant systems he thinks worthy of discussion. But they do not form a complete set in the technical sense of that phrase, and they allow for an enormous complication of higher-order modalities, e.g. the possibility of necessity and the necessity of possibility and so forth. O. Becker[1] and others have therefore suggested various supplements of which the most interesting are in Lewis's notation:

C10. $\sim\Diamond\sim p \dashv 3 \sim\Diamond\sim\sim\Diamond\sim p$    or    $\Diamond\Diamond p \dashv 3 \Diamond p$,

C11. $\Diamond p \dashv 3 \sim\Diamond\sim\Diamond p$    or    $\Diamond\sim\Diamond p \dashv 3 \sim\Diamond p$.

These have been called respectively the weak and the strong reduction principles, because they both serve to reduce the complexity of higher order modalities, though not to the same extent. In the presence of the basic axioms C11 is deductively equivalent to the conjunction of C10 with Brouwer's principle $p \dashv 3 \sim\Diamond\sim\Diamond p$. If we use $\Box$ as an abbreviation for $\sim\Diamond\sim$ (i.e. with the sense of 'it is necessary that') and make use of the principles of double negation and contraposition for strict implication, we can express them both without negations as follows:

C10. $\Box p \dashv 3 \Box \Box p$,

C11. $\Diamond p \dashv 3 \Box \Diamond p$.

For each the converse is provable, and so we may say that the first allows us to equate the necessity of any proposition with the necessity of its necessity, while the second allows us to equate the possibility of any proposition with the necessity of its possibility. The effect of adding the first or weaker principle to the basic axioms is to rule out all talk of necessities which are not themselves necessary but merely contingent, or rather to require that anyone who wishes to talk in that way should recognize he is not using the word 'necessary' in the same way as the sign $\Box$ is used in modal logic. The effect of adding the second principle is to require that all modal propositions shall be necessarily true or necessarily false. If we adopt it, we admit only four modalities (apart from truth and falsehood, which are sometimes included because necessity implies truth and truth implies possibility), namely those which make up the square of opposition

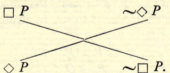

For on this assumption all second-order modalities collapse into first-order modalities. We have, for example, $\Diamond \Box P = \Box P$, which Becker finds slightly paradoxical. Lewis himself is inclined

[1] 'Zur Logik der Modalitäten, *Jahrbuch für Philosophie und phenomenologische Forschung*, xi (1930), pp. 497–548.

to reject both reduction principles and thus to allow the multiplication of higher-order modalities.

It has been proved by P. Henle[1] that the most economical system of modal logic, which Lewis calls S5 (i.e. the system determined by B1–7 and C11), is equivalent to the Boole–Schröder algebra (not the two-valued algebra) when the elements of the algebra are taken to be propositions and the modal sign ◇ is introduced by the rules:

$$\diamond P = \text{1} \ \textit{if and only if } P \neq \text{o},$$
$$\diamond P = \text{o} \ \textit{if and only if } P = \text{o}.$$

In short, this system, with its strong reduction principle, is the working out of what Boole had in mind when he suggested in his *Mathematical Analysis of Logic* that the sign 1 might be taken to represent the sum of all possibilities, which he called the Universe of the Proposition.

Although S5 is the tidiest of the systems Lewis considers, neither it nor any of the others gives a complete characterization of strict implication without Henle's rules, since all the axioms remain true if ◇P is regarded as equivalent to P and –3 taken to be merely a typographical variant for ⊃. It was apparently in order to exclude such an undesirable interpretation of his new sign that Lewis suggested the rather curious existential axiom:

B9. $(\exists p, q) \ [\sim(p \rightarrow 3 \ q) . \sim(p \rightarrow 3 \sim q)].$

This means that there are at least two propositions such that the first implies nothing about the truth or falsity of the second, and it holds for strict, though not for material implication. But it is radically different in kind from the other axioms. Whereas they, when taken with Lewis's principles of substitution, detachment, and adjunction, license all reasoning in certain specified patterns, this negates the universality which is expressed in other axioms by free variables, and its introduction amounts in effect to *rejection* of the formula $(p \rightarrow 3 \ q) \lor (p \rightarrow 3 \sim q)$. Perhaps the simplest way of achieving Lewis's purpose is to say in straightforward fashion that the schema

$$\frac{P \supset Q}{P \rightarrow 3 \ Q}$$

is not valid. And we need not be surprised that some provision of the kind is needed to exclude an undesired interpretation of a modal system in which –3 is undefined. Material implication can be characterized completely by the laying down of appro-

---

[1] Lewis and Langford, *Symbolic Logic*, p. 501.

priate rules of inference, but only because it is a truth-function. For strict implication taken as a primitive the best we can do in this way is to provide exhaustively and exclusively for the demonstration of those properties which it shares with material implication. On the other hand, with the definition of strict implication noticed above and Henle's rules S5 is complete and B9 unnecessary.

It will be noticed that in the presentation of his system Lewis writes $\rightarrow_3$ between propositional expressions (or rather between variables marking places for such) as though it were a sign of the same grammatical status as $\supset$, and similarly that he writes $\diamond$ before propositional expressions just as he writes $\sim$. If we wish to provide an English paraphrase in which each formula is represented by a sentence of approximately similar shape, we may perhaps read $P \rightarrow_3 Q$ as *If P then Q* and $\diamond P$ as *Possibly P*. For the conditional form of sentence was often used in antiquity both by Aristotle and the Stoics to indicate the deducibility of the consequent from the antecedent, which is what Lewis professes to symbolize with his fishhook sign, and in ordinary conversation we often prefix 'possibly' to expressions which are grammatically capable of occurring by themselves as complete sentences. But it is Lewis's main interest to maintain that the deducibility of conclusion from premiss in a valid argument depends on the holding between them of a relation called strict implication and that this relation cannot be defined truth-functionally. In order to emphasize this point we may, when it is convenient, read $P \rightarrow_3 Q$ as *The proposition that-P strictly implies the proposition that-Q*, but only if we suppose that Lewis had tacitly adopted a convention for his fishhook sign like that of our last section whereby the solidus can absorb the prefix which we put in front of propositional expressions to make propositional designations. And with a similar supposition about Lewis's diamond sign we may, when we wish, read $\diamond P$ as *It is possible that-P*. Lewis himself does not discuss the two different ways of reading his formulae, and his successors have often written as though the choice between them were merely a matter of literary taste. But it is important to realize that the second rendering gives a more explicit presentation of the various factors involved in Lewis's enterprise and is therefore preferable from a philosophical point of view.

When Whitehead and Russell spoke of $P \supset Q$ as a statement of material implication, they seem to have confused together two different questions, namely (i) 'What justifies inference from the proposition that-P to the proposition that-Q?' and (ii) 'What is the weakest additional premiss which in conjunction with the

premiss that-*P* suffices for inference to the conclusion that-*Q*?'
If inference from the proposition that-*P* to the proposition that-*Q*
is indeed justified, the first question may be answered by statement of a relation of implication between the two propositions,
but if a supplementary premiss is needed, there is no implication
in a strict sense between the two propositions first mentioned and
all we can do is to answer the second question by producing the
formula $P \supset Q$. This formula is constructed by use of the propositional signs $P$ and $Q$, but it is not *about* the propositions which
they express. We can, of course, replace it by the equivalent
sentence *Either not-P or Q* and then expand this to the form
*Either it is not the case that-P or it is the case that-Q*, which contains
the propositional designations *that-P* and *that-Q*. But the longer
sentence is not an analysis of the sense of the shorter, since it
merely fills out the same pattern with inflationary verbiage. On
the other hand, Lewis's formula $P \rightarrow\!3\, Q$ is supposed to be *about*
the propositions expressed by $P$ and by $Q$ precisely because it
is conceived as a proper answer to the first of the questions
noticed above. And when we render it by the paraphrase *The
proposition that-P strictly implies the proposition that-Q*, we may rightly
claim to have given an analysis of its sense, because our longer
version does not retain the same basic pattern as the original but
draws attention to a complexity of usage not immediately obvious
from consideration of that shape.

   Lewis's failure to make clear the point noticed in the last paragraph was perhaps due to the fact that he mistakenly agreed
with Whitehead and Russell in thinking it necessary to use implication statements as premisses for the *modus ponens*, and therefore followed their practice as closely as he could while maintaining the difference between strict and material implication. It
seems indeed that his chief motive for elaborating his theory as
he did was a desire to substitute strict implication for material
implication in the *modus ponens*, and so it is not surprising that his
attack on the system of material implication (as distinct from the
misleading name) involves argument at cross-purposes. Obviously
no one would dream of putting forward an argument in the form

$$\frac{P \quad P \supset Q}{Q}$$

if he had established the truth of the second premiss either by discovering the falsity of the other premiss or by establishing the
truth of the conclusion. For in the first case he would not be able
to assert the other premiss, and in the second case he would not
need an argument to reach the conclusion. When a Philonian

conditional of the form $P \supset Q$ appears as a premiss in *Principia Mathematica* it is accepted as necessary on logical grounds, and these are precisely the grounds on which it is possible to assert $P \rightarrow Q$. According to Lewis's definitions

$$(P \rightarrow Q) = \Box(P \supset Q)$$

where $\Box$ signifies logical necessity. He himself even goes so far as to assert that $P \rightarrow Q$ holds in his system when, and only when, $P \supset Q$ is a tautology.[1] If 'tautology' is supposed to mean here a truism of non-modal logic, the claim is incorrect, since axioms B6 and B7 furnish counter-examples. But it is certainly the case that $P \rightarrow Q$ never holds unless $P \supset Q$ is a truth of logic. The merit of his modal logic cannot, therefore, be, as he seems to suggest, that it provides an alternative method of reasoning which is superior in some way to that of Frege, but rather that it deals explicitly with the notion of necessity which all logicians, including Frege, have taken for granted.

In order to make clear the relationship between Lewis's logic and that of Frege or *Principia Mathematica* several authors have presented one or more of Lewis's systems as derivative from *Principia Mathematica* and certain supplementary axioms or rules of inference.[2] Thus for the derivation of Lewis's system with the weak reduction principle, i.e. S4, Gödel adds to the elementary logic of *Principia Mathematica* the three new axiom formulae

1. $\Box p \supset p$
2. $\Box p \supset [\Box(p \supset q) \supset \Box q]$
3. $\Box p \supset \Box \Box p$,

in which $\Box$ is to be taken as a primitive sign,[3] and a new rule that if $P$ is any thesis of the resulting system we may assert also $\Box P$. In the same notation the strong reduction principle of S5 would take the form

4. $\sim\Box p \supset \Box\sim\Box p$.

This version has an elegant simplicity, and the new rule which it contains brings out very well the interesting fact that the necessity studied in modal logic is a property of its own propositions. But it cannot be said that this presentation helps much to an understanding of the status of modal logic among deductive

[1] Lewis and Langford, *Symbolic Logic*, p. 244.
[2] e.g. K. Gödel, 'Eine Interpretation des intuitionistischen Aussagenkalküls', *Ergebnisse eines mathematischen Kolloquiums*, iv (1932), pp. 39–40. Cf. G. H. von Wright, *An Essay in Modal Logic*, appendix ii.
[3] Gödel himself uses 'B' (for *beweisbar*) because he offers the system in an article on intuitionistic logic, which will be noticed later.

theories. On the contrary, use of such an axiom system for modal logic seems to have led some philosophers to think that modal logic is logic only in a large and loose sense in which it may perhaps be permissible to speak also of deontic logic (when one wants to refer to the general axiomatic theory of obligation) or of tense logic (when one wants to refer to the general axiomatic theory of the relations which are expressed in many languages by tense inflexions) or even of spatial logic (when one wants to refer to pure geometry). This habit of thought is unfortunate because it directs attention away from those considerations which are most relevant to an appreciation of the logical character of modal logic and so to a decision on the question of reduction principles.

Lewis, as we have seen, is inclined to reject both reduction principles, but he confesses that he cannot bring forward any decisive argument in favour of his view. After distinguishing five systems which differ, as he maintains, in degree of strictness, he suggests that the interests of logical study would probably be served best by attention to those stricter systems which do not include reduction principles, but he says open-mindedly : 'Prevailing good use in logical inference—the practice in mathematical deduction, for example—is not sufficiently precise and self-conscious to determine clearly which of these five systems expresses the acceptable principles of deduction.'[1] This is a curious remark. If it is not yet possible to decide whether higher-order modalities can all be reduced to first-order modalities, how shall we ever be able to settle the question ? What sort of evidence should we seek and where ?

Von Wright, who works with a modal system something like that of Gödel, suggests that it may be helpful to compare alethic with epistemic modalities, that is to say, modalities such as Lewis and Becker had in mind with modalities expressed by phrases like 'it is known that', and he goes on to say :

'The equivalent to the Second Principle of Reduction for epistemic modalities states that if a proposition is not known to be false then it is known that the proposition is not known to be false. This deduction of knowledge from ignorance is plainly unacceptable, and should be considered at least a strong warning against assuming the Second Principle of Reduction to be true for the alethic modalities.'[2]

This again is curious. Why should the irreducibility of higher orders in expressions for what von Wright calls epistemic modalities furnish any presumption against the strong principle of reduction for pure logical modalities ?

[1] *Symbolic Logic*, pp. 501–2.        [2] *An Essay in Modal Logic*, p. 77.

In a later paper von Wright says:

'Our "logical intuitions", apparently, give no strong indication in favour of any definite answer to the question of truth here. One of the main reasons for this, it seems to me, is the fact that higher-order modal expressions like "possibly possible" or "possibly impossible" have hardly any *use* at all in ordinary or scientific discourse (outside modal logic). A problem of primary importance, therefore, is to *invent a use* or some kind of "equivalent" of a use for the expressions in question (outside modal logic). This done, the problem of truth mentioned above can be tackled on a firmer basis.'[1]

Then, having produced an interpretation in terms of natural processes which satisfies the basic axioms of his modal logic but neither reduction principle, he writes:

'It seems to me that the existence of such illustrations as these among natural processes shows that neither of the identities in question can claim universal validity for the concept of the possible (and the necessary) in modal logic, nor can either of them be rejected as contrary to the "true" nature of modality.'[2]

This is still more curious. From the invention of a model which satisfies some but not all of the axioms of a formal system we cannot reasonably conclude that the formal system as a whole is unsatisfactory for the totally different purpose for which it was designed. Anyone who accepts the strong reduction principle in modal *logic* does not thereby commit himself to defend the application of the principle to all actual uses of the words 'possible' and 'necessary', let alone its application to invented uses.

In order to get a proper appreciation of the status which modal logic has among deductive theories let us consider once more the nature of the logician's task. He wishes to present those rules or principles of inference which are valid for all subject-matters, but he cannot list them all independently because they do not form a finite set. He therefore puts down some very general principles and shows how others may be derived from these. Naturally he hopes to find a small number of general principles from which *all* other principles of logic can be derived, and we shall see later that this ambition was in fact achieved by Frege in the field of logic which he considered; but for the moment what interests us is the manner in which the logician derived lesser principles from greater.

In his reduction of all valid syllogistic principles to *Barbara* and *Celarent* Aristotle set the fashion of reasoning about principles by use of some of the principles studied. For what he did in effect

---

[1] 'Interpretations of Modal Logic', *Mind*, N.S., lvi (1952), pp. 153–77. The quotation is taken from p. 77 of the reprint in his *Logical Studies*.
[2] Ibid., p. 88.

was to prove the validity of each syllogistic principle other than *Barbara* or *Celarent* by showing that the result of applying that principle in any particular case could always be achieved, though in a more round-about way, by applying *Barbara* or *Celarent* together with some simple principles which were not syllogistic. In this procedure he did not generalize explicitly about all the particular cases, but assumed, correctly enough, that in any pattern in which he could produce a make-believe deduction with schematic letters he could also, if required, produce a genuine deduction with real terms. Chrysippus adopted the same plan when dealing with a field in which the number of patterns of valid reasoning is not finite, as it is in syllogistic theory, and what little we know of his work suggests that he applied the method with great proficiency. In the last section we saw that this technique had been used once more by Frege and his successors, though in their work the business of deriving new rules from old rules by help of the old rules was obscured by talk of first-order axioms and theorems. In Gentzen's system of natural inference schemata (and in the system of development schemata which we have obtained from this by some small modifications) the programme is carried out more clearly than ever before by the construction of proof trees which enable the reader to recognize at a glance how one rule is validated by others.

There can be no serious doubt about the propriety of the method followed by all these distinguished logicians, but it is possible also to present logic in another way, which is more explicit, though perhaps less easy to understand at first encounter. In this we deal with theses rather than with schemata of reasoning, but our theses are the principles corresponding to schemata of valid inference (or development), that is to say, they are second-order propositions concerning the relation of entailment (or involution), not first-order truisms like the axioms of Frege; and we derive some of them from others in accordance with a higher-order principle of transitivity. Lewis seems sometimes to have this programme in mind. For his axioms B1–5 are examples of initial principles, and B6 is a version of the transitivity of entailment. But instead of treating each of these propositions as a principle of inference he allows only that it may be used as a premiss for the *modus ponens* in place of the corresponding material implication. And conversely when he wishes to use the principle of his version of the *modus ponens* as a premiss for the deduction of further principles he adds it as a new axiom B7, regardless of the fact that it is contained already in his enunciation of the rule of the *modus ponens*.

If, as Lewis holds, strict implication, unlike material implication, *justifies* deduction, there can be no difference, except in vocabulary, between the assertion that one proposition strictly implies another and the assertion that inference from the first to the second is valid. Why then does Lewis present his calculus as he does? The reason seems to be that he takes for granted the necessity of the style of exposition which was introduced by Frege and brought to general notice by Whitehead and Russell. In the first place he apparently assumes from the beginning that his main task is to introduce a propositional connective which can properly appear in the *modus ponens* where Frege wrongly used the material implication (or Philonian conditional) sign. This prepossession naturally leads him to make a distinction in his own system between axioms and rules of inference and also to offer the definition

$$P \rightarrow Q =_{\text{def}} \sim\!\Diamond(P.\!\sim\!Q)$$

as a counterpart to the definition

$$P \supset Q =_{\text{def}} \sim\!(P.\!\sim\!Q).$$

Secondly, he assumes that a thesis of strict implication, like a thesis of material implication, must always have one implicant and one implicate. Since, however, it is impossible to present all logic as a theory of one-premiss inference, he finds himself compelled to introduce a rule of adjunction for which there cannot be any analogue among his theses of strict implication. Thirdly, he follows Frege in thinking that any statement to which he commits himself as a logician should be a universal thesis like $p.q \rightarrow p$ rather than an assertion that every proposition of a form such as $P.Q \rightarrow P$ is true. This belief naturally leads him to adopt a rule of substitution as something quite distinct in status from all his theses. In short, each of the rules of inference which he gives in addition to his axioms owes its place to the need for overcoming a restriction of thought which he accepted when formulating those axioms.

Let us then try to free our minds from the influence of a recently formed tradition and try to design a system of modal logic in which the notion of entailment is taken as fundamental and it is permissible to write $P, Q/P.Q$ as another version of the principle commonly expressed by introduction of the inference schema $\dfrac{P \quad Q}{P.Q}$. Or more generally, let us try to design a system in which principles of involution are derived in a natural (i.e. intuitively obvious) way from other such principles, themselves chosen for their naturalness. And in order to make the problem definite let us for our first attempt consider how to reproduce in an explicit form (i.e. with no covert assumptions) the argumentation exhibited in the following simple development schema

$$\frac{P \supset Q \qquad \overset{*}{\overline{P \qquad \overset{\textstyle\sim P}{}}} (5)}{\underset{*}{\underline{\underline{Q}}} \qquad \overset{\textstyle\sim Q}{} (6).} (8)$$

We may say that the principle $\sim Q, P \supset Q/\sim P$ is derived here from the principles indicated by the numbers at the ends of horizontal lines, namely $*/P, \sim P$ and $P \supset Q, P/Q$ and $Q, \sim Q/*$. But in talking like this we assume already that a statement of the form $\Gamma/\Delta$ (i.e. with a solidus) may be made correctly if and only if a development of the form $\dfrac{\Gamma}{\Delta}$ is valid. For convenience Greek capitals are used to represent *sequences* of formulae, including null sequences. Furthermore, we assume that the result of a development

$$\frac{\Gamma \qquad \overset{\Theta}{\overline{P}} \qquad \Lambda}{\Delta}$$

may be recorded in the form $\Gamma, \Theta/\Delta, \Lambda$, where $P$ is cut out because it is neither an initial formula nor an end formula of the whole arrangement. Again, in writing $\sim Q, P \supset Q/\sim P$ rather than $P \supset Q, \sim Q/\sim P$, we take it for granted that the order of the formulae in front of the solidus may be changed at will. If we try to take account of all such assumptions we may reformulate the argument as follows in explicitly second-order style

$$\frac{\dfrac{\dfrac{(6)}{Q, \sim Q/*} \text{ (solidus)}}{\sim Q, Q/*} \text{ (change)} \qquad \dfrac{\dfrac{(8)}{P \supset Q, P/Q} \text{ (solidus)} \qquad \dfrac{(5)}{*/P, \sim P} \text{ (solidus)}}{P \supset Q/Q, \sim P} \text{ (cut)}}{\sim Q, P \supset Q/\sim P} \text{ (cut).}$$

Here the words at the ends of lines refer, of course, to the licences by which we justify our transitions. In order to provide for the reformulation of more complicated arguments we must recognize also certain other licences, namely one whereby we may eliminate redundancies of any kind on either side of a solidus and two which allow us to pass over intermediate *classes* of formulae when stating the principles established by development schemata of general logic. And although it is not strictly necessary for the purpose of explicit reformulation, we may, if we wish, adopt also the obviously safe licence of adding items at will either before or after the solidus of a formula which expresses a correct principle. Similarly from any correct statement of principle $\Gamma/P$ taken together with the premisses $\Gamma$ we may safely conclude $P$.

Having come so far, we find, however, that we can simplify our task by no longer taking as axiomatic the principles corresponding to our original development schemata but adopting instead for each formal sign a single higher-order rule which fixes its use in relation to the solidus. For with such rules added to the general licences noticed above it is possible to derive all our original principles of involution from the single principle

$P/P$ corresponding to the trivial inference schema $\dfrac{P}{P}$.

Our new system takes the following form:

$$\alpha 1. \quad \frac{P}{P}$$

$$\alpha 2. \quad \frac{\Gamma/\Delta}{\Gamma,\ \Theta/\Delta,\ \Lambda} \qquad\qquad \alpha 3. \quad \frac{\Gamma,\ P/\Delta \quad \Theta/P,\ \Lambda}{\Gamma,\ \Theta/\Delta,\ \Lambda}$$

$$\alpha 4. \quad \frac{\Gamma/(\Delta/\Theta)}{\Gamma,\ \Delta/\Theta} \qquad\qquad \alpha 5. \quad \frac{\Gamma,\ (\Delta/\Theta)/(\Lambda/\Xi)}{\Gamma/[(\Delta/\Theta)/(\Lambda/\Xi)]}$$

$$\alpha 6. \quad \frac{\Gamma,\ \{Fx\}/\Delta \quad \{\Theta/Fx,\ \Lambda\}}{\Gamma,\ \Theta/\Delta,\ \Lambda} \qquad\qquad \alpha 7. \quad \frac{\{\Gamma,\ Fx/\Delta\} \quad \Theta/\{Fx\},\ \Lambda}{\Gamma,\ \Theta/\Delta,\ \Lambda}$$

$$\beta 1. \quad \frac{\left(\dfrac{\Gamma}{P}\right)}{\Gamma/P} \qquad\qquad \beta 2. \quad \frac{\Gamma/P}{\left(\dfrac{\Gamma}{P}\right)}$$

$$\beta 3. \quad \frac{\Gamma,\ \Delta,\ \Theta,\ \Lambda/\Xi,\ \Pi,\ \Sigma,\ \Phi}{\Gamma,\ \Theta,\ \Delta,\ \Lambda/\Xi,\ \Sigma,\ \Pi,\ \Phi} \qquad\qquad \beta 4. \quad \frac{\Gamma,\ \Delta,\ \Delta/\Theta,\ \Lambda,\ \Lambda}{\Gamma,\ \Delta/\Theta,\ \Lambda}$$

$$\gamma 1. \quad \frac{\Gamma,\ P.Q/\Delta}{\Gamma,\ P,Q/\Delta} \qquad\qquad \gamma 2. \quad \frac{\Gamma/P\vee Q,\ \Delta}{\Gamma/\ P,\ Q,\ \Delta}$$

$$\gamma 3. \quad \frac{\Gamma,\ \sim P/\Delta}{\Gamma/P,\ \Delta} \qquad\qquad \gamma 4. \quad \frac{\Gamma/P\supset Q,\ \Delta}{\Gamma,\ P/Q,\ \Delta}$$

$$\gamma 5. \quad \frac{\Gamma,\ (x)Fx/\Delta}{\Gamma,\ \{Fx\}/\Delta} \qquad\qquad \gamma 6. \quad \frac{\Gamma/(\exists x)Fx,\ \Delta}{\Gamma/\{Fx\},\ \Delta}$$

As before, each Greek capital is to be understood as an abbreviated reference to any sequence of propositions the reader may choose, including under 'sequence' for this purpose sets with one member and even null sets. This use of Greek letters and even the substance of some of the rules is suggested by the later part of the work of Gentzen cited in the last section, though the system which he elaborates there is different in kind from that considered here.[1]

With the exception of $\alpha 5$, which will be considered later, the rules of the first group are all connected with the licences introduced above, and none of them is very difficult to understand. In the expression of $\alpha 1$ we must use the italic letter $P$ rather than $\Gamma$ because $\dfrac{\Gamma}{\Gamma}$ would commit us to $\dfrac{*}{*}$, which is unacceptable. Rule $\alpha 2$ allows for addition of items on either side of the solidus in the expression of a principle. Since, however, either or both of the sequences represented by the letters $\Theta$ and $\Lambda$ may be null, it does not *require* any addition on either side. Here and in later rules the admission of null sequences makes for simplicity of presentation. Rule $\alpha 3$ allows the operation of cutting in primary logic, and $\alpha 4$ enables us to get Lewis's form of the *modus ponens* if we need it, while $\alpha 6$ and $\alpha 7$ do for general logic what $\alpha 3$ does for primary logic. As before, braces are used to indicate possibly infinite sets of propositions. Thus the set of propositions indicated by the complex sign $\{\Gamma/Fx, \Delta\}$ is that which we should establish by constructing a demonstration for the formula $\Gamma/Fx, \Delta$ with $x$ taken as a free variable.

In the next group $\beta 1$ and $\beta 2$ make clear the equivalence of two different ways of presenting principles of entailment. Here the expression $\left(\dfrac{\Gamma}{P}\right)$ may be taken to mean: *Any inference in accordance with the schema* $\dfrac{\Gamma}{P}$ *is valid.* Similarly $\beta 3$ allows rearrangement of formulae at will on either side of the solidus in the expression of a principle of involution, while $\beta 4$ allows elimination of redundancies from either side. As Leibniz said of one of his calculi, we take no account here of order or repetition. For although the signs we write on either side of a solidus must be ordered from left to right and may include some duplicates, these facts are of no importance for our theory. The relation of involution which interests us is one holding between *sets* of *propositions*, not between sequences of formulae considered in their own right, and these

---

[1] In the formulation of his second system Gentzen used some ideas and also some terms derived from P. Hertz's paper 'Über Axiomensysteme für beliebige Satzsysteme', *Mathematische Annalen*, ci (1929), pp. 457–514.

two rules serve merely to show the irrelevance of certain features in our symbolism. That is why they have been grouped together with $\beta 1$ and $\beta 2$.

In the third group we have a special rule for each of the various formal signs in common use. These are adapted in part from the rules of K. R. Popper,[1] and each has the form of a substitution licence which governs the use of a formal sign in association with the solidus.

Together these rules suffice for the reconstruction of the whole of logic as that is commonly understood. Here, for example, is a proof of a principle corresponding to one of the more complicated axioms of *Principia Mathematica*:

$$
\cfrac{\cfrac{\cfrac{(\alpha 1)}{Q \supset R/Q \supset R}(\beta 1)}{Q \supset R,\, Q/R}(\gamma 4) \quad \cfrac{\cfrac{\cfrac{\cfrac{(\alpha 1)}{P \vee Q/P \vee Q}(\beta 1)}{P \vee Q/P,\, Q}(\gamma 2)}{P \vee Q/Q,\, P}(\beta 3)}{}(\alpha 3)\ (\beta 3)}{\cfrac{\cfrac{\cfrac{Q \supset R,\, P \vee Q/P,\, R}{Q \supset R,\, P \vee Q/P \vee R}(\gamma 2)}{Q \supset R/(P \vee Q) \supset (P \vee R)}(\gamma 4)}{*/(Q \supset R) \supset [(P \vee Q) \supset (P \vee R)]}(\gamma 4).}
$$

It is interesting to notice that, while the principles which form the subject-matter of this system are principles of involution, the rules by means of which we construct our proofs are all rules of inference, i.e. rules for which the corresponding principles are principles of entailment. But even more interesting from our present point of view is the fact that this system without rule $\alpha 5$ is a generalization of Lewis's basic system by use of involution, which is a relation between classes of propositions, in place of his strict implication, which is a relation between propositions. For his axioms B1–5 and B7 can all be obtained from $\alpha 1$ by simple derivations like that we have just given, while B6 can be got by application of $\beta 1$ and $\gamma 1$ to a simplified version of $\alpha 3$. On the other hand, the schema $\dfrac{P \supset Q}{P/Q}$, which he rejects, does not represent a rule of this system. For it is certainly not the schema of any primitive rule of the system, and it cannot be the schema of a derivative rule, because its conclusion is of a higher order than its premiss, whereas our primitive rules, apart from $\alpha 5$, allow

[1] 'On the Theory of Deduction', *Proceedings of the Koninklijke Nederlandsche Akademie van Wetenschappen*, li (1948), pp. 173–83, 322–31.

only inferences to conclusions of an order not higher than the highest order among their premises.

When we add $\alpha5$, our system becomes a generalization of Lewis's S5. For $\alpha5$ is a generalization of the strong reduction principle. What our formulation says in effect is that there is no difference between strict implication and material implication when implicant and implicate are both propositions of involution (which includes strict implication or entailment as a special case). For, whatever the implicant and the implicate may be, every case of strict implication is likewise a case of material implication; and according to $\alpha5$ every case of material implication in which the implicant and the implicate are of the special kind indicated is also a case of strict implication. This may be seen from the following derivation:

$$\frac{\dfrac{(\alpha 1)}{(\varDelta/\varTheta) \supset (\varLambda/\varXi)/(\varDelta/\varTheta) \supset (\varLambda/\varXi)}\,(\beta 1)}{\dfrac{(\varDelta/\varTheta) \supset (\varLambda/\varXi),\ (\varDelta/\varTheta)/(\varLambda/\varXi)}{(\varDelta/\varTheta) \supset (\varLambda/\varXi)/[(\varDelta/\varTheta)/(\varLambda/\varXi)]}\,(\gamma 4)}\,(\alpha 5).$$

If we adopted instead of $\alpha5$ the simpler rule

$$\frac{\varGamma,\ \varDelta/\varTheta}{\varGamma/(\varDelta/\varTheta)}$$

which is the converse of $\alpha4$, we should be committed by a similar argument to the unacceptable thesis $P \supset Q/(P/Q)$. But by adopting $\alpha5$ we exclude only the baroque profusion of modalities to be found in Lewis's systems S1–4.

For a derivation of the strong reduction principle in a more familiar form we may define necessity by the rule $\dfrac{\square P}{*/P}$, where $*$ indicates the null class of premisses (contained as a sub-class in every class of premisses) and prove the derivative rule $\dfrac{Q/\square{\sim}Q}{\square{\sim}Q}$ as follows:

$$\frac{\dfrac{\dfrac{Q/\square{\sim}Q}{Q/(*/{\sim}Q)}\,(\text{def. }\square)}{Q,\ */{\sim}Q}\,(\alpha 4) \qquad \dfrac{\dfrac{(\alpha 1)}{{\sim}Q/{\sim}Q}\,(\beta 1)}{*/Q,{\sim}Q}\,(\gamma 3)}{\dfrac{*/{\sim}Q}{\square{\sim}Q}\,(\text{def. }\square).}\,(\beta 3)\ (\alpha 3)\ (\beta 4)$$

Then putting $\square P$ for $Q$ in our derivative rule (DR) we proceed as follows:

$$\frac{\dfrac{(\alpha 1)}{(*/P)/(*/P)}\ (\beta 1)}{\dfrac{\sim(*/P),\ (*/P)/(*/\sim\square P)}{\dfrac{\sim(*/P)/[(*/P)/(*/\sim\square P)]}{\sim\square P/(\square P/\square\sim\square P)}\ (\text{def } \square)}\ (\gamma 3)\ (\beta 3)\ (\alpha 2)\ (\alpha 5)} \qquad \frac{(\text{DR})}{(\square P/\square\sim\square P)/\square\sim\square P}\ {(\beta 1)\atop (\alpha 3)}.$$

$$\sim\square P/\square\sim\square P$$

According to our version of the strong reduction principle, any statement of involution (and therefore, of course, any statement of entailment) which is true is necessarily true, and any which is false is necessarily false. But when it is presented in this form, the principle can scarcely be doubted. For if anyone disputes it, he says in effect that the invalidity of a syllogism (or any other argument which purports to be deductive) may be a contingent matter of fact, and this seems plainly absurd. It is admittedly a contingent matter of fact that the sounds or marks used in presentation of an argument have the meanings customarily assigned to them, and it is therefore also a contingent matter of fact that they are used on a certain occasion in presentation of an invalid argument. But this is irrelevant to the question at issue. We assert only that the failure of one proposition or group of propositions to entail another is not contingent, and this thesis requires no more justification.

When a philosopher hesitates to accept the strong reduction principle, we may reasonably suspect that he has not understood the consequences of rejecting it because he has not kept his attention to appropriate examples of its application but allowed himself to be influenced by some of the many elliptical usages of modal words in ordinary speech, e.g. by that usage which led Frege to exclude modality from his logic. In discussion of a plausible but unproved proposition of mathematics (such as Goldbach's conjecture that every even number greater than two is the sum of two primes) it seems natural to say 'This may be a necessary truth, but we cannot at present assert that it must be'. On first consideration such talk may be thought to support the suggestion of irreducible higher-order modalities, but on further examination we find that it involves three different usages of the modal words within one sentence. For while the phrase 'necessary truth' is intended to convey the notion of necessity which interested Lewis when he formulated his calculus, 'may be' and 'must be' are used here to express relations to human knowledge, and 'cannot' brings in either moral or linguistic propriety. Such a mixture does not provide a genuine counter-example against the strong reduction principle, and it seems impossible that any should be found. For anyone who wishes to refute the principle in this way must indicate a proposition which is contingent in the strictly logical sense but in that same sense only contingently contingent.

Another possible source of doubt concerning reduction principles is a difficulty in the interpretation of the phrase 'necessarily true' as it occurs in ordinary discourse. In the chapter of his *Prior Analytics* where he deals with the third figure of syllogistic reasoning Aristotle says that the argument

| Every man is an animal | No man is a horse |
|---|---|
| Some horse is not an animal | |

is not a valid syllogism, or in other words that it is not necessary that some horse should not be an animal if every man is an animal and no man is a horse.[1] Now this pronouncement is obviously a truth of the form $\sim\Box P$ and therefore according to the strong reduction principle a necessary truth. But if we try to convey our judgement that it is a necessary truth by the sentence 'What Aristotle says is necessarily true' we may be taken to mean that the truth of Aristotle's remark follows necessarily from his having made it. For this reason it has been suggested by a distinguished modern logician that the reduction principles need to be stated with more care than they have usually received. He would, it seems, agree that *it is necessarily true that it is not necessary that some horse should not be an animal if every man is an animal and no man is a horse* but deny that *what Aristotle says in the passage mentioned above is necessarily true*, and he would give as his reason that the phrase 'necessarily true' can only be applied to a proposition as conceived in some particular way and must be understood in relation to that manner of conceiving the proposition.[2] This is obviously good sense, but it should not be held to throw doubt on the strong reduction principle as it is presented in the formula $\sim\Box P/\Box\sim\Box P$, and it should not make us forget that we can after all say what we want to say about Aristotle's pronouncement while referring to it as such. For there will be no danger of misunderstanding if we say simply 'Aristotle's pronouncement in his *Prior Analytics*, 28ᵃ30, is a necessary truth',

[1] *Analytica Priora*, i. 6 (28ᵃ30).
[2] A. Church, 'A Formulation of the Logic of Sense and Denotation', in *Structure, Method, and Meaning: Essays in Honor of Henry M. Sheffer*, 1951, pp. 3–24. He mentions only the weak reduction principle and naturally uses a different example.

though no one will be able to tell whether our judgement is correct until he knows the content of Aristotle's pronouncement.

In our desire to do justice to the notion of logical modality we have been led to present logic as the general theory of that relation between sets of propositions which we call involution. In the last section it became clear that the formal (or logical) signs of conjunction, disjunction, negation, Philonian junction, universality, and existence were those signs whose full sense could be given by the enunciation of rules of development for the propositions expressed by their help. But in our new version of logic the notion of involution is taken as fundamental and the formal signs of the more usual versions are introduced by means of rules which we may treat as definitions. Admittedly the rules of our third group do not allow by themselves for the elimination of the formal signs from all the contexts in which they may be used. But they determine the sense of the signs completely by fixing their roles in argument. No doubt the English word 'and' may have overtones of suggestion for which there is no allowance in $\gamma 1$, but the logician's use of the dot is intended to convey just the sense allowed by that rule, neither more nor less, and similarly each of the other formal signs has precisely the sense allowed by its special rule. Although each such rule deals only with the occurrence of a formal sign on one side of the solidus, each rule is in fact sufficient with the general rules given earlier to provide for the introduction or elimination of its sign either before or after the solidus. Thus the expression $\Gamma/P.Q, \Delta$ is equivalent in force to the pair of involution statements $\Gamma/P, \Delta$ and $\Gamma/Q, \Delta$; and $\Gamma/(x)Fx, \Delta$ can be replaced by the complex sign $\{\Gamma/Fx, \Delta\}$. In short, the formal signs are of special interest to the logician because they can be used as auxiliaries for the presentation of the theory of involution, and conversely signs which cannot be defined like these in association with the sign of involution have no place in logic.

Since there is a difference of the greatest importance between a set that can be specified by enumeration of its members and one that can be specified only by indication of some feature common to all its members, it is not surprising that general (or functional) logic, which deals with relations between possibly infinite sets of propositions specified by reference to propositional functions, should be a good deal more complicated than primary (or pro-positional) logic, which deals only with relations between finite sets of propositions. But our basic rules $\alpha 1-7$ are all simple and even trivial (if that word may be used without an implication of worthlessness). And this again is not surprising; for logic is concerned with the general features of involution, rather than with the holding of the relation between sets of propositions about special subject-matters, and it should be *fundamentally simple*.

## 5. *Suggestions for Alternative Logics*

In the version of logic we have just considered the basic notion is identified by the rules as a generalization of the relation which justifies inference, and there is therefore no room for doubt about the interpretation of the basic sign. But a system like that of Frege's *Begriffsschrift* or that of *Principia Mathematica* can be elaborated without regard to any interpretation of its signs, and when it is studied in this abstract fashion it may usefully be considered as one among a number of alternatives.

In the paper of 1921 in which he introduced truth-tables for elementary logic[1] E. L. Post suggested for consideration an alternative formal system in which each variable would be able to take not merely one or other of the two truth-values t and f but any one of m different values $t_1, t_2, \ldots t_m$. Since he had begun by examining the system of *Principia Mathematica* in which the signs $\sim$ and $\vee$ are taken as primitive, he presented this new system by means of value-tables for two new func-

| $P$ | $\sim_m P$ |
|-----|------------|
| $t_1$ | $t_2$ |
| $t_2$ | $t_3$ |
| . | . |
| . | . |
| . | . |
| $t_m$ | $t_1$ |

tions with the signs $\sim_m$ and $\vee_m$. For the first the value-table has the form indicated in the accompanying figure. That is to say, the sign $\sim_m$ is an operator which permutes values by one place. For the second function the value table is more complicated in appearance, but the principle of construction is simply that $P \vee_m Q$ always takes the higher of the two values belonging to $P$ and $Q$ (i.e. that which is indicated by a smaller subscript). In all this Post proceeds abstractly without suggesting that there are more than two truth-values conceivable for propositions, but he then goes on to show that the system which he has constructed can be interpreted within ordinary logic by the following stipulations: (i) each element (represented by a large letter) is to be taken to be not a proposition but an ordered set of m—1 propositions (represented here by small letters) such that if any one is true all that follow it in the sequence are true; (ii) an element is to have the value $t_r$ if exactly r—1 of its propositions are false; (iii) if the propositions of $P$ are expressed by $p_1, p_2, \ldots, p_{m-1}$ and those of $Q$ by $q_1, q_2, \ldots, q_{m-1}$, the propositions of $P \vee_m Q$

[1] 'A General Theory of Elementary Propositions', *The American Journal of Mathematics*, xliii (1921), pp. 163–85.

are to be expressed by $p_1 \vee q_1, p_2 \vee q_2, \ldots, p_{m-1} \vee q_{m-1}$; (iv) if the propositions of $P$ are expressed by $p_1, p_2, \ldots, p_{m-1}$, the propositions of $\sim_m P$ are to be expressed by $\sim(p_1 \vee p_2 \vee \ldots p_{m-1}), \sim(p_1 \vee p_2 \vee \ldots p_{m-1}) \vee (p_1.p_2 \cdots p_{m-1}), \ldots, \sim(p_1 \vee p_2 \vee \ldots p_{m-1}) \vee (p_{m-2}.p_{m-1})$.

Should Post's m-valued system be called an alternative logic? The answer to this question must depend on the sense we give to the word 'logic'. If we are content to apply the name to any system which has certain formal affinities with Frege's system, then we may say that this is logic. To do so is not patently absurd, since the word 'geometry' has been enlarged in just such a way. But if we allow ourselves this freedom, we should recognize that in our new technical usage a formal system called logic need have no connexion with reasoning. In particular we should not suppose that production of alternative logics in this sense of the word 'logic' does anything to show that Frege's system is inadequate for the purpose for which it was designed, nor yet that it is merely conventional.[1] If, on the other hand, we insist that the name 'logic' is to be reserved for systems which can be interpreted by reference to relations between propositions, we may say again that Post's m-valued system is logical in a large sense, but we must now maintain that it is not properly speaking an *alternative* to Frege's two-valued system, since the interpretation indicated above presupposes Frege's system (or that of *Principia Mathematica*) as an underlying theory. Post himself suggests at the end of his article that the entire argument might be translated into the language of some many-valued system, and that if this were done the many-valued system would then seem fundamental while the common two-valued system took on the appearance of an artefact. But he has not explained how his argument could be translated into the language of a many-valued system, and it seems difficult, if not impossible to attach any meaning to the suggestion.

About the same time J. Łukasiewicz conceived the idea of using a three-valued system of logic to solve Aristotle's problem of future contingents.[2] He explains his approach as follows:

'I can assume without contradiction that my presence in Warsaw at a certain moment of time next year, e.g. at noon on 21st December, is not settled at the present moment either positively or negatively. It is therefore *possible but not necessary* that I shall be present in Warsaw at the stated time. On this presupposition the statement "I shall be

[1] In their book of 1952 called *Many-valued Logics* J. B. Rosser and A. R. Turquette abstain from any attempt to interpret the formalisms which they consider.
[2] 'O logice trójwartościowej', *Ruch Filozoficzny*, v. (1920), pp. 169–71.

present in Warsaw at noon on 21st December next year" is neither true nor false at the present moment. For if it were true at the present moment my future presence in Warsaw would have to be necessary, which contradicts the presupposition, and if it were false at the present moment, my future presence in Warsaw would have to be impossible, which again contradicts the presupposition. The statement under consideration is therefore at the present neither true nor false and must have a third value different from 0, or the false, and from 1, or the true. We can indicate this by "$\frac{1}{2}$": it is "the possible" which goes as a third value with "the false" and "the true". This is the train of thought which gave rise to the three-valued system of propositional logic.'[1]

If there are to be three truth-values, the truth functions must be redefined, or rather their definitions must be extended in such a way as to provide for cases in which one or more arguments take the value $\frac{1}{2}$. In this context we shall introduce the sign $[P]$ as an abbreviation for the 'the truth-value of $P$', and for ease of comparison we shall use the Peano-Russell notation rather than that of Łukasiewicz himself. The definitions which he adopts for the Philonian conditional and for negation are given in the

| ⊃ | 1 | $\frac{1}{2}$ | 0 | ∼ |
|---|---|---|---|---|
| 1 | 1 | $\frac{1}{2}$ | 0 | 0 |
| $\frac{1}{2}$ | 1 | 1 | $\frac{1}{2}$ | $\frac{1}{2}$ |
| 0 | 1 | 1 | 1 | 1 |

accompanying matrix. The column at the extreme right indicates that for $[P] = 0$ and $[P] = 1$ there is no change in $[\sim P]$, and that for $[P] = \frac{1}{2}$ we have $[\sim P] = \frac{1}{2}$. Similarly in the definition of $P \supset Q$ the old cases are treated as usual and the new cases are settled on the principle that if the value of the antecedent is less than or equal to the value of the consequent the value of the conditional should be 1 but otherwise $\frac{1}{2}$.

It is important to realize that in this three-valued system the truth-functional signs cannot preserve exactly the same relations as they have in the two-valued system, and that formulae which are tautological in the two-valued system may cease to be so when considered as formulae in the three-valued system. Thus Łukasiewicz introduces disjunction by the definition

$$[P \vee Q] = [(P \supset Q) \supset Q].$$

This equivalence looks unfamiliar, but it is chosen to ensure that a disjunction in the three-valued system shall have the same value as its disjuncts if these have similar values but otherwise the higher of the two. Applying the definition to $P \vee \sim P$, we get 1 as the value of the whole only when one of the disjuncts has

---

[1] 'Philosophische Bemerkungen zu mehrwertigen Systemen des Aussagenkalküls', *Comptes rendus des séances de la Societé des sciences et des lettres de Varsovie*, Classe III, xxiii (1930), pp. 51–77.

that value, but otherwise $\frac{1}{2}$, which is presumably what Łukasiewicz wants. Unfortunately, however, the consequences of his definition of $P.Q$ are not so happy. For here he uses the De Morgan rule

$$[P.Q] = [\sim(\sim P \vee \sim Q)],$$

intending, no doubt, to make sure that a conjunction shall have the same value as its conjuncts if these have similar values, but otherwise the lower of the two; and the result is that for $P. \sim P$ we get the value 0 only when $P$ has one of the two extreme values, but otherwise $\frac{1}{2}$, which seems very strange.

Apart from the ordinary truth-functional signs Łukasiewicz introduces a new functional sign which is supposed to have the sense of 'possibly'. According to his usual practice he takes a capital letter for this purpose, namely the M of *möglich*. For convenience we shall use the diamond-shaped sign of Lewis, but we must add a caution that Łukasiewicz's notion of possibility is very different from that of Lewis.

The definition which Łukasiewicz adopted for his possibility sign (on the suggestion of his pupil A. Tarski) is given by the equivalence $[\diamondsuit P] = [\sim P \supset P]$. This is very surprising at first sight, because $\sim P \supset P$ is the antecedent of the *consequentia mirabilis* by which we can prove the truth of $P$ in the two-valued system of logic; but the paradox disappears when we remember that the definition belongs to a three-valued system. If a proposition can be derived from its own negation, then at least it cannot be false, whatever the number of the truth-values we recognize. In the two-valued system this property is enough to ensure truth, but in the three-valued system it guarantees only possibility. In other words Tarski's definition is thought suitable because the function which he equates with possibility takes the value 0 when the argument has that value but otherwise takes the value 1: what he has defined is possibility in that sense in which it may be said to exclude falsity.

Having succeeded so far in his endeavours, Łukasiewicz went on to generalize the notion of a many-valued system by laying down definitions for negation and the Philonian conditional which can be applied whatever the number of values, provided they are represented in the interval from 0 to 1. These definitions are as follows:

$$[\sim P] = 1-[P]$$
$$[P \supset Q] = 1 \text{ for } [P] \leqslant [Q]$$
$$[P \supset Q] = 1-[P]+[Q] \text{ for } [P] > [Q].$$

If we select as permissible values only the limits of the interval from 0 to 1, these definitions yield the ordinary two-valued system. If we add as a permissible value $\frac{1}{2}$, we get the three-valued system which has just been considered. According to Łukasiewicz it is possible also to construct a system of four or five or any desired number of truth-values; but when once we allow distinctions of degree within the possible and so go beyond the three-valued system, it seems most natural to allow for infinitely many degrees, as in the calculus of probability, and this consideration leads to the propositional calculus with infinitely many values, which he himself prefers. Perhaps he has in mind the idea that it may be used in presentation of the theory of probability. But it has not in fact been developed in this way, and it seems doubtful whether it could, since there seems to be no good interpretation for the possibility sign in this system. When it is applied here, Tarski's definition yields the curious result

$$[\Diamond P] = \text{I for } [P] \geqslant \tfrac{1}{2}$$
$$[\Diamond P] = 2[P] \text{ for } [P] < \tfrac{1}{2}.$$

The relations of the various systems to each other are as follows. The three-valued system is a proper part of the two-valued system in the sense that all its theorems are also theorems of the latter, and the infinitely-many-valued system is a proper part of the three-valued system in the same sense, though few of the theorems of *Principia Mathematica* which survive in the three-valued system are lost in the transition to the infinitely-many-valued system. The most important theorems of the two-valued system which are not valid in many-valued systems are those which have to do with apagogic argument (*reductio ad absurdum*) of the kind that seems to have given rise to trouble in the theory of sets, e.g.

$$(\sim p \supset p) \supset p,$$
$$(p \supset \sim p) \supset \sim p,$$
$$(p \supset q . \sim q) \supset \sim p.$$

Łukasiewicz has worked out his three-valued system in a fairly coherent fashion and supplied an interpretation which makes it look like logic according to the stricter requirement for the use of that word; but his system is not related to two-valued logic in the way he suggests. Throughout his discussions he has in mind that usage of the word 'possible' in which a man who is questioned about the future may say that it is possible there will be a naval battle on the next day. In a later essay, where he presents a different system of modal logic, he admits that other conceptions of possibility have been entertained, but continues to

argue from the assumption that $\Diamond P$ and $\sim P$ are incompatible.[1]
Now it would, of course, be dishonest for a man to say 'It is
possible that there has been a naval battle today' when he knew
for a fact that there had been no naval battle, because in this
context 'it is possible . . . ' means, as Frege said, that the speaker
knows nothing to the contrary. But this usage does not imply
that there is a third truth-value between truth and falsity. Nor
does it seem likely that anyone would want to interpret it in that
way unless he were worried by Aristotle's problem about future
contingents. We have already argued that the problem arises
from the confused notion that truth is a property which belongs
to a statement at a time, and it will be sufficient to add here
that Łukasiewicz's three values do not appear to be truth-values,
nor yet pure modal values, but rather certainty-values.

We have already noticed that with the principle of excluded
middle he has abandoned also the principle of non-contradiction.
This makes the system unacceptable as a whole. If, however, the
defect could be overcome by some adjustment that would satisfy
Łukasiewicz and those who are worried by the problem of future
contingents, the resulting system would, it seems, also admit
interpretation according to the table

$[P] = 1$   . . .   *It is certain that P.*
$[P] = \frac{1}{2}$   . . .   *It is not certain that P and not certain that* $\sim P$
$[P] = 0$   . . .   *It is certain that* $\sim P$.

But so far from requiring us to abandon our ordinary two-valued
logic, this interpretation presupposes the ordinary distinction of
truth and falsity and the ordinary use of the word 'not'. Applying
the device of the square of opposition, we can exhibit the relations
of the various expressions as follows:

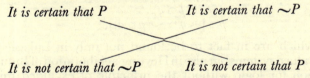

That is to say, the two claims to certainty are contraries, each of
which entails as its subaltern the contradictory of the other. On
the other hand, the two denials of certainty are sub-contraries,
which may both be true (according to the principles of ordinary
two-valued logic) but cannot both be false. These relations are
similar to those holding between the four modal expressions

[1] 'A System of Modal Logic', *The Journal of Computing Systems,* i (1953), pp.
111–49. Cf. also his book *Aristotle's Syllogistic,* 2nd edition, § 49.

'necessary', 'impossible', 'possible', and 'non-necessary'; and this is not surprising, since 'certain' may be taken as an abbreviation for 'necessary in relation to what we know'. But what is logical here is the general notion of necessity (or the notion of possibility, which may be taken instead as fundamental in the analysis), not the notion of knowledge, and although the pure modal functions cannot be defined by truth-tables, like the functions of two-valued primary logic, they do not require a theory which is alternative to that of two-valued primary logic.

In a later chapter we shall have occasion to consider an alternative to classical logic which has been suggested by L. E. J. Brouwer and A. Heyting for the purpose of eliminating paradoxes from the philosophy of mathematics. The peculiarity of this system is that it does not contain the principle of excluded middle either as an axiom or as a theorem. At least, that is what its authors say; but we shall see reason to believe that what they call the principle of excluded middle is not the law which commonly goes by that name.

If, starting with Frege's system of primary logic, we ask ourselves what must be retained in any abstract calculus which is to be called logic purely on account of its partial similarity in formal structure to Frege's system we can give no precise answer, because there is nothing but feeling to regulate such an extension of usage. But we may perhaps say that it is reasonable to expect the rules of substitution and detachment and formulae corresponding to some of the principal theses of Frege's system. If we assume that the new system is to have both Frege's constants, we may say, for example, that it should contain the four formulae

$$p \supset \sim\sim p$$
$$q \supset (p \supset q)$$
$$\sim p \supset (p \supset q)$$
$$p \supset [\sim q \supset \sim (p \supset q)],$$

all of which are in fact to be found not only in Łukasiewicz's many-valued systems but also in Heyting's elaboration of Brouwer's suggestion for logic without the principle of excluded middle. But A. Tarski[1] has shown that for any system which satisfies these conditions and is free from self-contradiction there can be only one consistent and complete enlargement, namely the ordinary two-valued system of logic. And he has also proved similar theorems with regard to alternative calculi which differ from

Frege's system either in employing only the sign of material implication or in containing signs of conjunction and disjunction together with signs of material implication and negation. It appears therefore that even from the purely formal point of view the ordinary two-valued system has a unique status among deductive systems which can plausibly be called logic, since it contains all the others as fragments of itself. In short, they are not alternatives to classical logic in the sense in which Lobachevski's geometry is alternative to Euclid's.

In the last section we tried to show that classical logic could be exhibited as the general theory of a relation between sets of propositions which has entailment as a special case. If our account is acceptable (and it seems to accord with the traditional conception of logic as the science of the principles of reasoning valid for all subject matters), anyone who advocates an alternative to classical logic must be understood to object in some way to the classical notion of entailment. For it now appears that we cannot tinker with the details of logic in any such ways as Łukasiewicz and Brouwer have suggested while still retaining the notion of entailment used in classical logic. But how can we abandon that notion and still reason? By what arguments could it be proved that our general conception of proof needs to be changed? No doubt it may be shown by reasoning that some particular argument on which we have relied is fallacious, but not that our whole conception of reasoning requires revision. And yet, if our analysis is correct, this is the task which the would-be reformer of logic sets himself.

# X

# THE PHILOSOPHY OF LOGIC
## AFTER FREGE

### 1. *Expression, Designation, and Truth*

FEW logicians wish to retain all Frege's philosophy of logic,[1] but his terminology of functions and truth-values has persisted and sometimes it seems to commit its users to Frege's doctrines even when they profess to have freed themselves from his theory. We must therefore begin this chapter with a discussion of his views on meaning and truth.

The peculiarity of Frege's theory of meaning is that he tries to explain the use of all words and other signs by consideration of what is involved in naming. He admits, of course, that verbs, common nouns, adjectives, prepositions, and symbols of various other sorts are not proper names or quasi-names, but he thinks that they are all merely devices for the construction of complex names such as 'the capital of Prussia' and 'the man who discovered the elliptical orbits of the planets'. In working out this line of thought he shows remarkable subtlety, and what he says about sense and reference seems very well adapted to the solution of his puzzle about statements such as 'The morning star is identical with the evening star'. It must be admitted, nevertheless, that there is something very strange in his doctrine that indicative sentences are names or designations for truth-values, and the fact that he comes to this conclusion should make us critical of his initial assumptions.

Frege's doctrine of truth-values is strange and unacceptable because he never succeeds in explaining clearly what these objects are. In one place he says that the truth-value of a sentence (*Satz*) is the circumstance that it is true or false as the case may be. This seems intelligible, but it is quite inconsistent with the suggestion that all true sentences designate one truth-value and all false sentences another. For the circumstance that '5 is a prime number' is true (if we may allow ourselves to speak in this way)

---

[1] The most faithful follower is A. Church, who has defended Frege's views in various places, e.g. in 'The Need for Abstract Entities in Semantic Analysis', *Proceedings of the American Academy of Arts and Sciences*, lxxx (1951), pp. 100–12, and in the introduction to the first volume of his *Introduction to Mathematical Logic*.

is not the same as the circumstance that '$2+2 = 4$' is true. In other places he talks simply of the True and the False. This phraseology is intended, no doubt, to suggest that he is dealing with two and only two objects; but what are they? In ordinary usage 'the true' would be taken to mean the same as 'that which is true', but the things that can be true in a primary sense are propositions, or, as Frege would say, thoughts (i.e. what sentences express, as distinct from what they are supposed to designate), and there may be infinitely many of these expressed by different sentences. Are we then to understand that his two truth-values are just the attributes truth and falsity? These are indeed a pair of objects in a large sense of the word 'object', and they can reasonably be called values in a sense which has nothing to do with mathematical talk about substitution for a variable. But it seems absurd to say that every true indicative sentence designates or stands for truth, since sentences are signs of a quite different kind from those which may properly be said to designate truth (e.g. the word 'truth' itself or the phrase 'what Pontius Pilate wished to have defined'). We might perhaps for certain purposes admit the convention of writing:

$$5 \text{ is a prime number} = \text{truth}$$

as a substitute for 'It is true that 5 is a prime number', but the possibility of re-making our language in this way can provide no justification for what Frege says. If we took to writing ' $=$ truth' after certain indicative sentences and ' $=$ falsity' after others, the two expressions would not retain their present meanings but come to be regarded in some other way, e.g. as like the tick and the cross which a schoolmaster uses in marking his pupils' answers to questions.

In his paper *Über Sinn und Bedeutung* Frege tries to make his theory plausible by arguing that it is involved in the distinction which we make between fiction and history. The sentences in an epic poem or a novel have sense, he tells us, but they are not ordinarily classified as true or false, because they are not thought to have reference. The sentences of an historian, on the other hand, are thought to have reference as well as sense. For if we seriously maintain that Odysseus was set ashore at Ithaca while sound asleep, we are prepared to insist that the word 'Odysseus' stands for an object, and this interest of ours in the reference of part of the sentence is intelligible only if we suppose that the sentence as a whole designates something. As in the understanding of any sentence, whether of fiction or of history, the sense of a part is relevant because it helps to determine the sense of the whole, so, it seems, in an inquiry about the truth of an historical statement the reference of a part is relevant because it helps to determine the reference of the whole, namely, its truth-value.

This argument is Frege's best defence, but it does not justify his attempt to distinguish between the sense and the reference of a statement. For if we suppose that an indicative sentence of fiction has precisely the same sense as it would possess in an historical narrative, we must suppose also that it is used to make a true or false statement. Nothing more is required according to Frege's own explanations, since a proposition, or complete thought expressed by an indicative sentence, is always something which must be true or false. There is, of course, an important distinction to be drawn between sentences in fiction and sentences in history, but it is not the case, as Frege assumes, that the former have sense without reference whereas the latter have both sense and reference. The fundamental difference is rather that historians make communications whereas story-tellers only pretend to make communications; and from this it follows that many sentences of fiction are meaningful only in the rather peculiar way in which 'John has the pen of the gardener's wife' is said to be meaningful when it occurs as an example in a grammar book. They are complex signs such as *might* be used for the making of communications in certain circumstances, and that is precisely why they *are* used by the story-teller when he pretends for our amusement to be in such circumstances. If anyone misunderstands the situation and thinks that the story-teller is making a genuine communication, he supplies in thought a complete sense for each sentence, and as Frege says, this commonly involves taking certain phrases to be genuine designations; but there is no good reason for saying that it involves treating the sentences of the story-teller as designations of truth-values.

The source of Frege's theory is his assumption that every complete sign must possess both sense and reference, and he was led to this by his preoccupation with names and quasi-names. When for one reason or another we become interested in the study of language and begin to ask questions about meaning, it is perhaps natural that we should look for clues in those situations in which we have enriched language by our own acts, and the most obvious of these is the giving of proper names. Certainly many philosophers before Frege have tried to explain the meaningfulness of words by saying that they stand for things in the way in which the name 'Socrates' stands for Socrates. But the suggestion is unfortunate, because proper names are by no means essential for communication.

Instead of 'Socrates died from drinking hemlock' we might say 'The snub-nosed philosopher who first asked for definitions of the virtues died from drinking hemlock'. Admittedly the sense of the second remark is not exactly the same as that of the first, since understanding of the second requires knowledge which is not required for understanding of the first; but in many contexts the second could do duty for the first, and there seems to be no imaginable context (other than that of compiling a dictionary of names) in which the purposes served by utterance of the first could not be served equally well by utterance of some paraphrase without a proper name. Nor is this all. In familiar contexts we could eliminate even definite descriptions and words such as 'I', 'you', 'this', 'that', 'here', and 'now', which are all treated by Frege as quasi-names. To do so we should need only a code like that which the post office uses in transmitting greetings telegrams. Corresponding to each frequently repeated sentence of English there would be a single expression without significant parts, and from constant use the latter would acquire the force which now belongs to the former. There are, indeed, examples of this in ordinary communication. When a golfer shouts 'Fore!', those in front take the cry for a warning that he is about to play his ball in their direction. And when a ship's wireless operator sends out the international distress signal, those who pick it up understand without translation that help is required urgently in the place from which the signal comes. No doubt it is impossible that we should conduct all our communication like this, but it is important to realize that the impossibility of the suggestion is connected with the way in which we learn languages, rather than with the way in which we use them when we have learnt them.

In the course of a day each of us has occasion to utter many sentences never heard before in the history of mankind. Thus even a child of ten might say 'I saw a walking doll and an electric lawn-mower in the shop next to the church where Grandfather dropped the collection plate after the sermon by the archbishop'; and if he did, we should not think that he had performed a great feat. But it is at least very unlikely that the English words of our example were ever put together in just that order until we constructed the example. Now clearly a language which allowed only unitary expressions would be inadequate to our needs, because it would provide no way of dealing with rare situations. Each expression we learnt would be appropriate only to situations of a certain kind, and while we might successfully extend the uses of some of them by analogy and metaphor, we should never be able to acquire a stock large enough for all the purposes now served by common speech. In a highly developed language, therefore, we must have syntax as well as vocabulary, though there is reason to believe that at the very beginning men may have had vocabulary alone. But whether we speak in simple standard phrases or in complex sentences, what we say is always something that could in principle be used on other occasions of the same kind, if there were any such. For though it is improbable, it is certainly not impossible that at various times and places dozens of children should utter the elaborate sentence we have constructed as an example, and each with the same linguistic propriety. Nor is the situation very different if we suppose that the language with which we are dealing contains proper names. It may be that in future no one except an actor or a grammarian will ever say 'Socrates is now drinking hemlock', but it is conceivable nevertheless that this sentence should be used to make a sincere and even a true statement. For at some time another Socrates (which means in this context another man called Socrates) may drink hemlock.

A unitary expression is something like a pattern of gesture or a variety of grimace. For saying 'Yes' and nodding the head are just two ways of signifying agreement; and saying 'Well!' with a falling intonation is an emphatic way of expressing what we sometimes express by raising our eyebrows. But a complex sentence with distinguishable subject and predicate may be regarded in the same way. For saying 'I am tired' is a piece of behaviour which we may use for our purposes in the same way as we sometimes use the dumb-show of closing the eyes and dropping the head. Can we then maintain that in all these cases our signs have both sense and reference? We must certainly distinguish between the general sense of a sign considered as a pattern of behaviour (i.e. what we learn when we learn how the sign is to be used) and the various communications which we may make by means of it on different occasions; and we may say correctly that the communications differ because they refer to different circumstances according to the occasion of utterance. But this is not the same as Frege's distinction. For the general sense of which we talk here is not, like his *Sinn*, a determinate proposition, and the reference of which we speak is not naming or designation. Use of words or phrases with a designating function may be involved, as when we say 'Socrates died from drinking hemlock' or 'The milkman called this morning'; but it is not essential, since reference of the kind we are now considering may be made by the use of signs which have no meaningful parts and it is at least conceivable that all signs should be of that sort. If we wish to use

Frege's terminology, we can say only that a particular utterance of a sentence expresses a sense; but for a proper understanding of this we must continue our analysis further.

Economy is the merit which has favoured the survival and development of syntax. Now the first and most obvious measure of economy that we can adopt in the construction of sentences is to use the same vocabulary for expressing statements, questions, commands, and the rest. In a language where no expression had any part or aspect that was separately meaningful, there could be no relevant similarity between a question and a statement that answered it, or between a request and a promise to fulfil it. But so far as we know, all human languages of which there is any record contain devices by which sentences containing the same words or word roots may nevertheless be distinguished as indicative, interrogative, imperative, or optative. In European languages the differences are very often shown by modifications of the special kind of word we call a verb, but even within this linguistic group there are other possibilities. Thus questions are commonly expressed by some adaptation of the indicative form, but this adaptation may be the addition of a particle (*Num venit?*), an inversion of word order ('Is he coming?'), or simply a special intonation ('He is coming?').

Sometimes for stylistic or rhetorical reasons the pattern normally appropriated to one kind of communication is used for a communication of a different kind, as when a military order is given by an indicative sentence in the future tense or an emphatic statement is made by means of an interrogative construction. But in every case there is some convention or implicit rule which makes a pattern suitable in its context for the speaker's purpose. And whatever the device of expression may be, it is safe to say that in a complex sentence there is always some feature which has the special function of manifesting the speaker's attitude or interest in speaking. For communication is essentially the deliberate manifestation of an attitude towards a proposition or thinkable state of affairs. The making of a statement is a manifestation of the speaker's belief, the putting of a question a manifestation of the speaker's curiosity or of his wish that the hearer should supply certain information, and so on. Only the commonest kinds of communications have received special names, but among those which are lumped together as exclamations we might, if we chose, distinguish many more varieties. Consider, for example, the differences between 'Thank God, that's over!', 'To hell with the Pope!', and 'Smith a bishop! Good heavens!' If we took account of uses of language for purposes other than communication (e.g.

for ritual), we should have other distinctions to draw, but we may safely ignore such complications here.

For the logician the chief interest of all this is that it involves a distinction between the manifesting of an attitude and the propounding of a proposition towards which that attitude is manifested. In some of our unitary expressions such as 'Yes', 'Well !', and 'Damn !', there is nothing to indicate the proposition towards which the speaker manifests an attitude, because the utterance of such an expression on a particular occasion is usually enough in itself to show the direction of the speaker's interest. Obviously the opposite case of a unitary expression which does not manifest an attitude cannot occur, since without manifestation of an attitude there would be no communication. But it is conceivable that the development of syntax should have produced purely propositional signs which in association with signs of attitude like Frege's judgement stroke would constitute complete sentences. We might, for example, have expressed statements in the form 'P yes' and questions in the form 'P query' where 'P' itself was neither declarative nor interrogative but simply a sign for propounding a proposition. In fact this has not occurred in any natural language of which we have heard; and so anyone who wishes to discuss a propositional sign in such a language must cite an expression which is also a complete sentence because it includes provision for the manifestation of an attitude. Usually logicians have taken indicative sentences as their examples without thinking of any alternatives. Perhaps they have done so because of some confusion in their minds between logic and epistemology, but there are nevertheless good reasons for the choice.

In the first place, indicative sentences tend to be simpler in construction than any others except imperatives. Secondly, the propositions propounded by statements may be of all sorts, whereas orders or requests always have to do with some possible future action of the hearer. Thirdly, in ordinary speech statements, unlike other communications, except perhaps questions, are often considered without regard to the attitude of any particular speaker. Presumably the reason is that belief enters into all sorts of complex situations, and many similar statements might conceivably be made by many people in various contexts. The usage is especially common in scientific discussions. But whatever the explanation may be, if anyone asks for the meaning of a statement which is considered in this way, we are content to reply with a phrase of the form 'that so-and-so', although we should consider it necessary to mention the attitude of the speaker if we were trying to give the meaning of an utterance of any other kind. It would perhaps be a little odd to say of any statement that it meant a proposition, but we can certainly say with Frege that statements are often conceived as expressions of thoughts in that sense in which thoughts can be entertained by many people with or without belief. Fourthly, and this is most important, indicative sentences, or rather the forms of words which in certain contexts would be called indicative sentences, may on some occasions be used without assertive force. When we say 'There will be a poor harvest if this weather continues' we do not commit ourselves to the belief that there will be a poor harvest, and so the opening phrase works in this context as a purely propositional sign. Admittedly it is only part of the sign for the proposition which is asserted, but the whole sentence could not do the work of propounding that proposition if this part were not recognizable as a propositional sign in its own right. All this is implicit in the Stoic formulation of inference patterns such as 'If the first then the second; but the first; therefore the second'.

Since it is difficult, if not impossible, to discuss these matters without some specialization of terms, let us agree to say that sentences and clauses like those to which we have just drawn attention are propositional expressions and that they express, propound, or signify propositions. But we must add that while some propositional expressions, such as '2+2 = 4' and 'Virtue is its own reward', express the same proposition on each occasion of utterance, most of those used in conversation express different propositions on different occasions according to the circumstances of utterance. Now it is obvious that if all our propositional expressions were unitary signs there would be no designations, but it is interesting to notice that these may be lacking also in propositional expressions which have some kind of internal structure. When a lift attendant shouts 'Going up!' the first word of his utterance conveys the idea of motion by his lift in the near future, and the second word supplements this by indicating a direction, but neither designates anything; and it is irrelevant to say that the remark is short for 'My lift is going up', since the attendant omits the first three words of this sentence precisely because they are unnecessary in the context. Why then were designations ever introduced during the syntactical development of language? It seems that the answer is to be found again in considerations of economy. No doubt there might be some way in which a lift attendant could tell a customer without the use of designations that the next lift going down would be found on the opposite side of the passage; but if all our propositional expressions were like workmen's cries, we should need a very great many of them, and

584 THE PHILOSOPHY OF LOGIC AFTER FREGE

some would be used very rarely indeed. There is an obvious advantage in building up sentences as we do from designations and functional signs, since by use of these elements we can cope with an almost unlimited variety of situations in a relatively easy fashion.

In saying this we do not intend to suggest that the subject-predicate pattern which we find in all highly developed languages is a merely arbitrary device. On the contrary, it seems evident that the usefulness of the device depends on the fact that many, though not all, of the propositions towards which we manifest attitudes are attributive or relational. It is always unsafe to base a metaphysical argument on the pattern of construction used in any particular propositional expression, but if anyone holds seriously that all syntax is a free construction of the human mind, the onus is on him to explain what he means by freedom in this connexion, and in particular to show by examples how the work could have been done in a radically different fashion. The point we wish to make here is quite different, namely that designation should not be taken as a paradigm of all sign-using, since when it occurs it has to be explained as something incidental to the making of communications. To say that 'Socrates' stands for Socrates is only to say that propositional expressions containing the name are appropriate for propounding propositions about Socrates towards which we may wish to manifest various attitudes. That names and quasi-names may be said to possess both sense and reference is a peculiarity of such signs which we must consider in the next section. The basic notion in the theory of meaning is not designation but rather what Frege called expression of a sense.

Once this point has been made clear, it is possible to use some of Frege's results for the formulation of a satisfactory theory of truth. In his account of indirect speech he says that a noun clause such as 'that the planetary orbits are circular' has for its reference the sense of the corresponding sentence 'The planetary orbits are circular'. In other words, by a suitable development of language propositions may be not only expressed but also designated. Naturally the designation of a proposition cannot be a propositional expression according to our technical usage; but it is not even necessary that it should be made from a propositional expression by the prefixing of 'that' or by the introduction of the accusative and infinitive construction as in Latin. For although designations made in this way by adaptation of propositional expressions have a certain priority, phrases like 'Pythagoras' theorem', 'the doctrine of original sin', and 'what Gladstone said in 1883', or even single words like 'materialism' may serve the same purpose. Indeed the variety of signs that may be used for this purpose is limitless, and in order to convince ourselves of the importance of being able to designate propositions we need only reflect how seriously our language would be impoverished if all such signs were lacking. Logic in particular could scarcely be studied without them, since the characteristic words of the logician, such as 'entails', 'inconsistent', 'necessary', and 'possible', are used primarily for making sentences in which the subject terms are designations of propositions. And for the same reason the word 'true' would cease to have that usage which interests philosophers.

In a passage which we quoted earlier Frege says that 'The thought that 5 is a prime number is true' is equivalent to '5 is a prime number', but he fails to see that the principle of this equivalence is a sufficient answer to the philosophical problem about truth. We need the adjective 'true' because we have designations of propositions and require also some way of saying by use of them what could only be said otherwise by means of expressions for the same propositions. If we think of the English word 'that' as a prefix which converts an expression of a proposition into a designation, we may perhaps say that addition of the phrase 'is true' reverses the operation. For when the two occur together they add nothing to what Frege would call the content of the utterance in which they appear, and we are inclined to say that the complex sign 'it is true that' serves only the same rhetorical purpose as the particle 'indeed', i.e. that of indicating a concession or marking the end of a dispute. We must not forget, however, that the word 'true' is often applied to propositions which have not been designated by clauses beginning with 'that' and sometimes even to propositions that could not be so designated by us now. Thus it has been said: 'Whatever a Pope may at any time declare *ex cathedra* concerning faith or morals is true.' Obviously the word 'true' cannot be eliminated from this context by the simple device of formulating expressions for all the papal pronouncements that may ever be made. But it can be eliminated nevertheless by a suitable use of propositional variables, as for example in the paraphrase, 'If a Pope speaking of faith or morals *ex cathedra* declares that p, then p'. And when this is done, it becomes clear that here too the role of the word 'true' is to provide a connexion between propositional designations and propositional expressions. For just as the letter 'p' in the apodosis of our new sentence marks a gap which may be filled by a propositional expression, so the phrase 'that p' in the protasis is a sign which would be converted into a propositional designation by substitution of a propositional expression for the letter 'p'. In formulating the paraphrase we have deliberately used a free, rather than a bound, variable to signify universality, because if we had begun our paraphrase with the quantifier 'for any p' the grammar of the English word 'any' would have suggested that the gaps marked by the letter 'p' were suitable only for designations, and that, of course, is not what we want here.

According to Frege each complete sign expresses a sense and designates something we have called its reference. But we have seen reason to believe that expression and designation are tasks performed by signs of different kinds, and this distinction seems to be important not only for the theory of truth but also for the solution of the difficulties which Frege finds in talking about functions. Just as the sentence 'The Pope is a man' may be said to express a proposition, so the contributory sign ' . . . is a man' may be said to express a propositional function. And though neither of these may properly be said to designate anything, we may, if it suits our convenience, construct signs to designate what they express. Thus 'humanity' and 'being a man' are common English designations for the attribute, or in Frege's terminology, the concept, which we assert of the Pope when we say that he is a man. Frege's troubles are due to the fact that he ignores the need for new signs and tries to use expressions like '$\xi$ is a man' for the purpose of designation in spite of their unsuitability for the role. Admittedly he does not often write anything so obviously unsatisfactory as 'the concept, $\xi$ is a man'; but in explanations of his script he often writes 'the concept $\Phi(\xi)$', and in general discussions he uses such awkward phrases as 'the concept *man*' or 'the concept "man"'. It is therefore not surprising that he sometimes feels uncomfortable and inclined to complain of the essential inadequacy of language. He assumes wrongly that the designation of a function should be incomplete or unsaturated like its expression, and yet he sees clearly that a sign which is appropriate for use as a predicate cannot also serve properly as a grammatical subject when we wish to talk about the function which it expresses.

In ordinary speech words such as 'humanity' work quite satisfactorily as designations of propositional functions, or attributes, because we are familiar with them and know well how to avoid all danger of confusing them with the corresponding expressions. When logicians suggest, as they sometimes do, that we ought to consider 'humanity' as an abbreviation for '$\xi$'s humanity', they make a mistake. Whereas it is permissible, though undesirable on stylistic grounds, to say 'Humanity is exemplified in the Pope', it is just nonsense to say '$\xi$'s humanity is exemplified in the Pope'. In a script such as Frege's, however, it is reasonable to expect rules more explicit than those of ordinary language, and if we wish to include designations of propositional functions we should try to show clearly how they are related to expressions. We can do this by adaptation of a device Frege uses in talking of ranges. Just as he writes $\grave{a}(a\ is\ a\ man)$ for 'the class of men', so we may write $\acute{a}(a\ is\ a\ man)$ for 'humanity' or 'the character of being a man'. Here it is obvious that the new sign is derived from a functional expression with one gap, but there is no danger of confusion, because the letter inside the bracket is tied to the letter outside and the whole complex sign is obviously a designation. Inverting Frege's membership sign in order to get an expression for having or exemplifying (i.e. what Frege calls falling under a concept), we may then write $\Delta \cup \acute{a} \Phi(a)$ as an equivalent in our new notation for $\Phi(\Delta)$. We do not suggest these innovations as the best possible symbolism for dealing with the problem, but simply in order to show that Frege's difficulties can be overcome quite easily with means like those he had at his disposal, provided always we recognize a clear distinction between expression and designation. Since $\Delta \cup \acute{a} \Phi(a)$ is a propositional expression of fairly complex construction, it naturally includes a functional expression, namely, . . . $\cup$ - - - , but this should not worry us. For it is no part of our reform to suggest that propositional expressions can be constructed from designations alone, and so we are untouched by the chief argument with which Frege tries to show the impossibility of talking directly about functions.

There is, however, a quite different consideration which should make us careful about talking of functions in logic. When Frege introduced the word, he thought of a logical function as one whose values were all truth-values. Those considered in primary logic were supposed by him to be from truth-values to truth-values, while those considered in general logic of the first level were supposed to be from objects of any kind to truth-values. In the later literature of logic the former have been called truth-functions and the latter propositional functions by many writers who do not accept Frege's theory of truth-values and perhaps have never examined it seriously. If, however, we come to the conclusion that Frege was wrong in describing an indicative sentence as the name of a truth-value, we deny in effect the analogy which led Frege to adopt his functional terminology. Some successors of Frege have tried to think of a function in logic as one from things in the widest possible sense (i.e. in a wider sense than that of Frege's 'object') to propositions, and others use the phrase 'propositional function' as though it were merely a convenient way of referring to a sentence fragment such as ' . . . is wise' or '...loves---'. Neither of these explanations would have seemed satisfactory to Frege, and neither is sufficient to justify retention of his terminology. For a function in the proper mathematical sense is a pattern of correlation, not an expression, as the second explanation suggests; and the application of the sign of such a function (e.g. '√') to a designation (e.g. '2') is supposed to produce another designation (e.g. '√2'), not an expression, as the first explanation suggests.

It might therefore be better to abandon Frege's terminology altogether and adopt in its place some way of speaking which does not suggest inappropriate analogies. We might, for example, talk of truth-dependencies instead of truth-functions and of attributes and relations instead of propositional functions of other kinds. If we were engaged in the presentation of logic without regard to its history, this is the course we should follow. But in the rest of this work we shall have occasion to notice the writings of many logicians who have used the word 'function' without accepting Frege's theory of truth-values, and for convenience of exposition we shall follow their practice, contenting ourselves with the caution that where the word occurs in our own text it is to be understood as equivalent to one or other of the substitutes proposed above.

In some respects the positive account of truth sketched above is like that of A. Tarski in his paper called 'The Concept of Truth in Formalized Languages'.[1] And we certainly wish to claim for our account, as he does for his, the authority of Aristotle's famous definition of telling the truth as saying of that which is that it is or of that which is not that it is not.[2] But there is a very important difference between our view and that of Tarski. We hold that the adjective 'true' is applicable primarily to propositions, whereas he assumes that it is applicable primarily to sentences. The sentence 'Snow is white' is true, he tells us, if and only if snow is white. Here the sign beginning and ending with quotation marks is to be understood as a name or designation, and the purpose of the whole remark is to show how the necessary and sufficient condition for the truth of the sentence thus *mentioned* can be given by a *use* of that same sentence (or rather of that form of words). In short the main difference between this theory

[1] First published in Polish in *Travaux de la Société des sciences et des lettres de Varsovie*, Class III, Math.-Phys., xxxiv (1933); German translation in *Studia Philosophica*, i (1936), pp. 261–405; English translation in *Logic, Semantics, Metamathematics*, pp. 152–278.    [2] *Metaphysica*, Γ, 7 (1011ᵇ25).

of truth and ours is that Tarski talks about sentences where we wish to talk about propositions. But, as Tarski himself points out, difficulties arise when an attempt is made to turn his paradigm of explanation into a general definition by use of a variable, i.e. by writing:

*For any p, 'p' is a true sentence if and only if p.*

For unless some special convention is made to the contrary effect (and it is very difficult, if not impossible, he says, to do this in a satisfactory manner), the sign which then begins and ends with quotation marks is not, as intended, a sort of functional sign which can be made into a name of a sentence by a suitable substitution for the letter within the quotation marks, but simply a designation of that letter. And he even goes on to argue that the possibility of constructing the paradox of the Liar within ordinary language shows that for this, as distinct from a formalized language of science, there can be no satisfactory definition of truth. This conclusion is so queer that it should make us suspicious of the assumptions from which it is derived; and the source of the trouble seems to be Tarski's unquestioned belief that truth is primarily a property of sentences.

When we are concerned with mathematical formulae (which especially interest Tarski) or with other phrases that resemble his example in not containing token-reflexive words (i.e. words which locate things or events by relation to the circumstances of their own utterance), Tarski's assumption leads to no serious difficulties. For we can certainly talk of the truth of mathematical formula, and it does not seem absurd to speak of the truth of the general sentence 'Snow is white'. In either case we have to do with a complex sign-type which propounds the same proposition on each occasion of its use, and that is why we can discuss the truth of the sign much as we discuss the truth of the proposition it expresses. But these are special cases. A sentence of the commonest kind may be uttered at different times and in different circumstances to express different propositions, some true and some false. What Jones asserts by saying 'I am hungry' is not the same proposition as that Smith asserts by uttering the words at the same time, nor yet the same as that Jones asserted by uttering the words yesterday. And when we say, as we sometimes do, that a sentence was true at the time of speaking or writing, we obviously mean that it was used then to express a true proposition though it could not be used to that effect now. When he was not immediately interested in putting forward his own theory of truth, Frege was well aware of this feature of language. Writing against psychologism in logic, he says that we may perhaps describe the sentence 'I am hungry' as true for some men and false for others, or true in some circumstances and false in others, but only because it is used to express different propositions on different occasions. 'All determinations of space, time, etc. belong', he says, 'to the proposition (*Gedanke*) whose truth is under consideration: being true is itself spaceless and timeless.'[1]

In order to escape from these difficulties those who are inclined to agree with Tarski may perhaps say that the sentences to which they ascribe truth in the basic or primary sense are token utterances, that is to say passing events of speech. These are certainly not what Tarski himself had in mind when he wrote his paper, since they cannot be designated by designations of the kinds he discusses, namely quotation-mark names and structural-descriptive names built up by use of such devices as spelling. But we do sometimes use the word 'sentence' to refer to a thing of this sort, as when, for example, we say that a speaker paused for breath in the middle of his first sentence; and if we ascribe truth to such a thing, we shall at least have no difficulty about its possibly becoming false later on. It is clear, however, that when a token sentence is supposed capable of truth, the condition for its truth cannot be given by Tarski's device of saying 'if and only if' and then repeating the sentence under consideration. For a token sentence is not a form of words but a passing event and so cannot be *used* in this way any more than it can be *mentioned* in any of the ways in which Tarski mentions the sentences that interest him. Nor do we in fact talk commonly of the truth of token utterances. When they are considered in this connexion, it is usually as expressions for propositions.

It is one of Tarski's main contentions that the paradox of the Liar is due to an inconsistency whereby ordinary language allows for the application of its own words 'true' and 'false' to its own sentences. And he seems to be right in thinking that *semantical* considerations (as he calls arguments of the kind produced in his paper) require a distinction of language levels. For there is obviously a good sense in which the possibility of constructing the sentence ' "Snow is white" is true' presupposes the possibility of constructing the sentence 'Snow is white'; and this reflection may be used to explain why the Liar's curious utterance fails to express any proposition at all. But it is a gratutitous paradox (in another sense of that word) to say that ordinary language is inconsistent because it claims universality or omnicompetence. Ordinary language is not a closed system, but whatever we make

[1] *Gg.*, vol. i, pp. xvi–xvii.

it in our talking; and if semantic considerations show the need for a distinction of language levels, the distinction will be made within ordinary language. For although natural languages such as English and French are in a certain sense alternatives to each other and to technical symbolism, ordinary language as Tarski discusses it is not an alternative to some extraordinary language which has been or may be devised by logicians for all the legitimate purposes now served by ordinary language. Rather, it is the matrix within which all other systems of communication are developed, and so not to be criticized like the unsuccessful production of a professional rival.

The anxiety of many logicians to insist that truth is an affair of sentences rather than of propositions is due to a phobia of abstract entities, and this in turn seems to arise from two sources. The first, which has been noticeable among philosophers ever since Plato aroused opposition by his talk of a supersensible world, is an obsessive desire to be economical in thought. The second, which belongs to more recent history, is a violent reaction against all attempts to talk about the structure of the world. When such a phobia has been diagnosed, the patient should be encouraged, and even urged, to carry out his programme of elimination systematically instead of merely making oracular pronouncements. If he can be induced to persevere for a sufficiently long time, he may in this way be brought to realize that it is impossible for him to say all he wants to say without speaking of qualities, relations, beliefs, hypotheses, conclusions, and the rest. The cure will be complete when he is ready to admit that, although Plato and his followers fell into the absurdity of talking about the supersensible as if it were something that might be observed by a kind of super-sense, this is a very poor reason for holding that all attempts to designate supersensible objects are in some way improper. For if we are to talk at all about our use of language, we must allow ourselves to say that a sentence or a predicate phrase expresses something. And in order to say what it is that such a sign expresses we require not another expression but a designation, since in any true expository statement of the form ' . . . expresses - - - ' the signs which fill the two blanks must both be designations, the first for an expression and the second for what that expression expresses. It is foolish therefore to deny ourselves this facility merely because it has sometimes been abused.

It is unlikely, however, that the programme of confining attention to sentences would ever have been widely adopted by logicians but for the fact that we have words which in some contexts mean the same as 'sentence' and in others the same as proposition'. In our examination of Bolzano's work we saw that the German word *Satz* is sometimes a grammatical term equivalent to 'sentence' or 'clause' but at other times indicates a law, theorem, principle, or proposition, i.e. something which can be expressed variously in different languages and described as true or false. In English the word 'sentence' is more narrowly specialized than *Satz* and not normally regarded as a proper subject for the adjectives 'true' and 'false'. But our word 'statement' is almost as versatile as *Satz* within a somewhat different range. For it can mean either an indicative sentence or what is affirmed by some utterance of an indicative sentence or the act of stating something; and apart from all these usages it can occur in the closely knit phrase 'make a statement', where it is not to be paraphrased separately. Those who find it plausible to ascribe truth to sentences seem to be influenced by the fact that 'indicative sentence' is linked as it is with 'statement' and through 'statement' with 'proposition'.

Sometimes, no doubt, mention of propositions arouses misgivings because writers such as Bolzano have assigned them to a queer limbo between language and reality. But it is a mistake to suppose that use of the word 'proposition' need commit us to any unacceptable novelty. As they are commonly used in modern times, the words 'sentence' and 'proposition' serve for the making of two different classifications among actual and possible events of speech. Each such event is an utterance of a sentence, that is to say the production of an instance of a certain form of words which might in principle have other instances. For it is impossible to speak without speaking in some language, i.e. using repeatable signs. But we have seen that the several utterances of one type sentence may express different propositions according to the circumstances of their occurrence; and it is obvious also that a single proposition may be expressed by utterances of many different type sentences, since there is not just one language in which we must say all that we have to say. When grammarians use the word 'sentence' (as they commonly do) for a form of words, they wish to refer to the common features of utterances that resemble each other almost completely in sound or some other perceptible character but may differ considerably as vehicles of communication. An example is the sentence 'I have the pen of the gardener's wife' which generations of schoolboys have tried to translate into French without bothering to ask themselves 'What pen?' or 'What gardener?' When, on the other hand, logicians use the word 'proposition', they wish to refer to the common feature of utterances that resemble each other completely as vehicles of communication (except in respect of attitude) but may differ completely in sound or other perceptual character. Anyone who is frightened by what Bolzano says may, if he wishes, ascribe truth and falsity to the determinate propositional signs we here call utterances. But if he takes this line, he must, like Leibniz, recognize that truth cannot be an affair solely of actual utterances, since it makes sense to talk of the discovery of previously unformulated truths. And with the concession of truth to possible utterances he allows all that is required in the modern view of propositions. In short, there is no more dangerous abstraction involved in logicians' talk of propositions than in grammarians' talk of sentences, though the latter sometimes seems more readily acceptable because the notion of resemblance in perceptual character is easier to grasp than that of resemblance in function. As we shall see in a later section of this chapter, there are some peculiar problems about the way in which references to propositions may occur in discourse, but for the solution of these it is not necessary to go beyond the account of propositions we have sketched here.

## 2. *The Theory of Descriptions and the Variety of Designations*

Frege introduced his distinction between sense and reference by consideration of the statement 'The morning star is identical with the evening star', and we have seen that it is well adapted to provide a solution for the question that worried him in this context. For while the two phrases 'the morning star' and 'the evening star' are designations of the same object, they obviously have different senses. But how is this admission to be reconciled with our attempt to show that expressions and designations are signs of radically different kinds? The answer is that these designations, like many others, are derivative from expressions and may therefore be said to have sense in a derivative way. When we use the phrase 'the morning star' as a subject in a sentence, we do not thereby express the proposition that there is one and only one star frequently visible in the morning, but our use of the phrase presupposes acceptance of that proposition. In the language of everyday life a sentence containing the phrase 'the morning star' is said to imply that there is one and only one star frequently visible in the morning. This is not a usage of 'implies' much discussed in treatises of logic, but it is interesting and rather complicated. In one way implication of this kind seems to be less than expression. For if a man who has used a phrase implying a certain proposition goes on to formulate that proposition, we think that he has added something. In another way, however, implication of this kind is more than mere expression. For a man may express a proposition without manifesting or purporting to manifest belief in it; but if he uses a phrase which implies that proposition, he is understood to have committed himself, even though the sentence in which the phrase occurs is not indicative. Thus if a man invites a new acquaintance to visit him and says 'Please bring your wife', he does not assert the proposition that the acquaintance is married, but he certainly lets it be understood that he believes that proposition. To designate anything is to mark it down or single it out for attention; and so when a speaker uses a definite description in the singular as though he were trying to designate something, it is natural to assume that he believes in the existence of one and only one thing answering to the description, since otherwise his procedure would be pointless. When a man is unsure of the truth of this existential proposition, he can qualify his remark in an appropriate way. When, for example, he is uncertain whether a new acquaintance is married, he may say 'If you are married, please bring your wife'. In this context the description does not seem to single out for attention a determinate thing which might perhaps have been described in some other way. For the conditional clause has the effect of cancelling the commitment which would otherwise be conveyed by use of the definite description. In view of what many logicians have said it is perhaps worth noticing also that a definite description may occur in the plural, i.e. with an implication of the existence of *more than one* thing answering to it. We say, for example, 'The original apostles were all Jews'.

Frege was well aware that in ordinary language the use of a definite description as subject in a singular statement presupposed acceptance of a proposition not explicitly asserted, and he saw that if the description failed to designate anything the statement as a whole could not be said to be true or false. But he thought it important to insist on the application of the principle of excluded middle to all well-formed formulae of his own script, and he therefore undertook, as we have seen, to provide a reference of some sort for every definite description in his system, while admitting that sometimes the reference would be quite independent of the normal intention of a person using the description. Later logicians have tried to cope with the difficulty in other ways.

Whitehead and Russell proceed in *Principia Mathematica* as though the proposition which is ordinarily said to be implied by the use of a description were stated explicitly in the sentence containing the description. According to their view 'The King of France is bald' is equivalent to $(\exists c)\{(x)[K(x) \equiv x = c]. B(c)\}$, or 'There is a thing, say $c$, such that (i) a thing is King of France if and only if it is identical with $c$, and (ii) $c$ is bald', which certainly expresses a false proposition if either there is no King of France or there are more than one.[1] But in order to maintain their view consistently they find it necessary to distinguish between primary and secondary occurrence of a description. Thus if anyone says 'The King of France is not bald' meaning $(\exists c)\{(x)[K(x) \equiv x = c]. \sim B(c)\}$, the description has primary occurrence, whereas if he uses the same form of words meaning $\sim(\exists c)\{(x)[K(x) \equiv x = c]. B(c)\}$, the description has secondary occurrence. It will be seen that in the first case the speaker is supposed to be committed to the existential implication of his description while in the latter case the whole sentence may express a true proposition even though there is no single King of France. In their own symbolism the distinction is made clear by a device something like the use of a quantifier to show the scope of a generalization. Thus our example of primary occurrence would be rendered by the formula $[(\imath x)K(x)]\{\sim B[(\imath x)K(x)]\}$ and our example of secondary occurrence by the formula $\sim[(\imath x)K(x)]\{B[(\imath x)K(x)]\}$. Here repetition of the description as a prefix to a bracketed expression is taken to indicate that the implication of the description belongs only to the bracketed expression. There is, however, a convention that for simplicity the prefix may be omitted when its scope would be the smallest bracketed expression in which the description occurs as a term.

Hilbert and Bernays, on the other hand, dispose of the difficulty by refusing to admit any definite description as a term until the proposition which it implies has already been proved.[2] From this ruling it follows that an arrangement of signs which is not admissible as a formula at one stage of development may nevertheless become admissible at another when more theorems have been demonstrated.

What are we to say of these three suggestions? Considered as rival proposals for legislation whereby the principle of excluded middle may be preserved in relation to formulae of the artificial language of mathematical logic, they are all alike respectable, but each has its peculiar advantages and disadvantages. Frege's scheme gives most liberty to the user of descriptions and is the easiest of the three to operate; but it is also the most arbitrary in its departure from ordinary usage. The scheme of Whitehead

---

[1] *Principia Mathematica*, i, *14.          [2] *Grundlagen der Mathematik*, i, § 8.

and Russell avoids extravagance and yet allows wide liberty to any user of descriptions who wishes to make everything explicit; but it does so only at the expense of a considerable complication of symbolism. The scheme of Hilbert and Bernays is very simple to operate and also very natural in the sense that it corresponds closely to the usage of natural languages; but it restricts the liberty of a user of descriptions, and it makes the notion of a well-formed formula relative to the degree of development of the system, which may be regarded by some as a defect. For our own part, we prefer the third suggestion, but we think it would be a mistake to talk as though either of the other two were wrong in the context of mathematical logic.

Unfortunately discussion of the technical merits of these proposals has often been confused by philosophers with debates on other questions. This is due to the fact that Russell presented his proposal as a contribution to philosophical analysis. He maintained in the first place that what he said about definite descriptions in his mathematical logic was also a correct account of the way in which definite descriptions were used in ordinary language, and secondly that there was a distinction between descriptions and logically proper names corresponding to the distinction between two kinds of knowledge which he called knowledge by description and knowledge by acquaintance. We have already seen that the first of these contentions is mistaken, and we need say no more about it, except that Russell was led into error by his very reasonable desire to find an escape from the doctrine of Bolzano and Meinong, according to which the phrase 'the present King of France', being significant, must stand for something, though not necessarily for an existent.[1] But the second raises an interesting problem which we must notice here.

According to Russell a *logically proper name* is one used to designate an object of which the speaker is directly aware at the time of speaking, e.g. something which he sees in a basic and unanalysable sense of the word 'see', and it designates what it does without saying or implying anything about it. Ordinary proper names do not satisfy these strict standards. Thus 'Homer' is to be understood as equivalent to 'the author of the *Iliad*' or something like that, and is really a description. We can sensibly say 'Homer did not exist', whereas we cannot sensibly say either 'A exists' or 'A does not exist' if 'A' is a logically proper name. Russell admits, indeed, that it is difficult to find anything in ordinary speech which is a logically proper name, but he thinks

[1] B. Russell, 'On Denoting', *Mind*, n.s. (1905), pp. 479–93; reprinted in *Logic and Knowledge*, pp. 41–56.

the words 'this' and 'that', used with reference to sense-data, may perhaps be cited as examples.[1] There is a good deal of dubious epistemology here which need not concern us, but it is interesting to notice that all three accounts of definite descriptions within mathematical logic seem to presuppose the possibility of designations which are not descriptions. For a definite description is constructed by use of functional expression and it fulfils the normal intention of the user only if there is something satisfying the function. But if all designations are descriptions, justification of the use of a description seems to involve an infinite regress. For a proof that something is the one and only so-and-so will presumably involve reference to the thing by means of another designation. As might be expected, this argument to show that there must be designations which are not descriptions is most impressive when presented in connexion with Russell's account of descriptions. For according to him every statement in which a definite description has primary occurrence is an abbreviation for a complex existential statement, and every existential statement is constructed by application of a quantifier to a functional expression derived from a statement of simpler pattern by omission of one of its constituents. But Frege before him and Hilbert and Bernays after him have also talked as though there must be elementary statements of the subject-predicate pattern in which the subject is not a definite description but a proper name, attached in some more direct way to what it designates. To Hilbert and Bernays the point is of no great importance, because they are content to treat statements like '$2+2 = 4$' as elementary for their purposes. But it should have worried Frege more than it did, because he maintained that every designation has a sense, which suggests at least that they are all descriptions.

In a footnote to his article *Über Sinn und Bedeutung* Frege writes:

'In the case of an actual proper name such as "Aristotle" opinions as to the sense may differ. It might for instance, be taken to be the following: the pupil of Plato and teacher of Alexander the Great. Anyone who does this will attach another meaning to the sentence "Aristotle was born in Stagira" than will a man who takes as the sense of the name: the teacher of Alexander the Great who was born in Stagira. So long as the reference remains the same, such variations of sense may be tolerated, although they are to be avoided in the theoretical structure of a demonstrative science and ought not to occur in a perfect language.'[2]

---

[1] *Principia Mathematica*, i, pp. 174–5; 'The Philosophy of Logical Atomism', *The Monist*, xxviii (1918), pp. 495–527, reprinted in *Logic and Knowledge* (see especially p. 201).
[2] *Über Sinn und Bedeutung*, p. 27.

598 THE PHILOSOPHY OF LOGIC AFTER FREGE

This is unsatisfactory, because it confuses the sense of the name with what it suggests to this or that hearer and so obscures the peculiar character of ordinary proper names. A man who had learnt the word 'Aristotle' from a classical dictionary but remembered nothing of the article there except that Aristotle was born in Stagira would not for this reason regard the statement 'Aristotle was born in Stagira' as a pointless remark like 'The man born in Stagira was born in Stagira'. On the other hand, he would certainly agree that it was useless to say 'Aristotle is called Aristotle'. The moral of this is obvious. An ordinary proper name works like a definite description which has for its implication or presupposition the existence of something called by that name in the circle of the speaker and the hearer. Some, such as the personal name 'Tommy', imply in addition that the thing so called is of a certain kind, e.g. a young male human being. And when necessary the selective power of any proper name may be reinforced by additional words, as in 'your Tommy', 'Jones minor', 'the London in Ontario'. Proper names, like descriptions, may admittedly be used sometimes without an implication of existence, i.e. when they are forced to commit suicide. But the fact that it seems slightly paradoxical to say 'Homer never existed' shows clearly that the normal use of a proper name pre-supposes the existence of something called by the name. Thus the words 'New College' became a proper name when they were first used by the inhabitants of Oxford as though they were equivalent to the phrase 'the college to which people here commonly refer when they say "New College" '.

To say, as Russell does, that ordinary proper names are a kind of definite descriptions may be confusing, but it is clear that ordinary proper names and definite descriptions raise the same problems, since their use implies, but does not guarantee, the existence of things of which they are designations. Is it then reasonable to look for what Russell calls logically proper names? According to his explanation, if 'A' is a logically proper name, it is not merely pointless, but senseless, to say 'A exists', because, although 'A' must designate something, it must do so without implying possession of any character by the thing. This seems to be an impossible requirement. For designation is essentially the selection of something for attention by means of a sign, and a sign which is to serve this purpose must have some implication, though this need be no more than the notion that there is something which it designates for a certain group of persons. When, however, Russell says that a word cannot be a logically proper name unless it designates something of which the speaker is immediately aware, he introduces another requirement of a very different sort. For this pronouncement suggests that what he wants is not a designation without any existential implication but rather a designation whose implication is guaranteed true. Now the theory of knowledge which he presents in this connexion may be wrong, and it must be admitted in any case that the knowledge which he ascribes to the speaker cannot furnish any guarantee to the hearer, but it is very interesting to note that there is at least one designation whose use does always guarantee the truth of its implication for the hearer as well as for the speaker. This is the word 'I'.

Not all token reflexive pronouns have this peculiar property. When a timid person thinks mistakenly that there is someone under his bed and summons up courage to say 'You had better come out', his token 'you' fails to designate anything, though he utters it sincerely. And when in the story of *The Emperor's New Clothes* a courtier is represented as saying 'This is fine stuff' though he cannot see any cloth in the hands of the rascally tailors, it is made clear that the word 'this' can be used for purposes of deception in such a way that it designates nothing. But neither false belief nor bad faith (as distinct from dramatic convention) can lead to a use of 'I' in which it fails to designate something. And that, of course, is why Augustine and Descartes were especially interested in the sentence 'I exist'. Whereas 'You do not exist' and 'This does not exist' are merely self-stultifying remarks, 'I do not exist' is self-refuting. For here the denial of existence is incompatible not only with the existential proposition implied by the use of the subject term, but also with the fact that the remark has been made. It would be a mistake, however, to suppose that the word 'I' enjoys a unique privilege among signs used for reference. Although the adverbs 'here' and 'now' can scarcely be called designations, their task is to help in the selection of objects for attention, and they cannot fail to do their part satisfactorily. If a man purports to speak of something that happened in Lyonnesse in the reign of King Arthur, he may believe mistakenly that there is a place called Lyonnesse and that there was once a king called Arthur, or he may conceivably intend to mislead others into such beliefs; but no use of the words 'here' and 'now' can be improper in either of these ways. The reason is obvious: 'here' and 'now', like 'I', presuppose in use no more than what must be the case because there is an utterance. In a language with well-developed syntax they appear as three signs among others used for the purpose of reference, but they are peculiar in adding nothing to what is implicit already in a unitary expression. When a man shouts 'Help!', he gives us to understand quite adequately by this single word that he the speaker wants help at the place and at the time of his speaking.

In the last resort all reference to particular things or events in space and time consists in the location of them by relation to the act of speech. For just as a proper name like 'Socrates' singles a thing out for attention as that which is called by the name in the circle to which speaker and hearer belong, so a description like 'the milkman' does its work by supplying enough detail to identify an object *in the context of speech*. And even more fundamental than either of these is the use of tenses or temporal particles to mark the time of an event by relation to the time of speaking. In an artificial language where the rules of usage of a symbol take no account of its context of utterance it is impossible to express any singular propositions about matters of fact, and so a script like Frege's can be no more than a supplement to a natural language, extremely useful for precise discussion of the relations of generalities in mathematics and natural science, but inadequate by itself for the ordinary purposes of life and also for metaphysical analysis. In fact the only designations ever used in mathematical logic by Frege and his successors are symbols for abstract entities such as universals, classes, and numbers. Like all designations, these do their work only because they have implications in the sense explained above, but their implications are of a sort that no one could reasonably deny, and so they usually pass unnoticed. Thus anyone who speaks of humanity, or of being a man, assumes quite naturally that there is something which all men have or would have in common. This presupposition of the usage has never been called into question except by persons who have an obsessive fear of metaphysics, and their caution is obviously misplaced, since the things to which a general term is applied must at the very least have in common the feature of being things to which the term is applied. Similarly anyone who uses the numeral '2' as a designation in sentences such as '2 is the smallest prime number' thinks that it stands for an object because he assumes that there is something common to all sets that have two members. In this case it is not so easy to explain the connexion of the noun with the adjective from which it has been derived in historical times, but it is clear at least that no one can attribute any meaning to a statement about a natural number without recognizing the possibility of using the corresponding numeral in the counting of objects of any kind.

The upshot of our discussion may be summarized as follows. The activity of designation is not the paradigm of all sign-using, but something incidental to the expression of propositions in languages which have reached the syntactical level of development. A sign called a designation may be said to have a sense, not because it is itself an expression of anything (for it is not), but because its use presupposes acceptance of an existential proposition. If it is singular it implies the existence of just one thing of a certain kind; if it is plural, it implies the existence of more than one thing of that kind. A designation of the sort for which Russell coined the technical term 'definite description' is a phrase derived in fairly obvious fashion from a functional expression which could be used in a formulation of the existential proposition it implies. An ordinary proper name, say 'Socrates', is equivalent in use to a description of the form 'the thing called Socrates', though it would be a mistake to treat it as an abbreviation for such a description, since it is presupposed by the phrase 'called Socrates' and is therefore obviously more primitive. Similarly token-reflexive words like 'you' and 'this' are equivalent in use to descriptions such as 'the person I am now addressing' and 'the thing to which I am now attending'. If the proposition implied by a designation is false, the designation fails to designate anything. But there is one designation, 'I', which cannot fail to designate something whenever it is used by a speaker in accordance with its grammatical conventions. It has this peculiarity because it serves only to make explicit something which is implicit already in any unitary expression. For a proper understanding of the role which designations of particular things and events play at the syntactical level of discourse, it is desirable indeed to remember at all times that complex sentences work as wholes in the same way as unitary expressions and may therefore express different propositions in different contexts. Designations which are supposed to stand for abstract entities raise special problems, but they too involve implications of existence, though this fact may be overlooked until the implications are debated by philosophers.

## 3. *Problems of Intensionality*

In modal logic we talk of propositions, ascribing to them attributes such as possibility and relations such as strict implication. It is therefore necessary that our symbolism should provide in some way for the designation, as well as for the expression, of propositions. Lewis and most other writers on the subject avoid the introduction of any special new symbolism by assuming tacitly that whenever a propositional expression occurs in a place appropriate for a designation of a proposition it shall be read as though it were preceded by some prefix such as 'the proposition that . . . '. Thus $\diamond P$ is taken as an abbreviation for *It is possible that* $-P$ and $P \rightarrow\!\!\!3\; Q$ as an abbreviation for *The proposition that* $-P$ *strictly implies the proposition that* $-Q$. In the last chapter we introduced the sign § as a prefix for converting the expression of a proposition into a designation, but stipulated that it could be omitted where it might conveniently be supposed to have been absorbed by a special modal sign such as that of Lewis. Obviously there is nothing to be gained from printing it in contexts where omission leads to no misunderstanding, though it may be useful on occasions as a reminder of the fact that the statements we make in modal logic are about propositions and have designations of propositions for their grammatical subjects and objects. The construction with which we have to deal here is like that of indirect speech. As Frege noticed in his article *Über Sinn und Bedeutung*, a clause beginning with 'that' has for reference that which would be the sense of the words if they appeared without 'that'.

Since the effect of the sign § is to convert expressions of propositions into designations of the same, it may be used also in the symbolism of logic to construct designations of propositional functions in a fashion that evades Frege's difficulties. That is to say, we may write §*xFx* when we wish to refer to the sense of the functional sign *Fx* and similarly §*xyG(x,y)* when we wish to refer to the sense of *G(x, y)*. Here a letter or letters must be inserted after § to bind the variable or variables in the functional expression which follows, and § can no longer be read as though it were an abbreviation for 'the proposition that', since the sense of the whole is rather that of 'the attribute which a thing has when it is *F*' or 'the relation which one thing has to another when the first is *G* to the second'.[1] But it is an advantage to have a symbolism which brings together propositions and propositional functions. For talk about them gives rise to similar problems. In philosophical discussions of logic they are often grouped together as intensions by way of contrast with truth-values (regarded as objects), classes, and individuals, which are all called extensions. The terminology of 'intension' and 'extension' was originally introduced, as we have seen, for discussion of general terms, but the modern usage has arisen by a natural development and may be accepted as a convenient way of discussing related topics. Sometimes it is said also that a definite description such as 'the

---

[1] In its use before a functional expression § resembles the lambda operator introduced by A. Church in his 'Set of Postulates for the Foundation of Logic', *Annals of Mathematics*, xxxiii (1932), pp. 341–66, but it is not clear there whether he thinks of his operator as a sign for the construction of designations. In later writings he treats λ*x* as equivalent to the class abstractor of Whitehead and Russell.

King of France' has an intension, namely an individual concept such as being the sole king of France.[1] Whether or not we like this terminology, we can agree that a description of the form $(\imath x)Fx$ must have a sense, and when there is occasion to talk directly of that sense we may, if we wish, designate it by a complex sign of the form $\S x[Fx.(y)(Fy \supset y = x)]$. In all three permissible cases the prefixing of $\S$ to an expression (delimited if necessary by brackets) makes a designation for the sense of that which follows, and so the prefix may perhaps be called an intensional abstractor.

A language as a whole may be said to be intensional if it allows for the designation of intensions where such designation is essential, i.e. not eliminable by deflationary translation like that from *It is true that* $-P$ to $P$. Obviously all the natural languages of civilized peoples qualify for this title. And so also does Lewis's symbolism, since it is a tacit convention of his script that a sign occurring as the grammatical subject of the predicate $\Diamond$ or as the subject or the object of the verb $\dashv$ shall be taken to be a designation of what it ordinarily expresses: we noticed earlier that there is a similar convention in ordinary English about clauses which follow the verb 'say' but are not introduced by 'that'. It is possible, however, to conceive languages in which intensions can be expressed but never designated: these are said to be extensional. The terminology is a little confusing, because those who are familiar with the history of the words naturally start by thinking of an intension as something expressed and an extension as something designated; but if we are to make use of the words in this context, we must free ourselves from that association and think of an extension as being either an individual, a class, or a truth-value and of an intension as being either an individual concept (if this rather queer phrase may be allowed), a propositional function, or a proposition. It is possible, as we have seen, to have a rudimentary language in which propositions can be expressed but nothing at all designated. According to the definition given above, such a language would be extensional. If it were enriched by functional expressions and designations of individuals and classes, it would still remain extensional. But if designations of propositions, propositional functions, and individual concepts were added, it would become intensional. In short, the difference is one in respect of the types of entities which languages admit as subjects of discourse, and an intensional language is essentially more complicated than an extensional, since it allows both expression and designation of that for which an extensional language would allow only expression.

[1] R. Carnap, *Meaning and Necessity*, pp. 41, 180–1.

In his article *Über Sinn und Bedeutung* Frege recognized clearly the possibility of taking propositions as subjects of discourse, but in his *Begriffsschrift* and again in his *Grundgesetze der Arithmetik* he made no provision for this or any other feature of intensional language. Presumably the reason for this omission was that he saw no need of intensional language for the presentation of mathematics. In the first edition of *Principia Mathematica* Whitehead and Russell follow the same course. While recognizing the possibility of intensional statements such as 'Socrates believed that his soul was immortal', they confine their discussion for the most part to the characteristics of extensional statements. But there appears in the *Begriffsschrift* and again in *Principia Mathematica* a logical principle

$$x = y \supset (fx \supset fy)$$

which appears at first sight to be inconsistent with the admission of intensional statements. It is in effect the converse of Leibniz's principle of the identity of indiscernibles, 'Eadem sunt quorum unum potest substitui alteri salva veritate', and it may perhaps be called the principle of the indiscernibility of identicals.[1] So far as we know, it has not been questioned even by those philosophers who find Leibniz's assertion unplausible, yet it seems to have extraordinary consequences. Let us suppose, for example, that we substitute '12' for $x$, 'the sum of the third and fourth prime numbers' for $y$, and 'the Pope knows that the number of the apostles is . . . ' for $f$. Then we get a true statement for $x = y$ and another true statement for $fx$, but two applications of the *modus ponens* yield the conclusion 'The Pope knows that the number of the apostles is the sum of the third and fourth prime numbers', which, to say the least, is very doubtful. By similar arguments we can prove paradoxes in the theory of modality, as for example that any true statement of identity is necessarily true. For the morning star is identical with the evening star and the morning star satisfies the function expressed by the words 'it is necessary that the morning star is identical with . . . '. Therefore, it seems, the evening star must also satisfy the function, i.e. it is necessary that the morning star is identical with the evening star.

How are we to deal with this awkward situation? In his *Tractatus Logico-Philosophicus* (5.54) Wittgenstein asserts that one propositional sign can occur in another only as an argument of

---

[1] This title was suggested by W. V. Quine in his book *From a Logical Point of View*, p. 139.

a truth-function. As it stands, this statement is clearly false, since the propositional sign 'it will rain tomorrow' does not appear as an argument of a truth-function in the sentence 'Brown thinks that it will rain tomorrow'. But it may perhaps be taken as an epigrammatic way of saying that every utterance made in an intensional language can be translated without loss into an extensional language. This Thesis of Extensionality, as it is now called, was adopted by Russell in the introduction to the second edition of *Principia Mathematica*, published in 1925, and defended at length by Carnap in his *Logical Syntax of Language*,[1] first published in 1934.

Complex signs of the kind we construct with our intensional abstractor can be eliminated very easily from some contexts where they occur together with expressions specially designed for reversing the work of the abstractor. Thus the sentence $§P$ *is true* can be replaced by $P$ and $X$ *has* (or *exemplifies*) $§yFy$ by $FX$. But these are special cases. In general Carnap relies on a method of reduction in which designations of intensions are replaced by designations of expressions while predicates which are appropriate to intensions are replaced by corresponding predicates appropriate to expressions. Thus 'Brown thinks that it will rain tomorrow' is reduced on his principles to 'Brown says to himself with a feeling of conviction "It will rain tomorrow" ', 'It is necessary that $7+5 = 12$' to 'The statement "$7+5 = 12$" is analytic', 'Plato wrote a book about justice' to 'Plato wrote a book containing the word "justice" or some equivalent', and so forth. When a sentence or phrase occurs in the translation within quotation marks, it is to be understood as forming part of a designation for itself, and must therefore not be construed as a grammatical constituent of the main sentence. In particular it must not be supposed that a word or phrase which occurs as part of such a sentence within quotation marks may be replaced at will by another which happens to have the same reference. For the conventions of quotation allow us to use ' "$7+5 = 12$" ' as a designation for the sentence '$7+5 = 12$', but they certainly do not allow us to use ' "$7+ 5 = $ the number of the apostles" ' as a designation for the sentence '$7+5 = 12$'. From this consideration, it seems, we can immediately obtain a solution for our puzzles. When, for example, we realize that the statement 'It is necessary that the morning star is identical with the morning star' means the same as 'The sentence "The morning star is identical with the morning star" is analytic', we can see that it is not about the morning star but about a certain set of words, and that there is

[1] §§ 67–71, 74–81.

no function expressed by the jargon phrase 'It is necessary that the morning star is identical with $x$' any more than there is by the words 'The sentence "The morning star is identical with $x$" is analytic'.

Objections may be raised to some of the reductions by which Carnap illustrates his thesis. We may doubt, for example, whether all thinking is speaking to oneself. But the thesis is undoubtedly very plausible. When we first hear of the paradoxes of intensionality, we feel inclined to say that being necessarily identical with the morning star is not a real attribute of independently existing objects, such as we had in mind when we first read Frege's principle of the indiscernibility of identicals, but rather something connected with human language; and the thesis of extensionality gives precision to this idea. If we reject the thesis, our reason should not be merely dissatisfaction with some of Carnap's illustrations, but rather an objection of principle to his way of dealing with intensional statements; and it is therefore best to take for critical examination a simple case of indirect speech, that is to say, a case in which it seems most plausible to say that the use of intensional language is only a substitute for a report of words actually uttered.

Let us consider, then, the statement 'Cavemen told their children that fire hurts'. This is easily understood, but no intelligent person who hears it supposes that cavemen said to their children the English words 'Fire hurts', or indeed any other words of any known language. If it is insisted that the statement must really be about the sounds which the cavemen uttered, the best reduction we can offer is 'Cavemen said to their children some phrase which meant in their language the same as "Fire hurts" now means in English'. This must be true if the original is true, and conversely if this is true the original must be true. It should be noticed, however, that the remark attributed to the cavemen is specified here by its equivalence in meaning to an English sentence. If we follow this method, we avoid an obvious return to intensional language such as would be involved in saying 'Cavemen said to their children some phrase which meant in their language that fire hurts'. And we do not even commit ourselves to any view about meaning which could conceivably be thought dangerous. For we say only that the phrase used by cavemen meant the same in their language as a certain English sentence means now, and it may be that the notion of having the same meaning can be explained satisfactorily without what is sometimes called abusively the reification or hypostatization of meaning. But the reduction we offer is nevertheless unsatisfactory because it introduces a reference to the English language which was not in the original.[1]

How can we avoid this unwanted reference without returning to the use of a 'that' clause? Only by allowing ourselves that looser use of direct speech which is common in translations. When a fundamentalist reads in his bible 'God said: Let there be light', he may possibly believe that God uttered certain words of Hebrew; but unless he is very silly, he does not assume that God said anything in English. So too if we produce the statement 'Cavemen said to their children "Fire hurts" ', persons of intelligence will not understand us to imply that cavemen spoke English, and anyone who takes the trouble to translate our remark into French will translate the words inside the quotation marks as well as the rest. But this device of quasi-quotation is itself a variety of intensional language. For in this context ' "Fire hurts" ' does not occur as a designation of the English sounds corresponding to the marks 'Fire hurts', but rather as an equivalent of the phrase 'that fire hurts'. Sometimes indeed the two devices approach so closely in spoken English that it is pointless to ask which has been used. If a small child who has been cautioned by a foreigner against playing with matches asks his mother 'What does he say?', the mother's reply may be represented in print equally well by 'He says "Fire hurts" ' or by 'He says fire hurts'. Nor is this surprising; for there can be little doubt that in all languages the main devices for designating intensions have evolved from quasi-quotation of words or phrases sufficient to express those intensions.

Carnap, who has been the most vigorous proponent of the thesis of extensionality, does not claim that it is a necessary truth, and the considerations which we have just put forward suggest that its plausibility is due to an important but little discussed ambiguity in our use of inverted commas. Although Carnap professes to replace intensional statements by statements that refer only to symbols, he cannot in fact make his translations seem acceptable except by allowing each symbol he mentions to retain its linguistic status. In short his quotation marks do not, as he thinks, indicate mention as distinct from use, but rather a special use which is founded on mention and amounts in effect to designation of the sense which the symbol would express if it occurred without quotation marks. It is possible, nevertheless, to learn something from the extensionalist attempt to deal with the paradoxes of intensionality. For an intensional abstractor works in some ways like inverted commas.

[1] Cf. A. Church, 'On Carnap's Analysis of Statements of Assertion and Belief', *Analysis*, x (1950), pp. 97–99.

In any propositional expression which contains a designation of any kind the sense of the whole depends on the sense of the designation as well as on the sense of the other signs occurring in the expression, but in the simple cases which are called extensional the truth-value of the proposition expressed by the whole does not depend on the sense of the designation as distinct from its reference. Thus the proposition that the morning star goes round the sun is distinguishable from the proposition that the evening star goes round the sun, but they have the same truth-value, because the morning star is identical with the evening star. This is the purport of the principle of the indiscernibility of identicals. On the other hand, in the more complicated cases which are called intensional the truth-value of the whole may well depend on the sense of some designation contained within a propositional designation which itself forms part of the whole. Thus it is true that it is necessary that the morning star is the morning star, but not true that it is necessary that the morning star is the evening star. In general, whatever the letters $F$, $G$, and $H$ may signify, the truth-value of the proposition expressed by $F\{§G[(\imath x)Hx]\}$ depends on the reference of $§G[(\imath x)Hx]$, and this depends on the sense of $G[(\imath x)Hx]$, and this in turn depends on the sense of $(\imath x)Hx$, so that from the equation

$$(\imath x)Hx = (\imath y)\mathcal{J}y,$$

which guarantees only identity of reference, we cannot safely conclude

$$F\{§G[(\imath x)Hx]\} \equiv F\{§G[(\imath y)\mathcal{J}y]\}$$

In such a case the intensional abstractor, which directs attention to the sense of the sign falling within its scope, serves also as a reminder against reliance on the principle of the indiscernibility of identicals to justify substitution within that scope.

Our task would be greatly simplified if we could go on to say that no expression of the form $F(§Gy)$ ever expresses a propositional function. For then we should have an almost exact parallel between the rules for the use of our intensional abstractor and those for the use of quotation marks: the principle of the indiscernibility of identicals could be accepted without qualification or restriction, and there would be no puzzles about quantifiers operating across intensional abstractors to bind variables within the scope of such abstractors, because there would be no meaningful expressions with quantifiers in that position. But the facts of ordinary usage are against this sweeping suggestion. In English the sentence 'There was one thing he said he liked' is clearly distinguishable in meaning from 'He said there was one thing he liked', and there can be no doubt that the first has the form $(\exists y)F(\S Gy)$. Being thought stupid by Lenin, being suspected of opportunism by Trotsky, being feared as a rival by Stalin—these are all intensional functions or attributes, and anyone who reads through a newspaper with an interest in the question at issue can easily find expressions for many more. In this connexion it is important, of course, to distinguish between $F(\S Gy)$ and $F(\S y Gy)$. Whereas the former expresses an intensional function which may have as a value the proposition expressed by $F(\S G \mathcal{Z})$, the latter expresses an intensional proposition about the function designated by $\S y Gy$; and it is precisely in order to preserve this distinction that the argument in the latter must be bound by another $y$ inserted immediately after the $\S$.

Our troubles arise from the fact that there are intensional functions and that some of them cannot be satisfied by an object as such but only by an object considered as falling under a certain description. Thus Oedipus wished to kill the haughty stranger who ordered him to give way on the narrow road from Delphi to Phocis, but he did not wish to kill his father, although the haughty stranger was in fact his father. If anyone says that functions like this have a special status in logic because their expressions occur only in second-order discourse (i.e. discourse that presupposes a simpler use of symbols in the sense of being about what they express, though not about them directly), we can agree very readily; but there seems no good reason for denying that they are functions, and once that point is conceded, it becomes clear that the only way out of our perplexities is to qualify the principle of the indiscernibility of identicals by making it apply only to extensional (i.e. non-intensional) functions.

To insist on the principle of the indiscernibility of identicals is to say in effect that for the context of our assertion we recognize none but extensional functions. To qualify it in the way just suggested is to admit that if $Fx$ expresses an intensional function we cannot argue *formally* from the two premisses $FX$ and $X = Y$ to the conclusion $FY$. Sometimes no doubt the nature of an intensional context shows clearly enough that one name or description can be substituted for another *salva veritate*, but it is a mistake to hope for rules of substitution valid in all such contexts. Let us suppose, for example, that there is no doubt of the truth of the statement 'St. Thomas Aquinas said that the Philosopher's doctrine of the soul was correct'. May we repeat it with 'Aristotle' substituted for 'the Philosopher'? Surely. For even if St. Thomas wrote the Latin word *Philosophus* rather than *Aristoteles* in the

passage which we profess to report, our substitution is well within
the bounds of the license permitted by custom to a user of indirect
speech. It may be argued, indeed, that for many readers our
new version will be preferable to the original, as being less open
to misunderstanding. May we, then, if we wish, substitute 'the
Stagirite' for 'the Philosopher'? It is impossible to give a simple
answer. In the eighteenth century there would probably have
been no harm in the change, because almost every reader would
have recognized the phrase as a modern description of Aristotle,
introduced for reasons of literary fashion, and therefore been
under no temptation to suppose that St. Thomas identified
Aristotle by reference to his birthplace. In the twentieth century
some readers would recognize the eighteenth-century mannerism,
but others might conceivably be misled into thinking that St.
Thomas mentioned Stagira, and others again who did not know
that Aristotle was born at Stagira might even suppose that
St. Thomas had in mind another person. There can be no formal
rules of substitution valid for all intensional contexts, because
the notions of saying, believing, knowing, wishing, intending, etc.,
which we often express by means of intensional language are not
formal notions. There are indeed conventions to be observed in
contexts of various kinds (for without conventions of some sort
there could be no communication such as we have in fact), but
it would be misleading to speak of these as subjects of study for
logic. Logic, as we consider it in this book, is concerned with
the forms of propositions as distinct from their subject-matter,
and the only part of the theory of intensional statements which
can properly be called formal is pure modal logic. It is not surprising therefore that this has aroused most interest among
logicians.

In a true modal statement, either of the form $\Box \S G[(\imath x)Hx]$
or of the form $\Diamond \S G[(\imath x)Hx]$, substitution of $(\imath y)Jy$ for $(\imath x)Hx$
may lead to falsity, or even to absurdity, if it cannot be authorized
by anything more than a contingent assertion

$$(\imath x)Hx = (\imath y)Jy.$$

Thus it would be ridiculous to argue from the modal premiss

$$\Box \S(12 < 13)$$

and the historical truth

$$12 = \textit{the number of the apostles}$$

to the modal conclusion

$$\Box \S(\textit{the number of the apostles} < 13).$$

Nor is it sufficient to say, as in Theophrastus' theory of modal syllogisms, that the conclusion must agree in modality with the weaker premiss. For it is equally ridiculous to argue from the modal premiss

$$\diamondsuit \S \sim (\textit{the number of the apostles} < 13)$$

and the historical truth

$$\textit{The number of the apostles} = 12$$

to the modal conclusion

$$\diamondsuit \S \sim (12 < 13).$$

On the other hand, substitution can be made in all such contexts *salva veritate* when the designation which is to be substituted has *necessarily* the same reference as that which it is to replace, e.g. when '7+5' is to be put for '12'. This is not to say that the result of substitution will then be an expression with exactly the same sense as the original, but simply that the change will make no difference to the truth-value of the whole. Two designations which have necessarily the same reference may nevertheless be different in sense, and so capable of making a difference in sense between two otherwise similar expressions in which they occur, but they must be so related that either can replace the other in a modal context without falsification. In order to understand why this is so let us consider once more the way in which designations occur in modal contexts.

If the proposition expressed by $\square \S G[(\imath x)Hx]$ is true, the reason must be either that the propositional function expressed by $Gy$ holds for all possible arguments or that it is entailed by the sense of the designation $(\imath x)Hx$. For an example of the first situation we may take the statement 'It is necessary that the last Stuart queen should be either dead or not dead'. Since everything must be either dead or not dead, we may replace 'the last Stuart queen' here by any other designation of the same general type without affecting the truth-value of the whole. For an example of the second situation we may take the statement 'It is necessary that the last Stuart queen was a woman'. Here the sense of the designation is all-important. If we wrote instead 'the last Stuart monarch', we should still succeed in referring to Queen Anne, but our new statement would not be true. Even in the second case, however, the existential presupposition of the designation used by the speaker is no part of what he declares to be necessary. He believes presumably that there was a last Stuart queen, but not that *this* is necessary, and he can if he wishes make the point

clear either by adding the words 'if indeed there was such a
queen' or by recasting the whole statement in the form 'The
last Stuart queen would necessarily be a woman'. For these
new ways of speaking leave the substance of the modal assertion
unaltered while cancelling the commitment ordinarily implied
by use of a designation. In logical symbolism we can produce
the same effect by introducing $H'x$ as an abbreviation for $Hx.(y)$
$[Hy \supset y = x]$, i.e. with the sense of $x$ is the only $H$ thing, and then
writing $\Box \S(x)[H'x \supset Gx]$ in place of $\Box \S G[(\imath x)Hx]$. Modal
assertions from which designations have been eliminated in this
way may be said to be in reduced form. If the propositional
function expressed by $Gx$ is truistic, $\Box \S(x)[H'x \supset Gx]$ must be
true, whatever $Hx$ may signify, and so the first of the two cases
we distinguished above may be subsumed under the second.

In this argument we have assumed, of course, that any designation which appears in a modal context may be treated as a definite
description or as an abbreviation for such, e.g. that 'Queen Anne'
may be treated as an abbreviation for 'the Queen called "Anne"'
and '12' as an abbreviation for 'the number common to all sets
which are equivalent in Cantor's sense to the set of numerals
$\{``1", ``2", ``3", \ldots, ``12"\}$'. This procedure is forced on us by the
need for attending in such contexts to the sense of our designations. In extensional contexts, for which the principle of the indiscernibility of identicals holds without restriction, proper names
may be used without much thought of their sense, so that substitution of 'Napoleon' for 'Bonaparte' or *vice versa* seems sometimes to be no more than a matter of style. But the situation is
very different in modal contexts. For it is said to be necessary that
Napoleon is identical with Napoleon but merely contingent that
Napoleon is identical with Bonaparte; and in order to understand this we must, as Frege argued, pay attention to differences
of sense, i.e. we must think of the two names as though they were
abbreviations for descriptions. It is certainly not necessary that
there existed a person called 'Napoleon'; but it is necessary that
the sole person called 'Napoleon', if there is any such, should be
identical with the sole person called 'Napoleon'.[1]

Returning now to the problem of substitution in modal contexts, let us suppose that we have for a datum

$$\Box \S [(\imath x)Hx = (\imath y)Jy].$$

[1] In *Principia Mathematica*, *14. 28, Whitehead and Russell say in effect that
$(\imath x)Hx = (\imath x)Hx$ is true if and only if $(\exists x)H'x$ is true. This restriction on substitution in the formula $x = x$ is required by their account of formulae containing definite descriptions. In ordinary English the problem of existential implication is
treated in the way indicated above.

From this there follows in accordance with ordinary rules for the use of definite descriptions the formula $\Box \S H'[(\imath x)\mathcal{J}x]$, and by the procedure explained above this in turn can be reduced to $\Box \S(x)[\mathcal{J}'x \supset H'x]$. But the statement

$$\Box \S G[(\imath x)Hx]$$

can be reduced to $\Box \S(x)[H'x \supset Gx]$, and so it is easy to see that with the supposition of necessary identity set out above it must entail the consequence $\Box \S(x)[\mathcal{J}'x \supset Gx]$, which itself is the reduced form of

$$\Box \S G[(\imath x)\mathcal{J}x].$$

By a similar argument it can be shown that necessary identity of reference in two designations is a sufficient condition for the replacement of either by the other *salva veritate* in a statement of possibility.

When we turn to consider the possibility of using quantifiers to operate across modal signs and therefore across intensional abstractors, it is natural to suppose that the relations between formulae which combine modal signs in various ways with quantifiers must be governed by rules like those for the relations between formulae which combine modal signs in various ways with signs of conjunction or disjunction. Now the latter are generally agreed and can be set out in the following diagram, where for brevity and ease of comparison we have introduced the convention of omitting from each formula the intensional abstractor which would follow in an unabbreviated version immediately after the modal sign:

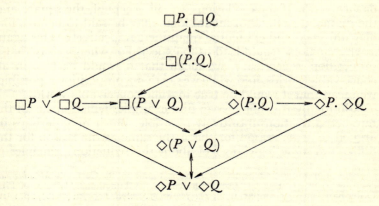

Obviously, therefore, analogy requires that the former should be as indicated in the corresponding diagram where universal quantification takes the place of conjunction and existential quantification the place of disjunction:

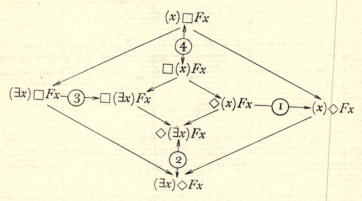

Formulae of the inner ring are those which raise no problem because their quantifiers occur within the scope of their modal signs, while those of the outer ring are the debatable formulae which have quantifiers operating across modal signs. The unnumbered arrows represent entailments guaranteed by generally accepted principles of logic, while those to which numbers have been assigned represent entailments suggested by the analogy mentioned above.[1] It will be noticed that entailments of the latter group are the only links between formulae of the two rings, and that they are not all mutually independent. By substitution and contraposition (3) can be derived from (1) and (4) from (2), or vice versa. If these relations are all accepted, the square and the diamond prefixes of modal logic may be said to behave like new universal and existential quantifiers respectively. This again is what analogy would lead us to expect. For when we say that a proposition is necessary, we mean that it would be true in all conceivable worlds, and when we say that a proposition is possible, we mean that it would be true in some conceivable world.

Admittedly it is not easy to find examples which make all the numbered relations intuitively plausible. But it may perhaps be argued that the reason for this is the same as the reason for the difficulties some logicians feel about the reduction principles of

[1] The four numbered principles may be found in R. Carnap's *Meaning and Necessity* (1947), p. 186. Cf. also Ruth Barcan, 'A Functional Calculus of First Order Based on Strict Implication', *The Journal of Symbolic Logic*, xi (1946), pp. 1–16.

modal logic. In natural languages modal words undoubtedly occur sometimes after quantifiers; but wherever they occur, they are nearly always used in elliptic fashion, i.e. to signify that something is necessary or possible, as the case may be, in relation to something else not explicitly indicated but easily identified by the hearer. In the technical symbolism of modal logic, on the other hand, everything is supposed to be made explicit. If, then, we try to render the sense of the technical symbolism in ordinary speech, we may find ourselves in difficulties because the words we use suggest supplementation where no supplementation is needed. Let us suppose, for example, that $(\exists x)\Diamond Fx$ is taken to mean 'There is something which may be on fire' and $\Diamond(\exists x)Fx$ to mean 'There may be something on fire'. Immediately we come on the difficulty that the two English sentences are certainly not equivalent. For the first can be used to state that something is inflammable, and the second to say that our information does not rule out the existence of a fire. But if these assertions were properly translated back into the symbolism of modal logic, the results would be much more complicated than the two formulae linked in our scheme by the relation (2). In modal logic the diamond signifies only self-consistency and according to this strict interpretation the two formulae just mentioned seem to be logically equivalent, at least for the non-empty universe which logicians commonly assume. Unfortunately no logician who adopts the strict interpretation has offered examples which make the relations numbered (1) and (3) seem thoroughly satisfactory.

None of the systems of modal logic considered by C. I. Lewis contains any provision for the operation of quantifiers across modal signs, and the development we have sketched in the last few paragraphs has not been accepted by all logicians. Those who object to it argue either that the innovation is useless or that it is senseless. Thus according to G. H. von Wright it is an unnecessary complication, because everything that can be expressed in this way can be expressed more simply otherwise.[1] He bases his case on the assumption that all attributes of things can be divided into two groups, the formal, whose presence in the things that have them and absence in the things that do not have them is necessary, and the material, whose presence in the things that have them and absence in the things that do not have them is merely contingent. Thus arithmetical attributes are supposed to belong to the first group, and colours to the second. From this assumption (which he calls the Principle of Predication) it seems to follow that, to anyone who can tell whether an attribute is

[1] *An Essay on Modal Logic*, p. 27.

formal or material, quantifiers operating across modal signs are useless. For if $Fx$ expresses a formal attribute, $(\exists x)\Box Fx$ and $(\exists x)\Diamond Fx$ are both equivalent to $(\exists x)Fx$; and if $Fx$ expresses a material attribute, the first is obviously absurd while the second is a truism.

Von Wright admits that there are apparent exceptions to his principle; but it is open to a general objection which he does not notice. Whether an attribute belongs necessarily to a subject which has it does not always depend solely on the nature of the attribute. Being less than 13 is an arithmetical attribute, and we may, if we like, say that it belongs necessarily to the number 12; but it is false that the number of the apostles is necessarily less than 13, although the number of the apostles is undoubtedly 12. It looks as though von Wright may have been misled here by the dubious distinction between modalities *de dicto* and modalities *de re* which he takes over from medieval writers. If the phrase *de re* is supposed to exclude dependence of the modality on the sense as distinct from the reference of the subject term, then paradoxically the only true modal statements *de re* are those in which the subject term can be replaced *salva veritate* by any other designation for a thing of the same category, i.e. statements like 'Queen Anne is necessarily dead or not dead', where the subject term contributes nothing of importance and the truth of the whole depends on the truistic character of the expression 'dead or not dead'.

W. V. Quine's objection to quantification across modal signs is more radical; for he says not merely that it is useless, but also that it is meaningless, and he even suggests that we should do well to abandon the whole theory of modality together with the talk of propositions and attributes which it seems to require. His arguments may be summarized freely as follows, with the help of an example we have used already. Those who allow the use of modal words and phrases think that $\Box(12 < 13)$ expresses a true proposition. If we accept this, we shall presumably admit also that the phrase $\Box(x < 13)$ expresses a function satisfied by the number 12, and then we can scarcely refuse to allow the formation of the existential sentence $(\exists x)\Box(x < 13)$. But how are we to understand this novelty? It cannot be just the assertion of the existence of a number possessing a certain property; for if there were such a number, anyone who put forward the assertion might properly be asked to justify it by stating explicitly which number had the property, and it would not matter for this purpose whether he replied by saying '12' or 'the number of the apostles', since these designations have the same reference. On the other hand, it is useless to suggest, as some logicians have done, that the variable $x$ may take as its values intensions of some sort. For if we admit intensions as possible values of our variables, we must abandon the principle of the indiscernibility of identicals, and then, because we have no clear criterion of identity, we shall be unable to say what we want to say about extensions:

'Intensional and extensional ontologies are like oil and water. Admission of attributes and propositions, along with free use of quantification and other basic idioms, rules out individuals and classes. Both sorts of entities can be accommodated in the same logic only with the help of restrictions, such as Church's, which serve to keep them from mixing, and this is very nearly a matter of two separate logics with a universe for each.'[1]

It cannot, we think, be the proper business of a philosopher to ban the mention of propositions and attributes or to say that we must drop the words 'possible' and 'necessary' from our logical vocabulary. There may perhaps be metaphysical puzzles about the status of propositions something like those that have been raised about the nature of political societies; but just as it would be wrong to protest against the extravagances of Hegel by saying 'There are no states' so it is a mistake to counter the queer assertions of Bolzano and Meinong by saying 'There are no propositions'. If, as Quine has shown, there is something wrong with the common attempts of logicians to make quantifiers operate across modal signs, we must look for the source of the trouble in the details of their symbolization rather than in any general fault of all talk about propositions and modalities. When we approach the problem in this way, we find in fact that it can be solved without much difficulty.

Construction of a formula such as $(\exists x)\Box Fx$ or $(x)\Diamond Fx$ presupposes that we know already what is meant by formulae like $\Box FY$ and $\Diamond FY$. Let us consider the first case in some detail. We have seen already that a designation occurring within a modal context can always be eliminated. If the designation is not a definite description but a proper name (e.g. 'Napoleon'), we first of all replace it by a definite description with the same sense (e.g. 'the person called "Napoleon" '). Next we extract from our description, say $(\imath x)Gx$, the predicate $G'x$ which means *x is the sole G thing*. And finally for $\Box F[(\imath x)Gx]$ we write $\Box(x)[G'x \supset Fx]$, or $(x)\Box[G'x \supset Fx]$, which is just another way of asserting together in the terminology of necessity all the propositions

[1] *From a Logical Point of View*, p. 157. The work of Church to which Quine refers is 'A Formulation of the Logic of Sense and Denotation' contributed to *Structure, Method, and Meaning: Essays in Honor of Henry M. Sheffer*, 1951.

expressible by entailment formulae of the form $G'Z/FZ$. Now when we meet the formula $(\exists x)\Box Fx$, we do not know what is the relevant description of the thing or things which are said to be necessarily instances of the character expressed by $Fx$, but there are only two possibilities to be considered. $(\exists x)\Box Fx$ may mean *There is something which under any description is necessarily F*, or it may mean *There is something which under some description is necessarily F*. If the first interpretation (*de re*) is that intended, $(\exists x)\Box Fx$ cannot express a true proposition unless $Fx$ is a truistic predicate and therefore entailed by any conceivable description. But this is as much as to say that the disputed formula is equivalent to $\Box(x)Fx$. If, on the other hand, the second interpretation is that intended, $(\exists x)\Box Fx$ cannot express a true proposition unless there is something which among its permissible descriptions has one entailing the predicate $Fx$. But this is as much as to say that the disputed formula is equivalent to $(\exists x)Fx$. Therefore $(\exists x)\Box Fx$ cannot on either interpretation represent a new kind of proposition. By a similar argument it can be shown that, if $(x)\Diamond Fx$ has any meaning at all, it must be equivalent either to $(x)Fx$ or to $\Diamond(\exists x)Fx$, and so here too it appears that there is no need to admit the operation of quantifiers across modal signs. We might indeed have avoided all this debate by retaining throughout the relational account of modality which we introduced in the last chapter; but in that case we should have overlooked the interesting development of language whereby it is possible to construct statements of the forms $\Box F[(\imath x)Gx]$ and $\Diamond F[(\imath x)Gx]$, and we should have been unable to give a plausible history of recent discussions about intensionality.

## 4. *Identity, Functions, and Classes*

In his *Begriffsschrift* and again in his *Grundgesetze der Arithmetik* Frege takes identity as a basic notion for which it is necessary to formulate special axioms. In *Principia Mathematica* (\*13·01), on the other hand, Whitehead and Russell avoid the need for special axioms of identity by introducing $X = Y$ as an abbreviation for $(f)[f!X \supset f!Y]$. The sign ! which they use here after the letter $f$ is intended to show that the functions under consideration are all *predicative* in a technical sense of that word. This restriction is required by Russell's Ramified Theory of Types, as we shall see in the next chapter, but the authors go on to point out that it involves no real loss of generality, since the Principle of Reducibility, which they introduce to modify the rigour of the Ramified Theory of Types, allows us to work with the definition as though it treated of all functions without qualification. Sometimes the distinction between predicative functions and others is said to be one of *order*, but this way of speaking is not the same as that usage in which discourse that requires intensional language may be said to be of higher order than discourse expressible in purely extensional language, and it is not sufficient to dispose of the difficulty connected with intensional language. If we admit the existence of intensional functions while using the definition just as it stands, we find ourselves committed to the curious conclusion that there can be no identity unknown to rational men. The morning star, it seems, cannot be identical with the evening star because there is at least one function, namely being known by all rational men to be identical with the morning star, which is satisfied by the former but not by the latter. For this reason what has been said above in reference to Frege's treatment of identity must be applied also *mutatis mutandis* to the treatment of the topic in *Principia Mathematica*. That is to say, the definition of identity given by Whitehead and Russell must be qualified in such a way that it refers only to extensional functions. Is there then any good reason for preferring one treatment to the other?

In Frege's system, as in *Principia Mathematica*, the theory of identity is supposed to be part of logic, but it is not quite clear why it is included, and a hostile critic might object that Frege has given us no general account of logic by which we can judge whether he has remained faithful to his programme at this point. When, however, the notion of identity is introduced by means of a definition, it seems evident at first sight that the theory must be part of logic. For now the signs of identity occur only as a device for the abbreviation of propositions which could be stated with signs that are all admittedly logical. But this apparent advantage can be gained only by use of the quantifier $(f)$ in the definition. It is true that according to his own explanations Frege's formula

$$x = y \supset (fx \supset fy)$$

should be treated as an abbreviation for

$$(f)[x = y \supset (fx \supset fy)].$$

But we have seen that the logician is entitled to use free variables of a special style for the expression of the universality which belongs to his own utterances. Taking advantage of this we can write

$$X = Y \supset (FX \supset FY)$$

in place of Frege's own formula, not indeed as a simple substitute, but rather as the expression of a truistic schema. In the system of

*Principia Mathematica*, on the other hand, the use of a *bound* functional variable is essential for the definition of identity. For while Whitehead and Russell wish us to understand that an expression of the form $X = Y$ may be regarded as an abbreviation for an expression of the form $(f)[f!X \supset f!Y]$, they certainly do not wish to suggest that any expression of the form $X = Y$ may be replaced wherever it occurs by an expression of the form $F!X \supset F!Y$, or vice versa. Now application of quantifiers to functional variables marks the transition to a calculus much more complicated than the simple or restricted calculus of propositional functions which we have considered so far in this chapter. If we think that this new calculus should be accounted part of logic, then we may say that Whitehead and Russell have reduced the theory of identity to logic, provided always that they can find some satisfactory way of qualifying their definition so that it deals only with nonintensional functions. But if for any reason we wish to talk of identity without raising for ourselves immediately all the difficulties of the new calculus, then we must return to Frege's course and present the theory of identity as a less comprehensive calculus in which two special axioms are added to the axioms and rules of the restricted functional calculus. One reason for doing this is precisely the fact that the theory of identity is closely bound up with the distinction of intensional and extensional language. Frege's distinction between *Sinn* and *Bedeutung* was first suggested to him by reflection on statements such as 'The morning star is identical with the evening star', and it may be the importance of this distinction in his thought which led him to introduce identity as a basic notion.

When he wrote his *Begriffsschrift*, Frege saw no need to make special provision for the enlarged calculus of functions in which quantifiers are applied to functional variables. But when he recast his system of logic for the purposes of his *Grundgesetze*, he added a new axiom of quantification which can be rendered in modern symbolism by the formula

$$(f)g_x(fx) \supset g_x(hx).$$

This means in effect that what holds for all functions of the first level with one argument holds for any of them. As in Frege's own script, the small letter written as subscript to the functional letter $g$ is supposed to show that any argument suitable for the succeeding bracket must be a function of the first level with one argument. It is a kind of binding prefix, though not a quantifier. Obviously the new axiom is very similar in character to the axiom of quantification for individual variables, namely,

$$(x)fx \supset fy.$$

But in Frege's system it is the only explicit authority for the application of quantifiers to functional variables, and is therefore by no means superfluous. Without this momentous innovation Frege could not even have made it seem plausible that arithmetic is reducible to logic. If he had thought it necessary to apply quantifiers to functional variables of the second and higher levels, he might perhaps have enunciated a separate axiom of quantification for each successive level. But we have seen that he felt ill at ease with formulae which involved functional variables of higher levels and that he tried to simplify his task by talking instead about classes and classes of classes.

It was probably the cumbrousness of his own notation that made Frege dislike formulae with bound functional variables. And this in turn was due to the contrast which he thought it necessary to make between functions and objects. But whatever we may think about Frege's general views about functions, we must admit that there is something new and strange in the use of bound functional variables. This becomes evident when we try to find a literal translation for the formulae in which they occur.

Although it is not easy to find strict equivalents in ordinary language for formulae with bound individual variables, that difficulty can usually be overcome by judicious use of 'thing' and various pronouns. Thus $(\exists x)[Fx.Gx]$ may be rendered as though it were an abbreviation of the near-English sentence *There is something such that it F's and it G's*. But when quantifiers are applied to functional variables, the grammar of the symbolism departs so far from that of ordinary language that it is no longer possible to give a literal, or word-for-sign, translation of the formulae. How, for example, are we to read $(\exists f)[fX.fY]$? When logicians construct a formula of this kind, they sometimes try to render it orally by the very-far-from-English sentence *There is some f such that Xf's and Yf's*. Such mixed jargon is obviously inelegant, but apart from that it is unsatisfactory because it fails to make clear the role of $f$. In the body of the formula the letter is taken properly enough to mark a gap that could be filled by a functional expression such as a verb, but in the prefix it is treated as though it were what mediaeval logicians called a general term of second intention, equivalent perhaps to 'function'. Having heard first the phrase 'there is some', we naturally expect to hear next a common noun, but later on we find that the letter which has been made to do duty as a noun must also take the place of a verb. Similar difficulties arise when quantifiers are applied to propositional variables. In each case the source of the trouble is the fact that, although English has words like 'somehow' and 'however', it contains no construction corresponding exactly to the use of a quantifier with a variable *expression* of the grammatical status of a verb or complete clause. If we want to say in natural language what is said in the symbolism of logic by the formula $(\exists f)[fX.fY]$, we can produce nothing nearer than *There is some character exemplified by X and also by Y*. This is indeed fairly close, but it is not a word-for-sign rendering of the logical symbols unless indeed we alter our conventions for the use of the latter, first by taking $f$ in the body of the formula as a gap sign which marks a place for a *designation* of a function and then by taking the ordering of the signs in any complex expression of the form $FX$ to mean that $F$ is exemplified by $X$.

Frege did not think it possible to talk about a function without grammatical impropriety, and for that reason he could not treat functional variables as signs which marked gaps to be filled by complete designations. In his view a function was essentially something incomplete, and he thought it inevitable that this peculiarity should be reflected in the form of the special axiom or axioms of quantification used for the enlarged calculus of functions. If we distinguish carefully between expression and designation, we can talk about functions without falling into Frege's perplexities, but the new interpretation of logical symbolism suggested in the last paragraph will not save us from the need for a special rule or axiom when we begin to apply quantifiers to functional variables. In the restricted calculus of functions we have rules for reasoning with expressions of the forms $(x)Fx$ and $(\exists x)Fx$, where $Fx$ is supposed to be an abbreviation for any functional expression containing $x$; but if we adopt the convention that $FX$ is short for $F$ *is exemplified by* $X$, our rules will no longer enable us to deal with formulae of such patterns as $(x)[Gx \supset Hx]$ and they will certainly not suffice to explain the application of quantifiers to variables in the position of $F$. There is nevertheless something unsatisfactory in the introduction of separate rules of quantification for different kinds of variables, and it seems desirable therefore to consider whether any simplification can be achieved by use of new symbolism.

One way out of the difficulty is to let $FX$ retain the sense it received from Frege but introduce a new functional constant $\eta$ with the meaning of 'exemplifies'. Since the new symbol is a kind of transitive verb, the signs which occur on the two sides of it in a simple formula must both be designations, and the meaning requires that the second at least should be a designation of a function. Thus as a variant for $FX$ we have $X\eta Y$, where $Y$ is short for §$xFx$. Sometimes indeed the first sign used with $\eta$ may designate an ordered sequence of two or more things while the second designates a character which can be exemplified if at all only in such a sequence. This will happen whenever a relational proposition is transcribed into the new notation. Instead of $G(X, Y)$ we then have $\langle X, Y \rangle \eta Z$, where $Z$ is short for $\S xyG(x, y)$. In yet other formulae both signs which go with $\eta$ may be designations of functions, i.e. when a function itself is said to exemplify some character. If, however, either or both of the designations which occur with $\eta$ in a simple formula is replaced by a variable, we get an expression which can serve as a matrix for general statements. Thus matrices of the forms $x\eta Y$ and $X\eta y$ will be equally open to quantification in accordance with the ordinary rules of quantification theory, and we may write for example $(\exists z)[X\eta z . Y\eta z]$ to express the proposition that there is some character which the things called $X$ and $Y$ both exemplify. Furthermore, apart from the simplification which it allows in the expression of general propositions about functions, the new notation has the great merit of making clear that the theory sometimes called the enlarged calculus of propositional functions is in effect the theory of exemplification. It would be foolish, of course, to suggest that $\eta$ should be taken as the sole functional expression of our language and used in the formulation of all propositions without exception. For when we wish to ascribe a definite attribute to a thing called $X$ there is obviously nothing to be gained from writing $X\eta \S yFy$ rather than $FX$; and in any case the possibility of designating a function always presupposes the possibility of expressing it. But it is an important fact that the enlarged calculus in which we talk of functions with complete generality can be presented as a system with one new sign not reducible to those of ordinary quantification theory. For this is as much as to say that it is the theory of the notion expressed by the sign.

When he discussed philosophical problems in German, Frege frequently spoke of a thing's falling under a concept, but for reasons which we have already examined he felt dissatisfied with such language and therefore never tried to develop a calculus of exemplification such as we have just suggested. On the other hand, the calculus of class-membership by which he tried to evade the difficulties of his own notation for applying quantifiers to functional variables is very similar in structure. For just as $FX$ may be rendered by $X\eta \S yFy$, so too it may be rendered by $X\epsilon \hat{y}Fy$, where $\epsilon$ is an abbreviation for 'is a member of'. And just as one thing's being related to another in a certain way can be regarded as the exemplification of a relational character by an ordered couple, so too it can be regarded as the membership

of that same ordered couple in a class of ordered couples.
Indeed the only important difference between the two calculi
is the condition of identity for their distinctive types of entity.
When he introduced a notation for classes in his *Grundgesetze*,
Frege laid down an axiom (V) which can be rendered in modern
symbolism by the formula

$$(\hat{x}Fx = \hat{y}Gy) \equiv (z)[Fz \equiv Gz].$$

This is as much as to say that for classes we have

$$(X = Y) \equiv (w)[w\epsilon X \equiv w\epsilon Y].$$

The corresponding proposition does not hold for characters or
attributes, and it would not even be correct to say for them

$$(X = Y) \equiv \square(w)[w\eta X \equiv w\eta Y].$$

For while it follows from the identity of two characters that they
must necessarily be exemplified by the same things, the converse
is not true. All equilateral triangles are necessarily equiangular
triangles, and vice versa, but the meaning of 'equilateral triangle'
is not the same as the meaning of 'equiangular triangle'.

Historically it is of some interest that the development of
mathematical logic, which began with the attempts of Leibniz to
formulate a calculus *de continentibus et contentis*, should reach its
culmination in the work of Frege, Whitehead, and Russell with
a theory of class-membership. But we must not attach too much
importance to a similarity in name. Leibniz did not distinguish
clearly between the relation of a member to a class and the
relation of a class to a super-class of which it is a part, but most
of what he had to say was appropriate only to the second relation. Certainly Boole's algebra of classes, which we regard as a
realization of Leibniz's project, is a theory of the interrelations
of classes whose members, if they have any, are all drawn from
a common domain of individuals called the universe of discourse.
In effect this calculus is a fragment of the restricted calculus of
propositional functions. Frege's calculus, on the other hand, is
concerned not only with relations of inclusion, exclusion, and
overlap, between classes of the same level, but also with the
membership of one class in another. In short it is Cantor's
theory of sets presented as derivative from the enlarged calculus
of propositional functions. Even if he had not been worried by
the application of quantifiers to functional variables, Frege
would probably have wished to talk about classes for the same
reason as led Cantor to talk of sets. For the carrying out of
his programme it is necessary to show (*a*) that arithmetic

can be elaborated within the theory of sets and (*b*) that the theory of sets can properly be described as part of logic. Whether or not these points can be established will be considered in the following chapters. Here we need only consider what is involved in talking of classes or sets rather than of functions.

Although Frege regarded statements about classes as substitutes in certain contexts for statements about functions, he did not think it possible that classes and functions should be the same. According to his explanations statements about classes can be substituted for statements about functions only when these latter statements are such as would hold true for all functions materially equivalent to those under consideration. This view was shared by Whitehead and Russell when they wrote the first edition of *Principia Mathematica*. But in the new introduction which he wrote for the second edition of that work Russell declared that he no longer found any need to distinguish between classes and functions because he thought that all functions were extensional, i.e. accepted every assertion of the form

$$(x)[Fx \equiv Gx] \supset [H(F\hat{x}) \equiv H(G\hat{x})],$$

where in accordance with his convention $F\hat{x}$ and $G\hat{x}$ are designations of functions.[1] If he means by this that there is no provision in his symbolism for expressing intensional functions, then what he says is no doubt correct, but it is not very important. If, however, he means that all functions of functions expressible in any symbolism whatever are extensional, his pronouncement is of great philosophical interest but highly controversial, to say the least. This is in fact the context in which the debate about intensionality started and from which the rather puzzling modern use of 'intensional' and 'extensional' is derived.

In the past many logicians have talked of classes because they hoped in this way to avoid difficulties about universals. They have supposed, for example, that a class of material things might be admitted as an entity even by the most hard-headed, because it could itself be regarded as a composite material thing even if its members were not all collected together in one place like the stones of a heap. But Russell and his followers are under no illusions on this score. Quine, for example, points out that the class of states of the U.S.A. is not the same as the class of counties of the U.S.A., although the territory comprised in the states is the same as the territory comprised in the counties.[2] If there is danger in talking of abstractions, we shall not escape from it by using the

---

[1] *Principia Mathematica*, 2nd ed., vol. i, p. xxxix.
[2] *Mathematical Logic*, § 22.

class notation, since classes are themselves abstractions. Nor shall we by this means avoid the need to use functional expressions other than $\epsilon$ at some level is our language. For every designation of a class is either a sign of the form $\hat{x}Fx$ or one whose meaning and reference are determined by recourse to a sign or signs of this kind. Sometimes, indeed, a class may be indicated by enumeration of its members, i.e. by construction of a class sign of the form $\hat{x}(x = Y \lor x = Z \lor \ldots)$, but it is evident that they cannot all be indicated in this way. For if they were, all true statements of class membership would be tautologous. In modern times logicians who prefer to talk of classes rather than of functions do so for the purpose of evading the problems of intensionality, and sometimes they even say that the classes of which they speak *are universals*.

In this connexion it is interesting to notice that logicians who agree in showing a preference for the class notation may nevertheless disagree much as philosophers of the past disagreed about universals. According to Quine realism, conceptualism, and nominalism are all to be found in the works of modern writers on the foundations of mathematics.[1] By 'realism' he means apparently a willingness to assume the existence of classes and classes of classes whenever our symbolism suggests the possibility of such assumptions, by 'conceptualism' a policy of admitting the existence of classes only when we are in a position to establish their constitution, and by 'nominalism' an attempt to dispense with any assumption of the existence of classes. In practice the three attitudes are supposed to show themselves in greater or less willingness to apply quantifiers to class variables. It is doubtful whether this use of the old labels can serve any good purpose, especially if (as often happens) realism is mistakenly identified with Platonism. But the fact that Quine and some others feel an inclination to talk in this way shows very clearly that they do not think it possible to dispose of all problems about universals merely by adopting a class notation. And here, of course, they are right.

When in a so-called higher-order functional calculus quantifiers are applied to variables which mark places for functional signs, the essential novelty of the resulting system may be overlooked because no new symbol has been introduced. On the other hand, if we present the system explicitly as a theory of exemplification or membership, we may perhaps overlook the fact that different sorts of basic entities are now assumed as possible values for the variables of our underlying general logic or quantification theory. In this connexion Hao Wang has written:

[1] *From a Logical Point of View*, pp. 127–9.

'The contrast between one-sorted and many-sorted quantification theories is more basic than that between first-order and higher-order predicate calculi. While higher-order predicate calculi and theories formulated therein all are many-sorted systems, there are many-sorted theories such as geometry dealing with points, lines, and planes which are not formulated in higher-order predicate calculi. While many-sorted quantification theories treat all predicates on an equal basis, higher-order predicate calculi reserve a special pedestal for the membership relation. Indeed, an $n$-th order predicate calculus is nothing but an $n$-sorted theory which contains a single axiom (the axiom of comprehension) asserting that every meaningful formula of the system defines a set.'[1]

A theory is many-sorted if it has variables of different kinds, each restricted to a different range of objects as possible values. Differences of kind among variables may be indicated typographically, but this is not essential; for it can be shown sufficiently by context. If in a version of plane geometry we see the phrase *x lies on y*, we know that the letter $x$ marks a place for designations of points and the letter $y$ a place for designations of lines. Nevertheless, if the theory is really many-sorted, it must be assumed that the rules of quantification are repeated for each separate kind of variable. They will, of course, be precisely the same in form for each kind; but the requirement that they should be repeated is irksome, and it is natural to ask whether we cannot do all we want to do with a one-sorted general logic in which rules of quantification are formulated once only.

The answer seems to be that we can transcribe every many-sorted theory into a standard one-sorted idiom if we allow our variables to take as their range of values the sum of all the categories of the theory under consideration and then re-introduce the distinction of categories by means of a number of categorial predicates (e.g. 'is a natural number', 'is a point', 'is a line') with which we can formulate conditions for the theorems of the system. Thus instead of saying:

$$x(y+z) = xy+xz,$$

where it is to be understood that the variables have for their range of values only the category of natural numbers, we say:

*If x, y, z are natural numbers, $x(y+z) = xy+xz$.*

This standardization (as it is sometimes called) is a procedure we follow without hesitation in ordinary speech, and it seems

[1] 'On Denumerable Bases of Formal Systems', *Mathematical Interpretation of Formal Systems* by Th. Skolem and others, (1955), p. 76. The term 'many-sorted' was introduced by A. Schmidt, 'Über deduktive Theorien mit mehreren Sorten von Grunddingen', *Mathematische Annalen*, cxv (1938), pp. 485–506.

unexceptionable. It is interesting also to notice that in many cases at least the transcription of a many-sorted theory into a standard one-sorted idiom can be carried through without the addition of any new categorial predicates. In these cases the distinction of categories can be made by the formulation of category conditions with the symbols already available.[1]

Among many-sorted theories that which deals with membership, i.e. the theory of sets, has a special importance, as mathematicians recognize when they use the title 'elementary' for those branches of their study which do not presuppose it. But it is by no means obvious that this is the only many-sorted theory required for the completion of science. Sometimes Russell and other philosophers who draw inspiration from his work have talked as though there can be only one basic category of individuals and apart from that various categories of sets. Conceivably their thesis may be correct. It is at least an interesting piece of philosophical speculation which may some day suggest a detailed programme for the unification of science. But we fall into error if we think that it is guaranteed by considerations of logic. In different contexts entities of different categories may be considered as individuals, and so the letters which logicians sometimes call individual variables mark gaps that may be filled with any names or designations which complete their formulae in significant fashion. If metaphysics is concerned, as Aristotle thought, with the nature of basic entities, its questions cannot be answered from considerations of formal logic, not because this latter study is independent of the structure of the world, but rather because it is concerned with patterns which may recur at different levels.

## 5. *Necessity and Language*

Although Frege had much to say about the principles of syntax and always thought of himself as the designer of a new language which would be especially suitable for scientific purposes, he did not, like many of his predecessors, regard logic as an *ars sermocinalis*, and he certainly did not hold the view of Hobbes and Berkeley that logical necessity is imposed by human rules for the use of words. On the contrary, when he said that arithmetic could be reduced to logic, he insisted that he did not mean to treat it either as a branch of psychology or as a branch of philology. For him logic was the most general of all sciences about reality, the *doctrina formarum* of which Leibniz had written, and only connected

---

[1] Hao Wang, 'Logic of Many-sorted Theories', *Journal of Symbolic Logic*, xvii (1952), pp. 105–16.

NECESSITY AND LANGUAGE        629

with grammar because it treated of the basic patterns which every natural language must be able to express. This was also the doctrine of Whitehead and Russell when they wrote *Principia Mathematica*. But in more recent times the conventionalist theory of necessity has been adopted by many philosophers, and logic is even treated by some as though it were identical with semantics, i.e. with the study of those linguistic rules or customs which give words their significance. The change seems to date from the publication of the *Tractatus Logico-Philosophicus* by Ludwig Wittgenstein in 1921, though it is almost certain that Wittgenstein did not at first intend anything of the kind.

In the years before 1914, when he was studying in Cambridge with Russell, Wittgenstein remarked that truths of logic could not be satisfactorily defined as all those expressible in a certain vocabulary but might be distinguished from others by a special character which he called tautology, meaning by this not repetitiousness but rather vacuity. Russell referred to this suggestion as follows in a work which he wrote while serving a sentence of imprisonment for his pacifist activities:

'We may take the axiom of infinity as an example of a proposition which, though it can be enunciated in logical terms, cannot be asserted by logic to be true. All the propositions of logic have a characteristic which used to be expressed by saying that they were analytic, or that their contradictories were self-contradictory. This mode of statement, however, is not satisfactory. The law of contradiction is merely one among logical propositions; it has no special pre-eminence; and the proof that the contradictory of some proposition is self-contradictory is likely to require other principles of deduction beside the law of contradiction. Nevertheless, the characteristic of logical propositions that we are in search of is the one which was felt, and intended to be defined, by those who said that it consisted in deducibility from the law of contradiction. This characteristic, which for the moment we may call tautology, obviously does not belong to the assertion that the number of individuals in the universe is $n$, whatever number $n$ may be. . . . Logical propositions are such as can be known *a priori*, without study of the actual world. . . . This is a characteristic, not of logical propositions in themselves, but of the way in which we know them. It has, however, a bearing upon the question what their nature may be, since there are some kinds of propositions which it would be very difficult to suppose we could know without experience. It is clear that the definition of "logic" also must be sought by trying to give a new definition of the old notion of "analytic" propositions. Although we can no longer be satisfied to define logical propositions as those that follow from the law of contradiction, we can and must still admit that they are a wholly different class of propositions from those that we come to know empirically. They all have the characteristic which, a moment ago, we agreed to call "tautology". This combined with the fact that they can be expressed wholly in terms of variables and logical constants (a logical constant being something which remains constant in a proposition when *all* its constituents are changed)—will give the definition of logic or pure mathematics. For the moment I do not know how to define tautology. (The importance of "tautology" for a definition of mathematics was pointed out to me by my former pupil Ludwig Wittgenstein, who was working on the problem. I do not know whether he has solved it, or even whether he is alive or dead.')[1]

Although he maintained that the truths of logic were in a certain sense vacuous, Wittgenstein did not think that they were unimportant, and at this stage in his development he was far from believing that they were arbitrary creations of mankind. In one of the more connected passages of his *Tractatus* he wrote:

'Logical sentences (*Sätze*) describe the scaffolding of the world, or rather they present it. They "treat" of nothing. They presuppose that names have reference and that atomic sentences (*Elementarsätze*) have sense. And this is their connexion with the world. It is clear that it must show something about the world that certain combinations of symbols—which essentially have a definite character—are tautologies. Herein lies the decisive point. We said that in the symbols which we use something is arbitrary, something not. In logic only the latter expresses: but this means that in logic it is not *we* who express, by means of signs, what we want, but in logic the nature of the essentially necessary signs itself asserts. That is to say, if we know the logical syntax of any sign language, then all the theses (*Sätze*) of logic are already given.'[2]

The tautological character of logical assertions was supposed to be made clear by the truth-table method of exposition, and it was thought to be a matter of no great importance that the truth-conditions of universal and existential assertions could not be presented in tables of finite complexity. The emphasis which Wittgenstein placed on his definitions of truth-functions by truth-tables was due, of course, to his conviction that logic did not deal with any special class of things or relations in the world but solely with the nature of what we might perhaps call logical complexity. In one place he writes:

'A truth-operation is the way in which a truth-function arises from atomic sentences . . . Every sentence is the result of truth-operations on atomic sentences . . . All truth-functions are results of the successive applications of a finite number of truth-operations to atomic sentences. Here it becomes clear that there are no such things as "logical objects" or "logical constants" (in the sense of Frege and Russell).'[3]

[1] *Introduction to Mathematical Philosophy* (1919), pp. 202–5.
[2] *Tractatus Logico-Philosophicus*, 6.124. Here and in later quotations we have departed occasionally from the English translation of Ogden and Ramsey.
[3] Ibid. 5.3–5.4.

But Wittgenstein was not content to say that logical truths were tautologies. He maintained also that the tautologies of logic were the only necessary truths and the whole realm of *a priori* knowledge:

'From the existence or non-existence of one state of affairs (*Sachverhalt*, i.e. possible atomic fact) we cannot infer the existence or non-existence of another. States of affairs are independent one of another.'[1]

'Logical research means the investigation of *all regularity*. And outside logic all is accident . . . A necessity for one thing to happen because another has happened does not exist. There is only *logical* necessity. At the basis of the whole modern view of the world lies the illusion that the so-called laws of nature are the explanations of natural phenomena.'[2]

The result is something like the philosophy of Hume, and it is not surprising that in the dozen years after the publication of the *Tractatus* the Logical Positivists of the Vienna circle led by Moritz Schlick tried to combine Wittgenstein's account of logic with the Humean tradition they had inherited from Ernst Mach. But there is an important difference between the two philosophical systems. Whereas Hume tried to recommend his conclusions by psychological analysis, Wittgenstein confined himself for the most part to oracular pronouncements without any supporting arguments except such as could be derived from consideration of the symbolism of *Principia Mathematica*. The explanation seems to be that he simply assumed without question the sufficiency of this symbolism as the syntactical apparatus for an ideal language. We have noticed already that he refused to recognize the possibility of an irreducibly intensional language which allows for the designation of propositions in contexts such as 'Jones believes that the earth is flat'. When he talks of logic as a set of tautologies and refuses to allow any importance to rules of inference such as Frege, Whitehead, and Russell had thought it necessary to add to their primitive propositions,[3] his reason seems to be that rules of inference which allow us to pass from one formula of *Principia Mathematica* to another cannot themselves be formulated within the special symbolism of that work. The way in which a language provides for what he sometimes calls 'the logic of the world'[4] can, he thinks, be shown in a language but never stated. This thesis must be untrue, if it is supposed to apply to all natural languages. For, as Wittgenstein himself admits at the end of the *Tractatus*, its truth would involve the senselessness of the pronouncement in which it was asserted.[5] But it is certainly correct that the special

---

[1] Ibid. 2.061–2.062.     [2] Ibid. 6.3–6.371.
[3] Ibid. 5.132 and 6.126.
[4] Ibid. 6.22.     [5] Ibid. 6.54.

symbolism of *Principia Mathematica* does not allow for the translation of all the English letterpress of that work.

Although Wittgenstein thought that the world consisted of independent atomic facts which could be pictured by atomic sentences (in that metaphorical sense of 'picture' in which the *fact* that the word 'out' appears after a man's name on a board at the foot of a staircase may perhaps be said to picture the *fact* that he is out of his room on that staircase at that time),[1] he never gave any examples or explained what kind of facts he had in mind. Some of his followers, wishing to connect his work with that of Hume for the reasons given above, jumped to the conclusion that atomic facts must be about sense-data and sensibilia. This was also the assumption of Russell in his lectures of 1918 on *The Philosophy of Logical Atomism*[2] and in a number of later works. But Wittgenstein did not commit himself to such a view, thinking apparently that the question was one to be settled empirically and therefore in some way below the dignity of his work:

'It is clear that we have a concept of the atomic sentence apart from its special logical form. Where, however, we can build symbols according to a system, there this system is the logically important thing and not the single symbols. . . . If we know on purely logical grounds that there must be atomic sentences, then this must be known by everyone who understands sentences in their unanalysed form. . . . It is the *application* of logic which decides what atomic sentences there are. What lies in its application logic cannot anticipate. . . . If I cannot indicate atomic sentences *a priori*, then it must lead to obvious nonsense to try to indicate them.'[3]

Clearly at this stage in his development Wittgenstein made a sharp distinction between the syntax and the vocabulary of science, thinking of the former as known *a priori* in a study of logic such as *Principia Mathematica* and of the latter as learnt only in connexion with particular experiences. He was right, no doubt, to try to defend the formal purity of logic, but there is something very strange in his refusal to consider more carefully the problem of its application. And it is this refusal which leads to his curious doctrine that there is no necessity outside of logic.

Like Frege, Wittgenstein introduces negation with a truth-functional definition, i.e. by saying that $\sim P$ is true if and only if $P$ is false, and sometimes he seems to think it is sufficient to say that $P$ is false if the state of affairs which it pictures is not realized.[4] But in one place he says:

---

[1] *Tractatus Logico-Philosophicus*, 1, 2.1, 2.14.
[2] *Logic and Knowledge*, ed. R. C. March, pp. 178–281.
[3] *Tractatus*, 5.555–5.5571.                    [4] Ibid. 2.06, 4.1.

'The negating statement (*der verneinende Satz*) determines a logical place *other* than that determined by the negated statement. The negating statement determines a logical place with the help of the logical place of the negated statement, by describing it as lying outside this latter.'[1]

Taken seriously, this implies that the possibility of using a negative particle significantly depends on the objective incompatibility of various thinkable states of affairs. For the otherness or exclusion of which Wittgenstein speaks here is presupposed by the construction of negative statements and must therefore be a relation independent of our use of a negative sign, though elsewhere he assumes that there can be no such incompatibility. Perhaps it was his loose use of the word 'logical' that blinded Wittgenstein to this inconsistency in his system. When he says that there is no necessity except that of logic, he seems to mean by 'logic' the theory of our use of signs; but when he talks of the logic of the world and speaks in particular of positions in logical space, he seems to mean something which might more properly be called metaphysics. If there is, as his words suggest, a system of alternatives within which we select items for affirmation or denial whenever we utter statements of contingent fact, the structure of that system must certainly embody all the principles of impossibility and necessity that can ever be formulated, but the study of the system will not be the restricted formal science which Frege called logic.

Apparently Wittgenstein was sometimes worried by misgivings about his doctrine of logical necessity. Towards the end of his *Tractatus* he wrote at unusual length:

'As there is only a *logical* necessity, so there is only a *logical* impossibility. For two colours, e.g., to be at one place in the visual field is impossible, that is, logically impossible, since it is excluded by the logical structure of colour. Let us consider how this contradiction presents itself in physics. Somewhat as follows: that a particle cannot at the same time have two velocities, i.e. that it cannot at the same time be in two places, i.e. that particles in different places at the same time cannot be identical. (It is clear that the logical product of two atomic sentences can neither be a tautology nor a contradiction. The assertion that a point in the visual field has two different colours at the same time is a contradiction.)'[2]

Critics soon noticed the insufficiency of this attempt to exhibit incompatibility of colours as a case of logical (i.e. formal) contradiction, and in 1929 Wittgenstein himself wrote with reference to this example: 'Atomic propositions, though they cannot

[1] Ibid. 4.0641.  [2] Ibid. 6.375–6.3751.

contradict, may exclude one another.'[1] This admission is fatal to the doctrine of the earlier work, but Wittgenstein was still so much under the influence of his own loose usage that he tried to present this change as a reform of *logic* rather than as an abandonment of his thesis that there is no impossibility outside logic.

It is evident on reflection that no statement can ascribe a character to a thing unless it thereby excludes some other character. Even Spinoza, who thought that there was only one substance, God or Nature, and might therefore be inclined to blur the outlines of things, said that all determination is negation ;[2] and it may be that no philosopher has ever tried to talk of a specification compatible with every other specification. But many philosophers have written as though they thought that contrary opposition of predicates was something instituted by human beings without consideration of the nature of things. Thus P. F. Strawson has said : 'It is ... our own activity of making language through using it, our determination of the limits of the application of words, that makes inconsistency possible.'[3] It is true, of course, that the inconsistency of words is established by human customs in the use of words; but our determination of the limits of the application of a general word is not selection of all the particular things to which we shall thereafter apply it. Rather it is selection of the specific varieties of character that may be exhibited by things to which we shall apply the word, and these specific varieties must be inconsistent in a non-linguistic sense. When definition is conceived as the fixing of boundaries (and that is the original sense of the word), the space within which it operates must be supposed to have for its points not individuals but perfectly specific universals which are mutually exclusive.

Although Wittgenstein presented formal logic in his *Tractatus* with an unnatural and misleading disregard for its application, he maintained there what might be called an absolutist view of logical truths. That is to say, he talked as though there was, and could be, only one system of logic, namely a simplified version of that presented in *Principia Mathematica*. But among some who might be called his followers the emphasis he had placed on the importance of symbolic conventions soon led to sympathetic consideration of the possibility of alternative logics such as those suggested by Post, Łukasiewicz, and Heyting. Thus we find Carnap writing in 1934:

'*In logic there are no morals*. Everyone is at liberty to build up his own logic, i.e. his own form of language, as he wishes. All that is required

[1] 'Some remarks on Logical Form', *Aristotelian Society, Supplementary Volume*, ix (1929), pp. 162–71, esp. p. 168.    [2] *Ep.* 50.    [3] *Introduction to Logical Theory*, p. 9.

of him is that, if he wishes to discuss it, he must state his methods clearly, and give syntactical rules instead of philosophical arguments. The tolerant attitude here suggested is, as far as special mathematical calculi are concerned, the attitude which is tacitly shared by the majority of mathematicians.'[1]

Inasmuch as it has encouraged the investigation of alternative formal systems and so helped to throw light on the structure of the generally accepted systems of two-valued formal logic, this conventionalist attitude has had good effects. For those who think of logic as an uninterpreted calculus it is indeed the proper attitude to adopt. But if logic is supposed to be connected, as Carnap implies, with language, i.e. if its formulae are to be interpreted as laws about negation, conjunction, universality, and the rest, conventionalism is a poor philosophy of logic, since it presupposes another view which it professes to reject. When, as Carnap urges, we set out explicitly a sequence of syntactical rules or conventions, we must use some language to formulate them, and reliance on this language inevitably carries with it acceptance of some logical principles which are not established by convention alone. Thus in order to express any rule for our new symbolism we must use some device for expressing universality, and for most we need also a device for expressing conditional dependence. With these we naturally take for granted the appropriate logical principles; and when we have finished, we do not call our new system logic in the ordinary sense unless it reproduces some of the principles we already assume.[2] In reply to Carnap's remark that there are no morals in logic we may therefore say (i) that logic in the proper sense consists essentially of restrictive laws about the possible combinations of propositions, and (ii) that such laws cannot be introduced by conventions made without knowledge of logical restrictions, any more than moral laws can be introduced by conventions made without knowledge of moral obligations. The conventionalist theory of logic is indeed strangely like the social contract theory of justice which Plato puts into the mouth of Glaucon in the second book of his *Republic*.

In the period of forty years after the first publication of his *Tractatus* Wittgenstein's views about logic became widely known and very influential among philosophers of a positivist or anti-metaphysical cast. During the process of popularization the master's doctrine was inevitably modified in various respects,

---

[1] *The Logical Syntax of Language* (English translation, 1937), § 17.
[2] This argument against conventionalism is presented with cogent detail by W. V. Quine in his essay, 'Truth by Convention' contributed in 1936 to *Philosophical Essays for A. N. Whitehead* and reprinted in *Readings in Philosophical Analysis* (ed. Feigl and Sellars), 1949, pp. 250–73.

partly through the efforts of admirers to systematize his oracular utterances and partly through the spread of reports about his later oral teaching, but a good deal also through the simplifying zeal of persons who were more interested in attacking metaphysics than in elucidating the theory of deduction. What has emerged is a new version of Hobbesian conventionalism in which not only the arithmetical theorems discussed by Frege but all truths ascertainable *a priori* are said to be analytic or logically necessary and therefore merely tautologies true by definition, that is to say, uninformative by-products of human activity in the making of rules for the use of symbols. Sometimes, however, those who declare that statements of necessary truth tell us nothing about the world go on to remark that tautological formulae may be used to give instruction about linguistic rules, as when, for example, a grownup says to a child 'An oculist is an eye-doctor', meaning thereby to teach the child the use of the comparatively rare English word 'oculist'. And so it is often maintained that an utterance of a tautological formula is informative if, and only if, it is taken as short for a remark about a language, namely for a remark to the effect that the rules of the language in which it is formulated are such as to make it tautological.

Any philosophical simplification which attains such wide popularity as this doctrine has achieved must contain some important truth, that is to say, some truth which requires emphasis at the time; and it is easy to see what the truth is in this case. Anything we come to know *a priori* is a second-order truth about the relations of propositions or a truism derivative from such a truth, and in either case it is learnt by reflection on the meanings of words or other symbols. An animal such as a dog may perhaps be said to know a contingent fact such as that there are two sheep in a field, but it seems absurd to say that a dog can know even a very simple truth of arithmetic such as the proposition that $2+2 = 4$; and the reason can scarcely be that all non-human animals lack the special kind of intuition which according to Kant enables us to learn arithmetical truths. Many misleading accounts of *a priori* knowledge have been inspired by Plato's notion of contemplation ($\theta\epsilon\omega\rho\acute{\iota}\alpha$) as a kind of intellectual gazing in which the soul may read off facts about super-sensible objects; and if we are to free ourselves from the influence of these, it is no doubt important that we should realize the connexion of *a priori* knowledge with the use of symbols. But the simplifying conventionalism of the twentieth century has produced other results which are by no means improvements in our intellectual apparatus. In particular it has lead to the blurring of two valuable distinctions.

First, those who adopt this view assume that the terms 'analytic', *a priori*, and 'necessary', taken respectively from logic, theory of knowledge, and metaphysics, are coextensive. No doubt every proposition which is analytically true can be known *a priori* and every proposition which can be known *a priori* is necessary. But it is by no means obvious that the converse relations hold. If 'analytic' is understood in the sense of Frege, there may well be truths known *a priori* which are not analytic because they do not follow from laws of formal logic even when explicit definitions are admitted as new transformation rules. An example which has often been discussed is the proposition that nothing can be both red and green all over at the same time. Another is the proposition that the relation of temporal precedence is transitive but irreflexive. Furthermore, if we can ever be sure that certain perceptible characters and relations provide a model satisfying the postulates of an abstract geometry, this too must be a piece of knowledge *a priori* but not analytic. It is not possible to show in the same way that there are necessary truths (i.e. truths without alternatives) which *cannot* be known *a priori*; for production of an example would clearly involve a claim to *a priori* knowledge. But it is at least conceivable that there are such. We commonly admit that there are truths of mathematics which no one in fact knows, and it does not seem absurd to suggest that there may be necessary truths about unperceived qualities or relations which no one can ever know because (as Locke might say) no one has the requisite ideas.

The situation is even worse when, as sometimes happens, the three terms 'analytic', *a priori*, and 'necessary' are assumed to be not only coextensive but also synonymous, so that any one of them may serve as contradictory to any of the three corresponding terms 'synthetic', 'empirical', and 'contingent'. For an example we may take A. J. Ayer's *definition* of analytic and synthetic propositions (i.e. in his usage, statements): 'A proposition is analytic when its validity depends only on the definitions of the symbols it contains, and synthetic when its validity is determined by the facts of experience.'[1] Obviously such confusion makes Kant's notion of synthetic *a priori* truths seem completely absurd, though this notion has been accepted in recent times by mathematicians as great as Frege, Poincaré, Brouwer, and Hilbert. It has in fact been suggested that the phrase 'synthetic *a priori*' is no better than a mystifying substitute for 'contingent necessary'.[2] But that is not all. At the same time Frege's thesis that truths of arithmetic

---

[1] *Language, Truth, and Logic* (1936), p. 103.
[2] P. F. Strawson, *Introduction to Logical Theory*, p. 263.

are analytic becomes indistinguishable from the triviality that such truths are known *a priori*. And even the positivist assertion that all *a priori* truths are analytic becomes a simple and therefore pointless tautology. Since, however, positivists do not all behave as though their main doctrine were a simple tautology, it seems that in this context some of them must commit a mistake like that which has been called in ethics the naturalistic fallacy, namely the mistake of equating in their theory words which are ordinarily used to perform different tasks and then going on to use the words as though they had not been equated.

Secondly, modern conventionalism confuses logical and linguistic rules in a way that leads to serious misunderstanding. We have seen an example of such confusion already in a quotation from Carnap, but we must now investigate the tendency a little farther. When philosophers say that necessary truths are all established by linguistic convention they seem to have at the back of their minds the notion that (as Wittgenstein said) the world consists of facts which are all independent and contingent and that what men call necessary truths are no more than shadows or projections of the rules they themselves have adopted for speaking and writing. So powerful is the influence of this simplified picture that conventionalists sometimes regret the prevailing use of the one word 'truth' for talk of contingent and necessary truths. In their view it would be better to keep the two notions clearly apart by talking instead of facts and conventions. If it is objected that there is something paradoxical in the equation of 'necessary' and 'conventional', they reply that in application to a truth the word 'necessary' expresses no more than the speaker's resolution to stand by a certain form of words in all circumstances. There are, they say, no alternatives to a necessary truth *within the speaker's language*, but only because he himself has limited his language in that way. Since they also maintain that (as Wittgenstein said) necessity is all logical necessity, they are naturally led on to say that logical statements are linguistic statements of a certain kind, namely statements about linguistic inconsistency (or relations definable by reference to this) which can be translated in full from one language to another.[1] The provision about translation is put in to meet the objection that logic is not commonly supposed to be concerned with any particular language. According to P. F. Strawson:

'The important thing is to see that when you draw the boundaries of the applicability of words in one language and then connect the words of that language with those of another by translation rules, there is no

[1] P. F. Strawson, *Introduction to Logical Theory*, p. 11.

need to draw the boundaries again for the second language. They are already drawn. This is why (or partly why) logical statements framed in one language are not just about that language.'[1]

If this means that logical rules are rules for all possible languages, it amounts in effect to an admission that they are not conventional and therefore not linguistic in any ordinary sense of that word but rather requirements to be satisfied in the making of what we ordinarily call linguistic rules. Sometimes, however, philosophers of this persuasion talk of the logic of ordinary language and even of the 'logical behaviour' of particular English words, as though they were engaged in some sort of *a priori* philology. It has been stated, for example, *as a point of logic* that attention is a polymorphous concept because the English word 'attend' may cover many different activities. No doubt the English word 'attend' has many different uses, but if logic is an *a priori* science it cannot claim this discovery, since the existence of the various uses is an historical accident. In German, as it happens, there is no single word with the same range of application as 'attend', though German is not a notably poorer language than English.

We have seen already that inconsistency of general words presupposes incompatibility of characters. From this it follows immediately that necessity cannot be merely a product of linguistic rules and customs. It is, of course, an historical accident that the sounds 'red', 'yellow', 'green', and 'blue' are used as they are in communication by speakers of the English language, and a truism that any language in which we can find exact renderings for the four English words must contain sounds subject to rules like those holding in English for 'red', 'yellow', 'green', and 'blue'. But it is neither an historical accident nor a truism (at least in the pejorative sense of that word) that there is a range of distinct hues which can be divided as we divide it by use of our colour words. Anyone who accepts conventionalism ignores this and thereby commits himself in practice to the view that general words are merely names with multiple denotations. John Stuart Mill recognized this mistake in the work of Hobbes and devised his theory of connotation to remedy it; but, as often happens in the history of philosophy, the error has reappeared in a new guise. Instead of saying 'The world consists of individuals: universals belong to language' modern conventionalists say 'The world consists of facts: necessities belong to language.'

If our argument is correct, the earlier heresy is implicit in the later. But apart from this, it is interesting to notice that the later

[1] Ibid., p. 12.

heresy can be refuted directly by a consideration like that which is generally admitted to be fatal to the earlier. Just as individuals are essentially correlative to universals and therefore inconceivable by themselves, so facts which are contingent in the sense of belonging to ranges of possible alternatives are essentially correlative to laws of necessity or impossibility and therefore inconceivable without the latter. This argument assumes a notion of possibility which is ignored by conventionalists, but even within their own assumptions it can be argued that, if convention makes necessary propositions necessary, convention must also make contingent propositions contingent, that is to say, non-necessary. Here the consequent is unacceptable to conventionalists—unless indeed they take it to be a version of the trivially true thesis that convention determines what forms of words shall express contingent propositions, in which case they must interpret the antecedent in an equally harmless fashion. For if it is not merely trivial, the consequent must mean that the facts of which the world consists are neither necessary nor contingent in themselves. We shall see later that some philosophers have defended such a view, but they do not call themselves conventionalists and they have been attacked by those who accept the title.

Wittgenstein's ideas have had more influence among philosophers than among mathematical logicians. Thus Tarski wrote in 1936: 'The concept of *tautology* (i.e. of a statement which "says nothing about reality") . . . to me personally seems rather vague . . . but has been of fundamental importance for the philosophical discussions of L. Wittgenstein and the whole Vienna circle.'[1] At this time it had recently been shown by Gödel (in a proof which we shall have occasion to notice later) that the ordinary notion of consequence does not coincide with that of formal derivability. With this new discovery in mind Tarski wrote:

'In every deductive theory (apart from certain theories of a particularly elementary nature), however much we supplement the ordinary rules of inference by new purely structural rules, it is possible to construct sentences which follow, in the usual sense, from the theorems of this theory, but which nevertheless cannot be proved in this theory on the basis of the accepted rules of inference. In order to obtain the proper concept of consequence, which is close in essentials to the common concept, we must resort to quite different methods and apply quite different conceptual apparatus in defining it.'[2]

The method which he then proposed was in essentials that of

[1] 'On the Concept of Logical Consequence', first published in Polish in *Przegląd Filozoficzny*, xxxix (1936), pp. 58–68, reprinted in English in *Logic, Semantics, Metamathematics* (1956), pp. 409–20, esp. pp. 419–20.    [2] Ibid., pp. 412–13.

Bolzano, though at the time of his first publication on the subject he knew nothing of this part of Bolzano's work.

Tarski himself has summarized his account of the consequence relation as follows:

'Let $L$ be any class of sentences. We replace all extra-logical constants which occur in the sentences belonging to $L$ by corresponding variables, like constants being replaced by like variables, and unlike by unlike. In this way we obtain a class $L'$ of sentential functions. An arbitrary sequence of objects which satisfies every sentential function of the class $L'$ will be called a *model* or *realization of the class L of sentences* (in just this sense one usually speaks of models of an axiom system of a deductive theory). If in particular the class $L$ consists of a single sentence $X$, we shall also call the model of the class $L$ the *model of the sentence X*. In terms of these concepts we can define the concept of logical consequence as follows:

*The sentence X follows logically from the sentences of the class K if, and only if, every model of the class K is also a model of the sentence X.*'[1]

Later he adds:

'We can agree to call a class of sentences *contradictory* if it possesses no model. Analogously a class of sentences can be called *analytical* if every sequence of objects is a model of it. Both of these concepts can be related not only to classes of sentences but also to single sentences . . . We can also show . . . that those and only those sentences are analytical which follow from every class of sentences (in particular from the empty class) and only those contradictory from which every sentence follows.'[2]

As Tarski himself insists, his essay is an attempt to work out clearly the implications of the old doctrine that the relation of logical consequence holds between statements in virtue of their forms. But his development of the doctrine has some curious features which deserve notice.

In the first place Tarski's explanation of logical consequence is given by reference to logical form as expressed by logical constants, and takes no account of the role which definitions have commonly been thought to have in this connexion. Thus according to him 'Socrates was a male' may be said to be a consequence of the pair of sentences 'Socrates was a father' and 'Every father is a male' but not of the first sentence alone; and the second sentence of the pair, namely 'Every father is a male', which Kant would certainly have described as 'analytic' does not qualify for that title in Tarski's classification, because the pattern 'Every — is . . . ' is not satisfied by every pair of objects. Apparently the reason for this strange result is that Tarski has tried to carry

[1] Ibid., pp. 416–17.   [2] Ibid., pp. 417–18.

through his analysis without reference to transformation rules and therefore can only take notice of definitions when they are presented in the form of true universal statements.

Secondly, although Tarski thinks of the relation of consequence as one holding between sentences and therefore tries to explain it by reference to forms of sentences (which he calls sentential functions), his account is not entirely syntactical, i.e. concerned solely with the relations of signs to each other, but involves the notion of satisfaction. According to the terminology of his essay 'The Concept of Truth', which we noticed in an earlier section, this is a fundamental concept of semantics, that is to say, of the science in which we consider the relations of signs to things and things to signs. We say that John and Peter satisfy the condition '$x$ and $y$ are brothers' if and only if John and Peter are in fact brothers. Now from this it follows that Tarski's definition of logical consequence involves reference to what is the case in the world. Thus to consider only the simplest possible example, in his theory the peculiarity of an analytic sentence (which follows from any class of sentences) is that all specimens of its form are in fact true statements. No doubt every analytic sentence has this characteristic, but philosophers may be surprised that it should be treated as the defining characteristic rather than as a consequential property.

Thirdly, although Tarski makes the notion of logical form central in his account of consequence, he, like Bolzano before him, finds himself unable to define it precisely, and therefore concludes:

'Underlying our whole construction is the division of terms of the language discussed into logical and extra-logical. This division is certainly not arbitrary. . . . If, for example, we were to include among the extra-logical signs the implication sign, or the universal quantifier, then our definition of the concept of consequence would lead to results which obviously contradict ordinary usage. On the other hand, no objective grounds are known to me which permit us to draw a sharp boundary between the two groups of terms. It seems to be possible to include among logical terms some which are usually regarded by logicians as extra-logical without running into consequences which stand in sharp contrast to ordinary usage. In the extreme case we could regard all terms of the language as logical. The concept of *formal* consequence would then coincide with that of *material* consequence.'[1]

We may add that in this extreme case the concept of the analytic would coincide with that of the true.

[1] *Logic, Semantics, Metamathematics* (1956), pp. 418–19.

Perhaps our three difficulties are interconnected. So long as we have no worry about the recognition of logical signs, Tarski's condition for the holding of the consequence relation seems to be sufficient, inasmuch as it does not obviously admit anything which would not ordinarily be called a case of logical consequence. But even at this stage in our reflection it does not seem to be necessary, since it excludes those cases of consequence which depend on connexion by definitions. If, however, as we commonly think, a definition is a stipulation that certain expressions shall be understood to be consequences of certain other expressions, the defect is not surprising. For in order to define the relation of consequence in such a way as to provide for connexions by definition it would be necessary to say among other things that a sentence was a consequence of a certain other sentence if there was a stipulation or rule of language to the effect that any sentence of a form exemplified by the one was to be accounted a consequence of a corresponding sentence of a form exemplified by the other. Such a provision would be no more circular than a legal provision that for the purposes of a certain act of parliament any establishment is a shop which belongs to a class of establishments in respect of which the competent minister has issued a certificate to the effect that they are to be treated as shops. But it would be very different from Tarski's account of consequence, since this latter is concerned solely with satisfaction of sentential functions by objects. When next we go on to consider Tarski's doubts about the possibility of drawing a clear line between logical and extra-logical signs and the conclusions which he says would follow from admission of the impossibility of drawing such a line, we see that the source of all the strangeness in his account of consequence is his assumption that the holding of the relation depends only on the truth of a universal proposition. For just as many philosophers who profess to follow Hume have said that the necessity with which an effect follows its cause is no more than the inclusion of this particular sequence in a constant natural association, so he says that the necessity with which a consequence follows in the logical sense from premisses is no more than the inclusion of this particular sequence in a universal fact about the satisfaction of certain sentential functions. If, following his own suggestions, we enlarge the range of sentential functions under consideration by including among the constant factors of our sentences not only the traditional logical constants but all unrestricted general terms such as 'man', 'iron', 'fire', &c., we find that Tarski's definition of consequence covers not only logical consequence but also all consequence in virtue of natural laws.

In short, the definition amounts to a generalization of the constancy theory of natural necessity. But the result can give no pleasure to followers of Hume, since it involves rejection of their view that there is a difference of kind between logical and natural necessity.

In defence of Tarski's definition it may perhaps be argued that for a sentential function such as *If p then not-not-p* we can know *a priori* that it is satisfied by every sequence of objects, whereas for a sentential function such as *If x has taken arsenic x will die* we can only conjecture universal satisfaction on empirical grounds. This is true, but there is nothing in Tarski's account of the matter to explain the difference, and he does not allude to it himself. Nor is it appropriate that a distinction of kinds of consequence should be made to depend on a distinction between cases in which we can and cases in which we cannot gain knowledge *a priori*. On the contrary, the epistemological distinction should be explained by an account of the differences of the cases; and it is just this which is lacking so far.

We have seen that conventionalism involves nominalism and that, if it is taken seriously, it can be made to yield the thesis that the world consists of facts which are not in themselves either necessary or contingent. We have seen also that Tarski's account of consequence excludes the possibility of one sentence's following from another by virtue of an explicit definition, and that his attempt to define the relation of consequence by reference to universality ends with a blurring of the distinction between the laws of logic and the laws of nature. To most logicians these results appear undesirable, and we have assumed that they are not desired by the authors of the theories under consideration. But there is at least one philosopher, W. V. Quine, who accepts them all.

His views can be summarized best in his own words:

'My present suggestion is that it is nonsense, and the root of much nonsense, to speak of a linguistic component and a factual component in the truth of any individual statement. Taken collectively, science has its double dependence upon language and experience; but this duality is not significantly traceable into the statements of science taken one by one. . . . The totality of our so-called knowledge or beliefs, from the most casual matters of geography and history to the profoundest laws of atomic physics or even of pure mathematics and logic, is a man-made fabric which impinges on experience only along the edges. Or, to change the figure, total science is like a field of force whose boundary conditions are experience. A conflict with experience at the periphery occasions readjustments in the interior of the field. . . . But the total field is so underdetermined by its boundary conditions, experience, that there is much latitude of choice as to what statements to re-evaluate in the light of any single contrary experience. . . . Any statement can be held true come what may, if we make drastic enough adjustments elsewhere in the system. Even a statement very close to the periphery can be held true in the face of recalcitrant experience by pleading hallucination or by amending certain statements of the kind called logical laws. Conversely, by the same token, no statement is immune to revision. Revision even of the logical law of the excluded middle has been proposed as a means of simplifying quantum mechanics; and what difference is there in principle between such a shift and the shift whereby Kepler superseded Ptolemy, or Einstein Newton, or Darwin Aristotle? . . . Ontological questions, under this view, are on a par with questions of natural science. Consider the question whether to countenance classes as entities. This, as I have argued elsewhere, is the question whether to quantify with respect to variables which take classes as values. Now Carnap has maintained that this is a question not of matters of fact but of choosing a convenient language form, a convenient conceptual scheme of framework for science. With this I agree, but only on the proviso that the same be conceded regarding scientific hypotheses generally. Carnap has recognized that he is able to preserve a double standard for ontological questions and scientific hypotheses only by assuming an absolute distinction between the analytic and the synthetic: and I need not say again that this is a distinction which I reject.'[1]

This is an agreeably bold attempt to present a unified account of the scientific enterprise, and especially impressive at a time when many professional philosophers talk as though an interest in synoptic philosophy were a form of mental illness. But, like the Absolute Idealists whose ways of thinking he has adapted to empiricism, Quine is too tolerant of paradoxes and too contemptuous of common sense. As we noticed in an earlier section, he rejects not only the whole theory of modality but also the notions of propositions, attributes, and relations. With these go even the notion of meaning, because it is traditionally connected with talk of analytic statements. To him the clearance seems no sacrifice, but rather a removal of dangerous rubbish. To many others, however, it seems like the act of captain who in fear of running his ship aground tries to lighten it by throwing the compass overboard. No doubt Quine is right to be dissatisfied with the suggestion that a statement may be made true by linguistic rules alone. For there is something absurd in talk of making truths. Dr. Zamenhof invented the rules for a language in which it is possible to construct infinitely many new sentences such as *Ĉiu patro estas viro*, but, unless they have been corrupted by bad philosophy,

---

[1] 'Two Dogmas of Empiricism' originally published in *The Philosophical Review* (1951), reprinted with modifications in *From a Logical Point of View*, pp. 20–46, esp. 42–43 and 45–46.

even the fondest admirers of his work do not claim that he made infinitely many new truths. It is a mistake, however, to suppose that because no statement is made true by linguistic rules alone, every statement must be related to experience in the same way. To assume this is to accept the basic thesis of conventionalism, that the world consists of facts without necessities. If we are candid in our consideration of the evidence, we must concede that the assertion that $2+2 = 4$ differs not only in degree but in kind from the assertion that Everest is higher than Mont Blanc. Geography and pure mathematics are indeed both parts of one great fabric elaborated by mankind, but they are not parts of the same sort.

The strongest point in favour of Quine's thesis is that many statements of unrestricted universality seem to hover in our theory of knowledge between empirical and *a priori* status. It was discovered empirically in comparatively recent times that iron can be magnetized; and yet, if a modern physical scientist were asked whether he could conceive the possibility of abandoning this generalization, he might feel puzzled and reply that he was half-inclined to treat it as something beyond empirical question. Many cases of this kind have been discussed by F. Waismann, who has suggested independently a view of science something like that of Quine,[1] and some of his most interesting examples are from common pre-scientific talk. Is the statement 'We see with our eyes' an empirical generalization, or is it a truth discoverable by reflection on the meanings of the words 'see' and 'eye'? We cannot answer such a question without deciding what custom has hitherto left undecided. For the most part we use general words satisfactorily by following analogies, much as judges settle cases under the common law; but when one of us is called upon to give a decision about the applicability of a word in an unfamiliar situation, then, like a judge who has no precedent to guide him, he must in effect legislate. Philosophers, with their tidy minds, have often refused to recognize these facts and discussed natural languages as though these were systems of rules and definitions rather than sets of customs. But for beings such as we are it is essential that our languages should grow as they do. It is not a defect of English that we have not decided whether the word 'eye' means properly an organ of vision or an object of a certain shape and chemical composition which may conceivably have nothing to do with vision. So long as we find only facts such as we have met, we can describe them adequately without making a choice

[1] 'Analytic-Synthetic', *Analysis*, x (1949), pp. 25–40; xi (1950–1), pp. 25–38, 49–61, 115–24; xiii (1953), pp. 73–89.

between these alternatives. Our word 'eye' is certainly not meaningless, but its meaning is not as fully determined as it could be,
and so there is a possibility for further legislation if this should be
required or suggested by the development of science. A similar
example of the complexity of ordinary usage is the statement
'Kittens are the offspring of cats'. We hold that we can recognize
kittens without any difficulty by their appearance alone, and
yet we feel inclined to say that being the offspring of a cat is involved in the meaning of the word 'kitten'. If anything turned up
which looked exactly like a kitten but was demonstrably not the
offspring of a cat, there would be need for a decision which
no one has hitherto found necessary.

A curious instance of additional specification of meaning during
the past few centuries may be noticed by any modern reader who
studies carefully the argument by which St. Thomas Aquinas tries
to prove the thesis that after the resurrection there will be no use of
foods (*quod in resurgentibus non erit usus ciborum*).[1] First the saint says
that with the end of the life of corruption there will no longer be
any need for food to replace material lost in the course of corruption. Next he makes the point that food will be unnecessary after
the resurrection for purposes of growth, since everyone will rise in
the right size (*in debita quantitate*). And then, moved perhaps by
consideration of his own figure, he goes on to remark that it would
be a denial of the good ordering of God to suppose that eating will
take place after the resurrection. For a man who eats without losing
anything by corruption will grow to an immoderate size (*perveniet
ad immoderatam quantitatem*). Indeed, if after the resurrection a man
continues to eat through the whole of his unending life, we must
suppose that he will grow to infinity (*oportet dicere quod corpus
hominis resurgentis in infinitum augeatur*). But that, he says, is
impossible. Now here we have an argument which is conducted
up to a certain point with scientific rigour. But when we consider
it seriously in the context of modern science, the saint's thesis
seems absurd. For, if it is sensible to talk about a resurrected body
as he does, it must be sensible also to inquire what happens
during the voluntary movements of this body. Obviously there
must be contraction of muscles. But this involves oxidation of
carbo-hydrates and a consequent wastage of muscular tissue,
unless the loss is made good by food, which St. Thomas refuses
to allow. More generally, a resurrected body as described by
St. Thomas would be a *perpetuum mobile* functioning contrary to
the laws of thermodynamics. To this it may perhaps be replied
boldly that resurrected bodies are not subject to the laws of nature

[1] *Summa contra Gentiles*, iv. 83.

which men have found applicable to corruptible bodies. But at this point it becomes clear to most of us that we no longer think of these laws of nature as purely empirical generalizations which might be abandoned without abandonment of the notion of an organic body. In our science, and therefore in the more highly evolved levels of our language, they are now linked by the theory of metabolism; and if anyone says there might be a living organism without metabolic processes, we feel inclined to say that he is putting words together in a meaningless fashion.

The Humean account of natural laws, which was until recently the orthodoxy of empiricists, arose from an imagist theory of meaning. Hume remarked quite rightly that it was always possible to imagine the contradictory of any supposed law of nature, and concluded from this that no such law could be a law of objective necessity. Later exponents of his doctrine, who think of meaning as determined always by initial conventions, point to the fact that the negation of a supposed law of nature is never a formal self-contradiction or reducible to such without assumption of the law itself. Neither argument proves what is required of it. It is true, of course, that we can imagine in the strict sense of that word (i.e. picture in the mind's eye) men living on and on without food. But this is irrelevant, since the question at issue is not about our powers of imagination. It is true also that before the development of physiology there was no obvious linguistic defect in the sentence 'A man will live for ever without food', and that even now, if we choose for a time to concentrate attention on the contexts in which we originally learnt the constituent words, we can give a sense of some sort to the remark. But this too is irrelevant, since a remark may be said to have sense merely because it is not excluded by any well-recognized rule of usage.

At any time the meanings of the words we use are fixed by two factors, namely, (i) their relations to perceptible features of certain situations which evoke their use and (ii) their relations to each other within the fabric of our language. Philosophers in the empiricist tradition have sometimes given their attention exclusively to relations of the first kind, but there are many words which have no such relations, and for all words (e.g. even colour words) relations of the second kind are at least equally important. Even before the development of science our language is a complex structure which touches experience only at certain places, but with the development of science the internal ties become more and more complex, and there appear new words such as 'electron' and 'gene' which are far removed from experience yet not necessarily far removed from all reality. The purpose of this tightening of the internal structure of a language is to make it fit the world more closely. So long as we can freely make sentences such as 'A man will live for ever without eating' there is an undesirable looseness in the linguistic garment we have made for the world, and so, like good tailors, we must take in the slack. Such deliberate adjustment, which has been attempted only within the last few centuries, is the method of empirical science, and the recognition of its peculiarity should remove the serious misunderstandings which have arisen about necessity and language.

Quine goes much too far when he tries to abolish the distinction of contingent and necessary truths. On the one hand, statements of history and geography always remain contingent because it would be pointless to exclude alternatives by linguistic legislation; and on the other hand, statements such as 'Nothing is both red and green all over at the same time' are necessarily true from the beginning, because they are guaranteed by the rules we follow from the beginning in distinguishing colours. But it is not always easy to determine the status of the propositions of unrestricted universality which we formulate in the empirical sciences. So long as we are prepared to allow that one of these may be refuted, we cannot claim to know its necessity *a priori*. If ever we accept one without reservation, then in so doing we claim such *a priori* knowledge. But here we must be prepared to distinguish cases according to the degree of insight involved. If we simply decide to regard iron as magnetic by definition, we exclude the possibility of ever using the word 'iron' for any non-magnetic metal, but we do not thereby increase our understanding of connexions in the physical world. And if we introduced this further specification of the meaning of the word 'iron' only in order to distinguish iron from some other metal with which it would otherwise be confused, we even make the statement 'Iron is magnetic' useless for purposes of inference. If, on the other hand, when able to recognize iron satisfactorily without testing it for this property, we succeed in deducing this property from a theory of the constitution of iron which not only covers a number of other generalizations about iron but is itself part of a much wider theory about matter in general, we think rightly that we have gained a great increase of understanding. In either case, however, we may be able to say that our unrestricted generalization is transformed by a development of language into a truism guaranteed by an assumed principle of necessary connexion. Logic, as we have tried to present it in our section on modal logic, is the theory of such necessary connexion—not the theory of all the several connexions that hold between various universals, but the theory of that kind of connexion in general, and that is why it must occupy a unique position in our account of science.

Quine recognizes that logic has a special place among the sciences, but insists that it too is subject to revision:

'Re-evaluation of some statements entails re-evaluation of others, because of their logical interconnexions—the logical laws being in turn simply certain further statements of the system, certain further elements of the field. Having re-evaluated one statement we must re-evaluate some others, which may be statements logically connected with the first or may be statements of logical connexions themselves.'[1]

This is an unfortunate piece of equalitarianism. For principles without which it is impossible to conceive any system such as he describes have a clear title to separate consideration. Being presupposed in the very concept of a system, they at least are absolutely *a priori*, whatever may be said of the contents of any particular system at any time.

For a correct account of science it is essential to admit that, in a division between the world and those features of language which are man-made, necessary connexions belong to the world no less than contingent facts. Unfortunately the influence of the conventionalist theory of necessity which has been derived from Wittgenstein's work is so strong that even K. R. Popper (who is not in general receptive to influences from that quarter) has written:

'I regard, unlike Kneale, "necessary" as a mere word, as a label for distinguishing the universality of laws from "accidental" universality. Of course any other label would do as well, for there is not much connection here with logical necessity. I largely agree with the spirit of Wittgenstein's paraphrase of Hume: "A necessity for one thing to happen because another has happened does not exist. There is only logical necessity." '[2]

Elsewhere, however, he has written:

'A statement may be said to be naturally or physically necessary if, and only if, it is deducible from a statement function which is satisfied in all worlds that differ from our world, if at all, only with respect to initial conditions.'[3]

This seems to mean that a natural law holds for all *possible* worlds that contain instances of the same attributes and relations as are exemplified in the actual world and of these only. But Popper compares his definition with Tarski's definition of analytic truth, failing to notice that when we speak of truth in all possible worlds

---

[1] *From a Logical Point of View*, p. 42.
[2] *The Logic of Scientific Discovery* (1959), p. 438.       [3] Ibid., p. 433.

with the same recurring features we introduce something radically new, namely just what the defender of objective necessity wishes. No necessity, whether logical or natural, can be reduced, as Popper seems to think, to bare universality, since it is conceivable that even a proposition of unrestricted universality should be true contingently. But there can be no objection to a definition of necessity as truth in all possible worlds, since the peculiarity of the concept to be defined is preserved here by the modal word 'possible'. Clearly the universality with which something holds even for worlds distinct from the actual world cannot be merely contingent.

What we propose, however, is not that the notion of necessity should be defined in this way, but rather that the more convenient notion of involution should be recognized as a fundamental concept in the description of nature and even in the explanation of the working of ordinary language. If the notion has indeed this role, the theory of it must occupy a privileged place among the sciences. In the two remaining chapters of this book we shall have occasion to consider again the relation of this theory to the studies called mathematical, and the result of the discussion should be a clearer understanding of its importance.

# XI

# THE PHILOSOPHY OF MATHEMATICS
# AFTER FREGE

## 1. *The Paradoxes of the Theory of Sets*

As early as 1895 Cantor found that his theory of sets contained an antinomy. This was the paradox published two years later by Burali-Forti, and it concerns transfinite ordinals, which we have not considered in our sketch of his system. Then in 1899 Cantor discovered the simpler and more fundamental paradox about sets which goes by his name. Let us suppose that S is the set of all sets. By his own theorem about power sets $\overline{\overline{\mathscr{U}S}} > \overline{\overline{S}}$. But since $\mathscr{U}S$ is a set of sets (namely the set of all subsets of S), it must be part of the set of all sets, that is, of S. And from this it follows that $\overline{\overline{\mathscr{U}S}} \leqslant \overline{\overline{S}}$, which is contradictory to the result we have just obtained.

Clearly there was something wrong with the rather naïve way in which Cantor assumed the existence of sets, but it was not until 1903 that the trouble became widely known. In that year Frege published the second volume of his *Grundgesetze* with a Postscript (dated October, 1902), which began:

'Hardly anything more unfortunate can befall a scientific writer than to have one of the foundations of his edifice shaken after the work is finished.

This was the position I was placed in by a letter of Mr Bertrand Russell, just when the printing of this volume was nearing its completion. It is a matter of my Axiom (V). I have never disguised from myself its lack of the self-evidence that belongs to the other axioms and that must properly be demanded of a logical law. And so in fact I indicated this weak point in the Preface to Vol. I (p. vii). I should gladly have dispensed with this foundation if I had known of any substitute for it. And even now I do not see how arithmetic can be scientifically established, how numbers can be apprehended as logical objects and brought under review, unless we are permitted— at least conditionally—to pass from a concept to its extension. May I always speak of the extension of a concept—speak of a class? And if not, how are the exceptional cases recognized? Can we always infer from one concept's coinciding in extension with another concept that any object that falls under the one falls under the other likewise? These are the questions raised by Mr Russell's communication.

*Solatium miseris, socios habuisse dolorum.* I too have this comfort, if comfort it is; for everybody who has made use in his proofs of extensions of concepts, classes, sets, is in the same position as I. What is in question is not just my particular way of establishing arithmetic, but whether arithmetic can possibly be given a logical foundation at all.

But let us come to the point. Mr Russell has discovered a contradiction which may now be stated.

Nobody will wish to assert of the class of men that it is a man. We have here a class that does not belong to itself. I say that something belongs to a class when it falls under the concept whose extension the class is. Let us now fix our eye on the concept: *class that does not belong to itself.* The extension of this concept (if we may speak of its extension) is thus the class of classes that do not belong to themselves. For short we will call it the class K. Let us now ask whether this class K belongs to itself. First, let us suppose that it does. If anything belongs to a class, it falls under the concept whose extension the class is. Thus if our class belongs to itself, it is a class that does not belong to itself. Our first supposition thus leads to self-contradiction. Secondly, let us suppose that our class K does not belong to itself; then it falls under the concept whose extension it itself is, and thus does belong to itself. Here once more we likewise get a contradiction.'

In the same year Russell gave his own account of the contradiction when he published his *Principles of Mathematics,* and two years later J. Richard announced yet another paradox which is especially interesting because it apes the diagonal procedure of Cantor.[1] First we consider all decimal fractions that can be defined by means of a finite number of words. Although they form an infinite set, they can be ordered in such a way that there is a first, a second, and so on. For we can sort them into groups according to the number of words used in defining them and then arrange them within these groups by the alphabetical order of their definitions. But when they are so arranged, it is possible to define a decimal by saying that its nth figure is the immediate successor in the ordinary scheme of figures to the nth figure of the nth decimal in the sequence or 0 if the nth figure of the nth decimal is 9. Obviously this new decimal is not identical with any of those in the sequence, and yet it ought to be included, since it is certainly defined in a finite number of words.

In an attempt to get out of the very unsatisfactory situation revealed to him by Russell, Frege considered first the suggestion that there might be concepts with no corresponding classes. If the concept of a class which is not a member of itself were such a one, Russell's paradox would naturally disappear, since there

---

[1] 'Les Principes de mathématiques et le problème des ensembles', *Revue générale des sciences,* xvi (1905), p. 541, reprinted in *Acta Mathematica,* xxx (1906), p. 295.

would then be no class of all classes which are not members of themselves. But Frege could not reconcile himself to this revolutionary novelty, and tried instead to evade the contradiction by a modification of his fifth axiom, about which he had always felt some misgivings. What he now proposed was that two concepts should be said to have the same extension if, and only if, every object which fell under the first *but was not itself the extension of the first* fell likewise under the second and vice versa. In an appendix to his *Principles of Mathematics* Russell recommended the suggestion to serious consideration; but he did not recur to it in his other writings, presumably because he became dissatisfied with it on closer examination, and later logicians have in fact proved that the modification is not enough to free Frege's system from inconsistencies.[1]

When he had time to think about the problem more carefully, Russell came to the conclusion that Frege's first suggestion was better. There were, he thought, some propositional functions which did not determine genuine classes, and the problem for the logician was to give rules by which these *non-predicative* functions, as he called them, could be distinguished from others. The contradictions seemed to result from the fact that logicians had incautiously admitted classes which turned out to be in a curious way *self-reproductive*. Perhaps such monstrosities might be excluded by special limitations on the use of the class notation, but he was strongly inclined to think that the problem could never be solved completely until all classes were eliminated from logical theory in the way in which infinitesimals had been eliminated from the theory of the differential calculus, and he therefore considered it important to find out how much of mathematics could be presented without the class notation.[2]

If Frege's symbolism for logic had been generally accepted, elimination of talk about classes would have been effective as a cure for the paradoxes by which mathematics was then afflicted. For his distinction of levels of functions makes it impossible to reproduce in his script any paradoxes about functions analogous to Cantor's and Russell's contradictions about classes. His disaster was due indeed to the self-indulgence by which he allowed himself to use a class notation without distinction of levels as a device for evading the complexities of his own theory of propositional functions. This is a very important point to which we must return later, but for the present it is enough to notice that when Russell

[1] W. V. Quine, 'On Frege's Way Out', *Mind*, n.s. lxiv (1955), pp. 145–59.
[2] 'On Some Difficulties in the Theory of Transfinite Numbers and Order Types' *Proceedings of the London Mathematical Society*, iv (1906), pp. 29–53.

put forward his 'no classes' theory he had already discovered a paradox which could be used to show that talk of classes was not the sole cause of difficulty. Instead of the class which is supposed to contain all classes that are not members of themselves let us consider the property of being a property which does not exemplify itself. If this property exemplifies itself, then it cannot exemplify itself; and if it does not exemplify itself, then it must exemplify itself. Clearly the nature of the trouble is the same here as in the original paradox, and yet there is no talk of classes.

When Russell published his suggestion that some propositional functions were non-predicative, Henri Poincaré was engaged in a hostile survey of the attempts by Peano and his followers to explain mathematical reasoning by the methods of symbolic logic.[1] He held that mathematical induction was the source of all excellence in mathematics and that it depended on an intuition of the possibility of infinite recurrence, i.e. on something that could never be reduced to a formal rule. Finding a new opponent in the field, he promptly produced another article, designed to show that the paradoxes resulted from a wrong conception of mathematics. Accepting Russell's distinction between predicative and non-predicative propositional functions, he said that the true explanation of the difference was to be found in Richard's note of the preceding year. After reporting his paradox Richard had gone on to say that there was really no contradiction, since the set of decimals definable in a finite number of words could not properly be understood to contain any decimal definable only by reference to the whole set. Generalizing from this, Poincaré wrote: 'Ainsi les définitions qui doivent être regardées comme non-prédicatives sont celles qui contiennent un cercle vicieux'. In later literature the expression 'non-predicative' (or 'impredicative') has frequently been used as though it were *defined* by this remark, i.e. as though 'non-predicative definition' were equivalent to 'definition which purports to distinguish an object under a concept by means of a reference to the totality of all possible objects falling under that concept'.[2] But it is clear from the context that Poincaré intended only to *explain* why some phrases which looked like definitions failed to define anything. It is clear also that in his view the vicious circle which gave rise to the paradoxes of the theory of sets was of a special kind and connected with the attempt to treat of an infinite set as a

---

[1] 'Les Mathématiques et la logique', *Revue de métaphysique et de morale*, xiii (1905), pp. 815–35; xiv (1906), pp. 17–34 and 294–317. The series is reprinted with some modifications in *Science et Méthode*.
[2] See for example, A. Fraenkel, *Einleitung in die Mengenlehre*, p. 248.

completed whole. For he went on to say: 'Il n'y a point d'infini actuel. Les Cantoriens l'ont oublié, et ils sont tombés dans la contradiction.'

In a reply published in the same year Russell agreed that the paradoxes were all due to vicious circles, and laid it down as a principle for the avoidance of such circles that 'whatever involves all of a collection must not be one of the collection'. But he said that Poincaré did not properly appreciate the difficulties of applying such a principle, and that Poincaré was wrong in supposing the source of the trouble to be some mistaken doctrine of infinity introduced by Cantor. He himself believed the contradictions of set theory must be logical rather than mathematical (in any sense in which the mathematical might be distinguished from the logical), since they were essentially of the same kind as the old paradox of Epimenides (or the Liar); and he thought it interesting to notice that the vicious circle in that example had been diagnosed already in the Middle Ages, according to the article on *Insolubilia* in Baldwin's *Dictionary of Philosophy and Psychology*.[1]

These exchanges led to a renewal of interest in logical paradoxes of all kinds, and in 1910 the Liar of Eubulides received the dignity of a whole treatise, *Der Lügner, Theorie, Geschichte und Auflösung*, by A. Rüstow. Among the new paradoxes invented at this time or shortly afterwards those of Berry and Grelling are perhaps the best known. Berry's paradox concerns *the least integer not nameable in fewer than nineteen syllables*. Although it seems obvious that any name of this integer must contain at least nineteen syllables, the words printed above in italics amount to a name for it and they contain only eighteen syllables. Grelling's paradox has to do with a newly invented word. Some adjectives such as 'short' and 'English' apply to themselves, others such as 'long' and 'German' do not. Let us call those of the second group *heterological*. Is the adjective 'heterological' itself heterological? If it is, then according to the definition just given it does not apply to itself, and so it cannot be heterological. On the other hand, if it is not heterological, then according to the definition it does apply to itself, and so it must be heterological. Since these sophisms bear a resemblance to the contradictions of Cantor and Russell but have nothing to do with infinity, their appearance did something to strengthen Russell's contention against Poincaré.

In his *Principles of Mathematics* published in 1903, Russell had arrived independently at a view of mathematics similar to that of Frege, and although he found the paradoxes disturbing, like

---

[1] 'Les Paradoxes de la logique', *Revue de métaphysique et de morale*, xiv (1906), pp. 627–50. The article on *Insolubilia* in Baldwin's *Dictionary* was by C. S. Peirce.

Frege, he still hoped for a satisfactory demonstration of the identity of arithmetic and logic. This was the reason why he thought it important to show that the paradoxes arose from a defect in the presentation of logic. It would not be sufficient to explain away the contradictions of the theory of sets by reflections on the peculiarity of infinite aggregates, nor yet to exclude them by *ad hoc* legislation about the use of symbols. For if he adopted either of these courses, he would no longer be able to say that arithmetic was identical with pure logic, and he would have no guarantee against the appearance of new contradictions. The only satisfactory solution of the problem would be to eliminate the paradoxes by a reform which recommended itself as a self-evident necessity of logic, once it had been propounded; and this, as we shall see, is what Russell attempted in his Theory of Logical Types. But in 1908, the year in which he gave the first account of this theory, there appeared also two other papers which suggested new ways of dealing with the crisis and new doctrines about the relation of mathematics to logic. In the next three sections we must consider these three proposals and their relations one to another.

## 2. *Russell's Theory of Logical Types*

In his article of 1908 with the title 'Mathematical Logic as based on the Theory of Types'[1] and again two years later in the second chapter of the introduction to the first edition of *Principia Mathematica* Russell presented his theory of logical types as a consequence of his vicious-circle principle and necessary for the solution of the paradoxes, but he recommended it also as consistent with common sense and inherently credible. Let us consider first the argument by which it was introduced and the form which it took when fully developed.

According to Russell a propositional function presupposes the totality of its values for a reason which he states as follows:

'When we speak of "$\phi x$", where $x$ is not specified, we mean one value of the function, but not a definite one. We may express this by saying that "$\phi x$" *ambiguously denotes* $\phi a$, $\phi b$, $\phi c$, etc., where $\phi a$, $\phi b$, $\phi c$, etc., are the various values of "$\phi x$". . . . It follows that "$\phi x$" only has a well-defined meaning (well-defined, that is to say, except in so far as it is of its essence to be ambiguous) if the objects $\phi a$, $\phi b$, $\phi c$, etc. are well-defined. . . . It follows from this that no function can have among its values anything which presupposes the function, for if it had,

---

[1] *American Journal of Mathematics*, xxx (1908), pp. 222–62, reprinted in *Logic and Knowledge*, pp. 59–102.

we could not regard the objects ambiguously denoted by the function as definite until the function was definite, while conversely, as we have just seen, the function cannot be definite until its values are definite. This is a particular case, but perhaps the most fundamental case, of the vicious-circle principle. A function is what ambiguously denotes some one of a certain totality, namely the values of the function; hence this totality cannot contain any members which involve the function, since if it did, it would contain members involving the totality, which, by the vicious-circle principle, no totality can do.'[1]

The phraseology of this passage is unfortunate. A function, not being a sign, cannot denote anything, and even a functional expression, which is indeed a sign, cannot properly be said to denote the values of the function, whether ambiguously or unambiguously. But the conclusion to which the argument leads is very interesting:

'Hence there must be no such thing as the value for $\phi\hat{x}$ with the argument $\phi\hat{x}$, or with any argument which involves $\phi\hat{x}$. That is to say, the symbol "$\phi(\phi\hat{x})$" must not express a proposition, as "$\phi(a)$" does if $\phi a$ is a value for $\phi\hat{x}$. In fact "$\phi(\phi\hat{x})$" must be a symbol which does not express anything: we may therefore say that it is not significant. Thus given any function $\phi\hat{x}$, there are arguments for which the function has no value, as well as arguments for which it has a value.'[2]

In his first article about the theory Russell says that a type may be defined as a range of significance, i.e. as the collection of arguments for which a given propositional function has values; but he also says later that propositional functions may be classified in types according to the entities which they admit as proper arguments. These two ways of describing matters are equivalent; for Russell's considerations require us to assume a hierarchy of entities. Thus if we take men as our individuals, or entities of type 0, wisdom, or being wise (i.e. the propositional function expressed by *x is wise*), is of type 1, because it can be asserted significantly, though not perhaps truly, of Socrates or Alcibiades, while being a cardinal virtue is of type 2, because it can be asserted significantly of wisdom; and in general every attribute is of a higher type than the entities of which it can be asserted or denied significantly. It is true that Russell's argument from his vicious-circle principle does nothing to prove that an attribute must always be of the *next* higher type to the entities of which it can be asserted or denied significantly; but this is what he assumes in the development of his theory, and it is necessary if, as he obviously thinks, entities of the same type are to be universally interchangeable in the sense that what can be asserted or denied significantly of one can be asserted or denied significantly of each of the others.

---

[1] *Principia Mathematica*, vol. i, p. 39.     [2] Ibid. p. 40.

So long as we deal only with attributive functions, we may think of the various types as arranged hierarchically in a simple ascending order; but when we take account also of relational functions, we must allow for a much greater complexity which cannot be represented adequately by the use of ordinal numbers alone. Thus a two-termed relation may perhaps hold between entities which are both individuals, and so may perhaps be said to be of the same level as an attribute of individuals, but it must be distinguished in type from such attributes and also from three-termed relations which hold between individuals. And again there may be relations, such as exemplification, which hold between entities of different types. Using the numeral 'o' still to represent the type of individuals, we may perhaps say that functions which take only individuals as proper arguments are of types (o), (o, o), (o, o, o), &c., that an attribute of an attribute of an individual is of type ((o)), that an attribute of a two-termed relation of individuals, as for example, the transitivity of the relation of being an ancestor, is of type ((o, o)), that an uneven relation such as exemplification may be of type (o, (o)), and so forth. It is a general rule, however, that no propositional function may take arguments from any but the appropriate lower type or types, i.e. from the type or types whose sign or signs in the notation just explained would be found by removing the outer brackets from the sign of the type of the propositional function in question.[1]

This theory is sufficient to exclude the paradox of the property of being a property which does not exemplify itself. For if the letter $F$ is supposed to signify the paradoxical property it must be introduced by some such definition as $F(g\hat{x}) =_{\text{def.}} \sim g(g\hat{x})$, where the combination of signs on the right-hand side is obviously at fault. In order to exclude the paradox of the class of all classes which are not members of themselves Russell finds it necessary, however, to use also his 'no classes' theory. This latter is rather unfortunately named, and it may perhaps be objected that the project of getting rid of paradoxes about classes by getting rid of classes is extravagant in the same way as a proposal to get rid of children's diseases by getting rid of children. But what Russell intends is something much more reasonable than his phraseology suggests. He holds that designations of classes are incomplete symbols, that is to say, symbols which cannot be defined alone but may be defined in company, since all the complexes in which they occur significantly can be replaced by equivalent complexes in which they do not appear. Thus

[1] R. Carnap, *The Logical Syntax of Language*, § 27.

whenever we have an expression of the form $A\epsilon\hat{x}(Fx)$, we may replace it by an expression of the form $FA$, and so too in more complicated cases class signs may be eliminated without loss. Sometimes he expresses all this by saying that classes are fictions which disappear on analysis, but such remarks are to be interpreted by reference back to what he says about incomplete symbols: they are suggested no doubt by lawyers' talk about the fictitious personality of corporations.

Now according to Russell's explanation, when we try to translate his paradox about classes in the manner required by the 'no classes' theory, the result to which we are led is a combination of symbols forbidden by the theory of types, and so it is evident that the paradox arises from the failure of ordinary grammar to meet all the requirements of logic. In his own words:

'A proposition about a class is always to be reduced to a statement about a function which defines the class, i.e. about a function which is satisfied by members of the class and by no other arguments. Thus a class is an object derived from a function and presupposing the function, just as, for example, $(x).\phi x$ presupposes the function $\phi$. Hence a class cannot, by the vicious-circle principle, significantly be the argument to its defining function, that is to say, if we denote by "$\hat{z}(\phi z)$" the class defined by $\phi\hat{z}$, the symbol "$\phi\{\hat{z}(\phi z)\}$" must be meaningless.'[1]

For the solution of other paradoxes, such as Berry's and the Liar, a further development is necessary, but one which seems to be required in any case by the vicious-circle principle. This is the ramified theory of types or the distinction of orders within types, and Russell explains the need for it as follows:

'Let $f(\phi\hat{z}, x)$ be a function of two variables $\phi\hat{z}$ and $x$. Then if, keeping $x$ fixed for the moment, we assert this with all possible values $\phi$, we obtain a proposition $(\phi).f(\phi\hat{z}, x)$. Here, if $x$ is variable, we have a function of $x$; but as this function involves a totality of values for $\phi\hat{z}$ it cannot itself be one of the values included in the totality, by the vicious-circle principle. It follows that the totality of values of $\phi\hat{z}$ concerned in $(\phi).f(\phi\hat{z}, x)$ is not the totality of all functions in which $x$ can occur as argument, and that there is no such totality as that of all functions in which $x$ can occur as argument.'[2]

For the sake of simplicity in our distinction of orders we may begin by supposing that we have to do only with functions which take individuals as proper arguments. If any such function can be defined without the application of quantifiers to any variables other than individual variables it may be said to belong to the

[1] *Principia Mathematica*, vol. i, pp. 62–63.    [2] Ibid., pp. 48–49.

first order. Taking men once more as our individuals, we may give as examples the functions expressed by *Socrates loves x* and *Everybody loves x*. Then according to Russell 'second order functions are such as contain variables which are first order functions but contain no other variables except (possibly) individuals'.[1] Strictly speaking, it is a functional sign, not a function, which contains a variable, but the sense of the definition is clear. Thus the phrase *x has all the first order qualities that make a great general* expresses a function of the first type but of the second order, because it takes individuals as its proper arguments but is equivalent in sense to $(f)[(y)(y\ is\ a\ great\ general \supset f\,!y) \supset f\,!x]$. In general, if the variable of highest order occurring in the expression of a function is one marking a gap for signs of functions of the nth order, then the function so expressed is of the $(n+1)$th order. And according to Russell's usage in *Principia Mathematica*, a function denoted by $F!\hat{x}$ is to be called *predicative* if, and only if, it is of the lowest order compatible with its having the argument or arguments it has.[2] Thus a predicative function in this new sense of the word involves no totality except the totality of its possible arguments and any totalities they presuppose.

The distinction of orders of functions helps to a solution of paradoxes like that of Berry by enabling us to split up illegitimate totalities. Thus we can say that in Berry's paradox the word 'name' is incorrectly taken to cover not only proper names in the ordinary sense, i.e. designations which involve no functions, but also descriptions involving functions of *all* orders. If we wish to talk correctly of descriptions, we must be prepared to specify the order or orders of functions which they involve. But then any description which refers to descriptions involving functions of order n will itself involve a function of order $n+1$ and so fail to apply to itself. Similarly the paradox of the Liar can be exposed as an attempt to use the description 'what I say' without regard to the need for a distinction of propositions by orders. These results of the ramified theory of types are very satisfactory, but unfortunately the limitation of discourse by which they are achieved is very drastic. Perhaps it does not matter that we must not say 'Napoleon had all the qualities that make a great general' unless we are prepared to add that the qualities in question are those of the first order, or at any rate of some finite set of orders. But it is important that we are apparently forbidden to formulate some well-known mathematical theorems and in particular the

[1] Ibid. p. 52.
[2] Ibid., p. 53. This sense of 'predicative' is different from that noticed in the last section.

theorem that any non-empty set of real numbers with an upper bound has a least upper bound.

It will be remembered that, according to the theory of Eudoxus and Dedekind, a real number is a cut or section among the rational numbers, or more precisely the lower of the two infinite sets into which the array of rational numbers may be divided by a cut. From this it follows that a set of real numbers is a set of sets of rational numbers. Now if S is a non-empty set of real numbers with an upper bound, the least upper bound of S is supposed to be a real number which is also the union or logical sum of all the real numbers in S, i.e. which has for its members all those rational numbers which are members of any of the members of S. Here there is something which looks like a violation of the ramified theory of types. For the set of rational numbers which constitutes a real number, being infinite, cannot be specified except by mention of a propositional function which all the members satisfy, and the functional expression which is supposed to specify the least upper bound of an infinite set of real numbers must apparently involve reference to the totality of propositional functions that specify real numbers, *including that function which it expresses*. If it is said that the least upper bound must belong to an order of real numbers distinct from the numbers of S and that there can be no completely general theorems about real numbers without restriction of order, mathematical analysis, as ordinarily understood, becomes impossible. How, if at all, can Russell evade this unpleasant consequence, while continuing to use his ramified theory of types for the exclusion of paradoxes?

He tries to have the best of both worlds by introducing the Axiom of Reducibility. This is the assumption that for every propositional function there is some predicative function (in the sense of *Principia Mathematica*) which is satisfied by all the same arguments and by no others,[1] or in symbols

$$(f)(\exists g)(x)[fx \equiv g!x].$$

If this is admitted, the difficulty about orders of real numbers can be overcome. For it may be said that the propositional functions specifying real numbers do indeed fall into distinct orders, but that for every propositional function of higher order specifying a real number there is a corresponding predicative function which specifies the same real number, because it is satisfied by the same rational numbers and by no others. We are still forbidden in principle to make generalizations about all propositional functions without regard to order, but in contexts like this we

[1] *Principia Mathematica*, vol. i, p. 56.

can be confident that if we talk of all predicative functions we shall not leave anything unsaid which needs to be said. Another example of the advantages to be drawn from the axiom is the possibility of defining identity (as we saw in the last chapter) by reference to predicative functions alone. At the same time paradoxes of the familiar kinds remain excluded, because they cannot be recast in terms of predicative functions alone. Thus if we try to reconstruct Berry's paradox, while talking only of integers nameable by first-order names (e.g. by names composed of English numerals in arrays such as 'five two nine'), we find that what we say gives rise to no contradiction.

Is there any reason, apart from convenience, for accepting the axiom of reducibility? Russell admits that it can scarcely be said to be a self-evident truth of logic, but he tries to explain it and render it plausible by showing its connexion with what logicians have said about classes. In his article of 1908 he suggests that it might be called the Axiom of Classes, but in the introduction to *Principia Mathematica* he writes more cautiously:

'If we admit the existence of classes, the axiom of reducibility can be proved. For in that case, given any function $\phi\hat{z}$ of whatever order, there is a class $a$ consisting of just those objects which satisfy $\phi\hat{z}$. Hence "$\phi x$" is equivalent to "$x$ belongs to $a$". But "$x$ belongs to $a$" is a statement containing no apparent variable, and is therefore a predicative function of $x$. Hence if we assume the existence of classes, the axiom of reducibility becomes unnecessary. . . . However, both on the ground of the contradictions, which require a more complicated treatment if classes are assumed, and on the ground that it is always well to make the smallest assumption required for proving our theorems, we prefer to assume the axiom of reducibility rather than the existence of classes.'[1]

When Russell says here that '$x$ belongs to $a$' is a predicative function of $x$ because it contains no apparent variable, he seems to be making no distinction between a function and a functional expression. But he can scarcely wish to suggest that introduction of the Greek letter $a$ as an abbreviation for $\hat{z}(\phi z)$ is enough to give us all the benefits of the axiom of reducibility, and so it must be assumed that he thinks of $a$ as a designation introduced without the help of $\phi x$ or any other functional expression of the same kind. It is not clear, however, why without assumption of the axiom of reducibility he should suppose it must be possible to provide such a new designation for the class previously designated by $\hat{z}(\phi z)$, unless indeed he mistakenly takes it for

[1] Ibid., p. 58.

granted that every class can be indicated by enumeration of its members.

In a later paragraph Russell produces another line of argument:

'The axiom of reducibility is equivalent to the assumption that any combination or disjunction of predicates (given intensionally) is equivalent to a single predicate, i.e. to the assumption that, if we assert that $x$ has all the predicates that satisfy a function $f(\phi!\hat{z})$, there is some one predicate which $x$ will have whenever our assertion is true, and will not have whenever it is false, and similarly if we assert that $x$ has some one of the predicates that satisfy a function $f(\phi!\hat{z})$. For by means of this assumption, the order of a non-predicative function can be lowered by one; hence, after some finite number of steps, we shall be able to get from any non-predicative function to a formally equivalent predicative function.'[1]

In effect this explanation amounts to the suggestion that an expression with a universal quantifier should be regarded as an abbreviation for a conjunction and an expression with an existential quantifier as an abbreviation for a disjunction, even though it may be impossible to write out either conjunction or disjunction in full. Thus 'Napoleon had all the qualities that make a great general' is to be taken as short for 'Napoleon was clever, alert, able to inspire confidence, quick at guessing the thoughts of others, . . . etc.' If we accept this account of the matter, we can go on to say that the distinction of orders of functions is not, like the hierarchy of types, something imposed by the nature of things, but rather a complication introduced by the exigencies of our language and useful only in connexion with problems concerning language. This is in fact the conclusion of F. P. Ramsey in his paper of 1925 on 'The Foundations of Mathematics',[2] and it has been accepted by most (but *not* all) of those who try to follow in the line of Frege, Whitehead, and Russell. As Ramsey pointed out, the simple theory of types is sufficient for the exclusion of those paradoxes which are of special importance to the logician and the mathematician (e.g. Cantor's and Russell's), and the ramifications of the theory of orders are not strictly necessary for the purposes of *Principia Mathematica*, because their only service is to exclude paradoxes about semantic or linguistic notions such as naming and defining, with which the mathematician has no concern in his professional capacity.

[1] *Principia Mathematica*, vol. i, p. 59. The phrase 'given intensionally' which is printed here within brackets occurs in a footnote.
[2] *Proceedings of the London Mathematical Society*, ser. 2, xxv (1926), pp. 338–84, reprinted in the volume *The Foundations of Mathematics and other Logical Essays*, pp. 1–61.

When Ramsey's point has been conceded, it seems more natural to deal with the semantic paradoxes by special semantic measures, and the suggestion which has won most favour is the distinction of language and metalanguage introduced by Tarski in his work on 'The Concept of Truth in Formalized Languages'.[1] According to this no consistent language can contain within itself the means for speaking about the meaning or the truth of its own expressions, and paradoxes such as the Liar and Berry's contradiction arise from failure to appreciate this limitation. If, for example, we speak of *the least integer not nameable in fewer than nineteen syllables*, it must be supposed that we are talking with reference to the re-sources of some particular language or languages. When this is understood, it will become clear that the phrase italicized above is not constructed out of the resources of the language or languages under reference, but belongs to a metalanguage which is essen-tially richer; and with this clarification the paradox will dis-appear. Unfortunately we often fail to understand the distinction when we talk of the use of a natural language such as English, because we are accustomed to think of it as omnicompetent, and this is the source of our troubles. If we wish to avoid contradictions, we must insist that what we ordinarily call English is in reality an infinite sequence of languages, namely, English$_1$ in which we can discuss sticks and stones and many other things but not English$_1$, English$_2$ in which we can discuss all the things we can discuss by use of English$_1$ but in addition English$_1$, English$_3$ in which we can discuss all the things we can discuss by use of English$_2$ but in addition English$_2$, and so on. Within this scheme English$_{n+1}$ is a metalanguage in relation to English$_n$.

Tarski recommends his distinction as necessary for the solution of the paradox of the Liar, but it is interesting to show that it can be derived from the simple theory of types. Let us suppose first that we try to use the words 'designate' and 'designation' without implicit reference to some particular language, and that we construct with their help the formula:

'Designation' designates designation.

Here there is an obvious violation of the simple theory of types, inasmuch as a relation is said to be one of its own terms. It is not enough, however, to say that in future we will always talk of designation-in-English. For precisely the same trouble arises when we construct the formula:

'Designation in English' designates in English
designation in English.

[1] *Logic, Semantics, Metamathematics*, pp. 152–278.

But the trouble ceases if we recognize the stratification explained in the last paragraph and write:

'Designation in English₁' designates in English₂ designation in English₁.

For then we make clear that the relation of which we speak is of a higher type than its terms. And this, it seems, is the only way out of the difficulty.

If we reject the distinction of orders we must reject also the vicious-circle principle from which it is derived. To do so is a relief rather than a loss, since the principle is dubious and difficult to apply. Why, for example, should we say with Russell that a function presupposes its values? But if we propose to retain the simple theory of types, while abandoning the vicious-circle principle with which Russell connected it, we must consider very seriously whether the simple theory has the intrinsic plausibility which he claimed for it, i.e. whether it is a theory we want to retain on its own merits, once we have realized its content. In order to prepare for a decision on this question, let us try once more to make clear what it involves and how it is related to the theory of propositional functions introduced by Frege.

The essential novelty of Russell's theory is a tightening of the rules of significance by which he excludes from the domain of well-formed formulae some combinations of signs that would otherwise pass for grammatically correct sentences, and in particular all combinations of the form $F(F\hat{x})$, or $F(\S xFx)$ in our notation. Instead of discussing whether these express true propositions or false propositions, he asserts that they express no propositions. In his account of functions of different levels Frege anticipated Russell's distinction of types, but it seems to be no more than an accident that his rules for the use of functional signs made it impossible to construct in his system the paradox of the property of being a property which does not exemplify itself. For he held that any *object* could occur as argument to any propositional function of the first level, so that the worst to be said of the complex '7 is wiser than the moon' would be that it expressed a false proposition; and if he could have satisfied himself that it was possible to talk about *functions* by means of designations which did not contain gaps, he would probably have been prepared to treat them in the same way. But he was convinced that any sign we use to talk of a function must contain a gap (which he marked by means of a small Greek consonant, not itself part of his script), and he therefore assumed that one function could occur as an argument to another function only if the expression of the second, say $—\mathbf{a}—\phi(\mathbf{a})$ would provide for the closing of the gap in the expression of the first, say $\Phi(\beta)$, and so produce a complete propositional expression, say $—\mathbf{a}—\Phi(\mathbf{a})$. This is clear from the way in which he deals with functions of the second level in his *Grundgesetze*.

If the only signs for functions were expressions such as ' . . . is wise', considerations of ordinary grammar would be enough to guarantee the truth of the theory of types. For ' . . . is wise is wise' is certainly not an English sentence, and no one will worry himself about the question whether it expresses a true proposition or a false proposition. When we write in our logical symbolism $F(Fx)$, we may perhaps be inclined to suppose for a moment that this can express a proposition, but we see that it is not a well-formed propositional expression when we remember that the letter $x$ is a mere gap sign. So far we may agree with Frege, and it has sometimes been suggested that this is the whole theory of types.[1] But in ordinary English we have gapless nouns such as 'wisdom' to designate functions, and it is possible, as we have seen, to introduce signs of the same kind into the symbolism of logic. The important question is whether any complex of the form $F(\S xFx)$ can express a proposition, and to this we can get no clear answer either from academic grammar or from a study of common usage. For 'Wisdom is wise' is not obviously ungrammatical, and although no one, except perhaps Plato, wants to offer it as a true statement, many may wish to say 'It is not the case that wisdom is wise', as though they thought that 'Wisdom is wise' had some meaning. How if at all can we settle the question?

Very often a sentence which contains a designation of a function can be replaced without loss by a sentence of a different shape in which there occurs no such designation but only an expression for the function. Thus instead of 'Socrates had wisdom' we can say 'Socrates was wise', and instead of 'The fear of the Lord is the beginning of wisdom' 'If a man fears the Lord he has already begun to be wise'. If it could be established that all significant sentences which contain designations of functions must be reducible in some way to sentences which contain no such designations, we could dismiss 'Wisdom is wise' and all similar complexes as insignificant, since it seems clear that they cannot be reduced. But no one has proved that it must always be possible to eliminate designations of functions from significant discourse, and it is not sufficient for our purposes to cite a multitude of examples in which they have been eliminated successfully, because

[1] This may perhaps be the sense of Wittgenstein's remarks in his *Tractatus Logico-philosophicus*, 3.332.

those who find the theory of types unplausible will retort that the question at issue cannot be settled by the methods of the natural sciences. The most we can achieve, then, by this line of argument is to show that the kind of complex to which the theory of types denies significance is in any case very peculiar. This consideration may well dispose us to accept the theory as a way out of our perplexities, but it is important to realize that there is a price to be paid for the advantages which it offers, and that it has its own difficulties.

In the first place, the theory produces an enormous complication in our account of logic, and not least in what we say about numbers. For we must not only distinguish in type between complex numbers, real numbers, rational numbers, signed integers, and natural numbers, but also between the natural numbers applicable to sets of different types. Thus according to Russell's elaboration of Frege's theory the number four which is the number of the cardinal virtues must be an entity of a different type from the number four which is the number of the English kings called William. Virtues are qualities which may belong to men, and so a set of virtues, determined by a character applicable only to such qualities, cannot properly be said to be in the same class with a set of men, determined by a character applicable only to men. It may be that, as Frege said, entities of all thinkable kinds can be counted, but it seems that there must be a different arithmetic for every distinguishable type, i.e. that the numerals in the equations 2 *men*+2 *men* = 4 *men* and 2 *virtues*+2 *virtues* = 4 *virtues* cannot signify the same numbers. Russell tries to get over this difficulty by saying that he uses the symbols of logic and mathematics with *systematic ambiguity*. According to him there are indeed different types of natural numbers (and so different types of rational numbers, &c.), but in the development of pure arithmetic we can safely overlook this complication because our formulae will be applicable without alteration to any type that may come under discussion in applied mathematics or even in those branches of pure mathematics where we count numbers themselves.

Secondly, the theory of types rules out the possibility of providing for the definition of an infinity of natural numbers in any way like that suggested by Frege. If 0 is said to be the set of all sets equivalent in Cantor's technical sense to the set of things not identical with themselves and 1 the set of all sets equivalent in the same sense to the set 0, it must be wrong to say that 2 is the set of all sets equivalent to the set whose members are 0 and 1. For according to the first two definitions 1 is of a higher type than 0, and so there can be no set of which these are both members. Frege made no distinctions of levels when dealing with the entities which he called objects; but if Russell is right, his definition of 2 is as curious as the assumption that Socrates and wisdom can have a character in common, and so his method of providing for an infinity of natural numbers must be abandoned. It is essential for mathematics, however, that there should be no end to the sequences of natural numbers, and so Russell finds himself driven to introduce a special Axiom of Infinity, according to which there is some type with an infinity of instances, and that presumably the type of individuals, which comes lowest in the hierarchy. Without this axiom, he tells us, we should have no guarantee against the disastrous possibility that the supply of numbers would give out at some highest number, i.e. the number of members in the largest admissible set.

There is something profoundly unsatisfactory about the axiom of infinity. It cannot be described as a truth of logic in any reasonable use of that phrase, and so the introduction of it as a primitive proposition of arithmetic amounts in effect to abandonment of Frege's project of exhibiting arithmetic as a development of logic. Nor is it a sufficient defence to suggest, as Russell has sometimes done, that we may treat it as a postulate or hypothesis rather than as an axiom in the old sense. For we want to assert that the series $1/2 + 1/2^2 + 1/2^3 + \ldots$ converges to 1 as a limit, not that it converges to 1 if there happens to be an infinity of individuals in the world. But even if we abandon all hope of carrying out Frege's programme in full and say boldly that Russell's axiom is required as an extra-logical premiss for mathematics, how can we justify our acceptance of it? What are the individuals of which Russell speaks, and how can we tell whether there are infinitely many of them? Russell says that he intends to refer to those things, whatever they may be, which can be named by logically proper names and cannot occur in propositions except as subjects. But he admits that it is difficult to indicate such things directly, and he even suggests that there may possibly be none because everything which appears to be an individual is in fact a class or complex of some kind. With regard to the second possibility, which seems very mysterious, he adds cheerfully that if it is realized the axiom of infinity must obviously be true for the types which there are in the world. But he does not profess to know for certain what the situation is, and he ends by saying that there is no known method of discovering whether the axiom of infinity is true or false.[1]

[1] *Introduction to Mathematical Philosophy*, p. 143.

Apart from these troubles, which even the simple theory of types involves for those who try to follow Frege in logicizing arithmetic, there is the more fundamental difficulty that it seems impossible to formulate the theory without violating its own provisions because words like 'function', 'entity', and 'type' must always remain free from type restrictions. If, for example, we say that no function may be asserted significantly of all entities without distinction of type, our own statement involves the unlimited generality which it declares to be impossible. And again there must be something wrong with any definition of a type according to which two entities are of the same type if a propositional function which can be affirmed or denied significantly of either can also be affirmed or denied significantly of the other. For when we try to apply such a definition in a particular case, and say, for example, that Plato is of the same type as Socrates but wisdom not of the same type, we find ourselves involved in a contradiction. From our pronouncement it follows that Plato is not of the same type as wisdom, and yet the pronouncement itself shows clearly that there is at least one function which can be affirmed truly of Plato and denied truly of wisdom, namely being of the same type as Socrates.

Such criticisms as these have led Russell to admit that he should have distinguished types of *symbols* rather than types of entities.[1] The words 'Plato' and 'wisdom', he now tells us, belong to different types because they are not interchangeable without loss of significance. For while 'Plato was younger than Socrates' makes good sense, 'Wisdom was younger than Socrates' is nonsense. On the other hand, when we construct names for these words by printing them within quotation marks, our new signs belong to the same type, because they are interchangeable without loss of significance. Thus if we replace 'Plato' by 'wisdom' in the sentence ' "Plato" is of the same type as "Socrates" ', the result is still meaningful though the proposition which it expresses is false.

With care this new version of the theory of types can be made to yield all the advantages that are derivable from the original, and it may perhaps be an improvement, not only because it saves us from new paradoxes, but also because it seems to offer better hope of an understanding of the situation. It is wrong, however, to suppose that by speaking about words instead of things we can escape from all metaphysical entanglements and base our distinctions on simple considerations of grammar. In particular it is a mistake to assume that difference in type is always an affair of

---

[1] See Max Black's criticism and Russell's reply in *The Philosophy of Bertrand Russell*, edited by P. A. Schilpp, pp. 235 and 691.

syntax according to the ordinary understanding of that grammatical term. There is indeed a syntactical difference between 'Plato' and ' . . . is wise', since the first is a designation and the second a functional expression; but there is no such difference between 'Plato' and 'wisdom', and it is by no means obvious that all significant remarks must be translatable into a simplified language which contains only designations of one type.

For the solution of the paradoxes which afflicted mathematicians and logicians at the beginning of this century, the important distinction of type is that between words like 'Plato' and words like 'wisdom' which may be said to stand for possible characters and relations of Plato. But under the influence of Russell it has become common for philosophers to talk of type or category distinctions in their attempts to solve problems of very different kinds. It has been suggested, for example, that there is a confusion of categories in talking of interaction between mind and body.[1] Whether such an extension of the theory of types is justifiable must be settled in each particular case by detailed examination of the ways in which we think and speak when we are at our best, but there are two general cautions to be borne in mind.

In the first place we must not assume that words of ordinary language are interchangeable *salva significatione* either in all contexts or in none. Although we cannot substitute 'wisdom' for 'Plato' in the sentence 'Plato was wise' without producing nonsense, we can make such a substitution in 'Socrates loved Plato' without evoking even a feeling of surprise. We must therefore be content to say that a difference of type is shown by failure of interchangeability in *some* context, and from this we may perhaps be led to doubt whether any two words are of the same type.

Secondly, when we leave the realm of logic and pure mathematics for the study of thoughts expressed in ordinary language, it is not always clear where we should draw the line between nonsense and scientific impossibility. Consider, for example, the following series of sign-complexes:

1. The parson believes in original sin.
2. The baby believes in original sin.
3. The cat believes in original sin.
4. The chair believes in original sin.
5. The rent believes in original sin.

Obviously the first may be uttered for the purpose of making a statement. And it seems reasonable to say that the last is nonsense. But what of the others? We have all heard of precocious children:

[1] G. Ryle, *The Concept of Mind.*

might not some child be so precocious that the parson felt obliged to instruct it in the doctrine of original sin while it was still a baby? Then, since some cats are more intelligent than others, might not the cat of this household, overhearing the parson's instruction, come to believe in original sin? And finally might not the chair on which the parson sat be all the while a true believer suffering from the enchantments of a wicked magician? Or at least does not all this make some sort of sense? Shall we then say that the line comes between the fourth and the fifth of our examples? But what sort of discovery is this? Suppose someone tells us that in Coptic fairy stories true believers are often said to be changed into rents and that Coptic children do not find such stories unintelligible. Shall we admit that any collection of words which is permissible according to customary syntax may make some sort of sense to someone? Or shall we reply dogmatically that we are not interested in Coptic fairy stories because we know *a priori* that there is a line to be drawn between the fourth and the fifth of the examples given above? In any case it seems clear that in contexts of the kind we have been considering the theory of types does not provide a simple rule for detecting otherwise unsuspected nonsense. On the contrary, those who talk of types in such contexts must allow that no one can discover a difference of type unless he is already able to detect nonsense without the help of the theory.

If our concern is solely to save the theory of sets from antinomies, we can get the benefit of Russell's theory of types without some of its difficulties by the technique of standardization noticed in the last chapter. That is to say, we can present the many-sorted theory of sets with variables which range over a single universe of discourse (containing entities of all types), provided (i) we qualify our theorems by conditions which distinguish entities according to their types and (ii) we introduce the new axiom schema

$$(x)(y)\{x\epsilon y \supset [T_n(x) \equiv T_{n+1}(y)]\}$$

in which the $T$-signs are supposed to be category or type predicates, themselves definable in terms of membership.[1]

### 3. *The Intuitionism of Brouwer*

In his controversy with Russell at the beginning of this century Poincaré suggested that the paradoxes of the theory of sets were due to the fundamental mistake of assuming actually infinite

---

[1] W. V. Quine, 'Unification of Universes in Set-Theory', *Journal of Symbolic Logic*, xxi (1956), pp. 267–79. Cf. Hao Wang, 'Logic of Many-Sorted Theories', *Journal of Symbolic Logic*, xvii (1952), pp. 105–16.

aggregates. He did not explain in detail why that assumption gave rise to contradictions; but he was right, of course, in thinking that if mathematicians abstained from talking of infinity in the manner of Cantor they would not have to face Cantor's peculiar puzzles, and he might perhaps have argued that it was useless to spend time on the detailed discussion of an assumption whose absurdity could be seen without reference to the paradoxes. In such an attitude he would have had the support of many distinguished mathematicians. At the beginning of the nineteenth century Gauss had said that there was no place in mathematics for talk of a completed infinity,[1] and more recently Kronecker had conducted a campaign against the Cantorian programme. But none of these had realized the full consequences of refusing to admit any infinity other than the potential infinity of a sequence which can be continued *ad libitum*, and it was not until the work of L. E. J. Brouwer in this century that the issue became clear—or at least clear enough to interest most mathematicians.

Like Kant and Poincaré, Brouwer holds that mathematical theorems are synthetic *a priori* truths. In his inaugural address of 1912 at the University of Amsterdam he admits that the development of non-Euclidean geometry has discredited Kant's view of space, but in opposition to Frege, Whitehead, and Russell he maintains that arithmetic, and with it all mathematics, must be derived from the intuition of time. In his own words, 'neo-intuitionism considers the falling apart of the moments of life into qualitatively different parts, to be re-united only while remaining separated by time, as the fundamental phenomenon of the human intellect'. From this 'intuition of the bare two-oneness' we get first the notion of the sequence of ordinal numbers, and then the notion of the linear continuum, i.e. 'of the betweenness which is not exhaustible by the inter-position of new units and therefore can never be thought of as a mere collection of units'. In so far as it assumes continuity, even geometry is dependent on the same intuition. There are no sets except the denumerable, and so there are no transfinite cardinals except $\aleph_0$, the cardinal of a set whose members can be correlated one-to-one with the sequence of natural numbers. In particular, there is no meaning to be given to any phrase such as 'the set of all real numbers between 0 and 1'.[2]

What Brouwer has to say about intuition in this manifesto is

---

[1] *Werke*, vol. viii, p. 216.

[2] 'Intuitionism and Formalism', Inaugural Address at the University of Amsterdam in 1912, translated and published in *The Bulletin of the American Mathematical Society*, vol. xx (1913), pp. 81–96.

obscure, and his other papers do not give much more light on that topic, interesting as it may be to philosophers; but he leaves no doubt that he repudiates everything connected with the notion of an actual (or completed or extensional) infinite, including even the liberty of talking about the set of real numbers in an interval. In his view even the sequence of natural numbers is to be conceived as an open manifold, always in growth and never brought to a finish: we can comprehend it only by understanding the law of its construction.

Sometimes Brouwer and his pupils say that the intuition of which they speak is just the mind's clear apprehension of what it has itself constructed, and they frequently assert that in mathematics all satisfactory proofs are constructive. It is difficult to know exactly what they mean by 'construction' and 'constructive' in this context, but the fact that they often deny the dependence of mathematical thought on any special sort of language and express distrust of the technique of formalization by which some other mathematicians hope to get security suggests that they think of a constructive proof as one which consists of the performance of an experiment in imagination. A. Heyting, who is a leading member of the school, has even gone so far as to say

'Intuitionistic mathematics consists . . . in mental constructions; a mathematical theorem expresses a purely empirical fact, namely the success of a certain construction. "$2+2 = 3+1$" must be read as an abbreviation for the statement "I have effected the mental constructions indicated by '$2+2$' and '$3+1$' and I have found that they lead to the same result".'[1]

But it can scarcely be his intention to reduce mathematics to psychological autobiography. For he quite obviously thinks that the theorems he has proved by reflection on his own powers of mental construction can be proved by anyone else who is sufficiently intelligent, and that it is not proper to say that each man has his own mathematics (unless that phrase means simply the stock of theorems he has personally discovered or verified). Presumably modern intuitionists agree with Kant that mathematical theorems are objective in the sense of being valid for all intelligent beings. If this is right, the symbolic expression of a theorem may perhaps be replaced in certain contexts by a statement that something is *provable*, but it cannot be treated as a record of the empirical fact that something has been *proved* by the writer. No doubt the writing of the symbolical expression can be cited as evidence of a mental achievement by the writer, but that is not sufficient reason for saying that the expression means something about the writer.

---

[1] *Intuitionism, An Introduction*, p. 8.

In practice the most important requirement of the programme of constructive proof is that no existential statement shall be admitted in mathematics unless it can be demonstrated by production of an instance. In Brouwer's view anyone who fails to observe this caution has only himself to blame if he falls into paradox; for he talks without insight. But it must be admitted that Brouwer too has been led to some surprising conclusions in his attempts to apply his programme rigorously. As early as 1908 he published a paper on the unreliability of the principles of logic,[1] and from 1918 onwards he produced a number of papers against the use of the principle of excluded middle in mathematics. In these he holds that mathematics, being derived directly from intuition, does not presuppose a system of logic, but is rather a source of logical principles, since these latter may be enunciated in general fashion only after their validity has been established by the appropriate intuition. There is, and can be, no completely safe language for mathematics, that is to say, no language which will eliminate all possibility of misunderstanding; and it is therefore vain to hope for a complete formalization of mathematics. This is shown strikingly by the history of the principle of excluded middle. In their daily concerns men commonly have to do with finite sets, and intuition shows that the rules of their ordinary logic are appropriate for reasoning about such sets. But these rules have been taken as absolute and applied without the warrant of intuition to reasoning about infinite sets. In this new context the principle of identity, the principle of non-contradiction, and the principle of syllogism are in fact once more appropriate; but the principle of excluded middle and the associated principle for the elimination of double negation are no longer sound.[2]

Let us consider an existential statement $(\exists x)[Fx.\!\sim\!Gx]$ and the universal statement $(x)\!\sim\![Fx.\!\sim\!Gx]$ which is ordinarily supposed to be its contradictory. If the set denoted by $\hat{x}Fx$ is finite, it is possible in principle to examine all the members, one after another, and so to decide in favour of one or other of the two statements. The task may be technically impracticable, but we have a clear conception of a method for deciding which of the alternatives is true. If, however, the set denoted by $\hat{x}Fx$ is denumerably infinite, the situation is different. Systematic enumeration is still quite satisfactory for proving the existential state-

---

[1] 'De onbetrouwbaarheid der logische principes', *Tijdschrift voor wijsbegeerte*, ii (1908), p. 152, reprinted in *Wiskunde, Waarheid, Werkelijkheid*. We have not seen this paper.
[2] See especially 'Mathematik, Wissenschaft und Sprache', *Monatshefte für Mathematik und Physik*, xxxvi (1929), pp. 153–64.

ment, since it must lead to a favourable instance in a finite number of steps if there is such an instance; but it is no longer an effective method of proving the universal statement, since it is senseless to talk of going through all the members. Thus anyone who succeeds in demonstrating Goldbach's conjecture that every even number greater than two is the sum of two primes must do so by showing that it is in the nature of a multiple of two to have this property. Now Brouwer and most intuitionists are prepared to concede that one way of proving a universal statement of this kind is to show, if we can, that the existential statement involves a contradiction and must therefore be rejected, i.e. they allow the logical thesis

$$\sim(\exists x)[Fx.\sim Gx] \supset (x)\sim[Fx.\sim Gx].$$

On the other hand they do not admit the thesis

$$\sim(x)\sim[Fx.\sim Gx] \supset (\exists x)[Fx.\sim Gx],$$

because they say that, if we succeeded in refuting the universal statement by showing that it involved a contradiction, we should be no nearer to discovering a thing called $A$ of which we could assert $FA.\sim GA$, and so should not be entitled to assert the existential proposition. In short, reasoning which involved the second thesis would be non-constructive, and anyone who asserted the existential proposition as a conclusion of such reasoning would be in intellectual danger, just as a man who runs in the dark is in physical danger. But rejection of the second thesis amounts in effect to abandonment of the principle of excluded middle and the associated principle for the elimination of double negation.

This conclusion is surprising enough to make many suspect a mistake in the intuitionistic philosophy of mathematics, but its oddity is somewhat disguised when Brouwer identifies it with rejection of the assumption that every mathematical problem is soluble.[1] For we must admit that problems about infinite sets cannot all be solved by a rule of thumb like that which leads infallibly to a solution of problems about finite sets. Although we can say something about the general form which a proof of Goldbach's conjecture must take, if one is ever obtained, we are unable to give effective instructions for the finding of such a proof. But why should Brouwer suppose that unqualified assertion of the principle of excluded middle is equivalent to claiming possession of a universal method for solving mathematical problems? One reason may be that his programme of constructive proof commits

---

[1] 'Intuitionistische Betrachtungen über den Formalismus', *Sitzungsberichte der Preußischen Akademie der Wissenschaften, Phys.-math. Klasse*, 1928, pp. 48–52.

him to the view that it is improper to assert any disjunctive statement unless one is prepared to assert one of the disjuncts. For
according to this very strict way of understanding a disjunction a
person who writes $p \vee \sim p$, using the letter $p$ as a free variable,
gives it to be understood that he is in a position to assert or deny
every proposition that may be suggested for consideration. It
seems likely, however, that Brouwer is influenced also by the
thought that in intuitionistic mathematics there is no difference
to be drawn between $\sim(\exists x)[Fx. \sim Gx]$ and $\triangle \sim (\exists x)[Fx. \sim Gx]$,
when $\triangle$ is used as an abbreviation for 'it is demonstrable that'.
We have noticed already that intuitionists talk of theorems as
statements of provability, and it is easy to see that any one who
dwells, as Brouwer does, on the requirements of constructive
proof may wish to assert emphatically that there is no place in
mathematics for merely accidental universality. Heyting has said
'In intuitionistic mathematics only falsity *de jure* can play a part :
the introduction of mere *de facto* falsity would conflict with the
principle of constructivity,'[1] and from this the view just mentioned
could easily be derived.

Whatever the precise meaning of his more philosophical pronouncements may be, there can be no doubt that for Brouwer
they have serious consequences in mathematics. For methods
which he calls non-constructive are unfortunately very common in
the theory of real numbers. It is difficult, indeed, to see how any
substantial part of classical analysis can be presented without
them. In Dedekind's theory a real number is considered to be
an actually infinite set of rational numbers, and even the simplest
theorems are then proved by the assumption of the principle of
excluded middle in relation to such sets. When, for example it is
desired to prove that for any two real numbers x and y either
$x > y$ or $x = y$ or $x < y$, it is first asserted that there either is or
is not a rational in x which does not belong to y. Brouwer and his
followers reject all this and try to reconstruct mathematics in
accordance with their own stricter standards of proof. The subtlety
and ingenuity which they bring to the work give aesthetic pleasure
to some mathematicians, but it is clear already that the structure
which they build must inevitably be more complicated than the
classical edifice which it is intended to replace.

For the study of intuitionistic logic, which especially concerns
us, the most important development within the school has been
the formulation of a calculus by Heyting in 1930.[1] Since it is one

---

[1] *Intuitionism, An Introduction*, p. 18.
[2] 'Die formalen Regeln der intuitionistischen Logik', *Sitzungsberichte der Preußischen Akademie der Wissenschaften, Phys. math. Klasse*, 1930, pp. 42–56. See also
*Intuitionism, An Introduction*, ch. vii.

of the intuitionistic tenets that there can never be any guarantee of the finality of a formal system, Heyting does not suggest that mathematical reasoning must be confined for all time to arguments of the patterns he records; but his system has been accepted by Brouwer as a correct digest of the logical principles used in intuitionistic mathematics at the present time, and it therefore deserves close attention. Its rules of deduction are the same as those of *Principia Mathematica*, but it has two distinctive features. In the first place the various logical signs (conjunctive, disjunctive, conditional, negative, universal, and existential) are all taken as undefined primitives;[1] and secondly the various sets of axioms given by Frege and others for the propositional calculus are all abandoned in favour of the following set of eleven:

1. $p \supset (p.p)$
2. $(p.q) \supset (q.p)$
3. $(p \supset q) \supset [(p.r) \supset (q.r)]$
4. $[(p \supset q).(q \supset r)] \supset (p \supset r)$
5. $q \supset (p \supset q)$
6. $[p.(p \supset q)] \supset q$
7. $p \supset (p \lor q)$
8. $(p \lor q) \supset (q \lor p)$
9. $[(p \supset r).(q \supset r)] \supset [(p \lor q) \supset r]$
10. $\neg p \supset (p \supset q)$
11. $[(p \supset q).(p \supset \neg q)] \supset \neg p$

It will be noticed that in the last two formulae the new sign $\neg$ occurs where we might have expected $\sim$. But apart from this, each of Heyting's axioms is similar in appearance to a thesis of classical logic, and together with the rules of substitution and detachment they allow for many of the ways of reasoning recognized in classical logic; but it is not possible to derive from them either of the two principles rejected by Brouwer, namely those expressible by the formulae $p \lor \neg p$ and $\neg \neg p \supset p$. Furthermore, the system has the peculiarity of admitting no disjunctive proposition unless one at least of its disjuncts is separately provable. An equivalent system of rules of 'natural inference' can be obtained by omitting rule (6b) from the version of Gentzen's system given in an earlier section.

What are we to say of Heyting's calculus? It is presented as though it were a formalization of that part of classical logic to which Brouwer raises no objection; and considered from one point of view, it is just that. On the other hand, it is not possible to abandon principles of classical logic, while giving all the logical signs their usual senses, since the sense of a logical sign is determined by the logical formulae in which it is introduced. And

---

[1] J. C. C. McKinsey has shown that none can be defined by reference to the other without alteration of the system, 'Proof of the Independence of the Primitive Symbols of Heyting's Calculus of Propositions', *Journal of Symbolic Logic*, iv (1939), pp. 155–8.

the intuitionists are not content to ignore the formula $p \lor \neg p$, but say explicitly that it has no place in their calculus of propositions. It seems, therefore, that if the sign $\lor$ retains its usual sense in intuitionistic logic, $\neg$ must mean something different from $\sim$. In his exposition of his theory Brouwer frequently writes 'it is absurd' where he might have been expected to say 'it is not the case', and Heyting, as we have seen, says that there is no merely *de facto* negation in intuitionistic mathematics. So it is not surprising that many critics here supposed the so-called negation sign of the intuitionistic calculus to be really a sign of impossibility and said in consequence that what is rejected is not, properly speaking, the principle of excluded middle but the obviously unacceptable thesis that every proposition is either true or impossible.[1] But this cannot be a sufficient account of the matter; for the last of the formulae of Heyting listed above is not a truth of logic if $\neg$ is taken to mean 'it is impossible that' and the other signs retain their usual senses. In reality the situation is more complicated, as K. Gödel showed in two papers of 1932.[2]

If Heyting's calculus is supposed to be part of classical logic, then paradoxically that part can be shown to contain in a certain way the whole. For although Heyting says that his signs are all to be taken as undefined primitives, there is nothing to prevent us from introducing a new disjunction signs, say $\oplus$, and a new implication sign, say $\rightarrow$, defined by the equivalences:

$$P \oplus Q = \neg (\neg P . \neg Q)$$
$$P \rightarrow Q = \neg (P . \neg Q).$$

And from these, taken together with the axioms and rules of inference given by Heyting, it is possible to obtain all the theses of the classical logic of propositions, including the principle of excluded middle in the form $p \oplus \neg p$ and the principle for the elimination of double negation in the form $\neg \neg p \rightarrow p$. For the two formulae just mentioned are merely abbreviations for $\neg(\neg p . \neg \neg p)$ and $\neg(\neg \neg p . \neg p)$, which can both be proved within Heyting's system. It should be noticed, however, that the new signs $\oplus$ and $\rightarrow$ are not to be equated with the intuitionist signs $\lor$ and $\supset$, and that the formula $\neg \neg p \rightarrow p$ cannot be used in the intuitionist calculus for the elimination of double negation, since the rule of detachment, or *modus ponens*, for that calculus refers to $\supset$, not to $\rightarrow$.

By an extension of the same procedure it has been shown that

---

[1] See, for example, W. Kneale, 'Are all Necessary Truths True by Convention?', *Aristotelian Society Proceedings*, sup. vol. xxi (1947), pp. 118–33.
[2] 'Zur intuitionistischen Arithmetik und Zahlentheorie' and 'Eine Interpretation des intuitionistischen Aussagenkalküls', *Ergebnisse eines mathematischen Kolloquiums*, Heft iv (1932), pp. 34–38 and 39–40.

the classical version of the restricted calculus of functions and classical elementary arithmetic can both be reconstructed within the corresponding intuitionistic systems, and it has even been conjectured that the same may be done for classical analysis.[1] Such reproduction of classical calculi within those of intuitionism amounts to a relative proof of consistency for the former, just as the modelling of a non-Euclidean geometry within Euclidean geometry proves that the former cannot be inconsistent unless the latter is so too. If intuitionistic mathematics is free from contradiction, then so too are those parts of classical mathematics which can be translated into parts of intuitionistic mathematics.

In the first of the two papers mentioned above Gödel draws the conclusion that the restrictions which Brouwer imposes on proofs in analysis and the theory of sets are not due, as Brouwer himself says, to abandonment of the principle of excluded middle, but rather to rejection of impredicative definitions (i.e. definitions which contain a vicious circle of the kind noticed by Poincaré). Whether this is correct or not, he has certainly proved that on the simplest interpretation Heyting's calculus includes the whole of classical logic, and that intuitionists who accept this interpretation cannot properly say that they have abandoned the principle of excluded middle, except in the sense of not using it for their own reasoning in mathematics.

It may be replied, however, that intuitionistic formulae always mean something different from classical formulae of the same shape, and there is good reason, as we have seen, for believing that this is true of Heyting's logical formulae. Here again Gödel has an interesting suggestion.[2] Starting from the intuitionists' own hints, he supposes in the second of the papers mentioned above that all four signs of Heyting's propositional calculus are different in sense from the signs of the classical calculus, but that expressions containing them may be regarded as abbreviations for more complicated expressions according to the following scheme in which $\triangle$ has the sense of 'it is demonstrable that' and the signs with which it occurs are classical:

| Heyting Expression | Classical Expansion |
|---|---|
| $\neg P$ | $\triangle \sim \triangle P$ |
| $P . Q$ | $\triangle P . \triangle Q$ |
| $P \vee Q$ | $\triangle P \vee \triangle Q$ |
| $P \supset Q$ | $\triangle P \supset \triangle Q$ |

[1] S. C. Kleene, *Introduction to Metamathematics*, § 87, and A. Heyting, *Intuitionism, An Introduction*, pp. 112–14.

[2] Cf. also J. C. C. McKinsey and A. Tarski, 'Some Theorems about the Lewis and Heyting Calculi', *The Journal of Symbolic Logic*, xiii (1948), pp. 1–15. The interpretation given here is the second of two suggested by Gödel.

The result is that all Heyting's axioms become theses in a system which differs from Lewis's modal system S4 only by its use of 'demonstrable' in place of 'necessary'. Moreover the thesis which Brouwer rejects under the name 'principle of excluded middle' turns out to be a version of the strong reduction principle. For its expanded form is $\Delta p \vee \Delta\Delta\sim\Delta p$, and this is equivalent to $\sim\Delta p \supset \Delta\sim\Delta p$. With the suggested interpretation it is easy to see why Brouwer says that the rejected thesis is equivalent to the principle of the solubility of all mathematical problems, and much easier to understand why he is prepared to reject it. For even those who believe in the strong reduction principle of ordinary modal logic do not all say that it seems to them as intuitively obvious as the principle of excluded middle, properly so called; and according to the suggested interpretation the rejected thesis is not concerned with the necessity of ordinary modal logic but with demonstrability in mathematics by constructive methods.

It is the basic idea of intuitionism that we should seek security in mathematics by accepting only constructive proofs, and it is therefore quite fitting that Heyting's calculus should be interpreted as an axiomatic theory of the notion of provability by constructive methods. So understood, it makes good sense; for we certainly do not wish to maintain that every mathematical conjecture is either demonstrably true or demonstrably indemonstrable by constructive methods. But according to this interpretation Heyting's calculus is not a system of logic in the strict sense, because it does not fix the sense of the logical signs that occur in its full formulation. On the contrary, it presupposes a classical calculus of logic, and it has only been mistaken for an alternative logic because of the intuitionists' unfortunate custom of talking of theorems as statements of provability. No doubt there may be theorems about the provability of theorems, but there must be others which are not of this kind although they involve logical notions such as those of conditionality and universality.

In practice anyone who decides to accept only constructive proofs in mathematics may have to reject arguments which employ the principle of excluded middle in relation to infinite sets (i.e. if he cannot explain the unsatisfactoriness of all non-constructive arguments in the way suggested by Gödel). But he should then content himself with the remark that such arguments do not yield the insight which he wants.

## 4. *Hilbert's Programme of Metamathematics*

In the year 1908, in which Russell published the first version of his theory of types and Brouwer first wrote against the reliability of the principles of logic, E. Zermelo produced a set of axioms designed to save the theory of sets from paradoxes.[1] Regarding this theory still as the most fundamental part of mathematics, he suggests that it should be rebuilt by the laying down of principles which are sufficient to support the generally accepted doctrine but so chosen that they do not give rise to contradictions. He admits that he cannot prove the consistency of his axioms, but he claims that he has at least excluded the antinomies discovered in recent years. The essential feature of his method is that he no longer talks of sets with the freedom of Cantor but admits in his theory only those sets whose existence is guaranteed by his axioms.

First in his Axiom of Definiteness (I) he lays it down that two sets are identical if whatever is a member of one is a member also of the other. Then in a number of axioms he provides for derivation of sets from others assumed to be given. Thus in his Axiom of Selection (III) he says that if there is a property such that for every member of a set S it is a determinate question whether that member has the property or not then there exists a second set whose members are just those members of S which have the property; in his Axiom of the Power Set (IV) that for any set S there exists a second set whose members are all the subsets of S; and in his axiom of the Union Set (V) that for any set S there exists a second set whose members are all the members of the members of S. These last three all correspond to implicit assumptions of Cantor, but Zermelo adds to the group a new assumption of his own called the Axiom of Choice (VI) according to which for every set S whose members are mutually exclusive sets all alike distinct from the null set there exists at least one subset of its union set which contains one and only member from each of the members of S. The independence of this axiom and even its admissibility have been much debated by later mathematicians. Finally, since none of the axioms mentioned so far provides *unconditionally* for the existence of any sets, Zermelo lays it down in his Axiom of Elementary Sets (II) and his Axiom of the Infinite (VII) that there exists in the domain of sets at least one set which contains the null set as a member and is so constructed that the inclusion in it of any member A implies also the inclusion in it of the unit class {A}, i.e. the class of which A is the sole member. Thus, to use a loose expression, all the sets required in this axiomatic presentation of the theory are generated in one way or another from the null set, and provision is made for infinity

---

[1] 'Über die Grundlagen der Mengenlehre', *Mathematische Annalen*, lxv (1908), pp. 261–81.

in the same way as by Frege. There is no distinction of types, but the known contradictions are avoided by the device of limiting talk to sets which are *not too large*. In particular the domain (*Bereich*) of sets is not itself admitted as a set. But J. von Neumann, who has himself produced a revised set of axioms for the theory of sets, argues conclusively that there is no additional danger in admitting very large sets such as this, provided always that no set as large as the set of everything in general is supposed capable of being a *member* of any set.[1]

Apart from the fact that it does not incorporate any distinction of types, Zermelo's version of the theory of sets differs from that of Whitehead and Russell in the role which it assigns to axioms. In *Principia Mathematica* the axioms are all supposed to be necessary truths, and the whole structure is conceived by its authors in the same way as Euclid conceived his elements. That is to say, there is no suggestion that there could be any alternative, except possibly a system of the same content in which some of the present axioms appeared as theorems and some of the present theorems as axioms. Admittedly Russell has misgivings about his axiom of reducibility and his axiom of infinity, but he still thinks that if they are to be accepted at all they are to be accepted as truths, and he therefore puts forward such considerations as he can produce to convince the reader or at least make him sympathetic. Zermelo, no doubt, also wishes that the axioms in his set should appear plausible, but he presents them rather as a modern geometer might present a set of axioms for a non-Euclidean geometry. If they are consistent, they delimit a system for study and provide an implicit definition of the membership sign which is used as a primitive symbol in the formulation of them.

The notion of implicit definition is as old as Gergonne, but the importance which formal, as opposed to material, axiomatics has in the thought of modern mathematicians is due largely to the work of Hilbert. In his *Grundlagen der Geometrie* of 1899 he produced the first really satisfactory set of axioms for Euclidean geometry, and in a paper of 1904 on the foundations of logic and mathematics he suggested a programme for eliminating the newly discovered paradoxes by axiomatizing logic, arithmetic, analysis, and the theory of sets.[2] He did not think that arithmetic could be reduced to logic, but rather that they should be

---

[1] 'Über eine Widerspruchsfreiheitsfrage in der axiomatischen Mengenlehre', *Journal für die reine und angewandte Mathematik*, clx (1929), pp. 227–41. In some later writings, e.g. *Axiomatic Set Theory* by P. Bernays and A. Fraenkel, 'set' is reserved for entities capable of membership, though 'class' is used in a wider way.

[2] 'Über die Grundlagen der Logik und Mathematik', *Verhandlungen des dritten internationalen Mathematiker-Kongresses in Heidelberg* (1904), pp. 174–85.

developed together in order that the whole system might then be shown to be free from inconsistency. The paper is a mere sketch, but it shows already some of Hilbert's guiding principles and in particular that faith in the axiomatic method which he expressed more fully in his later work and particularly in a paper of 1922:

'The axiomatic method is now and for all time the instrument suited to the human mind and indispensable for every exact enquiry, whatever its field may be. It is logically unassailable, and at the same time fruitful. It also preserves for the enquirer the most complete liberty of movement. To proceed axiomatically in this sense is simply to think with knowledge of what one is about. In earlier times, when they did not use the axiomatic method, men believed in various connexions with naïve dogmatism. Axiomatics removes this *naïveté*, but leaves us nevertheless the advantages of belief.'[1]

The explanation of the last-quoted sentence and the motive of all Hilbert's work on the foundations of mathematics can be seen most clearly in his essay of 1926 'On the Infinite'.[2] He tells us there that the role of the infinite in mathematics is that of an Idea of Reason in the Kantian philosophy: it transcends all experience and in a way completes it. That is to say, the theory of the actual infinite is radically different from constructive mathematics, but we must not reject it on that account. On the contrary we must welcome it as 'the most admirable flowering of the mathematical spirit' and try to preserve it by the greatest intellectual care. In short, 'we must let no one drive us from the paradise that Cantor has created for us'. These remarks are clearly directed against Brouwer, and so also is the assertion later in the same article that every mathematical problem is soluble. But for all that, Hilbert agrees with Brouwer about the primacy of intuition and constructive argument. He thinks that in mathematics the basic reasoning, which he calls *finitary*, is a kind of 'direct reflection on content that proceeds without axiomatic assumptions but by means of thought-experiments on objects imagined in full concreteness' and by use of mathematical induction, or the argument from recurrence to which Poincaré attached supreme importance.[3] Where he differs is in thinking that classical mathematics, with its 'ideal' theorems unattainable by finitary methods, may nevertheless be preserved as a valuable possession if the consistency of the axioms from which it is derivable can be proved by means of finitary argument. His programme has been described

---

[1] 'Neubegründung der Mathematik', *Abhandlungen aus dem mathematischen Seminar der Hamburgischen Universität*, i (1922), pp. 157-77.
[2] 'Über das Unendliche', *Mathematische Annalen*, xcv (1926), pp. 161-90.
[3] D. Hilbert and P. Bernays, *Grundlagen der Mathematik*, vol i, p. 20.

as a plan for reducing strict intuitionism to absurdity,[1] but it is not intended to be merely a polemic. On the contrary, according to Hilbert, the need for using intuitionistic methods in proving the consistency of classical arithmetic arises from the nature of the problem.

A system which is to be sufficient for the derivation of number theory, classical analysis, and the theory of sets must contain not only the rules and axioms of the restricted calculus of propositional functions, but also Frege's axioms of identity, axioms of number like those of Peano, and axioms of membership like those of Zermelo, or at any rate axioms equivalent in force to all these. Hilbert does not think it reasonable to call the whole amalgam logic, but it is clear that the name we use is of minor importance, and it is not even of very great concern that the axioms should all be independent. What is essential is that the system as a whole should be proved consistent, and for this purpose ordinary methods are useless. Since the system is intended to deal with the properties of actually infinite sets, we cannot give an absolute proof of its consistency by producing a set of objects whose relations satisfy all the conditions laid down in the axioms. For although our mathematical notion of continuity was originally suggested by reflection on continuity in the perceptual world, we have no guarantee that the requirements of the mathematical notion are all satisfied by any perceptibly continuous expanse or duration, and there is no other datum of experience in which it is even plausible to look for an actually infinite set of elements. Nor can we give a relative proof of the consistency of the set of axioms by showing that they can all be translated into statements of some other system, as axioms of non-Euclidean geometry may be translated into statements of Euclidean geometry. For there is no other system of known consistency which seems comprehensive enough to provide such a translation.[2] But we may conceivably be able to attain the goal in another way. To say that the system is consistent is to say that application of the rules of inference to the axioms can never lead to a pair of consequences one of which is the negation of the other. May it not be possible to prove this by reasoning at a higher level, i.e. not within the system but rather about the system, or to speak more strictly about the formulae in which the system is expressed? The axiomatic formulae are finite in number, and a derivation must

[1] J. von Neumann, 'Zur Hilbertschen Beweistheorie', *Mathematische Zeitschrift*, xxvi (1927), pp. 1-46.
[2] D. Hilbert and P. Bernays, *Grundlagen der Mathematik*, vol. i, pp. 14 ff. See, however, the conjecture of Kleene and Heyting mentioned in the last section.

be a finite sequence of steps taken in accordance with one or other of a finite number of rules; so it is not on the face of it absurd to suppose that the proof of consistency which we need may be attainable in this way by the use of finitary methods of argument. For just as in elementary number theory these methods are sufficient to prove the impossibility of finding two natural numbers m and n such that $m^2 = 2n^2$, so in this new study called *theory of proof* or *metamathematics* they may be sufficient to prove the impossibility of finding two derivations which lead from the given axioms to contradictory conclusions.

From 1917 onwards Hilbert worked on this project with various colleagues, and in 1934 and 1939 he published with P. Bernays the two volumes of *Grundlagen der Mathematik*, which explain the situation and set forth the results achieved up to the time of publication. In this work the authors admit that they are still far from a solution of the fundamental problem, and we shall presently see reason to believe that that problem can never be completely solved as it was originally conceived, but there is no doubt that the study started by Hilbert has been extremely fruitful. For, apart from the problem of consistency, there are many questions about deductive systems for which the technique he suggested seems appropriate, in particular questions about the completeness of axiom systems and about the possibility of devising decision procedures, or rules of thumb, for the solution of problems in various branches of mathematics. In all such investigations it is essential that the theory under investigation should be formalized by the help of a strict logical symbolism, and so it may be said that here at last the work of Leibniz and Frege has produced results of importance to the progress of mathematics, though not perhaps the results they expected.

Sometimes Hilbert's philosophy of mathematics is called formalism, and just as nineteenth-century formalists were attacked by Frege, so Hilbert is attacked by Brouwer for failure to appreciate the real *content* of mathematics. Frege's opponents maintained that new kinds of numbers could be introduced by creative definitions, and that if the definitions led to no self-contradictions it was pointless to ask for any further proof of the existence of the numbers. To this Frege replied that there could be no proof of freedom from contradiction except by production of an example, and that the converse inference was a fallacy. Hilbert now argues that the consistency of a postulate system may be established without the production of a model. To this Brouwer replies that intuitionism does not assume an inconsistency in the application of the principle of excluded middle to infinite sets, and that even if Hilbert succeeded in his enterprise he would have done nothing to prove the truth of his 'ideal' statements, because there is a vicious circle in the attempt to justify formalist mathematics through a proof of its consistency. We are asked to accept the correctness of a system of postulates when it has been shown that they do not lead to self-contradiction; but according to Brouwer this justification is of no value unless we can already accept the principle that the correctness of a proposition follows from the absurdity of its absurdity, and that is just another version of the law of excluded middle.[1] In his view a theory has no more title to be called true because it has been proved free from inconsistency than a wrongdoer has to be called an honest man because it has been found that his act cannot be punished by the existing law of the land. As Fraenkel has written

'To the thoroughgoing believer in axiomatics Hilbert's question counts as the supreme problem of all mathematics, and in the answer to it he would see one of the boldest, most original, and most profoundly important steps in the development of the problem of knowledge; but to the thoroughgoing intuitionist it is entirely without significance on the only point that matters.'[2]

This is a very curious dispute in which the parties seem to be arguing at cross purposes. Brouwer talks as though Hilbert were trying to prove the truth of his axioms, and so of what follows from them, by proving that they are self-consistent. But when Hilbert undertakes to axiomatize all mathematics he presumably thinks of his axioms as postulates which determine the sense of the otherwise undefined symbols which he uses. If this is right, a mathematical entity must be for him just what his axioms allow, neither more nor less, and every mathematical statement must have the same status as a statement of pure geometry, e.g. as the assertion that a Riemannian triangle has interior angles greater than two right angles. So interpreted, Hilbert's axiomatized mathematics is not open to Brouwer's objections. For anyone who talks of real numbers in the way Hilbert proposes will use the phrase 'real number' to mean any object satisfying certain conditions, and so his statements will be in effect assertions that his axioms have certain consequences in virtue of their form. In short, they will be truths of pure logic. On the other hand, it is not clear whether Hilbert is content with this conclusion, nor yet what he thinks about the ultimate relation of axiomatized

---

[1] 'Intuitionistische Betrachtungen über den Formalismus', *Sitzungsberichte der Preußischen Akademie, Phys.-math. Klasse*, 1928, pp. 48–52.
[2] *Einleitung in die Mengenlehre*, p. 381.

mathematics to constructive mathematics. Sometimes it seems that after a proof of the consistency of his axioms by constructive methods he would be content to forget the difference and treat non-constructive mathematics as a continuation of constructive mathematics. But this can scarcely be a correct attitude to adopt, if he and Brouwer are right in thinking that constructive mathematics involves insight into a special subject-matter. For there seems to be no guarantee that the theorems attained without this insight are about the same subject-matter. Thus a theorem which purports to be about natural numbers but is proved non-constructively (e.g. by a detour through classical analysis) may not really be about natural numbers in the original sense. This seems to be what Heyting has in mind when he says that the subject of intuitionistic mathematics, namely, constructive mathematical thought, 'places it beside, not interior to classical mathematics, which studies another subject, whatever that may be'.[1]

As we have already noticed, there is reason to believe that Hilbert's programme can never be carried out in full, but the stimulus which he gave to the study of axiom sets has led to some very interesting discoveries about the properties of logic and various other deductive systems. These will provide the subject for our last chapter.

[1] *Intuitionism, An Introduction*, p. 4.

# XII

## THE THEORY OF DEDUCTIVE SYSTEMS

### 1. *The Metatheory of Primary Logic*

IN 1926 P. Bernays, one of the collaborators of Hilbert, published an investigation of the axiomatization of the calculus of propositions in *Principia Mathematica*.[1] He had attained most of his results eight years before when he wrote his *Habilitationsschrift* (which dealt also with the possibility of replacing axioms by rules of inference), but some of them had been published meanwhile by E. L. Post, who had discovered them independently in his investigation of the properties of truth tables.[2] We have noticed in an earlier chapter that the three most important questions to be raised about a set of axioms are those of consistency, independence, and completeness, and in this section we shall see how they can be answered with reference to the axiomatization of the calculus of propositions in *Principia Mathematica*.

It may perhaps be thought superfluous to prove the consistency of the axioms and rules of inference set out by Whitehead and Russell in their primary logic (which they call the theory of deduction), since each is presented with an explanation which makes it seem acceptable on its own merits. But it is important for the formalist programme that it should be possible to prove the consistency of an axiomatized system without reliance on the customary interpretation, and it is interesting to see how this can be done in a very simple case where Brouwer and the intuitionists say that we are already in danger of being misled by our logical tradition. First of all, however, it is necessary to make clear what we understand by 'consistency' in this context. It is not enough here to say that the axioms must not contradict one another in their sense; for we are trying to think of them now in formalist fashion, and apart from that, the consistency which interests us is not a property of the set of axioms considered by itself, but rather of the system formed by the axioms and the rules of inference. What we wish to show is that the procedures of

---

[1] 'Axiomatische Untersuchungen des Aussagenkalküls der *Principia Mathematica*', *Mathematische Zeitschrift*, xxv (1926), pp. 305–20.
[2] 'Introduction to a General Theory of Elementary Propositions', *The American Journal of Mathematics*, xliii (1921), pp. 63–185.

substitution and detachment which are allowed within the calculus can never lead from the axioms

| $(p \lor p) \supset p$ | *Taut* |
|---|---|
| $q \supset (p \lor q)$ | *Add* |
| $(p \lor q) \supset (q \lor p)$ | *Perm* |
| $[p \lor (q \lor r)] \supset [q \lor (p \lor r)]$ | *Assoc* |
| $(q \supset r) \supset [(p \lor q) \supset (p \lor r)]$ | *Sum,* |

in which an expression of the form $P \supset Q$ is understood as an abbreviation for an expression of the form $\sim P \lor Q$, to a pair of formulae related as $P$ and $\sim P$. This account of the matter covers the requirement that no two axioms should be related one to another in the undesirable fashion, since any axiom may be said to be obtainable from itself in a trivial way by an identity substitution (i.e. one which leaves the original unaltered); but it is more comprehensive, and amounts in effect to saying that the calculus is consistent if, and only if, there is *some* formula *not* obtainable within it. For if it were possible to derive both $P$ and $\sim P$, then by an argument like that given by the Pseudo-Scot it would be possible also to derive any other formula $Q$.

Having made clear our objective, let us consider how it may be attained. Obviously we cannot examine in turn all derivations constructible within the calculus, since there is no limit to the number of these; but we may be able to prove what we want by reflection on the general nature of a derivation. Now to say that a certain formula can be reached by permitted transitions from the axioms is to say something about the calculus without reference to any special interpretation; but just for that reason the assertion should hold good for all satisfactory interpretations, and so it may be refuted by the production of such an interpretation for which it is patently false to say that the formula is derivable from the axioms. In this context, however, an interpretation is satisfactory if, and only if, the elements which it allows to serve as possible values for the variables $p$, $q$, $r$, &c., form a group,[1] say G, for which a singulary operation represented by $\sim$ and a binary operation represented by $\lor$ can be defined in such a way that (i) G is closed with respect to the operations, i.e. repetitions of the operations on the elements never lead outside G, (ii) all the axioms receive distinguished values, i.e. values falling within a proper subgroup of G, say G\*, and (iii) if any two elements represented by $P$ and $\sim P \lor Q$ are both in G\* then so too is the element represented by $Q$. In the ordinary interpretation intended by

---

[1] Bernays's use of this word should not be taken to imply that the class of values satisfies all the conditions of the mathematical theory of groups.

Whitehead and Russell $G = \{\text{truth, falsity}\}$ and $G^* = \{\text{truth}\}$, while $\sim$ has the sense of negation and $\vee$ that of disjunction. But we can, if we like, take $G = \{0, 1\}$, $G^* = \{0\}$, $\sim P = 1 - P$, and $P \vee Q = P \times Q$, where the formulae are not propositional but numerical and derivation is not inference but simply transition from one numerical sign to another in accordance with certain rules. The second interpretation is like Boole's algebra of 0 and 1, but with 0 instead of 1 as the distinguished value and multiplication instead of addition as the correlate of disjunction. In order to avoid entanglement with customary notions let us see what can be done with this numerical scheme.

By application of the definition of the horseshoe sign and use of the equations set out above for determining the sense of the signs $\sim$ and $\vee$ we can verify that all the axioms of the calculus have the distinguished or preferred value, whatever values from the group $\{0, 1\}$ may be assigned to the variables occurring in them. Thus we have, for example, $(p \vee p) \supset p = \sim(p \vee p) \vee p$, and if we put $p = 0$ this reduces to $\sim(0 \vee 0) \vee 0 = [1 - (0 \times 0)] \times 0 = 0$, while if we put $p = 1$ it reduces again to $\sim(1 \vee 1) \vee 1 = [1 - (1 \times 1)] \times 1 = 0$. Further, it is evident that neither substitution nor detachment can lead from an axiom or axioms of the calculus to a formula with the value 1. For since each axiom has the value 0, whatever may be the values assigned to the variables occurring in it, any formula derived from an axiom by substitution for its variables must retain the same value on the same condition. And it is already guaranteed that when $P$ and $\sim P \vee Q$ both have the value 0 the formula $Q$ must also have that value: in detail $0 = \sim P \vee Q = (1 - 0) \times Q = Q$. But these results are sufficient to establish the consistency of the calculus. For according to the interpretation we are considering all formulae derivable within the calculus must have the value 0, and so it is impossible that any two of them should be related as $P$ and $\sim P$, whose values are necessarily different according to the interpretation.

This proof has the great merit of being independent of the ordinary interpretation for which Whitehead and Russell designed the calculus, but the use of numerals which it involves may possibly give rise to misunderstandings. In the first place, it may perhaps be thought that the argument amounts only to a relative proof of consistency by the interpretation of logical axioms within arithmetic. Such an opinion is mistaken, because the axioms of propositional logic are not transformed here into *statements* of arithmetic, but into mere signs for numbers, and the subsequent reasoning is totally different from that by which a system of geometry may be shown to be consistent on the supposition that there is no self-contradiction in arithmetic. Nevertheless some students of logic have, it seems, been misled by the false analogy. Secondly, even if we escape from this danger, we may perhaps fall into the mistake of supposing that the introduction of numbers as values for variables is essential for the construction of a proof of the kind set out above. In fact all that is important is the number of values chosen and the manner in which they are connected, i.e. the *structure* of the interpretation, and so we may, if we wish, reformulate the proof in such a way that it involves reference to no special kind of entities like numbers but only to a group of values which satisfy certain formal conditions. Thus we may put $G = \{\alpha, \beta\}$ and $G^* = \{\alpha\}$ without specifying $\alpha$ and $\beta$ any farther than by the equations:

$$\sim\alpha = \beta, \quad \sim\beta = \alpha,$$
$$\alpha \vee P = P \vee \alpha = \alpha, \quad \beta \vee \beta = \beta.$$

This was in fact the device employed by Bernays in the article mentioned above, and we shall use it in what follows, except that for convenience we shall summarize the whole in a matrix like the accompanying table, with an asterisk attached to the symbol of a distinguished value at its first occurrence:

| $\vee$ | $\alpha$ | $\beta$ | $\sim$ |
|---|---|---|---|
| * $\alpha$ | $\alpha$ | $\alpha$ | $\beta$ |
| $\beta$ | $\alpha$ | $\beta$ | $\alpha$ |

When he turned to investigate the independence of the axioms of the calculus of propositions in *Principia Mathematica*, Bernays found that the thesis which Whitehead and Russell called *Assoc* could be derived from the other four axioms and was therefore redundant. As might be expected, the derivation is not very obvious; but it involves no novelty of principle, since it is constructed within the calculus itself. To prove that each of the remaining four axioms is independent of the others is a different matter. For here we must show in each case that the permissible transitions can never lead from three given formulae to a fourth, and we cannot proceed by examining all possible derivations from the three given formulae. But just as the axioms of a system of geometry may be shown to be independent by development of the technique of interpretation used in the same connexion for a proof of consistency, so here too the independence of any one axiom from the other three may be proved by production of an appropriate group or matrix for the other three. An example will make the method clear.

Let us suppose that we are trying to prove the independence of *Taut* from *Add*, *Perm*, and *Sum*. Our task is achieved if we can find a matrix satisfying the following conditions: (1) the elements form a group closed under the operations represented by the primitive signs; (2) with the interpretation, or scheme for interpretation, specified by the matrix the formulae *Add*, *Perm*, and *Sum* receive a distinguished value, whatever may be the values assigned to the variables occurring in them; (3) the elements are so disposed in the matrix that if $P$ and $\sim P \vee Q$ both have a distinguished value so too does $Q$, with the result that all formulae derivable from the three axioms mentioned above in accordance with the permitted procedures of substitution and detachment have a distinguished value; (4) with this interpretation the formula *Taut* does not always take a distinguished value. The first three requirements are exactly those we should lay down if we were trying to prove the consistency of the set containing just *Add*, *Perm*, and *Sum*, and the effect of the fourth is to make sure that the matrix shall be a counter-example sufficient to prove the impossibility of deriving *Taut* from that set by the rules of derivation of the calculus. All four conditions are in fact satisfied by the scheme:

| $\vee$ | $\alpha$ | $\beta$ | $\gamma$ | $\sim$ |
|---|---|---|---|---|
| *$\alpha$ | $\alpha$ | $\alpha$ | $\alpha$ | $\beta$ |
| $\beta$ | $\alpha$ | $\beta$ | $\gamma$ | $\alpha$ |
| $\gamma$ | $\alpha$ | $\gamma$ | $\alpha$ | $\gamma$ |

in which *Add*, *Perm*, and *Sum* always have a distinguished value, but not *Taut*, since $(\gamma \vee \gamma) \supset \gamma = \gamma$.

Each of the other three axioms may be proved independent of its companions in similar fashion. Appropriate matrices are:

| $\vee$ | $\alpha$ | $\beta$ | $\gamma$ | $\delta$ | $\sim$ |
|---|---|---|---|---|---|
| *$\alpha$ | $\alpha$ | $\alpha$ | $\alpha$ | $\alpha$ | $\beta$ |
| $\beta$ | $\alpha$ | $\beta$ | $\beta$ | $\beta$ | $\alpha$ |
| *$\gamma$ | $\alpha$ | $\beta$ | $\gamma$ | $\gamma$ | $\delta$ |
| $\delta$ | $\alpha$ | $\beta$ | $\gamma$ | $\delta$ | $\gamma$ |

in which *Taut*, *Perm*, and *Sum* always have a distinguished value, but not *Add*, since $\gamma \supset (\beta \vee \gamma) = \beta$;

| $\vee$ | $\alpha$ | $\beta$ | $\gamma$ | $\delta$ | $\sim$ |
|---|---|---|---|---|---|
| *$\alpha$ | $\alpha$ | $\alpha$ | $\alpha$ | $\alpha$ | $\beta$ |
| $\beta$ | $\alpha$ | $\beta$ | $\gamma$ | $\delta$ | $\alpha$ |
| $\gamma$ | $\alpha$ | $\gamma$ | $\gamma$ | $\alpha$ | $\alpha$ |
| $\delta$ | $\alpha$ | $\delta$ | $\delta$ | $\delta$ | $\gamma$ |

in which *Taut*, *Add*, and *Sum* always have a distinguished value, but not *Perm*, since $(\gamma \vee \delta) \supset (\delta \vee \gamma) = \delta$;

| ∨ | α | β | γ | δ | ~ |
|----|---|---|---|---|---|
| *α | α | α | α | α | β |
| β | α | β | γ | δ | α |
| γ | α | γ | γ | α | δ |
| δ | α | δ | α | δ | α |

in which *Taut*, *Add*, and *Perm* always have a distinguished value, but not *Sum*, since $(\delta \supset \beta) \supset [(\gamma \vee \delta) \supset (\gamma \vee \beta)] = \gamma$.

It is worth noticing that all the matrices used here to prove independence allow for more than two values and that one of them allows for more than one distinguished value; but it is a mistake to suppose, as some logicians have done, that these considerations lend support to the suggestion that logic itself may be many-valued—unless indeed the word 'logic' is intended to cover any abstract system originally constructed by modification of the calculus of propositions. No doubt the system which contains, apart from the rules of substitution and detachment, only the axioms *Add*, *Perm*, and *Sum* can be so interpreted, e.g. in arithmetic, that each variable admits three genuine values; but it cannot then be accounted logic in any ordinary sense of that word. And when it is treated as a part of logic in the ordinary sense, it is interpreted in such a way that *Taut* seems necessary, though independent. In short, the Greek letters in the multi-valued matrices given above do not stand for truth-values of proposition.

Apart from their importance in metalogic, these proofs of consistency and independence for a version of the calculus of propositions are interesting because they illustrate simply and clearly the way in which the notion of a model or interpretation can be used for investigating the properties of a deductive system. Instead of saying that the initial formulae of a calculus entail a consequential formula if, and only if, it is impossible for the first to be true without the latter's being also true, we may say that the initial formulae entail the consequential formula if, and only if, the latter is satisfied by all interpretations that satisfy the former. As we have seen, this way of looking at things has the merit of allowing for proofs of independence by production of counter-examples, but it can give rise to perplexities. So long as we are dealing with formulae in which some signs, and in particular those of logic, are assumed throughout to have a fixed sense, it is not difficult to understand what is meant by the assertion that a certain interpretation satisfies a formula. In geometry, for example, we say that a postulate is satisfied by a certain interpretation of its extra-logical signs if that interpretation converts it into a true statement. But when, as now in our investigation of the calculus of propositions, we have to treat *all* the signs occurring in our formulae as open to interpretation and reinterpretation, it is not immediately clear what can be meant by the satisfaction of a formula. If, as in one example we have considered, an interpretation turns a formula into a numerical designation rather than a propositional expression, it is plain that the result cannot be a true statement. What then is the point of talking here about satisfaction? In our exposition of the proofs we have evaded the difficulty by giving an *ad hoc* definition of a satisfactory interpretation, but it is desirable to consider the question more generally.

However great the effort we make to attain complete abstraction in the presentation of a calculus, we must still make clear by ordinary language that certain formulae take a distinguished value and can give rise by a determinate procedure to other formulae with a distinguished value. In short, the presentation of a calculus is essentially a second-order activity requiring signs not themselves accounted part of the calculus. In Frege's works and again in *Principia Mathematica* the assertion sign serves in practice as an indication that what follows is supposed to be a truism of logic, and the rules of inference are expressly said to be commitments which cannot themselves be formulated in the symbolism appropriate for such truisms.[1] Certainly we may, if we please, abstract from the notion of truth, which Whitehead and Russell take as the distinguished value in the presentation of their calculus, and even from the notion of a proposition, but we must still retain the idea of a distinguished value and talk in ordinary language of the transmission of such a value from some formulae to others. Thus what can properly be said to be satisfied by an interpretation are not strings of empty signs such as $(p \vee p) \supset p$ but rather postulates of such forms as 'If $p$ is in G, then $(p \vee p) \supset p$ is in G*'.

In an article of 1934 E. V. Huntington drew attention to the informal, or unofficial, part of the theory of deduction (i.e. calculus of propositions) in *Principia Mathematica* and showed that the whole theory (including the axioms and the rule of detachment) could be derived from the following eight postulates:[2]

1. If $P$ is in G and $Q$ is in G, then $P \vee Q$ is in G.
2. If $P$ is in G, then $\sim P$ is in G.
3. If $P$ is in G*, then $P$ is in G.
4. If $P \vee Q$ is in G*, then $Q \vee P$ is in G*.

[1] The distinction between rules and premisses was made clear by C. L. Dodgson (Lewis Carroll) in 'What the Tortoise said to Achilles', *Mind*, N.S., iv (1895), pp. 278–80.
[2] 'Independent Postulates for the "Informal" Part of *Principia Mathematica*', *Bulletin of the American Mathematical Society*, xl (1934), pp. 127–36.

5. If $P$ is in G\*, then $P \vee Q$ is in G\*.
6. If $P$ is in G and $\sim P$ is in G\*, then $P$ is not in G\*.
7. If $P$ is in G and $\sim P$ is not in G\*, then $P$ is in G\*.
8. If $P \vee Q$ is in G\* and $\sim P$ is in G\*, then $Q$ is in G\*.

Here the symbolism of *Principia Mathematica* (which Huntington does not use) has been retained for convenience of comparison, but it is to be understood that we are not thereby committed to the interpretation which Whitehead and Russell adopt and may accordingly suggest any interpretation which will help us to an understanding of the structure of the system determined by the eight postulates. The use of English words in the formulation of these postulates naturally carries with it the assumption of ordinary logical principles for use in the derivation of consequences, but this is inevitable. When we reason about reasoning, we must acknowledge some principles, and the only question to be decided is whether we should allow ourselves a weak or a strong apparatus of proof. The relative simplicity of Huntington's system of postulates is due to the fact that he admits not only 'if' and 'and' but also 'not' to the English vocabulary which he uses in the framing of postulates.

The set of axioms which Whitehead and Russell give for the calculus of propositions is complete, not only in the sense that it is sufficient for the proof of all formulae which are necessarily true by virtue of the special way in which they are composed with the truth-functional signs $\sim$ and $\vee$ (or signs, like the dot of conjunction, which are defined in terms of these), but also in the strong sense that a contradiction results from the addition to the axioms of any formula which is composed in truth-functional fashion with the signs of the calculus but not already derivable from the axioms. For the proof of this theorem of metalogic we must begin by establishing a number of lemmata.

First we prove within the calculus the following two-way Philonians (or material equivalences, as they are commonly called):

$$(1) \quad \sim\sim p \equiv p$$

$(2)\ p \vee p \equiv p$              $(3)\ p.p \equiv p$
$(4)\ p \vee q \equiv q \vee p$              $(5)\ p.q \equiv q.p$
$(6)\ p \vee (q \vee r) \equiv (p \vee q) \vee r$              $(7)\ p.(q.r) \equiv (p.q).r$
$(8)\ p \vee (q.r) \equiv (p \vee q).(p \vee r)$              $(9)\ p.(q \vee r) \equiv (p.q) \vee (p.r)$
$(10)\ \sim(p \vee q) \equiv \sim p.\sim q$              $(11)\ \sim(p.q) \equiv \sim p \vee \sim q.$

Here (1), (2), and (3) are principles of simplification by which we may eliminate certain repetitions, (4) and (5) commutative laws which permit variations of order, (6) and (7) associative laws which justify us in disregarding brackets in certain situations and writing if we wish $p \lor q \lor r$ or $p.q.r$, (8) and (9) distributive laws which allow us to proceed in certain circumstances from a disjunctive expression to one with the conjunctive sign as main connective, or vice versa, while (10) and (11) are De Morgan's rules which enable us to avoid the negation of complex expressions. All are so obvious, when interpreted according to the instructions of Whitehead and Russell, that it seems tedious to derive them from the four independent axioms of the calculus, and we shall not in fact go through the rather lengthy arguments here, but it is essential to the proof of completeness that they can be so derived.

Next we prove that, for any truth-function $\mathcal{F}$ of one argument, it is permissible to assert

$$(12) \quad (p \equiv q) \supset [\mathcal{F}(p) \equiv \mathcal{F}(q)].$$

Since all truth–functional expressions are reducible in *Principia Mathematica* to expressions which contain only the signs $\sim$ and $\lor$ with propositional letters, we start by proving the three special cases:

$$(p \equiv q) \supset (\sim p \equiv \sim q)$$
$$(p \equiv q) \supset [(r \lor p) \equiv (r \lor q)]$$
$$(p \equiv q) \supset [(p \lor r) \equiv (q \lor r)].$$

Here again the proofs are to be conducted in the calculus without the introduction of any new principle. But when we go on to assert (12) with full generality on the ground that it can be proved for any particular $\mathcal{F}$ by repeated application of the three simple rules in whatever order may be necessary to build up the complicated theorem, our reasoning, though obviously valid, is not conducted in the calculus. The proof for each determinate truth-function is indeed in the calculus, but not the proof of the generalization.

The importance of (12) is that it entitles us to use the principles (1) to (11) for the transformation of parts of formulae as well as for the transformation of whole formulae and so makes it possible for us to reduce any truth-functional expression to an equivalent expression in *conjunctive normal form*, that is to say, to a conjunction of disjunctions where each component of a disjunction is either an atomic propositional sign or the negation of one of these. For this purpose there are three main operations to be undertaken in the following order: (i) the elimination of $\supset$ and $\equiv$ from all positions by use of the customary definitions; (ii) the elimination of negation signs from in front of brackets by use of De Morgan's rules; (iii) the elimination of conjunction signs from inside brackets by use of the distributive law. But double negations are to be eliminated wherever they occur, and simplifications and re-arrangements may be made whenever they are convenient. For an example of such reduction we may take the following sequence of equivalent expressions in which all the various transformations are carried out separately:

$$(p \supset q) \equiv (\sim q \supset \sim p)$$
$$(\sim p \vee q) \equiv (\sim q \supset \sim p)$$
$$(\sim p \vee q) \equiv \sim \sim q \vee \sim p)$$
$$(\sim p \vee q) \equiv (q \vee \sim p)$$
$$[(\sim p \vee q) \supset (q \vee \sim p)].[(q \vee \sim p) \supset (\sim p \vee q)]$$
$$[\sim(\sim p \vee q) \vee (q \vee \sim p)].[(q \vee \sim p) \supset (\sim p \vee q)]$$
$$[\sim(\sim p \vee q) \vee (q \vee \sim p)].[\sim(q \vee \sim p) \vee (\sim p \vee q)]$$
$$[(\sim \sim p . \sim q) \vee (q \vee \sim p)].[\sim(q \vee \sim p) \vee (\sim p \vee q)]$$
$$[p . \sim q) \vee (q \vee \sim p)].[\sim(q \vee \sim p) \vee (\sim p \vee q)]$$
$$[(p . \sim q) \vee (q \vee \sim p)].[(\sim q . \sim \sim p) \vee (\sim p \vee q)]$$
$$[(p . \sim q) \vee (q \vee \sim p)].[(\sim q . p) \vee (\sim p \vee q)]$$
$$[(p \vee q \vee \sim p).(\sim q \vee q \vee \sim p)].[(\sim q . p) \vee (\sim p \vee q)]$$
$$[(p \vee q \vee \sim p).(\sim q \vee q \vee \sim p)].[(\sim q \vee \sim p \vee q).(p \vee \sim p \vee q)]$$
$$(p \vee q \vee \sim p).(\sim q \vee q \vee \sim p).(\sim q \vee \sim p \vee q).(p \vee \sim p \vee q).$$

Whatever the complication of the formula with which we start, it is clear that successive applications of the operations detailed above must lead finally to an expression in the desired normal form. In any particular case the reduction of a truth-functional expression can be performed within the calculus of propositions, but once more the generalization which we need for the proof of completeness must be established by reasoning outside the cal-culus.

There may be distinguishable expressions in conjunctive nor-mal form which are all alike logically equivalent to a given expression, but this is of no importance, since for the argument which follows any of them is as good as any other. If when a truth-functional expression has been reduced to an equivalent expression in conjunctive normal form, it is found, as in the example above, that each of the conjoined disjunctions contains some atomic expression together with its negation, the original expression must be necessarily true in virtue of its form and de-rivable from the axioms of the calculus of propositions through the derivation of its equivalent normal form. For it is easy to prove within the calculus (i) the disjunction of any formula with its negation, (ii) the disjunction of a truism so established with any other formula whatsoever, and (iii) the conjunction of any number of formulae already proved. But it is possible to go farther and assert that every statement which is necessarily true in virtue of its form as a truth-function can be derived in this way from the axioms of the calculus of propositions. For if one of the disjunctions in the conjunctive normal form of such a statement did not contain an atomic propositional expression together with its negation, it would be possible for that disjunction to be false, i.e. if each unnegated propositional sign in it were false and each negated propositional sign true. And this is as much as to say that the whole might be false, which is absurd.

In order to show that the calculus of propositions with which we are concerned is complete in the strong sense, let us suppose that the set of axioms is enlarged by addition of a formula composed of propositional variables and truth-functional signs but not derivable from the original axioms. In the conjunctive normal form of this new formula there must be at least one disjunction which does not contain a propositional variable both with and without a negation sign. Let us substitute $p$ for each letter of this disjunctive formula which is not preceded by a negation sign and $\sim p$ for each letter that is preceded by a negation sign. By elimination of double negations the new disjunction can be reduced to $p \vee p \ldots \vee p$ and this in turn can be reduced to $p$. It is therefore possible to derive $p$ from our enlarged set of axioms by means of the permitted transitions. But a system which allows this is self-contradictory.

The proofs of consistency, independence, and completeness which have been considered here all refer to the calculus of propositions as it is presented by Whitehead and Russell in *Principia Mathematica*, but by suitable modifications they can be adapted to show the consistency, independence, and completeness of other versions of propositional logic including those which involve only rules. As might be expected the proofs are especially simple for that version which employs only rules of development.

In order to prove consistency here it is sufficient to show that the rules do not enable us to demonstrate everything, and this we can do by finding an interpretation of the system which excludes the possibility of passing from some formula to some other formula by a legitimate derivation. In particular we take a group G for which operations represented by our various formal signs can be defined in such a way that G is closed with respect to them, and a proper sub-group G* such that if all the elements represented by the formulae above the line in any of our schemata of development belong to G* there must be at least one of the elements represented by a formula below the line in that same schema which also belongs to G\*. Since we have to do with several operational signs, such an interpretation can be set out most easily in tabular form as follows:

| $P$ | $Q$ | $P.Q$ | $P \vee Q$ | $\sim P$ | $P \supset Q$ |
|---|---|---|---|---|---|
| \*$\alpha$ | $\alpha$ | $\alpha$ | $\alpha$ | $\beta$ | $\alpha$ |
| $\alpha$ | $\beta$ | $\beta$ | $\alpha$ | $\beta$ | $\beta$ |
| $\beta$ | $\alpha$ | $\beta$ | $\alpha$ | $\alpha$ | $\alpha$ |
| $\beta$ | $\beta$ | $\beta$ | $\beta$ | $\alpha$ | $\alpha$ |

If the system of rules were inconsistent, it would be possible to demonstrate every formula and therefore a formula with the value $\beta$. Furthermore, such a demonstration would be a derivation in which the initial formulae could all be replaced by any formula whatsoever and therefore by a formula with the value $\alpha$. But such a derivation could not be a single application of any of our rules. Nor could it be any more complex development carried out in accordance with our rules. For when the initial formulae all have the value $\alpha$, a formula with the value $\beta$ cannot be introduced below the line except by application of one of the rules (4), (5), or (7a); and it can be shown by reference to the table that in each such case there is introduced also at the same time another formula with the value $\alpha$, so that it is impossible any succession of applications of our rules should constitute a development leading from an initial formula with the value $\alpha$ to a single end formula with the value $\beta$.

Given this interpretation, which may be called normal because it accords with our original intention, it is possible to prove the independence of the several rules by setting up for each of them in turn a modified or abnormal interpretation of its formal sign which leaves all the other rules unaffected (in the sense that they are still incapable of leading from a set of formulae that all have the value $\alpha$ to a set that all have the value $\beta$) but allows this rule to lead from a set of formulae that all have the value $\alpha$ to a set that all have the value $\beta$. Since there are never more than three rules concerned with a single formal sign, this is not a difficult matter. In the following list there is given for each rule an abnormal interpretation of its special sign which, taken together with the normal interpretation for all the other signs, suffices to prove the independence of that rule:

(1) $P.Q = \beta$      (2a) $P.Q = Q$ (2b) $P.Q = P$

(3a) $P \vee Q = Q$ (3b) $P \vee Q = P$      (4) $P \vee Q = \alpha$

(5) $\sim P = \beta$      (6) $\sim P = \alpha$

(7a) $P \supset Q = Q$ (7b) $P \supset Q = \sim P$      (8) $P \supset Q = \alpha$

For a direct proof of the completeness of our rules of development (1) to (8), considered as a system of propositional logic, it is necessary only to modify the proof of completeness given above by including arguments to show that the rules allow both for the reduction of all truth-functional formulae to conjunctive normal form and also for the reasoning by which an expression in that form can be proved true if each of its conjoined disjunctions contains some atomic expression together with its negation. We can then go on to show that addition of any new rule not derivable from those already present would commit us to acceptance of $*/P$.

Whatever the form of the calculus of propositions with which we are concerned, proofs of consistency, independence and completeness for its rules and axioms (if any) will inevitably involve reasoning that cannot be presented within the calculus itself. We have noticed examples of such reasoning in Post's proof of the completeness of the calculus presented in *Principia Mathematica*, but we might equally well have drawn attention to such reasoning in proofs of consistency or independence. For when it is shown that no legitimate derivation, however long, can lead from premisses with a distinguished value to a conclusion with an undistinguished value, the argument cannot be validated by principles of propositional logic alone. The reason for this is not simply that the theses which we prove are *about* the calculus of propositions (for some arguments about a calculus may exemplify principles of that calculus), but rather that the theses we prove are *general* and accessible only by reasoning which shows that a certain property belongs to all items of a sequence because it belongs to the first and is hereditary in the sequence, i.e. by mathematical induction. Since the principle of such reasoning transcends not only the resources of primary (or propositional) logic but also those of general logic (or quantification theory) it seems reasonable to say that even the elementary theorems of metalogic considered in this section do not belong to logic itself.

## 2. *The Metatheory of General Logic*

In our consideration of the metatheory of general logic let us assume for the sake of simplicity that we have to do with the following six rules:

(1) $P \supset Q, P/Q$

(2) $*/P \supset (Q \supset P)$

(3) $*/[P \supset (Q \supset R)] \supset [(P \supset Q) \supset (P \supset R)]$

(4) $*/(\sim P \supset \sim Q) \supset (Q \supset P)$

(5) $*/(x)Fx \supset FY$

(6) $P \supset Fx/P \supset (x)Fx$ provided that $x$ is not free in $P$.

Here the sub-system containing rules (1)—(4) is the primary part, and the whole is a simplified version of the system given by Frege in his *Begriffsschrift*, but with rules throughout in place of axioms.

In order to prove the consistency of these rules it is sufficient to show that they do not commit us to any two formulae related as $P$ and $\sim P$. For this purpose we adopt the interpretation used in the consistency proof of the last section, but with the additional proviso that universal quantifiers may be neglected and expressions of the form $Fx$ treated in the same way as propositional signs, i.e. regarded as capable of taking one of the two values $\alpha$ and $\beta$. It is then obvious that all formulae introduced by any of the rules (2)–(5) must have the distinguished value $\alpha$ and that this value will be retained by all formulae derived from formulae of the first group by use of rule (1) or rule (6). Since, according to the interpretation, no two formulae related as $P$ and $\sim P$ could both have the value $\alpha$, this establishes the consistency of the rules.

In this proof, first published by D. Hilbert and W. Ackermann in their *Grundzüge der theoretischen Logik* of 1928, the interpretation we provide for the symbolism of universality amounts in effect to the assumption that there is just one individual in the domain over which we generalize by means of that symbolism. For if there were just one individual and it had the name $Y$, the expression $(x)Fx$ would be equivalent to $FY$ and it would be evident that rules (5) and (6), which are proper to general logic, involve no risk of inconsistency. So far as our argument goes, assumption of some larger domain of individuals, in particular assumption of an infinite domain, might conceivably lead to a contradiction. But if it did, the contradiction would result from some absurdity introduced by that assumption and not from general logic considered in itself.

The trivial interpretation of the symbolism of universality by which we can prove consistency of the whole set of rules is useful also for a proof of the independence of rules (1), (2), (3), and (4). For this interpretation makes rules (5) and (6) equivalent respectively to

(5′)  $*/P \supset P$
(6′)  $P \supset Q /P \supset Q$

and it is possible to show by an adaptation of the methods of the last section that none of the first four rules can be derived from these taken together with the other three.

In order to show the independence of (5) we replace the universal quantifier $(x)$ wherever it occurs in our system by

$\sim(x)\sim$, i.e. by the combination of signs which we use as existential quantifier. Then rules (1)–(4) remain unchanged, and (6) goes over into the derivative rule $P \supset Fx/P \supset \sim(x)\sim Fx$. From this it follows that every rule derivable in the original system without recourse to (5) must either remain unchanged by the transformation or go over into another derivative rule. But (5) becomes $*/\sim(x)\sim Fx \supset FY$, which is not a derivative rule, since its addition to the original system would enable us to get $*/FX \supset FY$.

Similarly in order to show the independence of (6) we replace $(x)Fx$ wherever it occurs in our system by $(x)\sim(Fx \supset Fx)$. Then rules (1)–(4) remain unchanged, and (5) goes over into the trivial derivative rule $*/(x)\sim(Fx \supset Fx) \supset FY$. But (6) becomes $P \supset Fx/P \supset (x)\sim(Fx \supset Fx)$, which is certainly not a derivative rule.

These proofs of consistency and independence for the rules of a system of general logic without axioms are adapted from the proofs of consistency and independence which Bernays elaborated for a system with axioms, but the essential idea of the proof of consistency is contained in a paper of Herbrand.[1] A proof of completeness for a system of general logic was first published by Gödel in 1930.[2] This will be explained in what follows, but before considering it in any detail we must make clear the nature of the enterprise. For the situation with which we have to deal here is much more complicated than that discussed in the last section.

Our set of rules for general logic is not complete in the strong sense, since it can be enlarged without contradiction; that is to say, it is possible to conceive various rules consistent with those given above but not derivative from them. A simple example is the rule $*/\sim(x)Fx \supset (x)\sim Fx$, which, if suitable signs are available, can also be put in any of the following forms:

$$*/(x)Fx \lor (x)\sim Fx,$$
$$*/(\exists x)Fx \supset (x)Fx,$$
$$*/\sim[(\exists x)Fx.(\exists x)\sim Fx].$$

Addition of this to our set would amount to a stipulation in favour of the special interpretation which we used in the proof of consistency, i.e. to a restriction whereby the domain of individuals admissible as arguments to propositional functions is supposed to contain only one element. For, as the last version shows most clearly, the rule requires in effect that the formula

[1] 'Recherches sur la théorie de la démonstration', *Travaux de la Société des sciences et des lettres de Varsovie, Cl. III, math.-phys.*, xxxiii (1930), pp. 33–160.
[2] 'Die Vollständigkeit der Axiome des logischen Funktionkalküls, *Monatshefte für Mathematik und Physik*, xxvii (1930), pp. 349–60.

$(\exists x)Fx.(\exists x){\sim}Fx$ shall be false under all interpretations of $F$, and this is as much as to say that there are not as many as two individuals. By an extension of the same technique rules can be constructed as follows for the purpose of limiting the domain of individuals under consideration to two, three, or any desired number of individuals:

[1]   $*/(x)Fx \vee (x){\sim}Fx$
[2]   $*/(x)Fx \vee (x)({\sim}Fx \vee Gx) \vee (x)({\sim}Fx \vee {\sim}Gx)$
[3]   $*/(x)Fx \vee (x)({\sim}Fx \vee Gx) \vee (x)({\sim}Fx \vee {\sim}Gx \vee Hx) \vee$
        $(x)({\sim}Fx \vee {\sim}Gx \vee {\sim}Hx)$

. . . . . . . . . .

In each case the number indicated in brackets before a rule is the *upper limit* of size to the domains of individuals permitted by that rule. For while the propositional schema printed after the solidus in the second of these rules is not valid (i.e. necessarily true for any interpretation of its schematic letters) in any domain containing three or more individuals, it is valid in any domain containing two individuals or one; and similarly every schema valid for a domain of n+1 individuals is valid in any domain of n individuals, provided that n > o. This can be seen from consideration of what it means to say that a propositional schema with quantifiers is valid in a domain of n individuals.

When the domain over which quantifiers are used is finite, a universal expression may in principle be replaced by a conjunction and an existential expression by a disjunction. Thus we may write $F1.F2$ instead of $(x)Fx$ when this latter is applied to a domain of two individuals only and the individuals are designated arbitrarily by numerals. If, and only if, the result of making such replacements throughout an expression is a tautology according to the rules of propositional logic, the original expression with quantifiers may be described as necessarily true in the finite domain to which it has been applied. Similarly a propositional *schema* with quantifiers may be described as *valid* in a domain of specified finite size when for any interpretation of its schematic letters it can be turned into a necessary truth by elimination of its quantifiers in the manner explained above. Thus in relation to a domain of two individuals the schema which appears in the second of the restrictive rules noticed above can be reduced to

$$(F1.F2) \vee [({\sim}F1 \vee G1).({\sim}F2 \vee G2)] \vee [({\sim}F1 \vee {\sim}G1).({\sim}F2 \vee$$
$${\sim}G2)],$$

i.e. to

$$F1.F2 \vee {\sim}F1.{\sim}F2 \vee {\sim}F1.G2 \vee {\sim}F2.G1 \vee G1.G2 \vee {\sim}F1.{\sim}F2 \vee$$
$${\sim}F1.{\sim}G2 \vee {\sim}F2.{\sim}G1 \vee {\sim}G1.{\sim}G2$$

or

$$F_1.F_2 \vee \sim F_1.\sim F_2 \vee \sim F_1.(G_2 \vee \sim G_2) \vee \sim F_2.(G_1 \vee \sim G_1) \vee$$
$$G_1.G_2 \vee \sim G_1.\sim G_2,$$

which is tautological. If, however, the same schema is applied to a domain of one individual and reduced accordingly, the result is again a tautological pattern. And in general a schema which is valid in a domain of $n+1$ individuals must also be valid in a domain of n individuals, provided that $n > 0$. For if the application of the schema to a domain of $n+1$ individuals yields a reduced form which is tautological, another reduced form which is still tautological can be obtained by substituting the numeral 1 for $n+1$ throughout the first, and production of this second is obviously the same as application of the original to a domain of n individuals.

This law can be restated in terms of satisfiability. For just as a schema is said to be valid in a given domain if in application to that domain it yields a truth for every interpretation of its schematic letters, so a schema is said to be satisfiable in a given domain if it yields a truth for some interpretation of its schematic letters. And from this it follows that the validity of a schema in a domain can be identified with the non-satisfiability of its negation and satisfiability of a schema with the non-validity of its negation. It is therefore easy to show that a schema which is satisfiable in a domain of n individuals must be satisfiable also in a domain of $n+1$ individuals, provided that $n > 0$, and in some contexts this formulation of the law may perhaps be more useful than that given above.

If we confine our attention to the singulary (or monadic) functional calculus, i.e. to the part of general logic which deals only with propositional functions of one argument, we need not consider domains of more than a finite number of individuals. For it has been shown by P. Bernays and M. Schönfinkel that any schema of this calculus which is satisfiable at all (i.e. in some domain or other) is satisfiable in a domain of $2^n$ individuals where n is the number of different schematic function letters it contains.[1] In order to prove this we first suppose that the function letters of the schema have been interpreted as signs for various attributes $A_1, \ldots, A_n$. Then, however large the domain of individuals involved in this interpretation, it can be divided between at most $2^n$ classes in such a way that two individuals are members of the same class if and only if each has all the attributes

---

[1] 'Zum Entscheidungsproblem der mathematischen Logik', *Mathematische Annalen*, xcix (1928), pp. 342–72.

from our list which belong to the other. But these classes, say $K_1, \ldots, K_r$, where $r \leqslant 2^n$, may now be taken as a new domain of individuals for which we can define new attributes $A_1^*, \ldots,$ $A_n^*$ such that $K_i$ has $A_j^*$ if and only if the members of $K_i$ have $A_j$. And in this new domain our original schema must evidently be satisfied once more when its function letters are interpreted as signs for the attributes $A_1^*, \ldots, A_n^*$. If $r = 2^n$, this completes the required proof; and if $r < 2^n$, we need only invoke the law whereby the satisfiability of a schema in any finite domain entails its satisfiability in any larger finite domain.

So far we have considered only validity and satisfiability in finite domains. But in that part of general logic which deals with relations as distinct from attributes it is easy to produce schemata that cannot be satisfied in finite domains. One such is

$$(x)\sim F(x,x).(x)(y)(z)[F(x,y).F(y,z) \supset F(x,z)].(x)(\exists y)F(x,y).$$

If we take $F(x,y)$ to mean the same as $x < y$, the formula is satisfied in the infinite domain of natural numbers. But there cannot be any interpretation which allows for its satisfaction in a finite domain, and so its negation is valid in every finite domain. Is it perhaps possible to produce a schema which requires for its satisfaction a domain even larger than that of the natural numbers? We shall presently see reason to answer this question in the negative, but for the moment the important point to establish is that logic is not concerned with the distinction between finite and infinite domains. Our rules of general logic are not complete in the strong sense, precisely because they are rules which allow only for the demonstration of universally (or absolutely) valid schemata, that is to say according to the usual explanation, schemata valid in every non-empty domain.

The reservation by which empty domains are excluded from consideration may seem at first sight to be arbitrary, and it has in fact been criticized by some logicians as involving an assumption of existence which restricts the scope of their study and compromises its purity. The reason commonly urged in defence of the reservation is that it allows us to retain $(x)Fx \supset (\exists x)Fx$ as a universally valid schema derivative from $(x)Fx \supset FY$ and $FY \supset (\exists x)Fx$. According to this line of reasoning $(x)Fx$ would be true in an empty domain for every interpretation of $F$, being equivalent to $\sim(\exists x)\sim Fx$, but $(\exists x)Fx$ would be false, and with it the whole schema $(x)Fx \supset (\exists x)Fx$. This is, no doubt, a good argument for confining attention to non-empty domains, but it is not sufficient to remove the misgivings of those who fear an improper restriction of the scope of logic. In order to meet their objection it is necessary to show that the restriction is really no restriction at all because there can be no empty domains of individuals. Now in the technical terminology of logicians an individual is simply an admissible argument for the functions of lowest type under consideration at the moment, and it is therefore impossible to speak sensibly of a domain of individuals unless one is able to indicate some function or functions for which it is appropriate. Similarly it is absurd to suggest that there might conceivably be propositional functions appropriate to an empty domain. For there cannot be propositional functions without admissible arguments. Those which are inconsistent determine empty *classes*, but even these have non-empty *domains*, since there are arguments of which they may be denied with good sense. Indeed to say that a supposed domain of individuals was empty could be at best only a roundabout way of maintaining that some complex of signs which had been supposed to express a propositional function did not in fact express anything at all. Thus, for example, it may be said that there is nothing of which we can even deny sensibly that it is the square root of courage.

One reason for failure to appreciate this connexion between domains and functions may be the abstract fashion in which domain laws are commonly presented by logicians. But another source of confusion is a dogma that has become very common among empiricists in recent years. Having remarked correctly that the existence of a man or a horse is a contingent fact to be learnt only from experience, some of these philosophers have unfortunately gone on to say that no existential proposition can be established *a priori*. Their thesis can be refuted quite easily by the production of counter-examples from mathematics, such as the proposition that there is a prime number greater than a million, but it has been taken very seriously and used as an argument against the possibility of ontology. In this context it may lead to the view that logic, which is undoubtedly *a priori*, should not be based on the exclusion of empty domains.

Although for the reasons which have been explained the rules of general logic set out at the beginning of this section are not complete in the strong sense, they are complete in the weaker sense of being sufficient for the demonstration of all universally valid schemata. This in effect is what Gödel showed in the theorem of 1930 mentioned above, and we must now consider the plan of his proof. The main idea of the method by which he succeeds in relating validity in general logic to validity in primary or propositional logic was published first by Th. Skolem in 1928[1] and

---

[1] 'Über die mathematische Logik', *Norsk Matematisk Tidsskrift*, x (1928), pp. 125–42.

developed immediately after by J. Herbrand in an important dissertation to which we have already referred,[1] but his use of it is new, and with its help he is able to furnish incidentally a new proof of a very interesting theorem discovered by Löwenheim as early as 1915.

First of all it is necessary to show that for every universally valid formula of general logic there can be found a universally valid formula which is (a) demonstrable if and only if the original is demonstrable and (b) constructed in Skolem prenex normal form, that is to say, with all its quantifiers at the beginning and all its existential quantifiers, if any, in front of all its universal quantifiers, if any. This result, which was obtained by T. Skolem in 1920,[2] has the same place in Gödel's proof of his completeness theorem for general logic that the thesis of reducibility to conjunctive normal form has in Post's proof of his completeness theorem for propositional logic. Naturally the reduction of any given formula to Skolem normal form must be provable by argument within the calculus of propositional functions whose completeness is to be established in Gödel's theorem; but just as in the simpler case of reducibility to conjunctive normal form, so here mathematical induction is required for proof of the general thesis. We shall not attempt to reproduce the detail of the argument, but simply note the conclusion that it is sufficient for Gödel's purpose to show the demonstrability of all universally valid formulae that are in Skolem normal form.

Let us now introduce '$\mathscr{A}$' as a name for a well-formed formula of the Skolem form

$$(\exists x_1) \ldots (\exists x_k)(y_1) \ldots (y_m) M(x_1, \ldots, x_k; y_1, \ldots, y_m)$$

in which $M(x_1, \ldots x_k; y_1, \ldots, y_m)$ is itself an abbreviation for an expression without quantifiers and containing apart from the indicated variables only schematic function letters together with truth-functional connectives, brackets, and possibly schematic proposition letters. If $k = 0$, that is to say, if $\mathscr{A}$ contains no existential quantifiers, the whole may be universally valid because the full version of $M(y_1, \ldots, y_m)$ is tautological in pattern, e.g. of some such shape as $(Fy_1 \vee \sim Fy_1) . (Gy_2 \vee \sim Gy_2)$. If $k = 1$, that is to say, if there is only one existential quantifier in $\mathscr{A}$, the whole may again be universally valid because the full version of $M(x_1; y_1, \ldots y_m)$ is tautological in pattern. But if there is more than one existential quantifier, the situation is more complicated. For

[1] 'Récherches sur la théorie de la demonstration', *Travaux de la Société des sciences et des lettres de Varsovie, Classe III*, xxxiii (1930), pp. 33–160.

[2] 'Logisch-kombinatorische Untersuchungen über die Erfüllbarkeit oder Beweisbarkeit mathematischer Sätze etc.', *Skrifter utgit av Videnskapsselskapet i Kristiania*, I *Math.-nat. Klasse*, 1920, no. 4.

while the whole formula may still be universally valid because of the tautological character of the full version of $M(x_1, \ldots, x_k; y_1, \ldots, y_m)$, it may also be universally valid for another reason, namely, because there is some way of linking the existentially bound variables which gives to the full version of $M(x_1, \ldots, x_k; y_1, \ldots, y_m)$ a tautological character it would otherwise lack. Thus for the trivial case in which $k = 2$ and $m = 0$ the formula $(\exists x_1)(\exists x_2)(Fx_1 \vee {\sim}Fx_2)$ is universally valid because it is derivable from $FY \vee {\sim}FY$. In order to deal systematically with these complexities let us agree to denumerate as follows all the different k-tuples of the form $\langle z_{i_1}, z_{i_2}, \ldots, z_{i_k} \rangle$ which we can form from the infinite sequence of variables $z_0, z_1, z_2 \ldots$ by taking each as many times as we choose. First we group the k-tuples according to their index sums, putting earlier those for which $i_1 + i_2 + \ldots + i_k$ is smaller, and then we arrange them lexicographically within each such group. Thus the sequence begins $\langle z_0, z_0, \ldots, z_0 \rangle$, $\langle z_0, z_0, \ldots, z_0, z_1 \rangle$, $\langle z_0, z_0, \ldots, z_1, z_0 \rangle$, $\ldots$. Now let '$\mathscr{B}_n$' be a name for the expression $M(z_{n_1}, z_{n_2}, \ldots, z_{n_k}; z_{(n-1)m+1}, z_{(n-1)m+2}, \ldots, z_{nm})$ where $\langle z_{n_1}, z_{n_2}, \ldots, z_{n_k} \rangle$ is the nth of the k-tuples mentioned above. Thus, for example, if $k = 3$ and $m = 2$ we have

$$\text{'}\mathscr{B}_1\text{' as a name for } M(z_0, z_0, z_0; z_1, z_2)$$
$$\text{'}\mathscr{B}_2\text{'} \quad \text{,,} \quad \text{,,} \quad M(z_0, z_0, z_1; z_3, z_4)$$
$$\text{'}\mathscr{B}_3\text{'} \quad \text{,,} \quad \text{,,} \quad M(z_0, z_1, z_0; z_5, z_6)$$

. . . . . . . .

In each such expression the variables after the semicolon are different from all those before it, and also from all those in any earlier expression of the series, but except in the first expression of the series there are no variables before a semicolon which have not occurred in earlier expressions. Further let '$\mathscr{C}_n$' be a name for the disjunction of all the formulae $\mathscr{B}_1, \mathscr{B}_2, \ldots, \mathscr{B}_n$, and '$\mathscr{D}_n$' a name for the universal closure of $\mathscr{C}_n$, i.e. for the formula obtained by writing in front of $\mathscr{C}_n$ universal quantifiers for all the variables it contains. Then by use of the rules of the functional calculus under investigation together with the principle of mathematical induction it can be shown that, for every n, $\mathscr{D}_n$ entails $\mathscr{A}$. The detailed proof is rather tedious, but not difficult.

Now it may be that in our systematic denumeration of possibilities there is some number n for which $\mathscr{C}_n$ is tautological in the sense in which a schema such as $Fx \vee {\sim}Fx$ can be said to be tautological. If so, its universal closure $\mathscr{D}_n$ can be asserted, and from this, as we have noticed, $\mathscr{A}$ can be derived within the calculus under investigation. If, however, there is no number n for which $\mathscr{C}_n$ is tautological, $\mathscr{A}$ is not a universally valid formula, because it is possible to interpret its schematic letters in such a way as to make the whole false.

The last point is proved as follows. Since, according to the hypothesis, for every n, $\mathscr{C}_n$ is non-tautological, it is possible to assign truth-values to all its elementary parts (i.e. to its schematic proposition letters, if any, and to its part formulae of such patterns as $Fz_p$, $G(z_q, z_r)$, &c.) in such a way that the whole gets the value *falsity* by the rules of propositional logic. For any given n there can be only a finite number of such falsifying assignments, but altogether there must be infinitely many, since the sequence $\mathscr{C}_1, \mathscr{C}_2, \mathscr{C}_3$, &c., is infinite and each formula in it after the first contains some elementary part or parts which are not in its immediate predecessor. But for the same reason we may suppose all the elementary parts which appear in any of the formulae $\mathscr{C}_1, \mathscr{C}_2, \mathscr{C}_3$, &c., to be denumerable in the order of their first appearance, and on this basis we can make a master assignment of truth-values to them all as follows. The first elementary part is to receive the truth-value *truth* if and only if it has the value *truth* in infinitely many of the falsifying assignments mentioned above; the second is to receive the value *truth* if and only if it has the value *truth* in infinitely many of those falsifying assignments mentioned above which agree up to date with the master assignment; and so on. It is to be assumed, of course, that each elementary part gets the value *falsity* if it does not get the value *truth*. Clearly this master assignment falsifies simultaneously all the formulae $\mathscr{C}_1$, $\mathscr{C}_2, \mathscr{C}_3$, &c., and therefore all the formulae $\mathscr{B}_1, \mathscr{B}_2, \mathscr{B}_3$, &c., out of which they are constructed by disjunction. Next in each elementary part that is not a simple propositional letter we may suppose its variables $z_0, z_1, z_2$, &c., to be replaced by their own numerical indices so that we have expressions such as $F_0$, $G(1, 2)$, $F_1$, $G(5, 7)$, &c. If further we suppose that each of these new expressions retains the truth-value given to its original in the master assignment, we have in effect provided interpretations from within the theory of numbers for all the schematic function letters of the full version of $M(x_1, \ldots, x_k; y_1, \ldots, y_m)$. Thus if $F$ is such a letter with one argument place, it is now determined for which numbers $Fx$ is to be accounted true and for which false, and so on with each selected letter. Furthermore, these interpretations of the schematic letters with reference to the domain of natural numbers make $\mathscr{A}$ false, since it is obvious that there can be no k-tuple of natural numbers such as would now be required for the truth of

$$(\exists x_1) \ldots (\exists x_k)(y_1) \ldots (y_m)M(x_1, \ldots, x_k; y_1, \ldots, y_m).$$

The result then is this: either $\mathscr{A}$ is provable with the means of the calculus of propositional functions or it is not valid in the domain of natural numbers and so not universally valid. In short, if $\mathscr{A}$ is universally valid, it is provable. Admittedly the argument is not sufficient, as it stands, for the purposes of Hilbert, since it involves the principle of excluded middle in the assumption that there either is or is not a number n for which $\mathscr{C}_n$ is tautological. But it reveals the structure of general logic in a very interesting way, and it enables us to obtain as a corollary an important theorem first obtained independently by L. Löwenheim in 1915, namely, the theorem that a schema which is valid in the domain of natural numbers (or in any denumerably infinite domain) is universally valid.[1] For according to the result set out in disjunctive form at the beginning of this paragraph, if $\mathscr{A}$ is valid in the domain of natural numbers, it must be provable, and so universally valid. Writing 'U' for 'universally valid', 'D' for 'valid in a denumerably infinite domain', 'P' for 'provable by means of the rules of general logic', and an arrow for entailment, we can represent the relations of the various notions by a triangle

Gödel's completeness theorem is then of the form 'U→D→P' and Löwenheim's domain theorem, as presented here, of the form 'D→P→U'. The third circuit represented by 'P→U→D', would, of course, be a triviality.

The paper in which Löwenheim gave the first proof of his theorem (using the symbolism of Schröder) is the beginning of modern metalogic, but the importance of his result was not fully appreciated until some years after he published it. The theorem set out above is especially interesting because it shows that denumerably infinite domains are the largest which need ever be considered in logic. Perhaps its importance can be seen most clearly when it is recast as the statement that every schema satisfiable in some domain is satisfiable also in a denumerably infinite domain. For as Skolem pointed out in 1922, this leads to a new paradox in the theory of sets, and that, moreover, within the axiomatized theory which was designed to save us from the dangers of Cantor's unregulated pioneering.[2] From the axioms

---

[1] 'Über Möglichkeiten im Relativkalkül', *Mathematische Annalen*, lxxvi (1915), pp. 447–70.

[2] 'Einige Bemerkungen zur axiomatischen Begründung der Mengenlehre', *Wissenschäftliche Vorträge, gehalten auf dem Fünften Kongress der Skandinavischen Mathematiker in Helsingfors 1922*, pp. 217–32. We have not seen the original.

which are assumed it is possible to prove the existence of a non-denumerable infinity of sets: indeed any proposed system of axioms which did not allow this would be thought so narrow as to be worthless. But the axioms can be conjoined to make a single formula which, apart from the logical signs of the calculus of propositional functions, contains only the $\epsilon$ of membership; and according to Löwenheim's theorem, if it is possible to find any interpretation at all for $\epsilon$ which makes the formula true, it is possible to find some such interpretation in a denumerably infinite domain. In short, axioms designed for the purpose of focusing attention on a non-denumerable infinity must inevitably fail to achieve that purpose. Skolem has even shown that the difficulty cannot be overcome by the introduction of an infinity of axioms, since any *class* of formulae which are simultaneously satisfiable in any non-empty domain are satisfiable in a denumerably infinite domain.[1] The only possible way out of the difficulty seems to be Skolem's own suggestion that the distinction between denumerable and non-denumerable should be taken as relative to our axiom system. Thus the sub-sets of an infinite set may be non-denumerable within a given axiomatic system because denumeration of them would involve construction of another set (i.e. of pairs) not allowable within the theory though definable in some way from without by reference to the theory as a whole. This is a plausible hypothesis, but the establishment of it would scarcely be a vindication of Cantor. For it involves the thesis that there are no *absolutely* non-denumerable sets.

## 3. *The Incompletability of Formal Arithmetic*

The proofs of consistency, independence, and completeness which were noticed in the last section can be extended for application to the deductive system which contains Frege's two axioms for identity in addition to the apparatus of general logic. Within this system it is possible to define numerals as indices in existential statements. Thus for *There is exactly one F thing*, *There are exactly two F things*, &c., we may write:

$$(\exists_1 x)Fx =_{\text{def}} (\exists x)[Fx.(y)(Fy \supset x = y)],$$
$$(\exists_2 x)Fx =_{\text{def}} (\exists x)(\exists y)[Fx.Fy.{\sim}(x = y).(z)(Fz \supset x = z \lor y = z)],$$
. . . . . . . . . .

But we cannot do enough to make Frege's theory of arithmetic look plausible without introducing, as he did, variables of a higher

[1] 'Untersuchungen über die Axiome des Klassenkalküls, etc.', *Skrifter utgit av Videnskapsselskapet i Kristiania*, I *Mat.-nat. Klasse*, 1919, no. 3.

type. For it is only by their help that we can hope to define numbers as objects of a certain sort (namely, sets of concepts or sets of sets) and so to prove Peano's axioms. Introduction of variables of a higher type, when accompanied by the thesis of extensionality, amounts in effect to the passage from general logic to the theory of membership, or, as it is more commonly called, the theory of sets. Whether or not Peano's axioms can be derived within any acceptable version of the theory of sets is a question about which mathematicians may differ, but at the next step in the development of metamathematics it is possible to avoid this controversy by investigating the system $\mathscr{P}$ which results from dropping the questionable theses of *Principia Mathematica* and adding Peano's axioms instead. If Whitehead and Russell are right, $\mathscr{P}$ must be derivable from their own system, and there can be no doubt that it is also part of what Hilbert has in mind when he talks of the formalization of mathematics.

This is the subject of K. Gödel's study in his paper 'On Formally Undecidable Sentences of *Principia Mathematica* and related systems'.[1] His calculus of general logic is taken from *Principia Mathematica* without change, except that he writes $x\Pi F(x)$ in place of $(x)F(x)$. But of the rest he retains only the distinction of types, which he acknowledges by subscripts attached to his variables $x_1, y_1, x_2, y_2$, &c., and the principle of extensionality, which he presents in the form of an infinite sequence of formulae:

$$x_1\Pi(x_2(x_1) \equiv y_2(x_1)) \supset x_2 = y_2,$$
$$x_2\Pi(x_3(x_2) \equiv y_3(x_2)) \supset x_3 = y_3,$$

. . . . . . . . .

He introduces, however, two new primitive signs o and $f$ which he uses for the formulation of three special axioms of number theory:

1. $\sim(fx_1 = 0)$,
2. $fx_1 = fy_1 \supset x_1 = y_1$,
3. $x_2(0) . x_1\Pi(x_2(x_1) \supset x_2(fx_1)) \supset x_1\Pi(x_2(x_1))$.

If we take the sign o in its usual sense and $f$ as meaning 'the successor of', we have here versions of Peano's third, fourth, and fifth axioms. Since the sequence of natural numbers is taken for the domain of individuals of the system, it is unnecessary to introduce either of his other two axioms (i.e. o *is a number* and *If n is a number, so too is the successor of n*) and indeed impossible to do so, unless we regard *x is a number* as an abbreviation for $x = 0$ *or*

[1] Über formal unentscheidbare Sätze der Principia Mathematica und verwandter Systeme', *Monatshefte für Mathematik und Physik*, xxxviii (1931), pp. 173–98.

*x is the successor of something*. It is interesting to notice also that the principle of mathematical induction cannot be stated in a single axiom without use of a variable of higher type.

For convenience of reference Gödel distinguishes two kinds of meaningful formulae which may occur within the system. Formulae of the first kind are numerical signs, and they include not only numerals proper such as o, *fo, ffo*, &c., but also variables of the lowest type and complex signs which turn into designations of numbers when the variables which they contain are replaced by numerals. Formulae of the second kind are propositional expressions or expressions which can be turned into propositional expressions either by appropriate substitutions for variables or by the prefixing of quantifiers. Among numerical formulae special importance attaches to those which become designations of numbers when the variables which they contain are replaced by numerals. For these are the functional signs of ordinary mathematics, and Gödel finds it necessary to introduce a number of them in the development of his argument. Some of his definitions are explicit equivalences and some such as

$$\begin{cases} o! = 1 \\ (n+1)! = (n+1)n! \end{cases}$$

involve the recursive procedure of fixing the value of the function for the argument o and then showing how the value for any later argument can be obtained from the value for the preceding argument. But all alike are effective in the sense of providing equations from which in principle at least the values of the functions for any assigned arguments can be calculated by substitutions and replacements.

Within this system Gödel now constructs a formula that cannot be proved with the resources of the system, although it must be true unless the system is self-contradictory. In effect what the formula says is that it is itself unprovable. At first sight this seems paradoxical, and we are inclined to suspect that the formula must be faulty in the same way as the pseudo-statement 'What I am now saying is false'. But the self-reference of Gödel's formula is harmless. In order to see why this is so and how the self-reference is achieved, we must consider Gödel's arithmetization of syntax. As long ago as 1904 Hilbert remarked that symbolic logic could be treated as though it were a branch of elementary number theory,[1] but it was Gödel who first worked out such a corre-

---

[1] *Verhandlungen des Dritten Internationalen Mathematiker-Kongresses in Heidelberg*, 1904, pp. 174–85.

spondence in detail and made use of it for the investigation of the properties of a formalized deductive system.

In his article Gödel begins his arithmetization by correlating each of his primitive signs with one of the natural numbers according to the following scheme:

o with 1,          $\Pi$ with 9,
$f$ with 3,          ( with 11,
$\sim$with 5,          ) with 13,
$\vee$ with 7,     variables of type n with numbers of the form
                          $p^n$ where p is a prime greater than 13, e.g. $x_1$
                          with 17, $x_2$ with $17^2$, $y_3$ with $19^3$, &c.

Then if $s_1, s_2, \ldots, s_k$ are the numbers with which the k separate symbols of a formula have been correlated, he correlates the whole formula with the number $2^{s_1} \times 3 \times^{s_2} \ldots \times p_k{}^{s_k}$, where $p_k$ is the k-th prime. Thus the formula:

$$x_1\Pi(x_2(x_1) \vee \sim x_2(x_1))$$

is correlated with the number

$$2^{17}.3^9.5^{11}.7^{17^2}.11^{11}.13^{17}.17^{13}.19^7.23^5.29^{17^2}.31^{11}.37^{17}.41^{13}.43^{13}.$$

And finally if $f_1, f_2, \ldots, f_m$ are the numbers with which the m propositional formulae of a sequence such as a proof have been correlated, he correlates the sequence as a whole with the number $2^{f_1} \times 3^{f_2} \times \ldots \times p_m{}^{f_m}$. Clearly this method associates one and only one number with each possible formula or sequence of formulae, and does so in such a manner that for any number it is always possible in principle to find whether it has any associated expression, and if so, what that is. For it is a well-known theorem of arithmetic that there cannot be more than one way of decomposing a number into prime factors. There are other conceivable ways of associating signs with numbers to produce such a result, but Gödel's method has the advantage of making the next stage in the argument relatively simple.

Given an association between signs and numbers such as we have just considered, it is possible to construct a statement about the composition of a number corresponding to every statement we may wish to make about the structure of a formula or sequence of formulae in our system. Suppose, for example, that the formula printed above as a specimen were said to be a generalization containing a universal quantifier. In Gödel's version of the arithmetization of syntax, the corresponding arithmetical statement would be to the effect that the very large number indicated above (i.e. the number associated with the formula, or, as we may say for short, the number of the formula) is divisible by $3^9$ but not by any higher power of 3. This is a very simple case, but perhaps sufficient to illustrate the principle. In practice the arithmetical statements corresponding to detailed analyses of formulae and their relations tend to be very complicated, and Gödel therefore constructs a series of forty-six abbreviating definitions which enable him to bring all this complexity under control. One such definition introduces the sign $Z(n)$ which means in effect *the number ($Zahl$) associated with the numeral 'f f f . . . o' in which the letter 'f' occurs just n times.* Another introduces $Sb(x_v^y)$ for *the number of the formula which results from substituting the sign whose number is y for the sign whose number is v at all places where this latter sign occurs free in the formula whose number is x.* And the last of all introduces $Bew(x)$ as a predicate applicable to a number if and only if it is the number of a propositional formula provable (*beweisbar*) in the system, i.e. the number of the last formula in a sequence of formulae where each is either an axiom or an immediate consequence of one or two of its predecessors.

The functions and predicates introduced in this way are all, strictly speaking, functions and predicates of *numbers*, definable without reference to signs or formulae, and except for the last (whose peculiarity will be explained in the next section) all the definitions which Gödel gives are effective in the sense noticed above. That is to say, it is always possible to calculate in a finite number of steps what value one of the functions takes for a given number as argument, and similarly it is always possible to determine in a finite number of steps whether or not one of the predicates other than $Bew(x)$ applies to a given number. But it is obvious from the examples given that the functions and predicates of number theory which Gödel considers are chosen and named for their correspondence to notions required in the metatheory of the system $\mathscr{P}$. In fact he has directed attention to a fragment of number theory which corresponds in structure to the syntax of the system $\mathscr{P}$ but can nevertheless be presented within the system $\mathscr{P}$. It must be admitted, of course, that a relation between Gödel numbers is not *identical* with a relation between signs in $\mathscr{P}$. But it is not misleading to speak in this context of the arithmetization of syntax, since every statement we need to make about the relations of signs in $\mathscr{P}$ can be adequately *represented* by a statement about a relation between the Gödel numbers of the signs and conversely every formula that expresses a relation between Gödel numbers by means of Gödel's special symbolism can be safely *reinterpreted* as an expression for a relation between signs in $\mathscr{P}$. There is indeed a difference between talking about numbers and talking about signs of $\mathscr{P}$, but one and the same formalism, namely $\mathscr{P}$, can be used for the two purposes.

At this point it will be convenient to depart from Gödel's own exposition and to introduce two signs which he does not use (though they are suggested by his preliminary sketch of the argument). These are '$\mathscr{E}_N$', which is to mean 'the expression whose associated number is denoted by $N$', and $Diag(x)$, which is to be an abbreviation for $Sb\,(x^{17}_{z(x)})$. The first is not a sign of the system $\mathscr{P}$, since its sense is determined by the arbitrary associations of numbers and signs which we have established as a help to talking about the system $\mathscr{P}$, but it is useful as a supplementary device for quick transition between the two interpretations of the formulae. In our explanation the letter $N$ is, of course, a schematic letter. The second, on the other hand, is the sign of an arithmetical function that can be defined in the system $\mathscr{P}$ without mention of signs and formulae, though it may conveniently be read as an abbreviation for *the number of the formula which results from substituting the numeral denoting x for the free variable whose number is 17 in the formula whose number is x*. The name 'diagonal function' is intended to recall some remarks of Gödel in his preliminary sketch. If we consider only those propositional expressions, say $\mathscr{E}_A$, $\mathscr{E}_B$, $\mathscr{E}_C$, &c., which contain just one free variable and may therefore be said to express properties of numbers, we see that for each such expression it is possible to ask of each number, and in particular of each number associated with such an expression, whether it has the property expressed by the given expression. Writing '$[\mathscr{E}_N;M]$' to signify that the number denoted by $M$ satisfies $\mathscr{E}_N$, we can arrange the propositions under examination in a doubly infinite array

$$[\mathscr{E}_A;A]\quad[\mathscr{E}_A;B]\quad[\mathscr{E}_A;C]\ .\ \ .\ \ .$$
$$[\mathscr{E}_B;A]\quad[\mathscr{E}_B;B]\quad[\mathscr{E}_B;C]\ .\ \ .\ \ .$$
$$[\mathscr{E}_C;A]\quad[\mathscr{E}_C;B]\quad[\mathscr{E}_C;C]\ .\ \ .\ \ .$$
$$.\quad.\quad.\quad.\quad.\quad.\quad.\quad.\quad.\quad.$$

For all those arguments which are associated with propositional expressions containing just one variable, the numerical function expressed by $Diag(x)$ assumes as values the numbers of formulae that express propositions on the diagonal of the array. The full definition set out above provides also that it shall have values for other arguments, but these are of no interest to us here.

We are now in a position to construct a curious formula for which we shall introduce the name '$\mathscr{G}$' to indicate that it is made according to a prescription of Gödel. If $\mathscr{E}_N$ is $\sim Bew(Diag(x))$, then $\mathscr{G}$ is $\mathscr{E}_{Diag(N)}$ or $\sim Bew(Diag(N))$. What $\mathscr{G}$ says is that the number denoted by $Diag(\mathcal{N})$ has the arithmetical property expressed by $\sim\!Bew(x)$. But the number denoted by $Diag(\mathcal{N})$ is the number of $\mathcal{G}$ itself, and the arithmetical property expressed by $\sim\!Bew(x)$ is one that can belong only to the number of an unprovable formula. So $\mathcal{G}$ says in effect that it is unprovable. The nearest analogue that we can construct in ordinary English is 'It is impossible to prove the statement which results from completing with its own name the unfinished formula "It is impossible to prove the statement which results from completing with its own name the unfinished formula. . . . " '.[1] Here the notion of completing a formula with its own name corresponds to the diagonal function; and if a passage beginning and ending with quotation marks may be allowed to count for this purpose as a name of what occurs between the marks, the whole sentence may be described as the statement which results from completing the quoted formula with its own name. But in Gödel's theory the systematic correlation of numbers with formulae takes the place of naming and the notion of provability employed is one relative to the system $\mathscr{P}$: these differences are of great importance.

Gödel himself points to a similarity between $\mathcal{G}$ and the sentence which gives rise to the Liar paradox, but insists that $\mathcal{G}$ is in no way objectionable. $\mathcal{G}$ may in fact be unprovable, as it says, without being false, and so we cannot properly argue that, if it is unprovable, it must be provable. Nor would it be correct to argue that $\mathcal{G}$ is empty like the remark 'What I am now saying is true'; for given the correlation of numbers with signs in the manner explained above, $\mathcal{G}$ does succeed in saying something of itself. If a formula is provable within a fully formalized deductive system, it is derivable from the axioms by application of rules which refer only to the patterns of the formulae. Naturally the rules refer to patterns only in so far as these are significant. That is to say, the rules do not distinguish between the slightly different versions of the signs which may be spoken, written, or printed by different persons. But this means only that the rules take no account of variations to which no significance is assigned, not that the rules are themselves incomprehensible without reference to the significance of the signs. To employ a distinction which has become well known since Gödel wrote, we can say that in the presentation of a calculus we are concerned only with syntactical, as opposed to semantical, rules for the use of signs, or, roughly speaking, with rules about their relations to each other, as opposed to rules about their relations to the world. Now there is nothing to prevent a

---

[1] A somewhat similar example is given by J. N. Findlay in 'Goedelian Sentences: A Non-numerical Approach', *Mind*, li (1942), pp. 259–65.

statement from referring to its own pattern. If a man says 'The sentence I am now uttering contains nine words', his remark is not only free from paradox but true. The fault of 'What I am now saying is true' is not simply that it refers to itself; for as some medieval logicians saw, self-reference may be harmless. The fault is rather that it tries to talk about its own meaning, instead of merely expressing a meaning, and so has no meaning at all. When we construct a sentence which says that it is unprovable within a certain system, we avoid this trouble, because unprovability within a calculus, unlike truth and falsity, is a property that can be considered without reference to meaning. Such separation is indeed essential to the formalist procedure which Hilbert advocates in mathematics, though not in metamathematics. If, nevertheless, we find the syntactical interpretation of $\mathscr{G}$ curious and baffling, the reason may be that we are still trying to apply here the more common way of thinking according to which the property of being provable (and likewise the property of being unprovable) belongs to propositions rather than to formulae.

The importance of $\mathscr{G}$ is that it enables us to prove two very interesting theorems: (1) that if $\mathscr{P}$ is $\omega$-consistent, it must be incomplete, with $\mathscr{G}$ as an undecidable formula, and (2) that if $\mathscr{P}$ is consistent, the consistency of $\mathscr{P}$ cannot be proved within $\mathscr{P}$. We must now consider these in some detail.

(1) *If $\mathscr{P}$ is $\omega$-consistent, it must be incomplete, with $\mathscr{G}$ as an undecidable formula.* Let us first suppose that $\mathscr{G}$ can be proved within $\mathscr{P}$. Then there must be some number which is the number of a proof of $\mathscr{G}$. But what $\mathscr{G}$ asserts is precisely the non-existence of such a number, and so our hypothesis leads to a self-contradiction. By the principle of contraposition we are therefore entitled to say that, if $\mathscr{P}$ is consistent in the ordinary sense of not containing as theorems any formula together with the negation of that formula, $\mathscr{G}$ cannot be proved within $\mathscr{P}$. But there is nothing in what we have said so far to show that if $\mathscr{P}$ is consistent $\mathscr{G}$ cannot be disproved within $\mathscr{P}$. Let us then suppose that $\mathscr{G}$ can be disproved. This means in effect that it is possible to prove the negation of $\mathscr{G}$, which is equivalent to $(\exists x)P(x)$, where $P(x)$ is short for *x is the number of a proof of $\mathscr{G}$*. On the other hand, given any natural number, it is possible to prove within $\mathscr{P}$ that this is not the number of a proof of $\mathscr{G}$, i.e. we can prove $\sim P(1), \sim P(2),$ $\sim P(3),$ &c. For, although the investigation may often be tedious it must always be possible to reach a decision about a particular number in a finite number of steps; and the decision must always be negative, since otherwise it would be possible to construct a

proof of $\mathscr{G}$ within $\mathscr{P}$, contrary to what we have already established. Now a system within which we have $(\exists x)P(x)$ as a theorem together with $\sim P(1)$, $\sim P(2)$, $\sim P(3)$, &c., may not be inconsistent in the ordinary sense, but it is certainly unsatisfactory. The possibility of such a defect was first noticed by P. Finsler in 1926,[1] and the defect has been called $\omega$-inconsistency (after $\omega$, the first transfinite ordinal). Using once more the principle of contraposition, we may therefore say that if $\mathscr{P}$ is $\omega$-consistent, $\mathscr{G}$ cannot be refuted within $\mathscr{P}$. And then, since $\omega$-consistency is a stricter requirement than simple consistency, we may summarize our results by asserting that if $\mathscr{P}$ is $\omega$-consistent $\mathscr{G}$ is neither provable nor disprovable in $\mathscr{P}$, which is as much as to say that $\mathscr{P}$ is incomplete.[2]

(2) *If $\mathscr{P}$ is consistent, the consistency of $\mathscr{P}$ cannot be proved within $\mathscr{P}$.* In this connexion we need only consider simple consistency; for if it is impossible to prove simple consistency, then *a fortiori* it is impossible to prove $\omega$-consistency. Now we have already shown that if $\mathscr{P}$ is consistent $\mathscr{G}$ cannot be proved within $\mathscr{P}$; and from this it follows, of course, that if $\mathscr{P}$ is consistent $\mathscr{G}$ must be true, since what $\mathscr{G}$ says is that it cannot be proved. But the argument by which we have satisfied ourselves of this is informal. For the purposes of Gödel's second theorem it is necessary to show that, if $\mathscr{C}$ is a formula of $\mathscr{P}$ which asserts in syntactical interpretation the consistency of $\mathscr{P}$, the Philonian conditional with $\mathscr{C}$ as protasis and $\mathscr{G}$ as apodosis can be proved within $\mathscr{P}$. The demonstration is not difficult in principle, but it is inevitably tedious, and we shall not attempt to give it here. From the lemma which it establishes the second theorem follows immediately. For if it were possible to prove the consistency of $\mathscr{P}$ within $\mathscr{P}$, it would be possible also to prove $\mathscr{G}$; and that, as we have seen, is not the case. We may even say that $\mathscr{C}$ and $\mathscr{G}$ are equivalent, since $\mathscr{P}$ contains as a theorem not only the conditional mentioned above, but also its converse. In claiming that it is itself unprovable, $\mathscr{G}$ provides an example to show that $\mathscr{P}$ does not allow for the proof of all formulae; and that is as much as to say that $\mathscr{P}$ is not inconsistent in the ordinary way.

The second of these two theorems is interesting because it makes clear that Hilbert's programme can never be carried out as it was originally conceived. $\mathscr{P}$ seems to include provision for all arguments that have commonly been called finitary, and yet it does not allow for a metamathematical proof of its own

[1] 'Formale Beweise und die Entscheidbarkeit' in *Mathematische Zeitschrift*, xxv (1926), pp. 676–82.

[2] In his paper 'Extensions of Some Theorems of Gödel and Church', *Journal of Symbolic Logic*, i (1936), pp. 87–91, J. B. Rosser proved the stronger theorem that if $\mathscr{P}$ is simply consistent, it must also be incomplete.

consistency. Therefore *a fortiori* it cannot allow for a metamathematical proof of the consistency of any more ambitious system within which it is included as a part. No doubt there may be arguments outside the range of $\mathcal{P}$ by which $\mathcal{P}$ (and perhaps even richer mathematical systems) may be proved free, not only from simple inconsistency, but also from $\omega$-inconsistency. Since Gödel wrote, G. Gentzen has in fact produced such a proof by transfinite induction.[1] But there must always be some mathematical system which we accept as satisfactory without independent proof of its freedom from contradiction, and Gödel's argument shows that this must at least be richer than $\mathcal{P}$. After reflection on his results we may even suspect that there is something radically wrong in the formalist programme of trying to make a mathematical system respectable without finding an intuitively acceptable interpretation for it. Gödel, however, does not claim to have proved this. On the contrary, he says explicitly that his result is not inconsistent with Hilbert's programme, since there may be a finitary proof of consistency which cannot be presented in $\mathcal{P}$; but he does not explain his use of the word 'finitary' in this context.

While the second of the two theorems has the more obvious relevance to controversies about the foundations of mathematics, the first is of more fundamental importance, because it reveals a curious and hitherto unsuspected property of arithmetic, that it can never be completely formalized. In order to make this clear let us consider once more the construction of $\mathcal{G}$.

What the formula says in its syntactical interpretation is that it cannot be proved in $\mathcal{P}$; and since it cannot in fact be either proved or disproved in $\mathcal{P}$, it is useful as an example to prove the incompleteness of $\mathcal{P}$. What happens if we try to remove this defect of $\mathcal{P}$ by adding $\mathcal{G}$ as a new axiom? $\mathcal{G}$ then becomes provable in the trivial sense in which an axiom may be said to be provable because it follows from itself, but only within a new system $\mathcal{P}'$, and this new system can be shown to be incomplete by the construction of a new Gödel formula, say $\mathcal{G}'$. In the construction of $\mathcal{G}$ we used a predicate expression $Bew(x)$ which was defined by reference to the numbers associated with the axioms of $\mathcal{P}$. When we try to construct an undecidable formula in $\mathcal{P}'$, we must naturally use a new predicate expression, say $Bew'(x)$, which is defined by reference to the numbers associated with the axioms of $\mathcal{P}'$, including the number associated with $\mathcal{G}$. But otherwise we may proceed as in the construction of $\mathcal{G}$, and if $\mathcal{P}'$ is $\omega$-consistent the result will be undecidable in $\mathcal{P}'$ for reasons

---

[1] 'Die Widerspruchsfreiheit der reinen Zahlentheorie', *Mathematische Annalen*, cxii (1936), pp. 493–565.

like those given in the proof of theorem (1). Nor is this the end; for the manœuvre of adding the latest undecidable formula as a new axiom may be repeated *ad infinitum*, and always with the same result. In short, Gödel's argument proves not only that $\mathscr{P}$ is incomplete, but also that it is incompletable. This does not mean that there is any single formula of mathematics which can never be proved or disproved in any way, but only that it is vain to hope for a *formal system* which comprehends the whole of intuitive arithmetic.

The incompletability of formal arithmetic would be of no great importance if the formulae which eluded our efforts to provide proofs were always reflexive statements of the kind constructed by Gödel. But the possibility of constructing these peculiar undecidable statements is interesting only as a symptom of a special kind of incompleteness inevitable in an axiom set for the theory of numbers. Tarski has called it $\omega$-incompleteness because of its relation to $\omega$-inconsistency.[1] For if $P(x)$ is an abbreviation for *x is the number of a proof of $\mathscr{G}$*, it is possible, as we have seen, to prove within $\mathscr{P}$ every single formula of the series $\sim P(1)$, $\sim P(2)$, $\sim P(3)$, &c., but not $(x)\sim P(x)$ which is equivalent to $\mathscr{G}$ itself. That is to say, $\mathscr{P}$ makes no provision for generalization in a situation where generalization seems perfectly safe to unformalized common sense. If, instead of merely adding $\mathscr{G}$ as a new axiom, we enlarge our formalism by adding some new general apparatus of proof which enables us to obtain $\mathscr{C}$, and therefore $\mathscr{G}$, as a theorem, we have an instrument which is more powerful for the ordinary purposes of arithmetic. The novelty here is the use of axioms containing variables of higher type than those occurring in the number theory of $\mathscr{P}$; and Gödel has shown that this not only enables us to prove formulae that were hitherto unprovable, but allows very much shorter proofs for many of the previously obtainable formulae.[2] Within this new system it is possible, however, to construct a new undecidable formula, and so the whole process can be repeated *ad infinitum*.

In the theory of numbers there are some famous propositions which for centuries have eluded all attempts of mathematicians either to prove or to disprove them, e.g. Fermat's assertion that there are no natural numbers x, y, z, and n all greater than 0 and such that $x^{n+2}+y^{n+2}=z^{n+2}$, Goldbach's conjecture that every even number greater than 2 is the sum of two primes, and the hypothesis that there are infinitely many pairs of primes p and q such

[1] 'Einige Betrachtungen über die Begriffe der $\omega$-Widerspruchsfreiheit und der $\omega$-Vollständigkeit', *Monatshefte für Mathematik und Physik*, xl (1933), pp. 97–112.
[2] 'Über die Länge der Beweise', *Ergebnisse eines mathematischen Kolloquiums*, vii (1936), pp. 23–24.

that $p+2 = q$. Some of these may perhaps have escaped decision for reasons of the sort we have just considered, i.e. because they are true but require for their proof a formal system richer than any investigated hitherto. If, however, this is the status of any proposition, we cannot know that it is before we prove the proposition in some richer system. And however gloomy we may feel about the prospects of such progress, we must admit that none of these propositions can ever be proved *absolutely* undecidable. For in order to prove that one of them, say Goldbach's conjecture, was absolutely undecidable we should have to show that it was both indemonstrable and irrefutable. But it is impossible to prove that Goldbach's conjecture is irrefutable without at the same time giving a demonstration of it. The reason for this is that every formal system of number theory, however simple, provides a sure though tedious method whereby Goldbach's conjecture may be disproved some day if it is false, namely the method of comparing each number in turn with the sum of each pair of prime numbers smaller than itself. To show that Goldbach's conjecture cannot be disproved in any way is to show that it cannot be disproved even by this method, and therefore to show that it is true. On the other hand, it does not seem evident that a proof of the indemonstrability of Goldbach's conjecture would be at the same time a proof of the existence of a counter-example. This is the strong point in Brouwer's case.

In his original paper Gödel proved the very strong theorem that, for any $\omega$-consistent class $\kappa$ which contains only formulae of $\mathscr{P}$ and is recursive in a sense to be explained later, there exists a formula obtained by universal closure of a recursive predicate sign and such that neither it nor its negation can be derived from $\kappa$ within $\mathscr{P}$. In order to avoid introducing the notion of recursiveness before it is essential to do so, we have not tried to reproduce all the lemmata required for the proof of Gödel's comprehensive thesis, but confined our attention in the first instance to the special case where $\kappa$ adds nothing to the axioms of $\mathscr{P}$. As Gödel himself has pointed out, we may go even farther in the direction of simplification and assert the essential incompleteness of any system, such as *Principia Mathematica* or Zermelo's axiomatic theory of sets, within which it is possible to obtain Peano's axioms by means of suitable definitions for 'o' and 'successor'. For any such system will in fact contain $\mathscr{P}$, and therefore be incompletable as $\mathscr{P}$ is. This discovery has an important bearing on the claims of Frege and his followers.

In the last chapter of his *Introduction to Mathematical Philosophy* Lord Russell wrote:

'If there are still those who do not admit the identity of logic and mathematics, we may challenge them to indicate at what point, in the successive definitions and deductions of *Principia Mathematica*, they consider that logic ends and mathematics begins.'[1]

Since Gödel's discovery we may reasonably answer that logic extends no further than quantification theory. When we say that arithmetic, and with it all so-called higher functional calculi and all versions of the theory of sets, are essentially incomplete, we admit in effect that these theories involve a notion or notions which cannot be characterized exhaustively by the laying down of rules of inference; and this seems to be a very good reason for excluding them from the scope of logic. On any view logic must be the fundamental theory in the variegated family of deductive theories which we call mathematics, since it is presupposed by them all. But it seems pointless to assert that all mathematics can be reduced to logic, if at the same time we must maintain that logic involves all the diversity we find in mathematics. And yet this is what a follower of Frege must now say. When Frege wrote, the scope of logic had not been delimited precisely, and his thesis seemed plausible just because the reader could then make an easy transition in thought from quantification theory to the theory of sets and arithmetic. But Gödel has revealed a profound difference between quantification theory, which is complete, and the theory of sets, which is not. In the interests of clarity it therefore seems best to reserve the name 'logic' for the former, and this is in fact what most mathematicians do when they are engaged upon their ordinary concerns. In short, the study which we have called general logic because it deals with generality may also be said to deserve that title because it omits nothing proper to logic except the explicit treatment of modality introduced in the transition from first- to second-order rules.

## 4. *The Decision Problem*

For primary or propositional logic we have a decision procedure, or rule of thumb, by which we can determine whether any given schema is or is not valid. We reduce it to conjunctive normal form, and then if each of the conjuncts in this form is a disjunction containing something of the pattern $P \lor {\sim}P$, we say that the original is valid (or tautological), but otherwise that it is not valid. Alternatively we may construct a truth-table for the formula and look to see whether it receives the value *truth* for

[1] Op. cit., pp. 194-5.

all the truth-possibilities we enumerate. Obviously these techniques depend on the finitude of the range of possibilities to be
examined. No formula of primary logic can contain more than a
finite number of schematic letters; and if this number is n, we have
only $2^n$ truth-possibilities to consider when trying to determine the
validity of the formula. In general logic the situation is very
different, but it is natural to ask whether here too we can find a
decision procedure by which to determine (a) whether a given
formula is universally valid or not, and (b) if it is not universally valid for domains of what size, if any, it is valid. There are
analogous problems about the satisfiability of formulae, but for
reasons explained in an earlier section these need not be considered separately.

We shall see presently that there can be no general solution to
the decision problem of general logic, but decision procedures
have been found for a number of special cases, and the results
have been collected by W. Ackermann in his booklet of 1954
called *Solvable Cases of the Decision Problem*.[1] Although it is impossible to consider them all here in detail, it may be useful to set
out the main achievements with a few comments.

The problem has been solved for every well-formed schema that

(1) contains only monadic function letters,
or (2) can be reduced to a prenex normal form in which the
prefix contains:

    (a) no existential quantifier
   or (b) no universal quantifier
   or (c) no existential quantifier in front of a universal
       quantifier
   or (d) not more than one existential quantifier
   or (e) not more than two existential quantifiers and those
       not separated by any universal quantifier,

or (3) can be reduced to a prenex normal form in which

    (a) the matrix (i.e. the expression after the prefix) is a
       disjunction of elementary parts and the negatives
       of elementary parts or can be reduced to this form,
   or (b) the prefix is of the form $(\exists x_1) \ldots (\exists x_m)(y_1) \ldots (y_n)$
       and every elementary part of the matrix that con-
       tains any of the variables $x_1, \ldots, x_m$ contains either
       all the variables $x_1, \ldots, x_m$ or at least one of the
       variables $y_1, \ldots, y_n$,

[1] A summary of the discoveries may also be found in A. Church's *Introduction to Mathematical Logic*, i (1956), § 46, together with a number of historical notes.

or (c)   the prefix terminates in $(z_1) \ldots (z_n)$ and every elementary part of the matrix that contains any of the variables occurring in the prefix contains at least one of the variables $z_1, \ldots, z_n$,

or (d)   the prefix is of the form $(\exists x)(y)(\exists z_1) \ldots (\exists z_n)$ with $n \leqslant 4$ and the matrix is of the form $G(x, y) \supset H(z_1, \ldots, z_n)$, with the dyadic functional letter $G$ as the sole functional letter in the full version of $H(z_1, \ldots, z_n)$.

The decision problem for the monadic functional calculus has been solved independently by several authors, but the method of Bernays and Schönfinkel is perhaps the most interesting. According to a theorem of these authors which we noticed in an earlier section, any schema of the monadic functional calculus which is satisfiable at all is satisfiable in a domain of $2^n$ individuals, where $n$ is the number of different function letters it contains. But a schema is universally valid if and only if its negation cannot be satisfied in any domain, and so a schema of the monadic functional calculus containing $n$ function letters is universally valid if and only if its negation cannot be satisfied in a domain of $2^n$ individuals, i.e. if and only if the schema itself is valid in a domain of $2^n$ individuals. Since a universal quantification over a domain of $2^n$ individuals may be replaced by a conjunction of $2^n$ items and an existential quantification by a disjunction of $2^n$ items, we can always test a monadic functional schema by eliminating all its quantifications in favour of appropriate conjunctions or disjunctions and then applying the technique of truth-tables to the resulting formula. In practice, however, it may be easier to adopt H. Behmann's method and transform the original formula into a truth-functional complex of which each constituent is either an existential formula of some such form as $(\exists x)(Fx.\sim Gx.Hx)$, where $F$, $G$, and $H$ are a selection of the monadic function letters of the original schema, or the negative of such an existential formula.[1] The diagrammatic methods used by J. Venn in his *Symbolic Logic* of 1881 and by Lewis Carroll in his *Symbolic Logic* of 1896 for testing the validity of syllogisms are in effect anticipations of this technique.

With the admission of dyadic and other polyadic function letters general logic becomes more complex, but it is still possible to find some schemata which are universally valid if they are valid in a finite domain. Thus a schema $(x_1) \ldots (x_m)M(x_1, \ldots, x_m)$

[1] 'Beiträge zur Algebra der Logik, insbesondere zum Entscheidungsproblem', *Mathematische Annalen*, lxxxvi (1922), pp. 163–229.

with none but universal quantifiers is universally valid if it is valid in a domain of m individuals. For if it is not valid in any domain of more than m individuals, we can select from such a domain m individuals called $A_1, \ldots, A_m$ for which $M(A_1, \ldots, A_m)$ is false, contrary to the supposition that the original formula is valid for any domain of m individuals. Similarly a schema $(\exists x_1) \ldots (\exists x_m) M(x_1, \ldots, x_m)$ with none but existential quantifiers is universally valid if it is valid in a domain of one individual. For if it is not universally valid, then neither is the stronger formula $(\exists x) M(x, \ldots, x)$ and so there must be some domain of one element, called perhaps $A$, for which $M(A, \ldots, A)$ is false, contrary to the supposition that the original formula is valid for any domain of one individual. It should be noted, however, that, if the full version of $M(x_1, \ldots, x_m)$ contains part formulae of the pattern $\sim(x_p = x_q)$, there may be some number k such that the original formula is valid in all domains of k elements or more but not in any of fewer than k elements. To determine the number k in such a case is a more difficult task.

Furthermore, a schema $(x_1) \ldots (x_m)(\exists y_1) \ldots (\exists y_n) M(x_1, \ldots, x_m; y_1, \ldots, y_n)$ in which all the universal quantifiers precede all the existential quantifiers is universally valid if it is valid in a domain of m individuals. For if the original is valid for any domain of m individuals, so too must be the formula $(x_1) \ldots (x_m) N(x_1, \ldots, x_m)$ where $N(x_1, \ldots, x_m)$ is an abbreviation for the disjunction of all possible formulae $M(x_1, \ldots, x_m; x_{i_1}, \ldots, x_{i_n})$ in which the variables $y_1, \ldots, y_n$ of the original have been replaced in any way by variables of the set $x_1, \ldots, x_m$. But if $(x_1) \ldots (x_m) N(x_1, \ldots, x_m)$ is valid in a domain of m individuals, it must be universally valid by the first of the special cases noticed above, and with it the original which it entails.

The foregoing results are all contained in the paper of Bernays and Schönfinkel mentioned above. The other two cases of our second group are not so easy, but 2(d) was solved in 1928 by W. Ackermann[1] and T. Skolem[2] independently and 2(e) a little later by K. Gödel,[3] L. Kalmar,[4] and K. Schütte[5] independently.

[1] 'Über die Erfüllbarkeit gewisser Zählausdrücke', *Mathematische Annalen*, c (1928), pp. 638–49.
[2] 'Über die mathematische Logik', *Norsk Matematisk Tidsskrift*, x (1928), pp. 125–42.
[3] 'Ein Spezialfall des Entscheidungsproblems der theoretischen Logik', *Ergebnisse eines mathematischen Kolloquiums*, ii (1932) pp. 27–28;' Zum Entscheidungsproblem des logischen Funktionenkalküls', *Monatshfete für Mathematik und Physik*, xl (1933), pp. 433–43.
[4] 'Über die Erfüllbarkeit derjenigen Zählausdrücke welche in der Normalform zwei benachbarte Allzeichen enthalten', *Mathematische Annalen*, cviii (1933), pp. 466–84.
[5] 'Untersuchungen zum Entscheidungsproblem der mathematischen Logik'

For each the problem can be reduced by ingenious transformations to that of the monadic functional calculus. But these are the last cases that can be (i) described solely by reference to the composition of their prefixes in prenex normal form and (ii) solved by a proof of the sufficiency of a test in some finite domain. The reason, discovered by Schütte, is that for every prefix not already in our list (i.e. for every prefix having at least two existential quantifiers separated by at least one universal quantifier and for every prefix having at least three existential quantifiers followed, whether immediately or not, by a universal quantifier) there can be found schemata valid in any finite domain but not in a denumerably infinite domain. It has certainly not been shown to be impossible that there should be a solution of any kind for any of the excluded cases, but it is clear from Schütte's result that if there is any solution to be found it must be by another method.

In our third group we have collected some cases for which solutions may be found by attention to the patterns of matrices as well as to the composition of prefixes, but the list is neither systematic nor exhaustive. Indeed it could scarcely be so, since every success in the derivation of a mathematical theorem from axioms is in effect the discovery of a universally valid schema exemplified by $A \supset T$ where $A$ is the conjunction of the axioms and $T$ the theorem. What we have here are only a few cases interesting by virtue of their generality. Among them $3(d)$ is peculiar in covering schemata which are not valid in an infinite domain though valid in every finite domain.

Apart from solutions of the decision problem for special cases there have been discovered a number of reductions. Each of these is a procedure by which for a schema of any kind there can be constructed another schema of some prescribed class which is universally valid if and only if the first is universally valid, and a class of schemata to which all schemata can be reduced in this way is called a *reduction class*. The best known of these is the class of schemata in Skolem prenex normal form, but there are others, e.g. the class of schemata with only one function letter, the class of schemata containing only dyadic function letters, and even more narrowly defined classes such as that of schemata in Skolem prenex normal form with a prefix of the pattern $(\exists x_1) \ldots (\exists x_m)(y)$ and a matrix containing only one dyadic function letter.[1] Re-

*Mathematische Annalen*, cix (1934), pp. 572–603; 'Über die Erfüllbarkeit einer Klasse von logischen Formeln', ibid. cx (1934), pp. 161–94.
[1] The history of these and other reductions may be found in A. Church's *Introduction to Mathematical Logic*, i, § 47.

ductions may be useful in attacks on special problems, but in view of the discovery of A. Church to which we must now turn they are interesting also as indications of the limits of useful effort.

Under the influence of mistaken theories of logic philosophers have sometimes assumed that truisms of logic must all be certifiable as such by a simple procedure. Wittgenstein, for example, wrote:

'Our fundamental principle is that every question which can be decided at all by logic can be decided off-hand. . . . It is possible . . . to give at the outset a description of all "true" logical propositions. Hence there can *never* be surprises in logic. . . . Proof in logic is only a mechanical expedient to facilitate the recognition of tautology, where it is complicated.'[1]

And mathematicians for their part have sometimes thought that Frege's theory must be wrong because the problems of number theory are not all soluble by rules of thumb such as should in their opinion be sufficient for the settlement of all logical questions. In the paper in which he proved the incompletability of formal arithmetic Gödel made clear for the first time that discovery of a universal decision procedure for general logic would be sufficient for a solution of some famous unsolved problems of number theory such as that about Goldbach's conjecture. In the context in which it was written this remark was not intended to support any particular philosophy of mathematics, but rather to suggest the unplausibility of finding a universal decision procedure for general logic. Within a few years the impossibility of such a discovery was proved by a development of Gödel's own technique. In order to understand the argument leading to this conclusion we must consider his concept of a recursive function which was mentioned but not explained in the last section.

In the relevant part of his article of 1931 Gödel starts with a very general account of the familiar notion of recursive definition. A function of number theory $\phi(x_1, \ldots, x_n)$, i.e. a function whose arguments and values are all alike natural numbers, is *recursively defined* from the functions of number theory $\psi(x_1, \ldots, x_{n-1})$ and $\mu(x_1, \ldots, x_{n+1})$, he says, if for all natural numbers $x_2, \ldots, x_n$ and k

$$\phi(0, x_2, \ldots, x_n) = \psi(x_2, \ldots, x_n)$$
$$\phi(k+1, x_2, \ldots, x_n) = \mu(k, \phi(k, x_2, \ldots, x_2), x_2, \ldots, x_n).$$

Then he uses this notion to introduce a new concept. A function of number theory is *recursive*, he says, if there is a finite series of

[1] *Tractatus Logico-Philosophicus*, 5.551, 6.125, 6.1251, 6.1262.

functions of number theory $\phi_1, \phi_2, \ldots, \phi_n$ which ends with $\phi$ and is so constituted that every function in the series is either (a) recursively defined from two of the preceding functions in the series, or (b) derived from one or other of the preceding functions by employment of certain of the preceding functions as arguments to that one, e.g. in such a way that

$$\phi_k(x_1, x_2) = \phi_p(\phi_q(x_1, x_2), \phi_r(x_2))$$

where p, q, r < k, or (c) a constant, or (d) the successor function. The inclusion of the last two clauses in the definition of a recursive function makes it clear that Gödel has in mind here not only functions defined recursively (i.e. by recursion formulae) but also functions presupposed by such formulae. The interesting common feature of the functions he calls recursive is that each has its values fixed by initial equations, either directly, as in the last cases mentioned above, or indirectly, when the initial equations serve as premisses for the calculation of values by the two simple operations of substitution for variables and replacement of equals by equals. In this connexion recursions are important because they alone save the concept of a recursive function from triviality. On the other hand, no function could be defined by recursion formulae without mention of the constant o and the successor function.

With a further extension of usage Gödel goes on to say that a relation (propositional function) of n natural numbers $R(x_1, \ldots, x_n)$ may be called recursive if there is a recursive function of number theory $\phi(x_1, \ldots, x_n)$ such that

$$R(x_1, \ldots, x_n) \text{ if and only if } \phi(x_1, \ldots, x_n) = o.$$

In the special case where n = 1 we may call R a recursive property and say also that the class which it determines is recursive. But it is convenient to speak generally of recursive functions and recursive relations because the notion of a function is closely bound up in mathematical thought with that of a relation. Whenever it is proper to speak of a function $\phi$ such that $x = \phi(y)$, it is proper also to speak of a relation R such that $R(x, y)$.

Obviously the functions $x+y$, $x.y$, $x^y$ and the relations $x = y$, $x < y$ are all recursive. Thus writing 'n'' for 'the successor of n', we have for $x+y$ the equations:

$$\begin{cases} x+o = x \\ x+n' = (x+n)', \end{cases}$$

for x.y the equations:

$$\begin{cases} x.o = o \\ x.n' = xn + x, \end{cases}$$

for $x^y$ the equations:

$$\begin{cases} x^0 = 0' \\ x^{n'} = x^n.x. \end{cases}$$

Furthermore, the truth-functions of propositional logic may be correlated with recursive functions of number theory, and so they too are available for use in the definitions of recursive functions and relations. As might be expected, quantifiers present more difficulty, but Gödel shows that they can be used in the definition of recursive functions and relations provided they are accompanied by restrictions which make it possible in principle for us to work through all the relevant cases. Thus, given a recursive function expressed by $\phi(x)$ and a recursive relation expressed by $R(x, y)$, we can define another recursive relation by writing:

$$S(x, y) \equiv (\exists z)[z \leqslant \phi x.\, R(z, y)].$$

Whenever quantifiers are introduced in the definitions of his arithmetized syntax, they are accompanied by such restrictions, except in the last definition of all, that for the predicate $Bew(x)$, where it is essential for the development of the argument that the existential operator should appear without restriction. Similarly there is always a restriction on the number of cases to be investigated when we try to discover the number denoted by his sign $\epsilon_x F(x)$ which means *the least number x such that $F(x)$, if there is such a number, and otherwise* 0.

With the apparatus of his arithmetized syntax Gödel is able to prove that every recursive relation can be defined within his system $\mathscr{P}$, or more precisely that every recursive relational sign with n variables has in the system an associated number such that, if $r$ denotes this number and $u_1, \ldots, u_n$ denote the associated numbers of the variables, either the formula $Bew\ [Sb(r^{u_1, \ldots, un}_{Z(x_1), \ldots, Z(x_n)})]$ or the formula $Bew\ [Neg\ Sb(r^{u_1, \ldots, un}_{Z(x_1), \ldots, Z(x_n)})]$ is true for each n-tuple of natural numbers taken as values of the variables $x_1, \ldots, x_n$, according as the relation does or does not hold for that n-tuple.[1] For a recursive relation is said to be definable in a system if, and only if, the axioms of the system enable us to decide whether the relation holds for an appropriate set of numbers. In order to prove the theorem Gödel supposes each recursive relation of n arguments to be expressed in the form $x_1 = \phi(x_2, \ldots, x_n)$, where $\phi$ signifies a recursive function of n-1 arguments, and then uses mathematical induction over all the possible degrees of complexity in the structure of recursive functions. Later he shows that

---

[1] In order to preserve Gödel's expressions we have departed here from our own conventions of symbolism, but the sense is clear in the context.

all recursive functions can be defined within a simple version of Peano's arithmetic, which we may perhaps call $\mathscr{P}^0$, and conversely that any relation which this system enables us either to prove or to disprove for every appropriate sets of numbers is recursive.[1]

The most important difference between $\mathscr{P}$ and $\mathscr{P}^0$ is that the latter contains no provision for variables of different types. But this carries with it other differences. Identity can no longer be defined in the manner of *Principia Mathematica*, but must be introduced separately; and since neither the principle of extensionality nor the principle of mathematical induction can be formulated in a single statement, each must be replaced by an infinity of axioms falling under a schema. To put things positively in the notation most commonly adopted (i.e. with $x'$ for *the successor of $x$*, the signs $=, +$, and $\cdot$ in their usual arithmetical senses, and universality expressed wherever possible by free variables), $\mathscr{P}^0$ is the system obtained by adding to general logic the axioms:

A1. All instances of $x = y \supset (Fx \supset Fy)$
†A2. $x = x$
B1. $\sim(x' = 0)$
B2. $x' = y' \supset x = y$
B3. All instances of $[Fo. \ (x)(Fx \supset Fx')] \supset (x)Fx$
C1. $x + 0 = x$
C2. $x + y' = (x + y)'$
D1. $x.0 = 0$
D2. $x.y' = x.y + x.$

Here the axioms of group A correspond to Frege's axioms for identity, and those of group B to Peano's third, fourth, and fifth axioms, while the axioms of groups C and D are the recursion formulae for addition and multiplication respectively. A2 has been obelized because it can be derived from A1 and C1 taken together and is therefore redundant in this context, though not, of course, in all contexts.

Since it is inconvenient for certain purposes to have to deal with an infinite set of axioms, attempts have been made to find a still simpler system adequate for the definition of recursive functions, and it has been shown by A. Tarski, A. Mostowski, and R. M. Robinson in *Undecidable Theories* (1953)[2] that such a system, called $\mathscr{Q}$, can be obtained by dropping A1, A2, and B3 in favour of

---

[1] Strictly speaking, $\mathscr{P}^0$ is not Peano's but Skolem's arithmetic, since it does not contain a single axiom of mathematical induction, as we note below.
[2] The first publication seems to have been in the paper 'An Essentially Undecidable Axiom System' which R. M. Robinson contributed to the *Proceedings of the International Congress of Mathematicians* (Cambridge, Mass., 1950), i, pp. 729–30.

A11. $x = y \supset (x = z \supset y = z)$
A12. $x = y \supset x' = y'$
A13. $x = y \supset x+z = y+z$
A14. $x = y \supset z+x = z+y$
A15. $x = y \supset x.z = y.z$
A16. $x = y \supset z.x = z.y$
B31. $x = 0 \ \lor \ (\exists y(x = y'))$

while retaining all the other axioms of $\mathscr{P}^0$. Here the axioms A11–16, though special cases under the schema of A1, are sufficient together for the replacement of A1 and A2 in all proofs of $\mathscr{P}^0$. But $\mathscr{Q}$ as a whole is much weaker than $\mathscr{P}^0$, because B31 is by no means equivalent in power to the principle of mathematical induction which it replaces. On the contrary, B31 is the weakest possible result obtainable in $\mathscr{P}^0$ by the use of the principle; for it says no more than that each individual of the system is either identical with 0 or the successor of something, which means in effect that each individual is a natural number.

Gödel's discoveries directed attention to the class of functions that can always be evaluated systematically, and in 1936 Alonzo Church, following a suggestion made by Gödel in conversation, put forward the thesis that every effectively calculable function is recursive.[1] For centuries it had been a commonplace that certain mathematical questions could be answered by rules of thumb (or algorithms, as they are sometimes called in confused memory of the Arabian mathematician al-Khowarazmi), but this was the first attempt to give precision to the idea, and it soon won general acceptance. Church had conceived independently the plan of identifying effective calculability with a feature which he called λ-*definability*, but he discovered that this was equivalent to recursiveness, and a year later A. M. Turing proved the same of *computability-by-a-machine* which he had offered as another analysis of the notion of effective calculability.[2] The importance of the thesis is that it makes possible a new approach to the decision problem; and Church took advantage of this to prove first the impossibility of a universal decision procedure for a certain fragment of number theory and then, as a consequence, the impossibility of such a procedure for general logic.[3] Since his proof

[1] 'An Unsolvable Problem of Elementary Number Theory', *American Journal of Mathematics*, lviii (1936), pp. 345–63.
[2] 'On Computable Numbers, with an Application to the Entscheidungsproblem', *Proceedings of the London Mathematical Society*, xlii (1937), pp · 230–65; 'A Correction', ibid. xliii (1933), pp. 544–6; 'Computability and λ-Definability', *Journal of Symbolic Logic*, ii (1937), pp. 153–63.
[3] 'A Note on the Entscheidungsproblem', *Journal of Symbolic Logic*, i (1936), pp. 40–41; 'A Correction', ibid., pp. 101–2. These apply to logic the result obtained in the article mentioned in the last note but one.

of these conclusions is connected with his system of λ-conversion which has not been explained in this book, we shall not attempt to reproduce it here but consider instead a simpler argument constructed by Tarski, Mostowski, and Robinson on the basis of Tarski's earlier essay called 'The Concept of Truth in Formalized Languages'.[1]

If there is a universal decision procedure for $\mathcal{Q}$, it will enable us to decide whether any given formula of $\mathcal{Q}$ is true or not, and will do so, moreover, by reference to the pattern of the formula. So far there is nothing objectionable in the hypothesis. For although, as we have noticed earlier, truth is ascribed primarily to propositions, it is quite proper to speak of the truth of a mathematical formula, since by the rules of mathematical symbolism each such formula expresses the same proposition on every occasion of its use. And again it is quite proper to say that the truth of a mathematical formula may be recognized, if at all, from its pattern, since for the determination of the truth or falsity of a mathematical formula nothing can be relevant except its meaning, and under the rules of the symbolism this depends solely on its pattern. When we say that a formula of $\mathcal{Q}$ is true, we mean naturally that it is true *as a formula of* $\mathcal{Q}$, or for short *in* $\mathcal{Q}$.

Let us suppose, then, that there is a universal decision procedure for $\mathcal{Q}$. Since by Gödel's conventions every propositional formula of the system, whether true or false, has an associated number, there must be a number class consisting solely of the numbers of true formulae, and so our decision procedure is incidentally a rule of thumb for determining whether or not a number belongs to this class. But according to Church's thesis the existence of such a rule of thumb implies that the number class is recursive, and according to a discovery mentioned earlier this in turn implies that a predicate determining the class can be defined in $\mathcal{Q}$. Furthermore, if there is such a predicate, say $T(x)$, it is obvious that, when $\mathcal{N}$ denotes any number associated with a propositional formula in $\mathcal{Q}$, $T(\mathcal{N})$ must be deducible from $\mathcal{E}_N$ and vice versa. It is impossible, however, that these conditions should be satisfied together. For if $T(x)$ is a predicate formula of $\mathcal{Q}$, so too is $\sim T(x)$, and on the assumption that this latter is itself $\mathcal{E}_N$ we can construct in the system another formula $\mathcal{E}_{Diag}(\mathcal{N})$, or $\sim T(Diag(\mathcal{N}))$, which exhibits the peculiarities of the Liar paradox. This new formula, which we may call $\mathcal{L}$ for short, says that the number denoted by $Diag(\mathcal{N})$ has the character expressed by $\sim T(x)$, but that character can belong only to the number of a false formula, and the number denoted by $Diag(\mathcal{N})$

is the number of $\mathscr{L}$. So $\mathscr{L}$ says in effect that $\mathscr{L}$ is false. If it is true, it is false; and if it is false, it is true. In order to escape from this absurdity we must reject our original supposition and declare instead that if $\mathscr{Q}$ is consistent it has no universal decision procedure.

When we compare this ingenious reasoning with Gödel's proof of the incompletability of formal arithmetic, we find two points of great interest apart from the conclusions established. First, it is of fundamental importance for each argument that the system under investigation allows for the definition of the diagonal function through Gödel's device of arithmetization. The simplest known system of number theory in which this function can be defined, together with all other recursive functions, is one which Tarski, Mostowski, and Robinson[1] call $\mathscr{R}$. Its theoretical content is even less than that of $\mathscr{Q}$, but it cannot be presented with a finite set of axioms and is therefore less useful than $\mathscr{Q}$ in further investigations of the decision problem. Secondly, it is essential to the validity of the two arguments that there is a difference between provability and truth even for a completely axiomatized system where they coincide in application. Whereas the former may be defined with the symbols of the system to which it refers, though not in such a way as to make it recursive, the latter cannot be defined without the introduction of new concepts. In short, truth in mathematics is not to be equated with provability, any more than truth in empirical studies is to be equated with verifiability, and any philosophical doctrine which suggests the contrary must be mistaken.

We have seen that there can be no universal decision procedure for $\mathscr{Q}$ because this system allows for the definition of the diagonal function. But it is obvious that the addition of new axioms consistent with the old cannot produce a system in which it is no longer possible to define the diagonal function, and so we may go on to assert that there can be no universal decision procedure for any system, such as $\mathscr{P}^0$, $\mathscr{P}$, or the theory of sets, in which $\mathscr{Q}$ is a proper part. Tarski expresses this by saying that $\mathscr{Q}$ is an *essentially undecidable theory*. The name is rather unfortunate (since it might be used in other contexts to mean an hypothesis whose truth or falsity could never be known), but the notion is very important. For it has now been made clear that in any mathematical system which includes the very modest system $\mathscr{Q}$ absence of a decision procedure is not a defect we may conceivably remove by introduction of some new apparatus of proof, but a limitation we can never overcome. Hilbert may have been right in his faith

[1] Ibid., p. 52.

that all mathematical problems are soluble, but there is not, and cannot be, a method for the solution of all problems. No ingenuity in the design of calculating machines will ever make further ingenuity superfluous.

It would be wrong, however, to suppose that the system is interesting only because of what it enables us to prove about enlargements of itself. If $\mathscr{S}$ is any consistent system within which $\mathscr{Q}$ can be interpreted, then $\mathscr{S}$ and all its consistent enlargements lack a universal decision procedure. By 'interpretation' is meant here the establishment of a correlation of non-logical signs such as is commonly used in the investigation of axiom systems, and it is of great importance in this connexion that $\mathscr{Q}$ has only a finite number of axioms. By this indirect method Tarski and his collaborators have succeeded in proving the impossibility of a universal decision procedure for many formal systems, including the elementary theories of groups, rings, fields, and lattices.[1]

Important as these results are, it is even more interesting for the logician to notice that $\mathscr{Q}$ can be used to prove the impossibility of a universal decision procedure for general logic, which it contains as a part. For this purpose it is convenient to express all the propositions of $\mathscr{Q}$ in a new notation with

$Id(x, y)$       for $x = y$,
$Suc(x, y)$      for $x' = y$,
$Sum(x, y, z)$    for $x + y = z$,
$Prod(x, y, z)$    for $x.y = z$,

and new variables where necessary. At the same time all quantifiers should be restored, where they have been omitted for brevity. Thus for the last axiom of our set we get

D2. $(x)(y)(t)(u)(v)(w) [Prod(x, t, u) . Suc(y, t) . Prod(x, y, v) . Sum(v, x, w) \supset Id(u, w)]$.

Obviously the result is a set of very cumbrous expressions, much less useful for purposes of calculation than the expressions with term-functions which they replace; but the translation makes clear the role of general logic within the system. For when the letter $A$ is introduced as an abbreviation for the conjunction of the special axioms of the system expressed in the new notation and the letter $F$ as an abbreviation for any well-formed formula in the same notation, it is evident that the question whether $F$ can be proved within the system as a whole reduces to the question whether $A \supset F$ can be proved in general logic. If, therefore, it were possible to specify a universal decision procedure for general

[1] *Undecidable Theories*, pp. 5, 65 f.

logic, we should always be able to work out by rule of thumb whether or not $A \supset F$ was a truism of general logic and so to conclude whether $F$ was provable in $\mathcal{Q}$. But this would amount to the provision of a universal decision procedure for $\mathcal{Q}$, which has been shown to be impossible, and so it must be admitted that there can be no universal decision procedure for general logic.

It is not surprising that a system of formal arithmetic which is known to be incomplete should also lack a universal decision procedure. But it is remarkable that general logic, which has been proved to be complete (in the sense of being sufficient for the demonstration of all universally valid schemata expressible in logical symbolism) should nevertheless be found to lack such an algorithm. All the truisms of general logic are accessible to us, but there is no procedure by which for any given formula we can make sure of deciding within a finite number of stops whether or not it is a truism. That is to say, however long the time we have spent in systematic but unsuccessful search, a proof may yet be found.

## 5. *The Place of Logic among the Sciences*

It was a question much debated in antiquity whether logic should be accounted a branch of philosophy, as the Stoics said, or merely a preliminary to philosophical studies, as the Peripatetics maintained. But the dispute was little more than a quarrel about words. Both sides agreed that logic should come first in the education of a philosopher; and if the Stoics, unlike Aristotle, called it a part of philosophy, that was merely because they came later and were self-conscious in the presentation of their doctrines as a system. What most men in later centuries have called logic is the study of questions such as Aristotle discussed in the works of his *Organon*: and the novelty of the Stoic contribution, as we see it in retrospect, is not any new demarcation of subject-matter, but an emphasis on relations of propositions as distinct from relations of universals or concepts. But Aristotle gave no clear account of the province of logic, and for this reason important questions about its relation to other sciences have remained for discussion in modern times.

In the syllogistic doctrine of his *Prior Analytics* he enunciates a number of general principles about a relation between classes which he calls *inclusion in a whole* ($\dot{\epsilon}\nu$ $\ddot{o}\lambda\omega$ $\tau\hat{\omega}$ $A$ $\epsilon\hat{\iota}\nu\alpha\iota$) or a relation between universals which he calls *belonging* ($\dot{\upsilon}\pi\acute{a}\rho\chi\epsilon\iota\nu$) or *being predicated* ($\kappa\alpha\tau\eta\gamma o\rho\epsilon\hat{\iota}\sigma\theta\alpha\iota$), e.g. the principle *If A belongs to all B and B belongs to all $\Gamma$ then A belongs to all $\Gamma$*. But it is clear that he thinks of these principles as important because they guarantee the validity of certain patterns of argument for all possible subject-matters to which they may be applied. And he is interested in such patterns of argument primarily because he thinks they are required for the elaboration of science as he explains it in his *Posterior Analytics*. It is therefore not surprising that his successors have often connected logic with the theory of knowledge and the psychology of reasoning. In other parts of the *Organon* Aristotle deals with the ways in which terms can have meanings and the sorts of entities to which they can be applied. Among the preliminaries of his syllogistic also there is a good deal about the analysis of discourse and classification of statements. Again, therefore, it is not surprising that in later centuries logic has sometimes been classed with grammar and rhetoric as an *ars sermocinalis*. So long as men were content to take Aristotle's own works as their chief sources of logic, these differences of conception did not produce any great intellectual discomfort; by shifting their attention according to the part of the *Organon* with which they were concerned logicians could still think of logic as concerned alike with words, thoughts, and things. But the developments of the last century have made it impossible for us to remain content with a merely traditional grouping of themes. Following analogies suggested by the work of Aristotle and his successors, mathematicians and philosophers have used the word 'logic' in contexts of which older logicians never thought. The result is a confusion in which some usages of the word are so far removed from others that it no longer serves for clear communication between thinkers of diverse tendencies. In this situation we must first consider what is most central in our tradition and then try, if we can, to establish conventions which will make it easy for men to appreciate how this central core is related to all the matters with which it has been connected in the thought of various thinkers.

Although Boole called his most ambitious work on logic *The Laws of Thought* and sometimes wrote as though he supposed himself to be investigating the constitution of the human intellect, it is clear that his algebra has nothing to do with thought processes. In each of the interpretations which we call logical it is concerned with relations between entities that are entirely non-mental. In Frege's works there is even less possibility of confusion between logic and psychology, since the author makes an explicit contrast on many occasions. It is true that he called his concept-script 'a symbolic language of pure thought' (*eine Formelsprache des reinen Denkens*), but his explanations show that he does not mean by this phrase a language designed for talking about a special kind of thinking. On the contrary, when he asserts that arithmetic is identical with logic, he makes clear that he thinks of arithmetical statements as concerned with objects, namely numbers, which are not constructed by human thinking or in any way dependent upon human minds. The concept-script is a language of pure thought only in the sense that it is designed for expressing truths which we think when we abstract entirely from the special contents of our various experiences. This description is not precise enough to indicate that it is a language which provides only for the formulation of principles of logic. So far as the title goes, Frege's first book might be about a new symbolism for metaphysics; but there can be no doubt that he thinks of it as an aid to the development of the science which Aristotle began in his *Prior Analytics*. In his view arithmetic, which he identifies with logic, is the most fundamental of all sciences. But it is not about what philosophers commonly call the external world, i.e. the world of things in space. Nor, on the other hand, is it about minds. It is indeed about inferences which are made by minds, but only because it is concerned with connexions between thinkables. Its laws are not laws of nature, but laws of the laws of nature.[1]

We shall argue presently that this last remark, which Frege offers as an epigram rather than as a definition, may be taken seriously as a delimitation of the province of logic. But for the moment our chief purpose is to draw attention to the fact that Boole and Frege, like Leibniz before them, presented logic as a system of principles which allow for valid inference in all kinds of subject-matter, i.e. as the theory of relations such as Aristotle had considered in his doctrine of syllogisms and Chrysippus in his many books about derivative patterns of inference. There are, as we have seen, other elements in the tradition of logical teaching, but the greatest logicians of modern times have taken this as the central theme, and it seems reasonable to say that everything else in the corpus has its place there because of its connexion with the main enterprise of classifying and articulating the principles of formally valid inference. So much is clear; but two developments of the present century have produced some uncertainty and made it necessary to strive for greater precision in the characterization of logic.

The first of these is the discovery of paradoxes within the field which Cantor and Frege assigned to logic. This is disturbing because it shows that convictions which philosophers have sometimes dignified with the name of 'logical intuitions' may be misleading. To Brouwer it has even suggested that we ought to

[1] *Grundlagen der Arithmetik*, §§ 87 and 93.

deny the general validity of the principle of excluded middle. But, apart from that, it has introduced doubts about the correctness of trying to identify arithmetic with logic. Hilbert, as we have seen, prefers to think of arithmetic as derived from a set of special axioms which he adds to the apparatus of quantification theory. And although Whitehead and Russell continue to maintain the thesis of Frege, the expedients to which they are driven reveal the peculiarity of their usage of the word 'logic'. Russell's theory of logical types seems plausible to many philosophers, but even those who favour it have sometimes remarked that it looks more like metaphysics than like logic in the traditional sense, and there can be little doubt that the axioms of reducibility and infinity which he finds it necessary to introduce together with his theory of types are not what would ordinarily be called principles of logic.

The second event of the present century which has made it seem necessary to consider afresh the scope of logic is the debate about necessity and language which we noticed in our chapter on the philosophy of logic after Frege. Some of those who adopt a conventionalist view of logic wish to include under the title all *a priori* truths, thinking that these are all alike made true by linguistic rules. If their usage became general, it would be useless to ask whether Frege was right or wrong in thinking arithmetic a continuation of logic, since arithmetic would undoubtedly be the logic of numerals, just as geometry would be the logic of shape words, mechanics the logic of 'force', analytical economics the logic of 'price', philosophical theology (if such a science exists) the logic of 'God', and so forth. Such an enormous extension of the meaning of a technical term makes it useless for any but the coarsest classification, and it is therefore fortunate that the fashion is still confined to a relatively small school. But it is easy to see that the extension has been suggested by some elements in the old tradition. From the time of Aristotle onwards logicians have discussed the semantic rules or customs for the use of words such as 'all', 'if', 'or', 'possible'. When it is supposed that all principles of traditional logic such as those for the various syllogistic moods have been made true by semantic rules for the use of the words in which they are expressed, it is natural to remark that many other statements are made true in the same way, and it may even seem illuminating for a while to say that they all belong to logic. Already before this theory had been fully developed the word 'logical' was sometimes used in discussions of necessity to make a contrast with 'causal', as though between them the two covered the whole field.

When the word 'logic' has no agreed definition, the question

# LOGIC AND THE SCIENCES

whether the theory of sets or any other branch of *a priori* knowledge
should be accounted part of logic is one that can be settled only
by linguistic legislation. But such legislation may be well- or
ill-advised. For it is desirable that any new rules we adopt deliberately for old words should depart little, if at all, from previously
established customs, and that the distinctions on which they
depend should be distinctions important in the organization of
knowledge. Thus, if we think that the logic of tradition has been
concerned primarily with principles of inference valid for all
possible subject-matters, we must reject as unprofitable an extension of usage which allows such phrases as 'the logic of "God" '.
And if we think that the theory of sets is closely connected with
some topics of traditional logic but are nevertheless puzzled by the
devices needed to free it from paradox, we must consider carefully
the structure of the science of logic as it is presented by those who
wish to make it include the theory of sets. In this connexion the
discoveries recorded in the present chapter are obviously relevant.

The distinction between theories which admit a decision procedure and those which do not is very interesting philosophically,
and it may have great practical importance in an age of computers; but we can scarcely use it to delimit the province of logic.
For it would be contrary to long-established tradition to decide
that the name 'logic' should be reserved for the calculus of propositions, which we have called in this book primary logic, and
there is no clear line to be drawn within the restricted (or first-
order) calculus of propositional functions. We know that there
can be no decision procedure for the whole calculus, but we
cannot give a satisfactory general characterization of all that
part for which a decision procedure may be constructed. On the
other hand, it is easy to distinguish the restricted calculus of
propositional functions which is known to be deductively complete from the theory of sets (or the corresponding higher-order
functional calculus) which has been shown to be not only incomplete but incompletable, and it seems reasonable to say that
the former should be called logic but not the latter. For the word
'logic' is connected traditionally with discussion of rules of inference; and while it is strange to apply it to any axiomatic
system such as that of Frege, it is even more strange to apply
it to a system in which the consequences of the axioms are not all
accessible by inference from the axioms. Yet that, as we can now
see in the light of Gödel's theorem, is what Frege did when he
undertook to reduce arithmetic to logic. Where he noticed only
a difference of levels, there is in reality a gulf that may properly
be taken as the boundary of logic.

We might perhaps include the theory of identity within logic, since its basic notion is one of very high generality and its axioms can be added to quantification theory without loss of completeness for the resulting complex. But when once the theory of sets has been distinguished from the rest of Frege's system and based on axioms for membership, it seems most natural to present quantification theory in rules of inference like those of Gentzen or rules of development like those we have offered in an earlier section, and this technique cannot be extended to the theory of identity. We can, of course, replace axioms of identity by additional rules of inference; for that purpose we need only say that each axiom is a formula which may be inferred from the null class of premisses. But we cannot replace Frege's axioms of identity by paired rules of inference (or development) which provide between them for the introduction and the elimination of the identity sign. Nor can we define identity by means of a $\gamma$-rule within the system of higher-order rules which we have put forward in our section on modal logic. This implies that the notion of identity is not connected with the notion of entailment, or the more general notion of involution, in the same intimate way as the notions of conjunction, negation, universality, &c., which are commonly accounted logical. We therefore conclude that the theory of identity may be conveniently excluded from the scope of logic, and that our science is best defined as the pure theory of involution, that is to say, the theory of the general form of principles of involution without regard to the special natures of the propositions contained in the classes between which the relation holds. This account of the science agrees, as we have seen, very closely with an epigrammatic pronouncement of Frege about the way in which the laws of logic are related to the laws of other sciences, and it may be regarded also as a very strict interpretation of Bolzano's suggestion that logic is the science of sciences. No doubt in practice logic as we define it will always be studied together with other subjects which are relevant to the organization of knowledge, and in particular with those with which it has been associated by Aristotle, Chrysippus, Leibniz, Bolzano, and Frege. For we have seen that logic in our narrow sense is not even coextensive with the theory of deductive systems which has been developed by mathematicians out of Hilbert's suggestions. But however it may be named or described, this relatively simple study is central in the great tradition of European thought about science.

# SELECTIVE BIBLIOGRAPHY

MANY sources for the history of logic are listed in Bochenski's *History of Formal Logic*, noticed below, and a full bibliography of mathematical logic, covering not only books but articles in periodicals, can be found in *The Journal of Symbolic Logic*, vol. i (1936) and subsequent volumes.

ABELARD, PETER. *Ouvrages inédits d'Abélard*. Ed. V. Cousin. Paris, 1836.
—— *Peter Abaelards Philosophische Schriften*. Ed. B. Geyer. (*Beiträge zur Geschichte der Philosophie und Theologie des Mittelalters*, xxi.) Münster i. W., 1919–33.
—— *Scritti Filosofici: Editio super Porphyrianum*, &c. Ed. M. Dal Pra. Milan, 1954.
—— *Dialectica*. Ed. L. M. de Rijk. Assen, 1956.
—— *Abaelardiana Inedita*. Ed. L. Minio-Paluello. (*Twelfth Century Logic: Texts and Studies*, ii.) Rome, 1958.

ACKERMANN, W. *Solvable Cases of the Decision Problem*. Amsterdam, 1954.

ADAM OF BALSHAM. *Adam Balsamiensis Parvipontani Ars Disserendi* (*Dialectica Alexandri*). Ed. L. Minio-Paluello. (*Twelfth Century Logic: Texts and Studies*, i.) Rome, 1956.

ALBERT OF SAXONY. *Perutilis Logica*. Venice, 1522.

ALBERT THE GREAT. *Opera Omnia*, i and ii. Ed. A. Borgnet. Paris, 1890.

ALCUIN. *Poema de Pontificibus et Sanctis Eboracensis Ecclesiae* and *Dialectica*, in *Opera Omnia*, ii. Ed. J. P. Migne. (*Patrologia Latina*, ci.) Paris, 1863.

ALDRICH, H. *Artis Logicae Compendium*. Oxford, 1691.

ALEXANDER OF APHRODISIAS. *In Aristotelis Analyticorum Priorum Librum I Commentarium*. Ed. M. Wallies. (*Commentaria in Aristotelem Graeca*, ii (i).) Berlin, 1883.
—— *In Aristotelis Topicorum Libros Octo Commentaria*. Ed. M. Wallies. (*Commentaria in Aristotelem Graeca*, ii (ii).) Berlin, 1881.

AMMONIUS. *In Aristotelis Analyticorum Priorum Librum I Commentarium*. Ed. M. Wallies. (*Commentaria in Aristotelem Graeca*, iv (vi).) Berlin, 1899.

ANSELM OF CANTERBURY. *Monologion, Proslogion*, and *De Veritate*, in *Opera Omnia*, i. Ed. F. S. Schmitt. Edinburgh, 1946.
—— *De Fide Trinitatis = Epistola de Incarnatione Verbi*, in *Opera*, ii, 1946.

APULEIUS. *De Philosophia Rationali* = Περὶ Ἑρμηνείας, in *Opera*, iii. Ed. P. Thomas. Leipzig, 1908.

ARISTOTLE. *Categoriae et Liber de Interpretatione*. Ed. L. Minio-Paluello. Oxford, 1949.
—— *Topica et Sophistici Elenchi*. Ed. W. D. Ross. Oxford, 1958.
—— *Aristotle's Prior and Posterior Analytics*. A Revised Text with Introduction and Commentary by W. D. Ross. Oxford, 1949.
—— *Aristotle's Metaphysics*. A Revised Text with Introduction and Commentary by W. D. Ross. Oxford, 1924.

ARNAULD, A., and NICOLE, P. *La Logique, ou l'art de penser*. Paris, 1662.

AUGUSTINE, ST. *Principia Dialecticae* and *Categoriae Decem*, in *Opera Omnia*, i. Ed. J. P. Migne. (*Patrologia Latina*, xxxii.) Paris, 1861.

AVICENA (IBN SINA). *Opera*. Venice, 1508.

BACON, R. *Summulae Dialectices*. Ed. R. Steele. (*Opera hactenus inedita Rogeri Baconi*, fasc. xv.) Oxford, 1940.

BAUDRY, L. *La Querelle des futurs contingents* (*Louvain 1465–1475*), *Textes inédits*. Paris, 1950.

BECKER, A. *Die Aristotelische Theorie der Möglichkeitsschlüsse*. Berlin, 1933.

BECKER, O. *Zwei Untersuchungen zur antiken Logik*. (*Klassisch-Philologische Studien*, Heft 17.) Wiesbaden, 1957.

BOCHENSKI, I. M. *La Logique de Théophraste*. (*Collectanea Friburgensia*, N.S. fasc. xxxvii.) Fribourg, 1947.
—— *Formale Logik*. (*Orbis Academicus, Problemgeschichten der Wissenschaften in Dokumenten und Darstellungen*.) Freiburg and Munich, 1956.
—— *A History of Formal Logic*. English translation of the foregoing by I. Thomas. Notre Dame, Indiana, 1961.

BOETHIUS. *Opera Omnia*, ii. Ed. J. P. Migne. (*Patrologia Latina*, lxiv.) Paris, 1860.
—— *Commentarii in Librum Aristotelis* Περὶ Ἑρμηνείας. Ed. C. Meiser. Leipzig, 1877–80.

BOLZANO, B. *Wissenschaftslehre, Versuch einer ausführlichen und grösstenteils neuen Darstellung der Logik mit steter Rücksicht auf deren bisherige Bearbeiter*. 4 vols. Sulzbach, 1837.
—— *Paradoxien der Unendlichkeit*. Herausgegeben aus dem schriftlichem Nachlasse des Verfassers von Dr. Fr. Příhonský. Leipzig, 1851.
—— *Paradoxes of the Infinite*. English translation of the foregoing with an introduction by D. A. Steele. London, 1950.
—— *Funktionenlehre*. Herausgegeben und mit Anmerkungen versehen von K. Rychlík. Prague, 1930.

BOOLE, G. *The Mathematical Analysis of Logic*. Cambridge, 1847. Reprinted, Oxford, 1948.
—— *An Investigation of the Laws of Thought, on which are founded the Mathematical Theory of Logic and Probabilities*. London, 1854.
—— *Studies in Logic and Probability*. Ed. R. Rhees. London, 1952.

BOWDEN, B. V. *Faster than Thought, a Symposium on Digital Computing Machines*. London, 1953.

BURGERSDYCK, F. *Institutionum Logicarum Libri Duo*. First edition, Leyden, 1626.

BURIDAN, JEAN. *Sophismata*. Paris, undated, *per Johannem Lambert impressa*.

BURLEIGH, WALTER. *De Puritate Artis Logicae Tractatus Longior, with a Revised Edition of the Tractatus Brevior*. Ed. P. Boehner. (*Franciscan Institute Publications, Text Series*, No. 9.) St. Bonaventure, N.Y., 1955.

CANTOR, G. *Gesammelte Abhandlungen mathematischen und philosophischen Inhalts*. Ed. E. Zermelo. Berlin, 1932.

CARNAP, R. *Logische Syntax der Sprache*. Vienna, 1934.
—— *The Logical Syntax of Language*. English translation of the foregoing with additions. London, 1937.
—— *The Formalization of Logic*. Cambridge, Mass., 1943.
—— *Meaning and Necessity, a Study in Semantics and Modal Logic*. Chicago, 1947.

CARROLL, L. (DODGSON, C. L.). *Symbolic Logic, a Fascinating Mental Recreation for the Young*. Oxford, 1896.

CHURCH, A. *Introduction to Mathematical Logic*, i. Princeton, 1956.
—— and others. *Structure, Method, and Meaning: Essays in Honor of Henry M. Sheffer*. Ed. P. Henle, H. M. Kallen, and S. K. Langer. New York, 1951.

CICERO. *De Inventione, De Oratore*, and *Topica*, in *Scripta quae manserunt Omnia*, I i and ii. Ed. G. Friedrich. Leipzig, 1893.
—— *Academica* and *De Fato*, in *Scripta*, IV i and ii. Ed. C. F. W. Mueller. Leipzig, 1889–98.

COUTURAT, L. *La Logique de Leibniz d'après des documents inédits*. Paris, 1901.

CURRY, H. B., and FEYS, R. *Combinatory Logic*, i. Amsterdam, 1958.

DEDEKIND, J. W. R. *Stetigkeit und irrationale Zahlen*. Brunswick, 1872.
—— *Was sind und was sollen die Zahlen?* Brunswick, 1888.

DE MORGAN, A. *Formal Logic, or The Calculus of Inference, Necessary and Probable*. London, 1847.

DIELS, H. *Fragmente der Vorsokratiker*. 3 vols. Eighth edition by W. Kranz. Berlin, 1956.

DIOGENES LAERTIUS. *Lives of Eminent Philosophers*. Edited with an English Translation by R. D. Hicks. 2 vols. London, 1925.

DIONYSIUS OF HALICARNASSUS. *De Compositione Verborum*, in *Opuscula*, ii. Ed. H. Usener and L. Radermacher. Leipzig, 1904.

DIONYSIUS THRAX. *Grammatica*, in *Anecdota Graeca*, ii. Ed. I. Bekker. Berlin, 1816.

DUNS SCOTUS, JOHN. *Opera Omnia*, i. Ed. L. Wadding. Lyons, 1639.

EPICTETUS. *Dissertationes ab Arriano Digestae*. Ed. H. Schenkl. Leipzig, 1898.

EUCLID. *The Thirteen Books of Euclid's Elements*. Translated from the text of Heiberg with Introduction and Commentary by T. L. Heath. 3 vols. Cambridge, 1908.

EULER, L. *Lettres à une Princesse d'Allemagne*. 2 vols. St. Petersburg, 1768.

FRAENKEL, A. A. *Einleitung in die Mengenlehre*. Third edition, Berlin, 1928.
—— *Abstract Set Theory*. Amsterdam, 1953.

FREGE, G. *Begriffsschrift, eine der arithmetischen nachgebildete Formelsprache des reinen Denkens*. Halle, 1879.
—— *Die Grundlagen der Arithmetik, eine logisch-mathematische Untersuchung über den Begriff der Zahl*. Breslau, 1884.
—— *The Foundations of Arithmetic*. A reprint of the foregoing with an English translation by J. L. Austin. Oxford, 1950.
—— *Grundgesetze der Arithmetik, begriffsschriftlich abgeleitet*. Vol. i, Jena, 1893. Vol. ii, 1903.
—— *Translations from the Philosophical Writings of Gottlob Frege*. Ed. P. Geach and M. Black. Oxford, 1952.

GALEN. *Institutio Logica*. Ed. C. Kalbfleisch. Leipzig, 1896.
—— *De Hippocratis et Platonis Placitis*, in *Opera Omnia*, v. Ed. C. G. Kühn. Leipzig, 1823.

GARDNER, M. *Logic Machines and Diagrams*. New York, 1958.

GARLANDUS COMPOTISTA. *Dialectica*. Ed. L. M. de Rijk. Assen, 1959.

GEULINCX, A. *Logica Fundamentis Suis a quibus hactenus delapsa fuerat Restituta*, in *Opera Philosophica*, i. Ed. J. P. N. Land. The Hague, 1891.

GILBERTUS PORRETANUS. *Liber de Sex Principiis*. Ed. A. Heyse. Münster i. W., 1953.

GRASSMANN, H. *Die Lineale Ausdehnungslehre*. Leipzig, 1844.

HAMILTON, SIR WILLIAM. *Lectures on Logic*. 2 vols. Ed. H. L. Mansel and J. Veitch. Edinburgh, 1860.

HEATH, SIR THOMAS L. *Mathematics in Aristotle*. Oxford, 1949.

HEYTING, A. *Intuitionism, an Introduction*. Amsterdam, 1956.

HILBERT, D. *Grundlagen der Geometrie*. Leipzig, 1899.
—— and ACKERMANN, W. *Grundzüge der theoretischen Logik*. Third edition, Berlin, 1949.

HILBERT, D., and BERNAYS, P. *Grundlagen der Mathematik.* Vol. i, Berlin, 1934. Vol. ii, 1939.

HILLEBRAND, F. *Die neuen Theorien der kategorischen Schlüsse.* Vienna, 1891.

HOBBES, T. *Elements of Philosophy Concerning Body.* London, 1656.

HOWELL, W. S. *Logic and Rhetoric in England, 1500–1700.* Princeton, 1956.

JEVONS, W. S. *Pure Logic, or The Logic of Quality apart from Quantity.* London, 1864.
—— *Elementary Lessons in Logic, Deductive and Inductive.* London, 1870.
—— *The Principles of Science, a Treatise on Logic and Scientific Method.* London, 1874.

JOHN OF SALISBURY. *Metalogicon.* Ed. C. C. J. Webb. Oxford, 1929.

JUNGE, J. *Logica Hamburgensis.* Hamburg, 1638. Reprinted 1957.

KANT, I. *Critik der reinen Vernunft.* First edition, Riga, 1781.
—— *Prolegomena zu einer jeden künftigen Metaphysik die als Wissenschaft wird auftreten können.* Riga, 1783.
—— *Immanuel Kants Logik.* Ed. B. G. Jäsche. Königsberg, 1800.

KAUPPI, R. *Über die Leibnizsche Logik, mit besonderer Berücksichtigung des Problems der Intension und der Extension. (Acta Philosophica Fennica, fasc. xii.)* Helsinki, 1960.

KEYNES, J. N. *Studies and Exercises in Formal Logic, including a Generalization of Logical Processes in their Application to Complex Inferences.* London, 1884.

KLEENE, S. C. *Introduction to Metamathematics.* Amsterdam, 1952.

LAMBERT, J. H. *Logische und Philosophische Abhandlungen.* Ed. J. Bernoulli. Berlin, 1782.

LEIBNIZ, G. W. *Opera Omnia.* 6 vols. Ed. L. Dutens. Geneva, 1768.
—— *Leibnizens mathematische Schriften,* 7 vols. Ed. C. I. Gerhardt. Berlin, 1849–63.
—— *Die philosophischen Schriften von G. W. Leibniz.* 7 vols. Ed. C. I. Gerhardt. Berlin, 1875–90.
—— *Die Leibniz-Handschriften der Königlichen Öffentlichen Bibliothek zu Hannover.* Catalogue by E. Bodemann. Hanover, 1895.
—— *Opuscules et fragments inédits de Leibniz.* Ed. L. Couturat. Paris, 1903.

LEWIS, C. I. *A Survey of Symbolic Logic.* Berkeley, 1918.
—— and LANGFORD, C. H. *Symbolic Logic.* New York, 1932.

ŁUKASIEWICZ, J. *Aristotle's Syllogistic from the Standpoint of Modern Formal Logic.* Second edition enlarged, Oxford, 1957.

LULL, RAMÓN. *Raymundi Lullii Opera ea quae ad adinventam ab ipso artem universalem . . . pertinent.* Strassburg, 1617.

MAASS, J. G. E. *Grundriss der Logik.* Halle, 1793.

MCCOLL, H. *Symbolic Logic and its Applications*. London, 1906.

MAINZ, THE REGENT MASTERS OF. *Modernorum Summulae Logicales, a magistris Collegii Moguntini regentibus . . . innovatae*. Mainz, 1489.

MARTIANUS CAPELLA. *De Nuptiis Philologiae et Mercurii*. Ed. A. Dick. Leipzig, 1925.

MATES, B. *Stoic Logic*. (*University of California Publications in Philosophy*, vol. 26.) Berkeley and Los Angeles, 1953.

MILL, J. S. *A System of Logic, Ratiocinative and Inductive, being a Connected View of the Principles of Evidence and the Methods of Scientific Investigation*. London, 1843.

MONTUCLA, J. E. *Histoire des mathématiques*, i. Paris, 1758.

MOODY, E. A. *Truth and Consequence in Medieval Logic*. Amsterdam, 1953.

MOSTOWSKI, A. *Sentences Undecidable in Formalized Arithmetic, an Exposition of the Theory of Kurt Gödel*. Amsterdam, 1952.

OCKHAM, WILLIAM. *Super Quattuor Libros Sententiarum*. Lyons, 1495.
—— *Expositio Aurea et admodum utilis super Artem Veterem*. Bologna, 1496.
—— *Summa Totius Logicae*. Oxford, 1675. Parts i, ii, and iii (i) have appeared in a modern edition by P. Boehner, St. Bonaventure, N.Y., 1951–4.
—— *Tractatus de Praedestinatione et de Praescientia Dei et de Futuris Contingentibus*. Edited with a Study on the Medieval Problem of a Three-valued Logic by P. Boehner. (*Franciscan Institute Publications*, No. 2.) St. Bonaventure, N.Y., 1945.

PATZIG, G. *Die Aristotelische Syllogistik*. (*Abhandlungen der Akademie der Wissenschaften in Göttingen, Phil. Hist. Klasse*, III, No. 42.) Göttingen, 1959.

PAULUS NICOLLETUS VENETUS. *Logica Magna*. Venice, 1499.

PEANO, G. *Arithmetices Principia nova methodo exposita*. Rome, 1899.
—— *Notation de logique mathématique*. Turin, 1894.
—— *Formulaire de mathématiques*. Turin, 1895–1908.

PEIRCE, C. S. *Collected Papers*. 8 vols. Ed. C. Hartshorne, P. Weiss, and A. W. Burks. Cambridge, Mass., 1931–58.

PETER OF SPAIN. *Summulae Logicales*. Ed. I. M. Bochenski. Rome, 1947.

PHILOPONUS, JOHANNES. *In Aristotelis Analytica Priora Commentaria*. Ed. M. Wallies. (*Commentaria in Aristotelem Graeca*, xiii (ii).) Berlin, 1905.

PLATO. *Opera*. Ed. J. Burnet. Oxford, 1899–1906.

PLOUCQUET, G. *Sammlung der Schriften welche den logischen Calcul des Herrn Professor Ploucquet betreffen*. Ed. F. A. Bök, Tübingen, 1773.

PLUTARCH. *Libri contra Stoicos Scripti*, in *Moralia*, vi. 2. Ed. M. Pohlenz. Leipzig, 1959.

POINCARÉ, H. *Science et méthode*. Paris, 1908.

POPPER, K. R. *The Logic of Scientific Discovery*. London, 1959.

PORPHYRY. *Isagoge et in Aristotelis Categorias Commentarium*. Ed. A. Busse. (*Commentaria in Aristotelem Graeca*, iv (i).) Berlin, 1887.

PRANTL, C. *Geschichte der Logik im Abendlande*. 4 vols. Leipzig, 1855–70.

PRIOR, A. N. *Formal Logic*. Second edition, Oxford, 1961.

PRISCIAN. *Institutiones Grammaticae*, in *Grammatici Latini*, ii and iii. Ed. H. Keill. Leipzig, 1855–8.

PROCLUS. *In Primum Euclidis Elementorum Librum Commentarii*. Ed. G. Friedlein. Leipzig, 1873.

PSEUDO-SCOT (? JOHN OF CORNWALL). *See* DUNS SCOTUS.

QUINE, W. V. *Mathematical Logic*. First edition, New York, 1940. Revised edition, Cambridge, Mass., 1951.
—— *Methods of Logic*. First edition, New York, 1950. Revised edition, London, 1958.
—— *From a Logical Point of View*. Cambridge, Mass., 1953.

RAMSEY, F. R. *The Foundations of Mathematics and Other Logical Essays*. Ed. R. B. Braithwaite. London, 1931.

RAMUS, PETRUS (PIERRE DE LA RAMÉE). *Aristotelicae Animadversiones*. Paris, 1543.
—— *Dialecticae Partitiones*. Paris, 1543.
—— *Dialectique*. Paris, 1555.
—— *Dialecticae Libri Duo*. First edition, Paris, 1556. Last edition in his life, Paris, 1572.

REICHENBACH, H. *Elements of Symbolic Logic*. New York, 1948.

RIEMANN, G. F. B. *Über die Hypothesen welche der Geometrie zu Grunde liegen*. (*Abhandlungen der Königlichen Gesellschaft der Wissenschaften zu Göttingen*, xiii.) Göttingen, 1867.

ROBINSON, R. *Plato's Earlier Dialectic*. Second edition, Oxford, 1953.

ROSSER, J. B., and TURQUETTE, A. R. *Many-valued Logics*. Amsterdam, 1952.

RUSSELL, B. *A Critical Exposition of the Philosophy of Leibniz*. Cambridge, 1900.
—— *The Principles of Mathematics*, i. Cambridge, 1900.
—— *Introduction to Mathematical Philosophy*. London, 1919.
—— *Logic and Knowledge, Essays 1901–1950*. Ed. R. C. Marsh. London, 1956.
—— *The Philosophy of Bertrand Russell*. Ed. P. A. Schilpp. Evanston, Ill., 1946.

RÜSTOW, A. *Der Lügner, Theorie, Geschichte, und Auflösung*. Leipzig, 1910.

SACCHERI, G. G. *Logica Demonstrativa*. First edition (anonymous), Turin, 1697. Third edition, Cologne, 1735.

—— *Euclides ab Omni Naevo Vindicatus*. First edition, Milan, 1733. Reprinted with English translation and introduction by G. B. Halsted, Chicago and London, 1920.

SCHRÖDER, E. *Vorlesungen über die Algebra der Logik*. 3 vols. Leipzig, 1890–1905.

SCHUHL, P. M. *Le Dominateur et les possibles*. Paris, 1960.

SEXTUS EMPIRICUS. *Opera*. 3 vols. Ed. H. Mutschmann and J. Mau. Leipzig, 1912–54.

SIMPLICIUS. *In Aristotelis Categorias Commentaria*. Ed. C. Kalbfleisch. (*Commentaria in Aristotelem Graeca*, viii.) Berlin, 1907.

—— *In Aristotelis Physicorum Libros Quattuor Posteriores Commentarium*. Ed. H. Diels. (*Commentaria in Aristotelem Graeca*, x.) Berlin, 1895.

—— *In Aristotelis de Caelo Commentaria*. Ed. J. L. Heiberg. (*Commentaria in Aristotelem Graeca*, vii.) Berlin, 1894.

SKOLEM, T., and others. *Mathematical Interpretations of Formal Systems*. Amsterdam, 1955.

SOLMSEN, F. *Die Entwicklung der Aristotelischen Logik und Rhetorik*. Berlin, 1929.

STRAWSON, P. F. *Introduction to Logical Theory*. London, 1952.

STRODE, R., and others. *Consequentiae Strodi cum commento Alexandri Sermonetae, Declarationes Gaetani in easdem consequentias, Dubia magistri Pauli Pergolensis, Obligationes eiusdem Strodi, Consequentiae Ricardi de Ferabrich, Expositio Gaetani super easdem, Consequentiae subtiles Hentisberi, Quaestiones in consequentias Strodi perutiles eximii artis doctoris Antonii Frachantiani Vicentini*. Venice, 1517.

TARSKI, A. *Logic, Semantics, Metamathematics: Papers from 1923 to 1938*. Translated by J. H. Woodger. Oxford, 1956.

—— MOSTOWSKI, A., and ROBINSON, R. M. *Undecidable Theories*. Amsterdam, 1953.

TAYLOR, A. E. *Varia Socratica*. Oxford, 1911.

THOMAS AQUINAS, ST. *Summa Theologiae*. 4 vols. Ed. P. Caramelo. Rome, 1948.

—— *Summa contra Gentiles*. Editio Leonina manualis, Rome, 1934.

—— *De Veritate*, in *Quaestiones Disputatae*, i. Ed. R. Spiazzi. Turin, 1949.

VAILATI, G. *Scritti (1863–1909)*. Florence, 1911.

VENN, J. *Symbolic Logic*. London, 1881.

VINCENT FERRER, ST. *De Suppositionibus Dialecticis*, in *Œuvres*, i. Ed. P. Fages. Paris, 1909.

VON ARNIM, J. *Stoicorum Veterum Fragmenta*. 3 vols. Leipzig, 1903–5.

VON WRIGHT, G. H. *An Essay in Modal Logic.* Amsterdam, 1951.

WALLIS, J. *Institutio Logica.* Oxford, 1687.

WHITEHEAD, A. N. *A Treatise of Universal Algebra with Applications,* i. Cambridge, 1898.

—— and RUSSELL, B. *Principia Mathematica,* 3 vols. First edition, Cambridge, 1910–13. Second edition, 1925–7.

WILLIAM OF SHYRESWOOD. *Die Introductiones in Logicam des Wilhelm von Shyreswood.* Ed. M. Grabmann. (*Sitzungsberichte der Bayerischen Akademie der Wissenschaften, Phil. Hist. Abteilung,* Jahrgang 1937, Heft 10.) Munich, 1937.

WITTGENSTEIN, L. *Tractatus Logico-Philosophicus.* London, 1921.

ZABARELLA, J. *Opera Omnia quae ad perfectam Logicae cognitionem acquirendam spectare censentur utilissima.* Seventeenth edition, Venice, 1617.

# INDEX

Abbo of Fleury, 199.

Abelard, Peter, 200, 202, 203 ff.; on propositions, 205; on negation, 210; on copula, 207; on square of opposition, 210; on *proprietates nominum*, 209.

abstract entities, 591; in Plato, 20; Stoic *lekta* as, 156; in Abelard, 206; Ockham on, 270.

accident, 35, 36, 39, 82.

Ackermann, W., 515, 535 n., 546; on decision problem, 725, 727.

Ackrill, J. L., 22 n.

Adam of Balsham (Parvipontanus), 227, 440.

Adelard of Bath, 225.

adjunction, rule of, 550.

*a fortiori* argument, 42, 106.

Agrippa, Rudolphus, 300.

Albert of Saxony, 244, 270; *on consequentiae*, 294.

Albert the Great, 229, 235–6.

Alcuin, 198.

Aldrich, H., 298.

Alexander of Aphrodisias, 7, 23, 70, 77, 81, 87, 100, 102, 105, 107, 110, 111, 119, 154, 158, 164, 167, 169, 175, 177, 185, 191.

algebra, 309; of logic, 404 ff., 431.

'algorism', 225.

algorithms, 733.

al-Khowarazmi, 225, 733.

alternative logics, 568 ff.

Ammonius, 107, 198.

*ampliatio*, 261.

analytic and synthetic statements, Kant on, 356 ff.; Bolzano on, 365 ff.; Frege on, 445 ff., 637; Quine on, 644.

ancestral relation, 468, 493.

Anscombe. G. E. M., 48 n.

Anselm, 200; and the ontological argument, 201.

*antepraedicamenta*, 204.

antilogism, 278.

Antipater, 143, 163.

antisyllogism, 314.

ἀπαγωγὴ εἰς τὸ ἀδύνατον, 8.

ἀπόδειξις, ἀποδεικτική, 1 ff., 7.

Apollonius Cronus, 113.

ἀποφαντικὸς λόγος, 45–46.

*appellatio*, 144; in William of Shyreswood, 247; in Peter of Spain, 264.

Apuleius, 116, 159, 160, 169, 178, 181.

Archytas, 6.

Argall, J., 299.

Argand, J. R., 393.

Aristotle, 1, 6, 7, 12, 13, 15, 21, 22, 23–100, 115, 133, 134, 139, 158, 159, 173, 185, 187, 188, 196, 198, 206, 228, 257, 291, 478, 530, 557, 566, 588, 737.

arithmetization of syntax, 714 ff.

Arnauld, A., 315.

*ars combinatoria*, 162, 242, 321 f.

assertion sign, 478, 519.

Augustine, St., 174, 188, 239, 599.

Aulus Gellius, 145, 148.

*Ausdehnungslehre*, 337.

Austin, J. L., 435 n.

Averroes, 183, 229.

Avicenna, 229, 266.

*axioma*, 126, 145 ff.; truth of, 152.

axiomatics, 379 ff.

axiom schemata, 529.

Ayer, A. J., 637.

Bacon, F., 309.

Bacon, R., 234, 241; on *suppositio*, 251.

*Barbara Celarent*, 232.

Barcan, R., 614 n.

Barnes, W., 299.

Basilides, 142.

Baudry, L., 238 n.

Becker, A., 91 n.

Becker, O., 170 n., 551.

Bednarowski, W., 353 n.

Behmann, H., 726.

Bernard of Chartres, 239.

Bernays, P., 515, 526, 527, 535 595, 683 n., 684 n., 685 n., 686, 689, 690, 692, 703, 705, 726–7.

Berry's paradox, 656, 660–1, 665.

Bidez, J., 191 n.

bivalence, principle of, 47, 48, 52, 161, 214; applicability of, to conditionals, 136.

Black, M., 437 n., 670.

Blundeville, T., 299.

Bochenski, I. M., 91 n., 256 n., 288.

Bodemann, E., 321 n.

Boehner, Ph., 238 n., 271.

Boethius, 80, 105, 117, 122, 123, 125, 160, 161, 177, 186, 189, 198, 239; on conditionals, 192; on the nature of logic, 194; on universals, 196 ff.

Boethus, 182.

Bolzano, B., 358 ff., 400, 407, 440, 592, 596, 641, 742.

Bonaventura, St., 239.

PRINTED IN GREAT BRITAIN
AT THE UNIVERSITY PRESS, OXFORD
BY VIVIAN RIDLER
PRINTER TO THE UNIVERSITY

## DATE DUE

| | | |
|---|---|---|
| JUN 18 1964 | | |
| Jan 29, 1965 | | |
| MAY 7 - 1965 | | |
| JUN 3 0 1967 | | |
| JAN 3 0 1968 | | |
| MAR 5 1976 | | |
| OCT 1 0 1979 | | |
| NOV 1 5 1982 | | |
| NOV 2 3 82 | | |
| MAR 4 1985 | | |
| JUL 1 5 1985 | | |
| APR 2 1986 | | |
| JAN 1 3 1992 | | |
| | | |
| | | |
| | | |
| | | |
| | | |